W9-CXK-832

# STRATEGIC MANAGEMENT

# *STRATEGIC MANAGEMENT*
## PLANNING AND IMPLEMENTATION
## Concepts and Cases

SECOND EDITION

Lloyd L. Byars
**Graduate School of Business Administration**
**Atlanta University**

**HARPER & ROW, PUBLISHERS, New York**
Cambridge, Philadelphia, San Francisco, Washington,
London, Mexico City, São Paulo, Singapore, Sydney

1817

Sponsoring Editor: Jayne L. Maerker
Project Editor: Susan Goldfarb
Text Design Adaptation: Network Graphics
Cover Design: DanielsDesign Inc.
Text Art: Vantage Art, Inc.
Production Manager: Jeanie Berke
Production Assistant: Paula Roppolo
Compositor: ComCom Division of Haddon Craftsmen, Inc.
Printer and Binder: R. R. Donnelley & Sons Company

**STRATEGIC MANAGEMENT: Planning and Implementation, Concepts and Cases**
Second Edition

Copyright © 1987 by Harper & Row, Publishers, Inc.

All rights reserved. Printed in the United States of America. No part of this
book may be used or reproduced in any manner whatsoever without written
permission, except in the case of brief quotations embodied in critical articles and
reviews. For information address Harper & Row, Publishers, Inc., 10 East 53d Street,
New York, NY 10022.

**Library of Congress Cataloging-in-Publication Data**

Byars, Lloyd L.
  Strategic management.

  Includes bibliographies and index.
  1. Strategic planning.   2. Strategic planning—
Case studies.   I. Title.
HD30.28.B9     1987     658.4′012     86-22779
ISBN 0-06-041094-9

88  89  9  8  7  6  5  4  3  2

*To my wife, Linda*
*A good wife is her husband's pride and joy.*

*Proverbs 12:3*

# CONTENTS

*CASE CONTRIBUTORS*   xv

*PREFACE*   xvii


# part one
## Introduction   2

### chapter 1   STRATEGIC MANAGEMENT: AN OVERVIEW   4

STRATEGIC MANAGEMENT AND ORGANIZATIONAL SUCCESS   6

THE STRATEGIC MANAGEMENT PROCESS   8

Defining the Organization's Philosophy   9

Defining the Organization's Mission   12

Establishing Long- and Short-Range Objectives   14

Selecting a Strategy   16

INTEGRATING PHILOSOPHY, MISSION, OBJECTIVES, AND STRATEGY   17

STRATEGIC BUSINESS UNITS (SBUs)   17

MAKING STRATEGIC DECISIONS   18

*Review Questions   19   /   Discussion Questions   20   /   References and Additional Reading   20*


# part two
## Strategic Planning   22

### chapter 2   ANALYZING THE EXTERNAL AND INTERNAL ENVIRONMENT   24

ENVIRONMENTAL SCANNING   26

Economic Forces   26

Technological Forces   28

Political and Regulatory Forces   28

Social Forces   29

ESTABLISHING AN ENVIRONMENTAL SCANNING PROGRAM   30

ENVIRONMENTAL FORECASTING   31

Delphi Technique   31

Brainstorming   32

Scenarios   32

Trend-Impact Analysis  32
Economic Forecasting  32
COMPETITIVE ANALYSIS    34
INTERNAL ORGANIZATIONAL ANALYSIS    37
PROCEDURES    42
*Review Questions  44  /  Discussion Questions  44  /  References and Additional Reading  44*

**chapter 3    ORGANIZATIONAL CULTURE AND THE OBJECTIVE-SETTING PROCESS    46**

THE OBJECTIVE-SETTING PROCESS    48
ORGANIZATIONAL CULTURE    48
Origin of Organizational Cultures  50
Identifying and Classifying Organizational Cultures  51
Changing Organizational Cultures  54
MIX OF ORGANIZATIONAL OBJECTIVES    55
CASCADE APPROACH TO ESTABLISHING OBJECTIVES    58
*Review Questions  59  /  Discussion Questions  59  /  References and Additional Reading  59*

**chapter 4    IDENTIFYING STRATEGIC ALTERNATIVES    60**

STRATEGIC ALTERNATIVES    62
STABLE GROWTH STRATEGY    63
GROWTH STRATEGIES    64
Concentration on a Single Product or Service  66
Concentric Diversification  67
Vertical Integration  67
Horizontal Integration (or Diversification)  70
Conglomerate Diversification  71
ENDGAME STRATEGIES    72
RETRENCHMENT STRATEGIES    74
Turnaround Strategy  74
Divestment Strategy  75
Liquidation Strategy  76
COMBINATION STRATEGIES    76
BUSINESS UNIT OR CORPORATE STRATEGIES    77
Overall Cost Leadership Strategy  78
Differentiation Strategy  78
Focus Strategy  78
IMPLEMENTING STRATEGIES THROUGH MERGERS AND ACQUISITIONS    78
Reasons for Mergers and Acquisitions  78
Carrying Out Mergers and Acquisitions  80
Guidelines for Successfully Implementing Mergers and Acquisitions  81

IMPLEMENTING STRATEGIES THROUGH JOINT VENTURES    84

Reasons for Entering Joint Ventures  85
Strategies to Use in Joint Ventures  85
Considerations in Forming a Joint Venture  85
*Review Questions  87  /  Discussion Questions  87  /  References and Additional
Reading  87*

**chapter 5   STRATEGY EVALUATION AND SELECTION    90**

BUSINESS PORTFOLIO ANALYSIS    92
Growth-Share Matrix  92
Industry Attractiveness–Business Strength Matrix  97
Life-Cycle Approach  104
COMPETITIVE STRATEGY ANALYSIS    108
CLUSTER ANALYSIS    110
PIMS ANALYSIS    111
QUALITATIVE FACTORS IN THE STRATEGY EVALUATION AND SELECTION
PROCESS    112
Managerial Attitudes Toward Risk  112
Environment of the Organization  113
Organizational Culture and Power Relationships  114
Competitive Actions and Reactions  114
Influence of Previous Organizational Strategies  115
Timing Considerations  115
*Review Questions  115  /  Discussion Questions  116  /  References and Additional
Reading  116*

**part three**
**Strategy Implementation    118**

**chapter 6   MATCHING STRATEGY AND ORGANIZATIONAL STRUCTURE    120**

CONTINGENCY APPROACH TO ORGANIZING    122
Organizational Size and Growth Stage  123
Organizational Environment  124
Technology and Structure  125
Contingency Organizational Structures  125
ASSESSING AN ORGANIZATION'S STRUCTURE    126
GUIDELINES IN DESIGNING EFFECTIVE ORGANIZATIONAL
STRUCTURES    128
Simple Structures  128
Simple Form, Lean Staff  129
RESTRUCTURING AN ORGANIZATION    130
BOARD OF DIRECTORS    130

Composition of the Board   131
Structure of the Board   132
Legal Responsibilities of the Board   133
*Review Questions   134   /   Discussion Questions   135   /   References and Additional Reading   135   /   Appendix to Chapter 6: Strengths and Weaknesses of Organizational Structure Types   137*

**chapter 7    IMPLEMENTING STRATEGY: FUNCTIONAL STRATEGIES, BUDGETING, LEADERSHIP, AND MOTIVATION    142**

DEVELOPING FUNCTIONAL STRATEGIES    144
Marketing Strategies   145
Financial Strategies   147
Production/Operations Strategies   150
Human Resource/Personnel Strategies   151
Research and Development Strategies   152
DEPLOYMENT OF RESOURCES THROUGH BUDGETING    154
Flexible Budgets   156
Program Budgeting   157
Making the Budget Process Useful   158
ORGANIZATIONAL LEADERSHIP    159
MOTIVATIONAL SYSTEMS    160
*Review Questions   164   /   Discussion Questions   164   /   References and Additional Reading   164*

**chapter 8    STRATEGIC CONTROL PROCESS    166**

STRATEGIC CONTROL PROCESS    168
STRATEGIC CONTROL AND OTHER PHASES OF THE STRATEGIC MANAGEMENT PROCESS    170
THREE ELEMENTS OF CONTROL    170
Developing Criteria for Evaluation   170
Evaluating Performance   173
Feedback   174
EFFECTIVE CONTROL SYSTEMS    174
METHODS OF CONTROL    176
Budgets   176
Audits   176
Time-related Control Methods   179
Management by Objectives   180
STRATEGY AUDITS    181
MANAGEMENT INFORMATION SYSTEMS    181
Designing an MIS   181
Decision Support Systems   184
*Review Questions   184   /   Discussion Questions   185   /   References and Additional Reading   185*

# part four
**Useful Information for Analyzing Strategic Management Cases   186**

**Appendix A   PREPARING A CASE ANALYSIS   189**

**Appendix B   READING AND UNDERSTANDING FINANCIAL
STATEMENTS   199**

**Appendix C   BUSINESS FACTS FOR DECISION MAKERS: WHERE TO FIND
THEM   213**

# part five
**Case Studies in Strategic Management   252**

**Section A   Strategic Management: Planning and Implementation   255**

1   COCA-COLA COMPANY   255
    Lincoln W. Deihl, Kansas State University
    Thomas C. Neil, Atlanta University
2   LEVI STRAUSS & COMPANY: TAKING AN INDUSTRY GIANT PRIVATE   280
    Neil H. Snyder, University of Virginia
    Lloyd L. Byars, Atlanta University
3   JOHNSON PRODUCTS COMPANY, INC.: THE CHALLENGES OF THE 1980s   293
    Thomas L. Wheelen, Robert L. Nixon,
        Marian Hessler, Jan Hunter, Bob Bailey,
        and Tony Arroyo, University of South Florida
    Neil H. Snyder, University of Virginia
4   A NOTE ON THE BREWING INDUSTRY   314
    Michael D. Caputa, Virginia Polytechnic Institute and State University
5   IT'S MILLER TIME   336
    Thomas C. Neil and Lloyd L. Byars, Atlanta University
6   THE ADOLPH COORS COMPANY   351
    Jeffrey M. Miner and Larry D. Alexander, Virginia Polytechnic Institute
        and State University
7   XEROX CORPORATION PROPOSED DIVERSIFICATION   372
    J. David Hunger, George Mason University
    Thomas Conquest and William Miller, Iowa State University
8   A. H. ROBINS AND THE DALKON SHIELD   397
    Neil H. Snyder, University of Virginia

 9   THE AUTO INDUSTRY IN THE UNITED STATES: STRUCTURE AND STRATEGY   421
     Ernest R. Nordtvedt, Loyola University in New Orleans
10   LEE IACOCCA'S CHRYSLER   446
     Ernest R. Nordtvedt, Loyola University in New Orleans
11A  TURNER BROADCASTING SYSTEM, INC.   468
     William H. Davidson, University of Southern California
11B  TURNER BROADCASTING SYSTEM, INC.   486
     Neil H. Snyder, University of Virginia
12   NCNB CORPORATION   489
     Lloyd L. Byars and Debra Thompson, Atlanta University
13   McDONALD'S CORPORATION   511
     Lloyd L. Byars and Denise Murray, Atlanta University
14   BURGER KING'S BATTLE FOR THE BURGERS   529
     Larry D. Alexander and Thomas W. Ripp, Virginia Polytechnic Institute
       and State University
15   QUAKER OATS COMPANY   552
     Lloyd L. Byars and Wanda Benjamin, Atlanta University
16   MCI COMMUNICATIONS   568
     Lloyd L. Byars and Deirdre Creecy, Atlanta University
17   TANDY, INC.   592
     Sexton Adams, North Texas State University
     Adelaide Griffin, Texas Woman's University
18   CORPORATE PLANNING AT BORG-WARNER IN THE 1980s   617
     William C. Scott, Indiana State University
19   THE LINCOLN ELECTRIC COMPANY, 1984   626
     Arthur Sharplin, Northeast Louisiana University
20   7-ELEVEN STORES: CONVENIENCE 24 HOURS A DAY   647
     Jeremy B. Fox and Larry D. Alexander, Virginia Polytechnic Institute and State University
21   WAL-MART STORES, INC.   666
     Sexton Adams, North Texas State University
     Adelaide Griffin, Texas Woman's University
22   MARY KAY COSMETICS, INC.   682
     Sexton Adams, North Texas State University
     Adelaide Griffin, Texas Woman's University
23   MOBIL CORPORATION   706
     Robert R. Gardner and M. Edgar Barrett, Maguire Oil and Gas Institute,
       Southern Methodist University
24   KERR-McGEE CORPORATION   742
     Roger M. Atherton, Northeastern University
     Mark W. Bushell, University of Oklahoma
25   DELTA AIR LINES: WORLD'S MOST PROFITABLE AIRLINE   765
     Elizabeth Lavie and Larry D. Alexander, Virginia Polytechnic Institute
       and State University
26   WASTE MANAGEMENT, INC.   788
     Robert G. Wirthlin and James Kendrix, Butler University
27   NIKE, INC.   804
     Robert G. Wirthlin and Anthony P. Schlichte, Butler University
28   COMMUNITY MENTAL HEALTH CENTER   814
     E. R. Worthington, West Texas State University

# Section B    Small Business    826

29   CIRCUIT SERVICES NORTH     826
      Harriett Stephenson and Patrick Koeplin, Seattle University
30   HINES INDUSTRIES, INC.     835
      Robert P. Crowner, Eastern Michigan University
31   RAINBOW FOOD COMPANY     849
      Thomas M. Bertsch, James Madison University

# Section C    International Business Cases    855

32   FORD OF EUROPE AND LOCAL-CONTENT REGULATIONS     855
      H. Landis Gabel and Anthony E. Hall, INSEAD
33   NITROFIX GHANA     881
      William A. Stoever
34   MULTIQUIMICA DO BRASIL     894
      Mary Pat Cormack and M. Edgar Barrett, Maguire Oil and Gas Institute,
         Southern Methodist University

# Section D    Social Responsibility    901

35   UNION CARBIDE OF INDIA, LTD. (1985)     901
      Arthur Sharplin, Northeast Louisiana University
36   MANVILLE CORPORATION     915
      Arthur Sharplin, Northeast Louisiana University

      INDEX     931

# CASE CONTRIBUTORS

**Sexton Adams,** North Texas State University
**Larry D. Alexander,** Virginia Polytechnic Institute and State University
**Tony Arroyo,** University of South Florida
**Roger M. Atherton,** Northeastern University
**Bob Bailey,** University of South Florida
**M. Edgar Barrett,** Southern Methodist University
**Wanda Benjamin,** Atlanta University
**Thomas M. Bertsch,** James Madison University
**Donna Biemiller,** University of Virginia
**Alex Blair,** North Texas State University
**Elizabeth Bogdan,** University of Virginia
**Mark W. Bushell,** University of Oklahoma
**Lloyd L. Byars,** Atlanta University
**Michael D. Caputa,** Virginia Polytechnic Institute and State University
**Marlene Carle,** North Texas State University
**Robert Carle,** North Texas State University
**Thomas Conquest,** Iowa State University
**Mary Pat Cormack,** Southern Methodist University
**Tracy Cox,** University of Virginia
**Deirdre Creecy,** Atlanta University
**Robert P. Crowner,** Eastern Michigan University
**William H. Davidson,** University of Southern California
**Sally Dehaney,** North Texas State University
**Lincoln W. Deihl,** Kansas State University
**Gregg Dufour,** North Texas State University
**Richard Edwards,** North Texas State University
**Jeremy B. Fox,** Virginia Polytechnic Institute and State University
**H. Landis Gabel,** INSEAD
**Robert R. Gardner,** Southern Methodist University
**Elizabeth Ghaphery,** University of Virginia
**Monya Giggar,** North Texas State University
**Adelaide Griffin,** Texas Woman's University
**Gregg Gunchick,** North Texas State University
**Anthony E. Hall,** INSEAD
**Marisa Hausman,** University of Virginia
**Tim Hays,** James Madison University
**Marian Hessler,** University of South Florida
**J. David Hunger,** George Mason University
**Jan Hunter,** University of South Florida
**G. Rob Joseph,** University of Southern California
**James Kendrix,** Butler University
**Patrick Koeplin,** Seattle University
**Elizabeth Lavie,** Virginia Polytechnic Institute and State University

**Joan LeSoravage,** University of Virginia
**Michelle Little,** North Texas State University
**David Miller,** North Texas State University
**William Miller,** Iowa State University
**Jeffrey M. Miner,** Virginia Polytechnic Institute and State University
**Alan Moore,** North Texas State University
**Kerrie Morrison,** University of Virginia
**Denise Murray,** Atlanta University
**Thomas C. Neil,** Atlanta University
**Robert L. Nixon,** University of South Florida
**Ernest R. Nordtvedt,** Loyola University in New Orleans
**Michael Ratcliffe,** James Madison University
**Diane Reiff,** University of Virginia
**Thomas W. Ripp,** Virginia Polytechnic Institute and State University
**Larry Rosenberger,** University of Virginia
**Anthony P. Schlichte,** Butler University
**William C. Scott,** Indiana State University
**Arthur Sharplin,** Northeast Louisiana University
**Aseem Shukla,** Northeast Louisiana University
**Neil H. Snyder,** University of Virginia
**Harriett Stephenson,** Seattle University
**William A. Stoever**
**Debra Thompson,** Atlanta University
**Paul Trobaugh,** North Texas State University
**Paula Walters,** North Texas State University
**Laura Weiss,** University of Virginia
**Thomas L. Wheelen,** University of South Florida
**Robert G. Wirthlin,** Butler University
**E. R. Worthington,** West Texas State University

# PREFACE

The second edition of *Strategic Management: Planning and Implementation, Concepts and Cases* is designed to analyze the strategic management process and to give students practice in applying the process to actual organizations. The strategic management process is concerned with making decisions about an organization's future direction and implementing those decisions.

This book, which includes both text and case studies, has been structured around a simple logical framework for analyzing the strategic management process. Diagrams of this framework, which appear throughout the text, provide a visual display of the major components of the process and illustrate the interrelationships among the various components.

*Strategic Management* is divided into five major parts. Parts One through Four constitute the text portion of the book, and Part Five is a compilation of cases for use in studying the strategic management process. Part One introduces and defines the major components in the strategic management process. Part Two, which discusses strategic planning, focuses on establishing organizational objectives, defining organizational culture, identifying strategic alternatives, and selecting an appropriate strategy. Part Three, on strategy implementation, describes the processes of matching strategy and structure, implementing strategy, and exercising strategic control. In addition, each chapter contains an abundance of real-world examples showing how organizations apply the concepts presented in the chapter.

The three appendixes in Part Four provide information useful in analyzing strategic management cases. Appendix A discusses how to read and analyze cases; it also contains a summary of each text chapter with page number references. Appendix B, written by Johnnie L. Clark, former dean of the Graduate School of Business Administration of Atlanta University, provides an analysis of financial statements. Appendix C, adapted from an article by Jugoslav S. Milutinovich, is a guide to business reference sources.

The case studies in Part Five were systematically selected to serve as a cross section of a number of major industries and to provide opportunities for students to analyze all major aspects of the strategic management process. Several cases focus on studying strategic management in an international environment and on examining social issues in strategic management. The cases have been classroom tested to help ensure their readability and practicality.

I appreciate the valuable insights and contributions of the following individuals: Pierre A. David, Baldwin-Wallace College; Eliezer Geisler, Northeastern Illinois University; Peter M. Ginter, University of Alabama at Birmingham; Kenneth W. Olm, University of Texas at Austin; Joseph A. Schenk, University of Dayton; Scott A. Snell, Michigan State University; Wilma D. Strickland, Northern Illinois University; and Rajaram Veliyath, Virginia Polytechnic Institute and State University. I also greatly appreciate the research, suggestions, and encouragement of my editor, Jayne Maerker, as well as the assistance of the entire staff at Harper & Row.

I also want to thank the staff of the library at Georgia Tech, who provided access to and assistance in the use of that excellent library, and my colleagues and friends at Atlanta University, who provided an environment that encouraged me in the development of this book. I wish to express special thanks to Luther S. Williams, president of Atlanta University; Creigs C. Beverly, academic vice-president of Atlanta University; and Robert A. Lynn, acting dean of the Graduate School of Business Administration of Atlanta University. I also sincerely appreciate the help of my secretary, Gwendolyn Donaway, in preparing the manuscript.

LLOYD L. BYARS

# STRATEGIC MANAGEMENT

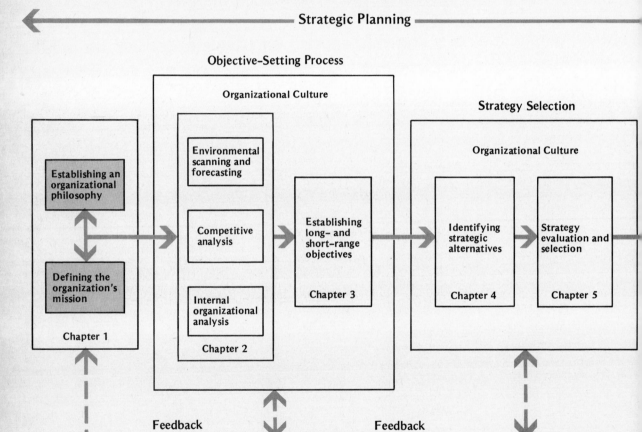

Strategic Management Process

Strategic Planning

Objective-Setting Process

Organizational Culture

Strategy Selection

Organizational Culture

Establishing an organizational philosophy

Defining the organization's mission

Chapter 1

Environmental scanning and forecasting

Competitive analysis

Internal organizational analysis

Chapter 2

Establishing long- and short-range objectives

Chapter 3

Identifying strategic alternatives

Chapter 4

Strategy evaluation and selection

Chapter 5

Feedback

Feedback

# PART ONE
# INTRODUCTION

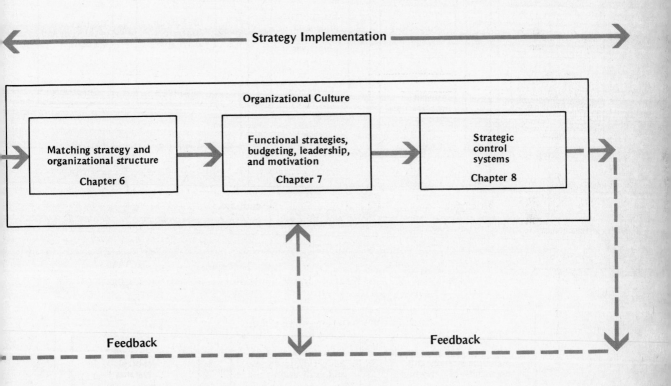

Strategy Implementation

Organizational Culture

| Matching strategy and organizational structure

Chapter 6 | Functional strategies, budgeting, leadership, and motivation

Chapter 7 | Strategic control systems

Chapter 8 |

Feedback                    Feedback

# Strategic Management Process

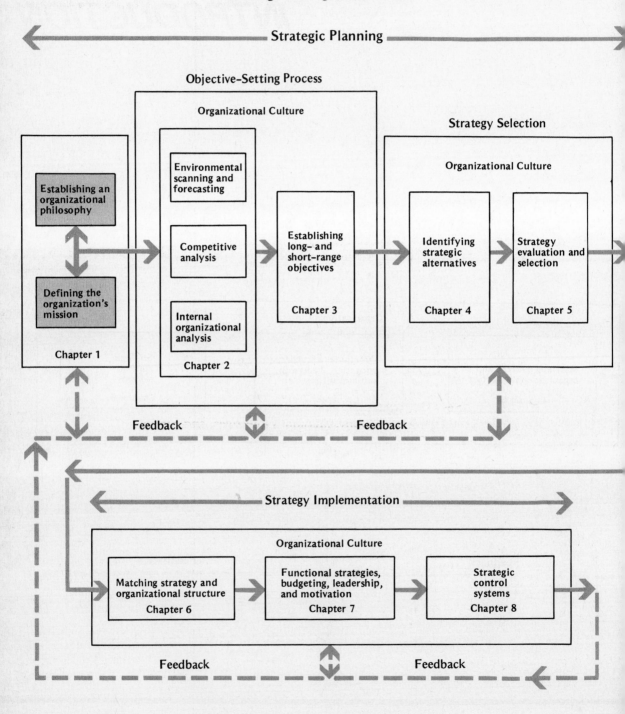

## Strategic Planning

### Objective-Setting Process

**Organizational Culture**

- Establishing an organizational philosophy
- Defining the organization's mission

Chapter 1

- Environmental scanning and forecasting
- Competitive analysis
- Internal organizational analysis

Chapter 2

- Establishing long- and short-range objectives

Chapter 3

### Strategy Selection

**Organizational Culture**

- Identifying strategic alternatives

Chapter 4

- Strategy evaluation and selection

Chapter 5

Feedback          Feedback

## Strategy Implementation

**Organizational Culture**

- Matching strategy and organizational structure

Chapter 6

- Functional strategies, budgeting, leadership, and motivation

Chapter 7

- Strategic control systems

Chapter 8

Feedback          Feedback

# 1 STRATEGIC MANAGEMENT: AN OVERVIEW

## STUDY OBJECTIVES

- To demonstrate the relationship between strategic management and organizational success
- To present an overview of the strategic management process
- To define strategic business units (SBUs)
- To describe the responsibilities of various levels of management in the strategic decision-making process

## CHAPTER OUTLINE

Strategic Management and Organizational Success
The Strategic Management Process
    Defining the Organization's Philosophy
    Defining the Organization's Mission
    Establishing Long- and Short-Range Objectives
    Selecting a Strategy
Integrating Philosophy, Mission, Objectives, and Strategy
Strategic Business Units (SBUs)
Making Strategic Decisions
Review Questions
Discussion Questions
References and Additional Reading

*Or suppose a king is about to go to war against another king. Will he not first sit down and consider whether he is able with ten thousand men to oppose the one coming against him with twenty thousand? If he is not able, he will send a delegation while the other is still a long way off and will ask for terms of peace.*—Luke 14:32

Over the years, some organizations have grown to be extremely large and profitable, while others have gone bankrupt. Some organizations have diversified into many new business activities, while others have not. Example 1.1 illustrates the changes that can occur in organizations from their initial date of incorporation.

In the decades to come, the increased rate of environmental, social, and technological change, the increased internationalization of business organizations, and the increased scarcity and cost of natural resources will make the environment of organizations even more complex. How do organizations make decisions about their future in this complex and changing environment? The process that is used is called *strategic management.* Specifically, *strategic management is concerned with making decisions about an organization's future direction and implementing those decisions.*

Strategic management is equally applicable to public, private, not-for-profit, and religious organizations. Strategic management concepts are as useful to a local restaurant, a small office supplies firm, or a college football team as to giant corporations such as Coca-Cola, IBM, or General Motors. Strategic management also applies to Georgia Tech, the Mayo Clinic, the Baptist church, Kiwanis International, the U.S. Department of Defense, the Ford Foundation, Sigma Mu Fraternity, and the NAACP. An attempt is made in this text to show the applicability of strategic management to all types of organizations. However, the main emphasis is on private enterprise organizations.

## STRATEGIC MANAGEMENT AND ORGANIZATIONAL SUCCESS

Many studies have examined a large number of organizations over different time periods, in different environments, and using different research methodologies to analyze the relationship between strategic management and organizational success.

One of the earliest and most comprehensive studies concerning the relationship between strategic management and success involved companies in the drug, chemical, machinery, oil, food, and steel industries.[1] The study divided the companies into one of two groups, depending on whether the company had a formal or informal strategic management system. Companies were classified as having a formal strategic management system if they determined objectives for at least three years ahead and if they established specific action programs, projects, and procedures for achieving the objectives. Companies that did not meet these requirements were classified as having an informal strategic management system. The performance of companies in each of these categories was then analyzed in

# STRATEGY IN PRACTICE

**Example 1.1** Experiences of Six Organizations

| Organization | Date of Incorporation and Initial Products/Services | Status as of 1986 |
|---|---|---|
| Beatrice Foods Company | Incorporated on November 20, 1924, as Beatrice Creamery Company. Primary product was milk. | Now called Beatrice Cos., Inc. Produces and distributes food-related products and a broad range of non-food-related products for use in consumer, commercial, and industrial products in both the U.S. and international markets.<br><br>Some of company's products include Samsonite luggage, Louver Drape window coverings, Cutty Sark, La Choy oriental vegetables, Tropicana orange juice, Wesson Oil, and Playtex tampons and brassieres. |
| Coca-Cola Company | Incorporated on September 5, 1919. Primary product was soft drink concentrates and syrups. | Largest manufacturer and distributor of soft drink concentrates and syrups.<br><br>Some of its other products include Minute Maid juices, Hi-C fruit drinks, and plastic packaging products. Acquired Columbia Pictures Industries, Inc., in 1982; produces and distributes motion pictures and television features.<br><br>Acquired Embassy Communications and Tandem Productions in June 1985; two television production companies which were privately owned. |
| Delta Air Lines, Inc. | Incorporated on December 31, 1930, as Delta Air Corp. Primary service was agricultural dusting operations in the South and Mexico. | Air carrier providing air transportation for passengers, freight, and mail over routes throughout the United States and abroad. |
| Federal Express | Incorporated on June 24, 1971. Primary service was delivery of packages and documents. | Company provides the same basic service. |
| IBM | Incorporated on June 15, 1911, as computing-tabulating-recording company. Primary products were time clocks and tabulating machines | Largest manufacturer of information-handling systems in world.<br><br>Some of its products include data processing machines and systems, information processors, electric and electronic typewriters, copiers, dictation equipment, and educational and testing materials. |
| W. T. Grant | Incorporated on November 27, 1937. Primary service was operating a chain of popular-priced department stores. | Company is bankrupt. The number of stores reached 1152. However, in 1976 the company declared bankruptcy and went out of business. |

terms of sales, stock prices, earnings per share, return on equity, and return on total capital. Those organizations with formal strategic management systems significantly outperformed the others on earnings per share, return on equity, and return on total capital. Although the sales and stock price appreciation for those organizations with formal systems were also greater, the figures were strongly influenced by a single company and therefore no inferences were drawn on those two items. A comparison was also made of the performance of the organizations with formal systems from the time they initiated the system to their performance over an equal period of time prior to the initiation of the formal system. Again, after the initiation of the formal system, the organizations surpassed their performance over prior years. A follow-up study of these same companies showed that those with formal strategic management systems continued to outperform those with informal systems and had, in fact, widened their margin.[2]

A study of 70 large commercial banks examined the financial performance (increase in net income and return on owner's equity) of those institutions with regard to whether they had a formal or informal strategic management system.[3] Again, those organizations with formal strategic management systems outperformed the other organizations. A study of 20 publicly listed firms in Australia concluded similarly that effective strategic management is significantly associated with higher levels of performance in profitability and return on invested capital.[4]

Some organizations, either through luck or the intuitive genius of their leadership, have been successful without formal strategic management systems. However, a study of 90 U.S. companies in the clothing, chemical, drugs and cosmetics, electronics, food, and machinery industries concluded that the management of any profit-seeking organization is delinquent if it does not engage in a formal strategic management process.[5]

## THE STRATEGIC MANAGEMENT PROCESS

A description of strategic management involves the use of various terms and expressions that have a variety of meanings and interpretations depending on the author and source. For example, some of the phrases used interchangeably with strategic management are *strategy and policy formulation, long-range planning,* and *business policy.* The purpose of this section is to define the terminology used in this text and to present a framework for analysis of the strategic management process.

As was stated earlier, *strategic management is concerned with making decisions about an organization's future direction and implementing those decisions.* Basically, strategic management can be broken down into two phases: strategic planning and strategy implementation. *Strategic planning* is concerned with making decisions with regard to

1. Defining the organization's philosophy and mission
2. Establishing long- and short-range objectives to achieve the organization's mission
3. Selecting the strategy that is to be used in achieving the organization's objectives

*Strategy implementation* is concerned with making decisions with regard to :

1. Developing an organizational structure to achieve the strategy
2. Ensuring that the activities necessary to achieve the strategy are effectively performed
3. Monitoring the effectiveness of the strategy in achieving the organization's objectives

## Defining the Organization's Philosophy

*An organizational philosophy establishes the values, beliefs, and guidelines for the manner in which the organization is going to conduct its business.* It establishes the relationship between the organization and its *stakeholders:* employees, customers, shareholders, suppliers, government, and the public at large. The importance of having an organizational philosophy was stated by Thomas J. Watson, Jr., former chairman of the board of IBM, as follows:

> This, then, is my thesis: I firmly believe that any organization, in order to survive and achieve success, must have a sound set of beliefs on which it premises all its policies and actions.
>
> Next, I believe that the most important single factor in corporate success is faithful adherence to these beliefs.
>
> And finally, I believe that if an organization is to meet the challenges of a changing world, it must be prepared to change everything about itself except those beliefs as it moves through corporate life.[6]

Watson went on to describe IBM's philosophy:

1. Respect for the individual. This is a simple concept, but at IBM it occupies a major portion of management time. We devote more effort to it than anything else.
2. We want to give the best customer service of any company in the world.
3. We believe that an organization should pursue all tasks with the idea that they can be accomplished in a superior fashion.[7]

Almost 20 years after Watson stated these three basic beliefs, IBM Board Chairman Frank Cary stated: "We've changed our technology, changed our organization, changed our marketing and manufacturing techniques many times, and we expect to go on changing. But through all this change, those three basic beliefs remain. We steer our course by those stars."[8] Example 1.2 shows the philosophy statements for Armstrong World Industries, J. C. Penney, SCANA (the holding company that owns South Carolina Electric & Gas Company), and the United States Copyright Office.

The philosophy of an organization is normally a rather permanent statement that is usually articulated by the chief executive officer. For small businesses, generally the owner establishes the philosophy either in writing or through his or her personal behavior. In many larger organizations, the founder of the business established the corporate philosophy and it is maintained throughout the life of the organization. For example, J. C. Penney and Thomas Watson, Sr., established philosophies for their organizations that are still in existence.

The content and specific wording of organizational statements of philosophy vary from organization to organization. However, Thomas Peters and Robert

## STRATEGY IN PRACTICE

**Example 1.2** Organizational Statements of Philosophy

**ARMSTRONG WORLD INDUSTRIES, INC.**

To respect the dignity and inherent rights of the individual human being in all dealings with people.

To maintain high moral and ethical standards and to reflect honesty, integrity, reliability, and forthrightness in all relationships.

To reflect the tenets of good taste and common courtesy in all attitudes, words, and deeds.

To serve fairly and in proper balance the interests of all groups associated with the business—customers, stockholders, employees, suppliers, community neighbors, government and the general public.

**J. C. PENNEY CO., INC.**

To serve the public, as nearly as we can, to its complete satisfaction.

To expect for the service we render a fair remuneration and not all the profit the traffic will bear.

To do all in our power to pack the customer's dollar full of value, quality, and satisfaction.

To continue to train ourselves and our associates so that the service we give will be more and more intelligently performed.

To improve constantly the human factor in our business.

To reward men and women in our organization through participation in what the business produces.

To test our every policy, method, and act in this wise: Does it square with what is right and just?

*Adopted 1913*

**SCANA (Holding company that owns South Carolina Electric & Gas Company)**

In pursuing our mission we realize that external events may create opportunities for us. Therefore, we encourage an entrepreneurial spirit among the employees of all SCANA companies in the pursuit of business opportunities within our purpose.

We believe that all business ventures and tasks within our organization should be pursued and accomplished with excellence.

We believe that present and future customers of our companies should receive superior service.

We also believe that the employees of our companies are our most valuable asset. Each employee will be treated with fairness, dignity, and respect.

We also intend to be open and honest in communications with our customers, regulatory bodies, stockholders, employees, and the public at large.

Finally, we recognize and intend to fulfill our corporate social responsibilities.

**UNITED STATES COPYRIGHT OFFICE**

All employees should treat one another with respect and dignity.

There should be an environment that encourages employee self-motivation and fulfillment.

The Copyright Office should aim to accomplish every task in a superior, professional, and responsible manner.

The public should be given the best and most courteous service possible.

*Source:* Public documents.

Waterman found that the philosophies of excellent companies included the following basic beliefs:

1. Belief in being the best.
2. Belief in the importance of the details of execution, the nuts and bolts of doing the job well.
3. Belief in the importance of people as individuals.
4. Belief in superior quality and service.
5. Belief that most members of the organization should be innovators, and its corollary, the willingness to support failure.
6. Belief in the importance of informality to enhance communication.
7. Belief in a recognition of the importance of economic growth and profits.[9]

If an organization's philosophy is to have meaning, it must be adhered to in all situations. Ignoring the organizational philosophy in crisis situations is a major mistake for the management of any organization. It is through the day-to-day decisions and actions of management that organizations and philosophies are confirmed and strengthened or become meaningless words on a piece of paper.

Finally, an organization's philosophy provides the general framework for the establishment of organizational policies. *Organizational policies provide guides to action for employees of the organization.* For example, after describing IBM's corporate policies, Thomas Watson, Jr., outlined one of IBM's corporate policies as follows:

> Open-door policy—Every employee has the right to talk to whomever they wish including any member of top management concerning problems, or concerns they have about management actions or decisions.[10]

Policies help to ensure that all units of an organization operate within the corporate philosophy. They also facilitate coordination and communication between various organizational units.

Several other factors influence the formulation of policies. One important factor has been federal, state, and local government. Government regulates organizations in areas such as competition (antitrust and monopoly), product standards (safety and quality), pricing (utilities), hiring practices (civil rights), working conditions (Occupational Safety and Health Administration, or OSHA), wages (minimum wages), accounting practices (income tax regulation), and issuance of stock (Securities and Exchange Commission, or SEC). Policies need to be developed in order to guide an organization's employees in meeting each of these regulations. For example, as a result of government regulation many organizations have developed a policy statement that declares the organization's unqualified opposition to all forms of discrimination.

Policies of competitors also influence an organization's policies. This is especially true with personnel policies such as employee wages and benefits and working conditions.

An extremely important consideration in policy formulation is that policies should facilitate the successful accomplishment of organizational objectives and implementation of strategy. All too frequently policies emerge from history, tradition, and earlier events. Changing environmental conditions and changed organizational objectives should trigger an evaluation of organizational policies to ascertain if they are still appropriate or should be changed.

**Defining the Organization's Mission**

An organization's *mission defines the current and future business activities of the organization.* Normally, it should include a broad description of the products, markets, and geographical coverage of the business today and within a time frame of three to five years. The establishment of an organization's mission is critical; without a concrete statement of mission it is virtually impossible to develop clear objectives and strategies.[11] It also provides a unifying force, a sense of direction, and a guide to decision making for all levels of management.

In recent years, many organizations have been troubled by the perception that they do not have a clear mission. For example, in 1983 Beatrice Foods, which was described in Example 1.1, announced that it was revising its strategy of growth through acquisition. With more than 400 companies within its corporate umbrella, the company had become unmanageable. Gulf + Western, ITT, U.S. Industries, and General Mills, Inc., have also been selling off many of their businesses at a rapid rate. Thomas Peters and Robert Waterman have concluded that most successful companies do have a sense of mission in that they stick to their knitting or, in other words, they make sure that things fit together.[12] A clear statement of mission is an essential first step in ensuring that all organizational activities do fit together.

Defining an organization's mission starts with a clear description of its customers. Questions that need to be answered in defining an organization's customers are as follows:

1. Who is the customer?
   a. Where is the customer located?
   b. How does the customer buy?
   c. How can the customer be reached?
2. What does the customer buy?
3. What does the customer consider value? (What does the customer look for when he or she buys the product?)[13]

Since a mission statement is also concerned with an organization's future business activities, its potential customers must also be described. Questions that need to be answered in describing an organization's potential customers include the following:

1. What are the market trends and market potential?
2. What changes in market structure might occur as a result of economic developments, changes in styles or fashions, or moves by the competition?
3. What innovations will alter the customer's buying habits?
4. What needs does the customer currently have that are not being adequately met by available products and services?[14]

One final question needs to be addressed in determining an organization's mission. Is the organization in the right business or should it change its business?[15] Example 1.3 illustrates several organizational mission statements.

An organization's mission not only must be defined at its inception but also must be reexamined regularly. For example, if the railroad companies had exam-

## JOHNSON CONTROLS, INC.

To be an industry leader in providing products, systems and services for control functions, the generation, management and storage of energy, and for the protection of life and property.

*Source:* Public company documents.

## McCORMICK & COMPANY

McCormick & Company will seek overall growth both from businesses in which it is now engaged, as well as new businesses. We define new businesses as products, services, customers, geography, or channels of distribution. However, these businesses will be relateable to and compatible with the areas or activity where we have strengths, are comfortable, and can perform well. Our "niche" will continue to be flavors, seasonings, and specialty foods, and the company will continue to pursue these opportunities within the food industry.

*Source:* Public company documents.

## COCA-COLA COMPANY

I perceive us by the 1990s to continue to be or become the dominant force in the soft drink industry in each of the countries in which it is economically feasible for us to be so. We shall continue to emphasize product quality worldwide, as well as market share improvement in growth markets. The products of our Foods Division will also continue to be the leading entries in those markets which they serve, particularly in the U.S. The Wine Spectrum will continue to be managed for significant growth with special attention paid to optimizing return on assets.

In the U.S. we will also become a stronger factor in the packaged consumer goods business. I do not rule out providing appropriate services to this same consumer as well. It is most likely that we will be in industries in which we are not today. We will not, however, stray far from our major strengths: an impeccable and positive image with the consumer, a unique franchise system second to none; and the intimate knowledge of, and contact with, local business conditions around the world.

In choosing new areas of business, each market we enter must have sufficient inherent real growth potential to make entry desirable. It is not our desire to battle continually for share in a stagnant market in these new areas of business. By and large, industrial markets are not our business.

Finally, we shall tirelessly investigate services that complement our product lines and that are compatible with our consumer image.

*Source:* Coca-Cola Company public document, "Strategy for the 1980s" by Robert C. Goizueta, adopted by board of directors on March 4, 1981.

## UNITED STATES COPYRIGHT OFFICE

To promote creativity in society, by administering the Copyright Law; creating and maintaining the public record through registration of claims and recordation of documents, including those related to compulsory licenses; providing technical assistance to Congress; providing information services to the public; serving as a resource to the domestic and international copyright communities; and supporting the Library of Congress by obtaining and making available deposits for its collections.

*Source:* Public documents.

ined and redefined their mission to be developing a firm position in the transportation business (rather than limiting themselves strictly to the rail business, which was their original mission), they might not be in the economic situation in which they find themselves today. In fact, the Southern Railway Company did define its corporate mission to be transportation services, and today it has the highest earnings per share of any company in the railroad industry. Southern achieved this position through careful acquisition of other railroads and by maintaining its stated mission of providing useful transportation services to its customers.

Several factors play a role in influencing a change in organizational mission. The most obvious is profitability considerations. Declining profits almost always force an organization to consider a change in its business activities. Changes in competitive position or top-level management personnel, new technologies, decreased availability or increased cost of resources, and changes in market demographics, government regulations, or consumer demand can also lead to a change in an organization's mission. A study in which 100 top managers in ten companies were interviewed over a period of several years outlined how the need for change in corporate mission is often recognized and should be implemented.[16] First, the need for change is often sensed by top management in quite vague or undefined terms (i.e., things just don't seem to be going right). Declining market share or profits often signal the need to reexamine an organization's mission. Next, top management should build an awareness of the need for change by forming study groups of company staff personnel and/or consultants to consider problems, options, contingencies, or opportunities posed by the need. Broadened support for the need to change is developed through consultation and participation by members of the top-management team. A clear focus can be gained by having an ad hoc committee formulate a position on the changed mission or by having the CEO express either in writing or verbally the changed position. The whole process of formulating an organization's mission is "a delicate art, requiring a subtle balance of vision, entrepreneurship, and politics."[17] Example 1.4 shows what can happen to a company when it doesn't change its mission.

Finally, it is important to note that organizational statements of philosophy and mission are not always separate and distinct documents. Often these statements are combined into one document, but that document still embodies the essential features of the philosophy and mission statements described in the previous paragraphs.

## Establishing Long- and Short-Range Objectives

*Long-range objectives specify the results that are desired in pursuing the organization's mission and normally extend beyond the current fiscal year of the organization. Short-range objectives are performance targets, normally of less than one year's duration, that are used by management to achieve the organization's long-range objectives.*

An organization's objectives depend on the particular organization and its mission. Although objectives can vary widely from organization to organization,

---

## STRATEGY IN PRACTICE

### Example 1.4 The Parable of the Ice Company

The Chicago Ice Company was a flourishing enterprise in the mid-1920s. If its CEO had been asked what business he was in, he very likely would have answered, "We make ice and haul it to homes."

This definition was predicated on what the company did—successfully. Suppose he had been asked about strategic challenges, "What are you going to do about the competitive challenge of those new-fangled refrigerators? What are you going to do about the changes in the market?"

Perhaps his answer would have been, "We're going to automate. We're going to put in centralized, high-technology, high-efficiency ice plants. We're going to double our efficiency in making ice. And we are going to get rid of our horses, which mess up the street anyway. We're going to buy trucks, and we're going to haul our ice more efficiently from our more efficient plants to the users. We have a sound technology plan and it is going to keep us doing what we are doing."

This was, in fact, what the company did, but alas, the Chicago Ice Company did not survive because there were some fundamental shifts in the marketplace, which management had not taken into account: Consumers simply found the new refrigerators, which did not depend on ice deliveries, far more convenient. In retrospect what was needed was a redefinition of the business—a new mission—rather than a piecewise automation of its functions.

Nowadays, the CEO might have said, in answer to the strategic challenge, that the firm was in the business of preserving food in homes. That response would allow management to look at other technologies for preservation of food. Or perhaps he might have said, "We are in the drayage business." Then maybe the firm would have concentrated on the trucking—not just [of] ice but other products as well.

*Source:* Adapted from James K. Brown, "Corporate Soul Searching," *Across the Board* 21 (March 1984): 47.

---

normally they can be categorized as follows: (1) profitability; (2) service to customers, clients, or other recipients; (3) employee needs and well-being; and (4) social responsibility.

The objectives of an organization are determined by the interaction among the following factors:

1.  Present condition of the organization as determined by an *internal organizational analysis.*
2.  External environment of the organization as determined by competitive analysis, environmental scanning, and environmental forecasting.
3.  *Corporate culture* of the organization. *Corporate culture is the values that set a pattern for an organization's activities and actions.*

The entire objective-setting process will be described in much more detail in Chapters 2 and 3.

**Selecting a Strategy**

The word *strategy* came from the Greek word *strategos,* which means "a general." Originally, strategy literally meant the art and science of directing military forces. Today, the term strategy is used in business to describe the steps taken by an organization in achieving its objectives and mission. Most organizations have several options available to them. Strategy is concerned with deciding which option is to be used. For example, in 1984, ITT sold the Continental Banking Company to Ralston Purina for $475 million. ITT's strategy was to divest itself of its business, while Ralston Purina felt that buying the business would better enable it to meet its objectives. *Strategy involves determining and evaluating alternatives available to an organization in achieving its objectives and mission and choosing the alternative that is to be pursued.* Strategy selection is examined in more depth in Chapters 4 and 5.

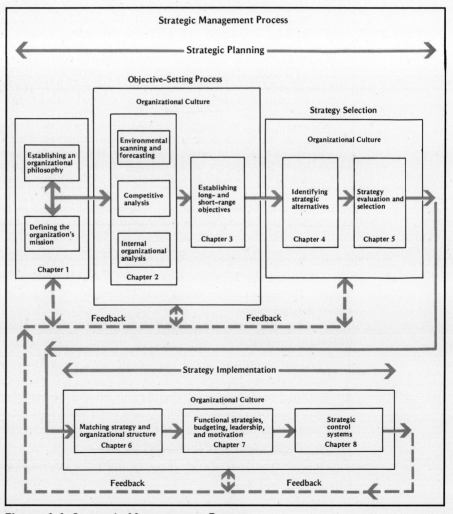

**Figure 1.1** Strategic Management Process

**INTEGRATING PHILOSOPHY, MISSION, OBJECTIVES, AND STRATEGY**

Figure 1.1 shows a framework that will be used throughout this text to analyze the strategic management process. Although the framework depicts a separate and sequential step-by-step process, the entire process requires considerable feedback among the various components. In fact, the components are inter-dependent and inseparable. For example, a change in an organization's environment could require a change in its mission and objectives. Furthermore, suppose a particular strategy has not achieved the objectives of the organization. Among other reasons, this could be a result of having established unrealistic objectives, having selected an inappropriate strategy, or having the wrong organizational structure. Thus, the dotted line in Figure 1.1 shows how feedback from each of the various components in the strategic management process has the potential to influence each of the other components in the process. Because this chapter defines a large number of terms, Figure 1.2 is presented in order to summarize these terms.

**STRATEGIC BUSINESS UNITS (SBUs)**

Before the various components in the strategic management process are examined, one final term needs to be defined. It is introduced here instead of later because it is used in discussions throughout the text.

---

*Long-range objectives* specify the results that are desired in pursuing the organization's mission and normally extend beyond the current fiscal year of the organization.

*Organizational mission* defines the organization's current and future expected business activities.

*Organizational philosophy* establishes the values, beliefs, and guidelines for the manner in which the organization is going to conduct its business.

*Short-range objectives* are performance targets, normally of less than one year's duration, that are used by management to achieve the organization's long-range objectives.

*Strategic management* is concerned with making decisions about an organization's future direction and implementing those decisions. It is composed of two phases: strategic planning and strategy implementation.

*Strategic planning* is concerned with making decisions with regard to determining an organization's philosophy and mission, establishing objectives, and selecting the strategy that is to be used in achieving the organization's objectives.

*Strategy* involves determining and evaluating alternatives available to an organization in achieving its objectives and mission and choosing the alternative that is to be pursued.

*Strategy implementation* is concerned with making decisions with regard to developing an organizational structure to achieve the strategy, staffing the structure, providing leadership and motivation to the staff, and monitoring the effectiveness of the strategy in achieving the organization's objectives.

---

**Figure 1.2** Definition of Terms

Normally, an organization's activities can be segmented into business units. *A business unit is an operating unit within an organization which sells a distinct set of products or services to an identifiable group of customers in competition with a well-defined set of customers.* [18] A business unit is normally referred to as a strategic business unit, or SBU for short.

William E. Rothschild, manager of corporate strategy development at General Electric, considers the following criteria in classifying an organizational unit as an SBU:

- First of all, an SBU must serve an external, rather than an internal, market; that is, it must have a set of external customers and not merely serve as an internal supplier.
- Second, it should have a clear set of external competitors, which it is trying to equal or surpass.
- Third, it should have control over its own destiny. This means that it must be able to decide for itself what products to offer, how and when to go to market, and where to obtain its supplies, components, or even products. This does not mean that it cannot use pooled resources such as a common manufacturing plant, or a combined sales force, or even corporate R&D. The key is choice. It must be able to choose, and not merely be the victim of someone else's decisions. It must have options from which it may select the alternative(s) that best achieves the corporate and the business objectives.
- Fourth, its performance must be measurable in terms of profit and loss; that is, it must be a true profit center.[19]

SBUs operate within the objectives and strategy that are set at the top management level. Within that framework, each SBU performs its own strategic management process. The SBU's operations are either strengthened or weakened depending on the resources that are allocated to it at the corporate level.[20] Example 1.5 shows how IBM has organized into independent business units which are analogous to strategic business units.

## MAKING STRATEGIC DECISIONS

Making strategic decisions is a function and responsibility of managers at all levels of the organization, but the final responsibility rests with top management. The top management of any organization has the final responsibility for developing the organization's philosophy and mission statements, establishing its objectives, and selecting its strategy. The strategic management responsibilities of managers at lower levels of the organization vary depending on the nature and size of the organization and their location within the organizational hierarchy.

In fact, most large organizations have a multilevel strategic management process.[21] Generally, the cycle of events goes as follows:

- Top management determines the corporate philosophy, mission, objectives, and strategy for the organization as a whole as well as guidelines for each of the businesses or SBUs.
- Each business unit or SBU then does its own strategic planning.

---

## STRATEGY IN PRACTICE

### Example 1.5 IBM's Independent Business Units

Early in the 1980s, IBM decided to set up independent business units (IBUs) to address specific business opportunities. Each IBU owns or controls all of the business functions essential for performance of its responsibilities. The development, manufacturing, marketing, service, and finance functions are contained within each IBU. An IBU is in effect its own business. Each IBU succeeds or fails on the basis of its own merit.

The IBUs report to an independent business unit committee which functions as a board of directors. In 1985 the following ten IBUs existed:

Academic Information Systems
Engineering Systems Products
Financial Services Business Unit
IBM Information Services
IBM Instruments
Low-end Storage Business Unit
Manufacturing Systems Products
Science Research Associates
Systems Products Business Unit
Work Station Business Unit

The number and exact composition of the IBUs change depending on market conditions. For example, an IBU was set up to develop IBM's personal computer. It has now been absorbed into IBM's normal structure.

---

- If the organization has a formal planning department, its function is to assist the business units or SBUs in their strategic planning or to supply information that the business unit or SBU may need.
- Top management then reviews and approves the strategic plans of each business unit or SBU.
- Each business unit or SBU then moves to develop a strategic plan for each of its functional areas (marketing, production, finance, R&D).
- After the development of strategic plans for each of the functional areas of the business or SBU unit, budgets are developed. As can be seen from this description, virtually all levels of management become involved in the strategic management process at some point.

## REVIEW QUESTIONS

1. What is strategic management?
2. Describe the relationship between strategic management and organizational success.
3. Define the following terms:
   a. Strategic planning
   b. Strategy implementation
   c. Organizational philosophy

    d. Organizational mission

    e. Long-range objectives

    f. Short-range objectives

✗ g. Strategy

4. Outline four criteria used in classifying an organizational unit as an SBU.

5. Describe the normal cycle of events in a multilevel strategic management process.

## DISCUSSION QUESTIONS

1. In 1985, United Airlines, Inc. (UAL) paid $587.5 million to purchase Hertz Corporation. What factors do you feel were considered by the top management of UAL in purchasing Hertz?

2. The final responsibility for strategic management decisions rests with top management. Since you are unlikely to enter an organization at the top management level, why is strategic management a required course at your college or university?

3. What do you feel would be the major differences in strategic management decisions made by a private enterprise and a not-for-profit organization?

4. What do you feel are the differences between a statement of corporate philosophy and corporate policies?

## REFERENCES AND ADDITIONAL READING

1. Stanley Thune and Robert House, "Where Long Range Planning Pays Off," *Business Horizons,* August 1970, pp. 81–87.

2. David Herold, "Long Range Planning and Organizational Performance: A Cross Validation Study," *Academy of Management Review,* March 1972, pp. 91–102.

3. Robley D. Wood, Jr., and R. Lawrence La Forge, "The Impact of Comprehensive Planning on Financial Performance," *Academy of Management Journal* 22, no. 3 (1979): 516–526.

4. David Burt, "Planning and Performance in Australian Retailing," *Long Range Planning,* June 1978, pp. 62–66. For another example of strategic management in a foreign country, see Egbert F. Bhatty, "Corporate Planning in Medium-Sized Companies in the U.K.," *Long Range Planning* 14 (February 1981): 60–72.

5. Delmar W. Karger and Zafar A. Malik, "Long Range Planning and Organizational Performance," *Long Range Planning,* December 1975, pp. 60–64. For other studies on the relationship between strategic management and organizational success, see C. B. Shrader, "Strategic Planning and Organizational Performance: A Critical Appraisal," *Journal of Management* 10 (Summer 1984): 149–71; and P. J. Carroll, "The Link Between Performance and Strategy," *Journal of Business Strategy* 2 (Spring 1982): 3–20.

6. Thomas J. Watson, Jr., *A Business and Its Beliefs* (New York: McGraw-Hill, 1963), p. 5.

7. Ibid., pp. 13, 29, 34.

8. Frank T. Cary, "The Remaking of American Business Leadership," *Think Magazine* 47, no. 6 (November–December 1981): 24.

9. Thomas J. Peters and Robert H. Waterman, Jr., *In Search of Excellence* (New York: Harper & Row, 1982), p. 285.

10. Watson, *A Business and Its Beliefs,* pp. 19–21.

11. For a more in-depth discussion on the importance of a mission statement, see J. A. Pearce, "The Company Mission as a Strategic Tool," *Sloan Management Review* 23 (Spring 1982): 15–24.

12. Peters and Waterman, *In Search of Excellence,* pp. 292–305.
13. Peter Drucker, *The Practice of Management* (New York: Harper & Row, 1954), pp. 52–54.
14. Ibid., p. 56.
15. Ibid., p. 57.
16. James B. Quinn, "Strategic Goals: Process and Politics," *Sloan Management Review* 19, no. 1 (Fall 1977): 22.
17. Ibid., p. 36.
18. Arnoldo C. Hax and Nicholas S. Majluf, "The Corporate Strategic Planning Process," *Interfaces* 14 (January–February 1984): 50.
19. William E. Rothschild, "How to Ensure the Continued Growth of Strategic Planning," *Journal of Business Strategy* 1 (Summer 1980): 14.
20. For additional information, see Boris Yavitz and William H. Newman, "What the Corporation Should Provide Its Business Units," *Journal of Business Strategy* 3 (Summer 1982): 14–19.
21. See, for instance, Jacques Horvitz, "New Perspectives on Strategic Management," *Journal of Business Strategy* 4 (Winter 1984): 19–33.

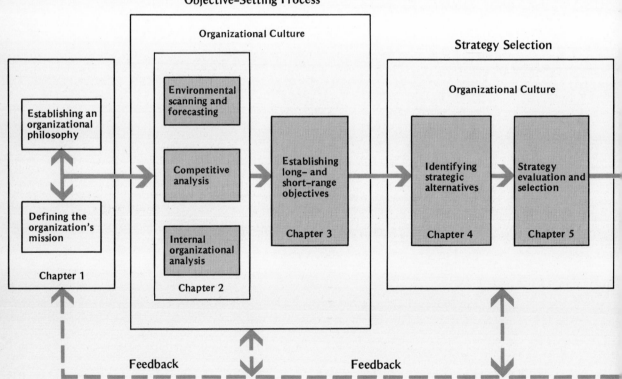

## Strategic Management Process

Strategic Planning

### Objective-Setting Process

**Organizational Culture**

**Strategy Selection**

**Organizational Culture**

Establishing an organizational philosophy

Defining the organization's mission

Chapter 1

Environmental scanning and forecasting

Competitive analysis

Internal organizational analysis

Chapter 2

Establishing long– and short–range objectives

Chapter 3

Identifying strategic alternatives

Chapter 4

Strategy evaluation and selection

Chapter 5

Feedback

Feedback

# PART TWO
# STRATEGIC PLANNING

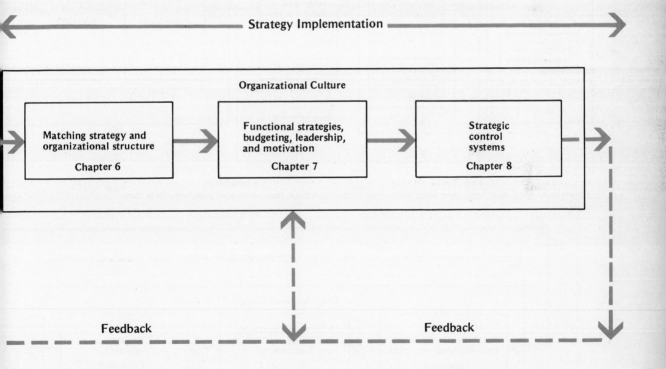

Strategy Implementation

Organizational Culture

| Matching strategy and organizational structure | Functional strategies, budgeting, leadership, and motivation | Strategic control systems |
|---|---|---|
| Chapter 6 | Chapter 7 | Chapter 8 |

Feedback          Feedback

# Strategic Management Process

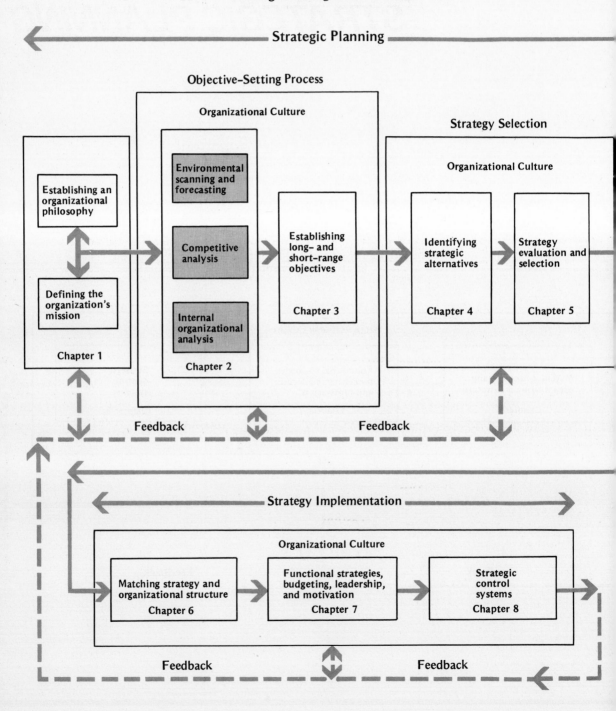

## Strategic Planning

### Objective-Setting Process

**Organizational Culture**

**Strategy Selection**

**Organizational Culture**

- Establishing an organizational philosophy
- Defining the organization's mission

**Chapter 1**

- Environmental scanning and forecasting
- Competitive analysis
- Internal organizational analysis

**Chapter 2**

Establishing long- and short-range objectives

**Chapter 3**

Identifying strategic alternatives

**Chapter 4**

Strategy evaluation and selection

**Chapter 5**

Feedback          Feedback

## Strategy Implementation

**Organizational Culture**

Matching strategy and organizational structure

**Chapter 6**

Functional strategies, budgeting, leadership, and motivation

**Chapter 7**

Strategic control systems

**Chapter 8**

Feedback          Feedback

# 2 ANALYZING THE EXTERNAL AND INTERNAL ENVIRONMENT

## STUDY OBJECTIVES

- To present methods and techniques used in environmental scanning and forecasting

- To discuss the methods used in performing a competitive analysis

- To describe the methods used in conducting an internal organizational analysis

- To outline a step-by-step procedure for conducting environmental scanning and forecasting, competitive analysis, and internal organizational analysis

## CHAPTER OUTLINE

Environmental Scanning
    Economic Forces
    Technological Forces
    Political and Regulatory Forces
    Social Forces
Establishing an Environmental Scanning Program
Environmental Forecasting
    Delphi Technique
    Brainstorming
    Scenarios
    Trend-Impact Analysis
    Economic Forecasting
Competitive Analysis
Internal Organizational Analysis
Procedures
Review Questions
Discussion Questions
References and Additional Reading

*The most reliable way to anticipate the future is by understanding the present.*—John Naisbitt, *Megatrends*

In making decisions about an organization's future direction, management must answer the following three basic questions:

1. Where are we now?
2. Where do we want to be (objectives)?
3. How do we get to where we want to be (strategy)?

Answering the first two questions is often called the objective-setting process. The purpose of this chapter is to describe the process used by organizations in answering the first question. Chapter 3 describes how organizations establish their objectives. Finally, the strategy selection process answers the third question and is described in detail in Chapters 4 and 5.

Answering the question "Where are we now?" should enable management to identify the organization's strengths and weaknesses as well as opportunities for and threats to the organization from its environment. The interaction among the following factors leads to this identification:

1. Environmental scanning and forecasting
2. Competitive analysis
3. Internal organizational analysis

Figure 2.1 illustrates the relationship among these factors. Environmental scanning and forecasting and competitive analysis identify threats to and opportunities for the organization. Competitive analysis and internal organizational analysis identify the strengths and weaknesses of the organization.

## ENVIRONMENTAL SCANNING

Organizations are also influenced by forces outside their industry. These forces may affect not only the success of particular organizations within the industry but also the industry as a whole. *Environmental scanning is the systematic methods used by an organization to monitor and forecast those forces that are external to and not under the direct control of the organization or its industry.* Organizations generally categorize environmental scanning into four areas: economic, political (including regulatory), social, and technological. The focus of scanning in each area is on trends that have organization-wide relevance.

## Economic Forces

Of the four areas, scanning in the economic area is probably considered the most significant. The general state of the economy (e.g., depression, recession, recovery, or prosperity), the level of interest paid by corporations and individuals, the unemployment rate, and the level of consumer income are key economic variables in corporate investment, employment, and pricing decisions. The rate of inflation and the growth rate of the gross national product (GNP) are additional economic variables that must be considered in the strategic planning process.

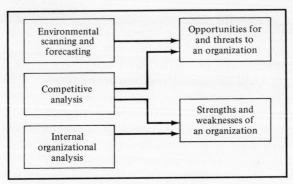

**Figure 2.1** Identifying Strengths, Weaknesses, Opportunities, and Threats

Economic factors that must be considered when an organization operates on a multinational basis include tariffs, payment for international transactions, government control over profits, and taxation. Tariffs are government-imposed taxes charged on goods imported into a country. They raise revenues for the country or protect the country's producers from the competition of imported goods.

International business also involves the exchange of currency between countries. Foreign exchange rates (the rate of exchange for one currency to another currency, e.g., eight French francs for one U.S. dollar) present problems because the rates can fluctuate dramatically in short periods of time. Furthermore, foreign governments sometimes limit the amount of profits that can be withdrawn from the country. Organizations operating in a foreign country are also subject to that country's tax laws.

Coalitions of cooperating countries are another economic force for multinational corporations. Two of the more important of these coalitions are the Organization of Petroleum Exporting Countries (OPEC) and the European Economic Community (EEC). The EEC or Common Market, as it is more frequently called, was organized in 1957. Its present membership includes Great Britain, Italy, France, West Germany, Denmark, Ireland, Greece, Belgium, Luxembourg, the Netherlands, Spain, and Portugal. The EEC's purpose is to reduce tariffs on goods sold among the member countries. OPEC is an oil cartel that includes most of the oil-producing countries of the world. Its purpose is to control oil prices and production levels among the member countries. The drastic increases in oil prices in the 1970s that resulted from OPEC pricing decisions significantly influenced the strategic decisions of many American companies. However, today the effectiveness and continued existence of OPEC has come under question since several of OPEC's member countries sell and produce at levels considerably different from official OPEC standards.

Other coalitions of cooperating countries have been formed by lesser developed countries (LDC). Two of these include the Organization of African Unity and the Latin American Integration Association. The purpose of these coalitions is to improve the economic conditions of the member countries.

## Technological Forces

*Technology is the systematic application of scientific or other organized knowledge to practical purposes and includes new ideas, inventions, techniques, and materials.* Technology has been traditionally associated with automated equipment or assembly lines, but this is an unnecessarily restrictive association. For example, a new method of planting trees could be considered new technology.

Technological forces influence organizations in several ways. First, technological developments can significantly alter the demand for an organization's or industry's products or services. Technological developments by an organization's competitors can make its products or services obsolete or overpriced. In international business, the use of more recent technological developments by an industry in one country often contributes to making the products produced in another country overpriced and noncompetitive. For example, the use of more sophisticated technology is one of the reasons that Japan is now a world leader in steel making, while the U.S. steel industry languishes. Technology itself cannot save the U.S. steel industry, but it can be an essential ingredient. New technology also influences organizations in that it can reduce costs ranging all the way from better utilization of raw materials to energy conservation.

## Political and Regulatory Forces

The political orientation (i.e., conservative versus liberal or Republican versus Democrat) of the U.S. House of Representatives, the Senate, and the presidency have an important influence on strategic planning decisions. For example, the Republican party has long been considered pro-business, and when it is in power both the legislative and executive branches of government are generally more favorably oriented toward business organizations.

In the regulatory environment, federal, state, and local governments have increasingly passed laws that influence how organizations operate. Federal laws have been passed that influence the hiring and firing of employees, compensation, working hours, and working conditions. Laws have also been passed that influence advertising practices, pricing of products, and corporate growth by mergers and acquisitions. In addition to these laws, governmental tax policies influence the financial structure and investment decisions of organizations.

Government agencies created by this legislation enforce most of the laws that make up the legal environment of organizations. Today, more than 75 federal agencies exercise some degree of control over business organizations. A brief examination of the function of just a few of these federal agencies, such as the FTC, the ICC, the FDA, the SEC, and the IRS, illustrates this impact.

The Federal Trade Commission (FTC) monitors the entire area of business competition and unfair trade practices, including such important aspects of business as advertising, pricing of products, and corporate growth by mergers and acquisitions. The Interstate Commerce Commission (ICC) licenses common carriers in interstate commerce and approves their rates. Similar agencies at the state level set rates and grant licenses for intrastate transportation and communication. Rates for telephone, water, gas, and electricity are set by these state agencies. The Federal Communications Commission (FCC) supervises all aspects of radio and

TV broadcasting, and the Food and Drug Administration (FDA) oversees the food, drug, and cosmetic industries. The FDA, for example, requires drug companies to submit proof that a drug is effective before it can be marketed. The Securities and Exchange Commission (SEC) oversees the issue and sale of investment securities. And the Internal Revenue Service (IRS) is responsible for the interpretation and application of the tax laws.

Not all government actions are restrictive in nature. Some have a direct and positive influence on organizations. For example, government purchases have a major influence in the aerospace, defense, and electronics industries. Government loans and subsidies have played a significant role in the farming industry and to companies such as Lockheed and Chrysler. The federal government can and does influence the level of foreign competition through the use of import quotas and tariffs.

During the 1980s, greater emphasis has been placed on the deregulation of business organizations. Budget cuts for many of the previously mentioned agencies have caused cutbacks in personnel, and these cutbacks have to some extent resulted in less government regulation. On the other hand, attempts have also been made to reduce federal subsidies for business by limiting Export-Import Bank funding, aid for synthetic-fuels development, and dairy industry price supports. These and other proposed initiatives make the assessment of political actions an essential element in strategic management.

In addition to the regulatory environment, a widening array of special-interest groups influence strategic decision making. The ethical investor movement, public interest groups, and the environmental protection movement are just a few of the groups that are moving strategic decision making from being merely a private management matter to more of a public interaction.[1]

Multinational organizations must also be aware of political risks and instability in foreign countries as well as political changes in the United States. Many multinational organizations now turn to consulting firms and private experts specializing in political risk forecasts that identify conditions that could lead to revolution or other types of turmoil.

## Social Forces

Social forces include factors that relate to the values, attitudes, and demographic characteristics of an organization's customers and employees. Dynamic social forces can significantly influence the demand for an organization's products or services and can alter its strategic decisions.

One recent, significant social change has been in the composition of the work force. Women now comprise over 44 percent of the work force and this percentage is forecast to increase through 1995.[2] Today the "traditional" household with a working father, nonworking mother, and dependent children represents only 15 percent of American households. Moreover, only 64 percent of American households have two adults.

Contrary to popular opinion, the 1980s should not be the age of the gray-haired revolution. The number of people over 65 has been forecast to grow only gradually from slightly under 25 million today to 30 million in 1990. Similarly, the number of people between ages 45 and 64 has been forecast to remain stable. The burgeoning growth for the 1980s is to be found in the group between ages 25 and 44. This group has been forecast to grow from 62 million in 1980 to 78 million by the 1990s.[3]

Another social change relates to the way people view work. Today, people are not as willing to work hard at boring jobs. People also want more in life than work. To most families the balancing of work and leisure is important. These values are likely to have a widespread impact on work scheduling, how work is organized, management practices, and pay systems. Determining the exact impact of social forces on an organization's objectives is difficult at best. Nevertheless, assessing the changing values, attitudes, and demographic characteristics of an organization's customers and employees is an essential element in establishing organizational objectives.

## ESTABLISHING AN ENVIRONMENTAL SCANNING PROGRAM

Three primary considerations in establishing an environmental scanning program are where the program should be located within the organizational structure, what sources of information should be scanned, and what system should be used in implementing the program. The location of the scanning program varies from organization to organization. Scanning programs have been placed in a separate corporate entity for scanning, the corporate strategic planning department, each individual strategic business unit, the legal department, the marketing research department, and the public affairs or public relations department.[4]

Daily newspapers are considered the most important sources of environmental information.[5] Trade publications are also useful in the environmental scanning of an organization's competition. Four other important sources of information are publications of research organizations such as the Brookings Institute and the Conference Board; business periodicals such as *Business Week, Fortune,* and *Forbes;* publications of consulting organizations such as the Hudson Institute, SRI International, and Data Research, Inc.; and government publications.[6]

Finally, the following guidelines have been proposed for implementing an environmental scanning program:

1. Place a senior manager in charge of scanning.
2. Identify a list of about 100 relevant publications.
3. Assign one publication per person to volunteers within the organization. Extremely important publications should be reviewed by the scanning manager.
4. Have each scanner review items in the publication that meet predetermined criteria based on the organization's mission.
5. Assign a predetermined code or keyword to the scanned information and prepare an abstract on the information in a few lines.
6. Submit the code and abstract to a scanning committee consisting of several managers to determine its relevance in terms of effect on the organization. The scanning committee should also add a relevance code.
7. Computerize the codes and abstract.

8. Prepare a newsletter to disseminate the information organization-wide. Encourage managers that are directly affected by the information to contact the scanning department for further analysis.[7]

## ENVIRON-MENTAL FORE-CASTING

No one can deny that economic, technological, political, and social change are a part of organizational life. Given that fact, the obvious question is, how can these changes be forecast?

To say the least, forecasting is a most difficult process. At this point it may be consoling to recall some humorous forecasting rules:

1. It is very difficult to forecast, especially the future.
2. Those who live by the crystal ball soon learn to eat ground glass.
3. The moment you forecast you know you're going to be wrong—you just don't know when and in which direction.
4. If you're right, never let them forget it.[8]

Regardless of the strong possibility of error, to be successful, organizations must forecast their future environment. Several studies have examined the impact of environmental analysis and forecasting on organizational performance. One study found that increased knowledge through environmental analysis and forecasting was positively correlated to profitability.[9] Furthermore, a study of 21 companies in the United Kingdom found that the companies that gathered and used more environmental information had a higher financial performance than those that used less information.[10] Several popular methods of forecasting are described in the following sections.

## Delphi Technique

The *Delphi technique* is a popular method of forecasting and can be used to forecast trends in economic, technological, political, and social forces. The Delphi technique can perhaps best be understood by examining it in the steps outlined below:

- *Step 1.* Experts on the subject being forecast are used.
- *Step 2.* The experts are kept apart and asked for their forecasts on the subject under study. The experts give their answers by a letter to a coordinating forecaster.
- *Step 3.* The coordinator determines the consensus opinion from the individual forecasts. Another questionnaire is then sent to the experts giving what the consensus opinion was and asking if they would like to change their opinion in light of the results. This step is repeated until the experts stop changing their opinions. When this happens, the final consensus opinion of the experts is used as a forecast for the subject under study.

Problems may arise in using the Delphi technique owing to the difficulty of accurately explaining the problem situation to the experts. Determining a consensus opinion from the individual forecasts may also be difficult.

**Brainstorming**

Brainstorming is a technique that is primarily used to produce creative ideas for solving problems, but it can also be used in forecasting. Basically, brainstorming involves presenting a particular subject to a group of people and allowing them to present their forecasts on the subject. Brainstorming generally consists of three phases. In phase one, members of the group are asked to present spontaneously their ideas on the future of the subject under study. The group is told that producing a large quantity of ideas is desired, and that they should not be concerned about the quality of their ideas. Four basic rules are observed in the first phase:

1. No criticism of forecasts is allowed.
2. No praise of forecasts is allowed.
3. No questions or discussion of forecasts is allowed.
4. Combinations and improvements of forecasts that have been presented are encouraged.

During the second phase, the merits of each forecast are reviewed, which often leads to additional alternatives. Alternatives with little merit are eliminated in this phase. In the third phase one of the alternatives is selected, normally through group consensus.

**Scenarios**

*Scenarios* (also sometimes called *scenario building*) are written narratives describing the future. Scenarios answer two kinds of questions: (1) What are the precise steps that might cause some hypothetical situation to develop? (2) What alternatives exist for preventing or facilitating the occurrence of the hypothetical situation? Normally, experts are asked to write scenarios that are then used by managers in examining contingencies that may face the organization in the future.

**Trend-Impact Analysis**

Trend-impact analysis is also used in environmental forecasting and is conducted along the following general steps:

1. Past history of a particular phenomenon is extrapolated with the help of a computer.
2. Panel of experts specifies a set of unique future events which could have a bearing on the phenomenon under study.
3. Panel of experts indicates how the trend extrapolation would be affected by the occurrence of each of these events.
4. Computer then modifies the trend extrapolation using these judgments.
5. Panel of experts then reviews the adjusted extrapolation and modifies the inputs.[11]

**Economic Forecasting**

Several approaches are used in economic forecasting. *Econometric models describe economic activity in terms of a system of mathematical equations.* These equations are designed to describe interrelationships among various sectors of the economy. The number of relationships specified in the model depends on many factors and determines how detailed a representation of the economy the model is. Of course, even the largest model in existence oversimplifies the workings of the actual economy. Econometric models are used not only to forecast economic variables but also to assess the impact of changes in government spending or proposed tax changes. Econometric forecasts are made by firms such as Chase Econometrics (Chase Manhattan Bank), Data Resources (McGraw-Hill, Inc.), and Wharton Econometric Forecasting Associates (Ziff-Davis Publishing Company).

*Leading indicators are also used in economic forecasting. A leading indicator is any measure of the economy that moves in the same manner as the economy but does so several months ahead of the economy.* Leading indicators are expected to give insight into questions such as: How many more months will the economy move upward? In what month will the economy begin to move downward? Some of the indicators that are used include plant and equipment expenditures, personal income, new orders for durable goods, and manufacturing inventories.

Surveys are also used in economic forecasting. Almost all economic data is compiled by means of surveys or interviews. Survey data is compiled by organizations such as the U.S. Department of Commerce, McGraw-Hill, Inc., *Fortune,* Dun and Bradstreet, and the Census Bureau. These organizations request and compile information from other organizations on such measures of economic activity as plant and equipment investment plans, sales expectations, and inventory plans. Generally, it is felt that surveys are more useful in short-term economic forecasting.

Most of the information already presented is concerned with forecasting variables for the economy as a whole. However, individual organizations must also be concerned with forecasting the demand for their industry's products or services and the demand for their specific products or services. One method of forecasting industry demand is trend analysis. *Trend analysis basically involves determining the pattern that exists in time-series data.* Trends can be either linear or exponential, and can be either increasing or decreasing. The major disadvantage to trend analysis is that it assumes that all of the major variables influencing the industry will remain constant. Dramatic changes in either political, social, or technological forces can change the trend projection.

Econometric models can also be used to forecast economic activity at the industry level. Industry econometric models use a set of mathematical equations to describe competing product demands, supplies, prices, general business conditions, promotional campaigns, and so on. These models are used to generate information on the elasticity of supply within the industry and the sensitivity of the demand for the industry's products or services to price, prices of competing products, and general economic conditions.

Multiple and linear regression and correlation analysis can also be used in industry forecasting. Linear regression expresses the statistical relationship that exists between two variables. Multiple regression attempts to link changes in the dependent variable to changes in two or more independent variables. Correlation analysis explains how closely two variables move together. Correlation techniques do not involve any implicit assumptions of causality, whereas regression techniques generally do.[12]

At the individual firm level, several methods are used in making economic

## STRATEGY IN PRACTICE

**Example 2.1** Executive Summary of Environmental Scanning and Forecasting for South Carolina Electric and Gas Company

Efforts to cut the federal deficit will be the major issue facing government at all levels in 1985 and beyond. Business will feel the results for many years of actions taken to bring about the reduction.

The recent trend of building energy-efficient homes and manufacturing energy-saving appliances will continue. Future electric-generating plants will be needed in smaller increments. More utilities will be announcing high-technology projects for future examination and development. The use of computers will continue to increase, helping to improve productivity. Fiber optics will be the premier communications technology in 10 years, but there is the potential of excess communication capacity. Increasing use of robots in the next decade will vastly improve the efficiency of industry but it could also displace thousands of workers.

Electricity is expected to have an increasing role in future energy markets. Its market share of delivered energy should increase from 13 percent in 1983 to 16 percent by 2000. The predominant share of generation growth will be in coal-fired capacity. Oil prices are expected to remain relatively stable through next year with no major increase expected until the end of the 1980s. If the United States should increase its use of foreign oil and prices are increased significantly, the role of natural gas becomes more attractive. Even with deregulation, gas prices are expected to remain relatively stable.

The Census Bureau has predicted that the U.S. population is likely to stop growing in the next century and may even decline. In the next five years the total population of the United States is expected to rise to approximately 250 million, reaching an estimated 260 million in 10 years. South Carolina's population is predicted to grow by 800,000 by the year 2000. Columbia is expected to be one of the fastest-growing metropolitan areas in the United States.

The trend in the future will be smaller households, meaning more meters but lower average usage. The consumer will increasingly demand reliable energy sources at low prices. The source or form of the energy will become even less important to consumers than today while sensitivity to price changes will grow. Other suppliers will try harder to gain market share so increased sophistication in marketing products will be required.

*Source:* Adapted from public company documents.

forecasts. First, informed estimates from an organization's managers and other personnel are frequently used to forecast specific economic variables. Trend analysis of internal company data is also used in forecasting for the individual firm. Finally, correlation analysis, multiple and linear regression, and econometric models can be used in forecasting economic variables for an individual firm. Example 2.1 is an executive summary of an environmental scanning and forecasting report for South Carolina Electric and Gas Company.

## COMPETITIVE ANALYSIS

Organizations do not exist in a vacuum. They operate within a competitive industry environment. Analyzing its competitors not only enables an organization to identify its own strengths and weaknesses but also helps to identify opportunities for and threats to the organization from its industry environment.

Michael E. Porter has postulated that the competitive environment within an industry depends on five forces: the maneuvering for position among the current competitors within an industry, the threat of new entrants into the industry, the bargaining power of customers, the bargaining power of suppliers, and the threat of substitute products or services being introduced into the industry.[13] Figure 2.2 diagrams these competitive forces.

One approach to competitive analysis is to use these five forces as a conceptual framework for identifying an organization's competitive strengths and weaknesses and threats to and opportunities for the organization from its competitive environment. For example, the "threat of new entrants" depends on the barriers to entry and reactions from existing organizations that the new entrant can expect. Porter identified the following six major barriers to entry:

1. Economies of scale—Here the basic notion is that as a plant or facility gets larger and volume increases, the average cost per unit of output drops because each succeeding unit absorbs part of the fixed costs, thus, new entrants would either have to make a large investment or enter at a cost disadvantage.
2. Product differentiation—Brand identification forces new entrants to spend heavily to overcome customer loyalty.
3. Capital requirements—The need to invest large amounts of capital in non-recoverable expenditures such as advertising and R&D creates a barrier to entry.
4. Cost advantages independent of size—Proprietary technology, assets purchased at preinflation prices, government subsidies, or favorable locations can also create barriers to entry.
5. Access to distribution channels—Limited wholesale or retail channels and the more that existing organizations have these tied up makes entry difficult.
6. Government policy—Licensing requirements and limiting access to raw materials are examples of government policies that can limit entry.[14]

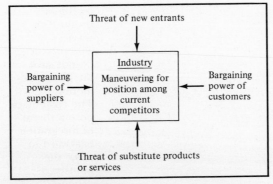

**Figure 2.2** Forces Governing Competition in an Industry

Figure 2.3 summarizes information about the five major forces that govern competition. Competitive analysis can then be conducted by collecting and assessing data about each of the subelements in Figure 2.3.

| Maneuvering for Position Among Competitors | Threat of New Entrants | Bargaining Power of Suppliers | Bargaining Power of Customers | Threat of Substitute Products or Services |
|---|---|---|---|---|
| Degree of competition depends on<br><br>1. Number of competitors and whether they are roughly equal in size.<br>2. Whether industry growth is slow.<br>3. Whether product/service lacks differentiation or switching costs. Switching costs are fixed costs buyers face in changing suppliers.<br>4. Whether fixed costs are high or product is perishable.<br>5. Whether exit barriers are high.<br>6. Whether rivals are diverse in stategies, origins, and culture. | Barriers to entry include<br><br>1. Economies of scale.<br>2. Product differentiation.<br>3. Capital requirements.<br>4. Cost advantages independent of size.<br>5. Access to distribution channels.<br>6. Government policy. | Power of suppliers is determined by whether<br><br>1. It is dominated by a few companies and is more concentrated than industry it sells to.<br>2. Its product is unique, differentiated, or has built up switching costs.<br>3. It poses a credible threat of integrating forward.<br>4. Industry is not an important customer of the supplier group. | A customer group is powerful if<br><br>1. It is concentrated and buys in large volume.<br>2. The products it purchases are standard or undifferentiated.<br>3. The products it purchases form a component of its product and represent a significant fraction of its cost.<br>4. It earns low profits.<br>5. The products are unimportant to the quality of the customer's product or service.<br>6. The products do not save the customer money.<br>7. The customers pose a threat of integrating backward to make the industry's product. | Substitute products that deserve the most attention from an organization are those that<br><br>1. Have trends improving their price performance trade-off with the industry's products.<br>2. Are produced by industries earning high profits. |

**Figure 2.3** Description of Forces Governing Competition
*Source:* Adapted from Michael E. Porter, "How Competitive Forces Shape Strategy," *Harvard Business Review* 57 (March–April 1979): 141.

Competitive analysis can also be conducted through the application of a comprehensive checklist of questions. Some of the key areas that might be examined about a particular industry include marketing practices, market structure, financial conditions, competitive conditions, operating conditions, and production techniques. Figure 2.4 gives typical questions that may need to be answered in performing a competitive analysis. Again, these questions are not intended to be all-inclusive. Other areas and questions may need to be added, depending on the nature of the industry.

Regardless of the method employed, the end result of a competitive analysis should give the management of an organization a comprehensive understanding of its competitive environment. This understanding should enable management to further assess its strengths and weaknesses and partially ascertain opportunities for and threats to the organization from its industry environment.

Example 2.2 gives some useful sources of competitive information. Appendix C in Part Four gives other sources for obtaining competitive information.

## INTERNAL ORGANIZATIONAL ANALYSIS

An *internal organizational analysis evaluates all relevant factors within an organization in order to determine its strengths and weaknesses.* One specific method used in performing an internal organizational analysis is through the application of a comprehensive checklist of questions.[15] This series of questions is normally developed for each functional area of the organization. A typical checklist might include the following areas:

1. Financial position
2. Organizational structure
3. Quantity and quality of both management and operative personnel
4. Product-market position
5. Condition of facilities and equipment
6. Marketing capability
7. Research and development capabilities
8. Past objectives and strategies

Figure 2.5 (p. 40) gives an example of a typical set of questions. Of course, the specific set of questions and the weight given to each question vary from organization to organization. Also, the specific set of questions must be tailored to each organization's unique requirements. However, the output that results from answering these questions should be a list of the most significant strengths on which the future of the organization should be built and the most significant weaknesses, which should either be corrected or avoided whenever possible. Appendix B gives useful information on how to analyze an organization's financial condition. Appendix C also provides useful sources of information to assist in performing an internal organizational analysis. Example 2.3 shows a strengths-weaknesses summary for a business unit of a large diversified company.

History
  1. What has been the nature of the industry: oligopoly, monopolistic competition, and so on?
  2. Is the industry declining, growing, stable?
  3. What unique features have made organizations in this industry successful?
  4. Are organizations in this industry conducting business on a regional, national, or multinational basis?

Marketing practices and market structure
  1. What is the sensitivity of this industry's products or services to fluctuations in the business cycle?
  2. What is the sensitivity of this industry's products or services to sudden shifts in customer desires?
  3. What channels of distribution are used in this industry?
  4. Have well-recognized brand names been developed in this industry? What are they?
  5. What pricing practices are used in this industry?
  6. Are there any specific packaging considerations?
  7. What are the industry practices on advertising and promotion expenditures?
  8. What major new products have been introduced within the past five years?
  9. Is there a large or limited number of customers for the industry's goods or services?
  10. Is new product development critical in this industry?
  11. What is the ease of entry or exit within this industry?
  12. Are there substitute products or services?

Financial conditions
  1. What are the capital requirements in this industry?
  2. What rates of return on investment are being achieved by organizations in this industry?
  3. What is the financial condition of organizations in this industry?
  4. What are the industry averages for financial ratios such as current ratio, acid-test ratio, inventory turnover, return on equity, earnings per share, and others?

**Figure 2.4** Questions for Developing a Competitive Analysis

## STRATEGY IN PRACTICE

### Example 2.2 Sources of Competitive Information

Annual reports and 10Ks are useful, but nonfocused, competitive information sources. Information can also be developed by research among sources such as distributors, end users, raw-material suppliers, substitute-product manufacturers, machinery suppliers, advertising agencies, investment bankers and analysts, and corporations formerly in the business at issue.

A sampling of other sources of pertinent data includes uniform commercial code filings; data available under the Freedom of Information Act, such as ERISA filings; state and local governmental agencies for such information as work force size, wage rates, productivity rates; court records involving matters of trade restraint; energy suppliers; IRS financial summaries for industries by company size.

*Source:* Adapted from R. E. MacAvoy, "Corporate Strategy and the Power of Competitive Analysis," *Management Review* 72 (July 1983):19.

Competitive conditions
1. What have been the pricing, advertising, and promotion policies of major competitors in this industry?
2. What have been the strategies of both successful and unsuccessful organizations?
3. Who are the industry leaders?
4. What is the market share of each organization in the industry?
5. Is competition in this industry based on price, service, availability of product, or quality of product?
6. Are there price leaders and price followers?
7. Does the industry have foreign competition? If so, what is the source of the competition and what significance does it play in this industry?

Operating conditions
1. What special skills and abilities are needed by an organization's employees in order to compete in this industry?
2. What is the union situation in this industry?
3. What raw materials are needed to produce this industry's products or services? Where are these raw materials located? Are they plentiful or in scarce supply? Are substitute raw materials readily available?
4. What is the nature and structure of the industry that supplies goods or services to this industry?

Production techniques
1. What production methods are used in this industry?
2. Are the production methods obsolete or state of the art?
3. Is there a minimum size for production facilities?
4. Have there been major innovations in production technology in this industry within the past five years?
5. Are organizations within the industry working at full capacity or do they have excess capacity?

## STRATEGY IN PRACTICE

**Example 2.3** Strengths and Weaknesses of a Business Unit of a Large Diversified Company

| Major Strengths | Major Weaknesses |
|---|---|
| Technical expertise in centrifugal area | Low market share |
| International sales force | Lack of product standardization |
| Heavy machinery capability | Fragmented product line |
| Business systems | Weak domestic distribution network |
| Puerto Rico facilities | High price image |
| Technically superior image among customers | |

*Source:* William R. King, "Integrating Strength-Weaknesses Analysis into Strategic Planning," *Journal of Business Research* 11 (December 1983): p. 483.

Financial position
1. What strengths or weaknesses emerge from an analysis of trends in financial figures such as earnings-sales ratio, earnings–tangible net worth ratio, earnings–working capital ratio, earnings per share, current ratio, acid-test ratio, inventory turnover, cash flow, and capitalization structure?
2. What do the trends in these financial figures indicate about the organization's financial position?
3. What percentage of profits comes from where?
4. Is there a program for increasing return on investment?
5. Does management understand the cost-of-capital concept?
6. Has management projected balance sheets and operating statements into the future?
7. Is there a cash management system?
8. Are capital expenditures appropriate for future operational needs?
9. Does management have the respect of the financial community?
10. Is the organization knowledgeable and aggressive in tax planning?

Organizational structure
1. What type of organizational structure currently exists?
2. Is there a formal organizational chart?
3. Are authority and responsibility relationships clearly established?
4. Are plans and controls in each organizational unit inadequate, adequate, or overdeveloped into a paperwork mill?
5. Is there a habit throughout the organization of reducing overhead, lowering break-even points, and improving quality?
6. Do all organizational units cooperate effectively in working toward organizational objectives?

Quality and quantity of management personnel
1. What person or group constitutes top management?
2. Has present top management been responsible for profit-and-loss results over the past few years?
3. What style of management is used by top management? (e.g., autocratic or participative?)
4. What influence or control does the board of directors exercise?
5. What are the capabilities of the members of the board of directors?
6. What is the dominant value system of top management?
7. What is the age of top management personnel, and how long are they expected to remain with the organization?
8. What is the quality of the middle management and supervisory personnel in terms of planning and controlling work, with regard to meeting schedules, reducing costs, and improving quality?

Quantity and quality of operative personnel
1. What are the skills and abilities of the work force?
2. Are these skills adequate for meeting today's and tomorrow's needs?
3. What is the general attitude and level of motivation of the employees?
4. Does the organization have enough skilled workers to meet its needs?
5. What is the wage policy of the organization? (e.g., are they paying the highest wages in their area or industry?)

Product-market position
1. What are the strengths and weaknesses in the organization's products or services: design problems, quality problems, delivery problems?
2. What is the pricing policy of the organization: price leader or price follower?

**Figure 2.5** Questions for Performing an Internal Organization Analysis

*Source*: Many of the questions were taken from or adapted from Robert B. Buchele, "How to Evaluate a Firm," *Management Review* 5, no. 1 (Fall 1962): 5–17; and David E. Hussey, "The Corporate Appraisal: Assessing Company Strengths and Weaknesses," *Long Range Planning* 1, no. 2 (December 1968): 19–25.

3. Does the organization hold any patents that give it a competitive edge over its competitors? When do these patents expire?
4. What share of the market does the organization's product(s) or service(s) currently hold? How firm is the hold on the market share?
5. Is the share concentrated with a small number of customers or is it diversified?
6. How do current and potential customers view the organization's products or services?
7. Are various product lines compatible marketing-wise, engineering-wise, and manufacturing-wise?
8. Is the market expanding or contracting and at what rate?
9. What is the trend in the organization's share of the market?
10. What is the product life-cycle stage of the organization's products or services?
11. Are the organization's products or services vulnerable to business cycle changes?
12. Are marketing research, research and development, and sales personnel working effectively toward the development of new products and services?

Condition of facilities and equipment
1. What is the nature of the production processes and the facilities? Are they appropriate to today's competition?
2. Are the organization's production facilities efficient?
3. Is there surplus capacity?
4. Is there room for expansion?
5. Are the equipment and facilities the most modern or are they obsolete?

Marketing capability
1. What channels of distribution are used?
2. How much of the total marketing job (research, sales, service, advertising, and promotion) is covered?
3. Is this capability matched with the nature and diversity of the organization's product line?
4. Is there a capability for exploiting new products and developing new markets?
5. Is market research capable of providing the organization with facts that will keep it customer-oriented?

Research and development (R&D) capability
1. What is the nature and depth of the R&D capability?
2. What has been the return on investment from R&D efforts?
3. Has R&D produced significant new products?
4. What is the nature and depth of engineering capability?
5. Have schedules been met by R&D and engineering for new product development?

Past objectives and strategies
1. What have been the major objectives over the past four years?
2. Have these objectives been achieved?
3. What strategies have been employed?
4. Have these strategies been successful?

Summary questions
1. Of all the factors studied, which, if any, is of overriding importance to the organization?
2. What factors are of major importance by virtue of the fact that they govern other factors?

Who is responsible for performing internal organizational analyses? Some organizations assign this responsibility to their planning department. Others contract with outside consulting firms. Recently, however, the trend has been toward having a team of line managers within the organization develop the analysis with technical assistance and coordination provided by the planning department. The premises for this trend are that if line managers develop the analysis, they will understand it, perceive its implications for the future direction of the organization, and use it as a guide for their own strategic planning decisions.[16] For example, if an organization has several strategic business units, a group of managers within each strategic business unit would be responsible for developing an internal organizational analysis for their unit. Each analysis would then be reviewed and approved by the top management of the particular business unit and by the top management of the organization as a whole.

**PROCEDURES**   The first part of this chapter dealt with suggestions for performing environmental scanning and forecasting, competitive analysis, and internal organizational analysis. The purpose of this section is to offer procedures that tie all of these suggestions together into a framework for analysis. Figure 2.6 shows this framework.

Environmental scanning and forecasting identify the key environmental forces and the trends in those forces in order to understand the threats to and opportunities for an organization. Competitive analysis partially indicates the threats to and opportunities for an organization. Competitive analysis and internal organizational analysis determine an organization's strengths and weaknesses. Answering the questions posed in Figures 2.4 and 2.5 provides a logical approach to developing a competitive analysis and internal organizational analysis.

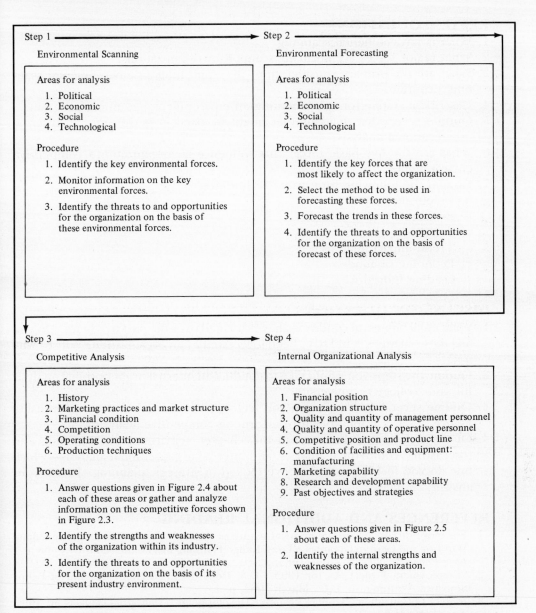

**Step 1** ────────────────────────────────→ **Step 2** ───────────────────────────────────→

Environmental Scanning

Areas for analysis

1. Political
2. Economic
3. Social
4. Technological

Procedure

1. Identify the key environmental forces.

2. Monitor information on the key environmental forces.

3. Identify the threats to and opportunities for the organization on the basis of these environmental forces.

Environmental Forecasting

Areas for analysis

1. Political
2. Economic
3. Social
4. Technological

Procedure

1. Identify the key forces that are most likely to affect the organization.

2. Select the method to be used in forecasting these forces.

3. Forecast the trends in these forces.

4. Identify the threats to and opportunities for the organization on the basis of forecast of these forces.

**Step 3** ────────────────────────────────→ **Step 4**

Competitive Analysis

Areas for analysis

1. History
2. Marketing practices and market structure
3. Financial condition
4. Competition
5. Operating conditions
6. Production techniques

Procedure

1. Answer questions given in Figure 2.4 about each of these areas or gather and analyze information on the competitive forces shown in Figure 2.3.

2. Identify the strengths and weaknesses of the organization within its industry.

3. Identify the threats to and opportunities for the organization on the basis of its present industry environment.

Internal Organizational Analysis

Areas for analysis

1. Financial position
2. Organization structure
3. Quality and quantity of management personnel
4. Quality and quantity of operative personnel
5. Competitive position and product line
6. Condition of facilities and equipment: manufacturing
7. Marketing capability
8. Research and development capability
9. Past objectives and strategies

Procedure

1. Answer questions given in Figure 2.5 about each of these areas.

2. Identify the internal strengths and weaknesses of the organization.

**Figure 2.6** Step-by-Step Procedures for Performing Environmental Scanning and Forecasting, Competitive Analysis, and Internal Organizational Analysis

## REVIEW QUESTIONS

1. What is environmental scanning?
2. What major forces are normally scanned by organizations?
3. What are the primary considerations in establishing an environmental scanning program?
4. Describe a system for implementing an environmental scanning program.
5. Outline a checklist of items that might be used in performing an internal organizational analysis.
6. What are the five basic forces that influence an organization's competitive environment?
7. Explain the following forecasting techniques:
   a. Delphi technique
   b. Brainstorming
   c. Scenarios
   d. Trend-impact analysis
   e. Econometric models
   f. Leading indicators

## DISCUSSION QUESTIONS

1. What environmental conditions have changed over the past five years? Do you feel these changes could have been forecasted by an organization? Why or why not?
2. Outline the steps you would take to conduct an internal organizational analysis for your college or university.
3. Outline several questions that you feel would need to be answered in using Figure 2.3 as a framework for performing competitive analysis.
4. Of the three areas discussed in this chapter—environmental scanning and forecasting, competitive analysis, and internal organizational analysis—which one do you feel is most often overlooked in strategic planning? Justify your answer.

## REFERENCES AND ADDITIONAL READING

1. For more discussion on the political nature of strategic decision making, see Duane Windsor and George Greanias, "Long-Range Planning in a Politicized Environment," *Long Range-Planning* 16 (June 1983):82–91.
2. "Employment Projections for 1995," U.S. Department of Labor, Bureau of Labor Statistics, Washington, D.C., March 1984, p. 1.
3. John C. O'Callaghan, "Human Resource Development," *Managerial Planning* 30 (July–August 1981):38–39.
4. Jeremiah J. O'Connell and John W. Zimmerman, "Scanning the International Environment," *California Management Review* 22 (Winter 1979):15–23.
5. Sabhash C. Jain, "Environmental Scanning in U.S. Corporations," *Long Range Planning* 17 (April 1984):122.
6. Ibid., p. 122.
7. Ibid., pp. 124–125.
8. Edgar R. Fiedler, "Fiedler's Forecasting Rules," *Reader's Digest,* March 1979, p. 100.
9. Joseph Wolf, "Learning Styles Rewarded in a Complex Simulation with Implications

for Business Policy and Organizational Behavior Research," *Academy of Management Proceedings,* August 1976, p. 167.

10. P. H. Grinyer and D. Norburn, "Planning for Existing Markets," *International Studies of Management and Organization* 7 (Fall–Winter 1977–1978):116.

11. Jain, "Environmental Scanning in U.S. Corporations," p. 126.

12. Dale G. Bails and Larry C. Peppers, *Business Fluctuations* (Englewood Cliffs, N.J.: Prentice-Hall, 1982), p. 161.

13. See Michael E. Porter, "How Competitive Forces Shape Strategy," *Harvard Business Review* 57 (March–April 1979):137–45; and Michael E. Porter, *Competitive Strategy* (New York: Free Press, 1980).

14. Porter, "How Competitive Forces Shape Strategy," pp. 138–139.

15. For additional information on checklists, see Stephen C. South, "A Competitive Advantage: The Cornerstone of Strategic thinking," *Journal of Business Strategy* 1 (Spring 1981):15–25; and Howard Stevenson, "Defining Strengths and Weaknesses," *Sloan Management Review* 17 (Spring 1976):51–68.

16. William R. King, "Integrating Strength-Weakness Analysis into Strategic Planning," *Journal of Business Research* 11 (December 1983):479.

# Strategic Management Process

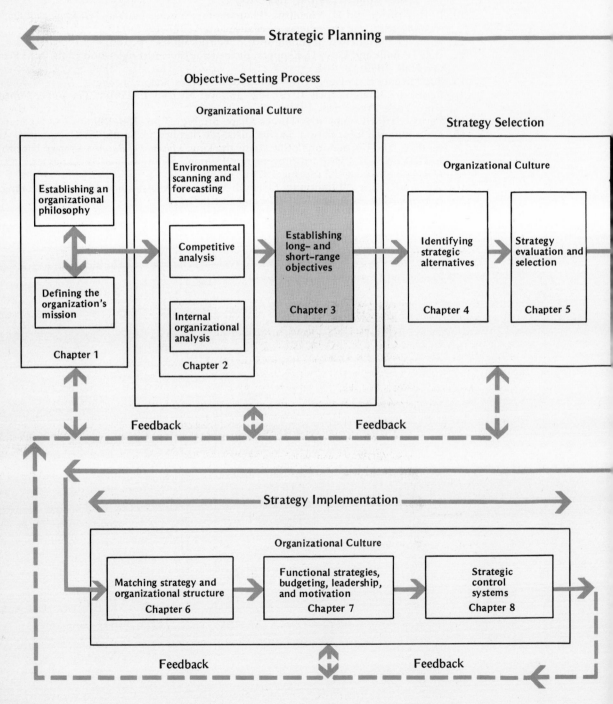

**Strategic Planning**

### Objective-Setting Process

Organizational Culture

**Strategy Selection**

Organizational Culture

Establishing an organizational philosophy

Defining the organization's mission

Chapter 1

Environmental scanning and forecasting

Competitive analysis

Internal organizational analysis

Chapter 2

Establishing long- and short-range objectives

Chapter 3

Identifying strategic alternatives

Chapter 4

Strategy evaluation and selection

Chapter 5

Feedback        Feedback

**Strategy Implementation**

Organizational Culture

Matching strategy and organizational structure

Chapter 6

Functional strategies, budgeting, leadership, and motivation

Chapter 7

Strategic control systems

Chapter 8

Feedback        Feedback

# 3 *ORGANIZATIONAL CULTURE AND THE OBJECTIVE-SETTING PROCESS*

## STUDY OBJECTIVES

- To describe the process of establishing objectives within an organization
- To define organizational culture and discuss its role in establishing objectives
- To provide potential areas for establishing objectives for most organizations
- To illustrate the cascade approach to objective setting

## CHAPTER OUTLINE

The Objective-Setting Process
Organizational Culture
    Origin of Organizational Cultures
        History
        Environment
        Staffing Process
        Socialization Process
    Identifying and Classifying Organizational Cultures
    Changing Organizational Cultures
Mix of Organizational Objectives
Cascade Approach to Establishing Objectives
Review Questions
Discussion Questions
References and Additional Reading

*Of course, objectives are not a railroad timetable. They can be compared to the compass bearing by which a ship navigates. The compass bearing itself is firm, pointing in a straight line toward the desired port. But in actual navigation the ship will veer off its course for many miles to avoid a storm. She will slow down to a walk in a fog and heave to altogether in a hurricane. She may even change destination in mid-ocean and set a new compass bearing toward a new port—perhaps because war has broken out, perhaps only because her cargo has been sold in mid-passage. Still, four-fifths of all voyages end in the intended port at the originally scheduled time. And without a compass bearing, the ship would neither be able to find the port nor be able to estimate the time it will take to get there.*—Peter F. Drucker, *The Practice of Management*

The compass bearing for organizations is their objectives. The purpose of the management of any organization is to lead and motivate the employees of the organization toward the accomplishment of the organization's objectives. *Long-range objectives specify the results that are desired in pursuing the organization's mission and normally extend beyond the current fiscal year of the organization.* Short-range objectives should follow logically from long-range objectives. *Short-range objectives are performance targets, normally of less than one year's duration, that serve to achieve the organization's long-range objectives.*

## THE OBJECTIVE-SETTING PROCESS

The objectives of an organization result from the interaction among the following factors:

1. Environmental scanning and forecasting
2. Competitive analysis
3. Internal organizational analysis
4. Organizational culture

Figure 3.1 shows the interrelationships among these factors in establishing organizational objectives. Internal organizational analysis and competitive analysis should identify the strengths and weaknesses of the organization. Competitive analysis and environmental scanning and forecasting should identify threats to and opportunities for the organization. All of these factors were described in detail in Chapter 2. However, overlapping these factors is the organizational culture, which has a crucial role in the selection of an organization's objectives. An organization's culture also has a significant influence on the strategy selection and strategy implementation processes.

## ORGANIZATIONAL CULTURE

Anthropologists have defined culture as a set of habitual and traditional ways of thinking, feeling, and reacting that are characteristic of the ways a particular society meets its problems at a particular point in time.[1] Organizations also have cultures. *Organizational culture is the pattern of beliefs and expectations shared by the organization's members which powerfully shape the behavior of individuals and groups within the organization.*[2] Organizational cultures provide a guide to how things are done

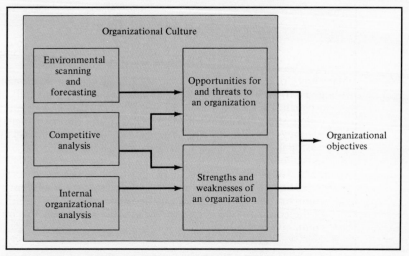

**Figure 3.1** Establishing an Organization's Objectives

---

## STRATEGY IN PRACTICE

### Example 3.1 Corporate Cultures

Atlantic Richfield—Emphasis on entrepreneurship encourages individual action. Lower-level employees have the authority to bid on promising oil fields without getting the advance approval of top management.

Delta Air Lines—Customer service and family feeling among employees produce a high degree of teamwork. Employees gladly substitute on other jobs to keep planes flying and baggage moving.

Digital Equipment—With emphasis on innovation, employees are allowed to set their own working style, but are also expected to demonstrate evidence of progress.

IBM—Emphasis on high-quality service has created an environment driven by the satisfaction of customer needs. IBM maintains a hot line around the clock, seven days a week, to service its products.

*Source:* Adapted from "Corporate Culture: The Hard to Change Values That Spell Success or Failure," *Business Week,* October 27, 1980, p. 148.

---

and how people relate within the organization. Example 3.1 summarizes cultural characteristics of some well-known companies.

Culture in an organization is analogous to personality in an individual. Just as people have relatively enduring and stable traits which influence their attitudes and behaviors, so do organizations. In addition, certain groups of traits or personality types can be identified because they consist of common elements. Organizations can be described in similar terms: warm, aggressive, friendly, open, innovative, conservative, and so forth. An organization's culture is transmitted in many ways, including long-standing and often unwritten rules, shared standards about what is important, prejudices, standards for social etiquette and demeanor,

---

## STRATEGY IN PRACTICE

### Example 3.2 Unusual Company Customs

Mary Kay Cosmetics—Cadillacs painted in a distinctive shade, called Mary Kay pink, are given to each year's top sales people; on their birthdays all company employees get a voucher for a free lunch for two and a birthday card; no one in the company is called Miss, Mrs., Mr., or Ms., or has a title on his or her door.

J. C. Penney—Employees who are promoted to a certain level are given a shiny black wastepaper basket instead of the drab-colored ones that are reportedly the lot of most Penney people.

Campbell Soup—Supervisors share their offices with their secretaries.

Reader's Digest—Employees at company headquarters can rent a garden plot from the company on company land. Furthermore, during the month of May, all employees of the company can garden or do anything else they like on Fridays; "TGIF" is a companywide holiday.

*Source:* Adapted from Susan Narod, "Off-Beat Company Customs," *Dun's Business Month* 124 (November 1984): 65–75.

---

established customs on how to relate to peers, subordinates, and superiors, and other traditions that clarify to employees what is and is not appropriate behavior. Example 3.2 shows some unusual customs in organizations that create and shape corporate culture. In summary, corporate culture communicates how people in the organization should behave by establishing a value system and conveying the value system through rites, rituals, myths, legends, and actions.

**Origin of Organizational Cultures**
Ideally, an organization's culture should develop and evolve from its statement of philosophy. However, it is not unusual for an organization's culture to be different from the ideals expressed in the corporate philosophy. The clearest understanding of an organization's culture comes from an examination of the practices of its management team. The day-to-day behaviors of management shape and determine the culture.

Many organizations trace their culture to an individual who personified the major values of the organization. Robert Wood Johnson of Johnson & Johnson, Harley Procter of Procter & Gamble, Walt Disney of Walt Disney Productions, and Thomas J. Watson, Jr., of IBM left their imprint on their organizations. In organizations that cannot point to such an influencial founder or other top manager, culture appears to develop in response to the specific environment in which the organization operates and to the needs of its employees. Four factors that contribute to the origin of an organization's culture have been identified: its history, environment, staffing process, and socialization process.

**History**  Employees are aware of the organization's past and this awareness builds culture. To a great extent, the way things are done is a continuation of the way things have always been done. The existing values, which may have been deliberately established, are continuously and subtly reinforced by experiences.

The status quo is also reinforced by the tendency of people to resist strongly changes in beliefs and values. For example, executives of Walt Disney Productions reportedly pick up litter unconsciously because of the Disney vision of an immaculate Disneyland.[3]

**Environment**   Because all organizations must interact with their environment, the environment plays an important role in shaping an organization's culture. Organizations that operate within a highly regulated environment, such as public utilities, develop cultures totally different from organizations that face fierce competition in industries with rapidly changing technology, such as the computer industry. In fact, since deregulation, many organizations in the communications, banking, and airlines industries are no longer sheltered by their regulated environment and must change their cultures. The question is whether the change can come fast enough to ensure their success and survival.

**Staffing Process**   Organizations tend to hire, retain, and promote people who are similar to current employees in important ways. A person's ability to fit in can be an important criterion in these processes. This criterion helps to ensure that current values are accepted and that potential challenges of "how we do things" are screened out.

**Socialization Process**   New employees also learn the organization's culture from their orientation program and their actual work experiences. Companies such as IBM, Procter & Gamble, and Morgan Stanley have formal orientation programs that teach the basic values of these companies. Furthermore, compensation systems, performance appraisal systems, and promotion systems communicate and reinforce the organization's culture.

**Identifying and Classifying Organizational Cultures**

Seven characteristics have been identified that, when taken together, capture the essence of an organization's culture:

1. *Individual Autonomy.*   Degree of responsibility, independence, and opportunities for exercising initiative that individuals in the organization have.
2. *Structure.*   Number of rules and regulations and amount of direct supervision that is used to oversee and control employee behavior.
3. *Support.*   Degree of assistance and warmth that managers give their subordinates.
4. *Identification.*   Degree to which employees identify with the organization as a whole rather than with their particular work group or field of professional expertise.
5. *Performance-Reward.*   Degree to which reward allocations in the organization (i.e., salary increases, promotions) are based on performance criteria.
6. *Conflict Tolerance.*   Degree of conflict present in relationships between peers and work groups as well as willingness to be honest and open about differences.
7. *Risk Tolerance.*   Degree to which employees are encouraged to be aggressive, innovative, and risk-seeking.[4]

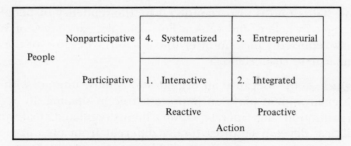

**Figure 3.2** Organizational Culture Grid
*Source:* Adapted from Robert C. Ernest, "Corporate Cultures and Effective Planning," *Personnel Administrator* 30 (March 1985):52.

Each of these characteristics should be viewed as lying on a continuum that ranges from low to high. One can form a picture of the overall organizational culture by appraising an organization on each of them.

Many distinct organizational cultures exist, and several methods have been proposed for classifying cultures. One approach is called the organizational culture grid.[5] The two dimensions on the grid used to identify culture are actions and people. Actions are the processes used by an organization in making decisions, organizing, monitoring, implementing plans, and generating ideas. In this dimension, organizations are classified as reactive (responding to the external environment) or proactive (actively shaping the external environment). The people dimension refers to the degree of interaction, relationship, and communication among both employees and customers. Participative cultures would be strong in communications and responsive to the needs, concerns, and ideas of both employees and customers. Organizations that are low on this dimension are likely to maintain nonparticipative relationships with employees and customers.

Four major organizational cultures emerge from this two-dimensional grid, as illustrated in Figure 3.2:

1. *Interactive Cultures.* These cultures are strongly oriented to satisfying the needs of employees and customers. Good service is an important aspect of these cultures. Interactive cultures respond to competition and new technologies rather than shaping the environment.
2. *Integrated Cultures.* These cultures are also strongly oriented to satisfying the needs of employees and customers, but are innovative in new products or services.
3. *Entrepreneurial Cultures.* Highly innovative in developing new products and services, these cultures generally have a low orientation toward people in that decision making tends to be nonparticipative.
4. *Systematized Cultures.* These cultures focus on maintaining procedures, policies, and systems of ongoing activities. Decision making is driven primarily by the external environment.

A classification of the corporate cultures of several organizations as they have been described in the media illustrates the use of the grid (see Figure 3.3). For example, Apple Computer has been designated as being proactive in the develop-

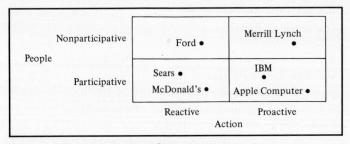

**Figure 3.3 Hypothetical Cultures**
*Source:* Adapted from Robert C. Ernest, "Corporate Cultures and Effective Planning." *Personnel Administrator* 30 (March 1985):54–55.

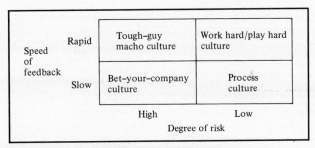

**Figure 3.4 Types of Organizational Cultures**

ment of new products and very high on people. Thus, it would be classified as strongly integrated. IBM would also be classified as integrated, but would probably be closer to the center due to a combination of other cultural elements. Sears and McDonald's are both hypothesized to be interactive and illustrate that companies in different industries can have similar cultures. Ford is hypothesized to have a systematized culture, whereas Merrill Lynch is hypothesized to have an entrepreneurial culture.

Another method of classifying cultures uses four categories which are determined by (1) the degree of risk associated with the organization's activities and (2) the speed with which organizations and their employees get feedback on whether their strategic decisions are successful.[6] Terrence Deal and Allan Kennedy, who developed this classification scheme, identified the four basic cultures as follows: tough-guy, macho culture; work hard/play hard culture; bet-your-company culture; and process culture. Figure 3.4 shows the four cultures in matrix form.

Terrence and Deal described the four cultures as follows:

1. *Tough-Guy Macho Culture.* This type of culture is characterized by individualists who regularly take high risks and get quick feedback on whether their decisions are right or wrong. Teamwork is not important and every colleague is a potential rival. In this culture the value of cooperation is ignored and there is no opportunity to learn from mistakes. It tends to reward individuals who are temperamental and shortsighted. Organizations that fall in this category include construction, cosmetics, management consulting, venture capi-

tal, advertising, television, movies, publishing, sports, and the entire entertainment industry.

2. *Work Hard/Play Hard Culture.*    This culture encourages employees to take
few risks and to expect rapid feedback. In this culture activity is the key to
success. Rewards accrue to persistence and the ability to find a need and fill
it. Because of the need for volume, team players who are friendly and outgoing thrive. Organizations in this category include real estate agents, computer
companies, automotive distributors, door-to-door sales companies such as
Mary Kay, mass consumer sales companies such as McDonald's, office equipment manufacturers such as Xerox, and retail stores.

3. *Bet-Your-Company Culture.*    These cultures require big-stakes decisions that
take considerable time before the results are known. Pressures to make the
right decisions are always present in this environment. Organizations in this
category include capital goods companies, mining and smelting companies,
oil companies, investment banks, architectural firms, and computer manufacturers.

4. *Process Culture.*    This culture involves low risk coupled with little feedback;
employees must focus on how things are done rather than the outcomes.
Employees in this atmosphere become cautious and protective. Those who
thrive are orderly, punctual, and detail-oriented. Organizations in this category include banks, insurance companies, financial-service organizations,
government, utilities, and pharmaceutical companies.

It should be obvious that no organization will precisely fit into either one of
these classification methods. In fact, within any organization there may be a mix
of cultures. For example, sales may be closer to the work hard/play hard category
and research and development may be closer to a bet-your-company category.
However, either one of the classification methods discussed in this section can be
a useful starting point in identifying an organization's culture.

## Changing Organizational Cultures

Organizational objectives are sometimes not achieved and strategies are ineffective because of their incompatibility with the organization's culture. However,
changing a corporate culture is a long, difficult process. In fact, massive cultural
reorientations are probably unreasonable in most situations. Allen Kennedy, an
expert on organizational culture, believes there are only five reasons to justify
large-scale cultural change: if the company has strong values that don't fit its
changing environment; if the industry is very competitive and moves with light-
ning speed; if the company is mediocre or worse; if the company is about to join
the ranks of the very largest companies; or if it is smaller but growing rapidly.[7]
Example 3.3 describes the cultural changes facing AT&T.

Although massive cultural reorientations may be unreasonable in most situations, it is still possible to strengthen or fine-tune the current situation. A statement of corporate philosophy that is consistently reinforced by the policies and
procedures of the company is a useful tool for strengthening the culture.[8]

On the other hand, many organizations that are hard-pressed to change their
culture seem to find it easier just to fire the senior management team and replace

---

## STRATEGY IN PRACTICE

### Example 3.3 Cultural Changes at AT&T

Before the court-ordered breakup of AT&T in January 1984, AT&T had a strong corporate culture that focused on delivering reliable, inexpensive phone service. Now AT&T is in the middle of what one insider termed "a cultural train wreck." The company culture that advocated consensus decision making, lifetime employment, promotion from within, and pride in service—all within the regulated environment guaranteed profits—is now suffering in the aftermath of the divestiture. The company is now having to come to terms with a highly competitive market, a declining reputation for quality service, poor employee morale, and a totally new organizational structure.

*Source:* Adapted from Jeremy Main, "Waking Up AT&T: There's Life After Culture Shock," *Fortune,* December 24, 1984, pp. 66–74.

---

them with a new team. This view is based on the assumption that most organizations promote people who fit the prevailing norms of the organization and, therefore, the easiest if not the only way to change the culture is to change the senior management.

## MIX OF ORGANIZA-TIONAL OBJECTIVES

No one mix or combination of organizational objectives is applicable to all organizations. The type of objectives that are established depends on the nature of the particular organization. For example, the Boy Scouts of America would have a set of objectives different from the American Express Company.

Ideally, an organization's objectives should be compatible with its culture and should

1. Match its strengths to opportunities
2. Minimize threats to the organization
3. Eliminate weaknesses in the organization

They should also support the organization's mission and need to be established for every area of the organization where performance and results directly influence the survival and success of the organization. The mix of organizational objectives is also influenced by the mix of objectives from prior years. The degree of achievement of prior objectives influences the aspiration level of the management team and often serves as a starting point for determining the mix and exact nature of the objectives for a future time period.

The following items provide potential areas for establishing objectives for most organizations:

1. *Customer Service.* Expressed in terms of delivery times or customer complaints. Example:
   a. To reduce the number of customer complaints by 40 percent over the next three years

2. *Financial Resources.* Expressed in terms of the capital structure, new issues of common stock, cash flow, working capital, dividend payments, and collection periods. Examples:
   a. To increase work capital to $10 million within five years
   b. To reduce long-term debt to $8 million within three years.

3. *Human Resources.* Expressed in terms of rates of absenteeism, tardiness, turnover, or number of grievances. Also can be expressed in terms of number of people to be trained or number of training programs that are to be conducted. Examples:
   a. To reduce absenteeism by 8 percent within three years
   b. To conduct a 40-hour supervisory development program for 300 supervisors at a cost not to exceed $400 per participant over the next four years

4. *Markets.* Expressed in terms of share of the market or dollar or unit volume of sales. Examples:
   a. To increase commercial sales to 85 percent of total sales and reduce military sales to 15 percent of total sales over the next three years
   b. To increase the number of units of product X sold by 500,000 units within four years

5. *Organizational Structure.* Expressed in terms of changes to be made or projects to be undertaken. Example:
   a. To establish a decentralized organizational structure within three years

6. *Physical Facilities.* Expressed in terms of square feet, fixed costs, or units of production. Examples:
   a. To increase storage capacity by 15 million units over the next three years
   b. To decrease production capacity in the West Coast plant by 20 percent within three years

7. *Product.* Expressed in terms of sales and profitability by product line or product or target dates for development of new products. Example:
   a. To phase out the product with the lowest profit margin within two years

8. *Productivity.* Expressed in terms of a ratio of input to output or cost per unit of production. Example:
   a. To increase the number of units produced per worker by 10 percent per eight-hour day over the next three years

9. *Profitability.* Expressed in terms of profits, return on investment, earnings per share, or profit-to-sales ratios. Example:
   a. To increase return on investment to 15 percent after taxes within four years

10. *Research and Innovation.* Expressed in terms of the amount of money to be spent or projects to be completed. Example:
    a. To develop an engine in the medium-price range within five years at a cost not to exceed $3 million

11. *Social Responsibility.* Expressed in terms of types of activities, number of days of service, or financial contributions. Example:

    **a.** To increase our contribution to United Way by 30 percent over the next three years[9]

Objectives can be expressed in both quantitative and qualitative terms. In both cases, they should be detailed enough so that the organization's personnel can clearly understand what the organization intends to achieve. Example 3.4 shows both qualitative and quantitative objectives for the J. C. Penney Company.

---

## STRATEGY IN PRACTICE

### Example 3.4 Objectives of the J. C. Penney Company

1. To achieve and maintain a position of leadership in the businesses in which we compete
2. To be a positive force that enhances the interests of our customers, associates, suppliers, investors, government, and the public at large
3. To be an attractive investment for our shareholders and creditors, and for this purpose:

    a. To achieve a return on equity in the top quartile of major competitors for the company as a whole and for each operating division

        At the present time, this will require us to achieve an after-tax return in excess of 15 percent, with each operating division achieving a minimum of 15 percent by 1986.

    b. To achieve consistent growth in earnings at a rate required to meet or exceed the return-on-equity (ROE) objective

        To achieve the minimum 15 percent ROE from our current level—and to exceed it once we've arrived there—will require a consistent earnings growth rate of approximately 12.5 percent.

    c. To maintain consistency and growth in dividend payout through increased earnings

        At the current time our objective is a payout of 33 percent of net income.

    d. To maintain a capital structure that will assure continuing access to financial markets so that we can, at reasonable cost, provide for future resource needs and capitalize on attractive opportunities for growth

        Specifically, we will maintain a minimum of A1/A+ ratings (Moody's/Standard & Poor's) on senior long-term debt and the A1/P1 ratings on commercial paper.
        Further, we plan to achieve a debt/equity ratio of no more than 1:1.

    e. To ensure that financing objectives governing the amount, composition, and cost of capital are consistent with and support other corporate objectives

*Source:* Adapted from public company documents.

## CASCADE APPROACH TO ESTAB- LISHING OBJECTIVES

An approach to setting objectives throughout the entire organization is to have the objectives "cascade" down through the organizational hierarchy. The steps involved in this approach are outlined below:

1. The objective-setting process begins at the top of the organization with a statement of mission.
2. Long-range objectives are then established from this statement.
3. Long-range objectives lead to the establishment of performance targets (short-range objectives) for the overall organization.
4. Long- and short-range objectives are then established for each strategic business unit (SBU), major division, or operating unit within the organization.
5. Long- and short-range objectives are then established for the functional areas (marketing, finance, production) within each strategic business unit (SBU), major division, or operating unit.
6. The process continues on down through the organizational hierarchy.[10]

The cascade approach to objective setting, as outlined above and as depicted in Figure 3.5, does not imply autocratic or "top down" management. It merely ensures that the objectives of individual units within the organization are in phase

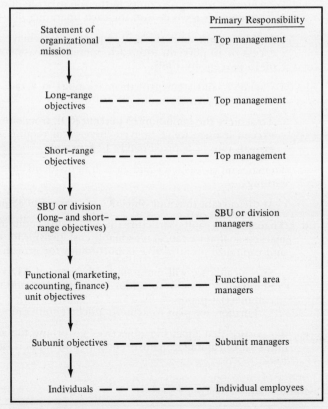

**Figure 3.5** Cascade Approach to Objective Setting

with the major objectives of the organization and that the entire objective-setting process is coordinated.

## REVIEW QUESTIONS

1. Distinguish between long-range and short-range objectives.
2. Outline the factors whose interaction determine an organization's objectives.
3. What is organizational culture?
4. Describe the major factors that influence an organization's culture.
5. What are the major characteristics that, when taken together, capture the essence of an organization's culture?
6. Describe the organizational culture grid.
7. Describe the four organizational cultures that result from categorizing cultures into degree of risk and speed of feedback.
8. Describe 11 potential areas for establishing objectives.
9. Discuss the cascade approach to establishing objectives.

## DISCUSSION QUESTIONS

1. Choose an organization of which you are a member and analyze its culture. How is your behavior shaped by the organization's culture? How are the cultural expectations transmitted to new members?
2. Choose any business organization and see if you can identify its objectives by researching business publications or public documents of the organization.
3. The only objective of business organizations is to make a profit. Do you agree or disagree? Be prepared to defend your choice.
4. Identify a business organization that you feel must change its culture in order to be successful in the future. Be prepared to explain the organization's culture and why you feel that it must change.

## REFERENCES AND ADDITIONAL READING

1. Robert C. Ernest, "Corporate Cultures and Elective Planning," *Personnel Administrator* 30 (March 1985): 49.
2. Howard Schwartz and Stanley M. Davis, "Matching Corporate Culture and Business Strategy," *Organizational Dynamics* 10 (Summer 1981): 33.
3. Bro Uttal, "The Corporate Culture Vultures," *Fortune,* October 17, 1983, p. 72.
4. Stephen P. Robbins, *Essentials of Organizational Behavior* (Englewood Cliffs, N.J.: Prentice-Hall, 1984), p. 171.
5. Robert C. Ernest, "Corporate Cultures and Effective Planning," p. 52.
6. Terrence E. Deal and Allan A. Kennedy, *Corporate Cultures* (Reading, Mass.: Addison-Wesley, 1982), pp. 107–127.
7. Bro Uttal, The Corporate Culture Vultures," p. 70. See also Terrence E. Deal and Allan A. Kennedy, *Corporate Culture: The Rites and Rituals of Corporate Life* (Reading, Mass.: Addison-Wesley, 1982).
8. For an interesting article on future corporate culture needs, see Meryl P. Gardner, "Creating a Corporate Culture for the Eighties," *Business Horizons* 28 (January–February 1985): 59–63.
9. Anthony Raia, *Managing by Objectives* (Glenview, Ill.: Scott, Foresman, 1974), p. 38.
10. Ibid., p. 30.

# Strategic Management Process

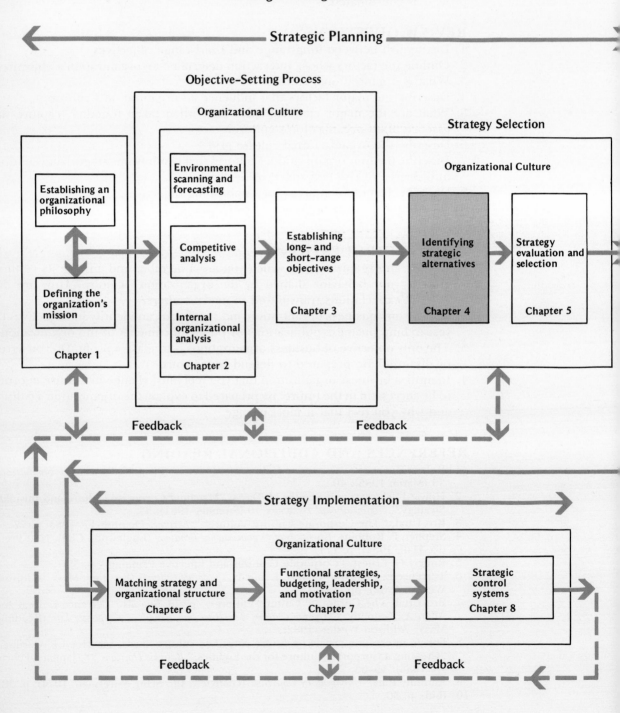

## Strategic Planning

### Objective-Setting Process

**Organizational Culture**

Establishing an organizational philosophy

Defining the organization's mission

**Chapter 1**

Environmental scanning and forecasting

Competitive analysis

Internal organizational analysis

**Chapter 2**

Establishing long- and short-range objectives

**Chapter 3**

### Strategy Selection

**Organizational Culture**

Identifying strategic alternatives

**Chapter 4**

Strategy evaluation and selection

**Chapter 5**

Feedback          Feedback

## Strategy Implementation

**Organizational Culture**

Matching strategy and organizational structure

**Chapter 6**

Functional strategies, budgeting, leadership, and motivation

**Chapter 7**

Strategic control systems

**Chapter 8**

Feedback          Feedback

# 4  *IDENTIFYING STRATEGIC ALTERNATIVES*

## STUDY OBJECTIVES

- To identify various corporate and business unit strategies used in achieving organizational objectives

- To discuss stable growth, endgame, combination, overall cost leadership, differentiation, and focus strategies

- To describe mergers and acquisitions, and reasons for carrying out mergers

- To present reasons for forming joint ventures and strategies used in joint ventures

## CHAPTER OUTLINE

Strategic Alternatives
Stable Growth Strategy
Growth Strategies
    Concentration on a Single Product or Service
    Concentric Diversification
    Vertical Integration
    Horizontal Integration (or Diversification)
    Conglomerate Diversification
Endgame Strategies
Retrenchment Strategies
    Turnaround Strategy
    Divestment Strategy
    Liquidation Strategy
Combination Strategies
Business Unit or Corporate Strategies
    Overall Cost Leadership Strategy
    Differentiation Strategy
    Focus Strategy
Implementing Strategies Through Mergers and Acquisitions
    Reasons for Mergers and Acquisitions
    Carrying Out Mergers and Acquisitions
    Guidelines for Successfully Implementing Mergers and Acquisitions
Implementing Strategies Through Joint Ventures
    Reasons for Entering Joint Ventures
    Strategies to Joint Ventures
    Considerations in Forming a Joint Venture
Review Questions
Discussion Questions
References and Additional Reading

*"Cheshire Puss," she [Alice] began, rather timidly. . . . "Would you tell me, please, which way I ought to walk from here?"*

*"That depends a good deal on where you want to get to," said the Cat.*

*"I don't much care where—" said Alice.*

*"Then it doesn't matter which way you walk," said the Cat.*

—Lewis Carroll, *Alice in Wonderland*

Strategy outlines the fundamental steps that an organization intends to take in order to achieve an objective or set of objectives. Management develops a strategy by evaluating options available to the organization and choosing one or more of the options.

Strategies exist at different levels in an organization and are classified according to the scope of their coverage. Strategies that address what businesses a multibusiness organization will be in and how resources will be allocated among those businesses are called *corporate strategies.* Corporate strategies are established at the highest levels of the organization and involve a long-range time horizon. *Business unit strategies* focus on how to compete in a given business. The scope of a business strategy is narrower than a corporate strategy and generally applies to a single business unit or SBU. A third level of strategy is the *functional-level strategy.* Functional strategies are narrower in scope than business strategies. Functional strategies are concerned with the activities of the different functional areas of a business such as production, finance, marketing, and personnel. Usually functional strategies are for a relatively short period of time—normally one year or less. Although functional strategies must support business level strategies, they are primarily concerned with "how to" issues. Corporate and business unit strategies are described in this chapter, and functional strategies will be described in Chapter 7.

## STRATEGIC ALTERNATIVES

In choosing corporate and business unit strategies, most organizations have a wide variety of options. The options described in this chapter are

### Corporate Strategies

1. Stable growth
2. Growth
   a. Concentration on a single product or service
   b. Concentric diversification
   c. Vertical integration
   d. Horizontal diversification
   e. Conglomerate diversification
3. Endgame strategies
4. Retrenchment
   a. Turnaround

      **b.** Divestment
      **c.** Liquidation
**5.** Combination

*Business Unit or Corporate Strategies*
**1.** Overall cost leadership
**2.** Differentiation of product or service
**3.** Focus of the organization

**STABLE GROWTH STRATEGY**

A *stable growth strategy* can be characterized as follows:

- The organization is satisfied with its past performance and decides to continue to pursue the same or similar objectives.
- Each year the level of achievement that is expected is increased by approximately the same percentage.
- The organization continues to serve its customers with basically the same products or services.

A stable growth strategy is a relatively low-risk strategy and is quite effective for successful organizations in an industry that is growing and in an environment that is not volatile. For many organizations, stable growth is probably the most effective strategy. Some of the reasons for the use of a stable growth strategy follow:

- Management may not wish to take the risk of greatly modifying its present strategy. Change threatens those people who employ previously learned skills when new skills are required. It also threatens old positions of influence. Furthermore, the management of a successful organization quite frequently assumes that strategies that have proved to be successful in the past will continue to be successful in the future.
- Changes in strategy require changes in resource allocations.[1] Changes in patterns of resource allocation in an established organization are difficult to achieve and frequently require long periods of time.
- Too-rapid growth can lead to situations in which the organization's scale of operations outpaces its administrative resources.[2] Inefficiencies can quickly occur.
- The organization may not keep up with or be aware of changes that may affect its product and market.

Generally, organizations that pursue a stable growth strategy concentrate on one product or service. They grow by maintaining their share of the steadily increasing market, by slowly increasing their share of the market, by adding new product(s) or service(s) (but only after extensive marketing research), or by expanding their market coverage geographically. Many organizations within the public utility, transportation, banking, and insurance industries follow a stable

---

## STRATEGY IN PRACTICE

**Example 4.1** Stable Growth at McIlhenny Company, the Maker of Tabasco Sauce

Tabasco sauce, first produced commercially in 1868 by E. L. McIlhenny & Company, has been manufactured and marketed in much the same way since the company's first factory opened in 1905. The overall strategy taken by the family firm has been one of stable growth. In fact, the second factory was not added until 1980. Between 1918 and 1928 McIlhenny consolidated its position through various legal actions fighting use of the name, Tabasco, and label by rivals. By 1931, the name and label were patented and remain uniquely their own. The sauce's ingredients and recipe, the way the sauce is manufactured (bottling, labeling, packaging, and materials handling), and distribution have remained stable. The company controls production of the basic ingredients and the formula, so quality control is no problem. McIlhenny has operated in international markets since its beginning. As a result of this stable growth strategy, Tabasco sauce has a 95 percent share of the market. Only one price increase was made between 1928 and 1980.

*Source:* Adapted from Phil Patton, "Tabasco Sauce: Hot Peppers and History in Every Bottle," *Companion* 3 (July 1977):8–11, and *Smithsonian*, May 1984, pp. 72–82.

---

growth strategy. In fact, for many industries and for many organizations, stable growth is the most logical and appropriate strategy. Example 4.1 describes one company that has been very successful in pursuing a stable growth strategy.

## GROWTH STRATEGIES

Organizations pursuing a *growth strategy* can be described as follows:

- They do not necessarily grow faster than the economy as a whole but do grow faster than the markets in which their products are sold.
- They tend to have larger-than-average profit margins.
- They attempt to postpone or even eliminate the danger of price competition in their industry.
- They regularly develop new products, new markets, new processes, and new uses for old products.
- Instead of adapting to changes in the outside world, they tend to adapt the outside world to themselves by creating something or a demand for something which did not exist before.[3]

A study of 53 growth companies found that they pursued one or more of the following strategies:

- They chose a general field of business that was expanding more rapidly than the economy as a whole.
- They chose a specific subsector that was growing even more rapidly than the general field of business.

- They chose a rapidly expanding market segment served by the specific subsector.
- They chose a specific subsector that was at an earlier stage of economic growth than the general field of business.
- They used internal expansion, mergers, and acquisitions to achieve growth.
- They entered foreign markets by using both foreign sales from the United States and foreign manufacture.[4]

It is important to note at this point, however, that organizations pursuing growth strategies are not confined to growth industries. They can be found in industries with relatively fixed markets and long-established product lines.[5]

Why does an organization decide to pursue a growth strategy? One of the most important reasons is the values held by either the top manager or the top-management team. Many top managers equate growth with their own personal effectiveness. In other words, growth of their business indicates their effectiveness as managers. Furthermore, many top executives have stock options as part of their compensation package. They know that if growth of the business leads to growth in the price of their organization's stock, then they will benefit directly through an increase in their own net worth.

In addition, some studies have shown that growth strategies lead to better organizational performance. One study found that companies pursuing growth strategies had substantially higher sales and profit increases than did other companies in the same general environment.[6] The PIMS (Profit Impact of Market Strategies) project sponsored by the Marketing Science Institute and the Harvard Business School studied 57 major North American companies and found a direct and positive relationship between growth strategy and return on investment.[7] Another reason given for employing a growth strategy is the so-called experience curve theory, which holds that as an organization grows in size and experience a corresponding increase in effectiveness results.[8]

Although growth strategies are often appealing to many managers, stockholders, and investment analysts, a word of caution seems appropriate at this point. Peter Drucker phrased it as follows:

> The securities market would be well advised to put a discount on growth stocks and growth industries rather than a premium. For growth is a risk.
>     . . . There is no virtue in a company's getting bigger. The right goal is to become better. Growth to be sound, should be the result of doing the right things. By itself, growth is vanity and little else.[9]

In fact, too much growth in the short run can result in inefficiencies that can prove disastrous in the long run.[10] It is for these reasons that management should answer the following three questions before embarking on a growth strategy:

1. Are company financial resources adequate?
2. If the company is stopped short in its strategy for any reason, will its position be competitively viable?
3. Will government regulators permit the company to follow the strategy it has chosen?[11]

Regardless of the cautions and potential problems, many companies have successfully implemented growth strategies. In fact, when a growth strategy is selected and properly implemented, it can be very effective for the stakeholders of the organization. In the following sections of this chapter, several growth strategy options are described.

**Concentration on a Single Product or Service**

Concentration on a single product or service entails increasing an organization's sales, profits, or market share of its current product or service faster than it has increased in the past. One approach in implementing this growth strategy is to identify reasons why an organization's sales, profits, or market share are falling short of their potential. Possible reasons might include

- Lack of a full product line within the relevant market (product line gap)
- Absent or inadequate distribution system to or within the relevant market (distribution gap)
- Less than full usage within the market (usage gap)
- Competitors' sales (competitive gap)

Some of the options available to an organization in filling these gaps include the following:

- Filling out the existing product line (e.g., new sizes, options, styles, or colors could be offered for the existing product line)
- Developing new products within the existing product line (e.g., Cherry Coke was a new product within an existing product line)
- Expanding distribution into new geographic areas either nationally or internationally
- Expanding the number of distribution outlets within a geographic area
- Expanding shelf space and improving the location of the product and displays of the product within present distribution outlets
- Encouraging nonusers to use the product and light users to use the product more frequently through the use of advertising, promotions, and special pricing campaigns
- Penetrating competitor's positions through pricing strategies, product differentiation, and advertising

An organization faces one major risk by adopting a growth strategy of concentrating on a single product or service. If the market for the organization's product or service declines, then the organization is in trouble. This is an especially important concern when one considers that it has been estimated that 80 percent of today's products will have disappeared from the market ten years from now, while an estimated 80 percent of the products that will be sold in the next decade are as yet unknown.[12] Several factors outside the control of any single organization can cause a decline in the demand for an organization's product or service. The increasing instability of consumer preferences, the growing intensity and sophistication of competition, technological change, and changes in government

---

## STRATEGY IN PRACTICE

### Example 4.2  McDonald's Corporation

Ray Kroc went to see the hamburger restaurant in San Bernardino, California, in 1954 because he sold multimixers and they were using eight (capable of making 40 milkshakes at a time) when virtually every restaurant or soda fountain customer of his was using one or two. He wanted to know why.

His objective was to sell more multimixers. He reasoned that by persuading the owners (two brothers) to expand he would assure himself a growing multimixer market. But when the brothers told him they preferred to devote their energies to running the San Bernardino restaurant, Kroc suggested that he franchise the restaurant business for them. They agreed to the arrangement, and at 52 years of age Ray Kroc started what we know today as McDonald's.

Today, there are over 8000 units in the United States and most foreign countries. The products served include hamburgers, cheeseburgers, fish, chicken, and pork sandwiches, french fries, pies, sundaes, cookies, and soft drinks. Most units also have a limited breakfast menu. All of this has been accomplished by concentrating in one business.

---

policy pose a major risk for an organization concentrating on a single product or service.[13] Example 4.2 shows how McDonald's has prospered by following this strategy.

**Concentric Diversification**

*Concentric diversification* is a growth strategy that involves adding new products or services that are similar to the organization's present products or services. In order for the strategy to be considered concentric diversification, the products or services that are added must lie within the organization's know-how and experience in technology, product line, distribution channels, or customer base. When an organization's industry is growing, concentric diversification is a viable strategy for strengthening its position in a field where it has knowledge and experience. For example, one study examined 460 corporations that account for nearly two-thirds of the U.S. corporate industrial assets and concluded that diversification that has led to relatively rapid rates of corporate growth has been to markets that are related to the entering organization's original markets.[14]

Many organizations have successfully adopted the concentric diversification strategy. Example 4.3 describes the concentric diversification strategy at Johnson & Johnson. After reviewing what they described as America's excellent companies, Thomas Peters and Robert Waterman concluded that organizations that do branch out but stick very close to their knitting outperform the others.[15]

**Vertical Integration**

*Vertical integration* is a growth strategy that involves extending an organization's present business in two possible directions. *Forward integration* moves the organization into distributing its own products or services. *Backward integration* moves

---

## STRATEGY IN PRACTICE

### Example 4.3 Johnson & Johnson

Johnson & Johnson (J&J) makes and sells a wide variety of products in the health care and related industries including such well-known products as baby shampoo, Tylenol, and Band-Aid adhesive bandages. Over the last ten years its earnings growth has averaged 13 percent annually. In 1983, it had over $6 billion in sales and $980 million in profits. All of this was accomplished by selling basically consumable or disposable health care related products.

However, since 1980 J&J has acquired 25 companies in high-technology health care markets such as surgical lasers and magnetic resonance scanners. Although this move would probably still be considered a form of concentric diversification, it is stretching the limits. It will be interesting to see if the company can be successful in these markets.

---

an organization into supplying some or all of the products or services that are used in producing its present products or services.[16]

Several factors, including the following, might cause an organization to pursue either forward or backward integration:

- Backward integration gives an organization more control over the cost, availability, and quality of the raw materials that go into its present products or services.
- When suppliers of an organization's products or services have large profit margins, the organization can convert a cost into a profit by integrating backward.
- Forward integration gives an organization control over sales and distribution channels, which can help in eliminating inventory buildups and production slowdowns.
- When the distributors of an organization's products or services have large markups, the organization may increase its own profits by integrating forward.
- Some organizations use either forward or backward integration in hopes of benefiting from the economies of scale available from the creation of nationwide sales and marketing organizations and the construction of larger manufacturing plants. They feel that these economies of scale result in lower overall costs and thus increased profits.
- Some organizations use either backward or forward integration to increase their size and power in a particular market or industry in order to gain some degree of monopolistic control.

Vertical integration is a reasonable and rational strategy in certain situations. However, organizations should adopt a vertical integration strategy with caution because integrated organizations have become associated with mature and less profitable industries.[17] At the same time, escape from these industries is particularly difficult for the large, vertically integrated organization. The reasons for this difficulty are twofold. First, the large size of vertically integrated organizations requires large investments in new businesses if significant changes in organizational performance are to be achieved. However, the low price-earnings ratios of vertically integrated organizations make such large investments difficult. In addition, it has been argued that vertically integrated businesses train few general managers and that the attitudes of management and the organizational structures they preside over tend to inhibit strategic change.[18] Another word of caution on forward integration comes from a study of 40 business organizations. This study concluded that organizations employing forward integration to enter a new product-market field performed worse than other companies using different strategies to enter the same product-market field.[19] Finally, a study examining the performance of 25 vertically integrated organizations found that these organizations had produced significantly lower price-earnings ratios than had organizations that had followed a concentric diversification strategy.[20]

Regardless of these cautions, organizations have made use of and will continue making use of vertical integration. The characteristics of the most profitable (as measured in pretax return on investment) businesses with high vertical integration has been described as follows:

- The corporation of which the business is a part is highly diverse (i.e., it is involved in many unrelated fields of business endeavor).
- The businesses belong to medium-size corporations (sales between $1 billion and $2 billion).
- The ratio of gross book value of plant and equipment to sales is low (below 37 percent). Integration should be accomplished with a minimum of investment. Investment per employee of highly profitable, highly integrated businesses is not more than $17,000.
- The products that these businesses sell are relatively "unimportant" to the immediate customer. To use an extreme example, most manufacturing operations would consider the purchase of light bulbs unimportant compared to the purchase of tooling or fixtures. Important products require customer scrutiny, adherence to strict specifications, and special or customized end products, all of which are costly.
- The degree of customer fragmentation is low. That is, 40 or less customers equal 50 percent of the sales of this business. Selling expenses are reduced with repeat business, and a lack of a variety of customers enables more product standardization.
- The ratio of new products as a percent of sales is low (less than 1 percent). Here again, standardization and repetition pay off for highly integrated businesses.[21]

Backward integration also seems to be more helpful in improving return on investment than forward integration because it enables a business to take advantage of production economies without having to tackle new marketing problems. Example 4.4 illustrates a forward vertical integration strategy at Coca-Cola.

---

> ### STRATEGY IN PRACTICE
>
> **Example 4.4** Forward Vertical Integration at Coca-Cola
>
> For many years, the Coca-Cola Company concentrated on manufacturing soft drink concentrates and syrups. The company sold these concentrates and syrups to independently owned, franchised bottling companies, which would then sell the bottled soft drinks to retailers and wholesalers.
>
> However, since the early 1980s Coca-Cola has spent almost $3 billion on buying out bottling companies. For example, in 1984 Coca-Cola purchased the bottling operations for southern England, which included the London market. In the United States, Coke purchased the Akron Coca-Cola Bottling Company and several other bottling operations contiguous to existing company-owned territories.
>
> *Source:* Public company documents.

**Horizontal Integration (or Diversification)**

*Horizontal integration or diversification* is a growth strategy that involves buying one of an organization's competitors. Horizontal integration and concentric diversification are similar strategies in that the new products or services that are added to the organization under both approaches are closely related to the organization's present products or services. However, under concentric diversification new products or services are added either through internal development or by the acquisition of an organization that is producing a product or service that is closely related to, but not directly competitive with, the acquiring organization's product or service. On the other hand, under horizontal diversification new products or services are added by the purchase of a competitive organization. As can be seen, there is little difference between these two strategies.

Horizontal diversification can be accomplished by the acquisition of a competitor's common stock, by the purchase of a competitor's assets, or by a pooling of interest of the two organizations. Horizontal diversification is normally accomplished through mergers, which are described later in this chapter.

The primary problem with employing a horizontal diversification strategy is that such a strategy eliminates the competition that has existed between the two organizations and may result in legal ramifications. In the 1950 Celler-Kefauver amendment to Section 7 of the Clayton Act, Congress prohibited mergers that substantially lessened competition or that tended to create a monopoly in any field of business in any section of the country. Some of the factors that are examined by the Antitrust Division of the U.S. Department of Justice in determining the legality of a merger are (1) the level of concentration in the industry (e.g., the market shares of the leading organizations and the increase in concentration that will be caused by the proposed merger), (2) whether the merger will give the resulting organization a competitive advantage over other organizations in the industry, (3) whether entry into the industry is difficult, (4) whether there has been a trend of mergers within the industry, (5) the economic power of the

---

> ## STRATEGY IN PRACTICE
>
> **Example 4.5** Horizontal Integration of Nabisco and Standard Brands
>
> In 1981, Nabisco, Inc., and Standard Brands, Inc., merged through an all-stock transaction at a book value of $2 billion to form Nabisco Brands, Inc. The basic intent of the merger was to exploit each corporation's geographic, distribution, technological, and management resources in order to be more competitive in the food industry.

merged organizations, (6) whether demand for the industry's products is growing, and finally (7) whether there is danger that the merger will trigger others.

Even with the risk of antitrust action, horizontal diversifications do occur. Example 4.5 illustrates a horizontal diversification strategy between Nabisco and Standard Brands.

## Conglomerate Diversification

*Conglomerate diversification* is a growth strategy that involves adding new products or services that are significantly different from the organization's present products or services. Conglomerate diversification can be pursued internally or externally. Most frequently, however, it is achieved through mergers and joint ventures, which are described later in this chapter.

A great many organizations prefer the conglomerate diversification strategy. In fact, the names of organizations employing this strategy would read like a who's who of American business. American Express, LTV, ITT, Gulf + Western, Textron, and others too numerous to mention are examples. The reasons for following such a strategy are also numerous. Some of the more important ones follow:

- Supporting some divisions with the cash flow from other divisions during a period of development or temporary difficulties.[22]
- Using the profits of one division to cover expenses in another division without paying taxes on the profits from the first division.[23]
- Encouraging growth for its own sake or to satisfy the values and ambitions of management or the owners.
- Taking advantage of unusually attractive growth opportunities.
- Distributing risk by serving several different markets.[24]
- Improving the overall profitability and flexibility of the organization by moving into industries that have better economic characteristics than those of the acquiring organization.
- Gaining better access to capital markets and better stability or growth in earnings.[25]
- Increasing the price of an organization's stock.
- Reaping the benefits of synergy. *Synergy* results from a conglomerate merger

when the combined organization is more profitable than the two organizations operating independently.

In choosing a conglomerate diversification strategy, an organization should proceed with caution and not diversify merely to be diversified. Conglomerate diversification brings with it bigness and the difficult management problems associated with bigness. In fact, companies with assets of less than $10 million have outperformed their larger counterparts in terms of return on stockholders' equity over the past decade. In addition, the rates of return on sales for large companies have been falling over that period while those of the smaller companies have been rising.[26] Furthermore, evidence has been found to show that under abnormal conditions, such as recession, conglomerate organizations have less staying power than concentric ones and hence suffer sharper reversals.[27] It is for these reasons that in order for conglomerate diversification to be successful it must utilize at least one, and generally more than one, of the four fundamental strengths of a business: financial resources, production capacity, access to a specific market, and technical capacity.

The basic elements in employing a successful conglomerate diversification strategy seem to be as follows:

1. A clear definition of organizational objectives
2. A determination of the organization's ability to diversify, which includes an analysis of its present operations (internal organizational analysis) and the resources available for diversification
3. Establishment of specific criteria for purchasing other organizations in line with points 1 and 2
4. A comprehensive search for organizations and their evaluation against the criteria[28]

Example 4.6 shows the results of a diversification strategy at Sears, Roebuck and Company.

## ENDGAME STRATEGIES

*Endgame strategies* are used by organizations in an environment of declining product demand where those environmental conditions make it unlikely that all the plant capacity and competitors put in place during the industry's heyday will ever be needed.[29] This condition can develop within a strategic business unit (SBU) or division of an organization or with a product line or separate product or brand.

Industry conditions within a declining industry influence the strategic options available to a company. Favorable industry characteristics include relatively low exit barriers, few "maverick" competitors who lapse into periods of cutthroat competition, or a low rate of technological change by users. Unfavorable industry characteristics include relatively high fixed costs, capital-intensive technologies, high exit barriers, many "maverick" competitors, or rapid standardization of the product. Within a particular industry, individual organizations can have relative

---

## STRATEGY IN PRACTICE

### Example 4.6 Sears, Roebuck and Company

Sears, Roebuck operates through the following principal business units:

Merchandise Group—One of the world's largest retailers of general merchandise selling by mail and through a nationwide chain of over 790 stores

Allstate Group—Engages in the property, liability, and life insurance business

Coldwell Banker & Company—Acts as a broker in residential and commercial real estate; invests in, develops and manages commercial real estate; and performs related services

Dean Witter—Provides a variety of financial services including brokerage services, investment banking services, and mortgage banking services

Sears Savings Bank (California), Greenwood Trust Company (Delaware), and Harley State Bank (South Dakota)—Provide banking services

Discover—Provides a financial services credit card to compete with Visa and Mastercard

Budget Rent-a-Car—Provides transportation rental services to compete with Hertz, Avis, and National

|  | Has competitive strengths | Lacks competitive strengths |
|---|---|---|
| Favorable industry conditions | Leadership or niche | Harvest or divest quickly |
| Unfavorable industry conditions | Niche or harvest | Divest quickly |

**Figure 4.1** Strategies for Declining Industries
*Source:* Kathryn Rudie Harrigan and Michael E. Porter, "End-game Strategies for Declining Industries," *Harvard Business Review* 61 (July–August 1983):119.

competitive strengths or weaknesses. Organizations with relative competitive strengths are described as being cost-efficient in producing the endgame product or are clearly identified as the industry leader. Figure 4.1 illustrates which strategies are most likely to be appropriate given endgame industry conditions and the individual organization's relative competitive strengths.

Basically, four strategic options exist for an organization in a declining industry. An organization using a *leadership strategy* tries to achieve above-average profitability by becoming one of the few companies remaining in the industry. The *niche strategy* attempts to identify a segment of the declining industry that will either maintain stable demand or decline slowly and that has favorable industry characteristics. Under a *harvest strategy* management reduces investments, cuts maintenance, and reduces advertising and research in order to cut costs and improve cash flow. Sales volume and/or market share are generally expected to decline, but the lost revenue is anticipated to be more than offset by reduced costs. Organizations following a harvest strategy ultimately sell or liquidate the business. *Quick divestment* involves selling the business in the early stages of the decline rather than harvesting and selling it later. Divestment is discussed more fully later in this chapter.

**RETRENCH-MENT STRATEGIES**

*Retrenchment strategies* are most frequently used during economic recessions and during times when the organization is having poor financial performance. Generally, organizations intend to pursue a retrenchment strategy only on a short-run basis. The basic purpose of the retrenchment strategy is to enable the organization to weather the storm and then return to using another strategic alternative. Three alternative retrenchment strategies employed by organizations are turnaround, divestment, and liquidation.

**Turnaround Strategy**

A *turnaround strategy* is an attempt to improve efficiency of operations during a decline in an organization's financial situation. Some of the more important reasons for declines in an organization's financial situation are

- Higher costs of wages and raw materials
- Decreased demand that can be the result of temporary demand dips (such as a lost government contract) or more general recessions
- Strikes
- Increased competitive pressures
- Management problems

Of course, the purpose of the turnaround strategy is to weather the bad times in hopes that the situation will change, and then a new strategy can be adopted during the upturn. Below are some of the actions that can be taken in a turnaround strategy:

- Change management personnel, both top and lower levels.
- Cut back on capital expenditures.
- Centralize decision making in an attempt to control costs.
- Cut back on hiring new personnel.
- Reduce advertising and promotion expenditures.
- Engage in general belt-tightening, including the firing of some personnel.
- Increase emphasis on cost control and budgeting.
- Sell off some assets.

- Tighten inventory control.
- Improve the collection of accounts receivable.

Another action that can be taken in a turnaround strategy is the use of Chapter 11 of the federal bankruptcy laws. Chapter 11 outlines the legal requirements for restructuring the financial affairs of an organization. Both voluntary and involuntary bankruptcy are permitted. Creditors can force a company into bankruptcy if it is not paying its debts when they come due. Chapter 11 gives an organization time to use some of the previously outlined strategies in an attempt to return the organization to a sound financial condition.

Almost every organization, at one time or another, must use a turnaround strategy. A study of 54 organizations concluded that the key to successful use of a turnaround strategy is a well-formulated concept of strategic management.[30] A company must decide whether the existing business activities must receive attention or whether the basic purpose of the business needs to be reformulated. Interestingly, this study of 54 organizations found that in over 72 percent of the firms involved in a turnaround strategy, significant changes were made in management personnel.[31]

**Divestment Strategy**

Divestment is a frequently used strategy when either endgame or turnaround strategies are not successful. *Divestment* involves selling off a major part of the business, which can be an SBU, a product line, or a division. Example 4.7 gives several divestments made over the past few years.

Divestment is a difficult decision for the management of any organization. The

| STRATEGY IN PRACTICE | | | | |
|---|---|---|---|---|
| **Example 4.7** Divestments | | | | |
| **Seller** | **Unit Sold** | **Buyer** | **Year** | **Price** |
| RCA | CIT Financial | Manufacturers Hanover | 1983 | $1.5 billion |
| RCA | Hertz | UAL | 1985 | $578 million |
| General Electric | Utah International | Broken Hill Proprietary | 1983 | $2.4 billion |
| General Electric | Family Financial Services | Philadelphia Saving Fund Society | 1984 | $600 million |
| Texaco | Employers Reinsurance | General Electric | 1984 | $1.1 billion |
| Husky Oil of Canada | Husky Oil (U.S. unit) | U.S. Steel | 1984 | $505 million |

barriers that impede an organization from following a divestment strategy have been described as follows:

1. *Structural (or Economic).*   Characteristics of a business's technology and its fixed and working capital impede exit.
2. *Interdependence.*   Relationships between the various business units within an organization may deter divestment of a particular business unit.
3. *Managerial.*   Aspects of a company's decision-making process inhibit exit from an unprofitable business. Such aspects may be
   a.   Company does not know that it is making an unsatisfactory return on its investment
   b.   Exit is a blow to management's pride
   c.   Exit is taken externally as a sign of failure
   d.   Exit threatens specialized manager's careers
   e.   Exit conflicts with social goals
   f.   Managerial incentive systems work against exit[32]

Special suggestions on overcoming exit barriers include the following:

- Have someone in the top-management team who has the responsibility of encouraging management to consider the divestment option.
- Design compensation and incentive systems so that they do not discourage sound exit decisions.
- Design management information systems that provide meaningful data to assist in the exit decision.
- Carefully plan answers to the questions of job security and easier progression for the middle managers affected by the divestment decision.
- Change top management periodically to overcome the commitments built up over time by incumbents.[33]

## Liquidation Strategy

*Liquidation* involves terminating an organization's existence either by selling off its assets or by shutting down the entire operation. Obviously, liquidation is a most unattractive strategy, and it is normally used only when all else fails. However, early liquidation may be a more appropriate strategy for an organization than pursuing a lost cause. The latter leads inevitably to bankruptcy, which in turn leaves less to liquidate.

## COMBINATION STRATEGIES

Most multibusiness organizations use some type of combination strategy, especially when they are serving several different markets. Certain types of strategies lend themselves to combination with other strategies. For example, a divestment strategy in one area of an organization is normally used in combination with one or more strategies in other parts of the organization. Combination strategies,

---

## STRATEGY IN PRACTICE

### Example 4.8  Holiday Inns

Holiday Inns was incorporated in 1954 and presently constitutes the largest hotel business in number of rooms in the world. During the 1960s and early 1970s, the company diversified by buying Trailways, Inc., a steamship company, a printing company, and a restaurant supply company.

However, in 1979 the company reversed this trend by selling Trailways for $94 million. Next it sold the printing company, the restaurant supply company, and in 1982 the steamship company.

During that same period, it purchased the Perkins Pancake-and-Steak chain for $80 million in 1979. It also acquired in 1980 the Harrah's Casino business for $196 million.

In addition to continuing support for the Holiday Inn hotels, it has recently developed the Holiday Inn Crown Plaza Hotels for the luxury hotel market and Hampton Inns for the low-priced hotel market segment.

---

which can be either simultaneous or sequential, are the norm. The following are just a few of the possible combination strategies:

*Simultaneous*

1. Divesting an SBU, product line, or division while adding other SBUs, product lines, or divisions
2. Retrenching in certain areas or products while pursuing a growth strategy in other areas or products
3. Using an endgame strategy on certain products and growth strategies on other products

*Sequential*

1. Employing a growth strategy for a specified time and then using stable growth for a specified time
2. Using a turnaround strategy and then employing a growth strategy when conditions improve

Example 4.8 describes a combination strategy pursued by Holiday Inns.

## BUSINESS UNIT OR CORPORATE STRATEGIES

By their very nature, business unit strategies, which focus on how to compete in a given business, are less generic than corporate-level strategies. Although almost all business-level strategies are tailored to some degree to the specific situation, it is nevertheless possible to categorize most business unit strategies as fitting into one of three major types: (1) overall cost leadership, (2) differentiation, and (3) focus.[34] It is important to note that each of these strategy types can also be a corporate-level strategy.[35]

**Overall Cost Leadership Strategy**

The overall cost leadership strategy emphasizes producing and delivering the product or service at a low cost relative to competitors, while not neglecting quality and service. This strategy requires the construction of efficient-scale facilities, vigorous pursuit of cost reductions, avoidance of marginal customer accounts, and cost minimization in areas such as R&D, service, sales force, and advertising.

**Differentiation Strategy**

A differentiation strategy requires that an organization create a product or service that is recognized industrywide as being unique, thus permitting the organization to charge higher-than-average prices.

**Focus Strategy**

A focus strategy involves concentrating on a particular group of customers, geographic markets, or product line segments in order to serve a well-defined but narrow market better than competitors who serve a broader market. Example 4.9 illustrates a focus strategy at Black & Decker.

Implementing these three generic strategies requires different skills, resources, and organizational requirements. Table 4.1 summarizes the requirements for each strategy.

**IMPLEMENT-ING STRATEGIES THROUGH MERGERS AND ACQUISI-TIONS**

Mergers and acquisitions are two frequently used methods for implementing the previously described diversification strategies. A *merger* takes place when two companies combine their operations, creating, in effect, a third company. An *acquisition* is a situation in which one company buys, and will control, another company.

*Horizontal mergers or acquisitions* involve a combination of two or more organizations that are direct competitors. *Concentric mergers or acquisitions* involve a combination of two or more organizations that have similar products or services in terms of technology, product line, distribution channels, or customer base. *Vertical mergers or acquisitions* involve a combination of two or more organizations that extends an organization into supplying products or services that are required in producing its present products or services or extends an organization into distributing or selling its own products or services. Finally, *conglomerate mergers or acquisitions* involve a combination of two or more organizations that are producing products or services that are significantly different from each other. Of course, it is entirely possible for mergers and acquisitions to take place between organizations in different countries.

**Reasons for Mergers and Acquisitions**

Organizations seek mergers and acquisitions for numerous reasons. One of the primary reasons is the potential benefit that can accrue to the stockholders of both companies. For example, if the earnings of two companies are valued differently in the stock market (i.e., they have different price-earnings ratios), a merger or

# STRATEGY IN PRACTICE

### Example 4.9 Focus Strategy at Black & Decker

Black & Decker has a built a worldwide reputation for quality products in the power tool business. The company diversified by buying the McCulloch gasoline chain saw company and developing a medical power tool product division. But in 1983, realizing that it had made a mistake, it began to refocus on its original business—power tools—by divesting itself of these two businesses.

**Table 4.1** Organizational Requirements for Generic Strategies

| Strategy | Commonly Required Skills and Resources | Common Organizational Requirements |
|---|---|---|
| Overall cost leadership | Substantial capital investment and access to capital<br>Process engineering skills<br>Intense supervision of labor<br>Products designed for ease in manufacture<br>Low-cost distribution systems | Tight cost control<br>Frequent, detailed control reports<br>Structured organization and responsibilities<br>Incentives based on meeting strict quantitative targets |
| Differentiation | Strong marketing abilities<br>Product engineering<br>Creative flair<br>Strong capability in basic research<br>Corporate reputation for quality or technological leadership<br>Long tradition in the industry or unique combination of skills drawn from other businesses<br>Strong cooperation from channels | Strong coordination among functions in R&D, product development, and marketing<br>Subjective measurement and incentives instead of quantitative measures<br>Amenities to attract highly skilled labor, scientists, or creative people |
| Focus | Combination of the above policies directed at the particular strategic target | Combination of the above policies directed at the particular strategic target |

*Source:* Michael E. Porter, *Competitive Strategy* (New York: Free Press, 1980), pp. 40–41.

acquisition can increase the market value of the stock of both organizations. This result is achieved if the acquiring company reports an increase in its earnings per share and if the multiple that is applied to its earnings rises as a result of the merger or acquisition.

Other reasons for mergers and acquisitions include the following:

- Providing a better utilization of existing manufacturing facilities.
- Selling in the same channels as existing channels to make the existing sales organization more productive.

- Getting the services of a proven management team in order to strengthen or succeed the existing staff.
- Smoothing out cyclical trends in present products or services.
- Evening out seasonal trends in present products or services.
- Providing new volume to replace static or shrinking volume in present products or services.
- Providing new products or services and better margins of profit in order to supplement older products or services still selling in good demand but at increasingly competitive levels.
- Entering a new and growing field.
- Securing or protecting sources of raw materials or components used in its manufacturing process (vertical integration).
- Effecting savings in income and excess profits taxes.
- Broadening the opportunities for using the managerial ability of the acquiring organization's personnel or its resources.
- Providing an avenue for the selling of the organization's stock. This is an especially important reason for an organization whose stock is not publicly traded and which is held by a small number of individuals. Selling out to a publicly owned organization facilitates the sale of the acquired company's stock.
- Providing resources for expanding the organization.
- Reducing tax obligations. In many situations the owner of a business may sell it and make substantial savings both in income taxes and in estate and inheritance taxes.
- Providing for management succession and the perpetuation or continuation of the business. Frequently, family-owned businesses or smaller businesses have few people capable of carrying on the business if the principal manager dies or is incapacitated. Merging with or being acquired by a larger organization helps to ensure the continuity of the organization.

Still, the primary reason for large mergers and acquisitions is the potential benefits that can accrue to the stockholders of both companies. Furthermore, mergers continue to be a popular technique for corporate growth strategies. Example 4.10 gives just a few of the largest mergers and acquisitions that have occurred in recent years.

**Carrying Out Mergers and Acquisitions**

Mergers and acquisitions can be carried out in either a friendly or a hostile environment. *Friendly mergers and acquisitions* are accomplished when the stockholders and management of both organizations agree that the combination will be good for both organizations, and then they work together to ensure its success. On the other hand, *hostile* (or, as they are frequently called, *takeover*) *mergers and acquisitions* result when the organization that is to be acquired (also sometimes called the *target company*) resists the attempt. Takeover attempts are often bitterly resisted by the management of the target organization. The reason for this is that if the takeover attempt is successful, the acquiring organization normally replaces the management of the target organization. Takeover mergers and acquisitions

## STRATEGY IN PRACTICE

### Example 4.10 Mergers and Acquisitions

| Acquiring Company | Acquired/Merged Company | Value $ Millions |
|---|---|---|
| Chevron Corp. | Gulf Corp. | 13,000 |
| Texaco Inc. | Getty Oil Co. | 10,125 |
| Mobil Corp. | Superior Oil Co. | 5,700 |
| Beatrice Cos., Inc. | Esmark Inc. | 2,710 |
| General Motors Corp. | Electronic Data Systems | 2,600 |
| IBM | ROLM | 1,260 |

usually come as a surprise to the target company. Generally, three conditions can make an organization a likely candidate for a takeover. First, the organization's stock may be selling for less than book value. Second, the organization may have a large cash surplus. Finally, the organization may be performing poorly compared to its competitors. In recent years, many companies have been installing antitakeover devices in corporate charters and bylaws and taking other defensive measures against hostile takeovers. Some of these measures include staggered terms for board members and stipulations requiring approval by two-thirds of the stockholders for a merger that is not approved by the board of directors.

Several methods are available for carrying out mergers and acquisitions. One method is the tender offer. A *tender offer* is a well-publicized bid made by a corporation for all or a prescribed amount of the stock of another organization. Tender offers are generally higher than the current trading price of the target organization's stock. Another option is for one company to purchase stock of the target organization in the open market. The acquiring company can also purchase the assets of the target company. Finally, the two organizations may agree to an exchange of stock. In agreeing to an exchange of stock, organizations use one of the following four yardsticks for determining the value of the stock: (1) book value per share, (2) earnings per share, (3) market price per share, or (4) dividends per share. Because so many terms are used in describing activities involved in mergers and acquisitions, Figure 4.2 is provided as a summary of the definitions of many of the terms.

**Guidelines for Successfully Implementing Mergers and Acquisitions**

Willard F. Rockwell, former chairman of the board of Rockwell International Corporation, outlined ten guidelines for successfully implementing mergers and acquisitions. The first four guidelines are critical and apply to any and all mergers and acquisitions. If any one of them is violated, then the chances of a successful merger or acquisition are very small. Rockwell's ten guidelines are

1. Pinpoint and spell out the objectives.
2. Specify the gains for the stockholders of both organizations.

**Acquisition:** Situation in which one company buys, and will control, another company.

**Arb or arbitrageur:** Professional stock trader who invests in stocks of companies that are takeover candidates, or rumored takeover candidates, hoping to make profits on price movements.

**Bear hug:** Offer for a company at so large a premium over the market price for the stock and with such favorable terms—such as all cash, with the financing in place—that the company has no choice but to accept it.

**Creeping tender offer:** Gradual accumulation of a company's stock through purchases on the open market. Law doesn't require disclosing holdings of a company's stock until 5% is acquired, then disclosure of each change in the holding is required.

**Friendly takeover:** Situation in which the management and directors of the target company support the takeover.

**Golden parachute:** Provisions in executives' employment contracts with their companies that guarantee substantial severance benefits if they lose their jobs or authority in a takeover.

**Greenmail:** Company purchase of its own shares from a suitor for more than the going market price to stop the threat of a hostile takeover.

**In play:** Term used by Wall Street deal makers to indicate a company is on the auction block and will be acquired, whether it wants to be or not.

**Junk bond:** Nickname derived years ago for bonds of corporations down on their luck. Now the name describes very high-yield, below-investment-grade bonds issued by many corporations to finance acquisitions and other activities. Corporate raiders have used them to finance hostile takeovers, but the Federal Reserve Board recently limited their use.

**Leveraged buy-out:** Acquisition of a public company by a small group of investors, typically including the company's management, which then makes the company private. Most of the purchase price is borrowed with the debt repaid from the company's profits or by selling assets.

**Lockup:** Agreement between two companies in a merger or acquisition designed to thwart a third-party suitor. A common lockup involves the acquirer receiving an option to buy the target's most valuable operations.

**Merger:** Situation in which two companies combine their operations, creating, in effect, a third company.

**Pac-man defense:** Tactic by which the target company in a hostile takeover bid becomes the aggressor and tries to take over the would-be acquirer.

**Figure 4.2** Terms of Business
*Source:* Adapted from Charley Blaine, "Terms of Business," *USA Today*, January 27, 1986, p. 3E. Used with permission.

**Poison pill:** Issue of securities by a target company, often preferred stock granted to holders of common stock, designed to thwart a hostile takeover. The shares are initially worthless, but their venom comes when a hostile bidder acquires a specified percentage of the target company's stock. Then the preferred shares can be converted into the target's common stock, forcing the bidder to extend an offer to a much larger number of shares and increasing the cost of the takeover so much that the bidder ends the takeover try.

**Raider:** Investor, often using his or her own money and that of other investors, who buys a big block of a company's stock attempting a hostile takeover. He or she may want to take the company over, or be bought out by the target company at a premium—a practice called greenmail.

**Self-tender offer:** Company offer to buy back its own shares, a move often used to keep the shares out of unfriendly hands.

**Shark repellent:** Measures taken in a company's bylaws to reduce the odds of a hostile takeover bid. These include staggering the terms of directors so a proxy fight can't result in taking over an entire board and requiring "super-majorities": approval by 75% or 80% of stockholders for takeovers.

**Standstill agreement:** Agreement between the bidder and the target company for the bidder to stop buying the target's stock or simply to leave the target alone for a specified period of time.

**Stock buy-back:** Company repurchase of its own stock, which reduces the number of shares outstanding. With earnings spread over fewer shares, the earnings per share increase, and so should the price of the company's stock. The move can deter a hostile takeover.

**Target company:** The company that is the takeover candidate.

**Ten-day window:** Federal law and Securities and Exchange Commission requirement that if 5% or more of a company's stock is bought by an individual or a company, the purchase must be made public within ten working days after the stock changes hands. Reason: To inform the company and investors of a possible change in control of the company.

**Tender offer:** Public offer to buy a company's stock. Usually priced at a premium above the market price to get shareholders to sell their shares to the bidder, the offer must remain open for 20 working days.

**Two-tiered tender offer:** Offer to pay cash for part of a company's shares, usually enough to give the bidder control. The bidder then offers a lower price, often in bonds, for the rest. The idea is to get shareholders to stampede their holdings into the cash offer.

**White knight:** Third party that takes over a hostile takeover target on a friendly basis, usually at the target's invitation, to avoid a hostile bid from another suitor.

3. Ensure that the management of the acquired company is or at least can be made competent.

4. Seek to ensure that the acquiring company's resources fit or mesh with the resources of the target company. This results in synergy.

5. Involve the chief executive officers of both the acquiring and the target organization in the entire merger program.

6. Clearly define the business of the acquiring company (organizational purpose).

7. Determine the strengths, weaknesses, and other key performance factors of both the acquiring and target organization.

8. Create a climate of mutual trust by anticipating problems and discussing them early with the target company.

9. Make the right advances. Avoid clumsy overtures, thoughtless actions, and carelessly voiced sentiments.

10. In assimilating a newly acquired company, exercise a minimum of control over the newly acquired organization. Maintain, and if possible improve, the status of the newly acquired management team.[36]

On the other hand, several factors need to be avoided in order to ensure a successful merger or acquisition. Some of these factors include

- Paying too much
- Straying too far afield
- Marrying disparate corporate cultures
- Counting on key managers staying
- Assuming a boom market won't crash
- Leaping before looking
- Swallowing too large a company[37]

Lessons learned from corporate mergers and acquisitions are that they work under the right circumstances. Understanding those circumstances and choosing the correct circumstances for a merger or acquisition are skills sorely needed by the top management of many organizations.

## IMPLEMENTING STRATEGIES THROUGH JOINT VENTURES

Another method used in carrying out diversification strategies is the joint venture. A *joint venture* is a separate corporate entity jointly owned by two or more parent organizations.[38] A joint venture combines the features of a partnership (which corporations cannot create) with those of a corporation (limited liability, indefinite life, and a familiar framework for funding and control). Thus, joint ventures represent one organizational form for achieving organizational objectives that neither organization could normally attain acting alone.

Joint ventures can take place between organizations within national boundaries or between private enterprise and government or not-for-profit organizations. Another frequent form of joint venture takes place between organizations in different countries.

## Reasons for Entering Joint Ventures

The major reasons for entering joint ventures include the following:

- Many countries have imposed formal and/or informal restrictions on foreigners doing business in their country. To deal with such restrictions, organizations form a joint venture with a local company.
- In many industries advantages connected with size of operations exist. Economies of scale can pertain to manufacturing, sales, and research and development. A joint venture can allow an organization to benefit from these economies of scale.
- Because of the tremendous risk involved in certain projects, many organizations find it appropriate to enter a joint venture in these situations.
- Certain resources and markets may not be available to an organization, and in such cases the need for access to these resources and markets can only be satisfied through a joint venture. A typical case occurs when one organization possesses a product that it wants to sell abroad. A joint venture with a partner abroad offers access to a distribution system together with a knowledge of local business practices, customs, and institutions.[39]

## Strategies to Use in Joint Ventures

Three basic strategies have been proposed for use in joint ventures.[40] They are called the spider's web, go together–split, and successive integration.

The *spider's web strategy* is employed in an industry with a few large organizations and several smaller organizations. One strategy for a smaller organization would be to enter a joint venture with one large organization and then, in order to avoid being absorbed, enter a new joint venture as quickly as possible with one or more of the remaining organizations. These different linkages thus form counterbalancing forces.

*Go together–split* is a strategy where two or more organizations cooperate over an extended period of time and then separate. This strategy is particularly appropriate on projects that have a definite life span, such as a construction project.

*Successive integration* starts with a weak joint venture relationship between the organizations, becomes stronger, and ultimately may result in a merger—either friendly or hostile.

## Considerations in Forming a Joint Venture

Three major considerations seem to be particularly important in forming a joint venture. The first consideration is choosing a partner. The issue of cultural difference arises almost immediately in that different approaches frequently are taken in selecting and appraising a joint venture partner. For example, an American organization's objective may be to enter a new market, whereas the objective of its joint venture partner (especially if it is in a developing country) may be to gain access to American technology. Different objectives have been documented to be one of the leading problems of Japanese-American joint ventures.[41] This problem can be resolved by having a formal agreement about the objectives for the joint venture.

Another consideration is the question of control over the joint venture. An organization can have a majority, an equal, or a minority participation in the equity capital of a joint venture. A foreign country may have legal restrictions (in its constitution, specific laws, or government policy) on the degree of control that organizations from other countries can hold in joint ventures. Negotiations between prospective joint ventures over the control issue have often resulted in failure. The major control consideration in a joint venture is to what extent control will contribute to the success of the joint venture.

A final consideration involves the management of the joint venture. Both parties to the joint venture should be interested in having the quality of management necessary to ensure its success. However, this can become a difficult problem, especially in joint ventures in foreign countries. One approach has been to allow staffing of all key positions in the joint venture to be limited to citizens of the country where the joint venture is located. Another approach involves requiring managers from the parent companies in joint ventures to become familiar with the language and culture of their partner. This facilitates adapting the managers to cross-cultural management decisions.[42]

## REVIEW QUESTIONS

1. Describe the characteristics of a stable growth strategy.
2. Outline the characteristics of a growth strategy.
3. What three questions should an organization's management answer before embarking on a growth strategy?
4. Define the following strategies:
   a. Concentric diversification
   b. Vertical integration
   c. Horizontal diversification
   d. Conglomerate diversification
5. Describe four endgame strategies.
6. Define the following strategies:
   a. Turnaround
   b. Divestment
   c. Liquidation
7. Describe the following business unit or corporate strategies:
   a. Overall cost leadership
   b. Differentiation
   c. Focus
8. What is a joint venture?

## DISCUSSION QUESTIONS

1. Select an organization in which you have been employed or with which you have some familiarity and identify the strategic alternatives available to it.
2. Many large companies have chosen conglomerate diversification as a strategy. Identify one of these companies and explain why you feel the company selected this strategy.
3. Identify a company that has used a growth strategy by concentrating on a single product or service. What are the risks to this company in using this strategy?
4. Select a merger that has recently occurred and identify the reasons for the merger.

## REFERENCES AND ADDITIONAL READING

1. Arnold Cooper, Edward Demuzzio, Kenneth Hatten, Elijah Hicks, and Donald Tock, "Strategic Responses to Technological Threats," *Academy of Management Proceedings,* 1973, p. 59.
2. Donald Gerwin and Francis D. Tuggle, "Modeling Organizational Decisions Using the Human Problem Solving Paradigm," *Academy of Management Review* 3, no. 4 (October 1978):770.
3. Peter L. Bernstein, "Growth Companies vs Growth Stocks," *Harvard Business Review* 34, no. 5 (September–October 1956):89.
4. Peter M. Gutmann, "Strategies for Growth," *California Management Review* 6, no. 4 (Summer 1964):31–36.
5. Isay Stemp, *Corporate Growth Strategies* (New York: American Management Association, 1970), p. 26.
6. Gutmann, "Strategies for Growth," pp. 34–35.

7. R. D. Buzzell, B. T. Gale, and R. G. M. Sultan, "Market Share—A Key to Profitability," *Harvard Business Review* 53 (January–February 1975):97–106.

8. Patrick Conley, "Experience Curves as a Planning Tool," in *Corporate Strategy and Product Innovation,* Robert Rothberg (ed.) (New York: Free Press, 1976), pp. 307–318.

9. Peter Drucker, *Management: Task, Responsibilities and Practices* (New York: Harper & Row, 1974), p. 772.

10. For studies on the potential consequences of too much growth, see Gerwin and Tuggle, "Modeling Organizational Decisions," pp. 762–773; and Paul Bloom and Philip Kotler, "Strategies for High Market Share Companies," *Harvard Business Review* 53, no. 6 (November–December 1975):63–72.

11. William E. Fruhan, Jr., "Pyrrhic Victories in Fights for Market Share," *Harvard Business Review* 50 (September–October 1972):107.

12. Eberhard E. Scheuing, *New Product Management* (New York: Dryden Press, 1974), p. 1.

13. Robert R. Rothberg, "Product Innovation in Perspective," in *Corporate Strategy and Product Innovation,* Robert Rothberg (ed.) (New York: Free Press, 1976), pp. 4–7.

14. Charles H. Berry, *Corporate Growth and Diversification* (Princeton, N.J.: Princeton University Press, 1975), p. 74.

15. Thomas Peters and Robert Waterman, Jr., *In Search of Excellence* (New York: Harper & Row, 1982), p. 15.

16. For an in-depth look at vertical integration strategies, see Kathryn Rudie Harrigan, "Formulating Vertical Integration Strategies," *Academy of Management Review* 9 (October 1984):638–652.

17. Richard P. Rumelt, *Strategy, Structure and Economic Performance* (Cambridge, Mass.: Harvard University Press, 1974), p. 139.

18. Ibid., p. 139.

19. E. Ralph Biggadike, *Corporate Diversification: Entry, Strategy, Performance* (Cambridge, Mass.: Harvard University Press, 1976), p. 194.

20. Theodore Levitt, "Dinosaurs, Bears, and Bulls," *Harvard Business Review* 53 (January–February 1975):43.

21. Joseph Vesey, "Vertical Integration: Its Effect on Business Performance," *Managerial Planning* 25–26 (May–June 1978):12.

22. Norman A. Berg, "What's Different About Conglomerate Management?" *Harvard Business Review* 47 (November–December 1969):118.

23. Ibid., p. 118.

24. Thomas A. Staudt, "Program for Product Diversification," *Harvard Business Review* 32 (November–December 1954):122–123.

25. H. Igor Ansoff, *Corporate Strategy* (New York: McGraw-Hill, 1965), pp. 136–137.

26. Fred R. Withnebert, "Big Equals Less Profitable (Still)," *Harvard Business Review* 53 (March–April 1975):18–20.

27. Ansoff, *Corporate Strategy,* p. 137.

28. Ansoff, *Corporate Strategy,* p. 137.

29. Kathryn Budie Harrigan and Michael E. Porter, "End-game Strategies for Declining Industries," *Harvard Business Review* 61 (July–August 1983):111.

30. Dan Schendel, G. R. Patton, and James Riggs, "Corporate Turnaround Strategies: A Study of Profit Decline and Recovery," *Journal of General Management* 3, no. 3 (Spring 1976):11.

31. For a discussion of turnaround strategies, see Donald C. Hambrick and Steven M. Schecter, "Turnaround Strategies for Mature-Industrial-Product Business Units," *Academy of Management Journal* 26 (June 1983):231–248.

32. Michael E. Porter, "Please Note Location of Nearest Exit: Exit Barriers and Planning," *California Management Review* 19, no. 2 (Winter 1976):21–25.

33. See also Surendra S. Singhvi, "Divestment as a Corporate Strategy," *The Journal of Business Strategy* 4 (Spring 1984):85–88.

34. Michael E. Porter, *Corporate Strategy* (New York: Free Press, 1980), pp. 34–46.

35. For an in-depth analysis of the effectiveness of these strategies, see Gregory G. Dess and Peter S. Davis, "Porter's (1980) Generic Strategies as Determinants of Strategic Group Membership and Organizational Performance," *Academy of Management Journal* 27 (September 1984):467–488.

36. Willard F. Rockwell, Jr., "How to Acquire a Company," *Harvard Business Review* 46, (September–October 1968):121–132.

37. Steven E. Prokesch and William J. Powell, Jr., "Do Mergers Really Work? *Business Week,* June 3, 1985, p. 90.

38. Sanford V. Berg and Philip Friedman, "Joint Ventures in American Industry," *Mergers & Acquisitions* 13, no. 2 (Summer 1978):39.

39. Staffan Gullander, "Joint Ventures and Corporate Strategy," *Columbia Journal of World Business* 11 (Spring 1976):105.

40. Ibid., pp. 106–108.

41. "How Companies Resolve Common Problems in Japanese Joint Ventures," *Business Asia,* September 10, 1976, pp. 289–291.

42. Richard B. Peterson and Justin Y. Shimada, "Sources of Management Problems in Japanese-American Joint Ventures," *Academy of Management Review* 3, no. 4 (October 1978):803–804.

# Strategic Management Process

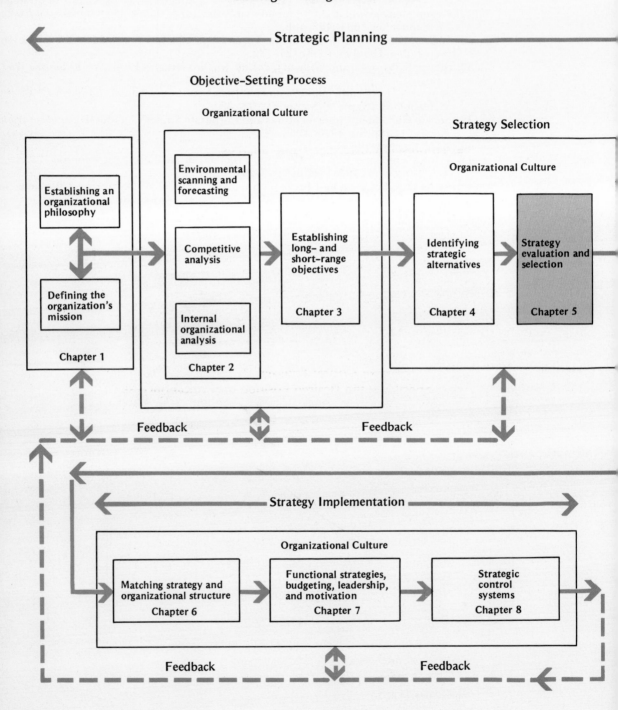

Strategic Planning

## Objective-Setting Process

Organizational Culture

### Strategy Selection

Organizational Culture

Establishing an organizational philosophy

Defining the organization's mission

Chapter 1

Environmental scanning and forecasting

Competitive analysis

Internal organizational analysis

Chapter 2

Establishing long- and short-range objectives

Chapter 3

Identifying strategic alternatives

Chapter 4

Strategy evaluation and selection

Chapter 5

Feedback          Feedback

## Strategy Implementation

Organizational Culture

Matching strategy and organizational structure
Chapter 6

Functional strategies, budgeting, leadership, and motivation
Chapter 7

Strategic control systems
Chapter 8

Feedback          Feedback

# 5

# *STRATEGY EVALUATION AND SELECTION*

## STUDY OBJECTIVES

- To describe methodologies used in business portfolio analyses including the growth-share matrix, the industry attractiveness–business strength matrix, and the life-cycle approach

- To discuss competitive strategy analysis

- To present cluster and PIMS analysis

- To discuss several qualitative factors that influence the strategy evaluation and selection process

## CHAPTER OUTLINE

Business Portfolio Analysis
  Growth-Share Matrix
    Strategy Selection
    Criticisms of the Growth-Share Matrix
  Industry Attractiveness–Business Strength Matrix
    Defining and Assessing Critical External Factors
    Defining and Assessing Critical Success Factors
    Forecasting Critical External Factors
    Specifying the Desired Position on Critical Success Factors
    Corporate-Level Strategies
    Business Unit Strategies
    Functional Area Strategies
    Criticisms of Industry Attractiveness–Business Strength Matrix
  Life-Cycle Approach
    Strategy Selection
    Product-Market Evolution Matrix
Competitive Strategy Analysis
Cluster Analysis
PIMS Analysis
Qualitative Factors in the Strategy Evaluation and Selection Process
  Managerial Attitudes Toward Risk
  Environment of the Organization
  Organizational Culture and Power Relationships
  Competitive Actions and Reactions
  Influence of Previous Organizational Strategies
  Timing Considerations
Review Questions
Discussion Questions
References and Additional Reading

*Gideon said to God, "If you will save Israel by my hand as you have promised—look, I will place a wool fleece on the threshing floor. If there is dew only on the fleece and all the ground is dry, then I will know that you will save Israel by my hand, as you said." And that is what happened. Gideon rose early the next day; he squeezed the fleece and wrung out the dew—a bowlful of water.*

*Then Gideon said to God, "Do not be angry with me. Let me make just one more request. Allow me one more test with the fleece. This time make the fleece dry and the ground covered with dew." That night God did so. Only the fleece was dry; all the ground was covered with dew.* —Judges 6:36–40

In what direction should an organization go? Ideally, an organization's strategy should be designed to take advantage of market opportunities and neutralize adverse environmental impacts. At the same time, it should reinforce the internal strengths of the organization and improve on its perceived weaknesses relative to its competition. Given these characteristics of an ideal strategy and considering the options available to most organizations, one can begin to understand why strategy selection is such a complex and difficult decision. Fortunately, several methodologies have been developed to assist organizations in making these decisions.

## BUSINESS PORTFOLIO ANALYSIS

One methodology developed to assist managers in the strategy evaluation and selection process is known as business portfolio analysis. Among the various approaches of this type, the most popular seem to be the growth-share matrix, the industry attractiveness–business strength matrix, and the life-cycle approach.

## Growth-Share Matrix

Originally developed by the Boston Consulting Group (BCG), the growth-share matrix approach postulates that all except the smallest and simplest organizations are composed of more than one business.[1] These businesses within an organization are called its *business portfolio.* The BCG approach proposes that a separate strategy be developed for each of these largely independent units.

In order to visually display an organization's business portfolio, BCG developed a four-quadrant grid as shown on Figure 5.1. The horizontal axis indicates the market share of the business relative to its major competitor and characterizes the strength of the organization in that business. The market share for any particular year is calculated as follows:

$$\text{Relative market share (current year)} = \frac{\left[\begin{array}{c}\text{Business unit sales}\\ \text{(current year)}\end{array}\right]}{\left[\begin{array}{c}\text{Leading competitor's sales}\\ \text{(current year)}\end{array}\right]}$$

The vertical axis indicates the percent of growth in the market in the current year and characterizes the attractiveness of the market for the business unit. The market growth rate is calculated as follows:

$$\text{Market growth rate} \atop \text{(current year)} = \frac{\left[\begin{matrix} \text{Total market} \\ \text{(current year)} \end{matrix}\right] - \left[\begin{matrix} \text{Total market} \\ \text{(previous year)} \end{matrix}\right]}{\left[\begin{matrix} \text{Total market} \\ \text{(previous year)} \end{matrix}\right]} \times 100$$

The lines that divide the matrix into four quadrants are somewhat arbitrarily set. A high market growth rate is taken to be in excess of 10 percent. The demarcation between high and low relative market share is set at 1.5. This means that if a particular business unit's current sales are 1.5 times or greater than its leading competitor's sales, then it is considered to have a high relative market share. These lines of demarcation are not absolutes and can be modified to fit the particular needs of an organization. Furthermore, in actual practice the market growth rate axis is plotted on a linear scale, whereas the relative market share is plotted on a logarithmic scale.

BCG describes the four quadrants of the growth-scale matrix as follows:

1. *Cash cows* have low growth and high market share. Because of high market share, profits and cash generation should be high. The low rate of growth means that the cash demands should be low. Thus, large cash surpluses are normally generated by cash cows. They provide the cash to meet the needs of the overall company and are thus the foundation of the company.
2. *Dogs* are business segments or units that have low market share and low market growth. The low market share normally implies poor profits. Because the growth rate is low, investments to increase market share are frequently

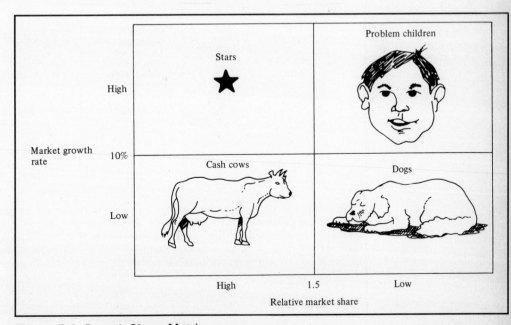

**Figure 5.1** Growth-Share Matrix

prohibitive. Unfortunately, the cash required to maintain a competitive position often exceeds the cash generated. Thus, dogs often become cash traps. Generally, dogs are harvested or divested.

3. *Problem children* are business units that have low market share and high market growth rate. Their cash needs are high because of their growth, and the cash generated is low because of their market share. Because growth is high, one strategy for a problem child is to make the necessary investments to gain market share and become a star. When the market growth rate slows, the unit can then become a cash cow. Another strategy is to divest the problem children that management feels cannot be developed into stars.

4. *Stars* are business units with high growth and high market share. Because of the high growth and high market share, stars use and generate large amounts of cash. Stars generally represent the best profit and investment opportunities. Obviously, the best strategy for stars is to make the necessary investments to maintain or improve their competitive position.

The labels used by BCG to classify the quadrants have often been criticized. After all, who would want to be known as the manager in charge of a dog? However, despite what some people feel are derogatory connotations, they have become widely accepted. Example 5.1 shows how the Mead Corporation named the four quadrants.

---

## STRATEGY IN PRACTICE

**Example 5.1** Growth-Share Matrix Categories for Mead Corporation

| | | Savings Account | Sweepstake |
|---|---|---|---|
| Market growth, % | High | Growing business<br>Self–financing<br>Medium risk<br>High profit<br>Cost–effective | Developing business<br>Net cash user<br>Extremely high risk<br>Low profit<br>Not cost–effective |
| 10% | | Bond | Mortgage |
| | Low | Mature business<br>Net cash generator<br>Low risk<br>High profit<br>Cost–effective | Mature business<br>Net cash generator<br>Medium risk<br>Low profit<br>Not cost–effective |

High    1.5    Low

Relative market share

The categories of sweepstake, savings account, bond, or mortgage businesses allow a general prediction of the behavior of the business unit and the way it should be managed; the hoped-for life cycle of a business unit is first as a sweepstake, then as a savings account, then as a bond. Business units with high market shares generally provide current earnings while those with high market growth generally provide future earnings; general characteristics of business units in the strategy matrix are also shown.

*Source:* Adapted from Francis J. Aguilar, *The Mead Corporation* (Boston: Intercollegiate Case Clearing House, 9-379-070).

The following steps are generally followed in using the growth-share matrix in strategy evaluation and selection:

1. Divide the company into its business units. Many organizations perform this step when they establish strategic business units (SBUs). On the matrix, a circle is used to depict individual business units.

2. Determine the business unit's relative size within the total organization. Relative size can be measured in terms of assets employed within the business unit as a percentage of the total assets or sales of the business unit as a percentage of total sales. On the matrix, the area within the circle indicates the business unit's relative size.

3. Determine the market growth rate for each individual business unit.

4. Determine the relative market share of each individual business unit.

5. Develop a graphical picture of the company's overall portfolio of businesses. Example 5.2 shows a business portfolio for individual markets within the packaging division (an SBU) of the Mead Corporation.

# STRATEGY IN PRACTICE

## Example 5.2 Growth-Share Matrix for Mead Packaging

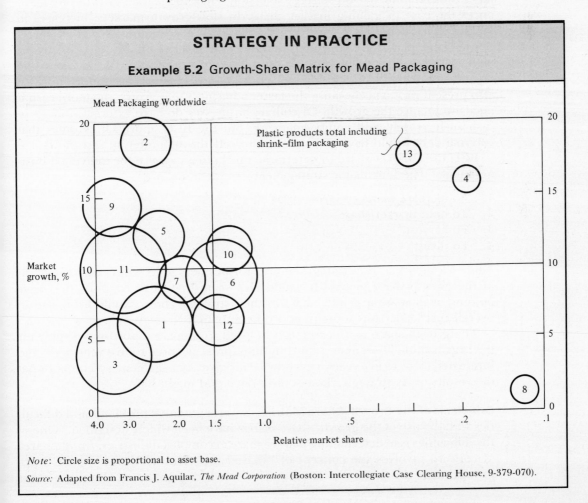

*Note*: Circle size is proportional to asset base.

*Source*: Adapted from Francis J. Aquilar, *The Mead Corporation* (Boston: Intercollegiate Case Clearing House, 9-379-070).

6. Select a strategy for each business unit based on its position in the company's overall portfolio of businesses.

**Strategy Selection**   Strategy selection using the growth-share matrix assumes that the primary objectives of the organization are growth and profitability.[2] The advantage of multibusiness organizations is that they can transfer cash from business units that are highly profitable but have low growth potential to other units that have high growth and high profit potential. Strategy selection among the various business units is designed to produce a balanced portfolio in terms of the generation and uses of cash.

Thus, relative market share and the market growth rate are the two fundamental parameters that influence strategy selection. Relative market share determines the rate at which the business unit generates cash. A business unit with a relatively high share of the market compared to its competitors should have higher profit margins and thus higher cash flows. On the other hand, the market growth rate has a twofold influence on strategy selection. First, the market growth rate influences the ease of gaining market share. In slow-growth markets, increases in market share generally come from decreases in a competitor's market share. Second, the market growth rate determines the level of opportunity for investment. Growth markets provide an opportunity for plowing cash back into the business unit and compounding the return on investment. This opportunity can also present problems because the faster a business unit grows, the more cash it needs to finance the growth. Of course, businesses do have external sources of cash such as debt and equity financing, but the BCG approach assumes that external debt would have to be met ultimately through internal cash flows.

BCG uses market share to determine the strategic choice for individual business units. The four major strategic choices identified are

1. To increase market share
2. To hold market share
3. To harvest
4. To divest

Table 5.1 identifies the strategic choices for business units within each quadrant of the growth-share matrix. It would also seem that business units that have holding or increasing market share as their strategic choice would likely use an overall cost leadership strategy or a differentiation strategy.

The growth-share matrix can also be used to prepare a portfolio display for the organization at separate points in time (present, three to five years ago, and forecasted three to five years from now). This gives management a picture of what the results of its strategic choices have been and might be.

**Criticisms of the Growth-Share Matrix**   Several potential problems and difficulties with the use of the growth-share matrix have been widely described.[3] One of the difficulties is in determining market share in complex industries. Another area of concern involves the concept of "shared experience." Under the BCG approach, dogs are generally harvested, divested, or liquidated. However, it has

**Table 5.1** Strategic Choices Using Growth-Share Matrix

| Quadrant | Strategic Choice | Business Unit Profitability | Investment Required | Cash Flow |
|---|---|---|---|---|
| Star | Hold or increase market share | High | High | Around zero or slightly negative |
| Cash cows | Add market share | High | Low | Highly positive |
| Problem children | Increase market share | None or negative | Very high | Highly negative |
| | Harvest/divest | Low or negative | Disinvest | Positive |
| Dogs | Harvest/ divest/ liquidate | Low or negative | Disinvest | Positive |

*Source:* Adapted from Arnoldo C. Hax and Nicholas S. Majluk, "The Use of the Growth-Share Matrix in Strategic Planning," *Interfaces* 13 (February 1983):51.

been pointed out that valuable experience may be gained in a low-profit business unit (dog) that can help in lowering costs in a related but more profitable business unit (star or cash cow).[4]

Furthermore, some research has indicated that well-managed dogs can become cash generators.[5] One study of 87 organizations that had low-market-share positions in slow-growth industries classified 40 of these organizations as being ineffective (i.e., a return on investment of less than 5 percent).[6] This research concluded that effective organizations tended to pursue a high-quality, medium-price strategy complemented by careful spending on marketing and R&D. On the other hand, ineffective dogs must still be considered candidates for harvesting, divestment, or liquidation.

**Industry Attractiveness–Business Strength Matrix**

General Electric (GE) found the visual display of the growth-share matrix appealing, but felt that using only two dimensions—market growth rate and relative market share—was inadequate for describing its portfolio of businesses. GE felt that a wider variety of factors needed to be identified and assessed in order to develop an effective display of its business units. Thus, GE asked McKinsey and Company to develop the portfolio approach that is now called the industry attractiveness–business strength matrix.

The industry attractiveness–business strength matrix is illustrated in Figure 5.2. The use of the matrix first requires an identification and assessment of both critical external factors and internal factors. Critical external factors are not directly controllable by the organization and determine the overall attractiveness of the industry in which the business unit operates. After identifying and assessing these critical external factors, top management makes a qualitative decision on

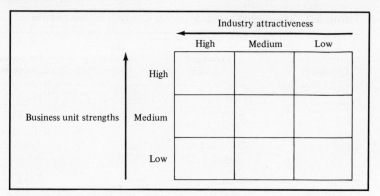

**Figure 5.2** Industry Attractiveness–Business Strength Matrix

whether the industry has a low, medium, or high attractiveness. Critical internal factors, or *critical success factors* as they are frequently called, are generally controllable by the organization and determine the business unit's strengths. Again, a qualitative decision is made on whether the business unit's strengths are low, medium, or high.

Identifying and assessing industry attractiveness and business unit strengths allows each business unit to be positioned on the nine-cell matrix. The following sections outline a methodology for using the industry attractiveness–business strength matrix.[7]

**Defining and Assessing Critical External Factors**  Critical external factors include the competitive characteristics of the industry of the business unit and the economic, technological, political, and social forces that influence the industry. Example 5.3 shows the actual assessment of critical external factors for a business unit of a Swiss organization in a high-technology industry. The management of this organization classified the industry attractiveness as being low largely because of the unattractive industry conditions.

**Defining and Assessing Critical Success Factors**  *Critical success factors* have a significant impact on the success of the particular business unit that is competing in an industry.[8] Some of the critical success factors that have been identified are market share, strength of the sales force, manufacturing capability, corporate image, breadth of product line, strength of financial resources, product quality and reliability, and managerial competence. The position that a particular business unit achieves on these factors, relative to its competition, determines its strength. Example 5.4 shows a chart assessing the critical success factors for the same Swiss firm shown in Example 5.3. The management of this firm decided that the business unit had medium business strengths. Example 5.5 shows the positioning of the business unit in the industry attractiveness–business strength matrix.

**Example 5.3** Assessment of Critical External Factors for a Business Unit of a Swiss Organization

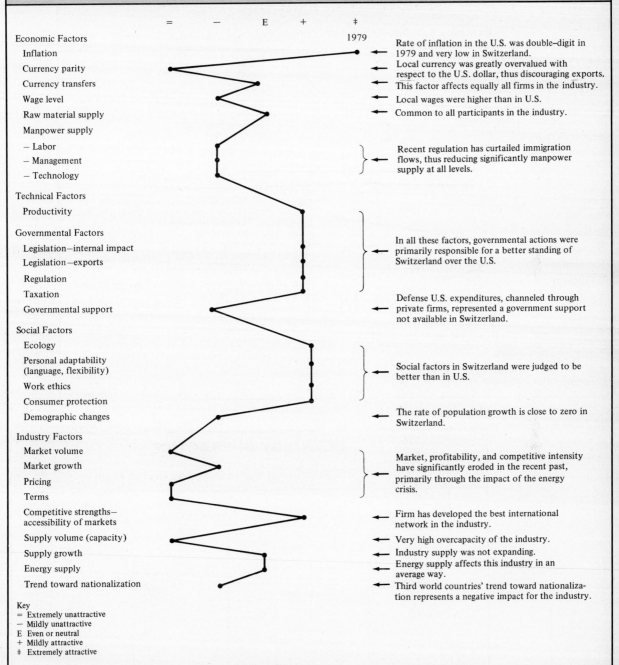

|  | = | − | E | + | ‡ |
|---|---|---|---|---|---|
|  |  |  |  |  | 1979 |

Economic Factors
  Inflation — Rate of inflation in the U.S. was double–digit in 1979 and very low in Switzerland.
  Currency parity — Local currency was greatly overvalued with respect to the U.S. dollar, thus discouraging exports.
  Currency transfers — This factor affects equally all firms in the industry.
  Wage level — Local wages were higher than in U.S.
  Raw material supply — Common to all participants in the industry.
  Manpower supply
    − Labor
    − Management — Recent regulation has curtailed immigration flows, thus reducing significantly manpower supply at all levels.
    − Technology

Technical Factors
  Productivity

Governmental Factors
  Legislation−internal impact
  Legislation−exports — In all these factors, governmental actions were primarily responsible for a better standing of Switzerland over the U.S.
  Regulation
  Taxation
  Governmental support — Defense U.S. expenditures, channeled through private firms, represented a government support not available in Switzerland.

Social Factors
  Ecology
  Personal adaptability (language, flexibility) — Social factors in Switzerland were judged to be better than in U.S.
  Work ethics
  Consumer protection
  Demographic changes — The rate of population growth is close to zero in Switzerland.

Industry Factors
  Market volume
  Market growth — Market, profitability, and competitive intensity have significantly eroded in the recent past, primarily through the impact of the energy crisis.
  Pricing
  Terms
  Competitive strengths− accessibility of markets — Firm has developed the best international network in the industry.
  Supply volume (capacity) — Very high overcapacity of the industry.
  Supply growth — Industry supply was not expanding.
  Energy supply — Energy supply affects this industry in an average way.
  Trend toward nationalization — Third world countries' trend toward nationalization represents a negative impact for the industry.

Key
= Extremely unattractive
− Mildly unattractive
E Even or neutral
+ Mildly attractive
‡ Extremely attractive

*Source:* Arnoldo C. Hax and Nicholas S. Majluk, "The Use of the Industry Attractiveness–Business Strength Matrix in Strategic Planning," *Interfaces* 13 (April 1983):57.

## STRATEGY IN PRACTICE

### Example 5.4 Assessment of Critical Success Factors

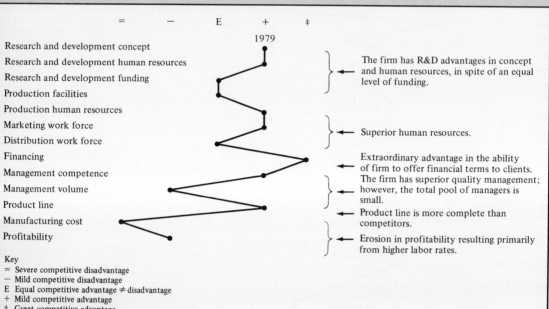

Research and development concept
Research and development human resources
Research and development funding
Production facilities
Production human resources
Marketing work force
Distribution work force
Financing
Management competence
Management volume
Product line
Manufacturing cost
Profitability

The firm has R&D advantages in concept and human resources, in spite of an equal level of funding.

Superior human resources.

Extraordinary advantage in the ability of firm to offer financial terms to clients. The firm has superior quality management; however, the total pool of managers is small.

Product line is more complete than competitors.

Erosion in profitability resulting primarily from higher labor rates.

Key
= Severe competitive disadvantage
− Mild competitive disadvantage
E Equal competitive advantage ≠ disadvantage
+ Mild competitive advantage
‡ Great competitive advantage

*Source:* Arnoldo C. Hax and Nicholas S. Majluk, "The Use of the Industry Attractiveness–Business Strength Matrix in Strategic Planning," *Interfaces* 13 (April 1983):58.

## STRATEGY IN PRACTICE

### Example 5.5 Position of Swiss Business Unit in Matrix

| | | Industry attractiveness | | |
|---|---|---|---|---|
| | | High | Medium | Low |
| Business strengths | High | | | |
| | Medium | | | 1979 position |
| | Low | | | |

*Source:* Arnoldo C. Hax and Nicholas S. Majluk, "The Use of the Industry Attractiveness–Business Strength Matrix in Strategic Planning," *Interfaces* 13 (April 1983):61.

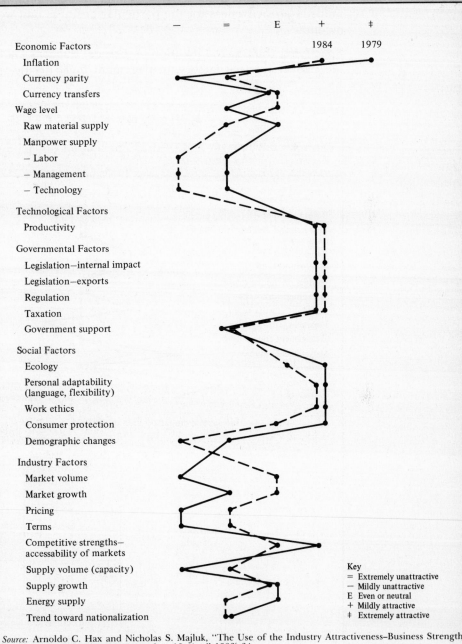

# STRATEGY IN PRACTICE

## Example 5.6 Forecast Critical External Factors

Source: Arnoldo C. Hax and Nicholas S. Majluk, "The Use of the Industry Attractiveness–Business Strength Matrix in Strategic Planning," *Interfaces* 13 (April 1983):64.

**Forecasting Critical External Factors**   Several techniques for forecasting external factors were described in Chapter 2. Any of those techniques can be used to assess the future trends of the critical external factors. Example 5.6 (p. 101) shows the forecast trends for the Swiss business unit. The management forecast that the industry attractiveness for the particular business unit would move from low to medium.

**Specifying the Desired Position on Critical Success Factors**   After forecasting the critical external factors, management must decide where it would like the

---

# STRATEGY IN PRACTICE

**Example 5.7** Present and Desired Position on Critical Success Factors and on the Matrix

Research and development concept
Research and development human resources
Research and development funding
Production facilities
Production human resources
Marketing work force
Distribution work force
Financing
Management competence
Management volume
Product line
Manufacturing cost
Profitability

Key
= Severe competitive disadvantage
− Mild competitive disadvantage
E Equal competitive advantage ≠ disadvantage
+ Mild competitive advantage
‡ Great competitive advantage

Present and desired position on critical success factors

Present and desired position on matrix

*Source:* Arnoldo C. Hax and Nicholas S. Majluk, "The Use of the Industry Attractiveness–Business Strength Matrix in Strategic Planning, *Interfaces* 13 (April 1983):64–65.

business unit to be at a future time period relative to the critical success factors. Example 5.7 illustrates where the management of the Swiss business unit decided they wanted to be in 1984. The management's desire is to move to a position of high business unit strengths. Example 5.7 also shows the matrix for the present and future position of the business unit.

**Corporate-Level Strategies**   Management can obtain an overall view of the corporate portfolio by placing the present and desired positions of all business units on the matrix. Because of the scarcity of money and other resources, the top management of most organizations must become selective and limit their investments to those business units that can provide an attractive payoff and in which they are strong. In addition, they must use some business units to finance the growth of others. Generally, when a business unit is high on industry attractiveness and business strengths, the natural corporate-level strategy is to invest heavily and pursue a growth strategy. Whenever attractiveness and business strengths are low, the strategy is normally to harvest or divest. In the intermediate positions, the strategy generally involves concentrating resources on the most attractive business units or in business units that have a unique competence. Obviously the choice of what units to fund is influenced by the organizational culture and other nonquantifiable factors which are discussed later in this chapter. Furthermore, changes in the external factors which can make the industry attractiveness of a business unit either high, medium, or low also influence the decision process. For example, the industry attractiveness of the business unit of the Swiss firm is forecast to change from low to medium. The strategic choice for corporate-level management is whether to harvest or divest the business unit or fund it based on the forecast industry attractiveness. Figure 5.3 illustrates the general corporate-level strategies available to an organization.

**Business Unit Strategies**   Obviously, the strategy of a particular business unit depends on the corporate-level strategy and the funding and resources provided to the business unit by corporate-level management. Nevertheless, after these

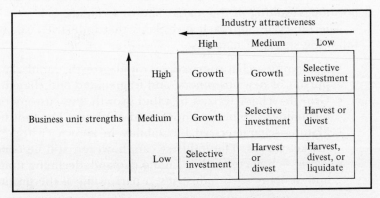

**Figure 5.3** Strategies Available to Organizations

decisions are made, the industry attractiveness–business strength matrix can be used to examine the performance of each of the product lines within the business unit and to identify those product lines that deserve either more or less support. It also can help identify the particular strategy—overall cost leadership, differentiation, or focus—that could be used for each product line.

**Functional Area Strategies**    As will be recalled, use of the industry attractiveness–business strength matrix requires an assessment and specification of the desired future position of the business unit on critical process factors; generally this provides a basis for the development of functional strategies. Most of the critical success factors fall either within functional areas of the business unit or across multifunctional areas. The development of functional strategies involves determining the actions that need to be taken within each functional area in order to move the functional area from its present position to its desired position. Of course, each functional area strategy is totally dependent on the strategies developed at the corporate and business unit level and the resources provided from these levels. Functional area strategies are described in more detail in Chapter 7.

**Criticisms of Industry Attractiveness–Business Strength Matrix**    Several problems or difficulties with the use of the industry attractiveness–business strength matrix have been identified and discussed. First, because it is often difficult to identify and agree upon standard lists of external and internal factors to be used by all business units within an organization, inconsistencies in the classification of business units can develop. It has also been argued that when applying the matrix, managers often do not agree and many categorize a business unit as medium because they cannot reconcile diverging opinions. Regardless of these difficulties, however, the industry attractiveness–business strength matrix is widely used in strategy evaluation and selection.

**Life-Cycle Approach**    The life-cycle approach, developed by Arthur D. Little, Inc., classifies business units within an organization by (1) industry maturity and (2) strategic competitive position, resulting in the matrix shown in Figure 5.4.

The life-cycle approach postulates that industries can be grouped into the following stages of maturity:

- Embryonic—characterized by rapid growth, rapid changes in technology, pursuit of new customers, and fragmented and changing shares of market.
- Growth—characterized by rapid growth, but customers, market share, and technology are better known and entry into the industry is more difficult.
- Mature—characterized by stability in known customers, technology, and market shares. The industry can, however, still be competitive.
- Aging—characterized by falling demand, declining number of competitors, and in many such industries, a narrowing of the product line.[9]

The determination of a business unit's strategic competitive position calls for a qualitative decision based on multiple criteria such as breadth of product line,

| Competitive position | Industry maturity | | | |
|---|---|---|---|---|
| | **Embryonic** | **Growth** | **Mature** | **Aging** |
| Dominant | | | | |
| Strong | | | | |
| Favorable | | | | |
| Tenable | | | | |
| Weak | | | | |

**Figure 5.4** Life-Cycle Matrix

market share, movement in market share, and changes in technology. The life-cycle approach maintains that as these criteria change over time, a business unit either gains or loses competitive advantage and can be classified as being dominant, strong, favorable, tenable, or weak.

**Strategy Selection**   After a business unit has been positioned within the matrix, a strategy can be formulated for the business unit. Table 5.2 illustrates a set of possible choices for business units within an organization. It also indicates the profit and cash implications for each option.

At the corporate level, resources are normally allocated among business units on a competitive basis. Business units are screened or ranked on criteria such as desirability of certain maturities, strength of competitive position, ability to produce positive cash flows in the short or long term, rates of return on investment or net assets, and degree of risk. This screening enables top management to decide which business units are to receive what resources.

**Product-Market Evolution Matrix**   Very closely allied with the life-cycle approach and only slightly different is the product-market evolution matrix.[10] Figure 5.5 illustrates the matrix in which business units are plotted in terms of their stage of product-market evolution and their competitive position. The circles represent the relative sizes of the industries. The wedges within the circles represent the market share of the business unit.

Several useful ideas concerning the strategic alternatives available to each business unit emerge from an analysis of Figure 5.5:

1. Business unit A appears to be a potential star. Its relatively large share of the market combined with being at the development stage of product-market evolution and its potential for being in a strong competitive position make it a good candidate for receiving more corporate resources.

2. Business unit B is somewhat similar to A. However, investments in B would be contingent on determining why B has such a relatively small share of the

**Table 5.2** Business Unit Strategy Choices

| Strategic Competitive Position | Industry Maturity | | | |
| --- | --- | --- | --- | --- |
| | Embryonic | Growth | Mature | Aging |
| **Dominant** | All-out push for share<br>Hold position:<br>  Invest slightly faster than market dictates<br>Probably profitable, but not necessarily<br>Net cash borrower | Hold position<br>Hold share:<br>  Invest to sustain growth rate and preempt new competitors<br>Profitable<br>Probably net cash producer (but not necessarily) | Hold position<br>Grow with industry:<br>  Reinvest as necessary<br>Profitable<br>Net cash producer | Hold position:<br>  Reinvest as necessary<br>Profitable<br>Net cash producer |
| **Strong** | Attempt to improve position<br>All-out push for share:<br>  Invest as fast as market dictates<br>May be unprofitable<br>Net cash borrower | Attempt to improve position<br>Push for share:<br>  Invest to increase growth rate (and improve position)<br>Probably profitable<br>Probably net cash borrower | Hold position<br>Grow with industry:<br>  Reinvest as necessary<br>Profitable<br>Net cash producer | Hold position<br>Harvest:<br>  Minimum reinvestment or maintenance<br>Profitable<br>Net cash producer |
| **Favorable** | Selective or all-out push for share<br>Selectively attempt to improve position:<br>  Invest selectively<br>Probably unprofitable<br>Net cash borrower | Attempt to improve position<br>Selective push for share:<br>  Selective investment to improve position<br>Marginally profitable<br>Net cash borrower | Custodial or maintenance<br>Find niche and attempt to protect:<br>  Minimum and/or selective reinvestment<br>Moderately profitable<br>Net cash producer | Harvest or phased withdrawal:<br>  Minimum maintenance<br>Investment or disinvest<br>Moderately profitable<br>Cash flow balance |
| **Tenable** | Selectively push for position:<br>  Invest very selectively<br>Unprofitable<br>Net cash borrower | Find niche and protect it:<br>  Selective investment<br>Unprofitable<br>Net cash borrower or cash flow balance | Find niche and hang on or phased withdrawal:<br>  Minimum reinvestment or disinvest<br>Minimally profitable<br>Cash flow balance | Phased withdrawal or abandon:<br>  Disinvest or divest<br>Minimally profitable<br>Cash flow balance |

**Table 5.2** Business Unit Strategy Choices (*continued*)

| Strategic Competitive Position | Industry Maturity | | | |
|---|---|---|---|---|
| | Embryonic | Growth | Mature | Aging |
| Weak | Up or out:<br>    Invest or divest<br>Unprofitable<br>Net cash borrower | Turnaround or<br>    abandon:<br>    Invest or divest<br>Unprofitable<br>Net cash borrower or<br>    cash flow balance | Turnaround or<br>    phased<br>    withdrawal:<br>    Invest selectively or<br>    disinvest<br>Unprofitable<br>Possibly net cash<br>    borrower or net<br>    cash producer | Abandon:<br>    Divest<br>Unprofitable<br>(Write-off) |

*Source:* Roger R. Osell and Robert R. V. Wright, "Allocating Resources: How to Do It in Multi-Industry Corporations," in *Handbook of Business Problem Solving,* Kenneth J. Albert (ed.) (New York: McGraw-Hill, 1980), p. 1–95.

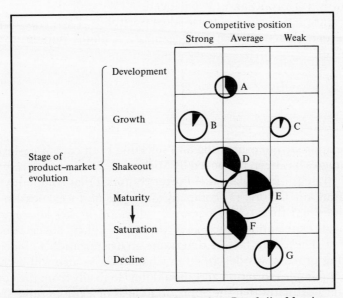

**Figure 5.5** Product-Market Evolution Portfolio Matrix
*Source:* Adapted from C. W. Hofer, *Conceptual Constructs for Formulating Corporate and Business Strategies* (Boston: Intercollegiate Case Clearing House, 9–378–754, 1977), p. 3.

market given its strong competitive position. A strategy would have to be developed to overcome this low market share in order to justify more investments.

3.  Business unit C has a small market share in a relatively small industry that is growing and has a weak competitive position. A strategy must be developed to overcome the low market share and weak competitive position in order to justify future investments. This might be a good candidate to divest in order to use the resources in either A or B.

4.  Business unit D is in a shakeout period, has a relatively large share of the market, and is in a relatively strong competitive position. Investments should be made to maintain the relatively strong competitive position. In the long run, D should become a cash cow.

5.  Business units E and F are cash cows and should be used for cash generation.

6.  Business unit G appears to be a dog within the corporate portfolio. It should be managed to generate cash in the short run, if possible; however, the long-run strategy will more than likely be divestment or liquidation.

Organizations can have a variety of mixes in their business portfolios. It has been suggested that most portfolios are variations of one of three ideal types: (1) growth, (2) profit, and (3) balanced.[11]

Figure 5.6 illustrates these ideal portfolios. Each type of portfolio represents different objectives that an organization might pursue in its allocation of resources.

## COMPETITIVE STRATEGY ANALYSIS

One approach to evaluating and selecting both corporate-level and business unit strategies has been proposed by Michael E. Porter and is referred to as "competitive strategy" formulation.[12] Porter contends that competitive strategies are built on four key factors: (1) company strengths and weaknesses; (2) industry opportunities and threats; (3) personal values of the key managers; and (4) broader societal expectations such as government policy, social concerns, and evolving mores. These four factors determine an organization's objectives. The objective-setting process was described in Chapter 2. As also will be recalled, policies are general guides to action and should flow logically from the corporate philosophy. Porter postulates that the appropriateness of a competitive strategy can be determined by testing the objectives and policies for consistency. Figure 5.7 provides questions that when answered determine the consistency between objectives and policies.

Porter's approach to selecting the optimal competitive strategy is summarized in Figure 5.8. Porter further contends that businesses and business units pursue basically three generic strategies (which can be used singly or in combination). These strategies are overall cost leadership, differentiation, and focus and were discussed earlier in Chapter 4. Performing the analysis required in answering the

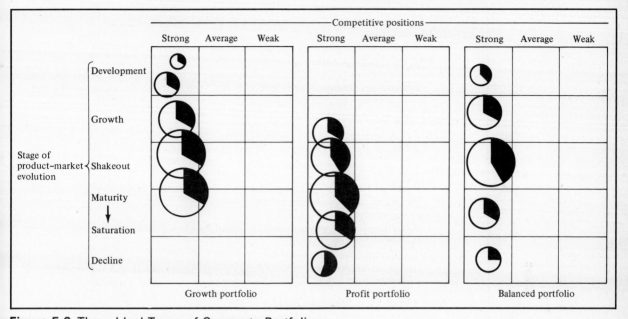

**Figure 5.6** Three Ideal Types of Corporate Portfolios
*Source:* Reprinted by permission of Charles W. Hofer and Dan Schendel from *Strategy Formulation: Analyical Concepts* (St. Paul, Minn.: West Publishing Company, 1978), p. 183. All rights reserved.

Internal Consistency
  Are the objectives mutually achievable?
  Do the key operating policies address the objectives?
  Do the key operating policies reinforce each other?

Environmental Fit
  Do the objectives and policies exploit industry opportunities?
  Do to the objectives and policies deal with industry threats (including the risk of
    competitive response) to the degree possible with available resources?
  Does the timing of the objectives and policies reflect the ability of the environ-
    ment to absorb the actions?
  Are the objectives and policies responsive to broader societal concerns?

Resource Fit
  Do the objectives and policies match the resources available to the company
    relative to competitors?
  Does the timing of the objectives and policies reflect the organization's ability to
    change?

Communication and Implementation
  Are the objectives well understood by the key implementers?
  Is there enough congruence between the objectives and policies and the values
    of the key implementers to insure commitment?
  Is there sufficient managerial capability to allow for effective implementation?

**Figure 5.7** Tests of Consistency for Objectives and Policies
*Source:* Adapted from Michael E. Porter, *Competitive Strategy* (New York: Free Press, 1980), p. xix.

A. What Is the Business (or Business Unit) Doing Now?
  1. Identification
     What is the implicit or explicit current strategy?
  2. Implied Assumptions
     What assumptions about the company's relative position, strengths and weaknesses, competitors, and industry trends must be made for the current strategy to make sense?

B. What Is Happening in the Environment?
  1. Industry analysis
     What are the key factors for competitive success and the important industry opportunities and threats?
  2. Competitor analysis
     What are the capabilities and limitations of existing and potential competitors, and their probable future moves?
  3. Societal analysis
     What important governmental, social, and political factors will present opportunities or threats?
  4. Strengths and weaknesses
     Given an analysis of industry and competitors, what are the company's strengths and weaknesses *relative to present and future competitors?*

C. What Should the Business Be Doing?
  1. Tests of assumptions and strategy
     How do the assumptions embodied in the current strategy compare with the analysis in B above? How does the strategy meet the tests in Figure 5.7?
  2. Strategic alternatives
     What are the feasible strategic alternatives given the analysis above? (Is the current strategy one of these?)
  3. Strategic choice
     Which alternative best relates the company's situation to external opportunities and threats?

**Figure 5.8** Process for Formulating a Competitive Strategy
*Source:* Adapted from Michael E. Porter, *Competitive Strategy* (New York: Free Press, 1980), pp. xix and xx.

questions shown in Figure 5.8 enables an organization to choose the most effective strategy or strategies not only for each business unit but also for the organization as a whole.

**CLUSTER ANALYSIS**

Cluster analysis suggests that several of the strategy evaluation and selection methods overlook the fact that often business units are interrelated and should not be viewed as separate district units for strategy selection purposes. The contention is that the realization of major opportunities or the avoidance of major threats does not lie with individual business units but in a grouping of business units. The grouping or clustering of business units into a broader context is normally done along some unifying theme such as shared production processes, allied technology underlying the product line, or control of a distribution system.[13]

In actual practice, cluster analysis merely involves developing corporate-level strategy for clusters of business units. The general steps involved include the following:

1. Identify clusters of business units based on some unifying theme such as shared production process.
2. Develop a corporate-level strategy for the cluster of businesses using any of the previously described methods such as the industry attractiveness–business strength matrix.
3. Develop individual business unit strategies based on the corporate-level cluster strategy. These business unit strategies can be developed using any of the previously described methods.

## PIMS ANALYSIS

The PIMS (Profit Impact of Market Strategies) project was initially developed at General Electric and later transferred to the Strategic Planning Institute (SPI). The basic idea behind PIMS was to provide insights and information on expected profit performance of different kinds of businesses under different competitive conditions using different strategies. About 200 organizations submit data annually on a total of about 2000 of their business units.[14] A business unit for the purposes of PIMS analysis is an operating unit which sells a distinct set of products to an identifiable set of customers in competition with a well-defined set of customers. Data that is submitted to PIMS include factors such as market share, total marketing expenditures, product quality, and R&D expenditures.

The submitted data are analyzed and several reports are regularly generated including the following:

- The *par report* is concerned with return on investment (ROI) and cash flow which is normal for the combination of circumstances that a particular business unit faces (market share, competition, market position, production process, capital/cost structure). The generated ROI figure is based on past performance of real business units under "comparable" conditions and assumes that managerial skills and decision abilities are at "average" levels.
- The *strategy report* analyzes short- and long-term effects of strategic changes on ROI. Usual strategic changes analyzed include changes in market share, changes in degree of vertical integration, and changes in capital intensity. The report summarizes the effect of these changes in several financial areas, including ROI.
- The *optimum strategy report* is concerned with isolating a particular combination of strategic moves which optimize a particular criterion (including profit, cash, or growth), again judging by the past experiences of others in similar situations.[15]

Companies pay a substantial amount of money to participate in PIMS. The data they submit and reports they receive provide them with reliable information for strategy evaluation and selection. Obviously, however, merely because a strategy has worked for another business in similar situations does not mean that the strategy is appropriate for all businesses in that same situation. Many other nonquantitative variables influence the strategy selection process.

## QUALITATIVE FACTORS IN THE STRATEGY EVALUATION AND SELECTION PROCESS

In actual practice, the strategy evaluation and selection process requires the decision makers to constantly reassess the future, find new congruencies as they unfold, and blend the organization's resources into new balances to meet the constantly changing conditions. The decision process is totally dynamic, with no real beginning or end. The methods discussed earlier in this chapter provide considerable guidance in the strategy evaluation and selection process, but ultimately several qualitative factors play a key role in this stream-of-decisions process.[16] Some of these are

1. Managerial attitudes toward risk
2. Environment of the organization
3. Organizational culture and power relationships
4. Competitive actions and reactions
5. Influence of previous organizational strategies
6. Timing considerations

These factors are discussed in the following sections.

## Managerial Attitudes Toward Risk

A common definition of risk is the chance of incurring loss or damage. In organizations, this translates into questions such as the following:

- What risks are involved in acquiring a new company?
- What risks are there in entering foreign markets?
- What risks are faced in enlarging plant capacity by 50 percent? Risk generally refers to those factors that can negatively influence planned results.

No amount of strategy evaluation can eliminate risk in the final strategy selection decision. Investing resources today in expectation of future conditions is in and of itself a risk-taking adventure.

Organizations and managers develop attitudes toward risk that influence the strategic choice decision. Some organizations seem to be eager to assume risk whereas others have a strong aversion to risk. Risk assumers generally adopt an offensive strategy in that they react to environmental change before they are forced to react. Risk avoiders generally adopt a defensive strategy in that they only react to environmental change when forced to do so by circumstances. Risk avoiders rely heavily on past strategies. Risk assumers look at a wider variety of options. Table 5.3 gives some general characteristics of risk-assuming and risk-avoiding organizations.

Many large organizations attempt to balance their business by having some

**Table 5.3** Characteristics of Risk-Assuming and Risk-Avoiding Organizations.

| General Characteristics of Risk-Assuming Organizations | General Characteristics of Risk-Avoiding Organizations |
| --- | --- |
| Operate in rapidly changing environments | Operate in stable industry environment |
| Seek high-risk/high-potential investment opportunities | Avoid high-risk/high-potential investment opportunities |
| Likely to pursue growth strategies | Likely to pursue stable growth strategies |
| Consider a wide range of strategic alternatives | Consider few strategic alternatives |
| Introduce totally new products or enter new markets frequently | Slow to introduce new products or enter new markets; generally follow risk assumers in this area |

## STRATEGY IN PRACTICE

### Example 5.8 Return of "Old" Coke

After extensive market testing, the Coca-Cola Company announced in April 1985 that it was introducing a "new" Coke and would no longer sell the "old" Coke. However, it did not anticipate the reaction of its customers. In fact, roughly 20 percent of its customers rejected the new product. And, in a remarkable turnaround, less than two months later the company announced that it was bringing back the "old" Coke under the name of Coca-Cola Classic.

risk-assuming business units and some risk-avoiding business units. In summary, the risk attitudes of the management of an organization reduce or expand the number of strategic alternatives considered and increase or decrease the likelihood that certain strategic options will be adopted.

**Environment of the Organization**

Organizations exist in an environment that is influenced by stockholders, competitors, customers, government, unions, and society in general. The degree of dependence that an organization has on one or more of the these environmental forces also influences the strategic choice process. A higher degree of dependence reduces the flexibility of the organization in its strategic choices. Example 5.8 shows how the Coca-Cola Company reacted to consumer pressure.

A study of several different organizations in such diverse fields as textbook publishing, electronics, food processing, and voluntary hospitals identified four basic organizational types based on their response to the environment.[17] These four types of organizations have the following general characteristics:

1. *Defenders* have a narrow product-market domain. Their top managers are experts in the limited area of product-market domain and generally do not search outside of their domain for new opportunities.
2. *Prospectors* almost continually search for new market opportunities. They are

the creators of change and uncertainty to which their competitors must respond.

3. *Analyzers* operate routinely. In the changing areas, they watch their competitors closely and rapidly adopt those ideas that appear to be the most promising.

4. *Reactors* frequently perceive change and uncertainty in their environments but are unable to respond effectively. Reactors are unstable and must either move to one of the other three organizational types or cease to exist.

This study concluded that patterns of adjustment to an organization's environment emerge, harden, and then tend to constrain management's future strategic choices.

## Organizational Culture and Power Relationships

*Organizational culture* is a term used to describe the values that set a pattern for an organization's activities and actions. Power is a relationship between people that consists of one individual's capacity to influence another individual or group of individuals to do something that would not be done otherwise. Both organizational culture and power relationships significantly influence the strategy evaluation and selection process.

As will be recalled from Chapter 2, all organizations have a culture. An organization's culture can contribute significantly to its success or can be an obstacle to future success. Matching an organization's culture to its environment and ensuring that it is a positive force is one of top management's key concerns in strategy evaluation and selection.

The power of the chief executive officer (CEO) is also a major influence on both the organization's culture and its strategic choices. Among large organizations, Henry Ford, Jr., at Ford Motor Company, Thomas Watson, Sr., at IBM, and Harold Geneen of ITT are just a few of the powerful CEOs who have dramatically influenced the culture and strategic choices of their organizations. In most organizations, when a powerful CEO favors a particular strategy, it generally becomes the strategy that is selected. Of course, if a powerful CEO selects a strategy that clashes with the present organizational culture, significant problems are likely to develop in the implementation of the strategy. In most highly successful organizations, however, the CEO and/or other top managers recognize and create the culture that is needed to implement the strategy.[18]

## Competitive Actions and Reactions

Another factor that influences strategy selection is the external coalition of competitive actions and reactions. This factor is of critical importance, especially in certain industries. For example, the actions and reactions of IBM strongly influence the strategic choices of all firms in the computer industry. Changes in product line, pricing, or organizational structure by IBM cause all firms in this industry to reexamine their strategic position. Another example is the pricing structure in the U.S. automobile industry. Pricing decisions made by General Motors almost always lead to changes by other automobile manufacturers.

**Influence of Previous Organizational Strategies**

For most organizations, past strategies serve as a beginning point in the strategy selection process. A natural result is that the number of strategic alternatives considered is limited based on past organizational strategies. Generally, managers commit the greatest amount of resources to a previously chosen course of action when they are personally responsible for the negative consequences of the chosen course of action. This may partially explain why changes in top management are often necessary to change strategy. The new management is less likely to be bound by the previous strategies.

**Timing Considerations**

Another factor influencing the strategy selection process is the amount of time available for making the decisions. Time pressures limit the number of alternatives that can be considered and also reduce the amount of information that can be gathered in evaluating the alternatives. When managers are placed under time pressures, they tend to place greater weight on negative rather than positive factors and consider fewer factors in making their decision.

On the other hand, determining the exact time to implement the strategy is also of critical importance. Waiting too long can be just as disastrous as jumping in too quickly.

## REVIEW QUESTIONS

1. What is a business portfolio?
2. Describe the four quadrants in the growth-share matrix.
3. Outline the steps followed in strategy evaluation and selection using the growth-share matrix.
4. Discuss the variables used in developing the industry attractiveness–business strength matrix.
5. Describe the variables used in developing the life-cycle approach.
6. What are growth, profit, and balanced portfolios?
7. What tests are used for determining the consistency of objectives and policies?
8. Outline the process for formulating a competitive strategy.
9. What is PIMS?
10. Describe the following reports:
    a. Par report
    b. Strategy report
    c. Optimum strategy report

11. Describe the influence of each of the following factors on the strategy evaluation and selection process:
    a. Managerial attitudes toward risk
    b. Environment of the organization
    c. Organizational culture and power relationships
    d. Competitive actions and reactions
    e. Previous organizational strategies
    f. Timing

## DISCUSSION QUESTIONS

1. Which variable or variables do you feel have the most influence in an organization's strategy evaluation and choice process? Why?
2. Which of the techniques discussed in this chapter do you feel is the most useful? Why?
3. Choose an organization with which you have some familiarity and describe its business using the business portfolio matrix.
4. Do you feel that most small organizations have a large number of strategic options? Why or why not?

## REFERENCES AND ADDITIONAL READING

1. For a discussion of the application of the growth-share matrix, see Bruce D. Henderson and Alan J. Zakon, "Corporate Growth Strategy: How to Develop and Implement It," in *Handbook of Business Problem Solving,* Kenneth J. Albert (ed.) (New York: McGraw-Hill, 1980), pp. 1.3–1.19.
2. See Arnoldo C. Hax and Nicholas S. Majluf, "The Use of Growth-Share Matrix in Strategic Planning," *Interfaces* 13 (February 1983):46–60.
3. See, for instance, Richard A. Bettis and William K. Hall, "The Business Portfolio Approach—Where It Falls Down in Practice," *Long Range Planning* 16 (April 1983): 95–104.
4. Richard Rumelt, "Evaluation of Strategy: Theory and Models," in *Strategic Management: A New View of Business Policy Planning,* Dan E. Schendel and Charles W. Hofer (eds.) (Boston: Little, Brown, 1979), p. 210.
5. For a discussion of effectively managing dog businesses, see H. Kurt Christensen, Arnold C. Cooper, and Cornelis A. DeKluyver, "The Dog Business: A Re-examination," *Business Horizons* 25 (November–December, 1982):12–18.
6. Carolyn Y. Y. Woo and Arnold C. Cooper, "Strategies of Effective Low Market Share Businesses," *Academy of Management Proceedings,* August 1980, pp. 21–25.
7. Much of the material in the following sections is adapted from Arnold C. Hax and Nicholas S. Majluf, "The Use of the Industry Attractiveness–Business Strength Matrix in Strategic Planning," *Interfaces* 13 (April 1983):34–71.
8. For other definitions, see Joel K. Leidecker, and Albert V. Brano, "Identifying and Using Critical Success Factors," *Long Range Planning* 17 (February 1984):23–32.
9. Roger R. Osell and Robert V. L. Wright, "Allocating Resources: How to Do It in Multi-Industry Corporations," in *Handbook of Business Problem Solving* Kenneth J. Albert (ed.) (New York: McGraw-Hill, 1980), pp. 1–92 and 1–93.
10. C. W. Hofer, *Conceptual Constructs for Formulating Corporate and Business Strategies* (Boston: Intercollegiate Case Clearing House, 9–378–754, 1977).
11. C. W. Hofer and Dan Schendel, *Strategy Formulation: Analytical Concepts* (St. Paul, Minn.: West Publishing Company, 1978), p. 182.

12. See Michael E. Porter, *Competitive Strategy* (New York: Free Press, 1980).
13. See Donald F. Heany and Gerald Weiss, "Integrating Strategies for Clusters of Businesses," *Journal of Business Strategy* 4 (Summer 1983):3–11.
14. Donald C. Hambrick, Ian C. MacMillan, and Diana L. Day, "Strategic Attributes and Performance in the BCG Matrix—A PIMS-Based Analysis of Industrial Product Businesses," *Academy of Management Journal* 25 (September 1982):515.
15. Carl R. Anderson and Frank T. Paine, "PIMS—A Reexamination," *Academy of Management Review* 3 (July 1978):603.
16. For a discussion of other qualitative factors in the strategy evaluation and selection process, see Michael A. McGinnis, "The Key to Strategic Planning: Integrating Analysis and Interaction," *Sloan Management Review* 26 (Fall 1984):45–52.
17. Raymond E. Miles and Charles C. Snow, *Organizational Strategy, Structure and Process* (New York: McGraw-Hill, 1978).
18. Edwin L. Baker, "Managing Organizational Culture," *Management Review* 69 (July 1980):10.

# Strategic Management Process

Strategic Planning

## Objective-Setting Process

### Organizational Culture

| | |
|---|---|
| **Establishing an organizational philosophy** | **Environmental scanning and forecasting** |
| | **Competitive analysis** |
| **Defining the organization's mission** | **Internal organizational analysis** |
| Chapter 1 | Chapter 2 |

**Establishing long- and short-range objectives**

Chapter 3

## Strategy Selection

### Organizational Culture

**Identifying strategic alternatives**

Chapter 4

**Strategy evaluation and selection**

Chapter 5

Feedback          Feedback

# PART THREE
# STRATEGY IMPLEMENTATION

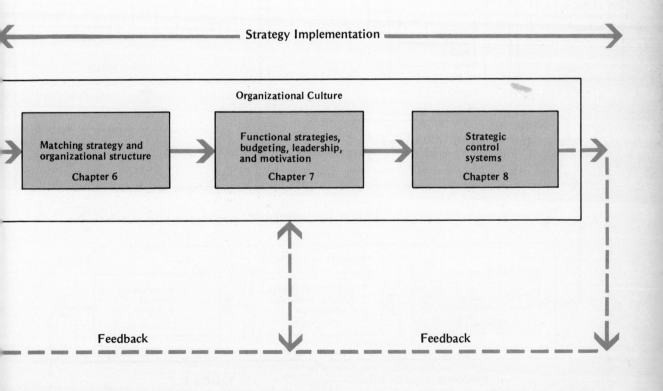

Strategy Implementation

Organizational Culture

| Matching strategy and organizational structure

Chapter 6 | Functional strategies, budgeting, leadership, and motivation

Chapter 7 | Strategic control systems

Chapter 8 |

Feedback

Feedback

# Strategic Management Process

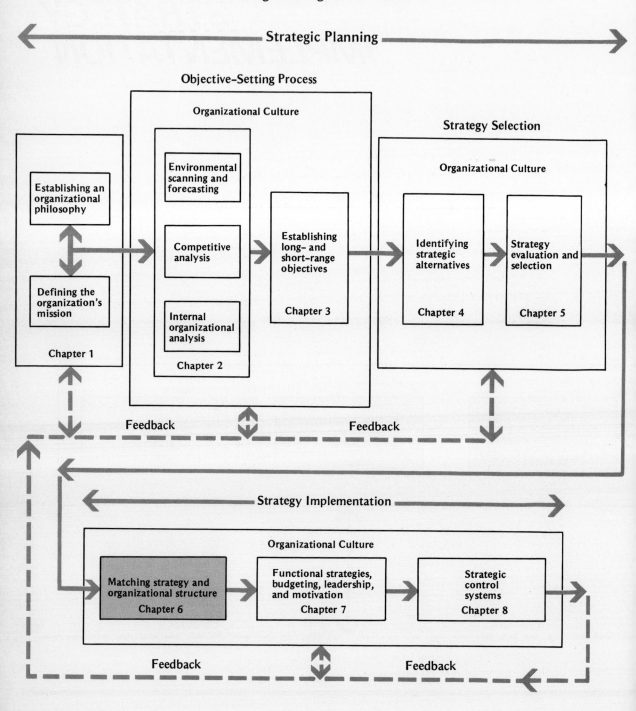

# 6 MATCHING STRATEGY AND ORGANIZATIONAL STRUCTURE

## STUDY OBJECTIVES

- To explain the relationship between organizational structure and strategy
- To discuss the contingency approach to organizing
- To offer guidelines in designing organizational structures
- To discuss the role of the board of directors

## CHAPTER OUTLINE

Contingency Approach to Organizing
    Organizational Size and Growth Stage
    Organizational Environment
    Technology and Structure
    Contingency Organizational Structures
Assessing an Organization's Structure
Guidelines in Designing Effective Organizational Structures
    Simple Structures
    Simple Form, Lean Staff
Restructuring an Organization
Board of Directors
    Composition of the Board
    Structure of the Board
        Executive Committee
        Audit Committee
        Compensation Committee
        Nominating Committee
        Finance Committee
        Corporate Responsibility Committee
        Planning Committee
    Legal Responsibilities of the Board
Review Questions
Discussion Questions
References and Additional Reading
Appendix: Strengths and Weaknesses of Organizational Structure Types

*In our western civilization only one formal organization, the Roman Catholic Church, claims a substantial age. A few universities, a very few national governments or formally organized nations, are more than two hundred years old. Many municipalities are somewhat older, but few other corporate organizations have existed more than one hundred years. Failure to cooperate, failure of cooperation, failure of organization, disorganization, disintegration, destruction of organization—and reorganization—are characteristic facts of human history*—Chester I. Barnard (former president of the Rockefeller Foundation and former president of the New Jersey Bell Telephone Company), *The Functions of the Executive*

Strategies are carried out through organizations. An *organization* is a group of people working together in a coordinated effort to attain a set of objectives that could not be achieved by individuals working separately. *Organizing* is the grouping of activities necessary to attain the set of objectives and the assignment of each grouping to a person who has the authority necessary to manage the people performing the activities. Thus, organizing basically is the division of labor accompanied by the delegation of authority. The framework that defines the boundaries of the organization and within which the organization operates is the organizational structure.

It has been widely advocated that structure follows strategy; that is, the organizational structure should be designed to facilitate the accomplishment of an organization's strategy.[1] However, it must be acknowledged that strategy and structure operate in a feedback system. Strategy definitely influences the resulting organizational structure, but the existing structure can and does influence the variety and type of strategic alternatives available to an organization.

Much research has been conducted on the relationship between organizational structure and strategy.[2] Generally, it has been found that strategy and structure must be properly aligned if the organization is to be successful in achieving its objectives and that an organization can seldom veer substantially from its current strategy without major alterations in its structure.

Most of these studies suggest that the relationship between strategy and structure is highly complex. Enough evidence does exist, however, to say with confidence that a chosen strategy cannot be effectively implemented without developing an organizational structure that complements and supports the strategy. Example 6.1 shows how Hewlett-Packard changed its organizational structure to meet its customers' needs.

## CONTINGENCY APPROACH TO ORGANIZING

Research studies seem to support what practicing managers have been saying for years: No organizational structure is applicable to all situations. Recognition by management practitioners and scholars that there is no universal best way to organize has led to the evolution of a contingency or situational approach to organizing. The situational approach recognizes that the most appropriate organ-

---

## STRATEGY IN PRACTICE

### Example 6.1 Reorganization at Hewlett-Packard

In the early 1980s, Hewlett-Packard (HP) had two different sales forces calling on major customers to sell instruments (measurement devices) and computers. Originally, computers and instruments involved different customers, technology, and buying decisions. Thus, having two sales forces made good sense. However, over time the needs of the customers changed in that they wanted both instruments and computers. As a result, in 1984 HP reorganized, and instead of selling its products with two field sales groups, it now sells with just one sales group. Sales are now oriented along geographic lines, according to major accounts.

---

izational structure depends primarily on the organization's objectives but also is influenced by the size and growth stage of the organization, the environmental conditions faced by the organization, and the technology employed by the organization.

**Organizational Size and Growth Stage**

The size and growth stage of an organization is a key variable in determining its organizational structure. For instance, the most appropriate structure for a small computer company would be considerably different from the most appropriate structure for the IBM Corporation. Thus, as an organization grows in size (both in terms of employees and product line) different organizational structures are required.

Several attempts have been made to develop a model for describing the various stages of organizational growth.[3] The basic idea behind these models is that organizations grow along a continuum from simple to complex. Furthermore, the models describe positions along the continuum and postulate that as an organization reaches a particular point on the continuum a different organizational structure should be implemented.

Many of the growth-stage models developed from the work of Alfred Chandler. Although Chandler did not specifically develop a growth-stage model, his work was one of the first to demonstrate the relationship between structure and growth or size of the organization.[4]

Later, J. Thomas Cannon proposed five stages of organizational growth.[5] These are

1. *Entrepreneurial Stage.*   Decisions are made mostly by the top person. The organizational structure is rather informal, with minimal coordination requirements. Communications are also on an informal basis.
2. *Functional Development Stage.*   Decisions are made more and more through other managers and less and less by the top manager. The organizational structure is based on specialization by functions, and problems of coordination among functions arise. Communications become more important and

more difficult. The problems associated with this stage move an organization into the third stage.

3. *Decentralization Stage.*   Management copes with the problems of a growing functional business by decentralizing. Organizational structures are developed on a division or product basis. The idea is to develop minibusinesses within the organization that can be managed under the conditions described earlier in the entrepreneurial stage. However, problems arise. Flexibility in shifting resources from one area to another in order to exploit new opportunities is reduced. Expenses are often increased from duplication of effort. Finally, top management may feel that they have lost control of the minibusinesses in the decentralization stage. These problems often cause an organization to move into one of the final two stages.

4. *Staff Proliferation Stage.*   This stage involves adding staff at the corporate level to assist top management in planning and control of the minibusinesses. Today, virtually all large organizations have corporate staffs. The greatest problem with adding staff is the inherent conflict that develops between line and staff and the time delays associated with staff review of proposals.

5. *Recentralization Stage.*   Sometimes, organizations resolve the problems of the decentralization and staff proliferation stages by recentralization. Recentralization is very similar to the functional development stage, with many of the same problems. Computerization of information and sophisticated control systems enable the management of organizations to move to this stage.

Obviously, all organizations do not move through these stages in sequence. They move through the stages in different and often unpredictable ways. However, it does appear that as organizations move from small, single-product organizations to large, multiproduct organizations, organizational structures change with this growth in size. Furthermore, it also appears that increasing organizational size fosters more rules, procedures, and job descriptions, which are all devices that formalize behavior.

**Organizational Environment**

A classic study relating organizational structure to environment examined 20 industrial organizations and identified two distinct organizational structure types.[6] One, labeled *mechanistic systems,* had a rigid delineation of functional duties, precise job descriptions, fixed authority and responsibility, and a well-developed organizational hierarchy. The other, labeled *organic systems,* had less formal job descriptions, greater emphasis on adaptability, more participation, and less fixed authority. The study found that successful organizations in stable and established industries tended to have "mechanistic structures." Successful organizations in dynamic and changing industries tended to have "organic structures." Another study that examined the relationship between organizational structure and environment concluded that, in order to be successful, organizations operating in a dynamic environment needed a relatively flexible structure, organizations operating in a stable environment needed a more rigid structure, and organizations operating in an intermediate environment needed a structure somewhere between the two extremes.[7]

Many other studies have been conducted on the relationship between environment and organizational structure.[8] In general, most have concluded that the most effective structure for a particular organization depends to some extent on the conditions of its environment.

**Technology and Structure**

One of the classic studies examining the relationship between organizational structure and the technology used by an organization analyzed 100 organizations in Great Britain.[9] These organizations were classified along a scale of "technical complexity" based on their method of production. The study also identified the following three methods of production: (1) unit or batch production (e.g., custom-made products), (2) large-scale or mass production (e.g., an assembly line operation), and (3) continuous-flow or process production (e.g., a chemical or paper plant). The unit-production method is at the lower end of the technical complexity scale whereas the continuous-flow method is at the upper end.

Each organization was classified into one of the above three categories, and a number of organizational variables was investigated. Some of the findings of this study which relate to organizational structures are summarized below:

- The number of levels of management increased as technical complexity increased.[10]
- Using the previously discussed definition of organic and mechanistic systems, organic systems predominated in organizations using unit- or continuous-flow production methods, whereas mechanistic systems predominated in organizations using a large-scale production method.[11]
- No significant relationship was found between technical complexity and organizational size.[12]
- The ratio of managers and supervisors to total personnel increased with technical complexity.[13]

The relationship between technology and structure was also analyzed in 43 other organizations. Those organizations were classified along a continuum from technical diffuseness to technical specificity. Technically diffused organizations were described as having a wider product line, producing products that vary from year to year, and producing more made-to-order products. Organizations described as having technical specificity produced products that had much less variation and change. Similar to the findings of earlier studies, this study found significant relationships between technology and organizational structure.[14]

Many additional studies have investigated the relationship between technology and structure.[15] Although much research has been concerned with whether size or technology is the more important variable, most studies have concluded that technology plays a key role in determining an organization's structure.

**Contingency Organizational Structures**

Using the results of much of the previously described research, Henry Mintzberg has proposed five structures that result from the variables that influence an organization.[16] Mintzberg views the organization as being pulled in five different directions, and to the extent that conditions favor one pull over the others the organization structures itself in one of five different configurations. The five different pulls on an organization are as follows:

1. Pull to centralize—a simple and dynamic operating environment enables top management (or more likely a top manager) to retain control over decision making.
2. Pull to standardize—a simple and stable operating environment that is large enough to have the volume of production needed for repetition and standardization and that is old enough to have established standards and procedures.
3. Pull to collaborate—a dynamic and complex operating environment that calls for innovative work and where change is accelerated.
4. Pull to professionalize—a stable and complex environment that requires the use of difficult procedures that can be learned only in extensive formal training programs but are used in an environment that is stable enough to enable these skills to become standardized.
5. Pull to balkanize—an environment that is neither very complex nor very dynamic but which has a market or product diversity.

The structures that result when conditions favor one of these pulls are shown in Table 6.1. Furthermore, Figure 6.1 describes each of the resulting structures in more detail. It is important to note at this point that, in general, contingency theory basically postulates that there is no one best structure for all situations. However, certain environmental forces that influence organizations do make certain structures more logical for particular organizations.

**ASSESSING AN ORGANIZATION'S STRUCTURE**

As can be seen from the previous discussion, many forces interact to influence organizational structure. However, an organization's structure cannot be changed every time one of these forces changes. If it did, the organization would be in a continuous state of reorganization. Unfortunately, some organizations do seem to be in a state of continuous reorganization, which generally only results in confusion and chaos. Changes in organizational structure cannot offset a bad strategy, poor product offerings, or having the wrong people in key positions.

However, there are several points at which the management of an organization should assess the appropriateness of its structure.[17] One obvious point is when the organization is having severe performance problems in achieving its objectives. Changes in leadership such as with retirements, resignations, or terminations almost always lead to changes in organizational structure. Finally, changes in organizational strategy should lead to an assessment of the appropriateness of the structure.

Many other symptoms also point to an ineffective organizational structure. According to Peter Drucker, the multiplication of management levels is the most common and most serious symptom.[18] Too many management levels make coor-

**Table 6.1** Contingency Structures

| Primary Pull | Structure | Centralization or Decentralization |
|---|---|---|
| Centralize | Simple structure | Vertical and horizontal centralization |
| Standardize | Machine bureaucracy | Limited horizontal decentralization |
| Professionalize | Professional bureaucracy | Vertical and horizontal decentralization |
| Collaborate | Adhocracy | Selective decentralization |
| Balkanize | Divisionalize | Limited vertical decentralization |

*Source:* Adapted from Henry Mintzberg, *The Structuring of Organizations* (Englewood Cliffs, N.J.: Prentice-Hall, 1979), pp. 301–302.

---

**Simple structure**—Has little or no structure, few support staff, loose division of labor, small managerial hierarchy; power is centralized in the hands of the chief executive. Most organizations pass through this structure in their formative years. Small organizations and entrepreneurial organizations generally have this structure. Organizations in crisis situations also frequently adopt this structure.

**Machine bureaucracy**—Mass production firms and service organizations that are mature in which work is simple and repetitive. Organizations that are externally controlled such as government agencies demonstrate this type of structure. Emphasizes reporting through the chain of command and centralized authority.

**Professional bureaucracy**—Organizations in this category hire trained professionals and give them considerable control over their own work. Employees work relatively independent of their peers, but closely with the clients they serve.

**Adhocracy**—Organic structure, high horizontal job specialization; groups specialists in functional units for housekeeping purposes but deploys them in small-market-based project teams to do their work; selective decentralization to and within these teams.

**Divisionalize**—Relies on the market basis for grouping units. Divisions control their operations and determine strategies for the markets that fall under their responsibility. Market diversity forces this type of structure. Organizations with SBUs have divisionalized structures.

---

**Figure 6.1** Contingency Structure Types
*Source:* Adapted from: Henry Mintzberg, *The Structuring of Organizations,* (Englewood Cliffs, N.J.: Prentice-Hall, 1979), Chapters 17–21.

dination and communication difficult, if not impossible. Another symptom of organizational ineffectiveness is too many meetings attended by too many people. Some organizations, unfortunately, seem to be structured in such a fashion that meetings are the norm and not the exception. In effective organizational structures, the need for meetings should be minimized. Another common symptom of an ineffective structure is when too much attention is directed toward following proper procedures or resolving interdepartmental conflicts. Effective organizational structures help resolve interdepartmental conflicts quickly. Other problems that often result from an inappropriate organizational structure include lack of opportunities for general management development, too much concentration on operational issues, lack of coordination among business units within the organization, neglect of special markets, excessive decision making at the top, and overworked key personnel.[19] In the final analysis, the effectiveness of an organization's structure is reflected in how well the organization achieves its objectives. An effective structure should facilitate the accomplishment of organizational objectives.

**GUIDELINES IN DESIGNING EFFECTIVE ORGANIZATIONAL STRUCTURES**

Unfortunately, no absolute guidelines exist for choosing the one best structure. For example, one of the oldest, largest, and most successful organizations is the Roman Catholic church. Its organizational structure, which has changed little over the years, is extremely simple. Basically, the parish priest reports to a bishop, and the bishop reports to a cardinal who, in turn, reports to the pope. On the other hand, large industrial organizations regularly change structures and often have many layers of management between the president and operative employees. However, the purpose of this section is to offer some general guidelines for use in designing organizational structures.

**Simple Structures**

Peter Drucker has proposed that the simplest organizational structure that will do the job is the best one.[20] He postulated that the following three questions need to be answered before an effective structure can be designed:

1. In what area is excellence required in order to obtain the organization's objectives?
2. In what areas would lack of performance endanger the results, if not the survival, of the organization?
3. What values are truly important to the company? Product quality? Product safety? Customer service?[21]

The answers to these three questions identify the key functions and activities of the organization that are essential for achieving organizational objectives. These activities should serve as the basis for developing an organizational structure. Other activities in the organization should be ranked according to the contribution they make in achieving organizational objectives. This contribution determines the ranking and placement of activities. Key activities should never be subordinate to non-key activities. Revenue-producing activities should never be subordinate to non–revenue-producing activities. Structuring the organization on the basis of the contribution made in achieving organizational objectives greatly enhances the likelihood that these same objectives will be achieved.

**Simple Form, Lean Staff**

As an organization grows and succeeds, it tends to evolve into a more and more complex structure. Just how this takes place varies; frequently, a major cause is an increase in staff positions, especially at high levels. Many managers seem to feel a need for more staff and a more complex structure as the organization grows; they seem inclined to equate staff size with success.

In their study, Thomas Peters and Robert Waterman found that many of the best-performing companies had managed to maintain a simple structure with a small staff (see Example 6.2).[22] One reason for this is that a simple form with a lean staff better allows an organization to adjust to a fast-changing environment. A simple form with a lean staff is also conducive to innovation. A simple form and a lean staff are naturally intertwined in that one breeds the other: A simple form requires fewer staff, and a lean staff results in a simple form.

Peters and Waterman outline four characteristics or practices that enable organizations to maintain a simple form and a lean staff:[23]

1. Extraordinary divisional integrity. Each division has its own functional areas, including product development, finance, and personnel.
2. Continual formation of new divisions and rewards for this practice.
3. A set of guidelines which determine when a new product or product line will become an independent division.
4. Moving people and even products among divisions on a regular basis without causing disruption.

Peters and Waterman postulate that the successful organizations of the future will be variations of the simple, divisionalized line and staff structure and that they will have the above characteristics.

---

### STRATEGY IN PRACTICE

#### Example 6.2 Companies with Lean Staffs

- Emerson Electric has 54,000 employees and fewer than 100 in its corporate headquarters.
- Dana employs 35,000 and reduced its corporate staff from about 500 in 1970 to around 100 in 1982.
- Schlumberger, the $6-billion diversified oil service company, has a corporate staff of 90.
- Intel, which enjoys $1 billion in sales, has virtually no staff; temporary staff assignments are given to line officers.
- ROLM manages a $200-million business with about 15 people in the corporate headquarters.

*Source:* Thomas J. Peters and Robert H. Waterman, Jr., *In Search of Excellence* (New York: Harper & Row, 1982), pp. 311–312.

## RESTRUC-
## TURING AN
## ORGANIZA-
## TION

After it has been determined that a particular organizational structure is inappropriate, certain steps need to be taken to move to a more appropriate structure. First, top management must decide what it is trying to achieve with the new structure. Some of the objectives of a reorganization may be to increase productivity, increase sales, improve service, control costs, eliminate overlaps in responsibilities, maximize utilization of critical staff skills, establish clearly defined functional units, or decentralize the decision-making process.[24]

Next, top management must decide on what structure is to be used. Organizational structures of all types and varieties exist. Each has its own potential strengths and vulnerabilities. The appendix at the end of this chapter provides a summary of the various organizational styles and outlines the potential strengths and weaknesses of each in terms of their competitive response, market response, and internal functioning. Example 6.3 illustrates how General Motors (GM) is restructuring its organizational structure and describes some of the results it hopes to achieve.

Finally, top management should establish a timetable for implementing the changes. This timetable should then be communicated to all levels of management.

For best results, the active participation of all levels of management should be encouraged throughout the restructuring process. Participation creates a feeling of "ownership" and leads to greater acceptance of the new structure when it is implemented. Top management should provide information to all levels of management on why it feels reorganization is necessary and should encourage open discussion of these reasons. Management should also attempt to explain how reorganization will benefit not only the organization but also the individuals who are involved in the changes.

## BOARD OF
## DIRECTORS

A *board of directors* is a group of people elected by the stockholders of an organization that serves primarily to see that the organization is well managed for all of the organization's stakeholders.[25] In serving the needs and interests of an organization's stakeholders, the primary responsibilities of the board include the following:

- Evaluating and approving the objectives, policies, and strategies of the organization
- Overseeing the capitalization, resource allocation, and other financial matters
- Approving or disapproving diversifications, mergers, aquisitions, and divestments
- Establishing the chief executive officer's compensation
- Appraising management's performance
- Ensuring that the organization is developing management talent
- Providing for succession to the chief executive officer's position

---

## STRATEGY IN PRACTICE

### Example 6.3 GM's Reorganization

Prior to 1984, GM had an organizational structure as shown below. GM operated with a corporate staff and operating divisions that shared some manufacturing resources (Fisher Body, AC-Delco, and so on). Superimposed on these divisions were projects that were formed and funded at the corporate level but were carried out by staff from all areas of the company.

Corporate staff (including planning, finance, and government relations)

Divisions (Chevrolet, Pontiac, Buick, and so on)

Common resources (Fisher Body, AC-Delco, diesel engine, and so on)

X-car project

Electric car project

Environmental projects

However, in January 1984, General Motors announced plans to reorganize its operations. Over the next few years, the seven divisions of GM—Fisher Body, assembly, and the five car divisions—will be consolidated into two: a small-car division and a large-car division. According to GM chairman Roger Smith, the major reason for the reorganization is to enable GM to concentrate on the difference between small and large cars. Other benefits of the reorganization include reducing duplication of effort, improving communications, forcing decision making and responsibility to lower levels in the organization, and creating true profit centers.

---

Basically, the board of directors is the body to whom the management of an organization is accountable for its actions. Example 6.4 shows how boards of directors can disagree with the management of organizations.

**Composition of the Board**

Most large, publicly owned organizations have both inside and outside directors. Inside directors are employees of the organization and include the chief executive and chief operating officers of the organization. Outside directors come from a wide variety of sources. Commercial bankers, investment bankers, attorneys, and chief executives of other companies are frequently used sources. In the past few

---

## STRATEGY IN PRACTICE

**Example 6.4** Board and CEOs Disagree on Merger Plans

In January 1985, Occidental Petroleum Corporation and Diamond Shamrock Corporation announced plans to merge. The merger was to involve a one-for-one stock exchange and the creation of a new holding company with Occidental's chairman Armand Hammer as the new chairman and chief executive officer. Diamond Shamrock's chairman and chief executive officer, William Bricker, and Armand Hammer had agreed to the merger and thought both boards would support it. However, when each board met to vote on the merger, there was very little support. Occidental's board reluctantly accepted the proposal over the adamant objections of two directors. Diamond Shamrock directors rejected the proposal unanimously. Within a few days of the initial announcement, all merger plans were canceled.

*Source:* Adapted from "Occidental, Diamond Shamrock Cancel Merger Plan Hours After Announcing It", *The Wall Street Journal,* January 8, 1985; "Diamond Shamrock Chief Says Concern Isn't for Sale but Notes Vulnerability," *The Wall Street Journal,* January 9, 1985.

---

years, it has become more common to have other interest groups represented on the board. Women, minorities, and public interest groups have slowly begun to appear on corporate boards.

The number of people on the board varies from organization to organization. However, it is not unusual for large organizations to have 15–20 members on the board.

## Structure of the Board

It is a fairly common practice in large organizations to have the chairman of the board also serving as the chief executive officer and concentrating on strategic planning and external relations. The chief operating officer (or president) is then concerned with day-to-day operations and reports to the chairman. This type of structure prevails in most large companies. Critics of this approach agree that it gives the chairman too much authority and undercuts the independence of the board. They feel that the chairman of the board should have authority over the board functions, but should not run the company.

Boards of directors normally have one or more standing or permanent committees of the board. Board committees have different functions but basically serve as the eyes and ears of the full board in particular areas of organizational activities. They keep the full board informed through reports or minutes of committee meetings. Some of the typical committees of the board include the following: executive, audit, compensation, nominating, finance, corporate responsibility, and planning.

**Executive Committee**   The executive committee is normally granted the power to act with the authority of the full board between board meetings. Typically, the executive committee is involved directly with the chief executive. A chief executive may use this committee as a sounding board on general management problems or issues that affect the organization as a whole.

**Audit Committee**   The audit committee has taken on added significance in recent years due to the pressure for greater exposure of company financial information, increased exposure of directors to legal liability, and legal actions in which public accounting firms have been charged with deficiencies in audits.[26] The most common responsibilities of audit committees are selecting or recommending auditors to the board and/or stockholders, determining the scope of the audit, reviewing the audit results, and reviewing internal accounting procedures. Normally the audit committee only consists of outside directors.

**Compensation Committee**   Compensation committees make recommendations to the board on the compensation (including salary, bonuses, fringe benefits, and stock options) for certain employees of the organization.[27] Normally, these employees include employee directors and officers of the organization.

**Nominating Committee**   The primary responsibility of the nominating committee is to recommend candidates for board membership to the full board.[28]

**Finance Committee**   The finance committee is concerned with the financial decisions of the organization. Its primary responsibilities include reviewing and making recommendations on the financial policies of the organization, monitoring the organization's financial condition and its requirements for funds, making recommendations on financing to be undertaken, reviewing and making recommendations on capital expenditure programs, and evaluating financial planning. As can be seen, the finance committee's role differs from the audit committee's role, which is to provide an independent check on financial reporting and controls. Thus, unlike the audit committee, the membership of the finance committee normally includes employee directors such as the chief executive officer and the chief financial officer.

**Corporate Responsibility Committee**   A relatively new committee for most boards, the corporate responsibility committee is primarily concerned with the effect of the organization on the community, its employees, consumers, the public, and the organization's natural environment.

**Planning Committee**   The planning committee is primarily concerned with the strategic planning process of the organization.[29] Its functions include reviewing mission statements, objectives, and strategies; monitoring performance against objectives; assessing the organization's strategic planning process; and advising the chief executive officer on strategic issues.

**Legal Responsibilities of the Board**

Most states have laws that require the board of directors to "manage" the business of the organization. Generally courts do not require that directors do this on a day-to-day basis. Rather, the board is primarily required to establish broad policies, approve major transactions, and provide general supervision of the management of the organization.

In handling these responsibilities, directors are charged with the duty of due care. _Due care_ requires that a director act with the degree of care, diligence, and skill which a prudent person would exercise under similar circumstances in like positions. Due care is a flexible standard that may have a wide latitude.

The law also recognizes that business decisions require the exercise of judgment and involve risks. Under what is frequently called the _business judgment rule_, theoretically short of fraud, self-dealing, or gross abuse of discretion, a court normally will not interject its own ideas about what should or should not have been done. However, a 1985 decision of the Delware Supreme Court _(Smith_ v. _Van Gorkom)_ held that the "business judgment rule" did not protect the directors of the Trans Union Corporation from personal liability in setting a price too low for the sale of the company. The court ruled that the directors were personally liable to the stockholders for the difference between the fair price that might have been received if the directors had acted properly and the lower actual sales price.[30] Interestingly, no charges were made that the directors acted fraudulently or profited personally at the expense of the stockholders. Thus, in minimizing problems of due care and business judgment a director would be wise to attend board and committee meetings regularly, read all material furnished by management, ask questions at meetings, study all SEC filings, review annual and quarterly reports to stockholders, discuss in full all major actions before the board, make independent inquiries regarding the organization, and register objections when appropriate.[31]

## REVIEW QUESTIONS

1. Explain the impact of the following variables on organizational structure:
   a. Size and growth stage
   b. Environment
   c. Technology
2. What are the five stages of organizational growth?
3. Define mechanistic and organic systems.
4. Describe five different contingency structures.
5. Name some symptoms that may indicate inappropriate organizational structure.
6. What general steps need to be taken in restructuring an organization?
7. Outline the primary responsibilities of a board of directors.
8. Describe the responsibilities of the following committees of a board of directors:
   a. Executive
   b. Audit
   c. Compensation
   d. Nominating
   e. Finance
   f. Corporate responsibility
   g. Planning

9. What is due care?
10. What is the business judgment rule?

## DISCUSSION QUESTIONS

1. Describe some of the ways in which an organization's structure can either positively or negatively influence the implementation of strategy.
2. Draw an organizational chart for your college or university. What type of structure does your college or university currently use? Do you feel that it is effective? How could it be restructured?
3. Choose an organization that has recently been reorganized. Be prepared to discuss why you feel the reorganization was necessary.
4. "Most of the organizations that I am familiar with are constantly reorganizing." Do you agree or disagree? Why do you feel that this statement is true?

## REFERENCES AND ADDITIONAL READING

1. Arnoldo C. Hax and Nicholas S. Majluf, "Organization Design: A Case Study on Matching Strategy and Structure," *Journal of Business Strategy* 4 (Fall 1983): 73.
2. For a discussion of several aspects of this research, see Paul C. Nystrom and William H. Starbuck (eds.) *Handbook of Organizational Design,* Volumes 1 and 2 (New York: Oxford University Press, 1981).
3. See, for instance, Malcolm S. Salter, "Stages of Corporate Development," *Journal of Business Policy* 1, no. 1 (Spring 1970): 23–27; Alan Filley and Robert House, *Managerial Process and Organizational Behavior* (Glenview, Ill.: Scott, Foresman, 1969), pp. 443–455; and Donald H. Thain, "Stages of Corporate Development," *The Business Quarterly,* Winter 1969, pp. 32–45.
4. Alfred D. Chandler, Jr., *Strategy and Structure* (Cambridge, Mass.: M.I.T. Press, 1962), p. 14.
5. J. Thomas Cannon, *Business Strategy and Policy* (New York: Harcourt Brace Jovanovich, 1968), pp. 525–528.
6. Tom Burns and G. M. Stalker, *The Management of Innovation* (London: Tavistock Institute, 1962).
7. Paul Lawrence and Jay Lorsch, "Differentiation and Integration in Complex Organizations," *Administrative Science Quarterly* 12 (June 1967): 1–47; and Paul Lawrence and Jay Lorsch, *Organization and Environment* (Homewood, Ill.: Irwin, 1969).
8. See, for instance, Jeffrey Pfeffer and Gerald Salancik, *The External Control of Organizations* (New York: Harper & Row, 1978); Michael Crozier and Jean-Claude Thoenig, "The Regulation of Complex Organized Systems," *Administrative Science Quarterly* 21 (1976): 547–570.
9. Joan Woodward, *Management and Technology* (London: H.M.S.O., 1958).
10. Ibid., p. 16.
11. Joan Woodward, *Industrial Organization: Theory and Practice* (London: Oxford University Press, 1965), p. 64.
12. Woodward, *Management and Technology,* p. 20.
13. Woodward, *Management and Technology,* pp. 16–17.
14. Edward Harvey, "Technology and the Structure of Organizations," *American Sociological Review* 33, no. 2 (April 1968): 247–259.
15. See for instance, Denise M. Rousseau and Robert A. Cooke, "Technology and Structure," *Journal of Management* 10 (Fall/Winter 1984): 345–361; Pradip N. Khandwalla, "Mass-Output Orientation of Operations Technology and Organization Structure," *Administrative Science Quarterly* 19 (1974): 74–97; and Peter M. Blau, Cecilia Falbe,

William McKinley, and Phelps K. Tracy, "Technology and Organization in Manufacturing," *Administrative Science Quarterly* 21 (1976): 20–40.

16. See Henry Mintzberg, *Structure in Fives: Designing Effective Organizations* (Englewood Cliffs, N.J.: Prentice-Hall, 1983).

17. See, for instance, John R. Kimberly, "The Anatomy of Organizational Design," *Journal of Management* 10 (Spring 1984): 123–125.

18. Peter Drucker, *Management: Tasks, Responsibilities and Practices* (New York: Harper & Row, 1974), p. 546.

19. Hax and Majluf, "Organization Design: A Case Study on Matching Strategy and Structure," p. 75.

20. Drucker, *Management,* pp. 601–602.

21. Ibid., pp. 530–531.

22. Thomas J. Peters and Robert H. Waterman, Jr., *In Search of Excellence* (New York: Harper & Row, 1982), pp. 306–318.

23. Ibid., p. 310.

24. Jack M. Kaplan and Eileen E. Kaplan, "Organizational Restructuring," *Management Review* 73 (January 1984): 15–16.

25. For an in-depth discussion of boards of directors, see Jeremy Bacon and James K. Brown, *Corporate Directorship Practices: Role, Selection and Legal Status of the Board* (New York: The Conference Board, 1975).

26. See Jeremy Bacon, *Corporate Directorship Practices: The Audit Committee* (New York: The Conference Board, 1979), Report No. 766.

27. See Jeremy Bacon, *Corporate Directorship Practices: The Compensation Committee* (New York: The Conference Board, 1982), Report No. 829.

28. See Jeremy Bacon, *Corporate Directorship Practices: The Nominating Committee and the Director Selection Process* (New York: The Conference Board, 1981), Report No. 812.

29. See James K. Brown, *Corporate Directorship Practices: The Planning Committee* (New York: The Conference Board, 1981), Report No. 810.

30. Jeremy Bacon and James K. Brown, *Corporate Directorship Practices: Role, Selection and Legal Status of the Board,* p. 77.

31. Richard M. Leisner, "Boardroom Jitters," *Barron's,* April 22, 1985, p. 34.

# APPENDIX TO CHAPTER 6: STRENGTHS AND WEAKNESSES OF ORGANIZATIONAL STRUCTURE TYPES

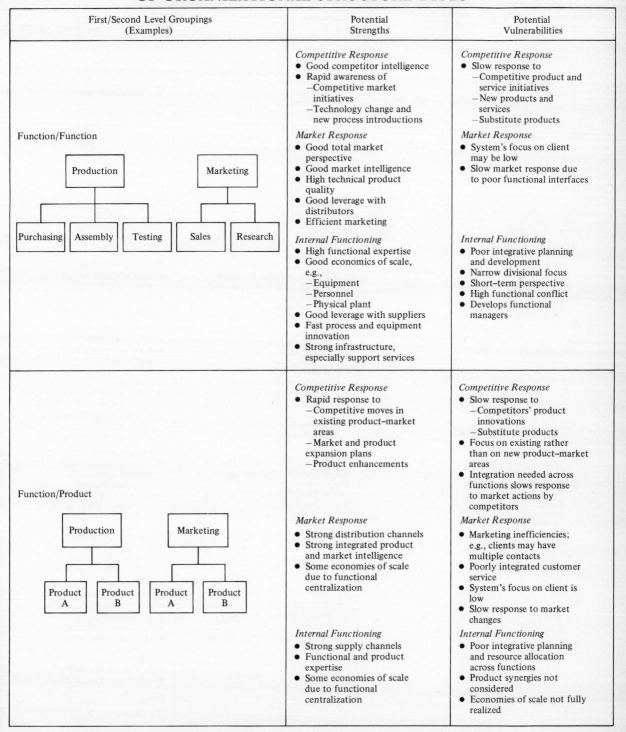

| First/Second Level Groupings (Examples) | Potential Strengths | Potential Vulnerabilities |
| --- | --- | --- |
| Function/Function | *Competitive Response*<br>• Good competitor intelligence<br>• Rapid awareness of<br>  —Competitive market initiatives<br>  —Technology change and new process introductions<br><br>*Market Response*<br>• Good total market perspective<br>• Good market intelligence<br>• High technical product quality<br>• Good leverage with distributors<br>• Efficient marketing<br><br>*Internal Functioning*<br>• High functional expertise<br>• Good economics of scale, e.g.,<br>  —Equipment<br>  —Personnel<br>  —Physical plant<br>• Good leverage with suppliers<br>• Fast process and equipment innovation<br>• Strong infrastructure, especially support services | *Competitive Response*<br>• Slow response to<br>  —Competitive product and service initiatives<br>  —New products and services<br>  —Substitute products<br><br>*Market Response*<br>• System's focus on client may be low<br>• Slow market response due to poor functional interfaces<br><br>*Internal Functioning*<br>• Poor integrative planning and development<br>• Narrow divisional focus<br>• Short-term perspective<br>• High functional conflict<br>• Develops functional managers |
| Function/Product | *Competitive Response*<br>• Rapid response to<br>  —Competitive moves in existing product–market areas<br>  —Market and product expansion plans<br>  —Product enhancements<br><br>*Market Response*<br>• Strong distribution channels<br>• Strong integrated product and market intelligence<br>• Some economies of scale due to functional centralization<br><br>*Internal Functioning*<br>• Strong supply channels<br>• Functional and product expertise<br>• Some economies of scale due to functional centralization | *Competitive Response*<br>• Slow response to<br>  —Competitors' product innovations<br>  —Substitute products<br>• Focus on existing rather than on new product–market areas<br>• Integration needed across functions slows response to market actions by competitors<br><br>*Market Response*<br>• Marketing inefficiencies; e.g., clients may have multiple contacts<br>• Poorly integrated customer service<br>• System's focus on client is low<br>• Slow response to market changes<br><br>*Internal Functioning*<br>• Poor integrative planning and resource allocation across functions<br>• Product synergies not considered<br>• Economies of scale not fully realized |

*Source:* This appendix is adapted from Ian C. MacMillan and Patricia E. Jones, "Designing Organizations to Compete," *Journal of Business Strategy* 4 (Spring 1984): 22–26.

| First/Second Level Groupings (Examples) | Potential Strengths | Potential Vulnerabilities |
|---|---|---|
| Function/Customer<br>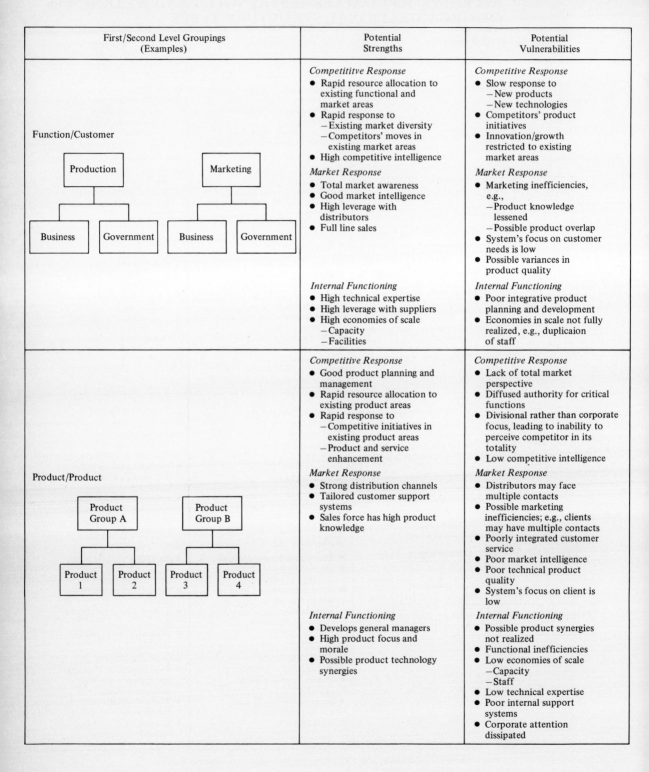 | *Competititve Response*<br>• Rapid resource allocation to existing functional and market areas<br>• Rapid response to<br>— Existing market diversity<br>— Competitors' moves in existing market areas<br>• High competitive intelligence<br><br>*Market Response*<br>• Total market awareness<br>• Good market intelligence<br>• High leverage with distributors<br>• Full line sales<br><br><br><br>*Internal Functioning*<br>• High technical expertise<br>• High leverage with suppliers<br>• High economies of scale<br>— Capacity<br>— Facilities | *Competitive Response*<br>• Slow response to<br>— New products<br>— New technologies<br>• Competitors' product initiatives<br>• Innovation/growth restricted to existing market areas<br><br>*Market Response*<br>• Marketing inefficiencies, e.g.,<br>— Product knowledge lessened<br>— Possible product overlap<br>• System's focus on customer needs is low<br>• Possible variances in product quality<br><br>*Internal Functioning*<br>• Poor integrative product planning and development<br>• Economies in scale not fully realized, e.g., duplicaion of staff |
| Product/Product | *Competitive Response*<br>• Good product planning and management<br>• Rapid resource allocation to existing product areas<br>• Rapid response to<br>— Competitive initiatives in existing product areas<br>— Product and service enhancement<br><br>*Market Response*<br>• Strong distribution channels<br>• Tailored customer support systems<br>• Sales force has high product knowledge<br><br><br><br><br><br>*Internal Functioning*<br>• Develops general managers<br>• High product focus and morale<br>• Possible product technology synergies | *Competitive Response*<br>• Lack of total market perspective<br>• Diffused authority for critical functions<br>• Divisional rather than corporate focus, leading to inability to perceive competitor in its totality<br>• Low competitive intelligence<br><br>*Market Response*<br>• Distributors may face multiple contacts<br>• Possible marketing inefficiencies; e.g., clients may have multiple contacts<br>• Poorly integrated customer service<br>• Poor market intelligence<br>• Poor technical product quality<br>• System's focus on client is low<br><br>*Internal Functioning*<br>• Possible product synergies not realized<br>• Functional inefficiencies<br>• Low economies of scale<br>— Capacity<br>— Staff<br>• Low technical expertise<br>• Poor internal support systems<br>• Corporate attention dissipated |

| First/Second Level Groupings (Examples) | Potential Strengths | Potential Vulnerabilities |
|---|---|---|
| **Product/Function** 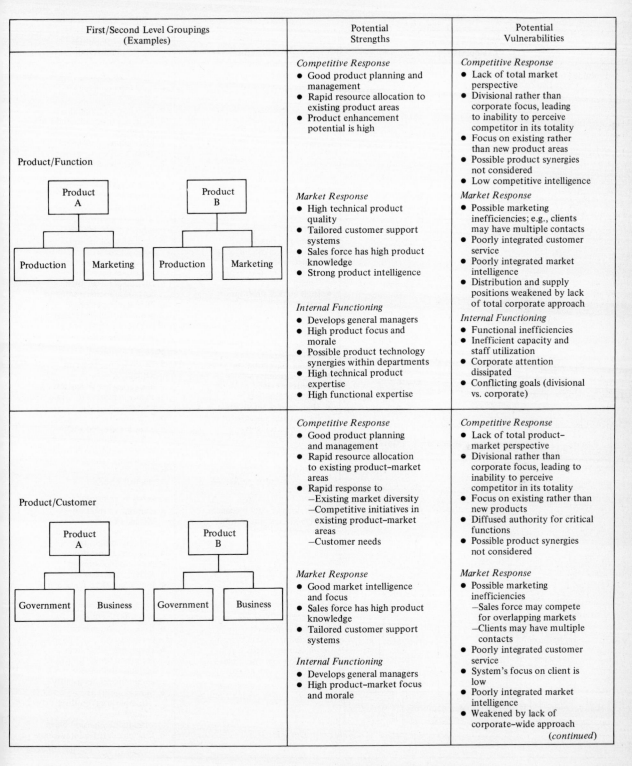 | *Competitive Response* <br> • Good product planning and management <br> • Rapid resource allocation to existing product areas <br> • Product enhancement potential is high <br><br> *Market Response* <br> • High technical product quality <br> • Tailored customer support systems <br> • Sales force has high product knowledge <br> • Strong product intelligence <br><br> *Internal Functioning* <br> • Develops general managers <br> • High product focus and morale <br> • Possible product technology synergies within departments <br> • High technical product expertise <br> • High functional expertise | *Competitive Response* <br> • Lack of total market perspective <br> • Divisional rather than corporate focus, leading to inability to perceive competitor in its totality <br> • Focus on existing rather than new product areas <br> • Possible product synergies not considered <br> • Low competitive intelligence <br><br> *Market Response* <br> • Possible marketing inefficiencies; e.g., clients may have multiple contacts <br> • Poorly integrated customer service <br> • Poorly integrated market intelligence <br> • Distribution and supply positions weakened by lack of total corporate approach <br><br> *Internal Functioning* <br> • Functional inefficiencies <br> • Inefficient capacity and staff utilization <br> • Corporate attention dissipated <br> • Conflicting goals (divisional vs. corporate) |
| **Product/Customer** | *Competitive Response* <br> • Good product planning and management <br> • Rapid resource allocation to existing product–market areas <br> • Rapid response to <br> —Existing market diversity <br> —Competitive initiatives in existing product–market areas <br> —Customer needs <br><br> *Market Response* <br> • Good market intelligence and focus <br> • Sales force has high product knowledge <br> • Tailored customer support systems <br><br> *Internal Functioning* <br> • Develops general managers <br> • High product–market focus and morale | *Competitive Response* <br> • Lack of total product–market perspective <br> • Divisional rather than corporate focus, leading to inability to perceive competitor in its totality <br> • Focus on existing rather than new products <br> • Diffused authority for critical functions <br> • Possible product synergies not considered <br><br> *Market Response* <br> • Possible marketing inefficiencies <br> —Sales force may compete for overlapping markets <br> —Clients may have multiple contacts <br> • Poorly integrated customer service <br> • System's focus on client is low <br> • Poorly integrated market intelligence <br> • Weakened by lack of corporate–wide approach <br> *(continued)* |

| First/Second Level Groupings (Examples) | Potential Strengths | Potential Vulnerabilities |
|---|---|---|
| **Product/Customer** (*continued*) | | *Internal Functioning*<br>• Poor internal support systems<br>• Functional inefficiencies<br>• Inefficient capacity and staff utilization<br>• Low technical product quality<br>• Low technical product quality<br>• Low functional expertise<br>• Corporate attention dissipated |
| **Geographic Area/Customer**<br><br>East Coast<br>— Business<br>— Government<br><br>West Coast<br>— Business<br>— Government | *Competitive Response*<br>• Rapid response to<br>—Existing market diversity<br>—Customer needs<br>—Existing market expansion plans<br>• High market preemption potential<br><br>*Market Response*<br>• Strong marketing and sales<br>• Good customer service<br>• Facilitates client planning and coordination<br>• High market intelligence<br>• Particularly suitable for key account strategies<br><br>*Internal Functioning*<br>• Develops general managers<br>• High market integration internally | *Competitive Response*<br>• Lack of total market perspective<br>• May not have authority over all critical functions<br>• Divisional rather than corporate focus, leading to inability to perceive competitor in its totality<br>• Innovation restricted to existing markets<br><br>*Market Response*<br>• Overresponse to client whims<br>• Marketing inefficiencies; e.g., clients may have multiple contacts<br>• Low product intelligence<br>• Sales force faced with broader product line and consequently lower product knowledge<br>• Weakened distribution channel position<br><br>*Internal Functioning*<br>• Corporate attention dissipated<br>• Market overlap may cause internal competition<br>• Low functional skills<br>• Poor internal support systems and integration<br>• Inefficient capacity and staff utilization |
| **Customer/Function**<br><br>Business<br>— Manufacturing<br>— Marketing<br><br>Government<br>— Manufacturing<br>— Marketing | *Competitive Response*<br>• Rapid response to<br>—Existing market diversity<br>—Customer needs<br>—Market expansion plans<br>—Competitors' market initiatives | *Competitive Response*<br>• Lack of total market perspective<br>• Divisional rather than corporate focus, leading to inability to perceive competitor in its totality<br>• Slow response to<br>—Competitors' product innovations<br>—Product expansion plans<br>• Low competitive intelligence<br>*(continued)* |

| First/Second Level Groupings (Examples) | Potential Strengths | Potential Vulnerabilities |
|---|---|---|
| Customer/Function (*continued*) | *Market Response*<br>• Strong marketing and full–line sales<br>• High leverage with distribution channels<br>• High product quality<br>• High market intelligence<br><br>*Internal Functioning*<br>• High function expertise<br>• Good internal support systems<br>• High leverage with suppliers | *Market Response*<br>• Marketing inefficiencies<br>—Product knowledge lessened<br>—Product priority conflict<br>—Possible market product overlap<br>• Low product intelligence<br><br>*Internal Functioning*<br>• Product priority conflict (if multiproduct)<br>• Low economies of scale (across divisions)<br>• Poor integration between functions |
| Customer/Product<br><br>Business — Product A, Product B<br>Government — Product A, Product B | *Competitive Response*<br>• Rapid response to<br>—Customer needs<br>—Market and product expansion plans<br>—Competitive moves in existing product–market areas<br>—Product enhancements<br>• Rapid resource allocation to product–market areas<br><br>*Market Response*<br>• Strong marketing and sales; e.g., sales force has high product knowledge<br>• Good market intelligence and expertise<br>• Good customer service<br><br>*Internal Functioning*<br>• Develops general managers<br>• High product and market focus and morale | *Competitive Response*<br>• Lack of total market perspective<br>• Divisional rather than corporate perspective, leading to inability to perceive competitor in its totality<br>• Low competitive intelligence<br>• Slow response to competitors' product innovations<br><br>*Market Response*<br>• Marketing inefficiencies; e.g., client may have multiple contacts<br>• System's focus on client is low<br>• Possibly overresponsive to client whims<br><br>*Internal Functioning*<br>• Low functional expertise<br>• Poor internal support systems<br>• Low capacity and staff utilization<br>• Product innovation/ enhancement overlaps<br>• Possible product synergies may be overlooked |

141

# Strategic Management Process

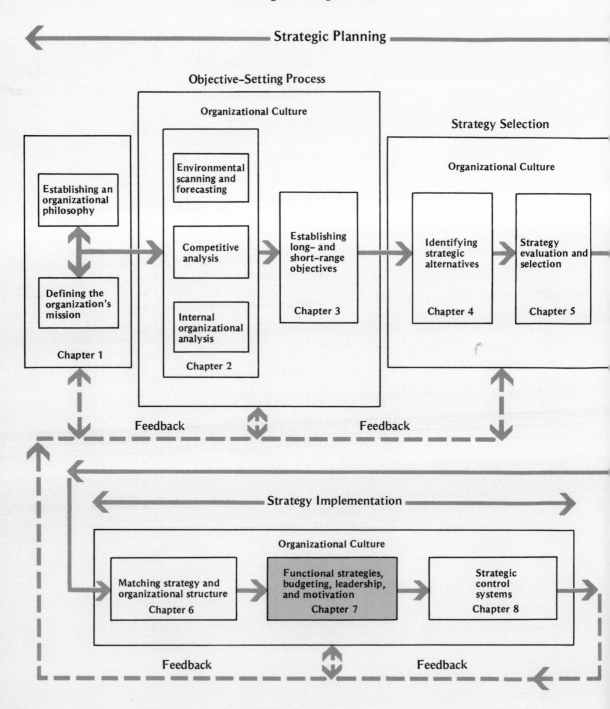

## Strategic Planning

### Objective-Setting Process

Organizational Culture

**Establishing an organizational philosophy**

**Defining the organization's mission**

Chapter 1

Environmental scanning and forecasting

Competitive analysis

Internal organizational analysis

Chapter 2

**Establishing long- and short-range objectives**

Chapter 3

### Strategy Selection

Organizational Culture

**Identifying strategic alternatives**

Chapter 4

**Strategy evaluation and selection**

Chapter 5

Feedback                    Feedback

## Strategy Implementation

Organizational Culture

**Matching strategy and organizational structure**

Chapter 6

**Functional strategies, budgeting, leadership, and motivation**

Chapter 7

**Strategic control systems**

Chapter 8

Feedback                    Feedback

# 7

# IMPLEMENTING STRATEGY: FUNCTIONAL STRATEGIES, BUDGETING, LEADERSHIP, AND MOTIVATION

## STUDY OBJECTIVES

- To describe the role, nature, and development of functional strategies
- To explain the role of the budgeting process in deploying resources in the pursuit of organizational objectives
- To emphasize the importance of leadership in strategic planning and strategy implementation
- To discuss the role of motivational systems in strategy implementation

## CHAPTER OUTLINE

Developing Functional Strategies
   Marketing Strategies
   Financial Strategies
      Capital Budgeting
      Cash Flow Analysis
   Production/Operations Strategies
   Human Resource/Personnel Strategies
   Research and Development Strategies
Deployment of Resources Through Budgeting
   Flexible Budgets
   Program Budgeting
   Making the Budget Process Useful
Organizational Leadership
Motivational Systems
Review Questions
Discussion Questions
References and Additional Reading

*The summits of the various kinds of business are, like the tops of mountains, much more alike than the parts below—the bare principles are much the same; it is only the rich variegated details of the lower strata that so contrast with one another. But it needs travelling to know that the summits are the same. Those who live on one mountain believe that their mountain is wholly unlike all others.*—Walter Bagehot, *The English Constitution,* as quoted by Anthony Jay, *Management and Machiavelli*

After objectives are established, corporate-level and business unit strategies are selected, and an organizational structure is chosen, several activities must take place in order to ensure that the strategy is successfully implemented. One of these activities is the development of strategies for each of the functional (marketing, finance, production, and so on) areas of the organization that complement each other and support the corporate-level or business unit strategy. Next, the resources of the organization must be allocated throughout the organization to ensure that each of the organizational units is adequately supported. This activity is normally accomplished through the budgeting process. Employees must be encouraged to direct their efforts toward the accomplishment of the organization's objectives. The leadership skills of the management team and the motivational systems used in the organization are two of the primary methods used to direct employees. The purpose of this chapter is to discuss each of these activities in more depth and describe their importance in the successful implementation of strategy.

## DEVELOPING FUNCTIONAL STRATEGIES

*Functional strategies* describe the means or methods that are to be used by each of the functional areas of the organization in carrying out the corporate-level or business unit strategy. Functional strategies differ from corporate or business unit strategies in several respects. First, functional strategies usually cover a much shorter time span than do corporate strategies. Second, functional strategies are much more specific and action-oriented than are corporate strategies. The corporate strategy is designed to give general direction; the functional strategy is designed to give more specific direction. Finally, functional strategy development requires much more active participation by lower levels of management. In fact, input by lower levels of management at the development stage is essential in the successful implementation of functional strategies. On the other hand, the development of corporate strategy is generally considered the private domain of top management, with little if any input from lower levels of management.

Functional strategies can be developed for any unit within an organization. However, the functional areas of organizations normally include most, if not all, of the following:

- Marketing
- Finance

- Production/operations
- Human resources/personnel
- Research and development

## Marketing Strategies

*Marketing* consists of those activities intended to move products or services from the producer to the consumer or market. The basic role of marketing in an organization is to have the right products or services in the right quantity at the right place at the right time.[1] When this role is performed effectively, profits are earned and customers are served efficiently. Marketing strategy is concerned with matching existing or potential products or services with the needs of customers, informing customers that the products or services exist, having the products or services at the right time and place to facilitate exchange, and assigning a price to the products or services. Example 7.1 illustrates some of the types of problems that are faced in developing a marketing strategy.

The marketing strategy selected by an organization is dependent on whether the organization is attempting to reach new or existing customers and whether the organization's products or services are new or already exist. A classification system for marketing strategies based on the type of customer and type of product or service is illustrated in Figure 7.1.

With a *marketing penetration strategy,* the organization attempts to gain greater control in a market in which it already has a product or service. Management must carefully consider several factors in using a market penetration strategy. These include

- The reaction of competitors
- The capacity of the market to increase usage or consumption and/or the availability of new customers
- The costs involved in gaining customers from competition, stimulating more usage or consumption, or attracting new customers

A *market development strategy* consists of introducing the organization's existing products or services to customers other than the ones it currently serves. Considerations in using a market development strategy include

- The reaction of competitors
- An understanding of the number, needs, and purchasing patterns of the new customers
- Determination of the organization's adaptability to new markets

An organization using a *product development strategy* creates a new product or service for existing customers. Considerations in a product development strategy include

- The competitive response
- The impact of the new product or service on existing products or services
- The ability of the organization to deliver the product or service

---

## STRATEGY IN PRACTICE

### Example 7.1 Marketing Scotch Whiskey

A problem facing the scotch whiskey industry in Scotland is determining the marketing strategy to be used. For the past decade, some companies in the industry have exported blended and malt whiskeys in bulk. Bulk blended scotch is bottled overseas and sold as scotch whiskey, but at a lower price than "bottled in Scotland" scotch. Bulk malt scotch is blended with indigenous whiskey and bottled at its destination and sold without "scotch whiskey" being mentioned.

Arguments have arisen claiming that these exports hurt both the Scottish economy and the industry. It is argued that bulk blend exports damage the economy because they compete with "bottled in Scotland" scotch and thus both potential jobs and foreign exchange earnings are lost. Bulk malt exports allegedly damage the industry because they allow local whiskey industries to build a reputation which could enable their products to compete with scotch whiskey.

Strategic options available to the scotch industry include the following: stop the export of bulk sales; compete freely against other whiskeys; enter into licensing agreements; or invest in local whiskey producers in export countries.

*Source:* Adapted from David Targett, "Marketing Strategies for Scotch Whiskey," *Long Range Planning,* 16 (April 1983):65–73.

---

|  |  | Customer | |
|---|---|---|---|
|  |  | Existing | New |
| Products or services | Existing | Market penetration | Market development |
|  | New | Product development | Diversification |

**Figure 7.1** Marketing Strategies by Customer and Products or Services.
*Source:* Adapted from H. Igor Ansoff, *Corporate Strategy* (New York: McGraw-Hill, 1965), p. 109.

With a *diversification marketing strategy,* an organization offers a new product or service to new customers. Considerations in using this strategy include

- Developing a considerable knowledge of the new customer's needs
- Making certain that the new product or service meets those needs
- Knowing that the organization has the human talent to serve the new customers

After the basic marketing strategy is determined, more specific strategies are required. These activities are often called the marketing mix. They include

- Determining the exact type of product or service that is to be offered (product strategy)

Consistency
1. Do the individual elements of the mix fit together to form a logical relationship, or are they fragmented?
2. Does the mix fit the organization, the market, and the environment into which it will be introduced?

Sensitivity
1. Are customers more sensitive to certain marketing mix variables than others?
2. Are customers more likely to respond favorably to a decrease in price or an increase in advertising?

Cost
1. What are the costs of performing the various marketing mix activities?
2. Do the costs exceed the benefits in terms of customer response?
3. Can the organization afford the marketing mix expenditures?

Timing
1. Is the marketing mix properly timed?
2. Is promotion scheduled to coincide with product or service availability?

**Figure 7.2** Questions in Determining the Appropriateness of a Marketing Mix
*Source:* Adapted from Roger A. Kerin and Robert A. Peterson, *Strategic Marketing Problems* (Boston: Allyn & Bacon, 1978), p. 7.

- Deciding how the product or service is to be communicated to customers (channel strategy)
- Selecting the method for distributing the product or service to the customer (channel strategy)
- Establishing a price for the product or service (price strategy)

Determination of the appropriate marketing mix is crucial in the success of any organization. Figure 7.2 outlines several questions that when answered give direction in determining the appropriate marketing mix for a particular organization.

Product positioning is often used as an aid in developing a marketing strategy. *Product positioning* uses marketing research techniques to determine where proposed and/or present brands or products are located in the market. Product positioning enables managers to decide whether they want to leave their present product and marketing mix alone or whether they want to reposition the product. Production positioning allows an organization to develop marketing strategies oriented toward target customers. Developing strategies of this type is frequently called target marketing. For example, an organization may develop a market segmentation strategy in which its products are aimed at a homogeneous submarket of a larger market. Another organization might develop a combining strategy that involves combining relatively homogeneous submarkets into a larger target market.

**Financial Strategies**

Financial management is primarily concerned with two functions. The first function, acquiring funds to meet the current and future needs of an organization, is normally the responsibility of the treasurer of the organization. The second function is recording, monitoring, and controlling the financial results of an organization's operations. This function is normally the responsibility of the controller of an organization.

The activities of financial management can be grouped into five categories:

1. Determining the magnitude and characteristics of funds necessary to conduct the business operations
2. Allocating resources in the most efficient manner
3. Serving as an interface with creditors and stockholders concerning the financial condition of the organization
4. Recordkeeping
5. Providing financial data to top management in determining the feasibility of various strategic alternatives.

Figure 7.3 outlines just some of the questions that need to be answered in developing a financial strategy.[2]

Two important considerations in financial management that influence all functional areas of an organization are capital budgeting and cash flows. Both are important to the implementation of strategies at all levels of the organization.

**Capital Budgeting** *Capital assets* are assets that are used in the physical process of producing an organization's goods or services and are normally used for a

---

Determining magnitude and characteristics of necessary funds
1.  What are cash flow requirements?
2.  How are credit and collections to be handled?
3.  Are long-term bonds, stock issues, or short-term bank borrowing to be used?
4.  How is inventory control to be handled?

Allocating resources
1.  Are the long-term benefits from the proposed project commensurate with the long-run costs?
2.  What types of budgets are to be developed?

Serving as an interface with creditors and stockholders
1.  What methods are to be used in paying dividends?
2.  What credit terms are going to be requested from suppliers?

Recordkeeping
1.  Are profit-center accountability systems to be established?
2.  Are financial statements to be prepared for each organizational unit?
3.  What reports are to be prepared for various levels of management, and when?

Providing financial data on various strategic alternatives
1.  What is the value of the company that is under consideration for acquisition?
2.  What are the financial implications of the proposed liquidation of a certain part of the organization?

**Figure 7.3** Potential Questions That Need Answering in Developing a Financial Strategy

number of years. Since the amount of money involved is so large, generally organizations carefully plan and evaluate expenditures for capital assets. Furthermore, an organization's current capital allocations directly affect its future strategic options. Inefficient capital allocation can slow an organization's growth, strain its financing capacity, and severely limit is strategic options.[3]

The process of determining how much to spend on capital assets and which assets to acquire is called capital budgeting. Capital budgets are developed on the basis of sales forecasts and the anticipated plant and equipment needed to meet those expected sales. Methods for evaluating various investment options are based on the marginal cash flow that results from each option. After the marginal cash flows have been estimated, several techniques can be used to evaluate the investment options. The primary techniques used are the present value, internal rate of return, payback period, and accounting rate of return.[4]

**Cash Flow Analysis**   Cash is essential to the survival, growth, and profitability of any organization. The cash flow process is basically an asset transformation process. Any organization must start with a certain amount of cash. It then purchases goods and services or invests in capital assets. The purchased goods and services and capital are then used to produce a product or service, which results in an inventory. Sale of the inventory results in an accounts receivable. The collection process then turns accounts receivable into cash. And, if the cash flow process works properly, the cycle repeats itself continuously.

Of course, the cash flow process is complicated by several factors. Credit from suppliers, outside financing, and retained earnings add to the resources in the cycle. On the other hand, debt reduction, dividends, and operating losses reduce the resources in the cycle. Furthermore, the periodic acquisition of large capital assets complicates the cycle. Actually, the cash flow cycle is often somewhat erratic and subject to disruptions.

The determination of the sources of cash flowing into an organization and the uses of that cash by the organization is called a sources and uses of funds analysis or funds flow analysis. This analysis is particularly useful in determining how well an organization is achieving its financial resource objectives. Example 7.2 describes the results of Fiat's cash management program.

---

## STRATEGY IN PRACTICE

### Example 7.2 Fiat's Cash Management Program

Over $54 billion in cash flowed through Fiat's operations in 1983. To keep track of this much money, Fiat has a centralized reporting system that allows it to determine the exact income and outflow positions of its companies over successive ten-day periods and to estimate the company's cash position over the next four months. This allows the company to use expected cash surpluses either by investing the money or to cover potential shortfalls.

*Source:* Adapted from "Clever Cash Management Revs Fiat's Finances," *Business Week,* April 30, 1984, p. 60.

---

---

## STRATEGY IN PRACTICE

### Example 7.3 Operations Management at GM

In January 1985, General Motors announced plans to set up a new company, Saturn Corporation, to produce a full line of subcompact cars. The Saturn line will be GM's attempt to seriously compete with the Japanese in the small-car market. The plant will use the latest automation techniques, which should reduce costs and provide better quality—the two areas where the Japanese currently have the advantage. According to GM's chairman, Roger Smith, the manufacturing process will be more important than any of Saturn's product innovations. "We hope this car will be less labor intensive, less material intensive, less everything intensive than anything we have done before."

*Source:* Adapted from "Saturn Makes Its Debut at GM," *Time*, January 21, 1985, p. 50.

---

**Production/ Operations Strategies**

Production/operations management, which evolved from the field of production or manufacturing management, is concerned with selecting, designing, and updating the systems that produce the organization's products or services and with operating those systems. Production or operating systems, which consist of the activities and processes necessary to transform inputs into products or services, exist in all organizations whether they are private, public, profit, nonprofit, service, or manufacturing. Generally, the operating system of an organization takes up the largest part of its financial assets, personnel, and expenses. It is being increasingly recognized that no amount of marketing, advertising, or financial manipulation can make an organization healthy if its products/services, facilities, technologies, and people are not of competitive quality.[5] Example 7.3 illustrates GM's emphasis on operations management.

The activities of production/operations management can be categorized into two main areas: (1) system design and (2) operations planning and control. *System design* starts with product or service design, which largely determines the production capabilities needed. Process selection, site location, layout of facilities, equipment selection, and design of work methods are all part of the design phase of operations management. Obviously, it is impossible to design efficient production systems and facilities without knowledge of the corporate objectives and strategies.

The *operations planning and control* phase involves planning production levels in light of demand forecasts, scheduling work through the operating system, and allocating employees throughout the system. This phase includes production control, inventory control, quality control, cost control and improvement, and facility maintenance. The operations planning and control activities must be closely coordinated with the design activities. For example, the design objectives of the operating system would most likely dictate the most appropriate control system. Similarly, the design objective would also affect the number and types of personnel needed. Figure 7.4 outlines some of the major considerations in developing a production/operations strategy.

It is important to note here that many of the activities involved in marketing,

| Birth of the system | What are the objectives and strategies of the organization?<br>What product or service will be offered? |
|---|---|
| Product design and process selection | What is the form and appearance of the product?<br>Technologically, how should the product be made? |
| Design of the system | What capacity do you need?<br>Where should the facility be located?<br>What physical arrangement is best to use?<br>How do you maintain desired quality?<br>How do you determine demand for the product or service?<br>What job is each worker to perform?<br>How will the job be performed, measured; how will the workers be compensated? |
| Start-up of the system | How do you get the system into operation?<br>How long will it take to reach the desired rate of output? |
| The system in steady state | How do you maintain the system?<br>How can you improve the system?<br>How do you revise the system in light of changes in corporate strategy? |
| Termination of the system | How does a system die?<br>What can be done to salvage resources? |

**Figure 7.4** Considerations in Developing a Production/Operations Strategy
*Source:* Richard B. Chase and Nicholas J. Aquilano, *Production and Operations Management,* 3rd ed. (Homewood, Ill: Richard D. Irwin, 1981), p. 13.

finance, and production/operations have considerable overlap. For example, product design is an operations activity that directly relates to marketing. Process design and equipment acquisition are operations activities that cannot be undertaken independently of finance. Thus, close coordination and cooperation are required in the development of functional strategies for all of these areas.

**Human Resource/ Personnel Strategies**

Human resource/personnel management includes those organizational activities that are concerned with determining the human resources (both quantity and quality) that the organization needs to achieve its objectives; recruiting, hiring, training, developing, and counseling employees; developing compensation systems; developing disciplinary systems; acting as a liaison with unions and government organizations; and handling other matters such as employee safety and corporate communications. The strategic alternatives of any organization are feasible from a human resource perspective if (1) the organization, business unit, or function has or can obtain the talent necessary to carry it out; and (2) the costs of acquiring, retaining, developing, and motivating the needed talent are economically feasible.[6]

In adapting a strategic perspective to human resource management, an organization should

1. Use its strategies (corporate-level, business unit, and functional) to identify what human resources are needed and how they should be allocated
2. Develop and implement personnel practices that select, reward, and develop employees that best contribute to the accomplishment of organizational objectives
3. Use its resources to compete for or retain employees who are needed to reach its objectives
4. Develop mechanisms that match employees' competencies to the organization's present and future needs as determined by the nature of the product or service and the market.[7]

Figure 7.5 poses several questions that must be addressed in developing a human resource strategy. Example 7.4 shows how Corning Glass developed a strategy to address one specific human resource problem.

## Research and Development Strategies

Products or services become obsolete—not only from a technical but also from an economic standpoint—more rapidly today than ever before. The same applies to methods of production. For example, one of the primary reasons for the economic difficulties faced by the steel industry in the United States is the technical obsolescence of its production facilities. An effective way for an organization to safeguard against either product or production process obsolescence is through research and development (R&D) efforts.

The R&D efforts of organizations can be divided into three basic categories:

1. *Basic Research.*   The objective of basic research is to enlarge technical knowledge without having a specific application of the knowledge. Colleges, universities, and several federal government agencies are active in performing basic research. Furthermore, an interesting trend is developing in which private enterprise organizations are funding basic research at colleges and universities in anticipation that useful, commercial applications can be developed from the basic research findings.
2. *Applied Research.*   The objective of applied research is to enlarge technical knowledge but in such a manner that a useful commercial application will result from the research.
3. *Development Research.*   The objective of development research is to use available knowledge in the introduction of new or improved products or services or production techniques.

Most private enterprise organizations devote a significant portion of their R&D budgets to applied and development research.

An important consideration in R&D strategy is the outlook or orientation that

1. Does the organization have methods for quantifying and expressing its human resource needs?
2. To what extent can human resources be transferred among business units or functions to meet the strategic plan?
3. To what extent can human resources be developed within business units or functional areas to implement the strategic plan?
4. Are there mechanisms for shifting resources among business units or functional areas, for example from a declining unit to a growing unit?
5. Are reward systems designed to encourage employees to contribute to accomplishing the strategic plan?
6. Are training and development programs oriented toward developing skills needed to implement the strategic plan?
7. Are performance evaluation and appraisal systems consistent with the objectives of the organization?
8. Are human resource policies and procedures consistent with the finance and marketing strategies?
9. Are human resource services such as employment, compensation, and training coordinated and directed toward the accomplishment of organizational objectives?

**Figure 7.5** Considerations in Developing a Human Resource Strategy
*Source:* Adapted from Lloyd Baird, Ilan Meshoulam, and Ghislaine DeGive, "Meshing Human Resources Planning with Strategic Business Planning: A Model Approach," *Personnel* 60 (September–October 1983):22–29.

## STRATEGY IN PRACTICE

### Example 7.4 Orientation Strategy at Corning Glass

Corning Glass Works primarily manufactures and sells products made from specialty glasses. It also produces a limited line of appliances, medical instruments, electronics devices, and special refractory materials. Its sales in 1984 were over $1.7 billion, and it has over 26,000 employees.

Hiring between 200 and 300 professionals each year, Corning felt that it was losing too many good people early in their careers. Management decided that they needed a new program to introduce their new employees to the company. The Corporate Education and Training Department was given the assignment of developing a new orientation program.

The objectives of the new orientation program were aimed at improving productivity and specifically were to cut losses of people in their first three years of employment by 17 percent and to shorten by 17 percent the time it takes a new person to learn the job.

*Source:* Adapted from Edmond J. McGarrell, Jr., "An Orientation System that Builds Production," *Personnel* 60 (November–December 1983):32–41.

an organization is going to assume in its R&D efforts. Basically, four orientations exist: innovative, protective, catch-up, or combination.

An *innovative R&D strategy* is primarily concerned with developing new products or services or production techniques. Most of the firms in the pharmaceutical and biomedical fields use the innovative approach.

A *protective R&D strategy* is concerned with improving present products and/or production techniques. The emphasis is primarily on maintaining the firm's present position.

Closely related to the protective R&D strategy is the *catch-up R&D strategy.* A firm that uses this strategy basically researches competitive products or services and incorporates their best features into its own products or services. This type of R&D strategy has been used by many foreign organizations and governments in developing products designed to compete with U.S. firms. On the other hand, U.S. firms have also used this strategy to catch up with foreign firms (e.g., the industrial application of robotics).

A final approach to an R&D strategy is a *combination* of any of the above three approaches. For example, IBM often uses a protective strategy for its existing products, but also uses an innovative strategy in developing new products.

The choice of what R&D strategy orientation is to be used by a particular organization depends on its size, its degree of technological leadership, its environment, and its competitors. Figure 7.6 outlines several questions that need to be considered in developing an R&D strategy. Example 7.5 shows the research and development strategies at Nippon Steel.

## DEPLOYMENT OF RESOURCES THROUGH BUDGETING

*Budgeting* is a process by which the management of an organization specifies the resources it will employ to obtain the organization's objectives. It also provides the means of measuring the successful accomplishment of the stated objectives within a specific time period, normally one year.[8] The following types of budgets can be developed: sales budget, production budget, capital budget, direct materials budget, direct labor budget, overhead budget, selling and administrative expense budget, cash flow budget, budgeted income statement, and a budgeted balance sheet. Each of these budgets can be prepared for the organization as a whole or for various components of an organization (e.g., business units or functional areas). Table 7.1 describes some of the more common types of budgets.

Although budgets may be expressed in other terms, the dollar is the most common denomination. Budgets that may be expressed in units other than dollars include equipment budgets (which can be expressed in numbers of machines) or material budgets (which can be expressed in pounds, pieces, and gallons). Budgets not expressed in dollars are normally translated into dollars for incorporation into an overall budget.

Budgets can also be classified as being participative or nonparticipative. Under a *nonparticipative budgeting process,* top management sets the budget, issues it to lower-level managers, and then holds these lower-level managers accountable for performance in accordance with the budget. Under a *participative budgeting process,* lower-level managers submit budgets for their organizational units, which top

1. Which technical know-how is available or has to be developed for the new product?
2. What kinds of research resources are required for the development of the new product, and are the resources available?
3. What research personnel are required or available?
4. What is the estimated applied research time?
5. What is the expected development time?
6. What is the earliest possible introduction time of the new product, and what is the latest one?
7. What additional labor and research resources are required for speeding up the research time?
8. What are the consequences (e.g., financial) of an earlier or better completion of the research phase compared with the optimal introduction time of the new product?
9. What synergy effects are likely to occur, taking into account other research projects?
10. Which technologies required for the development of this product are relevant for the research policy of the company in the long run?
11. What technological developments have been realized by competition in this area?
12. Are the technologies that are required to develop the product completely new to the organization?
13. What is the innovation value of the new product, and how long will this innovation value exist?
14. Will the new product require continuous defensive research to keep the product features up-to-date; what resources will probably be required for this?
15. What are the estimated design costs and production costs of a prototype or pilot plant?
16. Which additional research resources will make it possible to design a product essentially different from competitive products?
17. What is the probability of technical success?
18. How and with what additional resources could this probability of technical success be influenced?

**Figure 7.6** Checklist of Questions on Developing an R&D Strategy
*Source:* Adapted from T. Bemelmans, "Strategic Planning for Research and Development," *Long Range Planning* 12 (April 1979):41.

## STRATEGY IN PRACTICE

### Example 7.5 Research at Nippon Steel

Established in 1901, Nippon Steel is capitalized at $1.4 billion and employs 69,000 people. Nippon Steel's sales in 1982 amounted to $12 billion. Of this, steel products accounted for 84 percent, engineering business for 6 percent, chemical products for 6 percent, and welding rods for fabricated steel products for 4 percent. Roughly one out of every seven employees is an engineer or researcher. Research expenses are close to 2 percent of total sales.

Of the roughly 300 companywide research topics, 20 percent are basic research, 48 percent are concerned with manufacturing processes, and 27 percent pertain to steel products. About 14 percent of Nippon Steel's research projects are conducted jointly with other companies.

*Source:* Adapted from Azusa Tomiura, "How Nippon Steel Conducts Joint Research," *Research Management* 28 (January–February 1985):26.

**Table 7.1** Types and Purposes of Budgets

| Type of Budget | Brief Description or Purpose |
|---|---|
| Revenue and expense budget | Provides details for revenue and expense plans |
| Cash flow budget | Forecasts cash receipts and disbursements |
| Capital expenditure budget | Outlines specific expenditures for plant, equipment, machinery, inventories, and other capital items |
| Production, material, or time budget | Expresses physical requirements of production or material or the time requirements for the budget period |
| Balance sheet budgets | Forecasts the status of assets, liabilities, and net worth at the end of the budget period |

*Source:* Leslie W. Rue and Lloyd Byars, *Management: Theory and Application* 3rd ed. (Homewood, Ill.: Richard D. Irwin, 1983), p. 166.

management combines into an overall organizational budget. Some degree of participation in the budgeting process seems to exist in most organizations today.[9]

Budgets are not without their dangers. One of the greatest potential dangers is inflexibility. Inflexibility poses a special threat to organizations operating in an industry characterized by rapid change and/or severe competition. It can also lead to the subordination of organizational objectives to the budget. In this case, staying within the budget becomes more important than meeting objectives.

Budgets can hide inefficiencies. The fact that an expenditure was made in the past often becomes justification for continuing the expenditure, when in fact the situation may have changed considerably.

Budgets can also become inflationary and inaccurate. This often happens in a participative budgeting system when lower-level managers pad their budgets because they know they will be cut by upper levels of management. Since the lower-level manager is never certain of how severely the budget will be cut, the result is often an inaccurate and unrealistic budget. Some of the methods employed in the budgeting game, as it is often called, are budgeting a low sales figure or a high expense figure by exaggerating the problems faced by the business unit or functional area. In addition, money can be saved on the budget in the short run by not investing in research, ordering new equipment, or conducting training programs. Of course, cutting these budget items can have potential negative effects in the long run. In order to overcome some of the problems associated with game playing and inflexibility in budgets, organizations sometimes use flexible budgets and program budgets.

**Flexible Budgets**

*Flexible budgets* vary with the volume of sales or some other measure of output. Flexible budgets are generally limited in application to expense budgets. Under

**Table 7.2** Simplified Flexible Budget

|  | Sales (in units) | | | | |
|---|---|---|---|---|---|
|  | **10,000** | **11,000** | **12,000** | **13,000** | **14,000** |
| Material costs | $20,000 | $22,000 | $24,000 | $26,000 | $28,000 |
| Advertising | 10,000 | 11,000 | 12,000 | 12,500 | 13,000 |
| Shipping costs | 10,000 | 10,500 | 11,000 | 11,500 | 12,000 |
| Sales commissions | 5,000 | 5,500 | 6,000 | 6,500 | 7,000 |
| Budget expenses | $45,000 | $49,000 | $53,000 | $56,500 | $60,000 |

a flexible budget, material, labor, advertising, and other expenses are allowed to vary with the volume of output. Flexible budgets are more useful for evaluating what expenses should have been under a certain set of circumstances. Table 7.2 illustrates a simplified flexible budget.

**Program Budgeting**

*Program budgeting* allocates resources by programs instead of by functional areas as traditional budgets do. In a program budget, money is allocated to achieve a specific objective or objectives. Spending is classified by outputs tied to objectives rather than by inputs tied to functions. Program budgets extend far enough into the future to show the full resource requirements and spending implications of a program.

One of the largest users of program budgeting has been the U.S. Department of Defense; other government agencies also use program budgeting. The system used by these government agencies is called *program planning and budgeting (PPB)*. In general, a PPB system functions as follows:

1. Budgets are developed on a program basis.
2. Program expenditures are extended far enough into the future to show the full resource requirements and spending implications.
3. Each program is critically examined in terms of its cost effectiveness.

In examining each program in terms of its cost effectiveness, managers use the concept of *zero-based budgeting* (ZBB). The key difference between traditional budgeting and ZBB is that ZBB does not build from the previous year's budget. Traditional budgeting systems produce a set of numbers based on last year's budget. Those numbers do not necessarily justify the need for the activity or function or identify its effectiveness or priority.

ZBB requires managers to analyze each existing or newly proposed budget item as if no money had ever been allocated for the item. Each function or activity under a manager's control is identified, evaluated, and ranked in order of its importance. Then each year every function and activity in the budget is matched against all other claimants for an organization's resources. Theoretically, ZBB should enable an organization to react to changing conditions and to reallocate resources effectively to areas where the greatest return can be achieved.

## Making the Budget Process Useful

Unfortunately, many organizations and managers view the budgeting process as merely being a financial exercise rather than being a process to implement strategy. Some questions that management should ask itself to help in ensuring that the budgeting process does help in strategy implementation are

1. Does the business unit or functional area within the organization identify its objectives and contributions to the organization's objectives?
2. Are the objectives broken down within milestones for the next year so that management can review and control the progress?
3. Are the short-range objectives attainable, or will economic or business changes have an impact on the results?
4. Has the organization funded the objectives adequately in the form of a capital budget and human resources?[10]

Finally, Table 7.3 is offered to help in identifying a weak budgeting process. Example 7.6 shows how a church developed a new budgeting system and gained positive results.

**Table 7.3** Identifying a Weak Budgeting Process

| Symptom | Possible Cause |
|---|---|
| If, after the budgeting process is complete, the organization experiences the following symptoms: | Problems can possibly be traced to the following budgeting deficiencies: |
| • Programs and projects are having difficulty in getting established | • Short-range objectives are not synchronized with long-range objectives |
| • Shortly after the beginning of the year, much to the surprise of management, a hiring freeze or expenditure curtailment is imposed | • Key economic, business, or internal assumptions are either not considered or are faulty |
| • Organization experiences unexpected additional cash requirements | • Realistic cash flow analysis with varying assumptions was not prepared |
| • Key financial returns such as return on assets/return on investment are disappointing | • Organization did not consider steady or improved productivity, increased fixed cost more than required; or real growth expectations did not materialize |

*Source:* Adapted from Cosmo S. Trapani, "Six Critical Areas in the Budgeting Process," *Management Accounting* 64 (November 1982):55.

---

## STRATEGY IN PRACTICE

**Example 7.6** Budgeting at Northside Presbyterian Church of Blacksburg, Virginia

Like most churches, Northside does not secure enough cash to do everything it would like. In addition, Northside only prepared a budget for expenditures, not for receipts. In developing its system, the church established receipts accounts for undesignated offerings, designated offerings, building use fees, and other receipts. Its disbursements accounts included minister's salary, allowances, and benefits; church administration; worship; religious; utilities; buildings and grounds; financial commitments; and capital expenditures.

As a result of the budgeting system, Northside now publishes a funds flow statement. The statement begins with expenditures rather than receipts in order to focus attention on services rendered and their cost. In addition, the church now uses zero-base budgeting concepts in the development of their budget.

The results have been that some members of the congregation have stated that they now have more confidence in the church's ability to manage its financial affairs and have substantially increased their offerings.

*Source:* Adapted from Gary M. Cunningham and David E. Reemsynder, II, "Church Accounting: The Other Side of Stewardship," *Management Accounting* 65 (August 1983):58–62.

---

## ORGANIZA- TIONAL LEADERSHIP

Critical ingredients in strategic planning and implementation are the skills and abilities of the organization's leaders. A leader is an individual within an organization who is able to influence the attitudes and opinions of others within the organization; a manager is merely able to influence their actions and decisions. Leadership is not a synonym for management; it is a higher order of capability.[11] Example 7.7 describes in more detail this higher order of capability.

Influencing the attitudes and opinions of others in order to achieve a coordinated effort from a diverse group of employees is a difficult task. However, one of the key methods available to management is creating an overall sense of direction and purpose through strategic planning and implementation.

How is this accomplished? First, most employees have some idea about the performance of the organization and have some degree of understanding of the strengths, weaknesses, opportunities for, and threats to their organization. In other words, they have a general idea about what their organization should be doing. Next, each employee also has a concept of what the organization is presently doing. Finally, employees are influenced by the organizational structure and the organizational systems for planning, control, and motivation and develop a concept of what they should be doing to improve organizational performance and for their own self-interest.[12] Figure 7.7 graphically shows how employees develop these three perceptions. Obviously, the challenge of leadership within an organization is to develop systems which bring these three perceptions in line or as close as possible.

---

## STRATEGY IN PRACTICE

**Example 7.7** Martin Luther King, Jr., and the Southern Christian Leadership Conference

Martin Luther King, Jr., came to national attention in 1955 when the 26-year-old clergyman emerged as leader of the Montgomery bus boycott, the first massive and sustained black protest in the South following the Supreme Court's desegregation decision of May 1954. King and his associates went on to form the Southern Christian Leadership Conference in 1957 and lead the Birmingham protests of 1963, which contributed to the passage of the major civil rights legislation of 1964 and 1965. King's nonviolent philosophy won him the Nobel Peace Prize in 1965. He was recognized as one of the most important leaders of the civil rights movement.

Martin Luther King's leadership skills seemed to center around his faith in God, his vision of the future of the civil rights movement, and his ability to communicate. His "I have a dream" speech is well remembered for its eloquence in stating a vision for the future. On April 3, 1968, King stated:

> We've got some difficult days ahead. But, it really doesn't matter with me now. Because I've been to the mountain top. I won't mind. Like anybody, I would like to live a long life. Longevity has its place. But I'm not concerned about that now. I just want to do God's will.
>
>   And he's allowed me to go to the mountain. And I've looked over, and I've seen the Promised Land. I may not get there with you, but I want you to know tonight that we as a people will get to the Promised Land.

On April 4, 1968, Martin Luther King, Jr., was assassinated.

*Source:* Adapted from Martin Luther King, Jr., *The Measures of a Man* (Philadelphia: Pilgrim Press, 1968), p. 63; and Melvin Drimmer, *Black History: A Reappraisal* (Garden City, N.Y.: Doubleday, 1968), pp. 440–454.

---

Another area of interest in organizational leadership is the complementary relationship between manager selection and organizational strategy. Many contend that without a linkage between manager selection and strategy, an organization risks sacrificing a well-planned strategy to a manager who is ill suited to implement it or hiring a key manager but without a clear rationale for that particular choice.[13] The assumption here is that the style of managers can and does influence their effectiveness in carrying out particular strategies. On the other hand, matching managerial style to an organization's unique situation is a most difficult and challenging task. It is apparent, however, that certain organizational cultures and strategies are better suited for certain styles of management. Thus, when an organization is experiencing difficulties or is operating in a considerably different environment, it is not unusual for that organization to change its top management in anticipation that a new management team will better enable the organization to meet the situation.

**MOTIVA-TIONAL SYSTEMS**

Leadership and the level of motivation demonstrated by employees in an organization are complementary. In most instances the degree of motivation exhibited by employees is influenced by leader effectiveness. Furthermore, a highly moti-

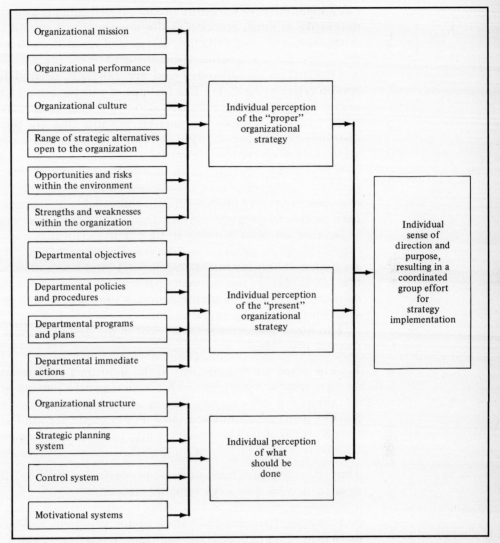

**Figure 7.7** Sources of the Individual Perceptions of Organizational Strategies
*Sources:* Adapted from LaRue Tone Hosmer, "The Importance of Strategic Leadership," *Journal of Business Strategy* 3 (Fall 1982):56.

vated management team in combination with highly motivated employees can bring about substantial increases in performance and can significantly increase the likelihood that organizational objectives will be achieved. Many variables influence the level of motivation of employees in an organization. However, the main variable explored in this section is the organizational reward system.

In most cases, the organizational reward system is one of the most effective motivational tools available to organizations. The design and use of the organizational reward system reflects management's attitude about performance and significantly influences the entire organizational climate. Few things in an organization evoke as much emotion as the organizational reward system.

*Organizational rewards* include all types of rewards, both intrinsic and extrinsic, that are received as a result of employment by the organization. Intrinsic rewards are internal to an individual and are generally derived from involvement in certain activities or tasks. The feelings of satisfaction and accomplishment that are derived from doing a job well are examples of intrinsic rewards. On the other hand, extrinsic rewards are tangible rewards that are directly controlled and distributed by the organization. An employee's pay and hospitalization insurance are examples of extrinsic rewards.

Many extrinsic benefits such as hospitalization and retirement programs depend only on an employee's continued employment with an organization. However, pay raises and promotions are controllable by management and should be used to encourage good performance on the part of all employees.

*Incentive pay plans* attempt to tie pay to performance and are used by many organizations to motivate employees. Unfortunately, most incentive programs are designed only for top management. Lower levels of management and operative employees do not normally participate. In order for pay to be an effective motivator in strategy implementation, it should be tied to performance and used at all levels within the organization.

Two major problems seem to exist in the design of most management incentive pay programs:

1.  The plans are not coupled to the industry's performance. Thus, managers may receive a high reward for achieving a 15 percent growth rate while the industry is growing at a rate of 25 percent.
2.  The plans are one-dimensional. For example, if compensation is based solely on return on assets, managers may be tempted to eliminate assets or investments critical to long-term growth.[14]

Thus, incentive programs must be properly designed or they can actually work against successful strategy implementation.

Some organizations, in an attempt to relate individual rewards to organization performance, have designed stock option programs in which all employees can participate. This indirectly ties individual rewards to organizational performance.

Many other factors within organizations influence the level of motivation of employees. Example 7.8 illustrates a unique motivational system. In the final analysis, the management team of an organization is the key element in determining the level of motivation within an organization. Peter Drucker has suggested several personal characteristics of managers that can significantly lower the level of motivation among employees:

*   Lack of integrity of character
*   Tendency to focus on people's weaknesses rather than on their strengths
*   Interest in who is right rather than what is right
*   Disposition to value intelligence more than integrity[15]

Motivated employees are something that some organizations have, and many others wish they had. In the final analysis, motivated employees play a significant role in the successful achievement of organizational objectives.

---

## STRATEGY IN PRACTICE

### Example 7.8 The "Golden Banana" Award

The Foxboro Company is a leading multinational manufacturer and distributor of instrumentation and control systems. In its early days, the company desperately needed a technical advance for its survival. Late one evening, a scientist rushed into the president's office with a working prototype. Dumbfounded at the elegance of the solution and bemused at how to reward it, the president bent forward in his chair, found something, leaned over the desk to the scientist, and said, "Here!" In his hand was a banana, the only reward he could immediately put his hands on. From that point on, the small "golden banana" pin has been the highest accolade for scientific achievement at Foxboro.

*Source:* Adapted from Thomas J. Peters and Robert H. Waterman, Jr., "How the Best-Run Companies Turn So-So Performers into Big Winners," *Management Review,* November–December 1982, p. 11.

---

## REVIEW QUESTIONS

1. What is the purpose of functional strategies?
2. Describe the following marketing strategies:
   a. Market penetration strategy
   b. Market development strategy
   c. Product development strategy
   d. Diversification marketing strategy
3. What are the primary activities of financial management?
4. What is capital budgeting?
5. Describe the cash flow process.
6. What are the main activities in production/operations management?
7. Outline several considerations in developing a production/operations strategy.
8. Outline several questions that need to be answered in developing a human resource strategy.
9. Describe the three basic categories of research and development.
10. What is a budget?
11. Describe the following budgeting systems:
    a. Flexible budgets
    b. Program budgets
12. What are some guidelines in identifying a weak budgeting process?
13. Briefly describe how leadership style influences strategy implementation.
14. Outline some of the organizational rewards that can influence the level of motivation in an organization.
15. Describe some of the personal characteristics of managers that can influence the level of motivation in an organization.

## DISCUSSION QUESTIONS

1. Do you think that the functional strategies in marketing, finance, and production are generally in conflict? Why or why not?
2. If you were the chief executive of a medium-size company, how would you ensure that all of the functional strategies interrelate and help the company achieve its overall objectives?
3. What system would you use to motivate functional area managers not only in achieving their objectives but also in working cooperatively with other functional area managers?
4. "The key to the successful implementation of a strategy is effective leadership." Do you agree? Discuss.

## REFERENCES AND ADDITIONAL READING

1. See Milton Leontiades, "The Importance of Integrating Marketing Planning with Corporate Planning," *Journal of Business Research* 11 (December 1983):457–473.
2. For a more in-depth look at problems in developing financial strategies, see Steward C. Myers, "Finance Theory and Financial Strategy," *Interfaces* 14 (January–February 1984):26–137.

3. Joseph V. Rizzi, "Capital Budgeting: Linking Financial Analysis to Corporate Strategy," *Journal of Business Strategy* 4 (Spring 1984):81.

4. For a discussion of the uses of these methods, see Lawrence D. Schall, Gary L. Sunden, and William D. Geijsbreek, Jr., *Journal of Finance* 33 (March 1978):281–287.

5. Wickham Skinner, "Getting Physical: New Strategic Leverage from Operations," *Journal of Business Strategy* 3 (Spring 1983):75.

6. Lee Dyer, "Bringing Human Resources into the Strategy Formulation Process," *Human Resource Management* 22 (Fall 1983):261.

7. Lloyd Baird, Ilan Meshoulam, and Ghislain DeGive, "Meshing Human Resource Planning with Strategic Business Planning: A Model Approach," *Personnel* 60 (September–October 1983):17.

8. Cosmo S. Trapani, "Six Critical Areas in the Budgeting Process," *Management Accounting* 64 (November 1982):52.

9. Carolyn Conn, "Budgets: Planning and Control Devices?" *Managerial Planning* 29, no. 4 (January–February 1981):37.

10. Trapani, "Six Critical Areas in the *Budgeting Process,*" p. 53.

11. LaRue Tone Hosmer, "The Importance of Strategic Leadership," *Journal of Business Strategy* 3 (Fall 1982):55.

12. Ibid., p. 57.

13. Milton Leontiades, "Choosing the Right Manager to Fit the Strategy," *Journal of Business Strategy* 3 (Fall 1984):69.

14. Ray Stata and Modesto A. Maidique, "Bonus System for Balanced Strategy," *Harvard Business Review* 58 (November–December 1980):157.

15. Peter F. Drucker, *Management: Tasks, Responsibilities, Practices* (New York: Harper & Row, 1974), p. 462.

# Strategic Management Process

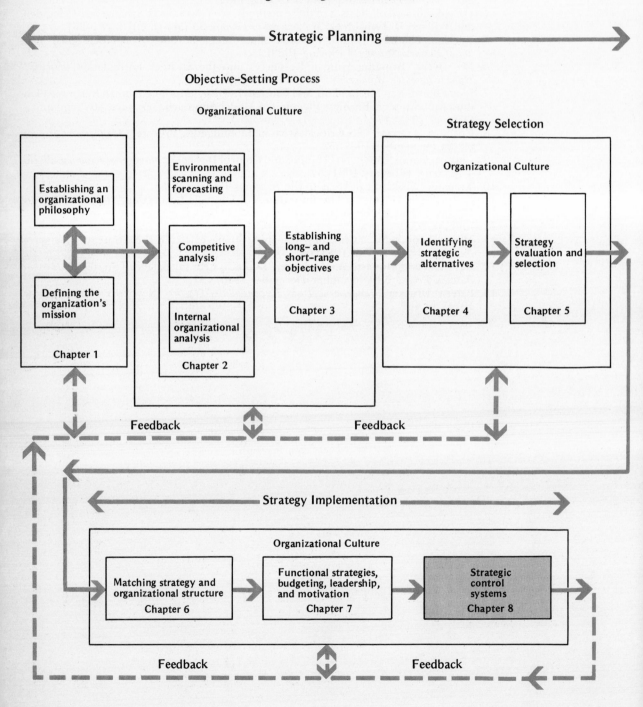

## Strategic Planning

### Objective-Setting Process

**Organizational Culture**

- Environmental scanning and forecasting
- Competitive analysis
- Internal organizational analysis

Chapter 2

Establishing long- and short-range objectives

Chapter 3

### Strategy Selection

**Organizational Culture**

- Identifying strategic alternatives

Chapter 4

- Strategy evaluation and selection

Chapter 5

- Establishing an organizational philosophy
- Defining the organization's mission

Chapter 1

Feedback    Feedback

## Strategy Implementation

**Organizational Culture**

- Matching strategy and organizational structure

Chapter 6

- Functional strategies, budgeting, leadership, and motivation

Chapter 7

- Strategic control systems

Chapter 8

Feedback    Feedback

# 8  *STRATEGIC CONTROL PROCESS*

## STUDY OBJECTIVES

- To discuss the major elements of the strategic control process

- To illustrate the relationship between strategic control and other phases of the strategic management process

- To describe several methods used in the strategic control process

- To present the role of the management information system (MIS) and the decision support system (DSS) in the strategic control process

## CHAPTER OUTLINE

Strategic Control Process
Strategic Control and Other Phases of the Strategic Management Process
Three Elements of Control
    Developing Criteria for Evaluation
        Qualitative Criteria
        Quantitative Criteria
    Evaluating Performance
    Feedback
Effective Control Systems
Methods of Control
    Budgets
    Audits
        Independent Auditors
        Government Auditors
        Internal Auditors
        Management Audits
    Time-related Control Methods
    Management by Objectives
Strategy Audits
Management Information Systems
    Designing an MIS
    Decision Support Systems
Review Questions
Discussion Questions
References and Additional Reading

*The best laid plans of mice and men sometimes go astray. This seems to be particularly true in managerial endeavors involving multiple individuals. In fact, the probabilities and possibilities for incorrect or inappropriate action seem to increase geometrically with an arithmetic increase in personnel. As a result, any person directing an overall undertaking must check on the actions of the participants as well as the results which they have achieved. If either the actions or results do not comply with preconceived or planned achievements, then planned and needed action must be communicated to the participants, for them either to correct what they have done or to take remedial action during subsequent events.*—Claude S. George, Jr., *The History of Management Thought*

The basic premise of strategic management is that the chosen strategy will achieve the organization's objectives. However, the possibility of this not occurring gives rise to the need for the strategic control process. In the *control process* top management determines how well or whether the chosen strategy is achieving the organization's objectives.

The strategic control process should alert management to a problem or potential problem before it becomes critical. Control is accomplished by comparing actual performance to predetermined objectives or standards and then taking action to correct any deviations from the objectives or standards. The need for control is essential. However, the nature and degree of strategic control is a complex and sensitive issue. The implementation of control systems often only leads to more controls which, in turn, lead to more controls. In order to avoid this trap, managers must remember that control is only one phase in the strategic management process and is not an end in itself. Control systems must be designed to provide information that facilitates the accomplishment of organizational objectives. Too much information can be as bad as or worse than not enough information.

## STRATEGIC CONTROL PROCESS

The strategic control and strategic planning processes are closely interrelated. Figure 8.1 illustrates the relationship. The desired results (objectives) of an organization are established during the strategic planning process. The development of criteria for evaluation can be viewed as a part of either strategic planning or strategic control. The criteria for evaluation are used as a point of reference for determining how well or whether an organization is achieving its objectives. The criteria for evaluation are derived from an organization's objectives. Budgets, which were discussed in the previous chapter, give criteria for evaluation.

Performance evaluation takes place when the outputs of the control system are compared to the criteria for evaluation. Control systems are designed to measure outputs from organizational activities. Finally, the information gained in the evaluation of performance must be used. Corrective action must be taken if the criteria for evaluation are not being met. Example 8.1 shows what can happen with a lack of control.

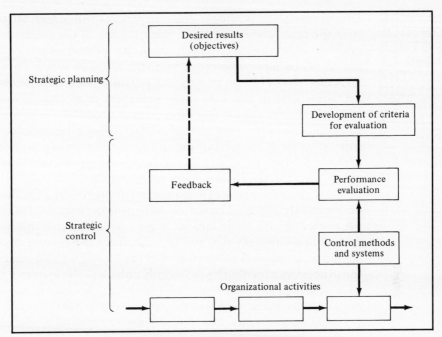

**Figure 8.1** Relationship Between Strategic Planning and
Strategic Control Process

## STRATEGY IN PRACTICE

### Example 8.1 Lack of Controls at DeLorean Motor Company

The collapse of DeLorean Motor Company was caused, in part, by a lack of basic
management control. From the beginning, the market for the DeLorean sports car was
substantially overestimated, and all financial matters were handled casually. The coordination of design and production engineering during the construction of the Belfast,
Ireland, plant was extremely poor. Lines of responsibility were abused, delegation was
minimal, and secrecy was encouraged. Company management failed to control costs
and to enforce quality standards. When it finally rolled off the line, the DeLorean sports
car was more expensive and of much lower quality than John DeLorean had said it
would be. Within 13 months of the plant start-up, the company was in receivership.

*Source:* Adapted from George Bikerstaff, "The Trashing of the DeLorean," *International Management,* May 1983,
pp. 23–30.

**STRATEGIC CONTROL AND OTHER PHASES OF THE STRATEGIC MANAGEMENT PROCESS**

Output from the strategic control process influences all other phases of the strategic management process. For example, if the profits for a particular SBU, division, or product are significantly below projections, then a complete reexamination of the unit's objectives and strategy is in order. However, the poor performance may only be due to the personal ineptness or negligence of certain managers, and in this case these managers must change or be replaced.

Furthermore, output from the control phase of strategy implementation provides information essential to the objective-setting process. As will be recalled from Chapter 2, answering the question "Where are we now?" is the first step in the objective-setting process. Properly designed control systems provide valuable information for answering this question.

Thus, the entire strategic management process is a feedback system that must be constantly adjusted based on information from the control system and from the organization's environment. Figure 8.2 illustrates this feedback system. The dashed lines indicate that information from the control process influences and should be used in all other phases of the strategic management process. Viewing the process as a feedback system only enhances the system's effectiveness. Otherwise, when performance deviations occur, piecemeal and often only stopgap measures are taken such as firing managers or reorganizing. These actions may very well be necessary, but they should be undertaken only after a review of the entire strategic management process.

**THREE ELEMENTS OF CONTROL**

The strategic control process has three basic elements: (1) developing criteria for evaluation, (2) evaluating performance, and (3) feedback. All three elements are essential in maintaining effective control.

**Developing Criteria for Evaluation**

The objectives of an organization should serve as an effective starting point in developing criteria for evaluation of the organization's effectiveness. Ideally, criteria for evaluation should be quantifiable and measurable. However, in actual practice all criteria for evaluation are not quantifiable.

**Qualitative Criteria**   An organization's objectives and strategy are based on a set of assumptions about the organization's future environment and its resources. If the environment and resources do not develop as forecast, then obviously the objectives and strategy may be inappropriate. It seems logical, therefore, that the strategic control process should focus, at least partially, on those areas.

Several key questions need to be addressed in developing this type of focus for a control system:

- What three or four basic assumptions underlie the objectives and strategy of the organization?
- Do these assumptions conform to the environmental trends and organizational resources?

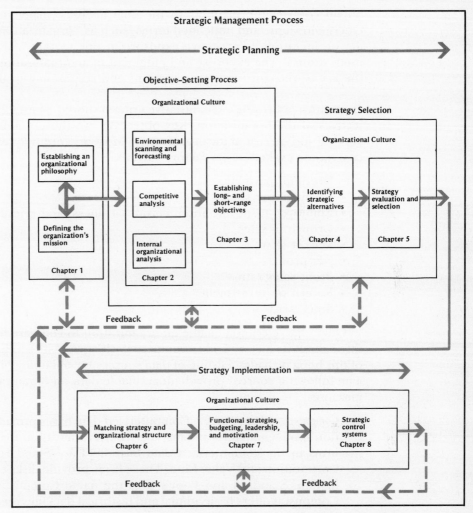

**Figure 8.2** Strategic Management Process as a Feedback System

- What are the three or four *key factors for success* of the organization? Key factors for success point out what an organization has to do well in order to succeed in an industry. Each industry and, in many cases, each organization within an industry have different key factors for success.
- Does the organization still possess the key factors for success?

Answering all of these questions calls for qualitative judgments. Top management can, and often does, use reports developed by staff personnel or outside consultants to assess and answer these questions. Reports developed for this purpose are a method of control.

Managers also often develop informal networks with other executives, customers, lower-level employees, suppliers, educators, and outside professionals to obtain control information.[1] In the final analysis, many strategic issues often emerge in vague and undefined terms, such as "organizational overlap," "product proliferation," "excessive exposure in one market," or "lack of focus and motivation."[2] The expertise and judgment of an organization's management are the key to recognizing these situations and responding to them.

**Quantitative Criteria**    Quantitative criteria should be established for all key objectives of the organization. Key objectives are those that are essential for the survival and success of the organization. Most organizations establish quantitative criteria for evaluation on factors such as

- Dividend payments
- Earnings per share
- Employee turnover, absenteeism, tardiness, and grievances
- Growth in sales
- Market share
- Net profit
- Profit-sales ratios
- Return on investment
- Stock price

Quantitative criteria enable an organization to compare how well it has done throughout its history and to compare itself against its competitors. Appendix C of this book provides a listing of data sources for obtaining business information. The following sources provide quantifiable data on organizational performance measures:

1. *Computerized Data Bases.*    Computerized data bases provide financial information about companies and markets from a variety of sources. Two of the major firms in the computerized data base field are Standard and Poor's (S&P) Corporation and Value Line. These firms provide disks containing the information. Standard and Poor's uses the name Compustat for its data base. Compustat offers basic annual and historical data files on over 5000 organizations. Some of the information provided by Compustat includes income statement data, balance sheet data, and information on stock prices. In addition, Compustat makes adjustments to the data to achieve comparability between time periods and companies.[3] The information provided by Value Line is similar to Compustat.

2. *Dun's Review.*    Each year (normally during November) Dun and Bradstreet publishes in *Dun's Review* key business ratios for the retailing, wholesaling, and manufacturing industries. Ratios in this listing include
   a. Current assets to current liabilities
   b. Net profits on net sales (percent)
   c. Net profits on tangible net worth (percent)
   d. Net profits on net working capital (percent)
   e. Net sales to tangible net worth
   f. Net sales to net working capital

    **g.**  Collection period (days)
    **h.**  Net sales to inventory
    **i.**  Fixed assets to tangible net worth (percent)
    **j.**  Current debt to tangible net worth (percent)
    **k.**  Total debt to tangible net worth (percent)
    **l.**  Inventory to net working capital (percent)
    **m.**  Current debt to inventory (percent)

    Furthermore, each year in December *Dun's Review* provides a qualitative evaluation of what it feels are the five best-managed companies for the year.

**3.** *Forbes.*   Each year in January, *Forbes* publishes its measures of performance for over 1000 organizations. *Forbes* measures these organizations on their profitability (in terms of return on stockholders' equity and total capital), growth (in terms of both earnings per share and sales), debt-equity ratios, net profit margins, and stock market performance. *Forbes* uses these measures to rank the organizations in terms of their profitability, growth, and stock market performance.

**4.** *Fortune.*   Each year in May, *Fortune* provides financial and other information on the 500 largest U.S. industrial corporations. The information provided includes sales, assets, net income, stockholders' equity, number of employees, net income as a percent of stockholders' equity, earnings per share, and total return to investors. In June, the same information is provided for the second 500 largest industrials.

    The use of quantitative criteria for evaluation raises several problems. First, most quantitative criteria are geared to the short-term profit objectives of the organization. Pressure is exerted by stockholders and the financial community for steady increases in earnings per share on a quarterly basis. Concern about immediate profit maximization makes it rather difficult to implement a strategy that cannot be immediately measured and has returns that are long-term in nature. A second problem with the use of quantitative criteria is that the set of criteria used at one particular point during the implementation of a strategy more than likely will change over time. For example, during the development phase of a new product, the most important criteria would probably relate to production efficiency and research and development. Later, criteria related to marketing and financial considerations would become more important. Finally, different accounting methods provide different results on many of the quantitative criteria. If quantitative measures are to be used in control, the accounting procedures used in the calculations must be consistently applied.

## Evaluating Performance

Unfortunately, performance evaluation is often viewed as being synonymous with the control process when in fact it is only part of the total control process. The overriding purpose of evaluating performance is to identify problem areas within an organization. Evaluating performance requires comparing actual performance to planned performance, that is, comparing the output from the control systems to the criteria for evaluation. Once the comparison is made between actual performance and the criteria for evaluation, proper corrective action can be taken. Obviously, the entire process of control is no better than the information on which it operates.

The major problems in evaluating performance are deciding when, where, and how often performance is to be evaluated. Performance must be evaluated often enough to provide adequate information. If it is overdone, however, the evaluation process can become expensive and can also result in adverse reactions when people feel that they are being evaluated too closely. All too frequently organizations lose sight of the purpose of control and start to enforce controls that become increasingly unrelated to any useful purpose. All the while, this increased control consumes more and more resources and produces less and less. Style and conformity become more important than performance. Another important consideration in evaluating performance is timing. Problem areas must be recognized in time to correct them.

## Feedback

All too often organizations develop criteria for evaluation and evaluate performance but do not follow up with appropriate actions. The first two steps are of little value if feedback is not provided to the appropriate managers and any necessary corrective action is not taken. Of course, no corrective action may be necessary if performance criteria are being met in a satisfactory manner.

Causes of deviations can range from unrealistic objectives to the wrong strategy being selected to achieve organizational objectives. Figure 8.3 lists some potential causes of deviations between desired and actual performance. If performance criteria are not being met satisfactorily, management must find the cause of the deviation and correct it. Feedback from the evaluation stage is an absolutely essential element in the entire strategic management process.

## EFFECTIVE CONTROL SYSTEMS

In today's environment, computer systems can be designed to control virtually anything that is happening within an organization. Floods of data and information can be generated to the point that the entire system becomes meaningless. In order to be effective, control systems must meet several basic requirements. The key requirements are as follows:

1. *Control Systems and Methods Must Be Economical.* In designing a control system for a particular area or function within an organization, management should always ask, What is the minimum information needed to have control over this area or function? Too much information can be just as bad as too little information.

2. *Control Systems and Methods Must Be Meaningful.* Controls must be related to the key objectives of the organization. At lower levels of management, control

Unrealistic objectives
Selection of wrong strategy to achieve organizational objectives
Use of wrong organizational structure to implement the strategy
Ineptness or negligence on the part of management and/or operative employees
Lack of motivation
Lack of communication within the organization
Environmental forces

**Figure 8.3** Potential Causes of Performance Deviations

systems should provide managers with useful information about the activities over which they have control and influence. A careful analysis should be made not only of what is needed but also of what is not needed.

3. *Control Systems and Methods Must Provide Timely Information.* Frequent and very rapid feedback of information does not necessarily mean better control. The key question that needs to be answered is whether the information is provided in time to be of use to the management team. At certain times and in certain areas, information is needed on an almost daily basis. For example, when an organization is test marketing a new product, rapid feedback on the results is almost essential. However, in a long-range research and development project, daily, weekly, or even monthly feedback on progress may be not only unnecessary but also counterproductive. Thus, control systems should be designed to correspond to the time span of the activity or function being measured.

4. *Control Systems and Methods Must Measure the True Character and Nature of the Activity or Function.* For example, reporting the number of grievances per thousand employees per month may be a valid control measure. On the other hand, the measure does not indicate the nature of the grievances and leaves the impression that the grievances are distributed throughout the organization in a random manner. However, if the grievances are negatively influencing the morale and productivity in one critical area of the business, then reporting the number of grievances per thousand employees may be very misleading control information. Control systems must be designed to provide a true picture of what is happening.

5. *Control Systems and Methods Should Provide Qualitative Information on Trends.* For example, knowing whether a particular product's market share is going up or down or remaining stable is probably as important as, if not more so than, knowing the actual percentage of market share. Knowing whether a new product is on schedule in terms of its market introduction is as important as knowing whether it is within budget. Qualitative information such as this can signal problem areas much more quickly than a mere presentation of quantitative data and thus can facilitate quicker action to solve the problem.

6. *Control Systems Must Facilitate Action.* Information from the control system must be directed to those people in the organization who can take action based on it. Providing a control report to a manager "for informational purposes only" usually means that the report will be ignored by the manager

and may, in fact, lead the manager to ignore other useful reports. Everyone within an organization does not have to receive all of the reports.

7. *Control Systems and Reports Need to Be Simple.*    Generally, it is safe to say that if someone needs to know the mechanics and methodology of the control system before it can be used, then more than likely the system needs to be redesigned. Complex control systems often only confuse people and accomplish little. The key to an effective control system is its usefulness, not its complexity.

Example 8.2 describes an effective system of financial control.

## METHODS OF CONTROL

Many methods are used in strategic control systems. Example 8.3 illustrates a hands-on method of control. Some of the other frequently used methods are described in the following sections.

### Budgets

Budgets are probably the most widely used control methods. Preparation of the budget determines how the resources of the organization are to be allocated among the various organizational units. On the other hand, the administration of the budget is a method of control.

After the budget is prepared, the controller's department in large organizations keeps records on expenditures and periodically prepares reports showing the budgets, actual expenditures, and differences (or variances, as they are frequently called). For smaller organizations, this function is often handled by the owner-manager, the office manager, or an independent service organization such as a bank or accounting firm. Table 8.1 shows a rather simplified example of a budget report. After the report is prepared, generally it is sent to the people responsible for the particular area or function covered by the budget. It is at this point that variances must be analyzed and corrective action taken, if necessary. Furthermore, in effective budgeting control systems, each manager meets with his or her subordinates to review variances and determine corrective actions. This process is repeated from the bottom to the top of the organization. At higher levels of management, written reports are often required that outline the reasons for variances and the corrective actions that are being taken.

Of course, it is entirely possible that the budget, which is actually only a forecast of expected results and requirements, may need revising. Normally, for larger organizations a budget review committee (generally composed of the top executives of the organization) meets regularly to review and revise the budget. In the final analysis, preparation, administration, and corrective action taken on budget variances are key elements in successful strategy implementation.

### Audits

Another frequently used method of control is an audit. *Auditing* has been defined by the American Accounting Association (AAA) to be "a systematic process of objectively obtaining and evaluating evidence regarding assertions about eco-

---

## STRATEGY IN PRACTICE

**Example 8.2** Du Pont's System of Financial Control

Du Pont's system of financial control (shown diagrammatically in the figure below) has received wide recognition.

The figure is divided into two main groupings. The upper group represents investment turnover, which is derived by combining current assets plus fixed investments in the form of property, plant, and equipment, and then dividing total investment into sales.

The lower group begins with an analysis of the income statement. Sales minus cost of sales gives earnings, and earnings divided by sales gives earnings as a percent of sales. Return on investment is calculated by multiplying turnover by earnings as a percent of sales.

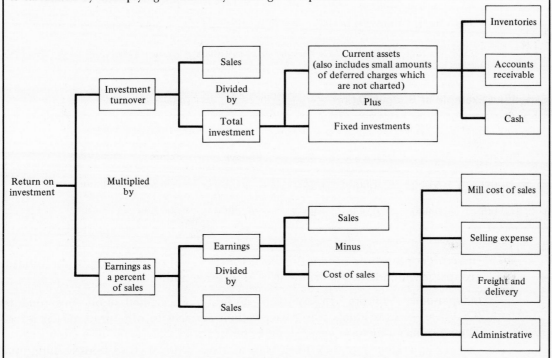

Return on investment is calculated for each operating division, department, or product. This has been called the *profit center approach* to looking at performance. Management compares division, department, or product performance not only to determine how to allocate additional resources but also to determine incentive bonuses for individual managers.

*Source:* Adapted from J. Fred Weston and Eugene F. Brigham, *Managerial Finance*, 7th ed. (New York: Dryden Press, 1981), p. 247.

---

nomic actions and events to ascertain the degree of correspondence between those assertions and established criteria and communicating the results to interested users."[4]

Basically, the audit process focuses on the financial assertions made by an organization and on how well these assertions represent events that have oc-

---

## STRATEGY IN PRACTICE

### Example 8.3 Hands-on Control at McDonald's

Ray Kroc, the founder of McDonald's Corporation, was involved in every aspect of the operations of the McDonald's fast-food business. Known as a "detail person," Ray Kroc was personally involved in setting quality and housekeeping standards, suggesting menu changes, making purchasing decisions, and performing store inspections. When potential new store sites were identified, Kroc would drive around the area and visit the local shops to see how a McDonald's store would do there. In the early 1960s, Kroc proposed that the company hold classes for new operators and managers to teach them "McDonald's method of providing services." According to Ray Kroc, "If I had a brick for every time I've repeated the phrase 'Q, S, C, and V' (quality, service, cleanliness, and value), I think I'd probably be able to bridge the Atlantic Ocean with them."

*Source:* Ray Kroc, *Grinding It Out: The Making of McDonald's* (Chicago: Regency, 1977), p. 85.

---

**Table 8.1** Simplified Example of Budget Report

|  | June | | | | 5 Months (year-to-date) | | | |
|---|---|---|---|---|---|---|---|---|
|  | Budget | Actual | Difference | % | Budget | Actual | Difference | % |
| Total cost | $ 4,000 | $ 5,000 | $ 1,000 | +25 | $ 20,000 | $ 20,500 | $500 | +2.5% |
| Total units produced | 100,000 | 120,000 | 20,000 | +20% | 1,000,000 | 1,000,000 | — | + 0% |

curred. People who perform the audit function can be divided into three basic groups: independent, government, and internal auditors.

**Independent Auditors**  Independent auditors or certified public accountants (CPAs) are professionals who provide their services to organizations for a fee. Their primary function is to examine the financial statements of a client. However, independent auditors also perform other work such as bookkeeping and accounting services, tax accounting, management consulting, and the preparation of financial statements for clients.

In order to offer their services to the public, CPAs must meet a series of standards as to education and experience and must pass a uniform national examination. The license to practice as a CPA is granted by individual states. Audits of financial statements by CPAs determine whether the statements have been prepared according to an objective set of rules, called generally accepted accounting principles (GAAP), and whether the statements fairly represent the activities of the organization. In making this determination, CPAs use a set of standards called generally accepted auditing standards (GAAS).

**Government Auditors**  Two government agencies—the General Accounting Office (GAO) and the Internal Revenue Service (IRS)—are primarily responsible for performing government audits of organizations. Government audits are conducted to determine the organization's compliance with federal laws, statutes, policies, procedures, and rules. Auditors from the GAO perform audits of other government agencies and companies with government contracts. The Internal Revenue Service, on the other hand, is primarily concerned with compliance with the federal tax laws (Internal Revenue Code) and, of course, can audit any private enterprise organization.

**Internal Auditors**    Internal auditors are employees within an organization whose primary responsibility is to determine whether organizational policies and procedures are being carried out correctly and to safeguard organizational assets. Internal auditors are also frequently called upon to assess not only the efficiency of various organizational subunits but also the efficiency of control systems within the organization. Top management and an organization's board of directors are the most frequent users of the information gained by internal auditors.

**Management Audits**    *Management audits* systematically examine, analyze, and evaluate the overall performance of an organization's management team. Management audits can be performed by outside consultants (the consulting division of independent certified public accounting firms often performs management audits) or by an organization's own internal audit staff. Management audits have been performed in organizations with such diverse interests as the Roman Catholic Church and the Procter & Gamble Company.[5] Example 8.4 describes the results of a management audit.

**Time-related Control Methods**    Several useful graphical and analytical methods have been developed that can serve as tools in the strategic control process. The primary purpose of such methods is to identify the work that is to be accomplished in performing a

---

## STRATEGY IN PRACTICE

**Example 8.4** Management Audits at Arkansas Power and Light Company

Two management audits have been conducted at Arkansas Power and Light Company (AP&L). AP&L's management audits can be characterized as highly successful because the company saved nearly $30 million as a result of implementing the recommendations of the audit. Initial audits focused on organizational structure, materials management, productivity, fleet management, personnel management, and industry-specific load forecasting, generation planning, and power plant operations. Later audits not only focused on these issues but also considered the capability of management to handle emerging issues in the electric utility industry, such as growth and entry into new businesses.

*Source:* Adapted from Ralph C. Mitchell and Richard J. Metzler, "The Second-Generation Management Audit," *Public Utilities Fortnightly* 111 (May 12, 1983):21–25.

particular project or task, to determine how the various segments of work interrelate, and to evaluate the overall progress being made.

The most popular methods are the critical path method (CPM) and program evaluation and review technique (PERT). These two methods were developed almost simultaneously in the late 1950s. CPM grew out of a joint study by du Pont and Remington Rand Univac to determine the best method for reducing the time required to perform routine plant overhaul, maintenance, and construction work.[6] PERT was developed by the Navy in conjunction with the Lockheed Corporation and the consulting firm of Booz, Allen, and Hamilton for use in the development and production of the Polaris weapons system. PERT is credited with shaving nearly two years from original completion date projections.[7]

CPM and PERT use graphical networks to depict the various segments of work that must be accomplished in the completion of a project or task. The graphical network consists of activities and events. An *activity* is the work necessary to complete a particular event and normally consumes time. An *event* denotes a point in time and signifies the completion of all activities leading into the event.

The path through the network which has the longest duration (based on a summation of individual activity times) is called the *critical path.* If any activity on the critical path requires more time than was originally estimated, then the completion time for the entire project or task increases.

The major differences between CPM and PERT concern the activity time estimates. CPM is used for projects whose activity durations are accurately known and whose variance in completion time is negligible. PERT, on the other hand, is used when the activity durations are more uncertain and variable. CPM is based on three time estimates for each activity: an optimistic (minimum) time, a most likely (modal) time, and a pessimistic (maximum) time.

CPM and PERT provide information for both project planning and control. Furthermore, knowing the critical activities necessary to complete a project or task enables the management of an organization to best allocate its limited resources.

**Management by Objectives**

Management by objectives (MBO) is another method used in both strategic planning and control. Based on the cascade approach to objective setting, MBO is a system under which objectives are established for the organization as a whole, for functional areas within the organization, for departments within functional areas, and finally for individuals within each department. In its most basic form MBO must meet the following three minimum requirements:

1. Objectives for individuals within an organization are jointly set by the superior and the subordinate.
2. Individuals are periodically evaluated and receive feedback on their performance.
3. Individuals are evaluated and rewarded on the basis of objective attainment.

Step 1 is used for planning purposes. Step 2 involves the control process. Step

3 is designed to encourage employees to direct their efforts toward the accomplishment of organizational objectives.

## STRATEGY AUDITS

Normally, an organization's board of directors is responsible for ensuring that the organization has an effective strategy. One of the methods it can use in carrying out this responsibility is the conducting of a strategy audit. A *strategy audit* involves nothing more than subjecting the strategy to a number of tests of its validity, consistency, and possible effectiveness.[8] An audit of this type can be an effective control mechanism for the board of directors.

The board or one of its committees (e.g., executive or planning committee) can perform the audit, assign responsibility for performing the audit to operating management, or arrange for a joint effort between operating management and the board. Figure 8.4 illustrates relevant questions for performing a strategy audit.

## MANAGEMENT INFORMATION SYSTEMS

A *management information system (MIS)* is a formal system designed to provide information to managers. The basic idea behind an MIS, regardless of its sophistication, is to provide managers with information in a systematic and integrated manner rather than in a sporadic and piecemeal manner. A good MIS enhances strategic control and strategic planning. Example 8.5 illustrates the uses that can be made of an MIS.

Although it is not absolutely essential, most MISs incorporate the use of computers. A frequently used acronym in computer terminology is EDP (electronic data processing). EDP refers to the hardware, software, and personnel that process data into information. *Hardware* is the computers and various input and output devices that make up a computer system. *Software* refers to the programs or sets of instructions that direct the hardware to perform its various functions. The personnel in an EDP system fall into three categories: systems analysts, programmers, and operators. *Systems analysts* design MISs. *Programmers* prepare computer programs based on the specifications of systems analysts. *Operators* run or operate the computer hardware.

## Designing an MIS

Unfortunately, many MISs have been failures. Careful design and implementation of an MIS is essential. Several crucial factors determine the success of an MIS:

- The information system must be designed and implemented to meet the needs of those managers who will use it in carrying our their day-to-day responsibilities.
- Designing and implementing an MIS is best accomplished through close cooperation between systems analysts and managers.

Is the company adequately informed about its markets? What further information would be worth the cost of getting? How should it be obtained?

How well informed is the company about its competitors? How well is it able to forecast what competitors will do under various circumstances? Is there a sound basis for such competitive appraisals? Is the company underestimating or over-estimating its competitors?

Has management adequately explored various ways of segmenting its market? To what extent is it addressing market segments in which the company's strengths provide meaningful advantages?

Are the products and services the company proposes to sell ones that it can provide more effectively than competitors? What is the basis for such a belief?

Do the various activities proposed in the strategy provide synergistic advantages? Are they compatible?

Does the proposed strategy adequately address questions of corporate objectives, financial policy, scope of operations, organization, and integration?

What specific resources (personnel, skills, information, facilities, technology, finances, relationships) will be needed to execute the strategy? Does the company already possess these resources? Has management established programs for building these resources and overall competence which will provide telling competitive advantages over the long run?

To what extent does the strategy define a unique and appropriate economic role for the company? How different is it from the competitors' strategy?

Has the issue of growth rate been raised? Are there good reasons to believe that investment in growth will pay off? Does the company's track record support such a conclusion?

Does the proposed dividend policy reflect the company's growth policy, based on a demonstrated ability or inability to reinvest cash flow advantageously? Or is it just a "safe" compromise, conforming to what others usually do?

Is management capable of implementing the strategy effectively? What leads to this conclusion?

How and to what extent is the strategy to be communicated to the organization? Is it to be distributed in written form? If competitors are aware of the company's strategy, will that help or hurt?

What provision is to be made for employing the strategy as a guide to operating decisions? To what extent is it to be used by the board? How?

How is it to be kept up to date? Are there to be regular reviews? How often and by whom?

Has a set of long-range projections of operations following the strategy been prepared? Have the possible results of following alternative strategies been prepared?

Does the strategy focus on the few really important key issues? Is it too detailed? Does it address genuine business questions (as opposed to "motherhood" statements)?

In its strategic thinking, has management avoided the lure of simplistic approaches such as

- Growth for growth's sake?
- Diversification for diversification's sake?
- Aping the industry leader?
- Broadening the scope in order to secure "incremental" earnings?
- Assuming it can execute better than competitors without objective evidence that such is the case?

Are there other issues, trends, or potential events that should have been taken into account?

**Figure 8.4** Relevant Questions for Performing a Strategy Audit

*Source:* Adapted from Milton Lauenstein, "The Strategy Audit," *Journal of Business Strategy* 4 (Winter 1984): 90–91.

---

## STRATEGY IN PRACTICE

**Example 8.5** Strategic Information Systems at American Express

The American Express Company is a diversified financial services company that provides American Express traveler's checks and charge cards, international banking, investments, and insurance. Annual revenues are over $8 billion and the company has approximately 60,000 employees.

American Express has nine major data processing centers, over 80 mainframes, some 380 main computers, and over 17,000 on-line terminals worldwide.

The information systems are used to improve the company's competitive position. Funds access services have been installed to give charge card holders easier access to funds while they are away from home. A nationwide network of automated traveler's check dispensing machines has been installed. Stolen traveler's checks are also replaced by use of the information system.

*Source:* Adapted from Richard G. Canning, *EDP Analyzer* 22 (May 1984):1–2.

---

- A good starting point in MIS design is an examination of the information systems that currently exist in the organization.
- Flexibility of design is a most desirable characteristic of an MIS.
- Output from the MIS must be presented in a form that is most appropriate for use by managers. Information overload must be avoided.

MISs must be designed to meet the needs of users and must be constantly evaluated in terms of changing user needs. The following ten questions should be posed regularly to users to ascertain the effectiveness of an organization's MIS system:

1. Do you feel that the information systems exist to provide service to you in your day-to-day work? How has it helped you in this respect?
2. Has the information system provided the service that you feel was promised at the start of its design and implementation? In which areas has it failed and excelled in your opinion?
3. Do you consider that the system has been implemented with due regard to costs and benefits? Are there any areas in which you consider costs excessive?
4. Do you feel comfortable using the system? Could more attention have been paid to matching the output of the system to your needs and if so, in what areas?
5. Is the system flexible enough in your opinion? If not, where should changes be made?
6. Do you still keep a personal store of information in a notebook or elsewhere? If so, will you share that information with the system? Do you see any benefits in so doing?
7. Do you think that the information system is still evolving? Can you influence this evolution and if not, why not?

8.  Does the system provide you with timely, relevant, and accurate information? Are there any areas of deficiency in this respect?

9.  Do you think that the information system makes too much use of complex procedures and models? Can you suggest areas in which less complicated techniques might be used to advantage?

10. Do you consider that there has been sufficient attention paid to the confidentiality and security of the information in the system? Can you suggest areas for improvement of these aspects of its operation?[9]

## Decision Support Systems

The *decision support system (DSS)* has gained prominence in recent years. Although some people use the term DSS as a synonym for MIS, certain distinct characteristics associated with DDSs make them much more useful in the strategic management process.

DSSs not only provide inputs to the decision process (MIS does this) but also actually become a part of the decision process. Thus, a DSS can be viewed as an extension of an MIS. It allows managers to use computers directly to retrieve information for decisions on semistructured problems. Normally, the DSS is made up of some combination of subsystems such as

- Decision models
- Interactive computer hardware and software
- A data base
- A data management system
- Graphical and other sophisticated displays
- A modeling language that is user-friendly[10]

Thus, a DDS is an interactive computer-based system that uses decision models, gives users easy and efficient access to a significant data base, provides various display possibilities, and incorporates a user-friendly modeling language that enables users to construct their own decision-making models.[11] DSSs provide the means for making decisions in areas such as site locations, product design, and production systems design.

Two of the most recent and significant developments in the area of DSS involves computer-integrated manufacturing (CIM) and computer-aided design systems (CAD). CIM enables management to track work that is planned or in process down to the smallest detail, thus giving management unprecedented control over the production/operations function. CAD enables engineers to sketch pictures of various assemblies and match them with existing or planned parts. In addition, CAD allows an engineer to specify parts and instantly determine if those parts are currently used in production.

## REVIEW QUESTIONS

1. Describe the relationship between strategic planning and strategic control.
2. What are the three basic elements in the strategic control process?
3. What questions need to be addressed in focusing an organization's control system on its future environment and resources?

4. Outline some typical areas in which organizations establish quantitative criteria for evaluation.
5. List several sources that provide quantifiable data on organizational performance measures.
6. Outline the characteristics of an effective control system.
7. Describe the following:
   a. Audit
   b. Independent auditors
   c. Government auditors
   d. Internal auditors
8. What are the minimum criteria of MBO?
9. What is a strategy audit?
10. Describe the following:
    a. MIS
    b. DSS
    c. CIM
    d. CAD

## DISCUSSION QUESTIONS

1. "Controls only necessitate the need for more controls." Discuss your views on this statement.
2. What are some of the major problems associated with using budgets as control devices?
3. Do you think that all organizations should have a team of internal auditors that reports directly to the board of directors? What are some of the possible negative consequences of having a group such as this?
4. When a strategy has not been successful, the most effective way to take corrective action is to change the management team. Do you agree? Why or why not?

## REFERENCES AND ADDITIONAL READING

1. James Brian Quinn, "Managing Strategic Change," *Sloan Management Review* 21 (Summer 1980): 4.
2. *Ibid.*, p. 4.
3. Edward I. Altman, *Financial Handbook,* 5th ed. (New York: Wiley, 1981), p. 16.10.
4. AAA *Committee on Basic Auditing Concepts,* 1971.
5. William T. Thornhill, *Complete Handbook of Operational and Management Auditing* (Englewood Cliffs, N.J.: Prentice-Hall, 1981), p. 73.
6. Joseph J. Moder and Cecil R. Phillips, *Project Management with CPM and PERT* (New York: Van Nostrand Reinhold, 1970), p. 6.
7. Darwin B. Close, "PERT Networks' Use Can Help Reduce BI Downtime," *Risk Management* 29, no. 3 (March 1982): 26.
8. Milton Lauenstein, "The Strategy Audit," *Journal of Business Strategy* 4 (Winter 1984): 90.
9. K. J. Radford, *Information Systems for Strategic Decisions* (Reston, Va.: Reston Publishing Company, 1978), pp. 220–221.
10. William R. King, "Planning for Strategic Decision Support Systems," *Long Range Planning* 16 (October 1983): 73.
11. *Ibid.*, p. 74.

# Strategic Management Process

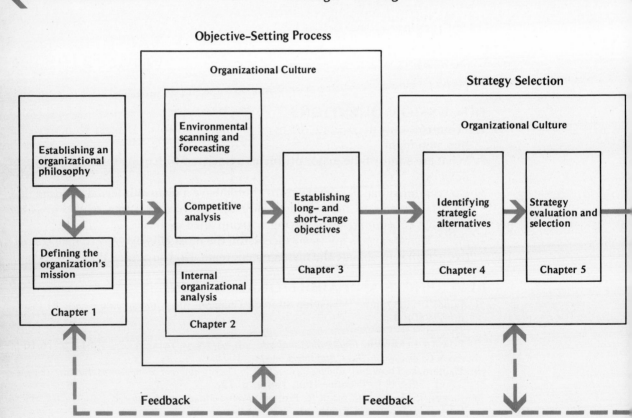

## Strategic Planning

### Objective-Setting Process

**Organizational Culture**

**Strategy Selection**

**Organizational Culture**

Establishing an organizational philosophy

Defining the organization's mission

**Chapter 1**

Environmental scanning and forecasting

Competitive analysis

Internal organizational analysis

**Chapter 2**

Establishing long– and short–range objectives

**Chapter 3**

Identifying strategic alternatives

**Chapter 4**

Strategy evaluation and selection

**Chapter 5**

Feedback

Feedback

# PART FOUR
# USEFUL INFORMATION FOR ANALYZING STRATEGIC MANAGEMENT CASES

APPENDIX A   Preparing a Case Analysis
APPENDIX B   Reading and Understanding Financial Statements
APPENDIX C   Business Facts for Decision Makers: Where to Find Them

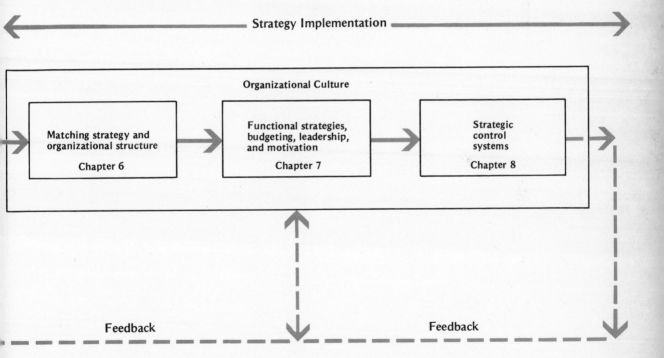

# APPENDIX _A_

# PREPARING A CASE ANALYSIS

A _case_ is a written description of an organization. A case generally contains a wide variety of information about the organization. Information that may be included in a case is the history of the organization, environmental forces affecting the organization, current operational data, a description of the management team, the organizational structure, and other general information. The primary reasons for using the case method for instructional purposes are to enable the student to see how actual organizations have performed the strategic management process and to allow students to practice and develop their skills in applying strategic management concepts to actual organizations.

Cases are developed from material taken from actual organizations. The cases in this text are about real organizations. Some cases are disguised in that the real name of the organization is not given. Nevertheless, the problems and challenges faced by the organization are real and should be viewed as such by the student.

## OBJECTIVES OF THE CASE METHOD IN STRATEGIC MANAGEMENT

The objectives of a course in strategic management (or business policy) are

1. To develop an appreciation for the interrelationships among the various functional (marketing, finance, production) areas of an organization
2. To understand the importance of timing and sequencing of strategic moves
3. To understand the complexity of the organization as a whole

In the most complete sense, a course in strategic management should cause students to apply the knowledge they have gained in their academic careers or personal experience to an analysis of how organizations develop a strategy for achieving organizational objectives within a changing environment.

The most frequently used vehicle for teaching strategic management is the case method. The following limerick describes what might happen to students without the benefit of cases:

> A student of business with tact
> Absorbed many answers he lacked
> But acquiring a job,
> He said with a sob,
> "How does one fit answer to fact?"[1]

Frequently, much of a student's academic career is devoted to listening to lectures. This, of course, is an essential part of the learning process. Cases, on the other hand, are designed to allow the student to learn by doing. Under the case method, both professors and students read the same basic materials and must determine what analyses are to be made and what decisions are required. Generally, there is no single, right answer to a case.

Under the case method, the professor's role is to assign cases, to participate actively as a member of the class in analyzing the case, to guide the class discussion by raising important questions or critical issues, and (if he or she chooses) to summarize the analysis of the case at the end of the class. The student's role is to analyze the assigned case and to participate actively as a member of the class in discussing the case. The case method of teaching results in total failure when either the professor or the student fails to perform his or her role.

When students come to class prepared, several benefits result. First, students learn the value of input from others in making strategic decisions. Students quickly learn that fellow students may have analyzed different issues and may have come to different conclusions. Other opinions must be analyzed and either accepted or rejected. Furthermore, a prepared student quickly learns that the professor does not have all of the correct answers. Each student should be free to present and hold his or her point of view. However, students and professors alike should be required to explain the reasoning and basis for their positions.

The case method's primary advantage is that it forces the student to think analytically and constructively. In forcing this type of thinking, the professor may pose such questions as the following:

- Given the available information, what trends do you see developing in the next decade that will affect the organization?
- What are the major opportunities for the organization?
- What are the major risks to which the organization will be exposed through changing social, economic, political, or technological forces?
- What is the current strategy?
- How well does this strategy match current resources?
- What organizational structure is being used?
- Are the control systems adequate?
- What noneconomic purposes are being served or should be served by the organization?
- Is the management team capable of handling the opportunities and risks?[2]

Of course, numerous other questions can and will be asked. Again, the primary purpose of the questions is to cause the student to think creatively.

## MISSING OR INCOMPLETE INFORMATION

A frequent criticism of the case method is the absence of or the incomplete nature of data and information contained in the case. Actually, these inadequacies contribute to the reality of the case. Managers who are responsible for making the strategic management decisions for organizations never have all of the information needed to make these decisions. And frequently the information available to the manager is contradictory. In these situations, the manager must decide what information is creditable and what information should be ignored.

The necessity to choose the most creditable information should in no way lead the student to feel that he or she might just as well ignore information in making strategy decisions. It is merely meant to emphasize that, even with available data and information, judgments and interpretations must be made.

One challenge in case analysis is for the student to supplement the data and information contained in the case through his or her own research. Appendix C is designed to provide a summary of available data and information to assist in case analysis. In addition, throughout the text numerous other sources of data and information are cited.

## ANALYSIS OF A CASE

The first step in the analysis of a case is a thorough reading of the case. A thorough reading of the case means that the student understands the overall organization and its components. Furthermore, the student should have a good understanding of all the data and information in the case. After a thorough reading of the case, the student is ready to begin his or her analysis.

One approach to case analysis is composed of five steps:

1. Defining the central issue of the case. Is the main issue strategy implementation or strategic planning? Is the main issue concerned with strategic control? Is the organizational structure the key issue?
2. Determining the pertinent areas of the strategic management process that need to be considered. For example, if an organization's strategy has not been successful, several pertinent areas could be causing this lack of success and would need to be analyzed.
3. Evaluating the available data, gathering and evaluating more data if necessary, drawing conclusions about the central issue, and drawing conclusions about and determining the relative importance of the other pertinent areas.
4. Investigating other, less critical, issues.
5. Drawing a final conclusion or developing an action plan for the organization.

## WRITING UP A CASE

Frequently, students are required to prepare a written analysis of a case. Sometimes the professor provides a specific format that is to be followed. On the other hand, quite frequently the student must develop his or her own format. No one format fits all case situations. However, a useful format results when the five steps to case analysis are followed.

Preparation is the key to the growth and development of the student in the use of the case method. Thorough preparation makes the case method one of the best and most enjoyable methods of learning.[3]

## CHAPTER SUMMARIES

The chapters in this text are designed to assist the student in successfully performing the five steps in case analysis. It is for this reason that the key points of each chapter are summarized in the following sections.

## Chapter 1: Strategic Management: An Overview

Strategic management is concerned with making decisions about an organization's future direction and implementing those decisions. Strategic management can be broken down into two phases: strategic planning and strategy implementation.

Strategic planning is concerned with making decisions with regard to

- Determining the organization's philosophy and mission
- Establishing long- and short-range objectives to achieve the organization's mission
- Selecting the strategy that is to be used in achieving the organization's objectives

Strategy implementation is concerned with making decisions with regard to

- Developing an organizational structure to achieve the strategy
- Ensuring that the activities necessary to accomplish the strategy are (effectively) performed
- Monitoring the effectiveness of the strategy in achieving the organization's objectives

An organizational philosophy establishes the values, beliefs, and guidelines for the manner in which the organization is going to conduct its business. The organizational mission defines the current and future business activities of the organization. Questions that need to be answered in defining an organization's purpose are outlined on p. 12.

Long-range objectives specify the results that are desired in pursuing the organization's mission and normally extend beyond the current fiscal year of the organization. Short-range objectives are performance targets, normally of less than one year's duration, that are used by management to achieve the organization's long-range objectives. Strategy involves determining and evaluating alternatives available to an organization in achieving its objectives and mission and choosing the alternative that is to be pursued. Figure 1.1 (p. 16) shows a framework that is used throughout this text to analyze the strategic management process. Figure 1.2 (p. 17) provides a summary of the definitions of major terms used throughout this text.

## Chapter 2: Analyzing the External and Internal Environment

The interaction among environmental scanning and forecasting, competitive analysis, and internal organizational analysis leads to an identification of an organization's strengths and weaknesses and opportunities for and threats to the organization from its environment.

Environmental scanning is the systematic methods used by an organization to monitor and forecast those forces that are external to and not under the direct control of the organization or its industry. Organizations generally categorize environmental scanning into economic, political (including regulatory), social, and technological. Several guidelines for establishing an environmental scanning program are given on pp. 30–31.

Organizations must also forecast their future environment. Several popular methods of forecasting include the Delphi technique, brainstorming, scenarios, trend-impact analysis, economic models, leading indicators, and trend analysis.

The competitive environment of an organization depends on the maneuvering for position among the current competitors within an industry, the threat of new entrants into the industry, the bargaining power of customers, the bargaining power of suppliers, and the threat of substitute products or services being introduced into the industry. Figure 2.3 (p. 36) summarizes information about these forces. Organizations can then conduct competitive analysis by collecting and assessing data about each of the elements on Figure 2.3. Figure 2.4 (p. 38) gives typical questions that need to be answered in performing a competitive analysis.

A checklist of factors to be considered in performing an internal organizational analysis is given on p. 37. Appendix B gives information on how to analyze an organization's financial condition. Appendix C provides sources of data to assist in performing an internal organizational audit. Figure 2.5 (pp. 40–41) provides a list of questions to be answered in performing an internal organizational analysis.

Figure 2.6 (p. 43) gives a step-by-step procedure for performing an internal organizational analysis, competitive analysis, and environmental scanning.

## Chapter 3: Organizational Culture and the Objective-Setting Process

Long-range objectives specify the results that are desired in pursuing the organization's mission and normally extend beyond the current fiscal year of the organization. Short-range objectives are performance targets, normally of less than one year's duration, that serve to achieve the organization's long-range objectives. The objectives of an organization result from the interaction among an internal organizational analysis, competitive analysis, environmental scanning and forecasting, and organizational culture. Figure 3.1 (p. 49) illustrates this interaction.

Organizational culture is the pattern of beliefs and expectations shared by an organization's members which powerfully shape the behavior of individuals and groups in the organization. Seven characteristics that shape an organization's culture are outlined on p. 51. Figure 3.2 (p. 52) and Figure 3.4 (p. 53) illustrate two methods for classifying organizational cultures.

No one mix or combination of organizational objectives is applicable to all organizations. Ideally, objectives should

- Match strengths to opportunities
- Minimize threats to the organization
- Eliminate weaknesses in the organization

Potential areas for establishing objectives are outlined and described on pp. 55–57. Furthermore, the cascade approach to setting objectives is summarized on pp. 58–59.

**Chapter 4: Identifying Strategic Alternatives**

Strategy outlines the fundamental steps that an organization intends to use in order to achieve an objective or set of objectives. Strategic alternatives available to organizations are outlined on pp. 62–63.

Stable growth strategy is defined on p. 63. Growth strategy is defined on p. 64. Three questions that should be answered before embarking on a growth strategy are

1.  Are company financial resources adequate?
2.  If the company is stopped short in its strategy for any reason, will its position be completely viable?
3.  Will government regulators permit the company to follow the strategy it has chosen?

Concentric diversification is a growth strategy that involves adding new products or services that are similar to the organization's present products or services. Vertical integration is a growth strategy that involves extending an organization's present business in two possible directions. Forward integration moves the organization into distributing its own products or services. Backward integration moves an organization into supplying some or all of the products or services that are used in producing its present products or services. Horizontal integration (or diversification) is a growth strategy that involves buying one of an organization's competitors. Conglomerate diversification is a growth strategy that involves adding new products or services that are significantly different from the organization's present products or services.

Endgame strategies are concerned with the actions of organizations in an environment of declining product demand where those environmental conditions make it unlikely that all the plant capacity and competitors put in place during the industry's heyday will ever be needed. Figure 4.1 (p. 73) outlines endgame strategies.

Three alternative retrenchment strategies employed by organizations are turnaround, divestment, and liquidation. A turnaround strategy is an attempt to improve efficiency of operations during a decline in an organization's financial situation. Divestment involves selling off a major part of the business. Liquidation involves terminating the organization's existence either by selling off its assets or by shutting down the entire operation.

Most large organizations do not pursue only one strategy. Combination strategies are the norm. Several possible combination strategies are outlined on pp. 76–77.

Business unit strategies focus on how to compete in a given business. Three major types of business unit strategies are overall cost leadership, differentiation, and focus. These three strategies are described on pp. 77–78.

A frequently used method for implementing diversification strategies is the merger. Several types of mergers are outlined on p. 78. Reasons for using mergers for both the acquiring and acquired organizations are outlined on pp. 78–80. Guidelines for successfully implementing mergers are given on pp. 81–84.

A joint venture is a separate corporate entity jointly owned by two or more parent organizations. Some of the major reasons for entering joint ventures are outlined on p. 85.

**Chapter 5: Strategy Evaluation and Selection**

Strategy should be designed to take advantage of market opportunities and neutralize adverse environmental impacts. At the same time, it should reinforce the internal strengths of the organization and improve on its perceived weaknesses relative to its competition. Several methodologies have been developed to assist organizations in evaluating and selecting an organizational strategy. Methods discussed in this chapter include the following:

1. Growth-share matrix (pp. 92–97)
2. Industry attractiveness–business strength matrix (pp. 97–104)
3. Life-cycle approach (pp. 104–105)
4. Product-market evolution matrix (pp. 105–108)

Another method used in evaluating and selecting strategies is called competitive strategy analysis. The approach to selecting the optimal competitive strategy is summarized in Figure 5.8 (p. 110).

Cluster analysis involves developing a corporate-level strategy for clusters of business units. The general steps involved are outlined on pp. 110–111.

PIMS (Profit Impact of Market Strategies) was developed to provide insights and information on the expected profit performance of different kinds of businesses under different competitive conditions using different strategies. Several reports generated using PIMS are summarized on p. 111.

Several qualitative factors that influence strategy selection are managerial attitudes toward risk, environment of the organization, organizational culture and power relationships, competitive actions and reactions, previous organizational strategies, and timing. These factors are discussed on pp. 112–115.

**Chapter 6: Matching Strategy and Organizational Structure**

Strategies are carried out through organizations. An organization is a group of people working together in a coordinated effort to attain a set of objectives. Organizing is the grouping of activities necessary to attain the organization's objectives and the assignment of each grouping to a person who has the authority necessary to manage the people performing the activities. The framework that defines the boundaries of the organization and within which the organization operates is the organizational structure. Size, environment, and technology are important variables that influence organizational structure. The influence of each of these variables is discussed on pp. 123–125. Table 6.1 (p. 127) summarizes several types of structures that can result from the interaction of size, environment, and technology.

Assessing the appropriateness of an organization's structure is discussed on pp. 126–128. Several guidelines for designing effective organizational structures are presented on pp. 128–129. Guidelines for restructuring an organization are presented on p. 130.

A board of directors is a group of people elected by the stockholders of an organization that serves primarily to see that the organization is well managed for all of the organization's stakeholders. The responsibilities of the board are outlined on pp. 130–131. The structure and composition of the board are described on pp. 131–132. Various committees of the board are described on pp. 132–133. The legal responsibilities of the board are described on pp. 133–134.

**Chapter 7: Implementing Strategy: Functional Strategies, Budgeting, Leadership, and Motivation**

Functional strategies describe the means or methods that are to be used by each of the functional areas of the organization (production, marketing, finance, and so on) in carrying out the corporate-level or business unit strategy. The functional areas of organizations normally include most, if not all, of the following: marketing, finance, production/operations, human resources/personnel, and research and development.

Marketing strategies are discussed on pp. 145–147. Figure 7.2 outlines questions used in determining the appropriateness of a marketing mix.

Financial strategies are discussed on pp. 147–148. Figure 7.3 outlines questions used in developing a financial strategy. Capital budgeting is discussed on pp. 148–149. Cash flow analysis is discussed on p. 149.

Production/operations strategies are described on pp. 150–151. Figure 7.4 (p. 151) outlines several considerations in developing a production/operations strategy.

Human resource/personnel strategies are discussed on pp. 151–152. Figure 7.5 (p. 153) outlines considerations in developing a human resource/personnel strategy.

Research and development strategies are described on pp. 152–154. Figure 7.6 (p. 155) provides a checklist of questions on developing a research and development strategy.

Budgeting is a process where the management of an organization specifies the resources it will employ to attain the organization's objectives. Table 7.1 (p. 156) describes types and purposes of budgets. Flexible budgets are described on pp. 156–157. Program budgeting is discussed on pp. 157–158.

A leader is an individual within an organization who is able to influence the attitudes and opinions of others within the organization; a manager is merely able to influence their actions and decisions. Leadership is critical to organizational success and is described on pp. 159–160.

Another important consideration in successfully achieving organizational objectives is the motivation of the organization's employees. Generally, the organizational reward system is one of the most effective motivational tools available to organizations. The design and use of the organizational reward system reflects management's attitude about performance and significantly influences the entire organizational climate. The role and importance of motivation in strategy implementation is discussed on pp. 160–163.

**Chapter 8:
Strategic
Control
Process**

Control is the phase of the strategic management process in which top management determines how well or if the chosen strategy is achieving the organization's objectives. Figure 8.1 (p. 169) illustrates the relationship between strategic planning and the strategic control process. Figure 8.2 (p. 171) shows the strategic management process as a feedback system. The three requirements of control are (1) developing criteria for evaluation (pp. 170–173), (2) evaluating performance (pp. 173–174), and (3) feedback (p. 174). Quantitative criteria for evaluation are discussed on pp. 172–173.

The requirements for an effective control system are described on pp. 174–176. Methods of control include budgets (p. 176), audits (pp. 176–179), time-related methods (pp. 179–180), and management by objectives (pp. 180–181).

A strategy audit subjects an organization's strategy to a number of tests of its validity, consistency, and probable effectiveness. Figure 8.4 (p. 182) illustrates relevant questions for performing a strategy audit.

A management information system (MIS) is a formal system designed to provide information to managers. Several guidelines for designing an MIS are offered on pp. 181–184. A decision support system (DSS) not only provides inputs to the decision process but also actually becomes a part of the decision process. Subsystems in a DSS are outlined on p. 184.

## REFERENCES AND ADDITIONAL READING

1. Charles I. Gregg, "Because Wisdom Can't Be Told," in Malcolm P. McNair (ed.), *The Case Method at the Harvard Business School* (New York: McGraw-Hill, 1954), p. 11.
2. Some of the questions on this list are adapted from Howard H. Stevenson, "Teaching Business Policy by the Case Method," in Bernard Taylor and Keith MacMillan (eds.), *Business Policy: Teaching and Research* (London: Bradford University Press, 1973), p. 122.
3. For more in-depth discussions of case analysis, see Malcolm P. McNair, *The Case Method at the Harvard University Business School* (New York: McGraw-Hill, 1954); Robert Ronstadt, *The Art of Case Analysis* (Dover, Mass.: Lord Publishing, 1980); and Bernard Taylor and Keith MacMillan (eds.), *Business Policy: Teaching and Research* (London: Bradford University Press, 1973).

# APPENDIX *B*

# *READING AND UNDERSTANDING FINANCIAL STATEMENTS*

*This appendix was written by Johnnie L. Clark, CPA, professor of accounting at the Graduate School of Business Administration, Atlanta University.*

Accounting has been variously defined as an art, as a science, as the language of business. Broadly, it is "the process of identifying, measuring, and communicating economic information to permit informed judgements and decisions by users of the information."[1] The end products of this process are financial statements which will tell us where the business has been and what its present position is, and indicate what its future portends.

This appendix attempts to facilitate an understanding of the meaning and purpose of financial statements. A typical set of financial statements of a manufacturing company are presented illustratively as an explanatory guide.

**COMMENTS ON FINANCIAL STATEMENTS**

In contemporary usage, a set of financial statements includes the balance sheet, the income statement, and a statement of changes in financial position. Generally, published statements are accompanied by an accountant's opinion. An opinion may be *clean, adverse,* or a *disclaimer.* Exhibit 1 presents a clean opinion which says that the financials present fairly the financial position and operating results of the enterprise. Further, the assumption is that this presentation is in accordance with generally accepted accounting principles applied on a consistent basis. Compliance deviations are disclosed and modify the opinion accordingly. Disclosures are reported in a middle paragraph between the scope and opinion paragraphs shown in Exhibit 1.

The amounts shown in the exhibits are expressed in round thousands of dollars (a typical presentation) in order to avoid the implication that accounting is a precise science. Computations of inventory value, reserves, intangible values, and liabilities are necessarily estimates and should not be expressed to the penny.

A basic assumption underlying financial statements is that they are presented on a going-concern basis. The values purport to be those that would be obtained in a liquidation. Normally, this would be set forth in the accountants' report.

Generally accepted accounting principles require that certain information regarding various financial statement amounts must be reported. It is usually too cumbersome to disclose this information in the body of the statements, so it is customary to append notes. Notes disclose the basis of accounting and expanded information about the content of the various financial statement captions and are of significance to the reader.

**Exhibit 1** Statement of Opinion

To the Board of Directors
XYZ Manufacturing Company, Inc.

We have examined the balance sheet of XYZ Manufacturing Company, Inc., as of December 31, 1985 and 1984, and the related statements of income, retained earnings, and changes in financial position for the years then ended. Our examinations were made in accordance with generally accepted auditing standards and, accordingly, included such tests of the accounting records and such other auditing procedures as we considered necessary in the circumstances.

In our opinion, the accompanying financial statements present fairly the financial position of XYZ Manufacturing Company, Inc., at December 31, 1985 and 1984, and the results of its operations and changes in its financial position for the years then ended, in conformity with generally accepted accounting principles applied on a consistent basis.

A, B, and C
Certified Public Accountants

February 9, 1986

Unless stated to the contrary, financial statements are presented on the accrual basis of accounting. It is assumed that the reader is familiar with this concept. Now let us take a look at the individual financial statements.

**Balance Sheet**  The balance sheet is a statement of the company's financial position as of a specific point in time. It sets forth the company's economic resources as well as the rights or claims of creditors and owners in those resources as subsumed in assets, liabilities, and owners' equity at a given moment. This moment is usually the end of a fiscal year. (See Exhibit 2.) For comparative purposes, prior year balances are usually presented.

The items in XYZ's balance sheet are the following:

*Current Assets*
- In general, current assets include cash and other resources that are reasonably expected to be converted into cash during the company's normal operating cycle.

*Cash*
- This asset represents cash on hand and money on deposit in banks to which the company has ready access.

*Marketable Securities*
- This asset represents a temporary investment of excess idle cash. It is usually invested in money market funds or other short-term securities that are easily converted into cash when needed.

**Exhibit 2** Balance Sheet

### XYZ MANUFACTURING COMPANY, INC.
#### Balance Sheet
#### For the Years Ended December 31

|  | 1985 | 1984 |
|---|---|---|
| **Assets** | | |
| Current assets | | |
|   Cash | $ 550,000 | $ 400,000 |
|   Marketable securities at cost (market value: 1985, $890,000; 1984, $480,000) | 950,000 | 560,000 |
|   Accounts receivable (less allowance for bad debts: 1985, $100,000; 1984, $95,000) | 2,000,000 | 1,900,000 |
|   Inventories (Note 1) | 2,700,000 | 3,000,000 |
|     Total current assets | 6,200,000 | 5,860,000 |
| Property, plant, and equipment (Note 2) | | |
|   Land | 550,000 | 450,000 |
|   Building | 3,900,000 | 3,800,000 |
|   Machinery | 950,000 | 850,000 |
|   Office equipment | 100,000 | 95,000 |
|  | 5,500,000 | 5,195,000 |
|   Less: accumulated depreciation | 1,800,000 | 1,500,000 |
|  | 3,700,000 | 3,695,000 |
| Prepayments and deferred charges | 100,000 | 90,000 |
| Intangibles (goodwill, patent, trademarks) | 100,000 | 100,000 |
|   Total assets | $ 10,100,000 | $ 9,745,000 |
| **Liabilities** | | |
| Current liabilities | | |
|   Accounts payable | $ 1,000,000 | $ 940,000 |
|   Notes payable | 950,000 | 1,200,000 |
|   Accrued expenses payable | 430,000 | 300,000 |
|   Federal income tax payable | 320,000 | 290,000 |
|     Total current liabilities | 2,700,000 | 2,730,000 |
| Long-term liabilities—first mortgage bonds; $1,000 denomination; 5% interest, due 1995 | 2,700,000 | 2,700,000 |
|     Total liabilities | 5,400,000 | 5,430,000 |
| **Stockholders' equity** | | |
| Capital stock | | |
|   Preferred stock, 5% cumulative, $100 par value per share; authorized, issued, and outstanding 6,000 shares | 600,000 | 600,000 |
|   Common stock, $5 par value per share; authorized, issued, and outstanding 300,000 shares | 1,500,000 | 1,500,000 |
| Additional paid-in capital | 900,000 | 900,000 |
| Accumulated retained earnings | 1,700,000 | 1,315,000 |
|   Total stockholders' equity | 4,700,000 | 4,315,000 |
|   Total liabilities and stockholders' equity | $ 10,100,000 | $ 9,745,000 |

### Accounts Receivable

- This asset indicates the amount not yet collected from customers to whom goods were shipped (or services rendered) prior to payment. Experience shows that some customers fail to pay their bills because of either financial difficulties or disputes with the seller. Therefore, in order to show the accounts receivable item at net realizable value, provision has been made for estimated bad-debt losses.

### Inventories

- Inventories of a manufacturer are in various stages of production and are of three types: purchased raw materials to be used in the product, partially finished goods in process of manufacture, and finished goods ready for shipment. There are several accepted methods of valuing inventories; the method used is explained in the notes to financial statements as well as the categories of inventories.

### Property, Plant, and Equipment

- Property, plant, and equipment is sometimes described as plant assets or operational assets. It represents those assets not intended for sale that are used to manufacture the product and bring it to the customer. Accordingly, this category includes land, buildings, machinery, equipment, furniture, automobiles, and trucks.

  The figure thus displayed is not intended to reflect either present market value or future replacement cost. Although the cost to replace plant and equipment at some future date may be higher, this is not recognized under conventional accounting principles.

### Depreciation

- Depreciation as used in accounting is the allocation of the cost of a tangible, operational asset over its estimated useful life. Each accounting period then will bear its fair share of that cost; therefore, costs and revenues will be equally matched. Often, as time passes, the original estimate of useful life will be found to have been inaccurate. (This can come about because of poor maintenance, excessive wear and tear, or technical obsolescence.) In this situation the periodic depreciation provision will be adjusted to reflect the new remaining useful life.

### Prepayments and Deferred Charges

- These assets represent expenditure outlays that will spare the future payment of cash and benefit more than one period. They should not be charged in their entirety to the current year's operations. A typical example is the purchase of a three-year fire insurance policy. Although cash has been expended for coverage at the policy's inception, the policy will continue to provide benefits for three years. Accordingly, the portion that will benefit future accounting periods is reflected as an asset in the balance sheet and will be written off over the periods that benefit. Prepayments are frequently classified as current assets since, in many cases, they can be converted back to cash by cancellation. Deferred charges, such as expenditures for the cost of obtaining financing of long-term debt, or for plant relocation, usually cannot be classified as current. The expenditure tends to be inextricably tied to the life cycle of the business and usually does not have a short-term cancellation value.

### Intangibles

- Intangibles can be defined as assets that have no tangible physical existence but have value to the company as economic rights or privileges. It is customary, when such an asset is produced internally, to charge the cost thereof to the current period's operations. However, when purchased from others, the cost is recorded as an asset and written off (amortized) over its estimated life. Patents, trademarks, franchises, and goodwill are examples of intangible assets.

### Current Liabilities

- This caption includes all financial obligations that are expected to be paid within the company's normal operating cycle (usually one year), and are expected to be paid out of current assets.

### Accounts Payable

- Accounts payable represent the amounts that the company owes to its business suppliers, and are expected to be paid within the current period.

### Notes Payable

- If money is owed to a bank or other lender, or if the company has issued a promissory note to suppliers or others, it appears on the balance sheet under the caption *notes payable* and as a current liability.

### Accrued Expenses Payable

- Accrued expenses payable are amounts due to others for which no formal invoice has yet been received. For example, a telephone bill may not yet have been received at the balance sheet date, yet the company can, and does, estimate and record the amount due. Similarly, salaries and wages earned by employees but unpaid at the balance sheet date would be included in this caption.

### Federal Income Tax Payable

- This is an amount due to the Internal Revenue Service but not yet paid. It is similar to other items included in accrued expenses payable. However, since it is usually significant in amount, it is generally stated separately.

### Long-Term Liabilities

- Long-term liabilities represent obligations due after one year from the date of the balance sheet. In the illustrative balance sheet, the 5 percent first mortgage bond due in 1995 represents money borrowed, which is due for repayment in 1995. Generally, interest is payable periodically during the term of the bond.

### Stockholders' Equity

- Stockholders' equity represents the initial and subsequent investments by the owners of the company (either in cash or other property), increased by earnings since the inception of the company, and decreased by losses and any distributions (dividends) paid by the company to the owners. It can also be described as the difference between the company's total assets and total liabilities. It is usually broken down into its legal elements.

### Capital Stock

- This represents ownership shares, evidenced by stock certificates, in the company. There may be several types or classes of shares issued by a corporation, each with different attributes.

### Preferred Stock

- Preferred shares have some preferential ownership rights over other shares. These rights usually relate to dividends, distribution of assets in case of liquidation, or other matters. The specific provisions with respect to any issues of stock can be determined from the provisions printed on the stock certificate. The preferred stock in the illustrative balance sheet is designated 5 percent cumulative, $100 par value, which means that each share is entitled to $5 a year in dividends (when declared by the board of directors) before any dividends are paid to the common stockholders. The word *cumulative* indicates that in any year the dividend is not paid it accumulates in favor of the preferred shareholders and must be paid to them before any dividends are distributed on the common stock. Sometimes preferred stockholders cannot vote unless the company fails to pay them dividends at the stated rate.

### Common Stock

- Common stock represents simple ownership. Unlike owners of the preferred stock, who are entitled to a dividend of $5 per share each year before owners of common stock receive anything, common stockholders have no such limit on dividends payable each year. Therefore, when company earnings are high, dividends may also be high. When earnings drop, so may dividends.

### Additional Paid-in Capital

- This is the amount paid by shareholders or contributed by others in excess of the par value of each share.

### Accumulated Retained Earnings

- Accumulated retained earnings is a measure of what the company has earned and retained for its shareholders since the inception of its business. Each year, the excess of income over expenses, reduced by losses and distributions to stockholders, is added to this caption. In the event that the company has a succession of losses and this amount is a negative number, it is usually captioned *deficit in retained earnings or accumulated loss.*

## Analyzing the Balance Sheet

As mentioned earlier, the balance sheet presents the company's financial position at a given point in time. What are the lessons to be learned by reviewing and comparing the various elements?

### Net Working Capital

- Clearly, an important factor in evaluating the prospects of XYZ is its ability to pay its bills as they become due. We have seen previously that current assets represent cash and items that will become cash within a year, and current liabilities represent debts that must be paid within a year. The difference is called net working capital; an excess of current assets is a healthy situation, whereas an excess of current liabilities represents potential trouble. To meet its obligations, the company must either dispose of part of its productive facilities or incur additional long-term debt with the interest expense that will follow.

  The current ratio, the relationship of current assets to current liabilities, may be more meaningful than the difference in dollars. Thus, it is more comfortable to have current assets that are 2 to 3 times current liabilities than a ratio of 1.2 to 1. Different industries, by the very nature of their businesses, may have higher or lower optimum ratios. Published sources provide information as to those that are typical of the major industries. Generally, businesses that operate with small inventories and rapid payment by customers should have a higher current ratio than those that carry large stocks or extend long credit terms.

  A variation of the current ratio is the quick asset ratio (sometimes called the acid-test ratio). This measures the company's "instant" debt-paying ability. It is determined by eliminating inventories from current assets and recomputing the ratio to current liabilities.

### Inventory Turnover

- This is a measure of the relationship between the volume of goods sold and the merchandise inventory. The computation of inventory turnover can provide information as to how effectively the company is managing and controlling its inventory position. Too high an inventory represents a drain on cash, whereas too low an inventory could mean an inability to fill customer orders. Inventory turnover is computed by dividing cost of sales by the average finished goods inventory. In the case of XYZ, using the total inventory figure, $9.2 million divided by $2.85 million equals 3.23. The 3.2 inventory turnover of XYZ means that the year-end inventory is sufficient for approximately four months' sales. In a comparison of similar companies, a higher inventory turnover rate is generally preferable to a lower one, since an overstocked inventory can lead to financial difficulty if sales should unexpectedly decline.

### Book Value of Securities

- Book value of securities is a commonly reported amount and represents the net assets available for each class of securities (bonds and stocks). The amounts relating to XYZ are computed as follows:

| | |
|---|---|
| Total assets | $ 10,100,000 |
| Less current liabilities | 2,700,000 |
| Net assets available for bond holders | $ 7,400,000 |

- Book value per $1,000 bond is $7,400,000 ÷ 2,700, or $2,740.

| | |
|---|---|
| Total assets | $ 10,100,000 |
| Less *all* liabilities | 5,400,000 |
| Net assets available for preferred stock | $ 4,700,000 |

- Book value per share of preferred stock is $4,700,000 ÷ 6,000, or $783.

| | |
|---|---|
| Total assets | $ 10,100,000 |
| Less liabilities and preferred stock | 6,000,000 |
| Net assets available for common stock | $ 4,100,000 |

- Book value as a concept typically refers to the per share value of common stock. Book value per share of common stock is $4,100,000 ÷ 300,000, or $13.66.

  It should be kept in mind that asset values in a going-concern balance sheet do *not* represent the amounts that could be realized and available to bondholders or shareholders if the company were to be liquidated. As discussed earlier, property, plant, and equipment are stated at cost less depreciation and might well bring far more in a liquidation sale than the amount stated in the balance sheet. Conversely, inventories, particularly work in process, can seldom be disposed of at book value in a distress sale.

### Capitalization Ratio

- Capitalization ratios represent the relative proportions of the securities issued by a company and, again, are useful in comparing the balance sheets of companies in similar businesses. A high proportion of debt securities to equity securities (often referred to as high leverage or trading on the equity) indicates that the company is financing its operations through the use of outsiders' money rather than that of the shareholders. In the case of XYZ, the ratios are as follows:

|  | Amount | Capitalization Ratio |
|---|---|---|
| Bonds | $ 2,700,000 | 36% |
| Preferred stock | 600,000 | 8 |
| Common stock | 4,100,000 | 56 |
|  | $ 7,400,000 | 100% |

**Statement of Income**

The income statement is a statement of operating results over a period of time. It is a summary of income-producing activities offset by their related expenses and losses for the period. (See Exhibit 3.) As a history, the statement of income can best be used to evaluate what the company's future might be. The presentation of two or more years enhances the ability to analyze the trend of the company's activities. The items in XYZ's statement of income are as follows:

**Exhibit 3** Statement of Income

### XYZ MANUFACTURING COMPANY, INC.
#### Statement of Income
#### For the Years Ended December 31

|  | 1985 | 1984 |
|---|---|---|
| Net sales | $ 12,000,000 | $ 10,200,000 |
| Less: |  |  |
| Cost of goods sold | 9,200,000 | 7,684,000 |
| Depreciation | 300,000 | 275,000 |
|  | 9,500,000 | 7,959,000 |
| Gross profit | 2,500,000 | 2,241,000 |
| Selling and administrative expenses | 1,500,000 | 1,325,000 |
| Operating profit | 1,000,000 | 916,000 |
| Other income | 150,000 | 27,000 |
|  | 1,150,000 | 943,000 |
| Other expenses | 135,000 | 135,000 |
| Income before provision for income taxes | 1,015,000 | 808,000 |
| Provision for income taxes (Note 5) | 480,000 | 365,000 |
| Net income | $ 535,000 | $ 443,000 |
| Common shares outstanding | 300,000 | 300,000 |
| Net earnings per common share | $1.68 | $1.38 |

### Net Sales

- Sales represent the company's basic source of revenue—where its resources come from. Since in most situations there will be minor amounts of price allowances or returned goods, these are deducted from total sales—hence the term *net* sales.

### Cost of Goods Sold

- This amount represents the production costs of the company's products that have been sold to its customers and includes labor, factory overhead, and the cost of raw materials used.

### Depreciation

- As discussed in connection with the balance sheet, the cost of the company's production facilities must be recovered over the period of their estimated use. Although depreciation is actually an element of cost of sales, it is often shown as a separate caption in the statement of income. It is the allocation of the cost of operational assets to the period of benefit.

### Gross Profit

- Gross profit is the difference between the cost of producing the company's products and the amount for which they are sold.

### Selling and Administration Expenses

- These expenses are the costs of getting the company's products into the hands of its customers and the costs of running the business. Accordingly, they include sales staff compensation, warehousing and shipping costs, travel and entertainment, executive and office salaries, and similar related items.

### Operating Profit

- This item represents the net results of the company's basic activity of producing and delivering goods to its customers at a profit.

### Other Income and Other Expenses

- Most companies have income or expense items that do not result from their normal operating activities. These items are usually reported separately so that operating profit is not distorted. Examples of such items are interest (paid or received), insurance proceeds, rent income, and burglary losses.

### Provision for Income Taxes

- Income taxes are a major expense of any successful company and are shown as a separate item in the income statement. Usually such taxes will be approximately 50 percent of income before taxes; the reasons for any significant variation from that percentage are explained in the notes to the financial statements.

### Net Income

- Net income is the excess of revenues over expenses for the period.

## Analyzing the Income Statement

Now that we understand the components of the income statement, what can we learn by analyzing its various elements? As with the balance sheet, comparisons with prior years can give us a picture of successful or unsuccessful trends in the company's business. Comparisons with other companies in the same business will give us a picture of how successfully the company is meeting its competition. To properly make these comparisons, various percentage relationships are developed.

### Earnings per Share

- Earnings per share are derived by dividing net income for the year less preferred dividends by the average number of common shares outstanding during the year. An increasing trend is an indication of a successful company. Keep in mind that, although earnings are the source of dividends, the company may or may not pay out its full earnings to its shareholders each year (few do). Earnings are often retained for use in the business, as we shall see later. Earnings per share are widely quoted for publicly held companies and have a strong influence on the market price of the company's stock.

### Profit Margins

- Gross profit, operating profit, and net profit can be expressed as a percentage of net sales, resulting in ratios that are useful for making comparisons.

### Bond Interest and Preferred Dividend Coverage

- For those interested in the company's bonds or its preferred stock, the statement of income lets us calculate the relative safety or "coverage" of such investments. In the case of XYZ, with its $2.7 million of bonds outstanding, an interest cost of $135,000 must be paid each year, no matter what the company's earnings are. Since the company has earned $535,000 in 1984, and has already included the bond interest expense in that amount, its earnings before bond interest are $670,000, or 4.96 times the bond interest. "Coverage" for the bond interest is said to be 4.96 times.

  Similarly, to compute the coverage for the preferred stock dividend, net income ($535,000) is divided by the required preferred stock dividend ($5 times 6,000 shares, or $30,000). In the case of XYZ, coverage is more than 17 times.

### Price-Earnings Ratio

- The market price of the common stock of publicly held companies varies with many factors. One frequently used factor in determining the desirability of purchasing (or retaining) the stock of a company is its price-earnings ratio, that is, the relationship between earnings per share and market price per share. If the price of XYZ stock were quoted at $16.80, its P-E ratio would be said to be 10 ($16.80 divided by per-share earnings of $1.68). If its market price were $33.60, its price-earnings ratio would be 20, which is to say that the stock would be selling at 20 times earnings. The price-earnings ratio is best used, not as an absolute amount, but rather as a basis for comparisons between companies or for year-to-year comparisons of the same company. For example, although XYZ common stock may have appeared to be a good buy at 10 times earnings, it would not be as attractive if selling at 20 times earnings.

**The Statement of Retained Earnings**

When presented formally, the retained earnings statement is a bridge between the income statement and balance sheet for the year. (Usually, it is subsumed under the balance sheet category of retained earnings at the end of the year.) Simply put, it tells us what the company did with the profit it earned. (See Exhibit 4.)

In the case of XYZ, the retained earnings balance at the beginning of the year is increased by the net income for the year ($535,000) and reduced by dividends paid during the year ($150,000), leaving a balance of $1.7 million at the end of the year.

The first thing to be noted is the dividend payout ratio. From the statement of income we have seen that the earnings per common share were $1.68. The common stock dividend of $0.40 represents 24 percent of that amount. This means that the company has retained 76 percent of its year's earnings for use in the business, a policy that is hoped will result in increased profitability in the future. Another observation to be made is that the company, even if no profits were to be made for several years, has sufficient retained earnings to declare both the preferred and common stock dividends, assuming that cash is available for this purpose.

**Exhibit 4** Statement of Retained Earnings

**XYZ MANUFACTURING COMPANY, INC.**

**Statement of Retained Earnings**

**For the Years Ended December 31**

|  | 1985 | 1984 |
|---|---|---|
| Balance, January 1 | $ 1,315,000 | $ 1,022,000 |
| Net income for year | 535,000 | 443,000 |
|  | 1,850,000 | 1,465,000 |
| Less: |  |  |
| Preferred stock dividends paid ($5.00 per share) | 30,000 | 30,000 |
| Common stock dividends paid ($0.40 per share) | 120,000 | 120,000 |
| Balance, December 31 | $ 1,700,000 | $ 1,315,000 |

**The Statement of Changes in Financial Position**

Typically, the statement of changes in financial position is prepared on a working capital basis. It may be prepared on a cash basis, a working capital basis, a financial resources basis, and an all resources basis. The discussion here assumes a working capital basis.

Just as the statement of retained earnings is a bridge between the income statement and the balance sheet caption retained earnings, the statement of change is a bridge between two successive balance sheets, subsuming changes in the income statement and the balance sheet. (See Exhibit 5.) In effect, one might say the statement of changes accounts for all changes between the balance sheet at the beginning of the year and the end of the year. From the statement of changes we see all the items that have added to or reduced the company's working

**Exhibit 5** Statement of Changes in Financial Position

**XYZ MANUFACTURING COMPANY, INC.**

**Statement of Changes in Financial Position**
**For the Years Ended December 31**

|  | 1985 | 1984 |
|---|---|---|
| **Sources of funds provided by** | | |
| Net income | $ 535,000 | $ 443,000 |
| Depreciation (charged to income, but not requiring funds) | 300,000 | 275,000 |
|    Total funds provided | 835,000 | 718,000 |
| **Use of funds** | | |
| Dividends on preferred stock | 30,000 | 30,000 |
| Dividends on common stock | 120,000 | 120,000 |
| Plant and equipment | 305,000 | 200,000 |
| Prepayments | 10,000 | — |
|    Total funds used | 465,000 | 350,000 |
| Increase in net current assets | $ 370,000 | $ 368,000 |
| **Analysis of changes in working capital** | | |
| Changes in current assets | | |
|   Cash | $ 150,000 | 40,000 |
|   Marketable securities | 390,000 | 200,000 |
|   Accounts receivable | 100,000 | 60,000 |
|   Inventories | (300,000) | 220,000 |
|    Total | 340,000 | 520,000 |
| Changes in current liabilities | | |
|   Accounts payable | 60,000 | 110,000 |
|   Notes payable | (150,000) | — |
|   Accrued expenses payable | 30,000 | (20,000) |
|   Federal income tax payable | 30,000 | (38,000) |
|    Total | (30,000) | 152,000 |
| Increase in net current assets | $ 370,000 | $ 368,000 |

capital during the year. In the past the statement of changes was sometimes jokingly referred to as the "where got—where gone" statement.

In most companies the major source of funds is net income for the year—in XYZ's case, $535,000. You will remember from the income statement that in arriving at the $535,000 an expense of $300,000 was deducted for depreciation. Although this is a proper charge against the year's operations, it does not require the use of working capital and, accordingly, it is added back to income in preparing the statement of changes in financial position, giving us total funds available for use in the business of $835,000. This amount, the sum of net income and depreciation for the year, is often referred to as *cash flow.*

The statement of changes then shows what was done with this influx of funds. In the case of XYZ for 1985, dividends of $150,000 were paid, plant and equipment of $305,000 were purchased, prepayments of $10,000 were made, and the remainder of the funds provided, $465,000, went to increase working capital.

The second part of the statement details the changes in the various elements of working capital. These amounts can be computed, if you want to take the time, by comparing XYZ's balance sheets at the beginning and end of the year.

This appendix has explained a typical set of financial statements such as would be found in most annual reports. Apart from the financials, much additional information is included. There are charts and graphs, photographs of facilities and products, and generally messages from key officers. It is the financial statements, however, that provide the data for an objective measure of the company's performance and its possibilities.

## REFERENCES

1. *A Statement of Basic Accounting Theory* (Evanston, Ill.: American Accounting Association, 1966), p. 1.

# APPENDIX C

# BUSINESS FACTS FOR DECISION MAKERS: WHERE TO FIND THEM

*This appendix is adapted from Jugoslav S. Milutinovich,* Business Horizons *28 (March–April 1985):63–80.*

This basic guide is a timely and cost-effective information resource for use by business executives, government officials, and academicians. In addition to classical sources of information, it includes the two newest, most popular sources: computerized on-line data bases and statistical sources.

Decisions are based on knowledge and information. The collection of relevant information is one of the most important steps in the decision-making process. Because knowledge is limited, relevant information is necessary to determine the scope of the problem and to select and implement the proper course of action. Gathering timely and precise information facilitates achievement of the desired result.

Information about the environment in which an organization operates is a vital asset and resource. Timely and reliable information about past and present conditions, constraints, and opportunities is a source of competitive power that will help an organization outperform its competitors with effective strategic decisions. Lack of information may result in great difficulties. Because decision makers operate with time and monetary constraints, there is a critical need for a selected list of available sources of information, properly annotated, which can be used in strategic decision making.

Data sources can be divided into four major categories:

1. Government publications
2. General reference sources of business information and ideas
3. Specialized sources of specific data
4. Statistical sources

Figure AC.1 presents the organization of government publications and Figure AC.2 presents the organization of general reference sources. Each of those figures starts with an index which is followed by selected basic sources.

Well-organized decision makers must know how to search for relevant facts and information. They should have some strategy for library information research. A modified version of the Auraria library model for library research is

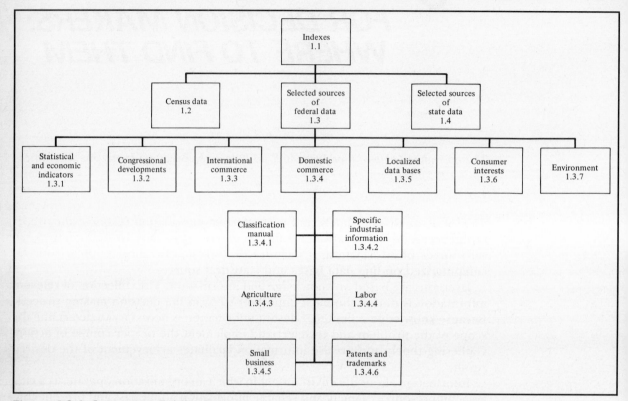

**Figure AC.1** Goverment Publications
*Source:* Adapted from Jugoslav S. Milutinovich, *Business Horizons* 28 (March–April 1985):63–80.

presented in Figure AC.3. This model presents the basic steps one should follow in searching for relevant information.

## 1. GOVERNMENT PUBLICATIONS

No other entity collects more business information than the United States government. Huge quantities of primary data, most collected for governmental use, become sources of secondary data for the business community. The various departments, bureaus, agencies, and committees issue reports, statistical publications, bibliographies, and periodicals. The countless publications are excellent sources for authoritative studies and official information vitally important to business. While many works are available for a nominal charge, they are also accessible at the Department of Commerce field offices' reference libraries and Government Depository libraries.

Because of its scope, this section could stand alone as a source book of business information (refer to Figure AC.1). Citations are divided into four categories:

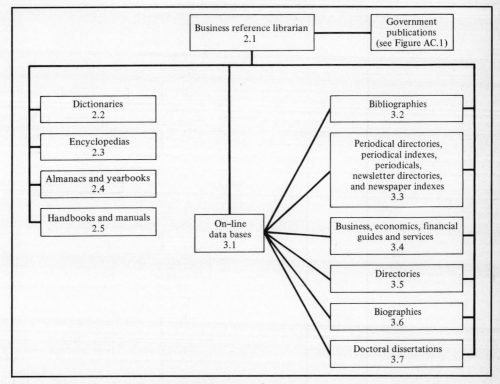

**Figure AC.2** General Business Reference Sources
*Source:* Adapted from Jugoslav S. Milutinovich, *Business Horizons* 28 (March–April 1985):63–80.

indexes; census data; selected sources of data generated by the federal government; and selected sources of data generated by the states.

## 1.1. Indexes

Adler, James B., *C/S/Index to Publications of U.S. Congress* (Washington, D.C.: U.S. Government). Published quarterly with annual cumulations, 1970 to present. Basic source for working papers of Congress. Information is in the form of abstracts of congressional documents (microfiche of actual documents available) covering the entire range of congressional publications. Two sections—indexes and abstracts. The subject title indexes use entry number referrals.

Andriot, John L., ed., *Guide to U.S. Government Publications* (McLean, Va.: U.S. Government, Documents Index). Published annually, 1973 to present. Annotated guide to publications of the various U.S. government agencies. Volume 1 contains a list of publications in existence as of January 1973; Volume 2 covers publications of abolished agencies and discontinued publications; Vol-

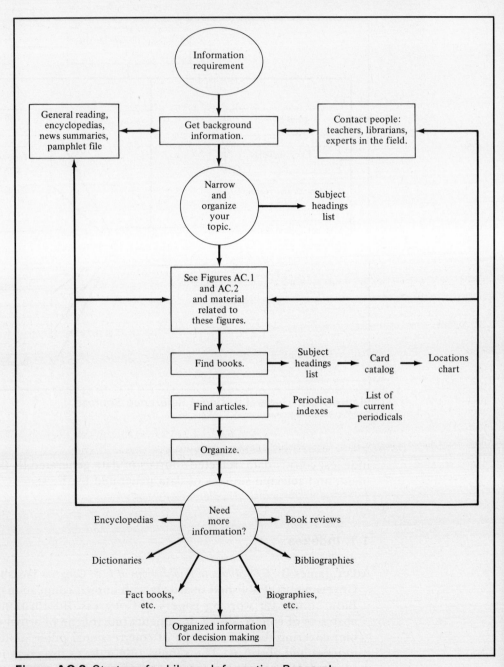

**Figure AC.3** Strategy for Library Information Research
*Source:* Adapted from Jugoslav S. Milutinvich, *Business Horizons* 28 (March–April 1985):63–80.

ume 3 explains and outlines the Superintendent of Documents classification scheme, by which Volumes 1 and 2 are arranged. Agency and title index.

*Business Service Checklist* (Washington, D.C.: Department of Commerce). Published weekly. Serves as a guide to U.S. Department of Commerce publications and to key business indicators.

*Business Services and Information: The Guide to the Federal Government* (New York: Management Information Exchange, Wiley, 1978). Guide used for identifying U.S. government publications. Divided into four parts: Introduction; Text, which is an annotated list of publications arranged by subject; Appendix with phone numbers and agency addresses; Index.

*The Federal Register* (Washington, D.C.: Division of the Federal Register, National Archives). Published daily. Contains all regulatory matter issued by all national agencies and governmental bodies. These listings are both complete and official, and are indexed.

*Code of Federal Regulations* (Washington, D.C.: Division of the Federal Register, National Archives). Published quarterly, revised yearly. A compilation of regulations first published in *The Federal Register.*

*Monthly Catalog of U.S. Government Publications* (Washington, D.C.: Government Printing Office [GPO]). Published monthly with annual cumulations. Most complete catalog available. Identifies and gives price and availability of federal documents in all subject areas. February issue includes "Directory of U.S. Government Periodicals and Subscription Publications." Includes subject, keyword, author/agency, title, and series report number indexes.

*Monthly Checklist of State Publications* (Washington, D.C.: Superintendent of Documents, GPO). Published monthly. A record of state documents and publications received by the Library of Congress.

*Selected United States Government Publications* (Washington, D.C.: Superintendent of Documents, GPO). Issued biweekly. Covers documents received by that office which are of some general interest and will be listed for sale. Each listing gives a short description of the contents of the publication, its price, and catalog number.

*United States Code Congressional and Administrative News* (St. Paul, Minn.: West Publishing Company). Published monthly with annual cumulations. Text of all Public Laws enacted by Congress, arranged by Public Law number, with a cumulative subject index. Includes legislative history, proclamations, executive orders, and an index of popular names of acts.

## 1.2. Census Data

The Bureau of the Census is by far the largest publisher of comprehensive statistical data. Its catalog, which is published monthly with annual cumulations, contains good, descriptive lists of all census publications.

The Census Bureau publishes only its most widely used censuses and surveys.

Much more information is available, usually on computer tapes. This information provides limitless possibilities for subject cross-classifications or area tabulations.

The following sampling of information available through the census surveys is divided into three parts: census data index; census of population data; and specific census data sources.

**1.2.1. Census Data Index**

*Bureau of the Census Catalog of Publications* (Washington, D.C.: Department of Commerce, Bureau of the Census). Published quarterly with monthly supplements and annual cumulations. Complete index of Census Bureau data, including publications and unpublished materials. Main divisions are Publications, Data Files, and Special Tabulations.

**1.2.2. Census of Population Data**

*Census of Population* (Series PC) (Washington, D.C.: Department of Commerce, Bureau of the Census). Published every ten years. Detailed characteristics of the population for states, counties, cities, and towns in a series of reports [PC(1)A–D] that give data on number of inhabitants, general population characteristics (age, sex, race, etc.), and general social and economic characteristics. Separate "Subject Reports," Series PC(2), cover statistics on ethnic groups, migration, fertility, marriage and living arrangements, education, employment, occupation and industry, and income.

**1.2.3. Specific Census Data Sources**

Produced and published to be used as major economic indicators.

*Census of Agriculture* (Washington, D.C.: Department of Commerce, Bureau of the Census). Published every five years. Reports data for all farms and for farms with sales of $2500 or more by county and by state.

*Census of Business* (Washington, D.C.: Bureau of the Census). Published every five years. Multivolume. Tables. Contains statistical data on retail and wholesale trade and on selected service industries for the United States, Guam, and the Virgin Islands. Arranged geographically and by Standard Industrial Classification (SIC) codes with subject reports. Issued for years ending in "2" and "7," the census is supplemented by "Monthly Retail Trade," "Selected Services Receipts," and the "Monthly Wholesale Trade" series.

*Current Business Reports: Monthly Retail Trade and Accounts Receivable* (Washington, D.C.: Bureau of the Census). Published monthly. Graphs, tables. Includes information on monthly sales for U.S. retail stores by kind of business, region, selected states, and Standard Metropolitan Statistical Areas (SMSAs). Also contains data on department stores and end-of-month accounts receivable. These reports are issued several weeks after the end of the month reported; a companion series, *Current Business Reports: Advance Monthly Retail Sales,* providing preliminary data, is issued one week after the month reported. These cumulate into an *Annual Retail Trade* series and finally into the quinquennial *Census of Business.*

*Current Business Reports: Monthly Wholesale Trade* (Washington, D.C.: Bureau of the Census). Published monthly. Graphs, tables. Contains monthly figures for wholesale inventories and sales arranged by kinds of business and geographic divisions. The reports are issued several weeks after the end of the month reported and cumulate into the quinquennial *Census of Business.*

*Census of Construction Industries* (Washington, D.C.: Bureau of the Census). Published every five years. Several volumes, maps, tables. Compiled using data from government and private organizations and reports from construction firms. Contains detailed data on construction establishments: number employed; payroll; payments and expenditures; assets; depreciation; and income. A comprehensive source of statistical data on the construction industry.

*Census of Governments* (Washington, D.C.: Bureau of the Census). Published every five years. Multivolume. Charts, graphs, tables. Important source for detailed statistics on governmental finance. Compiled using data from the Census Bureau, Census Advisory Committee on State and Local Government Statistics, and other federal agencies. Issued for years ending in "2" and "7". The following major subjects are included: governmental organization; taxable property values; public employment; governmental finance; local government; tax revenues; holdings of selected public-employment retirement systems; construction expenditures; and topical studies.

*Census of Housing* (Washington, D.C.: Bureau of the Census). Published every ten years. Multivolume.

*Volume I: States and Small Areas.* A presentation of detailed occupancy characteristics, structural characteristics, equipment and facilities, and financial characteristics for each state and several possessions, as well as a United States summary. The depth of information varies by area.

*Volume II: Metropolitan Housing.* A collection of data on SMSAs having 100,000 or more inhabitants, with cross-classifications of housing and household characteristics for analytical use.

*Volume III: City Blocks.* A collection of data that includes descriptions of conditions and plumbing facilities, average number of rooms, average contract monthly rents, average valuations, total population, number of housing units occupied by nonwhites, and number of persons per room.

*Volume IV: Components of Inventory Change.* A description of the physical changes that have taken place since the last census for the SMSAs with more than one million inhabitants.

*Volume V: Residential Financing.* Gives ownership and financial information.

*Census of Manufacturers* (Washington, D.C.: Bureau of the Census). Published every five years. Supplies data on U.S. manufacturing firms categorized under the headings of Final Area Reports and Final Industry Reports:

*Final Area Reports* presents statistics on value added by manufacturing, employment, payrolls, new capital expenditures, and number of establishments.

*Final Industry Reports* includes a series of separate reports on value of shipments, capital expenditures, value added by manufacturing, cost materials and employment for approximately 450 manufacturing industries. The data are classified by geographic region and state, employment size, class of establishment, and degree of primary products specialization.

*Census of Mineral Industries* (Washington, D.C.: Bureau of the Census). Published every five years. Tables. Compiled using data from surveys of establishments engaged in the extraction of minerals. Provides detailed data on the number of mineral industry establishments with data on employment, payrolls, assets, expenditures, consumption, costs, shipments, and receipts. This information is presented by industry, geographic area, and subject. Volume 5 of the 1972 *Census of Manufacturers* includes indexes of production for individual mineral industry groups. These data are not issued in any other form.

*Census of Retail Trade* (Washington, D.C.: Bureau of the Census). Published every five years. Compiles data for states, SMSAs and counties, and cities with populations of 2500 or more by type of business. Data include number of establishments, sales, payroll, and personnel.

*Census of Selected Services* (Washington, D.C.: Bureau of the Census). Published every five years. Includes data on hotels, motels, beauty parlors, barber shops, and other retail service organizations. Survey also includes information on number of establishments, receipts, and payrolls for states, SMSAs, counties, and cities.

*Census of Transportation* (Washington, D.C.: Bureau of the Census). Published every five years. Tables. Compiled using data from mail survey of carriers and Census of Population data. Issued for years ending in "2" and "7". Provides travel data on the civilian populations, truck inventory and use, and shipment of commodities by manufacturers. Most of these data are not publicly available elsewhere. This work is the most important cumulative general source for U.S. transportation data.

*Census of Wholesale Trade* (Washington, D.C.: Bureau of the Census). Published every five years. Presents statistics for states, SMSAs, and counties on number of establishments, sales, payroll, and personnel for kind of business.

*Census Tract Reports* (Washington, D.C.: Bureau of the Census). Published every ten years. Detailed report on population and housing.

*Construction Reports* (Washington, D.C.: Bureau of the Census). Tables. Each of the ten subseries in this series provides current statistical data on some specific aspect of the housing industry. Six of the most important periodicals: Vacant Housing Units in the U.S. (quarterly), Housing Starts (monthly), Housing Authorized by Building Permits and Public Contracts (monthly), Building Permits, Sales of New One-Family Homes (monthly), and Construction Expenditure of State and Local Tax Revenue (quarterly).

*Highlights of U.S. Export and Import Trade* (Washington, D.C.: Bureau of the Census). Published monthly. Tables. Compiled using data from the Bureau of Customs. Reports unadjusted and seasonally adjusted data on trade by commodity group, country and world area, U.S. customs regions and districts, method of shipment, and end-use category. Issued two months after month of coverage. The most comprehensive of several regular trade statistical series.

## 1.3. Selected Sources of Data Generated by the Federal Government

Categories include statistical and national economic indicators, congressional developments, international commerce, domestic commerce, localized data bases, consumer interests, and the environment. Pertinent publications for specific industries and activities are listed under "domestic commerce."

**1.3.1. Statistical and Economic Indicators**

*American Statistical Index* (Washington, D.C.: Congressional Information Service). Published monthly with annual cumulations, 1970 to present. Important source for identifying statistical publications published by the U.S. government. Indexes and abstracts statistics on numerous topics from the publications of many government agencies. Index volume contains four separate indexes that list publications by subject and name; by geographic, economic, and demographic categories; by title; and by agency report numbers. Abstract volume gives brief descriptions of the publications and their content.

*Business Conditions Digest* (Washington, D.C.: Department of Commerce, Bureau of Economic Analysis). Published monthly. Supplemented weekly by *Advance Business Conditions Digest.* Provides a look at many of the economic time series found most useful by business analysts and forecasters. Presents approximately 600 economic time series in charts and tables. Appendixes provide historical data, series descriptions, seasonal adjustment factors, and measures of variability. Economic measures listed include selected components of the national income and national product; measures of prices, wages, and productivity; measures of the labor force, employment, and unemployment; data on federal, state, and local government activities; measures of U.S. international transactions; and selected economic comparisons with major foreign countries. An essential economics reference tool.

*Economic Report of the President (together with the Annual Report of the Council of Economic Advisors)* (Washington, D.C.: GPO). Published annually. The annual report of the CEA comprises the major portion of this publication. Discusses economic policy and outlook and economic trends of the year. Includes statistical tables relating to income, employment, and publication.

*Economic Indicators* (Washington, D.C.: Superintendent of Documents, GPO). Published monthly. Charts, tables. A digest of current information on economic conditions of prices, wages, production, business activity, purchasing power, credit, money, and federal finance. Gives monthly figures for the past two years; frequently goes back as far as 1939.

*Measuring Markets: A Guide to the Use of Federal & State Statistical Data* (Washington, D.C.: Department of Commerce, GPO, 1974). Materials published by state and federal governments, which are useful in marketing research. Sources for population, income, employment, sales statistics, and some state taxes are included. Examples demonstrate the use of federal statistics in market analysis.

*Statistical Abstract of the United States* (Washington, D.C.: Department of Commerce, Bureau of the Census, GPO). Published annually, 1879 to present. Tables.

Arranged in 34 categories, it is a reliable source for statistical summaries of the economy, business, population, and politics. Emphasis is on information of national scope, plus tables for regions, states, and some local areas. Table of contents, introductory text to each section, source notes for each table, and bibliography of sources are extremely useful guides to additional material. Subject index.

*Historical Statistics of the U.S.: Colonial Times to 1970* (Washington, D.C.: Department of Commerce). Two volumes. A supplement to the *Statistical Abstract of the United States,* it correlates data.

*Survey of Current Business* (Washington, D.C.: Department of Commerce, Bureau of Economic Analysis, GPO). Published monthly, 1921 to present. Official source of gross national product, national income, and international balance of payments. Important reference for business statistics, including general economic and industrial statistics for specific products plus articles analyzing current business situations. Subject index. Statistics are indexed in *American Statistical Index* (see above). Companion publication: *Business Statistics,* weekly and biennial volumes that provide historical data for statistical series in surveys of current business.

**1.3.2. Congressional Developments**

These entries focus on activities of Congress and the federal government.

*Commerce Business Daily* (Washington, D.C.: Department of Commerce, Office of Field Operations). Published daily. Lists U.S. government procurement invitations, contract awards, subcontracting leads, sales of surplus property, and foreign business opportunities. Addresses are included. A code indicates which notices are intended wholly or in part for small businesses. The organization, by general subject categories, is not immediately apparent but can be grasped quickly by those searching regularly for particular kinds of contracts.

*Congressional Quarterly* (Washington, D.C.: Congressional Quarterly, Inc.). Published weekly, with quarterly cumulated index and an annual *CQ Almanac,* a compendium of legislation for one session of Congress. An excellent weekly service for up-to-date news on all activities of Congress and the federal government. Each issue includes the status of legislation and congressional voting charts. A record of the government for one presidential term is published every four years as *Congress and the Nation.*

*U.S. Government Manual* (Washington, D.C.: GPO). Published annually. An indispensable official handbook of the federal government. Describes personnel, purposes, and programs of most government agencies.

**1.3.3. International Commerce**

*Commerce Today* (Washington, D.C.: Department of Commerce). Published biweekly. Gives current information on commodities and foreign countries, especially those of interest to the foreign trader. Other phases covered include industrial developments, laws, and regulations of foreign countries.

*Foreign Commerce Handbook: Basic Information and Guide to Sources* (Washington, D.C.: U.S. Chamber of Commerce). Published every five years. Useful guide to foreign commerce sources.

*Foreign Economic Trends and Their Implications for the United States* (Washington, D.C.: Bureau of International Commerce). Pamphlets issued semiannually or annually for each country. Prepared by the U.S. Foreign Service/Embassies. Contains one summary table, a narrative of economic trends, and an analysis of possible implications of these trends for U.S. foreign trade.

*International Economic Indicators and Competitive Trends* (Washington, D.C.: Bureau of International Economic Policy and Research). Published quarterly. Graphs, tables. Compiled using data from the International Trade Analysis staff. Presents a variety of comparative economic statistics for the United States and seven major competitor nations, with an analysis of the economic outlook.

*Overseas Business Reports* (Washington, D.C.: Bureau of International Commerce). Published annually. Compiled using data from the Office of International Marketing. Each report deals with a group of countries' basic economic structure, trade regulations, practices and policies, market potential, and investment laws. Designed to aid business in gaining access to, and increasing its share of, foreign markets.

## 1.3.4. Domestic Commerce

### 1.3.4.1. *Classification Manual*

*Standard Industrial Classification Manual* (Washington, D.C.: GPO, 1973). Classifies establishments by type of activity in which engaged, to facilitate the collection, tabulation, presentation, and analysis of data, and to promote uniformity and comparability in presenting statistical data collected by various agencies of the U.S. government, state agencies, trade associations, and private research organizations. Covers entire range of economic activities.

### 1.3.4.2. *Specific Industrial Information*

This section is a sampling of reports on industrial information by many governmental departments, bureaus, agencies, and committees.

*Airlines*

*Handbook of Airline Statistics* (Washington, D.C.: Civil Aeronautics Board). Published annually. Data updated monthly by *Air Carrier Traffic Statistics* and quarterly by *Air Carrier Financial Statistics*. Maps, tables. Compiled using data from the Bureau of Accounts and Statistics and the U.S. Civil Aeronautics Board. Includes airline statistics for trends in passenger, freight, express, and mail revenues and traffic; flying operation expenses; aircraft expenses and depreciation; promotion, sales, and administrative expenses; and data on capital gains, interest expenses, income taxes, subsidies, dividends, investments, long-term debts, and rates of return on stockholders' equity. An essential source for background information and statistical data on the status of commercial air transportation in the United States.

*FAA Statistical Handbook of Aviation* (Washington, D.C.: Federal Aviation Administration). Published annually. Maps, tables. Compiled using data from federal government agencies and industry organizations. Statistical data on civil aviation activity such as airports, scheduled air carrier operations, and accidents. A convenient reference for current and retrospective statistics on the aviation industry.

### Banking and Finance

*Corporation Income Tax Returns* (Washington, D.C.: Internal Revenue Service). Published annually. Charts, graphs, tables. Compiled using data from estimates based on a sample of all tax returns filed during a specified period. Serves as a detailed report on corporate sources of income, assets, dividends, deductions, credits, income tax, and tax payments. Statistics are conveniently classed by industry, size of total assets, and size of business.

*Federal Reserve Bulletin* (Washington, D.C.: Board of Governors of the Federal Reserve System). Published monthly. A source of statistics on banking, deposits, loans and investments, money market rates, securities prices, industrial production, flow of funds, and various other areas of finance in relation to government, business, real estate, and consumer affairs.

*Statistical Bulletin* (Washington, D.C.: Securities and Exchange Commission). Published monthly. Charts, tables. Compiled using data from the NY and American Stock Exchanges, other registered U.S. exchanges, and periodic surveys by the SEC. Summarizes new securities offerings, trading, stock price indexes, and round-lot and odd-lot trading. Valuable to those interested in the operation and regulation of security exchange activities.

### Broadcasting

*Statistics of Communications Common Carriers* (Washington, D.C.: Federal Communications Commission). Published annually. Graphs, tables. Compiled using data from monthly and annual reports filed with the FCC. Contains detailed financial and operating data, by company, for all telephone and telegraph companies and communications holding companies engaged in interstate and foreign communication service, and for the U.S. Communications Satellite Corporation. Invaluable for information about specific utilities and the communications industry in general.

### Construction

*Construction Review* (Washington, D.C.: Bureau of Domestic Commerce). Published monthly. Tables. Compiled using data from federal, state, and local government agencies and trade associations. Provides current and retrospective statistical data on all aspects of the construction industry, by geographic area. Brings together virtually all current government statistics pertaining to the industry. Issues also include brief articles.

*Highways*

*Highway Statistics* (Washington, D.C.: Federal Highway Administration). Published annually. Data pertinent to motor fuel, motor vehicles, driver licensing, highway user taxation, state highway financing, highway mileage, and federal aid for highways. An important source for highway transportation data.

*Highway Transportation Research and Development Studies* (Washington, D.C.: Federal Highway Administration). Published annually. A compendium describing current highway research and development activities at the federal, state, industry, and university level.

*Highway Safety Literature* (Washington, D.C.: National Highway Traffic Safety Administration). Published semimonthly; no charge. Abstracts recent literature on highway safety. International coverage. Arranged topically.

*Marketing*

*Marketing Information Guide* (Washington, D.C.: Department of Commerce). Published monthly. Annotations of selected current publications and reports, with basic information and statistics on marketing and distribution.

*Mining and Petroleum*

*Minerals Yearbook* (Washington, D.C.: Bureau of the Mines). Published annually. Three volumes. Statistics on metals, minerals, and mineral products, along with economic and technical developments and trends in the United States and foreign countries. Volume 1: *Metals, Minerals, and Fuels;* Volume 2: *Domestic Reports;* Volume 3: *International Reports.* Data usually apply to information gathered two to three years before date of publication.

*Sales by Producers of Natural Gas to Interstate Pipeline Companies* (Washington, D.C.: Department of Energy). Published annually. Gives sales by size groups, states, and pricing areas; sales to individual purchasers; and pipeline companies' purchases from producers, as well as their own production.

*Statistics of Interstate Natural Gas Pipeline Companies* (Washington, D.C.: Department of Energy). Published annually. Statistical compendium of financial and operating information. Includes income and earned surplus, gas operating revenues, customers and sales, capital stock and long-term debt, gas utility plant, gas accounts, physical property, and number of employees for specific companies, with industry compilations.

*Mineral Industry Surveys* (Washington, D.C.: Bureau of the Mines). Published irregularly. Charts, graphs, maps, tables. Statistical data on metals, nonmetals, and fuels, regarding production, consumption, and shipments. Information also provided on fatal and nonfatal injuries, hours worked, and reports on developments in industrial safety and health programs.

*Printing and Publishing*

*Printing and Publishing* (Washington, D.C.: Bureau of Domestic Commerce). Published quarterly. Tables. Compiled using data from the Departments of Commerce and Labor. Statistical report on printing, publishing, and allied industries, issued four months after the month for which data are reported. Covers foreign trade by country and product, sales and profits, employment, and earnings by industry.

*Railroads*

*Rail Carload Cost Sales by Territories* (Washington, D.C.: Interstate Commerce Commission, Bureau of Accounts). Published annually. Includes data for rail carload mileage cost scales by district, region, and type of car, and unit costs for various weight loads by type of equipment, adjusted and unadjusted. Data grouped into seven regions of the United States by carriers with revenues of $5 million or more. An invaluable source of cost breakdowns for rail operations.

*Transportation*

*Transport Economics* (Washington, D.C.: Interstate Commerce Commission). Published quarterly. Tables. Provides analysis and summary of operating statistics, finances, equipment, and employment for carriers in interstate commerce (such as rail, motor, water, air, and pipeline). Supplements and cumulates into *Transport Statistics in the United States.*

*Transport Statistics in the United States* (Washington, D.C.: Interstate Commerce Commission). Published annually. Six parts issued separately. Maps, tables. Transport statistics on traffic operations, equipment, finances, and employment as they relate to railroads, water carriers, pipelines, motor carriers, freight forwarders, and private car lines.

*Utilities*

*Electric Power Monthly* (Washington, D.C.: Department of Energy). Tables. Statistics on production, fuel consumption, capacity, sales, and operating revenues and income. December issue includes data on peak loads, energy requirements, and system capacities for the previous ten years and estimates for the following ten years. Supplemented by and cumulated from *National Electric Power Generation and Energy Use Trends,* which is published quarterly.

### 1.3.4.3. *Agriculture*

*Agriculture Statistics* (Washington, D.C.: Department of Agriculture). Published annually. Tables. Compiled using data from USDA counts and estimates, census statistics, the Department of Labor, the Foreign Service, and other federal agencies. The annual agriculture reference book. Includes statistical data on acreage, yield and production of crops, commercial crops, prices paid and received by farmers, livestock production, market supplies and prices, imports and exports, farm resources, income and expenses, consumption and family living, and agricultural programs. Historical series limited to the last ten years. An indispensable tool for agribusiness. Well indexed for quick access to specific information.

*Statistical Summary* (Washington, D.C.: Department of Agriculture, Statistical Reporting Service). Published monthly. Designed for ready reference, this report summarizes statistical data estimated for or collected on prices, sales, stocks, and production of agricultural products, such as fibers, grains, vegetables, nuts, fruits, seeds, livestock, milk, and dairy products.

### 1.3.4.4. *Labor*

*Area Trends in Employment and Unemployment* (Washington, D.C.: Manpower Administration). Published monthly. Describes area labor market developments and outlooks for 150 major employment centers, with separate brief summaries for selected areas, including those with concentrated persistent unemployment and underemployment.

*Area Wage Surveys* (Washington, D.C.: Bureau of Labor Statistics). Published annually. Tables. Issued as a subseries of the *BLS Bulletin* series. Provides occupational earnings data for nearly 100 SMSAs, published separately for each SMSA. Useful information for wage and salary administration and collective bargaining, and for determining plant location.

*Directory of National Unions and Employee Associations* (Washington, D.C.: Bureau of Labor Statistics). Published biennially. Issued as a subseries of the *BLS Bulletin* series. Includes a listing of national and international unions, summary of significant labor developments, and appendixes.

*Employment and Earnings* (Washington, D.C.: Bureau of Labor Statistics). Published monthly. Charts and tables giving data on employment, hours, earnings, and labor turnover for states, metropolitan areas, and industries.

*Personnel Literature* (Washington, D.C.: Civil Service Commission, Library). Published monthly. Lists selected books, pamphlets, government documents, unpublished dissertations, microforms, and the contents of periodicals received in the CSC Library. Because the CSC Library comprehensively collects personnel literature, this is an exceedingly useful index-bibliography for research, but it is not cumulative.

*Handbook of Labor Statistics* (Washington, D.C.: Bureau of Labor Statistics). Published annually. Tables. The basic statistical reference book on U.S. labor characteristics and conditions. Includes retrospective data and assembles in one volume the major BLS labor statistical series. Ceased publication with 1981 annual.

*Labor Relations Reporter* (Washington, D.C.: Bureau of National Affairs, Inc.). Loose-leaf books with weekly updates. Covers labor laws, fair employment practices, wages and hours, and arbitration and court decisions.

*Employment and Training Report of the President* (Washington, D.C.: Manpower Administration). Published annually since 1963. Charts, graphs, and tables reporting the employment, earnings, size, and demographic characteristics of the labor force and Department of Labor manpower programs. Historical data and projections are included.

*Monthly Labor Review* (Washington, D.C.: Bureau of Labor Statistics). Published monthly. Reviews labor issues, including employment, wages, collective bargaining, industrial relations, labor law, and foreign developments. Contains statistics and book reviews.

### 1.3.4.5. *Small Business*

*Small Business Bibliographies* (Washington, D.C.: Small Business Administration). Published irregularly. Briefly describes particular business activities. Substantial bibliography includes federal, state, and nongovernmental publications. Preface to each issue may be helpful to those seeking career information.

### 1.3.4.6. *Patents and Trademarks*

*Index of Patents Issued from the U.S. Patent Office* (Washington, D.C.: Patent Office). Published annually. Two volumes. Volume 1 indexes patents listed in the year's issues of the *Official Gazette* by name of patentee. Entries include a general designation of the invention, patent number, date of issue, and classification code. Volume 2 indexes patents by subject of invention as indicated by the classification code number identified in the *Manual of Classification.* A convenient appendix is a list of libraries receiving current issues of U.S. patents and of depository libraries receiving the *Official Gazette.*

*Index of Trademarks Issued from the U.S. Patent Office* (Washington, D.C.: Patent Office). Published annually. Alphabetically indexes registrants of trademarks issued and/or published in the *Official Gazette* during the calendar year.

**1.3.5. Localized Data Bases**

*Congressional District Data Book* (Washington, D.C.: Department of Commerce, Bureau of the Census). Published irregularly. Various data from the census and election statistics for districts of the Congress. Includes maps of states with counties, congressional districts, and selected places.

*County and City Data Book* (Washington, D.C.: Department of Commerce, Bureau of the Census). Published irregularly. Various statistical information for counties, cities, SMSAs, unincorporated towns, and urbanized areas. For each county or county equivalent, 196 statistical items are given. Provides information supplemental to the *Statistical Abstract* (refer to 1.3.1, Statistical and Economic Indicators).

*County Business Patterns* (Washington, D.C.: Department of Commerce, Bureau of the Census). Published annually. Contains county, state, and U.S. summary statistics on employment number and employment size of reporting business units, and taxable payrolls for approximately 15 industry categories. Statistics are particularly suited to analyzing market potential, establishing sales quotas, and locating facilities.

**1.3.6. Consumer Interests**

*Consumer Legislative Monthly Report* (Washington, D.C.: Department of Health and Human Services, Office of Consumer Affairs). Published monthly when Congress is in session. Lists and briefly describes consumer-related bills introduced into the current Congress. Though summaries of bills are very brief, inclusion of bill sponsors and committees referred to gives access to further information. Topical arrangement and index are convenient to use.

**1.3.7. Environment**

*102 Monitor, Environmental Impact Statements* (Washington, D.C.: Council on Environmental Quality). Published monthly. Tables. Provides abstracts of environmental impact statements concerning proposed projects of federal agencies, as well as legislation relating to environmental impact statements.

## 1.4. Selected Sources of Data Generated by State Governments

This list categorizes sources of economic data. Much of the information generated at the state level is prepared by agricultural and/or business colleges of state universities.

Department of Geology or Conservation. Monographs are available from this department in most states, describing the geology of various geographic areas within the state in question. Water supply, fish and game conservation, and mineral resources of the state are also described.

Department of Health. Public health statistics are available on state births and deaths. Usually published monthly. Some states publish tracts on various diseases such as arthritis or skin infections; other publications may be available on such topics as disinfection of drinking water.

Department of Highways. Statistics, planning, and highway descriptions are available as maps and pamphlets. Data of this department will include road clearances of highway structures, public safety programs, and accident prevention projects.

Division of Insurance. Annual reports are based on the compilations of annual statements by insurance companies doing business in the state.

Division of Statistics. This division prepares monthly publications on labor statistics, such as employment, earnings, and labor supply of wage earners. Some assemble wholesale and retail trade information.

Industrial Commission. In most states, this commission puts out monthly bulletins on industrial safety and hygiene. Sometimes responsible for publicity to attract new industry to the states.

Public Utilities Commission. Statistical reports on railroads, express companies, and steam heat and telephone utilities. In many cases, annual reports provide excellent overviews of commission activities.

*Statistical Reference Index* (Washington, D.C.: Congressional Information Service). Published annually, 1980 to present. Indexes and abstracts statistical publications of state governments, associations, business organizations, commercial publishers, independent research organizations, and university research bureaus.

## 2. GENERAL REFERENCE SOURCES OF BUSINESS INFORMATION AND IDEAS

### 2.1. Business Reference Librarian

The business reference librarian should be consulted as a time-saving first step in gathering business facts. This specialist has the best sources at his or her fingertips and can give expert guidance. He or she compiles booklists concerning specific areas, identifies special library collections, and is aware of books scheduled for publication. The business reference librarian is a member of the Special Libraries Association, a formal group of librarians who meet monthly, keeping abreast of the best reference material available. Through networking, the librarian is aware of the holdings in all business reference libraries in the general area and in university, public, and corporate libraries open to the public.

The business reference librarian can also tap into the interlibrary loan system—a free, cooperative exchange system of books and periodicals from member libraries across the country.

### 2.2. Dictionaries

Dictionaries are useful to the business manager or student wanting to check the meaning, spelling, or pronunciation of words, terms, and phrases.

Crowley, Ellen T., ed., *Acronyms, Initialisms, & Abbreviations Dictionary,* 9th ed. (Detroit: Gale Research Co., 1985). A guide to alphabetical designations, contractions, acronyms, initialisms, abbreviations. Supplemented by *New Acronyms, Initialisms, & Abbreviations.*

Filkins, James F., and Donald L. Caruth, *Lexicon of American Business Terms* (New York: Simon & Schuster, 1973). Brief dictionary containing 3000 of the most common business terms.

French, Derek, and Heather Saward, *Dictionary of Management* (New York: International Publications Service, 1975). Defines about 4000 management and economic terms and techniques used by managers and writers about management. Includes abbreviations and brief descriptions of major associations and organizations.

Johannsen, Hano, and G. Terry Pag, *International Dictionary of Management: A Practical Guide* (Boston: Houghton Mifflin, 1975). Covers the entire area of business and management. Contains 5000 entries defining terms, concepts, initials, and acronyms in international usage, plus short descriptions on associations and organizations. Cross references.

Nemmers, E. E., *Dictionary of Economics and Business,* 4th ed. (Totowa, N.J.: Rowman & Littlefield, 1978). Paperback giving brief definitions for commonly used business terms.

Wood, Donna, ed., *Trade Names Dictionary,* 4th ed. (Detroit: Gale Research Co., 1985). Two volumes. A guide to trade names, brand names, product names, with addresses of their manufacturers, importers, marketers, or distributors. Supplemented periodically by *New Trade Names.*

## 2.3. Encyclopedias

Encyclopedias compile information on a wide range of topics and answer the need for basic, concise data. Entries are signed articles with frequent illustrations, plates, diagrams, maps, bibliographies, and indexes.

Akey, Denise, ed., *Encyclopedia of Associations* (Detroit: Gale Research Co.). Published annually. In-depth guide to associations. Four volumes: Vol. 1, National Organizations of the U.S.; Vol. 2, Geographic and Executive Index; Vol. 3, New Associations and Projects; Vol. 4, International Organizations.

*Exporters' Encyclopedia* (New York: Dun & Bradstreet). Published annually. Detailed facts on shipments to every country in the world. Covers regulations, types of communication and transportation available, foreign trade organizations, general export information, general reference tables, and listings of ports.

Schmittroth, John Jr., ed., *Encyclopedia of Information Systems and Services,* 6th ed. (Detroit: Gale Research Co., 1985). Two volumes: Vol. 1, International (excluding U.S.); Vol. 2, U.S. Describes approximately 1500 data bases. Describes more than 2000 organizations in U.S. and 60 other countries that produce, process, store, and use bibliographic and nonbibliographic information. Supplemented periodically by *New Information Systems and Services.*

Sullivan, Linda E., ed., *Encyclopedia of Governmental Advisory Organizations,* 3rd ed. (Detroit: Gale Research Co., 1980). Reference guide to presidential advisory committees, public advisory committees, and other government-related boards, panels, task forces, commissions, and conferences which serve in a consulting, coordinating, advisory, research, or investigative capacity.

Wasserman, Paul, C. Georgi, and J. Woy, *Encyclopedia of Business Information Sources,* 5th ed. (Detroit: Gale Research Co., 1983). Quick survey of basic information sources covering 1215 subjects. Provides specific citations, dealing with a single point, with the business manager in mind. Includes reference works, periodicals, trade associations, statistical sources, and on-line data bases.

## 2.4. Almanacs and Yearbooks

Almanacs are collections of current factual information covering a broad range of topics.

*World Almanac and Book of Facts* (New York: Newspaper Enterprise Association). Published annually. Facts on many diverse subjects.

Yearbooks are fact books providing current information. They usually give more information than almanacs.

*Commodity Year Book* (New York: Commodity Research Bureau). Published annually. Statistical yearbook with data on production, prices, stocks, exports, and imports for more than 100 commodities. Editorial comments on new developments affecting commodities.

*Statesman's Year Book* (New York: St. Martin's Press). Published annually. First three sections are factual data about international organizations, U.S. and Commonwealth countries. Final section provides descriptive data and statistics on other countries, including history, government, population, and commerce.

## 2.5. Handbooks and Manuals

Business handbooks and manuals are excellent reference tools that present concise introductions to the concepts, procedures, and techniques for specific managerial functions. These compendiums are well organized and indexed, providing easy access to the precise information needed.

Albert, Kenneth J., ed., *The Strategic Management Handbook* (New York: McGraw-Hill, 1983). Discusses concepts, principles, and practices of strategic management. Contains how-to material, highlighted with real-life cases and examples.

Written by experts from management consulting firms, Fortune 500 companies, and top business schools.

Davidson, Sidney, and Roman Weil, eds., *Handbook of Modern Accounting,* 3rd ed. (New York: McGraw-Hill, 1983). Illustrated. Defines important terms and procedures. Covers recent developments, their implications and applications.

Fettridge, Clark, and Robert S. Minor, eds., *Office Administration Handbook* (Chicago: Dartnell Corp., 1981). Discusses methods of handling office, personnel, and administrative problems.

Grikscheit, Gary M., Harold C. Cash, and W. J. E. Crissy, *Handbook of Selling: Psychological, Managerial, and Marketing Bases* (New York: Wiley, 1981). Discusses selling strategy and tactics. Deals with how to organize information about a customer and answer customer objections.

Makridakis, Spyros, and Steven C. Wheelwright, eds., *The Handbook of Forecasting: A Manager's Guide* (New York: Wiley, 1983). Explains which forecasting methods work and which do not. Divided into four sections: role and application of forecasting in organizations; approaches to forecasting; methods and forecasting challenges for the 1980s; and managing the forecasting function.

Scheer, Wilbert E., *Personnel Administration Handbook* (Chicago: Dartnell Corp., 1979). Reference book for personnel managers or administrators. Covers wage and salary administration, labor relations, interviewing, recruiting, hiring, measuring work performance, merit increases, and terminations.

Stansfield, Richard H., *Advertising Manager's Handbook* (Chicago: Dartnell Corp., 1982). Reference book on advertising strategies. Case studies included. Covers such topics as the campaign concept, copy, art, budgeting, and media selection.

Walmsley, Julian, *The Foreign Exchange Handbook: A User's Guide* (New York: Wiley, 1983). Provides an in-depth coverage of major currency markets. Discusses some of the economic and technical influences on currency and money markets. Other topics covered include financial futures and gold markets, payment systems, and exposure management and control. Provides standard foreign exchange calculations and money market formulas.

## 3. SPECIALIZED SOURCES OF SPECIFIC DATA

### 3.1. On-line Data Bases

The information explosion can be attributed to computer technology, which has revolutionized the search for business facts. By using a data base, which is an organized collection of information in a particular subject area, decision makers benefit from the accessibility and adaptability of massive resources now available. This tool is an expensive one, but is certainly cost-effective when measured by time savings. Total cost depends on the data bases selected for the search, the amount of time used, and the number of references retrieved.

The actual process of a computer search is a simple one. A questionnaire is completed, specifically describing the problem and indicating important authors, journals, or key facts useful in retrieving references. While the search is being completed, computer, librarian, and researcher interact in redirecting and re-defining. Citations can be printed immediately or mailed within five business days.

Three major vendors offer on-line interactive search access to hundreds of data bases. Bibliographic Retrieval Services (BRS), Scotia, New York, and DIA-LOG/Lockheed Informations Services in Palo Alto, California, store general bibliographic data; some of their data bases overlap. The third, SDC Search Service, System Development Corporation, Santa Monica, California, emphasizes technical and statistical information.

Listings of computer-based services can be found in the following directories.

*Directory of Computer Based Services* (Washington, D.C.: Telenet Communications Corp.). Published annually. Lists data banks, commercial service bureaus, educational institutions, and companies that offer interactive computer-based services to the public through the nationwide Telenet network. Lists data bases that may be accessed, a brief description of the contents, and who offers the data base.

*Directory of On-line Information Resources* (Rockville, Md.: CSG Press, 1980). Easy-to-use guide to selected, publicly accessible bibliographic and nonbibliographic on-line data bases. 225 data bases available, file descriptions, coverage, and size. Subject and source index; phone and address list of data base suppliers.

The business data bases are divided into three areas: bibliographies, statistics, and directories.

*Bibliographies:* On-line interactive search access to various bibliographic data bases.

*ABI/INFORM.* August 1971 to present, 134,636 records. All phases of business management and administration. Stresses general decision sciences information that is widely applicable. Includes specific product and industry information. Scans 400 primary publications in business and related fields.

*Management Contents* (Skokie, Ill.: Management Contents, Inc.). 1974 to present, with monthly updates. Current information on a variety of business- and management-related topics for use in decision making and forecasting. Articles from 200 U.S. and foreign journals, proceedings, and transactions are fully indexed and abstracted to provide up-to-date information in areas of accounting, design sciences, marketing, operations research, organizational behavior, and public administration.

*Monthly Catalog of U.S. Government Publications* (Washington, D.C.: GPO). Published monthly with annual cumulations (see entry under 1.1., government publications indexes); 101,401 records of reports, studies, fact sheets, maps, handbooks, and conferences.

*New York Times Information Bank* (see entry under 3.3, periodicals).

*PAIS International Bulletin* (New York: Public Affairs Information Service). Published monthly, 1976 to present. Worldwide coverage of more than 800 English-language journals and 6000 nonserial publications; 137,653 citations.

*Predicasts Terminal System* (Cleveland: Predicasts, Inc.). Bibliographic and statistical data base providing instant access to many business journals and other special reports for searches of current articles, statistics, geographic location of companies. Abstracts a wide range of periodical abstracts and indexes.

*Statistics:* In-depth statistics easily adapted for a wide variety of manipulations.

*Economic Time Series*

*Business International/Data Time Series* (Business International Corp.).
*PTS/U.S. Time Series* (Predicasts, Inc.).

*Marketing Statistics*

*BLS Consumer Price Index* (Department of Labor, Bureau of Labor Statistics).
*BLS Producer Price Index* (Department of Labor, Bureau of Labor Statistics).

*Financial Statistics*

*Disclosure II* (Washington, D.C.: Disclosure, Inc.). 1977 to present. Updated weekly. Extracts of reports filed with the U.S. Securities and Exchange Commission by publicly owned companies; 11,000 company reports provide a reliable and detailed source of public financial and administrative data. Source of information for marketing intelligence, corporate planning and development, portfolio analysis, legal and accounting research.

*Directories:* Arranged by subject, title, geographic location, and code number.

*CATFAX: Directory of Mail Order Catalogs.*
*EIS Industrial Plants* (Economic Information Systems, Inc.).
*Foreign Traders Index* (Department of Commerce).
*Trade Opportunities* (Department of Commerce).

## 3.2. Bibliographies

Bibliographies, lists of printed sources of information on a topic, are the most important starting point for business facts. They can quickly lead the business executive or student to original available sources of information on a specific topic.

*Bibliographic Index: A Cumulative Bibliography of Bibliographies* (Bronx, N.Y.: H. W. Wilson Co.). Published three times annually. Lists, by subject, sources of bibliographies containing 50 or more citations of books, pamphlets, and periodicals.

*Bibliography of Publications of University Bureaus of Business and Economic Research: The AUBER Bibliography* (Boulder, Col.: Association for University Business and Economic Research). Published annually. Bibliography of publications that do not appear in other indexes. Written by bureaus of business and economic research and members of the American Association of Collegiate Schools of Business. Includes books, series, working papers, and articles published by each business school. Divided into two parts: subject and institution. Author index.

Brownstone, David M., and Gorton Carruth, *Where to Find Business Information: A Worldwide Guide for Everyone Who Needs the Answers to Business Questions,* 2nd ed. (New York: Wiley, 1982). List of 5000 current foreign and domestic, private and public business information sources.

*Business Books in Print* (New York: Bowker). Published irregularly. (*Note:* same information available in the "Business" portion of the Subject Index of *Books in Print,* which is published annually.) Presents finding, ordering, and bibliographic data for more than 31,500 books and periodicals from U.S. publishers and university presses on business, finance, and economics. Indexed by author, title, and business subjects. Directory of publishers.

*Business Literature* (Newark, N.J.: Public Library of Newark, Business Library). Published ten times each year. Annotated lists of current business topics.

*Business and Technology Sources* (Cleveland: Cleveland Public Library). Published quarterly. Bulletin developed to cover one subject per issue; lists numerous other publications concerning the topic.

*Core Collection: An Author and Subject Guide* (Boston: Harvard University Baker Library). 1971 to present. Revised annually. Selective listing of more than 4000 English-language business books in the Harvard Business School Library. Lists books by author and subject.

Daniells, Lorna M., comp., *Business Reference Sources: An Annotated Guide for Harvard Business School Students,* rev. ed. (Boston: Harvard University Baker Library, 1979). Comprehensive annotated bibliography of entire field of business covering selected books and reference sources.

Figueroa, Oscar, and Charles Winkler, *A Business Information Guidebook* (New York: AMACAM, 1980). Useful first point of reference for locating sources of business and economic information.

*Management Information Guides* (Detroit: Gale Research Co.). A group of bibliographic references to business information sources in many fields. Each volume includes general reference works, film strips, government and institutional reports. Two examples of this source are

Norton, Alice, *Public Relations Information Sources* [Management Information Service Guide #22] (Detroit: Gale Research Co., 1970). Annotated bibliography of general sources, public relations tools, and international public relations.

*Service to Business and Industry* (New York: Brooklyn Public Library, Business Library). Published ten times each year. Annotated bibliographies covering current business topics.

*Subject Catalogue: A Cumulative List of Works Represented by Library of Congress Printed Cards* (Washington, D.C.: U.S. Library of Congress). Published quarterly, with yearly and five-year cumulated editions, 1950 to present. Comprehensive current annotated bibliography on every subject from all parts of the world. Cross-reference of subject headings is an important guide suggesting many different appropriate headings on subjects in several standard sources, opening up new resources. A good starting point in an information search.

Tega, Vasie G., *Management and Economics Journals: A Guide to Information Sources* (Detroit: Gale Research Co., 1977). Bibliography of periodicals in the fields of management and economics.

Vernon, K.D.C., ed., *Use of Management and Business Literature* (Woburn, Mass.: Butterworths, 1975). Bibliography of information published in the English language on business and management. Includes a description of British publications and library practices, forms of business information, and surveys of literature in corporate finance, management, accounting, organizational behavior, manpower management and industrial relations, marketing, computers, and quantitative methods and production.

Wasserman, Paul, C. Georgi, and J. Woy, *Encyclopedia of Business Reference Sources,* 5th ed. (Detroit: Gale Research Co., 1983). Survey of basic information tools covering 1215 subject sources (see 2.3, Encyclopedias). Includes reference works, periodicals, trade associations, statistical sources, and on-line data bases.

## 3.3. Periodical Directories, Periodical Indexes, Periodicals, Newsletter Directories, and Newspaper Indexes

Periodical directories are helpful reference tools for finding major industry publications relevant to a specific area.

*Business Publication Rates and Data* (Skokie, Ill.: Standard Rate and Data Service, Inc.). Published monthly. Index to business, trade, and technical publications arranged by "market served" classifications.

*Ulrich's International Periodicals Directory* (New York: Bowker). Published annually. Subject index of more than 55,000 entries for in-print periodicals published worldwide. Contains "Abstracting and Indexing Services" chapter.

Periodical indexes are valuable sources of current information for a broad scope of subjects. Abstracts provide the added feature of descriptive notation.

*Accountants Index* (New York: American Institute of Certified Public Accountants). Published quarterly with annual cumulations. Comprehensive index of English-language books, pamphlets, government documents, and articles on accounting and related fields. Author, title, and subject listing.

*Business Periodicals Index* (New York: Wilson Company). Published monthly with quarterly and annual cumulations, 1958 to present. Cumulative subject index covering 270 business periodicals in the English language. Subject categories are very specific. Separate book review index follows subject index in the annual volume.

*Cumulative Index* (New York: Conference Board). Published annually. Useful subject index for wide range of studies, pamphlets, and articles that the Conference Board research firm has published in the areas of business economics, corporate administration, finance, marketing, personnel, international operations, and public affairs. Covers material published during the past 20 years, with emphasis on the most recent 10 years.

*Current Contents: Social and Behavioral Sciences* (Philadelphia: Institute for Scientific Information). Published weekly, 1961 to present. Reproduces the tables of contents of journals in business, management, economics, computer applications, and other disciplines in social and behavioral sciences. Worldwide coverage of 1330 journals. Subject, author, and publishers' address indexes.

*Predicasts' F&S Index United States* (Cleveland: Predicasts, Inc.). Published weekly, with monthly, quarterly, and annual cumulations, 1960 to present. Index covering company, industry, and product information from business-oriented periodicals and brokerage house reports in the United States. Information arranged by company name, SIC number, and company according to SIC groups.

*Predicasts' F&S Index International.* Same as above, except that it gives information about the rest of the world, excluding Europe.

*Predicasts' F&S Index Europe.* Same as *F&S International,* but with coverage of European continent only.

*Index of Economic Articles* (Homewood, Ill.: Irwin). Published annually. Bibliographies from 200 English-language journals on articles, communications, papers, and proceedings discussions. Classified index and author index.

*Management Contents* (Skokie, Ill.: G. D. Searle & Co.). Published biweekly. Reproduction of the tables of contents of a selection of 150 of the best business/management journals. Each issue can be scanned for significant articles. Now available as on-line data base.

*Public Affairs Information Service Bulletin (PAIS)* (New York: Public Affairs Information Service). Published weekly, 1915 to present. Cumulations five times each year and annually. Selective subject index of current books, yearbooks, directories, government documents, pamphlets plus 1000 periodicals relating to national and international economic and public affairs. Factual and statistical information. Brief annotations of entries. Now available as on-line data base.

*Work Related Abstracts* (Detroit: Information Coordinators). Published monthly with annual indexes, 1972 to present. Abstract of articles, dissertations, and books concerning labor, personnel, and organizational behavior. Loose-leaf format. Arranged by subject in 20 categories. Subject index. Subject headings list published annually.

Business periodicals feature articles of use and interest to business managers and students. Specialized journals report new research findings and developments. Two examples of general business periodicals are

*Business Week* (New York: McGraw-Hill). Published weekly. Business news magazine with concise articles on new business trends and developments. Special issues: Survey of Corporate Performance and Investment Outlook. Indexed in BPI, F&S, PAIS (see indexes).

*Fortune* (New York: Time, Inc.). Published monthly. Topics of general interest cover new products and industries, politics and world affairs, biographical information. May issue: Fortune 500/500 largest U.S. industrial corporations. Indexed in BPI, F&S, and PAIS (see indexes).

Other general business periodicals include *Across the Board; Barron's National Business and Financial Weekly; Business Briefs; Boardroom Reports; Columbia Journal of World Business; Commerce Business Daily; Commercial and Financial Chronicle; Dun's; Forbes; Nation's Business;* and *Supervisory Management.*

Academic journals are also important periodicals. Three examples are

*Business Horizons* (Bloomington: Indiana University Graduate School of Business). Published bimonthly. Readable articles, balanced between practice and theory, of interest to management and academicians. Indexed in BPI, F&S, and PAIS.

*Harvard Business Review* (Boston: Harvard University Graduate School of Business Administration). Published bimonthly. Professional management journal featuring practical articles on all aspects of general management and policy. Indexed in BPI, F&S, and PAIS.

*Journal of Business* (Chicago: University of Chicago Business School). Published quarterly. Scholarly journal geared to professional and academic business and economic theory and methodology. Includes short subject list of books. Indexed in BPI, F&S, and PAIS.

Each major industry issues publications containing specific information concerning its field. Some examples are

*Advertising Age* (Chicago: Crain Communications, Inc.). Published weekly. February issue, "Agency Billings," provides data on advertising agencies ranked by billings for the year. August issue, "Marketing Profiles of the 100 Largest National Advertisers," provides data on leading product lines, profits, advertising expenditures, and names of marketing personnel.

*Sales Management* (New York: Bill Communications, Inc.). Published semimonthly. "Survey of Buying Power," published in July and October issues, is a prime authority on U.S. and Canadian buying income, buying power index, cash income, households, merchandise line sales, population, and retail sales information. National and regional summaries, market ratings, and metro-market and county-city market data by states.

Some important management journals are *The Journal of Creative Behavior; California Management Review; Human Relations; Administrative Science Quarterly; Academy of Management Review; Sloan Management Review; Academy of Management Journal; Organizational Behavior and Human Performance; Industrial and Labor Relations Review; Personnel Psychology.*

Newsletters of trade associations and professional societies can provide valuable business facts and services. The following directories are useful in finding the appropriate newsletter:

*National Directory of Newsletters and Reporting Services* (Detroit: Gale Research Co. 1981). Lists and provides information on newsletters and publications closely akin to newsletters issued regularly by business associations, societies, clubs, and government agencies. Features reference guide to national and international services, financial services, association bulletins, and training and educational services. Cumulative subject, publisher, and title indexes.

*Oxbridge Directory of Newsletters* (New York: Oxbridge Communications, Inc.). Published annually. Lists 5000 U.S. and Canadian newsletters in 145 subject areas along with advertising and subscription rates, description of contents, names of key personnel, and names, addresses, and telephone numbers of the publishers.

Newspaper indexes are helpful sources of information about current events and newsworthy materials not appearing in other types of periodicals.

*New York Times Index* (New York: The New York Times Co.). Published every two weeks with annual cumulations. Dates back to 1851. Detailed index summarizing and classifying news alphabetically by subject, persons, and organizations. Cross-references. Also on-line data base from January 1969.

*Wall Street Journal Index* (New York: Dow Jones Company, Inc.). Published monthly with annual cumulations, 1958 to present. Complete report on current business. Subject index of all articles that have appeared in the *Journal,* grouped in two sections: Corporate News and General News.

## 3.4. Business, Economics, and Financial Guides and Services

Business services are information agencies that compile, interpret, and distribute data on specific subjects. These guides are kept up to date by revised and supplemental data issued on various schedules.

*Babson's Business Service* (Babson Park, Mass.: Business Statistics Organization, Inc.). Issued in three bulletins:

*Business Inventory—Commodity Price Forecasts.* Published monthly. Pertinent discussions on business topics as well as short sketches of supply, demand, price, and buying advice of major commodities.

*Business Management—Sales and Wage Forecasts.* Published monthly. Covers current problems on labor and wages; keeps abreast of current developments in sales and buying power. *Babson's Washington Service* is published by the same organization.

*Babson Weekly Staff Letter* covers current trends and business problems.

*Business and Investment Service* (New York: International Statistical Bureau, Inc.). Published weekly. Analyses of production in basic industries. Includes political analyses of interest. Section entitled "Selected Securities Guide" presents stock market trends and indexes, as well as earnings and prices of stocks in selected industries. Additional services available are a quarterly security list, a monthly trend of distribution, a foreign newsletter, and postwar reports.

*Chase Manhattan Foreign Trade Service* (New York: Chase Manhattan Bank). Published annually with additional supplements. Service for Chase Manhattan Bank customers gives foreign exchange and export trade information for many countries.

*Dun and Bradstreet Credit Service* (New York: Dun and Bradstreet). Published every two months. Collects, analyzes, and distributes credit information on manufacturers, wholesalers, and retailers. Includes general information on the character, experience, and ability of the enterprise, plus a highly detailed statement covering the antecedents, methods of operation, financial statement analysis, management progress, and payment record for each entry. Also operates a foreign division.

Grant, Mary M., and Norma Cote, eds., *Directory of Business and Financial Services,* 7th ed. (New York: Special Libraries Association, 1976). (*Note:* new edition planned for 1985.) Guide to existing national and international business, economic, and financial services describing 1051 publications issued by 421 publishers. Each listing includes coverage, frequency, price, and addresses. Arranged alphabetically by title; publisher and subject index use referral numbers.

*John Herling's Labor Letter* (Washington, D.C.: John Herling's Labor Letter). Published weekly. Gives current information on labor topics, legislation, and opinions in Washington.

*The Kiplinger Washington Letter* (Washington, D.C.: Kiplinger Washington Agency). This is a condensed and confidential letter to subscribers. It analyzes economic and political events and attempts some forecasting. The news service features continuous events and reports from the "grass roots" membership. Additional publications include *Kiplinger Tax Letter,* published biweekly, which reviews federal tax legislation, and *Kiplinger Agricultural Letter,* published biweekly, which gives pertinent developments affecting agriculture.

*Moody's Bond Record* (New York: Moody's Investors Service). Published weekly. Provides statistics, prices, and other information for bonds of all types, including municipals.

*Moody's Dividend Record* (New York: Moody's Investors Service). Published weekly. Gives current information on dividend declarations, payment dates, ex-dividend dates, dividend dates, income bond interest payments, payments on bond and default, stock split-ups, stock subscription rights, and preferred stocks called.

*Moody's Handbook of Common Stocks* (New York: Moody's Investors Service). Published quarterly. Covers more than 1000 selected common stocks listed alphabetically. Each company page has a 10-year statistical history, a 15-year price chart, the company's background, recent developments, and investment quality. Industry cross-index.

*Moody's Manuals* (New York: Moody's Investors Service). Published semiweekly with annual cumulations, 1900 to present. Major investment service composed of seven financial manuals: *Moody's Transportation Manual; Moody's Public Utilities Manual; Moody's Bank and Finance Manual; Moody's Industrial Manual; Moody's OTC Industrial Manual; Moody's International Manual; Moody's Municipal and Government Manual.* Provides corporate news and financial information on American, Canadian, and foreign companies listed on U.S. stock exchanges. Loose-leaf news reports, covering corporate news releases, are issued twice each week. Annual volumes include brief company history, subsidiaries, plants, officers and directors, products, and financial data. Special features pertinent to subject area. All titles indexed in *Moody's Complete Corporate Index* (pamphlet).

*Moody's Stock Survey* (New York: Moody's Investors Service). Published weekly. Presents data on stocks including recommendations for purchase, sale, or exchange of individual stocks. Discussions on industry trends and developments.

*Standard and Poor's Corporation Services* (New York). Offer comprehensive investment data weekly, with annual cumulations. Their publications include *American Exchange Stock Reports; Bond Outlook; Called Bond Record; Convertible Bond Reports; Daily Dividend Record; Facts and Forecast Service* (daily); *Industry Issues; The Outlook; Stock Reports: Over-the-Counter and Regional Exchanges; Standard NYSE Stock Reports.*

*Standard Rate and Data Service* (Wilmette, Ill.). Issues 12 volumes of publishing rates and data on the following areas: Business Publications (monthly); Canadian Advertising (monthly); Consumer Magazine and Farm Publications (monthly); Direct Mail Lists (semiannually); Networks (bimonthly); Newspapers (monthly); Print Media Production Data (semiannually); Spot Radio (monthly); Spot Television (monthly); Transit Advertising (quarterly); Weekly Newspaper (semiannually); plus a Newspaper Circulation Analysis.

*Trading Areas and Population Data in Eastern United States* (New York: Hagstrom). Issues a number of maps of the metropolitan New York, Philadelphia, and adjacent areas. These are city, county, and special area maps giving detailed information useful to marketing and forecasting.

*United Business and Investment Report* (Boston). Published weekly. This investment service offers a commentary on the current situation with a forecast of business, financial, and economic conditions.

Loose-leaf services offer efficient, up-to-date information, especially for business law topics and taxes. Laws, regulations, rules, orders, and decisions, along with explanations and interpretations, are set up in loose-leaf volumes. Weekly or biweekly packets include new revisions in an effort to keep the business community current with frequent changes in the federal and state laws. The following are the major loose-leaf services.

Bureau of National Affairs, Inc., Washington, D.C. Issues reports on government actions which affect labor, management, and legal professions. Some of its reports are

*Daily Report for Executives.* Overnight service. Discusses such topics as legislation in Congress, tax rulings and decisions, transportation rulings, and price and cost trends.

*Daily Labor Report.* Overnight service. Discusses important labor-management agreements, major NLRB and court decisions.

Business International Corporation, New York. Publishes information about worldwide business problems and opportunities, emphasizes international management, laws, regulations, and business forecasts. Its loose-leaf services are

*Financing Foreign Operations* (New York: Business International). Published weekly. Eight-page weekly report for managers of worldwide operations.

*Investing, Licensing and Trading Operations Abroad* (New York: Business International). Published monthly. Current information for each country on foreign investment, competition, and price.

Commerce Clearing House Services, Chicago. Publishes more than 100 loose-leaf reports, covering various topics in the fields of tax and business regulatory law. Publications include *Federal Banking Law Reports, Government Contracts Reports, Contract Appeals Decisions, Insurance Law Reports.*

Prentice-Hall Services, Englewood Cliffs, N.J. Publishes loose-leaf reports covering the latest laws and regulations. Gives comments and interpretations of the laws. Publications include *American Federal Tax Reports, Tax Court Service, Tax Ideas, Prentice-Hall Management Letter.*

## 3.5. Directories

Directories provide brief data on companies, organizations, or individuals. They are used for a variety of purposes: to determine the manufacturer of a specific product; to check companies located in a particular area; to verify company names, addresses, and telephone numbers; and to identify company officers.

Benjamin, William A., ed., *Directory of Industry Data Sources: U.S. and Canada,* 2nd ed. (Cambridge, Mass.: HARFAX, 1982). Three volumes. Includes more than 15,000 annotated entries describing a wide range of information sources on 60 industries. Arranged in five parts: general reference sources; industry data sources; directory of all publishers mentioned in part 2; extensive subject and title indexes.

*Consultants and Consulting Organizations Directory,* 6th ed. (Detroit: Gale Research

Co., 1984). Indexes over 8000 firms, people, and organizations involved in consulting. Main arrangement is geographic, with subject, personal name, and organization name indexes.

*Corporate 500: The Directory of Corporate Philanthropy,* 2nd ed. (Detroit: Public Management Institute, 1982). Data about corporate philanthropy of the nation's 500 largest corporations. Lists eligible activities, corporate headquarters, board and committee members, contact people, and grant recipients.

Darnay, Brigitte, T., ed., *Directory of Special Libraries and Information Centers,* 8th ed. (Detroit: Gale Research Co., 1983). Three volumes: Special Libraries and Information Centers in the United States and Canada; Geographic and Personnel Indexes; New Special Libraries. Provides information about holdings, services, and personnel of more than 16,000 special libraries, information centers, and documentation centers.

*Directory of Corporate Affiliations* (Skokie, Ill.: National Register Publishing Co., Inc.). Published annually with quarterly updates titled *Corporate Action.* Lists 3000 American parent companies with their 16,000 divisions, subsidiaries, and affiliates.

Ethridge, James M., ed., *The Directory of Directories,* 3rd ed. (Detroit: Gale Research Co., 1985). Nearly 7000 informative, up-to-date listings of current directories; 2100 subject headings and cross references.

Kruzas, Anthony T., and Robert C. Thomas, eds., *Business Organizations & Agencies Directory,* 2nd ed. (Detroit: Gale Research Co., 1984). Supplies exact names to write, phone, or visit for current facts, figures, rulings, verifications, and opinions on business matters. Names agencies, associations, groups, federations, organizations, and, whenever possible, authorized contact people.

Kruzas, Anthony T., and Kay Gill, eds., *Government Research Centers Directory,* 2nd ed. (Detroit: Gale Research Co., 1982). Identifies research and development facilities funded by the government. Describes research centers, bureaus and institutes, testing and experiment stations, and statistical laboratories.

Kruzas, Anthony T., and Kay Gill, eds., *International Research Centers Directory,* 2nd ed. (Detroit: Gale Research Co., 1984). Identifies and describes research and development facilities throughout the world (excluding the United States). Includes government, university, and private installations.

*Million Dollar Directory* (New York: Dun and Bradstreet). Published annually in three volumes. Lists 39,000 U.S. companies worth $1 million or more. Gives officers and directors, products or services, SIC number, sales, and number of employees. Division, geographic, and location indexes. Also available as on-line data base.

*National Trade and Professional Associations of the U.S. and Canada and Labor Unions* (Washington, D.C.: Columbia Books, Inc.). Published annually. Listing of trade and professional organizations and labor unions with national memberships. Key word, geographic, and budget size indexes.

*Rand McNally International Banker's Directory.* Published semiannually. Multivolume. Referred to as the "Blue Book." Contains names of officers and directors of all banks in the world. Details include basic principles and practices of banking, with the latest information on all domestic and foreign banks, statements, personnel, U.S. banking, and commercial laws. Also includes the most accessible banking points for 75,000 nonbanking towns and Federal Reserve Districts and banks.

*Reference Book* (New York: Dun and Bradstreet Marketing Services Division). Published every two months. Available only to customers of D&B Business Information Reports. Detailed lists of names and addresses of U.S. firms by state, city, SIC code, line of business, estimated financial strength, and credit appraisal. Information can be retrieved in any desired sequence.

*Research Centers Directory,* 9th ed. (Detroit: Gale Research Co., 1984–1985). Listings include research institutes, centers, foundations, laboratories, bureaus, experiment stations, and similar nonprofit research facilities, activities, and organizations in the United States and Canada. Identifies special research facilities and their availability for use by outsiders. Contains sections on business, economic, and multidisciplinary programs. Subject research center and institutional indexes.

*Research Services Directory,* 2nd ed. (Detroit: Gale Research Co., 1982). Lists for profit organizations providing research services on a contract or fee-for-service basis to clients. Covered research activities include business, education, energy and the environment, agriculture, government, public affairs, social sciences, art and the humanities, physical and earth sciences, life sciences, and engineering and technology.

Schmittroth, John, Jr., ed., *Telecommunications Systems and Services Directory* (Detroit: Gale Research Co., 1983). Three parts. Four indexes, cumulative in each part. Provides descriptions of communications systems serving the need for rapid and accurate transmission of data, voice, text, and images. Covers voice and data communications networks, teleconferencing, videotex and teletext, electronic funds transfer, telex, facsimile, and two-way cable television.

*Standard and Poor's Corporation Records* (New York: Standard and Poor's Corp.). Published semimonthly in loose-leaf format, 1925 to present. Corporate news and financial information on American, Canadian, and foreign companies. Provides company history, officers, and product data. *Daily News* covers current corporate developments. Indexes to main entry and subsidiaries.

*Standard and Poor's Register of Corporations, Directors and Executives* (New York: Standard and Poor's Corp.). Published annually, 1928 to present. Volume 1: Alphabetical list of U.S. and Canadian corporations includes product or line of business, SIC code, and number of employees. Volume 2: Alphabetical list and brief biography of executives in United States and Canada. Volume 3: Indexes corporations by SIC code, geographic area, new individuals, obituaries, and new companies.

*Surveys, Polls, Censuses, and Forecasts Directory* (Detroit: Gale Research Co., 1983). Describes studies conducted in many areas including economics, business, science, and technology.

*Thomas Register of American Manufacturers* (New York: Thomas Publishing Co.). Published annually. Comprehensive U.S. directory restricted to manufacturing firms. Volumes 1–7 are indexes to manufacturers by product. Volume 7 includes a list of trade names. Volume 8 lists manufacturers by company name, including information similar to Standard & Poor's *Register.* Volumes 9–12 are compilations of manufacturers' catalogues.

Wasserman, Paul, and Marek Kaszubski, eds., *Law and Legal Information Directory,* 2nd ed. (Detroit: Gale Research Co., 1982). Guide to national and international organizations, bar associations, the federal court system, federal regulatory agencies, law schools, continuing legal education, paralegal education, scholarships and grants, awards, prizes, special libraries, information systems and services, research centers, legal periodical publications, book and media publishers.

Wasserman, Paul, and Janice McLean, eds., *Training & Development Organizations Directory,* 3rd ed. (Detroit: Gale Research Company, 1983). Contains profiles on 1967 individuals and organizations that conduct training and development programs for business, industry, and governments.

## 3.6. Biographies

Biographical reference books are useful sources of information regarding people, living or deceased. They provide dates of birth and death, nationality, and information about occupations.

*Dun and Bradstreet's Reference Book of Corporate Management* (New York: Dun and Bradstreet). Published annually. Directory of top executives arranged by company, birthdate, college, and employment history.

*Who's Who in America* (Chicago: Marquis Who's Who, Inc.). Published every two years. Biographies of prominent living Americans.

*Who's Who in Consulting* (Detroit: Gale Research Co., 1983). Reference guide to professional personnel engaged in consultation for business, industry, and government.

*Who's Who in Finance and Industry* (Chicago: Marquis Who's Who, Inc.). Published every two years. Contains brief biographies of financial and industrial, national and international leaders.

*Marquis Who's Who Publications/Index to All Books* (Chicago: Marquis Who's Who, Inc.). Published annually. An index to 250,000+ biographical sketches currently contained in Marquis' *Who's Who* volumes.

## 3.7. Doctoral Dissertations

Somewhat obscure sources of research are the unpublished doctoral dissertations required in university Ph.D. programs. These are clearly indexed and available on photocopies or microfilm:

*American Doctoral Dissertations* (Ann Arbor, Mich.: University Microfilms International). Published annually. A complete listing of all doctoral dissertations accepted at American and Canadian universities. Arranged by broad subject classification and, under each heading, alphabetically by name of university. Author index. Publication is slow.

*Dissertation Abstracts International* (Ann Arbor, Mich.: University Microfilms International). Published monthly. Section A: The Humanities and Social Sciences; Section B: The Sciences; Section C: European Dissertations. Informative abstracts of dissertations submitted by more than 345 cooperating institutions. Arranged in same categories as *American Doctoral Dissertations;* each issue is a detailed "Keyword Title Index." *DATRIXII* offers a personalized search service for all past and current dissertations.

## 4. STATISTICAL SOURCES

Statistics are an absolute necessity to decision makers. They are becoming increasingly valuable and available through computer on-line data bases. The most comprehensive compilations are provided by governmental agencies, universities, and trade associations. These statistics determine U.S. and regional business trends. Data are also gathered for specific industries. Examples are banking and monetary statistics; labor and marketing statistics; and plant and equipment expenditures studies. Other sources concentrate on important international statistics and foreign economic trends.

Statistical sources are divided into two major sections: indexes and selected statistical sources for general information, and international and industrial marketing statistics.

### 4.1. Indexes

Predicasts, Inc., *Predicasts Forecasts* (Cleveland: University Circle Research Center). Published quarterly, cumulated annually. Abstracts business and financial forecasts for specific U.S. industrial products and the general economy. Presents composite data for economic, construction, energy, and other indicators.

*Standard and Poor's Trade and Securities Statistics* (New York: Standard and Poor's Corp.). Loose-leaf, with monthly supplements. Current and basic statistics in the following areas: banking and finance; production and labor; price; indexes (commodities); income and trade; building and building materials; transportation and communications; electric power and fuels; metals; auto, rubber and tires; textiles, chemicals, paper; agricultural products; security price index record.

Wasserman, P., J. O'Brien, and K. Clansky, *Statistics Sources: A Subject Guide to Data on Industrial, Business, Social, Educational, Financial and Other Topics for the U.S. and*

*Internationally,* 9th ed. (Detroit: Gale Research Co., 1984). Finding guide to statistics indexes information from domestic and international sources. Arranged dictionary style; includes selected bibliography of key statistical sources.

## 4.2. Selected Statistical Sources

**4.2.1. General**    Levine, Sumner N., ed., *The Dow Jones–Irwin Business and Investment Almanac* (Homewood, Ill.: Dow Jones–Irwin). Published annually. Tables and graphs. Most basic, comprehensive statistical information on various aspects of business, finance, investments, and economics for recent trends. Includes articles on tax, accounting, and labor developments. Subject index.

**4.2.2. Industry**    Many business projects involve gathering statistical and/or investment data on a particular industry. The following sources provide useful statistics on leading industries and analyze current trends and future projections:

Balachandran, M., *A Guide to Trade and Securities Statistics* (Ann Arbor, Mich.: Pierian Printing, 1977). Specialized guide of composite statistical data available in 30 of the most widely used loose-leaf services and statistical yearbooks. Analyzed on an item-by-item basis, using a subject/keyword approach. Sources are listed and described at the front of the volume.

*Real Estate Analyst Reports* (St. Louis: Wenzlick Research Co.). Published monthly. Loose-leaf real estate analyses include *The Agricultural Bulletin; As I See* (commentary); *Construction Bulletin; Mortgage Bulletin; Real Estate Analyst.*

*Yearbook of Industrial Statistics* (New York: United Nations). Published annually. Supplemented monthly in *Monthly Bulletin of Statistics.* Volume 1: General Industrial Statistics. A body of international statistics on population, agriculture, mining, manufacturing, finance, trade, and education. Volume 2: Supplies internationally comparable data on the production of industrial commodities internationally.

**4.2.3. Marketing**    Access to current statistical data is essential to those engaged in market research. Marketing departments attempting to determine sales potential, set sales quotas, or establish effective sales territories are interested in details such as population, number of households, age, sex, marital status, occupation, education level, income, and purchasing power. Much of this information is available from U.S. government sources. Individual states also publish statistical series, often on a more timely basis than the federal government. Private companies also generate data applicable to marketing functions.

*Commercial Atlas and Marketing Guide* (Chicago: Rand McNally Services). Published annually, 1884 to present. Includes maps for each state in the U.S. and a section of maps of foreign countries. Marketing statistics for states and some world-wide data, such as airline and steamship distances, are provided. Also included are population statistics and figures for retail sales, bank deposits, auto registrations, etc., for principal cities.

*Editor and Publisher Market Guide* (New York: Editor and Publisher). Published annually, 1884 to present. Market data are provided for more than 1500 U.S. and Canadian cities in which newspapers are published. Included are figures for population, households, principal industries, and retail outlets. Estimates are given by country and newspaper city, and strategic market segment analysis is performed for such items as population and personal income. Total retail sales are arranged by state.

*Survey of Business Power Data Service* (New York: Sales and Marketing Management). Published annually, 1977 to present. A spin-off of the July and October statistical issues of *Sales and Marketing Management* magazine. Arranged in three volumes: Volume 1, county and city population characteristics, such as household distribution, effective buying income, total retail store sales, and various buying power indexes. Volume 2, retail sales by individual store groups and merchandise line. Volume 2 includes retail sales by individual store groups and merchandise line categories for the current year. Volume 3, TV market data, metro area and county projections for population, effective buying income, and retail sales.

**4.2.4.**
**International**

*International Marketing Handbook* (Detroit: Gale Research Co., 1981). Provides a marketing profile of 138 nations. Data regarding transportation and utilities, credit, foreign trade outlook, investment, industry trends, distribution sales, advertising and research, trade regulations, and market profile. 1983 supplement.

*Consumer Europe 1982,* 4th ed. (Detroit: Gale Research Co., 1982). Provides data on the production, sales, and distribution of more than 150 consumer product categories. Focuses on Western Europe.

*European Marketing Data and Statistics* (London: Euromonitor Publications Ltd.). Published annually. The volume's 70,000 statistics provide current marketing data on the population, employment, production, trade, economy, consumer expenditures, market sizes, retailing, housing, health and education, culture and mass media, and communications of Europe's 26 major countries.

*Handbook of the Nations,* 3rd ed. (Detroit: Gale Research Co., 1983). Provides political and economic data for 190 countries. Economic data include statistics on the GNP, agriculture, major industries, electric power, exports, imports, major trade partners, and the budget.

*Index to International Statistics* (Washington, D.C.: Congressional Information Service). Published monthly, with quarterly and annual cumulations. Indexes publications of international intergovernmental organizations, such as the U.N., the Common Market, and the World Bank. Geographic index is included.

*International Marketing Data and Statistics* (London, Euromonitor Publications Ltd.). Published annually. Handbook that supplies statistical tables and latest data for 45 countries in the Americas, Africa, Asia, and Australia. Information is geared toward marketing use.

*Japanese Trade Directory* (Tokyo: Japan External Trade Organization, 1984–1985). Provides information about 1700 Japanese companies and their 8500 products and services. Three sections: products and services, prefectures and companies, advertising.

Stopford, John M., ed., *World Directory of Multinational Enterprises,* 2nd ed. (Detroit: Gale Research Co., 1982). Two volumes. Provides information on 550 multinational corporations, with five-year financial summaries. Ranks corporations according to sales, diversification, and other criteria.

Wasserman, Paul, and Jacqueline O'Brien, *Statistics Sources,* 9th ed. (Detroit: Gale Research Co., 1984). Facts and figures on 12,000 subjects for nearly every country in the world. Arranged in dictionary style with cross-references, it cites annuals, yearbooks, directories, and other publications.

*World Bank Annual Report* (Washington, D.C.: World Bank). Published annually. Tables. Summarizes the activities of the World Bank and International Development Association. Reviews economic trends in developing countries, capital flow, and external public department.

*World Business Cycles* (London: The Economist Newspapers Ltd., 1982). Provides business and economic data for three decades (1950–1980) for many countries worldwide. Also provides longer-term data for Great Britain and the United States.

*World Trade Annual* (New York: Walker & Co.). Published annually. Five volumes offering statistics and detailed information on various aspects of the world trade situations.

Sources from which this article was compiled:

Bernard Bernier, Katherine Gould, and Humphrey Porter, *Popular Names of U.S. Government Reports* (Washington, D.C.: Library of Congress, 1976).

David M. Brownstone and Gorton Carruth, *Where to Find Business Information. A Worldwide Guide for Everyone Who Needs the Answers to Business Questions* (New York: Wiley, 1979).

Lorna M. Daniells, *Business Information Sources* (Berkeley: University of California Press, 1976).

Oscar Figueroa and Charles Winkler, *A Business Information Guidebook* (New York: AMACOM, 1980).

C. R. Goeldner and Laura M. Dirks, "Business Facts: Where to Find Them," *MSU Business Topics,* Summer 1976, pp. 23–36.

Andrew S. Grove, *High Output Management* (New York: Random House, 1983).

Richard L. King, ed., *Business Serials of the U.S. Government* (Chicago: American Library Association, 1978).

Linda J. Piele, John C. Tyson, and Michael B. Sheffey, *Materials and Methods for Business Research,* Library ed. (New York: The Libraryworks, 1980).

Paul Wasserman, C. C. Georgi, and J. Woy, *Encyclopedia of Business Information Sources,* 4th ed. (Detroit: Gale Research Co., 1980).

## Section A  Strategic Management: Planning and Implementation

**1**  COCA-COLA COMPANY
  Lincoln W. Deihl, Kansas State University
  Thomas C. Neil, Atlanta University

**2**  LEVI STRAUSS & COMPANY: TAKING AN INDUSTRY GIANT PRIVATE
  Neil H. Snyder, University of Virginia
  Lloyd L. Byars, Atlanta University

**3**  JOHNSON PRODUCTS COMPANY, INC.: THE CHALLENGES OF THE 1980s
  Thomas L. Wheelen, Robert L. Nixon, Marian Hessler, Jan Hunter, Bob
    Bailey, and Tony Arroyo, University of South Florida
  Neil H. Snyder, University of Virginia

**4**  A NOTE ON THE BREWING INDUSTRY
  Michael D. Caputa, Virginia Polytechnic Institute and State University

**5**  IT'S MILLER TIME
  Thomas C. Neil and Lloyd L. Byars, Atlanta University

**6**  THE ADOLPH COORS COMPANY
  Jeffrey M. Miner and Larry D. Alexander, Virginia Polytechnic Institute
    and State University

**7**  XEROX CORPORATION PROPOSED DIVERSIFICATION
  J. David Hunger, George Mason University
  Thomas Conquest  and William Miller, Iowa State University

**8**  A. H. ROBINS AND THE DALKON SHIELD
  Neil H. Snyder, University of Virginia

**9**  THE AUTO INDUSTRY IN THE UNITED STATES: STRUCTURE AND STRATEGY
  Ernest R. Nordtvedt, Loyola University in New Orleans

**10**  LEE IACOCCA'S CHRYSLER
  Ernest R. Nordtvedt, Loyola University in New Orleans

**11A**  TURNER BROADCASTING SYSTEM, INC.
  William H. Davidson, University of Southern California

**11B**  TURNER BROADCASTING SYSTEM, INC.
  Neil H. Snyder, University of Virginia

**12**  NCNB CORPORATION
  Lloyd L. Byars and Debra Thompson, Atlanta University

**13**  McDONALD'S CORPORATION
  Lloyd L. Byars and Denise Murray, Atlanta University

# PART FIVE
## CASE STUDIES IN
## STRATEGIC MANAGEMENT

14 BURGER KING'S BATTLE FOR THE BURGERS
   Larry D. Alexander and Thomas W. Ripp, Virginia Polytechnic Institute
      and State University
15 QUAKER OATS COMPANY
   Lloyd L. Byars and Wanda Benjamin, Atlanta University
16 MCI COMMUNICATIONS
   Lloyd L. Byars and Deirdre Creecy, Atlanta University
17 TANDY, INC.
   Sexton Adams, North Texas State University
   Adelaide Griffin, Texas Woman's University
18 CORPORATE PLANNING AT BORG-WARNER IN THE 1980s
   William C. Scott, Indiana State University
19 THE LINCOLN ELECTRIC COMPANY, 1984
   Arthur Sharplin, Northeast Louisiana University
20 7-ELEVEN STORES: CONVENIENCE 24 HOURS A DAY
   Jeremy B. Fox and Larry D. Alexander, Virginia Polytechnic Institute
      and State University
21 WAL-MART STORES, INC.
   Sexton Adams, North Texas State University
   Adelaide Griffin, Texas Woman's University
22 MARY KAY COSMETICS, INC.
   Sexton Adams, North Texas State University
   Adelaide Griffin, Texas Woman's University
23 MOBIL CORPORATION
   Robert R. Gardner and M. Edgar Barrett, Maguire Oil and Gas Institute,
      Southern Methodist University
24 KERR-McGEE CORPORATION
   Roger M. Atherton, Northeastern University
   Mark W. Bushell, University of Oklahoma
25 DELTA AIR LINES: WORLD'S MOST PROFITABLE AIRLINE
   Elizabeth Lavie and Larry D. Alexander, Virginia Polytechnic Institute
      and State University
26 WASTE MANAGEMENT, INC.
   Robert G. Wirthlin and James Kendrix, Butler University
27 NIKE, INC.
   Robert G. Wirthlin and Anthony P. Schlichte,
      Butler University
28 COMMUNITY MENTAL HEALTH CENTER
   E. R. Worthington, West Texas State University

### Section B  Small Business

29  CIRCUIT SERVICES NORTH
   Harriett Stephenson and Patrick Koeplin, Seattle University
30  HINES INDUSTRIES, INC.
   Robert P. Crowner, Eastern Michigan University
31  RAINBOW FOOD COMPANY
   Thomas M. Bertsch, James Madison University

### Section C  International Business Cases

32  FORD OF EUROPE AND LOCAL-CONTENT
   REGULATIONS
   H. Landis Gabel and Anthony E. Hall, INSEAD
33  NITROFIX GHANA
   William A. Stoever
34  MULTIQUIMICA DO BRASIL
   Mary Pat Cormack and M. Edgar Barett, Maguire Oil
   and Gas Institute, Southern Methodist University

### Section D  Social Responsibility

35  UNION CARBIDE OF INDIA, LTD. (1985)
   Arthur Sharplin, Northeast Louisiana University
36  MANVILLE CORPORATION
   Arthur Sharplin, Northeast Louisiana University

# Section A   Strategic Management: Planning and Implementation

# 1   Coca-Cola Company

Lincoln W. Deihl
Kansas State University

Thomas C. Neil
Atlanta University

Before the United States put its first space vehicle into orbit, foreign cartoonists had assumed that American satellites would be built along the familiar lines of a Coca-Cola bottle. In their eyes, as in the eyes of many people abroad, Coca-Cola is a fluid that, like gasoline, is responsible for, and symbolic of, the American way of life. The two legends, indeed, are often thought of as compatible, even though gasoline is one of the few solutions around that has not yet been mixed with Coke. An English cartoon showed the space shuttle fueled in flight by a pair of aerial tankers, one furnishing gas to the engines, the other Coca-Cola to the crew.[1]

**HISTORY**   Coca-Cola entered the market originally as one of thousands of exotic medicinal products belonging to the nationwide patent medicine industry. Coca-Cola was created by founder Dr. John Styth Pemberton in May 1886. The extract of "Coca" was blended with the "Cola" extract to form a syrup base for a new and wondrous "Brain Tonic."

Dr. Pemberton sold 25 gallons of syrup the first year and spent $46, or about 90 percent of his receipts, for advertising. In 1886, Asa Candler purchased all the rights to the product. In 1892, the Coca-Cola Company was formed as a Georgia corporation with capital stock of $100,000. In 1893, the trademark Coca-Cola was registered in the U.S. Patent Office. In the same year, the company paid its first dividend. Candler, a firm believer in advertising, laid the foundation of promotion through coupons and souveniers. The bottling of Coca-Cola started in 1894 in Vicksburg, Mississippi, and continued until 1899, when the company granted rights to bottle and sell Coca-Cola in practically the entire continental United States.

By 1904 the annual sales for Coca-Cola syrup reached one million gallons, and there were 123 plants authorized to bottle the finished drink. The Coca-Cola Company was the first to introduce the glass containers in 1915 and the cans in 1954. The cans have been found well suited for the overseas shipment of the finished drinks.

In 1919, the company was sold to Ernest Woodruff, an Atlanta banker, and an investor group for $25 million. Robert W. Woodruff was elected president succeeding Howard Candler. Moving aggressively, the company established a foreign sales department. A concentrate for the syrup was developed which reduced transportation costs. At the present time, Coca-Cola is served in 155 countries.

Since 1960, the company has acquired more than 13 different kinds of businesses ranging from food, wine, and bottling to entertainment in the form of movies. In 1984, Coca-Cola decided to license its trademark to a complete line of leisure wear. The company has divested itself of selected businesses, the latest being its Wine Spectrum, Taylor California Cellars, in 1983.

## GENERAL ORGANIZATION AND MANAGEMENT

Roberto C. Goizueta is the chairman of the board of directors and the chief executive officer of the Coca-Cola Company. His appointment as CEO was an important step forward, signaling an end to what many expected to be a messy fight to succeed Austin (former CEO), orchestrated by the CEO himself. Austin, who was not known for his gentle methods ("He is the ice man," said a competing bottler), set up an intense competition for Coke's number two spot after he suddenly forced popular president Lucin Smith out of office in 1979. By creating an office of the chairman, made up of six vice-chairmen plus the chief financial officer, he forced the contenders to "tough it out" for the right to be president and, presumably, move on to the top spot.

Roberto C. Goizueta, was born in Cuba and came to the United States when he was 18 to study chemical engineering at Yale University. A year later, Goizueta completed his prep-school studies at Cheshire Academy as class valedictorian. After Yale, Goizueta returned to Havana, joining Coke in 1954 as a quality control chemist at $500 a month.

Fidel Castro nationalized Coke's Cuban business in 1961. By then Roberto C. Goizueta had been transferred to Coke's Carribean area headquarters in Nassau. His background was mainly technical, and many of Coke's 551 independent U.S. bottlers wish he had had direct experience with marketing soft drinks. Goizueta noted, "Mr. Austin was Coca-Cola's first lawyer and Mr. Woodruff didn't finish college." In any case, Goizueta preferred to describe his role as one of "an orchestra conductor," not "a first violinist."[2]

"Selecting Goizueta, a foreign born executive, is welcome recognition that Coke is truly an international company," said Kevin B. Skislock, investment officer of Brown Brothers Harriman, noting that almost all of Coca-Cola's earnings growth during 1970–1982 came from overseas. Timothy Griffith of Merrill Lynch pointed out that Goizueta's inexperience in soft drinks can work to his advantage. "He has a free hand in that he didn't come through any special branch of the company—he's not a soft drink man or a coffee man or whatever. Executives have a tendency to stay overly loyal to operations they once ran."[3]

Some observers thought that his appointment as chairman and CEO of the company was beneficial. Economic conditions in the United States were rough. They were very similar to conditions which many foreign countries had faced in the past: double-digit inflation, declining productivity, and escalating costs. Goizueta was one executive who had firsthand knowledge of dealing with these problems and managing successfully in spite of them. In addition, he brought a conciliatory brand of management philosophy to what was the world's largest beverage firm and to what, until his promotion, suffered from diffused executive management.

Discussing the operation of the company, for example, he stressed:

> . . . and yet, our business is truly multilocal in nature, because our products are produced and sold for the most part by local, independent entrepreneurs—our 1500 franchised bottlers of Coca-Cola. In the U.S. we are associated with over 500 of the best American Companies—our partners—our Coca-Cola bottlers. And that's where the real strength of our business system lies.[4]

Roberto C. Goizueta is a man of very definite opinions, "but only if they are right," and he takes the time to find out if they are right, commented a long-time supplier to the industry who knew the new chairman from his days in Latin America.[5]

In January 1980, Goizueta made what was at that time the most important decision in the 47-year history of the product: allowing its bottlers to substitute high-fructose corn-based syrup for sucrose. "Our bottlers are absolutely delighted," Goizueta said.[6] Fructose is roughly 40 percent cheaper than sugar, and Coke used 15 percent of the fructose consumed in the United States in 1982. He, naturally, wanted something in return. "It gives the bottlers a nice edge, which I hope they will use to promote the product."

At a New York press conference on April 23, 1985, Coca-Cola said they had made the best better in a new formula. After a taste test of over 190,000 persons, with 55 to 45 percent preferring the new taste, Coke was changed. Eighty-eight days later, in response to a tidal wave of protest by devout Coke drinkers, the company brought back the old formula, renamed Coca-Cola Classic.

Roberto C. Goizueta has ruled out the possibility of acquiring fast-food businesses. "We will not compete with our customers, which include the fast food people and their fountain business," said Goizueta, aiming a swipe at rival PepsiCo and its ailing Pizza Hut restaurant chain.[7]

He was not altogether content with Coke's existing business either. Coffee, for instance, where Coke made Butter-Nut and Maryland Club, was not safe from his axe. Even though coffee was profitable, it had not been percolating. "It provides

$400 million (sales) which helped with the overhead, but it was not growing," he observed.[8]

Donald R. Keough was elected president, chief operating officer, and director of the Coca-Cola Company in March 1981. At age 56, he moved up from senior executive vice-president, with responsibility for all operating units and the corporate marketing division. He had also been president of the company's food division and Coca-Cola U.S.A.

Sam Ayoub, age 63, was senior executive vice-president and chief financial officer of the company. He was treasurer of the company from May 1976 to November 1977, and vice-president from May 1976, to March 1979. From March 1979, to May 1980, he served as senior vice-president of the company. On May 30, 1980, he was selected executive vice-president, general operations, of the company, and served in that capacity until August 1981, when he assumed his present position, senior executive vice-president and chief financial officer.

## Employees

The company and its subsidiaries employed approximately 39,000 persons, of whom approximately 17,000 were located in the United States. Through its divisions and subsidiaries, the company had entered into numerous collective bargaining agreements and management had no reason to believe it would not be able to renegotiate any such agreements on satisfactory terms. Management of the company generally believed that its relations with its employees were satisfactory.

## SOFT DRINK OPERATIONS

Coca-Cola began a dynamic new advertising campaign with the introduction of its caffeine-free versions of Coca-Cola, Tab, and Diet Coke brands. Coca-Cola was extremely successful with its ad themes. The important changes in attitudes and behavior occurring among the country's young people were carefully researched by the company, with expenditures totaling nearly $3.5 million.

Exhibit 1.1 illustrates the 1984 rankings by market share and sales of the top ten soft drinks in the industry. Coke was leading the market percentages with 24.8 percent of the total industry. The total volume of sales (millions of cases) had Coke heading the list with 1584 million cases.

Coca-Cola plunged into no-caffeine cola, introducing no-caffeine versions of its Coke and Diet Coke brands, predicting that demand for decaffeinated colas would equal May 1983 levels of diet drink sales by 1985. Coke was capitalizing on its trademark name to catch up in the market. The company's strategy was to introduce the no-caffeine versions as line extensions in order to avoid the "cannibalization" of the company's main cola drinks.

A new marketing innovation gave the company a competitive edge, with the introduction of talking vending machines, each costing over $3000 and equipped with computerized voice synthesizers to converse with consumers. Other new designs included energy-efficient machines and vendors equipped with electronic games for play after purchase.

**Exhibit 1.1** Coca-Cola Company: The Top Ten Soft Drink Brands

| Brand | 1984 Market Percent | 1984 Sales (millions of cases) |
|---|---|---|
| Coke | 24.8 | 1,584.6 |
| Pepsi | 18.1 | 1,155.6 |
| Diet Coke | 6.9 | 439.8 |
| 7UP | 5.3 | 335.9 |
| Dr. Pepper | 4.7 | 298.0 |
| Sprite | 3.3 | 214.0 |
| Diet Pepsi | 3.1 | 198.5 |
| Mountain Dew | 2.8 | 176.6 |
| RC | 2.2 | 140.1 |
| Tab | 2.1 | 131.3 |
| Top ten total | 74.3 | 4,674.4 |
| Other brands | 26.7 | 1,720.3 |
| Total industry | 100.0 | 6,394.7 |

*Source: Beverage World,* March 1985.

The number of soft drink vending machines in use throughout the United States ranged from 1.1 million to 1.8 million in late 1983. Of these, 600,000 to 800,000 were Coca-Cola's. PepsiCo was gaining a substantial footing in the race for the vending market share.

**Diet Coke** The 1982 annual report highlighted Diet Coke as the "Company's most significant new product entry in 96 years," with greater than 60 percent of its volume coming from sales of competitive products or from new soft drink consumers. Extending its precious trademark to a new product in 1982, the company was committing itself to the rapid expansion of the new worldwide market for low-calorie beverages.

The commitment to Diet Coke returned tenfold with its movement into position number three in 1984. It appears, however, that this growth was supported in part by the decline by Tab from number five in 1982 to number ten in 1984.

**Cherry Coke** With a bow to nostalgia, longtime soda fountain favorite Cherry Coke was introduced in April 1985 into four U.S. test markets. The product is an extension of the Coke line rather than a new product, and the company is anticipating a 2 percent market share. Cherry Coke is being positioned as an alternative cola taste with a target market of males and females aged 12 to 29.

**Advertising** Since the slogan "Delicious and Refreshing" was first used in 1886, advertising for Coca-Cola has reflected the pleasant things in life. Advertising expenditures were over $11,000 by 1882, and by 1920 had reached $2 million. Radio has been used since 1927 and television since 1950. (See Exhibits 1.2 and 1.3.)

In 1929, the company's first universal slogan "The Pause That Refreshes" appeared and set a standard that was not matched until 1963. In 1963, "Things Go Better with Coke" emerged as a worthy successor to the pause. In the early seventies, riding the tide of concern for world harmony, the jingle "I'd Like to Give the World . . ." sung by a multinational group of young people was presented.

The company's commitment to wholesome, high-quality advertisement has a history incorporating the works of Norman Rockwell and Hoddin Sundblom's "portraits" for holiday ads. Begun in the 1930s, Sundblom's pictures established the standard for the rosy-cheeked, red-suited Santa Claus. Famous names in Coke advertising included Jean Harlow, Johnny Weissmuller, Cary Grant, Clark Gable, and Bill Cosby. In an award-winning television commercial, "Mean" Joe Greene and a small admirer raised a lump in the throat and a tear in the eye.

Exhibit 1.4 shows the company's popular soft drink brands available in the United States

## Bottlers and Can Containers

Attempts to design a can for Coca-Cola originated in 1940, but it was only after the end of World War II, when steel became more plentiful, that the company made significant progress distributing the cans in the domestic markets. The sale of Coke in cans increased sharply between 1969 and 1976. After 1970, the dynamic contour design with the trademarks "Coca-Cola" and "Coke" was featured on all cans for Coca-Cola.

## Distribution Channels

The company manufactures soft drink syrups and concentrates which it sells to bottling and canning operations and to approved fountain wholesalers. Syrups are comprised of sweetener, water, and flavoring concentrate. The bottling and canning operations, whether independent or company-owned, combine the syrup with carbonated water and package the final product for sale to retailers. Packaged soft drinks are distributed to consumers in cans, returnable and nonreturnable glass bottles,and plastic packaging. Fountain wholesalers sell soft drink, syrups to fountain retailers, who sell soft drinks to consumers in cups and glasses. Some syrups and concentrates, however, are completely processed for sale to the ultimate consumer by the canning and bottling operations of the company's susidiaries.

During 1984, the company sold about 70 percent of its soft drink syrup and concentrate gallonage in the United States to approximately 500 bottlers who prepared and sold the products for the food store and vending machine markets. The remaining 30 percent was sold to approximately 4000 authorized fountain retailers. The parent company provided promotional and marketing support to its bottlers and developed and introduced new products, packages, and equipment in order to assist its bottlers. Coca-Cola continued its bottler restructuring

**Exhibit 1.2** Coca-Cola Company: Estimated 1981 Total Media Spending

|  | Total (Millions) | Per Gallon |
|---|---|---|
| Coca-Cola | $ 72.0 | $ 2.40 |
| Dr. Pepper | 14.2 | 2.58 |
| PepsiCo | 56.3 | 2.57 |
| Royal Crown | 10.2 | 2.67 |
| 7UP | 36.9 | 6.80 |

*Source: Beverage World Periscope,* May 1983, p. 8.

**Exhibit 1.3** Coca-Cola Company: Soft Drink Market, 1981–1982 Media Expenditures (in thousands of dollars)

|  | Media Dollars | |
|---|---|---|
|  | 1981 | 1982 |
| Magazines | $ 350,000 | $ 276,000 |
| Supps. | — | — |
| Newspapers | 2,191,000 | 2,535,000 |
| Network TV | 15,203,000 | 17,197,000 |
| Spot TV | 20,446,000 | 26,878,000 |
| Network radio | — | — |
| Spot radio | 6,231,000 | 6,123,000 |
| Outdoor | 2,458,000 | 2,602,000 |
| Total | $ 46,879,000 | $ 55,611,000 |

*Source:* "Coca-Cola Soft Drink," brand report, *Marketing and Media Decisions,* July 1983, p. 90.

**Exhibit 1.4** Coca-Cola U.S.A.: Soft Drink Products of the Coca-Cola Company

| | |
|---|---|
| New Coca-Cola | Fresca |
| Coca-Cola Classic | Mr. Pibb |
| Diet Coke | Sugar-free Mr. Pibb |
| Caffeine-free Diet Coke | Mello-Yello |
| Tab | Fanta |
| Caffeine-free Tab | Hi-C soft drinks |
| Sprite | Ramblin' Root Beer |
| Sugar-free Sprite | Sugar-free Ramblin' Root Beer |

*Source:* Consumer Information Center, Coca-Cola U.S.A., a division of Coca-Cola Company, Atlanta, Ga.

begun in 1981. In 1984, bottlers were acquired in Ohio, Michigan, Oregon, and California.

Coca-Cola is pushing ahead with technological changes. Bag-in-box non-returnable fountain syrup packing systems, first tested on the West Coast, were made available nationally in 1984. The bag-in-box does away with the cumbersome metal cylinders, is cheaper to manufacture, and does away with pickup and recycling.

The third-generation vending machine with video display, voice simulation, and coupon dispensing is in the final testing phase. This machine will be unique in that it will offer a choice of products in several prices and sizes.

In the food sector, the company continues to push aseptic packaging. Aseptic packaging, especially for the fruit juices, is seen as opening previously untapped consumer consumption.

## COMPETITION

Among Coca-Cola's leading competitors are PepsiCo, Seven-Up, Dr. Pepper, and Royal Crown.

## PepsiCo

Pepsi-Cola U.S.A. had been playing the numbers game again, asserting that Pepsi-Free was the third-largest-selling cola in 1983. Pepsi-Free, it was claimed, held more than 50 percent of the caffeine-free segment and was the number-three cola in the United States (considering both sugar and sugar-free versions). (This lead was lost to Diet Coke in 1984.) The Diet Pepsi commercials were found to be more traditional, warmer—targeting women, with increased focus on taste rather than low-calorie content.

The Pepsi-Free commercials focused on moods of celebration. The ads showed all sorts of people drinking Pepsi-Free, offering bottles and cans to TV viewers and singing, "We are Pepsi-Free."[9] The success of Pepsi-Free and Sugar-free Pepsi-Free, however, was due to fundamental shelf positioning. Sugar-free accounted for 40 percent to 50 percent of Pepsi-Free's total sales. Health consciousness was the reason cited for its popularity. The lemon-flavored Pepsi Light was repositioned to appeal to men. Pepsi was making every effort to be the leader in the decaffeinated beverage market—the fastest-growing segment of the domestic soft drink industry.

PepsiCo netted sales of $7,499,000,000 for the year ending December 31, 1982. The projected sales for the calendar year 1984 was $8.3 billion. "The new advertising strategy calls for an approach based on segmentation," said the Pepsi vice-president of advertising. The company had slated an ad budget of $40 million for brand Pepsi.

Mountain Dew was sold mostly on a single-drink basis in cold boxes and vendors. The target market was the American teenager, particularly the male teenager.[10]

**Seven-Up**   Seven-Up Company, a division of Philip Morris, Inc., continued its assault on the soft drink industry with increased emphasis on the "no artificial flavoring or coloring" aspect, through commercials. Competitors did not feel good about Seven-Up.

In 1982, Seven-Up garnered 5 percent of the total market, superseding and pushing Dr. Pepper to the fourth position. Estimated sales for 1982 were $11,-716,000,000, an increase from $10,886,000,000 over the previous year. A change in Seven-Up's advertising approach in 1983 resulted in increased market share and shipment gains, but with less than significant increases in earnings (as reflected in its remaining number four at 5.3 percent in 1984). Promotional outlays had been stepped up. Seven-Up used a new advertising approach—antiadditive for Like (caffeine-free) positioned against Coke and Pepsi, which had not been received well in the soft drink circles.

**Dr. Pepper**   The discounting effect by Coca-Cola and PepsiCo in many of Dr. Pepper's prime areas had an adverse effect on the company's unit volume. Dr. Pepper lost unit volume in 1982, and Sugar-free Dr. Pepper continued to lose market share. The company netted sales of $516.1 million in 1982, an increase from $364 million the previous year.

To compete with Coke and Pepsi, Dr. Pepper initiated a new marketing approach, seeking out "new markets" of opportunity. New markets of opportunity meant attempting to strengthen areas that were already strong, and not to do more than they were capable of doing. Dr. Pepper cut back on network television advertising for 1983, favoring regional spots funded jointly by the company and its bottlers. It introduced a caffeine-free product, Pepper-Free, during January 1983, with the idea of extending the life cycle of its products. It was acclaimed as a nationwide leader in the mixer category with Canada Dry, USA, which Dr. Pepper acquired in 1982, doing well in fiscal 1983.

Canada Dry, the popular ginger ale, increased its unit volume a sound 15 percent in the first six months of 1982 and boasted a 37 percent share of the domestic ginger ale business in late 1983. The increase of 1982 sales by Dr. Pepper was primarily due to the Canada Dry acquisition.

**Royal Crown**   In 1983, Royal Crown was still a small factor in the highly competitive soft drink business, although it was the nation's fifth largest soft drink manufacturer in 1982. It introduced decaffeinated and sugarless RC 100 in the spring of 1980. The parent company recorded sales of $469.8 million in 1982, with sales of 18 million cases in 1981 and 35 million cases in 1982.

Royal Crown entered a new soft drink category with the distribution of Diet Rite Cola, which contained neither salt nor caffeine. Catering to the U.S. consumer's concern with health, RC's "no-salt" approach was geared to attack Seven-Up's marketing approach of combating others for containing artificial flavors or colors. In 1981, 33.1 million cases of Diet Rite were sold; in 1982, 32.1 million cases were sold.

**FOODS BUSINESS SECTOR**

The Foods Business Sector includes citrus products, Minute Maid and Hi-C, coffee, spring water, and household consumer goods. In 1984, the net operating revenues were $1.5 billion with operating income of $150 million.

**Foods Division**

The Coca-Cola Company Foods Division products mainly include Minute Maid fruit juices and ades; Hi-C fruit drinks and Five-Alive beverages; two regionally marketed coffees, Maryland Club and Butter-Nut brands; spring water; and nonedible products. In 1983, the operating income was $121 million in revenues of $1,285,000,000.

**Citrus Products**

Harvested at the peak of flavor, fresh fruit is quickly processed and the juice extracted and concentrated under strict quality controls at the division's processing plants. The concentrate is used to make Minute Maid juices and ades as well as Five-Alive fruit beverages, and as the basis for many Hi-C fruit drinks.

Keeping abreast of changing consumer needs is vital to the success of the Foods Division. Before a new product is introduced nationally, it has been tested extensively. This testing is a lengthy process—sometimes taking as long as seven or eight years.

The division faced difficulties when a freeze in January 1982 was followed by a devastating freeze on December 25, 1983. Approximately 40 percent of Florida's orange crop as well as its trees were destroyed. Also occurring in 1983 was the introduction of competitive brands backed by significant promotion. In response, Coca-Cola worked out an agreement with Brazilian fruit growers to supply concentrate and began an intense advertising campaign in 1984.

Minute Maid brand orange juice gained both record volume and record market in 1982. Overall unit sales for the division's frozen products increased 7 percent. Chilled products increased 3 percent. Despite the problems of 1983, Minute Maid remained the industry leader that year with 24 percent of the market.

Snow Crop Five-Alive, introduced in 1979, had become one of the division's strongest brands. This product ranked second in sales among all frozen products, surpassed only by Minute Maid brand orange juice.

The division extended the Minute Maid line with new products. Minute Maid frozen concentrated orange juice with more pulp was introduced successfully, and Minute Maid reduced-acid orange juice was tested in selected markets. It also introduced Hi-C in the Drink Box, teaming aseptic packaging with the nation's number one fruit drink, in January 1983. In 1984, aseptic packaging was used for Minute Maid orange juice and then for a fruit punch. The division was the first

U.S. firm to market an aseptic-packaged fruit drink nationwide. The innovative package was sterilized to require no refrigeration or preservatives. From 1977 to 1982, the Foods Division introduced 35 new items or products in test markets, with 50 percent becoming successful. Continuing its aggressiveness learned from the cola fountain service, the division placed Minute Maid orange juice into Denny's, Days Inns, and Marriott.

**Other Products**

Coffee production is another facet of the division's operations. Unroasted coffee beans purchased from around the world are roasted to perfection, specially blended, and ground to the desired fineness at two Foods Division plants. Maryland Club is processed in Houston for distribution primarily in the Southwest, and Butter-Nut is processed in Omaha for Midwest distribution. The division maintained market share for its coffee products although both suffered from the U.S. decline in coffee consumption from 38 gallons per capita in 1966 to 27 gallons in 1982. In order to combat this downturn, decaffeinated was introduced under both brands while emphasis was given to the coffee food service business. In 1984, unit volume for coffee grew 2 percent. Exhibit 1.5 shows the division's market share of the regular coffee market.

Also in the Foods Division are pasta foods, spring water, and plastic wraps and films. In line with the strategy of developing or acquiring new product bases, the division acquired Ronco Foods Company, its first venture into the marketing of solid foods. Ronco manufactures high-quality pasta products, marketed primarily in the Southwest.

Belmont Spring Water Company, Inc., continued to grow in 1984 as consumer demand for bottled water increased in the company's greater Boston market. Sales volume rose to 25 percent in 1984.

Presto Products, Inc., in Appleton, Wisconsin, is a leading private-label supplier of plastic wraps and films. In 1984, unit volume and revenue growth continued to be favorable, with revenues up 14 percent.

**WINE SPECTRUM**

The Coca-Cola Company announced on September 26, 1983, the sale of its Wine Spectrum, Taylor California Cellars, to the New York subsidiary of the world's

**Exhibit 1.5** Coffee Market Shares

|                          | 1982 |
|--------------------------|------|
| General Foods            | 34.8 |
| Procter & Gamble         | 23.0 |
| Coca-Cola Maryland Club  | 1.0  |
| Butter-Nut               | 2.4  |

Source: *Advertising Age,* May 9, 1983, p. 82.

largest distiller, the Montreal-based Seagram Company, for about $210 million. Coke sold out for only marginally more than it had invested—probably about $150 million in terms of their Wine Spectrum operations.

**Operations**

In 1975 and 1976, the Coca-Cola Company wanted to move into endeavors where there would be opportunity for growth. Since the fastest-growing beverage was wine, and Coke was a beverage company, a wine company seemed a natural choice. Coke took over the 97-year-old Taylor Wine Company in early 1977 and renamed it Taylor California Cellars in November 1977.

Wine Spectrum grew more quickly than any of its rivals during 1980–1982 (Exhibit 1.6), moving from 9.3 million 9-liter cases to 13.5 million. After Heublein Wines decided in 1983 to sell its lower-priced United Vintners brands back to its growers, Coke's unit rose to number two from number three in the industry. But growth and size alone were not enough for Coke.

According to Chairman Roberto C. Goizueta, Coke decided to "concentrate our resources in the areas of our business where the returns on assets are highest."[11] In 1982, the company had a net income of $512 million on $6.2 billion in revenues, but its wine business was estimated to have earned only $6 million on $220 million in sales.

A number of observers suggested that Coke's sale was at least prompted by pressure from Wall Street. Marvin Shanken, publisher of *Impact,* said, "They were influenced by Wall Street's desire for immediate returns, and that made Coke unwilling to make the kind of long-term investment spending that was necessary to build the brands."[12] It expanded long-term contracts with growers and invested $34 million in its Gonzales Winery, the largest investments in a production facility Coke has made in its 97-year history. Part of the problem was that Coke banked on nonstop growth and "the market failed to keep up," says wine consultant Ed Everett.[13]

**Exhibit 1.6** Six Largest American Wineries—Total Wine Shipments (millions of 9-liter cases)

| 1982 Rank | Winery | 1980 | 1981 | 1982 |
|-----------|--------|------|------|------|
| 1 | E & J Gallo | 51.3 | 55.3 | 57.8 |
| 2 | Heublein Wines | 22.1 | 21.2 | 20.2 |
| 3 | The Wine Spectrum | 9.3 | 11.7 | 13.5 |
| 4 | Almaden | 13.5 | 12.8 | 12.1 |
| 5 | The Wine Group | 9.1 | 9.1 | 9.1 |
| 6 | Paul Masson (Seagram) | 7.4 | 7.8 | 8.1 |
| | Total | 112.7 | 117.9 | 120.8 |

*Source: Marketing & Media Decisions,* August 1983, p. 116.

**Market and Competition**

California table wine shipments flattened at 273 million gallons in 1982 after a decade of 10 percent annual growth. Wine inventories soared 16 percent to 685 million gallons between 1981 and 1982.

But California's main problem mirrored that of Detroit and Pittsburgh. While domestic sales flattened, wine imports grew 6.5 percent, continuing their steady climb of the past decade. Their market share reached almost 24 percent compared with 13 percent in 1975. American producers reacted by offering the deepest discounts in memory. Prices of magnum-size jugs plunged by half after 1981.

If the future belongs to the low-cost producer, nobody was better positioned than E & J Gallo. Gallo enjoyed operating economies at every stage of making wine. Analysts admitted that their estimates of the dollar volume of its sales were $650 million to $700 million a year. One rival firm insisted, "Gallo has everything, just loves selling more wine, and earns a zero rate of return on sales." Few in the wine business took seriously the idea that the Gallo winery did not make money.[14]

Almaden's parent, National Distillers and Chemical Corp., reported that the winery's operating profits fell in 1981 and 1982 by 50 percent, to $10.5 million on revenues of $180.6 million in 1982. Its case sales dropped 5.3 percent in 1982.

In October 1982, R. J. Reynolds bought Heublein, which was facing a 6.6 percentage point drop in market share since 1975. Robert M. Furek, president of Heublein's wine division, said, "Profits had become the biggest issue in the business."[15]

Lower prices seem destined to become permanent in the California wine business. The companies which survive are likely to be the efficient and aggressive wine makers who can keep costs down and spend heavily to build their brands.

**COLUMBIA PICTURES INDUSTRIES, INC.**

The Coca-Cola Company entered the dynamic and fast-growing entertainment industry on June 22, 1982, with the acquisition of Columbia Pictures Industries, Inc.

Columbia was a major producer and distributor of motion pictures and television programming. In addition, Columbia had become an important factor in the growing pay-television, videocassette, and videodisk markets. Throughout its 62 years of existence, it had built a vast library of more than 1800 film titles and thousands of hours of television programs.

Columbia's activities reflected its dedication to fulfill a well-defined strategy which called for an increase in annual volume of filmed entertainment, expansion of outside financing of film production costs, continued control of distribution of its products, maintenance of the properties in its library, establishment of profitable market share in the video game business, and formation of new lines of business. The record box-office receipts achieved by Columbia in 1982 clearly underscored the long-term growth potential of the newly formed entertainment business sector of the Coca-Cola Company.

## The Motion Picture Industry

Most indications pointed to a continuing high in box-office receipts for the motion picture industry topping the 1982 record year.

Through the first half of 1983, receipts totaled $1.74 billion (based on data reported by *Industry Surveys*), 8.5 percent above year-earlier figures. Optimistic expectations for the year were based on the success of summer releases. Between Memorial Day and Labor Day, receipts rose about 8.1 percent to $1.50 billion. Although this approximately equaled the increase in ticket prices for 1983, the number of tickets sold remained at 1982 levels—when attendance set records by wide margins. In 1982, summer ticket sales totaled about 470 million, some 8 percent higher, year to year. Dollar volume exceeded the 1981 figure by 15 percent and the average for 1978–1980 by 40 percent.

The summer and Christmas seasons are critically important because they are periods of relative leisure for the principal movie audience—persons under 24 years of age. During 1978–1983, 37.5 percent of annual box office receipts were generated during the summer months.

## Megahits Capture the Market

The heavy box office for the summer of 1983 followed a customary pattern: The bulk of consumer spending went to a few megahits, with relatively smaller amounts spread among all the rest. The big winners for the year shaped up as *Return of the Jedi, Tootsie, Trading Places, War Games,* and *Flashdance.* During 1984, the blockbuster was *Ghostbusters,* Columbia's all-time box-office attraction grossing over $88 million in just 19 weeks. Although not as dramatic in income, *Karate Kid,* grossing $25 million between September 1984 and April 1985, was acclaimed as a warm, sensitive picture.

The movie industry is characterized by inherent earnings volatility, reflecting changing public tastes, the individual nature of each film project, and the lack of continuity in the business. As a relatively inexpensive form of entertainment, motion pictures had historically exhibited little correlation to economic fluctuations. It had even been argued that box-office totals were helped by unfavorable economic conditions, since people tended to reduce outlays for other, more expensive diversions; films provided a convenient method of escaping unpleasant realities.

## Production and Budgets Rise

In 1982, 184 films were produced by major studios and independents—compared with 205 in 1981, 209 in 1980, and 248 in 1979—largely due to rising production costs. During 1973–1983, however, rising costs caused a substantial drop in total production. In 1972, the average production cost $1.5 million to complete. By 1982, rising inflation, increasing studio overhead, rising interest rates, and large single-picture guarantees for stars pushed the average cost to $10 million.

However, in the first eight months of 1983, the number of films in production rose 31 percent to 145, from 111 in the comparable 1982 period. The record year had an impact and everyone wanted to be on the bandwagon.

**Independent Production Continues to Grow**

Rising costs had for some time prompted the major producer/distributors to spread their risk by increasingly distributing films made by outside production companies and by attracting capital from outside sources.

The major companies had various sources of cofinancing for in-house productions. Although tax shelter financing was largely eliminated by changes in U.S. tax laws in the mid-1970s, some were available in foreign countries. Other cofinancing arrangements included foreign sale and lease backs, joint ventures with nonentertainment companies, advances from pay-television exhibitors, and publicly sold limited partnerships.

Examples of the last were the Delphi I and Delphi II partnerships organized and marketed through syndicates of major underwriters. Each of these partnerships had raised $60 million through minimum subscriptions of $5000 for investment in Columbia Pictures productions.

**Diversification Spreads Risk**

Most film entertainment companies had diversified into other fields in recent years, either by making acquisitions or being acquired themselves. For example, MCA, Inc. (Universal Pictures) were active in the production of television programs and records, music publishing, retailing, mail order and book publishing, as well as its Universal Studio tour and other tours and services. Walt Disney Productions (Buena Vista) had a dominant position in the theme park area, while Warner Communications (Warner Bros.) had interests in recorded music, cable television, book publishing, traditional and electronic games, and direct-response marketing. Paramount Pictures was a part of Gulf + Western Industries, and Columbia Pictures was a 1982 purchase of the Coca-Cola Company.

**Operations of Columbia**

The 1978–1983 periods had been good ones for Columbia. It had seen its revenues advance at a compound growth rate of 17 percent to $780 million in the fiscal year which ended June 30, 1982. In 1984, the entertainment sector earned $121 million, an increase of 34 percent over 1983.

A vital element of Columbia's aggressive strategy was its library of some 1800 film titles and thousands of hours of television programming. The tremendous growth rate in the entertainment industry had enormous implications for Columbia because pay television had a virtually insatiable demand for programs, a demand which was being filled largely by showing movies produced by Columbia and other studios.

Its strategy was to increase the number of movies to catch up with its competitors (illustrated in Exhibit 1.7), improving its chances of producing more successful and profitable films. Toward that goal, Columbia planned to increase motion picture production levels to meet the full capacity of the excellent distribution system. It also continued its efforts to attract the best producers and creative talent to its studios to ensure further success.

**Exhibit 1.7** Coca-Cola Company: U.S. Film Distributors—Market Share Breakdown

| Company | 1980 | | 1981 | | 1982 | |
|---|---|---|---|---|---|---|
| | Rank | Share % | Rank | Share % | Rank | Share % |
| Universal (MCA, Inc.) | 1 | 20 | 3 | 14 | 1 | 30 |
| Paramount (Gulf & Western Inc.) | 2 | 16 | 2 | 15 | 2 | 14 |
| 20th Century-Fox | 2 | 16 | 4 | 13 | 2 | 14 |
| MGM/UA[a] | 6 | 7 | 6 | 9 | 4 | 11 |
| Warner Brothers | 4 | 14 | 1 | 18 | 5 | 10 |
| Columbia Pictures | 4 | 14 | 4 | 13 | 5 | 10 |
| Walt Disney Productions (Buena Vista) | 7 | 4 | 8 | 4 | 7 | 4 |
| Embassy | 8 | 3 | 7 | 5 | — | — |

[a]MGM acquired UA from Transamerica Corp. in July 1981; prior to that, UA distributed MGM's films domestically.

*Source: Industry Surveys,* October 13, 1983.

In 1984, Columbia Pictures Television group, producer of prime-time and daytime series, miniseries, and made-for-television movies was the largest contributor to the entertainment sector's earnings.

## INTERNATIONAL OPERATIONS

When Robert W. Woodruff was elected president of the Coca-Cola Company on April 28, 1923, the amount of Coca-Cola being sold outside the United States, Canada, and Cuba was infinitesimal. And that's why, as the 33-year-old Woodruff took office, he quickly became concerned as to the reason for such a poor showing. He was convinced that there was rewarding market potential the world over for a product of such demonstrated consumer appeal.

So it was logical that in 1926, President Woodruff launched the first organized effort to sell Coca-Cola overseas through establishment of a Foreign Department in New York City. At that time, there were fewer than a dozen plants bottling Coca-Cola offshore. By 1950, when the Foreign Department became the Coca-Cola Export Corporation, there were 65 bottlers of Coca-Cola in 30 offshore countries.

In 1983, seven of the world's ten largest bottling plants were offshore. The largest bottler of Coca-Cola and allied products in the world was in Buenos Aires, Argentina. The second largest bottler was in Mexico City. Exhibit 1.8 shows the total consumption and per capita consumption in selected countries.

In 1984, non-U.S. operating earnings increased 4 percent, with good perform-

**Exhibit 1.8** Coca-Cola Company: Soft Drinks Are
International Favorites

| Country | 1981 Total Consumption (million liters) | 1981 Per Capita Consumption (liters) |
|---|---|---|
| United States | 31,000 | 147 |
| West Germany | 4,310 | 70 |
| Japan | 2,680 | 54 |
| United Kingdom | 2,000 | 36 |
| Canada | 1,990 | 89 |
| Spain | 1,810 | 52 |
| Benelux | 1,750 | 63 |
| Italy | 1,350 | 24 |
| Colombia | 1,300 | 49 |
| Venezuela | 1,260 | 91 |
| Australia | 950 | 65 |
| South Africa | 800 | 27 |
| Malaysia | 260 | 19 |
| Puerto Rico | 230 | 69 |
| Singapore | 130 | 29 |

*Source: Beverage World Periscope,* December 4, 1982.

ance in Europe, Africa, the Pacific, and Canada; earnings in Latin America declined primarily due to the economic environment. The modest increase was due to the strong dollar.

Coca-Cola was sold in over 155 countries through more than 900 local independent and company-owned bottlers in 1982. In 1982 also, markets outside the United States and Puerto Rico accounted for 64 percent of total unit sales of the soft drink operations.

In March 1982, a massive international rollout of the new Diet Coke was begun. By August 1982 Diet Coke was in 35 countries. By 1984, 41 markets had been penetrated with a unit volume increase of 105 percent. Diet Coke contributes an average of 8 percent of Coca-Cola sales on the international scene. In Japan, introduced as Coca-Cola light, the beverage has garnered a 68 percent share of the low-calorie market.

The long-term strategic objective for Coca-Cola is to achieve growth in the international market by increasing per capita soft drink consumption. Outside the United States, soft drink consumption is only 15 percent of the U.S. total. Focusing on increasing frequency of use, emphasis is placed on product availability, product variety, and product positioning. Consumption increase is encouraged through occasion use, vending machine availability, and enlarging fountain outlet use. In 1985, Coca-Cola moved into the 275-million-person market of the Soviet Union. During the ten years ending in 1984, Coca-Cola experienced an average growth in unit volume of 6 percent.

**Latin America**    In Mexico, the company's second largest world market by sales volume, a 10 percent unit volume gain outperformed the industry in 1982. In 1984, the unit volume increase was a modest 3 percent in response to a slight easing of price controls. The company increased its share of the fountain segment, launched Tab in cans, and increased coverage of both Coke and Sprite. Economic pressures affected a unit sales decline of 7 percent in Brazil and more than 20 percent in Argentina. Rebounding in 1984, Coca-Cola experienced a 17 percent volume gain in Brazil, where the economy had improved. In Argentina, a 33 percent volume gain was due to the low prices of Coca-Cola products being held in place by price controls. In Ecuador, unit sales had doubled from 1977 to 1982. In 1982, Colombia became the seventh largest market for Coca-Cola worldwide.

In December 1982, a wave of poisonings in which caustic soda was put in bottles of Coca-Cola, and which involved threats of more poisons being added to other beverages—similar to the Tylenol poisonings in the United States—swept Brazil. Sales of Coke temporarily dropped an estimated 10 percent in the Rio area.

In the Diet Coke segment, the main barrier to Diet Coke's entry in Brazil was a tough government regulation that maximum recommended consumption of the diet beverage clearly be stated on the label. "You have to give maximum intake a day, not more than half a liter a day," said Coca-Cola Brazil's marketing director Jorge Giganti. "It's like a medicine. You can't launch it as a diet product."[16]

In Argentina, three years after the introduction of Tab in 1980, category sales accounted for 55 percent of the overall soft drink market. Tab was soon followed by Coca-Cola's low-calorie Sprite in May 1981 and Seven-Up Company's Diet 7UP in September 1982.

But Seven-Up president Ruben Roys was not optimistic about the potential for growth in the segment in Argentina, since "market studies show that even the most emancipated diet drink consumer will seldom ask for such a drink at restaurants and pubs, and that diet drinks will continue to appeal mostly to women."[17]

**Europe**    The introduction of Diet Coke (called Coca-Cola Light in certain countries) in Germany, Great Britain, and other countries in 1983 spearheaded aggressive marketing that in 1982 earned an outstanding unit volume increase of approximately 10 percent for company products in Europe.

West Germany, the company's largest market in Europe, achieved 9 percent unit growth and an increase in corporate market share in 1982. Sluggish economic conditions in 1984 held volume gains to less than 3 percent. Germany had an underdeveloped diet-drink category that posed problems for Diet Coke. One reason was heavy mineral water consumption, and another was that laws permitted only limited use of sweeteners.

In Spain, the second largest European market, 1984 unit sales increased slightly. Aiding the sales effort were expanded availability of Sprite and growth in the fountain segment. In Italy, sales of Sprite continued strong following its

1981 introduction; overall unit volume gained 10 percent in 1982 but slipped to 5 percent in 1984 again due to slow economic growth.

Coca-Cola continued to lead the cola segment in Great Britain, where the company's unit sales rose 12 percent in 1982. Diet drinks accounted for 5 percent of Britain's total soft drink market, but as much as 45 percent of that was accounted for by Schweppes's slim line range and only 20 percent by colas. However, the diet cola segment grew by 30 percent in volume in 1982 with little promotional support, and many observers believed that it was ripe for expansion. Diet Pepsi held 55 percent of this business, with Tab trailing at 15 percent. The Diet Coke introduction could mean the end of Tab, or at a least dramatic cut in sales. In order to improve per capita consumption the southern United Kingdom bottler was purchased. New management was installed and directed to aggressively pursue increasing product availability and awareness.

In the Soviet Union, new bottling operations in the city of Tallin supported a good performance in 1982 by Fanta Orange. In 1985, the Moscow market became available. In France, there was no chance of introducing Diet Coke because of stiff rules preventing the use of all artificial sweeteners (including aspartame) except through pharmacies. The country's powerful sugar beet interests had been successful in their fight to prevent France from conforming with EEC standards, which permit the use of artificial sweeteners.

In Norway, artificial sweeteners were forbidden except for use by diabetics, and the term diet or low calorie could not appear on labels; drinks like Tab were technically only for use by diabetics. Still, the irony was that 11 percent of soft drinks sold in Norway were diet; only the United States and Canada rank higher. In countries like Norway and Germany, where the word diet connotes illness, Diet Coke became Coke Light, but that may cause problems, too. Authorities warned that if there was a sharp increase in consumption of these drinks, they would ban the "Light" name and maybe diet drinks as well.

**Africa**  In Egypt, the company's business more than doubled during 1982 as new plants were brought into production. Unit volume was up 13 percent in South Africa, following the introduction of the 1.5-liter bottle, a new tangerine flavor for Fanta, and the launch of the 500-milliliter nonreturnable bottle. South Africa's continuing problems with apartheid influenced economic vitality and resulted in a volume growth of 3 percent. The company saw potential for growth and profits from Tab and the low-calorie segment in South Africa. Diet Coke was introduced in the market in June 1982. The diet segment held 4 percent of the soft drink market. Coke had to address image problems in South Africa, largely due to the race issue.

In this segmented market, where soft drinks were expected to grow 12 percent in 1983, blacks consumed 70 percent of the soft drinks. But only 4 percent of that was low-calorie. Among whites, however, 20 percent of the soft drinks consumed were in that category. In 1982, Tab held 80 percent of the diet segment, with Diet Pepsi (which was still not available nationwide) covering the rest.

In Nigeria, governmental import restrictions caused erratic shipment patterns and a 59 percent lower volume. The company hopes that new markets in the Sudan and Congo can lead to an overall upswing in volume in the African market.

**Far East**    For the Far East, excluding Japan, unit volume rose 8 percent. The standout performance came in the Philippines, where unit volume rose 16 percent. This market growth was fueled by introductions of the 12-ounce returnable bottle for Coke, the 1-liter resealable returnable bottle, and Mello Yello. In Korea, the company achieved a 3 percent gain in unit growth.

In Australia, where the diet segment was 12 percent of the total soft drink market in 1982, Tab had well over 50 percent of the cola category, with Diet Pepsi holding a smaller share. The company introduced Diet Coke in the Australian market in June 1982. A strengthening economy in 1984 led to a 7 percent volume gain.

The entire soft drink market had been undergoing a slow but steady decline in Australia, with diet drinks static over 1982, following the introduction and success of mineral waters (including new flavored varieties). Fortunately for the soft drink industry, this trend appears to be reversing.

**Canada**    Historically, the diet segment of the Canadian soft drink market ranged from around 8 percent to 10 percent of the total market until 1977, when saccharin was banned. By 1979, the diet share of the market had shrunk to 2 percent. In 1982, the first full year aspartame was available, the diet segment had not only regained historical levels, it had grown to 15 percent of the total market by year's end, while the total market itself had doubled.

Figures for April–May 1982 showed food store sales of diet soft drinks at a new high of 21.4 percent of the total and still growing. Roy Lockyer, president and CEO, Canada Dry Ltd., said, "It's 21% already and it could go to 30% by the end of 1983. It's heading that way."[18] Exhibit 1.9 shows the diet drink market as a percent of the total soft drink market. Coca-Cola Ltd. showed a 6 percent unit volume gain in 1984, double the Canadian industry growth rate of 3 percent. During the third quarter of 1984, Minute Maid orange soda was introduced in markets covering 40 percent of the Canadian population.

**Coca-Cola Export Corporation**    The Coca-Cola Export Corporation is a rare blend. On the one hand, it is thoroughly decentralized with as much decision making as possible pushed down through a hierarchy of zone, area, and regional offices to the person on the scene. On the other hand, its progress is increasingly the concern of Coke's people at the top.

Since most of the bottlers are local nationals, the company likes to think it is

**Exhibit 1.9** Diet Drink Market as
Percent of Total Soft Drink
Market

| Country | Percentage |
|---|---|
| United States | 20.0 |
| Canada | 13.0 |
| Australia | 12.0 |
| Norway | 11.0 |
| Argentina | 5.5 |
| Germany | 5.3 |
| England | 5.0 |
| South Africa | 4.0 |
| Japan | 0.1 |

Source: *Advertising Age*, March 14, 1983.

relatively immune to the dangers of expropriation. "It's a franchise business; if they nationalize the assets, they're nationalizing their own people," said J. Paul Austin, the former chairman of Coca-Cola Company.[19] Nevertheless, Coke was not entirely free of overseas hazards. Several Arab states shut them out some years ago because Coke refused to stop selling to Israel.

**BUSINESS OBJECTIVES AND STRATEGY**

Coca-Cola's core strategy is to increase shareholder value by achieving growth in earnings per share in excess of inflation and by increasing return on equity. The strategy will be achieved by focusing on the following:

1. *Increases in Unit Volume at Rates in Excess of Industry Rates for the Soft Drink and Foods Sectors.* Within the United States, the soft drink sector will accomplish this through marketing strength, positioning in the growing low-calorie segment, and the strengthening of the bottler system. The international focus will be on increasing per capita consumption through the mechanism of availability. The foods sector strategy will be one of product and package segmentation. Increases in unit volume will focus on layering new products into existing distribution systems.

The entertainment sector has as its key objective leveraging its distribution system through increased product flow without significantly increasing invested capital. Risk will be reduced through the use of equity and prelicensing agreements with such entities as Home Box Office and CBS, Inc.

2. *Profit Margins.* Coca-Cola's objective is to improve real profits per unit. This can be accomplished through tight controls over pricing, operating expenses, and operating effeciencies. In 1984, 91 percent of the bottlers agreed to give Coca-Cola more pricing flexibility in return for additional marketing expenditures.

**Exhibit 1.10** Selected Financial Data (dollars in millions except per share data)

| Year Ended December 31, | 1984 | 1983 | 1982^b | 1981 | 1980 | 1979 | 1978 | 1977 | 1976 | 1975 | 1974 |
|---|---|---|---|---|---|---|---|---|---|---|---|
| **Summary of operations^a** | | | | | | | | | | | |
| Net operating revenues | $7,364 | $6,829 | $6,021 | $5,699 | $5,475 | $4,588 | $4,013 | $3,328 | $2,928 | $2,773 | $2,425 |
| Cost of goods and services | 3,993 | 3,773 | 3,311 | 3,188 | 3,103 | 2,521 | 2,203 | 1,836 | 1,614 | 1,633 | 1,462 |
| Gross profit | 3,371 | 3,056 | 2,710 | 2,511 | 2,372 | 2,067 | 1,810 | 1,492 | 1,314 | 1,140 | 963 |
| Selling, administrative, and general expenses | 2,313 | 2,063 | 1,830 | 1,725 | 1,635 | 1,378 | 1,167 | 922 | 806 | 693 | 616 |
| Operating income | 1,058 | 993 | 880 | 786 | 737 | 689 | 643 | 570 | 508 | 447 | 347 |
| Interest income | 129 | 83 | 106 | 71 | 40 | 37 | 35 | 29 | 29 | 22 | 21 |
| Interest expense | 124 | 73 | 75 | 39 | 35 | 11 | 7 | 6 | 6 | 6 | 6 |
| Other income (deductions)—net | 5 | (3) | 7 | (23) | (9) | (3) | (14) | (9) | (4) | (8) | 5 |
| Income from continuing operations before income taxes | 1,068 | 1,000 | 918 | 795 | 733 | 712 | 657 | 584 | 527 | 455 | 367 |
| Income taxes | 439 | 442 | 415 | 355 | 329 | 318 | 300 | 268 | 245 | 218 | 170 |
| Income from continuing operations | $ 629 | $ 558 | $ 503 | $ 440 | $ 404 | $ 394 | $ 357 | $ 316 | $ 282 | $ 237 | $ 197^e |
| Net income | $ 629 | $ 559 | $ 512 | $ 482 | $ 422 | $ 420 | $ 375 | $ 331 | $ 294 | $ 249 | $ 204^e |
| **Per share data^c** | | | | | | | | | | | |
| Income from continuing operations | $ 4.76 | $ 4.10 | $ 3.88 | $ 3.56 | $ 3.27 | $ 3.18 | $ 2.89 | $ 2.56 | $ 2.29 | $ 1.93 | $ 1.60^e |
| Net income | 4.76 | 4.10 | 3.95 | 3.90 | 3.42 | 3.40 | 3.03 | 2.68 | 2.38 | 2.02 | 1.65^e |
| Dividends | 2.76 | 2.68 | 2.48 | 2.32 | 2.16 | 1.96 | 1.74 | 1.54 | 1.325 | 1.15 | 1.04 |
| **Year-end position** | | | | | | | | | | | |
| Cash and marketable securities | $ 782 | $ 611 | $ 261 | $ 340 | $ 231 | $ 149 | $ 321 | $ 350 | $ 364 | $ 389 | $ 241 |
| Property, plant, and equipment—net | 1,623 | 1,561 | 1,539 | 1,409 | 1,341 | 1,284 | 1,065 | 887 | 738 | 647 | 601 |
| Total assets | 5,958 | 5,228 | 4,923 | 3,565 | 3,406 | 2,938 | 2,583 | 2,254 | 2,007 | 1,801 | 1,610 |
| Long-term debt | 740 | 513 | 462 | 137 | 133 | 31 | 15 | 15 | 11 | 16 | 12 |
| Total debt | 1,363 | 620 | 583 | 232 | 228 | 139 | 69 | 57 | 52 | 42 | 69 |
| Shareholders' equity | 2,778 | 2,921 | 2,779 | 2,271 | 2,075 | 1,919 | 1,740 | 1,578 | 1,434 | 1,302 | 1,190 |
| Total capital^d | 4,141 | 3,541 | 3,362 | 2,503 | 2,303 | 2,058 | 1,809 | 1,635 | 1,486 | 1,344 | 1,259 |

## Financial ratios (percent)

| | | | | | | | | | | | |
|---|---|---|---|---|---|---|---|---|---|---|---|
| Income from continuing operations to net operating revenues | 8.5 | 8.2 | 8.4 | 7.7 | 7.4 | 8.6 | 8.9 | 9.5 | 9.6 | 8.5 | 8.1 |
| Income from continuing operations to average shareholders' equity | 22.1 | 19.6 | 19.9 | 20.2 | 20.2 | 21.5 | 21.6 | 21.0 | 20.6 | 19.0 | 17.1 |
| Long-term debt to total capital | 17.9 | 14.5 | 13.7 | 5.5 | 5.8 | 1.5 | .8 | .9 | .7 | 1.2 | 1.0 |
| Total debt to total capital | 32.9 | 17.5 | 17.3 | 9.3 | 9.9 | 6.8 | 3.8 | 3.5 | 3.5 | 3.1 | 5.5 |
| Dividend payout | 58.0 | 65.3 | 62.8 | 59.5 | 63.2 | 57.6 | 57.4 | 57.5 | 55.7 | 56.9 | 63.0 |

## Other data

| | | | | | | | | | | | |
|---|---|---|---|---|---|---|---|---|---|---|---|
| Average shares outstanding[c] | 132 | 136 | 130 | 124 | 124 | 124 | 124 | 123 | 123 | 123 | 123 |
| Capital expenditures | $ 391 | $ 384 | $ 382 | $ 330 | $ 293 | $ 381 | $ 306 | $ 264 | $ 191 | $ 145 | $ 154 |
| Depreciation | 166 | 154 | 144 | 133 | 127 | 106 | 88 | 77 | 67 | 64 | 57 |

[a] In June 1982 the company acquired Columbia Pictures Industries, Inc., in a purchase transaction.

[b] In 1982 the company adopted Statement of Financial Accounting Standards No. 52, "Foreign Currency Translation." See Note 10 to the Consolidated Financial Statements.

[c] Adjusted for a two-for-one stock split in 1977.

[d] Includes shareholders' equity and total debt.

[e] In 1974 the company adopted the last-in, first-out (LIFO) accounting method for certain major categories of inventories. This accounting change caused a reduction in net income of $31.2 million (25 cents per share) in 1974.

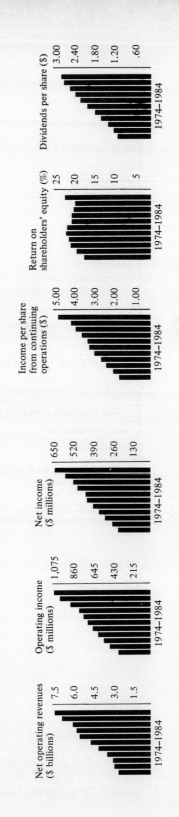

Net operating revenues ($ billions) — 1974–1984 (7.5, 6.0, 4.5, 3.0, 1.5)

Operating income ($ millions) — 1974–1984 (1,075, 860, 645, 430, 215)

Net income ($ millions) — 1974–1984 (650, 520, 390, 260, 130)

Income per share from continuing operations ($) — 1974–1984 (5.00, 4.00, 3.00, 2.00, 1.00)

Return on shareholders' equity (%) — 1974–1984 (25, 20, 15, 10, 5)

Dividends per share ($) — 1974–1984 (3.00, 2.40, 1.80, 1.20, .60)

**Exhibit 1.11** Consolidated Statements of Income (in thousands except per share data)

| Year Ended December 31, | 1984 | 1983 | 1982 |
|---|---|---|---|
| **Net operating revenues** | $ 7,363,993 | $ 6,828,992 | $ 6,021,135 |
| Cost of goods and services | 3,992,923 | 3,772,741 | 3,310,847 |
| **Gross profit** | 3,371,070 | 3,056,251 | 2,710,288 |
| Selling, administrative, and general expenses | 2,313,562 | 2,063,626 | 1,830,527 |
| **Operating income** | 1,057,508 | 992,625 | 879,761 |
| Interest income | 128,837 | 82,912 | 106,172 |
| Interest expense | 123,750 | 72,677 | 74,560 |
| Other income (deductions)—net | 5,438 | (2,528) | 6,679 |
| **Income from continuing operations before income taxes** | 1,068,033 | 1,000,332 | 918,052 |
| Income taxes | 439,215 | 442,072 | 415,076 |
| **Income from continuing operations** | 628,818 | 558,260 | 502,976 |
| Income from discontinued operations (net of applicable income taxes of $414 in 1983 and $4,683 in 1982) | — | 527 | 9,256 |
| **Net income** | $ 628,818 | $ 558,787 | $ 512,232 |
| **Per share:** | | | |
| Continuing operations | $ 4.76 | $ 4.10 | $ 3.88 |
| Discontinued operations | — | — | .07 |
| Net income | $ 4.76 | $ 4.10 | $ 3.95 |
| **Average shares outstanding** | 132,210 | 136,222 | 129,793 |

In 1984, high-fructose corn syrup was increased to the 100 percent level for Coca-Cola sold in bottles and cans. By January 1985, all diet drinks went to the use of 100 percent aspartame.

In 1984, the percentage of administrative and general expenses to gross profits was 16.8 percent compared to 17.7 percent in 1983. This reduction resulted in an operating income increase of over $30 million.

3. *Resource Management.* Coca-Cola attempts to achieve its goals by concentrating its resources in consumer markets offering a strategic fit, attractive returns, and high growth potential. For investments with risk characteristics similar to the soft drink industry, cost of capital is estimated to be 14 percent after taxes.

In 1984, Coca-Cola reinvested $339 million excluding fixed assets of purchased companies. Reinvestment was allocated among the sectors as follows: soft drink, 72 percent; foods, 12 percent; entertainment, 9 percent; corporate, 7 percent. Additionally, Coke acquired over $100 million in soft drink bottling territories and product lines.

## CAPITAL STRUCTURE

Coca-Cola attempts to maintain a strong financial position by using prudent amounts of long-term debt. During 1984, there were three $100 million long-term debt offerings with interest rates of 12.75, 11.75, and 11.375; at the close of 1984, long-term debt represented 17.9 percent of total capital. Future policy regarding the use of long-term debt will be on funding attractive investment opportunities. Exhibit 1.10 (pp. 276–277) details the financial review for 1974–1984. Exhibit 1.11 (p. 278) gives consolidated statements of income for 1982–1984.

## FUTURE OUTLOOK

Top management at Coca-Cola will no longer hide under the blanket of brand popularity. Goizueta stated, "With the exception of putting out a fire here and there, I'm devoting 90% of my time to strategic planning." The clear implication is that Coke is looking hard for acquisitions. Will he buy big and will the spending be in the United States?

## NOTES

1. E. J. Kahn, Jr., *The Big Drink, The Story of Coca-Cola* (New York: H. Wolff Manufacturing Co., 1960).
2. "Coca-Cola Cuban Libre," *Fortune,* September 8, 1980, pp. 15–16.
3. Neal Gaff, "Coke Fights Back," *Financial World,* September 15, 1980, pp. 17–20.
4. Paul E. Mullins, "Goizueta Clear Priorities at 'Multilocal' Coca-Cola," *Beverage Industry,* November 7, 1980.
5. Ibid.
6. Ibid.
7. Ibid.
8. Maurice Barnfather, "Coke's Cultural Revolution," *Forbes,* December 22, 1980, pp. 32–33.
9. Nancy Giges, "Colas Intensify Share Fight as Key Selling Season Heats," *The International Newspaper of Marketing,* August 8, 1983, Section I, pp. 1–2.
10. Larry Jabbonsky, "Segregating the Pepsi Generation," *Beverage World,* May 1983.
11. Michael Emerson, "Why Coca-Cola and Wine Didn't Mix," *Business Week,* October 10, 1983.
12. Ibid.
13. Ibid.
14. Gilbert T. Sewall, "Trouble for California Wine Makers," *Fortune,* April 18, 1983.
15. Ibid.
16. Carolyn Hulse, "Diet Coke Faces Hurdles as It Spreads World Wide," *Advertising Age,* March 14, 1983, pp. 68–72.
17. Ibid.
18. Special Report, "Canadian Bottlers See Diets at 30% of Market," *Beverage Industry,* September 1983, p. 1.
19. "How Coke Runs a Foreign Empire," *Business Week,* August 25, 1973.

# 2 Levi Strauss & Company: Taking an Industry Giant Private

Neil H. Snyder
University of Virginia

Lloyd L. Byars
Atlanta University

Levi Strauss & Company, founded in 1850, is the world's largest brand-name apparel manufacturer. It designs, manufactures, and markets a diversified line of apparel for men, women, and children including jeans, slacks, shirts, jackets, skirts, and hats. Most of the company's products are marketed under the Levi's trademark and are sold in the United States and in many foreign countries throughout North and South America, Europe, Asia, and Australia.

**BACK-GROUND**

Levi Strauss, a Bavarian immigrant who was lured to the West during the gold rush in search of prosperity, did not strike it rich in gold, but he found his fortune in jeans. His first pair of jeans was sold in 1853 to a San Francisco gold digger who wanted a sturdy pair of pants which would hold up in the mines. In time, his jeans became so popular that young Strauss set up a shop in San Francisco. Today the headquarters of Levi Strauss & Company (L. S. & Co.) stands near the same location as young Strauss's shop.

It was not until the 1930s that Levi's jeans reached the eastern market. Although attempts were made to promote jeans for resort wear, the basic clientele continued to be limited. World War II, however, created a sharp increase in demand, and jeans were sold only to individuals engaged in defense work. It also marked a turning point for Levi Strauss. The company had been largely a wholesale operation prior to World War II, but after the war, it began concentrating on manufacturing and direct sales. Before the war, L. S. & Co.'s annual sales were around $8 million, but by 1961 sales reached $51 million, mainly because of aggressive product diversification.

In 1981 L. S. & Co. was the largest manufacturer of jeans in the world, controlling about one-third of the jeans market. Additionally, it was the largest firm in the apparel industry, with products in virtually every product line and with sales and profits by far the greatest in the apparel industry. According to L. S. & Co. Chairman of the Board Peter E. Haas, "We'd like to outfit people from the cradle to the grave."

The authors would like to thank Debie Alford, Karen Davis, Allison Gillum, Jim Tucker, and Jeff Walker for their work on an earlier version of this case and Earlinda Elder for her work on this case.

Levi's success has resulted in part from the company's skill in sensing an emerging new market and responding quickly and in part from its strong management and exceptional brand-name acceptance. In addition, a focus on identifying market opportunities through segmentation in recent years has aided a diversification strategy. As a result, the company's growth and success have been strong despite the extreme competitiveness and cyclical nature of the apparel industry.

**OPERATIONS**    In November 1984, the company reorganized certain domestic operations. As a result its three major operating entities are now identified as the Jeans Company, Levi Strauss International, and Battery Street Enterprises. The company also has a corporate staff which performs financial, legal, and administrative functions.

**The Jeans Company**    The Jeans Company, the company's largest operating unit in terms of sales and profits, is the leading manufacturer of jeans in the United States. It consists of marketing units, each with specialized sales personnel. In addition to basic jeans for men and women, this entity markets a broad line of western wear and knit and woven shirts. It is also one of the world's largest brand-name manufacturers of children's clothing, including basic and fashion jeans, slacks, shirts, knit and woven tops, jackets, blouses, vests, and active wear. In 1984 approximately 21 percent of the Jeans Company's apparel production was provided by independent contractors.

The Jeans Company serves the domestic jeans market which consists primarily of young men and women aged 14 to 30 years old. Due to demographic changes in the 1980s, this market is forecast to decrease as a percentage of the population.

**Levi Strauss International**    Levi Strauss International is structured along geographic lines and primarily consists of the European, Canadian, Asia/Pacific, and Latin American divisions. These divisions are generally divided into countries, each considered a separate market. Each country within the European Division is generally responsible for sales, distribution, and finance activities. The headquarters in Europe coordinates merchandising and production activities. With few exceptions, Canada and each country in Latin America and Asia/Pacific is staffed with its own merchandising, production, sales, and finance personnel.

Levi Strauss International is substantially independent of the Jeans Company and Battery Street Enterprises in terms of manufacturing and distribution. Sales are derived primarily from basic lines of jeans, shirts, and jackets, although women's fit jeans, youth wear, menswear and related tops are also marketed in most areas. In 1984, approximately 28 percent of Levi Strauss International's apparel production was provided by independent contractors.

**Battery Street Enterprises**

Battery Street Enterprises consists primarily of Koret of North America, Menswear, and Battery Street Sportswear Divisions. In addition, Battery Street Enterprises includes several smaller operations. The manufacturing and distribution activities of Battery Street Enterprises are substantially independent of the Jeans Company and Levi Strauss International. In 1984, approximately 43 percent of Battery Street Enterprises' production was provided by independent contractors.

The Koret of North America Division manufactures and markets coordinates and related separates for women including skirts, pants, jackets, blouses, and other tops in misses, petite, and larger sizes in the United States and Canada. The Menswear Division manufactures and markets men's casual and dress slacks, sport coats and vests, including the Levi's Action garments. The Battery Street Division markets lines of casual sportswear under the Levi's brand, including pants, skirts, tops, and jackets. Size ranges are misses, large, petite, and tall.

Other business units within Battery Street Enterprises provide a variety of apparel lines. The Resistol Division produces western and fashion hats. The Oxxford Division produces fine men's and women's clothing under the Oxxford trademark. The David Hunter Division produces fine men's jackets, blazers and slacks. The Perry Ellis America Division markets a collection of men's and women's casual clothes designed by fashion designer Perry Ellis. The fashion Portfolio Division markets a collection of fashionable men's casual apparel under the Tourage SSE and CMA trademarks. The Frank Shorter Running Gear Division manufactures and markets athletic competition apparel.

**EXECUTIVE OFFICERS OF THE COMPANY**

Listed below are the executive officers of the company as of November 26, 1984.

| Name | Office and Position | Age |
|------|---------------------|-----|
| Peter E. Haas[a,b,c] | Chairman of the board | 65 |
| Robert D. Haas[a,b,c] | President and chief executive officer | 42 |
| Walter A. Haas[a,b,c] | Chairman of the executive committee | 68 |
| Leo P. Isotalo | Senior V.P. and president of Battery Street Enterprises | 48 |
| David K. Lelewer | Senior V.P. human resources | 44 |
| Karl F. Slacik[a] | Senior V.P. of finance and chief financial officer | 55 |
| Lee Smith | Senior V.P. and president of Levi Strauss Intl. | 42 |
| Peter Thigpen[a] | Senior V.P. and president of Jeans Company | 45 |
| Thomas W. Tusher[a,b] | Executive V.P. and chief operating officer | 43 |

[a]Member of the board of directors.
[b]Member of the executive committee.
[c]Walter A. Hass, Jr., is the father of Robert D. Haas and the brother of Peter E. Haas.

**Background of Executive Officers**

*Mr. Peter E. Haas* joined the company in 1945. He was appointed president in 1970 and chief executive officer in 1976. He assumed his present position as chairman of the board in 1981. He has served as a director since 1948.

*Mr. Robert D. Haas* joined the company in 1973. He was elected senior vice-president—corporate planning and policy in 1978 and was appointed president of the new Business Group in January 1980. He became president of the Operating Groups in December 1980. He was named executive vice-president and chief operating officer in 1981 before assuming his current position as president and chief executive officer in 1984. He has served as a director since 1980. He is the son of the great-nephew of Levi Strauss.

*Mr. Walter A. Haas, Jr.,* joined the company in 1939 and served as its president from 1958 to 1970 and as its chief executive officer from 1958 to 1976. He was chairman of the board from 1970 to 1981 and has been chairman of the executive committee since 1976. He has served as a director since 1943. He is the great-grandnephew of Levi Strauss.

*Mr. Leo P. Isotalo* joined the company in 1975. In 1978 he became vice-president and general manager of the Continental European Division and in 1980 was named its president. In 1982, he became a vice-president of the company and executive vice-president of Group II—Levi Strauss International. His current position, which he assumed in 1984, is senior vice-president and president of Battery Street Enterprises.

*Mr. David K. Lelewer* joined the company in 1980 as director of special projects and assistant to the chief executive officer. In June 1981 he became director of personnel—Levi Strauss USA, and in November 1981 was elected a vice-president of the company and director of personnel. He became director of human resources in 1984. Prior to joining the company, he was vice-president and manager of employee relations at Wells Fargo Bank.

*Mr. Karl F. Slacik* joined the company in 1978 as vice-president—financial operations and was appointed to the additional position of treasurer in 1979. He became vice-president—finance in January 1980, and retained the title of treasurer until he assumed his present position as senior vice-president—finance and chief financial/Officer in May 1980. He has served as a director since 1982.

*Mr. Lee Smith* joined the company in 1966. From 1978 to 1980, he served as division president, Levi Strauss International. In 1981, he was named a vice-president of the company and in 1984, executive vice-president of Levi Strauss International.

*Mr. Peter Thigpen* joined the company in 1967. In 1980 he was appointed executive vice-president of Group I—Levi Strauss International and became president of Group I—Levi Strauss USA in 1981. He became president of Levi Strauss USA and was elected a senior vice-president of the company in 1982. He assumed his present position as president of the Jeans Company in 1984. He has served as a director since 1983.

*Mr. Thomas W. Tusher* joined the company in 1969. In 1976, he served as executive vice-president of the International Group and was elected a vice-president of the company. In 1977, he was elected a senior vice-president of the company. From 1980, he held the position of president of Levi Strauss International before he assumed his present position as executive vice-president and chief operating officer in 1984. He has served as a director since 1979.

## COMPETITION IN THE APPAREL INDUSTRY

The apparel industry is characterized by ease of entry and is therefore highly competitive. In its traditional market for jeans in the United States, the L. S. & Co. has a large market share. Competition in this market includes a large number of domestic and foreign concerns who manufacture and sell jeans and other lines of apparel. Outside of the jeans market, competition includes numerous manufacturers of all sizes. Neither the company nor any of its competitors has a large share of these highly diverse and shifting consumer apparel markets.

Outside of the United States, the company typically has a smaller share of the jeans market, but is generally either the major or one of the major brands in each country where it has an established market. There are numerous domestic and multinational competitors in most of the company's principal markets.

According to Standard and Poor's, the U.S. apparel market has been saturated by both foreign and domestic producers. Imports of apparel have been growing gradually since the 1950s, and in recent years they have captured a large portion of the domestic market. Imports have continued to increase. Thus, domestic producers have found it increasingly difficult to pass along to their customers the increased costs of raw materials, labor, and energy. In response to this trend, domestic manufacturers are turning toward mechanization, adoption of a global view of the business, diversification toward products that are more import-resistant, and a reliance on brand-name marketing and product exclusivity to counteract pressures on price.

## TRADEMARKS

The company has registered the Levi's trademark, one of its most valuable assets, in over 150 countries. The company owns other trademarks which it utilizes in marketing its jeans and other products. Of these other trademarks, the most important in terms of product sales are the Pocket "Tab" device, 501, the Two-Horse Brand, and Arcute Design. The company also markets products under other trademarks, including Koret, Resistol, Oxxford, Tourage SSE, CMA, and David Hunter. The company vigorously defends its trademarks against infringement and, when necessary, initiates litigation to protect such trademarks.

## ADVERTISING

In the United States, the company advertises on radio and television and in national publications. It also participates in local cooperative advertising programs under which the company shares with retailers the cost of advertising Levi's products.

Internationally, the company has similar advertising programs, modified as required by market conditions and applicable local laws.

In 1984 L. S. & Co. boosted its advertising expenditure by more than 20 percent to $150 million.

**MARKETING**   The marketing orientation of Levi Strauss has undergone significant change since the company's inception in the 1850s. Originally, Levi's jeans were worn almost exclusively by gold miners who considered them essential equipment because they were both rugged and durable. However, in the 1950s jeans became a trend. Thus, L. S. & Co. adjusted their marketing orientation to take advantage of this trend. Currently, Levi's products are oriented toward the more fashion-conscious consumer. At this time Levi is moving toward a market for men, women, and children. This is evident in that for the first time the company has formed an alliance with a well-known designer, Perry Ellis, to produce a line of sportswear.

**BRAND AWARENESS**   Levi Strauss & Company is the leading producer in the apparel industry. Much of their success can be attributed to the marketing strengths they developed over many years of producing and selling jeans. The most important and competitive advantage L. S. & Co. has, and their most important marketing strength as well, is wide consumer acceptance of the Levi's brand. Levi Straus sells high-quality products at reasonable prices, and this fact is recognized throughout the world.

**DISTRIBU-TION**   The Jeans Company sells primarily to department stores; specialty stores for men, women, and children; pants-only stores; and two national retail stores, Sears, Roebuck and Company and J. C. Penney Company. At the end of 1984, retail accounts were serviced by approximately 400 sales representatives.

Levi Strauss International sells directly to retailers in its established markets, although elsewhere in the world it has other distribution arrangements. At the end of 1984, retail accounts were serviced by approximately 400 sales representatives.

Battery Street Enterprises sells principally to department stores and men's and women's specialty stores. The Menswear and Battery Street Sportswear Divisions also sell to Sears, Roebuck and Company and J. C. Penney Company. At the end of 1984, retail accounts were serviced by approximately 300 sales representatives.

No single customer accounts for more than 10 percent of the company's net sales.

**RESEARCH AND DEVELOP-MENT**   Research is considered one of L. S. & Co.'s most important competitive advantages. Their Product Research and Development Department is responsible for the company's progress in new fabrics and garments and their goal is to improve functional performance. Additionally, an Equipment Research and Development Center is maintained by L. S. & Co. so that it can remain a leader in automated and semiautomated production equipment. Further, Corporate Marketing Research has an on-line computerized data bank to monitor major fashion directions, general apparel pricing, retail point-of-sale trends, the company image, and consumer attitudes toward products currently offered. Research also pretests the effectiveness of proposed advertisements and receptivity of the marketplace to new products.

## PERSONNEL

The company employs approximately 37,000 persons, a majority of whom are production workers. A significant number of the production workers are employees in plants where the company has collectively bargained agreements with recognized labor unions. The company considers its relationship with its employees to be generally satisfactory.

## PRODUCTION FACILITIES

Levi Strauss & Company has numerous plants and distribution centers in North America and throughout Asia, Latin America, and Europe. Due to the downturn in the market for jeans apparel, Levi Strauss began a painful revamping of its production operation in 1984. In recent years the company closed 23 of its 128 factories.

## MARKETING PROBLEMS

Despite its numerous marketing strengths and its position in the apparel industry, Levi Strauss & Company is having its share of problems. First, the company has been battered by a downturn in the market for jeans apparel. Levi Strauss International has been plagued by the drop in demand for jeans abroad and a strong dollar. Second, the company's pricing policy is subject to Federal Trade Commission (FTC) regulations. Specifically the FTC does not permit forced price maintenance by manufacturers at the retail level. In recent years, this has cost L. S. & Co. millions of dollars for out-of-court settlements of cases in which they were accused of price maintenance. As a result L. S. & Co. is susceptible to price wars. Retailers will drastically cut the price of Levi products to attract customers to their stores from their competitors. This may pose a possible threat to the quality image of a branded product.

## OUTLOOK FOR THE DOMESTIC APPAREL MARKET

The future of the domestic apparel industry looks good for various product lines such as designer fashions, active wear, sportswear, women's wear, jeans, and western styles. Clothing purchases remain remarkably stable and unchanged since 1980 according to the MRCA Information Services. At present, there is an emphasis on designer fashions and leisure fashions.

Many firms who are surviving the effects of increased competition are doing so primarily because of diversification into various segments of the apparel market. By broadening their scope and focusing on different markets, firms find it easier to avoid the potentially serious negative effects resulting from rapid style changes which characterize the industry.

**OUTLOOK FOR THE INTERNATIONAL MARKET**

As the U.S. apparel market has become more saturated, growth-oriented apparel producers in the United States have directed their attention toward the market potential overseas. United States clothing makers are increasingly being forced into overseas production because of higher domestic labor costs and competition from other big importers, all resulting in imports of about 20 percent or 11.5 billion of their brand-name products.

**FINANCIAL MATTERS AT LEVI STRAUSS**

The following exhibits describe Levi Strauss & Company: consolidated statement of income (Exhibit 2.1), consolidated balance sheets (Exhibit 2.2), consolidated statement of changes in financial position (Exhibit 2.3), financial highlights (Exhibit 2.4), comparative sales data (Exhibit 2.5), and financial summary (Exhibit 2.6).

**Exhibit 2.1**

### CONSOLIDATED STATEMENT OF INCOME[a]
#### Levi Strauss & Company and Subsidiaries

| | Year (52 weeks) Ended | | |
|---|---|---|---|
| | November 25, 1984 | November 27, 1983 | November 28, 1982 |
| Net sales | $ 2,513,536 | $ 2,731,273 | $2,572,172 |
| Cost of goods sold | 1,652,476 | 1,648,502 | 1,635,539 |
| Gross profit | 861,060 | 1,082,771 | 936,633 |
| Marketing, general, and administrative expenses | 674,322 | 710,442 | 665,660 |
| Operating income | 186,738 | 372,319 | 270,973 |
| Interest expense | 28,763 | 39,793 | 42,766 |
| Other (income) expense, net | 46,612 | (44,287) | (21,614) |
| | 111,363 | 376,823 | 249,831 |
| Income before taxes | 111,363 | 376,823 | 249,831 |
| Provision for taxes on income | 69,976 | 182,300 | 113,256 |
| Net income | 41,387 | 194,523 | 116,575 |
| Net income per share | 1.07 | 4.61 | 3.05 |
| Average common and common equivalent shares outstanding | 38,517,526 | 42,206,980 | 41,553,553 |

[a]Dollars in thousands.

**Exhibit 2.2**

## CONSOLIDATED BALANCE SHEET[a]
### Levi Strauss & Company and Subsidiaries

| | November 25, 1984 | November 27, 1983 |
|---|---|---|
| **Assets** | | |
| Current assets | | |
| Cash | $ 37,452 | $ 16,967 |
| Temporary investment of cash | 225,937 | 449,351 |
| Trade receivables (less allowance for doubtful accounts: 1984—$8,676; 1983—$9,682) | 334,798 | 425,464 |
| Inventories | | |
| Raw materials and work-in-process | 170,510 | 183,734 |
| Finished goods | 217,150 | 180,427 |
| Other current assets | 51,731 | 70,995 |
| | 1,042,579 | 1,427,443 |
| Total current assets | 1,042,579 | 1,427,443 |
| Property, plant equipment (less accumulated depreciation: 1984—$208,217; 1983—$182,573) | 330,455 | 347,150 |
| Other assets | 48,068 | 57,282 |
| | $1,421,103 | $1,831,875 |
| **Liabilities and stockholder's equity** | | |
| Current liabilities | | |
| Current maturities of long-term debt | $ 9,354 | $ 32,440 |
| Short-term borrowing | 21,077 | 58,429 |
| Accounts payable | 83,361 | 128,658 |
| Accrued liabilities | 123,023 | 96,496 |
| Compensation and payroll: taxes | 72,923 | 74,508 |
| Pension and profit sharing | 4,257 | 26,397 |
| Taxes based on income | 40,235 | 73,724 |
| Dividend payable | 17,070 | 19,375 |
| Total current liabilities | 371,305 | 504,017 |
| Long-term debt less current maturities | 199,017 | 225,045 |
| Deferred taxes and other items | 43,339 | 44,094 |
| Stockholder's equity | | |
| Common stock—$1 par value: authorized 100,000,000 shares; issued 43,998,808 shares | 43,999 | 43,999 |
| Additional paid-in-capital | 63,266 | 63,063 |
| Retained earnings | 1,066,068 | 1,093,417 |
| Translation adjustment | (81,051) | (56,993) |
| Employee stock ownership plan shares | (38,638) | (36,499) |
| Purchased with debt | | |
| Treasury stock at cost: 1984—7,091,288 shares; 1983—3,108,120 | (246,203) | (53,278) |
| Total stockholder's equity | 807,441 | 1,053,709 |
| | $1,421,102 | $1,831,875 |

[a]Dollars in thousands.

**Exhibit 2.3**

## CONSOLIDATED STATEMENT OF CHANGES IN FINANCIAL POSITION[a]
### Levi Strauss & Company and Subsidiaries

|  | November 25, 1984 | November 27, 1983 | November 28, 1982 |
|---|---|---|---|
| **Working capital increased by** | | | |
| Operations | | | |
|   Net income | $ 41,387 | $ 194,523 | $ 126,575 |
| Add items not requiring working capital | | | |
|   Depreciation and amortization | 47,832 | 44,524 | 43,219 |
|   Other net | 6,492 | 6,837 | 7,957 |
| Working capital provided by operations | 95,711 | 245,884 | 177,751 |
| Increases in long-term debt | 5,083 | 125,542 | 31,116 |
| Payment of debt by ESOP | — | 10,419 | — |
| Common stock issued to employees | 6,970 | 12,384 | 6,067 |
| Reductions in long-term deposits | 9,611 | 42 | 1,453 |
|  | 117,375 | 394,271 | 216,387 |
| **Working capital reduced by** | | | |
| Purchase of treasury stock | 199,693 | — | — |
| Additions to property, plant, and equipment | 41,398 | 50,937 | 54,171 |
| Cash dividends declared | 68,736 | 73,111 | 68,292 |
| Reductions in long-term debt | 30,391 | 61,562 | 18,472 |
| Effect of exchange rate changes on working capital items | 20,175 | 10,814 | 30,705 |
| Purchase of shares by ESOP with company-guaranteed debt | 2,139 | 46,918 | — |
| Other, net | 1,986 | (2,653) | 6,863 |
|  | 364,517 | 240,684 | 178,503 |
| Increase (decrease) in working capital | $ (247,142) | $ 153,582 | $ 37,884 |
| **Increase (decrease) in working capital, represented by change in** | | | |
| Cash and temporary investments of cash | $ (202,924) | $ 113,056 | $ 179,571 |
| Trade receivables, net | (85,666) | 31,301 | (50,387) |
| Inventories | (77,006) | 68,633 | (117,184) |
| Other current assets | (19,263) | 6,844 | 1,111 |
| Current maturities of long-term debt and short-term borrowings | 60,433 | (20,511) | (28,176) |
| Accounts payable and accrued liabilities | 18,770 | (25,289) | 14,987 |
| Other current liabilities | 58,519 | (20,452) | (18,390) |
| Increase (decrease) in working capital | $ (247,142) | $ 153,582 | $ 37,884 |

[a]Dollars in thousands.

**Exhibit 2.4**

### FINANCIAL HIGHLIGHTS[a]
#### Levi Strauss & Company and Subsidiaries

|  | 1984 | 1983 | (Decrease)/increase (%) |
|---|---|---|---|
| Net sales | $ 2,513,536 | $ 2,731,273 | $ (8.0) |
| Net income | 41,387 | 194,523 | (78.7) |
| Dividends declared | 68,736 | 73,111 | (6.0) |
| Stockholder's equity | 807,441 | 1,053,709 | (23.4) |
| Working capital | 671,274 | 918,416 | (26.9) |
| Property, plant, and equipment—net | 330,455 | 347,150 | (4.8) |
| Average common and common equivalent shares outstanding | 38,517,526 | 42,206,980 | (8.7) |
| Per Share |  |  |  |
| Net income | 1.07 | 4.61 | (76.8) |
| Dividends declared | 1.85 | 1.75 | 5.7 |

[a]Dollars in thousands except per share accounts.

**Exhibit 2.5** Comparative Sales Data[a]

|  | 1984 | 1983 | Increase (dollars) | Decrease (units) |
|---|---|---|---|---|
| The Jeans Company | $1,432.6 | $1,497.5 | (4.3) | (4.2) |
| Battery Street Enterprises | 485.1 | 529.2 | (8.3) | (7.4) |
| Levi Strauss International |  |  |  |  |
| European Operation | 321.7 | 416.4 | (22.7) | (15.8) |
| Latin American Operations | 87.2 | 94.1 | (7.4) | (14.3) |
| Canada Division | 93.3 | 95.4 | (2.2) | — |
| Asia/Pacific Division | 89.0 | 94.8 | (6.0) | (5.2) |
| Total Levi Strauss | 591.2 | 700.7 | (15.6) | (13.2) |
| International | 4.6 | 3.9 | 18.1 | 12.2 |
| Other operations |  |  |  |  |
| Consolidated | 2,513.5 | 2,731.3 | (8.0) | (6.7) |

[a]Dollars in millions.

**FUTURE** Levi Strauss & Company directors have proposed a $1.45 billion buyout to take the company private. The Strauss families currently control about 40 percent of the company's 36.9 million common shares outstanding. The families are seeking to take Levi Strauss & Company private in part so that management can broaden a corporate reorganization now under way without having to answer to shareholders, Wall Street analysts, or the media. The company intends to sharpen the focus of its jeans business domestically and internationally and review the performances of its 11 fashion apparel units. The tender offer for all outstanding Levi shares started August 2, 1985. The buyout is virtually guaranteed. The family group will then own between 80 and 92 percent of the company.

**Exhibit 2.6**

### FINANCIAL SUMMARY[a]
#### Levi Strauss & Company and Subsidiaries

|  | 1984 | 1983 |
|---|---|---|
| Net sales | $ 2,513.5 | $ 2,731.3 |
| Gross profit | 861.1 | 1,082.8 |
| Interest expense | 28.8 | 32.8 |
| Income before taxes | 111.4 | 376.8 |
| Provision for taxes on income | 70.0 | 182.3 |
| Net income | 41.4 | 194.5 |
| Earnings retained in the business | (27.3) | 121.4 |
| Cash retained in the business | 27.0 | 172.8 |
| Income before taxes as % of sales | 4.4 | 13.89 |
| Net income as % of sales | 1.6 | 7.1 |
| Net income as % of beginning stockholders equity | 3.9 | 20.1 |
| Current assets | $ 1,042.6 | $ 1,427.4 |
| Current liabilities | 371.3 | 509.0 |
| Working capital | 671.3 | 918.4 |
| Ratio of current assets to current liabilities | 3.8/1 | 2.8/1 |
| Total assets | $ 1,421.1 | $ 1,831.9 |
| Long-term debt less current maturities | 199.0 | 225.0 |
| Stockholders equity | 807.4 | 1,053.7 |
| Capital expenditures | 41.4 | 50.9 |
| Depreciation expense | 42.6 | 40.0 |
| Property, plant, and equipment, net | 330.5 | 347.2 |
| Number of employees | 37,000 | 44,000 |
| Per share data |  |  |
| Net income | $ 1.07 | $ 4.61 |
| Dividends declared | 1.85 | 1.75 |
| Book value (of shares outstanding at year's end) | 21.88 | 25.15 |
| Market price range | $43\frac{1}{6}$–23 | $56$–$32\frac{2}{8}$ |
| Average common and common equivalent shares outstanding | 38,517,516 | 42,206,980 |

[a]Dollars in millions except per share data.

The family has arranged $2.1 billion in financing for the proposed buyout. San Francisco–based Wells Fargo and Company has agreed to lead a bank syndicate that will lend the group $1.7 billion, the remainder coming from other "major money centers." About $1.45 billion will be used to finance the leveraged buyout and $250 million will be used for working capital. However, paying off the debt used to finance the $2 billion leveraged buyout will pose a heavy burden. Net interest expense is estimated at $182.6 million in 1986, $174.2 million in 1987, $166 million in 1988, and $157.5 million in 1989.

The company expects operating earnings to be up 136 percent in 1985. The company projects net income will shoot up to $82 million in 1986 aided by "other income" of 64 million. Net income is projected to drop 18 percent in 1987, but to increase by 20.4 percent in 1988 and 21.7 percent in 1989 as interest expense declines and operating income rises.

Levi anticipates sales growth of 2.6 percent in 1986, 5.5 percent in 1987, and 5.6 percent in 1988 and 1989. After the strong operating income recovery in 1985, the company expects an additional 20 percent gain in 1986, to $322.7 million. For the next three years the company projects more modest gains of 6.4 percent in 1987, 5.7 percent in 1988, and 7.4 percent in 1989.

Battery Street Enterprises is expected to show the strongest sales gains of the three divisions. Battery Street Enterprises, which includes Levi's non-jeans designer operations such as Perry Ellis, is expected to gain 11.5 percent, which would bring 1985 sales to $540.9 million.

The Jeans Company is expected to gain 4.1 percent in sales in 1986 and grow steadily at 4% annually for the following three years.

Sales for the International Division are expected to drop 2.4 percent in 1986, but the company expects them to grow after that: 5.4 percent in 1987, 7.2 percent in 1988, and 7 percent in 1989.

The assumptions used to formulate the projections include a decline in corporate expenses to 1.8 percent of sales in 1989, from 2.1 percent in 1985, and capital expenditures to range between $43.2 million and $48.6 million over the 5-year period.

If the projections pan out, the company's debt-to-equity ratio will go from 8 to 1 in 1985 to 2.4 to 1 in 1989, and the book value of each common share will increase from $23.69 to 54.77. Total long-term debt will shrink from $1.5 billion in 1985 to $1.24 billion in 1989.

# 3  Johnson Products Company, Inc.: The Challenges of the 1980s

Thomas L. Wheelen/Robert L. Nixon/Marian Hessler/Jan Hunter/
Bob Bailey/Tony Arroyo
University of South Florida

Neil H. Snyder
University of Virginia

**HISTORY**  Johnson Products Company, Inc., the largest manufacturer of personal grooming products for black consumers in the world, was formed in 1954. The company was organized as an Illinois corporation in 1957, and in 1969 its state of incorporation was changed to Delaware.

George E. Johnson started the business after he became aware that blacks were unhappy with their naturally coarse, thick hair. Many blacks wanted their hair straightened so that they would have more flexibility in their hair styling. Johnson was not the first to enter the black hair-care products market, but his company became a leading firm because of his efforts to satisfy the needs of the black consumer.

George E. Johnson began his career as a door-to-door salesman in Chicago for Fuller Products, a black cosmetics company. Some time later, he had an opportunity to work as an assistant chemist with Dr. Herbert Martini in the lab at Fuller Products. During the ten years Johnson worked with Martini, he learned the basics of the cosmetic industry. On these foundations, he built his own cosmetics business. The beginning of Johnson Products can be traced back to a particular day on which Johnson met a barber who had visited the managers at Fuller Products to seek help in formulating an improved hair straightener. Fuller Products was not interested, but Johnson was.

Johnson spoke with the barber, Orville Nelson, about his problem and later visited his shop to explore the matter further. At the shop Johnson found customers standing in line to have their hair straightened, but the straightener being used simply did not work. Johnson and Nelson formed a short-lived partnership by putting up $250 each in capital. Johnson sought the assistance of Dr. Martini in solving the problem with existing hair straighteners, and the Johnson Products Company was under way.

In order to obtain as much information as he could about the demand for hair straighteners, Johnson visited many black beauty shop owners. He found that the

Prepared by Professors Thomas L. Wheelen and Robert L. Nixon, and Marian Hessler, Jan Hunter, Bob Bailey, and Tony Arroyo of the University of South Florida; and Professor Neil H. Snyder of the McIntre School of Commerce at the University of Virginia. Copyright © 1985 by Thomas L. Wheelen, Robert L. Nixon, and Neil H. Snyder. Reprinted by permission.

problem was universal: Blacks were dissatisfied with the poor performance of the available hair straighteners. In a *New York Times* article, Johnson was quoted as saying, "Black beauticians used a hot comb and grease on the hair of black women. Dr. Martini and I agreed that the smoke was bad for the health and the grease was no good for the hair, so we worked on a process to eliminate the grease and smoke, and came up with a cream press permanent, cream shampoo, and Ultra-Sheen conditioner that could be applied at home between visits to the beauty shop."[1] With the hot-comb technique, an individual's hair had to be redone constantly, and rain or moisture would destroy the arrangement.

The emergence of black nationalism in the 1960s popularized the Afro and presented a dilemma for makers of hair straighteners. "I didn't know if it was a fad or not," said Johnson, "so I took a wait-and-see attitude until I was sure it was a trend. Then we developed Afro Sheen for the natural. But I always felt the natural wouldn't last. It's too monotonous and sure enough, women are moving from it."[2]

Historically a vigorous, competitive hair-care products and cosmetics manufacturing enterprise, Johnson Products is also an important black institution and a growing American business. For example, Johnson Products Company, Inc., was the first black-owned firm to be listed on a major stock exchange. Through innovative product development and promotional techniques, it has rapidly become one of the success stories of American business.

The Johnson story nearly ended one day in October 1964 when a devastating fire swept through the plant on Green Street in Chicago and destroyed nearly all of the production facilities. Instead of abandoning the business, Johnson and his employees salvaged what they could, and with the help of suppliers and Fuller Products Company, the company was operating from temporary headquarters within a week.

Following the fire, the company's growth was steady but unspectacular until product innovations in 1965 ushered in a period of rapid sales growth. From 1971 to 1975, gross sales increased from $13 million to $39 million. Since 1975, however, the firm has experienced a series of setbacks. Its first attempt to expand its market with an expensive men's cologne, Black Tie, was a disaster. The failure was attributed to improper distribution channels and poor shelf space and displays at retail establishments. Coinciding with this setback was the mounting pressure exerted by major competing firms, primarily Revlon, which viewed the fast-growing black cosmetics market as an untapped well. Then, in February 1975, the firm's public image was damaged seriously when management felt obligated to sign a consent order issued by the Federal Trade Commission (FTC) requiring that warning labels be placed on its best-selling hair straightener, Ultra Sheen Permanent Creme Relaxer. Johnson claims that the FTC assured him that competitors would also have to put these warning labels on their products. However, Revlon did not place this label on two of their products until nearly two years later. Compounding these problems were the generally poor state of the economy and high level of black unemployment in the late 1970s and early 1980s. The firm experienced its first operating loss in 1980 and saw a loss again in 1982. It again returned to profitability in 1983, but the firm's future now seems uncertain.

**COMPANY HIGHLIGHTS**

1954—Company founded
1957—Ultra Sheen Conditioner and Hair Dress introduced
1958—Ultra Sheen line entered professional beauticians' market
1960—Ultra Sheen line introduced in retail market
1964—Fire destroys production facilities
1965—Ultra Sheen No Base Cream Relaxer introduced
1966—Completed first phase of new headquarters
1968—Afro Sheen products introduced
1968—Established the George E. Johnson Foundation
1969—Sponsored its first nationwide TV special, ". . . & Beautiful"
1969—Completed second phase of new headquarters
1969—Company made its first public stock offering
1970—Ultra Sheen cosmetics introduced
1971—Began sponsorship of "Soul Train," nationally syndicated TV show
1971—Johnson Products Company listed on American Stock Exchange
1972—Established the George E. Johnson Educational Fund
1973—Completed third phase of new headquarters
1974—Purchased 11 adjoining acres with building
1975—Entered men's fragrance market with Black Tie cologne and splash-on
1975—Started exporting to Nigeria
1975—Acquired the Debbie's School of Beauty Culture
1978—Established its first overseas corporation in Nigeria to manufacture its products
1979—Reformulated cosmetics lines
1979—Acquired Freedom Distributors, who distributed the company's and competitors' products on the eastern seaboard
1980—Established Johnson Products of Nigeria
1980—Introduced Ultra Sheen Precise, first of 42 innovative product lines
1981—Undertook overseas expansion by establishing a sales and service center in Eastbourne, England
1981—Introduced new products: Gentle Treatment, Tender Treatment, and Bantu Curl
1982—Established Debbie Howell Cosmetics, direct sales line in key black market areas
1982—Introduced 19 new products
1983—Formed Mello Touch Labs, Inc., to manufacture, market, and distribute a line of consumer products
1983—Introduced two lines of cosmetics: Ultra Sheen and Moisture Formula
1983—Sold Freedom Distributors

**OFFICERS AND DIRECTORS**

*George E. Johnson,* 56, serves as the chairman of the board and president. Mr. Johnson's business affiliations include board positions with Commonwealth Edison Company; Metropolitan Life Insurance Company; American Health and

Beauty Aids Institute (Chairman); and the Cosmetic, Toiletry, and Fragrance Association. He is also a member of a number of civic, charitable, professional, and social organizations.

*Dorothy McConner,* 54, serves as the executive vice-president, administration, and corporate secretary. She was elected to the board of directors in 1969. Mrs. McConner has been with the company for approximately 25 years and was selected *Blackbook*'s 1975 Business Woman of the Year.

*David N. Corner,* 53, joined the company in December 1978 as vice-president, finance, and chief financial officer. In the preceding five years he was with Libby, McNeil & Libby, Inc., most recently as vice-president, finance, and treasurer.

*Marilynn J. Cason,* 40, has served as corporate counsel and was elected a vice-president in 1977. Before joining the company in 1975, she spent three years as an attorney for Kraft, Inc., three years as an associate attorney for Kraft, Inc., and three years as an associate attorney with the Denver law firm of Dawson, Nagel, Sherman, and Horwald.

*Tehsel S. Dhaliwal,* 42, has been with the company since 1973. He served previously as director of manufacturing operations. He was promoted to vice-president of operations in 1983.

*Michael J. Guthrie,* 33, vice-president of corporate planning, has served as senior attorney on the company's legal staff since joining the company in 1979. He was appointed to his present position in 1983. Prior to joining the company, Mr. Guthrie was a staff attorney with Sonnenschein, Carlin, Nath, and Rosenthal.

*Ezzat N. Khalil,* 49, joined the company in 1975 as director of cosmetics. He was elected vice-president, research and development, in 1978. In the five years preceding 1975, Mr. Khalil held the following positions: vice-president of research and development with Chromex Chemical Company; director of new products with Kolmar Laboratories, Inc.; laboratory manager with Estee Lauder; director of research and development with Maybelline, Inc.; and general manager of Essencial Ohio International.

*Alan N. Sym-Smith,* 52, has served as vice-president, international, during the past five years and is responsible for coordinating the company's international sales and marketing activities. He joined the company in 1975. From 1971 to 1975 he served as vice-president, international, of Helene Curtis Industries, Inc.

*Joan B. Johnson,* 54, wife of George E. Johnson, shared in the founding of the company in 1954. She presently serves as treasurer and director.

Except for Tehsel S. Dhaliwal and Michael J. Guthrie, each executive officer was last elected as such on December 8, 1982, and will serve until a successor is appointed and qualified. Mr. Dhaliwal was appointed a vice-president in March 1983 and Mr. Guthrie in September 1983. Deborah A. Howell serves as president of Debbie's School of Beauty Culture, which is a wholly-owned subsidiary.

The three internal directors are George E. and Joan B. Johnson, and Dorothy McConner. A brief account of the experiences of each director who is not an officer is set forth below:

*John T. Schriver* has served as a first vice-president of Shearson/American Express, Inc. (formally Loeb, Rhoades, Shearson, a Division of Shearson Hayden Stone, Inc.), investment bankers, during the past five years.

*Alvin J. Bouette* has served as president of the Independence Bank of Chicago,

Illinois, during the past five years and was made chairman of the board of Independence Bank in 1980.

*Melvin D. Jefferson* is owner and president of Superior Beauty and Barber Supply Company (Detroit, Michigan), a full-service distributor of beauty and hair care products.

*Jesse L. Howell* has served as vice-president of Debbie's School of Beauty Culture, Inc. (a wholly-owned subsidiary of the company since 1975). He has served as a director of the company since 1977.

**OWNERSHIP**   Because of their direct and indirect ownership of shares of the company's stock, George E. Johnson and Joan B. Johnson may be deemed to be controlling persons of the company for the purposes of the federal securities law. The Johnson family controls 66.5 percent of the company. (See Exhibit 3.1.)

**SUBSID-IARIES AND FACILITIES**   The company's corporate offices and manufacturing facilities are located at 8522 South Lafayette Avenue in Chicago. The building encompasses approximately 64,000 square feet of office space and 176,000 square feet for manufacturing and warehousing purposes.

To support its continued growth, the company acquired additional property adjacent to the South Lafayette facilities in November 1974 at a cost of $1 million. This property consists of approximately 11 acres of land (compared to the 12-acre tract of the old facility) and a 200,000-square-foot building. This building currently houses the administrative offices of Johnson's subsidiary, Debbie's School of Beauty Culture, Inc., and selected administrative offices of the company and warehousing.

The company's wholly owned subsidiary, Debbie's School of Beauty Culture, operates nine training facilities for beauticians. In 1977 the Johnson Product Company purchased a Chicago building totaling 12,000 square feet. This facility now houses one of Debbie's schools. The other eight locations are leased. The locations and terms of the leases are outlined in Exhibit 3.2.

Since its acquisition by Johnson in 1975, Debbie's has operated profitably with the exception of fiscal 1982. Its poor performance in that year was attributed to the economic recession and curtailment in federal funding for certain types of education. The school's staff currently includes more than 100 administrators and instructors. The school's curriculum includes anatomy, hairdressing, hair weaving, personal appearance, skin and nail care, shop management, and product education. The program is 1500 hours over nine and one-half months. In 1983, Debbie's graduated a record 1000 students; the previous class was only 455 students. Johnson Products intends to continue expansion of Debbie's schools, taking advantage of the scarcity of black beauty schools nationwide (there were fewer than 75 in operation in 1981). Plans call for opening a school in St. Louis, Missouri, in 1984.

**Exhibit 3.1** Stock Ownership

| Title of Class | Names and Addresses of Beneficial Owner | Amount Beneficially Owned | Percent of Class |
|---|---|---|---|
| Common stock | George E. Johnson, trustee of personal trust[a] | 2,016,775 | 50.7 |
| Common stock | Joan B. Johnson, trustee of personal trust[b] | 180,000 | 4.5 |
| Common stock | Joan B. Johnson, trustee for children[a,b] | 254,000 | 6.4 |
| Common stock | Joan B. Johnson, under 11 irrevocable trusts granted by George E. Johnson[a,b] | 48,200 | 1.2 |
| Common stock | George E. Johnson and Joan B. Johnson as trustees of The Johnson Products Co., Inc., Employees Profit Sharing and Plan and Trust[a,b] | 2,700 | 0.07 |
| Common stock | Total shares owned by George E. and Joan B. Johnson | 2,501,675 | 62.9 |

[a]Mrs. Johnson disclaims beneficial ownership in these shares.
[b]Mr. Johnson disclaims beneficial ownership in these shares.

As of November 1, 1983, directors and officers of the company (14 in group) beneficially owned the following shares:

| Title of Class | Amount Beneficially Owned | Percent of Class |
|---|---|---|
| Common stock | 2,528,610[a] | 63.5 |

[a]Includes 5,470 shares under options exercisable within 60 days.

By virtue of their direct and indirect ownership of shares of the company's common stock, Mr. Johnson and Mrs. Johnson may be deemed to be controlling persons in the company for purposes of the federal securities laws.

**Exhibit 3.2** Facilities of Johnson Products

| Location | Approximate Square Footage | Lease Expires |
|---|---|---|
| Chicago, Illinois | 25,000 | December 31, 1984[a] |
| Chicago, Illinois | 12,000 | December 31, 1984[a] |
| Chicago, Illinois | 8,000 | December 31, 1984[a] |
| Harvey, Illinois | 10,000 | December 31, 1984 |
| East St. Louis, Illinois | 12,000 | August 31, 1984 |
| Detroit, Michigan | 7,200 | July 31, 1984 |
| Birmingham, Alabama | 7,000 | April 30, 1984 |
| Indianapolis, Indiana | 9,000 | June 30, 1984 |

[a]The Chicago leases that expired in December 1984 are renewable at the option of the company, and the East St. Louis lease contains a purchase option exercisable 60 days after expiration of the lease.

Debbie's operates a salon division which consists of three Ultra Precise Beauty Boutiques in Chicago, one of which is situated in a Sears department store. The other two are operating from leased space in Chicago. These leases are up for renewal in September 1987. The salons, thus far, have been only marginally profitable. All of Debbie's schools and salons use Johnson Products predominately.

In 1982, Debbie's established Debbie Howell Cosmetics, a direct-sales organization to promote Johnson's new line of cosmetics. This division currently employs consultants in about 30 cities that the firm believes are in key black consumer markets. Losses in its first year of operation approximated $147,000, due primarily to initial start-up costs. The parent company is optimistic about the future of the endeavor because consultants have proven to be a very successful sales technique for Avon and Mary Kay Cosmetics. There are plans to expand further in existing markets and other key black consumer market areas.

## INTERNATIONAL SUBSIDIARIES

At the present time, Johnson Products has subsidiaries in Nigeria, Great Britain, and Jamaica.

### Nigeria

Johnson Products owns a 40 percent interest in Johnson Products of Nigeria, Ltd., a manufacturing affiliate established in 1980. Johnson was the first U.S. company to manufacture hair-care products in Nigeria. The Nigerian partners represent various segments of that nation's business community. The facilities include a 36,000-square-foot manufacturing and warehousing building located just outside the capital of Lagos. An additional 18,000-square-foot facility is available for expansion. Mr. Johnson said of the Nigerian investment:

> We have been exporting to Nigeria since 1975, but actually our products have been sold there since the 1960s. Consequently, we have excellent corporate and product name recognition. . . . By manufacturing in Nigeria we are taking what we believe is the best approach to building on our well-established reputation and maximizing the opportunities available in a developing country.

Initial investment for the Nigerian operation was $1.6 million. First-year losses totaled $380,000 and were attributed to extremely heavy living costs in accommodating a team of Johnson Products representatives from headquarters, who supervised the plant setup and the early stages of operations. Johnson Products' managers have grown more pessimistic about the potential profitability of this venture as it has continued to operate in the red. Total losses in fiscal 1981 were $466,000. In fiscal 1982 losses were $1,802,000, including losses from operations and write-down of investment (net foreign exchange gains).

In 1983, the Nigerian operation recorded its first profitable year. Initially, problems stemmed from smuggling activities that forced Johnson Products of Nigeria, Ltd., to compete with its own product being manufactured in the United States and being sold on the black market at well below retail prices. Then, in

1981, in an effort to stave off illegal imports, the Nigerian government severely restricted the flow of goods, both raw materials and products, entering the country. As a result, the Nigerian plant was forced to suspend operations on several occasions due to difficulties in receiving shipments of raw materials and other goods. This operation manufactures more than 30 different products under the Ultra Sheen and Afro Sheen brands.

The main problem for the past few years centers around the Nigerian government's lack of foreign exchange, which causes prolonged delays in the acquisition of raw materials. Import licenses have been granted. Therefore the company will maintain some degree of production in Nigeria despite the enduring basic raw materials problem.

In 1983, Nigeria "remains the largest market in black Africa, as well as the one most likely to provide business opportunities for American firms in the medium and long term."[3] (Foreign Economic Trends and Their Implications for the United States, November 1983) Nigeria is an untapped ethnic consumer market that numbers 90 million people with an annual growth rate of 3.2 percent.

## Great Britain

Johnson Products continued its overseas expansion by establishing a sales and service center in Eastbourne, England (40 miles south of London), in October 1981. This is essentially a low-overhead central distribution center for the Great Britain and Western European markets (primarily France, Germany, Belgium, and Holland). This 3000-square-foot facility has allowed the company to offer a broader range of its professional and retail product lines to European consumers. In fiscal 1983, this distribution center "made a positive contribution" toward profit. Personal income in England increased in 1983, which promoted a 2 percent growth in personal consumption. These markets will be supported by an expanding advertising and promotion campaign.

## Jamaica

In 1981, after seven consecutive years of decline, the Jamaican economy had a growth rate of approximately 2.0 percent. Future growth rates were estimated in the 2.0 to 3.0 percent range. So in 1981, Johnson Products entered into its first licensing agreement with a Jamaican firm. The licensee currently manufactures Ultra Sheen brand products out of its facility in Kingston, Jamaica's capital city. Johnson Products supplies the raw materials as well as technical and marketing support. In return, the company receives royalties based on a percentage of sales. Although strict import regulations limit Johnson's ability to tap most of the Caribbean islands as well as Central and South America, the Jamaican licensee is expected to be able to sell its products to the English-speaking islands, formerly the British West Indies. Puerto Rico is Johnson's biggest market in that area of the world.

## Future Plans

In addition to its present activities, Johnson Products is planning to establish distributorships in the Spanish-speaking islands, in order to fully develop these markets. Johnson Products is experiencing heavy competition throughout the Caribbean and Canadian markets. In the future, the company will open new markets in those Central and South American countries with the fewest import restrictions. The company's net sales and other operating revenue from international operations were $2,151,000 in 1983, $1,514,000 in 1982, and $2,690,000 in 1981.

**INDUSTRY AND COMPETITION**

In 1983, consumers spent $11,857,000,000 on toiletries and cosmetics. Although continued gains are expected, the industry's real growth rate is expected to fall to an annual increase of 2 to 3 percent. (See Exhibit 3.3.) This is well below that experienced in the 1960s and 1970s, for the increase in multi-income families may have run its course and stabilized. Currently the country is experiencing a normal growth rate in the employment of women.

One of the fastest-growing areas in the toiletries and cosmetics industry is the ethnic market. A study by Fairchild Publications estimates the ethnic toiletries and cosmetics market is growing at an annual rate of 20 percent through 1986. The ethnic market consists of an estimated 40 million blacks, Hispanics, and other minorities. Of Johnson's sales, 30 percent are accounted for by minorities other than blacks. Minority women are estimated to spend three times more on cosmetics than white women. In the 1980 U.S. census, the black population numbered approximately 26 million with a median age of 25. (See Exhibit 3.4.) The ethnic market has potential sales of $5 billion according to estimates made by the Commerce Department.

**Exhibit 3.3** Toiletries and Cosmetic Industry Financial Information

| Financial Indicators | 1985[a] | 1984[a] | 1983 | 1982 | 1981 | 1980 |
|---|---|---|---|---|---|---|
| Sales (millions) | $13,700 | $12,750 | $11,857 | $11,507 | $10,851 | $10,166 |
| Operating Margins (%) | 15.5 | 15.5 | 14.9 | 15.0 | 15.9 | 16.4 |
| Net profits (millions) | $ 875.0 | $ 790.0 | $ 737.3 | $ 714.1 | $ 761.1 | $ 768.1 |
| Net profit margins (%) | 6.4 | 6.2 | 6.2 | 6.2 | 7.0 | 7.6 |
| Percent earned to total capital | 13.0 | 13.0 | 13.8 | 13.5 | 15.9 | 16.4 |
| Percent earned to net worth | 16.0 | 16.0 | 16.4 | 15.5 | 18.2 | 19.0 |
| Percent retained to common equity | 7.5 | 7.0 | 7.2 | 6.4 | 8.5 | 10.0 |

[a]Estimated.

Source: *Value Line* Investment Survey, January 25, 1985, p. 812.

**Exhibit 3.4** Black Demographics

**LABOR FORCE BY PERCENT**

| Age | 1977 | 1978 | 1979 | 1980 | 1981 | 1982 | 1983 |
|---|---|---|---|---|---|---|---|
| 16–19 | 8.5 | 8.8 | 8.4 | 8.0 | 7.5 | 7.3 | 7.0 |
| 20–24 | 16.0 | 16.0 | 16.1 | 15.8 | 16.0 | 16.3 | 16.1 |
| 25–34 | 27.9 | 28.0 | 28.6 | 29.5 | 31.0 | 30.8 | 31.5 |
| 35–44 | 19.5 | 19.4 | 19.5 | 19.7 | 20.0 | 20.3 | 20.6 |
| 45–54 | 16.2 | 15.8 | 15.7 | 15.6 | 14.5 | 14.2 | 14.0 |
| 55–64 | 9.3 | 9.2 | 9.1 | 9.0 | 9.0 | 9.0 | 9.0 |
| 65+ | 2.6 | 2.8 | 2.6 | 2.4 | 2.0 | 2.1 | 1.9 |

**MEAN INCOME**

| Age | 1978 | 1979 | 1980 | 1981 | 1982 | 1983 |
|---|---|---|---|---|---|---|
| 14–24 | $ 6,673 | $ 7,738 | $ 7,898[a] | $10,350[a] | $10,487[a] | $ 9,019[a] |
| 25–34 | 11,815 | 12,916 | 14,018 | 15,079 | 16,256 | 15,871 |
| 35–44 | 14,021 | 15,277 | 16,788 | 18,350 | 19,172 | 20,376 |
| 45–54 | 14,983 | 16,933 | 18,013 | 19,286 | 19,812 | 21,404 |
| 55–64 | 11,976 | 14,741 | 16,301 | 17,089 | 18,093 | 19,105 |
| 65+ | 8,363 | 8,713 | 10,472 | 10,650 | 11,566 | 12,272 |

[a]These figures represent the age category of 15–24.

**POPULATION PERCENTAGE**

| Age | 1977 | 1978 | 1979 | 1980 | 1981 | 1982 | 1983 |
|---|---|---|---|---|---|---|---|
| 16–19 | 9.4[a] | 9.3[a] | 9.1[a] | 11.3[c] | 10.8[c] | 10.5[c] | 10.1[c] |
| 20–24 | 14.3[b] | 14.4[b] | 13.5[b] | 10.3 | 10.5 | 10.5 | 10.5 |
| 25–34 | 14.1 | 14.5 | 15.0 | 17.1 | 16.6 | 17.0 | 17.4 |
| 34–44 | 10.1 | 10.3 | 10.4 | 10.2 | 10.3 | 10.6 | 10.9 |
| 45–54 | 9.1 | 9.0 | 9.0 | 8.6 | 8.4 | 8.3 | 8.1 |
| 55–64 | 7.0 | 7.1 | 7.1 | 7.2 | 7.1 | 7.1 | 7.1 |
| 65+ | 7.7 | 7.8 | 7.9 | 7.9 | 7.9 | 8.0 | 7.9 |

[a]These figures represent the age category of 14–17.
[b]These figures represent the age category of 18–24.
[c]These figures represent the age category of 15–19.

*Source: Statistical Abstracts of U.S., 1985.*

The black consumer is experiencing an increase in disposable income greater than that of the population at large. Between 1972 and 1979, blacks' aggregate income expanded 194 percent from $30 billion to $88.2 billion and in 1983 was in excess of $100 billion. According to an industry analyst, blacks account for an increasing percentage (currently 13 percent) of the nation's population. The 24–35 age group—heavy toiletry and cosmetics consumers—will by the mid-1980s represent 17.4 percent of the total black population.

With statistics like these, the ethnic consumer is being sought after as never before. The major national competitors of Johnson Products Company are (1) Revlon, with its Realistic hair straightener and Polished Amber lines; (2) Avon, with Shades of Beauty and Earth and Fire lines of makeup products for black women; and (3) Cosmair's L'Oreal of Paris, which has a product line called Radiance consisting of hair colors and formula hair relaxers. (See Exhibit 3.5.)

In 1983, the market penetration of the larger national companies may have peaked. The competition has added a new facet in the market. The large companies such as Revlon, Avon, and Fashion Fair are still in pursuit of the ethnic dollar, but they face new competition from the small regional manufacturers. These competitors offer a restricted product line while competing for the same shelf space. For example, M&M Products—with their product Sta-Sof-Fro—was founded in 1973. The company's sales reached approximately $47 million in 1983, and it employed 383 people. This firm has earned a reputation as a major competitor in the black hair-care industry. In 1982, Pro-Line—another competitor—had sales of approximately $23 million and had 200 employees. Pro-Line is an innovative black hair-care firm that is constantly introducing new products such as Perm Repair and Cherry Fragrance Oil Shampoo.

## PRODUCTS

Johnson Products currently manufacturers over 100 different products. Since January 1980, the company has introduced more than 45 new products, including 19 in 1982. Most new products introduced by Johnson Products were matched by similar new products from their competitors. Products lines fall into two categories: those marketed to the professional industry, and those sold to the general public. (See Exhibit 3.6.) Johnson's retail sales are the company's largest segment.

Before the introduction of Ultra Sheen Precise in 1980, the company had not introduced a single innovative product in over 15 years. As a result, the firm's public image had waned and its reputation among professional beauty operators had faltered. Each successive new product introduction in the following four years has been designed to portray the firm as an industry innovator, "personally concerned with solving the beauty problems of Black consumers."[4] (Black Enterprise; June 1980).

According to Mr. Johnson, "In assessing why our business [1980] had slacked we learned several things. For one, we were no longer thought of as an innovative, sophisticated organization. We found also a low level of loyalty from professional beauticians and salon operators. In addition, there was an apparent lack of understanding among many large retail buyers that Johnson Products is a large, substantial organization."[5]

Johnson also cited other problems, including

1. Increased competition from large and small regional competitors
2. Competition for shelf space
3. Changing buying habits of the consumer due to economic conditions
4. Bad economy which caused retailers to carry smaller inventories, causing higher stock-out conditions and loss of customer goodwill

**Exhibit 3.5** Selected Financial Information on Competitors

| Company | Sales[a] | | Operating Margins (%) | | Net Profit[a] | | Net Profit Margins (%) | | EPS | | % Earned to Total Capital | | % Earned to Net Worth | | % Retained to Common Equity | |
|---|---|---|---|---|---|---|---|---|---|---|---|---|---|---|---|---|
| | 1983 | 1982 | 1983 | 1982 | 1983 | 1982 | 1983 | 1982 | 1983 | 1982 | 1983 | 1982 | 1983 | 1982 | 1983 | 1982 |
| Alberto-Culver | 313.7 | 320.4 | 5.2 | 6.0 | 3.9 | 6.6 | 1.3 | 2.1 | 1.01 | 1.17 | 5.6 | 8.9 | 5.7 | 9.8 | 2.7 | 7.0 |
| Avon Products | 3,000.1 | 3,000.8 | 13.6 | 15.7 | 164.4 | 196.6 | 5.5 | 6.6 | 2.21 | 2.75 | 11.9 | 14.2 | 13.7 | 16.1 | 1.3 | 1.8 |
| Gillette | 2,183.3 | 2,239.0 | 18.1 | 17.7 | 145.9 | 135.1 | 6.7 | 6.0 | 4.78 | 4.45 | 15.3 | 14.6 | 19.3 | 18.7 | 9.9 | 9.9 |
| Helene Curtis | 330.4 | 243.2 | 8.3 | 5.2 | 10.4 | 3.6 | 3.2 | 1.5 | 2.84 | 0.98 | 13.7 | 7.1 | 19.5 | 8.4 | 19.5 | 8.4 |
| Johnson Products | 45.8 | 42.4 | 9.5 | loss | 1.6% | (3.6) | 3.6 | loss | 0.41 | (0.91) | 7.5 | loss | 7.5 | loss | 7.5 | loss |
| Mary Kay | 323.8 | 304.3 | 22.2 | 22.0 | 36.7 | 35.4 | 11.6 | 10.3 | 1.22 | 1.18 | 27.2 | 35.6 | 27.8 | 37.1 | 25.1 | 33.8 |
| Noxell Corp. | 304.3 | 261.9 | 14.5 | 13.7 | 23.2 | 18.5 | 7.6 | 7.1 | 2.33 | 1.88 | 20.0 | 18.7 | 20.0 | 18.7 | 14.0 | 12.9 |
| Redken Labs | 86.3 | 84.6 | 15.7 | 16.2 | 6.4 | 6.5 | 7.4 | 7.6 | 2.95 | 2.25 | 14.0 | 16.0 | 14.9 | 17.6 | 12.0 | 15.0 |
| Revlon, Inc. | 2,378.9 | 2,351.0 | 13.6 | 12.9 | 111.2 | 111.1 | 4.7 | 4.7 | 5.01 | 4.44 | 9.9 | 8.7 | 12.3 | 9.3 | 4.1 | 2.8 |

[a]These figures are stated in millions of dollars.

Source: *Value Line* Investment Survey, January 25, 1985, pp. 813, 814, 819, 820–825.

**Exhibit 3.6** Major Product Lines Introduced in the Last Four Years

|  | **Year Introduced** |
| --- | --- |
| **Professional lines** |  |
| 1. Ultra Sheen brand |  |
|     Precise Conditioning Relaxer | 1980 |
|     Precise Curl System | 1980 |
|     Precise No-Lye Relaxer | 1983 |
| 2. Bantu Curl brand (8 products) | 1981 |
| 3. Ultra Sheen II | 1983 |
| **Retail lines** |  |
| 1. Afro Sheen brand | 1980 |
| 2. Ultra Sheen brand |  |
|     Natural Body Formula | 1980 |
|     Ultra Sheen No-Lye Relaxer | 1983 |
| 3. Classy Curl brand | 1980 |
| 4. Tender Treatment brand | 1980 |
| 5. Gentle Treatment brand |  |
|     Gentle Treatment Instant Conditioner | 1983 |
|     Super Setting Lotion | 1983 |
|     No-Lye Condition Relaxer | 1983 |

Hair-care products and cosmetics accounted for 94 percent of net sales and other operating revenue in 1983. The firm also manufactures two lines of cosmetics: Ultra Sheen and Moisture Formula.

**MARKETING**

The sales effort of Johnson Products Company is directed almost entirely toward reaching black consumers. The company's products and marketing are strategically positioned to concentrate on the ethnic markets. In 1975, Johnson Products deviated from this pattern when it introduced a men's fragrance line, Black Tie, which was marketed to the general consumer. In keeping with this marketing strategy, Johnson focuses its sales efforts in areas where there is a concentration of the black population. Therefore, most consumer purchases of Ultra Sheen, Afro Sheen, and other company products originate in the East, Midwest, West Coast, and South, with few sales being made in the Northeast, Great Plains, and Rocky Mountain regions of the United States.

**Sales Organization**

Johnson Products distributes its lines mainly through retail outlets by utilizing a company/distributor/retailer channel. Johnson's professional lines are sold to barber shops and beauty salons. Although an intermediary is usually involved in product distribution, a substantial number of company sales are made directly to national and regional drug, grocery, and mass merchandising chains. Freedom distributed Johnson's and competitors' products on the eastern seaboard.

With the introduction of Black Tie, Johnson's top management contracted an outside sales organization adept in the men's fragrance market to distribute the new line. Through its marketing tactics, Johnson Products hoped to create for Black Tie an image which is appealing to both the ethnic and general markets. The fragrance was perceived in the marketplace as an ethnic product and failed to achieve a profitable sales level.

Prior to 1969, all contacts with Johnson's sales organization emanated from the company's home office in Chicago. In an effort to improve the effectiveness of its sales programs, Johnson Products developed a district sales structure in 1969 to aid the control and development of its sales force and to improve its recruiting efforts. In the nine sales districts, salespeople now demonstrate the importance and profitability of ethnic products to distributors and retailers and assist them in merchandising the company's products.

Johnson Product's sales force marketing division has grown steadily over the life of the company. Each sales representative undergoes an intensive sales training program which continues after he or she is assigned to various districts for work in the field.

Johnson's salespeople function in various capacities, all aimed at increased retail and professional sales. Some conduct store demonstrations of Johnson's facial cosmetics. Others conduct clinics in the proper use of Ultra Sheen Creme Relaxers and products designed for beauticians and barbers.

In the area of international marketing, Johnson Products Company exports to selected foreign markets. George E. Johnson's stated philosophy is that he plans to sell personal-care products wherever there are blacks to buy them. It was in this spirit that Johnson Products began exporting to Nigeria in 1975. (See the section entitled International Subsidiaries.)

**Consumer Market**

In an effort to improve consumer perception, Johnson Products had introduced innovative products backed by elaborate promotional campaigns. In 1980, for example, the Ultra Sheen Precise line was introduced. This was the first hair relaxer to contain a substantive conditioner, and it was so unique the company was issued a patent. A marketing plan, "The Precise System of Success," was developed to introduce the Precise line. Stage presentations were made in about ten cities, with more than 10,000 beauticians attending. This was followed by more than 100 day-long seminars in some 30 cities attended by about 20,000 professionals. Also, the Classy Curl line was introduced for the younger market segment. For the professional market, Johnson Products introduced Natural Body Formula, Ultra Sheen Conditioning Plus Shampoo, and Curl System.

In 1981, new product introductions were Gentle Treatment, Tender Treatment, and Bantu Curl. The Tender Treatment brand includes conditioning detangling shampoo, super penetrating conditioner, and creme hair dress. Gentle Treatment has a built-in conditioning agent similar to the successful Precise brand. In addition, this product line had a significant product attribute: a calcium hydroxide base instead of the sodium hydroxide base which had prompted the FTC in 1975 to intervene with a consent decree to place a warning on its product.

Along with these product introductions, the company has experimented with several extensive promotional campaigns. The "Win A Date" contest offering a male and female winner a weekend date in Jamaica with the two Classy Curl models was used in the Classy Curl campaign. In promoting the Gentle Treatment Conditioning Creme Relaxer, the "Great Model Search" was conducted. More than 7000 people entered this contest. The winners were used as models in promotional campaigns in 1983. Soon after these promotions, an A. C. Nielson audit survey showed an increase in market share in both product categories.

In the cosmetics lines, advertising is done mostly in magazines based on demographic and psychographic analysis. Earlier in 1979, Johnson's cosmetics line was being reformulated. The Ultra Sheen line was being designed to appeal to women under 25, while Moisture Formula was directed toward the more sophisticated segment. The company accomplished the segmentation of the market by price differentials. This reformulation was done by William Pinkney, director of marketing cosmetics in 1979. Mr. Pinkney joined the company after developing the Polished Amber lines for Revlon. Moisture Formula was advertised in such magazines as *Cosmopolitan, Ebony, Essence, Glamour,* and *Jet.* TBWA of New York was handling the advertising of the cosmetics lines.

In 1982, Johnson Products commissioned a study to research consumer opinions and/or perceptions of the company. Results from the study were (1) a high level of name recognition (93 percent), (2) a feeling that its products guarantee quality (68 percent), and (3) a belief that the firm is reliable and trustworthy (70 percent).

Advertising and promotion expenses increased from 1979 through 1981. From 1982 through 1983, advertising was reduced. However, as a percentage of net sales, these expenditures have varied. (See Exhibit 3.7.)

**Exhibit 3.7** Advertising and Promotion Expenditures

| Year | Amount | Percentage of Net Sales |
|------|--------|------------------------|
| 1971 | $2,830,000 | 20 |
| 1972 | 3,097,000 | 18 |
| 1973 | 3,733,000 | 15 |
| 1974 | 4,202,000 | 13 |
| 1975 | 4,498,000 | 12 |
| 1976 | 5,608,000 | 14 |
| 1977 | 5,731,000 | 18 |
| 1978 | 6,211,000 | 17 |
| 1979 | 6,019,000 | 18 |
| 1980 | 7,243,000 | 21 |
| 1981 | 8,076,000 | 17 |
| 1982 | 7,467,000 | 18 |
| 1983 | 7,226,000 | 16 |

## Professional Market

In 1983, one of the company's product development goals was to increase its professional market share, which constitutes about 15 percent of Johnson's total hair-care business. Over the past six years, sales have been increasing between 15 and 20 percent annually. These increases show an expanding ethnic market. The first market introduction in 1983 was the Precise No-Lye Relaxer, which was followed by improved versions of earlier lines, Ultra Sheen II and Bantu. Special promotions and training programs are being aimed at the professional market segment.

On the retail side, the Gentle Treatment No-Lye Conditioning Creme Relaxer was influenced by the "Great Model Search" campaign in 1982. The 1983 promotion plans included a 15-market concert tour schedule featuring the Gap Band. This tour was sponsored by the Ultra Curl brand. Extensive couponing and sampling were conducted concurrent with the concert tour.

## RESEARCH AND DEVELOPMENT

Since January 1980, the Johnson Products Research Center has introduced, for both the retail and professional markets, more than 50 new products and line extensions. These new products contributed more than 60 percent of the company's sales in 1983, compared to 48 percent in 1982 and 36 percent in 1981.

The Johnson Products Research Center is considered the largest laboratory of its kind devoted exclusively to the research and development of beauty-care products for black consumers. A staff of more than 30 technicians and scientists representing a variety of scientific disciplines works with the latest sophisticated equipment in a 7000-square-foot research laboratory. Approximately one-third of the research and development man-hours are spent on quality control; the rest are spent on new product development and the improvement of existing products. Research and development expenditures are shown in Exhibit 3.8. In-house capabilities are supplemented through the use of outside consultants and technical services in developing concepts and packaging design and researching the characteristics of ethnic skin and hair.

One significant aspect of the company's efforts is the capability to perform basic scientific research, which has enabled Johnson Products to develop unique technologies for producing a variety of beauty-aid products. During the past three

**Exhibit 3.8** R&D Expenditures

| Year | R&D Expenditures |
|------|------------------|
| 1983 | $799,000 |
| 1982 | 868,000 |
| 1981 | 870,000 |
| 1980 | 782,000 |
| 1979 | 690,000 |
| 1978 | 763,000 |
| 1977 | 739,000 |
| 1976 | 525,000 |
| 1975 | 467,000 |

years, the company has received four patents for products presently on the market; several other patents are pending.

**FINANCE**  Since 1969, Johnson Products has been a public corporation. The initial stock offering was 300,000 shares at $15 per share. Johnson was authorized to issue a total of 7,504,400 shares. The company was listed on the American Stock Exchange and the stock split 2-for-1 in January 1973. The par value of the stock changed from $1 to $.50. On August 31, 1983, the market price per share of stock was $9.75. (See Exhibit 3.9.)

During the fiscal years 1980, 1981, 1982, and 1983, the company sustained losses in 8 of the 16 quarters. In 1980 and 1982, the company suffered yearly losses of $2,379,000 and $3,623,000, respectively. Johnson Products' return to profitability in 1983 was facilitated by the development of new products along with significant decreases in labor, material, and overhead costs. Some previously contracted activities (e.g., building maintenance and silk-screening of plastic bottles) were done in-house. In 1982, total staff was cut by approximately 10 percent by increasing employee productivity and eliminating certain jobs.

A decrease in short-term borrowing also helped improve working capital and overall liquidity. Short-term borrowings were $963,000 in August 1983, compared to $3.5 million at the end of 1982. During 1983, the company replaced its existing line of credit with a three-year loan agreement which guarantees availability of funds if needed. The old agreement was set up so that credit was granted at the bank's option. The amounts of the loans are to be based on eligible trade accounts receivables as defined in the agreement. Collateral under the agreement consists of Johnson Products' trade accounts receivables and inventories. Other restrictions include provisions regarding recapitalization, mergers, consolidations, and minimum net worth requirement.

In August 1983, the unused portion of this agreement was $4,037,000. Borrowings under the agreement bear interest at 2½ percent above the prevailing prime interest rate. The maximum outstanding borrowings were $3.5 million at a weighted average interest rate of 15 percent in both fiscal 1982 and 1983.

To meet operational efficiency goals, the company spent $1 million in both 1983 and 1982 on fixed-asset additions. More than $600,000 was allocated for capital expenditures in 1984. Investment in fixed assets at year end was $17.6 million compared to $16.6 million in 1982. Trade accounts receivable increased $1.1 million to $11.1 million in 1983 as a result of higher enrollments in the beauty school subsidiary. The allowance for doubtful accounts increased by $229,000. The company's net sales and other operating revenue for 1983 increased 8 percent to $45.7 million from $42.4 million in 1982, primarily reflecting an approximately 77 percent increase in beauty school revenues.

Owing to significant operating losses at Johnson Products of Nigeria, Ltd., and other external factors, the Johnson investment and advances to the Nigerian operation were written down in 1982. Previously, Johnson's 40 percent interest in this venture was carried at acquisition cost adjusted for equity in losses through

**Exhibit 3.9** Ten-Year Financial Review[a]

| Years Ended August 31, | 1983 | 1982 | 1981 |
|---|---|---|---|
| **Summary of operations** | | | |
| Net sales | $40,937 | $39,177 | $43,197 |
| Other operating revenue | 4,838 | 3,270 | 3,710 |
| Total net sales and other operating revenue | 45,775 | 42,447 | 46,907 |
| Cost of sales | 16,649 | 18,191 | 19,528 |
| Selling, general and administrative (exclusive of advertising and promotion) | 18,490 | 19,122 | 17,866 |
| Advertising and promotion | 7,226 | 7,467 | 8,076 |
| Equity in losses and write-down of investment in Nigerian affiliate | — | 1,802 | 466 |
| Interest, net | 424 | 414 | 48 |
| Income (loss) before income taxes | 2,986 | (4,549) | 923 |
| Income taxes (benefit) | 1,358 | (926) | 538 |
| Net income (loss) | 1,628 | (3,623) | 385 |
| Net income (loss) per share (EPS) | 0.41 | (0.91) | 0.10 |
| Dividends per share | — | — | — |
| **Other financial data** | | | |
| Current assets | 19,894 | 20,082 | 20,112 |
| Current liabilities | 7,186 | 9,022 | 6,683 |
| Working capital | 12,708 | 11,060 | 13,429 |
| Property, net | 9,210 | 9,133 | 8,988 |
| Total assets | 29,785 | 29,659 | 30,860 |
| Capital lease obligations | 299 | — | — |
| Shareholders' equity | 21,715 | 20,062 | 23,660 |
| Shareholders' equity per share | 5.46 | 5.05 | 5.96 |
| Capital expenditures | 987 | 1,076 | 791 |
| Ratios | | | |
| Income (loss) before income taxes to net sales and other operating revenue | 6.5% | (10.7%) | 2.0% |
| Net income (loss) to net sales and other operating revenue | 3.6% | (8.5%) | .8% |
| Return on average shareholders' equity | 7.8% | (16.6%) | 1.6% |
| Advertising and promotion to net sales and other operating revenue | 15.8% | 17.6% | 17.2% |
| Average common and common equivalent shares outstanding[b] | 3,980,000 | 3,973,000 | 3,972,000 |
| Stock price range–High | $11\frac{3}{8}$ | $3\frac{1}{2}$ | $5\frac{1}{8}$ |
| —Low | $3\frac{1}{8}$ | 2 | $2\frac{5}{8}$ |
| Sales per share (dollars) | 11.50 | 10.68 | 11.81 |
| Number of employees | 550 | 541 | 568 |

[a]In thousands of dollars except per share data, percentages, and employee data.

[b]Common equivalent shares consist of class B common shares for the years 1984 through 1976.

*Source:* 1984 Annual Report and *Value Line* Investment Survey, April 19, 1985, p. 821.

| 1980 | 1979 | 1978 | 1977 | 1976 | 1975 | 1974 |
|---|---|---|---|---|---|---|
| $32,294 | $31,337 | $37,246 | $32,380 | $39,428 | $37,660 | $31,585 |
| 2,842 | 1,801 | 1,416 | 920 | 703 | — | — |
| 35,136 | 33,138 | 38,662 | 33,300 | 40,131 | 37,660 | 31,585 |
| 15,250 | 12,291 | 14,854 | 13,071 | 14,327 | 12,993 | 9,877 |
| 16,773 | 14,657 | 13,776 | 12,812 | 12,232 | 9,431 | 7,917 |
| 7,243 | 6,019 | 6,211 | 5,731 | 5,608 | 4,498 | 4,202 |
| 380 | — | — | — | — | — | — |
| (270) | (450) | (416) | (237) | (234) | (372) | (404) |
| (4,240) | 621 | 4,237 | 2,553 | 8,198 | 11,110 | 9,993 |
| (1,861) | 300 | 2,000 | 1,150 | 3,950 | 5,460 | 4,991 |
| (2,379) | 321 | 2,237 | 1,403 | 4,248 | 5,650 | 5,002 |
| (0.60) | 0.08 | 0.56 | 0.35 | 1.05 | 1.40 | 1.24 |
| 0.18 | 0.36 | 0.36 | 0.36 | 0.30 | 0.25 | 0.20 |
| 18,573 | 18,658 | 22,632 | 20,026 | 21,751 | 18,800 | 15,689 |
| 5,396 | 2,989 | 5,510 | 3,250 | 4,125 | 3,382 | 3,433 |
| 13,177 | 15,669 | 17,122 | 16,776 | 17,626 | 15,418 | 12,256 |
| 9,062 | 9,400 | 9,346 | 9,533 | 8,907 | 7,506 | 5,734 |
| 29,205 | 29,886 | 33,505 | 30,900 | 31,621 | 27,126 | 22,049 |
| — | — | — | — | — | — | — |
| 23,257 | 26,355 | 27,433 | 27,018 | 27,038 | 23,415 | 18,396 |
| 5.86 | 6.63 | 6.87 | 6.67 | 6.67 | 5.79 | 4.56 |
| 528 | 1,008 | 864 | 1,508 | 2,082 | 2,184 | 669 |
| (12.1%) | 1.9% | 11.0% | 7.7% | 20.4% | 29.5% | 31.6% |
| (6.8%) | 1.0% | 5.8% | 4.2% | 10.6% | 15.0% | 15.8% |
| (9.6%) | 1.2% | 8.2% | 5.2% | 16.8% | 27.0% | 31.1% |
| 20.6% | 18.2% | 16.1% | 17.2% | 14.0% | 11.9% | 13.3% |
| 3,972,000 | 3,976,000 | 3,995,000 | 4,051,000 | 4,051,000 | 4,044,000 | 4,037,000 |
| $5\frac{5}{8}$ | $6\frac{3}{4}$ | $11\frac{1}{4}$ | $8\frac{7}{8}$ | $20\frac{5}{8}$ | 28 | $25\frac{3}{4}$ |
| $2\frac{7}{8}$ | $3\frac{1}{2}$ | $8\frac{7}{8}$ | $4\frac{3}{4}$ | $7\frac{5}{8}$ | $12\frac{1}{2}$ | $14\frac{1}{2}$ |
| 8.85 | 8.34 | 9.73 | 8.22 | 9.91 | 9.32 | 7.83 |
| 563 | 516 | 553 | 470 | 490 | 420 | 410 |

**Exhibit 3.10**

# JOHNSON PRODUCTS CO.
## Last Five Years Balance Sheets[a]

|  | 1983 | 1982 | 1981 | 1980 | 1979 |
|---|---|---|---|---|---|
| **Assets** | | | | | |
| Current assets | | | | | |
| Cash and certificates of deposit | $ 1,418 | $ 1,324 | $ 1,388 | $ 550 | $ 1,915 |
| Receivables | | | | | |
| Trade less allowance for doubtful accounts of $500,000 in 1983 and $271,000 in 1982 | 11,120 | 9,962 | 11,423 | 8,061 | 7,149 |
| Commercial paper | — | — | — | — | 2,654 |
| Other | 183 | 232 | 169 | 137 | 605 |
| Refundable income taxes | — | 1,170 | — | 2,310 | 749 |
| Inventories | 6,579 | 6,850 | 6,067 | 6,624 | 4,727 |
| Prepaid expenses | 594 | 544 | 1,065 | 891 | 859 |
| Total current assets | 19,894 | 20,082 | 20,112 | 18,573 | 18,685 |
| Property, plant, and equipment | 17,590 | 16,603 | 15,527 | 14,735 | 14,363 |
| Less accumulated depreciation and amortization | 8,380 | 7,470 | 6,539 | 5,673 | 4,963 |
|  | 9,210 | 9,133 | 8,988 | 9,062 | 9,400 |
| Other assets | | | | | |
| Cash value, officers' life insurance | 339 | 90 | 164 | 35 | 1,226 |
| Investments | 244 | 244 | 1,453 | 1,361 | 395 |
| Miscellaneous receivables | 57 | 49 | 63 | 733 | 86 |
| Unamortized excess cost over net assets of business acquired | 41 | 61 | 80 | 101 | 121 |
|  | 681 | 444 | 1,760 | 1,570 | 1,828 |
| Total assets | $29,785 | $29,659 | $30,860 | $29,205 | $29,886 |
| **Liabilities and shareholders' equity** | | | | | |
| Current liabilities | | | | | |
| Short-term bank loans | $ 963 | $ 3,500 | $ — | $ 625 | $ — |
| Accounts payable | 3,376 | 4,556 | 4,971 | 3,829 | 1,917 |
| Current capital lease obligations | 133 | — | — | — | — |
| Dividends payable | — | — | — | — | 357 |
| Income taxes | | | | | |
| Current | 638 | — | 499 | 82 | — |
| Deferred | 440 | — | — | — | — |
| Deferred income | 303 | 182 | 321 | 243 | 402 |
| Accrued expenses | 1,333 | 784 | 892 | 617 | 313 |
| Total current liabilities | 7,186 | 9,022 | 6,683 | 5,396 | 2,989 |
| Capital lease obligations | 299 | — | — | — | — |
| Deferred income taxes | 585 | 575 | 517 | 552 | 542 |

**Exhibit 3.10** (continued)

|  | 1983 | 1982 | 1981 | 1980 | 1979 |
|---|---|---|---|---|---|
| Shareholders' equity | | | | | |
| Capital stock | | | | | |
| Preferred stock, no par; authorized 300,000 shares; none issued | | | | | |
| Common stock, $.50 par; authorized 7,504,400 shares; issued 4,052,722 shares | 2,027 | 2,027 | 2,027 | 2,027 | 2,027 |
| Additional paid-in capital | 649 | 670 | 646 | 628 | 634 |
| Retained earnings | 19,430 | 17,784 | 21,425 | 21,040 | 24,132 |
| Treasury stock, 72,360 shares in 1983 and 77,520 shares in 1982, at cost | (391) | (419) | (438) | (438) | (438) |
| | 21,715 | 20,062 | 23,660 | 23,257 | 26,355 |
| Total liabilities and shareholders' equity | $29,785 | $29,659 | $30,860 | $29,205 | $29,886 |

[a]Dollar figures in thousands.

*Sources:* Johnson Products Company, Inc., Annual Reports 1983, 1981, and 1979.

July 31 of each year. Under Nigerian law, Johnson's ownership is limited to 40 percent. Because this affiliate is still in operation, Johnson may be required in the future to advance significant amounts of working capital to this venture.

The above financial data can be found in Exhibits 3.9 and 3.10.

## NOTES

1. *New York Times,* June 6, 1978.
2. Ibid.
3. *Foreign Economic Trends and Their Implications for the United States,* November 1983.
4. *Black Enterprise,* June 1980.
5. Ibid.

# 4  A Note on the Brewing Industry

Michael D. Caputa
Virginia Polytechnic Institute and State University

**INTRODUC-
TION**

American brewers were facing sobering times indeed. Americans' changing life-styles and tastes, along with public concern about alcohol abuse and drunk driving and federal pressure to raise the drinking age to 21, appeared likely to leave industry growth flat in upcoming years. Already, per capita consumption of most alcoholic beverages was falling.

For the U.S. brewing industry 1984 was an especially rough year. Total domestic shipments were down almost 2 million barrels (one barrel equals 31 gallons). Unfortunately, it appeared that things would be much the same in 1985. Declining volume would probably cause the breweries to more aggressively advertise and promote their products to hold on to market share. In fact, advertising and promotional spending were soaring and price cutting had become commonplace. Brewers needed to decide how to maintain their profitability in a shrinking market dominated by fierce competition.

**HISTORICAL
BACK-
GROUND**

No one knows who invented beer—it just happened. The beverage occurred when water, mashed grains, and yeast cells, which were found floating freely in the air, came in contact.[1] Beer has been a part of mankind's existence since its beginnings. It was known to most ancient peoples—the Babylonians, the Assyrians, the Egyptians, the Hebrews, the Chinese, the Incas, and the Caucasian tribes of western Asia and Europe. The oldest written record of beer making dates back 6000 years to ancient Babylonia.[2]

The colonists who arrived in America in the seventeenth century were well acquainted with brewing. Puritanism did not ban the consumption of beer and ale. In fact, most of the prominent figures of early America thought highly of beer. George Washington, Thomas Jefferson, James Madison, and Patrick Henry favored beer as a "temperate beverage." During the early days of the republic, many states passed acts exempting commercial brewers from various taxes as an attempt to encourage the young industry. By 1810, there were 129 breweries in the United States producing 182,690 barrels of beer worth $955,791. With the introduction of lager beer—a lighter, more palatable beer—in the first half of the nineteenth century, the brewing industry got the lift that was needed to make it

This case was written by Michael D. Caputa (M.B.A. in marketing from V.P.I. in June 1985) under the direction of Larry D. Alexander (assistant professor of strategic management), Department of Management, College of Business, Virginia Polytechnic Institute and State University. Copyright © 1985 by Michael D. Caputa and Larry D. Alexander.

one of the great industries of the country.[3]

During the latter half of the nineteenth century, the brewing industry mainly concerned itself with the technical problems of the brewing process. Temperature control, pasteurization, improvements in barley and hop yields, new methods of malting, and other technical developments helped to turn the craft of brewing into a business. As in all businesses, there was a constant pressure to make and sell more product. But even as plants grew larger and business expanded, breweries remained largely local operations that were well known only within the communities they served. Toward the end of nineteenth century, the industry began to undergo increasing consolidation. For example, in 1873 there were 4,131 breweries producing 9,633,223 barrels—an average of 2,332 barrels per brewery per year.[4] In 1914, however, there were only 1,392 breweries producing 66,189,473 barrels—an average of 47,535 barrels per brewery per year.[5]

Even as the industry boomed in the early part of the twentieth century there was growing pressure from the forces of temperance. Despite the opposition of President Wilson, Congress finally succumbed to the will of the "Drys" and enacted the Eighteenth Amendment, Prohibition, effective January 16, 1920. For the next 13 years the country was plagued with underworld violence brought on by illegal bootlegging. In addition, there were billions of dollars in lost tax revenues and millions spent attempting to enforce an unworkable law. Public sentiment finally convinced Congress to relegalize malt beverages on April 7, 1933. In the intervening years, however, hundreds of small breweries had gone out of business.

Since the end of Prohibition, the brewing industry has increasingly become a business of large national companies. Although 750 breweries opened in the two years after 1933, only 163 remained by 1968. By 1976, that number had dwindled to 97. This shrinking number of breweries has led to the dominance of a few large firms. Today over 90 percent of the beer market share is controlled by the six largest breweries (see Exhibit 4.1).

## The Brewing Process

Beer production begins with barley malt. Malted barley is grain that has been allowed to germinate. This releases enzymes that convert starches into sugars. Originally, beer was made entirely of barley malt. But large U.S. brewers usually add rice, corn, or other cereal grains to their beers because it is cheaper and makes a lighter beer. The grains are then mixed with water to yield "mash." The mash is cooked at controlled temperatures to convert the cereal starches to fermentable sugars.

After cooking, the solid parts of the mash are removed by straining and the remaining liquid, called wort, is boiled with hops. Hops add flavor and bitterness to beer. After the mixture has been cooled, yeast is added to begin the fermentation process. Yeast converts the sugars in the wort into carbon dioxide and alcohol.

After fermentation, the beer is filtered and aged. Most beers are pasteurized before packaging. This process destroys microorganisms that could cause spoil-

**Exhibit 4.1** Top Ten Domestic Brewers

As A-B and Miller hold tight to their number one and two spots, respectively, increased activity has come from Stroh, Heileman, and Coors, which round out the big five and continue to expand geographically.

| Rank 1983 | Brewery | Brands | Distribution | 1983 Barrel Sales (millions) |
|---|---|---|---|---|
| 1 | Anheuser-Busch, Inc. (St. Louis, Mo.) | Budweiser, Budweiser Light, Michelob, Michelob Light, Busch, Natural Light, L.A., others | National | 60.5 |
| 2 | Miller Brewing Company (Milwaukee, Wis.) | Miller High Life, Lite, Lowenbrau, Milwaukee's Best, Meister Brau, Sharp's L.A., others | National | 37.5 |
| 3 | The Stroh Brewery (Detroit, Mich.) | Stroh's, Stroh Light, Old Milwaukee, Schlitz, Signature, Shaefer, Old Milwaukee Light, Piels, Goebel, others | National | 24.3 |
| 4 | G. Heileman Brewing (LaCrosse, Wis.) | Old Style, Old Style Light, Special Export, Blatz L.A., Schmidt's, Rainier, Blatz, others | Regional | 17.5 |
| 5 | Adolph Coors Company (Golden, Col.) | Coors, Coors Light, Herman Josephs, George Killian's Golden Lager, others | National | 13.5 |
| 6 | Pabst Brewing Company (Milwaukee, Wis.) | Pabst Blue Ribbon, Jacob Best, Olympia, Hamm's, Pabst Extra Light, Andeker, Low Alcohol Gold, others | National | 12.8 |
| 7 | Genesee Brewing Company (Rochester, N.Y.) | Genesee, Genesee Cream Ale, Genesee Light, 12 Horse Ale | Regional | 3.2 |
| 8 | C. Schmidt & Sons, Inc. (Philadelphia, Pa.) | Schmidt's, Bavarian, Rheingold, others | Regional | 2.9 |
| 9 | Falstaff Brewing Corporation (Vancouver, Wash.) | Falstaff, Ballantine, Ballantine Ale, Lucky Lager, others | Regional | 2.7 |
| 10 | Pittsburgh Brewing Company (Pittsburgh, Pa.) | Iron City, Iron City Light, Robin Hood Cream Ale, Old German, others | Regional | 1.0 |

*Source: Beverage World,* September 1984, p. 10.

age during shipping and handling. Keg or draught beer is not pasteurized, but it must be kept refrigerated until it is drunk. Although all beers contain roughly the same ingredients, brewers can vary the quality and quantity of ingredients and the timing of the process to separate average beers from superior ones.

**THE MARKET FOR BEER**

Americans consume nearly 184 million barrels of beer each year—that is almost 35 gallons per legal drinking age adult. Of this volume, 177.5 million barrels are produced domestically and 6.3 million barrels are imported. Out of approximately 240 million Americans, 80 million regularly drink beer. Beer is far and away the most popular alcoholic beverage in this country. American beers generally contain between 3 and 5 percent alcohol—much lower than either wine or distilled spirits. Americans consume about 12 times as much beer as distilled spirits and 11 times as much beer as wine. About 80 percent of all American beer sold is drunk by men (although women actually account for 40 percent of all beer sales according to marketing studies).[6]

American breweries produce more beer than any other nation. However, Americans do not lead the world in per capita consumption. Several of the nations of central Europe surpass U.S. consumption by a wide margin. For example, annual U.S. consumption is about 25 gallons per capita (based on total population). In Germany, Czechoslovakia, and Austria, per capita consumption is 38, 37, and 27 gallons, respectively.

In the United States, California leads all states in beer consumption at approximately 20 million barrels per year. At 52 gallons per capita, individual consumption levels are highest in Nevada, although this number is undoubtedly inflated by tourists. The lowest per capita consumption is in Utah, where 22.5 gallons of beer per legal age adult are drunk annually.[7]

**Market Segments**

The American beer market is generally segmented into six distinct categories: generic beers, price beers, premium beers, superpremium beers, reduced-calorie beers, and malt liquors (see Exhibit 4.2). A seventh segment, imports, is captured by all beers not domestically brewed.[8]

Generic beers, often called plain-label beers, do not carry any type of brand identification, although they sometimes may carry the name of the retailer. Generic beers are generally the lowest-priced beers available. However, they also tend to be of highly variable quality. They are usually produced by a regional brewer as a means of utilizing excess capacity. As far as the American beer market is concerned, generic beers do not appear to be a real threat to the more established segments.

Price beers are priced below premium brands and often enjoy success in specific sales regions. Some price beers have been marketed nationally with good results. The price beer segment, comprised of both the popular- and

**Exhibit 4.2** 1983 Percent of Market
Beer Consumption

| Brand | Percent of Market |
|---|---|
| Premium | 47 |
| Popular | 23 |
| Low-calorie | 18 |
| Superpremium | 6 |
| Import | 3 |
| Malt liquor | 3 |

*Source:* Miller Brewing Co., *Fact Book*, p. 7.

budget-priced beer categories, represents about 23 percent of the American beer market—approximately 43 million barrels in 1983. During the 1970s, sales in this segment were down sharply. The depressed economy of the early 1980s, however, helped to boost the sales of price beers.

Premium beers, the largest beer category, represent the standard of American brewing. Premium beers are more heavily advertised than the other segments and are usually distributed nationally. Most American beer drinkers drink a premium beer. In fact, nine out of the the top ten U.S. beers are premium brands. Premium beers are most noted for providing high quality and full-bodied taste at a moderate price. American breweries produced 86.7 million barrels of premium beer in 1983. Twenty-five years ago, however, premium beers held only a minority share of the U.S. market.

Superpremium beers represent the very best quality the brewer has to offer. These brands are usually the most expensive domestic beers available, but are generally priced below imports. Examples of superpremium beers are Anheuser-Busch's Michelob and Miller's Lowenbrau. American breweries produced 10 million barrels of superpremium beer in 1983.

Reduced-calorie beer is a relatively new segment in the beer market. It literally did not exist until Miller introduced its Lite beer in 1975. Before Lite beer came along, several brewers had tried and failed with reduced-calorie beers. Today, this category is the fastest-growing segment in the industry. With more than 18 percent of the beer market, it is already the third largest segment behind premium and price beers. In 1983, 34.1 million barrels of reduced-calorie beer were brewed in America.

Malt liquor is a beer with a higher alcohol content, usually 5 to 9 percent. It represents a relatively small segment and is popular mainly among young urban males, particularly in the South. In 1983, 5.7 million barrels of malt liquor (about 3.1 percent of the beer market) were produced.

Imports make up the seventh segment. These are beers imported into the United States from such countries as Canada, the Netherlands, Germany, Mexico, and the United Kingdom. Imports make up about 3 percent of the U.S. beer market. They tend to be substantially more expensive than domestic brands owing in part to shipping costs. About 6.3 million barrels of imported beer were consumed in the United States in 1983.

Finally, low-alcohol beers should be mentioned. This is a potential segment in the beer market that has emerged during the mid-1980s. Low-alcohol beers, now generically called LAs, generally contain between 1 and 2 percent alcohol. Several breweries test marketed LAs in 1984, but the verdict is still out on whether these will prove to be widely accepted.

## COMPETI-TION AND CONCENTRA-TION

The malt beverage industry today is composed of two types of breweries: national and regional. As the total number of breweries declines, regional brewers are becoming less important with respect to their share of the total market. The nationals are gaining larger market shares and are enjoying greater economies of scale in production, distribution, and marketing. Over the past 20 years, the larger companies have invested heavily in cost-saving technologies. Smaller plants that lacked such investment remained labor-intensive and experienced higher costs.

## Consolidation of the Industry

As operating costs increase and profitability declines, many companies have turned to consolidation to achieve greater efficiency.[9] As one brewing executive noted, "We all know that to win nationally you probably have to be in the top five—and for many of us the only way to get there is through acquisition."[10]

Until the second half of this century, breweries were largely family-owned businesses. After Prohibition, 750 independent breweries emerged to satisfy demand. Most of these had a single plant located in a fairly well protected geographic market. Customer loyalty to the local brand was extremely high. The company's name was a household word within the community, but virtually unknown outside it. However, as operational requirements became more sophisticated and transportation and marketing capabilities improved, consolidation of the industry began.[11]

Brewing industry consolidation has occurred at a surprisingly consistent rate. The number of plants has dropped in half every 15 years since 1935. At the company level, however, the rate of consolidation has been taking place at an increasing rate. In 1935 there were 750 independent brewing companies, but by 1980 there were only 43.[12] In 1984, the top six brewers—Anheuser-Busch, Miller, Stroh, Heileman, Coors, and Pabst—controlled 90.1 percent of the total beer market share. Despite this high level of concentration, competition is fierce among these major companies. Success is a determined by market share, which is a function of price, image, advertising, and new product development.[13]

 Acquisitions in the brewing industry have occurred largely in three distinct stages. The first stage is the acquisition of small brewers by other small or regional brewers. National companies also make acquisitions during this stage to acquire internal resources in new markets. In the next stage, regionals acquire other regional brewers to form superregionals. This is largely a consolidation among the weak. Finally, acquisition of regionals by nationals occurs. Prior to 1980, almost none of the acquisitions was priced over $100 million. However, between 1980 and 1983 a large percentage of the deals were for prices in excess of $250 million. Examples of these larger acquisitions include Stroh's purchase of Schlitz and Schaefer and Pabst's purchase of Olympia brewery.

**Anheuser-Busch**

Anheuser-Busch is a diversified corporation whose subsidiaries include the world's largest brewery and the country's second largest producer of baked goods. The company was founded in 1852 by Georg Schneider. Five years later, the tiny brewery on St. Louis's South Side faced insolvency but was saved by a loan from businessman Eberhard Anheuser. In 1860, Anheuser bought all interests in the firm and became sole owner. Anheuser's daughter married a young brewery supplier named Adolphus Busch, who later became president of the company. It was Busch's dream to market a national beer that appealed to all taste preferences. Busch also had a flair for advertising. He used only the finest horses to draw his shiny red and green delivery wagons through the city streets.[14]

The company grew and prospered under Busch and his son, who became president in 1913. By 1901, the brewery was producing one million barrels of beer annually. The company survived the Prohibition years by producing corn products, yeast, ice cream, soft drinks, and commercial refrigeration units. Since the end of Prohibition, the corporation has diversified into can manufacturing, malt production, transportation, and family entertainment.

Anheuser-Busch's well-known family of beers includes eight nationally distributed products. Budweiser, brewed and sold since 1876, is the company's principal product and the largest-selling beer in the world. The company also produces Michelob, its superpremium brand, and Busch, a premium beer developed in 1955 to appeal to a particular taste market. The newest product additions are the light beers. Natural Light was first introduced in 1977. It was followed by Michelob Light in 1978 and Bud Light in 1982. Anheuser-Busch has also recently introduced Michelob Classic Dark, a superpremium dark beer, and LA Brand, a reduced-calorie brand with a traditional beer taste. It is hoped that this beer will be popular with consumers who are concerned with their alcohol consumption.

 Anheuser-Busch produces its beers at 11 strategically located breweries throughout the country. The oldest and largest is located in St. Louis and is capable of producing 12.7 million barrels annually. Other major plants are located in Tampa, Jacksonville, Newark, Los Angeles, Williamsburg, Houston, Columbus, Ohio, and Baldwinsville, New York. Total capacity is currently approximately 66 million barrels per year. Plants are presently under construction to expand capacity to 75 million barrels by the mid-1980s.[15]

Distribution of the beer is the responsibility of 960 beer wholesalers. Anheuser-Busch grants its wholesalers exclusive territories to distribute the product wherever permitted by law. It is felt that this action enhances brewer-wholesaler relations.

Anheuser-Busch has recently diversified into several beer-related operations.

Metal Container Corporation, the company's can manufacturing subsidiary, is a significant factor in both company brewing operations and the U.S. can and lid industry. During 1984, Metal Container Corporation produced 3.9 billion cans, providing approximately 33 percent of Anheuser-Busch's total can requirements and 12 percent of all beer cans produced in the United States. Busch Agricultural Resources processes barley into barley malt at plants in Wisconsin and Minnesota. These plants supplied the company with 32 percent of its barley requirement in 1984. The subsidiary also operates rice milling and storage facilities in Arkansas and Missouri.

For the past 26 years, Anheuser-Busch has led all beer producers in nearly every category. In 1982, the company established a new industry record by brewing, packaging, and selling 59.1 million barrels of beer. This record was shattered the following year when the company's volume increased to 60.5 million barrels. In 1984, the nation's leading brewer sold a record 64 million barrels for a 5.8 percent year-to-year gain. This volume is close to the company's 66 million barrels per year capacity. Anheuser-Busch today has a market share of about 35 percent. Its total sales for 1984 were $9.1 billion, up from $6.6 billion in 1983 (see Exhibit 4.3). Net income for 1984 was $391.5 million or $7.40 per share. In contrast to Anheuser-Busch's glowing performance, a flat U.S. beer market left five of the top seven domestic producers with volume declines in 1984.[16]

**Miller Brewing Company**

Miller Brewing Company, headquartered in Milwaukee, Wisconsin, is a subsidiary of Philip Morris, Incorporated. Frederic Miller, a German immigrant, founded the brewery in 1855. Miller began his operation in a small abandoned facility called the Plank Road Brewery. Although Miller only produced 300 barrels his first year, the beer proved so popular in the Milwaukee area that capacity was expanded to 30,000 barrels per year by 1870. Miller also built his own bottling plant in 1883. He insisted on putting his beer in clear bottles so that people would be able to see the quality of his product.

During the late 1800s and early 1900s, Miller's brewing company expanded in capacity, sales volume, product line, and popularity. The company was kept alive during Prohibition by producing such lines as cereal beverages and soft drinks. The brewery reopened after Prohibiton and began to expand rapidly. By the early 1950s, Miller was the ninth largest brewer in the United States in terms of volume.[17]

In 1966, W. R. Grace and Company purchased a controlling interest in the company. This was followed over the next three years by acquisition of plants and rapid expansion of capacity. Philip Morris purchased Miller in 1970 for $130 million. Since that time, Miller's sales have grown from 5.2 million barrels to 37.5 million barrels. Its market share increased from 4 percent in 1970 to 22 percent by 1981.

Miller's premium brand has been brewed since 1855. However, it was not until 1903 that it was first marketed as Miller High Life. This theme was to continue for the next 67 years. When Philip Morris acquired the company in 1970, its

**Exhibit 4.3**

### CONSOLIDATED STATEMENT OF INCOME

**Anheuser-Busch Companies, Inc., and Subsidiaries (in millions, except per share data)**

| Year Ended December 31, | 1984 | 1983 | 1982 |
|---|---|---|---|
| Sales | $7,158.2 | $6,658.5 | $5,185.7 |
| Less federal and state beer taxes | 657.0 | 624.3 | 609.1 |
| Net sales | 6,501.2 | 6,034.2 | 4,576.6 |
| Cost of products sold | 4,414.2 | 4,113.2 | 3,331.7 |
| Gross profit | 2,087.0 | 1,921.0 | 1,244.9 |
| Marketing, administrative, and research expenses | 1,332.3 | 1,220.2 | 752.0 |
| Operating income | 754.7 | 700.8 | 492.9 |
| Other income and expenses | | | |
| Interest expense | (102.7) | (111.4) | (89.2) |
| Interest capitalized | 46.8 | 32.9 | 41.2 |
| Interest income | 22.8 | 12.5 | 17.0 |
| Other expense, net | (31.8) | (18.8) | (8.1) |
| Gain on sale of Lafayette plant | — | — | 20.4 |
| Income before income taxes | 689.8 | 616.0 | 474.2 |
| Provision for income taxes | | | |
| Current | 118.4 | 133.7 | 92.4 |
| Deferred | 179.9 | 134.3 | 94.5 |
| | 298.3 | 268.0 | 186.9 |
| *Net Income* | $391.5 | $ 348.0 | $ 287.3 |
| Earnings per share | | | |
| Primary | $7.40 | $ 6.50 | $ 5.97 |
| Fully diluted | 7.40 | 6.50 | 5.88 |

*Source:* Anheuser-Busch, Inc., 1984 Annual Report, p. 42.

managers decided to change the marketing strategy for Miller High Life. Philip Morris felt that the brand had enormous potential for growth, but that it was failing to grow in 1970 due to its "country club" image.[18] The corporation's marketing managers felt that Miller was targeting the wrong segment. They immediately began working on a new advertising campaign for the beer. The "Miller Time" slogan, one of America's most successful marketing programs, was soon developed. Miller Time soon became synonymous with fun and relaxation after a hard day's work. The Miller Time commercials were modified to "Welcome to Miller Time" in the early 1980s. This new campaign projected an upbeat image that Miller High Life was the beer for good times. According to the company,

Philip Morris did more than transform Miller High Life into a top-selling brand. What it did with Miller caused upheaval throughout the industry. Miller started a marketing revolution, applying modern marketing techniques, including product and package segmentation, target advertising and promotion, and emphasis on distribution. . . . As the Miller-led revolution in marketing progressed, it carried [other] premium brands with it. . . . Along the way, many local and regional brewers . . . closed their doors or became part of larger brewers. Though four of the top five brewers in 1957 are gone today, each of their flagship brands survives as part of another brewer's product family.[19]

Before 1975, the reduced-calorie or light beer segment went unexploited—though a few brewers had tried and failed. Today, this category makes up 18 percent of the beer market. Miller's Lite beer was never marketed as a diet beer. The idea of a diet beer had failed to win any consumer support in the past. Instead, Miller stressed the image that Lite was a flavorful beer, which also had fewer calories. One 12-ounce bottle of Lite has 96 calories, about one-third less than most regular beers. Miller backed its Lite beer with heavy advertising using well-known sports figures in humorous settings. Since Lite's introduction, other national and regional brewers have flooded the market with about 65 reduced-calorie beer brands.[20]

Miller brews two variations of its superpremium beer, Lowenbrau Special and Lowenbrau Special Dark. Lowenbrau had originally been a very popular import beer in America. In 1974, Miller negotiated an agreement with Lowenbrau Munich (a respected brewer since 1393) to first import Lowenbrau, then test-market a domestically brewed version of the beer. Test marketing of the American-made Lowenbrau proved so favorable that Miller went to national distribution in 1975.

Miller also brews two price beers: popular-priced Meister Brau and budget-priced Milwaukee's Best. Both of these beers, introduced in 1983 and 1984, respectively, are targeted at budget-conscious consumers. These brands have helped to "maintain brewery capacity, to satisfy the volume requirements of . . . distributors, and to safeguard shelf and cooler space within retail outlets" during a time of declining volume.[21]

Since Philip Morris acquired Miller in 1970, the brewery has moved from seventh place to number two in the industry. In the late 1970s, Miller even began to appear to threaten Anheuser-Busch's number one position. Despite Miller's longtime goal of gaining this top spot, its potential profit leadership is in serious doubt today. Although Miller's output increased 8.3 percent to 40.3 million barrels in 1981, its operating income fell 20 percent to $145.6 million on sales of $2.8 billion. Miller gained back some lost ground in 1982 and 1983 with an operating income of $158.8 million and $227.3 million, respectively. But in 1984, this figure plunged to $116.2 million on operating revenues of nearly $3 billion. Perhaps even more disastrous has been Miller's drop in unit profitability. Miller earned $5.06 per barrel in 1979 compared with $3.10 in 1984. Anheuser-Busch earned approximately $6.50 per barrel in 1984.[22,23]

Miller's current weak profit showing has been attributed in part to poor pricing decisions in the early 1980s. Miller substantially boosted its prices twice just as the economy was heading into a recession. According to Lauren S. Williams,

Miller's executive vice-president, "At that time we saw a significant slowing of our momentum, particularly with [top selling] High Life."[24] In 1981, Miller decided not to take a price leadership position; the company instead returned to following Anheuser-Busch's price moves.

Another factor contributing to Miller's weak profit is overcapacity. Miller's volume increases from its aggressive marketing campaign beginning in 1982 have not kept pace with the company's massive capital expansion program. As a result, Miller presently has a newly completed 10 million barrel per year plant in Trenton, Ohio, sitting idle.

**Stroh Brewery**   Stroh Brewery is a conservative, family-owned business that has been brewing beer in Detroit for 132 years. The company is currently under the management of sixth-generation Strohs. Because Stroh is still a closely held corporation, information about the company is somewhat limited.

As recently as 1979 the company ranked eighth in the beer industry. Today it ranks third with a sales volume of over 24 million barrels in 1984. To a large extent, this dramatic increase can be attributed to Stroh's purchase of Schlitz and F. & M. Schaefer breweries in 1982. The Schlitz deal cost Stroh about $340 million and put the company deep into debt. Despite this burden, Stroh still earned a profit of $1.5 million in 1982. These acquisitions also helped Stroh strengthen its position in the brewing industry. Now armed with 15 brands, seven breweries, six can plants, 1250 wholesalers, and 7000 employees, Stroh seems fortified against any brewing industry shakeouts for years to come.[25] Stroh's brewing capacity presently stands at over 29 million barrels per year. Its seven breweries are strategically located throughout the country and offer products in every price category.

Stroh has rapidly expanded the distribution of its products throughout the country. The company's premium brands, Stroh and Stroh Light, are now distributed in all 50 states. In 1983, the company began test marketing its Signature superpremium brand. Stroh also has a strong following in the price-beer segment with its Old Milwaukee and Old Milwaukee Light.

Stroh's two new major brands, Schlitz and Schaefer, have been experiencing mild turnarounds since their acquisition. Both brands had had rapidly eroding market shares before they were acquired. For both of these brands, Stroh's first move was to make changes in pricing, packaging, and promotion to bring about a new awareness of these products. This new approach seems to have been modestly successful. In 1983, Schaefer's sales were up 141 percent over the previous year. Schlitz's sales have stabilized and management soon hopes to expand distribution of the product.[26]

One major advantage that Stroh has over its primary competitors is its privately held status. The top managers have no outside investors, board of directors, or Wall Street analysts to answer to. Because of this, Stroh has a little more room to take risks (as in the highly levered Schlitz acquisition) than most firms. In addition, there are no public stockholders to demand high short-run returns on investments. According to Chris Lole, Stroh's vice-president of corporate planning and development: "If returns remain small . . . the only issue is the Stroh family. As long as the family is committed to those returns, [Stroh] will make it. The nice part about being privately held is that we have a small group of shareholders, all of whom are the Stroh family, and we don't have to keep a Wall Street analyst happy."[27]

## G. Heileman Brewing

G. Heileman Brewing Company, the country's fourth largest brewer, sold over 17.5 million barrels in 1984. The company was founded by Gottlieb Heileman, in La Crosse, Wisconsin, over 125 years ago. Gottlieb Heileman's motto was: "We don't aim to make the most beer, only the best."

Heileman has been unusually successful at marketing its more than three dozen regional beer brands. Principal brands include Old Style, Blatz, Rainier, Schmidt, Wiedeman, Black Label, Red White and Blue, Lone Star, Colt 45, and Mickeys [sic] Malt Liquor. These brands along with Heileman's two super-premium brands, Special Export and Henry Weinhard's, account for more than 80 percent of the company's beer sales. The company's present annual brewing capacity stands at about 26 million barrels. Heileman's brands reach all 50 states from plants located throughout the country. The company is also engaged in the wholesale bakery business, the production and sale of snack foods, and the manufacture of metal parts for jet engines.[28]

Heileman has aggressively pursued acquisitions in the brewing industry over the past several decades. In the late 1950s, the company was just another regional brewer trying to maintain its market share against increasing competition. Heileman's survival can largely be attributed to its strategy of expansion by acquiring regional brewers. By following this program, the company has increased its distribution base, added new wholesalers and brands, and expanded sales throughout the United States. The company has risen from thirty-ninth place in the industry in 1959 to number four today.

For Heileman and the brewing industry, 1984 was a troubled year. Heileman was the target of new premium competitive brand introductions in the midwestern and northwestern states—its major marketing region. Miller also attacked Heileman's market by introducing its Meister Brau and Milwaukee's Best at unrealistically low prices. According to Russell Cleary, president and chairman of the board of Heileman, this was done in some instances "undoubtedly below cost."[29] In addition, Stroh slashed prices on its Schaefer and Old Milwaukee brands. These factors, combined with the industry's first major volume decline since 1957, left Heileman's 1984 earnings off 20 percent from the previous year. Earnings per share were $1.73 in 1984 versus $2.15 in 1983.

Despite Heileman's problems, industry analysts believe that the company's leadership will carry it through the hard times. For example, *Forbes* magazine ranked Heileman number one for the second consecutive year in its Yardsticks of Management Performance ratings of beverage companies (see Exhibit 4.4). The company has outpaced Anheuser-Busch in terms of its five-year average return on equity and sales growth. Because of the company's overall record, the Wall Street Transcript honored President Cleary in 1984 with a gold medal for the outstanding CEO in the brewing and distilling industry.

Since 1983, Heileman has unsuccessfully attempted to acquire Pabst Brewing Company, the sixth largest brewery in the country. It was hoped that this acquisition would expand Heileman's capacity to a level more competitive with the top three. However, at the present time it appears fairly certain that Pabst will be sold to Mr. Paul Kalmanowitz, a West Coast brewer and investor.

## Adolph Coors Company

In 1873, Adolph Coors established his golden Brewery in the Clear Creek Valley outside Golden, Colorado. Coors concentrated all his effort on brewing and marketing one premium beer, a tradition the company had continued to follow until very recently. Coors also reinvested virtually all of his company's profits for expansion and equipment. The beer proved to be very popular in the area and the company thrived. Production increased from 3,500 barrels in 1880 to 48,000 barrels by 1900.[30]

Prohibition became a reality for Colorado in 1914. However, the family was

**Exhibit 4.4** Forbes Brewing Industry Yardsticks of Management Performance

| | Profitability | | | | Growth | | | |
|---|---|---|---|---|---|---|---|---|
| | **Return on Equity** | | | Net Profit Margin (%) | **Sales** | | **Earnings Per Share** | |
| Company | 5-Year Average (%) | 5-Year Rank | Latest 12 Months (%) | | 5-Year Average (%) | 5-Year Rank | 5-Year Average (%) | 5-Year Rank |
| G. Heileman Brewing | 31.9 | 1 | 21.3 | 5.0 | 24.6 | 1 | 23.0 | 1 |
| Philip Morris[a] | 23.9 | 2 | 24.7 | 9.5 | 13.8 | 3 | 15.9 | 3 |
| Anheuser-Busch Cos. | 20.8 | 3 | 20.4 | 5.8 | 20.6 | 2 | 22.0 | 2 |
| Adolph Coors | 9.1 | 4 | 5.9 | 8.0 | 10.7 | 4 | 1.9 | 4 |
| Pabst Brewing | — | NR[b] | — | 0.5 | — | NR[b] | — | NR[b] |
| Alcoholic beverage medians | 18.3 | | 13.9 | 5.8 | 14.6 | | 18.3 | |
| All-industry medians | 15.1 | | 13.4 | 3.7 | 10.2 | | −0.6 | |

[a]Classified as tobacco company.
[b]NR—not ranked.

Source: Forbes, January 14, 1985.

determined to keep the company in business. Between 1914 and 1933, Coors produced porcelain, cement, and a variety of popular food products including a nonalcoholic malt beverage. In addition, Coors was authorized by the government to keep the brewery open on a limited scale for the production of pharmaceutical-grade alcohol.[31]

After Prohibition ended, Coors's beer grew rapidly in popularity. By 1970, the brewery was selling its single beer product in 11 western states. In spite of its regional status, Coors was the fourth largest brewer in the United States in the early 1970s. Since that time, the company has expanded its product line to meet new market opportunities. In 1984, Coors was selling its flagship premium brand in most of the United States. The company also brews Coors Light, the second best selling reduced-calorie beer. A superpremium beer, Herman Joseph's, was test marketed in 1984 with mixed results. The company plans to test market a new superpremium beer, Coors Extra Gold, in 1985.

Because of Coors's high-quality image and the fact that the product was only available west of the Mississippi, the beer developed a devoted following among some easterners. In an effort to capitalize on the beer's mystique, the company began expanding distribution in the mid-1970s. By 1975, sales were $520 million, up $270 million from 1971. Furthermore, Coors's profit per barrel was approximately $9, almost twice as high as Anheuser-Busch's.

Coors's enormous success was not to last long. By the late 1970s, several factors began to hurt Coors's market share in many of its marketing regions. Probably the most significant of these factors was Coors's low per barrel advertising expenditure. The company relied too heavily on its unique image to sell its product. In 1977, for example, it spent only $.25 per barrel even though the industry average at the time was over $1.00. Coors was also hurt by heavy marketing pressure from Miller Brewing, which was using aggressive advertising targeted at specific segments in its battle with Anheuser-Busch.

Coors also suffered a serious blow to its image in 1977. A 20-month strike sparked by alleged abusive treatment at the plant led to a national AFL-CIO boycott of Coors's beers. This boycott continues [in 1985]. In addition, President Joseph Coors has infuriated a number of women, blacks, Latinos, and gays because of his outspoken right-wing philosophy. The Coors brothers are also founders of the ultraconservative Heritage Foundation and are strong supporters of Jerry Falwell's Moral Majority.

Coors lost considerable market share from the late 1970s to the early 1980s. In California, formerly the company's largest market, its share fell from 40 percent to 20 percent over the period. Coors also lost substantial market share in former stronghold Texas. By 1984, volume was 13.5 million barrels per year—the same volume as in 1976—and the company had fallen into fifth place, well behind G. Heileman and only slightly ahead of Pabst.

## Pabst Brewing

Pabst Brewing Company of Milwaukee is the sixth largest brewery in the United States. The company is the successor to Pabst Brewing and Olympia Brewing, both of which were previously separate companies run independently for over 80 years. Pabst brewed 12.8 million barrels in 1983, about 6 percent of the industry total. The company's principal products include Pabst Blue Ribbon, Jacob Best's, Olympia, Hamm's, Pabst Extra Light, and Andeker.

Despite its declining profits and volume over the past several years, Pabst has been the focus of takeover attempts by several brewers, most notably G. Heileman Brewing. By early 1985, however, it seemed likely that the company would be purchased by Mr. Paul Kalmanowitz of California. If he succeeds, Mr. Kalmanowitz has indicated that he would consider selling the Pabst Blue Ribbon brand and three breweries to G. Heileman. The major feature Pabst has to offer is capacity, which could be acquired by a company like Heileman for a relatively cheap price. Furthermore, the additional volume would help a company like Heileman to increase economies of scale through a more efficient utilization of its brewing facilities.[32]

## MAJOR INPUTS

The primary raw materials required in the brewing process are the grains and hops for brewing and containers for packaging. Grain and hops are commodities and are generally out of the control of beer producers. In principle, commodity prices are set by supply and demand. Whereas demand tends to remain fairly stable in the short run, supply can fluctuate wildly each year due to a variety of reasons. Factors such as rainfall, temperature, and sky cover can all affect crops and significantly alter their yields.

The principal grain ingredient in the brewing process is barley malt. In the United States, barley production is generally concentrated in the northern plains states and the Northwest. Barley malt for brewing is the second most important use for barley (livestock feed is the primary use of barley). In 1984, barley malt accounted for over one-third of all domestically produced barley. Trends in barley production from 1960 to 1982 as related to the brewing industry can be seen in Exhibit 4.5. The rising trend in barley production since 1960 has closely tracked the per capita increase in beer consumption over the period. This trend is likely to diminish over the next few years as a result of a flat beer market and the increasing popularity of light beer. Light beer relies more heavily on other grains such as rice in its production.

The second most commonly used grains in beer production are rice and corn. Anheuser-Busch and Coors use only rice as their second grain source, whereas Miller, Pabst, and Stroh use corn grits. However, rice and corn use by brewers actually constitute a small proportion of total starch input. In any case, rice and corn prices and production are functions of beer consumption and the two grains compete with one another in this market.

In the United States, hops are produced principally in Washington and California. Like any commodity, hop prices are generally set by supply and demand. However, in 1983, the Justice Department filed a civil suit against the five largest hop producers charging them with price fixing. Together, these five producers

**Exhibit 4.5** Production and Tax-Paid Withdrawals of Malt Beverages and Use of Barley Malt by the Brewing Industry, 1960–1982

| Fiscal Year Ended June 30 | Production of Malt Beverages (million barrels) | Total Barley Malt Used (million pounds) | Barley Malt Used per Barrel[b] (pounds) | Taxpaid Withdrawals[a] | |
|---|---|---|---|---|---|
| | | | | Total (million barrels) | Per Capita (gallons) |
| 1960 | 94.5 | 2,697 | 28.5 | 88.9 | 15.4 |
| 1965 | 108.0 | 3,016 | 27.9 | 100.3 | 16.0 |
| 1970 | 134.7 | 3,721 | 27.6 | 122.6 | 18.7 |
| 1975 | 157.9 | 4,225 | 26.8 | 146.9 | 21.3 |
| 1976 | 160.7 | 4,158 | 25.9 | 148.8 | 21.5 |
| 1977 | 172.2 | 4,310 | 25.0 | 156.9 | 22.4 |
| 1978 | 171.6 | 4,392 | 25.6 | 157.3 | 23.1 |
| 1979 | 183.5 | 4,890 | 26.6 | 168.2 | 23.8 |
| 1980 | 188.4 | 5,039 | 26.7 | 168.8 | 24.3 |
| 1981[c] | 194.5 | 5,160 | 26.4 | 176.6 | 24.6 |
| 1982[c] | 194.0 | 4,993 | 25.5 | 176.5 | 24.4 |

[a]IRS taxes paid on sales leaving a brewery.
[b]One barrel equals 31 gallons.
[c]Fiscal year ended September 30.

*Source:* U.S. Brewers Association, Inc., *Brewers Almanac,* 1983 and earlier issues.

accounted for over 80 percent of the $250 million sales in 1981. Domestic hops also compete with foreign hops grown in Germany, Yugoslavia, Czechoslovakia, and other European countries. Some brewers such as Anheuser-Busch and Coors use a blend of domestic and imported hops in their premium beers.[33]

The final primary input in brewing is packaging for the finished product. On a per unit basis, this input also represents the most expensive factor in the process. As a result, many brewers have attempted to gain some control over packaging costs through backward vertical integration. For example, Anheuser-Busch's Metal Container Corporation produced about 33 percent of its total can requirement in 1984, or about 3.8 billion cans. Adolph Coors is strongly vertically integrated. The company meets all its container requirements through its container manufacturing facilities. The company has manufactured cans since the 1950s in its can subsidiary, and it was the first to develop an energy-efficient recyclable container.

**RELATIONS WITH DISTRIBU-TORS**

Despite the present lag in beer sales, distributors as a whole appear satisfied with their brewer relations. In a recent survey by *Beverage World,* 150 wholesalers were asked for their feelings on such subjects as brewer responsiveness to wholesaler requests, advisory services, consumer advertising, new products, product pricing, contract terms, and quality control standards.[34] Although brewers appear willing to listen and communicate with wholesalers, the survey found that follow-through on requests is somewhat lacking.

Wholesalers consider quality control standards to be brewers' strongest point. However, they also feel that beer producers should pay more attention to existing product lines rather than constantly flooding the market with experimental brands. Many wholesalers seem to think that breweries are spreading themselves too thin, especially in light of the tough times the industry has been facing lately. With the exception of Anheuser-Busch's Budweiser, wholesalers said that flagship brands are being hurt by the deluge of newly created labels, in particular those in the light segment.

With the exception of top-selling brands, wholesalers expressed concern that advertising has become increasingly ineffective. For brands with declining sales, advertising was almost always cited as the reason. However, the complaint was with the quality of advertising rather than the quantity.

## ADVERTISING

Many consider advertising the most important factor in selling beer. Domestic brewers spent an estimated $482 million in 1983 for advertising. The overwhelming majority of this spending came from the top six brewers making spot and national television time purchases. With the recent increase in new brands, the level of advertising expenditures is expected to accelerate in upcoming years.

Most of beer advertising is focused on building a brand image, and most of the ads are directed at males between the ages of 21 and 35. If the ads mention women at all, they are usually seen as girlfriends or waitresses. The general theme running throughout beer commercials emphasizes the idea that what you drink says something about you in the presence of your peers.[35] For example, Anheuser-Busch's Budweiser continues to maintain the number one spot by linking itself with the hard-working man. Most recently, the company has been offering "salutes" to blue collar workers through its advertisements.

Miller also aims at the "hard-working premium man" with its "Welcome to Miller Time" campaign. In these advertisements, men are shown leaving work after a hard day to unwind with the boys down at the corner tavern. In spite of the company's recent weak performance, management believes that these advertisements will help stimulate a turnaround.

Popular-priced beer advertisements are targeted at the fun-loving man who is a little short of cash. Stroh's Old Milwaukee is the leader in this segment. In these commercials, for example, characters are seen bass fishing in Louisiana followed by a night of partying with Old Milwaukee. Miller has recently taken a different approach to advertising in this segment. Meister Brau is currently being backed by a hard-hitting ad that compares its quality with Budweiser at a cheaper price.

The light beers are another segment that has been heavily advertised over the past several years. This segment is comprised of a combination of young blue-collar and upwardly mobile males. These ads avoid the idea of a diet beer—a product that has failed to capture any consumers in the past. Miller has been the most successful in this category with its use of well-known former athletes in its commercials. Bud Light has also achieved some degree of success with its "Bring Out Your Best" series of ads.

**INDUSTRY THREATS AND TRENDS**

The increased popularity of imported beers and a decline in the consumption of alcoholic beverages (except for some wines), as opposed to a rise in the consumption of soft drinks, are trends that pose a challenge to the brewing industry in this country.

**Imported Beers**

There are about 300 imported beer brands available in the United States today and the number is still growing. Imported beers presently account for only 3 percent of the total U.S. market. However, imports are actually gaining momentum even as domestic beer market growth has come to a virtual halt in the mid-1980s.

Of the top ten imported beers, six of them—Heineken, Beck's, Moosehead, Dos Equis, St. Pauli Girl, and Tecate—are distributed in all 50 states.[36] A seventh extremely popular brand, Guiness Extra Stout, is distributed in 48 states. Molson, a Canadian beer, nearly doubled its distribution between 1979 and 1984 and currently distributes its product in 42 states. Labatt, another Canadian beer with a sizable market share, covers 32 states in its distribution.

Imported beers have traditionally been strong with the on-premises market. But in recent years, the off-premises market has strengthened significantly. Most imported beers are now sold through liquor stores and supermarkets. The latter have grown increasingly more important to the distribution of imported beer as grocers realize the potential for improved profit margins. Margins on imported brands are generally 2 percent higher than domestic brands. Imports now receive about 20 to 25 percent of total beer shelf space even though they presently make up a much smaller proportion of the total market.

**Changing Attitudes and Demographics**

Americans are becoming increasingly concerned with alcohol consumption and drinking-related problems. Per capita consumption of most kinds of alcoholic beverages has been declining for the past several years. For example, the popularity of liquor has been falling rapidly since 1978. Beer consumption has also fallen every year since 1981. The only alcoholic beverages that have not experienced any significant volume declines are white table wines and sparkling wines.

According to sociologists, the decline in alcohol consumption is due to changing demographics—the baby-boomers are now reaching middle age. Traditionally, when people reach this stage in life they begin to switch from beer to distilled spirits. Instead, the trend is now toward drinking in moderation or total abstinence. Middle-aged people are increasingly interested in self-improvement and health, and excessive alcohol consumption does not fit into this picture.[37]

Another major factor in the slump in alcoholic beverage sales is the growing outrage over drunk driving—especially among teenagers. As a result of this concern, Congress passed legislation in 1984 to pressure states into raising the drinking age to 21. In addition, groups such as Mothers Against Drunk Driving (MADD) and Students Against Drunk Driving (SADD) have spread nationwide in an effort to combat the problem and lobby for stricter laws.

In 1985, there is a growing movement to ban beer and wine commercials from TV and radio. A group calling itself Project Smart (*Smart* stands for Stop Marketing Alcohol on Radio and Television) is heavily lobbying Congress to keep alcoholic beverage commercials off the airwaves. Members of this group include the 24,000-chapter National Congress of Parents and Teachers and a variety of religious groups including the Methodist and Seventh-Day Adventist churches.

Although distillers of hard liquor have had to limit their advertisements to print for decades now, beer and wine producers spent $700 million on TV and radio ads in 1984. If Smart is successful and convinces the government to ban beer and wine ads on the air, more than just these two industries will be affected. Football, baseball, networks, and ad agencies are just a few of the industries that would suffer. For example, In the 1984–1985 season, the National Football League received almost $415 million from the networks for the right to carry games. It is doubtful that a network would be willing to pay such a fee without the backing of the big brewers.[38]

Brewers have argued that advertising is not encouraging people to drink abusively. The companies contend that their commercials influence brand preference but not the decision whether or not to drink. Alan Easton of Miller Brewing states: "We don't want our product abused any more than General Motors wants people to speed."[39] In early 1985, Smart appeared to be gaining increasing support on Capitol Hill. Many lawmakers are becoming interested in the relationship between advertising and alcohol consumption. However, at the present time it does not appear likely that an outright ban will be made in the near future. In the meantime, it is fairly certain that the controversy will remain alive.

**Substitute Products**

Virtually every type of drink—including water—could be considered a substitute product for beer. However, the most reasonable substitutes can probably be grouped into two categories: soft drinks and other alcoholic beverages.

Soft drink consumption reached a record level in 1984. American consumers guzzled approximately 42 gallons per capita during the year—by far the highest per capita consumption in the world. Soft drink purchases have more than doubled in the past 20 years. The top two soft drink producers—Coca-Cola and PepsiCo—both reported record profits in 1984. The growth of this industry during the past year can be attributed to diet soft drinks. Diet drinks now account for 25 percent of the entire market. Only four years ago diet drinks were only 14 percent of industry sales. Soft drink producers greatly benefit from this switch because diet brands have a considerably higher profit margin than regular sugar-sweetened drinks. The recent introduction of aspartame has also helped to fuel the rapid growth in soft drink consumption. For example, Diet Coke, introduced in 1982, is now the third largest selling soft drink on the market—the most successful new beverage ever introduced by the industry. Increasing domestic consumption combined with the expanding foreign markets should help to make 1985 the best year ever for American soft drink producers.[40]

In contrast to the growing U.S. soft drink market, American liquor producers experienced their worst year in over two decades. Per capita liquor consumption was down to 2.52 gallons in 1984. This is a significant drop from 1978, when liquor consumption reached 2.85 gallons per capita.

At the present time, wine is the only alcoholic beverage experiencing a steady growth in consumption. Per capita wine consumption was 2.25 gallons in 1984, up from 1.31 gallons in 1970. Part of this rise can be attributed to a trend that has made wine a more fashionable beverage. White and sparkling wines are especially in vogue now.

**INDUSTRY OUTLOOK**

The upcoming years look rough and tough for the American brewing industry. Declining volume in the total market will continue to spark heated marketing battles among the top brewers. Changing demographics, competition from imports, the higher drinking age, and the threat of more adverse legislation will all hurt the brewing industry's growth rate. The industry should continue to consolidate, but at a much slower pace than in the past. In 1984, the top ten brewers already controlled over 99 percent of the 184 million barrel per year market.

In light of these changes in the industry and in consumers' attitudes, it should be apparent that brewers will be forced to make changes in products and promotion if the industry is to continue growing. Several options are already being explored. For example, most of the larger breweries are offering a low-alcohol beer. It is hoped that this product will appeal to those who like to drink, but are concerned about their alcohol consumption. Given the proper promotion, this new segment may someday achieve the phenomenal success the light beers have had.

Another potential segment might be the nonalcoholic or "near beers." G. Heileman is already the nation's leading producer in this market. The company is currently brewing Kingsbury, Schmidt Select, and Zing; all are nonalcoholic with approximately 60 calories per 12-ounce can. Anheuser-Busch may soon sell a similar near beer product. In fact, the company actually test marketed a nonalcoholic brand called Chelsea in 1978. The company withdrew the product after loud public outcry that this was an attempt to encourage children to drink. In the future, brewers must promote this sort of product as a beer and not as a soft drink. Sales of near beer reached $14 million in 1984. This figure is expected to triple in 1985.

One very promising note in an otherwise clouded future is the overseas beer market. The size of this market is gigantic—about 550 million barrels in 1984. Budweiser is already the leading beer in Japan and is gaining popularity in

England as well.[41] In the future, American brewers will need to make a greater effort marketing the American mystique that is so popular in foreign countries. According to Miller's vice-president Alan Easton: "Anyone who is really serious about being in the beer industry is going to have to seriously consider how to participate in the non-U.S. markets."[42]

One final note: Beer makers may now be able to cash in on evidence that drinking in moderation is healthful. In 1985, several scientific studies linked moderate alcohol intake—about two drinks per day—with a significantly lower chance of coronary heart disease. The protective role alcohol plays will probably not be understood for years. However, alcoholic beverage producers have wasted no time in promoting this protective side of alcohol despite the numerous complaints from critics.

## NOTES

1. Adolph Coors Co., *The Adolph Coors Story,* 1985.
2. United States Brewers Association, *Brewers Almanac* (Washington, D.C.: 1980).
3. John P. Arnold, *History of the Brewing Industry and Brewing Science in America* (Chicago: G. L. Peterson Co., 1933).
4. Ibid.
5. Adolph Coors Co., 1984 Annual Report.
6. Miller Brewing Co., *Fact Book,* 1985.
7. Anheuser-Busch, Inc., *Fact Book,* 1984.
8. Miller Brewing Co., *Fact Book,* 1985.
9. M. Laureano, *The American Beer Industry* (Merrick, N.Y.: The Merrick Research Corp., 1978).
10. J. A. Bleeke, "Banking on Brewing: How to Play the Acquisition Game," *Bankers Magazine* 167 (July–August 1984): 24.
11. W. J. Lynk, "Interpreting Rising Concentration: The Case of Beer," *Journal of Business* 57 (January 1984): 43–55.
12. Bleeke, "Banking on Brewing," pp. 22–28.
13. Ibid.
14. Anheuser Busch, Inc., *Fact Book,* 1984.
15. Ibid.
16. Anheuser-Busch, Inc., 1984 Annual Report.
17. Miller Brewing Co., *Fact Book,* 1985.
18. Ibid.
19. Ibid., p. 8.
20. Ibid.
21. Philip Morris, Inc., 1984 Annual Report.
22. Ibid.
23. "What Blew the Head Off Miller's Profits," *Business Week,* February 15, 1982, pp. 39–40.
24. Ibid., p. 39.
25. Ann M. Morrison, "Betting the Barn at Stroh," *Fortune,* May 3, 1982, pp. 118–121.
26. J. Lucasick, "Where There's Stroh, There's Fire," *Beverage World* 102 (October 1983): 23–28.
27. Ibid., p. 27.
28. G. Heileman Brewing Co., 1984 Annual Report.
29. Ibid., p. 2.
30. Adolph Coors Co., *The Adolph Coors Story,* 1985.

31. Ibid.
32. "Pabst," *Value Line,* March 1, 1985, p. 1554.
33. Robert H. Bork, "Technobrew," *Forbes,* December 5, 1983, pp. 236–242.
34. "What Wholesalers Think of the Brewers," *Beverage World,* October 1984, p. 27.
35. Robert Reed, "Satisfying a Thirst for Images," *Advertising Age,* January 16, 1984, pp. M-9–M-11.
36. Phil Fitzell, "Imported Beers: Bulls in Bear Country," *Beverage World,* June 1984, p. 74.
37. Gail Bronson, "Times Are Changing the Liquor Business," *U.S. News & World Report,* September 3, 1984, p. 56.
38. C. C. Carter, "Sudless Sports?" *Fortune,* January 21, 1985, p. 84.
39. Ibid., p. 84.
40. "Brewing/Soft Drink Industry," *Value Line,* March 1, 1985, p. 1543.
41. "Bud Is Making a Splash in the Overseas Beer Market," *Business Week,* October 22, 1984, p. 52–53.
42. Fitzell, "Imported Beers," p. 75.

# 5  It's Miller Time

Thomas C. Neil and Lloyd L. Byars
Atlanta University

Miller Brewing Company was founded in 1855 by Frederic Miller, a 31-year-old former German brewmaster. Miller toured America for almost one year before selecting Milwaukee as the location to start his brewery. Miller purchased a small idle brewery located west of Milwaukee. This small brewery was originally built in 1850 and was called the Plank Road Brewery. The brewing operation was discontinued in 1853 and the plant had been idle until Frederic Miller bought it in 1855 for $8000. The plant had a capacity of 1200 barrels per year, but during its first year of operation Miller produced only 300 barrels of beer.

Frederic Miller's philosophy on brewing was to produce a product of uncompromising and unchanging quality. Miller also sought to expand the availability of Miller beer into beer gardens and taverns throughout the Milwaukee area and also in eight surrounding states. Beer was dispensed on tap in these popular social centers, and thus Miller became a familiar fixture. Miller's strategy was to encourage people to gather together to share the events of the day and savor the rich, good taste of Miller Beer.

Due to the popularity of his beer and the growing demand, Miller expanded his output capacity in 1870 by building a new brick brewery. By 1880, the plant was producing about 30,000 barrels a year. In 1883, Miller established his first bottling plant; within three years this plant was bottling 5000 of Miller's 80,000 barrels per year. Miller also constructed seven icehouses in the Chicago, Waukesha, and Milwaukee areas for the storage of his beer.

After Fredric Miller's death in 1888, his eldest son Ernest and a son-in-law, Carl A. Miller, took over the management of the company and effectively continued Frederic Miller's philosophy of business. The brewery continued to grow in size, capacity, product line, and sales volume.

In 1903, a contest was held to name Miller's premium beer. The result was the name Miller High Life and the slogan "The Champagne of Bottled Beer." The name remains today, but the slogan has since been phased out. Miller High Life's fame was also aided by the introduction of the girl-in-the-moon symbol for the beer. Much speculation surrounds the reason for the use of this symbol. However, the primary reason seems to be that it gave beer drinkers the impression that Miller High Life was the beer that was in keeping with the "high times" that existed at the turn of the century.

By the beginning of Prohibition in 1920, Miller was producing more than 0.5 million barrels a year. However, with the ratification of the Eighteenth Amendment, production of alcholic beverages ceased and Miller faced a major crisis in its corporate life. The Miller family decided to keep the name of the company alive and began producing a line of products that included a cereal beverage, malt tonic, health drink, and carbonated soft drinks. All of these products carried the Miller label.

During the Prohibition era, Ernest Miller died and his younger brother, Frederic A. Miller, assumed the presidency of the company. With the aid of his sister and subsequent successor, Elsie Kay John, Frederic A. Miller reopened the brewery at the end of Prohibition. They immediately recognized that the end of Prohibition would open up new markets for beer and also realized that these new markets would require new marketing and production techniques. Under their leadership the company moved to adapt to the changed conditions, but it never sacrificed the quality of its products. In fact, management described its task to be positioning Miller High Life as one of America's favorite pastimes.

In 1947, Frederic C. Miller, the grandson of the founder, became president of the company. He succeeded Harry G. John, Jr., who followed his mother as president but only served for a short period of time. Under Frederic C. Miller's leadership, the company developed a major expansion program, including the construction of a brewhouse and three aging and fermenting cellars. He developed an aggressive merchandising and advertising campaign targeted primarily at the home consumption market segment; as a result, the home consumption market was a significant factor in the growth of the company during the late forties and fifties. During this time, Miller also implemented policies that resulted in Miller Brewing Company becoming actively involved in community affairs projects. Miller High Life's sales increased dramatically, output nearly quadrupled, and the company moved from twentieth to ninth place nationwide. In December 1954, Frederic C. Miller and his son, Fred, Jr., died in an airplane crash.

Norman R. Klug succeeded Frederic C. Miller as president of the Miller Brewing Company. This was the first time in the history of the company that the president of the company was not directly related to the Miller family. Klug continued Miller Brewing Company's fundamental growth strategy by expanding the brewery's production facilities. This was accomplished largely through the acquisition of General Brewing Corporation's plant in Azusa, California. Despite this expansion program, production remained relatively constant and the company experienced very little real growth.

In September 1966, W. R. Grace & Company purchased controlling interest in the Miller Brewing Company, and following the death of Norman Klug, later that year Charles W. Miller (unrelated to the original family) was named president. Also during 1966, the company purchased Carling Brewing Company located in Fort Worth, Texas. Throughout the next three years, renovation and expansion of the newly acquired plant increased Miller's production capabilities to over 1 million barrels per year. In May 1969, J. Peter Grace, president of Grace, told the annual stockholders' meeting that W. R. Grace had decided to sell its Miller interest because at the time of purchase, it had expected to acquire the remaining 47 percent interest in Miller; however, in the intervening period, it concluded that this holding would not be sold to Grace at any time. Grace decided the situation was undesirable. The remaining 47 percent of the shares of Miller Brewing was owned by the De Rance Foundation in Milwaukee.

Later that same month, PepsiCo offered W. R. Grace $120 million for its 53 percent interest in Miller. W. R. Grace initially accepted the offer, but in early June the company did an about-face and rejected the offer. On June 12, 1969, Philip Morris, Inc., purchased W. R. Grace's 53 percent ownership in Miller for $130 million. PepsiCo filed suit in the District Court for the Southern District of New York challenging the sale of Miller Brewing to Philip Morris. PepsiCo charged that Philip Morris and W. R. Grace had violated Securities and Exchange Commission (SEC) rules by failing to disclose material facts about their negotiations. PepsiCo asked that the sale be voided so that it could purchase Miller. W. R. Grace stated that the suit was "utterly without substance."

In January 1970, a federal judge dismissed the PepsiCo suit against W. R. Grace. In a statement, the judge said that PepsiCo had failed to prove its contention that the sale of the 53 percent interest in Miller to Philip Morris had violated the SEC laws. Later that year, Philip Morris acquired the remaining 47 percent interest in Miller from the De Rance Foundation for $97 million, making Miller a wholly owned subsidiary of Philip Morris.

In late 1971, John A. Murphy became chief executive officer of Miller. Philip Morris also replaced the experienced beer managers at Miller with "homegrown cigarette marketers." The philosophy of these cigarette people was that beer and cigarettes have a great deal in common. Their philosophy on the beer and cigarette business was as follows: Both are low-priced, pleasurable products made from agricultural commodities that are processed and packaged on high-speed machinery. Both are advertised the same way and are sold to many of the same end use customers through similar distribution channels. Your beer drinker and your cigarette smoker are often the same guy.

Since the purchase of Miller by Philip Morris, Miller's sales have grown from 5.2 million barrels to a high of 36.7 million barrels in 1981 and a slight decrease to 36.3 million barrels in 1984. Miller's market share has increased from 4.0 percent in 1972 to 20.7 percent in 1984 down from a high of 22 percent in 1981. (See Exhibit 5.1.)

**Exhibit 5.1** Market Share of Top Ten Brands

| | |
|---|---|
| Budweiser | 23.1% |
| Miller High Life | 9.7 |
| Miller Lite | 9.7 |
| Coors | 5.3 |
| Pabst | 4.1 |
| Old Milwaukee | 4.1 |
| Michelob | 3.8 |
| Old Style | 3.1 |
| Stroh | 2.9 |
| Bud Light | 2.0 |

*Source:* Lehman Bros., Kuhn Loeb Research. Copyright © *Beverage Industry,* January 1984.

In 1982, William K. Howell, president of Miller Brewing Company, characterized the growth and development that began in 1971 as follows:

> The change in the brewing industry began in October, 1971, when Philip Morris, Inc.
> changed the management of Miller Brewing Company. But it took about two years for
> the change to show up as a real change in direction of the company and the industry.
> When the change was finally felt, beginning in 1973, it was explosive.
>
> Miller quickly shot up in sales and position, moving from seventh in the industry in
> 1972 to second place in 1977. Since 1972, we've increased shipments by 566 percent.*

In mid-1984, a new management team assumed responsibility for Philip Morris
Incorporated. A continuing commitment was given to the principles that have
characterized Philip Morris, as stated in the 1984 Annual Report:

- We are committed to make and market products of the highest quality and to develop
  new products that satisfy consumers' present demands and anticipate their needs. To
  do that, we will continue to invest in the best and most productive facilities, machinery, and equipment as well as in research and development activities oriented to the
  marketplace;
- We are committed to profitable growth. We intend to continue to gain sales and
  market share through innovative marketing, and to broaden the base of our business
  through investment or acquisition in fields compatible with our experience. We will
  use our growing financial strengths and resources to improve the value of our
  stockholders' investment;
- We are committed to defending the legitimate interests of our business against
  discriminatory taxation and critics' proposals to impose unreasonable restrictions on
  the use of our products and on some of our competitive marketing tools;
- We are committed to continue our programs in the public interest and to recognize
  our obligations to the society that supports us, in particular to the communities
  where we work and invest.

**PRODUCT
LINE
(1972–1984)**

Beginning in the seventies, the management of the revitalized Miller's has followed a strategy of introducing several new brands. In June 1983, Calgary, a
Canadian-produced beer, was introduced into three markets. Calgary is to compete with Molson Golden and Moosehead and is priced lower than the popular
import Heineken. In late 1983, Meister Brau, a bargain label that is supposed to
taste as good as the costlier Budweiser, was introduced. Meister Brau was followed by Milwaukee's Best, positioned to compete against the low-priced beers
of Stroh's and Pabst. This strategy is, in part, due to the goal of garnering the
greater share of the entire beer spectrum. However, additional reasons are to
maintain brewery utilization, satisfy the volume requirements of distributors, and
safeguard shelf and cooler space within retail outlets. The product line now
consists of Miller High Life, Lite, Lowenbrau, Miller Special Reserve, Magnum
Malt Liquor, Calgary, Meister Brau, and Milwaukee's Best.

*Quotes in this case are drawn from public documents.

Miller High Life is Miller's leading brand of beer and currently generates the second largest revenue of national premium brands in the industry. Initially marketed as the "Champagne of Bottled Beers," Miller was targeted to occasional beer drinkers—the beer-drinking elite. However, the new management at Miller changed the positioning strategy to include a new group of beer drinkers and not just the "country club set." The "Champagne of Bottled Beers" slogan was changed to "Time to Relax" with the purpose of positioning the beer to sports-oriented and blue-collar types of drinkers: "an audience of the 30 percent of the consumers who drink 80 percent of the beer." High Life is presented to the new target market in TV advertising featuring "real people doing real jobs—and being rewarded at the end of their day with Miller Time: a time to relax and enjoy the best tasting beer you can find—If you've got the time, we've got the beer." In 1972, High Life was offered in the 7-ounce pony bottle. High Life is also offered in 12-ounce returnable and nonreturnable bottles, 12- and 16-ounce cans, 1-quart bottles, and on draft.

Lite Beer from Miller has been acclaimed to be the most successful beer ever introduced in the history of the brewing industry. The Lite brand name was acquired in 1972 when Miller bought the trade name and distribution network of Meister Brau, Inc., of Chicago. Meister Brau Lite was one of the first low-calorie beers. Miller modified Meister Brau's formula, and according to the management of Miller, the big difference is that Lite actually tastes like beer.

Previous attempts to introduce low-calorie beers into the marketplace were characterized by appeals aimed at the diet-conscious consumer. Miller's sales pitch communicated its message through the use of "convincing beer-drinking personalities" such as Mickey Spillane; baseball's Whitey Ford, Mickey Mantle, and Billy Martin; and football's Dick Butkus and Bubba Smith. "The typical beer drinker is not dietetically oriented, but when he sees a football player drinking this low-calorie beer, he figures he shouldn't be ashamed to drink it." The Lite Beer promotion (with "a third less calories than one regular beer") also suggests that the beer is not as filling as other beers; therefore, more Lite Beer can be consumed.

Since its introduction in 1973, Lite has become the second-best-selling brand of beer in the United States. Packaging for Lite includes 7-ounce nonreturnable bottles, 12-ounce returnable and nonreturnable bottles, 12- and 16-ounce cans, 1-quart bottles, and on draft. Lowenbrau Special and Dark Special are two other Miller products. The Lowenbrau brands were first brewed in Munich, Germany, in 1383 in the Lowenbrau Brewery, one of the most highly recognized names in the world. In April 1974, Miller Brewing Company entered into an agreement with the German brewery and acquired importation rights for Lowenbrau in the United States. Lowenbrau was then introduced nationally in 1977. As a super-premium beer, Lowenbrau is marketed as a beer "to be enjoyed on special occasions shared with special friends—Tonight, let it be Lowenbrau." Both the Special and Dark Special are packaged in foil-wrapped, 12-ounce nonreturnable bottles and on draft. In addition, the Special is distributed in 7-ounce bottles, called the cub.

In 1984, the strong American dollar resulted in price advantages for imported beers. This adversely affected Lowenbrau, resulting in a 1984 decline in sales.

Magnum Malt Liquor was Miller's first entry into the special market segment of malt liquor drinkers. In February 1981, Miller began testing the product in Atlanta and Savannah, Georgia; Portland, Oregon; Birmingham, Alabama; and Greensboro, North Carolina. The test results indicated that Magnum had the potential to capture a sizable portion of the malt liquor market and had strong acceptance by loyal malt liquor drinkers.

Magnum is primarily targeted at 18- to 25-year-old males. This audience accounts for nearly two-thirds of the total malt liquor drinkers. Its current sales theme suggests to malt liquor drinkers "to get on the M-train . . . it's your ticket to ride."

Miller's decision to go after the malt liquor market was based on their increased production capacity. President William Howell stated:

> It is not a new market for the company. We had Miller Malt out there in the early 1970s, but had to discontinue it during our rapid growth years to provide additional capacity for Miller High Life and Lite brands. In fact, the basic formula for Miller Malt proved very successful against current competition in our tests, and it was refined to produce Magnum. We are going back after that business because we now have the capacity to deliver Magnum at the highest consistent quality to this special market wherever it exists.

In 1981, Miller introduced another superpremium beer, Miller Special Reserve. At the launching of Miller Special Reserve, Miller Executive Vice-President Lauren Williams stated:

> It was those millions of beer drinkers who want the full, rich taste and extra quality of a super-premium brand on a regular basis. We feel that Miller Special Reserve will add a new dimension to our existing line of high-quality brands. Its entry into the market will enable us to cover the entire spectrum of the super-premium segment, one of the fastest growing segments in the beer industry.

Miller's advertising theme for Special Reserve is "Taste the Best in Life."

Meister Brau and Milwaukee's Best, the last additions to the stable, are direct responses to the blitz of the low-price market by G. Heileman Brewing, Pabst, and Stroh's. The focus on the low-price-brew drinker appears to be the result of "Joe Six-pack's" taste acceptance of lower-priced beers during the three-year recession. In 1982, the beer industry experienced its first slump in 25 years and a growth of about one percent in 1983. Miller's recognizes the difficulty with the low-priced beers, low profit margins, but seeks to maintain a high image in the industry while keeping production up. Miller's has two premium-priced brands in test markets and others under development.

Between 1979 and 1981, Miller test marketed Munich Oktoberfest, an imported dark beer. This beer is brewed by Lowenbrau Brewery, which is the same company from which Miller had originally obtained Lowenbrau. Oktoberfest was test marketed in Boston and Washington, D.C. The test results were disappointing and, as of today, no decision seems to have been made on what to do with Oktoberfest. Exhibit 5.2 summarizes the principal brands of the major brewers by market segment.

**PRODUCTION AND DISTRIBU-TION**

Miller has breweries in Milwaukee, Wisconsin; Fort Worth, Texas; Fulton, New York; Eden, North Carolina; Albany, Georgia; and Irwindale, California. A brewery was completed in Trenton, Ohio, in 1984. Canning facilities are located in Milwaukee, Wisconsin; Fort Worth, Texas; Fulton, New York; Reidsville, North Carolina; and Moultrie, Georgia. A bottling plant is located in Sennett, New York.

### Description of Breweries

- *Milwaukee, Wisconsin.*   Oldest brewery and has a capacity of 9 million barrels annually.
- *Fort Worth, Texas.*   Purchased from Carling Brewing Company in 1966 and has a capacity of 8 million barrels annually.
- *Fulton, New York.*   Capacity of 10 million barrels annually.
- *Eden, North Carolina.*   Capacity of 10 million barrels annually.
- *Albany, Georgia.*   Capacity of 10 million barrels annually.
- *Trenton, Ohio.*   Capacity of 10 million barrels annually.

**Exhibit 5.2** Principal Brands of Major Brewers

| Company | Premium Brands | Super-premium Brands | Light Brands | Imported Brands |
|---|---|---|---|---|
| Anheuser-Bush | Budweiser | Michelob | Michelob Light Natural Light | Wurzburger Holbrau |
| Miller | Miller High Life | Lowenbrau | Lite | Calgary |
| Stroh | Schlitz Stroh's | Erlanger | Schlitz Light Old Milwaukee Light Stroh Light | — |
| Pabst | Pabst Blue Ribbon | Andeker | Pabst Extra Light | Fuerstenberg |
| Coors | Coors | Herman Joseph's 1868 | Coors Light | Stella Artois |
| Heileman | Old Style Rainier | Special Export | Several entries | Beck's |

*Source:* Company reports.

The slowdown in industry beer sales with improved productivity in operating brewers resulted in a decision to write Trenton down to its net realizable value and postpone for the foreseeable future its opening.

Miller products are sold and delivered to retailers by a network of 800 independent distributors. Miller products can be purchased in all 50 states, Puerto Rico, St. Thomas, and 82 foreign countries. Miller also has its own company-owned distributorships in Milwaukee, Wisconsin; New Orleans, Louisiana; Los Angeles, California; Salt Lake City, Utah; and Poughkeepsie, New York.

Distributors receive their beer shipments by truck and rail and use their own fleet of trucks to service retail accounts. To help its distributors, Miller has a sales force of 150 area managers operating from 12 regional headquarters. The sales force personnel help the distributors maintain proper inventories, work with retailers to obtain adequate shelf space for greatest product visibility, and conduct in-house training programs for the distributors' sales personnel.

One innovative technique developed by Miller marketing personnel is the Vertibrand system. The Vertibrand system is basically a method of arranging beer vertically by brand and horizontally by package. This provides an appealing arrangement for the customer, makes brand selection easier, and, more importantly, enables the retailers to utilize shelf space more effectively.

## ADVERTISING

Before 1976, only certain brands such as Miller High Life and Anheuser-Busch's Michelob had very high per-barrel advertising expenditures. In 1976, however, the nature of advertising expenditures, particularly by the larger brewers, changed dramatically. Advertising on many major brands doubled, and with the introduction of large numbers of new brands, particularly in the light beer market, overall advertising expenditures increased dramatically. Miller's advertising for Miller High Life increased 230 percent to $29.7 million in 1976. High Life became the most heavily advertised brand in 1979. Miller Light advertising increased between 1976 and 1978 by 58 percent, making Lite the third most heavily advertised beer. Advertising on Lowenbrau increased from $11.3 million in 1978 to $17 million in 1979. This is an almost unbelievable $16.97 per barrel.

Introducing the low-priced Meister Brau cost Miller $10 million. In 1983, for the second year in a row, the Lite beer commercials were voted the outstanding television campaign. In 1983, Miller High Life and Lite were among the top five most advertised beers, accounting for over 40 percent of the industry total. Miller's president, William Howell, stated in 1981:

> We have built our success by doing our homework, finding out what beer consumers want and then delivering it. We have worked hard. We have been innovators in product, merchandising and advertising. Our most visible competitive act has been to advertise on television. Those commercials have been called some of the highest quality in American advertising history. We believe that just as American consumers deserve the

highest quality beer, they ought to have those beers presented to them with the highest quality advertising. Our television commercials broke a new ground in this industry because they were filmed with the same high quality film technique as a feature length film. No expense was spared.

**FINANCES**

Philip Morris, Miller's parent company, conducts business through six operating companies: Philip Morris U.S.A.; Philip Morris International; Miller Brewing Company; the Seven-Up Company; Philip Morris Industrial; and Mission Viejo Company. Exhibit 5.3 gives a brief description of each of the subsidiaries and the operating revenues and income for each. Exhibit 5.4 gives a 15-year financial review for Philip Morris and its subsidiaries.

Over the last ten years, Miller's operating revenues have increased at an average annual compound rate of 29 percent. During 1978, an increase in beer revenue resulted from both volume and price increases. Miller's income was reduced in 1980 due to the industry's competitive pricing environment and brewery start-up costs.

**MARKET ANALYSIS**

The coming decade is forecasted to be a highly competitive one in the brewing industry. During 1983, the domestic segment of the industry increased production by an estimated 0.7 percent, or 177.9 million barrels versus 176.6 million barrels in 1982. Projected annual growth rates of 1 to 2 percent indicate that the market is both static and mature. Various other factors have contributed to the industry's slight gains.

The increasing concern over alcohol abuse coupled with more severe drunk driving penalties have affected sales adversely. Alcoholics Anonymous reported record enrollment during 1983. Campus officials are discouraging the use of alcohol at student gatherings such as fraternity parties. In 1984 a law was passed to raise the legal drinking age throughout the United States to 21. This would be phased in over three years.

Competition in the brewing industry has reached its fiercest level since 1969 when Philip Morris first entered into the brewing industry. The top nine brewers in the industry dominate over 95 percent of total market share (see Exhibit 5.5). Industry experts feel that segmentation of the market with light beer and other product introductions has increased competition. In addition, brewers increased prices above inflation rates, affecting sales in various categories.

Of the six major beer segments, growth occurred among the light, popular, and imported brands. As people are becoming more health conscious, they are increasing purchases of light beer brands. In 1983, the light beer segment captured 18.5 percent of the industry's market share with a production level of 34 million barrels. Popular brands showed a 1.2 percent increase over 1982 levels,

**Exhibit 5.3** Financial Review of Subsidiaries (in millions of dollars, except per share amounts)

| | 1984 | 1983 | 1982 | 1981 | 1980 |
|---|---|---|---|---|---|
| Operating revenues | $13,813.7 | $12,975.9 | $11,586.0 | $10,722.3 | $9,649.5 |
| Net earnings | 888.5 | 903.5 | 781.8 | 659.7 | 549.1 |
| Earnings per common share | 7.24 | 7.17 | 6.23 | 5.28 | 4.41 |
| Dividends declared per common share | 3.40 | 2.90 | 2.40 | 2.00 | 1.60 |
| Funds from operations per common share | 12.61 | 10.70 | 9.24 | 7.81 | 6.29 |
| **Percent increase over prior year** | | | | | |
| Operating revenues | 6.5 | 12.0 | 8.1 | 11.1 | 18.4 |
| Net earnings | (1.7) | 15.6 | 18.5 | 20.1 | 8.1 |
| Earnings per common share | 1.0 | 15.1 | 18.0 | 19.7 | 8.1 |
| Dividends declared per common share | 17.2 | 20.8 | 20.0 | 25.0 | 28.0 |
| **Operating revenues** | | | | | |
| Philip Morris U.S.A. | $6,133.3 | $5,519.9 | $4,330.1 | $3,761.6 | $3,272.1 |
| Philip Morris International | 3,741.0 | 3,646.7 | 3,563.7 | 3,400.3 | 3,205.4 |
| Miller Brewing Company | 2,928.2 | 2,922.1 | 2,928.7 | 2,837.2 | 2,542.3 |
| The Seven-Up Company | 734.0 | 649.9 | 530.6 | 432.1 | 353.2 |
| Philip Morris Industrial | 277.2 | 237.3 | 232.9 | 291.1 | 276.5 |
| Consolidated Operating Revenues | $13,813.7 | $12,975.9 | $11,586.0 | $10,722.3 | $9,649.5 |
| **Operating income** | | | | | |
| Philip Morris U.S.A. | $1,745.2 | $1,337.8 | $1,101.6 | $905.7 | $786.1 |
| Philip Morris International | 420.9 | 366.0 | 446.0 | 396.6 | 318.0 |
| Miller Brewing Company | 116.2 | 227.3 | 158.8 | 115.6 | 144.8 |
| The Seven-Up Company | 5.3 | (10.8) | (1.2) | (1.7) | (7.1) |
| Philip Morris Industrial | 29.5 | 13.6 | 7.6 | 18.9 | 16.9 |
| Mission Viejo Realty Group Inc.[a] | 17.2 | 19.6 | 2.0 | 11.1 | 14.7 |
| P.M. Credit Corporation[a] | 11.3 | 4.5 | 0.9 | | |
| Consolidated operating income | $2,345.6 | $1,958.0 | $1,715.7 | $1,446.2 | $1,273.4 |
| **Compounded average annual growth rate** | | 1984–1979 | 1984–1974 | 1984–1969 | 1984–1959 |
| Operating revenues | | 11.1% | 16.5% | 18.1% | 14.2% |
| Net earnings | | 11.8% | 17.6% | 19.9% | 16.5% |
| Primary earnings per share | | 12.2% | 16.4% | 17.6% | 15.2% |

[a]Represents equity in net earnings of these unconsolidated subsidiaries.
Operating companies' income is income before corporate expense, interest, and other nonoperating income and deductions. The amortization of previously capitalized interest is included in operating companies' income.
 A write-down of the completed but inactive Miller Brewing Company facility in Trenton, Ohio, reduced 1984 net earnings and earnings per share by $145.6 million and $1.19, respectively.

*Source:* Annual Report, 1984.

**Exhibit 5.4** Fifteen-Year Financial Review (in millions of dollars, except per share amounts)

| | 1984 | 1983 | 1982 | 1981 | 1980 | 1979 |
|---|---|---|---|---|---|---|
| **Summary of operations** | | | | | | |
| Operating revenues | $13,813.7 | 12,975.9 | 11,586.0 | 10,722.3 | 9,649.5 | 8,149.1 |
| Cost of sales: | | | | | | |
| Cost of products sold | 5,516.6 | 5,342.8 | 5,315.4 | 5,024.2 | 4,446.7 | 3,655.5 |
| Federal excise taxes | 2,040.9 | 1,983.3 | 1,180.0 | 1,168.5 | 1,105.3 | 1,036.8 |
| Foreign excise taxes | 1,635.0 | 1,527.0 | 1,434.5 | 1,410.8 | 1,388.7 | 1,122.0 |
| Operating income | 2,345.6 | 1,958.0 | 1,715.7 | 1,446.2 | 1,273.4 | 1,179.4 |
| Interest expense | 299.1 | 233.9 | 267.2 | 258.5 | 215.0 | 205.5 |
| Earnings before income taxes | 1,606.9 | 1,584.8 | 1,300.2 | 1,068.1 | 924.4 | 894.5 |
| Pre-tax profit margins | 11.6% | 12.2% | 11.2% | 10.0% | 9.6% | 11.0% |
| Provision for income taxes | $718.4 | 681.3 | 518.4 | 408.4 | 375.3 | 386.6 |
| Net earnings | 888.5 | 903.5 | 781.8 | 659.7 | 549.1 | 507.9 |
| Summary earnings per common share | 7.24 | 7.17 | 6.23 | 5.28 | 4.41 | 4.08 |
| Fully diluted earnings per common share | 7.24 | 7.17 | 6.23 | 5.28 | 4.41 | 4.08 |
| Dividends declared per common share | 3.40 | 2.90 | 2.40 | 2.00 | 1.60 | 1.25 |
| Weighted average shares-primary | 122.7 | 126.0 | 125.6 | 124.9 | 124.6 | 124.5 |
| Weighted average shares— fully diluted | 122.7 | 126.0 | 125.6 | 124.9 | 124.6 | 124.5 |
| Capital expenditures | $298.1 | 566.2 | 918.2 | 1,018.5 | 750.8 | 629.4 |
| Annual depreciation | 340.5 | 293.8 | 249.9 | 210.5 | 178.0 | 132.6 |
| Property, plant, and equipment (gross) | 5,580.5 | 5,698.7 | 5,284.2 | 4,513.6 | 3,573.8 | 2,803.9 |
| Property, plant, and equipment (net) | 4,013.9 | 4,381.2 | 4,178.1 | 3,583.2 | 2,806.4 | 2,214.0 |
| Inventories | 2,653.5 | 2,599.2 | 2,833.8 | 2,921.8 | 2,499.2 | 2,234.8 |
| Current assets | 3,640.1 | 3,452.8 | 3,598.8 | 3,733.1 | 3,189.3 | 2,881.3 |
| Working capital | 1,288.6 | 1,116.5 | 1,989.2 | 1,797.5 | 1,662.0 | 1,727.7 |
| Total assets | 9,339.2 | 9,667.0 | 9,622.1 | 9,115.1 | 7,301.7 | 6,322.1 |
| Total debt | 2,588.6 | 3,074.9 | 3,745.8 | 3,804.2 | 2,800.1 | 2,507.1 |
| Stockholders' equity | 4,092.9 | 4,033.7 | 3,662.9 | 3,233.7 | 2,837.0 | 2,471.0 |
| Net earnings reinvested | 472.3 | 538.1 | 480.3 | 407.8 | 350.3 | 352.3 |
| Common dividends declared as % of net earnings | 46.8% | 40.5% | 38.6% | 37.9% | 36.3% | 30.6% |
| Book value per common share | $33.72 | 32.27 | 29.10 | 25.79 | 22.74 | 19.84 |
| Market price of common share high-low | 83¼-62⅛ | 72⅜-54 | 67¾-44⅛ | 55⅛-42 | 48½-29⅛ | 38⅝-31⅛ |
| Closing price year-end | 80⅝ | 71¾ | 60 | 48¾ | 43¼ | 36 |
| Price/earnings ratio year-end | 11 | 10 | 9 | 9 | 9 | 8 |
| Number of common shares— actual outstanding year-end | 121.4 | 125.0 | 125.9 | 125.4 | 124.8 | 124.5 |

Operating companies' income is income before corporate expense, interest, and other non-operating income and deductions. The amortization of previously capitalized interest is included in operating companies' income. A write-down of the completed but inactive Miller Brewing Company facility Trenton, Ohio reduced 1984 pretax earnings, net earnings, and earnings per share $280.4 million, $145.6 million, and $1.19, respectively.

*Source:* Annual Report, 1984.

| 1978 | 1977 | 1976 | 1975 | 1974 | 1973 | 1972 | 1971 | 1970 |
|---|---|---|---|---|---|---|---|---|
| 6,632.5 | 5,202.0 | 4,293.8 | 3,642.4 | 3,011.0 | 2,602.5 | 2,131.2 | 1,852.5 | 1,509.5 |
| 3,072.1 | 2,401.7 | 1,966.9 | 1,656.8 | 1,290.3 | 1,060.8 | 832.9 | 700.0 | 577.1 |
| 960.8 | 862.1 | 778.2 | 686.3 | 619.5 | 558.9 | 494.8 | 441.1 | 372.1 |
| 702.8 | 490.4 | 381.1 | 392.1 | 349.4 | 334.5 | 228.2 | 201.4 | 147.1 |
| 968.1 | 782.7 | 634.5 | 492.8 | 403.6 | 329.5 | 287.5 | 241.1 | 203.2 |
| 149.8 | 101.6 | 102.8 | 99.0 | 82.7 | 51.0 | 37.9 | 35.5 | 35.4 |
| 745.5 | 625.5 | 471.9 | 360.8 | 297.5 | 255.6 | 229.6 | 189.8 | 150.0 |
| 11.2% | 12.0% | 11.0% | 9.9% | 9.9% | 9.8% | 10.8% | 10.2% | 9.9% |
| 336.9 | 290.6 | 206.2 | 149.2 | 122.0 | 107.0 | 105.1 | 88.3 | 72.5 |
| 408.6 | 334.9 | 265.7 | 211.6 | 175.5 | 148.6 | 124.5 | 101.5 | 77.5 |
| 3.38 | 2.80 | 2.24 | 1.81 | 1.58 | 1.35 | 1.17 | 1.00 | .84 |
| 3.38 | 2.80 | 2.24 | 1.81 | 1.53 | 1.30 | 1.09 | .91 | .71 |
| 1.025 | .781 | .575 | .463 | .388 | .337 | .316 | .303 | .263 |
| 120.7 | 119.6 | 118.8 | 116.9 | 111.3 | 109.6 | 106.0 | 100.3 | 91.2 |
| 120.7 | 119.6 | 118.8 | 116.9 | 114.7 | 114.6 | 114.5 | 113.1 | 113.2 |
| 566.2 | 279.8 | 220.2 | 244.5 | 215.8 | 174.7 | 120.0 | 68.0 | 39.6 |
| 105.5 | 78.5 | 64.9 | 49.9 | 38.0 | 30.2 | 26.6 | 21.5 | 17.7 |
| 2,217.3 | 1,594.9 | 1,323.9 | 1,129.8 | 899.8 | 728.7 | 571.1 | 447.1 | 394.1 |
| 1,737.6 | 1,202.4 | 993.9 | 851.1 | 659.5 | 510.3 | 373.4 | 274.1 | 236.7 |
| 2,188.6 | 1,817.6 | 1,657.5 | 1,448.4 | 1,269.2 | 1,009.4 | 801.1 | 670.2 | 568.4 |
| 2,756.8 | 2,221.0 | 2,005.7 | 1,788.1 | 1,557.9 | 1,245.9 | 989.7 | 826.5 | 728.8 |
| 1,585.1 | 1,415.9 | 1,202.2 | 890.8 | 725.0 | 515.3 | 524.8 | 417.6 | 347.7 |
| 5,608.2 | 4,048.0 | 3,582.2 | 3,134.3 | 2,653.3 | 2,108.4 | 1,701.5 | 1,392.0 | 1,239.4 |
| 2,372.2 | 1,563.5 | 1,525.6 | 1,443.3 | 1,239.3 | 947.4 | 681.0 | 553.9 | 557.7 |
| 2,114.7 | 1,690.1 | 1,430.0 | 1,227.8 | 974.7 | 815.0 | 695.5 | 579.1 | 452.8 |
| 283.8 | 253.7 | 197.2 | 157.1 | 131.9 | 111.4 | 89.9 | 69.7 | 52.2 |
| 30.6% | 27.9% | 25.7% | 25.7% | 24.8% | 25.0% | 27.2% | 30.6% | 31.6% |
| 17.00 | 14.08 | 12.00 | 10.32 | 8.48 | 7.33 | 6.28 | 5.36 | 4.47 |
| 38⅜-28 | 32½-25¾ | 31⅝-24⅞ | 29⅝-20½ | 30¾-17⅛ | 34¼-24⅜ | 29⅝-17 | 17¾-11¾ | 12⅝-7 |
| 35¼ | 31 | 30⅞ | 26½ | 24 | 28¾ | 29⅝ | 17⅝ | 12⅜ |
| 10 | 11 | 13 | 14 | 15 | 21 | 25 | 17 | 14 |
| 124.3 | 119.8 | 119.0 | 118.7 | 114.5 | 110.8 | 108.9 | 104.7 | 96.6 |

**Exhibit 5.5** Estimated Market Share of Top Ten Brewers (percent)

|  | 1980 | 1981 | 1982 | 1983E |
|---|---|---|---|---|
| Anheuser-Bush | 28.2 | 30.0 | 33.0 | 33.5 |
| Miller | 20.9 | 22.2 | 22.0 | 20.9 |
| Stroh | 13.9 | 12.9 | 12.8 | 13.4 |
| Heileman | 7.5 | 7.7 | 8.1 | 9.7 |
| Coors | 7.8 | 7.3 | 6.6 | 7.5 |
| Pabst | 11.9 | 10.5 | 9.8 | 7.3 |
| Genesee | 2.0 | 2.0 | 1.9 | 1.7 |
| Schmidt | 2.0 | 1.6 | 1.8 | 1.7 |
| Pittsburgh | 0.6 | 0.5 | 0.5 | 0.5 |
| Others, net[a] | 5.2 | 5.3 | 3.5 | 3.8 |
| Total | 100 | | | |

[a]Includes imports

*Source:* Lehman Brothers, Kuhn Loeb Research. Copyright © *Beverage Industry*, January 1984.

producing 39.3 million barrels. Price consciousness has affected premium and super premium segments, which continued to show a decline in both production and market share (see Exhibit 5.6).

Anheuser-Busch continues to occupy the number one position among the nation's brewers in brand market share and brewery production and market share. Its 1982 promotional campaign behind Bud Light helped strengthen its position and provide increasing competition for Miller's Lite beer. Busch and Natural Light are also expected to be competitive in 1984.

G. Heileman and Stroh have become fierce competitors due to acquisitions. Stroh's acquisition of Schlitz has placed the company among the top three domestic brewers. The firm increased production by 1.3 million barrels in 1983. Much of its growth is due to sales of Schaefer's Old Milwaukee and Old Milwaukee Light brands.

Coors increased production to 13.6 million barrels in 1983. Coors Light showed growth of 0.9 million barrels produced to 3.6 barrels during the same year. An aggressive expansion campaign into the southeastern market was launched by Coors in 1982 and 1983. Territorial expansion increased Coors's market share by nearly one full percent. Growth in the future will be determined by each major brewer's ability to take away market share from its competitors.

**POSITION STATEMENT**

John A. Murphy, group executive vice-president of Philip Morris and chairman and chief executive officer of Miller Brewing Company, summarized Miller's position in 1981 as follows:

> The brewing industry produced and sold about 3 percent more than in 1979. Per capita consumption also went up. Behind the leadership of its President, Bill Howell, Miller

**Exhibit 5.6** Market Breakdown by Product (millions of barrels and percent market share)

| | Superpremium | Premium | Light | Popular | Malt Liquor | Imported | Total |
|---|---|---|---|---|---|---|---|
| 1981 | 12.6 | 93.8 | 25.1 | 38.8 | 6.4 | 5.2 | 181.9 |
| | 6.9% | 51.6% | 13.8% | 21.3% | 3.5% | 2.9% | |
| 1982 | 12.4 | 88.5 | 32.4 | 36.7 | 6.6 | 5.8 | 182.4 |
| | 6.8% | 48.5% | 17.8% | 20.1% | 3.6% | 3.2% | |
| 1983 | 11.6 | 86.4 | 34.0 | 39.3 | 6.6 | 6.3 | 184.2 |
| | 6.3% | 46.9% | 18.5% | 21.3% | 3.6% | 3.4% | |

*Source: Beverage Industry.* Copyright © John Maxwell, January 1984.

again outperformed the brewing industry and in the process earned an industry share of 21 percent.

Miller's total volume was up 4 percent to more than 37 million barrels, while retail sales were up 6 percent. The difference represents a reduction of field inventories which was good for our wholesalers in this inflation period and which was made possible by the commencement of production at our newly-completed breweries at Albany, Georgia, and Irwindale, California.

Because of this new capacity, our production has become more orderly and efficient. And with six breweries now in operation around the country, our trans-shipping costs are coming down. The picture will improve still further when our Trenton, Ohio, brewery, now under construction, is completed.

Finally, in addition, the output of our sixth and newest container plant, opened early this year in Moultrie, Georgia, is already being put to good use. In making a substantial portion of our containers, we are realizing significant production cost savings.

Miller's policy continues to be one of combining traditional brewing methods with the most modern brewing equipment and technology, helping ensure the quality, freshness and uniformity of our products. And, being a part of Philip Morris, we are particularly proud that we continue to outspend the industry in quality control.

Because of the extremely high quality of Miller products, we believe they should be priced to ensure a return of all costs plus a good profit. Our experience shows that consumers will willingly pay that kind of price for that kind of beer.

Last year, despite the healthy consumer demand for beer, some in the industry decided to reach out for still more sales by not increasing their prices to cover what we know to be the increased costs of production. In some cases they reduced prices.

Miller resisted. We lost some sales. This, combined with the heavy start-up costs of the new breweries—which of course had been anticipated—led to a 20 percent decline in operating income.

We remain convinced that our traditional price policy is correct. The brewing industry has not been keeping up with the cost increases caused by inflation. Price promotions only make the situation worse by lowering profit margins. However, Miller is in a better position than most to make do in this environment.

The adverse impact of 1980's pricing environment was felt by our flagship brand, Miller High Life, the industry's second-largest seller. However, we expect these effects to be temporary. High Life is a strong brand and its "Miller Time" theme is as current today as it was when we introduced it.

In the meantime Lite, which dominated the lower-calorie segment of the industry since its introduction in 1975, continued to grow strongly and last year became the industry's third-largest selling brand. Lite is clearly no longer a specialty item but has become a mainstream brand with a large and loyal following.

Our super-premium brand, domestically brewed Lowenbrau, is meeting sales objectives and doing well.

With these three brands Miller is well-positioned in the key segments of the industry for volume, profit, and potential.

Let me now touch briefly on some other matters.

We continue to oppose efforts to enact more forced-deposit laws. These are currently on the books in six states. They raise beverage prices to the consumer considerably without significantly reducing litter. Yet bottle bill proponents persist and have introduced legislation in both houses of the Congress again this year, as well as in some 30 states.

The beer business continues to be penalized by outdated and needless regulations, of which forced deposits constitute only one set. These regulations are imposed by the Federal Government as well as the 50 states, each with its own particular—I should say peculiar—set of restrictions. The cost of compliance is heavy on the states and thus on the taxpayer.

With economy in government at all levels now the order of the day, surely the time has come to abandon these wasteful anachronisms—to the benefit of both beer-drinkers and taxpayers, who are one and the same.

We also continue to be mindful of the potential dangers of alcohol abuse. Beer is an adult drink and a drink of moderation. Miller regularly supports the American Council on Alcoholism and other groups which work to check the spread of alcohol abuse through education and the encouragement of responsible use of all alcoholic beverages, beer included.

This is another aspect of Miller's commitment to quality—in this case quality of life for the society which permits us to be in business. It is an essential and permanent element in the Philip Morris way of doing things.

# 6 The Adolph Coors Company

Jeffrey M. Miner and Larry D. Alexander
Virginia Polytechnic Institute and State University

**INTRODUC-TION**

Coors had been very profitable and had grown by emphasizing a single premium brand of beer. It was the only major brewer located in the Rocky Mountains, with one large production facility located in Golden, Colorado. Although it had expanded into other states and was the sixth largest brewer in 1982, it was still a regional brewer.

In the 1980s, Coors faced increasingly stronger competition from two national brewers, Anheuser-Busch and Miller. Given the slow industry growth rate for beer sales in recent years, some industry analysts felt that an industry shakeout would occur. Regional brewers would be the most susceptible to going bankrupt or being acquired during such a consolidation. Even though Coors had been strong up through the 1970s, could it remain successful as just a regional brewer in the 1980s? Thus, two distinct strategic alternatives presented themselves to the Coors family, who held tight control of the firm. Should the firm remain as a regional brewer or go nationwide in the production and marketing of beer?

**HISTORY**

Adolph Herman Joseph Coors, a German immigrant, and Jacob Schueler, a Denver businessman, began brewing in an old tannery in the Clear Creek Valley of Golden, Colorado, in 1873. They called it the Golden Brewery. Coors was attracted to the area because of the numerous springs flowing from the Rocky Mountains. In 1880, Coors bought out Schueler and renamed the successful venture Coors Golden Brewery.

The company thrived until Prohibition; then it survived by selling near beer and malted milk. It also developed several manufacturing operations for producing cement and porcelain during that same period. While Coors did well, such was not the case for breweries in general. From 1910 to 1933, the number of breweries was cut in half from 1568 to 750.

After Prohibition, Coors Company experienced phenomenal growth. Still, it remained a regional brewery that produced only one type of beer from a single brewery. Its beer was sold in 11 western states in 1970, with California being its largest market. By 1970, this regional brewer also became the nation's fourth largest brewer.

This case was prepared by Jeffrey M. Miner (M.B.A. in finance from V.P.I. in December 1983; employee of IBM) and Larry D. Alexander (assistant professor of strategic management, Department of Management, College of Business, Virginia Polytechnic Institute and State University).

Copyright © 1985 by Jeffrey M. Miner and Larry D. Alexander.

Coors beer began to develop a mystique in the early 1970s, perhaps because it was the only beer brewed with pure Rocky Mountain spring water. Many people thought it was of higher quality than other beers. Coors conveyed environmental purity and a western image, which were in vogue at that time. Also, since easterners could not get the beer except at very high prices, this added to its mystique. The movie *Smokey and the Bandit* illustrated the degree to which some people would go to get Coors beer, and celebrities such as Paul Newman and Clint Eastwood regularly drank Coors beer on movie sets. Even President Jerry Ford carried the beer on board Air Force One.

Coors, the market leader in 9 of the 11 states it served including California, then turned to geographical expansion. The company began selling beer in Texas and other nearby states, where it quickly gained market share. Its 1975 sales of $520 million represented a $270 million increase over 1971. Operating margin was 28 percent in 1975, the highest in the industry, and profit per barrel averaged almost $9, almost twice that of the industry leader, Anheuser-Busch. As a Coors marketing vice-president put it at that time, "You could have sold Coors beer in Glad bags."[1]

Coors's tremendous success did not last and it started to lose market share for several reasons. First, Coors suffered from a negative public image. A brewery workers' union strike in 1977 led to a boycott of Coors beer by numerous AFL-CIO unions. Second, Joe Coors's ultraconservative philosophy alienated a number of minorities, including women, blacks, Hispanics, and gays. Third, Coors failed to realize that the industry was changing. Miller Brewing, which was acquired by Philip Morris in 1970, was the first to recognize that beer drinkers were not a single market, but rather a number of differentiated segments. Whereas Anheuser-Busch used price and lower costs to compete with Schlitz in the 1960s, Miller shifted that emphasis toward heavy advertising and promotion and development of new products to appeal to these segments in the 1970s. This new strategy helped Miller jump from eighth at the start of the decade to second by 1977.

Unfortunately, Coors ignored the signs for quite a while, continued with its production orientation, and brewed only one beer, Coors Premium. Conversely, Coors's advertising expenditures were the lowest in the industry. In 1977, they were only about $.25 per barrel compared to an industry average of over a $1.00. A marketing battle ensued as Miller attempted to unseat Anheuser-Busch from the number one spot, and Coors suffered from it.

Coors's loss in market share was most dramatic in California, its traditional stronghold. Share dropped from 40 percent in the mid-1970s to under 20 percent by 1982. The loss for Coors was a gain for Anheuser-Busch, which then controlled about 47 percent of that market. Coors also lost share to Miller in Texas, which was another former stronghold. Overall, Coors dropped from fourth place brewer in the early 1970s to sixth place in 1982. Volume was 13.5 million barrels in 1976, a 9.1 percent market share, and earnings were $76 million on sales of $594 million. In 1982, however, volume dropped to 11.9 million barrels, which represented only a 6.6 percent share, while earnings were only $40 million on sales of $915 million.

## MANAGE- MENT

Adolph Coors Company had sustained itself for over 100 years as a family owned and managed business. The Coors family had a pervasive influence over all aspects of company operations. Since 1970 the top spot had actually been shared by two brothers, William and Joseph Coors. Their late brother, Adolph Coors III, would have been chief executive had he not been killed in 1960. Adolph Coors II retained control of the company until he died in 1970, when control was passed on to Bill and Joe. In the early 1980s, Joe's two oldest sons, Jeff and Peter, were added to the management team supposedly to provide a transition between the two generations of management.

Bill Coors, age 66, was the elder of the two and his official position was chairman and chief executive officer. He handled the technical side of the business and had a reputation for being a genius in the brewing industry. Joe Coors, age 65, was the president and chief operating officer and oversaw the financial and administrative functions. In reality, each brother acted in any capacity they wanted and there were no formal lines of authority. Their apparent lack of rivalry amazed outsiders. Both men were lean, tall, rugged westerners who were very open and personal with employees. In fact, they were referred to as Bill and Joe by all employees, rather than by their famous last name.

The brothers devoted themselves to brewing the finest quality beer that they could. Bill and Joe did not put much faith in that mystique bit. They genuinely believed they simply made a better product and that was why it sold so well. Bill was well respected for his technical know-how and was chairman of the United States Brewers Association. The brothers shunned the public eye in the past; however, the company's more recent unfavorable public image had forced them to be more open with the public. Joe, a longtime conservative, was very outspoken and his views tended to alienate a number of minority groups.

The brothers realized that in the new competitive brewing industry of the 1980s, maintaining market share and survival were key goals. This was one reason that they decided to infuse fresh thinking in the management team when they brought Jeff and Peter into top management in 1982.

Peter Coors, age 36, and Jeff, age 38, were named division presidents in 1982 when an expanded four-man office of the presidency was created. They both had engineering degrees from Cornell. Peter also had an M.B.A. degree and was involved in the sales and marketing aspect of the company. He initiated the company's first market research in the early 1970s, which his father disapproved of at the time. However, since he realized that the low-calorie beer market segment was growing rapidly, he proved instrumental in developing Coors Light. Both Joe and Bill opposed this move at first. Peter was heir apparent to the presidency and more easily handled the pressures of being a public figure. Jeff oversaw research and development operations and was a one-man research team in the early 1970s. By the early 1980s, that department had grown significantly in size and importance. Jeff also headed up all new product development efforts at Coors in the 1980s.

Both were responsible for shifting the emphasis toward advertising, price competition, and new product introduction. These actions probably helped the company to survive. The pair disagreed with each other and also with Bill and Joe, but the differences tended to be constructive.

**PRODUCTION**    Coors was considered a maverick among brewers because its brewing process defied industry norms. However, the company was very highly regarded in the industry as a quality and technologically superior brewer. With Coors's single brewery, which had a 20-million-barrel capacity, uniformity and quality were easier to maintain. The drawback, however, was that transportation costs were quite high and there were significant logistics problems in producing and packaging different kinds of beer in the same brewery.

All raw materials and finished products were constantly monitored for uniformity and quality. Coors used the highest-quality ingredients possible. The water was pure Rocky Mountain spring water from over 40 springs located on the brewery grounds. Rarely was water in its pure form suitable for brewing, but no chemical alterations of this water were necessary. Coors supplied its own special barley seed, Moravian III, to contract farmers in the West. Coors bought its hops from growers in Washington and Idaho and imported two types from Germany. Coors also had its own malt house to ensure that proper aging of the barley was adhered to. Rice, grown for Coors in California and Arkansas, was used to give the beer its light body. A computer was used extensively to monitor many steps in the brewing operation, and flavor checks were performed regularly at each step. In addition, trained personnel routinely evaluated the quality of all ingredients and the final product.

Coors's brewing process was unique because it was entirely natural. No artificial ingredients were used. Since all biochemical processes were allowed to occur naturally, Coors had one of the longest brewing processes in the industry, which took an average of 68 days to brew and package the beer. Coors Light took even longer to produce because extra time had to be allowed for enzymes to dissolve the sugars.

In keeping with its natural brewing philosophy, Coors approached the problem of germ control in a unique way—the beer was not pasteurized. In 1959, company scientists discovered a better way which involved a series of filters combined with controlled conditions. The filling process was so germfree that it was likened to a sterile operating room.

Coors's filling process was designed to keep the beer cold at all times. This was supposed to enhance the flavor since heat was thought to take away some of the beer's body and flavor. Packaging was a completely computerized operation to maintain Coors's goals of uniformity and quality. The computer told the forklift drivers which pallets to pick up and where to put them. Because of this system, Coors did not require a warehouse. Beer that came off the line was sent almost immediately to trucks and railcars for distribution.

Coors was trying to minimize pollution caused by its packaging materials. The company was the founder and leader of used aluminum can recycling. In 1979, 80 percent of its aluminum cans used in packaging were recycled. Coors paid out over $33 million for them. The major sources for these cans were the recycling centers located at Coors's distributorships. Also, 50 can banks, which were reverse vending machines for aluminum cans, were being test marketed. This approach helped to make recycling more convenient for consumers. This program also enabled the company to be less dependent on the aluminum market. Recycling was not only cost-effective for the company, it also provided consumers with supplemental income.

Brewery wastes were always a problem, but Coors had developed a method to transform much of this waste into animal feed. An average of 4 million gallons of industrial wastes were processed daily at Coors. The company was a leader in the efficient use of wastewater, yielding only 3.5 barrels of it per barrel of beer, compared to 8 for most brewers.

Coors was also committed to energy conservation. The company began converting to coal in 1976 and by 1980 was virtually 100 percent coal-dependent. This move was relatively risk-free since Coors sat in the middle of America's most plentiful coal supply. Also, recycling saved about 95 percent of the energy required to produce new aluminum from bauxite.

Clearly, Coors was the most energy-efficient brewer in America, with the lowest B.T.U.-per-barrel ratio in the industry. Its engineering capabilities enabled the company to become nearly energy self-sufficient while maintaining rigid pollution control standards. For example, Coors had been able to remove 99.5 percent of the pollutants caused by burning coal.

## MARKETING

In the 1980s, Coors marketing capabilities were improving but still did not compare to many of its major competitors. However, it had come a long way since the mid-seventies when the company brewed only one product, did no market research, and spent next to nothing on advertising. By the early 1980s, Coors was trying to remedy this through extensive advertising, promotion, and development of new products to cater to different segments of the beer-drinking population.

Coors switched its emphasis from producing one beer of superior quality to producing products of superior quality. Until 1978, Coors Premium was the only beer that the company produced. Management felt that this was a superior beer and they simply did not need another brand. Coors Premium was considered a rich and light-bodied beer and contained 138 calories per 12 ounces. This beer was still the staple for the company and the fourth best-selling brand of beer in the nation. The company sold 8.4 million barrels of Premium in 1982, but this was down some 19 percent from 1981, mainly due to increased competition and the recession. By 1983, however, Coors also marketed other brands of beer to different market segments.

Coors Light was introduced in 1978 in response to the fast-growing light-beer segment. The company had earlier insisted that Coors Premium was light enough, but later realized the importance of developing a new product for this important growth segment. Coors Light contained 105 calories per 12 ounces. In an effort to provide a light beer with quality taste, Coors spent a great deal of time developing this product. Not surprisingly, it also used all natural ingredients. The brand grew substantially since its introduction, but remained far behind the leader, Lite beer from Miller. The company sold 3.2 million barrels of Coors Light in 1982, an increase of 2.1 million over 1980. However, many analysts felt that this growth had been at the expense of Coors Premium, which was another reason for Premium's sales decline.

In 1983, Coors started test marketing a new premium brew called Golden Lager 1873 because the company recognized that both Coors Premium and Light appealed to basically the same type of beer drinkers. Company research showed that many drinkers wanted a heartier-tasting beer. Coors hoped that Golden Lager would compete effectively with the national leaders in this category, Anheuser-Busch's Budweiser and Miller's High Life. The company tried to add credibility to the brand by linking it with its Rocky Mountain heritage. Initially, it was being tested in selected cities in the South and West. Coors also hoped that the new beer would help fill the brewery's excess capacity.

Coors had also tried to appeal to the growing import and superpremium-beer-drinking segment. George Killian's Irish Red Ale from France had been sold to Coors, which began testing the product in 1980. Successful results prompted a marketwide rollout in 1982. The company claimed that high initial sales indicated that the product had already developed a strong following.

Earlier in 1980, Coors began testing its first superpremium brand, Herman Joseph's 1868. It was very rich and full-bodied, which was achieved through a longer brewing and aging cycle. Coors hoped that the beer would be able to compete with Anheuser-Busch's Michelob, the leader in that segment. In 1982, the beer was still being tested in six states, but it had not yet been very successful. As a result, Herman Joseph's was periodically reformulated, repackaged, and readvertised, but it had never topped 100,000 barrels.

In an industry as competitive as brewing, it was important for Coors to generate a strong following for its products. Advertising and promotional skills were a great concern, probably because the firm had grown complacent in its century of operation. Fortunately, Coors management realized that it could no longer rely on its product's mystique to cure marketing problems. Since 1975, advertising expenditures increased dramatically as shown in Exhibit 6.1. However, Coors made frequent ad theme changes over the past few years, which had given the company a branding identity problem.

To complement its own marketing department, Coors also enlisted the aid of two top advertising agencies. Advertising for Coors Premium emphasized its purity, freshness, and superiority. The campaign was supported by in-store point-of-purchase displays which cost much less than television and were probably fairly effective. On television, Coors depicted its beer being drunk in traditional beer-

**Exhibit 6.1** Coors
Advertising Expenditures
(1975–1983)

| Year | Expenditure (in millions) |
|------|---------------------------|
| 1975 | $     1.2 |
| 1976 | 2.0 |
| 1977 | 15.5 |
| 1978 | 33.5 |
| 1979 | 46.4 |
| 1980 | 66.8 |
| 1981 | 85.8 |
| 1982 | 88.1 |
| 1983 | over 88.1 |

*Source:* Adolph Coors Company 1980 Annual Report and 1982 Annual Report. Also see Robert F. Hartley's "Coors—We Are Immune to Competition," in his *Management Mistakes* (Columbus, Ohio: Grid Publishing Co., 1983), pp. 139–153.

drinking settings, such as bars and parties, and was targeted at those who drank three or four beers at a time. Coors Light had an energetic new campaign to attract more consumers in the low-calorie segment. It focused on the unsurpassed taste in informal active settings.

Coors used outdoor billboards as a secondary medium, which was not standard for the industry. Billboards were used to depict the image of the snow-covered Rockies. This medium was used mainly for Coors Premium. Although Coors used radio advertising to a rather limited extent, it was being used more extensively in the 1980s for Coors Light.

Advertising and promotional efforts were increased in 1982 to the young-adult segment which, while declining in absolute numbers, was usually where brand loyalty was established. Campaigns to improve Coors product awareness among blacks and Hispanics, who accounted for a significant proportion of the target market, had been initiated. Corporate messages aimed at these groups tried to persuade them to give the company a chance to dispel Coors' negative image, which still lingered on. Coors felt, however, that its new open, straightforward public relations efforts would help win these consumers over to its side.

Perhaps the most important way in which brewers advertised their products was through sports promotions, especially on television. Coors focused on both participative and spectator sports events, and selected these events based on a sports activity study performed by the company. Its recent sports emphasis had been on motor sports and cycling. In 1980, many Coors distributors registered sizable sales increases before, during, and after various Coors-sponsored sporting events. Sports promotion also helped Coors gain valuable national exposure. However, it should be pointed out that Coors and other smaller brewers had some difficulty finding available spots on nationally televised sports due to exclusive arrangements that Anheuser-Busch and Miller had established with the networks.

Coors had over 350 distributors in its marketing territory. These distributors usually had to be large because Coors insisted that its products be refrigerated during distribution. This required both the company and its distributors to undertake added expenses and pains to keep the beer cold so that the flavor of the beer was preserved until it got to retailers. All beer was shipped from Coors in insulated railcars or refrigerated trucks. Distributors, in turn, were required to keep the beer refrigerated in their warehouses. Coors thus usually only took on veteran wholesalers who could make the necessary investments in refrigeration and insulation. The beer was placed in special vaults and kept at a constant 35 degrees. Because of this requirement, distributors had to pay an additional $100,000 or more each year just to keep Coors beer cold.

Retailers were encouraged to keep Coors beer refrigerated at all times, but because of increased promotions, there were often floor displays at room temperature. The company claimed that it would not harm Coors beer or cause it to lose its flavor any faster than any other beer on the market. To further ensure that flavor was preserved, the distributors were required to rotate retailer stocks every 60 days. This 60-day rotation rule was the strictest in the industry.

The distributors also played a vital role in marketing the product. They set up point-of-purchase displays in retail outlets, prepared local advertising, and developed customer relations. In order to maintain better relations with its distributors, Coors established its own television network, Second Century, in 1980. Stories were periodically done on different wholesalers. Distributors had to purchase the equipment to view the films, but over 90 percent had already done so. Brewery employees also viewed what the distributors were doing on this network.

The company also owned six of its own distributorships, not to compete with the independent wholesalers, but to give Coors's management firsthand knowledge of actual conditions in the field. It also enabled the company to analyze local and regional consumer patterns, train management in marketing and sales, and test new programs before they were introduced everywhere.

Approximately 78 percent of Coors's products were shipped by rail. The remaining 22 percent were shipped by truck. Of this, 14 percent went by common carrier or trucks owned by Coors distributors, and 8 percent went by the Coors Transportation Company. This wholly owned subsidiary had grown in the last couple of years since only 3 percent of Coors' products used it in 1980. The company was formed in 1971 to provide hauling flexibility. It operated 132 temperature-controlled trailers and 52 tractors. Each truck traveled about 215,-000 miles a year. The purpose was to reach distributors who did not have rail service, to handle emergency loads, and to haul to areas where profitable backhauls were available. Backhauls usually brought food products into the Denver area. The company was also formed as a reaction to rising railroad rates.

The advantage of having this flexibility was exemplified in 1980, when Coors was entering Arkansas. Thousands of extra cases were needed because demand had been underestimated. It could have turned into embarrassing shortages just when the company was trying to establish itself in a new territory. Fortunately, it turned into extra sales because of quick backup trucking by Coors's trucks.

Coors had recently begun a two-pronged approach to gain market share. One way was to expand further into the east, and the other was to reverse share losses in its traditional 20-state territory, most notably in California and Texas. Neither way promised to be an easy task. The effort would mean head-to-head competition with leaders Anheuser-Busch and Miller and would require huge marketing expenditures. Coors had been trying to meet advertising expenditures, but aggressive marketing was still a relatively new experience for Coors.

In 1983, Coors's biggest expansion campaign yet was undertaken to enter the Southeast market. This region was considered to be a growth area by many brewers. It appeared that the mystique was still alive in the Southeast, where there had been strong initial customer acceptance of Coors Premium and Light. Initial sales were going well in 1983 for both brands in this region. Although competition in this area was intense, Coors had selected large distributors who were well established in their markets to help implement this effort.

This expansion was also supported by heavy advertising on radio and television which stressed the fact that Coors could finally be purchased in the region. With that expansion, Coors marketed its products in 26 states and the District of Columbia. However, the good news was tempered by two points. First, some analysts feared that the sales in the Southeast perhaps increased so very rapidly because of the novelty factor. Thus, they suggested that more time would be needed to determine if Coors's success would be maintained. Second, Coors's transportation costs to the Southeast were very high. One estimate was that the cost of shipping from Golden, Colorado, to the Southeast was $7 to $8 per barrel, compared to an industry average of $3 per barrel.

Coors had purchased land options for the possible erection of another brewery in Virginia or Tennessee. However, there were no plans to begin building any time soon. If the company were to acquire or build another plant, a marketing problem could arise, since Coors's identity was associated with pure Rocky Mountain spring water. Jeff Coors remarked, "Now . . . you can make good water out of anything. We haven't crossed the hurdle of what impact we'd suffer if we dropped the Rocky Mountain water theme. But you never know. We might produce an entirely different beer for the East."[2] However, one analyst suggested that the delaying of the plant would only allow the competition time to solidify their hold even further on eastern and southeastern markets.

**FINANCE**    Coors had always been strong financially. Exhibits 6.2 and 6.3 show the consolidated balance sheets and consolidated income statements for the years 1980 through 1982. The company went public in 1975, only because it needed to raise

**Exhibit 6.2**

## ADOLPH COORS COMPANY
### Consolidated Balance Sheets (dollars in thousands)

|  | 12/28/80 | 12/27/81 | 12/26/82 |
|---|---|---|---|
| **Assets** | | | |
| Cash | $ 87,883 | $ 76,614 | $ 71,251 |
| Accounts/notes receivable | 57,930 | 66,667 | 64,909 |
| Inventories | 149,504 | 115,677 | 118,658 |
| Prepaid expenses | 28,856 | 34,282 | 34,614 |
| Income tax prepayments | 6,036 | 2,215 | 4,236 |
| Total current assets | 330,209 | 295,455 | 293,668 |
| Properties, net | 556,419 | 652,090 | 702,769 |
| Excess of cost over net | 2,649 | 2,567 | 3,029 |
| Other assets | 5,108 | 6,272 | 8,448 |
| Total assets | $894,385 | $956,384 | $1,007,914 |
| **Liabilities and equity** | | | |
| Accounts payable | $ 48,923 | $ 40,033 | $ 45,601 |
| Salaries, vacation | 25,677 | 27,488 | 25,543 |
| Taxes (not income) | 19,872 | 18,494 | 17,252 |
| Income taxes | 3,427 | 9,922 | 2,789 |
| Accrued expenses | 18,195 | 21,577 | 28,820 |
| Total current liabilities | 116,094 | 117,514 | 120,005 |
| Deferred income taxes | 60,149 | 75,968 | 95,097 |
| Other long-term liabilities | 6,042 | 9,335 | 9,600 |
| Capital stock: | | | |
| Class A common, voting | 1,260 | 1,260 | 1,260 |
| Class B common, nonvoting | 11,000 | 11,000 | 11,000 |
| Total | 12,260 | 12,260 | 12,260 |
| Paid-in capital | 2,011 | 2,011 | 2,011 |
| Retained earnings | 724,284 | 765,751 | 795,396 |
| Total | 738,555 | 780,022 | 809,667 |
| Less treasury shares | 26,455 | 26,455 | 26,455 |
| Total equity | 712,100 | 753,567 | 783,212 |
| Total liabilities and equity | $894,385 | $956,384 | $1,007,914 |

*Source:* Adolph Coors Company 1982 Annual Report, pp. 12–13.

money to pay inheritance taxes on the estate of Adolph Coors II. These public shares were traded over the counter and there were some 9000 shareholders in 1983. However, this public stock was class B nonvoting, so outsiders did not have a say in management decisions. The Coors family owned 35 percent of the class B shares and 100 percent of the 1.26 million shares of class A voting stock. Thus, the Coors family controlled their stock to such an extent that no other firm would be able to acquire it unless management allowed it. That didn't appear very likely, given the history of this maverick brewery.

Exhibit 6.3

# ADOLPH COORS COMPANY
## Consolidated Income Statements (dollars in thousands)

|  | 12/26/80 | 12/27/81 | 12/26/82 |
|---|---|---|---|
| Sales | $ 1,012,198 | $ 1,060,345 | $ 1,032,297 |
| Less excise taxes | 133,301 | 130,429 | 117,039 |
| Net sales | 887,897 | 929,916 | 915,258 |
| Costs and expenses |  |  |  |
| Cost of goods sold | 629,758 | 659,623 | 659,033 |
| Marketing, G&A | 146,293 | 181,348 | 185,076 |
| Research and development | 14,256 | 16,848 | 15,230 |
| Total | 790,307 | 857,819 | 859,339 |
| Operating income | 97,590 | 72,097 | 55,919 |
| Other |  |  |  |
| Interest income | (16,514) | (13,788) | (10,411) |
| Interest expense | 1,563 | 1,601 | 2,480 |
| Miscellaneous | 6,764 | 4,651 | (1,298) |
| Total | (8,187) | (7,536) | (9,229) |
| Income before taxes | 105,777 | 79,633 | 65,148 |
| Income taxes | 40,800 | 27,663 | 25,000 |
| Net income | 64,977 | 51,970 | 40,148 |
| Beginning retained earnings | 668,939 | 724,284 | 765,751 |
|  | 733,916 | 776,254 | 805,899 |
| Cash dividends | 9,632 | 10,503 | 10,503 |
| End retained earnings | $   724,284 | $   765,751 | $   795,396 |

*Source:* Adolph Coors Company 1982 Annual Report, p. 10.

Another aspect of Coors's financial approach was the company's refusal to borrow money. This was a family tradition which dated back to the company's beginnings. Coors's capital structure consisted almost entirely of common stock. Also, since the company did not plan to issue any more stock, all future expansion would have to be financed through internally generated cash. Its normal cash balance was around $70 million, but Coors planned to increase this. Although lack of debt was a sign of financial strength, this avoidance of debt financing altogether sometimes caused the company to bypass attractive opportunities. One was the addition of an eastern plant, which the company agreed was necessary to offset huge transportation costs of shipping to eastern markets. Another example related to Coors's can manufacturing facility, which developed the technical process for making the two-piece aluminum can. However, the company sold the process to Continental Can Company and American Can Company because Coors would have had to borrow money to begin production.

## RESEARCH AND DEVELOP- MENT

Coors was often considered the most technically advanced brewery in the world. The company had Colorado's single largest engineering crew for any private-sector firm. Research and development was concerned with developing new products, brewing techniques, and packaging techniques. Coors had developed technical superiority in ceramics and aluminum cans. There was an extensive barley R&D program, which had genetically developed Coors's own special variety called Moravian III. Yeast cells, used in the brewing process, were specifically selected by Coors for testing to develop new and better strains to upgrade the quality of its beer. Farmers wanted a higher yield for their crops and Coors wanted reliable sources of supply, so much of the company's research dealt with counseling farmers on how to get higher yields while maintaining Coors's standards. The company also did research on how to get more out of the grain in the production process. They were now reusing many things that used to be thrown away.

Not all R&D efforts had been successful, however. The press tab can was developed to stop pollution from ring pull tabs. The idea was good, but it failed because the can was hard to open and consumers often cut their fingers in the process.

Jeff Coors, who was responsible for R&D, became the first American in a quarter century to present a technical paper at the European Brewing Convention in 1979. Research and development was a relatively minor part of the company's operations before Jeff became involved in the early 1970s. Although many advancements in the industry occurred in the 1960s and 1970s, Jeff did not see any major technical breakthroughs on the horizon in the 1980s. Research appeared to have taken a distant back seat to marketing; however, Coors remained committed to R&D. Bill Coors's credo was, "If technology exists, use it. If it doesn't, develop it."[3]

## HUMAN RESOURCES

Coors employed about 8600 people in 1983, down some 850 from just 1981. Company officials blamed the layoffs on the recession, which reduced industry demand. Coors tried to develop its own personnel so they could later be promoted from within. This required extensive educational and training programs. The company's television network, Second Century, had also been used to produce in-house training programs.

Coors was committed to equal employment opportunity and supported an active affirmative action program. Minority employment agencies were used to recruit minorities, which represented 13.4 percent of the work force in 1979. Coors also had an employee opportunity training program which hired ex-convicts, disabled veterans, and the disadvantaged and trained them for responsible positions within the firm.

An average salary for a Coors production worker was $20,000 a year and Coors offered fringe benefits totaling an additional $5800 per employee per year.

Clearly, these wages and benefits were considerably higher than the average for Golden, Colorado, a city of approximately 11,000 people.

Coors's management maintained that business should operate as a free enterprise; thus, the company was philosophically opposed to unions. Unfortunately, Coors's brewery workers were unionized and represented a large proportion of the work force. They went out on strike in 1977. The issue was not money but rather that the company was forcing employees to take lie detector tests. A boycott of the company's products ensued, but Coors management stood its ground, replaced many of the striking workers, and rehired those who wanted to return.

In 1978, Coors's brewery workers voted out the union and the boycott's effect diminished. In 1982, the "60 Minutes" television show did a story on Coors to try to uncover human rights violations. The show, often noted for its revealing stories, found no such violations, which somewhat helped to ease Coors's negative image. As of 1983, Coors was still operating without a union.

Coors was very concerned about employee health and well-being. In 1982, the American Center for Occupational Health, a Coors subsidiary, continued to be committed to safer working conditions. The company provided health care tests and services to Coors's employees and other businesses, and it was currently completing the development of a lightweight, compact health testing machine.

Coors opened a wellness center on its brewery property in 1981. All employees, retirees, spouses, and dependents were allowed to use the facility, which contained a track, trampolines, weight sets, stationary bicycles, and other equipment. The center also sponsored programs in physical fitness, nutrition, stress management, weight control, stopping smoking, and alcohol education. The staff was comprised of experts in each field. Thus far, it had been very successful. Bill Coors was not worried whether the center could be cost justified, but whether it promoted health and happiness. Coors also funded participation in various sports for a number of employees, and many were sent to survival training courses. In sum, management regarded physical fitness as very important.

**COORS'S VERTICAL INTEGRATION AND DIVERSIFICATION EFFORTS**

In keeping with Coors's philosophy of independence in all aspects of operations, it became the most vertically integrated firm in the industry. Exhibit 6.4 shows a map of Coors operations throughout the United States. Coors had attempted to control its raw materials supply by having contract farmers grow its barley and rice and maintaining its own malt house. Coors also had its own supply of packaging materials. It owned a can manufacturing plant, which was the largest single such plant in the industry, a glass manufacturing plant, and a paper mill. Coors Energy Company owned a coal mine, 249 natural gas and oil wells, and leased rights to 330,000 acres. Coors owned its own truck fleet and waste treatment facility, and company engineers designed and constructed most of its own machinery and equipment. This was all very important for cost control, stability, and

**Exhibit 6.4** Map of Coors Operations

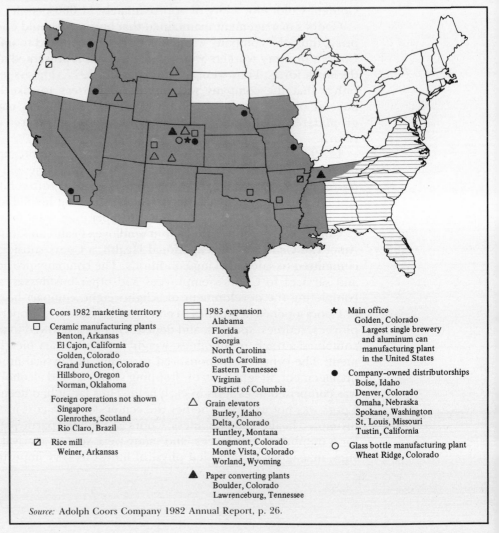

| | | |
|---|---|---|
| ■ Coors 1982 marketing territory | ▨ 1983 expansion | ★ Main office |
| ☐ Ceramic manufacturing plants | Alabama | Golden, Colorado |
| Benton, Arkansas | Florida | Largest single brewery |
| El Cajon, California | Georgia | and aluminum can |
| Golden, Colorado | North Carolina | manufacturing plant |
| Grand Junction, Colorado | South Carolina | in the United States |
| Hillsboro, Oregon | Eastern Tennessee | |
| Norman, Oklahoma | Virginia | ● Company-owned distributorships |
| | District of Columbia | Boise, Idaho |
| Foreign operations not shown | | Denver, Colorado |
| Singapore | △ Grain elevators | Omaha, Nebraska |
| Glenrothes, Scotland | Burley, Idaho | Spokane, Washington |
| Rio Claro, Brazil | Delta, Colorado | St. Louis, Missouri |
| | Huntley, Montana | Tustin, California |
| ▨ Rice mill | Longmont, Colorado | |
| Weiner, Arkansas | Monte Vista, Colorado | ○ Glass bottle manufacturing plant |
| | Worland, Wyoming | Wheat Ridge, Colorado |
| | ▲ Paper converting plants | |
| | Boulder, Colorado | |
| | Lawrenceburg, Tennessee | |

*Source:* Adolph Coors Company 1982 Annual Report, p. 26.

independence from supplier price hikes and shortages. Clearly, Coors believed in vertical integration, both forward and backward.

Coors had also diversified into companies not directly related to brewing, though they complemented the primary product. Coors Porcelain Company was one of the world's foremost suppliers of technical ceramics, mainly for the computer industry and energy firms. The company was trying to decide whether to compete in the $1-billion-a-year dental restoration industry. Coors Food Products Company did well in 1982, acquiring a snack food company which made potato chips. The Coors subsidiary also packaged rice and competed in the rice flour and cereal markets. They were experimenting with bread products made from brewers grain 28, a high-protein by-product of the brewing process. Variety breads were growing by 15 percent yearly. They also made cocomost, a cocoa substitute derived from brewer's yeast.

**COORS'S COMPETI-TION**

Since Miller Brewing's effect on the industry was already discussed earlier, only Anheuser-Busch, Stroh, and Heileman are profiled here. While Anheuser-Busch was the industry's giant, these two second-tier brewers were similar to Coors in size but followed different strategies. Exhibit 6.5 contains a list of the top six brewers and their major products in order of volume sold. Then, Exhibit 6.6 shows the top brewers' market shares for 1979 through 1982. Finally, Exhibit 6.7 shows the top ten domestic beer brands along with their 1982 market shares.

**Exhibit 6.5** Top Six Brewers and Their Major Brands (1982)

| | |
|---|---|
| 1. Anheuser-Busch | 4. Heileman |
| Budweiser | Old Style |
| Michelob | Schmidt's |
| Busch | Blatz |
| Michelob Light | Black Label |
| Bud Light | Colt 45 Malt Liquor |
| Natural Light | Old Style Light |
| | Blatz Light |
| | Black Label Light |
| | |
| 2. Miller | 5. Pabst |
| High Life | Pabst |
| Lite | Red, White & Blue |
| Lowenbrau | Olde English Malt |
| | Blitz |
| | Pabst Light |
| | Jacob Best |
| | Andeker |
| | |
| 3. Stroh/Schlitz | 6. Coors |
| Old Milwaukee | Coors Premium |
| Stroh's | Coors Light |
| Schlitz | George Killian's Ale |
| Schaefer | Herman Joseph's 1868 |
| Schlitz Malt Liquor | |
| Old Mil Light | |
| Stroh Light | |
| Goebel | |
| Schlitz Light | |
| Erlanger | |

*Source:* Paul Mullins, "Brewing Industry Has Flat Growth in '82," *Beverage Industry,* January 28, 1983, p. 31.

**Exhibit 6.6** Brewers' Estimated Market Shares (percent)

| Brewer | 1979 | 1980 | 1981 | 1982 |
|---|---|---|---|---|
| Anheuser-Busch | 26.8 | 28.2 | 30.0 | 32.3 |
| Miller | 20.8 | 20.9 | 22.2 | 21.8 |
| Stroh/Schlitz | 15.3 | 13.9 | 12.9 | 12.8 |
| Heileman | 6.6 | 7.5 | 7.7 | 7.9 |
| Pabst | 8.8 | 8.5 | 7.4 | 6.8 |
| Coors | 7.5 | 7.8 | 7.3 | 6.6 |
| Olympia | 3.5 | 3.4 | 3.1 | 2.8 |
| Genessee | 2.0 | 2.0 | 2.0 | 1.9 |
| Schmidt | 2.2 | 2.0 | 1.6 | 1.8 |
| General | 1.7 | 1.4 | 1.2 | 1.0 |
| Pittsburgh | 0.4 | 0.6 | 0.5 | 0.5 |
| Others | 4.4 | 3.8 | 4.1 | 3.8 |

*Source:* Paul Mullins, "Brewing Industry Has Flat Growth in '82," *Beverage Industry,* January 28, 1983, p. 34.

**Exhibit 6.7** Top Ten Beer Brands in 1982

| Brand | Market Share (percent) | Volume (million barrels) |
|---|---|---|
| Budweiser | 22.0 | 40.0 |
| Miller High Life | 11.0 | 20.0 |
| Lite from Miller | 9.6 | 17.5 |
| Coors | 4.6 | 8.4 |
| Michelob | 4.6 | 8.3 |
| Pabst | 4.5 | 8.1 |
| Old Milwaukee | 3.1 | 5.7 |
| Stroh's | 3.0 | 5.6 |
| Old Style | 3.0 | 5.5 |
| Schlitz | 2.6 | 4.7 |

*Source:* "Many Top Brews Give Ground to Other Brands," *Beverage World,* April 1983, p. 33.

**Anheuser-Busch**

Anheuser-Busch was the number one brewer in the United States ever since it took over that spot from Schlitz in the late 1950s. The giant lumbered along until the 1970s, when an onslaught by Miller to knock it out of its top position caused August Busch III, the company's chief strategist, to rethink his game plan. In large part, he began to copy Miller's methods. He determined that Miller's success was a direct function of heavy advertising in sports media, product diversification, and a switch in emphasis to the beer-drinking young-adult segment. This strategy change occurred in 1977 and had often been seen as the turning point in the industry. From then on, Anheuser-Busch steadily pulled away from Miller. It was the best-performing brewer in 1982, with a market share of 32.7 percent. Its 59.1 million barrels sold topped Miller's by almost 20 million.

By 1983, the firm was pursuing a total marketing effort, continuing to focus on the young-adult segment with a well-balanced line of quality beers. The Budweiser brand, by far the nation's best-selling beer and leader in the premium segment, represented an amazing 40.7 million of total barrels sold. Michelob was the leader in the superpremium segment. While Miller controlled 60 percent of the light-beer segment with its best-selling Lite, Anheuser-Busch had set its sights on taking over that market. It marketed three light beers with different tastes, prices, and images, and controlled 28 percent of the segment. Budweiser Light, introduced in 1982, had become the second best-selling light beer already. This brewing giant also had its sights on international expansion. Budweiser was already the best-selling import in Japan, and it was also strong in Canada.

The firm was the nation's biggest sponsor of sporting events. It had the twenty-second largest advertising budget among all U.S. firms, and it far outdistanced all competitors in television advertising. Furthermore, Anheuser-Busch was locked into many exclusive contracts, as was Miller. The company's operating efficiency was outstanding, and it boasted the highest profit per barrel in the industry. It had the best distribution system in the industry and its plants were located strategically throughout the United States. It was committed to new capacity increases, especially in Los Angeles. Like Coors, the company had vertically integrated to better control raw material supplies and costs. The firm's growth was expected to continue, and recent capacity expansions would increase pressure to capture more market share. Some industry observers felt that Anheuser-Busch might control 40 percent of the market by 1990.

## Stroh Brewing Company

Stroh saw merger as the only way to survive against the two industry giants. In 1982 the company acquired Schlitz, which had been suffering vast market declines. The merger put Stroh in the third spot in the brewing industry. Management was quite strong and had done a good job with its Stroh brand. However, the company had put itself at a disadvantage because it had leveraged itself so heavily with debt. Key problems for Stroh's were how to successfully integrate its acquisitions into the company and how to reverse the sales decline of its Schlitz brand.

Stroh was not advertising the Schlitz brand very much in 1983, although there were plans to step it up in the near future. The company appeared to be using cash flow from the brand to finance marketing expenditures for its best-selling brand, Old Milwaukee. It was being promoted with heavy television advertising and cents-off coupons, which were fairly new to this industry. Many analysts attributed the success of Old Milwaukee, a popular-priced brand, to the 1981–1983 recession.

## G. Heileman Brewing Company

Heileman, like Coors, had been very successful as a regional brewer. It was targeted for markets in the Midwest and Northwest, but was presently the fourth largest brewer in the United States. The company had increased barrelage dramatically over the past few years, from 4.5 million barrels in 1975 to 14.9

million in 1982. It was the only major brewer except Anheuser-Busch to register a sales gain in 1982.

In 1982, Heileman took a big step toward long-term viability by acquiring Pabst and its 49 percent share of Olympia. However, because of objections raised by the Department of Justice, a new Pabst entity was spun off to the remaining Olympia shareholders. Heileman strongly believed that continued consolidation of second-tier and small brewers needed to take place to more effectively compete. As a side note, 7 of the top 11 brewers were involved in acquisitions or attempted acquisitions in 1982.

Heileman also had very good management. The company was unusually adept at being able to market more than three dozen regional beers, of which Old Style was the best selling. It also had a very good cost structure which was quite competitive with that of Anheuser-Busch. To remain competitive, Heileman knew it had to expand into new markets. But having regional products might have helped the company to target some of its products to local market conditions.

There were two potential problems for Heileman. First, it served only the popular-priced market segment. This was one of the reasons that the company did so well in the face of a recession. Lack of brand loyalty may be in Heileman's favor, however, if people continued to trade down from higher-priced brands. Second, Heileman tried to remain well under Anheuser-Busch's prices; unfortunately, the industry giant had not raised prices in Heileman's market for about two years. If an increase did not come shortly, profit margin pressures might reduce Heileman's profitability.

**LEGAL AND POLITICAL ISSUES**

A number of legal and political issues facing the brewing industry were becoming more prevalent in the 1980s. First, the vast number of traffic deaths related to alcohol had increased dramatically. There had been a number of bills introduced in the U. S. Congress to raise the legal drinking age nationally to 21, and such bills were gaining increasing support. Raising the age would cause a decrease in beer sales. Perhaps substitutes, such as near beer, would crop up. Also, a number of consumer groups were asking the Consumer Protection Agency to look into the advertising practices of brewers. They claimed that brewers were encouraging the consumption of alcohol by highly vulnerable younger groups, which brought about heavy drinkers.

The company even started distributing counter cards and posters to bars throughout its marketing area with a message from E.T., the extraterrestrial. E.T. advised, "If you go beyond your limit, please don't drive. Phone home."[4] Coors had a longstanding policy against alcohol abuse. They sponsored alcohol awareness classes at their wellness center and supported many organizations that dealt with alcohol abuse.

Another major issue was the threat of mandatory deposits for bottles and cans. This would increase the price of beer and decrease customer convenience, possibly affecting demand. The difficulties in handling, shipping, and selling beer under this law were well known, as 18 percent of the beer sold in the United States in the early 1980s was covered by such laws. The law's rationale was to cut down on litter along the roadside, in the city, or out in the country. However, recycling might be an alternative means to accomplish this. Coors had a vigorous program for recycling both bottles and cans.

A third issue was excise taxes. Various state legislatures currently had bills to raise the excise tax on beer. There had also been some activity at the federal level. A number of groups had advocated taxing all alcoholic beverages by their alcohol content, which would result in drastically higher taxes on malt beverages. This, too, would result in increased prices for the consumer.

## PRODUCT-MARKET OPPORTUNITIES

Under market penetration, Coors could more heavily advertise its products on television. Radio might also be a promising medium for beer advertising. One survey revealed that beer drinkers spent only about 33 percent of their media time watching television, whereas 47 percent of their time was spent listening to radio, which was less expensive for advertisers.[5] Another method could be increased price competition through such means as price cuts, cents-off coupons, and rebates. Coupons might attract more women who presently did not buy much beer. Finally, Coors could merge with other brewers, which could help it penetrate existing markets with a wider selection of products.

Under market development, Coors could continue to expand nationally. This could be done by expanding its own facilities or by acquiring another brewery to give it additional capacity. A list of the top 40 breweries in the United States is shown in Exhibit 6.8. Expansion abroad might also be a viable alternative, especially since Anheuser-Busch was doing well in Japan. Clearly, this later option would require additional plants to make it feasible.

Under product development, Coors could develop near beer or other nonalcoholic beverages in response to a raising of the mandatory drinking age. Near beer was one product that helped Coors survive during prohibition. It could also sell bottled spring water. Coors could also develop plastic containers for beer products, which would be a response to the threat of mandatory deposits and a way to lower transportation costs with lighter plastic containers. Another alternative would be to develop a beer product for the popular-priced segment for a more complete line of products. Coors could also import a name brand to compete more effectively in that segment. Coors's engineers could do consulting jobs for area firms. Coors Porcelain Company could accelerate its plans to get into the lucrative billion-dollar-a-year dental restoration market.

Finally, under diversification, Coors could consider other glass products, such as test tubes. Also, the company could get into other areas related to the beverage industry, such as soft drinks or distilled spirits.

## THE FUTURE

The Coors family remained confident of their firm's success in the future. Bill and Joe Coors felt their firm had survived because of the superior quality of its

**Exhibit 6.8** Top 40 U.S. Commercial Brewers

| | 1983 Sales (31-gallon barrels) | Gain or Loss in Percent Over 1982 | Location |
|---|---|---|---|
| 1. Anheuser-Busch, Inc. | 60,500,000 | 2.4 | St. Louis, Mo. |
| 2. Miller Brewing Co. | 37,500,000 | −4.6 | Milwaukee, Wis. |
| 3. The Stroh Brewery Co. | 24,300,000 | 6.1 | Detroit, Mich. |
| 4. G. Heileman Brewing Co. | 17,549,000 | 20.9 | LaCrosse, Wis. |
| 5. Adolph Coors Co. | 13,719,000 | 15.1 | Golden, Colo. |
| 6. Pabst Brewing Co. | 12,804,000 | [c] | Milwaukee, Wis. |
| 7. Genesee Brewing Co. | 3,200,000 | −5.9 | Rochester, N.Y. |
| 8. Christian Schmidt & Sons | 3,150,000 | 0.0 | Philadelphia, Pa. |
| 9. Falstaff Brewing Co. | 2,704,884 | −15.1 | Vancouver, Wash. |
| 10. Pittsburgh Brewing Co. | 1,000,000[a] | 1.0 | Pittsburgh, Pa. |
| 11. Latrobe Brewing Co. | 700,000[a] | 0.0 | Latrobe, Pa. |
| 12. Champale Products Corp. | 450,000[a] | 4.7 | Trenton, N.J. |
| 13. Hudepohl Brewing Co. | 400,000[a] | 0.0 | Cincinnati, Ohio |
| 14. The F. X. Matt Brewing Co. | 400,000[a] | 0.0 | Utica, N.Y. |
| 15. Eastern Brewing Co. | 350,000[a] | 0.0 | Hammonton, N.J. |
| 16. The Schoenling Brewing Co. | 315,000[a] | 5.0 | Cincinnati, Ohio |
| 17. Joseph Huber Brewing Co. | 272,000 | −1.1 | Monroe, Wis. |
| 18. The Lion Inc.—Gibbons | 230,000 | 0.0 | Wilkes-Barre, Pa. |
| 19. D. G. Yuengling & Son | 143,000 | 0.0 | Pittsburgh, Pa. |
| 20. Jones Brewing Co. | 122,000 | −2.9 | Smithton, Pa. |
| 21. Dixie Brewing Co., Inc. | 113,000 | −24.7 | New Orleans, La. |
| 22. Jacob Leinenkugel Brewing | 67,000 | −1.5 | Chippewa Falls, Wis. |
| 23. Fred Koch Brewery | 60,000 | −7.7 | Dunkirk, N.Y. |
| 24. Stevens Point Brewery | 48,900 | 0.8 | Stevens Point, Wis. |
| 25. Cold Spring Brewing Co. | 40,000[a] | 0.0 | Cold Spring, Minn. |
| 26. Spoetzl Brewery, Inc. | 36,000 | −3.0 | Shiner, Tex. |
| 27. August Schell Brewing Co. | 35,000 | 0.0 | New Vim, Minn. |
| 28. Straub Brewery, Inc. | 35,000 | 0.0 | St. Mary's, Pa. |
| 29. Anchor Steam Brewery Co. | 33,500 | 16.6 | San Francisco, Calif. |
| 30. Walter Brewing Co. | 26,800 | −3.9 | Eau Claire, Wis. |
| 31. Dubuque Star Brewing | 5,400[b] | −75.3 | Dubuque, Iowa |
| 32. Old New York Beer Co. | 3,629[a] | — | New York, N.Y. |
| 33. Geyer Brothers | 3,500 | −12.5 | Frankenmuth, Mich. |
| 34. Redhook Ale Co. | 3,000 | — | Seattle, Wash. |
| 35. William S. Newman Brewing | 2,800 | 12.0 | Albany, N.Y. |
| 36. River City Brewing Co. | 2,500 | 108.3 | Sacramento, Calif. |
| 37. Sierra Nevada | 2,200 | 25.7 | Chico, Calif. |
| 38. Yakima Brewing | 1,400 | — | Yakima, Wash. |
| 39. Boulder Brewing Co. | 500 | 25.0 | Longmont, Colo. |
| 40. Thousand Oaks Brewing | 232[a] | — | Berkerly, Ariz. |

[a] Estimate.
[b] Less than a full year's production.
[c] Due to Pabst-Olympia merger, 1983 figures are not comparable to 1982.

*Source: MBA Blue Book, 1984,* pp. 6, 8, 10, 168.

product. But would Coors's quality and its Rocky Mountain mystique be enough to survive a changing industrial structure?

It appeared that slow growth would continue to plague the U.S. brewing industry. This meant that any significant increase in sales by one brewer would be at the expense of competitors. In addition, increased concentration among brewers—via acquisitions, mergers, and bankruptcies—would continue and it was predicted that the top three firms could have up to 80 percent of the market by 1990.[6] As a result, a major strategic decision faced Coors management in the mid-1980s. Could Coors remain a regional brewer and be successful? If so, what would it need to do differently as a regional brewer to compete against the national breweries and other regional firms? Conversely, should Coors go into nationwide production and distribution? These two clear strategic alternatives presented themselves to the Coors family members in top management.

Over the years, Coors had increased its territory to 26 states and Washington, D.C. It had announced that it would add Alaska and Hawaii by the end of 1983 and move into Maryland in early 1984. But would this be enough to compete against the two national giants, Anheuser-Busch and Miller? Could one production facility serve a nationwide distribution, or would Coors have to operate additional breweries? Which alternative—remain regional or go nationwide—that Coors management would select remained undetermined as 1983 came to a close.

## NOTES

1. "A Test for the Coors Dynasty," *Business Week,* May 8, 1978, p. 69.
2. Bob Lederer, "Can Coors Survive Its Image?" *Beverage World,* April 1979, p. 49.
3. Bob Lederer, "Coal Power," *Beverage World,* September 1978, p. 58.
4. Ibid., p. 47.
5. "Industry News," *Beverage Industry,* April 10, 1983, p. 58.
6. Michael C. Bellas, "Beer Wholesaler Sales Concentration: Implications for the 80's and Beyond," *Beverage Industry,* January 28, 1983, p. 30.

# 7  Xerox Corporation Proposed Diversification

J. David Hunger
George Mason University
Thomas Conquest and William Miller
Iowa State University

In the autumn of 1982, David Kearns was facing some difficult problems as the new chief executive officer of the Xerox Corporation. His company had recently posted a 39 percent drop in third-quarter earnings. This was Xerox's fourth quarterly decline in a row and the picture did not appear any brighter for the current quarter. Much of the profit decline had been attributed to narrower profit margins brought on by steep price cutting on many copier models in response to increasing competition, especially from the Japanese. In addition, profits had been reduced by the severance costs of trimming its work force; by the strength of the dollar, which eroded dollar values of sales made abroad; and particularly by the sluggish economy. Xerox had been forced to reduce its work force by 2,174 in 1981, down to 120,981 people worldwide. This was the first such reduction in the company's history. Further reductions occurred in 1982, with more predicted for the coming year. Kearns had watched Xerox's share of the plain paper copier market slip from 95 percent in the early 1970s to about 45 percent in 1982. In addition, Xerox stock, which had traded for as high as $172 in 1972, was selling for less than $40 in 1982.

Xerox's attempt to lessen its dependence on the competitive copier market by moving into the broader office automation arena had proved less than spectacular. The Office Products Division has had only one profitable quarter in its seven-year history and it racked up losses in 1981 totaling approximately $90 million. Kearns recently admitted to analysts that he did not expect the unit to be profitable until 1984.[1] The division had recently been reorganized in an attempt to deal more effectively with some of these problems. Shortly after the reorganization, however, two of the key executives of the Office Products Division resigned to form their own company. Industry reaction to these resignations and Xerox's proposed acquisition of an insurance company has given rise to reports that Xerox may be somewhat less than enthusiastic about the office automation marketplace and its strategies to garner a piece of the market.

Wall Street analysts were puzzled over Xerox's recent offer to acquire Crum & Forster, an insurance holding company, for about $1.65 billion in cash and securities. The proposed acquisition thrusts Xerox, with a mixed record in diversification efforts, into the property-casualty insurance field, where it has no experience. Kearns defended the proposed acquisition by saying that it could eventu-

This case was prepared as a basis for class discussion rather than to illustrate either effective or ineffective organizational practices. It was presented at the Midwest Case Writers Association Workshop in July 1984. Address reprint requests to J. David Hunger, Associate Professor, College of Business Administration, Iowa State University, 300 Carver Hall, Ames, IA 50011.

Used with permission of *Journal of Management Case Studies*, vol. 1, no. 1, Spring 1985, pp. 13–35. © J. David Hunger, Thomas Conquest, and William Miller, 1985

ally produce a lot of cash, which Xerox needs to support its vigorous research efforts in its core businesses. He maintained that Xerox's entry into the insurance business would not alter its commitment to the office automation market, nor would it sap resources from Xerox's basic businesses.[2,3] Some analysts felt, however, that the acquisition may have been a reaction to a rumored offer by GTE in late summer 1982 to acquire Xerox Corporation. The offer had apparently been made on a very quiet, friendly basis. The mere existence of such an offer, nevertheless, might have prompted top management to consider more seriously making Xerox less attractive to an acquiring firm by diversifying out of the high-tech industry and taking on more debt.[4]

## HISTORY

Xerography is basically a process that uses static electricity to make copies instantly on plain paper. Every office worker today takes it for granted, but it took Chester Carlson, a patent attorney and amateur physicist, several years of dabbling in his kitchen to discover the fundamental principles of what he called "electrophotography." By 1927 he had enough of a process to patent it, and he set up a small lab behind a beauty parlor in Astoria, Long Island, to pursue his experiments. His breakthrough came on October 22, 1938, when he duplicated a glass slide on which he had written "10-22-38 ASTORIA."

Selling his process was more difficult and frustrating than inventing it. During the next six years Carlson was turned down by more than 20 companies, including such notables as IBM, RCA, and General Electric. Finally, in 1944, the Battelle Memorial Institute, a nonprofit research organization in Columbus, Ohio, became interested. It signed a royalty-sharing contract with Carlson and began to develop the process. In 1947 Battelle entered into an agreement with a small photographic paper company in Rochester, New York, called Haloid, giving the company the right to develop an "electrophotography" machine. Chester Carlson joined Haloid as a consultant.

Haloid's president, Joseph C. Wilson, had grown up with the business. His grandfather had been one of the company's founders in 1906, and his father had worked for the firm from the start. As Haloid and Battelle continued to develop electrophotography, Wilson decided that the process needed a more distinctive name. A Greek scholar from Ohio State University suggested *xeros* (dry) and *graphien* (writing) to form the word *xerography*. The machine itself, they decided, would be called Xerox.

Haloid introduced its first copier in 1949, but it was slow and complicated. Haloid found the early models to be better for making lithography masters than for copying documents, but management was sure they were on the right track. In 1958, the changed the name of the company to Haloid Xerox, and in 1959 the firm marketed the first dependable, easy-to-use document copier. The 914 copier, so named because it could copy sheets as large as 9 by 14 inches, was very successful, and within three years the company was ranked among the Fortune 500. In 1961, management changed the name of the company to Xerox.

Between 1959, when Xerox introduced the world's first convenient office copier, and 1974, its sales exploded from $33 million a year to $3.6 billion; its profits mushroomed from $2 million to $331 million; and the price of its stock soared from $2 a share to $172. The company had grown 100 times in 15 years. In that same short period, photocopying machines dramatically transformed the nature of office work. Xerography made carbon paper and mimeograph machines obsolete and drastically reduced typing time. By year-end 1970, Xerox held a dominant position in the worldwide office plain-paper copier marketplace with more than a 95 percent share of the market.

This monopolistic market share was seriously eroded in the 1970s because of increased competition from many sources. Xerox had built its business by creating the plain-paper copying market and then protecting it with a solid wall of patents, a classic entry barrier to keep out competition. In 1975, however, the company signed a consent decree with the Federal Trade Commission, which forced Xerox to license other companies wanting to use its process. The 17-year patent protection was also expiring and Xerox's technology could be increasingly used by anyone. Recognizing the mature state of the reprographics industry, Xerox has positioned itself, through both horizontal and vertical integration, to become a major competitor in the "office of the future" marketplace. In 1981, Xerox executives stated to stockholders in the company's annual report that the overriding corporate objective over the next decade is to be one of the leading companies in providing productivity in the office. "In order to accomplish this," asserted top management, "Xerox must maintain and strengthen its position of leadership in reprographics—as we refer to our total copying and duplicating business—*and* emerge from the 1980s as a leading systems company that is a major factor in automating the office."[5]

## MANAGEMENT

David T. Kearns, who had previously served as president and chief operating officer of Xerox, succeeded C. Peter McColough as chief executive officer in May 1982. McColough, who had joined Xerox in 1954 and served as chief executive since 1968, continued as chairman of the board. Other key executives and related information are shown in Exhibit 7.1. Xerox's top management has generally been promoted from within. Outside help has been recruited when the company has had to deal with significant changes in strategy or the introduction of new products.

There are 19 directors on the Xerox board, 8 of whom are officers of the corporation. The 11 outside directors include a retired executive vice-president of Xerox, two university professors (one from Europe), the chairman of the board of Prudential Insurance, a retired chairman of American Express, the president of the Children's Television Workshop, a managing director of Deutsch Bank AG, the chairman of an investment firm, a president of a university, and two partners in a Washington-based law firm. Together, the corporation's directors and officers own about 1 percent of the common stock of the firm.

**Exhibit 7.1** Xerox Corporation 1982 Top Management

| Name | Title | Years with Xerox | Jobs Prior to Xerox | Expertise |
|---|---|---|---|---|
| D. T. Kearns[a] | Chief executive officer | 11 | IBM: V.P. data processing | Marketing |
| W. F. Glavin[a] | Executive V.P. | 12 | IBM: V.P. operations | Operations |
| W. F. Souders[a] | Executive V.P. | 18 | | Marketing |
| J. V. Titsworth[a] | Executive V.P. | 3 | Control Data: executive V.P., systems | |
| M. H. Antonini | Group V.P. | 7 | Eltra Corp.: group V.P. Kaiser Jeep Int.: V.P. | Operations |
| R. D. Firth | Group V.P. | 13 | IBM: various positions | Personnel |
| M. Howard[a] | Senior V.P., chief financial officer | 12 | Shoe Corp. of America; V.P. | Finance |
| F. J. Pipp | Group V.P. | 11 | Ford Motor Co. | Manufacturing |
| R. M. Pippitt[a] | Senior V.P. | 21 | | Marketing |
| R. S. Banks | V.P. and general counsel | 15 | E. I. du Pont: attorney | Legal affairs |
| E. K. Damon | V.P. and secretary | 33 | | Accounting |
| S. B. Ross | V.P. and controller | 16 | Macmillan Publishing Co.: D.P.A. Harris, Kerr & Forster: accountant | Finance |
| J. S. Crowley[a] | Executive V.P. | 5 | McKinsey & Co.: senior partner and director | Administration |
| J. E. Goldman[a] | Senior V.P. | 14 | Ford Motor Co. | Engineering |

[a]Also serve on the board of directors.

*Source:* Xerox Form 10-K Annual Report, 1981.

The corporation introduced an executive long-term incentive plan in 1976 under which approximately 5.4 million shares of common stock have been reserved for issue. In December 1981, the board of directors amended the plan to provide for the issuance of incentive stock options as defined in the Economic Recovery Tax Act of 1981. Under the plan, eligible employees may be granted incentive stock rights, incentive stock options, nonqualified stock options, stock appreciation rights, and performance unit rights. Performance rights entitle the employee to receive the value of the performance unit in cash, in shares of common stock, or in a combination of the two at the company's discretion. The value of a performance unit is determined by a formula based on the achievement of specific performance goals. Performance unit rights are payable at the end of a five-year award period.

## BUSINESS SEGMENTS

Although Xerox Corporation is organized around a set of groups and divisions, it primarily defines itself in terms of its various businesses. Xerox's principal business segment is reprographics, consisting of the development, manufacture, and marketing of xerographic copiers and duplicators, electronic printing systems, and providing related service. Another significant segment is paper, consisting primarily of the distribution of paper related to reprographic products. The other business segments include electric typewriters, word processors, small computers, facsimile transceivers, toner and other supplies, and the publishing of education-related materials. Estimated revenues and profits for each product line are shown in Exhibit 7.2.

## Reprographics

Xerox manufacturers and markets reprographic equipment for lease or purchase. Leasing accounted for over 55 percent of the company's revenues in 1981. The revenues and profits from this segment depend principally on the number of units of xerographic equipment leased and the usage of these units. In 1981, the reprographics segment accounted for 72 percent of revenues.

**Copiers.** Copying machines have been and still are the largest segment of Xerox's business. However, Xerox has experienced problems in this segment over the past few years. Increased competition from IBM and Kodak in the medium-volume market and from Japan in the lower-volume market has significantly decreased Xerox's market share. Competing now with 40 companies selling at least 240 different models, Xerox's share of the plain-paper copier industry in the United States has dropped from 67 percent to 43 percent over the past five years. The market, however, has grown in terms of total revenues from $2.8 billion in 1976 to $7.5 billion in 1981. Competitors imported more than a million units into the country in 1981. Analysts expected this number to increase by 50 percent in 1982.[6] Xerox faces similar competition worldwide. Current estimates of market share data are presented in Exhibit 7.3.

"We really should have been thinking about the market on a much broader basis," said Kearns.[7] Xerox ignored the low-cost coated-paper copier that dominated the world copier market before Xerox introduced the first plain-paper copier. But the coated-paper copiers served a market much larger than anyone knew. Xerox has clearly fought back to regain some of its lost market share. It has cut prices on its lower-volume models, concentrating on cutting costs to improve profit margins, and decentralized the management of the reprographics group to enable more timely and market-oriented decision making. Two desktop

**Exhibit 7.2** Xerox Corporation Revenues, Operating Profit, and Operating Margins by Product Line, 1981 ($ million)

| Product line | Revenues | Operating Profit | Operating margin (%) |
|---|---|---|---|
| Copiers | | | |
| Rentals | 4,805 | | |
| Sales | 1,135 | | |
| Paper and supplies | 795 | | |
| Total | 6,735 | 1,400 | 20.8 |
| Office products | | | |
| Word processing and small comp. | 310 | (22) | — |
| Facsimile | 95 | 11 | 11.6 |
| Total | 405 | (11) | — |
| Peripherals | | | |
| Printing | 125 | (15) | — |
| Xerox computer services | 90 | 10 | 11.1 |
| Shugart | 200 | 25 | 12.5 |
| Century Data | 110 | 10 | 9.1 |
| Diablo | 130 | 13 | 10.0 |
| Versatec | 75 | 7 | 9.3 |
| Kurzweil | 5 | 0.5 | 10.0 |
| Total | 735 | 50.5 | 6.9 |
| Other products | | | |
| Publishing | 320 | 30 | 9.4 |
| WUI | 175 | 26 | 14.9 |
| Other | 310 | 25 | 8.1 |
| Total | 805 | 81 | 10.1 |
| Total | 8,680 | 1,520.50 | 17.5 |

*Source:* Northern Business Information Estimates, January 1982.

**Exhibit 7.3** Xerox Corporation Copier Revenues and Market Share by Geographic Area, 1981 ($ million)

| | Market Size | Xerox Revenues | Xerox Market Share (%) |
|---|---|---|---|
| United States | 7,350 | 3,160 | 43 |
| Europe | 4,900 | 2,200 | 45 |
| Japan | 1,510 | 620 | 41 |
| Canada | 725 | 410 | 56 |
| Other | — | 525 | — |

*Source:* Northern Business Information Estimates, January 1982.

copiers, the 2350 and the 2830, were introduced in 1982 with a selling price of around $3500 each. A new line of low- and medium-volume copiers labeled the "10" series was introduced in January 1983. These copiers were imported from Fuji Xerox Co. in Japan. "If you can't beat 'em, join 'em," stated Peter McColough.[8] Xerox will also bring in parts and subassemblies from the Japanese affiliate to help lower costs. The new 10 series costs between 40 percent and 50 percent less to produce than earlier machines.

Another technique used by Xerox to stay competitive is called competitive benchmarking. This means looking carefully at the lowest-price competing copier, determining exactly how it is being produced for less, and developing a plan to make and sell a competitive product.

In large copiers, Xerox still dominates the industry with a 70 percent market share. This is due mainly to Xerox's large and experienced sales and service staff. Japanese companies currently lack extensive service support and are not seen to offer Xerox much competition in the higher-priced copier market in the near future. Xerox has many models in this market with high output rates and sorting capabilities. Prices range from $25,000 to $125,000.

In a maturing market with high competition, Xerox management realizes that the copier segment will not provide growing profits in the long run the way the company would like. This realization underlies the company's diversification into office automation. Eugene C. Glazer of Dean Witter Reynolds stated, "Eventually the company won't make it if they have to depend only on copiers."[9] In the company's annual report, David Kearns noted, "To continue to succeed in the face of strong competition, Xerox must undergo major and lasting change." Robert D. Firth, however, president of the reprographics group, maintained, "Our copier business is and will remain the main business of Xerox for the projectable future."[10]

**Electronic Printing.** Listed under Peripherals in Exhibit 7.2, this segment became a dominant product line in 1977 with the introduction of the 9700 electronic printer. Until March 1982, the electronic printing segment reported to U.S. copier operations in Rochester. Now established as the Printing Systems Division, it reports directly to corporate headquarters in Stamford, Connecticut. The traditional computer printout method has been impact printing with ink ribbons and mechanical printing heads on 11- by 17-inch fan-fold computer paper. Although this printing serves many purposes, Xerox management believes that for periodic reports, forms, proposals, or other information stored on electronic computer data files, nonbulky and clear printouts would provide a better alternative. With its electronic printer, Xerox has combined computer technology, lasers, and xerography to design a printer that can print exceptionally clear text on standard 8½- by 11-inch paper. In addition, this printer can print graphics that cannot be done on most traditional printers, and it has multiple-copy and sorting capabilities. Xerox management sees electronic printing as playing a large role in the company's future. Customers seem to agree. Jack Jones, vice-president of the Southern Railway System, stated that "the quality of the print is such that everybody is enthusiastic about the smaller page."[11]

In 1980 Xerox developed the 5700 printing system. Priced at $66,000, this unit is designed to be used in an office environment, whereas the 9700 is geared more toward a computer room. The 5700 has the same basic technology as the 9700 but is extremely easy to use with a touch control screen to eliminate operator confusion. It can also be connected to Xerox's Ethernet network system to provide printing from various word processors or computer terminals on the network. A lower-priced model has been released on a limited basis with many of the same features as the 9700 and 5700. The 2700, priced at $19,000, is marketed for the small business that can't afford some of the more expensive models.

Xerox has approximately 40 percent of the global market for electronic printing—slightly behind IBM, with Honeywell a distant third in market share. The market in electronic printing may soon be crowded with heavy competition from Japanese companies, such as Canon and Fujitsu. It is also a market where new technology may change things drastically. Ink jet printing and heat transfer processes are already being considered as printing alternatives.

Currently, electronic printing accounts for only 15 percent of the $8.7 billion computer printing market. Predictions for electronic printing are for a $5.8 billion market by 1986. According to Robert Adams, president of Xerox's Printing Systems Division, "The majority of information generated from host computers and word processors will someday be produced by electronic printers."[12] Although Xerox revenues in 1981 from electronic printing were estimated at $125 million by Northern Business Information, Inc., a New York-based research firm, the newly established Printing Systems Division was hoping for $300 million in revenues in 1982 and $2 billion annually in revenues by 1987.[13]

## Office Products

The Office Products Division (responsible for electronic typewriters, word processors, and facsimile telecopiers) and the Office Systems Division manufacture and market information-processing equipment for use in the "office of the future." Although office products accounted for only 10 percent of the company's revenues in 1981, the commitment was made several years ago to steer Xerox away from a copier-only company to an information company capable of supplying many types of office information and equipment. Current estimates of market share data for both divisions are provided in Exhibit 7.4.

The 860 Information Processing System first marketed in 1979 is a word-processing workstation with full text-editing capability. It is medium-priced and designed for use by professional and clerical personnel. It has limited program-

**Exhibit 7.4** Xerox Corporation Office Products Revenues and Market Share by Geographic Area, 1981 ($ million)

| Segment | Total Xerox Revenues | U.S. Xerox Revenues | U.S. Market Size | U.S. Xerox Share (%) | International Xerox Revenues |
|---|---|---|---|---|---|
| Word processing | 295 | 180 | 1,385 | 13 | 115 |
| Facsimile telecopiers | 95 | 50 | 165 | 30 | 45 |
| Small business systems | 15 | 10 | 1,300 | 1 | 5 |

*Source:* Northern Business Information Estimates, January 1982.

ming capability. Xerox introduced its 8010 Star Professional workstation in 1981 for a price of $17,000. It is designed for use by managers and professionals to perform word- and data-processing tasks with a minimum of training. Its ease of use makes it very desirable in preparing presentations and reports.

In 1981, the 820 Information Processor was developed to service a broad range of needs. It can be used as a limited professional workstation for small businesses that cannot afford the Star. It can also be used as a business or personal computer or a word processor. Prices for the microcomputer system start at $3000 and options for word-processing capability bring the price up to $6500. These prices make the model very competitive with the Apple II or Radio Shack TRS Model III personal computer and also with the IBM Displaywriter and Wang Wangwriter word processors. Xerox also introduced in 1981 a new line of electronic typewriters, called Memorywriters, and an inexpensive (under $1000) personal computer.

Probably the biggest gamble that Xerox is taking in the office product segment is its Ethernet concept. Ethernet is a communication network designed for short physical distances (intrabuilding) that will connect many pieces of office equipment by coaxial cable together into one information system. This concept allows several word processors or professional workstations to use common data banks or printing facilities in different physical locations within the building. Xerox's marketing strategy is to force its Ethernet network as an industry standard so that all manufacturers of office equipment will be pressured to make their equipment compatible.

Peter McColough described the development this way: "We can go into your company and tell you that you don't have to stick with Xerox. You can go to DEC, Intel, or anybody else. The IBM approach says: We'll put our system in there with IBM equipment, but you won't be able to get much else."[14] This compatibility argument is an extremely effective marketing tool for customers leery of total commitment. The automated office product market is highly competitive and expanding. Major competitors include IBM, Wang, Exxon, Hewlett-Packard, and dozens of smaller companies.

Many problems currently face Xerox's office product divisions. Contributions to profits have been nonexistent for the last several years. Although Xerox has intentionally sacrificed profits to get a jump on competitors, the new products are not selling as management had hoped they would by this time. Of the 300 Ethernet system installations planned for 1981, only 45 were completed. Marketing may be to blame. The company acknowledged the 820 had met with little success in the retail sales environment because many had perceived the machine as an entry into the home computer market, not the office market. Software development problems created delays for the full-scale production of the 8010 Star. In addition, the country's prolonged recession has prevented companies from making commitments in office automation.

Disagreements between top management and division management resulted in the resignations of Donald Massaro, president of Xerox Office Systems, and David E. Liddle, vice-president. The 39-year-old Massaro had founded Shugart Associates, a leading computer memory manufacturer that had been acquired by

Xerox in 1977. Liddle, a ten-year Xerox veteran, had worked closely with Massaro to develop the Star and Ethernet. In an interview with *Business Week,* Massaro asserted that he resigned because he wanted complete control of Xerox's office systems effort. He conceded, however, that in a corporation like Xerox, where 75 percent of the revenues and almost all the profits came from copiers and duplicators, "it was frustrating trying to get the attention of top management."[15] Analysts felt that Massaro's resignation was an expected result of the battle between the "old" Xerox, epitomized by the conservative East Coast copier group, and the "new" Xerox, epitomized by the freewheeling California-type entrepreneur, Massaro. A consultant who had worked extensively with Xerox suggested that a real schism had developed. "The copier people didn't like the idea they were being used as a cash cow and Xerox's office systems people could spend all this money without making any."[16]

In a report from Strategic, Inc., before the Office Products Division was split, the company's president, Michael Killen, boldly predicted, "Xerox will fail because the Office Products Division will fail; and the Office Products Division will fail because Ethernet will fail."[17] Killen's rationale is that Ethernet is built on base-band modulation techniques that limit information over the network to interactive data. Broad-band modulation techniques, on the other hand, although more complex with which to interface components, allow video and voice communications as well as interactive data.

Ethernet may not become the formal industry standard supported by the Institute of Electrical and Electronics Engineers. Much squabbling is still going on over this issue. Hewlett-Packard, for example, has dropped its support of Ethernet in favor of the slightly different IEEE 802 proposed local-area-networking (LAN) standard. Nevertheless, Xerox management plans to continue working to get Ethernet accepted by the industry as an informal standard even though IBM is said to be working on its own version of Ethernet.

Many people continue to believe that Ethernet is a viable system. John W. King, an industry analyst, said, "Ethernet is alive and well and has excellent prospects through the 1980s." King sees Ethernet and broad-band networks working together.[18] Many new electronic components have been developed to simplify connecting equipment to Ethernet. Digital Equipment Corporation and Intel agreed to a joint venture with Xerox in May 1980. Digital Equipment's role was to provide design expertise in the area of communication transceivers and computer networks. Intel provided expertise in integrated circuits for communications functions. Because Xerox has based all its products in the office segment around Ethernet, its future is of vital strategic importance.

**Other Segments**

Xerox is one of the largest distributors in the world of standard cut sheet paper used for writing, typing, copying, and other office needs. It also distributes many types of office chemicals for use with its machines.

Xerox's peripheral subsidiaries are generally composed of acquisitions that helped to integrate the company vertically. Shugart Associates manufactures floppy disk drives, Diablo Systems, Inc., manufactures daisy wheel printers (a substitute technology for IBM's famous typewriter ball), Century Data Systems manufactures rigid disk drives, Versatec manufactures electrostatic printers and plotters, and Kurzweil makes optical scanners. Xerox Computer Services was established in 1970 as an outgrowth of its Scientific Data Systems acquisition and offers time-sharing and software packages. Other products and services include published materials, information services, medical systems, and a credit service.

**MARKETING**     In the past, Xerox has traditionally been a single-product company, selling copiers to large businesses through its own sales and service force. This has changed over the past several years as Xerox has diversified its product lines and redefined its customers. All the company's product lines have been revamped to offer a wide range of products, not only to larger companies but to smaller businesses as well. With the advent of Ethernet, a systems approach to marketing has become necessary.

To better meet the distribution problems associated with the company's new concepts, Xerox is experimenting with new distribution techniques. Independent distributors and dealers have been contracted to sell products not only to end users but also to original equipment manufacturers who resell the products as part of a larger system. These distribution channels reduce the company's expenses, thereby increasing profit margins while unburdening the company's own sales force. Xerox also plans to use retail chains as well as its own retail stores to reach small-business people. It has already opened approximately 30 retail stores throughout the United States, and management has plans to open more nationwide. All outlets are named "The Xerox Store" and are designed to make the small-business person comfortable in a store with a familiar name and reputation. In addition to selling Xerox's equipment, these retail outlets also carry brand-name equipment of other manufacturers (including competitors) for home and office use. Most of this other equipment complements Xerox's own product line. This supermarket approach includes the selling of Apple computers, Hewlett-Packard calculators, Matsushita dictating machines, as well as a host of other products.[19]

Xerox is also using new promotions as part of its marketing strategy. Management has cut prices on many products to better compete with Japanese firms for the small-business person's dollar. Mail order and telephone campaigns are also being used to reach smaller firms. For the larger customers, Xerox has been offering quantity discounts as an incentive to buy total systems.

According to industry analysts, Xerox has three major marketing strengths. First, its sales and service staff is the largest in the industry. These people have excellent sales skills and are well known in most major companies. Second, the company has large financial resources to fund challenging new product developments. No other company, with the possible exception of IBM, could have tackled the highly complex Star workstation project. Third, the Xerox name is a household word and gives the business person a feeling of confidence when it comes to getting the product serviced.

If there is any weakness in the company's marketing department, analysts agree it is its lack of expertise in marketing complex office products and systems. There is apparently a world of difference between marketing stand-alone copying machines and marketing technically more involved information handling and processing systems. In addition, retailing is a new field for Xerox in which it has no previous experience. There appears to be some confusion among customers as to the purpose of several particular products. For example, Xerox's efforts to sell the 820 to the retail market through Xerox stores as well as distributors has been costly and somewhat ineffective. Jack Darcy, senior vice-president of Kierulff Distributors, an independent distributor who sells equipment from many manufacturers to industrial users, said, "There is such a difference in the mentality to run a successful retail operation and to run a successful industrial business. At Kierulff, we're pointing our effort totally toward the industrial. Xerox, as I understand it, is a consumer product. We're not interested."[20]

**FINANCE**   Consolidated income statements and balance sheets for the five-year period 1977–1981 are shown in Exhibits 7.5, 7.6, and 7.7. Although Xerox management considers the firm to be strong financially, it can be seen that both revenues and profits have been increasing at a decreasing rate. From 1964 to 1974, net income had grown 24 percent a year on 30 percent annual revenue gains. From 1975 to 1981, revenues increased 15 percent, compounded annually, while earnings for the same period increased by slightly over 12 percent a year. In the first nine months of 1982, Xerox's net income was $370 million, down 24 percent from the same period the year earlier. Revenues were $6.24 billion, slightly down from $6.28 billion during the same period in 1981.

Data outlining Xerox's common stock performance are given in Exhibit 7.8. The company's stock, which made millionaires of several early investors, has recently traded as low as $27 per share, bringing its P/E ratio to an all-time low. In addition, Xerox stock reacted negatively to the news of the proposed acquisition of Crum & Forster, falling over $3 per share. Investment analysts have recently advised customers to postpone purchases of Xerox stock "until current operations show some sign of life."[21]

Xerox attributes much of the earnings decline to greatly reduced profit margins, as shown in Exhibit 7.9. The company's after-tax profit margin in the third quarter of 1982 was equal to 4.7 percent of sales, down from 7.9 percent a year earlier. In the first nine months of 1982, the profit margin was 5.9 percent, compared with 7.7 percent in 1981. Xerox top management attributes the squeeze on profit margins to several factors:

1. Increased competition has forced price reductions on many copier models, especially in the low-volume segment where competition has been the fiercest. Reductions of up to 27 percent have been seen on many models.
2. Increased revenues have occurred in the low-volume copier segment where margins are traditionally lower (see Exhibit 7.10).
3. There have been increasing expenditures for research and development, and

**Exhibit 7.5** Xerox Corporation Consolidated Income Statements, 1977–1981 ($ in million, except per share data)

|  | 1981 | 1980 | 1979 | 1978 | 1977 |
|---|---|---|---|---|---|
| Operating revenues |  |  |  |  |  |
| Rentals and services | 5,279.6 | 5,151.6 | 4,606.3 | 4,130.5 | 3,713.8 |
| Sales | 3,411.4 | 3,044.9 | 2,390.1 | 1,887.5 | 1,368.2 |
| Total operating revenues | 8,691.0 | 8,196.5 | 6,996.4 | 6,018.0 | 5,082.0 |
| Costs and expenses |  |  |  |  |  |
| Cost of rentals and services | 2,269.5 | 2,167.5 | 1,905.0 | 1,691.6 | 1,477.1 |
| Cost of sales | 1,570.8 | 1,435.6 | 1,075.1 | 770.6 | 579.8 |
| Research and development | 526.3 | 435.8 | 378.1 | 311.0 | 269.0 |
| Selling, administrative, and general | 3,095.0 | 2,882.1 | 2,432.9 | 2,089.0 | 1,760.9 |
| Total costs and expenses | 7,461.6 | 6,921.0 | 5,791.1 | 4,862.2 | 4,086.8 |
| Operating income | 1,229.4 | 1,275.5 | 1,205.3 | 1,155.8 | 995.2 |
| Other income less interest expense | (49.5) | 3.6 | 1.7 | (64.6) | (82.4) |
| Income before income taxes | 1,179.9 | 1,279.1 | 1,207.0 | 1,091.2 | 912.8 |
| Income taxes | 454.4 | 611.8 | 587.2 | 528.0 | 440.5 |
| Income before outside shareholders' interests | 725.5 | 667.3 | 619.8 | 563.2 | 472.3 |
| Outside shareholders' interests | 127.3 | 102.4 | 104.8 | 86.7 | 68.3 |
| Net income | 598.2 | 564.9 | 515.0 | 476.5 | 404.0 |
| Average common shares outstanding | 84.5 | 84.4 | 84.1 | 84.1 | 83.9 |
| Net income per common share | 7.08 | 6.69 | 6.12 | 5.91 | 5.15 |

*Source: Moody's 1982 Industrial Manual,* p. 4672; and 1981 Annual Report, Xerox Corporation, p. 29.

capital expenditures. In 1981, Xerox spent $526 million and $1.4 billion for these items, respectively. Of the 1981 total for capital expenditures, $1.1 billion was for additions to rental equipment and related inventories, and the balance was for additions to land, buildings, and equipment.

4.  Revenues and net income from foreign operations represented 44 percent and 41 percent, respectively, of the company's 1981 total. Because of the strong dollar, it is estimated that foreign currency translations created a $64.5 million loss to Xerox in 1981. If unfavorable current impacts were excluded, international revenue growth would have been 13 percent in 1981 over 1980, slightly higher than domestic growth.

5.  The reduction of overhead cost the company $63 million in severance costs in 1981.

**Exhibit 7.6** Xerox Corporation Consolidated Balance Sheets, 1977–1981 ($ million)

|  | 1981 | 1980 | 1979 | 1978 | 1977 |
|---|---|---|---|---|---|
| **Assets** | | | | | |
| Current assets | | | | | |
| Cash | 45.2 | 86.8 | 42.2 | 57.7 | 73.3 |
| Bank time deposits | 234.0 | 228.8 | 267.7 | 412.0 | 338.4 |
| Marketable securities | 148.0 | 207.3 | 447.7 | 269.8 | 280.3 |
| Trade receivables | 1,245.3 | 1,163.8 | 1,120.4 | 927.5 | 731.0 |
| Receivable from Xerox Credit Corp. | 178.2 | 196.3 | — | — | — |
| Accrued revenues | 403.3 | 376.8 | 259.3 | 211.3 | 191.6 |
| Inventories | 1,131.9 | 1,090.2 | 785.8 | 601.8 | 525.3 |
| Other current assets | 230.2 | 210.0 | 180.5 | 158.7 | 128.7 |
| Total current assets | 3,616.1 | 3,560.0 | 3,103.6 | 2,638.8 | 2,268.6 |
| Trade receivables due after one year | 245.5 | 199.4 | 274.2 | 216.2 | 104.9 |
| Rental equipment and related inventories | 1,905.1 | 1,966.8 | 1,736.4 | 1,501.2 | 1,397.7 |
| Land, buildings, and equipment | 1,438.7 | 1,410.4 | 1,222.3 | 1,111.3 | 1,029.2 |
| Investments, at equity | 319.6 | 226.6 | 105.7 | 67.9 | 63.2 |
| Other assets | 149.4 | 150.6 | 111.4 | 137.7 | 183.0 |
| Total assets | 7,674.4 | 7,513.8 | 6,553.6 | 5,765.7 | 5,046.6 |
| **Liabilities and shareholders' equity** | | | | | |
| Current liabilities | | | | | |
| Notes payable | 224.2 | 208.4 | 96.3 | 64.5 | 109.6 |
| Current portion of long-term debt | 96.3 | 80.0 | 40.2 | 52.4 | 57.5 |
| Accounts payable | 340.2 | 315.8 | 325.1 | 273.2 | 209.4 |
| Salaries, profit-sharing, other accruals | 909.9 | 907.3 | 689.5 | 600.7 | 475.1 |
| Income taxes | 346.5 | 425.4 | 426.0 | 328.8 | 232.3 |
| Other current liabilities | 163.7 | 147.8 | 102.2 | 81.3 | 61.7 |
| Total current liabilities | 2,080.8 | 2,084.7 | 1,679.3 | 1,400.9 | 1,145.6 |
| Long-term debt | 869.5 | 898.3 | 913.0 | 938.3 | 1,020.0 |
| Other noncurrent liabilities | 145.0 | 133.0 | 127.9 | 97.2 | 46.1 |
| Deferred income taxes | 247.0 | 142.7 | 110.4 | 62.7 | — |
| Deferred investment tax credits | 108.9 | 85.6 | 70.1 | 63.2 | 59.6 |
| Outside shareholders' interests in equity of subsidiaries | 495.6 | 539.5 | 431.5 | 349.0 | 315.2 |
| Shareholders' equity | | | | | |
| Common stock, $1 par value Authorized 100,000 shares | 84.3 | 84.3 | 83.9 | 83.8 | 80.1 |
| Class B Stock, $1 par value Authorized 600,000 shares | 0.2 | 0.2 | 0.2 | 0.3 | 0.3 |
| Additional paid-in capital | 306.0 | 304.9 | 286.8 | 286.0 | 257.3 |
| Retained earnings | 3,500.1 | 3,155.4 | 2,866.2 | 2,501.3 | 2,142.0 |
| Cumulative translation adjustments | (150.1) | 98.8 | — | — | — |
| Total | 3,740.5 | 3,643.6 | 3,237.1 | 2,871.4 | 2,479.7 |
| Deduct class B Stock receivables | 12.9 | 13.6 | 15.7 | 17.0 | 19.6 |
| Total shareholders' equity | 3,727.6 | 3,630.0 | 3,221.4 | 2,854.4 | 2,460.1 |
| Total liabilities and shareholders' equity | 7,674.4 | 7,513.8 | 6,553.6 | 5,765.7 | 5,046.6 |

*Source: Moody's 1982 Industrial Manual,* p. 4673; and 1981 Annual Report, Xerox Corporation, pp. 30–31.

**Exhibit 7.7** Xerox Corporation Business Segment Data, 1979–1981[a]
($ million)

|  | 1981 | 1980 | 1979 |
|---|---|---|---|
| **Reprographics** | | | |
| Rentals and services | 4,974.2 | 4,840.9 | 4,313.1 |
| Sales | 1,419.2 | 1,224.1 | 990.6 |
| Total operating revenues | 6,393.4 | 6,065.0 | 5,303.7 |
| Operating profit | 1,355.6 | 1,326.1 | 1,243.0 |
| Identifiable assets | 5,172.2 | 5,212.4 | 4,544.9 |
| Depreciation | 717.9 | 718.6 | 664.6 |
| Capital expenditures | 1,202.3 | 1,108.0 | 1,004.0 |
| **Paper** | | | |
| Operating revenues (sales) | 554.5 | 573.6 | 446.4 |
| Operating profit | 34.9 | 44.2 | 34.9 |
| Identifiable assets | 202.6 | 220.9 | 185.5 |
| Depreciation | 8.0 | 8.3 | 7.7 |
| Capital expenditures | 11.0 | 13.1 | 11.3 |
| **Other businesses** | | | |
| Rentals and services | 449.3 | 409.1 | 357.1 |
| Sales | 1,437.7 | 1,247.2 | 953.1 |
| Transfers between segments | 37.4 | 34.0 | 16.6 |
| Total operating revenues | 1,924.4 | 1,690.3 | 1,326.8 |
| Operating profit | 107.8 | 124.7 | 106.1 |
| Identifiable assets | 1,511.2 | 1,398.0 | 1,171.5 |
| Depreciation | 96.8 | 98.3 | 90.3 |
| Capital expenditures | 188.1 | 192.4 | 179.7 |

[a]Figures do not sum to data in consolidated income statements because of various adjustments and expenses due to foreign currency gains and losses and general expense items not included in this exhibit.

*Source:* 1981 Annual Report, Xerox Corporation, p. 36.

**Exhibit 7.8** Xerox Corporation Stock Performance, 1973–1982

|  | 1982 | 1981 | 1980 | 1979 | 1978 | 1977 | 1976 | 1975 | 1974 | 1973 |
|---|---|---|---|---|---|---|---|---|---|---|
| High price ($) | 41.8 | 64.0 | 71.8 | 69.1 | 64.0 | 58.8 | 68.4 | 87.6 | 127.1 | 170.0 |
| Low price ($) | 27.1 | 37.4 | 48.6 | 52.6 | 40.5 | 43.1 | 48.8 | 46.4 | 49.0 | 114.8 |
| Book value ($) | 46.45 | 44.11 | 42.90 | 38.29 | 34.72 | 30.76 | 27.30 | 23.97 | 22.14 | 18.89 |
| Earnings per share ($) | — | 7.08 | 7.33 | 6.69 | 5.77 | 5.06 | 4.51 | 3.07 | 4.18 | 3.80 |
| P/E ratio | — | 7.1 | 8.2 | 9.0 | 8.9 | 9.9 | 13.2 | 20.8 | 22.3 | 39.0 |
| Dividends per share ($) | 3.00 | 3.00 | 2.80 | 2.40 | 2.00 | 1.50 | 1.10 | 1.00 | 1.00 | 0.90 |
| Earnings yield (%) | — | 14.1 | 12.2 | 11.1 | 11.2 | 10.1 | 7.6 | 4.8 | 4.5 | 2.6 |
| Dividend yield (%) | — | 5.9 | 4.7 | 4.0 | 3.9 | 3.0 | 1.9 | 1.6 | 1.1 | 0.6 |
| Common shares (million) | 84.55 | 84.51 | 84.48 | 84.14 | 80.24 | 80.37 | 79.83 | 79.57 | 79.24 | 27.17 |

*Source:* Value Line Investment Survey, November 12, 1982.

**Exhibit 7.9** Xerox Corporation After-Tax Margins, 1967–1982 (%)

| Year | Net Income/ Sales (%) | Year | Net Income/ Sales (%) |
|------|------|------|------|
| 1967 | 13.9 | 1975 | 6.0 |
| 1968 | 13.0 | 1976 | 8.2 |
| 1969 | 10.9 | 1977 | 8.0 |
| 1970 | 10.9 | 1978 | 8.4 |
| 1971 | 10.9 | 1979 | 7.5 |
| 1972 | 10.3 | 1980 | 7.0 |
| 1973 | 10.1 | 1981 | 7.0 |
| 1974 | 9.4 | 1982 | 5.0 |

*Source: Moody's Industrial Manual, 1972, 1978,* and *1983;* and *The Wall Street Journal.*

**Exhibit 7.10** Xerox Corporation Copier Revenues and Operating Profit by Market Segment, 1981 ($ million)

| Segment | Revenue | Operating Profit | Operating Margins |
|---------|---------|------|------|
| Low volume | 2,020 | 300 | 14.9 |
| Medium volume | 2,265 | 700 | 30.9 |
| High volume | 1,835 | 365 | 19.9 |
| Paper and supplies | 795 | 70 | 8.8 |
| Totals | 6,915 | 1,435 | 20.8 |

*Source:* Northern Business Information Estimates, January 1982.

**RESEARCH AND DEVELOPMENT**

The Xerox research and development program is directed primarily to the development of new and improved copying and duplicating equipment and supplies, facsimile and digital communications equipment, and computer peripheral equipment and services, as well as to the development of new products and capabilities in other areas related to the broad field of information systems.

The company's Palo Alto Research Center (PARC) was established in Palo Alto, California, in 1969 by then-President Peter McColough to provide the technology Xerox needed to become "an architect of information" in the office. Flourishing under a hands-off policy by corporate headquarters, PARC soon developed an excellent reputation within the research community. The center developed technology in computer-aided design, artificial intelligence, and laser printers. Xerox's ability to design custom chips for use in future copiers comes largely from PARC. Nevertheless, analysts contend that Xerox has been unable to really take advantage of PARC's research on computerized office systems, its original reason for being. Arguing that Xerox's sheer size slows decision making, analysts state that the corporation has trouble translating first-rate research into profitable products. It is simply unable to move quickly into small, rapidly changing markets.

Loose management by headquarters may have also encouraged PARC to go into the development of products not necessarily in line with the corporation's needs. For example, PARC worked in the mid-1970s to develop the Alto, a computer with some of the attributes of a personal computer, which was supposed to serve as a research prototype. Alto and its software became so popular inside Xerox that some researchers began to develop it as a commercial product. This put PARC into direct conflict with Xerox's product development group, which was developing a rival machine called the Star. Because the Star was in line with the company's expressed product strategy of developing complete office systems, the Alto was ignored by top management and emphasis was placed on the Star and the Ethernet concept. The conflict between PARC and Xerox top management has resulted in a number of researchers leaving PARC for firms such as Atari and Apple.

Jack Goldman, Xerox's former research chief, suggested that a big company like Xerox wants every product to be a "home run" in order to justify the costs of marketing and development. Another former employee said that top management "followed the big-bang strategy. They wanted to build absolutely the best office system instead of taking things bit by bit."[22]

In 1981, Xerox incurred $526 million in research and development expenses, approximately 6 percent of total revenues. Less than $35 million went to PARC. The $526 million represents less than the average percentage of research and development to sales of some of Xerox's major competitors (Hewlett-Packard, 9.7 percent; Apple Computer, 6.3 percent; Burroughs, 6.5 percent; Commodore, 5.9 percent; Digital Equipment Corp., 9.0 percent; Honeywell, 7.0 percent; IBM, 5.5 percent; Wang, 7.5 percent; CPT, 5.0 percent).[23]

## OPERATIONS AND INTERNATIONAL INTERESTS

Xerox's principal xerographic facilities are located on a 1047-acre site owned in Webster, New York, a suburb of Rochester. Corporate headquarters were moved to Stamford, Connecticut, in 1969 so that corporate attention would be given not only to xerography but to xerography overseas, to computers, data processing, education, and other extensions of activity generated by acquisitions, mergers, and related research. The Office Products Division, recently reorganized into Office Products and Office Systems, is located in Dallas, Texas. The Office Systems Division, located in Palo Alto, California, is responsible for marketing local network-based office systems to end users. In forming these two divisions, Xerox retained centralized marketing, sales, and manufacturing functions with the Office Products Division in Dallas.

Xerox's largest interests outside the United States are the Rank Xerox Companies—comprising Rank Xerox Limited of London, England, and Rank Xerox Holding B.V. of the Netherlands and their respective subsidiaries—and the other subsidiaries jointly owned by Xerox and the Rank Organization. Approximately 51 percent of the voting power of Rank Xerox Limited and Rank Xerox Holding B.V. is owned directly or indirectly by Xerox and 49 percent is owned directly or indirectly by the Rank Organization Limited. The earnings of the Rank Xerox Companies are allocated according to an agreement between Xerox and the Rank Organization. For 1981, approximately 66 percent of the earnings of Rank Xerox was allocated to Xerox. Rank Xerox Limited manufactures and markets most xerographic copier/duplicator products developed by Xerox. Its manufacturing operations are located principally in the United Kingdom.

Fuji Xerox Co., Ltd., of Tokyo, Japan, equally owned by Fuji Photo Film Co., Ltd., of Japan and by Rank Xerox Limited, manufactures in Japan various copiers, duplicators, and supplies marketed principally in Japan and in other areas of the Far East. They are also marketed by Xerox in the United States and by Rank Xerox Limited in Europe.

## THE PROPOSED CRUM & FORSTER ACQUISITION

In September 1982, Xerox announced an agreement to acquire Crum & Forster, an insurance holding company, for about $1.65 billion in cash and securities. Crum & Forster, the nation's fifteenth largest property-casualty insurer with 1981 premium volume of $1.6 billion, is largely involved in writing insurance for businesses. In 1981, it drew 83 percent of its premiums from commercial insurance lines. Its biggest line is workers' compensation insurance, which generated 28 percent of premiums last year. Other lines include commercial casualty, commercial automobile, multiple-peril, and fire insurance. In 1981, its operating income was $171 million, up 17 percent over 1980. Its net income of $176 million increased 24 percent over 1980 (see Exhibits 7.11 and 7.12). This increase in net income, however, was due almost entirely to an increase in net investment income of $270 million. Pretax underwriting losses of over $70 million were somewhat larger than in 1980 (see Exhibit 7.13). In effect, although insurance premiums were insufficient to cover claims and expenses, interest from the investment of these premiums enabled the firm to make a profit. In the first half of 1982, Crum & Forster's operating profit was down 30 percent to $64.8 million ($2.25 a share) from $92.1 million ($3.24 a share) a year earlier.

Xerox offered $55 for each Crum & Forster share, giving holders the choice of receiving either cash or a combination of Xerox common and a new Xerox preferred stock. At $55 a share, Crum & Forster shareholders will receive about 1.7 times book value, which was $32.33 a share in June 1982. The Xerox offer is double the preoffer price and also 40 percent above the stock's 15-year high price.

Xerox planned to finance the cash part of the acquisition, about $800 million, through existing revolving-credit agreements and short-term bank loans without touching any cash holdings set aside for its office products businesses. Xerox claimed that the acquisition would be self-funding in that interest costs associated with the takeover would be covered by Crum & Forster's earnings.[24]

**Exhibit 7.11** Crum & Forster and Subsidiaries Consolidated Statement of Income for the Years Ended December 31 ($ thousand)

| | 1981 | 1980 | 1979 | 1978 | 1977 |
|---|---|---|---|---|---|
| **Income** | | | | | |
| Net premiums written | 1,624,614 | 1,660,636 | 1,585,022 | 1,436,061 | 1,283,149 |
| Increase (decrease) in unearned premiums | 15,522 | (4,473) | 50,742 | 69,891 | 60,210 |
| Premiums earned | 1,609,092 | 1,665,109 | 1,534,280 | 1,366,170 | 1,222,939 |
| Net investment income | 270,199 | 220,957 | 171,967 | 132,526 | 103,400 |
| Commission income | 45,203 | 44,306 | 38,280 | 26,564 | 11,870 |
| Rental income on operating properties | 591 | 627 | 541 | 876 | 566 |
| Total income | 1,925,085 | 1,930,999 | 1,745,068 | 1,526,136 | 1,338,775 |
| **Expenses** | | | | | |
| Losses | 954,844 | 988,041 | 881,070 | 769,907 | 722,228 |
| Loss expenses | 173,907 | 187,377 | 183,995 | 144,423 | 131,252 |
| Acquisition costs | 496,328 | 507,847 | 450,936 | 400,257 | 339,075 |
| General expenses | 65,505 | 46,315 | 39,843 | 26,102 | 17,509 |
| Dividends to policyholders | 62,940 | 55,371 | 26,866 | 24,622 | 21,895 |
| Total expenses | 1,753,524 | 1,784,951 | 1,582,710 | 1,365,311 | 1,231,959 |
| Operating income before federal and foreign income taxes | 171,561 | 146,048 | 162,358 | 160,825 | 106,816 |
| Provision for (recovery of) federal and foreign income taxes | | | | | |
| Current | 593 | 3,497 | 1,032 | 11,991 | 1,107 |
| Deferred | (5,185) | (8,911) | 13,275 | 22,912 | 20,615 |
| Operating income | 176,153 | 151,462 | 148,051 | 125,922 | 85,094 |
| Net realized capital (losses) gains | (160) | (19,790) | (5,968) | (6,627) | 4,385 |
| Discontinued operations | | 9,886 | 1,265 | 979 | 1,135 |
| Net income | 175,993 | 141,558 | 143,348 | 120,274 | 90,614 |
| **Earnings per common share** | | | | | |
| Primary | | | | | |
| Operating income | 6.16 | 5.39 | 5.36 | 4.69 | 3.23 |
| Net realized capital (losses) gains | (.01) | (.70) | (.22) | (.25) | .17 |
| Discontinued operations | | .35 | .04 | .04 | .04 |
| Net income | 6.15 | 5.04 | 5.18 | 4.48 | 3.44 |
| Fully diluted | | | | | |
| Operating income | 6.02 | 5.26 | 5.20 | 4.52 | 3.11 |
| Net realized capital (losses) gains | (.01) | (.68) | (.21) | (.24) | .16 |
| Discontinued operations | | .34 | .04 | .04 | .04 |
| Net income | 6.01 | 4.92 | 5.03 | 4.32 | 3.31 |
| Cash and accrued dividends per share | | | | | |
| Preferred Series A | 2.40 | 2.40 | 2.40 | 2.40 | 2.40 |
| Common | 1.54 | 1.35 | 1.15 | .905 | .80 |

*Source:* 1981 Annual Report, Crum & Forster, p. 19.

**Exhibit 7.12** Crum & Forster and Subsidiaries Consolidated Balance Sheet at December 31
($ thousand)

|  | 1981 | 1980 |
|---|---|---|
| **Assets** | | |
| Fixed maturities | | |
|   Bonds, at amortized cost (market $1,648,849 and $1,575,439, respectively) | 2,376,859 | 2,118,257 |
|   Preferred stocks, at amortized cost (market $87,705 and $93,895, respectively) | 120,344 | 119,976 |
| Equity securities | | |
|   Preferred stocks, at market (cost $28,486 and $36,383, respectively) | 21,486 | 27,746 |
|   Common stocks, at market (cost $350,119 and $286,841, respectively) | 413,016 | 455,070 |
| Short-term investments, at cost (market $270,139 and $361,450, respectively) | 270,136 | 361,472 |
| Investment in real estate (net of accumulated depreciation of $13,702) | | 15,417 |
| Cash | 11,689 | 9,740 |
| Receivables | | |
|   Premiums (net of allowance for uncollectible accounts of $6,245 and $6,019, respectively) | 439,356 | 372,904 |
|   Other | 192,008 | 99,294 |
| Equity in assets of insurance associations | 5,204 | 8,339 |
| Acquisition costs applicable to unearned premiums | 144,939 | 146,919 |
| Land, buildings, and equipment used in operations (net of accumulated depreciation of $40,832 and $38,492, respectively) | 75,591 | 65,249 |
| Other assets | 89,480 | 60,602 |
| Total assets | 4,160,108 | 3,862,985 |
| **Liabilities** | | |
| Unearned premiums | 661,759 | 646,237 |
| Unpaid losses | 1,672,510 | 1,510,458 |
| Unpaid loss expenses | 402,978 | 300,645 |
| Dividends to policyholders | 65,189 | 54,320 |
| Accounts payable and accrued liabilities | 314,981 | 295,496 |
| Mortgages payable | 19,372 | 12,104 |
| Deferred federal and foreign income taxes | | |
|   Unrealized appreciation of equity investments | 16,984 | 46,571 |
|   Other | 60,945 | 65,338 |
| Other liabilities | 22,000 | 12,312 |
| Total liabilities | 3,236,718 | 3,003,481 |
| **Commitments and contingent liabilities** | | |
| Stockholders' equity | | |
| Preferred stock (liquidating value $4,804 and $5,467, respectively) | 480 | 547 |
| Common stock (issued 28,487,085 and 28,071,639 shares, respectively) | 17,804 | 17,545 |
| Additional paid-in capital | 39,175 | 31,858 |
| Retained earnings | 827,084 | 649,911 |
| Net unrealized appreciation of equity investments | 38,913 | 115,021 |
| Less treasury stock at cost (4,000 and 16,000 shares, respectively) | (66) | (378) |
| Total stockholders' equity | 923,390 | 859,504 |
| Total liabilities and stockholders' equity | 4,160,108 | 3,862,985 |

*Source:* 1981 Annual Report, Crum & Forster, p. 20.

**Exhibit 7.13** Crum & Forster and Subsidiaries Business Segments ($ thousand)

|  | 1981 | 1980 | 1979 |
|---|---|---|---|
| **Revenues** | | | |
| Workers' compensation | 443,086 | 431,257 | 376,349 |
| Casualty | 304,454 | 358,882 | 357,622 |
| Automobile—commercial | 171,586 | 175,714 | 161,874 |
| Automobile—personal | 167,493 | 166,699 | 137,989 |
| Commercial multiple-peril | 218,389 | 217,564 | 208,049 |
| Fire and allied | 133,056 | 171,154 | 164,255 |
| Homeowners' | 95,246 | 85,532 | 77,722 |
| Marine | 95,169 | 79,781 | 69,743 |
| Fidelity and surety | 25,816 | 23,666 | 18,957 |
| Investments | 277,931 | 229,383 | 178,064 |
| Other | 591 | 627 | 541 |
| Total | 1,932,817 | 1,940,259 | 1,751,165 |
| **Operating profit (loss)** | | | |
| Workers' compensation | 14,241 | 2,796 | (1,935) |
| Casualty | 9,615 | (10,431) | 12,386 |
| Automobile—commercial | (17,342) | (12,602) | 1,760 |
| Automobile—personal | (20,671) | (15,568) | (11,842) |
| Commercial multiple-peril | (44,775) | (7,303) | 3,141 |
| Fire and allied | (6,912) | (5,952) | 6,084 |
| Homeowners' | (8,265) | (9,291) | (3,284) |
| Marine | (1,324) | (6,978) | (8,781) |
| Fidelity and surety | 2,937 | 2,919 | 3,148 |
| Investments | 270,199 | 220,957 | 171,967 |
| Other | 591 | 627 | 541 |
| Total | 198,294 | 159,174 | 173,185 |
| General corporate expenses | (26,733) | (13,126) | (10,827) |
| Operating income before federal and foreign income taxes | 171,561 | 146,048 | 162,358 |

*Source:* 1981 Annual Report, Crum & Forster, p. 29.

Responding to industry puzzlement over Xerox's choice of diversification, Kearns cited the following reasons for the acquisition:

- Xerox believes the property-casualty insurance lines offer the best growth opportunities in the insurance business. Crum & Forster's lines are not heavily dominated by a few industries, as in auto coverage.
- Xerox perceives the acquisition as an expansion of Xerox's commercial financial services, pioneered by Xerox Credit Corporation. Formed in 1979, Xerox Credit expected to report a profit of about $35 million in 1982, about double 1981's profits.
- The acquisition will provide investment income that Xerox needs to support its vigorous research efforts in copiers, duplicators, electronic typewriters, and other office equipment.

- Xerox foresees a reduction of its tax rate during the down phase of the insurance cycle. Crum & Forster's current underwriting losses, which totaled $110 million before taxes in the first half of 1982, offer potential tax benefits to Xerox. The insurer currently pays relatively little in taxes and says its effective federal income tax rate has ranged from 12 percent to 14 percent of operating profit.[25]

Xerox watchers, however, wonder whether the company has lost confidence in its office automation business. Amy Wohl, president of Advanced Office Concepts Corp., responded to the announcement by saying, "This says Xerox doesn't feel its current set of investments gives enough return."[26] "My hunch," said office automation analyst Patricia Seybold, "is that office products may never be profitable for them. They've lost momentum."[27] Kearns, however, disagreed: "This is a very aggressive strategy to grow this business more rapidly with two market segments very different from each other." As he explains it, Xerox management believes they can maintain their total commitment to office automation and still diversify into a self-funding, high-growth area. "We concluded we could leverage the balance sheet at this time to branch out to other areas for a better return to our shareholders."[28]

But Xerox has had a mixed record in previous diversification attempts. In 1969, for example, the company purchased Scientific Data Systems (SDS), a manufacturer of mainframe computers, for 10 million shares of Xerox stock worth approximately $908 million. Hoping to compete with IBM, Xerox management hoped that SDS's expertise in computers would be worth giving the SDS stockholders a 73 percent premium over the stock's market price. Renamed Xerox Data Systems (XDS), the new division's sales fell below $100 million in 1970 and failed to show a profit. By 1972, XDS had lost $100 million before taxes. Losses ranging from $25 to $44 million annually continued until 1975, when the company wrote off the division at an $84 million loss. After six years of effort, XDS still had less than one percent of the mainframe computer market. Analysts reported that Xerox management had been surprised by the lack of R&D capability in Scientific Data Systems.[29]

In 1979, Xerox purchased Western Union International (WUI), an international communications carrier, for $212 million. This represented Xerox's first entry into telecommunications and operating in a regulated environment. Before it purchased WUI, Xerox already had a proposal before the Federal Communications Commission for a domestic data communications network called XTEN. This project was subsequently cancelled because Xerox felt the funds could be better used elsewhere. In December 1981, Xerox announced that it had reached an agreement to sell WUI to MCI Communications Corp. for $185 million, a $27 million loss. Other recent acquisitions, such as Shugart Associates, have been of a smaller nature, less than $50 million, and represent Xerox's attempt to diversify, both horizontally and vertically, in the information-processing industry in order to bolster its position in the office automation marketplace.

Just as the current recession has had a negative impact on Xerox's business, the weak economic climate has hurt the insurance industry. Pressures on pricing have cut underwriting profits for property and casualty insurance companies and, with interest rates declining, investment profits may drop. In the last quarter of 1982, the industry looked forward to record underwriting losses offset by also record income from investments. Insurers in recent years have been willing to cut their rates and write policies at a loss in order to generate policyholders' premiums for investment activities. Analysts fear, however, that the industry's underwriting losses may be growing faster than its investment income.[30]

On the other hand, declining interest rates have several positive effects on the insurance business. First, the bonds that comprise the bulk of the companies' portfolios are worth more when rates come down. Second, the insurers' reserves for future claims liabilities are more likely to be adequate when interest rates (and by association, inflation) are lower. Third, lower interest rates raise the prospect of an end to the destructive three-year price war still raging in the industry. Finally, with rates coming down, general economic prospects may brighten enough to increase demand for insurers' services.

Once a turnaround in pricing occurs, industry analysts expect profits to show strong growth over the next three to five years. Between 1975 and 1979, after the last recession, industry profits increased almost eight times. The rebound is not expected to be as strong this time, but considerable growth is predicted. Lower inflation, reduced interest rates, and generally improved economic conditions are predicted to boost the demand for insurance by the mid-1980s.[31]

In reaction to the announcement of the proposed acquisition of Crum & Forster by Xerox, Moody's Investors Service lowered its ratings of several debt issues of Xerox. Moody's said its action "reflects the anticipated additional claim on existing cash flow in support of debt to be issued to acquire Crum & Forster, and the effect of competitive conditions in the company's key markets."[32]

## THE OFFICE OF THE FUTURE

The high costs of management, professional, and clerical workers, in combination with continued favorable trends for electronic systems capabilities and costs, establishes office automation as a major growth market in the 1980s. The powerful basic reason for automating offices is that white-collar salaries are a huge and intractable cost of doing business. In 1980, 60 percent of the $1.3 trillion paid out for wages, salaries, and benefits in the United States went to office workers. Meanwhile the prices of electronics have been falling. Computer memory has become cheaper at a compound annual rate of 42 percent over the last five years, and the price of the logic chips that give computers their intelligence has dropped about 28 percent a year.

Although in theory office automation makes sense, the market has not developed as quickly as vendors had hoped. According to Wang Laboratories, only 60 or so of the largest industrial corporations have acquired as many as 100 office work stations. A much smaller number have linked them into pervasive networks. Demand has simply developed more slowly than anyone thought it would a few years ago. The current market is so narrow that profits may not appear for years.[33]

Vendors give many reasons for the slow growth of this market. First of all, the recession has cut back capital spending plans of many organizations. Second, the lack of convincing studies on the savings associated with office automation has heightened customers' reluctance to purchase. Third, in developing automation for managers and professionals, there is a problem in specifying exactly what steps or processes these individuals go through in doing their jobs. Fourth, top management does not yet feel comfortable with a computer terminal on the desk. Fifth, the confusion over which networking system will prevail, broad-band or base-band, has made buyers slower to purchase networks. Finally, despite the universal desire of business people to find better ways of doing work, office automation remains poorly understood.[34]

Dataquest, Inc., a California-based market research firm, estimates that U.S. shipments of equipment that can be linked to form electronic offices should grow 34 percent a year through 1986. Total revenues are predicted to grow between $12 and $15 billion by 1986.[35] Exhibit 7.14 describes the predicted growth in the U.S. market for office automation equipment.

This anticipation of a booming market for office automation has brought dozens of companies into the competition. AT&T, IBM, and Xerox have declared the market a key to their futures. In 1981, the top three minicomputer companies—Digital Equipment, Hewlett-Packard, and Data General—launched office automation systems within 30 days of one another. The most successful vendors court the end user and are actually encouraged to do so by most corporate customers. Buyers will designate "preferred" vendors but leave the final decisions to the line managers and secretaries who have to use the gear. Analysts see IBM, Wang, Digital Equipment, and Xerox as being in the best position to capture large pieces of the growing market. Yet there appear to be enough profitable niches to reward any company that can fill a particular customer need.

Xerox's thrust in office automation has been in directing its equipment to professionals and managers and in selling complete systems. Its strategy in gaining a share of this market is characterized by the following:

- Sacrifice profits for market share until the mid-1980s.
- Aim automation at the executive rather than at clerical workers.
- Design machines with a multitude of uses.
- Provide buyers with the opportunity to use the best available equipment from a range of suppliers.

**Exhibit 7.14** The U.S. Market for Office Automation Equipment ($ million)

|                            | 1981  | 1986  |
|----------------------------|-------|-------|
| Word processors            | 2,200 | 6,000 |
| Electronic typewriters     | 275   | 1,200 |
| Professional work stations | 5     | 250   |
| Intelligent copiers        | 185   | 900   |
| Digital PBXs               | 220   | 4,100 |

*Source:* Dataquest, Inc. *Fortune*, May 3, 1982, p. 184.

- Be the first to enter new markets.
- Make products easy and nonfatiguing to use.

Although it has been the traditionally routine tasks that have been automated so far, manufacturers of this equipment must reach beyond the secretary to managers and professionals for office automation to reach its true potential. These individuals account for 80 percent of white-collar salaries. The more complex products, such as professional workstations and intelligent copiers, may not come into their own for some time. Analysts estimate that in 1985 only 6 percent of managers and professionals are likely to be using sophisticated workstations.[36]

## NOTES

1. *Electronic News,* October 4, 1982, p. 22.
2. *Time,* November 1, 1982, p. 67.
3. *Wall Street Journal,* September 22, 1982.
4. *Datamation,* February 1983, pp. 90–98.
5. Xerox Corporation, Annual Report, 1981, p. 3.
6. *Sales and Marketing Management,* February 8, 1982, p. 24.
7. *Forbes,* July 7, 1980, pp. 40–41.
8. Ibid.
9. *Sales and Marketing Management,* February 8, 1982, p. 24.
10. Ibid.
11. *Infosystems,* January 1981.
12. Ibid.
13. *Business Week,* August 23, 1982, p. 80.
14. *Forbes,* July 7, 1980, pp. 40–41.
15. *Business Week,* October 18, 1982, p. 134M.
16. *Datamation,* February 1983, pp. 90–98.
17. *Infosystems,* February 1982, p. 26.
18. *Mini-Micro Systems,* February 1982.
19. *Business Week,* April 21, 1980, p. 130.
20. *Electronic News,* December 7, 1981, p. 18.
21. *Value Line,* November 12, 1982.
22. *Fortune,* September 5, 1983, pp. 97–102.
23. *Value Line,* November 12, 1982.
24. *Wall Street Journal,* September 22, 1982.
25. Ibid.
26. *Business Week,* October 4, 1982, p. 52.
27. Ibid.
28. Ibid.
29. *Electronics,* March 29, 1981, p. 86.
30. *Wall Street Journal,* December 30, 1982, p. 20.
31. *Value Line,* October 22, 1982, p. 637.
32. *Wall Street Journal,* October 1982.
33. *Fortune,* May 3, 1982, p. 176.
34. Ibid.
35. Ibid.
36. Ibid.

# 8 A. H. Robins and the Dalkon Shield

Neil H. Snyder
University of Virginia

Founded in 1866, A. H. Robins is a diversified multinational company with base operations in Richmond, Virginia. Robins is primarily a manufacturer and marketer of two types of pharmaceuticals: those marketed directly to the consumer and those dispensed solely through the medical profession (commonly known as ethical pharmaceuticals). However, Robins is more than a pharmaceutical company. Pet care products, health and beauty aids, and perfumes are among the many products manufactured by the company under brand names which include Robitussin* cough syrup, Sergeant's* pet care products, Chap Stick* lip balm, and Caron* perfumes.

In 1866, Albert Hartley Robins opened a tiny apothecary shop for the purpose of providing to the medical profession research-formulated, clinically proven, and ethically promoted pharmaceuticals. Over a century later, the Robins philosophy remains unchanged. After three generations of operation, Robins is still led by members of the Robins family. Currently, the company has almost 6000 full-time employees. Making employees feel like family has long been recognized as important to the overall success of the company. The ability to "converse as decision makers and to be treated as first-class" causes Robins's employees to take great pride in their company and to demonstrate a very high degree of loyalty to the firm. As an example of this concern for the views of employees, one Robins salesman said "that his advice often carries greater weight than that of the firm's market research department."[1]

This sense of family extends beyond work, too. The company sponsors activities that include a company softball team and company trips, and it offers employees little things that tend to make a big difference, such as free coffee and birthday holidays. Claiborne Robins believes that "his greatest assets are the people that work for him."[2] According to the *Richmond Times-Dispatch*, "When a person is employed by A. H. Robins, it's almost for life. Only on rare occasions do people not reach retirement with this company."[3]

*Trademarks of A. H. Robins.

© 1985 by Neil H. Snyder. All rights reserved. This case was prepared by Elizabeth Bogdan, Tracy Cox, Joan LeSoravage, Elizabeth Ghaphery, Marisa Hausmann, and Larry Rosenberger under the direction of Neil H. Snyder of the McIntire School of Commerce, University of Virginia. It is designed to be used as a basis for discussion rather than to illustrate either effective or ineffective handling of an administrative situation.

**THE INTRA-UTERINE DEVICE ENVIRON-MENT**

The market for birth control devices in the 1970s was very volatile. Before the inception of intrauterine devices (IUDs), several artificial methods of birth control were available to consumers. Included in this group were the diaphragm, the condom, and the pill. Each of these methods offered women significantly better birth control protection than afforded by natural measures. However, the diaphragm and the condom lacked what women seemed to want most from birth control devices—spontaneity. Thus, the pill was viewed by consumers as the ultimate form of contraception. Unquestioned, because it solved the perennial problem of birth control, the pill enjoyed a prosperous existence. The pill was convenient and safe, and it offered exceptional birth control protection.

The discovery of the pill's harmful side effects caused many women to lose confidence in oral contraceptives. The realization of problems such as an increased risk of heart disease, dramatic mood swings, and excessive weight gain gave rise to a national concern over the safety of the pill. This concern was the focus of the Gaylord Nelson hearings of the early 1970s. These hearings publicly exposed the harmful side effects of oral contraceptives. "It is estimated . . . that within six months of the Gaylord Nelson hearings . . . up to one million women went off the birth control pills."[4]

Since the pill was no longer viewed as the ultimate answer to birth control, women returned to traditional methods of contraception. However, they refused to sacrifice convenience and almost foolproof protection. What could have been better than a device—not a "dangerous" drug—that offered the same protection as the pill at a comparable price with more convenience? The stage was set for the introduction of the IUD. Previously, IUDs had been used only on a small scale in various Planned Parenthood clinics. It was not until the harmful side effects of the pill were made public that IUDs were viewed as commercially viable.[5]

An IUD is a "small, flexible piece of sterile plastic which is inserted into the uterus by the physician to prevent pregnancies."[6] The minute the device is inserted it is effective. "Once an IUD has been inserted, it entails no further costs, no daily protective procedures. It works only inside the uterus—without effects on your body, blood, or brain; it doesn't cause you to gain weight, have headaches or mood changes. And it provides the user with a most satisfying method of contraception."[7]

Because of the simplicity of the device, manufacturing costs are low and profits can be high. When volume is sufficient, an IUD can be manufactured, sterilized, and packaged for 35 to 40 cents, and it can be sold for $3.00 to $3.50.[8] Owing to the size and profit potential of the birth control market, the manufacturers of IUDs were well positioned to reap a bountiful harvest, but competition was tough. The secret to success was timing, and the winners would be the first in the market. Firms competing in the market realized that "unlike most consumer products, new drugs and delivery devices must first gain acceptance among a small group of specialists. If the specialists accept this their patients will too."[9] Therefore, the marketing effort was directed at physicians, knowing that they would refer the device to their patients.

## THE DALKON SHIELD

Dr. Hugh Davis, an assistant professor of medicine at John Hopkins University and an expert in birth control, was instrumental in developing the Dalkon Shield. Dr. Davis conducted research on patients using the shield, and he reported a pregnancy rate of 1.1 percent (comparable with the pill). The competitive advantage the Dalkon Shield had over other IUDs was the "larger surface area designed for maximum coverage and maximum contraceptive effect."[10] The potential of the Dalkon Shield was great, and drawing from its already established reputation and distribution channels in the pharmaceutical industry, the IUD seemed to be a logical addition to Robins's product offerings.

On June 12, 1970, A. H. Robins paid $750,000, a royalty of 10 percent of future net sales, plus consulting fees to acquire the Dalkon Shield. At the time of purchase, Robins had no expertise in the area of birth control. Although they did hire consultants, Robins had neither an obstetrician nor a gynecologist on its staff.[11] They assigned assembly of the shield to the corporate division of the company that manufactures Chap Stick lip balm. Before buying the product, however, Robins's medical director, Frederick A. Clark, Jr., reviewed statistical tests performed by Dr. Davis on the shield.[12] These tests showed that in 832 insertions, 26 women became pregnant. Dr. Davis' tests, however, were done on the original shield, not the one ultimately sold by Robins. The major difference between the original shield and the one sold by Robins was the addition of a multifilament tail.[13]

When they went to the market, Robins was excited about their product. "Possibly no other IUD has received the benefit of such ecstatic claims by its developer, its manufacturer, and the admiring multitude."[14] Robins used promotional methods that were designed especially for acceptance of the shield within the medical profession. Foremost among these promotions was a text written by Dr. Davis, *Intrauterine Devices for Contraception—The IUD.* The appendix of his book lists complications reported with the use of ten major IUDs (page 140). The Shield was presented in a very good light, with only a 5.4 percent complication rate. The complication rate of the competition ranged from 16.9 to 55.7 percent.

## DIFFICULTIES DEVELOP

A. H. Robins began selling the Dalkon Shield on January 1, 1971. On June 22, 1971, when a doctor reported that his shield-wearing daughter suffered a septic spontaneous abortion, miscarriage caused by infection, the company was particularly concerned about the safety aspects of the shield. The main concern was the shield's unique multifilament tail, which has since been accused of actually drawing infection from the vagina into the normally sterile uterus.[15] Ironically, the product that was thought to be the ultimate form of birth control turned sour (36 alleged deaths and 13,000 alleged injuries), and it had a devasting effect on A. H. Robins.

## DIFFICULTIES WITH RESEARCH*

Although the text written by Dr. Davis had been accepted by the medical profession as a major textbook on IUDs, the problems with IUDs raised many concerns, and the text was referred to as a "thinly disguised promotion of the Shield."[16] Examination revealed that Robins possessed data on five formal studies based on the experience of about 4000 shield users. Three of these five studies were perormed by people with financial interests in the shield. The foremost of these studies was done by Dr. Davis. He claimed a pregnancy rate of 1.1 percent, an expulsion rate of 2.3 percent, a medical removal rate of 2.0 percent, and a total complication rate of 5.4 percent. However, another study conducted over an 18-month period that was dated October 25, 1972, showed a 4.3 percent pregnancy rate.

In an interview broadcast on the CBS television show "60 Minutes" on August 5, 1984, Paul Rheingold, a New York attorney who has represented 40 Dalkon Shield users, said that "this IUD got on the market with no animal tests, and with whatever minimal clinical . . . or testing on human subjects . . . the company wanted to do, which turned out to be practically nothing."

## FINANCIAL IMPLICATIONS

Approximately 4.5 million Dalkon Shields were sold by Robins, producing an estimated profit of $500,000.[17] "The product generated total revenues to the company of $13.7 million in 4.5 years. But during the first six months of 1985, Robins paid out $61.2 million in Dalkon-related expenses."[18] By June 30, 1985, Robins and Aetna Life and Casualty Company (Robins's insurance company) had paid $378.3 million to settle 9230 Dalkon Shield cases. This exhausted all but $50 million of Robins's product liability insurance. Legal fees and other costs related to the shield have totaled $107.3 million. Robins's portion of the total Dalkon claims has been $198.1 million. Robins announced an anticipated minimum cost to handle future Dalkon expenses of $685 million excluding punitive damages.

Exhibits 8.1 through 8.12 present financial information on the company contained in its 1984 annual report.

## BANKRUPTCY

On August 21, 1985, A. H. Robins filed for bankruptcy under Chapter 11 of the Federal Bankruptcy Code. "When it filed its request for reorganization on August 21, Robins listed $2.26 in assets for each $1 in debts and talked publicly about the strengths of the company when items related to the Dalkon Shield birth control device were excluded."[19]

Robins noted that it had a profit of $35.3 million from net sales of $331.1 million in the first six months of 1985. What the sales and profits did not show was the extent to which Robins was having to dip into its retained earnings to pay

---

*Most of the information in this section was taken from Dr. Thomsen's testimony before the Committee on Government Operations, House of Representatives, May 30–31, 1973; June 1, 12–13, 1973.

**Exhibit 8.1** Net Sales (in millions of dollars)

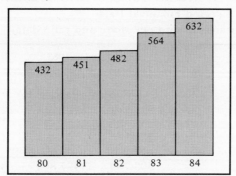

**Exhibit 8.2** Net Earnings or Loss (in millions of dollars)

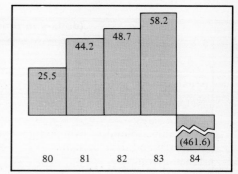

**Exhibit 8.3** Earnings or Loss per Share (in dollars)

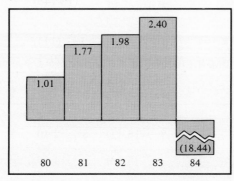

**Exhibit 8.4** Dividends per Share (in dollars)

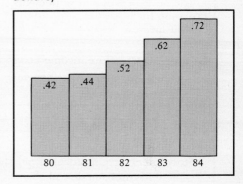

**Exhibit 8.5** Worldwide R&D Expenditures (in millions of dollars)

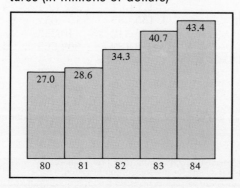

**Exhibit 8.6** Capital Additions (in millions of dollars)

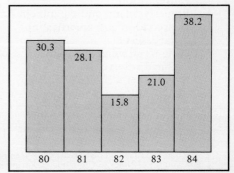

401

**Exhibit 8.7**

## A. H. ROBINS COMPANY, INCORPORATED, AND SUBSIDIARIES
### Selected Financial Data
#### (dollars in thousands except per share and ratio data)

|  | 1984 | 1983 | 1982 | 1981 |
|---|---|---|---|---|
| **Operations** | | | | |
| Net sales | $ 631,891 | $563,510 | $482,324 | $450,854 |
| Cost of sales | 237,508 | 220,628 | 195,008 | 190,759 |
| Marketing, administrative, and general | 222,939 | 196,495 | 168,963 | 157,852 |
| Research and development | 43,352 | 40,686 | 34,279 | 28,572 |
| Total operating costs and expenses | 503,799 | 457,809 | 398,250 | 377,183 |
| Operating earnings | 128,092 | 105,701 | 84,074 | 73,671 |
| Interest income | 7,560 | 8,350 | 8,085 | 8,437 |
| Interest expense | (3,240) | (5,441) | (10,308) | (3,564) |
| Litigation settlement income | 1,205 | 2,256 | 3,135 | 3,379 |
| Reserve for Dalkon Shield claims | (615,000) | | | |
| Litigation expenses and settlements | (77,950) | (18,745) | (7,091) | (3,318) |
| Provision for losses on disposition of businesses | | | | |
| Other, net | (13,190) | (144) | (3,740) | (4,997) |
| Earnings (loss) before income taxes | (572,523) | 91,977 | 74,155 | 73,608 |
| Provision for income taxes (benefits) | (110,910) | 33,756 | 25,462 | 29,380 |
| Net earnings (loss) | $(461,613) | $ 58,221 | $ 48,693 | $ 44,228 |
| **Per share data** | | | | |
| Earnings (loss) per share | $ (18.44) | $ 2.40 | $ 1.98 | $ 1.77 |
| Dividends per share | .72 | .62 | .52 | .44 |
| Stockholders' equity (deficit) per share | (5.23) | 14.69 | 13.29 | 12.52 |
| Weighted average number of shares outstanding | 25,037 | 24,295 | 24,552 | 25,015 |
| **Balance sheet data** | | | | |
| Cash and cash equivalents | $ 91,627 | $133,381 | $ 79,986 | $ 89,024 |
| Working capital | 122,344 | 229,525 | 200,810 | 177,259 |
| Current ratio | 1.7 to 1 | 3.2 to 1 | 4.0 to 1 | 3.1 to 1 |
| Property, plant, and equipment, net | $ 135,685 | $107,651 | $ 98,079 | $ 96,457 |
| Depreciation and amortization | 16,310 | 10,253 | 10,384 | 10,096 |
| Total assets | 648,129 | 509,663 | 439,983 | 443,942 |
| Long-term obligations, exclusive of Dalkon Shield reserve | 25,330 | 48,322 | 51,040 | 48,232 |
| Stockholder's equity (deficit) | (127,851) | 355,837 | 321,085 | 310,201 |

[a]Results preceded adoption of Statement of Financial Accounting Standards No. 52 which revised the method of translating foreign currency.
[b]Results were computed on a FIFO basis.

Amounts for 1983 and prior years have been reclassified to conform to 1984 presentation.
See Note 12 of Notes to Consolidated Financial Statements for information on litigation.

| 1980[a] | 1979[a,b] | 1978[a,b] | 1977[a,b] | 1976[a,b] | 1975[a,b] | 1974[a,b] |
|---|---|---|---|---|---|---|
| $432,328 | $386,425 | $357,070 | $306,713 | $284,925 | $241,060 | $210,713 |
| 187,496 | 157,895 | 146,636 | 122,374 | 108,519 | 89,304 | 71,233 |
| 160,477 | 139,782 | 131,195 | 114,490 | 101,568 | 85,378 | 77,128 |
| 27,033 | 20,522 | 18,951 | 16,107 | 12,729 | 10,690 | 9,568 |
| 375,006 | 318,199 | 296,782 | 252,971 | 222,816 | 185,372 | 157,929 |
| 57,322 | 68,226 | 60,288 | 53,742 | 62,109 | 55,688 | 52,784 |
| 5,614 | 5,767 | 3,469 | 2,033 | 2,355 | 1,726 | 2,465 |
| (4,741) | (4,194) | (3,469) | (2,106) | (1,719) | (1,189) | (1,134) |
| 3,590 | 28,934 | | | | | |
| (4,616) | (6,005) | (9,560) | (3,331) | (1,146) | (5,065) | |
| (9,129) | | | | | | |
| (4,112) | (13,539) | 901 | (2,675) | (2,710) | (2,518) | (1,209) |
| 43,928 | 79,189 | 51,629 | 47,663 | 58,889 | 48,642 | 52,906 |
| 18,458 | 34,443 | 21,713 | 20,862 | 27,534 | 23,095 | 25,989 |
| $ 25,470 | $ 44,746 | $ 29,916 | $ 26,801 | $ 31,355 | $ 25,547 | $ 26,917 |
| $ 1.01 | $ 1.71 | $ 1.15 | $ 1.03 | $ 1.20 | $ .98 | $ 1.03 |
| .42 | .40 | .34 | .32 | .30 | .27 | .26 |
| 11.16 | 10.52 | 9.20 | 8.39 | 7.69 | 6.79 | 6.04 |
| 25,314 | 26,107 | 26,127 | 26,127 | 26,127 | 26,127 | 26,126 |
| $ 49,705 | $ 69,381 | $ 72,058 | $ 43,611 | $ 50,769 | $ 41,763 | $ 29,228 |
| 146,258 | 153,411 | 156,632 | 128,838 | 126,904 | 100,387 | 89,459 |
| 3.0 to 1 | 2.9 to 1 | 3.7 to 1 | 3.5 to 1 | 4.1 to 1 | 3.5 to 1 | 4.5 to 1 |
| $ 80,511 | $ 59,994 | $ 55,350 | $ 49,751 | $ 39,066 | $ 34,640 | $ 30,418 |
| 10,950 | 8,806 | 8,427 | 6,837 | 6,076 | 5,007 | 4,322 |
| 390,570 | 379,597 | 326,073 | 287,045 | 262,668 | 223,544 | 190,263 |
| 35,346 | 26,518 | 27,809 | 16,718 | 20,412 | 6,740 | 5,620 |
| 280,394 | 272,673 | 240,275 | 219,242 | 200,802 | 177,275 | 157,695 |

**Exhibit 8.8**

### A. H. ROBINS COMPANY, INCORPORATED, AND SUBSIDIARIES
#### Consolidated Statements of Operations
#### (dollars in thousands except per share data)

| Year Ended December 31, | 1984 | 1983[a] | 1982[a] |
|---|---:|---:|---:|
| Net sales | $ 631,891 | $563,510 | $482,324 |
| Cost of sales | 237,508 | 220,628 | 195,008 |
| Marketing, administrative, and general | 222,939 | 196,495 | 168,963 |
| Research and development | 43,352 | 40,686 | 34,279 |
| Total operating costs and expenses | 503,799 | 457,809 | 398,250 |
| Operating earnings | 128,092 | 105,701 | 84,074 |
| Interest income | 7,560 | 8,350 | 8,085 |
| Interest expense | (3,240) | (5,441) | (10,308) |
| Litigation settlement income | 1,205 | 2,256 | 3,135 |
| Reserve for Dalkon Shield claims | (615,000) | | |
| Litigation expenses and settlements | (77,950) | (18,745) | (7,091) |
| Other, net | (13,190) | (144) | (3,740) |
| Earnings (loss) before income taxes | (572,523) | 91,977 | 74,155 |
| Provision for income taxes (benefits) | (110,910) | 33,756 | 25,462 |
| Net earnings (loss) | $(461,613) | $ 58,221 | $ 48,693 |
| Earnings (loss) per common share | $ (18.44) | $ 2.40 | $ 1.98 |
| Average number of shares outstanding | 25,037 | 24,295 | 24,552 |

[a]Reclassified to conform to 1984 presentation.
The Notes to Consolidated Financial Statements are an integral part of these statements.

Dalkon-related bills. "Dalkon payments had taken away only 1.7 cents from each $1 in Robins sales from 1974 through 1983, but then jumped to 12.3 cents in 1984. And when it jumped to 18.5 cents in the first six months of this year [1985] there wasn't enough left from sales to meet other expenses."[20]

"The petition in Bankruptcy court stops the flow of Dalkon payments. A perceived advantage for Robins in seeking the Chapter 11 route is that the company's reorganization plan would likely stretch out Dalkon payments so that a cash-flow problem wouldn't recur."[21] "The action was taken [in bankruptcy court] in an effort to ensure that the economic vitality of the company, which is of course, critical to our ability to pay legitimate claims to present and future plaintiffs."[22]

A. H. Robins's petition in bankruptcy court has been at the center of a heated debate. Those in support of the company have argued that "A. H. Robins' move into bankruptcy court could ensure that there is money for all who are suing the company instead of letting 'the first wolves who tear at the carcass' get it all."[23] On the other hand, Aaron M. Levine, a lawyer for women filing against Robins, believes that "this is a company that's saying, 'We'll pay our suppliers and we'll pay for TV ads and we'll pay for the syrup for the Robitussin and we'll pay our

**Exhibit 8.9**

## A. H. ROBINS COMPANY, INCORPORATED, AND SUBSIDIARIES
### Consolidated Statements of Stockholders' Equity (Deficit)
#### (dollars in thousands except per share data)

| | Common Stock ($1 par value) | Additional Paid-in Capital | Retained Earnings (deficit) | Cumulative Translation Adjustments | Treasury Stock (at cost) | Total |
|---|---|---|---|---|---|---|
| Balance—January 1, 1982 | $26,127 | $ 700 | $ 295,851 | 84 | $(12,561) | $ 310,201 |
| Net earnings | | | 48,693 | | | 48,693 |
| Cash dividends—$.52 per share | | | (12,696) | | | (12,696) |
| Translation adjustment for 1982 | | | | (16,559) | | (16,559) |
| Purchase of treasury stock—644,000 shares | | | | | (8,844) | (8,844) |
| Issued for stock options—24,550 shares | 24 | 266 | | | | 290 |
| Balance—December 31, 1982 | 26,151 | 966 | 331,848 | (16,475) | (21,405) | 321,085 |
| Net earnings | | | 58,221 | | | 58,221 |
| Cash dividends—$.62 per share | | | (14,997) | | | (14,997) |
| Translation adjustment for 1983 | | | | (9,250) | | (9,250) |
| Issued for stock options—61,900 shares | 62 | 716 | | | | 778 |
| Balance—December 31, 1983 | 26,213 | 1,682 | 375,072 | (25,725) | (21,405) | 355,837 |
| Net loss | | | (461,613) | | | (461,613) |
| Cash dividends—$.72 per share | | | (17,936) | | | (17,936) |
| Translation adjustment for 1984 | | | | (10,051) | | (10,051) |
| Purchase of treasury stock—1,040,404 shares | | | | | (17,070) | (17,070) |
| Issued for stock options—20,300 shares | 21 | 201 | | | | 222 |
| Shares reissued with acquisition—1,243,707 shares | | 9,427 | | | 13,333 | 22,760 |
| Balance—December 31, 1984 | $26,234 | $11,310 | $(104,477) | $(35,776) | $(25,142) | $(127,851) |

The Notes to Consolidated Financial Statements are an integral part of these statements.

405

**Exhibit 8.10**

## A. H. ROBINS COMPANY, INCORPORATED, AND SUBSIDIARIES
### Consolidated Balance Sheets
### (dollars in thousands)

| December 31 | 1984 | 1983 | 1982 |
|---|---|---|---|
| **Assets** | | | |
| *Current assets* | | | |
| Cash | $ 1,792 | $ 1,534 | $ 5,792 |
| Certificates of deposit and time deposits | 13,426 | 57,700 | 14,349 |
| Marketable securities | 76,409 | 74,147 | 59,845 |
| Accounts and notes receivable—net of allowance for doubtful accounts of $2,613 (1983—$2,560, 1982—$2,473) | 111,313 | 112,260 | 107,790 |
| Inventories | 84,611 | 82,714 | 72,219 |
| Prepaid expenses | 5,643 | 6,674 | 5,136 |
| Deferred tax benefits | 15,800 | | 3,537 |
| Total current assets | 308,994 | 335,029 | 268,668 |
| *Property, plant, and equipment* | | | |
| Land | 6,313 | 6,552 | 6,940 |
| Buildings and leasehold improvements | 106,165 | 89,374 | 75,933 |
| Machinery and equipment | 90,260 | 70,169 | 68,453 |
| | 202,738 | 166,095 | 151,326 |
| Less accumulated depreciation | 67,053 | 58,444 | 53,247 |
| | 135,685 | 107,651 | 98,079 |
| *Intangibles and other assets* | | | |
| Intangibles—net of accumulated amortization | 82,502 | 50,201 | 53,140 |
| Note receivable, less current maturity | | | 8,044 |
| Deferred tax benefits | 106,700 | | |
| Other assets | 14,248 | 16,782 | 12,052 |
| | 203,450 | 66,983 | 73,236 |
| | $648,129 | $509,663 | $439,983 |

The Notes to Consolidated Financial Statements are an integral part of these statements.

| December 31 | 1984 | 1983 | 1982 |
|---|---|---|---|
| **Liabilities and stockholders' equity (deficit)** | | | |
| *Current liabilities* | | | |
| Notes payable | $ 16,129 | $ 7,116 | $ 5,419 |
| Long-term debt payable within one year | 21,600 | 3,225 | 1,325 |
| Current portion of reserve for Dalkon Shield claims | 51,000 | | |
| Accounts payable | 23,855 | 23,989 | 20,807 |
| Income taxes payable | 11,850 | 28,589 | 12,269 |
| Accrued liabilities: | | | |
|   Dalkon Shield costs | 22,653 | 11,094 | 2,134 |
|   Other | 39,563 | 31,491 | 25,904 |
|     Total current liabilities | 186,650 | 105,504 | 67,858 |
| Long-term debt | 11,400 | 33,000 | 36,225 |
| Reserve for Dalkon Shield claims, less current portion | 564,000 | | |
| Other liabilities | 13,930 | 12,270 | 14,022 |
| Deferred income taxes | | 3,052 | 793 |
| *Stockholders' equity (deficit)* | | | |
| Preferred stock, $1 par—authorized 10,000,000 shares, none issued | | | |
| Common stock, $1 par—authorized 40,000,000 shares | 26,234 | 26,213 | 26,151 |
| Additional paid-in capital | 11,310 | 1,682 | 966 |
| Retained earnings (deficit) | (104,477) | 375,072 | 331,848 |
| Cumulative translation adjustments | (35,776) | (25,725) | (16,475) |
| | (102,709) | 377,242 | 342,490 |
| Less common stock in treasury, at cost—1,793,347 shares (1983) | | | |
|   —1,996,650 shares, 1982—1,996,650 shares) | 25,142 | 21,405 | 21,405 |
| | (127,851) | 355,837 | 321,085 |
| | $ 648,129 | $509,663 | $439,983 |

**Exhibit 8.11**

### A. H. ROBINS COMPANY, INCORPORATED, AND SUBSIDIARIES
#### Consolidated Statements of Changes in Financial Position
#### (dollars in thousands)

| Year Ended December 31 | 1984 | 1983[a] | 1982[a] |
|---|---|---|---|
| **Cash provided by operations** | | | |
| Net earnings (loss) | $(461,613) | $58,221 | $48,693 |
| Noncash expenses | | | |
|    Depreciation and amortization | 16,310 | 10,253 | 10,384 |
|    Deferred tax benefit, reserve for Dalkon Shield claims | (125,933) | | |
|    Reserve for Dalkon Shield claims | 615,000 | | |
|    Other, net | 6,140 | 2,477 | 3,201 |
| | 49,904 | 70,951 | 62,278 |
| **Operating requirements, (increase) decrease** | | | |
| Accounts and notes receivable | 1,686 | (7,212) | (18,172) |
| Inventories | 125 | (10,424) | (4,647) |
| Accounts payable, income taxes payable and accrued liabilities | (147) | 36,279 | (13,936) |
| Other, net | 2,955 | 4,910 | 5,477 |
| | 4,619 | 23,553 | (31,278) |
| **Investments** | | | |
| Capital additions | (38,155) | (20,955) | (15,815) |
| Acquisitions | (51,809) | (5,700) | (2,035) |
| | (89,964) | (26,655) | (17,850) |
|    Cash flow from operations | (35,441) | 67,849 | 13,150 |
| **Cash provided by (utilized in) financial activities** | | | |
| Notes payable and long-term debt | 5,933 | 543 | (648) |
| Purchase of treasury shares | (17,070) | | (8,844) |
| Issuance of treasury shares for acquisition | 22,760 | | |
| | 11,623 | 543 | (9,492) |
| Less cash dividends paid | 17,936 | 14,997 | 12,696 |
| Net increase (decrease) in cash and cash equivalents | $(41,754) | $53,395 | $(9,038) |

[a]Reclassified to conform to 1984 presentation.
The Notes to Consolidated Financial Statements are an integral part of these statements.

workers, but as far as this one particular group of creditors—the women we have maimed—we won't pay."[24]

    Levine pointed to Robins's own estimates that it has $466 million in assets and only $216.5 million owed to creditors. " 'Certainly this is far from the usual type of debtor who files a bankruptcy court petition.' According to Levine's motion,

**Exhibit 8.12**

## A. H. ROBINS COMPANY, INCORPORATED, AND SUBSIDIARIES
### Notes to Consolidated Financial Statements

### 1. SIGNIFICANT ACCOUNTING POLICIES

#### Consolidation

The consolidated financial statements include the accounts of A. H. Robins Company, Incorporated, and all majority-owned subsidiaries. Accounts of subsidiaries outside the U. S. and Canada are included on the basis of a fiscal year beginning December 1 (or date of acquisition) and ending November 30. All significant intercompany accounts and transactions have been eliminated.

#### Inventories

Inventories are valued at the lower of cost or market. The cost for substantially all domestic inventories is determined on the last-in, first-out (LIFO) method, while cost for foreign inventories is based on the first-in, first-out (FIFO) method.

#### Property, Plant, and Equipment

Property, plant, and equipment are recorded at cost and are depreciated over their estimated useful lives. Depreciation for all companies is computed on the straight-line method for assets acquired after 1979. Depreciation on assets acquired in 1979 and prior years is computed on the declining-balance method for domestic companies and on the straight-line method for foreign companies.

#### Intangible Assets

Excess of cost over net assets of subsidiaries acquired after October 31, 1970, is being amortized over a period of 40 years or less. Excess cost of $17,357,000 relating to companies acquired prior to that date is not being amortized. Expenditures for development of patents are charged to expense as incurred. Patents purchased and trademarks are being amortized over their determinable lives.

#### Income Taxes

The company provides for deferred income taxes on items of income or expense reported for tax purposes in different years than for financial purposes. The investment tax credit is included in earnings in the year the credit arises as a reduction of any provision for income taxes.

    The company files a consolidated Federal income tax return with its domestic subsidiaries. Income taxes, if any, are provided for on earnings of foreign subsidiaries remitted or to be remitted. No provision is made for income taxes on undistributed earnings of foreign subsidiaries reinvested in the companies.

#### Retirement Plans

The company and certain of its subsidiaries have retirement plans for their employees. Costs of the plans are funded when accrued except for the plans of certain foreign subsidiaries. Unfunded prior-service costs are provided for over periods not exceeding 40 years. Certain medical and life insurance benefits are provided for qualifying retired employees. The annual costs for these programs are not material and are expensed when paid.

(continued)

**Exhibit 8.12** (continued)

**Earnings (Loss) Per Share**

Earnings (loss) per share are based on the weighted average number of common shares and common share equivalents outstanding during each year.

## 2. ACQUISITIONS AND DIVESTITURES

On January 5, 1984, the company acquired all of the outstanding stock of Quinton Instrument Company, Inc. for which the company issued 1,243,707 shares of its common stock valued for accounting purposes at $18.30 per share and paid $20.1 million in cash. The total acquisition cost was $42.9 million, which consisted of the assigned value of the above-mentioned shares, the cash paid, and acquisition expenses. The company accounted for the acquisition as a purchase and accordingly has included Quinton's results of operations in its financial statements beginning January 5, 1984. On an unaudited pro forma basis, assuming the acquisition had occurred on January 1, 1983, the company's net sales, net earnings, and earnings per share would have been $587,328,000, $56,992,000, and $2.23, respectively. The pro forma amounts reflect estimated adjustments for goodwill amortization, depreciation, and interest expense. Goodwill of $27,118,000 is being amortized on a straight-line basis over a period of 40 years.

On April 2, 1984, the company acquired substantially all of the assets associated with radio stations WRQK-FM and WPET-AM in Greensboro, North Carolina. The acquisition price was $7.6 million.

In December 1984, the company acquired all of the outstanding stock of Lode B. V., an established ergometer manufacturer located in the Netherlands. Lode B. V., an addition to the company's Medical Instruments Division, has been accounted for by the purchase method and did not result in a significant impact on 1984 financial results.

In March 1983, the company acquired substantially all of the assets of Scientific Protein Laboratories, a company primarily engaged in the manufacture of animal-derived pharmaceutical products.

Also in March 1983, the company sold its Quencher cosmetics line at an after-tax gain of $801,000.

In November 1982, the company acquired the assets of U. S. Clinical Products, Incorporated, located in Richardson, Texas. U. S. Clinical Products engages primarily in the manufacturing and marketing of tamper-resistant seals used in hospitals on intravenous containers after the manufacturer's closure has been removed.

## 3. FOREIGN OPERATIONS

At December 31, 1984, undistributed earnings of foreign subsidiaries totaled approximately $70,981,000 including amounts accumulated at dates of acquisition. Of this amount, $14,600,000 might be subject to net additional federal income taxes if distributed currently. No provision has been made for income taxes on these undistributed earnings.

Foreign currency exchange losses included in earnings amounted to $1,187,000 in 1984 (1983—$938,000, 1982—$2,436,000). Net foreign assets included in the consolidated financial statements at December 31, 1984 were $75,098,000 (1983—$93,011,000, 1982—$101,271,000).

## 4. INVENTORIES

| | (Dollars in thousands) | | |
| --- | --- | --- | --- |
| | 1984 | 1983 | 1982 |
| Finished products | $41,814 | $43,462 | $38,467 |
| Work in process | 18,425 | 16,186 | 8,221 |
| Raw materials and supplies | 24,372 | 23,066 | 25,531 |
| | $84,611 | $82,714 | $72,219 |

Substantially all domestic inventories were valued on the last-in, first-out (LIFO) method while most foreign inventories were valued on the first-in, first-out (FIFO) method. Approximately 68% of inventories was valued under LIFO in 1984 (1983—70%, 1982—65%) and the remainder under FIFO. Current cost (FIFO method) of inventories exceeded the LIFO values by $3,281,000 in 1984; $4,424,000 in 1983; and $3,546,000 in 1982.

## 5. LONG-TERM DEBT

Long-term debt, net of amounts payable within one year, is summarized as follows:

| | (Dollars in thousands) | | |
| --- | --- | --- | --- |
| | 1984 | 1983 | 1982 |
| 8¾% promissory note due annually to 1988 | | $19,700 | $21,025 |
| Bonds, interest rate 55% of prime, due annually from 1984 to 1991 | 11,400 | 13,300 | 15,200 |
| | $11,400 | $33,000 | $36,225 |

Annual maturities of long-term debt for the next five years are 1985—$21,600,000; 1986—$1,900,000; 1987—$1,900,000; 1988—$1,900,000; and 1989—$1,900,000.

The 8¾% promissory note was redeemed at par subsequent to year end and therefore has been reclassified as long-term debt payable within one year.

Interest incurred during 1984 of $2,500,000 was capitalized and included in property, plant, and equipment. No interest was capitalized in 1983 or 1982.

## 6. LINES OF CREDIT

At December 31, 1984, unused lines of credit which do not support commercial paper or similar borrowing arrangements and may be withdrawn at the banks' option amounted to $12 million with domestic banks. Aggregate compensating balances were not material.

(continued)

**Exhibit 8.12** (continued)

## 7. STOCK OPTIONS

The company has stock option plans for officers and certain key employees. The qualified stock option plan of 1973 as amended in 1982 was terminated on January 31, 1983, except as to outstanding options. A new incentive stock option plan was approved by the stockholders on April 26, 1983, under which 1,000,000 shares of common stock were made available for the granting of options. The plans are administered by a committee, subject to certain limitations expressly set forth in the plan, with authority to select participants, determine the number of shares to be allotted to a participant, set the option price, and fix the term of each option.

Transactions of the qualified and nonstatutory stock option plans are summarized below:

| | Shares Available for Option | Options Outstanding | |
| --- | --- | --- | --- |
| | | Shares | Price per Share |
| Balance—Dec. 31, 1981 | 1,355,300 | 241,350 | $ 10.19 to $11.38 |
| Exercised | | (24,550) | 10.19 to 11.38 |
| Canceled and expired | 4,150 | (4,150) | 10.19 |
| Balance—Dec. 31, 1982 | 1,359,450 | 212,650 | 10.19 to 11.38 |
| Terminated—1973 plan | (602,450) | | |
| Exercised | | (61,900) | 10.19 to 11.38 |
| 1983 plan | 1,000,000 | | |
| Balance—Dec. 31, 1983 | 1,757,000 | 150,750 | 10.19 to 11.38 |
| Granted | (488,500) | 488,500 | 13.69 |
| Exercised | | (20,300) | 10.19 to 13.69 |
| Canceled and expired | 13,700 | (13,700) | 11.38 |
| Balance—Dec. 31, 1984 | 1,282,000 | 605,250 | 10.19 to 13.69 |

The options are exercisable at any time until their expiration dates, which are in 1986 (136,550 shares) and 1994 (468,700 shares).

## 8. PROVISION FOR INCOME TAXES

The provision for income taxes includes

|                          | (Dollars in thousands) | | |
|--------------------------|-----------:|----------:|----------:|
|                          | 1984       | 1983      | 1982      |
| Currently payable        |            |           |           |
| Domestic                 | $ (4,061)  | $13,563   | $ 1,572   |
| State                    | 1,580      | 2,745     | 3,639     |
| Foreign                  | 9,234      | 10,947    | 11,859    |
|                          | $ 6,753    | $27,255   | $17,070   |
| Deferred                 |            |           |           |
| Domestic                 | $(110,009) | $ 5,917   | $ 8,238   |
| State                    | (8,648)    | 270       | 292       |
| Foreign                  | 994        | 314       | (138)     |
|                          | $(117,663) | $ 6,501   | $ 8,392   |
| Total provision          | $(110,910) | $33,756   | $25,462   |
| Earnings (loss) before income taxes consist of |  |  |  |
| Domestic                 | $(590,925) | $71,613   | $52,974   |
| Foreign                  | 18,402     | 20,364    | 21,181    |
|                          | $(572,523) | $91,977   | $74,155   |

Note 12 in the Notes to Consolidated Financial Statements discusses a minimum reserve established by the company in 1984 for pending and future claims related to the Dalkon Shield. These claims are deductible for tax purposes as incurred by the company. It is the company's belief that the currently recognized claims will be fully deductible against its future taxable income. However, generally accepted accounting principles limit the recognition of future tax benefits to those amounts assured beyond any reasonable doubt. Accordingly, the company has recognized for financial statement purposes only those benefits arising from the carryback of product liability expenses against income tax expenses previously recognized by the company. At December 31, 1984, the company had, for financial statement purposes only, unrecognized loss carry-forward deductions in the amount of $138,132,000 and unrecognized foreign and investment tax credits carryforward of $86,939,000.

Should the realization of product liability claims produce a taxable loss in a future period, the company is permitted under provisions of the U.S. Internal Revenue Code to carry such loss back as a deduction against previous taxable income for a period up to 10 years. Such loss may also be used to reduce future taxable income for a period up to 15 years.

In 1984, the company realized net tax benefits of $5,206,000, primarily in the form of investment tax credit and depreciation, from its investment in tax benefit leases under the "safe harbor" leasing provisions enacted in 1981 and 1982. These benefits reduced the 1984 provision for domestic taxes currently payable and increased the provision for deferred taxes. As current tax benefits are realized, the company has

(continued)

413

**Exhibit 8.12** (continued)

reduced its purchase cost of the leases and established a deferred tax liability for the leases' future taxable income. Interest income is accrued on the unrecovered purchase cost. The excess of the purchase cost and accrued interest over the cumulative tax savings expected is amortized on an interest method during the years temporary excess tax savings are produced. The interest accrued and investment amortized during the lease terms have no material effect on earnings. At December 31, 1984, the balance of unrecovered investment and accrued interest was $1,071,000.

Deferred income taxes result from tax leases and from income and expense items reported for financial accounting and tax purposes in different periods. The source of these differences and the tax effect of each is shown below:

|  | (Dollars in thousands) | | |
|---|---|---|---|
|  | 1984 | 1983 | 1982 |
| Reserve for Dalkon Shield claims | $(125,933) | | |
| Discounted portion of installment note receivable | 574 | $1,106 | $1,520 |
| Tax depreciation in excess of books | 2,134 | 1,480 | 1,096 |
| Other | 356 | 988 | 585 |
| Tax benefit from tax leases | $   5,206 | 2,927 | 5,191 |
|  | $(117,663) | $6,501 | $8,392 |

Reconciliation of the effective tax rate and the federal statutory rate is as follows:

|  | Percent of Pretax Income (Loss) | | |
|---|---|---|---|
|  | 1984 | 1983 | 1982 |
| Statutory federal tax rate | (46.0) | 46.0 | 46.0 |
| Product liability claims in excess of amounts carried back | 15.2 | | |
| Foreign, investment, and other tax credits not recognized after loss carryback | 11.1 | | |
| Federal tax on foreign earnings | 1.4 | (1.1) | (3.1) |
| State taxes on income, net of federal tax benefit | (1.3) | 2.8 | 3.6 |
| Investment and other tax credits | | (2.1) | (2.8) |
| Foreign earnings taxed at higher (lower) effective tax rate | .1 | | .3 |
| Puerto Rican earnings exempt from tax | (1.1) | (6.7) | (9.0) |
| Tax-exempt interest | (.1) | (.3) | (1.2) |
| All other, net | 1.3 | (1.9) | .5 |
|  | (19.4) | 36.7 | 34.3 |

A wholly owned subsidiary in Puerto Rico operates under partial income tax exemptions granted for periods through 1999. The estimated tax saving from the Puerto Rican operation was $6,200,000 in 1984 (1983—$6,200,000, 1982—$6,700,000). Puerto Rican withholding taxes are provided on those earnings expected to be repatriated prior to expiration of the exemptions.

During 1983, the Internal Revenue Service completed its examination of the company's tax returns for the years 1978 through 1980 and proposed a deficiency of income taxes of approximately $6,400,000. The company is contesting the proposed deficiency which arises from a proposed reallocation of income from the company's Puerto Rico subsidiary. It is likely that a similar deficiency will be proposed for the years 1981 and 1982.

Management believes that any additional income taxes that may result from the proposed deficiency, and from the probable proposed deficiency related to the same issues for the years 1981 and 1982, should not have a material adverse effect on the consolidated financial position of the company.

## 9. BUSINESS SEGMENT INFORMATION

Information about operations in different business segments and in various geographic areas of the world is included on page 32 of this report and incorporated herein by reference.

## 10. RETIREMENT PLAN

The company and certain of its subsidiaries have retirement plans covering substantially all of their employees. The total retirement expense for 1984 was $6,908,000 (1983—$6,246,000, 1984—$5,435,000). The actuarial present value of accumulated plan benefits, assuming a weighted average rate of return of 8% in 1984 (1983—8%, 1982—6.5%), and plan net assets available for benefits of domestic defined benefit plans as of January 1, 1984, 1983 and 1982 are as follows:

| | (Dollars in thousands) | | |
| --- | --- | --- | --- |
| | 1984 | 1983 | 1982 |
| Actuarial present value of accumulated plan benefits | | | |
| Vested | $40,895 | $35,601 | $30,925 |
| Nonvested | 3,472 | 3,250 | 4,351 |
| | $44,367 | $38,851 | $35,276 |
| Net assets available for benefits | $55,621 | $47,287 | $36,017 |

Assets available for benefits and the actuarial present value of accumulated benefits have not been determined for several minor foreign pension plans which are not required to report such information to government agencies.

(continued)

415

**Exhibit 8.12** (continued)

Other liabilities include $6,635,000 of accrued pensions and severance benefits in foreign subsidiaries (1983—$7,063,000, 1982—$7,100,000).

## 11. COMMITMENTS

Rentals of space, vehicles, and office and data processing equipment under operating leases amounted to $6,718,000 in 1984 (1983—$6,428,000, 1982—$5,843,000).

Minimum future rental commitments under all noncancelable operating leases at December 31, 1984 with remaining terms of more than one year are as follows:

|  | (Dollars in thousands) |
| --- | --- |
| 1985 | $2,515 |
| 1986 | 1,804 |
| 1987 | 1,634 |
| 1988 | 1,265 |
| 1989 | 822 |
| Later years | 1,853 |
| Total minimum future rentals | $9,893 |

The company has agreed to repurchase, at the option of the shareholder until such time as the securities are registered, the shares of the company issued to the former Quinton Instrument Company, Inc. shareholders. Upon tender of the shares, the company will repurchase the shares at the current market price. At December 31, 1984, there were 1,017,103 shares subject to this agreement.

As of December 31, 1984, the company had outstanding commitments of $8 million for the construction of plant, office, and research and development facilities.

## 12. LITIGATION

Dalkon Shield—In June 1970, the company acquired the rights to the Dalkon Shield, an intrauterine contraceptive device. Approximately 2.8 million devices were sold in the U.S. through June 1974. Approximately 1.7 million of the devices were sold abroad.

Numerous cases and claims alleging injuries claimed to be associated with use of the device have been filed against the company in the U.S. ("claims"). Only a few claims have been filed in foreign jurisdictions. The alleged injuries fall under the following general groups: perforation of the uterus or cervix, infection of the female reproductive system, pregnancy, ectopic pregnancy, spontaneous abortion which may be accompanied by sepsis, death, sterility, fetal abnormality and premature delivery, painful insertion and removal, and miscellaneous injuries. In addition to compensatory damages, most cases also seek punitive damages.

As of December 31, 1984, there were approximately 3800 claims pending against the company in federal and state courts in the U.S. The company expects that a substantial number of new claims will be filed against the company in the future.

Through December 31, 1984, the company had disposed of approximately 8300 claims. In disposing of these claims, the company and its insurer have paid out approximately $314.6 million. Prior to 1981, substantially all disposition costs (including legal expenses, but excluding punitive damages) were charged to applicable products liability insurance carried by the company. The company incurred costs in excess of insurance in the following amounts: 1981—$3.3 million; 1982—$7.1 million; 1983—$18.7 million; and 1984—$78.0 million (exclusive of the reserve described below).

Of the claims disposed of prior to December 31, 1984, 50 were tried to conclusion.

Of that number, 27 resulted in verdicts for compensatory damages in favor of plaintiffs and 23 in verdicts in favor of the company. Seven of the plaintiff verdicts (involving compensatory awards aggregating approximately $5 million) and one verdict in favor of the company are the subject of pending appeals. Eight of the plaintiff verdicts also included awards of punitive damages in an aggregate amount of $17,227,000. Six of these punitive awards aggregating $8,827,000 have been paid; two are the subject of appeals. Punitive damage awards are not covered by insurance and are payable by the company.

The company is unable to assess its potential exposure to additional punitive damage awards. It has recently filed a motion in the United States District Court for the Eastern District of Virginia seeking certification of a class of present and prospective claimants in both federal and state courts for the purpose of determining and finally resolving in a single proceeding whether the company should be liable for punitive damages by reason of the Dalkon Shield and, if so, the aggregate amount of additional punitive damages that should be awarded.

The company had product liability insurance covering compensatory awards with respect to the Dalkon Shield for pertinent periods prior to March 1978. In October 1984, the company settled its suit, commenced in 1979, against its insurer concerning coverage of Dalkon Shield liability. From existing coverage and some additional coverage resulting from the settlement of this suit the company had at December 31, 1984, approximately $70 million of insurance coverage that it expects to be able to use.

In anticipation of the conclusion of the insurance coverage suit, the company commissioned a study, the purpose of which was to provide management of the company with data to establish a loss reserve for the future costs in compensatory damages and legal expenses of the disposition of pending and future claims. The study estimated the amount of this future disposition cost based on the following: (1) an estimate of total injuries based on an epidemiological analysis of published literature regarding the Dalkon Shield and other IUDs; (2) a statistical analysis of all claims filed during the period 1981 through 1983 which constitute 51% of all claims filed since the inception of the litigation through December 31, 1983; and (3) a statistical analysis of disposition timing and costs of all claims filed during the period January 1, 1979, through December 31, 1983, and disposed of prior to October 1, 1984. The information on claims filed and disposition timing and costs was extracted from a data base which contains information on claims filed through December 31, 1983. The study utilized information from the periods discussed above, which was believed to be more representative of future experience, rather than the entire litigation period which would have produced a materially higher estimate of disposition cost.

Based on the study's estimate of disposition cost and a review of 1984 fourth-quarter settlement cost data, management established a reserve, net of insurance, of $615 million against 1984 earnings in the accompanying consolidated financial statements. Management believes this represents a reasonable estimate of a minimum reserve for compensatory damages and legal expenses for pending and future claims. The reserve does not provide for any punitive damages or damages from Dalkon Shield litigation abroad since there is no substantive basis to quantify such exposures. In taking into account 1984 fourth-quarter settlement cost data, management excluded the cost of a single group settlement which, management believes is reasonable to assume, is not representative of the expected future disposition of claims. If the excluded settlement cost had been factored as an increasing trend into projected future cost of disposition of claims, the reserve would have been increased by a material amount.

Based on the study's projected schedule of disposition of pending and future claims, the payout of the reserve will take place over many years. The company has reduced

(continued)

**Exhibit 8.12** (concluded)

its 1984 provision for income taxes by $125.9 million, representing the expected minimum tax benefit to be realized by loss carrybacks to 1983 and prior years, plus reductions in deferred taxes expected to turn around in the tax loss carryforward period. The net effect of the reserve, less estimated tax benefits, is $489.1 million or $19.53 per share.

Continuing uncertainties associated with the litigation preclude a determination of the ultimate cost of the Dalkon Shield litigation to the company. There has been a significant increase in the number of new claims filed per month and additional pressure on and a resulting increase in some settlement values which, if continued, would result in a greater claim disposition cost than the amount estimated by the study. Whether this represents a long-term trend or is, as management believes is reasonable to assume, the temporary result of publicity associated with several Dalkon Shield related events in 1984 and 1985 causing a temporary acceleration in the rate of filing of claims with a subsequent leveling to those shown in the study will only be determined by future experience.

In addition to these uncertainties, there are other factors which could affect, either favorably or unfavorably, the ultimate outcome of the Dalkon Shield litigation and the resulting financial impact on the company. Among them are

· The Dalkon Shield removal campaign initiated on October 29, 1984
· The types of injuries alleged in future claims
· The effect of the passage of time, including the effect of statutes of limitations
· The level of litigation activity relating to devices sold abroad
· The method of disposition of claims
· The class action intended to resolve the question of punitive damages.

Accordingly, the reserve may not necessarily be the amount of the loss ultimately experienced by the company. It is not likely, however, that the ultimate loss will be less than the amount reserved. Further, the exposure of the company for additional compensatory and punitive damages awards over and above this reserve, although not presently determinable, may be significant and further materially adversely affect the future consolidated financial condition and results of operations of the company.

Other—In December 1982, the United States District Court for the Southern District of New York determined that the suit filed in 1977 by Kalman and Anita Ross, stockholders of the company, should be certified as a class action for damages on behalf of persons who purchased the company's common stock during the period March 8, 1971, through June 28, 1974. In addition to the company, certain of its present and former officers and directors are defendants. This suit alleges dissemination of false and misleading information and failure to disclose other information concerning the Dalkon Shield. After completion of discovery, an agreement was reached under which the company will pay $6.9 million in settlement of this class action. This agreement is subject to final judicial approval. The action against the individual defendants will be dismissed, subject to final judicial approval. A provision for this settlement has been recorded in 1984 and included in Other, Net.

In March 1980, Zoecon Corporation filed a civil action against the company and Miller-Morton Company, a subsidiary since merged into the company, alleging unfair competition (a claim since abandoned) and patent infringement in connection with the marketing of the Sergeant's Sentry V flea and tick collar. The company counterclaimed, alleging patent invalidity on the part of Zoecon Corporation. The case has now been disposed of by way of a settlement having no material financial impact on the company.

Robins's petition was instituted not to benefit a corporation in distress, as the laws are intended, 'but to enable the petitioner to escape the jurisdiction of another court when the day of reckoning for their alleged acts of misconduct was at hand.' "[25] The National Woman's Health Network, for instance, said at a news conference that the company is financially healthy, but is trying to duck its responsibility to women who have filed lawsuits. On the other hand, Roscoe E. Puckett, Jr., a spokesman for Robins, contends, "The best hope for all concerned is for A. H. Robins to remain financially healthy. To do that, we had to stop the financial hemorrhaging that threatened to destroy the company to the detriment of everyone, including the legitimate Dalkon Shield claimants."[26] "Other factors include our desire to ensure that all persons to whom the company has an obligation are treated fairly, to preserve the assets of the company and maintain its current operations."[27]

To supplement Dalkon expenses and to alleviate the tight cash flow position that Robins has experienced recently, they requested a $35 million credit limit "to meet $25 million of cash needs of its U.S. operations, $2 million in letters of credit for foreign suppliers, and $8 million of credit for its foreign units."[28] This credit limit was the subject of heated debate among the Internal Revenue Service, the attorneys for more than 10,000 women who have filed suit against Robins, and various Robins creditors. "The IRS contends that Robins owes about $61 million in corporate income taxes from as far back as 1978. Arguing on behalf of the agency, Assistant U.S. Attorney S. David Schiller told the judge that Robins had failed to prove that it needs the entire $35 million of credit or that it couldn't get the loans elsewhere under more favorable terms."[29] The credit line requested by Robins was ultimately approved by a federal court judge. "Under the agreement, Robins will receive $23 million from Manufacturers Hanover Trust Co., New York, and $12 million from Bank of Virginia. The arrangement, which was opposed vigorously by the Internal Revenue Service and others with claims pending against Robins, assigns the two banks priority for payments among all Robins creditors."[30]

"In approving the credit agreement, Judge Robert R. Merhige Jr. acknowledged that some of the terms 'could be questioned.' But he said he felt compelled to 'give way to the business judgment' of the company's managers. He also expressed concern that denying the request might harm the company's prospects for obtaining credit."[31]

**THE FUTURE**  "In October (1984), the Company filed in Federal District Court in Richmond a motion seeking a class action to resolve all punitive damage claims arising from Dalkon Shield litigation. The goal is a single trial for the purpose of determining if A. H. Robins should, in fact, be liable for punitive damages and, if so, the amount of those damages in respect to all present and future Dalkon Shield claimants. It is our view that this is the only fair means of settling this issue. In addition to the class action, the court has been requested to establish a voluntary opt-in proceeding to dispose of claims for compensatory damages on a facilitated basis. Such a proceeding would allow those plaintiffs who so desire to advance their claims with a minimum of delay and expense."[32]

Additionally, the company initiated an advertising campaign for the purpose of persuading women using the shields to have them removed at the company's expense. As of the publication date of the company's 1984 Annual Report, "More than 18,250 inquires [had] been received, . . . the Company [had] paid for 777 examinations and 4,437 removals."[33]

## NOTES

1. *Product Management,* October 1972.
2. A. H. Robins, *75th Anniversary Book.*
3. *Richmond Times-Dispatch,* June 23, 1985.
4. Subcommittee hearing before Congress, June 13, 1973, Dr. Thomsen's testimony.
5. Subcommittee hearing, Thomsen testimony.
6. SAF-T-COIL informational pamphlet.
7. Ibid.
8. Subcommittee hearing, Thomsen testimony.
9. Ibid.
10. Ibid.
11. *Richmond Times-Dispatch,* June 23, 1985.
12. Ibid.
13. Ibid.
14. Subcommittee hearing, Thomsen testimony.
15. *Richmond Times-Dispatch,* June 23, 1985.
16. Subcommittee hearing, Thomsen testimony.
17. *Richmond Times-Dispatch,* August 25, 1985.
18. *Richmond Times-Dispatch,* August 22, 1985.
19. *Richmond Times-Dispatch,* September 1, 1985.
20. Ibid.
21. *Richmond Times-Dispatch,* August 24, 1985.
22. *Richmond Times-Dispatch,* September 1, 1985.
23. *Richmond Times-Dispatch,* August 25, 1985.
24. *Richmond Times-Dispatch,* August 24, 1985.
25. Ibid.
26. Ibid.
27. *Richmond Times-Dispatch,* August 22, 1985.
28. *Wall Street Journal,* October 2, 1985.
29. *Wall Street Journal,* October 10, 1985.
30. *Wall Street Journal,* October 2, 1985.
31. Ibid.
32. A. H. Robins 1984 Annual Report.
33. Ibid.

# 9 The Auto Industry in the United States: Structure and Strategy

Ernest R. Nordtvedt

Loyola University in New Orleans

**INTRODUC-
TION**

The past 15 years have been turbulent ones for the auto industry in the United States and have seen the emergence of trends which have produced fundamental and lasting changes in its structure. These trends include the following:

- Consumer demand has shifted away from larger, full-sized luxury cars toward smaller, more fuel-efficient vehicles which prior to 1979 found only a limited market in the United States. Some evidence exists, however, that consumer demand for larger cars is enjoying a comeback in the mid-1980s.
- World trade in motor vehicles has expanded dramatically without a corresponding expansion in the distribution (by country) of consumer demand. The primary reason for this expansion has been the export of Japanese autos to existing markets in Europe and the United States. The primary effect of the expansion has been felt by U.S. automakers, whose production dropped by about 45 percent between 1979 and 1981.
- United States automakers have been exposed to growing pressures from consumers to improve quality and reliability, control costs and sticker prices, and to develop new products to compete with the smaller, more efficient imports while modernizing and adjusting production facilities and capacities to reflect changes in consumer preferences, lower industrywide sales volume, and slower domestic market growth.
- Auto-producing countries have responded to increased exports by the Japanese with a variety of restrictions designed to protect their indigenous industries from the effects of the new competitive environment while giving their automakers time to adjust to the changes.

The Arab oil embargo of 1973 and the resulting long gas lines were the original impetus for the trends. These events generated an immediate demand for smaller, more fuel-efficient cars for a relatively short period of time and resulted in the passage of the Energy Policy and Conservation Act of 1975, which mandated Corporate Average Fuel Economy goals for auto manufacturers. However, the memory of the American car owner is short and the severity of the experience soon faded. The government did not help by keeping gasoline prices

"The Auto Industry in the United States: Structure and Strategy" was prepared by Ernest R. Nordtvedt, professor of management, Loyola University, New Orleans. It is based on public documents and other published information and is intended as a basis for classroom discussion and not as an illustration of effective or ineffective management action.

Copyright © 1985 by Ernest R. Nordtvedt.

below worldwide market levels. It was not until 1979 and the shortages induced by the revolution in Iran that the trends became indelibly etched in the U.S. marketplace and in the minds of U.S. consumers.

To its observers, the response of the domestic auto industry to these trends initially seemed out of step with the realities of the marketplace. Not only was this an embarrassment to the industry, but it had most serious implications for an economy whose dependency on the industry could be illustrated by a series of observations regarding this relationship as it existed in 1980:

- About one in every six jobs in the United States was related to the auto industry, and more than four million jobs were in areas directly dependent on the auto.
- The auto industry used significant portions of other industry outputs, for example, steel, 21 percent; synthetic rubber, 60 percent; primary aluminum, 11 percent; ferrous castings, 30 percent; glass, 25 percent; machine tools, 20 percent; and a growing share of plastics and electronics outputs.
- The manufacturing process involved over 100 plants, and the industry purchased over $40 billion annually in equipment and materials from thousands of suppliers.

As a result of the 1979 gasoline shortage and price shock coupled with a worldwide recession, the U.S. auto industry entered a period during which smaller shares of lower overall demand resulted in enormous financial losses. The problem was exacerbated by the fact that the demand was shifting to a new product—smaller, more fuel-efficient autos—which required substantial outlays for tooling for new models and modernization of facilities to produce them. In two years (1980 and 1981) four U.S. automakers—General Motors, Ford, Chrysler and American Motors—suffered combined operating losses of about $5.5 billion. In 1980, General Motors registered its only loss since 1921.

Chrysler had appealed for and had received federal assistance in the form of loan guarantees. Even with that help, its continued existence was far from assured. Imports, to whom the domestic manufacturers had previously ceded the small-car market in the United States, claimed 26.7 percent of the market in 1980, 27.3 percent in 1981, and 27.9 percent in 1982. This happened despite the voluntary export restraints announced by the Japanese government in March 1981. The image of the industry was one of poor workmanship and disregard for consumer concerns. Government regulations aimed at preserving the environment and the quality of life had added substantively to manufacturing costs and sticker prices. Government control of gasoline prices had muddied the picture for consumers and manufacturers alike by keeping the price at the pump artificially low. Capital requirements were increasing just at the time when interest rates were at historic highs and company debt capacity and ability to raise equity funds were limited by financial losses and loss of market share and sales to the imports. Worldwide forecasts for the decade of the 1980s promised a replacement market with little overall growth in auto sales. An uncertainty in domestic and international economies around the world compounded all of these problems. From their historic worldwide employment high in 1977, the four U.S. manufacturers had dropped 424,000, or almost 28 percent, by 1982.

Major restructuring of the industry, its products, and the competitive positions of its members in recognition of the new environment was inevitable.

This study will examine first the industry structure, including pertinent competitive factors and market segmentation, and the recent performance and current strategy of each major domestic competitor. Additional factors indicating general changes and/or problems in the industry, such as productivity, break-even, capacity utilization and labor trends will also be covered. Finally, government regulation will be discussed in terms of its impact on the competition and the consumer. Although most of the automakers manufactured and marketed vans, trucks, and/or specialty vehicles, this study will concentrate on the passenger-car segment of the industry. This was the area of greatest visible competition and was the area of greatest interest to the observer. The other products in the product lines are mentioned, but detail and impact are not discussed.

## STRUCTURE

The auto industry in the United States can be characterized as a race which many started but few finished. The early 1900s found almost 200 manufacturers producing cars for varying periods of time. By 1927, 137 companies had disappeared. Only two new companies have tried to enter the business since the beginning of World War II, and both have gone the way of the others. In 1981, only four major companies remained, and all four suffered heavy financial losses between 1979 and 1982. A fifth company in the United States, Volkswagen of America, imported about 40 percent (based on the value of parts and labor) of its components to its Pennsylvania assembly plant and was classified as an import by the Department of Transportation despite its classification as domestic for retail purposes.

Domestic manufacturers assembled and sold their products in both domestic and foreign markets. In 1982, they accounted for 73 percent of domestic auto sales. The remainder was filled by imports, mostly from Japan with smaller numbers coming from West Germany, Italy, France, Great Britain, and Sweden. The imports first claimed more than 20 percent of the U.S. market in 1979.

The inroads into the U.S. marketplace by imports led predictably to calls for protection for domestic industries and for the jobs that were endangered by loss of sales by American manufacturers. An alternative to such protection was the opening of manufacturing facilities by Japanese companies in the United States. Nissan opened a truck-manufacturing facility in Tennessee in 1983, and made plans to begin manufacturing autos there in 1985. Honda opened a facility in Ohio in late 1983, and passed Volkswagen of America to become the fifth largest domestic manufacturer of autos in 1984. The industry was indeed undergoing dramatic change.

**Barriers to Entry**

**Economies of Scale**   Among the most important barriers to entry was the economic efficiency which can and must be achieved by size through volume production and sales. Volume was essential to recover the fixed costs of the large, continuing capital investment required in the industry. This was a major consideration in the recovery strategy of Chrysler. Becoming a specialized or partial line manufacturer or autos was specifically rejected in favor of maintaining the full line because of the need for a larger volume that could not have been attained with a partial line.

Integration of component manufacture needed in the assembly process also provided some absolute cost advantage. Integration was a practice of the healthiest, relatively larger volume manufacturers, with General Motors manufacturing about 62 percent of its component parts, Ford about 54 percent, and Chrysler less than half. Chrysler was required to divest itself of its non–auto-manufacturing activities and component-manufacturing facilities in order to raise operating funds in the early 1980s. This contributed to the reduction of Chrysler's break-even in its North American operations from 2.61 to 1.1 million units between 1979 and 1982. It later planned to resume some of its own parts manufacturing in an effort to reduce its unit variable costs, thus providing a higher variable margin. Maintaining such facilities raised the break-even (along with potential exposure and profit), which may explain why smaller manufacturers sourced more component parts.

**Capital Requirements**   Facilities, machinery, equipment, tooling, organizational expenses, and advertising were enormously expensive on inital entry as well as with occurrence of model and option changes. The high interest rates of 1979–1982 raised this barrier even higher. Capital investment needs over the 1980–1985 time frame were projected to be two to three times the historic trend levels. The primary reason was the need to design and develop the capacity to produce small, more efficient front-wheel-drive cars to compete with the imports in the growing small-car market segment. Capital investment of the domestic auto companies is shown in Exhibit 9.1.

**Product Differentiation**   New cars historically have been differentiated on the basis of physical differences, image, and distribution networks.

*Physical Differences.*   During the mid- and late 1950s, all of the American new-car producers introduced features on their traditionally low-priced models (Chevrolet, Ford, and Plymouth) which made them essentially as large as their largest cars. Luxury interiors, tail fins, high gross weight, long wheelbase, and comfort were among the physical attributes advertised. Through the mid-1970s, Ford continued to state in its annual reports that "superior styling [would] continue to be a major factor in car sales," while placing less emphasis on economy, reliability, workmanship, and safety. This is the same period when imports were stressing economy and reliability, and government regulations began to address safety, economy, and environmental controls.

Other features which traditionally have been tools in the differentiation process include transmissions (Hydramatic, Fluid Drive, DynaFlow), engines (the

**Exhibit 9.1** Domestic Auto Company Worldwide Capital Investment, 1975–1984 ($ millions)

| Year | General Motors | Ford | Chrysler | American Motors | Total (current $) | Total (1983 $) |
|------|------|------|------|------|------|------|
| 1975 | 2,237 | 956 | 384 | 89 | 3,666 | 6,303 |
| 1976 | 2,307 | 1,055 | 424 | 52 | 3,838 | 6,279 |
| 1977 | 3,647 | 1,762 | 723 | 47 | 6,179 | 9,529 |
| 1978 | 4,522 | 2,542 | 671 | 41 | 7,776 | 11,182 |
| 1979 | 5,366 | 3,440 | 749 | 62 | 9,597 | 12,700 |
| 1980 | 7,761 | 2,769 | 835 | 97 | 11,462 | 13,854 |
| 1981 | 9,741 | 2,227 | 456 | 186 | 12,610 | 13,928 |
| 1982 | 6,212 | 2,968 | 374 | 335 | 9,889 | 10,304 |
| 1983 | 4,007 | 2,333 | 1,057 | 261 | 7,658 | 7,658 |
| 1984[a] | 2,531 | 1,125 | 502 | 63 | 4,224 | NA |

[a]Numbers for 1984 are for net additions to property for the first six months of the year (through June); actual expenditure data are available on annual basis only.

*Source:* Motor Vehicle Manufacturers Association, company annual reports, and Economic Report of the President, 1984.

Rocket engine), suspension (independent), steering (power, rack and pinion), and brakes. Targeted segments and products were brought together through carefully researched and executed advertising campaigns.

Product feature emphasis began to change as a result of the gasoline shortage and price increases sparked by revolution in Iran and the resulting shortage of oil. Lee Iacocca, chairman and chief executive officer of Chrysler, appeared personally in his company's ads to convey a message of economy as well as trust, quality, reliability, and workmanship in Chrysler products, a change in emphasis which has been emulated by his competitors in recent years.

However, change is constant and the memory of the consumer is short. Consumers who became very fuel-efficiency-minded in the 1979–1980 period forgot quickly as they became accustomed to the unlimited availability of gasoline, albeit at higher prices. According to *Automotive Consumer Profile,* fuel economy has been replaced by dependability and workmanship as the most important decision points to the consumer. As sticker prices have steadily increased, so has the cost of the auto assumed greater importance to the consumer. Physical appearance seems to be important only when it is a negative to the consumer. Product differentiation strategies have reflected these trends.

*Image.* Product attributes were not the only ideas that advertising campaigns attempted to convey to the consumer. An evaluation by the potential buyer of the claims heard or visualized in advertising messages was based on a preconceived image of the manufacturer. Buyer loyalty is based in part on the reputation of the producer, and unsatisfactory experiences quickly bring about a change in buying patterns. Among the domestic producers, Chrysler's share of the total U.S. passenger-car production declined from 17.8 percent in 1969 to 10 percent in 1980.

Part of that decline was due to an image of a product with lesser overall quality than products produced by its competitors. A major obstacle to Chrysler's recovery was overcoming the image of a loser, of a manufacturer of inferior products that might not be around for long. When the purchase decision was between a foreign or domestic auto, it might be made on such perceptions of the domestic industry as seeming out of step with market realities, producing products with poor workmanship and reliability, but with high sticker prices. Concern for profits and unconcern for the consumer seems to be the message. As it was with Chrysler, the image problem is a continuing one for all domestic auto manufacturers as they vie with foreign producers in an increasingly competitive milieu.

Recall data and company statements seemed to indicate that progress in quality and workmanship was being made by American auto producers. However, negative consumer perceptions had not been overcome and continued to hamper efforts to create a positive image of domestic auto products.

*Distribution Networks.*   A well-financed, well-located, well-trained, responsive and aggressive national system of established dealers is essential to the well-being of the auto industry. Sales capability is important but after-market service is also important to customer satisfaction and loyalty. Both are functions of the dealer. For most auto purchasers, the dealer is their only contact with the manufacturer. A dealer who is successful in handling consumer problems before or after the sale can be a major attribute in developing the consumer's perception of the manufacturer and the product.

Despite various dealer assistance programs conducted by the auto manufacturers and $400 million earmarked by the Small Business Administration, almost 7 percent (1654) of the domestic auto dealers closed in 1980, as shown in Exhibit 9.2. Chrysler led the list, losing 13.5 percent and 600 of its dealers, followed by Ford (8 percent, 529), General Motors (3.2 percent, 365), and American Motors (7 percent, 163). However, the shakeout seemed to start and stop early in the period of crisis, and the dealer network was in place and operating as the recovery got under way in 1983.

## RECENT PERFORMANCE: TRENDS

Several trends have impacted the recent performance of the entire auto-manufacturing industry. These are of general import and will be discussed prior to the individual industry competitors.

## Japanese-American Cost Differential

One of the most serious problems faced by U.S. automakers was a significant production cost differential, particularly in small-car manufacture. Estimates of the differential magnitude varied but seemed to fall mostly around $2000, which gave the Japanese an advantage in the price to the U.S. consumer of about half that amount. This was an enormous advantage in a most important market seg-

**Exhibit 9.2** U.S. Car Dealers in Operation, 1979–1983

| Manufacturer/Dealer | 1979 | 1980 | 1981 | 1982 | 1983 |
|---|---|---|---|---|---|
| Chrysler | 4,434 | 3,834 | 3,693 | 3,645 | 3,864 |
| Ford | 6,582 | 6,053 | 5,685 | 5,414 | 5,508 |
| General Motors | 11,425 | 11,060 | 10,655 | 10,160 | 10,040 |
| American Motors | 2,317 | 2,154 | 1,579 | 1,564 | 1,526 |
| Volkswagen of America | 1,015 | 1,018 | 1,006 | 934 | 906 |
| Total | 25,773 | 24,119 | 22,618 | 21,717 | 21,844 |

*Source: Ward's Automotive Yearbooks.*

ment. Production causes could be found in productivity of the average worker, labor wage rates, component inventory management, and workmanship/quality control. Some additional part of the differential was due to the dollar-yen exchange rate. The best efforts of U.S. automakers to reduce or to eliminate the differential had been unsuccessful through mid-1985. Substantial progress in cost reductions through process automation and management techniques were matched by similar Japanese efforts with the result that the net difference remained essentially unchanged.

**Productivity of Labor**

According to company annual reports for 1980–83, productivity in U.S. auto-manufacturing operations showed an increase in per-worker output of 23 percent, while Japanese per-worker output dropped by about 15 percent. The improvement in U.S. worker productivity was due mostly to improved production processes and machinery and could probably be considered a continuing trend. The Japanese decline might have been due to lower capacity utilization and therefore could be short-term in nature.

Another factor affecting industry productivity was the number of models and options which the assembly line had to satisfy. The more required, the more complex and expensive was the production process. Yet another was the number of job/work classifications present in the production process. The Japanese had relatively fewer, which made it possible for workers to perform more than one function on the assembly line. American labor unions had historically negotiated many classifications and more labor specialization, resulting in more costly production.

Despite the factors which adversely affected productivity, U.S. motor vehicle industry output per hour had grown at a 2.5 percent long-term annual rate while the growth in the overall economy had been just 2.0 percent. The rate of capital investment and research and development had been higher in the auto industry and was probably responsible for the higher productivity. More variability was also noted in the output of the motor vehicle industry. Exhibit 9.3 compares the output per hour in the motor vehicle industry with the private sector, and both durable and nondurable goods manufacturing.

**Exhibit 9.3** Industry Output per Hour (1977 dollars), 1975–1983

| Year | Motor Vehicle Industry | Private Sector | Total Manufacturing | Durable Goods Manufacturing | Nondurable Goods Manufacturing |
|---|---|---|---|---|---|
| 1975 | 47.5 | 21.1 | 29.9 | 25.8 | 35.8 |
| 1976 | 53.1 | 22.0 | 31.3 | 27.2 | 37.3 |
| 1977 | 55.5 | 22.3 | 32.4 | 28.2 | 38.6 |
| 1978 | 55.2 | 22.4 | 32.5 | 28.3 | 38.9 |
| 1979 | 53.2 | 22.4 | 32.4 | 28.2 | 39.1 |
| 1980 | 49.4 | 21.9 | 32.2 | 27.8 | 39.0 |
| 1981 | 47.9 | 22.1 | 32.5 | 27.9 | 39.4 |
| 1982 | 48.9 | 21.8 | 32.2 | 27.0 | 39.8 |
| 1983 | 53.5 | 22.6 | 34.3 | 29.4 | 41.4 |

*Source:* U.S. Department of Labor, Bureau of Labor Statistics.

## Compensation Trends

Union and nonunion labor contributed heavily in forgone wages and salaries from existing contract and salary levels toward the $1.43 billion stakeholder contribution to nonfederally guaranteed assistance required by the Chrysler Corporation Loan Guarantee Act of 1979. This produced a labor cost advantage in Chrysler's favor of about $5 per hour and about $600 per unit manufactured. Some of this had been regained by labor, but the trends in recent labor settlements in the auto industry had essentially been neutral in their impact on productivity. That is, the additional cost was expected to be overcome by other productivity improvements such as more automated processes. Additionally, contracts negotiated by Ford and General Motors in the fall of 1984 provided for modest wage increases augmented by bonuses and profit sharing. This was expected to reverse a trend that saw real output exceeded by real compensation from 1979 through 1983. (See Exhibit 9.4.) The new contracts also required General Motors to contribute $1 billion and Ford $280 million to job security programs which provided protection to workers laid off because of technology or productivity improvements, but not because of demand decreases.

## Capacity Utilization

Trends in capacity utilization are shown in Exhibit 9.5. As with output per hour shown in Table 3, the variability in the motor vehicle and parts industry was greater than in all manufacturing.

## Resurgence of Larger Car Sales

One of the trends during the mid- and late 1970s emphasized the consumer demand for smaller, more efficient cars. This was caused in large part by the two oil shocks of 1973 and 1979. However, as the price of gasoline stabilized and its availability was no longer a problem, larger cars increased in sales. The memory

**Exhibit 9.4** Change in Real Output and Compensation in Motor Vehicle Manufacturing, 1960–1983.

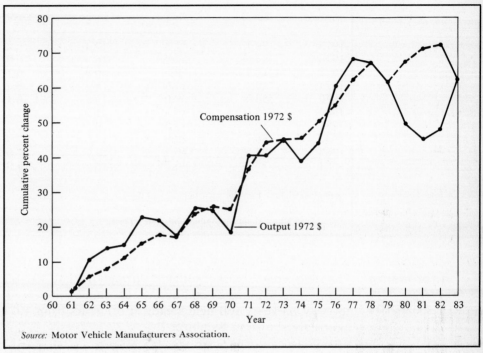

*Source:* Motor Vehicle Manufacturers Association.

**Exhibit 9.5** Capacity Utilization of Motor Vehicles and Parts Manufacturers, 1975–1984

| Year | All Manufacturing | Motor Vehicles and Parts | Year | All Manufacturing | Motor Vehicles and Parts |
|------|------|------|------|------|------|
| 1975 | 72.9 | 66.6 | 1980 | 79.6 | 60.3 |
| 1976 | 79.6 | 82.7 | 1981 | 79.4 | 62.0 |
| 1977 | 82.2 | 89.2 | 1982 | 71.1 | 56.2 |
| 1978 | 84.7 | 89.4 | 1983 | 75.3 | 71.6 |
| 1979 | 86.0 | 82.1 | 1984 | 81.7 | 86.0 |

*Source:* Motor Vehicles Manufacturers Association, First Quarter 1985 Economics Indicators.

of the auto owner in the United States is indeed a short one. This factor served to complicate the capital investment and product plans of the domestic manufacturers in that they had to offer a full line in order to achieve needed volume and satisfy the vagaries of consumer demand. Exhibit 9.6 traces the demand trends in the various retail segments.

**Exhibit 9.6** U.S. New Car Retail Sales by Market Segment, 1975–1984 (percent)

| Year | Small | Middle | Large | Luxury |
|------|-------|--------|-------|--------|
| 1975 | 29.1 | 47.3 | 17.4 | 6.2 |
| 1976 | 24.8 | 50.7 | 18.5 | 6.0 |
| 1977 | 27.1 | 46.5 | 20.3 | 6.1 |
| 1978 | 29.4 | 45.5 | 18.7 | 6.4 |
| 1979 | 38.5 | 39.9 | 15.2 | 6.4 |
| 1980 | 43.0 | 40.5 | 11.1 | 5.4 |
| 1981 | 40.8 | 42.3 | 10.4 | 6.5 |
| 1982 | 38.2 | 42.9 | 11.6 | 7.3 |
| 1983 | 33.3 | 46.1 | 13.0 | 7.6 |
| 1984 | 32.0 | 46.7 | 13.4 | 7.9 |

Definitions: Small—compact, subcompact; middle—intermediate, standard.

*Source:* Ford Motor Company Annual and 10-K reports.

## Increasing Average Age of Autos

The replacement market suffered through the late 1970s and early 1980s as the average age of autos owned by U.S. consumers increased. In 1970, the average age was 5.5 years and held steady at 5.7 years from 1971 through 1974. Later trends are shown in Exhibit 9.7.

## Break-Even

The reductions in break-even by the domestic manufacturers were difficult to determine simply because their operations were spread so widely and operations results were reported in aggregate form. However, it appears clear that break-even points were reduced substantially between 1979 and 1984. Actions taken included plant closures, reduction in union and nonunion labor, delaying product introduction, better matching of production and inventory needs, requiring suppliers to carry inventory, wage, and salary concessions, and work rule changes. Enormous investments in new and updated facilities, automated equipment, and management techniques have all contributed to more efficient operation.

## RECENT PERFORM-ANCE: CORPORATE STRATEGIES

The imports' overall share of the U.S. market fluctuated within a narrow range between 1980 and 1983 (high in 1982, 27.9 percent; low in 1983, 26.0 percent). In 1984, the share of an increasing market declined to 23.8 percent because of the absolute number limit imposed by the voluntary restraints. During the same time period, General Motors' share of the domestic market declined slightly while Ford and Chrysler shares increased slightly. AMC recovered about 0.5 percent of the market share lost in 1976.

Exhibits 9.8, 9.9, and 9.10 provide comparative figures on sales, income, and

**Exhibit 9.7** Average Age of Passenger Cars in Use in the U.S., 1974–1983

| Year | Years Old | Year | Years Old |
|------|-----------|------|-----------|
| 1974 | 5.7 | 1979 | 6.4 |
| 1975 | 6.0 | 1980 | 6.6 |
| 1976 | 6.2 | 1981 | 6.9 |
| 1977 | 6.2 | 1982 | 7.2 |
| 1978 | 6.3 | 1983 | 7.4 |

*Source:* Motor Vehicle Manufacturers Association and R. L. Polk and Co.

**Exhibit 9.8** Net Sales for U.S. Automakers, 1975–1984 ($ millions)

| Year | General Motors | Ford | Chrysler | American Motors |
|------|----------------|------|----------|-----------------|
| 1975 | 35,725 | 24,009 | 11,598 | 2,282 |
| 1976 | 47,181 | 28,839 | 12,240 | 2,315 |
| 1977 | 54,961 | 37,841 | 13,059 | 2,237 |
| 1978 | 63,221 | 42,784 | 13,618 | 2,585 |
| 1979 | 66,311 | 43,514 | 12,002 | 3,117 |
| 1980 | 57,728 | 37,085 | 9,225 | 2,553 |
| 1981 | 62,698 | 38,247 | 9,971 | 2,600 |
| 1982 | 60,026 | 37,067 | 10,040 | 2,900 |
| 1983 | 74,582 | 44,500 | 13,240 | 3,300 |
| 1984 | 83,648 | 51,911 | 19,508 | 3,750 |

*Source: Standard & Poor's Industry Surveys;* Motor Vehicle Manufacturers Association; company annual reports.

**Exhibit 9.9** Net Income (Loss) for U.S. Automakers, 1975–1984 ($ millions)

| Year | General Motors | Ford | Chrysler | American Motors |
|------|----------------|------|----------|-----------------|
| 1975 | 1,253 | 227 | (207) | (27) |
| 1976 | 2,903 | 983 | 328 | (46) |
| 1977 | 3,338 | 1,672 | 163 | 8 |
| 1978 | 3,508 | 1,589 | (205) | 37 |
| 1979 | 2,893 | 1,169 | (1,097) | 84 |
| 1980 | (763) | (1,543) | (1,710) | (198) |
| 1981 | 333 | (1,060) | (476) | (137) |
| 1982 | 963 | (658) | 170 | (154) |
| 1983 | 3,730 | 1,867 | 701 | (147) |
| 1984 | 4,517 | 2,907 | 2,380 | 15 |

*Source: Standard & Poor's Industry Surveys;* Motor Vehicle Manufacturers Association; company annual reports.

**Exhibit 9.10** U.S. Car Production, 1975–1984 (percent of domestic market)

| Year | General Motors | Ford | Chrysler | American Motors | Volkswagen of America | Honda of America |
|------|------|------|------|------|------|------|
| 1975 | 54.75 | 26.96 | 13.46 | 4.83 | — | — |
| 1976 | 57.60 | 24.18 | 15.70 | 2.52 | — | — |
| 1977 | 57.13 | 27.75 | 13.42 | 1.70 | — | — |
| 1978 | 57.61 | 27.88 | 12.28 | 1.79 | 0.44 | — |
| 1979 | 60.46 | 24.26 | 11.03 | 2.19 | 2.06 | — |
| 1980 | 63.79 | 20.51 | 10.02 | 2.59 | 3.09 | — |
| 1981 | 62.46 | 21.12 | 11.99 | 1.75 | 2.68 | — |
| 1982 | 62.55 | 21.76 | 11.84 | 2.16 | 1.66 | 0.03 |
| 1983 | 59.22 | 22.95 | 12.98 | 2.97 | 1.29 | 0.59 |
| 1984 | 58.82 | 21.50 | 14.40 | 2.56 | 1.28 | 1.44 |

*Source: Ward's Automotive Yearbooks.*

production for the domestic competitors discussed below. Exhibit 9.11 shows the distribution of market share among all competitors. Trends in each of the areas are important to the discussion which follows.

**Chrysler**  Chrysler was a full-line manufacturer of passenger cars, light trucks, and vans sold under the Plymouth, Dodge, and Chrysler nameplates. It also imported and sold passenger cars and pickup trucks manufactured in Japan by Mitsubishi. Other corporate activities included Chrysler Financial, a credit company which financed the sales of Chrysler products. Chrysler had been forced to divest itself of most of its other subsidiaries, including a marine engine company, real estate, and Chrysler Defense, which manufactured tanks for the U.S. Army. Of its foreign operations, only those in Mexico and Canada remained. Divestiture was required to raise cash or reduce losses, or to meet the provisions of the Chrysler Loan Guarantee Act of 1979, a federal statute enacted to provide financial assistance to the company in the form of loan guarantees to a total of $1.5 billion. At the end of 1982, Chrysler was essentially a North American company without overseas operations.

Chrysler lost its position as the number two manufacturer of cars to Ford in 1948. From that time until 1962, Chrysler's trend was generally downward. This was the period when American Motors made its dramatic comeback and other independents enjoyed a short-lived modicum of success. In 1962, Chrysler began a climb which ended in 1969 with over 17 percent of total domestic production, then began another downward slide to its 1980 levels and near bankruptcy. The years 1978 through 1981 were years to forget as the company lost a total of $3,488,000,000 and was forced to appeal to the federal government for assistance. Initial requests were for loans or tax concessions, but little enthusiasm was found in either the administration or the Congress for this form of assistance, and the request was modified to loan guarantees.

Chrysler's predicament generated shock waves not only through the auto

**Exhibit 9.11** U.S. Car Market Share, 1975–1984 (percent of total market)

| Year | General Motors | Ford | Chrysler | American Motors | Volkswagen of America | Honda | Other Imports |
|------|------|------|------|------|------|------|------|
| 1975 | 43.83 | 23.61 | 12.25 | 3.73 | 3.10 | 1.19 | 12.29 |
| 1976 | 47.61 | 22.62 | 13.67 | 2.45 | 2.00 | 1.49 | 10.16 |
| 1977 | 46.31 | 23.40 | 12.00 | 1.65 | 2.35 | 2.00 | 12.29 |
| 1978 | 47.79 | 23.54 | 11.05 | 1.51 | 2.14 | 2.43 | 11.54 |
| 1979 | 46.26 | 20.81 | 10.13 | 1.52 | 2.77 | 3.31 | 15.20 |
| 1980 | 45.86 | 17.20 | 8.77 | 1.98 | 3.00 | 4.18 | 19.01 |
| 1981 | 44.49 | 16.56 | 9.85 | 1.97 | 2.87 | 4.35 | 19.91 |
| 1982 | 44.06 | 16.87 | 9.95 | 1.88 | 2.00 | 4.58 | 20.66 |
| 1983 | 44.15 | 17.11 | 10.36 | 2.47 | 1.77 | 4.37 | 19.77 |
| 1984 | 44.15 | 19.05 | 9.49 | 1.83 | 0.71 | 1.29 | 23.50 |

*Source: Ward's Automotive Yearbooks;* company annual reports.

industry but throughout related independent industries, and state and local governments as well. The impact of a Chrysler failure on communities with substantial Chrysler activity and employment could easily be imagined. The terms of the Chrysler Corporation Loan Guarantee Act required Chrysler to obtain contributions from all entities with a stake in its continued existence. Concessions were obtained from the Canadian government, and financial aid from the states of Indiana, Michigan, Illinois, and Delaware. The United Auto Workers and nonunion employees, both salaried and hourly, were required to make concessions from contracts already negotiated and signed. Suppliers delayed collections and payments of interest on debt and accepted equity in place of some debt. Banks, foreign and domestic, and other creditors allowed debt restructure at least twice.

In order to receive the government loan guarantees, Chrysler pledged the entire assets of the company as collateral securing the loans. Of the estimated asset total of $2.4 billion, the company pledged $2.1 billion to the U.S. government and the remainder to other lenders. The Canadian assets were pledged to the Canadian government. Had the company defaulted on its loans, the interesting and perhaps unprecedented situation of several government entities owning a major U.S. industrial corporation would have occurred. The UAW was granted a seat on the Chrysler board of directors in return for its concessions. UAW President Douglas Fraser was the first occupant of the seat, a position he temporarily relinquished when the company and the union entered into labor negotiations. Although not uncommon in Europe, labor membership on large corporate boards is rare in the United States. The trends in labor contracts toward profit sharing and bonuses, job security provisions, and bonuses based on corporate performance may whet labor's interest in retaining and enlarging its participation in management.

In all, Chrysler found it necessary to take down $1.2 billion in loan guarantees in 1980–1981. The year 1982 represented a moral victory for the company as it posted $170 million in net income, despite the fact that the entire amount was due to gain on the sale of Chrysler Defense to General Dynamics. Economic recovery and growth became strong realities in 1983 and the company was able to repay all loans which had been guaranteed by the federal government, make early repayment of loans made by Michigan and Illinois, offer a successful equity issue, and post a net income of $701 million. Its performance was even better in 1984, when it posted a net income of $2,380,000,000.

Chrysler's survival strategy rested on an improving economy, increasing demand for autos, regaining part of its lost market share, and dramatic cost reduction measures. Its primary product was to be the K-car, a new four-cylinder, front-wheel-drive platform which was to serve as the model for the entire Chrysler line. Two models, the Aries and the Reliant, were introduced in October 1980 and immediately failed to attract sales because of high sticker prices. The latter was due to a marketing mistake which loaded the cars with options when the consumer was expecting something to compete in the lower-price segment. The success of the K-car can be illustrated by the fact that it serves as the platform for the 1985 model line, including LeBaron, Chrysler E Class, Dodge 400/600, New Yorker, Daytona, and Laser. The practice of using derivatives from the same basic platform has saved Chrysler the $1 billion investment which normally accompanies the development of each new model.

The other elements on which Chrysler's strategy rested cooperated also. The economy rebounded in terms of real growth, lower inflation and interest rates, and higher employment.

Concessions from union and nonunion labor pursuant to the Chrysler Corporation Loan Guarantee Act saved the company almost $600 per unit manufactured from 1980 to 1983. Concessions from vendors through delayed payments and acceptance of equity for debt, delay in new product development, and plant closure added millions more in cost reduction. The net result was a reduction in break-even in its North American operations from 2.61 million units in 1979, a level above its production capacity, to 1.1 million in 1981. Chrysler attained these reductions earlier than its domestic competitors, probably because of the requirements of the Loan Guarantee Act.

Having survived as a full-line manufacturer of autos, Chrysler entered the second half of the 1980s with an optimistic outlook. Chrysler would continue to do much as it did during the 1981–1984 period. The company intended to continue its relationship with Mitsubishi, importing as many small cars as it could for sale under the Chrysler nameplates. The Omni and Horizon were scheduled for replacement in 1986–1987, and could be replaced by a new subcompact produced either in the United States, in Korea, or in Japan. The K-car platform, however, will continue to form the base for its line. As other manufacturers have found, the rear-wheel-drive intermediate was still popular. Chrysler will manufacture its entry, the Fifth Avenue, as long as a market remains.

**Ford**    The principal business of the Ford Motor Company was the manufacture, assembly, and sale of cars, trucks, and accessories. These activities constituted 90 to 93 percent of sales revenue between 1970 and 1984. Ford had foreign manufacturing at assembly plants in West Germany, Great Britain, Canada, Spain, Brazil,

Australia, Argentina, and Mexico, in addition to other countries. It enjoyed 14.4 percent of the worldwide sales of cars and trucks. Ford's foreign operations in 1980 brought a net profit of $475 million, but its North American operations produced a $2,018,000,000 loss. In 1984, both foreign and domestic operations were profitable, contributing to a net income of $2,907,000,000.

Ford was a full-line manufacturer of passenger autos sold under the Ford, Mercury, and Lincoln nameplates. It was also the second leading domestic manufacturer of trucks, with a market share hovering between 30 and 32 percent between 1975 and 1983, but dropping to 28 percent in 1984. Ford's declining truck market has been accompanied by a corresponding increase in foreign imports and a consumer demand shift to the compact-truck segment, where Ford's market share is smaller than its share of other segments.

During the 1970s, Ford's production levels averaged between 25 and 29 percent of total U.S. production. However, industry observers commented that the sharp decrease to 20.5 percent in 1980 might represent a lasting erosion of its U.S. market position. Ford lagged behind General Motors in downsizing and revising its product line to position itself for retention of its historical market share. Ford was the last of the Big Three domestic manufacturers to return to profitability, losing $3,261,000,000 between 1980 and 1982, before posting large profits in the recovery years 1983–1984. Ford's tardiness in downsizing was aggravated by these losses, which retarded its ability to make the huge capital investments necessary to make new fuel-efficient autos. Its capital outlay in 1979–1980 was $6.2 billion, but its 1981–1985 needs were projected at $4 billion per year. Ford's credit rating was lowered to A in October 1980.

Ford was carried throughout 1982 by its subcompact, Escort, the best-selling domestic car in the United States during the model year. The most significant product line action taken by Ford in 1983 was the introduction of the new aerodynamically styled Tempo and Thunderbird. Together with continued good sales of Escort and a much leaner, more efficient management, Ford was able to return to profitable operations. Ford did, however, seem to be the last of the Big Three to actively cut its break-even and introduce new models in response to new consumer demand for more efficient, front-wheel-drive autos. Continuation of full-size Grand Marquis Mercury and Continental autos was again in recognition of the resurgence of demand for larger autos.

Ford lowered the break-even on its North American operations from approximately 3.6 million units in 1979 to about 2.5 million in 1983, and to 2.3 million in 1984. Between 1979 and 1984, Ford closed seven plants and reduced its payroll by 60,000 workers.

As it had in its response to the development of the small-car demand, Ford continued to show uncertainty in its further product strategy. The company seemed to be stressing the import of cars for sale in the United States with Ford nameplates in its plans to build a 130,000-capacity plant in Mexico to assemble a Mazda-designed subcompact. The Tempo seemed to be the choice in the compact market for the next few years. A new front-wheel-drive intermediate was slated for 1986 introduction to accompany the Thunderbird in that market. Luxury/full-size car production would continue as long as demand warranted.

**General Motors**

General Motors was a highly integrated business, primarily operating in the auto industry as a manufacturer, assembler, and vendor of autos, trucks, and related accessories. Nonauto products included diesel engines, locomotives, turbines, aircraft engines, ordnance transmissions, and inertial navigation, guidance, and control systems. Historically, more than 90 percent of its annual net revenue had come from automotive products. General Motors also operated a financial group comprised of the General Motors Acceptance Corporation and General Motors Insurance Corporation. It had overseas operations in 33 countries with plants in Canada, Australia, Brazil, West Germany, and the United Kingdom. Contributions to 1975–1979 net income from foreign operations ranged from a low of 11 percent in 1977 to a high of 21 percent of 1979.

General Motors was a full-line manufacturer of passenger autos sold under Chevrolet, Pontiac, Buick, Oldsmobile, and Cadillac nameplates. It also manufactured trucks, vans, and specialty vehicles and marketed a small pickup truck manufactured in Japan until it introduced its own model in 1982.

General Motors had been the market share and production leader in the U.S. auto industry since displacing Ford in the early 1930s. Between 1962 and 1984, General Motors had manufactured more than half of the autos produced in the United States every year except 1970 (45.5 percent) and 1974 (48.8 percent). Steadily increasing unit sales accompanied the production record through 1979. These trends are observable in Exhibits 9.10 and 9.11. However, the increasing volume was accompanied by decreasing profit margins. The year 1980 saw a substantially reduced production and sales volume performance, resulting in a net loss of $762.5 million, the first since 1921. General Motors blamed inflation, economic sluggishness, high interest rates, and a shift in consumer preference to smaller cars for the loss. A return to profitable operations did occur in 1981, two years ahead of its primary domestic competitors, but profit levels generated were considered insufficient to generate the capital needed for long-term success. But the relative strength of General Motors did seem to be indicative of its higher levels of previous capital investment and earlier downsizing of its line.

General Motors had reduced its break-even using the same cost reduction methods its competitors had found successful. Its break-even had been lowered from the 1982 level for its worldwide operations of 6.5 million units to 5.6 million in 1984. General Motors' break-even was estimated to be as high as 8.4 million units in 1979.

General Motors' product line strategy appeared to be better defined than that of its domestic competitors. It had begun a joint venture with Toyota to jointly manufacture autos in one of GM's closed plants in Fremont, California. The company position seemed to be that it needed Toyota's technology in order to successfully produce a small car at a competitive price. The product was called the Nova, and the first models appeared in showrooms around the country on June 13, 1985. Other U.S. automakers were not overjoyed with the prospect of a joint venture between two of their largest competitors. Chrysler sued to stop the venture as a violation of antitrust statutes. As of mid-1986, however, such attempts to obstruct the GM-Toyota venture had not proved successful.

General Motors also announced the Saturn project, in which the company planned to invest more than $1 billion. General Motors created a new division to develop and produce a small car using totally redesigned management and production processes and techniques. The apparent goal was to improve its ability to compete with the Japanese on a cost basis.

General Motors also had plans to exploit its partial ownership of Suzuki and Isuzu to import substantial numbers of small cars for sale in the U.S. market.

It was in its major acquisitions of Electronic Data Systems and Hughes Aircraft that General Motors had confirmed its intent to become a diversified holder participating in several industries. The two new members of the GM family cost the automaker almost $8.5 billion. Another investment in a Japanese manufacturer of industrial robots was producing machines for GM's updated, efficient assembly lines.

A major reorganization of its auto manufacturing divisions was announced by GM in January 1984. In an effort to avoid duplication in its firm, GM established two new groups, one for small-car development and the other for large-car development. The small-car group included Chevrolet, Pontiac, and General Motors of Canada, and the large-car group included Oldsmobile, Buick and Cadillac. Better response to rapidly changing consumer buying patterns and better in-house coordination and communications were also expected from the new organization.

**American Motors Corporation**

American Motors was a manufacturer and seller of compact and subcompact cars, and specialty vehicles. It ceased production of intermediate-size autos in 1978. The company lost a total of $635 million between 1980 and 1983 before completing 1984 with a modest profit ($15 million).

In December 1980, American Motors shareholders approved a financing plan which made the French automaker, Renault, a 46 percent partner. Options included in the plan could make Renault a majority owner with up to 59 percent of the equity.

The centerpiece of American Motors' future product plans and its strategy was a new-generation fuel-efficient subcompact designed by Renault and built by AMC in its Kenosha, Wisconsin, plant. The Alliance, as it was called, began production in June 1982 and, along with increasing sales of the company's venerable Jeep, helped soften its 1983 performance and turn in a marginal gain in 1984.

The future of American Motors as a U.S. auto manufacturer was very much in doubt. Despite improving sales, the company's 1984 performance was marginally profitable. Labor problems at the Kenosha plant made uninterrupted production of its major attraction, the Alliance, questionable. Renault was having trouble of its own in its domestic markets. Clearly, the survival of the company as a U.S. auto manufacturer depended on Renault's willingness and ability to provide the continuing cash infusions and capital investment essential to modernization and updating of both the AMC product line and its manufacturing facilities.

**Imports**  Retail sales of imported autos had increased from 29,000 in 1952 to 2.9 million in 1980 and 2.5 million in 1984. The import share of the U.S. market had risen from less than 1 percent to more than 27 percent in 1982, dropping slightly to 23.5 percent in 1984. The first significant numbers of imports to sell here were produced in West Germany, primarily by Volkswagen. In 1957, West German imports held 57.4 percent of the import market and 8.7 percent of the total sales in the United States. These figures slipped to 12 percent and 3.4 percent, respectively, in 1980 as Japanese imports came on strong. In 1980, Japanese imports garnered about 80 percent of the U.S. import market, but they dropped slightly in 1984 due to voluntary restraints on exports to the United States.

The import market has gone through three phases. Before 1948, only expensive imports were sold in the United States. From the mid-1950s until 1975 when Toyota assumed leadership, Volkswagen held over half of the import market. The generally accepted explanation given by industry observers for the ascendance of the Japanese import included an accurate reading of the U.S. consumer's reaction to the gasoline shortages of 1973–1974, the increasing cost of fuel, and the production of high-mileage, efficient, quality small cars. The corollary was the misreading of the same market by U.S. automakers, who continued to make big cars while giving lip service to the production of small cars. Until 1979, no effective large-scale effort to counter that penetration of the small-car market was attempted by U.S. car manufacturers. It was in fact ceded to the Japanese and others. A major reason for the disinterest of the U.S. automakers was the smaller profit margin on smaller cars.

The sporadic efforts of the U.S. manufacturers to compete in the small-car market included Ford's Pinto, Maverick, and Bobcat; Chevrolet's Vega; and Chrysler's Aspen and Volare. None was marketed or advertised heavily and all had frequent, substantial maintenance or other problems which produced a negative product image to the customer. This image of poor design and workmanship in small cars, when superimposed on a worsening overall image of the auto industry as held by the American consumer, contrasted dramatically with the widely held favorable perception of quality in imports, especially in Japanese imports.

Much pressure was exerted by the U.S. government on the Japanese government and car manufacturers to voluntarily limit exports to the United States in 1981. The catalyst for the effort was of course the deteriorating U.S. economy and the accompanying decline in demand for autos. The domestic automakers were not equipped to fight the Japanese in an open market because their facilities were not as efficient, nor were they designed to produce large numbers of small cars. Efforts to establish U.S. trade barriers were resisted despite heavy pressure from lawmakers from states which depended heavily on auto manufacture. The Japanese agreed to voluntary restraints in 1981 and continued them for four years. The Reagan administration did not ask for renewal when they expired on March 31, 1985.

Additional pressures were exerted on foreign companies, particularly the Japanese, to establish manufacturing facilities in the United States. Initially, the companies expressed some reluctance to do so because of high labor rates, poor workmanship, frequent work stoppages by unionized workers, distance from suppliers located overseas, the high capital investment required, and the fluctating dollar-yen relationship. However, Nissan opened a plant in 1983 for the assembly of trucks and planned to begin assembly of autos there in 1985. Honda opened a car assembly plant in Marysville, Ohio, in 1983. Volkswagen had an assembly plant in Westmoreland, Pennsylvania, and a stamping plant in Charleston, West Virginia. A second assembly plant in Sterling Heights, Michigan, which was never opened due to lagging U.S. sales, was sold to Chrysler in 1983 for $150 million.

The Japanese had a very strong competitive position in the world auto markets but had made particularly deep inroads into the American market, which U.S. automakers had considered their own for 70 years. In addition to reading the U.S. consumer correctly and being the beneficiary of domestic automakers' mistakes, the Japanese had developed some important comparative advantages which produced the per-unit cost advantage discussed earlier. These are summarized here:

- *Greater Productivity.* Management systems and production techniques resulted in less waste in the use of all resources including labor and materials. Fewer work classifications also increased worker productivity.
- *Lower Wage Rates.* Japanese production workers were paid about two-thirds of the wages paid Americans for similar work.
- *Closer Government Relations.* Government and business in Japan and other countries were not cast in the roles of adversaries, but instead coordinated on key issues such as taxes, trade, and other regulation.

Exhibit 9.12 indicates the depth of import penetration into the U.S. car market.

**Exhibit 9.12** Domestic and Import Sales, 1975–1984 (units 000)

| Year | Domestic | Imports[a] | | Total | Share of U.S. Market (%) | |
| | | From Japan | Total | Total | Japan | Total Import |
|------|----------|-----------|-------|-------|-------|-------------|
| 1975 | 7,053 | 808 | 1,571 | 8,624 | 9.4 | 18.2 |
| 1976 | 8,611 | 942 | 1,499 | 10,110 | 9.3 | 14.8 |
| 1977 | 9,109 | 1,388 | 2,074 | 11,183 | 12.4 | 18.5 |
| 1978 | 9,312 | 1,357 | 2,002 | 11,314 | 12.0 | 17.7 |
| 1979 | 8,341 | 1,770 | 2,332 | 10,673 | 16.6 | 21.9 |
| 1980 | 6,581 | 1,906 | 2,398 | 8,979 | 21.2 | 26.7 |
| 1981 | 6,209 | 1,859 | 2,327 | 8,536 | 21.8 | 27.3 |
| 1982 | 5,759 | 1,802 | 2,223 | 7,982 | 22.6 | 27.9 |
| 1983 | 6,795 | 1,916 | 2,387 | 9,182 | 20.9 | 26.0 |
| 1984 | 7,952 | 1,906 | 2,439 | 10,391 | 18.3 | 23.8 |

[a]Includes captive imports made by foreign companies and sold in the United States under U.S. manufacturers' nameplates.

*Source:* First-quarter 1985 economic indicators, Motor Vehicle Manufacturers Association; *Ward's Automotive Reports.*

**GOVERN-**
**MENT REGU-**
**LATIONS**

In addition to its direct involvement in the recovery of Chrysler through the guarantee of loans, the federal government played a primary role in the regulation of the industry. Not surprisingly, the industry placed major responsibility on government regulation for the problems it had encountered in the late 1970s and early 1980s. The impact and importance of current regulations to the industry are discussed below in consumer protection categories. Exhibit 9.13 indicates the retail price impact of improvements in emission control, safety, and other categories of consumer protection.

**Environmental**

The Clean Air Act of 1970 together with its 1977 amendments was administered by the Environmental Protection Agency and had as a prime purpose the curbing of specific air pollutants emitted by motor vehicle engines. The big offender was the automobile and the areas of most severe pollution from autos were urban, for example, the Los Angeles basin. The pollutants were hydrocarbons, carbon monoxide, and nitrogen oxides. Allowable levels of emission were expressed in grams of pollutant per mile traveled (GPM) as measured by a standard federal test procedure. Emission standards had to be met over the first 50,000 miles or five years of operation, whichever came first. California had been permitted to impose more stringent controls than those required by the federal legislation, necessitating the installation of additional emission control equipment on cars destined for delivery in that state. The standards required of all three pollutants became progressively more stringent, with new lower levels required in 1978–1979, 1980, and 1981. Chrysler requested and received a two-year waiver from the 1981 carbon monoxide standards, and other manufacturers had been granted waivers on an engine-by-engine basis. Major industry concerns seem to center on continual tightening of emission standards, shifting emphasis from initial certification to in-use certification for engines after extended use periods, and emissions and fuel economy test procedures used by the EPA. Concern for acid rain, chlorofluorocarbons, asbestos, and other hazardous air pollutants is present also. The cost of emission controls totals $1223.28 (1983 dollars) per unit, as estimated from Bureau of Labor Statistics data.

**Energy**

Congress enacted the Energy Policy and Conservation Act in 1975. Title III, Part A, established passenger-car average fuel economy standards at 18 miles per gallon for model year 1978, and at 27.5 for model year 1985 and thereafter. The secretary of transportation was given the responsibility for setting post-1985 standards subject to Congressional approval. The Energy Tax Act of 1978 imposed a progressive tax on passenger cars whose combined miles-per-gallon rating was generally 5 miles per gallon below the standard. These actions were taken in the aftermath of the gasoline shortages and oil embargos of 1973–1974 as part of a program to lessen oil consumption and limit dependence on foreign

**Exhibit 9.13** Average Retail Price Increase of New Car Quality Improvements, 1968–1984 ($ per unit)

| Model Year | Initial Value (dollars) | | | | 1983 Dollars Total |
| | Federal Requirements | | Other[b] | Total | |
| | Safety | Emissions | | | |
|---|---|---|---|---|---|
| 1968 | 29.65 | 16.00 | −00.70 | 44.95 | 88.10 |
| 1969 | 14.00 | .00 | −13.00 | 1.00 | 1.93 |
| 1970 | 7.50 | 5.50 | 33.00 | 46.00 | 86.05 |
| 1971 | .00 | 19.00 | −25.00 | −6.00 | −10.74 |
| 1972 | 2.00 | 6.00 | 12.00 | 20.00 | 36.20 |
| 1973 | 85.60 | 27.70 | 10.50 | 123.80 | 224.08 |
| 1974 | 107.60 | 1.40 | 8.90 | 117.90 | 201.60 |
| 1975 | 10.70 | 119.20 | .00 | 129.90 | 205.25 |
| 1976 | −4.60 | 7.60 | −5.40 | −2.40 | −3.55 |
| 1977 | 6.95 | 14.30 | 37.90 | 59.15 | 83.39 |
| 1978 | .00 | 9.99 | 40.13 | 50.12 | 65.67 |
| 1979 | 5.75 | 12.10 | 28.50 | 46.35 | 56.08 |
| 1980 | 13.29 | 118.04 | 110.18 | 241.51 | 270.47 |
| 1981 | 4.29 | 465.65[a] | 59.91 | 530.85 | 562.69 |
| 1982 | .00 | 84.68[a] | 41.64 | 126.32 | 128.84 |
| 1983 | .00 | 64.65[a] | 63.39 | 128.04 | 128.04 |
| 1984 | −12.09 | 58.89[a] | 63.28 | 110.08 | 110.08 |
| Total | 271.64 | 1,031.70 | 465.23 | 1,767.57 | 2,234.18 |

[a]Includes changes to improve fuel economy and emissions control.
[b]Includes improved warranties, corrosion protection, changes in standard equipment.
*Note:* Because of limitations in BLS methodology, annual figures may not be additive year to year (e.g., models selected may change). Annual figures do not necessarily indicate that manufacturers fully recovered the cost of federal requirements in a particular year. Figures do not include data for import sources or the cost of California emissions requirements.

*Source:* Computed by Motor Vehicles Manufacturers Association from Bureau of Labor Statistics data.

oil. Gasoline consumption accounted for almost 40 percent of oil used in the United States, and imports accounted for 50 percent of our overall consumption.

Through 1985 no domestic cars for consumer use have been taxed for not meeting the goals; however, 1986 requires tax on cars with EPA ratings less than 22.5 miles per gallon.

**Safety**　Congress enacted the National Traffic and Motor Vehicle Safety Act of 1966 in an effort to reduce traffic accidents and resulting deaths and injuries. In the period 1961–1966, the death rate per million miles traveled rose from 4.92 to 5.48, an increase of 11 percent. The act charged the secretary of transportation with setting federal motor vehicle safety standards. The government addressed not only motor vehicles as part of a highway safety program but also developed programs to improve driver performance and eliminate roadway hazards. The safety requirements for new autos issued between 1968 and 1984 increased the retail price of a new auto by an average of $465.23 (1983 dollars), as estimated from Bureau of Labor Statistics data.

The issue of mandatory passive restraints for passengers has elicited the most controversy from consumer advocates, government, and industry. The industry position is that properly worn seat belts offer the best immediate means for reducing injury and death in auto accidents. Consumer advocates take the position that auto users cannot be relied upon to use seat belts and need the protection of a passive restraint, such as an air bag. The status of the issue is that the Transportation Department has published a final rule that will require the installation of passive restraints unless states with two-thirds of the U.S. population pass mandatory seat belt laws before April 1, 1989.

Other safety issues include five-mile-per-hour bumper standards, truck safety standards, and penalties for safety act violation.

**Economy**   The sensitivity of auto industry performance to overall economy performance was illustrated by the 1979–1981 recession's impact on auto sales. Various federal policies such as monetary and fiscal, budget deficits, and tax reform are of concern to the auto industry as they impact both the consumer and industry.

**International Policy**   Perhaps the most important of the international policy issues facing the auto industry is the degree to which protection of the industry will be afforded by government policy. For four years beginning in 1981, Japanese exports to the United States were limited voluntarily by action of the Japanese government. These voluntary restraints expired on March 31, 1985, and the Reagan administration did not request their renewal. Instead, the position was taken that the transition to health of the domestic automakers had been completed and it was time to return to an open market. The restraints had benefited the automakers but had cost the consumer in terms of higher auto prices. However, there is still strong sentiment in Congress to retaliate in some measure against the Japanese for keeping many of their markets closed to foreign competition. In addition to further limiting imports, another possible action by Congress could require a certain level of domestic content in products sold in the United States. The prevailing notion is that opening the U.S. market to unlimited competition has led to job losses with resulting damage to the U.S. economy.

**Industry Attitude Toward Regulation**

Auto manufacturers predictably argue for regulation where they perceive that protection of the industry will result, and against regulation where they perceive the result as confining or damaging to their competitive position. Some specific criticisms of government action are outlined below.

- *Regulation Hurts Smaller Companies.*  The financial burden imposed on large or small companies is about equal. Smaller companies must spread the burden over smaller volume with a resulting higher compliance cost per unit, which in turn raises the market price of the smaller company's product.
- *Capital Requirements.*  Substantial capital requirements are necessary to ensure compliance. This again penalizes the smaller company, whose access to capital markets may be more limited. Periods of high interest exacerbate this problem.
- *Capital Is Limited.*  Allocation of resources to regulation compliance lessens the amount available for other purposes, such as research and development. The loss of comparative advantage may be the result.
- *General Motors/Toyota Venture.*  Chrysler sued to stop the joint GM-Toyota venture in building the Nova. This is an example of the sort of government action which would be regarded as friendly by some members of the industry but unfriendly toward others. The Chrysler Loan Guarantee Act of 1979 was another example of regulation seen as friendly by Chrysler but not as friendly to other auto companies.

**Reagan Administration Attitude Toward Regulation**

When President Reagan assumed office in 1981, he signaled a major effort to lessen industry regulation. The auto industry expected less avid enforcement of safety, environmental, and efficiency regulations and some change in the overall regulatory environment. This has not occurred to the extent that the initial rhetoric and flurry of activity indicated it would, and certainly not to the extent hoped for by the auto industry. Part of the problem has been the mixed attitude of industry, as indicated above. Not all industry is opposed to all regulation; opposition is limited to those areas where individual benefits can be realized by deregulation. Where regulation protects or enhances advantages in the marketplace, then support for change is not forthcoming. Generally, the administration favored a market as free from government intervention as possible.

**THE FUTURE**

Considerations for the future include import restrictions, energy, image, labor, government regulation, worldwide demand, and the ability of labor, industry, and government to address these problems.

**Import Restrictions**  Voluntary restraints, tariffs, export-import quotas, and domestic content are all considerations which will affect the future performance of the domestic auto industry.

**Energy**  Consumer buying patterns have been greatly affected by the availability and cost of energy. The shortage of gasoline was responsible for the large increases in import market share and the investment programs of domestic automakers to produce efficient front-wheel-drive cars. But the memories of the consumer are short and their loyalties to market segments fickle. Should energy prices remain stable, consumer preference for larger cars in the U.S. market may be expected to develop further. However, the next oil shock will produce a reversal toward smaller cars again.

**Image**  The perceptions of quality, price, and consumer satisfaction are important factors in purchase decisions. American automakers have made important progress toward retooling their image. They must not allow that progress to reverse itself.

**Labor**  Labor has contributed much toward the recovery of the U.S. auto industry in terms of forgone compensation and unemployment. A larger voice in management, more profit sharing, retraining in case of technological obsolescence, and other job security measures may be in the autoworker's future. Labor must not, however, forget that one of the reasons for the landed-price disparity between Japanese imports and American cars is the high wage paid to labor and the lesser productivity of the American worker. If the U.S. auto industry is to enjoy long-term prosperity, some of these differences must be narrowed or eliminated entirely.

**Government Regulation**  Regulation of the auto industry in terms of safety, environmental, and efficiency considerations will probably continue. These appear to be valid interventions by government in the marketplace.

**Worldwide Demand**  Expansion of the worldwide industry seems to rest on the development of demand in countries where demand is now minimal. This development will depend on the rate of infrastructure and road development, and the regulatory environment in the developing country.

**Problem Solving**

The solution to these and other problems faced by the auto industry probably depends on the ability of the interested parties—labor, industry, and government—to work together in addressing them, not as adversaries but as partners with overlapping interests in the development of the marketplace.

# 10  Lee Iacocca's Chrysler

Ernest R. Nordtvedt
Loyola University in New Orleans

*I am happy to tell you today that in the second quarter of this year (1981) just completed, Chrysler earned a net profit of $12 million. . . . Now if we had returned to profitability in a booming car market it would have been a remarkable achievement. But to do it against all the odds, in spite of double-digit inflation and a 20 percent prime rate, in the most depressed market in 50 years, is maybe a little miracle. . . . We've been accused of adjusting the books just a little. Let me say this is a genuine operating profit. . . . Chrysler has fought its way back to profitability, and everyone associated with this company has reason to be proud.*—Lee Iacocca, chairman and chief executive officer, Chrysler Corporation, at the National Press Club, Washington, D.C., July 22, 1981.

**INTRODUC-TION**  Much white water has passed under the bridge since Lee Iacocca was elected chairman of the board and chief executive officer of the Chrysler Corporation on September 20, 1979, after John Riccardo's sudden retirement amid the rising crescendo of Chrysler's financial problems. A quarterly net profit of $12 million (actually $11.6 million) on sales of $3 billion is not usually an event that sees a CEO proclaiming it as something of which "everyone associated with this company has reason to be proud." The excitement is placed in perspective, however, when Chrysler's record of the previous seven years is examined: American market share declining from 16 percent to 8.8 percent, net losses exceeding net profit by $2.7 billion, and loss per share of common stock totaling $46.72 in the period 1978 through 1980 alone.

Much has changed at Chrysler in Mr. Iacocca's tenure, and for the first four years, many of the changes were beyond his control. The overriding control mechanism in Chrysler's management picture between January 1980 and August 1983 was the Chrysler Corporation Loan Guarantee Act of 1979 (the act), which provided loan guarantees by the federal government up to a total of $1.5 billion and was the centerpiece of a massive effort to ward off Chrysler's bankruptcy. Along with the guarantees, however, came a variety of preconditions that in themselves produced some far-reaching changes. Relationships between the company and the federal, state, and other jurisdictions where Chrysler does business, and between the company and its suppliers, banks and other lenders, its shareholders, and its major union have all changed substantively as a result

"Lee Iacocca's Chrysler" was prepared by Ernest R. Nordtvedt, professor of management, Loyola University, New Orleans. It is based on public documents and other published information, and is intended as a basis for classroom discussion and not as an illustration of effective or ineffective management action.

Copyright © 1985 by Ernest R. Nordtvedt.

of the act's provisions. In all likelihood, many of the changes will become permanent. Spillovers could impact on other firms in the auto and other industries, and on the reindustrialization and changes which are occurring in the U.S. industrial base.

At Chrysler, most operations not involved with auto manufacture were divested. Survival as a full-line manufacturer of autos was the goal. Cost reductions, increased production efficiency, new smaller and more efficient cars, intense marketing efforts, concessions from Chrysler stakeholders, and government loan guarantees were the tools to be used in attaining the goal.

This study first examines briefly Chrysler's history including the stages of product and product line strategy and development. The focus then narrows to the circumstances and conditions which led to the crisis at Chrysler. Discussion of the survival plan centers on the terms and implementation of the act. A comparison is made between projections submitted to the Chrysler Loan Guarantee Board and subsequent actual performance. Finally, current and future long-term problems facing Chrysler as it attempts to adjust to a rapidly changing competitive environment are indicated. Little reference is made to competitors or other environmental elements found within the industry. These are covered in Case 9, "The Auto Industry in the United States: Structure and Strategy," and are introduced here only as necessary to the discussion of Chrysler.

## HISTORICAL PERSPECTIVE

The Chrysler Corporation grew out of the efforts and talents of Walter P. Chrysler, truly one of the giants of the U.S. auto industry, who left General Motors in 1920 and assumed control of Maxwell-Chalmers, an ailing manufacturer of autos. He incorporated the new company, giving it his name in 1925. The Dodge Company was absorbed in 1928. The third major nameplate, Plymouth, was also added in 1928 as an entrant into the low-price field to compete with Ford and Chevrolet, the latter being the General Motors entrant. The Chrysler Corporation enjoyed solid success throughout the 1930s, and when Walter Chrysler died in 1940, the company held a quarter of the domestic market and was the number two auto manufacturer in the world behind General Motors.

After World War II, Plymouth and Dodge autos were downsized in an effort to lock onto the small-car market. However, Chrysler's smaller cars did not achieve widespread market acceptance, and its place in the market began to slip. In 1948, Ford assumed second place among the domestic manufacturers, a position Chrysler has never regained. By 1954, Chrysler's market share dropped to 12 percent from over 20 percent and has not risen above 18 percent since.

In 1958, American Motors Corporation introduced the Rambler, a compact similar to those Chrysler had manufactured for several years. The AMC entrant achieved much greater market penetration and product acceptance. Under pressure from the large cars of General Motors and Ford, Chrysler again began to emphasize large cars in the late 1950s. The company also continued in the small-car market, with the Dodge Dart and the Plymouth Valiant competing with the Rambler. Compacts comprised about a quarter of Chrysler's production throughout the 1960s compared with Ford's 18 percent and General Motors' 13 percent. Although the decade of the 1960s was a period of modest market share growth and profitability was consistent, Chrysler's relatively heavier concentration on lower-margin smaller cars made the company less profitable than its market share and volume indicated, and also less profitable than its two major competitors.

## CURRENT BACK-GROUND

In 1969, General Motors introduced the Chevrolet Vega and Ford introduced the Pinto as new subcompact models. Chrysler, long a champion of the compact, had a choice to make. It could follow the other two manufacturers into the subcompact market, or it could push for a bigger share of the more profitable larger-car market. Owing to limited resources, the company could not afford the investment in tooling and facilities required to do both. The decision was made to emphasize larger cars. That decision set in motion a series of events that found Chrysler out of step with the economy, the market, and its competitors—or all three simultaneously—until Mr. Iacocca's leadership reversed the trend. Examples of those events include the following:

- Chrysler's investment program for 1969–1970 was increased on the basis of optimistic projections of population growth and improved highways. The decision coincided with the 1969–1970 recession.
- Intermediate-sized models were restyled in 1971 as the economy emerged from the recession and demand swung back to full-sized cars.
- New full-sized cars were introduced in 1974, just in time to join the gas lines brought about by the Arab oil embargo and to face the resultant demand shift to smaller cars. The $450 million that Chrysler invested on this series of large cars represented a costly decision which seemed to plague Chrysler through 1981.
- Tentative downsizing of cars began with the new intermediate in 1975, as the memory of the gas lines dimmed and consumer preference shifted back toward larger cars. Government control of gasoline prices gave the consumer little incentive to buy smaller, more efficient cars, and even less to the producer to make good ones.
- The 1975 enactment of the Energy Policy and Conservation Act introduced the Corporate Average Fuel Economy (CAFE), a government-mandated goal for the average fuel economy for an auto manufacturer's entire auto production. The subcompact, which was missing from the Chrysler line, would have contributed to meeting the mandate.

## Foreign Operations

Chrysler's unprofitable forays into the European market were late and its acquisitions unfortunate. Its intent was to supplement small-car offerings in the U.S.

market while gaining entry to the European market. In 1957, Chrysler acquired a major stake in Simca, a French automaker, followed in 1963 by an additional 38 percent and the remainder in 1971. In 1964–1965, it acquired two-thirds of the voting and nonvoting stock of the Rootes Group, a British automaker. Neither investment was successful. The primary products, the Simca and the Hillman autos, did not achieve market acceptance in the United States and suffered steady declines in local markets as well. The British government provided an infusion of $329 million to Chrysler–U.K. in 1976, but its market share continued to dwindle. Both operations were subsequently disposed of and Chrysler found itself in 1981 as largely a North American firm, essentially without overseas operations. Ford and General Motors, by contrast, shared almost 21 percent of the European market.

The company's agreement with Mitsubishi, a Japanese firm, had been much more successful. Mitsubishi manufactured autos for sale in the United States under the Dodge and Plymouth nameplates. While these captive imports had helped Chrysler financially, the Energy and Conservation Act permitted inclusion of imports in the computation of CAFE for 1978 and 1979 only.

## Recent Performance

Chrysler's decline in the late 1970s and early 1980s appeared to have begun in earnest in 1976, when the last big-car boom started. Chrysler's resources were inadequate to cover the wide product spectrum indicated by rapidly changing economic conditions and the confusing signals sent out by consumers and government alike. The consumer had been greatly impressed in 1974 by shortages and increases in the cost of gasoline—increases, however, which were limited by government control of oil prices. But the alarm sounded by the oil embargo of 1973–1974 was forgotten by 1976. Sales of full-sized and intermediate cars were brisk that year, and General Motors had a six-month supply of Vega subcompacts on hand. Sales of American subcompacts declined from 12.3 percent of the 1975 market to 7.4 percent in 1976. Imports were down to 14.8 percent, their lowest share of the U.S. market in five years. Chrysler was unable to satisfy its big-car demand. Its strength was in compact cars, a market segment that was declining. Chrysler lost money in 1974 and 1975, and again in 1978, losses that turn into a hemorrhage in 1979, 1980, and 1981.

General Motors began marketing downsized Chevrolet Chevettes and Cadillac Sevilles in 1976 as part of a $15 billion investment directed at the ultimate downsizing of its entire fleet by 1985. Consumers resisted the downsizing. Ford and Chrysler began marketing downsized cars in 1978 in an effort to avoid federal penalties to be assessed if CAFE standards were not met. Both brought out new subcompacts that sold well, although Chrysler had to source the needed four-cylinder engines for its Omni and Horizon autos. Chrysler's subcompacts were hurt badly, however, by a *Consumer Reports* story that reported the steering to be unsafe. And the consumer continued to buy large cars.

**Image**    Chrysler's image as a producer of quality products was also becoming tarnished in the eyes of the consumer. Ralph Nader, in a statement before the Senate Committee on Banking, Housing and Urban Affairs on November 20, 1979, gave lack of consumer confidence as a key to Chrysler's problems:

> The company is not selling the volume of vehicles it must in order to be profitable. Year after year, Chrysler has been acting in ways to diminish or shatter consumer confidence in its products. Recent years have been vintage for Chrysler lemons—and lemons of the most unsettling kinds. Volares and Aspens for instance. . . . Judging by letters which we receive, owners of Chrysler cars are among the most bitter. . . .

In a study of 1975–1977 consumer complaints, the Center for Auto Safety reported in a letter to the Chrysler board chairman on August 26, 1977, findings that "reflect disturbing safety and consumer problems as well as poor quality control within the Chrysler Corporation." The report detailed carburetor, brake, transmission, and steering problems of the Volare and Aspen, as well as others in the Cordoba. Other minor problems encountered by consumers with Chrysler products were also described. A general perception held by the American consumer was that U.S.-made autos in general and Chrysler autos in particular were inferior products, especially when compared to foreign models. Whether statistically supportable or not, the perception still persisted into mid-1985 and helped import sales at the expense of Chrysler and other U.S. auto manufacturers.

## THE CRISIS

Despite a 1978 loss of $204.6 billion, Chrysler's management expressed an optimistic outlook to its stockholders as it entered 1979. A fourth-quarter 1978 profit of $43.2 million had been registered. Although its annual production and unit sales were down in 1978, production of the Omni and Horizon autos had begun, thus filling the gap in the subcompact part of the product line. These new cars were selling well, although limited in number by the availability of sourced four-cylinder engines. New full-sized and luxury cars also entered production. Passenger vans and recreational vehicles, a market segment at which Chrysler directed substantial emphasis and resources, were moving well after recovery from a slowdown in 1973 and 1974. A new line of subcompact trucks manufactured by Mitsubishi was introduced to the U.S. market. For the first time in many years, Chrysler seemed to have all of the bases in the marketplace covered. Although economists were predicting a slowdown in the economy and its growth rate, early 1979 sales were strong. Industry forecasts indicated a good year was at hand.

It was not to happen. The Shah of Iran was overthrown in January and the revolution resulted in interruption of oil supplies from that country. The memories of 1973–1974 gas lines became all too vivid in the minds of consumers again. Inventories of large cars grew as demand for them diminished sharply. This was accompanied by an increase in small-car demand, and long waiting lists quickly developed. All manufacturers were caught short, and Chrysler, with availability of subcompacts limited by the supply of its purchased four-cylinder engines, was again unable to satisfy demand for its products, this time at the end of the product spectrum which historically had been its strength—the small-car segment. Overall, for 1979, sales by U.S. manufacturers declined by more than 10 percent from 1978, whereas the imports claimed a market share larger by 4.2 percent. Chrysler's sales declined by more than 200,000 units, and its share of a shrinking market decreased by a full point to 11.3 percent. The market for inefficient trucks, vans, and recreational vehicles, which had been a profitable part of Chrysler's market, almost evaporated as spot gasoline shortages began to appear.

Many of the factors that came together to damage the U.S. auto manufacturers in general and Chrysler in particular were beyond the control of management. These included increasing interest rates, inflation, fear of recession, and decreasing consumer confidence in the economy. However, one Chrysler management practice contributed substantially to company problems. Most auto manufacturers matched production with dealer order levels, thereby minimizing or at least controlling the level of finished-goods inventory. This practice resulted in more variation in production levels but minimized the enormous cost of carrying the inventory. Chrysler had adopted the policy of leveling production numbers, thereby producing for inventory. This policy proved disastrous in the face of declining demand. In late 1979, Chrysler had an unsold backlog of vehicles totaling more than 80,000 units worth $750 million, many of which were large cars and vans for which demand neither existed nor could be generated. The storage, handling, and interest charges alone approached $2 million per week. The marketing effort to eliminate this inventory continued even after the introduction of 1980 models, and saw the use of factory rebates and other costly marketing innovations. Not only did the company suffer because of high inventory costs, but it also sold the units at or below cost simply to move them.

By early 1979, it became apparent that Chrysler faced a serious cash flow problem which limited its ability to finance its programs fully and perhaps even threatened its survival. Despite a reduction in costs, improvements in internal operations, and a new production planning system which matched production with dealer orders, deterioration in the company's financial position accelerated. In July 1979, Chrysler approached the federal government with a request for financial assistance.

**THE RECOVERY PLAN: DEBATE**

On July 24, 1979, Chrysler Corporation made its initial request to the Department of the Treasury for $1 billion in cash loans or tax concessions over the ensuing 18 months. Secretary William Miller quickly rejected the request but did indicate a willingness to explore loan guarantees as a means of helping Chrysler. In its October 17 revision, Chrysler asked for up to $750 million in loan guarantees, and on November 1, Treasury sent a preliminary draft of the Chrysler Corporation Loan Guarantee Act of 1979 to Congress. The measure passed the Congress on December 21 and was signed into law by President Carter on January 7, 1980. As might be expected, rhetoric and positions espoused in the hearings revolved around the free-enterprise capitalistic system and government's proper role therein. Major considerations raised are summarized below.

**Debate: For Assistance**

**Cost to the Federal Government**   Chrysler's demise would produce losses of revenue, additional unemployment and welfare payments, and costs to the Pension Guarantee Corporation. These totaled an estimated $3 billion. State and local governments would incur substantial added costs of a similar nature.

**Employment/Unemployment**   Secretary Miller estimated that unemployment would increase by about 100,000 during 1980–1981, primarily among the 400,000 Chrysler and Chrysler dealer and supplier employees. The impact would be especially hard in the Detroit area, where unemployment, already above 7 percent, would increase to about 11 percent. Other pockets of Chrysler activity throughout the Midwest and Northeast would suffer heavy local impact.

**Industry Concentration**   With a Chrysler failure, only General Motors and Ford would remain as major producers of domestic-make autos, representing a narrow competitive base. With high entry barriers already limiting new competition, concern about the effectiveness of the competitive process arose. Chrysler's efforts in the compact market in recent years were cited as providing added competition to General Motors and added choice to the consumer.

**Balance of Payments**   Current import penetration of the U.S. car market would be expected to increase and partially fill the vacuum left by a Chrysler failure. The impact on U.S. balance of payments would be negative.

**Lower Economic Activity**   Congressional testimony estimated that a Chrysler collapse would lessen real economic growth by 0.5 to 1.0 percent in 1980, together with an increase in unemployment. This would only deepen the recession already in process at the time.

**Precedent**   The Lockheed loan guarantee was cited as the most applicable precedent, although loan guarantees provided for homes, rural electrification, shipbuilding, medical facilities, railroads, steel, and by the Small Business Administration were also cited. The total of outstanding government loan guarantees was estimated at about $240 billion in October 1979.

**Debate: Against Assistance**

**Intervention in Capital Markets**   Government loan guarantees would alter the pattern of resource allocation to the most efficient use, a pattern that theoretically occurs in the free capital markets. Loan guarantees would upset the discipline imposed by the free marketplace, which requires adjustment to strategy and operations by firms unsuccessful in selling their products and competing in the market.

**Rewarding Failure**   A free marketplace penalizes failure by requiring liquidation or bankruptcy, not by providing access to additional financing through loan guarantees. Chrysler's management had not reflected the necessary sensitivity to consumers or to changing trends in the marketplace and should not be rewarded with support to avoid bankruptcy.

**Impact on Auto Demand**    Retail sales of autos would not be changed appreciably by Chrysler's failure. Its sales would in part be picked up by the other domestic manufacturers and in part by the imports. But the same number of jobs would be available in the long term because the demand for autos would remain unchanged.

**Government Aid Historically Has Been Unsuccessful**    The British experience with British Leyland and Chrysler–U.K. had shown that cash infusions to the automakers by the government had not produced long-term viability. Conditions that led to the initial difficulties were not corrected with the provision of financial aid because the pressures of the marketplace are missing in such bailouts.

**RECOVERY PLAN: THE CHRYSLER CORPORATION LOAN GUARANTEE ACT OF 1979**

A summary of events involving the enactment and implementation of the Chrysler Corporation Loan Guarantee Act of 1979 may be found in Exhibit 10.1. An outline of the act's provisions is found in Exhibit 10.2, but some provisions are mentioned here as pertinent to the immediate discussion of Chrysler's performance in the period since the implementation of the act.

The act created a Loan Guarantee Board with authority to issue $1.5 billion in federal loan guarantees prior to December 31, 1983, to be repaid by the end of 1990. Loan guarantees were to be made available if credit was unavailable to the company elsewhere on reasonable terms, if there was reasonable assurance of repayment, and if failure of the company to secure such funds would adversely affect the economy or employment in any region of the country. Annual submission of satisfactory operating and financial plans covering four fiscal years was required. Actual balance sheet and operating statement data, and actual and forecast market penetration data are found in Exhibits 10.3, 10.4, and 10.5.

In a major provision, the act made obtaining the federal loan guarantees contingent on the provision of $1.43 billion in nonfederally guaranteed assistance by stakeholders in Chrysler's continued existence. The act also specified that there had to be reasonable assurance of corporate viability beyond December 31, 1983, without additional federal loan guarantees.

**Nonfederally Guaranteed Assistance**

The act specifies that there must be "$1 of nonfederally guaranteed assistance in place for each dollar of guarantee." Although not specified, the implication was that assistance had to be accrued against the amount of guarantees outstanding at any one time. Chrysler obtained concessions from a variety of stakeholders and also sold a portion of corporate assets to achieve the levels of nonfederally guaranteed assistance specified by the act. Although included initially, a requirement for sale of new equity to the public was modified by the Loan Guarantee

**Exhibit 10.1** Chrysler Corporation Loan Guarantee Act of 1979: Chronology of Events in Passage and Implementation, 1979–1984

| 1979 | July 24 | Chrysler outlined proposal for financial aid (loans, tax concessions) to the Treasury Department |
|---|---|---|
| | September 20 | Lee Iacocca elected chairman and chief executive officer of the Chrysler Corporation |
| | October 17 | Chrysler submitted revised request for up to $750 million in federal loan guarantees |
| | November 1 | Treasury sent draft bill to Congress |
| | December 21 | Congress passed the bill |
| | December 31 | Chrysler reported 1979 loss of $1,097,000,000 |
| 1980 | January 7 | President Carter signed the bill into law |
| | April 29 | Chrysler Loan Guarantee Board met to begin consideration of issuing commitments for $1.5 billion in loan guarantees |
| | | Chrysler submitted plan in justification of first takedown |
| | May 10 | Chrysler submitted plan revisions |
| | June 24 | First takedown of $500 million approved by board |
| | July 10 | Chrysler submitted plan in justification of second takedown |
| | July 31 | Second takedown of $300 million approved by board |
| | October 16 | New K-cars, Ares and Reliant, introduced |
| | December 31 | Chrysler reported 1980 loss of $1,710,000,000 |
| 1981 | January 15 | Chrysler submitted plan in justification of third takedown |
| | February 2 | Third takedown of $400 million approved by board |
| | March 31 | Chrysler reported a first-quarter 1981 loss of $298.4 million |
| | June 30 | Chrysler reported second-quarter 1981 profit of $11.6 million; year to date: $286.8 million loss |
| | December 31 | Chrysler reported 1981 loss of $475.6 million |
| 1982 | March 14 | Chrysler sold Chrysler Defense, Inc., to General Dynamics at a gain of $239 million |
| | December 31 | Chrysler reported 1982 profit of $170.1 million |
| 1983 | March 12 | Twenty-six million shares of common stock sold for $432 million; $400 million of guaranteed loans paid off with proceeds |
| | July 13 | Chrysler announced decision to pay off remainder of guaranteed loans |
| | August 15 | Chrysler paid off remaining obligation under loan guarantees of $813,487,500; early repayment of $38.5 million in loans from Michigan and Illinois |
| | December 31 | Chrysler reported 1983 profit of $701 million |
| 1984 | December 31 | Chrysler reported 1984 profit of $2,380,000,000 |

Board as unrealistic in light of Chrysler's current financial condition. (A highly successful equity offering was put on the market in the spring of 1983.)

**Labor** Both union and nonunion labor agreed to forgo raises or other monetary-related employment benefits, such as cost-of-living allowances. This was particularly difficult for the UAW, which had completed negotiations with Chrysler on a new three-year contract in the fall of 1979. The union did, however, forgo certain of the benefits contained in that contract to achieve their share of the targeted contribution.

**Exhibit 10.2** Chrysler Corporation Loan Guarantee Act of 1979: Major Provisions

---

**LOAN GUARANTEE BOARD**

*Voting members:* Secretary of the treasury, comptroller general, chairman of the Federal Reserve Board
*Nonvoting members:* Secretaries of labor and transportation

**AUTHORITY**

Authorized $1.5 billion in loan guarantees for Chrysler Corporation
Authority terminated December 31, 1983; loans to be repaid by end 1990
Requires security (collateral) for loans

**FEES**

Requires minimum of 0.5 percent per year on daily balance
(Treasury Secretary Donald Regan set fee at 1.0 percent on assuming office in January 1981)

**CONDITIONS OF LOANS**

Satisfactory energy savings plan
Certification that failure to secure funds would adversely affect economy or employment in any region of the country
Required satisfactory operating and financial plan submission to board
Nonfederally guaranteed assistance in amount of $1.43 billion from Chrysler stakeholders, sale of assets, and issuance of $1 billion in common stock to its employees

**LOAN GUARANTEE REQUIREMENTS**

Credit not otherwise available to company on reasonable terms
No substantial likelihood of merger or sale of company to foreign entity
No stock dividends to be paid while guaranteed loans outstanding

**NONFEDERALLY GUARANTEED ASSISTANCE**

At least $500 million from domestic banks, financial institutions, or other creditors; $400 million must be new loans or credits and $100 million concessions on outstanding debt
At least $150 million from foreign banks, financial institutions, and other creditors in the form of new loans or credits
At least $300 million from the sale of corporate assets
At least $250 million from state, local, and other governments
At least $180 million from suppliers and dealers, with at least $50 million in the form of capital
At least $50 million from additional sale of stock
Board may modify individual components as long as total reaches $1.43 billion

**EMPLOYEE CONTRIBUTIONS**

Unionized employees reduce current wage contract with company by $462.5 million (effective dates of contract: 9/14/79 to 9/14/82).
Nonunion employees make at least $125 million in wage concessions over the same three years.

**Exhibit 10.3** Summary of Company Market Penetration and Net Income, 1974–1984 (includes imports)

| Year | Industry Unit Sales (millions) | Chrysler Market Share (percent) | Chrysler Net Income ($ millions) |
|------|------|------|------|
| 1974 | 8.9 | 13.6 | (52) |
| 1975 | 8.6 | 11.5 | (207) |
| 1976 | 10.1 | 11.7 | 328 |
| 1977 | 11.2 | 10.9 | 163) |
| 1978 | 11.3 | 10.1 | (205) |
| 1979 | 10.7 | 8.9 | (1,097) |
| 1980 | 9.0 | 8.8 | (1,710) |
| 1981 | 8.5/9.6 | 9.9/9.1 | (476)/(253) |
| 1982 | 8.0/10.6 | 10.0/9.7 | 170/319 |
| 1983 | 9.2/11.4 | 10.4/9.7 | 701/587 |
| 1984 | 10.4/11.6 | 10.4/9.5 | 2,380/1,089 |

*Note:* Where two numbers are shown for years 1981–1984, the first is actual and the second is the forecast.

*Source:* Findings of the Chrysler Corporation Loan Guarantee Board, January 19, 1981 (forecast data); company annual reports; *Ward's Automotive Yearbooks; Standard & Poor's Industry Surveys.*

**Pension Deferral**   Although not an original funding source, Chrysler deferred pension contributions totaling $187 million in September 1981, with the agreement of the UAW. The financing benefit of the deferral was allowed as a contribution in meeting the requirements of the act. Additionally, the expiration date on the employee profit sharing plan was moved up from 1985 to the end of 1983.

**Vendors**   Original equipment vendors provided price concessions totaling about $72 million against a target of $230 million.

**State and Local Governments**   Four states (Michigan, Indiana, Delaware, and Illinois) approved loans to the company. The government of Canada and the province of Ontario contributed assistance to help sustain Chrysler's Canadian operations.

**The January 1981 Financing Plan**   Because sales were lower than had been expected when the initial loan guarantees were issued in June and July 1980, a significant portion of the planned financial margin had been used or was expected to be used when the third (and final) takedown request was prepared in January 1981. The new operating plan provided details of additional nonfederally guaranteed financing that had been obtained above the July plan and were not anticipated in any of the previous submissions. This financing is outlined in Exhibit 9.7, but the details of the institutional lenders' concessions are of sufficient import to the discussion to be presented here.

In accordance with an override agreement in effect with most of its institutional lenders, Chrysler restructured $1,109,000,000 in debt on February 1, 1981. The

**Exhibit 10.4** Chrysler Corporation Consolidated Statement of Operations, 1975–1984 ($ millions)

| | 1975 | 1976 | 1977 | 1978 | 1979 | 1980 | 1981 | 1982 | 1983 | 1984 |
|---|---|---|---|---|---|---|---|---|---|---|
| Total revenues | 11,567 | 15,559 | 16,745 | 13,670 | 12,004 | 9,169 | 10,824 | 10,049 | 13,388 | 19,717 |
| Costs other than items below | 10,538 | 13,625 | 15,083 | 12,640 | 11,632 | 9,694 | 10,275 | 9,255 | 11,666 | 16,516 |
| Selling and admin. expenses | 466 | 566 | 613 | 572 | 599 | | | | | |
| Depreciation and amortization | 294 | 402 | 388 | 352 | 401 | 567 | 451 | 432 | 457 | 554 |
| Pension plans | 281 | 277 | 297 | 262 | 261 | 302 | 297 | 272 | 255 | 267 |
| Interest expenses, net | 168 | 130 | 140 | 129 | 215 | 276 | 262 | 158 | 82 | (51) |
| Earnings (loss) before taxes | (181) | 541 | 218 | (286) | (1,102) | (1,670) | (460) | (68) | 704 | 2,430 |
| Taxes on income (credit) | 26 | 212 | 94 | (81) | (5) | 40 | 16 | — | 402 | 934 |
| Extraordinary item | — | 94 | 38 | — | — | — | — | — | 399 | 884 |
| Discontinued operations gain (loss) | (75) | — | — | — | — | — | — | 238 | — | — |
| Effect of accounting change gain (loss) | 23 | — | — | — | — | — | — | — | — | — |
| Net earnings (loss) | (259) | 423 | 163 | (205) | (1,097) | (1,710) | (476) | 170 | 701 | 2,380 |

**Exhibit 10.5** Chrysler Corporation Consolidated Balance Sheet, 1975–1984 ($ millions)

| | 1975 | 1976 | 1977 | 1978 | 1979 | 1980 | 1981 | 1982 | 1983 | 1984 |
|---|---|---|---|---|---|---|---|---|---|---|
| **Assets** | | | | | | | | | | |
| Current assets | | | | | | | | | | |
| Cash | 151 | 168 | 208 | 123 | 188 | 104 | 121 | 110 | 112 | 75 |
| Marketable securities and time deposits | 76 | 404 | 201 | 400 | 286 | 194 | 283 | 788 | 958 | 1,625 |
| Accounts receivable | 642 | 798 | 897 | 848 | 610 | 476 | 430 | 248 | 291 | 332 |
| Inventories | 2,069 | 2,354 | 2,623 | 1,981 | 1,874 | 1,916 | 1,600 | 1,133 | 1,301 | 1,626 |
| Other | 178 | 155 | 225 | 210 | 162 | 172 | 167 | 91 | 92 | 322 |
| Total current assets | 3,117 | 3,878 | 4,153 | 3,562 | 3,121 | 2,861 | 2,601 | 2,369 | 2,754 | 3,980 |
| Investments and other assets | 997 | 1,071 | 1,052 | 1,396 | 1,184 | 1,237 | 1,222 | 1,421 | 964 | 1,370 |
| Net property, plant, equipment | 2,115 | 2,087 | 2,425 | 2,023 | 2,349 | 2,520 | 2,447 | 2,474 | 3,055 | 3,713 |
| Cost of investments in consol. subs. in excess of equity | 38 | 38 | 37 | — | — | — | — | — | — | — |
| Total assets | 6,267 | 7,074 | 7,668 | 6,981 | 6,653 | 6,618 | 6,270 | 6,264 | 6,772 | 9,063 |
| **Liabilities and shareholders' investment** | | | | | | | | | | |
| Current liabilities | | | | | | | | | | |
| Accounts payable | 1,400 | 1,763 | 1,912 | 1,725 | 1,530 | 1,405 | 1,023 | 898 | 1,579 | 2,323 |
| Short-term debt | 374 | 172 | 250 | 49 | 601 | 151 | 164 | 79 | 361 | 7 |
| Payments due within one year on long-term debt | 60 | 69 | 91 | 12 | 276 | 166 | 62 | 16 | 56 | 43 |
| Other | 628 | 822 | 837 | 699 | 825 | 1,307 | 1,170 | 1,120 | 1,458 | 1,743 |
| Total current liabilities | 2,462 | 2,826 | 3,090 | 2,486 | 3,232 | 3,029 | 2,419 | 2,113 | 3,454 | 4,116 |
| Other liabilities and deferred credits | 312 | 367 | 382 | 361 | 567 | 646 | 997 | 971 | 849 | 882 |
| Long-term debt | 1,067 | 1,048 | 1,240 | 1,189 | 977 | 2,483 | 2,059 | 2,148 | 1,104 | 760 |
| Obligations under capital leases | — | — | 13 | 15 | 15 | — | 15 | 41 | — | — |
| Minority interest in net assets of consolidated subsidiaries | 16 | 19 | 19 | 5 | 38 | — | — | — | — | — |
| Shareholder's investment | 2,410 | 2,815 | 2,925 | 2,927 | 1,824 | 459 | 780 | 991 | 1,365 | 3,306 |
| Total liabilities and shareholders' investment | 6,267 | 7,074 | 7,668 | 6,981 | 6,653 | 6,618 | 6,270 | 6,264 | 6,772 | 9,063 |

*Source:* Company annual reports.

terms of those agreements allowed conversion of $685.9 million in debt in two installments (February 27 and June 12, 1981) into preferred stock, with a redemption value of $1,097,400,000. Chrysler had an option to redeem most of the remainder ($623.1 million) at thirty cents cash on the dollar. This option was exercised on March 31 when $233.8 million was redeemed for $71.3 million. The debt restructure helped the cash flow situation substantially by eliminating fixed charges and converting debt to equity.

The nonfederally guaranteed assistance in Exhibit 10.7 also shows additional concessions from both union and nonunion labor. The impact of all new assistance was to be accrued through the years 1981–1985.

**Summary**    Exhibits 10.6 and 10.7 summarize nonfederally guaranteed assistance as projected by the company through 1985.

## RECOVERY PLAN

Certain of the underlying assumptions were most critical to the success of the recovery plan. All impacted directly on net profit.

### Product Strategy

Chrysler stated an intention to remain a full-line producer of automobiles in the U.S. market and resisted suggestions that it should specialize or find a particular product or market niche in which it could excel. The argument against specialization maintained that profit margins in a highly competitive small-car market and the volume associated with specialty products were insufficient to sustain a major competitor. Additionally, increased industry concentration would accompany Chrysler's withdrawal from markets shared with General Motors and Ford. Chrysler later modified this position publicly, but published product plans seemed to leave no doubt that full-line competition was intended.

### Volume, Mix, and Market Penetration

Volume is essential to reach break-even and to recover the high-capital-investment characteristic of the auto industry. Chrysler's break-even volume for all North American operations was estimated at 2.61 million units in 1979 by the staff of the Chrysler Loan Guarantee Board. The break-even goal for 1983 in the same market was set at 1.65 million units. The importance of Chrysler's market penetration can be illustrated by the fact that a one-percentage-point variation in market share was estimated to produce a $200 million variation in annual income before taxes, based on 1980 volume and unit margins. The continued market acceptance of an increasingly heavier mix of fuel-efficient autos accompanied by a switch to consumer purchase of U.S. autos were both important factors in Chrysler's plans to regain the market share lost in recent years. An improving economy with larger overdemand would also increase company sales. Maintenance of the existing dealer network as a sales and service outlet and consumer contact was also essential.

**Exhibit 10.6** Nonfederally Guaranteed Assistance, 1980–1981 ($ millions)

| Assistance Category | Initial Target | Approved | | |
|---|---|---|---|---|
| | | 5/15/80 | 7/10/80 | 1/15/81 |
| Lender | $650 | $642 | $655 | $911 |
| State/local government | 250 | 357 | 357 | 357 |
| Suppliers | 180 | 63 | 150 | 195 |
| Asset sales | 300 | 628 | 730 | 730 |
| Pension deferral | 0 | 342 | 342 | 342 |
| Additional equity | 50 | 0 | 0 | 0 |
| Other | 227 | 0 | 0 | 0 |
| Labor unions | 463 | 463 | 463 | 1,370 |
| Labor (nonunion) | 125 | 125 | 125 | |

*Source:* Findings of the Chrysler Corporation Loan Guarantee Board, May 12, 1980, and January 19, 1981; Report of the Chrysler Corporation Loan Guarantee Board, July 15, 1980.

**Exhibit 10.7** Projected Nonfederally Guaranteed Assistance, 1981–1985[a] ($ millions)

| Year | Reduced Planned Expenditures | Concessions | | | | Total New |
|---|---|---|---|---|---|---|
| | | Lender Interest[b] | Supplier | Employee | Personnel Other | |
| 1981 | $ 670 | $25 | $45 | $293 | $97 | $ 1,130 |
| 1982 | 603 | 58 | — | 490 | 35 | 1,186 |
| 1983 | 441 | 61 | — | — | 41 | 543 |
| 1984 | 354 | 56 | — | — | 44 | 454 |
| 1985 | (180) | 56 | — | — | 48 | (76) |

[a]Cash impact of actions in January 1981 plan not previously anticipated.
[b]The low end of the range estimating the cash impact of lender interest concessions is indicated. In addition to the cash interest savings, Chrysler planned to avoid additional charges paid in notes instead of cash, 1981–85.

*Source:* Findings of the Chrysler Corporation Guarantee Board, January 19, 1981.

## Fixed-Cost Reduction

Reductions in manufacturing burden, general, administrative, and sales expenses were targeted for completion by the end of 1981. These were expected to have permanent impact on future break-even levels.

## Cash Flow

The ability to fund operations and future programs involved increasing revenue and accompanying profit margins, and obtaining concessions from stakeholders and loan guarantees from the federal government. One of the symptoms of Chrysler's problem had been day-to-day cash flow shortages leading to occasional doubts regarding ability to meet the payroll. At times, during the recovery period, working capital was virtually nonexistent.

**Variable Margin Improvement**

Programmed efforts to increase the unit variable margin included better targeting of standard options and design of new ones taking advantage of technology (trip computers, electronic/digital instrumentation), product action (new styling, design, front-wheel drive), design cost reduction (value engineering), manufacturing efficiency through new production techniques and facilities (paint processes, robots), making rather than purchasing more components, improved warranty and quality control programs to decrease the incidence and necessity of recalls, purchasing programs to reduce material costs, and a better reading of market, consumer, and environmental changes. Exhibit 10.8 indicates the desired variable margin improvement in monetary terms per unit for these programs.

**RECOVERY PLAN VERSUS ACTUAL PERFORMANCE**

Chrysler's recovery plan, then, assumed continuation as a full-line auto manufacture, reduced fixed costs and increased variable margins, an improving economy with increased demand for autos in general and Chrysler products in particular, all resulting in higher sales which in turn would allow higher capital expenditures and produce positive cash flow and a return to profit.

The company was required to submit periodically detailed operating and financial plans to the Loan Guarantee Board, and specific submissions were required to support requests to receive loan guarantees against the $1.5 billion authorized by the act. Three takedowns were requested and received in April and July 1980, and the last in January 1981. The following sections examine critical area forecasts made by the company in its plans submitted in support of the takedown requests and compare them with subsequent actual performance. (See Exhibits 10.9–10.12).

**Industry Sales Forecasts**

In each instance except the July–April 1980 forecasts for 1983, Chrysler's forecasts were more optimistic than those of the independent forecasters (see Exhibit 10.9). Another pattern shows the 1981 and 1982 forecasts made by both sources decreasing substantially as the year 1980 progressed because performance did not live up to expectations.

Industry sales volume was of great significance to Chrysler and its forecasts were of central import to the recovery plan. In a shrinking or level sales volume market, the company could improve its share only at the expense of an industry competitor, most of whom were much stronger than Chrysler. In the expanding market apparent in Chrysler's forecasts, concurrent growth for all, including Chrysler, was a possibility.

In none of the recovery years was the industry sales volume forecast put forth by Chrysler or the independent forecasters reached, despite the strong recovery

**Exhibit 10.8** Variable Margin Improvements per Unit by
Type of Program, 1980–1984 Model Years

| Program | Amount per Unit |
|---|---|
| Product action | $ 112 |
| Options and equipment changes | 91 |
| Design cost reductions | 126 |
| Manufacturing improvements | 204 |
| Component insourcing | 41 |
| Warranty improvements | 67 |
| Purchasing programs | 125 |
| Market demand changes | (112) |
| Total variable margin improvement | $ 654 |

*Source:* Report of the Chrysler Corporation Loan Guarantee Board, July 15, 1980.

**Exhibit 10.9** U.S. Car Forecast and Actual Sales Performance, 1980–84 (million units)

| Date of Forecast | 1980 | 1981 | 1982 | 1983 | 1984 |
|---|---|---|---|---|---|
| April 1980 | | | | | |
| Chrysler | 9.8 | 11.0 | 12.1 | 10.8 | — |
| Independent (avg.)[a] | 9.7 | 10.1 | 10.9 | 11.4 | — |
| July 1980 | | | | | |
| Chrysler | 8.8 | 11.0 | 12.1 | 10.8 | 11.7 |
| Independent (avg.) | 8.8 | 9.4 | 10.4 | 11.4 | 11.5 |
| January 1981 | | | | | |
| Chrysler | — | 9.6 | 10.6 | 11.4 | 11.6 |
| Independent (avg.) | — | 9.4 | 10.4 | 11.0 | 11.3 |
| Actual | 9.0 | 8.5 | 8.0 | 9.2 | 10.4 |

[a]Independent (avg.) is a composite of several independent forecasts.

*Source:* Findings of the Chrysler Corporation Loan Guarantee Board, May 12, 1980; July 15, 1980; January 19, 1981; and U.S. Department of Commerce, Bureau of Economic Analysis.

of the economy. The pent-up-demand theory which provided a strong rationale for most of the forecasts simply did not materialize. The replacement market continued to suffer as the average age of the U.S. automobile continued to increase from 6.6 years in 1980 to 7.4 years in 1983.

**Market Penetration**   An optimistic pattern of forecast market penetration similar to that found in the industry sales forecast was apparent. (See Exhibit 10.10.) The optimism was based on significant quality improvements, emphasis on front-wheel-drive vehicles, and a steady stream of new products. The basic K-car was the first of these and was to be followed by larger K-car derivatives for entry in

**Exhibit 10.10** Chrysler Market Share Projection/Actual, 1980–1984 (percent) (includes imports)

| Date of Forecast | 1980 | 1981 | 1982 | 1983 | 1984 |
|---|---|---|---|---|---|
| October 1979 | 10.2 | 11.1 | 11.6 | 11.9 | — |
| April 1980 | 9.5 | 11.1 | 11.1 | 12.4 | — |
| July 1980 | 10.1 | 11.1 | 11.1 | 12.4 | 11.3 |
| January 1981 | — | 9.1 | 9.7 | 9.7 | 9.5 |
| Actual | 8.8 | 9.9 | 10.0 | 10.4 | 10.4 |

*Source:* See Exhibit 10.9.

the middle-market segment. A station wagon and a new sport specialty car were planned for 1982 and 1983, respectively. Chrysler suggested that by the mid-1980s, fuel economy would no longer be the primary tool for product differentiation because only small differences in economy would then exist among competing products. Instead, the passenger capacity would become more important to the consumer.

Although Chrysler's product and market penetration strategies depended heavily on introduction of new products, execution of the strategy would not be possible without a reliable source of financing from internal or external sources. Growth in both total industry sales and Chrysler market share were critical to the recovery plan. Just as important were the loan guarantees.

The Chrysler share of a slightly increasing market rose somewhat faster than the latest projections made in January 1981. This single factor attested to the effectiveness of the recovery plan elements: lower costs induced by stakeholder concessions, lower break-even, and success of the K-car concept. Had the economic recovery occurred earlier, Chrysler's performance probably would have been even better.

**Net Income** Shortfalls in total industry growth and Chrysler's increased share of the resulting larger market clearly show in the revised net income forecasts prepared for successive loan guarantee takedown applications. For reasons of unfavorable economic conditions and product nonacceptance, Chrysler's outlook became progressively worse in 1980 and into 1981 (see Exhibit 10.11). The deterioration was a major factor in the company's decision to ask for a third takedown in December 1980, a request which was granted the following month. Actions taken by Chrysler to improve its cash flow and financial condition included the following:

- Decreased planned expenditures by $1,888,000,000 between 1981 and 1985
- Obtained an additional $622 million in concessions from the UAW
- Negotiated $72 million in price and other concessions from suppliers
- Reduced fixed costs by reducing management personnel by 3000
- Sought infusion of capital through merger or joint venture

**Exhibit 10.11** Chrysler Net Income Forecast/Actual, 1980–1984 ($ millions)

| Date of Forecast | 1980 | 1981 | 1982 | 1983 | 1984 |
|---|---|---|---|---|---|
| April 1980 | (781) | 304 | 642 | 368 | 890 |
| July 1980 | (1,225) | 78 | 508 | 21 | 482 |
| January 1981 | — | (253) | 320 | 587 | 1,089 |
| Actual | (1,710) | (476) | 170 | 701 | 2,380 |

*Source:* See Exhibit 10.9; company annual reports.

The projected net income figures as presented to the Chrysler Loan Guarantee Board were not met until the fourth and last year under the act (1983).

**Planned Expenditures** The questions of long-term competitive viability and market acceptance of its product were very real to Chrysler and required the simultaneous evaluation of the impact of deferral and/or cancellation of product changes and new product introduction. Forecasts for new product and capital expenditures made in October 1979 covering the period through 1985 were reduced by 40 percent in the succeeding 15 months owing to the lower than projected sales and associated financial performance figures. Simply put, Chrysler's need for cash and investment funds was being met by loans guaranteed by the federal government under the act.

As indicated earlier, the K-car was the centerpiece of the recovery strategy. As Mr. Iacocca put it, "The K-car was the last train in the station. If we failed here, it was all over." Most of Chrysler's capital expenditures supported the tooling and production necessary to produce the original K-cars, the Aries and the Reliant. Several derivatives have been spun off from the original platform and in mid-1985 still formed the core of the Chrysler product line—LeBaron, Chrysler E Class, Dodge 400/600, New Yorker, Daytona, and Laser. This concept has allowed Chrysler to avoid the $1 billion investment associated with the development of each new model.

**Other Factors**    **Merger** Booz, Allen & Hamilton, management consultants, stated in an attachment to Chrysler's third takedown application that results of actions in the new plan gave the company a reasonable prospect of recovery. The consultant cautioned that a basic assumption underlying that opinion was that unforeseen outside factors (e.g., abnormally high interest rates, disruption of oil supplies) would not hold back the recovery of the industry. Booz, Allen also commented that the major cash shortfall would appear in the first quarter of 1981. (Chrysler successfully passed that milestone.) Nevertheless, another major caveat in the consultant's opinion was that the company faced a major long-term risk that its competitive position in the worldwide automotive industry might be impaired and that alternatives such as merger and joint venture should be examined. In 1982, Chrysler secretly drew up a proposal for a merger with Ford. The proposal was presented in confidence to Ford management but was publicly rejected out of hand for reasons partly business and economic, and partly emotional. No anti-trust obstacle had been placed in its way during preliminary discussions with the Justice Department.

**Dealer Network**   Although not a specific forecast area, the retention of a healthy dealer network was essential to the revitalization of the company and was implicit in its recovery plans. Survival of the dealer network was contingent on the basic strength of the individual dealership, consumer acceptance of Chrysler products, support provided by the manufacturer, and, in some instances, assistance provided by the Small Business Administration. Grass-roots confidence in Chrysler's recovery was important to the continued local financing of dealers by local investors and creditors. In 1980, Chrysler lost 600 dealers, more than any other U.S. automaker (see Exhibit 10.12). The shakeout, however, was largely complete by the end of 1983 and the network was in place when the recovery begin in earnest in 1983.

**Cost Reduction**   By the end of 1981, Chrysler's break-even point had been reduced from 2.61 million units to 1.1 million units. This had been achieved by a combination of fixed-cost reduction actions which included closing facilities, sourcing parts and components, selling almost all divisions except those producing autos, and thinning the ranks of salaried workers.

**Voluntary Export Restraints**   For four years beginning April 1, 1981, the Japanese government adhered to voluntary restraints on exports. The purpose was to give time for the U.S. market to improve and domestic manufacturers to transition successfully to smaller cars. For the first three years passenger-car exports were limited to 1,762,500. In the year ending March 31, 1985, the limit was placed at 1,940,850. Renewal of the restraints was not sought by the Reagan administration. This restraint was an important contributor to the recovery by Chrysler and other U.S. manufacturers.

**The Economy**   The prime interest rate peaked at 22 percent in 1980 and had declined steadily to the 9.5 percent level in mid-1985. Consumer interest rates experienced similar declines. Unemployment had dropped over the same period

**Exhibit 10.12** U.S. Car Dealers in Operation, 1979–1983

| Manufacturer/Dealer | 1979 | 1980 | 1981 | 1982 | 1983 |
|---|---|---|---|---|---|
| Chrysler | 4,434 | 3,834 | 3,693 | 3,645 | 3,864 |
| Ford | 6,582 | 6,053 | 5,685 | 5,414 | 5,508 |
| General Motors | 11,425 | 11,060 | 10,655 | 10,160 | 10,040 |
| American Motors | 2,317 | 2,154 | 1,579 | 1,564 | 1,526 |
| Volkswagen of America | 1,015 | 1,018 | 1,006 | 934 | 906 |
| Total | 25,773 | 24,119 | 22,618 | 21,717 | 21,844 |

*Source: Ward's Automotive Yearbooks.*

from an average of 9.7 percent to 7.3 percent. Annual Consumer Price Index increases declined from double digits to 3.9 percent in 1984. These changes made it easier for consumers to buy big-ticket items such as autos.

**Quality of Projections**   Any projection is necessarily subject to error. However, the magnitude and constant direction of the errors in the projections provided to the Chrysler Loan Guarantee Board and their acceptance by the board led to speculation regarding the objectivity of the analysis and the purpose of reports generated under the act.

## RECOVERY: EPILOGUE

*We at Chrysler borrow money the old-fashioned way. We pay it back.*—Lee Iacocca, announcing the payback of loans to Chrysler under the Chrysler Corporation Loan Guarantee Act at the National Press Club, July 13, 1983.

The first $400,000 repayment of funds borrowed under government guarantee was made from proceeds of an equity issue offered in the spring of 1983. The entire offering was sold almost immediately. In August of the same year, the remaining $813,487,500 owed was repaid and the company no longer was subject to the constraints—or the protection and assistance—of the act. Chrysler was on its own.

Chrysler's return to profitability is clearly indicated in the material presented above. The securities market also expressed confidence in the company's future as indicated by the fact that Chrysler common stock was traded at $36.75 per share on June 7, 1985, up from a low of about $3 reached in the darker days. Capacity utilization in the motor vehicle and equipment manufacturing industry hit a low of 52.9 percent in 1982, but stood at 86 percent in 1984. However, the long-term viability of the company and the industry is still the topic of some debate. That the industry and its members have not returned to full health is indicated by the fact that unemployment in the industry still totals 90,000, or about 6.6 percent of the work force. Many problems remain to be solved.

## THE FUTURE

The Motor Vehicle Manufacturers Association of the United States identified 40 issues, 18 of which were described as "key" to the industry in that important governmental action was expected in 1985. They included environmental, energy, safety, economic, and international policy issues. Many other problems of corporate strategy, financing, market penetration, new products, labor relations, and supplier relationships must be addressed by management on a continuing basis. Specifically:

- Honda emerged as the fifth largest domestic manufacturer of autos in 1984 after its first full year of operation at its Marysville, Ohio, plant. The effect of this and Nissan's plan to begin manufacturing autos at its Smyrna, Tennessee, truck plant was an open question.

- The consumer image of Chrysler (and the other domestic manufacturers as well) was still largely negative. The image of foreign manufacturers was one of greater quality.
- Strong sentiment existed for the erection of trade barriers to protect the domestic auto industry from foreign competition. The expiration of the voluntary restraints on Japanese exports, which had been in place from 1981 to 1985, had done little to lessen this sentiment. The Japanese marketplace still raised substantial barriers to U.S. products and producers.
- A continuing conflict still existed between environmentalists and the auto industry. Both had socially desirable goals but different perceptions of how they should be brought into consonance. About half of the issues identified by the Motor Vehicle Manufacturers Association fell into safety or environmental categories. The cost to the consumer in addressing these types of issues was substantial.
- A major responsibility of government is to ensure a degree of certainty in the business environment. Provision of assistance and the act of regulating seem to produce a basic conflict and uncertainty. How far can government go in assisting business and industry? What is the role of government in business? Protector? Helper? Decision maker? Owner?
- High concentration existed in the auto industry. Basic economics tells us that this limits consumer choice and adversely affects prices. Government substitutes its regulation for competition. In Chrysler's case, government subsidized a company to keep it in business at the expense of its competition.
- Should we protect specialty manufacturers because they provide an alternative to the larger producers?
- Labor was being asked to give back more and more of what it had gained through years of negotiations. These concessions may lead to a larger voice in management for labor. The form of future compensation increments was very much in doubt.
- Increases in demand for autos over the next decade were forecast to occur mostly in currently low-demand countries as their road mileage increased, as fuel became more easily available and as government trade and regulations became less restrictive. Chrysler had no foreign divisions currently in operation.

Government, labor, lending institutions, and suppliers joined with management in preventing the probable demise of a major U.S. manufacturer. How the players interacted in addressing Chrysler's problems, however, could not be considered a model for the future. Their roles and relationships in making policy and solving the problems of the U.S. economy were undergoing fundamental change and were far from established or defined by the Chrysler case.

## 11A Turner Broadcasting System, Inc.

William H. Davidson
University of Southern California

In October 1983, Ted Turner, Bill Bevans (vice-president of finance), Steven Korn (deputy counsel) and Tench Cox (senior partner, Troutman and Sanders), were discussing Turner Broadcasting's plans to acquire the Satellite News Channel (SNC) from American Broadcasting Co. and Westinghouse Electric Corp. The purchase could boost Turner Broadcasting System's (TBS) revenues by adding up to 7 million SNC subscribers to the 23 million who already received Cable News Network (CNN) or CNN Headline News in their homes. Not only would TBS collect more in subscriber fees, but advertisers would pay higher sums to buy airtime on the 24-hour-a-day all-news stations. And if Turner acquired SNC, it would put an end to the ruinous price war that had eroded TBS revenues over the past 18 months.

But TBS had finished 1982 with its third consecutive net loss, and the company's balance sheet showed liabilities totaling $153 million on assets of only $135 million. Turner wondered whether adding more debt to buy SNC was realistic, and if so, what price he should pay.

**TURNER BROADCASTING**

Robert Edward "Ted" Turner III first came to national attention in the summer of 1977, when he skippered the 12-meter yacht *Courageous* to win the America's Cup off Newport, Rhode Island. An outsider to the northeastern yachting elite, he was portrayed by the sports media as a newcomer who beat the established champions at their own game, providing Turner with an underdog image that suited him well for his later battles with the television networks.

Although the America's Cup spectators hadn't seen anyone like Turner before, around Atlanta Turner had been considered a local hero for some time. The stories about Turner made him larger than life: his maneuvering to rescue his father's billboard business from a consortium of northern businessmen, rambunctious telethons to gain viewers for his Atlanta television station, and his purchase of the Atlanta Braves to keep them from moving to Toronto. When Turner announced in 1979 that he planned to build an international 24-hour-a-day news network for cable television, there were skeptics—but few of them lived in Atlanta.

In 1963, when Turner was 24, his father took his own life. Turner's father had left his son the family billboard business, Turner Outdoor Advertising, which operated in Atlanta, Macon, and Columbus, Georgia, and Norfolk, Richmond,

This case was written by G. Rob Joseph under the supervision of Professor William H. Davidson.

and Roanoke, Virginia. But Ed Turner also had sold the company to a trio of businessmen from Minneapolis. Ted Turner asked the buyers to nullify the purchase agreement for the business, but the buyers insisted the deal was final. Before the property was transferred, however, Turner fired all the employees of his father's company, rehired them to work for a subsidiary over which he had control, and transferred the billboard location leases to the subsidiary. The consortium agreed to accept $200,000 worth of stock in Ted Turner's billboard company and return control of the company to him.

Turner's billboard company soon became a cash generator, and with the proceeds Turner bought a radio station in Chattanooga. Soon after, he acquired four more radio stations, and by 1969 he also owned a sailboat manufacturer, a direct-marketing enterprise, and a silk-screening company. In 1970 he sold most of these companies to buy Channel 17, an unprofitable UHF television station in Atlanta.

It took one year before the television station too became profitable. Turner's strategy was to "counterprogram" the network affiliates in Atlanta, starting all shows five minutes past the hour or half hour to attract viewers as they flipped their channel selectors during the first network commercial break. Turner ran "Star Trek" when the networks were running the national news. The station showed old movies and Atlanta Braves baseball games, and soon had a substantial local audience.

Turner bought the Atlanta Braves in January 1976 and the Atlanta Hawks basketball team in December 1976 to ensure that sports programming would continue to be available. Although the baseball team had consistently finished nearly last in its division for years, he attracted new players with large contracts. A team owner with a high profile, Turner was known for leaping onto the playing field when one of the Braves hit a home run so that he could shake the player's hand as he crossed home plate.

In December 1976, Turner Broadcasting beamed the Channel 17 signal onto RCA's communications satellite. The signal was made available free of charge to cable TV operators, making SuperStation WTBS, as Turner renamed it, the first advertiser-supported cable television network. A year earlier, Home Box Office, the first programming service to offer uninterrupted current movies to cable subscribers, had begun satellite broadcast, so cable systems were already installing satellite receiver dishes when the SuperStation went "on the bird." The installation of satellite antennas accelerated rapidly after the SuperStation became available.

## CABLE NEWS NETWORK

In 1979, Turner announced he would broadcast a second satellite-distributed cable programming service, Cable News Network. On June 1, 1980, CNN originated its first day of programming. Broadcasting from a converted private clubhouse on Atlanta's near north side, CNN relied on satellite technology both to distribute its programming to cable subscribers around the nation and to receive reports from news bureaus in major American and European cities.

The main studio of CNN, located on the first level of the Atlanta headquarters, resembled a cross between a newspaper newsroom and a commodity trading floor. Islands of desks arranged together by functions—reporting, editing, reviewing incoming videotape and satellite transmissions, and reading the news to a camera and national audience—filled an area the size of two basketball courts with computer monitors, television cameras, lighting equipment, typewriters, control panels, and telephones. By combining the studio and work areas, CNN achieved a look on camera that seemed improvised but in fact was meant to enhance its atmosphere of up-to-the-minute timeliness: in the foreground, the anchors read the latest news while viewers could see reporters, editors, and graphics technicians scurrying about behind the main CNN logo.

Since CNN broadcast around-the-clock, the editorial team had continuous deadlines to meet. Most videotape footage, text, and telephone "voicers" arrived through the assignment desk, an elevated platform where three to five coordinators selected stories for broadcast, told reporters in bureaus around the world when their deadlines were, and routed the flow of news within the CNN studio. From the assignment desk, a story went to videotape and copy editors, who polished and timed each piece and then submitted it to the producer. The producer set the order in which stories would appear on the air, made sure the scripts appeared in front of the anchormen and anchorwomen at the right time, and supervised the technicians. In the background, graphic artists created the letters and backgrounds that accompanied stories, and special staffs prepared the daily business, sports, and interview shows. The Atlanta headquarters employed about 600 people. Across the hall, another 100 technicians, anchors, editors, and producers summarized CNN's broadcasts into a half-hour short form for CNN Headline News.

## SUBSCRIBER REVENUE

WTBS was offered "free" to cable systems—the cable operators paid no fee to TBS for carrying the service, although they had to pay 10 cents per subscribing household per month to the company that beamed WTBS to the satellite, as required by FCC regulations.

For CNN, however, Turner charged 20 cents per subscriber household per month from cable operators. This subscriber revenue augmented the advertising fees that CNN collected. That gave Turner Broadcasting two major sources of revenue—advertising sales for airtime on the two channels and subscriber fees. Since the SuperStation cost relatively little to operate, the cash flow it generated helped to cover the considerable expense of running CNN (Exhibit 11A.1).

Turner had been the first entrepreneur to put together a national cable network that cable systems could carry on their basic channels. TBS, therefore, provided a valuable marketing tool for the cable operators, because they didn't have to charge their customers extra for a service that was available only on cable.

**Exhibit 11A.1**

## TURNER BROADCASTING SYSTEM, INC.
### Statement of Operations, Itemized by Business Unit
### (unaudited, figures in thousands)

|  | 1983 | 1982 |
|---|---|---|
| Revenue, net of commissions |  |  |
| Management services | $ 1,473 | $ 2,717 |
| WTBS | 109,797 | 78,323 |
| TB sales | 7,884 | 6,393 |
| TPS (program syndication) | 11,486 | 6,393 |
| CNN | 51,073 | 41,787 |
| CNN Headline News | 5,526 | 1,677 |
| Braves | 22,456 | 17,386 |
| Total net revenues | $209,695 | $155,609 |
| Expenses |  |  |
| Management | $ 3,373 | $ 3,139 |
| WTBS | 60,416 | 43,308 |
| TB sales | 10,066 | 7,297 |
| TPS | 13,265 | 9,487 |
| TBS Productions | 1,549 | — |
| Turner Educational Services | 111 | — |
| CNN | 54,085 | 47,035 |
| CNN Headline News | 14,331 | 10,775 |
| Braves | 22,193 | 17,049 |
| Total expenses | $179,389 | $138,090 |
| Operating income | 30,306 | 17,519 |
| Interest | 14,383 | 13,084 |
| Income before noncash charges and equity in ltd. partnerships | 15,923 | 4,435 |
| Depreciation and amortization | 5,763 | 5,869 |
| Equity in ltd. partnerships | (3,313) | (2,698) |
| Net income (loss) | $ 6,847 | $ (3,350) |

*Source:* TBS controller.

This innovation, combined with Turner's swashbuckling image, contributed to his favorable relations with cable operators. As a result, the two Turner services were the most widely carried cable services in the United States except for ESPN, the sports network. Turner was consistently one of the most requested speakers at cable conventions.

**THE CABLE TELEVISION INDUSTRY** The first cable TV system began operations in 1948 in rural Pennsylvania, where hills blocked out TV signals. To sell more television sets, a local store owner erected an antenna on top of a hill and connected it to the neighborhood's television sets with copper wire. Jack Benny's monologues and Milton Berle's slapstick came in more clearly in those Pennsylvania homes than on the flickering TV sets sold to the rest of the nation, and cable systems began to spring up around the country. Thereafter hundreds of entrepreneurs built community antenna television (CATV) systems in areas that had poor over-the-air television reception, and the cable industry grew rapidly.

Cable television systems generally operated under a franchise license from the local community, which regulated their fees. As the number of subscribers climbed, the Federal Communications Commission (FCC) became increasingly involved as it became apparent that CATV systems were competing with broadcast stations under the FCC's authority. The regulatory environment was influenced partly by lobbying from the major networks and their broadcast affiliates. At first NBC, ABC, and CBS welcomed the growth of cable systems, since more viewers could see their programming. But they objected when cable systems began carrying independent broadcast stations that took viewers away from the networks.

By 1983, cable systems could carry independent broadcast signals provided they paid a fee to the common carrier (the telephone line, microwave, or satellite system that delivered the signal) (Exhibit 11A.2). Independent stations could beam their signals to cable systems around the country, but they were required to pay a royalty for the shows they broadcast to the Copyright Tribunal, a government agency set up to distribute these royalties to the syndicators that owned the TV shows.

The cable industry was highly fragmented; for the most part local entrepreneurs built the systems. Almost 6000 cable systems operated in the United States in 1983. Increasingly, small systems were being purchased and operated by conglomerates, called multisystem operators (MSOs). The largest MSO, Telecommunications Inc., owned 270 cable systems and served 2.5 million subscribers, or 8.6 percent of all the cable households in the nation. The trend toward consolidation of cable systems was accelerating. In 1983, the top 73 MSOs accounted for 20 percent of the cable subscribers in the country (Exhibit 11A.3).

The chief advantage that an MSO held over the small cable system operator was marketing expertise. The corporate headquarters commonly sent marketing managers to visit the smaller systems and inform them of techniques for boosting the number of subscribers and viewership of their systems. On a street that already was served by the cable company, the cost of adding an additional household was low. By increasing penetration (the ratio of cable households to total households available), the cable operator could increase revenues and profitability (Exhibit 11A.4).

## THE ROLE OF ADVERTISING

Another source of revenue for cable operators was available from sales of advertising on their systems (Exhibit 11A.5). Most advertiser-supported national ser-

## Exhibit 11A.2 Twenty-five Largest Cable Satellite Services, 1983

| Video Service | Programming | Subscribers | Percent of U.S. Homes |
|---|---|---|---|
| ESPN<br>Briston, Conn. | Sports events | 28.5 million | 34.2 |
| WTBS<br>Atlanta, Ga. | Independent station | 27.7 million | 33.3 |
| Cable News Network<br>Atlanta, Ga. | News/special features | 22.6 million | 27.1 |
| CBN Cable Network<br>Virginia Beach, Va. | Religious/family<br>programming | 22.2 million | 26.7 |
| USA Cable Network<br>Glen Rock, N.J. | Sports/entertainment | 20.0 million | 24.0 |
| C-SPAN<br>Washington, D.C. | House of Representatives<br>& political<br>programming | 15.7 million | 18.8 |
| MTV Music Television<br>New York, N.Y. | Video rock music | 15.0 million | 18.0 |
| Cable Health Network<br>New York, N.Y. | Health programming | 14.0 million | 16.8 |
| Financial News Network<br>Santa Monica, Calif. | Financial programming | 12.8 million | 15.4 |
| ARTS<br>New York, N.Y. | Cultural programming | 12.6 million | 15.1 |
| Home Box Office<br>New York, N.Y. | Movies/specials | 12.5 million | 15.0 |
| WGN<br>Chicago, Ill. | Independent station | 10.9 million | 13.1 |
| The Nashville Network<br>Nashville, Tenn. | Country music | 10.0 million | 12.0 |
| The Weather Channel<br>Atlanta, Ga. | National and local<br>weather | 10.0 million | 12.0 |
| Daytime<br>New York, N.Y. | Programming for women | 9.5 million | 11.4 |
| Satellite Program<br>Network<br>New York, N.Y. | Variety | 8.8 million | 10.6 |
| MSN—The Information<br>Channel<br>New York, N.Y. | Variety | 8.7 million | 10.4 |
| PTL Satellite Network<br>Charlotte, N.C. | Religious | 8.5 million | 10.2 |
| CNN Headline News<br>Atlanta, Ga. | News cycles | 7.8 million | 9.4 |
| Black Entertainment<br>Television<br>Washington, D.C. | Programming for black<br>audiences | 5.1 million | 6.1 |

(continued)

**Exhibit 11A.2**   (continued)

| Video Service | Programming | Subscribers | Percent of U.S. Homes |
|---|---|---|---|
| Showtime<br>New York, N.Y. | Movies/specials | 4.7 million | 5.6 |
| WOR<br>New York, N.Y. | Independent station | 4.3 million | 5.2 |
| ACSN—The Learning<br>  Channel<br>Washington, D.C. | Education/community<br>  programming | 3.8 million | 4.6 |
| Trinity Broadcasting<br>  Network<br>Santa Ana, Calif. | Religious | 3.4 million | 4.1 |

*Source: NCTA Satellite Services Book,* December 1983.

**Exhibit 11A.3** Systems and Subscribers by Number of Subscribers

| Number of Subscribers | Systems | Percent of All Systems | Basic Subscribers | Percent of All Subscribers |
|---|---|---|---|---|
| 0–1,000 | 2518 | 43.29 | 1,126,153 | 3.88 |
| 1,001–5,000 | 1916 | 32.94 | 4,622,469 | 15.91 |
| 5,001–10,000 | 551 | 9.47 | 3,980,607 | 13.70 |
| 10,001–20,000 | 384 | 6.60 | 5,373,067 | 18.49 |
| 20,001–50,000 | 249 | 4.28 | 7,639,286 | 26.29 |
| 50,000+ | 73 | 1.26 | 5,591,355 | 19.58 |
| Not available | 125 | 2.15 | 627,819 | 2.16 |
| Totals | 5816 | | 29,060,756 | |

*Source:* ICR, Titsch Communications, September 1983.

vices, including CNN, ESPN, USA, CBN, and Lifetime, made a certain number of time slots each hour available for local advertising. For example, at 23 minutes past the hour, CNN ran a public service announcement on its national feed, and cable operators had permission to preempt the spot with a 30-second commercial from the local community. The cable operator would put a videotape cassette with the commercial recorded on it into a playback machine that would automatically start when it heard the computerized "cue tone" come over the national network. By setting the machine on automatic, the cable operator could collect advertising fees with little incremental labor cost.

The advertising rates charged at the local level followed the same principle that had governed television since the beginning of the networks. Advertisers paid rates that were based on the number of households that were tuned into a certain channel at a given time. Television audience sizes were measured by the A. C.

**Exhibit 11A.4** Pro Forma Income Statement of a Typical Cable System (figures in thousands)

| Assumptions | | |
|---|---|---|
| Miles of cable | 900 | |
| Basic subscriber penetrations | 0.455 | |
| Basic monthly fee | $7.00 | |

| Pay-TV | Price | Pay-TV Penetration |
|---|---|---|
| HBO | $7.00 | 0.33 |
| Showtime | $7.00 | 0.12 |
| PRISM | $9.00 | 0.26 |
| Cinemax | | |
| $4      .00 | | 0.08 |

| Revenues | |
|---|---|
| Basic | $6,139.5 |
| Installation fees | 28.6 |
| Pay-TV (net) | 2,962.4 |
| Total revenues | $9,130.5 |

| Expenses | |
|---|---|
| Basic expense | $3,095.3 |
| Franchise fee | 456.5 |
| Depreciation | 1,658.4 |
| Total | $5,210.2 |

| Profit before tax | $3,920.3 |
|---|---|

| Taxes | $2,254.2 |
|---|---|
| Investment tax credit | $1,692.8 |

*Source:* G. Kent Webb, *The Economics of Cable Television* (Lexington, Mass.: Lexington Books, 1983), pp. 134–35.

Nielsen Co. and Arbitron, among others. In sample households, a meter connected to the television sent information about the time and channel that the set was tuned to through telephone lines to a central computer. Other households reported their viewing with diaries that contained time schedules for family members to record the shows they watched and the time they spent viewing. Meter data were considered more accurate, but diary data provided demographic information about the audiences for various shows. Viewership data were used to determine fees for advertising slots. Broadcasters, ad agencies, and advertisers used Nielsen and Arbitron ratings to calculate the size of the viewing audience for any ad slot. The expected audience size was multiplied by a revenue rate, expressed as a cost per thousand households, to determine fees. For example, if the rating services estimated that NBC delivered 6.7 million households for an episode of "Cheers," and the cost per thousand was $2.50, then a 30-second national commercial would cost $16,750.

**Exhibit 11A.5** Estimated Cable TV Network Advertising Revenues (figures in millions)

| Network | 1982 Gross Ad Revs. | 1983 Gross Ad Revs. | 1984 Proj. Ad Revs. |
|---|---|---|---|
| ARTS | $ 2.1 | $ 1.5 | $ 1.3 |
| BET | 1.8 | 2.5 | 4.3 |
| CBN | 6.5 | 12.5 | 26.0 |
| CHN | 1.9 | 6.8 | — |
| Country Music TV | — | — | 0.8 |
| CNN | 24.0 | 31.5 | 45.0 |
| CNN Headline | 1.5 | 2.0 | 7.5 |
| Daytime | 1.5 | 2.2 | — |
| ESPN | 26.0 | 41.0 | 60.0 |
| FNN | 1.8 | 3.6 | 10.5 |
| Lifetime | — | — | 21.0 |
| MSN | 0.5 | 0.3 | 0.5 |
| MTV | 6.8 | 24.0 | 36.0 |
| Nashville | — | 5.9 | 17.5 |
| SIN | 1.5 | 1.8 | 2.2 |
| SNC | 1.5 | 1.9 | — |
| SPN | 0.7 | 0.9 | 1.8 |
| USA | 18.5 | 29.5 | 41.6 |
| Weather Channel | 0.9 | 2.5 | 4.1 |
| WGN | 8.0 | 10.0 | 12.0 |
| WOR | 5.0 | 5.0 | 5.0 |
| WTBS | 85.0 | 117.0 | 148.0 |
| Totals | $ 195.2 | $ 302.6 | $ 448.7 |

*Source:* Paul Kagan Associates, Inc.

Audience size was critical in determining broadcasting revenues, but the revenue rate also varied sharply. The major networks, who established prevailing price levels, set very different rates for different times of day and individual programs. A typical rate for daytime programming would be in the $2 range. Rates during prime time averaged about $5 per thousand households. Shows with high ratings had the highest cost per thousand households. Advertisers would pay a premium for a show with a 30 rating (30 percent of all viewing households) to ensure a broader audience for their commercials. The purchase of three slots with 10 ratings would not reach as many unique households because of overlap among the viewer populations. The higher the show's rating, the more attractive and expensive ad slots became.

CNN used revenue rates that were slightly lower than the major networks. Although ad fees on WTBS or CNN were negotiable, the pricing schedule was not highly flexible. Turner Broadcasting had a rigid policy of enforcing integrity in pricing for ad slots. The advertising sales department frequently had to reject business because of pricing considerations.

Cable networks were in competition with the national networks and independent broadcasters for ad revenues. Before the boom of cable service, the networks had enjoyed a 95 percent share of household viewership. But by 1977, the networks' share had declined to 86 percent, and by 1983, it was estimated that only 77 percent of the viewing audience was tuned to the networks during prime time. The networks were losing viewers to the national cable networks, to local independent stations, and to the public broadcasting system. However, the major networks' share of advertising revenues remained at over 90 percent of total spending on television media.

**NEW TECHNOLOGIES**

Both the networks and the cable services were threatened by the advent of new television technologies. Although still experimental in 1984, direct-broadcast satellite television (DBS) opened the possibility that homeowners could buy their own three-foot-diameter satellite dish antennas to receive the same programming that the cable services provided—but without the monthly subscription charge. A second technology, low-power television, was being encouraged by the FCC. Local stations broadcasting at low wattage would be able to program their signals without the usual requirements that the FCC required of larger stations: public service programming, news programming, and local access that added to the overhead expense of regular television stations. An additional development, satellite master antenna television (SMATV), allowed owners of hotels and apartment complexes to buy their own seven-meter-diameter satellite dish antennas and receive cable programming, which they could provide to living units through a small-scale cable system. Already widespread in 1984, SMATV systems provided the same service as the local cable franchise but without the monthly charge. They had resulted in substantial erosion of cable system revenues.

Cable itself promised to change rapidly during the next few decades. Since 1974, most new cable laid was designed for two-way communication, under the expectation that consumers could shop, bank, and even subscribe to magazines and data bases at home. Some industry analysts foresaw an age of electronic mail, where paper documents would be replaced by communication over television. And although the divestment of AT&T's operating subsidiaries had injected considerable ambiguity into the role that the telephone company would play in the future, there was speculation that by the end of the century telephone and television service would have merged.

**OUTLOOK**

Despite these competing technologies, the number of households wired for cable television was forecast to increase through the end of the decade. Industry forecasts projected that the number of cable households would reach 58.9 million in 1990, an annual growth rate of 9.8 percent. That would represent 62 percent of all U.S. television households (Exhibit 11A.6).

**Exhibit 11A.6**

| PENETRATION OF TBS SERVICES | | |
|---|---|---|
| | December 1982 | December 1983 (est.) |
| Superstation WTBS | | |
| Homes (000s) | 24,990 | 28,492 |
| Percent of U.S. | 0.30 | 0.34 |
| Number of systems | 4,885 | 5,803 |
| Cable News Network | | |
| Homes (000s) | 17,493 | 25,140 |
| Percent of U.S. | 0.21 | 0.30 |
| Number of systems | 3,240 | 4,278 |
| CNN Headline News | | |
| Homes | 2,393 | 9,860 |
| Percent of U.S. | 0.03 | 0.12 |
| Number of systems | 340 | 983 |

**SUBSCRIBER FORECASTS THROUGH 1990**

| | Estimated Households | U.S. TV Households | Percent of U.S. TV Households |
|---|---|---|---|
| Cable Penetration | | | |
| 1985 | 40,619 | 84,800 | 48 |
| 1986 | 44,359 | 85,800 | 52 |
| 1987 | 48,348 | 86,800 | 56 |
| 1988 | 52,241 | 87,800 | 60 |
| 1989 | 55,944 | 88,800 | 63 |
| 1990 | 59,537 | 89,800 | 66 |
| SuperStation WTBS | | | |
| 1985 | 33,750 | 84,800 | 40 |
| 1986 | 36,894 | 85,800 | 43 |
| 1987 | 40,796 | 86,800 | 47 |
| 1988 | 44,778 | 87,800 | 51 |
| 1989 | 48,840 | 88,800 | 55 |
| 1990 | 52,084 | 89,800 | 58 |
| Cable News Network | | | |
| 1985 | 32,817 | 84,800 | 39 |
| 1986 | 38,009 | 85,800 | 44 |
| 1987 | 42,359 | 86,800 | 49 |
| 1988 | 46,358 | 87,800 | 53 |
| 1989 | 50,438 | 88,800 | 57 |
| 1990 | 53,700 | 89,800 | 60 |

*Source:* TBS research.

The increasing popularity of cable meant that advertisers could no longer reach their intended audiences merely by buying time on the three networks, as they had done for decades. In 1982, the advertising industry spent $12.7 billion for national and local spot television advertising. Cable programmers received $200 million of that total. By 1990, according to projections by RCA Corp., advertising expenditures would reach $32.3 billion, of which the cable industry would receive $3.5 billion. The network and network-affiliated stations would receive a total of $24.6 billion in 1990, up from $11.1 billion in 1982, according to RCA. The projections assumed that the advertising industry would shift substantial portions of their budgets to cable.

To advertisers, cable presented the advantage of reaching an audience with more buying power per person than the American public as a whole. Surveys showed that cable households tended to be younger, more affluent, and more disposed toward owning household appliances, sports equipment, and other consumer durables.

Cable programmers like Turner Broadcasting used these superior demographics to sell advertising. For example, they argued that companies that made sports equipment, nutritional supplements, and other health-oriented products would reach the right consumers by advertising on Cable Health Network. ESPN, a national network that broadcasts sports events, pitched its airtime as appealing to males aged 25–54, and attracted advertising from automobile, beer, and tool companies. MTV, a station that presented rock-and-roll videos, attracted a teen-aged audience. The Financial News Network, on the other hand, broadcast only during business hours and advertised subscriptions to business publications like the *Wall Street Journal.*

In addition to SuperStation WTBS, two other "superstations" were reaching subscribers outside their broadcast areas. WOR in New York City and WGN in Chicago both transmitted a satellite signal that could be carried by cable systems. But they were "passive" superstations. Station management placed almost no emphasis on attracting a national audience. The impetus for national distribution came instead from the common carrier that collected a subscriber fee for providing the satellite link. Thus viewers in places like Portland, Oregon, found they were frequently urged to bring their car repair needs to West Diversey Street in Chicago, or to buy tickets to the latest Broadway hits.

Although most national cable networks hoped to attract specific audiences, Turner Broadcasting had aimed its programming at the general public. SuperStation WTS showed old movies and television series that had previously succeeded on network television, including "Hogan's Heroes," "The Andy Griffith Show," "The Munsters," and "Rat Patrol." Together with its sports events (Atlanta Braves baseball, Atlanta Hawks basketball, and Big Time wrestling), WTBS positioned itself as classic family entertainment. CNN, on the other hand, broadcast news and features that viewers could tune in for up-to-the-minute reports of major happenings. Nielsen research showed that CNN viewership increased dramatically whenever an unpredicted major news event took place, such as the assassination attempt on President Reagan. While the channel showed news all day and night, however, its programming was not confined to breaking news. The schedule included a daily talk and news show at 12 noon, an evening business report at 7 P.M. eastern time, and an interview show at 10 P.M.

Since viewership ratings determined the advertising sales revenue that Turner services would receive, the company was concerned with two components of viewership. First was the number of households that could receive WTBS and CNN, that is, the number of cable systems that allocated a channel to each service. Since WTBS had been available to cable systems for a longer time than CNN, it was available in more households: 28.5 million in October 1983 on 5803 cable systems, representing 74 percent of all cable homes and 34 percent of all television homes. CNN was available in 25.1 million cable homes via 4278 cable systems.

The second component of viewership was the number of households that were actually tuned into one of the two services during a given hour. Exhibit 11A.7 shows an itemization of ratings by time of day, revealing that WTBS reached its highest viewership levels during weekend afternoons, when it ran old movies.

These viewership ratings were dwarfed by the networks, however. On a typical evening, more than half of all the televisions in the United States were tuned to the networks. However, the number of households watching network program-

**Exhibit 11A.7**

| **WTBS RATINGS BY DAY PART** | | | | |
|---|---|---|---|---|
| | **Day Part** | **Rating** | **Households Delivered (thousands)** | **Programming** |
| M–Su | 8 A.M.–11 P.M. | 4.0 | 1173 | Prime movies |
| M–F | 7 A.M.–9 A.M. | 2.8 | 821 | Kids' sitcoms |
| M–F | 9 A.M.–3 P.M. | 2.2 | 645 | Movies/soaps |
| M–F | 3 P.M.–6 P.M. | 3.1 | 909 | Kids' programs |
| M–F | 6 P.M.–8 P.M. | 3.8 | 1115 | Sitcoms |
| M–F | 11 P.M.–1 A.M. | 1.3 | 381 | Catlins/Late Show |
| Sa | 8 A.M.–1 P.M. | 3.4 | 997 | Morning Movies |
| Sa | 1 P.M.–6 P.M. | 5.4 | 1584 | Afternoon Movies |
| Su | 8 A.M.–1 P.M. | 5.3 | 1554 | Sitcoms/Academy Award Theater |
| Su | 1 P.M.–6 P.M. | 6.2 | 1818 | Afternoon Movies |
| Sa–Su | 6 P.M.–8 P.M. | 4.7 | 1379 | Wrestling |

| **WTBS RATINGS PERFORMANCE 24-HOUR AVERAGES** | **January 1984** | **January 1983** |
|---|---|---|
| Households using TV | 36.6 | 4.9 |
| Rating | 2.6 | 2.5 |
| Share | 7 | 7 |
| Households delivered (thousands) | 763 | 625 |

ming was estimated to be 13 percent lower in cable homes than in noncable homes (Exhibit 11A.8).

Cable News Network attracted considerably fewer viewers (Exhibit 11A.9). Since the average cost per thousand for a 30-second national commercial was $2.00 on CNN, the company was concerned about the low ratings. They calculated that a gain of 0.1 of a rating point would result in $10 million in additional advertising revenue over the course of a year.

Turner Broadcasting advertised its services through two main channels. National advertising appeared in general-circulation magazines such as *Time, Esquire,* and *TV Guide.* These ads were administered by the Advertising and Promotion Department. Also, each Turner network ran commercials for the other networks during regular programming. For example, CNN devoted two minutes an hour to promotions for WTBS, featuring upcoming movies and sports events.

The second mechanism for advertising the services was carried out by Turner Cable Sales, the division charged with signing up cable systems to carry the

**Exhibit 11A.8** Network Ratings in Cable vs. Noncable Homes

| | Prime-Time Ratings 8–11 P.M. M–Su | | | |
|---|---|---|---|---|
| | U.S. Homes | Cable Homes | Non-cable Homes | Percentage Difference Cable/Noncable |
| ABC | 16.6 | 15.3 | 17.6 | −13 |
| CBS | 18.2 | 16.9 | 19.3 | −12 |
| NBC | 15.6 | 14.4 | 16.5 | −13 |
| Combined networks | 50.4 | 46.6 | 53.4 | −13 |

*Source:* A. C. Nielsen Co.

**Exhibit 11A.9** Cable News Network Ratings by Day Part/Program

| | Time | Program | Rating | Households (thousands) |
|---|---|---|---|---|
| M–F | 6 A.M.–9 A.M. | Daybreak | 0.3 | 75 |
| M–F | 9 A.M.–12 N | Daywatch | 0.7 | 176 |
| M–F | 12 N–2 P.M. | Take Two | 0.7 | 176 |
| M–F | 2 P.M.–5 P.M. | Afternoon News | 0.5 | 126 |
| M–F | 5 P.M.–7 P.M. | Newswatch | 0.8 | 201 |
| M–F | 7–7:30 P.M. | Moneyline | 1.0 | 251 |
| M–F | 7:30–8 P.M. | Crossfire | 1.3 | 327 |
| M–F | 8 P.M.–10 P.M. | Prime News | 1.7 | 176 |
| M–F | 10 P.M.–11 P.M. | Freeman Reports | 0.6 | 151 |
| Sa–Su | 6 A.M.–12 N | Weekend News | 0.9 | 226 |
| Sa–Su | 12 N–6 P.M. | Weekend News | 1.1 | 277 |

*Source:* A. C. Nielsen Co.

services. As a sales incentive, Turner Cable Sales provided funds to each cable system, based on the number of subscribers it had, for spending or local advertising. Turner Cable Sales also provided free marketing materials to cable systems, including radio scripts, newspaper advertising layouts, T-shirts, baseball caps, direct-mail inserts to be included with monthly cable system bills, coffee mugs, and even copies of a biography of Ted Turner. The two advertising and promotion departments were budgeted to spend $11.8 million in 1984.

**SATELLITE NEWS CHANNEL**

Despite these efforts, Turner Broadcasting had been unprofitable since the start-up of CNN in 1980 (Exhibits 11A.10 and 11A.11). CNN had lost $2 million per month in 1983. One factor that contributed to CNN's continuing losses was the advent of a competitor, Satellite News Channel. A joint venture of the American Broadcasting Company and Group W Communications (the media subsidiary of Westinghouse Electric Co.), Satellite News Channel began broadcasting on June 1, 1982. The channel provided 24-hour-a-day news reports in 18-minute segments.

ABC and Group W had announced in late 1981 that they would form Satellite News Channel. One month later, Ted Turner announced that his company would begin a new programming service, CNN Headline News, which would broadcast half-hour summaries of the latest news in a format similar to SNC's. Turner's new service began broadcasting on December 31, 1981. When SNC came on line six months later, the two companies found themselves competing head-to-head for limited channel capacity on the nation's cable systems.

The Turner Cable sales force, faced for the first time with competition from another all-news channel, stepped up the pace of signing on new cable systems to carry the Turner services. While Turner Broadcasting had charged cable systems 20 cents per subscriber per month for CNN, it offered to provide CNN Headline News for free. The rate for CNN was 15 cents for cable systems that also carried SuperStation WTBS on its basic selection channels, providing an incentive for the operator to carry both services at once. SNC, however, offered to pay each cable system that carried it as much as 25 cents per subscriber. SNC also offered large sign-up bonuses to new cable customers. The consequence was an erosion in the price that cable systems were willing to pay for CNN. Where Turner Broadcasting had intended to collect an average of between 16 and 18 cents per subscriber, the average monthly rate per subscriber stood at only 7 cents by September 1983. These price cuts usually took the form of fixed-fee contracts where large multisystem operators were guaranteed a maximum total charge for CNN regardless of the number of households served. Where CNN had been budgeted to bring $30 million in subscribers fees in 1983, the actual number was estimated to be $21 million.

At the same time, it was difficult to trim CNN's costs because of the high broadcast standards that the station strove to uphold. CNN's budget for 1983 had been $59.1 million. The CNN budget for 1984 was $70.9 million.

In March 1983, Turner launched a legal salvo against SNC and its corporate

**Exhibit 11A.10**

## TURNER BROADCASTING SYSTEM, INC.
### Consolidated Income Statement
**(figures in thousands, except per share data)**

|  | 1983 | 1982 | 1981 | 1980 |
|---|---|---|---|---|
| Revenues |  |  |  |  |
| Broadcasting | $136,217 | $ 96,647 | $ 55,329 | $ 35,495 |
| Cable productions | 65,169 | 49,708 | 27,738 | 7,201 |
| Professional sports | 21,401 | 16,263 | 8,840 | 9,211 |
| Management fees from affiliated company | 1,462 | 2,717 | 2,835 | 2,473 |
| Other | 283 | 306 | 305 | 230 |
|  | $224,532 | $165,641 | $ 95,047 | $ 54,610 |
| Cost and expenses |  |  |  |  |
| Cost of operations | $105,685 | $ 81,187 | $ 49,036 | $ 33,391 |
| Selling, general, and administrative | 80,722 | 60,343 | 37,067 | 26,951 |
| Amortization of player, film, and other contract rights | 8,674 | 7,497 | 4,010 | 4,013 |
| Depreciation | 4,706 | 4,182 | 3,469 | 2,172 |
| Interest expense and amortization of debt discount, restructing fees, and imputed interest | 14,383 | 13,084 | 9,673 | 4,437 |
|  | $214,170 | $166,293 | $103,255 | $ 70,964 |
| Operating income (loss) | 10,362 | (652) | (8,208) | (16,354) |
| Equity in losses of limited partnerships | (3,350) | (2,698) | (8,208) | (2,905) |
| Income (loss) before gains on dispositions of properties | 7,012 | (3,350) | (13,423) | (19,259) |
| Gains on dispositions of properties | — | — | — | 15,684 |
| Income (loss) before provision for income taxes | 7,012 | (3,350) | (13,423) | (19,259) |
| Provision for income tax | — | — | — | 200 |
| Net income (loss) | $ 7,012 | $ (3,340) | $ (13,423) | $ (3,775) |
| Net income (loss) per common share | .34 | (.16) | (.66) | (.19) |
| Common shares outstanding | 20,393 | 20,402 | 20,358 | 20,062 |

parents. It sued Group W for allegedly preventing Turner access to cable systems owned by Group W cable, an MSO owned by Westinghouse. These systems totaled about 2 million subscribers in 1983 and included several key markets, such as most of Manhattan. Turner Broadcasting charged Group W with restraint of trade, and charged that it was forcing cable systems it owned to carry SNC rather than the Turner News Services.

Lawyers for both sides spent the spring of 1983 in the discovery phase, photo-

## TURNER BROADCASTING SYSTEM, INC.
### Consolidated Balance Sheet
### (in thousands, except per share data)

| | 1983 | 1982 | 1981 | 1980 |
|---|---|---|---|---|
| **Assets** | | | | |
| Cash | $ 594 | $ 538 | $ 504 | $ 489 |
| Accounts receivable | 31,768 | 23,731 | 17,701 | 9,869 |
| Current portion of film contract rights | 12,613 | 4,516 | 3,495 | 2,521 |
| Prepaid expenses | 2,177 | 3,868 | 1,086 | 552 |
| Other current assets | 4,965 | 2,585 | 1,433 | 1,591 |
| Total current assets | $ 51,667 | $ 35,238 | $ 24,222 | $15,022 |
| Property, plant and equipment | 71,505 | 33,555 | 28,698 | 26,647 |
| Intangible assets | 25,567 | 34,000 | — | — |
| Film contract rights, less current portion | 26,057 | 15,633 | 9,464 | 5,660 |
| Player and other contract rights, less amortization | 1,246 | 1,583 | 2,084 | 2,784 |
| Investment in limited partnerships | 1,633 | 1,900 | 900 | 2,027 |
| Deferred charges | 13,926 | 6,585 | 9,623 | — |
| Deferred program production costs | 11,432 | 4,460 | — | — |
| Other assets | 2,805 | 2,232 | 1,970 | 1,878 |
| Total assets | $205,838 | $135,186 | $ 76,961 | $54,018 |
| **Liabilities and stockholders' deficit** | | | | |
| Current liabilities | | | | |
| Short-term borrowings | $— | $ 49,924 | $ 42,783 | $17,907 |
| Accounts payable | 6,954 | 7,548 | 3,926 | 2,079 |
| Accrued expenses | 22,551 | 16,750 | 11,152 | 7,196 |
| Deferred income | 7,083 | 7,220 | 2,226 | 700 |
| Current portion of long-term debt | 14,473 | 4,266 | 3,005 | 8,430 |
| Current portion of obligations for film contract rights | 11,317 | 5,613 | 3,465 | 2,456 |
| Current portion of debt restructuring fees | 3,650 | 3,000 | 2,253 | — |
| Total current liabilities | $ 66,028 | $ 94,321 | $ 68,810 | $38,931 |
| Long-term debt, less current portion | 122,404 | 42,802 | 7,165 | 9,825 |
| Obligations for film contract rights, less current portion | 13,959 | 7,379 | 3,943 | 2,662 |
| Obligations under employment contracts, net of imputed interest | 5,201 | 3,442 | 2,560 | 2,221 |
| Deferred income | 562 | 646 | 1,313 | — |
| Debt restructuring fees | 650 | 3,000 | 4,207 | — |
| Other liabilities | 7,507 | 1,097 | 3,117 | 1,201 |
| Total liabilities | $216,311 | $152,687 | $ 91,115 | $54,840 |
| Stockholders' deficit | | | | |
| Common stock | 2,663 | 2,663 | 2,663 | 2,663 |
| Capital in excess of par value | 1,508 | 1,508 | 1,508 | 602 |
| Accumulated deficit | (12,734) | (19,746) | (16,396) | (2,973) |
| Less 906,000 shares of common stock in treasury | (754) | (474) | (474) | (605) |
| Notes receivable from sales of common stock in treasury | (1,156) | (1,452) | (1,455) | (509) |
| Total treasury stock | (1,910) | (1,926) | (1,929) | (1,114) |
| Total stockholders' deficit[a] | $ (10,473) | $ (17,501) | $(14,154) | $ (822) |
| Total liabilities and stockholders' deficit | $205,838 | $135,186 | $ 76,961 | $54,018 |

[a]Approximately 87 percent of TBS stock was owned by Ted Turner.

copying internal documents and analyzing details of each other's businesses. At the same, Turner filed a second suit against Group W, charging them with failure to pay overdue fees and cancellation payments owed to Turner Broadcasting from cable systems acquired by Group W. This suit had become the focal point of the confrontation between SNC and Turner by June 1983. In July, Griffin Bell (former attorney general under President Carter), as the chief lawyer for SNC, suggested that the two parties search for a "larger settlement." In September, Dan Ritchie, chairman of Group W, suggested that Mr. William Daniels mediate the negotiations between Turner and SNC. Mr. Daniels, chairman of Daniels and Associates, was an ex-marine who was considered the founding father of the cable TV industry. Daniels conducted shuttle diplomacy between New York and Atlanta to communicate offers and counteroffers as they developed.

On September 16, the *Wall Street Journal* reported that Turner Broadcasting was negotiating the acquisition of SNC. The TBS stock price rose 5¾ points to 31 in the first three hours before trading was halted by the Securities and Exchange Commission. Turner's lawyers met with the SEC to establish that no leak or insider trading had occurred. They also met with officials of the Regulated Industries Section of the Anti-Trust Division to review plans for the acquisition.

By early October, a preliminary agreement had been worked out in the ongoing sessions between SNC and Turner lawyers and management. All major obstacles had been cleared except the issue of acquisition price. It was difficult to establish a value for the company, since it was unclear when the service would become profitable. SNC had lost an estimated $80–90 million since its founding. SNC had generated less than $3 million in ad revenue during that period. In addition, field salesmen from the TBS Cable Sales Division were reporting that cable system operators had begun to inquire about switching from SNC to CNN. With these issues in mind, the Turner team began their strategy session to prepare for the final round of negotiations with the SNC representatives resident in Atlanta.

# 11B Turner Broadcasting System, Inc.

Neil H. Snyder
University of Virginia

**AN ABORTED TAKEOVER ATTEMPT**

For many years, Ted Turner's interest in acquiring a major television network was widely known. Finally, in late April 1985, Ted Turner made his move and announced his intention to purchase CBS, a goal that seemed unattainable since CBS is 17 times bigger than TBS. In preparation for this action, CNN had been offered for sale to the three major networks in 1981. CBS offered $250 million and NBC $200 million. One of Turner's stipulations about the sale of CNN was that he was to be paid in stock. When the networks realized that this deal would make Turner the largest single stockholder of the company acquiring CNN, they promptly withdrew their offers. As recently as March 1985, Turner was still trying to entice CBS into a deal that would enable Turner to gain control of CBS in a friendly manner, but his attempts failed. Undaunted, Ted Turner, together with the aid of E. F. Hutton & Company, made an offer to the shareholders of CBS to gain control of the network by exchanging debt for stock in a hostile takeover attempt.

Turner's plan was to acquire 73 percent of CBS's 30 million outstanding shares of stock (5 percent more than the 67 percent required by New York State for the merger to take place). To do this, TBS would have had to borrow heavily and offer a variety of high-risk debt securities in exchange for the CBS stock. At the time of the offer, CBS's net worth was estimated at $7.6 billion, or $254 a share. The face value of Turner's offer was for $175 a share in securities, but estimates of the market value of the offer ranged from $155 to $130 a share.

Besides TBS stock, the other securities offered to CBS shareholders were low-quality, high-risk junk bonds paying 15 percent interest or higher and zero coupon bonds which require the payment of the principal and interest in a lump sum at maturity. Zeros would have allowed Turner to borrow $600 million and pay nothing until 1990. In addition, each share of TBS offered to CBS shareholders would have had only one-tenth of a vote. Thus, Turner would have maintained control of 73 percent of the voting rights in TBS stock.

If Turner's offer had been accepted, he would have acquired the broadcast network and four of the five CBS owned and operated television stations. Turner had planned to sell one station, the CBS records group, the CBS publishing group, radio stations, and various other holdings for $3.1 billion and to apply the proceeds from these sales to the debt. Selling off these pieces of CBS would have

© 1986 by Neil H. Snyder. All rights reserved. This case was prepared by Donna Biemiller, Kerrie Morrison, Diane Reiff, and Laura Weiss under the direction of Neil H. Snyder of the McIntire School of Commerce, University of Virginia. It is designed to be used as a basis for discussion rather than to illustrate either effective or ineffective handling of an administrative situation.

reduced the total cost of the deal from $7.6 billion to $4.5 billion. Exhibit 11B.1 presents a financial summary of the offer to CBS.

From the perspective of CBS stockholders, the proposed offer would result in the exchange of a $3 per year CBS dividend for $21.71 in interest and preferred stock dividends from TBS. Although the offer sounds very appealing, Wall Street analysts expressed concern about the security of the TBS assets.

**THE CBS RESPONSE**   To ward off the hostile takeover attempt, CBS had several alternatives. One option was to find a "white knight," a more suitable and friendly merger partner. Another possibility, and the one preferred by CBS directors, was to increase their debt and buy back their own stock. By raising additional debt, CBS would make their acquisition by Turner even riskier, because the combined debt of CBS and TBS after the merger would virtually guarantee failure. Additionally, the stock repurchase would leave fewer shares available for purchase by Turner.

Subsequently, CBS purchased 6.4 million shares of their stock, roughly 21 percent of the shares outstanding, at a cost of $960 million. The price paid by CBS for the stock was $40 per share in cash, plus $110 per share in senior notes at 10⅞ percent interest due to mature in 1995. A "poison pill," a maneuver designed to make CBS an unattractive takeover target in the future, was added by the placing of limits on the amount of debt CBS can carry. The plan also included the sale of $123 million in new convertible preferred shares to institutional investors.

To prevent the repurchase plan, Turner filed a suit against CBS accusing its directors of a breach of fiduciary duty. The complaint alleged that the board was motivated by self-interest and that it was attempting to insulate the CBS shareholders from Turner's offer. On July 30, both the FCC and a federal judge in Atlanta ruled that the board had acted in a fair and reasonable manner and in the best interest of the company. Because he lacked both sufficient cash to compete

**Exhibit 11B.1** A Summary of the Offer Made by Ted Turner to Acquire CBS

|  | Face Value | Estimated Market Value |
|---|---|---|
| Interest-bearing "junk bonds"[a] | $ 122.00 | $ 105.00 |
| Zero coupon notes[b] | 20.00 | 19.00 |
| TBS stock[c] | 16.50 | 15.00 |
| 1 share preferred ¾ share class B common |  |  |
| Total | $ 175.50 | $ 150.00 |

Estimated total market value of offer—$4.5 billion

[a]15% senior notes due 1992; 15.5% senior debenture due 2000; 16.25% senior subordinated debenture due 2005.
[b]Four series with maturity range 1990–1994 with effective interest rate of 15%.
[c]One share preferred $2.64.

with the CBS stock repurchase offer and the ability to wage a proxy battle, these rulings ended any hope Ted Turner had of gaining control of CBS.

**REPER-CUSSIONS**   TBS reported that it lost $6.7 million on revenues of $99.3 million in the second quarter of 1985. In total, the takeover attempt cost TBS $18.2 million. According to *Newsweek,* (April 29, 1985), it may have been worth it to Turner just to be in the spotlight for a few weeks.

The cost of the failed merger attempt to CBS was very high. They purchased approximately 21 percent of their stock at a cost of $960 million. Since the takeover attempt ended, CBS has had serious financial difficulties and several members of its top management group have been dismissed.

# 12 NCNB Corporation

Lloyd L. Byars and Debra Thompson
Atlanta University

**INTRODUC-TION**

NCNB Corporation is a diversified financial corporation with consolidated total assets of $15.679 billion on December 31, 1984. The corporation operates through separate banking subsidiaries in Florida and North Carolina and two nonbanking subsidiaries that provide additional financial services. NCNB's services include general, international, and merchant banking; consumer and commercial finance; leasing; factoring; trust and investment management services; corporate finance; cash management; and discount brokerage services. The 596 offices of the corporations are located in ten states, the United Kingdom, Hong Kong, Australia, Brazil, South Africa, the Channel Islands, and the Cayman Islands.

**PART I. INTERNAL ORGANIZA-TIONAL AUDIT**

NCNB, with assets of $15.7 billion, is currently the largest regional multistate bank holding company in the Southeast. It has 222 banking offices in North Carolina and 155 in Florida and operates wholesale banking offices in New York, Chicago, Nashville, and Rockville, Maryland.[1]

As shown in Exhibit 12.1, net per share has compounded at 10.1 percent over the last five years and 14.3 percent over the last ten years. In addition, earnings have advanced in each of the last 10 years and 14 of the last 15. Dividend growth over the last ten years has compounded at 8.4 percent.

Despite NCNB's aggressive middle-market lending, credit quality has been an important criterion. As shown in Exhibit 12.2, net chargeoffs as a percent of average loans have averaged 50 basis points over the last nine years. As a result of the real estate problems during the mid-1970s, nonperforming assets were high in the late 1970s. However, they showed a downward trend to under 2 percent in 1983. The net charge-offs of 0.38 percent in 1983 compared favorably with the regional index of 1.04 percent.

Strengthened credit quality procedures—including the allocation of loan losses to the company's various profit centers—are expected to contribute to an improved corporate credit quality outlook. In addition, loan proposals must be screened by NCNB's seven regional executives—four in Florida and three in North Carolina—as well as by members of the company's credit review committee.[2]

Exhibit 12.3 shows how improved profitability and a high retention rate in the late 1970s built the equity base to a high of 5.7 percent in 1982. The internal growth rate averaged 11 percent over the last eight years. It is anticipated that

**Exhibit 12.1** Historical Share Data, 1969–1985E[a]

| Year | IBST | Net Income | Dividend | Payout (%) | Median Yield (%) | Price Range |
|------|------|------------|----------|------------|------------------|-------------|
| 1969 | $ 0.82 | $ 0.79 | $ 0.36 | 45.6 | 2.9 | NA |
| 1970 | 0.98 | 0.98 | 0.38 | 38.8 | 2.7 | NA |
| 1971 | 1.19 | 1.18 | 0.42 | 35.6 | 2.0 | NA |
| 1972 | 1.36 | 1.37 | 0.44 | 32.1 | 4.4 | NA |
| 1973 | 1.60 | 1.54 | 0.48 | 31.2 | 1.3 | 40–4 |
| 1974 | 1.05 | 1.08 | 0.52 | 48.1 | 2.2 | 40–7 |
| 1975 | 1.10 | 1.09 | 0.52 | 47.7 | 4.8 | 14–8 |
| 1976 | 1.20 | 1.20 | 0.52 | 43.3 | 4.7 | 13–9 |
| 1977 | 1.42 | 1.41 | 0.52 | 36.9 | 4.5 | 13–10 |
| 1978 | 2.02 | 2.00 | 0.58 | 29.0 | 4.0 | 17–11 |
| 1979 | 2.46 | 2.53 | 0.62 | 24.5 | 4.6 | 17–11 |
| 1980 | 2.61 | 2.60 | 0.76 | 29.2 | 5.7 | 17–11 |
| 1981 | 2.88 | 3.22 | 0.82 | 25.5 | 5.9 | 18–13 |
| 1982 | 3.22 | 3.18 | 0.91 | 28.6 | 5.6 | 21–12 |
| 1983 | 3.66 | 3.68 | 1.03 | 28.0 | 4.3 | 30–19 |
| 1984E | 4.08 | 4.10 | 1.17 | 28.5 | 4.3 | 35–22 |
| 1985E | 4.70 | 4.70 | 1.35 | 28.7 | NA | NA |

**Compound growth (%)**

| | | | | | | |
|------|------|------|------|------|------|------|
| 1979–1984 | 10.7 | 10.1 | 13.5 | | | |
| 1974–1984 | 14.5 | 14.3 | 8.4 | | | |

[a]IBST and net income are on an originally reported, primary basis; IBST, after 1982, is computed by GS&Co.; dividends are those paid in a calendar year; and the payout ratio is on a net income basis.

*Source:* Goldman Sachs Research.

**Exhibit 12.2** Historical Credit Quality Data, 1975–1984

| | | As % of Period End Loan | |
|------|----------------------------------------|---------|----------------------|
| Year | Net Charge-offs as % of Average Loans | Reserve | Nonperforming Assets |
| 1975 | 0.71 | 1.07 | 7.10 |
| 1976 | 0.50 | 1.15 | 7.50 |
| 1977 | 0.50 | 1.03 | 5.60 |
| 1978 | 0.47 | 1.10 | 3.40 |
| 1979 | 0.53 | 1.08 | 2.49 |
| 1980 | 0.43 | 1.16 | 2.23 |
| 1981 | 0.40 | 1.16 | 2.47 |
| 1982 | 0.56 | 1.16 | 2.66 |
| 1983 | 0.38 | 1.10 | 1.70 |
| 1984 | 0.29[a] | 1.11[b] | 1.59[b] |

[a]Nine months ended September 1984, annualized.
[b]September 30, 1984.

*Source:* Goldman Sachs Research.

**Exhibit 12.3** Components of Internal Growth Rate, 1974–1985E (percent)

| Year | Return on Assets | | Equity as % of Total Assets = | Return on Equity × | Earnings Retention Rate = | Internal Growth Rate |
|------|------|------|------|------|------|------|
| | IBST | Net Income ÷ | | | | |
| 1974 | 0.43 | 0.42 | 4.84 | 8.7 | 51.9 | 4.5 |
| 1975 | 0.48 | 0.47 | 5.26 | 8.9 | 52.3 | 4.7 |
| 1976 | | 0.50 | 5.22 | 9.6 | 56.7 | 5.4 |
| 1977 | 0.54 | 0.53 | 5.00 | 10.6 | 63.1 | 6.7 |
| 1978 | 0.73 | 0.74 | 5.08 | 14.6 | 71.0 | 10.3 |
| 1979 | 0.80 | 0.81 | 5.05 | 16.0 | 75.5 | 12.1 |
| 1980 | | 0.74 | 4.95 | 14.9 | 70.8 | 10.6 |
| 1981 | 0.82 | 0.90 | 5.23 | 17.2 | 74.5 | 12.8 |
| 1982 | 0.91 | 0.90 | 5.69 | 15.8 | 71.4 | 11.3 |
| 1983 | 0.79 | 0.80 | 4.88 | 16.3 | 72.0 | 11.8 |
| 1984E | 0.82 | 0.82 | 5.20 | 15.8 | 71.5 | 11.3 |
| 1985E | 0.86 | 0.86 | 5.35 | 16.1 | 71.3 | 11.5 |

*Source:* Goldman Sachs Research.

NCNB will sell some of its assets from a less desirable market, which in turn would improve its primary capital and loan loss reserve ratio.

NCNB's financial structure is comprised mostly of consumer deposits as a source of funds, and loans and leases as a use of funds (see Exhibit 12.4). The dramatic change in consumer deposits held was due primarily to both deregulation and the Florida acquisitions. It is also evident that NCNB decided to hold a greater proportion of liquid assets in the form of investment securities rather than time deposits.

NCNB's cash management services, from account reconciliation to lockbox and disbursing, have become highly recognized for their efficiency and speed.

**Organizational Structure**

The organizational structure, shown in Exhibit 12.5, is rather decentralized. The number of signatures required on a loan depends on the size of the loan. At least two signatures are needed on every loan. The greater the size of the loan, the greater the chances that the loan would have to be reviewed by a city or regional committee. If the loan is of a special type (e.g., real estate), it is also reviewed by a specialty lending department before being sent to the committee.

Hugh L. McColl, chairman of NCNB, established a six-member executive management team to assure profitable growth within NCNB. According to Mr. McColl, the structure is intended to shorten the distance from policymakers to line officers, reduce administrative costs, provide better communications throughout the organization, and allow them to take advantage of a broad range of knowledge and expertise at the executive management level.[3]

**Exhibit 12.4** Funding Sources as a Percent of Assets, 1982–1984

| | Quarter Ended | |
|---|---|---|
| | 6/30/82 | 6/30/84 |
| Consumer deposits | 23.0 | 38.6 |
| Non–interest-bearing funds | 20.8 | 19.6 |
|   Core funds | 43.8 | 58.2 |
| Market rate wholesale funds | 48.5 | 34.3 |
| Long-term debt and capital leases | 1.8 | 2.5 |
| Equity | 5.9 | 5.0 |
|   Total sources of funds | 100.0 | 100.0 |
| **Percent composition of assets, 1982–1984** | | |
| Loans and leases | 56.7 | 56.1 |
| Investment securities | 11.4 | 16.0 |
| Time deposits placed | 10.5 | 6.0 |
| Other earning assets | 5.9 | 7.2 |
| Other assets | 15.5 | 14.7 |
|   Total assets | 100.0 | 100.0 |

*Source:* Goldman Sachs Research.

**Quality and Quantity of Management Personnel**

The board of directors for NCNB Corporation consists of 25 members—listed in Exhibit 12.6—ranging from presidents of retailing chains to insurance company presidents. There are 14 members on the board of directors for NCNB National Bank of Florida and 16 for NCNB National Bank of North Carolina. They are responsible for formulating, changing, and evaluating the strategy of NCNB.

**Quality and Quantity of Operative Personnel**

As of December 31, 1984, NCNB had 9329 full-time employees,[4] people who top management feel should be intelligent, self-motivated, energetic, aggressive, and entrepreneurial. The level of education ranges from high school to graduate school and other special training schools. NCNB offers an intense training program for the majority of its employees where they receive technical as well as leadership training. NCNB pays competitively when compared with the industry. NCNB's basic philosophy is that progress and rewards should be based on individual performance instead of on a set pattern or schedule.[5]

**Competitive Position and Product Line**

NCNB is the largest regional bank holding company in the Southeast, the largest in North Carolina, and the fourth largest in Florida. It has a 26 percent market share in the 50 North Carolina counties in which it operates, or 20.6 percent of the state total.[6] In Florida, NCNB operates in 27 counties with a market share of 7.5 percent, or 6.5 percent of the state total. Florida is the seventh largest state

**Exhibit 12.5** Organizational Chart

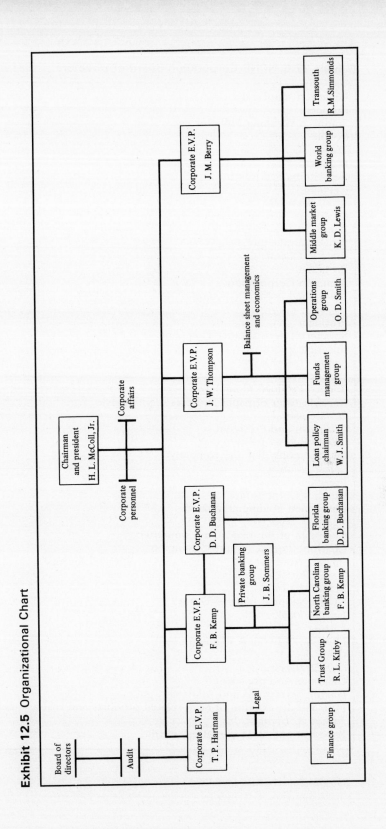

**Exhibit 12.6** NCNB Corporation Board of Directors

*William M. Barnhardt*
President
Southern Webbing Mills Inc.
(textiles)
*Thomas M. Belk*
President
Belk Stores Services Inc.
(retailing)
*W. C. Boren III*
Chairman
Pomona Corporation
(brick manufacturer)
*Bruce B. Cameron*
President
Cameron Corporation
(diversified holding company)
*Wilbur L. Carter, Jr.*
President
Southern Life Insurance Company
(insurance)
*Charles W. Coker, Jr.*
President
Sonoco Products Company
(manufacturer of paper and plastic products)
*H. L. Culbreath*
Chairman and President
TECO Energy Inc.
(electric utility holding company)
*Alan T. Dickson*
President
Ruddick Corporation
(diversified holding company)
*W. Frank Dowd, Jr.*
Chairman of the Executive Committee
Charlotte Pipe & Foundry Company
(manufacturer of cast iron and plastic pipe and fittings)
*A. L. Ellis*
Senior chairman
NCNB National Bank of Florida
*Foy B. Fleming*
Partner
Fleming, O'Bryan & Fleming
(law)
*C. Felix Harvey*
Chairman and president
Harvey Enterprises and Affiliates
(sale and distribution of farm-related products and real estate)
*Edward A. Horrigan, Jr.*
President and chief operating officer

R. J. Reynolds Industries Inc.
(consumer products)
*William A. Klopman*
Chairman and chief executive officer
Burlington Industries Inc.
(textiles)
*Hugh L. McColl, Jr.*
Chairman
NCNB Corporation
*H. Smith Richardson, Jr.*
Chairman
Richardson-Vicks Inc.
(health care and consumer products)
*Charles E. Schmidt*
(private investor)
*John C. Slane*
President
Slane Hosiery Mills Inc.
(textiles)
*Albert F. Sloan*
Chairman
Lance Inc.
(snack food products)
*W. Roger Soles*
President
Jefferson-Pilot Corporation
(insurance)
*C. D. Spangler, Jr.*
President
C. D. Spangler Construction Company
(construction)
*Robert H. Spilman*
Chairman, president, and chief executive officer
Bassett Furniture Industries Inc.
(furniture manufacturer)
*Colin Stokes*
Retired chairman
R. J. Reynolds Industries Inc.
(consumer products)
(deceased December 1984)
*Thomas I. Storrs*
Retired chairman
NCNB Corporation
*Dr. Otto Sturzenegger*
Chairman and chief executive officer
CIBA-GEIGY Corporation
(specialty chemicals company)

*Source:* NCNB Annual Report 1984.

**Exhibit 12.7** Rank by Population, 1983 (thousands)

| State | Amount |
|---|---|
| California | 21,174 |
| New York | 17,667 |
| Florida and North Carolina | 16,762 |

*Source:* Goldman Sachs Research.

and North Carolina the tenth. Together, they rank third in population (see Exhibit 12.7).[7]

Florida has ranked first in growth rate from 1970 to 1983, with an annual growth rate of 3.54 percent (see Exhibit 12.8).

The services offered by NCNB include a variety of checking and savings accounts which pay interest, a nationwide 24-hour banking service (Plus System), and a highly personalized Private Banking Program. In a private survey of southern companies with sales of $50–$250 million, NCNB was acknowledged as the bank with (1) the most customer relationships, (2) the most aggressive program of soliciting new business, (3) the greatest market coverage, (4) the most effective domestic loan solicitation, and (5) the most effective marketing of cash management services.[8]

**Marketing Capability**

NCNB has concentrated on improving branch management and cultivating a sales-oriented environment. NCNB National Bank of North Carolina has also improved the productivity of its retail delivery system by bundling services and adopting profit center accountability at the branch level.[9] The establishment of a credit card bank in Fairfax County, Virginia, in May 1985 was designed to heighten the bank's retail-based sources of noninterest income. By the end of 1985 NCNB National Bank of North Carolina had $233 million in credit card outstandings and was the largest bank card lender in the state.[10] The opportunities in marketing areas of the bank include marketing research, marketing planning, advertising, branch planning, and regional marketing planning and implementation.

NCNB's reputation as an innovator of services stems from being the first bank in the state to introduce such services as 24-hour banking machines, a debit card, and a comprehensive package of banking services. NCNB has actively promoted its advertising theme, "We want to be the best bank in the neighborhood."[11]

**Acquisition Strategy**

During 1982, 1983, and 1984, NCNB bought five banks in Florida and made a major acquisition in North Carolina. Exhibit 12.9 lists each of the banks, along with their asset sizes and the purchase prices.

**Exhibit 12.8** Rank by Population Growth (among the 20 largest states)

| Rank | State | 1970–1983 Compound Annual Growth Rate (%) |
|------|-------|-------------------------------------------|
| 1 | Florida | 3.54 |
| 2 | Texas | 2.65 |
| 3 | California | 1.80 |
| 4 | Washington | 1.79 |
| 5 | Georgia | 1.73 |
| 6 | Louisiana | 1.53 |
| 7 | North Carolina | 1.39 |
| 8 | Tennessee | 1.37 |
| 9 | Virginia | 1.37 |
| 10 | Maryland | 0.71 |
| 11 | Wisconsin | 0.56 |
| 12 | Missouri | 0.47 |
| 13 | Indiana | 0.41 |
| 14 | New Jersey | 0.31 |
| 15 | Illinois | 0.26 |
| 16 | Michigan | 0.16 |
| 17 | Massachusetts | 0.11 |
| 18 | Ohio | 0.06 |
| 19 | Pennsylvania | 0.06 |
| 20 | New York | (0.25) |
| Total | | 1.09 |

*Source:* Goldman Sachs Research.

**Exhibit 12.9** Acquisition Activity, 1982–1984

| Bank | Date Acquired | Assets at Acquisition (millions) | Consideration (millions) | | Price to | |
|------|---------------|----------------------------------|--------------------------|-----------|-----------|-----------|
| | | | Cash | Com. Shs. | Book Value[a] | Earnings[b] |
| First National Bank of Lake City | 1/8/82 | $    23 | $  6.0 | — | 2.50X | NM[c] |
| Gulf Stream | 9/3/82 | 787 | 92.0 | — | 1.85 | 17.8X |
| Bancshares of North Carolina | 12/23/82 | 425 | — | 2.1 | 1.54 | 7.8 |
| Exchange Bancorp | 12/31/82 | 1,590 | 135.0 | — | 1.78 | 17.2 |
| A Miami branch of Peoples Downtown National Bank | 12/31/82 | 9 | 6.0 | — | [d] | NM |
| Ellis Banking | 3/16/84 | 1,830 | 68.6 | 4.0 | 1.73 | 14.6 |

[a] At date of acquisition.
[b] Based on four quarters prior to completion of acquisition.
[c] NM—Not meaningful
[d] Purchased assets and a charter, no equity.

*Source:* Goldman Sachs Research.

**Past Objectives and Strategies**

NCNB management set two primary goals for the corporation: to continue as the dominant financial institution in the Southeast, and to become a significant competitor among the world's major banks. To achieve these goals, a three-phase strategic plan was developed for the 1980s:[12]

*Phase I:* To utilize every reasonable opportunity to improve the corporation's capital position, managerial depth, and technical expertise.

*Phase II:* To expand the geographic coverage of the corporation to achieve economies of scale, offer innovative products to a broader market, and eliminate limitations based on size.

*Phase III:* To achieve profitable internal growth by managing products, pricing, and markets for increased market shares.

Phase I was accomplished from 1980 to mid-1982. Shareholder's equity was increased by 50 percent—from $300 million at the beginning of 1980 to more than $450 million on June 30, 1982.[13] The company raised additional equity by the private sale of stock, the exchanging of stock for debt, the acquiring of equity through a merger with Carolina First National Bank, its dividend reinvestment program, and an employee stock purchase plan. NCNB also intensified personnel recruiting efforts and expanded in-house training and management development programs.

Phase II was started when the Florida law prohibiting acquisitions by out-of-state banks did not apply to NCNB, who owned the Trust Company of Florida in Orlando before the law was written. On January 8, 1982, NCNB acquired the First National Bank of Lake City in northern Florida. As a member of the Florida banking community, NCNB had already accomplished a major part of phase III.

Ranked by retail sales and sales growth, Florida and North Carolina were second and fourth, respectively, in 1983 (see Exhibit 12.10).

**Summary**

Out of the factors discussed above, the most important factor to NCNB is its competitive position. As a result of a less regulated banking environment, NCNB must be able to compete against other money center banks and nonbanks in order to survive. However, in order to gain or maintain its market share, NCNB must be financially sound. Capital adequacy and credit quality are essentials for expanding and improving its operations. Top management must have the expertise necessary to move the organization forward and the willingness to delegate authority to competent lower-level managers. The line employees must know how to sell the services offered, and the staff should be willing to provide the support necessary. All factors link together one way or another, therefore. As the saying goes, "United we stand, divided we fall."

**PART II. INDUSTRY PROFILE**

The American banking system is known as a dual banking system because its main feature is side-by-side federal and state chartering and supervision. The National Banking System was established in 1863 and 1864 when Congress passed the

**Exhibit 12.10** Rank by Retail Sales and Sales Growth, 1970 and 1983 (billions)

| State[a] | Retail Sales | | Compound Growth Rate | |
|---|---|---|---|---|
| | 1970 | 1983 | Rate | Rank |
| California | $ 39.3 | $ 140.5 | 10.3% | 7 |
| Texas | 19.3 | 88.3 | 12.4 | 1 |
| New York | 33.2 | 81.6 | 7.2 | 20 |
| *Florida | 13.3 | 59.1 | 12.2 | 2* |
| Illinois | 21.7 | 56.4 | 7.6 | 19 |
| Pennsylvania | 20.3 | 54.4 | 7.9 | 18 |
| Ohio | 18.7 | 50.8 | 8.0 | 17 |
| Michigan | 15.8 | 44.7 | 8.3 | 14 |
| New Jersey | 13.0 | 40.5 | 9.1 | 12 |
| Massachusetts | 10.8 | 34.7 | 9.4 | 11 |
| Virginia | 7.3 | 29.1 | 11.2 | 3 |
| *North Carolina | 7.8 | 28.8 | 10.6 | 4* |

[a]Ranked by 1983 retail sales.

*Source:* Goldman Sachs Research.

National Bank Acts, which set up a system of privately owned banks chartered by the federal government. The Federal Reserve Act provided a way for the federal government to control bank reserves and to adjust the money supply to meet the nation's needs. The Great Depression in 1929 created a run on the banks which, in turn, caused approximately 2000 bank failures a year during the years 1930–1933. The Glass-Steagall Banking Act of 1933 created the FDIC to insure bank deposits and restrict risky banking practices. Originally passed in 1927 and amended in 1933, the McFadden Act still prohibits interstate branching by nationally chartered banks. The Douglas Amendment to the Bank Holding Company Act of 1956 allows bank holding companies to acquire banks across state lines if the potential acquiree resides in a state whose legislation specifically allows out-of-state holding companies to acquire in-state banks. The Depository Institutions Act of 1982 (Garn–St Germain) was enacted into law on October 15, 1982, with the purpose of furthering the long-term process of deregulating depository institutions. Moreover, the Garn–St Germain Act enables banks and savings and loan associations to acquire failing institutions across state lines.

**Marketing Practices and Market Structure**

The banking industry provides a number of services to consumers, corporations, other banks, etc. Among the many services provided are the following:[14]

- Safeguarding deposits
- Providing a means of payment
- Making loans

- Electronic banking (automated teller machines; automated clearinghouses; point-of-sale terminals)
- Trust services
- Individual retirement accounts

Interest-rate sensitivity plays a major role in the banking industry. The spread between interest paid on deposits and interest earned on loans must be wide enough to cover the cost of services while generating a profit for the bank.

Over the last decade, the banking system has spent billions on computer hardware and software for electronic funds transfer systems.[15] Automated teller machines provide 24-hour cash management services at the bank and other convenient locations. Point-of-sale systems allow customers to pay for their purchases by electronically debiting their checking accounts.

Most banks have started to emphasize full-service banking for corporate and retail customers. Commercial banks are requesting to be allowed to offer mutual funds, insurance, and brokerage services in order to be able to compete in the growing deregulated environment.

**Financial Conditions**

The most comprehensive measure of profitability is return on assets (ROA) (see Exhibit 12.11). The ROA of most banks falls within a range of 0.60–1.40 percent.[16] Banks with a large proportion of non–interest-bearing assets, such as those with extensive branch networks, usually have an ROA that is nearer the lower end of the range, whereas those with only one or two offices tend to be on the higher end. Accordingly, ROA for money center and large regional banks tends to be below that of small community banks. Another measure of profitability is return on equity (ROE), which is usually between 10 and 20 percent.[17] Those banks that rely heavily upon debt to support assets will tend to have a higher ROE than those that do not.

The principal source of a bank's revenues is interest on earnings assets, which is measured by the gross yield on earnings assets (GYEA). The cost of funds is measured by the rate paid on funds (RPF). The difference between GYEA and RPF is the net interest margin.

In order to cover possible future loan losses, banks are required to maintain a reserve for loan losses. The reserve at most banks falls within a range of 0.80–1.5 percent of total loans outstanding. Net charge-offs, measured as a percentage of average loans outstanding, usually range from 0.25 to 0.50 percent.[18]

Banks are required by regulators to maintain minimum levels of capital in order to protect depositors from losses sustained by the bank. Smaller banks are required to maintain capital at 6 percent of assets and larger banks at 5 percent.[19] In general, the higher the capital ratio, the more conservative the bank.

In terms of financial leverage, the debt to equity-and-debt ratio for banks is generally 30–35 percent. A bank that is "loaned up" has a high ratio of loans to assets: 65 percent and up would be considered high.[20]

**Exhibit 12.11** Performance Measures for Selected Banks, 1983 (in percent)

## MEASURES OF PROFITABILITY

| | Return on Assets | Return on Equity | Gross Yield on Earning Assets | Rate Paid on Funds | Net Interest Margin | Nonint. Income Total Income | Nonint. Expense Total Income |
|---|---|---|---|---|---|---|---|
| **Money center banks** | | | | | | | |
| BankAmerica | 0.3 | 7.5 | 11.60 | 8.15 | 3.45 | 9.2 | 27 |
| Bankers Trust | 0.6 | 15.6 | 11.09 | 8.24 | 2.85 | 11.0 | 20 |
| Chase Manhattan | 0.5 | 12.8 | 11.81 | 8.27 | 3.54 | 10.1 | 24 |
| Chemical New York | 0.6 | 14.0 | 11.50 | 7.64 | 3.86 | 9.2 | 25 |
| Citicorp | 0.7 | 16.6 | 13.84 | 10.1 | 3.74 | 10.8 | 22 |
| First Chicago | 0.5 | 11.2 | 11.04 | 8.47 | 2.57 | 10.4 | 19 |
| Manufacturers Hanover | 0.5 | 13.4 | 11.63 | 8.37 | 3.26 | 9.4 | 22 |
| J. P. Morgan & Co. | 0.8 | 15.2 | 11.20 | 8.17 | 3.03 | 9.7 | 14 |
| **Regional banks** | | | | | | | |
| Bank of Boston | 0.7 | 14.1 | 15.09 | 10.93 | 4.16 | 10.2 | 23 |
| Barnett Banks | 1.0 | 18.6 | 12.74 | 6.84 | 5.90 | 11.7 | 36 |
| First Interstate | 0.6 | 12.9 | 12.01 | 7.20 | 4.81 | 10.7 | 32 |
| InterFirst | NM | NM | 11.64 | 7.70 | 3.94 | 7.3 | 23 |
| Mellon Corp. | 0.7 | 12.8 | 11.62 | 8.02 | 3.60 | 11.6 | 25 |
| *NCNB Corp. | 0.7 | 15.7 | 12.05 | 7.76 | 4.29 | 10.0 | 27 |
| Northwest Corp. | 0.7 | 11.5 | 12.63 | 8.09 | 4.54 | 14.0 | 30 |
| Texas Commerce | 0.9 | 18.6 | 11.74 | 7.42 | 4.32 | 6.6 | 21 |

## MEASURES OF FINANCIAL CONDITION

| | Loan Loss Reserve Total Loans | Charge-offs Avg. Loans | Non performing Loans Total Loans | Capital Total Assets | Long-Term Debt Equity + L-T Debt | Loans Assets |
|---|---|---|---|---|---|---|
| **Money center banks** | | | | | | |
| BankAmerica | 1.25 | 0.90 | 4.3 | 5.1 | 32 | 67 |
| Bankers Trust | 1.13 | 0.20 | 2.4 | 5.6 | 19 | 58 |
| Chase Manhattan | 1.01 | 0.47 | 3.3 | 5.5 | 28 | 68 |
| Chemical New York | 1.10 | 0.35 | 2.6 | 5.5 | 23 | 65 |
| Citicorp | 0.85 | 0.51 | 2.4 | 5.1 | 68 | 67 |
| First Chicago | 0.98 | 0.63 | 3.7 | 5.6 | 15 | 61 |
| Manufacturers Hanover | 0.90 | 0.35 | 1.7 | 5.0 | 48 | 74 |
| J. P. Morgan & Co. | 1.43 | 0.31 | 1.9 | 7.0 | 14 | 57 |
| **Regional banks** | | | | | | |
| Bank of Boston | 1.14 | 0.40 | 2.7 | 5.9 | 23 | 60 |
| Barnett Banks | 1.30 | 0.29 | 0.9 | 6.1 | 23 | 54 |
| First Interstate | 1.36 | 0.86 | 3.9 | 5.5 | 41 | 57 |
| InterFirst | 1.93 | 3.28 | 4.4 | 6.3 | 30 | 66 |
| Mellon Corp. | 1.56 | 0.22 | 2.9 | 6.1 | 29 | 58 |
| *NCNB Corp. | 1.10 | 0.38 | 1.4 | 5.4 | 27 | 54 |
| Northwest Corp. | 1.36 | 0.93 | 1.9 | 5.9 | 56 | 61 |
| Texas Commerce | 1.11 | 0.38 | 1.9 | 5.9 | 5 | 59 |

*Source: S & P Industry Surveys, 1984.*

**Competition**    Commercial banks compete with each other as well as with thrift institutions—savings and loan associations, mutual savings banks, and credit unions—and also with other participants in the money and capital markets. The largest financial institutions as of September 30, 1984, according to *Standard & Poor's Industry Surveys,* are shown in Exhibit 12.12.

Other financial companies, such as Merrill Lynch, Shearson/Lehman, American Express, and Sears, are offering banking as well as other financial services. On the other hand, many commercial banks, such as BankAmerica, have already entered the discount brokerage business. Although prohibited by law from underwriting insurance, some banks provide space in their branch lobbies for sales kiosks operated by independent insurance companies.[21]

During the 1970s, many private investment companies began to offer money market funds. These funds paid interest rates on their deposits that exceeded the rates offered by banks and thrifts. As a result, many people began to withdraw money from lower-yielding bank and thrift accounts and deposit it in money market funds. This finally gave rise to the Garn–St. Germain Act in 1982.

Many of the bank failures have been caused by bad energy loans, the deregulation of interest rates on deposits in 1982, and risky foreign loans to Latin American countries. For example, the FDIC rescued Continental Illinois from $3.5 billion of bad loans during 1984. While about 800 banks were on the FDIC's problem list, it was estimated that 75 or 80 banks would fail by the end of 1984, compared with four bank failures in 1974.[22]

**Operating Conditions**    Bankers today have to be self-motivated, aggressive, energetic, intellectually bright, and able to communicate well with people. They must be creative and able to attract new customers as well as sell the products and services offered by the bank. Most banks have an intense training program where they teach their employees the technical and leadership skills that are necessary to compete in the banking industry.

The structure of the banking system can be classified as unit, branch, or group banking. Commercial banks may also be classified as a regional, community, or money center bank. Banks can be members or nonmembers of the Federal Reserve System. Presently, there are approximately 14,500 commercial banks in existence. Half of all banks in the United States still operate only one office, and three-quarters have assets of $50 million or less.[23] The future structure of banking is leaning toward a multioffice banking system on a broad geographic scale.

**Technological Innovations**    Technology is reducing the need for branch offices and is introducing interstate banking for retail and commercial customers. The three services that most financial institutions consider as retail electronic services are automated teller machines (ATMs), point-of-sale services (POSs), and home banking.[24] The ATMs are the first of the retail electronic banking services to achieve market success. As a result of the establishment of national network systems such as Cirrus and Plus, the question is now whether or not ATM and POS terminals are branch banks.

**Exhibit 12.12** Largest Financial Institutions, September 30, 1984
(in millions of dollars)

| Companies (ranked by assets) | Assets | Equity | 1983 Earnings | Est. 1984 Earnings |
|---|---|---|---|---|
| Citicorp | $144,731 | $6,264 | $860 | $863 |
| BankAmerica | 120,547 | 5,171 | 390 | 415 |
| Chase Manhattan | 87,471 | 3,940 | 430 | 389 |
| Manufacturers Hanover | 73,344 | 3,233 | 337 | 340 |
| J. P. Morgan | 62,165 | 3,600 | 460 | 496 |
| Chemical New York | 55,244 | 2,470 | 306 | 327 |
| First Interstate | 44,653 | 2,229 | 247 | 275 |
| Bankers Trust | 45,091 | 2,017 | 257 | 300 |
| Security Pacific | 42,741 | 1,908 | 264 | 290 |
| First Chicago | 40,066 | 1,890 | 184 | 88 |
| Continental Illinois | 31,488 | 1,675 | 101 | d1,125 |
| Mellon Bank | 28,249 | 1,460 | 187 | 167 |
| Wells Fargo | 27,194 | 1,348 | 155 | 166 |
| Marine Midland | 22,390 | 1,092 | 101 | 107 |
| Crocker National | 21,859 | 1,113 | d10 | d101 |
| First Bank System | 21,838 | 1,084 | 130 | 136 |
| Norwest | 21,565 | 1,146 | 125 | 68 |
| Bank of Boston | 21,342 | 1,121 | 136 | 128 |
| Republic Bank | 21,006 | 1,111 | 130 | 137 |
| Irving Bank | 19,668 | 866 | 93 | 102 |
| Interfirst | 19,648 | 1,136 | d172 | 48 |
| Texas Commerce Bancshares | 19,519 | 1,134 | 177 | 185 |
| First City Bancorp. of Texas | 16,989 | 977 | 50 | 86 |
| *NCNB | 14,527 | 782 | 92 | 120 |
| NBD Bancorp. | 14,408 | 851 | 82 | 91 |

*Source: S & P Industry Surveys.*

The retail financial service of the future is home banking. Delivering banking services to customers' personal computers or home terminals offers a wider variety of services and a greater sense of control.

**Summary**   One of the most important factors in the banking industry today will be determining the nature and structure of the banking system for the future. Will there be regional or nationwide banking? Will the money center banks control the political and banking environment? How large will they be allowed to get? These and many other questions must be answered by Congress in the near future.

**PART III. PRESENT ENVIRON-MENT**   **Political**   Commercial banks in the United States must have a state or federal charter, and they may choose which they want. The choice of a charter determines not only whether state or federal officials supervise the bank, but also many of the rules that govern the operation of the institution. There are about 10,000 state-chartered banks and about 4500 federally chartered banks, called national banks.[25]

Regulation of a state-chartered bank is directed by a state official who is called the bank commissioner or superintendent of banks. Regulation of national banks is administered by the comptroller of the currency, an official of the U.S. Department of the Treasury. All national banks must belong to the Federal Reserve. As a member of the Federal Reserve System, NCNB has the opportunity to use the system's lending and check-clearing services, and each deposit account is insured for a maximum of $100,000 by the Federal Deposit Insurance Corporation (FDIC).

In 1968, Congress passed the Consumer Credit Protection Act, often called the Truth in Lending Act, which requires banks and other lenders to state clearly the actual annual interest on loans. The Equal Credit Opportunity Act, enacted in 1974 and amended in 1976, forbids discrimination on the basis of race, color, religion, national origin, or age. The Community Reinvestment Act of 1977 affects a bank's application to open a new branch or to merge with another bank.

Presently, banking is developing into a new industry called financial services. NCNB's ability to offer a wide variety of services will determine its ability to compete in today's banking environment.

**Economic**    In February 1985, the index slipped below 50 percent for the first time since January of 1983. A reading below 50 percent indicates the economy is in a declining phase, whereas a reading above 50 percent indicates an expanding economy.[26] Despite a slip in production, employment levels improved slightly for the third consecutive month. On the other hand, inventory levels declined and prices decreased during March 1985. This was due to the increasing strength of the dollar. A survey by Dun & Bradstreet of 1400 executives found that business leaders are positive about the outlook for sales, profits, and employment in the second quarter of 1985. According to the consensus, economic growth averaged about 5.9 percent in 1984.

At year-end 1984, NCNB had foreign exposure totaling $1.691 billion.[27] During 1984, some countries such as Mexico and Brazil were unable to obtain adequate U.S. dollars to make payments of interest and/or principal on their loans. As a result of restructuring agreements supported by the International Monetary Fund, NCNB is committed to provide an additional $1.2 million to Mexico in 1985. Although foreign transactions are highly risky, NCNB's loan portfolio is diversified and the company is not dependent on just one or two market segments.

**Social**    A key factor in NCNB's success is its regional and national markets. With a combined population of more than 17 million people and deposits of more than $150 billion, Florida—the seventh largest state in the nation—and North Carolina—the tenth largest—provide excellent markets for NCNB's growing menu of products and services (see Exhibit 12.13).[28] Florida offers many profitable market segments for NCNB, including boat financing.

NCNB supports the neighborhoods where it does business in Florida and North Carolina. For example, during 1984, NCNB contributed to construction of

**Exhibit 12.13** Market Penetration by County, North Carolina and Florida

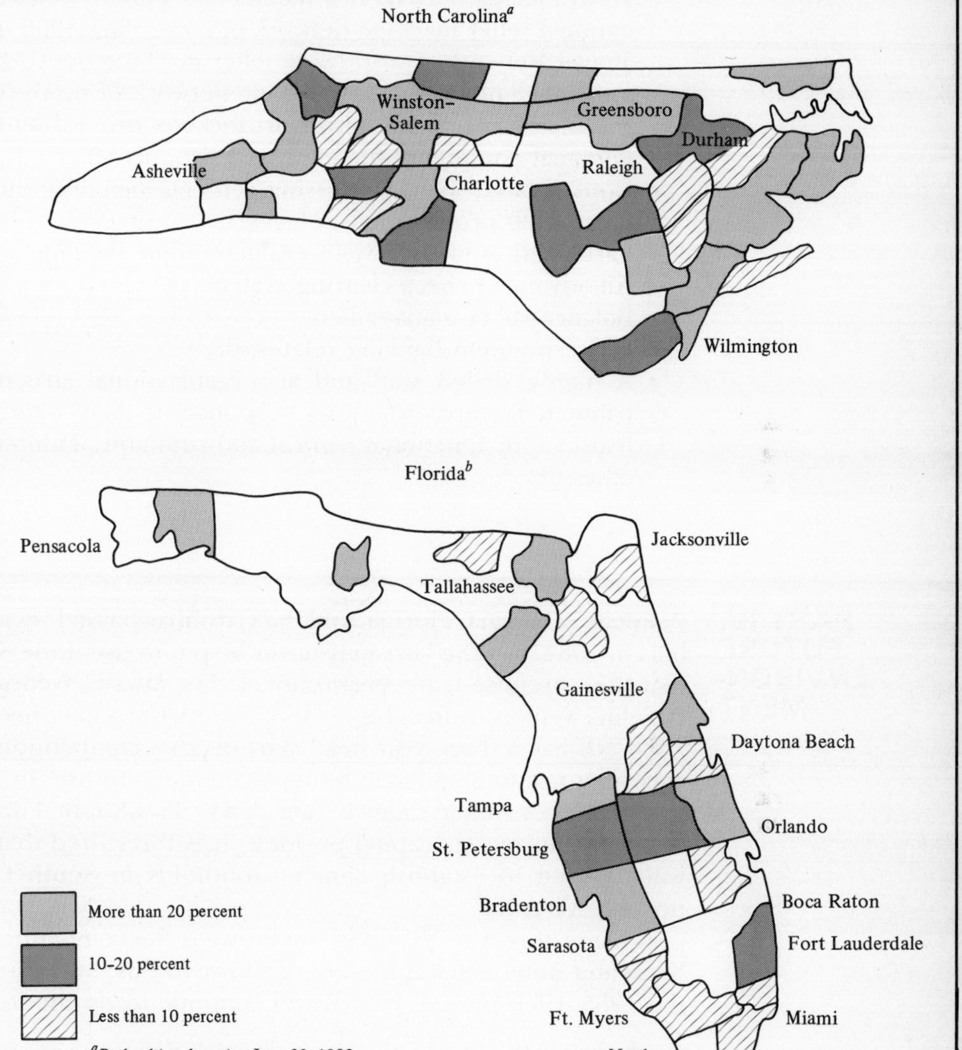

North Carolina[a]

Winston-Salem
Greensboro
Durham
Asheville
Raleigh
Charlotte
Wilmington

Florida[b]

Pensacola
Jacksonville
Tallahassee
Gainesville
Daytona Beach
Tampa
Orlando
St. Petersburg
Bradenton
Boca Raton
Sarasota
Fort Lauderdale
Ft. Myers
Miami
Naples

More than 20 percent

10–20 percent

Less than 10 percent

[a] By banking deposits, June 30, 1983.
[b] By banking deposits, March 31, 1984.

*Source:* Goldman Sachs Research.

a new performing arts center in Tampa and helped sponsor statewide tours by the Florida Orchestra and other performing arts groups. NCNB's style is an aggressive, no-nonsense, professional approach to banking.

During February 1985, NCNB adopted a policy that precludes further loans to the South African government or its agencies.

**Technological** One of the fundamental operations of a bank is transferring funds from buyers to sellers of goods and services. Examples of NCNB's use of technology in the changing world of banking include the following:[29]

- More than 100 automated teller machines in North Carolina and more than 70 in Florida. NCNB is a member of Plus System, Inc., which operates a national teller machine network of more than 3000 machines, and the Visa Travel Network, a worldwide teller machine network. In Florida, NCNB is a member of Honor, a statewide network of more than 1700 machines.
- Installation of a state-of-the-art lockbox processing system.
- Personal computers for improved productivity.
- Consolidated word processing centers, including one in Charlotte serving nearly 200 professionals.
- Participation in a study to evaluate home banking.
- An advanced check clearing system.
- Balance sheet management.
- Correspondent banking relationships.
- A highly skilled staff and an organizational structure that includes distributed features for quick response in daily operations and centralized features for functional control and common planning, as well as operating efficiency.

**PART IV. FUTURE ENVIRON- MENT**

**Political**   Georgia, Florida, and the Carolinas passed regional interstate banking bills in 1984, but the laws may never be put to use if the Supreme Court decides that their premise is unconstitutional. The laws in Georgia, Florida, and North Carolina went into effect July 1, 1985. South Carolina's becomes effective in 1986.

NCNB has a three-year head start over its competition with a two-state franchise that would be difficult to duplicate in the future. In 1984, NCNB proposed to sell its consumer finance subsidiary, TranSouth Financial Corporation, in order to improve its capital position. It is forecasted that the additional capital will be used to establish banking footholds in South Carolina, Georgia, and possibly Virginia.

A major threat to NCNB in the future is the competition by nonbanks such as Sears and American Express. In response to this threat, it is anticipated that over the 1985–1986 period, NCNB will continue to do the following:[30]

1. Enhance the productivity of its branch delivery systems by streamlining operations and emphasizing the cross-selling of consumer products
2. Become the primary banker for more of its middle-market clients by promoting a broadened array of innovative products and cash management services
3. Reshape its corporate-based activities to emphasize merchant banking, trade-related, and fee-based services

**Economic**   The U.S. economy faces either a revival of inflation or a great crash in the future. The fiscal 1985 deficit reached a record of $200 billion-plus (see Exhibit 12.14). To achieve $34 billion in savings, David Stockman—then Office of Management & Budget director—had to cut federal pay by 5 percent, eliminate the Small Business Administration and all direct lending by the Export-Import

**Exhibit 12.14**

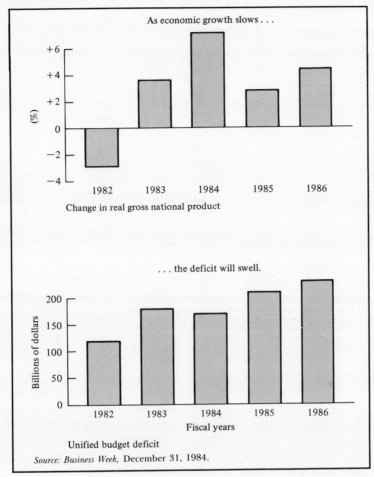

As economic growth slows . . .

Change in real gross national product

. . . the deficit will swell.

Unified budget deficit

*Source: Business Week,* December 31, 1984.

Bank, and cut farm support payments in half. All the domestic cuts assembled by Stockman left the White House $35 billion short of its goal of halving the deficit to $100 billion by 1988.

White House economists expect interest rates to fall steadily, with the yield on short-term Treasury bills dropping to 5 percent by 1989.[31] According to Goldman Sachs Research, net interest margins for NCNB should be relatively stable, with a slight uptrend for the next two years, as assets are redeployed (see Exhibit 12.15). Improving profitability, coupled with strong earning asset growth, will provide NCNB with the capability of a 15 percent compound growth rate over the three years 1985–1987.

**Social** Consumer financial relationship management has emerged as the dominant retail financial strategy in the 1980s. One of the key pressures now acting

**Exhibit 12.15** Earnings Projections, 1984–1987

|  | 1984 | 1985 | 1986 | 1987 |
|---|---|---|---|---|
| As % of earning assets |  |  |  |  |
| Net interest income | 4.39 | 4.40 | 4.45 | 4.40 |
| Loan loss provision | 0.39 | 0.36 | 0.36 | 0.35 |
| Net funds revenue | 4.00 | 4.04 | 4.07 | 4.05 |
| Other income | 1.21 | 1.19 | 1.20 | 1.23 |
| Other expense | 3.43 | 3.36 | 3.34 | 3.30 |
| Net noninterest expense | 2.22 | 2.17 | 2.14 | 2.07 |
| Net income | 0.98 | 1.01 | 1.04 | 1.07 |
| Earning asset growth (%) | 26.0 | 16.0 | 15.0 | 12.0 |
| Earning assets (millions) | $12,244 | $14,200 | $16,360 | $18,325 |
| Net income (millions) | 119.5 | 143.3 | 170.1 | 196.0 |
| Average shares outstanding (millions) | 29.1 | 30.5 | 31.0 | 31.0 |
| Net per share | $4.10 | $4.70 | $5.50 | $6.30 |
| Year-to-year % incr. | 11.3 | 14.7 | 17.0 | 14.5 |

on the environment of financial services is competition for the pool of household assets.

In November 1982, Electronic Banking, Inc., asked consumers, "If it were possible to obtain nearly all financial services such as checking, savings, loans, insurance, investments and tax planning from one provider, would you be inclined to consolidate your services?"[32] Nearly 50 percent of the respondents answered yes (see Exhibit 12.16).

NCNB began moving toward a relationship management approach in 1980 when deregulation and increasing competition led to a number of new products and services. Regardless of the increasing competition, many consumers continue to prefer traditional financial relationships. In a recent survey, more than half of the U.S. households questioned stated that they are unlikely to try a new financial product unless someone they know recommends it.[33]

**Technological** Technology is the key to unit growth in financial services. It increases transactions-processing capacity and improves quality without increasing unit cost (see Exhibit 12.17).

A team of more than 100 people, including NCNB employees and outside consultants, is dedicated exclusively to new systems development, which is separate from the support and maintenance of existing systems.

New systems being developed for NCNB include an international system to automate letters of credit, foreign exchange trading, foreign-currency-denominated lending, and noncredit services, and to tie NCNB's international operations together in Florida, North Carolina, and around the world; a funds transfer system including automated clearinghouse, wire transfers, and other money movement functions, and a bank card system for more flexible Visa and MasterCard processing.[34] All of NCNB's basic operating systems, including loans and trust, are to be replaced as part of the long-range effort.

**Exhibit 12.16**

| ATTITUDES TOWARD DESIRABILITY OF ONE-PLACE FINANCIAL SERVICE | |
|---|---|
| Not at all desirable | 16% |
| Somewhat undesirable | 14% |
| Neither desirable nor undesirable | 20% |
| Somewhat desirable | 26% |
| Very desirable | 24% |
| Total number of respondents | 2804 |
| **CONVENIENCE AND WILLINGNESS TO CONSOLIDATE SERVICES** | |
| No | 36% |
| Don't know | 14% |
| Yes | 50% |
| Total number of respondents | 1092 |

*Source: Economic Review,* May 1984.

**Exhibit 12.17** Cost of Teller Transaction Versus ATM Transaction

| | 1979 | 1985E | % Change |
|---|---|---|---|
| Teller-activated transaction at main branch bank | 45¢ | 72¢ | 60 |
| Automated teller machine transaction | 26¢ | 29¢ | 12 |

*Source:* Paine Webber Mitchell Hutchins Inc., August 1983.

## CONCLUSION AND RECOMMEN- DATION

According to the Boston Consulting Group's business portfolio concept, NCNB is definitely a star.* NCNB selected a growth strategy with concentric and horizontal diversification. Having already gained a lead on its competitors, NCNB is in a position to build up its capital in order to take advantage of the opportunity to expand.

Looking to 1985 and beyond, NCNB's strategic orientation should continue to be on profitability and growth. This focus has positioned NCNB as the Southeast's leading bank and will enable the company to continue to respond to a changing political, social, technological, and economic climate.

## NOTES

1. Goldman Sachs, *Investment Research—NCNB Corp.,* Financial Services Research Group, December 19, 1984, p. 5.

*See Figure 5.1, p. 000.

2. Thomas H. Hanley, *Bank Weekly—NCNB Corp.,* Salomon Brothers, Inc., December 7, 1984, p. 7.
3. NCNB Annual Report 1983, p. 13.
4. NCNB Annual Report 1984, p. 14.
5. NCNB brochure, 1983.
6. Goldman Sachs, op. cit. p. 19.
7. Ibid., p. 19.
8. Ibid., p. 23.
9. Salomon Brothers, Inc., op. cit., p. 6.
10. Ibid., p. 6.
11. NCNB brochure, 1983.
12. Ibid.
13. Ibid.
14. *World Book Encyclopedia,* vol. 2 (Chicago: World Book–Inc., 1984), pp. 58–60.
15. *Standard & Poor's Industry Surveys* 1 (January 1985): B19.
16. Ibid., p. 27.
17. Ibid., p. 27.
18. Ibid., p. 28.
19. Ibid., p. 28.
20. Ibid., p. 28.
21. Ibid., p. 18.
22. Ibid., p. 15.
23. Richard W. Nelson, "Large Banks' Strengths and Weaknesses," *Economic Review,* January 1985, Federal Reserve Bank of Atlanta, p. 22.
24. Veronica M. Bennett and Charles R. Haywood, "Technology and Interstate Banking," *Economic Review,* May 1983, Federal Reserve Bank of Atlanta, p. 56.
25. *World Book Encyclopedia,* 1984, p. 61.
26. *Wall Street Journal,* April 1, 1985, p. 7.
27. NCNB Annual Report 1984, p. 29.
28. Ibid., pp. 6–7.
29. NCNB Third Quarter Report 1984, p. 6.
30. Salomon Brothers, Inc., op. cit., p. 9.
31. Stephen B. Wildstrom, "Investment Outlook 1985," *Business Week,* December 31, 1984/January 7, 1985, p. 63.
32. Veronica M. Bennett, "Consumer Demand for Product Deregulation," *Economic Review,* May 1984, Federal Reserve Bank of Atlanta, pp. 29–30.
33. Ibid., p. 38.
34. NCNB Annual Report 1984, p. 13.

# 13  McDonald's Corporation

Lloyd L. Byars and Denise Murray
Atlanta University

Thirty years ago, Ray Kroc opened his first McDonald's franchise in Des Plaines, Illinois. Currently, McDonald's is a billion-dollar business whose existence is often cited as the embodiment of the American dream. How was McDonald's able to achieve its success? The following pages will answer this question as the McDonald's Corporation is explored and analyzed.

**HISTORY**  Contrary to popular belief, McDonald's was not created by Ray Kroc. McDonald's was founded in 1948 by Dick and Maurice McDonald, two brothers from San Bernardino, California. At that time Mr. Kroc was selling Multimixers, a machine that could make five milkshakes at one time. The McDonald brothers had purchased eight Multimixers for their hamburger drive-in restaurant. Mr. Kroc was amazed that a small hamburger drive-in had enough business to make 40 milk shakes at a time.

Upon reaching the restaurant, Mr. Kroc became more bewildered because he could see nothing obvious to attest to the attraction. The place was spotlessly clean, but it had no particular angle. The menu was basic—hamburgers, french fries, and something to drink—and people were practically running to get in line. All of this piqued Ray's curiosity, so he got in line and began to talk to the people around him. Ray questioned the excitement for what was basically a hamburger joint. The answers were pretty much the same. Although there wasn't much variety (as mentioned above), the food was the best you could get anywhere.

At the time, Ray Kroc had no vision of a billion-dollar business. However, he thought that if he could talk the McDonald brothers into opening a few more restaurants he could sell more Multimixers. The McDonald brothers had little ambition and were not particularly interested in opening other restaurants (they didn't want to leave their home). Ray next suggested allowing other people to open more of these drive-ins. The McDonald brothers said they had already tried selling the rights to other people and had failed. There were about ten McDonald-like drive-ins scattered around California and Arizona that had been licensed to operate like the San Bernardino McDonald's. However, not all of these drive-ins had the same high quality as the original, and anything lower in quality tended to reflect on the brothers' San Bernardino drive-in.

Exasperated, Ray gave it one more try. He suggested finding one person who would run the whole operation. This person would maintain the high quality, find the operators, find places for the operators to set up business, build the drive-ins, and make sure all the operators adhered to standards. The McDonald brothers liked this idea, and questioned where to find such a man. Ray Kroc volunteered, and McDonald's Corporation was founded. The year was 1954.

Ray Kroc left San Bernardino with a franchise agreement and knowledge of everything about the McDonald brothers' operation. The agreement gave Ray Kroc the power to organize a McDonald's System. The contract provided for the following:

1. There would be a $950 charge to each person who wanted a license to duplicate the McDonald's restaurant.
2. Ray Kroc would collect 1.9 percent of all the money that the new store owners took in. The McDonald brothers would collect 0.5 percent of Ray's 1.9 percent.
3. A clause was included guaranteeing that the new drive-ins would be exactly like the San Bernardino drive-in.
4. Ray Kroc agreed not to deviate from any detail of the San Bernardino drive-in without obtaining the agreement of both brothers in writing and having it sent to him by registered mail.[1]

On April 15, 1955, Ray Kroc opened his first McDonald's. The restaurant was highly successful, and Ray Kroc was in the hamburger business. The company symbol was a little hamburger man named Speedee. By 1956 McDonald's restaurants appeared in Illinois, Indiana, and California. In 1957 McDonald's became known for the motto "Quality, Service, and Cleanliness (QSC)." There was a cloud, however, in front of this silver lining.

In the process of expansion Ray Kroc had made some changes to the original San Bernardino restaurant. Even though Ray had gotten a verbal agreement for all these changes, he was still in violation of his original contract with the McDonald brothers. Ray was legally liable to the McDonald brothers, and they could sue and put him out of the business (this does not mean that the brothers would sue, only that they could sue). This left Ray Kroc in a very insecure position. As luck would have it, word came that the McDonald brothers wanted to retire from running the San Bernardino store. Ray took advantage of the situation. He offered to buy the McDonald brothers' rights to McDonald's. The brothers had a price—one million dollars each, after taxes. Ray figured the total to be about $2.7 million, taxes included. In 1961 Ray Kroc became the owner of McDonald's.

The company has flourished. Today, it holds a 7 percent share of the U.S. restaurant market, an 18 percent share of the domestic fast-food market, and a 45 percent share of the fast-food hamburger market.[2] McDonald's attracts about 10 million Americans per day. The International Division alone is large enough to qualify as one of the United States' ten largest restaurant systems. Systemwide sales and sales from company-owned stores in 1983 totaled over $8 billion. A detailed listing of the historical highlights of the McDonald's Corporation is shown in Exhibit 13.1.

**Exhibit 13.1** Historical Highlights of the McDonald's Corporation

| | |
|---|---|
| 1948 | Dick and Maurice McDonald established the first McDonald's in San Bernardino, California, on December 20. They founded the McDonald's System. |
| 1955 | On April 15, Ray Kroc opened his first McDonald's in Des Plaines, Illinois.<br>In July, Ray Kroc's second McDonald's opened in Fresno, California.<br>Total company sales were $235,000.<br>A little hamburger man called Speedee was the company symbol. |
| 1956 | Ray Kroc hired Fred Turner to head up operations. |
| 1957 | McDonald's became known for the motto "QSC for Quality, Service, and Cleanliness."<br>At year's end, sales for McDonald's 21 restaurants totaled $4,466,860. |
| 1961 | Ray Kroc bought out the McDonald brothers for $2.7 million.<br>Hamburger University opened in the basement of the Elk Grove, Illinois, restaurant and conferred Bachelor of Hamburgerology degrees to the first graduating class. |
| 1962 | Speedee was replaced by a new logo—the symbol of the golden arches, a modernistic M. |
| 1963 | The five hundredth McDonald's restaurant opened, in Toledo, Ohio.<br>Ronald McDonald made his debut in Washington, D.C.<br>Filet-O-Fish sandwich became the first menu addition to the original menu. |
| 1965 | McDonald's celebrated its tenth anniversary with the first public stock offering at $22.50 per share. |
| 1966 | In April, McDonald's had it first stock split—3 for 2.<br>On July 5, McDonald's was listed on the New York Stock Exchange with the ticker symbol MCD. |
| 1967 | First McDonald's All-American High School Band was organized.<br>Indoor seating was introduced.<br>First McDonald's restaurants opened in Canada and Puerto Rico.<br>First home television network advertising. |
| 1968 | Fred Turner became president and chief executive officer.<br>Big Mac and Hot Apple Pie were added to the menu.<br>One thousandth store opened, in Des Plaines, Illinois. |
| 1969 | International Division was formed.<br>McDonald's listed on the Midwest and Pacific exchanges. |
| 1970 | Fifteen hundredth store opened, in Concord, New Hampshire. |
| 1971 | World headquarters opened in Oak Brook, Illinois.<br>First McDonald's opened in Japan, Germany, and Australia. |
| 1972 | Ten billionth hamburger was sold.<br>Two thousandth store opened in Des Plaines, Illinois.<br>Introduction of the Quarter Pounder sandwich. |
| 1973 | Twenty-five hundredth store opened, in Lockport, New York.<br>Egg McMuffin was introduced. |
| 1974 | Three thousandth store opened, in Woolwich, England.<br>McDonald's opened it first store in a zoo in Toronto, Canada.<br>First Ronald McDonald House opened in Philadelphia, Pennsylvania.<br>The company sold its 15 billionth hamburger. |
| 1975 | The first drive-through was established in Oklahoma City, Oklahoma.<br>McDonald's celebrated its twentieth anniversary. |
| 1976 | Four thousandth store opened, in Montreal, Canada.<br>Fred Turner was named chairman of the board, Ray Kroc was named senior chairman, and Ed Schmitt was named president and chief administrative officer.<br>Twenty billionth hamburger was sold. |

(continued)

**Exhibit 13.1**  (continued)

| | |
|---|---|
| 1977 | McDonald's added a complete breakfast line to its national menu. |
| 1978 | The five thousandth store opened, in Fujizawa City, Japan. |
| 1980 | McDonald's celebrated its twenty-fifth anniversary.<br>The first floating McDonald's launched on the historic Mississippi riverfront in St. Louis, Missouri.<br>Mike Quinlan was elected to the newly created position of president of McDonald's U.S.A. and chief operating officer.<br>Six thousandth store opened, in Munich, Germany. |
| 1981 | There were 5558 stores in the U.S. and 1183 internationally, totaling 6741 stores worldwide with sales of $7 billion.<br>First McDonald's restaurants open in Spain, Denmark, and the Philippines. |
| 1982 | McDonald's opened its seventh thousandth restaurant.<br>Edward H. Schmitt was elected vice-chairman of the corporation and continues as chief administrative officer.<br>Michael R. Quinlan was promoted to president and chief operating officer of McDonald's Corporation and continues as president—McDonald's U.S.A..<br>Chicken McNuggets introduced into all domestic restaurants. |
| 1983 | McDonald's served its forty-fifth billionth hamburger.<br>Eight thousandth store opened, in Atlanta, Georgia. |
| 1984 | January 14, founder and senior chairman of the board Ray Kroc died. |

## MANAGEMENT

The management of the McDonald's Corporation can be looked at as two groups—the group that works for the company, and the franchisees and affiliates. The group working for the company, the Oak Brook, Illinois, group, will be discussed first.

Exhibit 13.2 shows the top management of the McDonald's Corporation. Ray Kroc's legacy is firmly established in the Oak Brook management. Fred Turner, who is chairman of the board and chief executive officer, has been with McDonald's since 1956. Turner was hired by Ray Kroc, went to work grilling hamburgers, moved up the rapidly growing corporation, and became president in 1968.[3] Turner runs the company in the same manner as his predecessor and is often referred to as the son Ray Kroc never had.

McDonald's top management is well indoctrinated with Ray Kroc's motto of "Quality, Service, Cleanliness, and Value." Except for Executive Vice-President and Chief Financial Officer Jack Greenberg, all of McDonald's top-management people have risen through the ranks. The 64 executive officers of McDonald's Corporation have a total of over 892 years of experience with the company, or an average of 14 years each.[4] The executives above the level of vice-president have an average of 17 years with the company. Ray Kroc insisted upon "sticking to the knitting" and instilled this trait in the current management team.

The franchisees are the other group of McDonald's managers. At year-end 1983, franchised and affiliated restaurants accounted for 74.9 percent of all McDonald's restaurants; this translates into over 5000 restaurants. The McDonald's name is synonymous with franchising. Exhibits 13.3 and 13.4 give detailed information for the conventional franchise and the Business Facilities Lease for the McDonald's Corporation.

**Exhibit 13.2** Top Management of McDonald's Corporation

*Fred L. Turner* (53)—Chairman of the board and chief executive officer. Joined the company in 1956.

*Edward H. Schmitt* (59)—Vice-chairman of the board and chief administrative officer. Started as a manager trainee.

*Michael R. Quinlan* (39)—President and chief operating officer, and president—McDonald's U.S.A. Started as a mail clerk at headquarters.

*Jack M. Greenberg* (41)—Executive vice-president and chief financial officer.

*Edward H. Rensi* (40)—Senior executive vice-president and chief operations officer. Started as a member of a Columbus, Ohio, kitchen crew.

*Steven J. Barnes*—Executive vice-president and chairman—International Division.

*Source:* McDonald's Corporation Annual Report 1983.

## Exhibit 13.3 Conventional Franchise Information

The following table represents the fees and approximate costs of a new McDonald's restaurant. Size of the restaurant facility, area of the country, and style of decor and landscaping will affect costs. Forty percent of the total cost must be funded from nonborrowed personal resources. The remainder may be financed from traditional sources. McDonald's does not provide financing or loan guarantees, nor does it permit absentee investors.

| | |
|---|---|
| Term | 20 years |
| Ongoing fees | A monthly fee based upon the restaurant's sales performance (currently 3% of monthly sales) plus a minimum monthly fee, or 8% of monthly sales, whichever is greater. |

Initial costs

| | |
|---|---|
| $12,500 | Paid to McDonald's.<br>Initial fee earned by McDonald's at the time the McDonald's restaurant is ready for occupancy. |
| $15,000 | Paid to McDonald's and subject to refund.<br>Interest-free security deposit for the faithful performance of the franchise, refundable at the expiration of the franchise. |
| $135,000 | Paid to supplier.<br>Approximate cost of kitchen equipment not including taxes, delivery, and installation. |
| $35,000 | Paid to supplier.<br>Approximate cost of seating and decor not including taxes, delivery, and installation. |
| $18,000–$26,000 | Paid to supplier.<br>Approximate cost for taxes, delivery, and installation of the signage, equipment, seating, and decor. (Amount varies depending on state and local taxes, distance, etc.) |
| $10,000–$31,000 | Paid to supplier.<br>Approximate cost of cash register system.<br>The lower figure is for mechanical registers; the higher figure is for computerized registers. |
| $50,000–$75,000 | Paid to suppliers.<br>Approximate cash requirements for miscellaneous equipment, franchisee's construction options, landscaping, operating cash, safe, first month's rent, training, preopening expenses, etc. |
| $298,500–$352,000 | Approximate total cost. |

*Source:* McDonald's Corporation Information Package.

**Exhibit 13.4** Business Facilities Lease Information

The company makes its Business Facilities Lease Program available to a limited number of its outstanding candidates (registers applicants), who excel in their qualifications but are unable to meet the financial requirements of the conventional franchise program.

The costs of developing and equipping the restaurant are the same as a conventional franchise. The total initial investment (approximately $60,000) must be funded from nonborrowed personal resources.

| | |
|---|---|
| Initial costs | The following costs will vary depending on individual circumstances. This list does not include living expenses prior to opening the restaurant. |

$15,000 Security deposit
 12,000 Inventory
  3,400 First month rent
  5,000 Moving expense
  6,000 Management training
  7,000 Crew training
  3,000 Uniforms
  3,600 Preopening advertising
  5,000 Landscaping
―――――――――――――――
$60,000 Total

| | |
|---|---|
| Term | 3 years |
| Ongoing fees | A monthly fee based upon the restaurant's sales performance (currently 16% of monthly sales). |
| Purchase option | Available in the second and third year of the term (assuming full compliance with the franchise). |
| Option price | The higher of<br>a. $325,000 or<br>b. a percentage of annual sales calculated as follows: |

| Sales Volume | Percent of Sales |
|---|---|
| Less than $899,999 | 40 |
| $900,000–$999,999 | 41 |
| $1,000,000–$1,099,999 | 42 |
| $1,100,000 and higher | 44 |

plus
c. the cost of any additional equipment or leasehold improvements purchased by McDonald's leased to the franchisee and installed after the restaurant has opened for business.

The terms upon exercise are as follows:

| | |
|---|---|
| Term | Normally 20 years from the beginning date of the Business Facilities Lease. |
| Ongoing fees | Reduced to those in effect for conventional franchises. |

*Source:* McDonald's Corporation Information Package.

**Exhibit 13.5** Number of McDonald's Restaurants by Operation

| Operated by | 1983 | 1982 | 1981 | 1980 |
|---|---|---|---|---|
| Company | 1949 | 1846 | 1746 | 1608 |
| Franchisees | 5371 | 4911 | 4580 | 4302 |
| Affiliates[a] | 458 | 502 | 413 | 353 |

[a]Affiliates refers to those operators under the Business Facilities Lease.

*Source:* Standard NYSE Reports, December 28, 1984.

In 1955 it cost $950 to obtain a McDonald's franchise. Today, the cost is in excess of $350,000. Despite the high cost people line up to get a McDonald's franchise. Why? Because the average store does about $1.5 million in sales every year. A McDonald's franchise is as close to a sure thing as they come in the restaurant industry, which is why thousands of people apply every year for the 100 or so new licenses available.[5]

Another contributing factor to the success of the McDonald's franchise system "is that the franchisees are, for the most part, highly successful businessmen and businesswomen who are committed to the rigorous controls and standards of the parent."[6] Franchisees are expected to give 100 percent of their business time and efforts to their McDonald's operation. In addition to the start-up costs, the franchisee gives the parent 11.5 percent of its gross annual sales for rental and service fees. Above all, franchisees are expected to adhere to the "Quality, Service, Cleanliness, and Value" motto. "An extensive McDonald's field operation checks on each store continually to make sure the franchisee is minding his QSCVs."[7] Exhibit 13.5 gives the breakdown of company-owned, franchised, and affiliated restaurants for the years 1980–1983.

The Oak Brook management and the franchisees depend on one another to keep the highly successful McDonald's machine running smoothly. The franchisees brings complaints and suggestions to the Oak Brook people for their concern (over problems) and their okay (for suggestions). In fact, the Filet-O-Fish sandwich, the Big Mac sandwich, and the Egg McMuffin were all invented by franchisees.[8] The idea for McSnack—a scaled-down McDonald's for shopping malls—came from the head of the Minneapolis region. These examples show that McDonald's management and franchisees work together for the good of all concerned.

## OPERATIONS

"Quality, Service, Cleanliness, and Value" also applies to the operation of McDonald's restaurants. The restaurants are known for being spotlessly clean. The "McDonald's Family" is how the company sees all who work for McDonald's— from the kitchen crews to the franchisees to the Oak Brook management team.

**Exhibit 13.6** Net Profit Margins of Big Three, 1984

| Company | Net Profit Margin (%) |
|---|---|
| McDonald's | 11.4 |
| Wendy's International | 7.7 |
| Burger King | 4.1 |

*Source: Forbes,* January 14, 1985, p. 198.

The "McDonald's Experience" refers to the inviting aura of group—preferably family and friends—dining.[9]

Net profit margin measures a firm's ability to control its level of costs, or expenses, relative to the revenues it generates. McDonald's has always had an enviable net profit margin. In fact, McDonald's net profit margin "has become an annual tradition on the Forbes Yardsticks."[10] Exhibit 13.6 gives the profit margins for McDonald's and its nearest hamburger competitors, Burger King and Wendy's International, for the year 1984.

Few people in or out of the fast-food industry dispute the fact that McDonald's operates its restaurants exceptionally well. McDonald's is known for satisfying the market for speed, convenience, and good values. This has led to McDonald's large market share and number one ranking in the fast-food hamburger market. A former executive of Burger King was asked why McDonald's is number one in hamburgers. His answer was the following:

> Do they have great French fries? Yes. Is the service quick? The fastest. Are the restaurants clean? Immaculate. You have to give McDonald's credit for knowing exactly what they are doing.[11]

Finally, McDonald's puts much of its money back into the business. The company often chooses to refurbish its stores before such practice is necessary. The company also uses funds for new equipment and design improvements. Examples of this are the eat-in restaurants, the drive-thrus, and the McDonald's playlands.

**HAMBURGER UNIVERSITY**

Hamburger University is McDonald's worldwide management training center. The first Hamburger University was located in an Elk Grove Village, Illinois, restaurant in 1961. Hamburger University was relocated in 1968 and expanded in 1973 to accommodate the increasingly larger classes. In October 1983, Hamburger University moved to its present campus in Oak Brook, Illinois.

Hamburger University consists of eight classrooms, eight seminar rooms, a library, and four fully equipped labs. It also has the latest audiovisual equipment, as well as restaurant equipment to help the student make the transition from the classroom to actual restaurant application.

The curriculum is designed to instruct McDonald's personnel in the various aspects of their business. Upon completion of the program, students receive a Bachelor of Hamburgerology degree. Presently, there is a resident teaching staff of 20 persons. "The American Council of Education recommends to universities and colleges that 18 McDonald's courses and programs qualify for a total of 40 hours of college credit."[12] In addition to the basic curriculum, informational seminars are conducted on a continuous basis.

## PRODUCT

McDonald's main product is the hamburger, complemented by the french fry and a soft drink or a shake. In 30 years of business McDonald's has added only three products—the Filet-O-Fish sandwich, Chicken McNuggets, and the Egg McMuffin (and other breakfast items)—that are not hamburger to the menu (other items such as the McChicken and McRib sandwiches have been tested on the market and subsequently removed). "McDonald's is sticking overwhelmingly to burgers and fries. Its management doesn't know anything else and doesn't want to learn."[13] Quoting President Mike Quinlan, "McDonald's hamburgers is what we are."[14]

McDonald's is facing a problem with its product. The problem is one of quality. Most people who eat McDonald's hamburgers aren't enthusiastic about the taste.[15] The problem of quality is a perception problem. "There is no question that McDonald's food is clean, pure and of high quality. The eggs in the Egg McMuffin are grade A. The hamburger is 100 percent beef."[16]

To combat the public's misconceptions about its quality, McDonald's has been aggressive in promoting the nutritional value and good taste of its food. McDonald's current advertising campaign announces: "It's a good time for the great taste of McDonald's!" However, changing the public's mind may prove a difficult thing to do.

McDonald's can rely on its most popular product—the french fry—to offset some of its quality problems. The Chicken McNugget and the breakfast menu are also drawing people back to the golden arches. The Chicken McNuggets accounted for about 8 percent of total sales in 1983.[17] The breakfast menu caters to about one-quarter of all Americans who eat breakfast out and accounted for more than 15 percent of total sales in 1983.[18] Currently, McDonald's is testing various new menu items to support it present menu. The company will try many things; however, if it does not improve Q, S, C, or V, it doesn't fit.[19]

## INTERNATIONAL DIVISION

McDonald's International Division deserves special attention. In 1981 McDonald's international sales alone were enough to qualify the division for fifth place on the list of top U.S. restaurant systems.[20] Sales from international operations in 1983 totaled $1.6 billion, or 19 percent of total sales.

**Exhibit 13.7** Number of International Restaurants by Country, 1983

| Country | Number of Restaurants | Country | Number of Restaurants |
|---|---|---|---|
| Australia | 147 | Japan | 393 |
| Austria | 12 | Malaysia | 5 |
| Bahamas | 2 | Netherlands | 27 |
| Belgium | 9 | Netherlands Antilles | 2 |
| Brazil | 21 | New Zealand | 17 |
| Canada | 442 | Nicaragua | 1 |
| Costa Rica | 3 | Norway | 1 |
| Denmark | 7 | Panama | 6 |
| El Salvador | 3 | Philippines | 5 |
| England | 133 | Puerto Rico | 5 |
| France | 15 | Singapore | 9 |
| Germany | 190 | Spain | 10 |
| Guam | 2 | Sweden | 15 |
| Guatemala | 3 | Switzerland | 8 |
| Hong Kong | 24 | Virgin Islands | 3 |
| Ireland | 5 | | |

*Source:* McDonald's Corporation Annual Report 1983.

McDonald's opened its first restaurant outside the United States in 1967 in Canada. The International Division was created in 1969, and today McDonald's operates restaurants in 31 countries outside the United States. Exhibit 13.7 gives the number of international restaurants by country. Although McDonald's restaurants are located all over the world, the company has concentrated on six countries—Canada, Japan, Australia, Germany, France, and England—where it does the majority of its business (by sales).

Management of the international restaurants is very similar to the management of the U.S. stores. It is company policy to hire, train, and develop local management. There are four types of McDonald's ownership within the International Division:

1. Wholly owned by McDonald's Corporation.
2. Joint venture between McDonald's Corporation and a local corporate organization.
3. Developmental license—an individual is granted a license to develop several McDonald's restaurants within a specified city or country.
4. Licensee—similar to the license system in the United States where a license for one store is granted to an individual entrepreneur. This system may be implemented under either of options 1 or 2 above.[21]

All international restaurants must follow the "Q, S, C, and V" motto. This means that quality products must be used (for example, 100 percent beef), the service should be fast, and the prices should be low. Most of the food is purchased from local suppliers. Use of local contractors and banks is also encouraged. The international franchisees and affiliates must conform to the company standards.

**MARKETING AND ADVERTISING**

Marketing and advertising have been a staple in McDonald's Corporation. Although marketing and advertising are currently considered separate disciplines, the terms have been used interchangeably throughout McDonald's history. Therefore, this section will discuss both marketing and advertising.

"More than anything else, the McDonald's story is a success in story in marketing."[22] In its early years, McDonald's advertised in local markets exclusively through the print medium. In 1962 McDonald's began local radio advertising. In 1967 McDonald's began its first nationwide advertising on network television (local markets integrated their advertising with the national plan).

Since its inception, McDonald's advertising has been highly successful. "In the advertising community, McDonald's is practically held in awe. Its tear-jerking 'heart sell' ads and catchy jingles consistently rank among the most memorable ads on TV, and its cast of McDonaldland characters is as familiar to most children as the cast of Sesame Street."[23] The advertising reflects the company's character, "food, folks, and fun." The success of McDonald's advertising can be seen in how often the commercials come to the mind of the consumer: "For example, in the February 1983 Adwatch survey published in *Ad Age,* McDonald's of all fast food chains came first to the minds of 43.6 percent of American consumers, with a commanding 30-point lead over its nearest rival, Burger King."[24]

In 1983, McDonald's Corporation's systemwide advertising expenditure was $423 million. It was money well spent. Exhibits 13.8 and 13.9 compare McDonald's sales and market share to Burger King and Wendy's International (sales include company-owned and franchised restaurants).

Part of the cost for McDonald's national advertising and marketing campaigns is paid by the operators of U.S. restaurants. The Operators National Advertising Fund (OPNAD) was founded in 1967. The individual operators voluntarily con-

**Exhibit 13.8** Comparison of Total Sales—McDonald's, Burger King, and Wendy's International

| Company | Sales (millions) |
|---|---|
| McDonald's | $8,700 |
| Burger King | 3,100 |
| Wendy's Int. | 1,900 |

*Source: Fortune,* November 12, 1984, p. 34.

**Exhibit 13.9** Percentage of Market Share (1983) for McDonald's, Burger King, and Wendy's International.

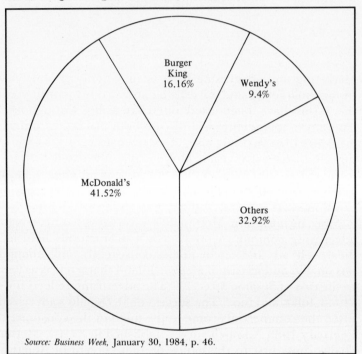

Source: *Business Week*, January 30, 1984, p. 46.

tribute a percentage of their gross sales to the fund for the purchase of national advertising.[25]

It takes many people to maintain this massive advertising campaign. The following is a list of advertising and promotional agencies employed by the McDonald's Corporation.

- *Leo Burnett* is McDonald's national advertising agency. Their responsibilities include the development of all national television, radio, print, and outdoor advertising.
- *Burrell Inc.* is McDonald's national black consumer advertising agency and is responsible for marketing plans targeted toward the black community. They also develop all black television, radio, and print advertising for McDonald's.
- *Conill, Inc.,* is McDonald's Hispanic consumer advertising agency and is responsible for the development of all Hispanic television, radio, and print advertising.
- *Golin-Harris Communications,* McDonald's national public relations agency, is responsible for helping to develop effective public relations programs.
- *Frankel and Company* is McDonald's national promotional agency.

**Exhibit 13.10** McDonald's Corporation Public Service Programs

*Ronald McDonald House*—A facility that provides low-cost housing for parents and families of children being treated for serious illnesses. The facilities are located near local hospitals. In 1983 there were 50 Ronald McDonald Houses in the United States.

*McDonald's All-American High School Basketball Team*—25 high school stars from around the nation are selected and given all-American status. In 1983 the team played in Atlanta, Georgia, and raised over $70,000 for the Ronald McDonald Childhood Cancer Clinic at Emory University.

*McDonald's All-American High School Band*—The students in the 50 states and Puerto Rico compete for the two state spots in the band. The 102 members then perform in the Macy's Thanksgiving Day and the Tournament of Roses parades.

*The 1984 Olympics*—McDonald's was a national sponsor of the 1984 Olympic Games. The McDonald's Olympic Swim Stadium was funded by contributions of individual restaurant operators.

*Muscular dystrophy*—In 1983 McDonald's raised $1.5 million for muscular dystrophy. McDonald's has been contributing for 12 years and has raised over $15 million during this time.

*"Make It Click"*—Through commercials Ronald McDonald encouraged entire families to "buckle up" for safety. The McDonald's restaurants distributed some 10 million "Make It Click" bumper stickers.

**PUBLIC SERVICE**

Ray Kroc believed that his hamburger restaurants could be a community resource, so McDonald's gives something back to the communities where it does business.[26] Exhibit 13.10 lists many of the public service programs conducted by the McDonald's Corporation.

**FINANCES**

"Financially, McDonald's is one of the great success stories in all of American business, never mind the restaurant business."[27] McDonald's has been a stockholder's dream. Since McDonald's went public in 1965, the corporation has never reported quarterly earnings that were less than the comparable period the year before.[28] Stockholders' equity has averaged a return of more than 20 percent for the last ten years. Dividends have increased consistently since their initiation. The best way to see how well McDonald's is doing financially is through the following series of exhibits. Exhibits 13.11, 13.12, 13.13, and 13.14 show the financial highlights of the McDonald's Corporation for the year 1983.

A reproduction of the balance sheet for McDonald's Corporation is shown in Exhibit 13.15.

**FUTURE TRENDS**

The retail fast-food hamburger market is reaching a saturation point and the McDonald's Corporation is taking a series of steps to offset the slower growth. The International Division is one way that McDonald's is protecting its future.

**Exhibit 13.11** Total Revenues, 1981–1983
(in millions of dollars)

| Quarter | 1983 | 1982 | 1981 |
|---------|------|------|------|
| March | 663 | 617 | 562 |
| June | 787 | 725 | 650 |
| September | 830 | 738 | 668 |
| December | 783 | 690 | 636 |
| Total | 3,063 | 2,770 | 2,516 |

*Source:* Standard NYSE Reports, December 28, 1984.

**Exhibit 13.12** McDonald's Common Share Earnings
Data

| Quarter | 1983 | 1982 | 1981 |
|---------|------|------|------|
| March | $ 0.73 | $ 0.65 | $ 0.57 |
| June | 1.07 | 0.96 | 0.83 |
| September | 1.12 | 0.97 | 0.83 |
| December | 0.90 | 0.76 | 0.67 |
| Total | $ 3.83 | $ 3.33 | $ 2.91 |

*Source:* Standard NYSE Reports, December 28, 2984.

**Exhibit 13.13** Three-Year Financial Summary of McDonald's Corporation
(dollars in millions)

| | 1983 | 1982 | 1981 |
|---|------|------|------|
| Systemwide sales | $ 8,687 | $ 7,809 | $ 7,129 |
|   United States | 7,069 | 6,362 | 5,770 |
|   International | 1,618 | 1,447 | 1,359 |
| Sales by company-operated restaurants | 2,297 | 2,095 | 1,916 |
| Revenues from franchised restaurants | 704 | 620 | 561 |
| Total revenues | 3,063 | 2,770 | 2,516 |
| Income before taxes | 628 | 546 | 482 |
| Net income | 343 | 301 | 265 |
| Funds generated from operations | 580 | 528 | 447 |
| Net property and equipment at end of year | 3,183 | 2,765 | 2,497 |
| Total assets at end of year | 3,727 | 3,263 | 2,899 |
| Long-term debt at end of year | 1,171 | 1,056 | 926 |
| Per common share | | | |
|   Net income | $ 5.74 | $ 5.00 | $ 4.36 |
|   Dividends declared | 0.97 | 0.79 | 0.63 |
|   Stockholders' equity at end of year | 29.58 | 25.51 | 22.72 |
|   Market price at end of year | 70½ | 60⅜ | 43⅝ |

*Source:* McDonald's Corporation Annual Report 1983.

**Exhibit 13.14** Consolidated Statement of Income of McDonald's Corporation (dollars in thousands)

| Year end | 1983 | 1982 | 1981 |
|---|---|---|---|
| **Revenues** | | | |
| Sales by company-operated restaurants | $ 2,297,430 | $ 2,094,805 | $ 1,915,908 |
| Revenues from franchised restaurants | 703,718 | 620,413 | 561,321 |
| Other revenues—net | 61,774 | 54,321 | 38,607 |
| Total revenues | 3,062,922 | 2,769,539 | 2,515,836 |
| **Costs and expenses** | | | |
| Company-operated restaurants | | | |
| Food and paper | 845,620 | 776,929 | 720,293 |
| Payroll | 501,199 | 473,018 | 431,031 |
| Rent | 30,454 | 26,054 | 23,873 |
| Depreciation and amortization | 93,297 | 78,769 | 72,161 |
| Other operating expenses | 412,692 | 386,742 | 341,921 |
| Franchises restaurants | | | |
| Rent | 38,274 | 33,552 | 31,069 |
| Depreciation and amortization | 69,365 | 59,621 | 54,214 |
| General, administrative, and selling expenses | | | |
| Interest expense | | | |
| Total interest charges | 122,774 | 109,230 | 103,580 |
| Less amounts capitalized | 14,280 | 15,029 | 12,263 |
| Total costs and expenses | 2,434,882 | 2,223,495 | 2,034,202 |
| Income before provision for income taxes | 682,040 | 546,044 | 481,634 |
| Provision for income taxes | 285,400 | 245,400 | 264,834 |
| Net income | $ 342,640 | $ 300,644 | $ 264,834 |
| Net income per share | $ 5.74 | $ 5.00 | $ 4.36 |
| Dividends per share | $ .97 | $ .79 | $ .63 |

One-third of all McDonald's restaurants are located outside of the United States. Analysts predict the international restaurants will make up 50 percent of all McDonald's restaurants by the end of the 1980s.[29] McDonald's will expand this market to its fullest potential.

In addition to expanding the international stores, McDonald's is cultivating what it calls semicaptive markets—toll roads, military bases, museums, and hospitals—where there are lots of people and very few places to eat.[30] Exhibits 13.16 and 13.17 give a synopsis of some of these developments.

Diversification may also be in McDonald's future. The company realizes that hamburger sales will eventually become stable and decline. Also, McDonald's is predicted to have $1 billion in cash by the year 1990.[31] The company will be cash heavy (a cash cow), and may have to diversify to avoid a takeover.

**Exhibit 13.15** Consolidated Balance Sheet (in thousands of dollars)

| | December 31, 1983 | 1982 |
|---|---|---|
| **Assets** | | |
| Current assets | | |
| Cash and equivalents | $   66,479 | $   44,076 |
| Accounts receivable | 64,099 | 66,768 |
| Notes receivable | 24,863 | 21,234 |
| Inventories, at cost, which is not in excess of market | 26,632 | 23,502 |
| Prepaid expenses | 42,490 | 31,332 |
| Other current assets | 6,848 | 13,145 |
| Total current assets | 231,411 | 200,057 |
| Other assets and deferred charges | | |
| Notes receivable due after one year | 71,785 | 104,563 |
| Investments in and advances to affiliates | 49,133 | 36,456 |
| Miscellaneous | 47,714 | 46,561 |
| Total other assets and deferred charges | 168,632 | 187,580 |
| Property and equipment | | |
| Property and equipment, at cost | 4,005,186 | 3,456,534 |
| Less accumulated depreciation and amortization | 822,014 | 691,061 |
| Net property and equipment | 3,183,172 | 2,765,473 |
| Intangible assets, net | 144,092 | 109,701 |
| Total assets | $3,727,307 | $3,262,811 |
| **Liabilities and stockholders' equity** | | |
| Current liabilities | | |
| Notes payable | $   55,582 | $   44,334 |
| Accounts payable | 179,371 | 153,756 |
| Income taxes | 66,321 | 59,640 |
| Other taxes | 27,745 | 26,772 |
| Other accrued liabilities | 55,453 | 37,902 |
| Current maturities of long-term debt | 45,463 | 55,883 |
| Total current liabilities | 429,935 | 378,287 |
| Long-term debt | | |
| Long-term debt | 1,100,390 | 980,376 |
| Obligations under capital leases | 70,892 | 75,546 |
| Total long-term debt | 1,171,282 | 1,055,922 |
| Security deposits by franchisees | 72,865 | 67,739 |
| Deferred income taxes | 298,084 | 232,303 |
| Stockholders' equity | | |
| Common stock, no par value, authorized—200,000,000 shares at December 31, 1983 and 100,000,000 shares at December 31, 1982 | 6,818 | 6,802 |
| Additional paid-in capital | 120,794 | 109,416 |
| Retained earnings | 1,827,653 | 1,543,049 |
| Equity adjustment from foreign currency translation | (90,940) | (73,302) |
| | 1,864,325 | 1,585,965 |
| Less treasury stock, at cost | 109,184 | 57,405 |
| Total stockholders' equity | 1,755,141 | 1,528,560 |
| Total liabilities and stockholders' equity | $3,727,307 | $3,262,811 |

**Exhibit 13.16** McDonald's Semicaptive Expansions

---

*Toll roads*—McDonald's won a contract to put ten stores on the Connecticut Turnpike. Contract included a guarantee of $37 million in royalties.

*Military bases*—McDonald's won a bid to put up to 300 stores on naval bases around the world. Deal should net company up to $600 million. Restaurant also located at Camp Pendleton Marine base in California.

*McSnack*—A scaled-down McDonald's for shopping malls, serving McNuggets, fries, hamburgers, and drinks. Currently, locations in Minneapolis, Minnesota, and La Jolla, California.

*McStop*—McDonald's entry into the truck stop business. Two stores in planning and construction phase.

*Hospitals*—McDonald's recently opened store in hospital in Phoenix, Arizona. See Exhibit 13.17 for related article.

*Source: Fortune,* November 12, 1984, p. 36.

---

**Exhibit 13.17** Article from April 17, 1985, *USA Today*

---

**BIG MACS IN HOSPITALS: JUST WHAT DOC ORDERED**

McDonald's Corp. tells customers, "You deserve a break today." And who deserves a break more than hospital patients and their relatives?

So it might be no surprise that the fast-food chain's latest untraditional location is in the midst of the wards at St. Joseph's Hospital and Medical Center in Phoenix, Arizona.

Other unusual sites include military bases, college campuses, Miami International Airport, the Toronto Zoo, a Philadelphia train station and a riverboat in St. Louis.

McDonald's also has a restaurant at Children's Hospital in Philadelphia, but that one's on the ground floor and readily accessible to the public, restaurant spokesman Robert Keyser said.

The St. Joseph's McDonald's is a second-story affair with a balcony that caters primarily to hospital workers, patients and their relatives, said Bill Byron, spokesman for the 624-bed hospital. Patients embraced the ever-familiar purveyor of burgers and fries as a welcome alternative to the hospital cafeteria, Byron said.

"There's a familiarity and comfort going to someplace you know."

Reported by Wayne Beissert, Jon Friedman, John Hillkirk, Julie Morris, and John Reilly.

---

## NOTES

1. William Barry Furlong, "Ray Kroc: Burger Master," *The Saturday Evening Post,* March 1981.
2. Walter Sublette and Ted Rodewig, "McDonald's Corporation in the Year 2000," *Restaurant Hospitality,* May 1983, p. 52.
3. Monci Jo Williams, "McDonald's Corporation Refuses to Plateau," *Fortune,* November 12, 1984, p. 34.
4. Sublette and Rodewig, "McDonald's in the Year 2000," p. 52.
5. Ibid., p. 86.

6. Ibid.

7. Williams, "McDonald's Refuses to Plateau," p. 35.

8. Ibid., p. 40.

9. W. David Gibson, "Did McDonald's Deserve a Break? Wall Street to the Contrary, the Company Is Doing Just Great," *Barron's,* September 5, 1983, p. 7.

10. "Services," *Forbes,* January 14, 1985, p. 198.

11. Williams, "Mcdonald's Refuses to Plateau," p. 38.

12. McDonald's Corporation Annual Report 1983, p. 33.

13. Williams, "McDonald's Refuses to Plateau," p. 34.

14. Ibid., p. 40.

15. Ibid., p. 34.

16. Sublette and Rodewig, "McDonald's in the Year 2000," p. 58.

17. Williams, "McDonald's Refuses to Plateau," p. 38.

18. Gibson, "Did McDonald's Deserve a Break?" p. 7.

19. Williams, "McDonald's Refuses to Plateau," p. 35.

20. Sublette and Rodewig, "McDonald's in the Year 2000," p. 54.

21. McDonald's Corporation Information Package.

22. Sublette and Rodewig, "McDonald's in the Year 2000," p. 52.

23. Ibid., p. 54.

24. Ibid.

25. McDonald's Corporation Information Package.

26. McDonald's Corporation Annual Report 1983, p. 14.

27. "What to Do with a Billion Dollars," *Restaurant Hospitality,* May 1983, p. 70.

28. Williams, "McDonald's Refuses to Plateau," p. 36.

29. Ibid.

30. Ibid.

31. "The Fast-Food War: Big Mac Under Attack," *Business Week,* January 30, 1984, p. 46.

# 14 Burger King's Battle for the Burgers

Larry D. Alexander and Thomas W. Ripp
Virginia Polytechnic Institute and State University

**INTRODUC-TION**

In 1985, J. Jeffrey Campbell, Burger King Corporation's chief executive officer since 1983, was still trying to put together a winning formula. With four different CEOs since 1977, it was not surprising that Burger King had made a number of strategic changes in recent years. More changes were probably necessary as Burger King prepared itself for the rest of the 1980s and beyond. How should it position itself in the fast-food industry? What could it do to dethrone McDonald's, the number one firm in the industry? How could Burger King convince the public that its hamburgers were really superior to McDonald's? What could be done to hold off the challenge from Wendy's, Hardee's, and a number of other chains that were growing in size and competitive power? These and other questions came to mind as Burger King's Campbell tried to develop a winning strategy and bring stability to Burger King.

**HISTORY**

Burger King Corporation started when David R. Edgerton obtained the Miami area rights to a fast-food concept called Insta/Burger King. He opened the first restaurant in March 1954. Three months later, James W. McLamore joined the venture and the pair built three more Insta/Burger Kings. Hamburgers were sold for just 19 cents and french fries for 10 cents. Edgerton invented a chain broiler during 1956 which moved the hamburgers along a chain conveyor over the broiler until done. They changed their name to Burger King because they were no longer using the broilers sold to them but rather their own chain broilers.

In 1957, McLamore invented the Whopper and claimed it was the first fast-food jumbo hamburger. Although Burger King had expanded to only five restaurants by 1959, Edgerton and McLamore still envisioned someday becoming a chain of restaurants located throughout the United States. At that time, the fast-food industry was still very fragmented and no national or significant regional chains existed. In 1961, Burger King made its first move outside of Florida when it opened a franchise in McLamore's hometown of Wilmington, Delaware.

Burger King's initial franchise agreements were relatively inexpensive and contained few restrictions. The franchisee paid only $25,000 for an exclusive franchise to a specified region, where he or she had a Burger King monopoly. The

This case was written by Larry D. Alexander (assistant professor of strategic management) and Thomas W. Ripp (M.B.A. student in management science), Department of Management, College of Business, Virginia Polytechnic Institute and State University, Blacksburg, Virginia 24061.

Copyright © 1985 by Larry D. Alexander and Thomas W. Ripp.

franchisee could decide how many Burger King restaurants, if any, could be opened and where to locate them, and could even decide to sell off part of the region to other people. Such an unencumbered franchise agreement attracted many franchisees, particularly because they paid only a modest 1 percent of sales to Burger King.

The year 1967 was a historic one for Burger King, which had already grown to 274 restaurants. That was when McLamore and Edgerton sold their chain to Pillsbury for $18 million. The two founders sold out to Pillsbury to obtain the financial resources Burger King needed to expand further and to increase its market share. McLamore agreed to continue on as Burger King's CEO.

Pillsbury bought Burger King primarily because of the high growth potential for the fast-food industry. As Paul S. Gerot, then president of Pillsbury, noted: "We view Burger King as an opportunity to participate in the rising trend toward more away from home meals. Burger King has demonstrated the ability of a franchise operation to grow in the most rapidly expanding segment of the food business, where quality, convenience, and economy are important."[1]

In 1970, Burger King had over 700 franchised and company-owned restaurants. In addition, it was opening new restaurants at the rate of ten per month. To handle this rapid expansion, it restructured its marketing organization. A new position of director of advertising and merchandising was created. Three advertising and merchandising coordinators, which reported to this position, handled advertising and sales promotional activities for seven newly established districts, each headed up by a district manager. Finally, a new position of advertising and merchandising planner was created which handled new products.

One of Burger King's franchisees, Chart House Inc., had been increasing its size and power over the years. Unlike many other franchisees, it owned the land and buildings itself for each restaurant. Chart House had grown so big under Burger King's franchise agreement that it began competing with Pillsbury for territorial expansion. For example, in 1970 Pillsbury wanted to buy out five franchisees who held 99-year rights to a territory that included Chicago. Chart House, however, beat them to it and by 1971 owned 100 Burger King restaurants. Later, in 1972, Chart House offered $100 million to purchase Burger King, but Pillsbury turned it down. Chart House still continued to acquire smaller franchises. When it bought 9 restaurants in Boston and 13 in Houston, Pillsbury sued both Chart House and the Boston franchisee for disregarding Pillsbury's right of first refusal. Later, Pillsbury and Chart House reached a compromise whereby Chart House gave up its Boston franchise in exchange for keeping its Houston restaurants.

Pillsbury subsequently took action to make Burger King restaurants more profitable. In 1974, it required all new restaurants to be equipped with multiple-order-taking lines and requested franchisees to shift to multiple lines in their existing restaurants. Chart House refused to change to multiple lines and claimed that the additional cash registers would cost more than the increased sales they would generate. Many smaller franchisees followed Chart House's lead by refusing to switch to multiple lines until sales increased enough to make the change profitable.

In 1977, Burger King began to remake its franchise system on the basis of McDonald's model. New franchisees had to agree not to own any other fast-food business and had to live within an hour's drive of all their Burger King restaurants. This greatly reduced the potential size and power of future franchisees. An exception to this rule was made for Chart House. It was allowed to continue to build as many restaurants as it liked in its Illinois territory, but it had to agree not to expand elsewhere without Pillsbury's approval.

## THE COMPANY'S CURRENT OPERATION

Burger King was an operating unit within Pillsbury's Restaurants Group. The other operating unit within this group was the S & A Restaurant Corporation, which was comprised of Steak and Ale, Bennigan's restaurants, and JJ. Muggs. Burger King had such a high priority, however, that it reported directly to William H. Spoor, Pillsbury's CEO, rather than to a group vice-president. Pillsbury had four other major groups, which included Agri-Products, Dry Grocery Products, Frozen and Refrigerated Products, and International.

## MARKETING AND SALES

Burger King's name itself appropriately reflected the wide variety of hamburgers that were included in its menu. Its various hamburgers included a hamburger, cheeseburger, double hamburger, double cheeseburger, bacon double cheese-burger, the Whopper, the Whopper with cheese, Whopper Jr., and Whopper Jr. with cheese. Amazingly, more than 600 million Whoppers were sold annually. Burger King's menu didn't stop there, as Exhibit 14.1 clearly shows. It also included various specialty sandwiches, soft drinks, french fries, and onion rings. A salad bar was even added in 1983, following Wendy's tremendous success with its earlier one.

In 1979, Burger King restaurants started opening early for breakfast. By 1983, the breakfast menu included eggs, bacon, omelets, and pancakes. Its Croissand-wich, which was added later that same year, was a crescent-shaped flaky roll with eggs, cheese, and bacon, sausage, or ham inside. Its morning topping station was also added that same year.

Burger King relied heavily on a number of advertising campaigns in recent years, as shown in Exhibit 14.2. One of its famous early campaigns was "Have It Your Way." The catchy words to the tune in this television advertisement stated, "Hold the pickles, hold the lettuce, special orders don't upset us. All we ask is that you let us serve it your way." A number of other advertising campaigns were used since then.

In early 1982, Burger King launched a new campaign with the slogan "Aren't You Hungry?" which again used a song to make its point. This theme was introduced because Burger King's CEO, Norman Brinker, wanted improved ads with more imagination. Brinker's new philosophy brought about Burger King's various "Battle of the Burgers" advertisements. In September 1982, Burger King launched an ad campaign that for the first time directly compared its hamburgers

**Exhibit 14.1** Burger King's Menu Items

**Breakfast Items Only**

Croissandwich (bacon, egg, and cheese; ham, egg, and cheese; or sausage, egg, and cheese)
French toast
Scrambled egg platter with bacon or sausage
Hash browns
Danish pastry (cinnamon, apple, or raspberry)
Orange juice

**Hamburgers for Lunch, Dinner, or Snack**

Hamburger
Cheeseburger
Double hamburger
Double cheeseburger
Bacon double cheeseburger
Bacon double cheeseburger deluxe
Whopper junior
Whopper junior with cheese
Whopper
Whopper with cheese

**Specialty Sandwiches and Salads**

Chicken
Whaler
Ham & cheese
Salad bar

**Side Orders**

French fries (small or large order)
Onion rings

**Beverage (served anytime, except for shakes)**

Soft drinks (Pepsi, Diet Pepsi, Mountain Dew, Dr. Pepper in small, medium, or large)
Shakes
Iced tea (small or large)
Coffee (small or large)
Milk

**Desserts**

Pies (apple, cherry, and pecan)

to McDonald's and Wendy's hamburgers. The attacking ads claimed that the Whopper won nationwide taste tests over McDonald's and Wendy's hamburgers. Burger King also claimed that its hamburgers were bigger and prepared better than its competitors' hamburgers.

Wendy's and McDonald's each filed suit against Burger King. When Burger King agreed to phase out its ads, Wendy's and McDonald's dropped their lawsuits. Still, the ads paid off for Burger King. Its fourth-quarter 1982 sales increased by 10.8 percent, up 3.8 percent from a 7 percent sales growth rate before the ad campaign started. This was the first time that Burger King had achieved

**Exhibit 14.2** Some of Burger King's Major Ad Campaigns

| Advertising Theme | Year(s) |
|---|---|
| "Have It Your Way" emphasized the fact that Burger King was willing to make special orders. | Late 1973 |
| "Magical Burger King" aimed advertising at the kids. A Ronald McDonald–type costumed man magically made french fries and other Burger King products appear before a group of children. | Late 1978 |
| "Aren't You Hungry?" moved Burger King away from its life-style themes to more aggressive advertising. | Early 1982 |
| "Battle of the Burgers" launched Burger King's first round of ads that compared itself directly to McDonald's and Wendy's. Later, Burger King agreed to stop ads and McDonald's dropped its lawsuit. | Late 1982 |
| "Battle of the Burgers" launched another round of comparative advertising which focused on flame broiling versus frying, and which only mentioned competitor McDonald's. | 1983 |
| "Aren't You Hungry?" theme was returned to as its major theme, but Burger King also continued to compare flame broiling to frying. | Early 1984 |
| "Battle of the Burgers" was used again to compare Burger King's hamburgers against both McDonald's and Wendy's. | Mid-1984 |
| "Battle of the Burgers" was taken overseas by Burger King to Europe to try to educate Europeans about the difference between flame broiling and frying. | Late 1984 |
| "Eight Simple Words That Can Change Your Life" showed hamburger eaters tasting their first flame-broiled hamburger and then stating, "I'll never eat another fried Quarter Pounder again." | Late 1984 |

a double-digit growth rate, which was almost twice McDonald's 5.8 percent increase during 1982.

The 1982 settlement between Burger King, McDonald's, and Wendy's, according to Pillsbury's Vice-Chairman Winston Wallin, did not prohibit Burger King from launching future comparative advertisements. Burger King later undertook another round of comparative ads in 1983. This time, Burger King focused on its flame-broiled hamburgers versus its competitors' fried hamburgers. The ads stated that Burger King had won another taste test that found hamburger eaters preferred flame-broiled to fried hamburgers. Consumer comments on flame broiling being better were also included in the ads to drive the point home. This time, the ads mentioned only Burger King's arch rival, McDonald's. Unlike the previous ones, these ads did not claim that Burger King served bigger hamburgers than its competitors.

Burger King tried to link all of its ads to its ongoing "Aren't You Hungry?" theme since then. During the summer of 1983, Burger King's ads concentrated on its new salad bar and emphasized that many of its drive-through order windows were open until 4 A.M. That summer's campaign seemed aimed at countering Wendy's restaurants, which all had salad bars and drive-through windows.

In the fall of 1983, Burger King's commercials reverted back to attacking McDonald's. A supposedly real-life family coincidentally named the MacDonalds talked about why they switched to Burger King. The entire family, plus their dog, masked their identities by wearing false glasses, noses, and moustaches. Burger King hoped this ad campaign would match the success of its earlier "Battle of the Burgers" theme.

Burger King took its "Battle of the Burgers" to Europe in the fall of 1984. The campaign first began in West Germany, where Burger King had 22 restaurants compared to McDonald's 200. The idea behind this campaign was to be as aggressive as possible without violating comparative advertising restrictions. West Germany's regulations said that ads (1) could not be dishonest or misleading, (2) could not degrade another product, and (3) must serve a consumer need. Burger King first used outdoor billboards and newspaper ads to make German customers aware of the difference between flame broiling and frying. Later, television and radio commercials were used which featured female models eating a Whopper with the captions "All like it hot" or "Love at first bite." Burger King conducted similar campaigns later in the ten other European countries where it operated.

In late 1984, Burger King launched another domestic advertising campaign that attacked fried hamburgers. Burger King's new ad said that it would like to introduce "eight simple words that can change your life." In the ad, hamburger eaters tasted a flame-broiled Burger King hamburger for the first time and then uttered the eight key words, "I'll never eat another fried Quarter Pounder again."

Burger King used television as its chief advertising medium. It spent nearly $40 million on its spring 1984 television ad campaign alone. This used up about 40 percent of its annual ad budget. Unfortunately, McDonald's outspent Burger King by about three to one on network advertising and had an annual budget of nearly $400 million. Because Burger King's advertising budget was much smaller, it felt that its television ads needed to be deliberately combative.

Burger King had opened restaurants in poor locations in recent years. As a result, Burger King's top management stated it would start concentrating on increasing its penetration in important metropolitan areas where it was already located. For example, in early 1984, Burger King bought 11 Arby's in Kansas City and St. Louis and indicated it planned to add more restaurants there as well as in other growth areas.

Burger King had also established a long-term objective of placing restaurants in new and unique locations. One such nontraditional location was military bases, which Burger King first entered when it won a bid to open a franchise at the Pearl Harbor naval base in 1982. That new Burger King restaurant was built by the navy and leased to the franchisee, who also ran 11 other Burger Kings on the Hawaiian islands. Burger King later opened restaurants at a navy base in Norfolk, Virginia, and a Coast Guard station at Governor's Island, New York. In May 1984, Burger King announced it had beat out Mcdonald's in competitive bidding to open fast-food restaurants at selected U.S. Army and Air Force bases in the United

States, Germany, Korea, and selected Pacific islands. Under the terms of the agreement, Burger King could open as many as 185 military restaurants by 1989. All of the restaurants on U.S. military bases would be operated by the Army and Air Force Exchange Service. Still, Burger King expected to earn more than $13 million a year from the 6 percent royalties collected from the restaurants.

Later, in 1984, Burger King linked itself with Woolworth's, a large national retailer. Under the agreement, Burger King would convert at least 50 in-store food service units into Burger King restaurants over the next five years. Woolworth's would operate the restaurants itself, but employees would be trained by Burger King. Some of the restaurants would serve a mix of Woolworth's old menu items and Burger King's fast-food items. The Burger King in-store restaurants could be entered from inside the Woolworth's stores and also by a separate street entrance. This would let the restaurants open earlier and close later than Woolworth's retail stores.

In 1983, Burger King switched from Coke to Pepsi soft drinks in its U.S. restaurants. Pepsi had been trying to get Burger King to serve its other soft drinks ever since Burger King added Diet Pepsi in 1979 and Mountain Dew in 1980 to its otherwise Coca-Cola soft drink line. Burger King's switch to Pepsi made it Pepsi's number one fast-food account. This change was made in hopes that it would result in better service than being Coca-Cola's number two fast-food account, behind McDonald's. Management felt that by bringing together its "Battle of the Burgers" ads with Pepsi's similar "Pepsi Challenge," they might help convince consumers to switch to their products. Burger King's top management also hoped that being Pepsi's number one account might give it first crack at any licensing rights for Pepsi products in the future. Despite Burger King's switch to Pepsi in the United States, it stayed with Coca-Cola products overseas because of their better customer recognition and more efficient foreign distribution.

Two Burger King franchises began experimenting with local delivery. In early 1984, a Burger King franchisee named Consumer Food Service announced that it would offer free delivery to the immediate area. Since all of its restaurants were located in downtown Manhattan, the cost of free delivery was minimized. Uniformed employees made the deliveries using hot-box equipment to keep the orders warm. Later that year, another Burger King franchisee in Columbus, Ohio, started offering local delivery. A five-dollar minimum order was required for this service, but only a five-cent delivery fee was added on. Deliveries were to any home, business, or other location within a three-mile radius of the restaurant. Top management at Burger King was closely watching both of these delivery attempts to evaluate their potential use at other Burger King restaurants.

**OPERATIONS**   Burger King operated 3827 fast-food restaurants in all 50 states and 25 foreign countries by 1984. Only 301 of its restaurants, however, were located in foreign countries. Some 109 restaurants were in Canada, 49 in Puerto Rico, 37 in Australia, 22 in West Germany, 18 in Spain, 9 in England, 8 in Venezuela, and fewer restaurants in all the other foreign countries. Burger King opened 356 new restaurants in fiscal year 1984, and a similar number were scheduled to open the next year. Approximately 86 percent of all its restaurants worldwide were owned by independent franchise holders. These franchise holders still were required to follow Burger King's policies and procedures in running their restaurants.

The typical Burger King restaurant had a seating capacity for 86 customers and parking for 40 cars. A floor plan of one typical Burger King restaurant is shown in Exhibit 14.3. In recent years, Burger King has also opened smaller restaurants with a 60 seating capacity and larger ones with a 100 seating capacity.

All Burger King restaurants featured eat-in as well as carry-out service. In addition, 95 percent of its freestanding restaurants had a drive-through service for customers who did not want to leave their cars. Some Burger King restaurants had even added an outdoor playground similar to those McDonald's had placed outside some of its restaurants.

Burger King painstakingly analyzed what effect new product introductions would have on operations in its restaurants. For example, it studied various data

**Exhibit 14.3** Typical Floor Plan of a Burger King Restaurant

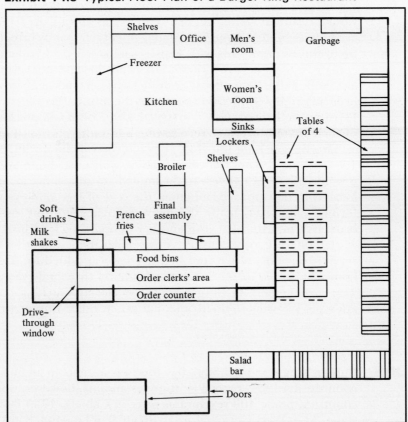

for more than two years before deciding to switch from Coke to Pepsi. Burger King even sent employees on undercover missions to Jack-in-the-Box restaurants to clock how much time was wasted on informing customers who asked for Coke that the chain only served Pepsi. Burger King even used a computer to predict how much labor a new product would require, what effect it would have on sales for other items, and how much total profits it would generate. Finally, Burger King considered the logistics of national distribution, supplier availability, and price stability for the new ingredients.

Burger King made a number of other changes to handle more customers in less time. It installed computerized french fry machines which sounded a warning when done. Television terminals linked to the cash register were placed in the kitchen. This let the cooks read incoming orders on a screen, rather than relying on verbal orders that were sometimes misunderstood. Burger King also installed soft drink dispensers that only required the push of a button to dispense the desired amount of drink. All of these improvements were first simulated on a computer, then tested at Burger King's research and development restaurants in the Miami area.

Top management encouraged individual restaurant managers to make productivity suggestions. If their suggestions proved useful, they were given a cash reward. Management used this approach to tap the ideas of the restaurant managers who were right on the firing line.

Burger King franchisee John Diab developed the Whopper Express to meet the challenge of doing business in high-cost urban areas. Consumer Food Service, which Diab was a partner in, opened five Whopper Expresses in Manhattan in early 1984 and had two under construction in Philadelphia. The Whopper Express served a scaled-down menu in a smaller restaurant. For example, only one size of drink and fries was served. Although breakfast was still served at these restaurants, all specialty sandwiches and the small hamburger were eliminated. Consumer Food Service planned to open up to ten Whopper Expresses per year through 1989.

The Whopper Express restaurant generated about twice the hourly sales of the larger traditional Burger King restaurants. Some 900 customers per hour were served, which generated sales of up to $3000 per hour. The Whopper Express had two complete service areas, each with its own broiler. The average Whopper Express was only 1300 square feet. Its kitchen took up only 200 square feet of that space, versus 500 square feet for a traditional Burger King kitchen. Burger King was able to reduce the kitchen size by eliminating unnecessary equipment and scaling down most of the remaining equipment. Although a Whopper Express restaurant employed the same number of people, most of them worked just during the lunch hours. Whopper Expresses did not have tables and chairs for customers; instead, they had eating bars where the customers stood. As a result, most customers were there for take out food.

Burger King also had increased the efficiency of site development for its restaurants. Burger King's computers contained a software program to make site selections which included key decision-making criteria. This cut down the average site approval time from two weeks to one day. Burger King also added a construction specialist in each of its ten regional offices. These specialists knew the various building codes in their regions and were able to cut the average time spent on the design of each restaurant from six to two weeks. Regional staff people were also taught how to negotiate real estate deals to save both time and money.

When Jeffrey Campbell took over as Burger King's CEO in 1983, he launched "Operation Shapeup." It was initiated to improve the efficiency of its restaurant employees up through all levels of management. A crash training program for restaurant managers and their employees was started to address the issue of uneven franchise performance. Campbell also started tackling the tough task of reining in the franchisees and convincing them that they had to follow policy and procedures developed by corporate headquarters.

Campbell tried to emphasize better communications throughout Burger King. He met with corporate employees in Miami. He held meetings with the regional staffs and then gave them 30 days to come up with three-year plans for their regions. He also relocated some corporate staff out into the field to be closer to the divisions and districts they served. He moved two regional managers out of Miami and placed more authority with the division managers.

Campbell also tried to get more media coverage for Burger King. He was personally interviewed by the *Washington Post, Chicago Tribune,* and *Business Week.* One reason for this effort to get more public attention was to boost the morale of Burger King employees and franchise holders.

Burger King had established DISTRON to serve its domestic restaurants. This independently operated supply and distribution division handled food, paper products, and other supplies utilized by its restaurants. DISTRON's operations in the United States were run through three decentralized divisions, overseeing 11 regions.

**FINANCE**     Burger King had gross sales of $3.43 billion for fiscal year 1984, which ended May 31, 1984. That amounted to over one and a half billion hamburgers for the year. Sales averaged $944,000 per restaurant, which was a 13 percent increase over the previous year. Company-operated restaurants had significantly higher yearly sales at $1.04 million, whereas domestic franchises averaged $928,000. Burger King's goal for 1985 was to get the average domestic restaurant's sales near $1 million, with a 17.4 percent operating profit per restaurant.

Pillsbury's consolidated statement of earnings for fiscal years 1982–1984 is shown in Exhibit 14.4. The consolidated sales for Pillsbury for 1984 amounted to $4,172,300,000. Net earnings after taxes were $169,800,000, a substantial increase over the previous two years. The consolidated balance sheets for Pillsbury for fiscal years 1983 and 1984 are shown in Exhibit 14.5. It must be emphasized that Pillsbury does not give detailed financial reports for individual strategic business units such as Burger King. However, Pillsbury does provide a financial summary by industry segment, as shown in Exhibit 14.6.

**Exhibit 14.4** Consolidated Statements of Earnings

| | Year Ended May 31[a] | | |
|---|---|---|---|
| | **1984** | **1983** | **1982** |
| Net sales | $4,172.3 | $3,685.9 | $3,385.1 |
| Costs and expenses | | | |
|   Cost of sales | 2,952.5 | 2,589.5 | 2,389.7 |
|   Selling, general, and administrative expenses | 871.9 | 826.8 | 728.1 |
|   Interest expense, net | 44.2 | 39.4 | 39.3 |
| | 3,868.6 | 3,455.7 | 3,157.1 |
| Earnings before taxes on income | 303.7 | 230.2 | 228.0 |
| Taxes on income | 133.9 | 91.3 | 91.7 |
| Net earnings | $169.8 | $ 138.9 | $ 136.3 |
| Average number of shares outstanding | 43.5 | 43.5 | 43.3 |
| Net earnings per share | $3.91 | $ 3.20 | $ 3.14 |

[a]Dollars in millions except per share amounts.

*Source:* Pillsbury Annual Report 1984, p. 35.

**INNOVATION** Burger King had introduced a number of innovations to the fast-food industry. An early innovation by Burger King was the continuous chain broiler. This breakthrough was accomplished in 1956 by David Edgerton, one of Burger King's two founders. It enabled Burger King to efficiently and evenly broil its burgers and gave fast-food customers an alternative to the typical fried hamburger.

Burger King also introduced several firsts in its restaurants' format. It was the first fast-food chain to offer inside sit-down eating for what had previously been all take-out food. The company also pioneered the addition of drive-through window service for customers not wanting to leave their cars.

Burger King had also made various menu innovations. In 1982, it introduced the bacon double cheeseburger, which was the first new hamburger from a major chain in ten years. Later, it introduced the bacon double cheeseburger deluxe, whose toppings included bacon, lettuce, tomato, and mayonnaise. In the fall of 1983, Burger King introduced a morning topping station in test markets in Miami, Florida, Hartford, Connecticut, and Savannah, Georgia. Cheese, tomatoes, and salsa were available for customers to add to their omelets. Similarly, hot apple fruit topping, whipped cream, and various syrups could be added to customers' pancakes. Orange juice, sliced fruit, individual boxes of cereal, and freshly ground coffee were also available at its morning topping station and breakfast bar. Also in the fall of 1983, Burger King tested its new Croissandwich, which was later made available at all of its restaurants that served breakfast.

**Exhibit 14.5** Consolidated Balance Sheets

| | May 31[a] | |
| --- | --- | --- |
| | 1984 | 1983 |
| **Assets** | | |
| Current assets | | |
| Cash and equivalents | $142.5 | $ 129.6 |
| Receivables, less allowance for doubtful accounts of $11.5 million and $12.9 million, respectively | 355.8 | 350.6 |
| Inventories | | |
| Grain | 75.5 | 52.9 |
| Finished products | 214.1 | 204.1 |
| Raw materials, containers and supplies | 150.6 | 133.7 |
| | 440.2 | 390.7 |
| Advances on purchases | 107.7 | 128.4 |
| Prepaid expenses | 25.6 | 22.3 |
| Total current assets | 1,071.8 | 1,021.6 |
| Property, plant and equipment | | |
| Land and improvements | 199.2 | 179.3 |
| Buildings and improvements | 885.1 | 788.2 |
| Machinery and equipment | 692.5 | 600.3 |
| | 1,776.8 | 1,567.8 |
| Less accumulated depreciation | 583.8 | 514.6 |
| | 1,193.0 | 1,053.2 |
| Net investment in direct financing leases | 184.0 | 178.7 |
| Intangibles | 83.2 | 21.6 |
| Investments and other assets | 76.3 | 91.5 |
| | $2,608.3 | $2,366.6 |
| **Liabilities and stockholders' equity** | | |
| Current liabilities | | |
| Notes payable | $17.3 | $ 10.5 |
| Current portion of long-term debt | 94.3 | 32.8 |
| Trade accounts payable | 369.2 | 279.6 |
| Advances on sales | 136.0 | 136.7 |
| Employee compensation | 83.8 | 72.4 |
| Taxes on income | 16.5 | 20.8 |
| Other liabilities | 169.3 | 152.1 |
| Total current liabilities | 886.4 | 704.9 |
| Long-term debt, noncurrent portion | 503.1 | 572.4 |
| Deferred taxes on income | 149.3 | 108.5 |
| Other deferrals | 23.3 | 24.4 |
| Stockholders' equity | | |
| Preferred stock, without par value, authorized 500,000 shares, no shares issued | | |
| Common stock, without par value, authorized 80,000,000 shares, issued 43,516,019 shares and 43,462,156 shares, respectively | 306.2 | 284.1 |
| Common stock in treasury at cost, 322,785 shares and 180,318 shares, respectively | (11.7) | (4.6) |
| Accumulated earnings retained and used in the business | 792.4 | 704.9 |
| Accumulated foreign currency translation | (40.7) | (28.0) |
| Total stockholders' equity | 1,046.2 | 956.4 |
| | $2,608.3 | $2,366.6 |

[a]In millions.

*Source:* Pillsbury Annual Report 1984, pp. 36–37.

**Exhibit 14.6** Financial Summary by Industry Segment

Pillsbury is a diversified international food company operating in three major segments of the food industry.

Net sales by segment include both sales to unaffiliated customers, as reported in the consolidated statements of earnings, and intersegment sales made on the same basis as sales to unaffiliated customers.

Operating profit of reportable segments is net sales less operating expenses. In computing operating profit, none of the following items has been included: interest income and expense; general corporate income and expenses; equity in net earnings (losses) of unconsolidated affiliates; and income taxes.

|  | Year Ended May 31[a] | | |
|---|---|---|---|
|  | **1984** | **1983** | **1982** |
| Net sales |  |  |  |
| Consumer Foods | $1,793.9 | $1,652.1 | $1,635.7 |
| Restaurants | 1,768.7 | 1,494.6 | 1,279.3 |
| Agri-Products | 694.8 | 627.5 | 568.6 |
| Less Agri-Products intersegment sales | (85.1) | (88.3) | (98.5) |
| Total | 4,172.3 | 3,685.9 | 3,385.1 |
| Operating profit |  |  |  |
| Consumer Foods | 146.8 | 139.4 | 134.8 |
| Restaurants | 187.4 | 135.3 | 116.3 |
| Agri-Products | 34.5 | 16.4 | 28.6 |
| Total | 368.7 | 291.1 | 279.7 |
| General corporate expense, net | (20.8) | (21.5) | (12.4) |
| Interest expense, net | (44.2) | (39.4) | (39.3) |
| Earnings before taxes on income | 303.7 | 230.2 | 228.0 |
| Identifiable assets |  |  |  |
| Consumer Foods | 836.3 | 725.4 | 747.9 |
| Restaurants | 1,191.2 | 1,025.7 | 993.3 |
| Agri-Products | 498.2 | 486.1 | 536.6 |
| Corporate | 82.6 | 129.4 | 150.5 |
| Total | 2,608.3 | 2,366.6 | 2,428.3 |
| Capital expenditures |  |  |  |
| Consumer Foods | 59.4 | 48.7 | 50.0 |
| Restaurants | 197.4 | 164.0 | 126.8 |
| Agri-Products | 13.8 | 20.9 | 15.8 |
| Corporate | 11.8 | 10.3 | 15.9 |
| Total | 282.4 | 243.9 | 208.5 |
| Depreciation expense |  |  |  |
| Consumer Foods | 36.1 | 33.0 | 30.3 |
| Restaurants | 59.5 | 54.7 | 48.6 |
| Agri-Products | 14.2 | 13.6 | 11.5 |
| Corporate | 4.8 | 4.2 | 2.4 |
| Total | 114.6 | 105.5 | 92.8 |
| Foreign operations included in the above categories are as follows: |  |  |  |
| Net sales | 355.5 | 360.1 | 357.9 |
| Operating profit | 16.2 | 18.0 | 22.8 |
| Identifiable assets | 241.8 | 212.8 | 241.8 |
| Capital expenditures | 20.4 | 16.3 | 22.6 |
| Depreciation expense | 9.7 | 10.3 | 8.8 |

[a] In millions.

*Source:* Pillsbury Annual Report 1984, p. 32.

Several of Burger King's new products were made in response to innovations by competitors. For example, in the spring of 1983, Burger King began to test a new one-third pound hamburger. This was done to compete more effectively against the growing number of gourmet hamburger chains that specialized in large hamburgers with fancy toppings. Burger King's new hamburger, however, soon had to be put on hold because of equipment problems that caused uneven broiling during the tests. Also in 1983, Burger King introduced a salad bar in response to Wendy's salad bar, which had done very well.

New menu innovations at Burger King were the result of its extensive ongoing research and development program at Burger King's Miami headquarters. For example, Burger King was testing new toppings in 1984 for its hamburgers in Milwaukee, Detroit, Pittsburgh, and Houston that were first developed at its research and development center. The toppings offered for its double hamburger included pizza sauce with mozzarella cheese, taco sauce with jalapeños and cheese, and a mushroom and Swiss cheese topping. Other new breakfast, lunch, dinner and dessert items were being tested. If successful, they would become a part of each restaurant's menu offerings in the future.

## HUMAN RESOURCES

Burger King employed approximately 38,500 people worldwide. An additional 161,000 people were employed in franchised restaurants; however, they were not considered Burger King employees. Burger King's corporate headquarters staff in Miami, made up of 550 people, ran a variety of functional areas such as finance, marketing, operations, and personnel.

Burger King conducted many training programs on an ongoing basis. It operated Burger King University, a $2 million training center near its Miami corporate headquarters. In addition, it ran ten regional training centers, known as Whopper Colleges, throughout the United States. These 11 facilities provided initial training and ongoing educational classes for Burger King restaurant franchisees and managers.

Burger King, along with other fast-food restaurants, had been having problems with its work force. Burger King's average restaurant had a staff of 35 workers. Unfortunately, the average Burger King employee lasted only a couple of months, resulting in a very high employee turnover ratio. In addition, the declining number of youths in the United States made it difficult to attract and retain employees willing to work at or near minimum wage. Furthermore, it was estimated that the 37 million young workers in 1980 would dwindle to only 24 million by 1990. Burger King had already taken efforts to retain its employees by paying them up to $4.50 an hour, $1.15 above the minimum wage in 1984.

Burger King also took actions to increase the productivity of its employees and their equipment. This was particularly important during peak meal times. Every movement of the employees was studied and changes made to eliminate needless motion. For example, productivity experts found that it took Burger King order takers 11 seconds just to answer customers whose cars had tripped the bell hose at the drive-through window. When they relocated the bell hose back 10 feet, the order taker was ready to serve the customer by the time the customer's car had stopped. This and other small changes allowed the drive-through window to handle an extra 30 cars per hour.

Burger King's franchisees had also tried various programs to improve worker productivity and service. In 1982, Greyhound Food Management, a franchisee of Burger King, sponsored a promotion called "Beat the Clock." The employees of its Burger King restaurants competed in a service time race. Cash prizes of $1,500, $1,000, and $500 were to be awarded to the top three Burger King restaurants. Any customer who was not served in three minutes or less was entitled to a free meal on his or her next visit to the same restaurant. The rules of the competition were changed when only 26 out of 62,151 customers were awarded a free meal because they waited more than three minutes. The next competition cut the serving time to two and a half minutes, to two minutes the following week, and to one and a half minutes the week after that. Even then, 10 of the 28 restaurants still had not awarded any free meals. According to Greyhound Food Management, the employees and their customers were enthusiastic about this promotion.

Another franchisee, Dennis C. Erwin, had been promoting "The Pride of Burger King" in his seven restaurants since 1979. At the start of each day, he had the employees sign stickers for their individual stations. As orders were prepared during the day, an employee would attach a sticker to the food item that he prepared. One typical sticker read as follows:

> The Pride of Burger King. Hello from the drink person. I check everything daily before we serve you. It's my job to serve you a quality drink. Thank you.[2]

The goal of Erwin's program was to restore employees' pride in their work and to let Burger King's customers know of that pride. The customers reacted favorably to the program, and employee mistakes were reduced by more than 90 percent.

Burger King hired an outsider to fill a newly created position of vice-president of human resources in 1984. This was done because Burger King had not done much to make its key managers and hourly employees remain at Burger King. Career ladders were developed for senior managers, who were also given pay incentives and chances for personal development that would, it was hoped, make them want to stay.

## MANAGE-MENT

The company was organized on a geographic basis. A handful of restaurants reported to a district manager who visited each restaurant at least once a month. District managers in turn reported to an area manager, who reported to a regional manager. Regional managers reported to a division manager in Miami, New York, or Denver. Finally, these three division managers reported directly to the chief executive officer of Burger King.

Burger King's big advances against McDonald's started after Donald N. Smith became Burger King's chief executive officer in 1977. To combat its number one foe, Pillsbury Chairman Spoor had hired away Smith, the number three man at McDonald's, to McDonaldize Burger King right down to the french fries. Despite his being only 36 years old at the time, many of Smith's actions were just what Burger King needed.

One of Smith's first actions was to decentralize the management structure. He established four major operating units. They were (1) Burger King U.S.A., (2) Burger King Canada, (3) Burger King International, and (4) Distribution. Smith also quickly broadened Burger King's menu to include more than just hamburgers. Unfortunately, he left Burger King in mid-1980 to head up Pizza Hut.

Pillsbury then had Louis P. Neeb head up Burger King. Neeb, age 43, had been head of another Pillsbury unit, Steak & Ale. He introduced breakfast at Burger King restaurants and opened approximately 500 new restaurants. Unfortunately, he also left in mid-1982.

Pillsbury again went inside to find Burger King's next CEO, Norman E. Brinker. Brinker, age 50, was moved from the presidency of Pillsbury's Restaurant Group. Within his first two weeks as CEO, Brinker made several top-management changes. After the management changes, Brinker's strategy was to go back to the basics. He remarked, "We're going back to emphasizing the hamburger, back to being the home of the Whopper."[3] Brinker was openly critical of his predecessor Neeb and felt he had not been aggressive enough for the fast-food industry. Unfortunately, in June of the next year, Brinker announced that he was leaving Burger King to become chairman of Chili's Inc., a gourmet burger firm.

J. Jeffrey Campbell, age 39, was appointed the new chairman and CEO of Burger King in June 1983. Campbell had worked his way up through the management ranks of Burger King. When Brinker was still CEO, he had promoted Campbell to president of Burger King U.S.A. As CEO, Campbell's early strategy was to focus on hamburgers and emphasize quality control. For his longer-term strategy, Campbell said, "We're not out to simply make plans or have a good year. We're out to change the competitive environment of the fast-food industry and that's a three to five year job."[4] To achieve this objective, Campbell launched an effort to improve operations, media coverage, market development, and management.

Campbell also wanted to restore the confidence that employees had in top management. Burger King had been plagued by top-management turnover since 1977. Surprisingly, Campbell was the first CEO promoted from within Burger King. By early 1984, eight of the top ten executives had been with Burger King for at least five years. Campbell hoped that he could provide stability among the senior management ranks, which would help calm the franchisees down.

## THE FAST-FOOD INDUSTRY

The fast-food industry was actually a segment of the food service industry. Sales for just the hamburger part of this segment were growing so rapidly that its $24.6 billion total sales in 1979 were expected to rise to $42 billion in 1985. This phenomenal increase was facilitated by an annual 10 percent growth in the amount that Americans spent on meals away from home.

The fast-food industry was composed of many national and regional chains located throughout the United States. In addition to these chains, numerous independent fast-food type restaurants could be found many places. Exhibit 14.7 shows a list of the top 30 franchise restaurants systems in the United States, ranked according to total sales. Exhibit 14.8 shows the market share and sales of

**Exhibit 14.7** Sales of the Top 30 Franchise Restaurant Systems

| Franchise System | 1983 Sales | Percentage Increase Over 1982 |
|---|---|---|
| 1. McDonald's | $8,600,000,000 | 10 |
| 2. Burger King[a] | 2,810,000,000 | 19 |
| 3. Kentucky Fried Chicken | 2,623,000,000 | 10 |
| 4. Wendy's | 1,800,000,000 | 10 |
| 5. Hardee's[a] | 1,718,000,000 | 54 |
| 6. Pizza Hut | 1,671,000,000 | 19 |
| 7. Dairy Queen[a] | 1,288,000,000 | 8 |
| 8. Big Boy | 1,000,000,000 | 6 |
| 9. Taco Bell | 693,000,000 | 20 |
| 10. Arby's | 650,000,000 | 12 |
| 11. Church's[a] | 613,900,000 | 22 |
| 12. Long John Silver's[a] | 554,500,000 | 7 |
| 13. Ponderosa[a] | 554,000,000 | 7 |
| 14. Jack-in-the-Box[a] | 546,700,000 | 13 |
| 15. Dunkin' Donuts[a] | 475,800,000 | 9 |
| 16. Western Sizzlin'[a] | 473,800,000 | 5 |
| 17. Baskin Robbins[a] | 455,000,000 | 8 |
| 18. Howard Johnson's | 435,100,000 | (4)[b] |
| 19. Godfather's Pizza | 400,000,000 | 28 |
| 20. Bonanza[a] | 389,000,000 | 6 |
| 21. Domino's Pizza | 365,700,000 | 58 |
| 22. Sizzler[a] | 353,700,000 | 9 |
| 23. Roy Rogers | 341,700,000 | 33 |
| 24. Perkin's Cake & Steak | 287,900,000 | 6 |
| 25. Sonic Drive Ins[a] | 262,600,000 | 4 |
| 26. Popeyes Famous Fried Chicken[a] | 240,000,000 | 39 |
| 27. Pizza Inn[a] | 236,600,000 | 3 |
| 28. International House of Pancakes | 226,000,000 | 8 |
| 29. Captain D's[a] | 215,700,000 | 10 |
| 30. Chi-Chi's[a] | 198,500,000 | 72 |

[a]Indicates figures are for the firm's 1983 fiscal year. All other figures are for calendar year 1983.

[b]( ) indicates a loss in percentage for the year.

*Source:* "Restaurant Franchising in the Economy," *Restaurant Business,* March 20, 1984, p. 170.

**Exhibit 14.8** Market Share by Sales (dollars in millions) and Percent for the Top 30 Fast-Food Chains

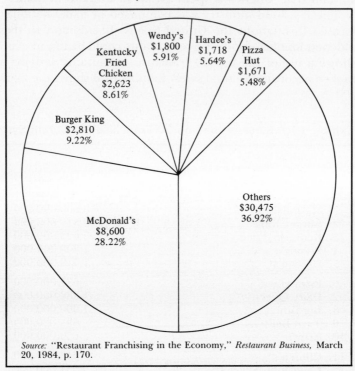

*Source:* "Restaurant Franchising in the Economy," *Restaurant Business,* March 20, 1984, p. 170.

the top six fast-food chains. Each firm's market share is calculated as a percent of the total sales for the 30 leading restaurant chains, rather than as a percent of total industry sales.

**Competitor Profiles**

**McDonald's** McDonald's was clearly number one in the fast-food industry. It was started in 1949 by Maurice and Richard McDonald in San Bernardino, California, selling 15-cent hamburgers. It had net sales of $8 billion for 1983. McDonald's 1983 sales from only its company-owned restaurants plus licensing fees from the franchised restaurants were $3,062,922,000. McDonald's had a staggering 7778 restaurants, of which 68 percent were franchised rather than owned by itself. Some 6251 of its restaurants were located in the United States, 442 were located in Canada, and the remaining 1085 were located in 30 other countries.

McDonald's product offerings focused on hamburgers. They included a simple hamburger, cheeseburger, double cheeseburger, Big Mac, and Quarter Pounder. These main-dish items were complemented with french fries, soft drinks, milk shakes, ice cream cones, sundaes, and Danish pastries.

McDonald's had a history of introducing new products over the years. Filet-O-Fish sandwiches were added in 1962. Later, Egg McMuffin was introduced when its restaurants started opening early for breakfast in 1973. McDonald cookies were added the next year. More recently, Chicken McNuggets were offered in 1982.

The four P's of marketing—product, price, promotion, and place—were clearly emphasized at McDonald's. Its product was a standardized, reasonably priced array of hamburgers, drinks, french fries, etc. Service was so fast that its customers only had to wait a minute or two to place and pick up their orders. Its prices had always been kept low in order to stimulate customer demand. Although the Quarter Pounder and Big Mac were priced over a dollar in late 1984, its plain hamburgers cost only about half as much. McDonald's promotion of its product was one of its greatest strengths. It spent nearly $400 million on advertising in 1983 alone, relying heavily on national television using its Ronald McDonald costume character. McDonald's spent heavily on major television events. For example, it spent about $35 million for ads during two weeks of the 1984 Summer Olympics in Los Angeles alone. Finally, its restaurants were seemingly located everywhere. With thousands of restaurants located in all 50 states and numerous foreign countries, and 500 new restaurants being opened each year, this generalization seemed fairly justified.

Its overall marketing strengths helped McDonald's achieve a 28.2 percent market share of the total sales for the top 30 food franchise systems, whereas second-place Burger King had only a 9.2 percent market share.[5] Not surprisingly, the four P's at McDonald's created a large fifth P called profit. Its profits after taxes for 1983 were a whopping $342,640,000, for an 11.1 percent return on sales ratio.

In recent years, McDonald's had been trying to expand into new and different market segments. In 1976, McDonald's opened its first restaurant in a high school cafeteria. In 1984, McDonald's experimented with restaurants in office buildings, and it also won a ten-year contract with the navy to open as many as 300 restaurants at navy bases throughout the world.

**Kentucky Fried Chicken**   Although Kentucky Fried Chicken (KFC) sold no hamburgers, it was still ranked third in the fast-food industry. A division of R. J. Reynolds Industries, KFC had total sales of $2,623,000,000 in 1983, which was a 10 percent increase over the previous year. There were 4471 domestic KFC restaurants, of which 998 were company-owned. Internationally, KFC had already placed approximately 1500 restaurants in 47 foreign countries. Its largest overseas market was Japan, which had 413 KFC restaurants.

KFC's principal products were fried chicken, prepared in accordance with methods first developed by Colonel Harland Sanders. Customers could choose from regular or extra crispy chicken, which could be bought in 2-, 3-, or 5-piece dinners and 9-, 15-, or 21-piece bucket sizes. Although most KFC restaurants had some tables for customers to eat their meals, most customers took their chicken dinners home.

**Wendy's**   Wendy's, which ranked fourth among fast-food restaurants, tried to appeal to a more discriminating customer. Its more expensive hamburgers, salad bar, chili, and stuffed baked potatoes were aimed at "Wendy's kind of people."

Its customers had to pay more, but Wendy's felt its higher-quality products clearly justified somewhat higher prices.

Although considerably smaller than McDonald's, Wendy's had a net income after taxes of $55,220,000 on total sales of $1.8 billion for 1983. Its average restaurant volume was $754,000 per year; however, Wendy's hoped that it would top $1 million by 1985. At a cost of approximately $75,000 per restaurant, Wendy's was installing glass-enclosed extensions to several hundred restaurants each year. In many respects, this made efficient use of earlier outdoor patios that were not used by very many customers.

In mid-1984, Wendy's launched its famous "Where's the Beef?" commercials. These various commercials featured Clara, who could never find the beef in competitors' skimpy hamburgers. These humorous commercials were so popular that 1984 Democratic candidate Walter Mondale even asked "Where's the beef?" of his opponent President Reagan's campaign promises. Wendy's future commercials will undoubtedly emphasize new upscale menu items it was continuing to develop.

**Pizza Hut**   In sixth place was Pizza Hut, a division of PepsiCo Inc. As its name suggests, its menu focused heavily on pizza, but it also had a salad bar. Like Kentucky Fried Chicken, however, Pizza Hut did not sell any hamburgers. It had some 1900 company-owned restaurants and 2090 franchises in 1983. For 1983, the total revenues for the overall parent corporation were $7,093,587,000, with a net income of $284,111,000. Pizza Hut sales for that same year were $1,671,000,000, which was a 19 percent increase over 1982.

Pizza Hut had become more competitive ever since Donald Smith was lured away from Burger King. Some industry analysts felt that Smith's prior experience at both McDonald's and Burger King might help to further strengthen Pizza Hut in coming years.

Pizza Hut's recent actions had substantially improved its position in the fast-food industry. It was trying to move away from being a fast-food chain to being more of a family restaurant. More private booths and wood decor were being used to give the restaurants a cozier atmosphere.

**Other Competitors**   In addition to these top national chains, Burger King also had to compete with a variety of other types of restaurants. The next largest segment was the steak and full-menu segment. This included places such as Western Sizzlin', Ponderosa, and Bonanza. The third largest segment was the pizza segment. This segment was headed by Pizza Hut, Godfather's Pizza, and Domino's Pizza. In addition, there were restaurants like Kentucky Fried Chicken, which catered to the chicken segment, and Long John Silver's, which catered to the fish segment. Some of the restaurants in these other segments were also fast-food restaurants. Finally, Burger King had to compete against restaurants such as Big Boy, Denny's, and Howard Johnson's, which straddled most of the different segments in family-style restaurants. Exhibit 14.9 shows a comparison of how Burger King's lunch and dinner menu compares with those of many of its major competitors.

**Exhibit 14.9** Lunch and Dinner Menu Comparison

| | Restaurant[a] | | | | | | | |
|---|---|---|---|---|---|---|---|---|
| | A | B | C | D | E | F | G | H |
| **Main-dish items** | | | | | | | | |
| Hamburgers | x | x | x | x | x | | | |
| Chicken | x | x | x | x | x | x | | x |
| Fish | x | x | | x | x | x | | |
| Pizza | | | | | | | x | |
| Turkey | | | | x | x | | | |
| Ham & cheese | x | | | x | x | | x | |
| Roast beef | | | | x | x | | | |
| Hot dog with chili | | | | x | | | | |
| Bacon, lettuce & tomato | | | x | | | | | |
| Meatball | | | | | | | x | |
| Spaghetti | | | | | | | x | |
| Cavatini | | | | | | | x | |
| Ham, salami, & cheese | | | | | | | x | |
| Baked potato | | | x | x | x | | | |
| Scallops | | | | | | x | | |
| Shrimp | | | | | | x | | |
| **Side orders** | | | | | | | | |
| French fries | x | x | x | x | x | x | | |
| Potato cakes | | | | x | | | | |
| Mashed potatoes | | | | | | | | x |
| Onion rings | x | | | | | | | |
| Chili | | | | x | | | | |
| Cole slaw | | | | | | x | | x |
| Potato salad | | | | | | | | x |
| Chicken livers | | | | | | | | x |
| Gizzards | | | | | | | | x |
| Baked beans | | | | | | | | x |
| Hush puppies | | | | | | x | | |
| Corn on the cob | | | | | | x | | x |
| Clam chowder | | | | | | x | | |
| **Salads** | | | | | | | | |
| Garden salads | x | | x | x | | x | x | |
| Seafood salads | | | | x | | x | | |
| Taco salads | | | x | | | | | |

[a]Codes are as follows:

A = Burger King  C = Wendy's  E = Arby's    G = Pizza Hut
B = McDonald's  D = Hardee's  F = Long John Silver's  H = Kentucky Fried Chicken

(continued)

**Exhibit 14.9** (continued)

| | Restaurant | | | | | | | |
|---|---|---|---|---|---|---|---|---|
| | A | B | C | D | E | F | G | H |
| **Desserts** | | | | | | | | |
| Pies/turnovers | x | x | x | x | x | x | | x |
| Cookies | | x | | x | x | | | |
| Sundaes | | | x | | | | | |
| Cones/frosty | | | x | x | | | | |
| **Beverages** | | | | | | | | |
| Soft drinks | x | x | x | x | x | x | x | x |
| Coffee | x | x | x | x | x | x | x | x |
| Milk shakes | x | x | | x | x | | | |
| Iced tea | x | x | x | x | | x | x | x |
| Hot tea | | | x | | | x | | |
| Milk | x | x | x | x | x | x | x | x |
| Hot chocolate | | | x | | | x | | |
| Orange juice | x | x | | x | x | | | |
| Beer | | | | | | | x | x |

<sup>a</sup>Codes are as follows:

A = Burger King   C = Wendy's   E = Arby's   G = Pizza Hut
B = McDonald's   D = Hardee's   F = Long John Silver's   H = Kentucky Fried Chicken

**BURGER KING'S FUTURE BATTLE FOR THE BURGERS**

One and a half years had passed since Jeffrey Campbell became CEO in mid-1983. A lot had been done in recent years to improve the firm's performance. Still, a lot more could be done. Shortly after becoming CEO, Campbell remarked, "Three to four years from now, I want a little more than half the restaurants of McDonald's, about half the market share, higher average sales, higher [restaurant] operating profits, and as good if not better return on investment for the operator."[6]

Burger King had been trying to tap new locations to continue growing in a saturated market. The Greyhound Food Management franchisee had even opened Burger King restaurants in some of its downtown bus terminals. In 1983, Burger King reached an agreement with Howard Johnson's to be its sole franchise at all of its turnpike service plazas. Clearly, Burger King's recent move onto military bases and in-store restaurants at Woolworth's retail stores were good moves. However, Burger King still needed to identify other nontraditional locations to counter the growing maturity of the fast-food industry.

Burger King had used new product offerings in recent years to increase its sales. Expanded menus had the potential to attract customers who were going elsewhere to get these offerings. New product introductions were also a key to maintaining market share and stealing customers from its competitors. Burger King had some success with new menu items such as the Croissandwich, the bacon double cheeseburger, and the salad bar. However, it also had been plagued by the failure of other new products in the past, such as the veal parmigiana specialty sandwich, pizza, and a one-third pound hamburger. Future new product items could be an asset to Burger King's sales growth if they were successful, but they would also be a costly drain on cash if a number of them failed.

Burger King's ad campaigns had been successful in stealing customers away from competitors in recent years. Its "Battle of the Burgers" theme was clearly appropriately named, given the intense competition in the fast-food industry. As its flame-broiling-versus-frying theme grew old and less effective, Burger King needed to develop new ad campaigns to draw customers away from its competitors. What form and theme they would use remained to be seen. Future ads, it was hoped, would help win more converts to Burger King while not turning off some customers who did not like the knocking-of-competitors nature of its ads. In addition, Burger King hopefully could find a way to counter a finding in a recent *Consumer Reports* survey. It found that more people preferred Burger King's hamburgers to McDonald's, yet they were more likely to eat at McDonald's.[7]

In another effort to maintain growth, Burger King had been considering new market concepts. Pillsbury had given Burger King the go-ahead to shop for new alternative restaurant concepts. Burger King might possibly acquire one or more existing smaller restaurant chains that were not intensely focused on fast-food hamburgers. At the same time, totally new restaurant concepts had already been ruled out. Italian and other ethnic foods are distinct possibilities. Pillsbury's Totino's and Fox Deluxe lines of frozen pizza could represent a substantial resource for Burger King to draw upon if it decided to enter a Burger King–owned pizza venture. Another possibility was a chain serving Mexican food, which was enjoying the highest yearly increase in sales of any ethnic food.

Finally, Burger King needed to bring about more stability, from its top management down to its hourly employees in its restaurants. Four different CEOs since 1977 had caused too many changes in Burger King's strategy. Similarly, the high turnover in its individual restaurants made any ongoing relationship between customers and Burger King employees almost impossible. Furthermore, new employees usually made more mistakes in handling customer orders and were less productive.

These and other strategic issues may need to be addressed as Burger King prepares for the rest of the 1980s. It is hoped that the decisions and actions that Jeffrey Campbell makes will bring Burger King closer to challenging McDonald's and maybe even someday becoming the leader in the fast-food industry.

## NOTES

1. "Pillsbury Co. Says It Agreed 'in Principle' to Buy Burger King," *Wall Street Journal,* January 20, 1967, p. 12.
2. "Beat the Clock," *Restaurant Business,* November 1, 1982, p. 330.
3. "The Pride of Burger King," *Restaurant Business,* May 1, 1982, p. 62.
4. Ibid.
5. "Restaurant Franchising in the Economy," *Restaurant Business,* March 20, 1984, p. 170.
6. David Kohn, "J. Jeffrey Campbell, Burger King," *Restaurant Business,* April 10, 1984, p. 90.
7. "Fast Foods," *Consumer Reports,* July 1984, p. 370.

# 15 Quaker Oats Company

Lloyd L. Byars and Wanda Benjamin
Atlanta University

**HISTORY**  The Quaker Oats Company was established in 1891 by three entrepreneurs. Ferdinand Schumacher, Henry Cromwell, and Robert Stuart were regional millers who decided they could benefit by uniting. Their union resulted in the world's largest oatmeal company, which was first known as the American Cereal Company. Realizing the limitations of a single-product company, the founders began looking for other opportunities. Shortly thereafter they embarked upon a strategy of growth through concentric diversification coupled with geographic expansion that has permeated the company's strategic management throughout its history. In 1900 the company went international by beginning to conduct business in Canada, Holland, and the United Kingdom. In the next decade the company launched two ready-to-eat cereals, Puffed Wheat and Puffed Rice, both of which are still in Quaker's product line. The company continued its growth strategy with the acquisition of the Mother's Oats brand. This was the first of many Quaker acquisitions.

Although the company had its beginning as a breakfast food manufacturer, it has since diversified into other food areas, pet foods, toys, tools, clothing, eye wear, and crafts. Quaker was also involved in the chemical business as well as the restaurant business. The restaurant business consisted of three separate chains, namely Magic Pan, Proud Popover, and Engine House Pizza restaurants. In fiscal 1982 the company completed a series of divestitures. Among those businesses divested were the Restaurant Division, the Biscuit Group of the Burry Subdivision of Food Service, the Mexican chemical business, the Needlecraft Division, and the company's Mexican toy-manufacturing business. The result of these divestments was a move back to Quaker's basic business, grocery products. William Smithburg, the company's chairman, was quoted in the *Advertising Age* August 1, 1983, issue as saying, "We are re-emphasizing our dependence on the strengths and growths of our U.S. grocery products operations." To that end the company has come full circle in its strategic management. In the process of growth, Quaker has moved from a single breakfast food product company to a diversified international corporation. (See financial statements, Exhibits 15.1 and 15.2.)

Exhibit 15.3 gives a brief synopsis of the company's growth strategy. Essentially this growth strategy was achieved via geographic expansion, new production innovations, concentric diversification, conglomerate diversification, and subsequent divestments.

**Exhibit 15.1** Consolidated Balance Sheet (millions of dollars)

| | 1984 | 1983 | 1982 |
|---|---|---|---|
| **Assets** | | | |
| June 30 | | | |
| Current assets | | | |
|   Cash & short-term bank deposits | $ 60.1 | $ 23.1 | $ 7.2 |
|   Marketable securities | 5.0 | 2.9 | 4.2 |
|   Receivables—net of allowances | 484.9 | 361.3 | 363.1 |
|   Inventories | | | |
|     Finished goods | 232.7 | 176.1 | 215.0 |
|     Grain & materials | 105.4 | 91.9 | 106.8 |
|     Supplies | 18.5 | 18.1 | 22.8 |
|     Total inventories | 356.6 | 286.1 | 344.6 |
| Other current assets | 32.3 | 88.0 | 45.8 |
|     Total current assets | 938.9 | 761.4 | 764.9 |
| Other receivables & investments | 22.2 | 23.1 | 27.8 |
| Plant, property, & equipment | 1,073.3 | 906.2 | 909.7 |
| Less accumulated depreciation | 342.7 | 289.9 | 291.3 |
|     Properties net | 730.6 | 616.3 | 618.4 |
| Intangible assets, less amortization | 115.1 | 62.9 | 65.6 |
| Total | $1,806.8 | $1,463.7 | $1,476.7 |
| **Liabilities & equity** | | | |
| June 30 | | | |
| Current liabilities | | | |
|   Short-term debt | $ 214.3 | $ 178.0 | $ 174.7 |
|   Current portion of long-term debt | 2.8 | 12.2 | 13.6 |
|   Trade accounts payable | 196.1 | 140.0 | 177.4 |
|   Accrued payrolls, pensions, & bonuses | 82.1 | 66.4 | 72.4 |
|   Accrued advertising & merchandising | 48.8 | 30.6 | 24.1 |
|   Income taxes payable | 11.9 | 18.4 | 19.7 |
|   Other current liabilities | 66.1 | 53.9 | 46.4 |
|     Current liabilities | 622.1 | 499.5 | 498.3 |
| Long-term debt | $ 200.1 | $ 152.8 | $ 162.2 |
| Other liabilities | 62.1 | 21.0 | 23.6 |
| Deferred income taxes | 163.9 | 109.7 | 116.7 |
| Redeemable preference stock, without par value, $100 stated value,   $9.56 cumulative | 38.5 | 41.3 | 45.3 |
| Common shareholders' equity | | | |
|   Common stock, $5 par value, authorized 35 shares; issued   20,997,349 shares | 105.0 | 105.0 | 105.0 |
| Additional paid-in capital | 26.3 | 23.1 | 22.8 |
| Reinvested earnings | 703.2 | 612.8 | 544.6 |
| Cumulative exchange adjustment | (89.9) | (68.2) | (53.5) |
| Treasury common stock, at cost | (24.5) | (33.3) | (43.4) |
|     Common shareholder's equity | 720.1 | 639.4 | 630.5 |
| Total | $1,806.8 | $1,463.7 | $1,476.7 |

*Source:* Annual reports.

**Exhibit 15.2** Consolidated Statement of Income (Millions of dollars except share data)

| Year Ended June 30 | 1984 | 1983 | 1982 |
|---|---|---|---|
| Net sales | $ 3,344.1 | $ 2,611.3 | $ 2,576.2 |
| Cost of goods sold | 2,073.1 | 1,576.3 | 1,634.4 |
| Gross profit | 1,271.0 | 1,035.0 | 941.8 |
| Selling, general, & administrative expenses | 952.9 | 758.7 | 689.5 |
| Interest expense—net | 59.9 | 41.9 | 45.9 |
| Other (income) expense | (1.9) | 14.5 | (0.5) |
| Income from continuing operations before income taxes | 260.1 | 219.9 | 206.9 |
| Provision for income taxes | 121.4 | 100.6 | 89.6 |
| Income from continuing operations | 138.7 | 119.3 | 117.3 |
| Discontinuted operations | | | |
|   (Loss) from operations—net of income taxes | — | (7.0) | — |
|   (Loss) on disposal—net of income taxes | — | (55.5) | (20.4) |
| Total (loss) from discontinued operations | — | (62.5) | (20.4) |
| Net income | 138.7 | 56.8 | 96.9 |
| Preference dividends | 3.9 | 4.1 | 4.3 |
| Net income available for common | $ 134.8 | $ 52.7 | $ 92.6 |
|   Income from continuing operations | $ 6.71 | $ 5.83 | $ 5.81 |
|   (Loss) from discontinued operations | — | (.35) | — |
|   (Loss) on disposal | — | (2.82) | (1.05) |
| Net income | $ 6.71 | $ 2.66 | $ 4.76 |
| Dividends declared | 2.20 | 2.00 | 1.80 |

*Source:* Annual Report 1984, p. 38.

**Exhibit 15.3**

| Decade | Activity |
|---|---|
| 1890s | Three regional millers (Schumacher, Cromwell, and Stuart) form an independent milling company, and the original Quaker Man trademark is registered in 1897. |
| 1900s | Schumacher, Cromwell, and Stuart start the American Cereal Company. ACC starts conducting business in Canada, Holland, and the United Kingdom. The company pays its first dividend. A major fire nearly destroys the company's mill in Cedar Mills, Iowa. |
| 1910s | Cromwell becomes president of the Quaker Oats Company (successor to the American Cereal Company). Quaker launches ready-to-eat cereals, Puffed Wheat and Puffed Rice. Company begins advertising its products. |
| 1920s | Mother's Oats brand acquired. |
| 1930s | John Stuart (Robert's son) becomes president. Aunt Jemima brand acquired and Quick Quaker Oats introduced. |
| 1940s | Quaker sales pass $50 million. Quaker shares are publicly traded. |
| 1950s | Quaker sales pass $100 million. Douglas Stuart (John's brother) and later Donald B. Loune become president. The Ken-L Ration brand is acquired. Quaker is awarded the Army/Navy 'E' in World War II. |
| 1960s | Puss 'n Boots cat food brand and Wolf brand chili acquired. Quaker's Latin American business expanded. Quaker shares listed on the New York Stock Exchange. |
| 1970s | Quaker sales pass $500 million. Robert D. Stuart, Jr., becomes president. Quaker introduces new hot ready-to-eat cereals. The company acquires Celeste brand frozen pizza, Fisher-Price Toys, Magic Pan restaurants, Louis Marx & Company. In 1976, the Marx toy company is sold. The company expands internationally. |
| 1980s | Quaker sales pass 2 billion. Kenneth Mason and later William Smithburg become president. Major international expansion for both grocery and toys. Fourth quarter fiscal 1984 hails an unprecedented number of new product introductions. Assets of the Restaurant Division and the Mexican Chemical Company are sold. Stokely–Van Camp, Jos. A. Bank Clothiers, Inc., The Brookstone Company Inc., Herrschners Specialty Tools Inc., Eyelab Inc., and U.S. Games are acquired. Quaker sells its interest in Artefactos Plasticos, a Mexican toy maker; U.S. Games (a California-based maker of video game cartridges) is also sold. The company sells all of the assets of the Biscuit Group of the Burry Division and the business of the Needlecraft Division. |

*Sources:* Annual Report 1982, *New York Times*, July 21, 1983.

## MANAGE-
## MENT TEAM

Quaker has basically been a family-operated business since its beginnings. Although the company was started by three entrepreneurs (Schumacher, Cromwell, and Robert Stuart) the business has primarily been run by the Stuart family. During the 1930s, John Stuart, Robert's son, became president; later, during the 1950s, John's brother, Douglas, took over the presidency. The last Stuart to hold the reins of the business was Robert D. Stuart, Jr., who became president in 1972. He left the company in 1983 after President Reagan nominated him as U.S. ambassador to Norway. Stuart relinquished the presidency to the current CEO, William Smithburg, but remains actively involved in the company's operations. He is currently a member of the board of directors, where he serves as the chairman of the finance committee.

The current CEO, William Smithburg, was described in the *Wall Street Journal* (November 11, 1983) as being "a breath of fresh air" at Quaker. He joined Quaker in 1966 as the Aunt Jemima Frozen Waffle brand manager. He is a former Leo Burnett advertising executive. Smithburg can best be described as young, energetic, aggressive, and a risk taker. In 1981, when he became chairman, he was 45 years old, making him one of Quaker's youngest chairmen in recent years. Since his move into the company's top position, Quaker has dramatically increased advertising expenditures, introduced an unprecedented number of new

### Exhibit 15.4

Frank J. Morgan, age 59, chief operating officer. Joined Quaker in 1964. Elected to present office in November 1983.

Michael J. Callahan, age 45, senior vice-president finance. Joined Quaker in 1982 in his present position from Exxon Corporation, where he served as assistant general manager of Exxon U.S.A. and treasurer and corporate planning manager of Esso Eastern, Inc.

Richard H. Glantz, age 62, senior vice-president management services. Joined Quaker in 1942. Elected to present office in 1982.

Luther C. McKinney, age 53, senior vice-president law, corporate affairs and corporate secretary. Joined Quaker in 1974. Elected to present office in 1977.

Paul E. Price, age 50, executive vice-president International Grocery Products. Joined Quaker in 1972. Elected to present office in November 1983.

Robert N. Thurston, age 52, executive vice-president U.S. and Canadian Grocery Products. Joined Quaker in 1966. Elected to present office in November 1983.

Richard D. Jaquith, age 43, vice-president and treasurer. Joined Quaker in 1969. Elected to present office in 1973.

Donald G. Wittmer, age 49, vice-president and corporate controller. Joined Quaker in 1965. Elected to present office in 1976.

R. Bruce Sampsell, age 43, president Fisher-Price. Joined Quaker in 1964. Elected to present position in February 1983.

Richard Chollot, age 42, executive vice-president Specialty Retailing. Joined Quaker in 1980 from Brookstone, where he served as president (1980–April 1984) and general manager (1971–1980). Elected to present office in April 1984.

*Source:* Annual Report 1984, pp. 63–65.

products, made a controversial major acquisition (Stokely–Van Camp, 1983), and completed a series of divestitures. He has moved the company back toward its basic business, grocery products.

Smithburg was cited in the November 11, 1983, *Wall Street Journal* as saying "that most of Quaker's top executives have spent most of their time in the grocery products division." As a result of this, many outsiders feel "Quaker's lack of top-management talent may restrict fast growth in unfamiliar nonfood businesses."[1] Analysts believe this to be a major factor in Smithburg's decision to divest several of Quaker's nonfood business segments. Exhibit 15.4 shows the balance of the management team at Quaker.

**OPERATIONS**

The operations of the company are carried out through its four major divisions, U.S. Grocery Products Division, International Grocery Products Division, Fisher-Price Toy Division, and Specialty Retailing Division (see Exhibit 15.5). The U.S. Grocery Products Division is the largest profit contributor to company earnings. In fiscal 1983 this division produced about 64 percent of Quaker's total operating income. It is closely followed by the International Grocery Products Division, the second largest contributor to Quaker profits. The Fisher-Price Toy Division is the third largest business segment as well as the third largest profit contributor. The Specialty Retailing Division is the smallest business segment; it contributes approximately 5 percent to the company's total profits.

If one were to apply the Boston Consulting Group business portfolio concept to Quaker's major divisions, one could possibly deduce the following: The U.S. Grocery Products Division is Quaker's cash cow; the Specialist Retailing Division is Quaker's star, as is the Fisher-Price Division; and possibly International Grocery Products Division is Quaker's problem child. (See Exhibit 15.6.) For a more detailed look at the individual divisions, each division will be described fully, starting with U.S. Grocery Products.

**U.S. Grocery Products**

Quaker's largest and most profitable business, U.S. Grocery Products is headquartered in the company's corporate office in Chicago. The division employs over 8,000 of Quaker's 28,400 employees.[2] U.S. Grocery Products is further segmented into three subdivisions—Foods, Pet Foods, and Food Service. The Foods Subdivision had sales in fiscal 1984 of over a billion dollars.[3] The Pet Foods Subdivision had a sales volume of more than $300 million in fiscal 1984. The Food Service Subdivision is currently "a $100 million plus business."[4] In sum, U.S. Grocery Products manufactures and markets a wide range of hot ready-to-eat cereals, corn goods, baking mixes, frozen products, syrup, snacks, canned goods, beverages, and pet foods.

**Exhibit 15.5** Industry Segment and Geographic Area Information (millions of dollars)

### INDUSTRY SEGMENT INFORMATION

| | Identifiable Assets | | | | Capital Expenditures | | | |
|---|---|---|---|---|---|---|---|---|
| | 1984 | 1983 | 1982 | 1981 | 1984 | 1983 | 1982 | 1981 |
| U.S. Grocery Products | $ 769.8 | $ 483.8 | $ 457.6 | $ 450.2 | $ 20.2 | $ 58.2 | $ 30.1 | $ 41.2 |
| International Grocery Products | 459.0 | 482.5 | 432.6 | 409.8 | 29.1 | 45.2 | 60.0 | 58.7 |
| Fisher-Price | 318.1 | 305.8 | 315.4 | 296.2 | 13.7 | 17.1 | 21.3 | 21.2 |
| Specialty Retailing | 91.4 | 65.2 | 52.2 | 14.4 | 7.1 | 3.5 | 2.1 | 1.6 |
| Total existing business | 1,638.3 | 1,337.3 | 1,257.8 | 1,170.6 | 118.4 | 124.0 | 113.5 | 122.7 |
| Other | 34.3 | — | 12.8 | 20.1 | 1.7 | 0.2 | 0.6 | 4.1 |
| Corporate | 134.2 | 126.4 | 206.1 | 263.4 | — | — | — | — |
| Total consolidated | $1,806.8 | $1,463.7 | $1,476.7 | $1,454.1 | $ 120.1 | $ 124.2 | $ 114.1 | $ 126.8 |

### GEOGRAPHIC AREA INFORMATION

| | Sales | | | | Operating Income | | | |
|---|---|---|---|---|---|---|---|---|
| | 1984 | 1983 | 1982 | 1981 | 1984 | 1983 | 1982 | 1981 |
| United States | $2,164.0 | $1,623.5 | $1,580.7 | $1,367.2 | $ 249.5 | $ 210.6 | $ 183.7 | $ 163.0 |
| Canada | 160.3 | 151.3 | 148.3 | 135.6 | 12.4 | 10.7 | 8.7 | 7.2 |
| Europe | 614.4 | 581.0 | 525.8 | 533.0 | 22.0 | 34.8 | 30.5 | 31.6 |
| Latin America & Pacific | 226.4 | 245.2 | 303.3 | 288.1 | 34.3 | 32.2 | 33.3 | 28.3 |
| Total existing business | $3,165.1 | 2,601.0 | 2,558.1 | 2,323.9 | 318.2 | 288.3 | 256.2 | 230.1 |
| Other | 179.0 | 10.3 | 18.1 | 61.2 | 7.8 | (2.2) | 4.9 | 1.9 |
| Corporate | — | — | — | — | — | — | — | — |
| Total consolidated | $3,344.1 | $2,611.3 | $2,576.2 | $2,385.1 | $ 326.0 | $ 286.1 | $ 261.1 | $ 232.0 |

*Source:* Annual Report 1984, pp. 46, 47.

**International Grocery Products**

International Grocery Products employs more than 9000 people who "are responsible for producing the wide array of food and non-food items that range from hot and ready-to-eat cereals to pet foods, chocolate candy and corn oil."[5] "International Grocery Products (IGP) operates more than 30 manufacturing facilities in 16 different countries in Europe, Canada, Latin America, Australia and Taiwan."[6] The division represents Quaker's second largest business seg-

**Exhibit 15.6** The Four Major Divisions

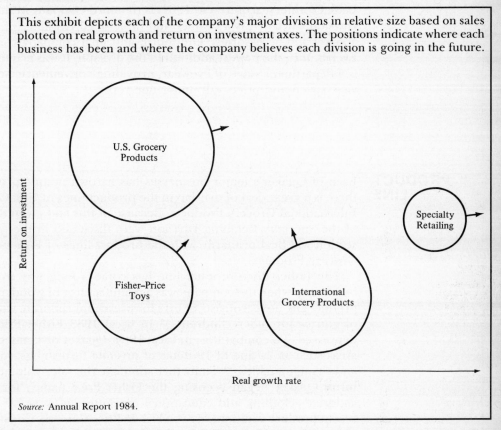

This exhibit depicts each of the company's major divisions in relative size based on sales plotted on real growth and return on investment axes. The positions indicate where each business has been and where the company believes each division is going in the future.

*Source:* Annual Report 1984.

ment. Its sales were just under $1 billion during fiscal 1984. IGP has grown primarily through a series of acquisitions which occurred within the last ten years.

**Fisher-Price Toys**

Fisher-Price "is the world's largest producer of infant and preschool toys and is the third largest manufacturer of traditional toys in the U.S."[7] Fisher-Price manufactures approximately 50 million toys yearly and sells in almost 100 countries.[8] It is headquartered in East Aurora, New York, and employs 6000 people at peak employment periods.

**Specialty Retailing**

Consisting of four separate companies, the Specialty Retailing Division came into being with the 1972 acquisition of Herrschners, "the oldest art needlework mail-order house in the U.S."[9] A second company, the Brookstone Company, was acquired in 1980. Brookstone is a "marketer of hard-to-find tools, homeware and energy-saving products through mail-order catalogs and retail stores."[10] Jos. A. Bank Clothiers, acquired in 1981, is the third company in the Specialty Retailing Division (SRD). It is a retailer and direct-mail marketer of men's and women's apparel and accessories. The fourth and final company comprising the SRD is Eyelab, Inc., the newest addition to the division. It was acquired in 1983. "Eyelab is a department store of eyewear, providing convenience, selection, quality, service, speed and price—all under one roof."[11]

**PRODUCT LINE**

Each of Quaker's major businesses has its own unique product line. However, there is a great deal of overlap in the product lines of U.S. Grocery Products and International Grocery Products. Because of this and given that the product lines of the Specialty Retailing Division were discussed in the previous section, this section will deal primarily with the product lines of Fisher-Price Toys and U.S. Grocery Products.

The Fisher-Price product line has come a long way from its humble 1930 beginning, when the company was a manufacturer of wooden push-pull toys. The product line now "consists of toys for preschool children, with a growing number of entries for older children."[12] In fiscal 1983 Fisher-Price sales volume was depressed. To combat this, in fiscal 1984, Quaker diversified into several nontoy areas such as "a line of 19 items of juvenile furnishings, including a high chair and changing table."[13] To further stimulate the sales volume of the toy manufacturer, Quaker began licensing the Fisher-Price name "for the manufacture of children's clothing and educational computer software."[14] Among Fisher-Price recent product additions are the Fisher-Price Camera, Construx building sets for older children, Fisher-Price roller skates, and a new zoo playset.[15]

Just as the Fisher-Price product line has grown through new product introductions and expansion into other markets, so has the product line of U.S. Grocery Products. U.S. Grocery Products has coupled the above growth strategies with horizontal diversification. As previously stated, Quaker Oats started in 1891 with one product, rolled oats. Since that time the product line has expanded to 50 different widely recognized consumer brands. These brands fall into several categories: hot cereals, ready-to-eat cereals, mixes, syrup, corn products, grain-based snacks, Stokely–Van Camp, frozen foods, and other foods. Quaker's "well-known brand names include Quaker Oats, Cap'n Crunch, Aunt Jemima, Mother's, Life, Celeste, Flako, Van Camp's, Gatorade, Ken-L Ration and Puss'n Boots."[16] Some of lesser known brands are Wolf Chili, Mr. T. Cereal, Chewy Granola Bars, 100% Natural Cereal, Pounce cat treats, and Moist Meals cat food.

The fourth quarter of fiscal 1984 hailed an unprecedented number of new product introductions and product restages for the company. Among the recent product introductions are Mr. T. Cereal, Granola Dipps, three flavor additions to the Chewy Granola snack line, two flavor additions to the Instant Oats line, Snausages (Quaker's first entry into the premium dog snack segment), Puppy

Kibbles 'n Bits (Quaker's first entry into the puppy food segment), Raisin Life, and Choco Crunch. Among the product restages (a restage occurs when a product is reformulated, repackaged, and advertised in a manner different from previously presented) were Kibbles 'n Bits 'n Bits 'n Bits, Ken-L Ration canned dog food, and Puss 'n Boots canned cat food.

**ADVERTISING TRENDS**

The advertising and merchandising expenditures for Quaker have changed dramatically with the onset of new products. In order to successfully launch these new products and restages, Quaker increased advertising and merchandising by 28 percent over fiscal year 1983. In actual dollars, the company spent $575 million on advertising and merchandising (A&M) in fiscal 1984;[17] of this amount approximately $66 million was spent mainly on new product introductions. Quaker has consistently increased its A&M expenditures as evidenced by the percentage of sales spent on advertising over the last 11 years. These expenditures ranged from as low as 6.7 percent of sales in fiscal 1974 to an all-time high of 17.2 percent of sales in fiscal 1984. (See Exhibit 15.7.) The 17.2 percent of sales in fiscal 1984 marked a 257 percent increase of the fiscal 1974 figure of 6.7 percent of sales. According to the Corporate and Industry Research Report's (CIRR) *Food Industry Spotlight,* "Trends in advertising are important in food companies for two reasons. An increase in spending, first of all may signal the beginning of a marketing effort that would lead to a better competitive position and faster growth in the future. Moreover, because advertising is a discretionary cost, to a certain extent, in the short term, it can influence the quality of reported earnings."[18] Also in this issue of the *Food Industry Spotlight* was a list of the top 25 advertisers in the food manufacturing business. The Exhibit 15.8 is an abbreviated list of those advertisers.

The trend toward increased advertising and merchandising expenditures appears to be deeply set in the food industry as evidenced by the abbreviated listing in Exhibit 15.8. The increased percentage of sales A&M now consumes is also indicative of this trend.

**PRODUCTION FACILITIES**

As of June 30, 1984, Quaker Oats operated 68 manufacturing plants in 16 states and 16 foreign countries.[19] The company has a total of 18 elevator grain storage facilities, 3 plants are located in the U.S. and the remaining 15 plants in foreign countries throughout the world. Three of these facilities have capacity in excess of 1.0 million bushels. They are Cedar Rapids, Iowa (10 million bushels), St. Joseph, Missouri (4.5 million bushels), and Peterborough, Ontario, Canada (1.3 million bushels). Along with the previously mentioned manufacturing operations, the company also has 46 retail locations scattered throughout the continental

**Exhibit 15.7** Eleven-Year Selected Financial Data (millions of dollars except share and percent data)

| Financial Statistics | 5-Year Compounded Growth Rate (%) | 10-Year Compounded Growth Rate (%) | Year Ended June 30 | | |
|---|---|---|---|---|---|
| | | | 1984 | 1983 | 1982 |
| Current ratio | | | 1.5 | 1.5 | 1.5 |
| Working capital | 4.8 | 5.6 | $ 316.8 | $ 261.9 | $ 266.6 |
| Working capital turnover | | | 11.6 | 9.9 | 9.9 |
| Property, plant, & equipment | 7.6 | 8.6 | 730.6 | 616.3 | 618.4 |
| Depreciation expenses | 15.6 | 11.7 | 70.0 | 52.3 | 46.3 |
| Total assets | 9.8 | 8.8 | 1,806.8 | 1,463.7 | 1,476.7 |
| Long-term debt | 4.9 | 1.6 | 200.1 | 152.8 | 162.2 |
| Redeemable preference stock | | | 38.5 | 41.3 | 45.4 |
| Common shareholders' equity | 7.0 | 7.9 | 720.1 | 639.4 | 630.5 |
| Book value per common stock | 6.5 | 8.2 | 35.57 | 32.07 | 32.17 |
| Return on avg. shareholder equity (%) | | | 19.8 | 18.1 | 18.2 |
| Gross profit as a percent of sales | | | 38.0 | 39.6 | 36.6 |
| Advertising & merchandising as a percent of sales | | | 17.2 | 16.6 | 14.7 |
| Research & development as percent of sales | | | 0.9 | 1.0 | 1.0 |
| Income as a percent of sales | | | 4.1 | 4.6 | 4.6 |
| Long-term debt ratio (%) | | | 20.9 | 18.3 | 19.4 |
| Total debt ratio (%) | | | 35.5 | 33.5 | 34.1 |
| Common dividends as a percent of income available for common stock | | | 32.9 | 34.3 | 31.2 |
| No. of common shareholders | | | 26,785 | 27,943 | 29,552 |
| No. of employees worldwide | | | 28,400 | 25,200 | 26,000 |
| Market price range of common stock—High | | | $64\frac{5}{8}$ | $51\frac{3}{4}$ | $43\frac{1}{2}$ |
| Low | | | $42\frac{3}{4}$ | $35\frac{1}{4}$ | $41\frac{1}{4}$ |

*Source:* Annual Report 1984, pp. 34–35.

| | | | Year Ended June 30 | | | | |
|---|---|---|---|---|---|---|---|
| 1981 | 1980 | 1979 | 1978 | 1977 | 1976 | 1975 | 1974 |
| 1.5 | 1.6 | 1.8 | 1.8 | 2.0 | 2.0 | 2.4 | 1.8 |
| $ 252.4 | $ 250.9 | $ 250.7 | $ 223.11 | $ 233.2 | $ 215.5 | $ 208.7 | $ 184.5 |
| 9.2 | 8.5 | 7.5 | 6.6 | 6.4 | 6.5 | 6.6 | 6.8 |
| 633.3 | 572.8 | 507.4 | 458.0 | 406.7 | 373.6 | 358.2 | 319.3 |
| 42.3 | 37.1 | 33.9 | 30.2 | 29.0 | 30.4 | 27.4 | 23.1 |
| 1,454.1 | 1,334.2 | 1,131.5 | 1,008.8 | 924.3 | 854.9 | 765.1 | 776.4 |
| 165.2 | 151.7 | 157.5 | 159.4 | 151.8 | 148.7 | 158.3 | 171.4 |
| 46.7 | 50.0 | 50.0 | 50.0 | 50.0 | 50.0 | 50.0 | — |
| 612.6 | 582.9 | 513.6 | 461.5 | 434.3 | 386.0 | 350.1 | 335.2 |
| 31.98 | 28.85 | 25.94 | 23.13 | 20.75 | 18.62 | 16.91 | 16.91 |
| | | | | | | 6.4 | 11.6 |
| 16.7 | 16.6 | 15.9 | 15.3 | 16.8 | 12.2 | 25.2 | 25.4 |
| 34.2 | 33.8 | 33.9 | 33.7 | 32.1 | 31.2 | 8.5 | 6.7 |
| 13.8 | 12.7 | 12.3 | 11.7 | 10.3 | 9.8 | 1.1 | 1.2 |
| 1.0 | 0.9 | 1.0 | 1.2 | 1.0 | 1.1 | 1.8 | 3.3 |
| | | | | | | 28.0 | 33.4 |
| 4.4 | 4.4 | 4.6 | 4.9 | 5.1 | 3.6 | 31.5 | 45.9 |
| 20.0 | 19.3 | 21.8 | 23.8 | 23.9 | 25.1 | 75.5 | 42.2 |
| 36.8 | 33.1 | 30.7 | 33.0 | 30.9 | 30.8 | | |
| 32.0 | 30.8 | 30.7 | 31.2 | 27.7 | 39.2 | | |
| 30,418 | 30,818 | 31,567 | 31,853 | 31,830 | 24,747 | 25,064 | 22,320 |
| 30,900 | 31,400 | 31,400 | 29,600 | 27,800 | 23,900 | 25,100 | 25,400 |
| $37\frac{3}{4}$ | $34\frac{1}{2}$ | $27\frac{1}{2}$ | 26 | $27\frac{3}{4}$ | $28\frac{3}{8}$ | $24\frac{3}{8}$ | $39\frac{7}{8}$ |
| $25\frac{7}{8}$ | $23\frac{1}{2}$ | 22 | 20 | $20\frac{7}{8}$ | 45 | 11 | $49\frac{3}{4}$ |

**Exhibit 15.8** Fourth Quarter and Annual Media Advertising, 1978–1981 (millions of dollars)

| | Annual Expenditures | | | | 1981 % Change From | |
|---|---|---|---|---|---|---|
| | **1981** | **1980** | **1979** | **1978** | **1980** | **1979** |
| General Foods | $ 367.5 | $ 345.5 | $ 362.1 | $ 297.0 | +6 | +2 |
| General Mills | 186.9 | 157.0 | 173.4 | 152.4 | +19 | +8 |
| Pillsbury | 97.9 | 91.0 | 99.8 | 77.2 | +8 | −2 |
| Ralston Purina | 96.9 | 108.1 | 100.5 | 81.9 | +10 | −4 |
| Quaker Oats | 329.8 | 278.6 | 217.4 | 175.9 | +18 | +51 |

*Source: Food Industry Spotlight,* May 15, 1982.

United States. The Foods Subdivision of U.S. Grocery Products has 13 plants in the following cities:

Cedar Rapids, Iowa
Chattanooga, Tenn.
Dallas, Tex.
Danville, Ill.
Haines City, Fla.
Indianapolis, Ind.
Jackson, Tenn.

Kissimmee, Fla.
Newport, Tenn.
Oakland, Calif.
Pekin, Ill.
St. Joseph, Mo.
Shiremanstown, Pa.

The Pet Foods Subdivision has plants in the following locations: Lawrence, Kansas; Marion, Ohio; and Rockford, Illinois. Exhibits 15.9 and 15.10, taken from the 1984 Annual Report, summarize Quaker's production and retail facilities.

The company also owns a research and development laboratory in Barrington, Illinois, and a pet food nutritional facility in Lake County, Illinois.[20]

**SALES FORCE ORGANIZATION**

The sales force organization of the Quaker Oats Company is composed of approximately 700 people.[21] This field sales force handles the sale of all retail grocery products in the United States. Also included in this number is a separate sales force which handles the frozen foods and confectionary products separately from other grocery products. This arrangement exists because the frozen and confectionary products have a different distribution channel from that of the other grocery products. The frozen and confectionary products are sold primarily through broker representatives who sell not only Quaker products but a host of other manufacturers' products as well.

The field sales force organization is further divided into four geographic regions, which in turn are broken down into zones.[22] These zones are segmented

**Exhibit 15.9**

| Industry Segment | Total No. of Mfg. Locations | | Total Mfg. Area (in sq ft) | |
|---|---|---|---|---|
| | U.S. | Foreign | Owned | Leased |
| U.S. Grocery Products | 18 | — | 6,313,000 | — |
| International Grocery Products | — | 37 | 4,495,000 | 51,700 |
| Fisher-Price | 5 | 4 | 2,084,000 | 253,000 |
| Specialty Retailing | 4 | — | 35,000 | 110,000 |

**Exhibit 15.10**

| Retail Locations (all U.S.) | 1984 | 1983 | 1982 | 1981 | 1980 |
|---|---|---|---|---|---|
| Brookstone | 20 | 15 | 9 | 7 | 7 |
| Jos. A. Bank | 19 | 15 | 13 | — | — |
| Eyelab | 7 | — | — | — | — |

into districts. Normally 13 to 17 salespeople, with individual territories, comprise a sales district. There is yet another separate sales force of 50 people within the Quaker system for Food Service sales.[23]

The 700 figure has remained relatively constant through the past several years. It was thought to be an adequate number of salespeople to maintain Quaker's customer service standards until the acquisition of Stokely–Van Camp in 1983. In that year, in an effort to ascertain the adequacy of the current sales force, Quaker decided to embark upon an experimental project with its Jacksonville (Florida) Zone. This zone was to be divided into two separate sales teams. The project, slated to begin before the close of fiscal 1984, would attempt to determine if indeed the product line had expanded to the point where it justified two separate sales teams to service the retail grocers. One of the sales teams would handle Stokely–Van Camp and Pet Foods exclusively, whereas the second sales team would handle the remainder of Quaker's product line. The service level to retailers and increases or decreases in sales volume was to be closely monitored to determine if the benefits of the project outweigh the costs. The outcome of the experimental project would no doubt have far-reaching effects on future manpower decisions for the sales organization.

## PRESENT AND FUTURE FACTORS

The Quaker Oats Company has been marketing grain-based consumer foods for over 105 years.[24] Although it has enjoyed a long successful history and currently holds an enviable position in the grocery industry, there are several factors which could affect the company's current position. Among those factors are the following: There is a growing trend among American consumers to eat breakfast away from home; the primary target market of Fisher-Price is the slowest-growing age group in the general U.S. population; the majority of Quaker's products are in the mature market stage; and there are major competitive threats to the Quaker product line.

The first factor mentioned, a growing trend among Americans to eat breakfast away from home, is one that has serious implications to a business where 82 percent of its annual sales are from breakfast grocery products.[25] In an effort to assure its stability and survival, Quaker began (over ten years ago) a series of acquisitions into nonfood business. However, the company's success outside the food segment has been dismal, and the company has at times sold recently acquired businesses at a loss. Quaker's lack of management expertise in areas other than grocery products has been cited as the primary reason for the company's dismal nonfood track record. Another move by the company to adapt to the trend was to beef up its Food Service Subdivision which supplies restaurants with breakfast foods for people who eat away from home.

Ways to combat the second factor, the shrinking target market of Fisher-Price Toys, has baffled Fisher-Price management for some time. After fiscal 1983's depressed sales volume, Fisher-Price's management seems to have found a solution to this problem. In fiscal 1984 Fisher-Price began to diversify into nontoy areas such as juvenile furnishings; Fisher-Price also started to license its name to children's computer software and clothing. As a result of these moves, Fisher-Price enjoyed a 14 percent increase in sales. "Fisher-Price has continued to grow through expansion into older age categories, which now represent one-third of Fisher-Price U.S. sales."[26]

The third factor, that most of Quaker's products are in the mature market stage, has both negative and positive implications for Quaker. The negative implication is that these markets may be fully saturated, so increased consumption, hence increased sales volume, may not be possible. The positive implication is that because these products are in the mature stage they are also cash generators for the company. Since these mature products require little capital expenditures for maintenance, the excess cash generated can be used to finance new product introductions, growth products, and growth areas. The mature Quaker products are standard oats, mixes, syrup, corn goods, frozen foods, canned and semimoist pet foods, beans, and chili. The growth products and growth areas are instant oatmeal, ready-to-eat cereals, snacks, dry dog food, Gatorade, and the foods service area. Since fiscal 1979 the mature categories have decreased in total U.S. Grocery Products tonnage from 66 percent of total tonnage to 52 percent of total tonnage in fiscal 1984.

The fourth and final factor, major competitive threats to Quaker's product line, is not unique to Quaker alone. Competitive threats are the norm in the grocery products industry. However, during 1984 some of Quaker's cash generators, stars, and flagship brands were challenged by major competitors with resources strong enough to cause problems. In the fourth quarter of fiscal 1984 Ralston Purina posed a serious threat to one of Quaker's flagship brands, instant oats, with a nationwide introduction of instant oats licensed under the Sun-Maid Raisin name. General Mills recognized the dollar value of the grain-based snack category when Quaker sales of Chewy Granola Bars reached $100 million within four years and when Granola Dipps gained national consumer acceptance beyond all Quaker expectations. The Minnesota-based food manufacturer is now in hot pursuit of a share of this snack category. Likewise, Ralston Purina recently introduced a line of granola snack bars to compete against both Quaker and General Mills. Coke Foods, the Houston, Texas, division of the soft drink giant Coca-Cola, is primed to introduce an isotonic drink targeted to compete against Quaker's newly acquired Gatorade franchise. The franchise is a star within the Quaker product line with sales of about $100 million in 1982.[27] The aforementioned companies are but a few of the many who have smelled the sweet success Quaker has experienced with these brands. These companies in particular have adequate financial, marketing, and production resources to become serious competitive threats to the Quaker product line.

## NOTES

1. Sue Shellenbarger, *Wall Street Journal,* November 11, 1983, p. 25.
2. *Quaker!* (company document).
3. Ibid.
4. Ibid.
5. Ibid.
6. Ibid.
7. Ibid.
8. Ibid.
9. Ibid.
10. Ibid.
11. Ibid.
12. Ibid.
13. Quaker Oats Company Annual Report 1984, p. 24.
14. Ibid.
15. Ibid.
16. *Quaker!* (company document).
17. Quaker Oats Company Annual Report 1984, p. 31.
18. CIRR *Food Industry Spotlight,* May 15, 1982, p. 11.
19. Quaker Oats Company Annual Report 1984, p. 54.
20. Ibid.
21. *Quaker!* (company document).
22. Ibid.
23. Ibid.
24. Ibid.
25. Shellenbarger, *Wall Street Journal,* p. 25.
26. Quaker Oats Company Annual Report, 1984, p. 3.
27. Jay McCormick, *Advertising Age,* August 1, 1983, p. 4.

# 16 MCI Communications

Lloyd L. Byars and Deirdre Creecy
Atlanta University

**HISTORY**     MCI began in the early 1960s when a group of northern Illinois mobile radio distributors tried to solve a common problem for trucking companies hauling goods between Chicago and St. Louis. The freight companies were having difficulty maintaining communications between their dispatchers and the trucks on the road.

The mobile radio distributors formed a company called Microwave Communications, Inc. (MCI), led by Jack Goeken. They proposed a microwave radio system from Chicago to St. Louis permitting the dispatchers and trucks to remain in contact throughout their route. Microwave Communications, Inc., applied to the Federal Communications Commission (FCC) in late 1963 for permission to build nine microwave stations linking the two cities. From the start, the application met strong resistance from Illinois Bell.

In Washington, D.C., in August 1968, William McGowan, a financial and management consultant, and Goeken founded Microwave Communications of America, Inc., to provide a wide range of services on a nationwide basis. The FCC had traditionally awarded one license to service a specific region. In order to compete for the license, several independent, locally financed regional carriers were formed. These carriers could later be interconnected to create a national network. MCI Communications, Inc., was originally formed to be a regional carrier. The Washington headquarters was to sponsor and serve as consultant to the regional carriers and was to take a minority stock position in each regional operation. In 1972, MCI Communications became the parent corporation and MCI Telecommunications Corporation was formed as a subsidiary.

In August 1969, the FCC approved the company's application for its Chicago–St. Louis route. Following the landmark "MCI Decision," the FCC was flooded with applications from companies seeking to offer similar services in various parts of the country. In June 1971, the FCC ruled that any business which was financially, technically, and legally qualified could enter the specialized telecommunications transmission market. MCI could then develop from the regional system into a strong national network.

In January, 1972, MCI inaugurated Private Line service between Chicago and St. Louis. MCI extended its Private Line service to 13 additional cities by 1973. At that time, AT&T refused to provide MCI with some of the local interconnections needed to connect customers with the MCI terminal in each city. By mid-1973, the problem became critical, affecting business plans and staffing. MCI presented the problem to the FCC, the Department of Justice, and the Federal District Court of Philadelphia. On December 31, 1973, the court decided in favor of MCI and ordered AT&T to give MCI the local interconnections it needed to provide Private Line service. As a result of AT&T's actions, MCI filed its first antitrust suit in March 1974.

In November, the U.S. Justice Department filed a suit against AT&T for abuse of its monopoly over the telephone industry by keeping competitors (including MCI) out of the markets for equipment and long-distance phone service.

During 1974, MCI continued to expand by building its network to increase radio capacity. In an effort to increase revenues, MCI began to explore the ideas of a "dial-up" service or a service to compete against Bell's Direct Dial service. The first metered service to develop from this idea was Execunet, which allowed a customer to dial an MCI computer and gain access to the MCI network to make long-distance calls at a rate significantly lower than that of the Bell system.[1] A tariff was filed in late 1974 and was approved by the FCC in January 1975. AT&T contended that MCI was not authorized to provide this service. MCI had to rely on vital local interconnections from AT&T to provide Execunet, and once again, AT&T refused to provide them.

The objections prevented MCI from providing the service until early 1978, when the courts required AT&T to provide the interconnections, AT&T froze MCI's growth efforts for nearly two years and, as a result, MCI filed a second antitrust suit against AT&T. Although MCI could not market Execunet, it continued to sell Network Service.[2]

In June 1980, MCI won a major victory in its first antitrust suit against AT&T, originally filed in 1974. The jury awarded MCI $600 million in damages because of AT&T's anticompetitive actions between 1971 and 1975. Under provisions of the antitrust laws, the award was tripled to $1.8 billion. The decision was under appeal by AT&T. In 1983, the appeals court upheld AT&T's guilt but suggested that the damage portion of the verdict be retired.

While the activities were taking place relative to Execunet, MCI expanded its Private Line service to additional cities.[3] MCI posted its first profitable month in September 1976, and has shown a profit for each quarter ever since. AT&T long-distance revenues account for 95 percent of all long-distance revenues, with MCI accounting for 3 percent and all other common carriers, 2 percent. At the end of the 1982 fiscal year, MCI grossed over $500 million.

In early 1980, MCI expanded its customer base to include the residential market. MCI's Residential service was enthusiastically received from the outset and has continued to grow since 1980.

In early January 1982, the U.S. government announced a proposed consent decree to settle the government's antitrust suit filed against AT&T in 1974. The proposed consent degree would require AT&T to divest itself of its operating companies.

The divestiture degree, a decision announced by Judge Harold H. Greene, sets up an industry framework which is extremely procompetitive and has been MCI's objective over the past decade. MCI first suggested to the FCC and Congress nearly ten years ago that AT&T should be forced to divest itself. The consent decree has been agreed upon by both the U.S. government and AT&T. Now that the consent decree has been implemented, the users of telecommunication services and companies that provide them are benefiting.

In accordance with MCI's philosophy to buy technology and market services in the telecommunications area, in late June 1982 MCI purchased Western Union International, Inc. (WUI) and its subsidiaries from Xerox Corporation. WUI is a leader in international telecommunications, offering a range of subscriber services to the United States and more than 100 foreign countries.

In September 1983, MCI formed a new company, MCI Digital Information Services Company, to provide electronic postal service to the continental United States. The first system introduced by the company is MCI mail, which subscribers use to transmit time-sensitive mail.

MCI Communications is now comprised of four distinct wholly owned subsidiary companies:

1. MCI Telecommunications, which provides domestic long-distance service
2. MCI International, which includes Western Union International, and which provides data, record, telex, message, and voice services
3. MCI Airsignal, which provides cellular mobile radio paging
4. MCI Digital Information Services Company, which provides nationwide electronic postal service.

These operating subsidiaries and the organizational overview are shown in Exhibit 16.1.

**CORPORATE ORGANIZA-TIONAL STRUCTURE**

In 1981, MCI created a region headquartered in St. Louis, Missouri, with sales and operations responsible for Minnesota, Iowa, Nebraska, Kansas, Missouri, Oklahoma, and Tennessee. MCI increased its employee base 26 percent by adding 400 employees.

In 1982, MCI formed a new functional group called Corporate Development. It had eight functional groups, each headed by a senior vice-president. The groups were law, regulation and industry relations, network operations, sales and marketing, transmission systems, corporate development, planning and administration, and finance.

Also, two new field regions were created. The Southeast region (headquartered in Atlanta) was responsible for North Carolina, South Carolina, Georgia, Florida, Alabama, Mississippi, and Tennessee. A formal organizational chart and reporting relationships are shown in Exhibit 16.2. The Northwest region (headquartered in San Francisco) had responsibility for northern California, Nevada, Utah, Colorado, Wyoming, Montano, Idaho, Washington, and Oregon. This was done as part of MCI's continuing process of decentralizing the functions which could be performed more efficiently at the field locations.

Responsibility relationships for the functional area of sales and marketing are delineated in Exhibit 16.3. The director of marketing services, the director of marketing, and the director of marketing major accounts all report to the senior

**Exhibit 16.1** MCI Communications Corporation Organizational Overview and Operating Subsidiaries

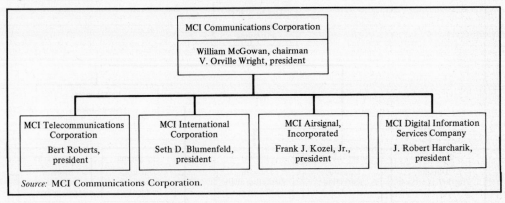

Source: MCI Communications Corporation.

**Exhibit 16.2** MCI Telecommunications Corporation Functional Organization

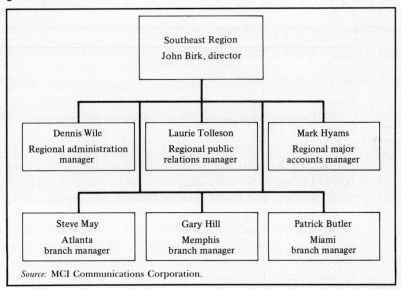

Source: MCI Communications Corporation.

vice-president of marketing. All other marketing functions work together as a group and also report to the senior vice-president of marketing.

**PHILOSOPHY AND OBJECTIVES**

MCI's corporate philosophy is to be a market-driven, responsive, full-service telecommunications company. MCI believes that past successes are just in the past, and that it is the future that really counts.[4] Also, as stated earlier, MCI's

**Exhibit 16.3** MCI Marketing

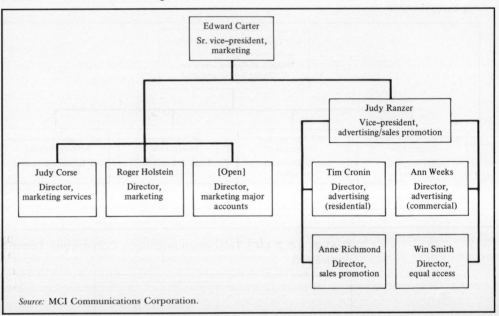

*Source:* MCI Communications Corporation.

philosophy is to buy technology and market services in the telecommunications area.

MCI's main purpose is to be a comprehensive provider of telecommunications services. In order to fulfill this goal, MCI has undergone and will continue to undergo many fundamental technological and capacity improvements that will strengthen its ability to meet the rapidly expanding need for information in future years. Today, its services include intercity voice and data communications, international voice and data communications, and paging, and mobile telephone services.

Short-term operations are planned and implemented to provide maximum growth and profitability in the future. MCI has specified several objectives that will enable it to achieve its purpose. The company's 1983 general report stated its objectives as follows:

1. MCI expects to generate increased market share as equal access is extended across the United States during the next few years.
2. MCI will continue to be the most efficient and low-cost supplier of telecommunications services.
3. MCI will continue to be market-driven, responding to proven demand with the latest technology, combined with its own imprint of productivity and innovation.
4. MCI will continue to invest in its own network.
5. MCI will continue to bring diversity to its company.

**SUBSIDI-ARIES**   MCI's subsidiaries include MCI Telecommunications, the company's long-distance business; MCI Airsignal, a national leader in personal communications; MCI Digital Information Services Company, a time-sensitive message delivery system that can reach anyone in the United States; and MCI International, which serves the international voice market.

**MCI Telecommuni-cations**   MCI Telecommunications is the largest and most profitable division of MCI. It also has the largest active customer base with 1,650,000 customers.[5] For these reasons, this section will focus primarily on this division.

**Organizational Structure.**   On January 1, 1985, MCI Telecommunications Corporation realigned its sales, customer service, and network operations to expedite the transition to equal access. (Since The AT&T divestiture of 1984, local Bell operating companies must offer their customers equal access to all long-distance carriers.) The decentralization brought MCI senior management closer to its customers and closer to the local telephone companies that are providing access.

MCI has been divided into seven operating divisions covering the same geographical areas as the seven Bell regional holding companies. Each of the new divisions will be responsible for all aspects of sales, operations, and service within its own territory. The seven new regions will be headed by senior vice-presidents of MCI Telecommunications Corporation, each of whom will serve as the president and chief operating officer of his division. The backgrounds of the presidents are shown in Exhibit 16.4. The new divisions are

1.   The Pacific Division, which is headquartered in San Francisco, covers California, Nevada, and Hawaii.
2.   The West Division, headquartered in Denver, covers a 15-state area stretching from Minnesota to Washington and Alaska in the Northwest to Arizona and New Mexico in the Southwest.
3.   The Southwest Division, headquartered in St. Louis, covers the states of Texas, Missouri, Oklahoma, Kansas, and Arkansas.
4.   The Midwest Division, headquartered in Chicago, covers Illinois, Indiana, Ohio, Michigan, and Wisconsin.
5.   The Southeast Division, headquartered in Atlanta, is responsible for Florida, Georgia, Alabama, Mississippi, Louisiana, Tennessee, Kentucky, North Carolina, and South Carolina.
6.   The Mid-Atlantic Division, headquartered in Washington, D.C., covers Pennsylvania, New Jersey, Maryland, Delaware, Virginia, West Virginia, and the District of Columbia.
7.   The Northeast Division, headquartered in New York, is responsible for New York and the six New England States.

**Service.**   Before 1982, MCI was a single-product supplier—it offered intercity voice telecommunications services. In July 1982, MCI introduced its Omni-Call feature that permitted its dial-up commercial and residential customers to com-

**Exhibit 16.4** Presidents of the Seven Regional Divisions

*Eugene Eidenberg,* president, Pacific Division. Mr. Eidenberg is senior vice-president for regulatory and public policy at MCI Communications Corporation. Prior to joining MCI in November 1982, Eidenberg was director of the Democratic National Committee. He also held a series of government posts during the Carter administration, including deputy under secretary of HEW, secretary to the Cabinet, and assistant to the president for intergovernmental affairs. Eidenberg was a 1981 fellow at the Institute of Politics at Harvard's JFK School of Government. He holds M.A. and Ph.D. degrees from Northwestern University.

*Gerald H. Taylor,* president, West Division. Mr. Taylor, president of MCI Airsignal, joined MCI Communications Corporation in 1969 as the executive assistant to the president. Prior to his appointment as president of Airsignal in 1982, Taylor served in a variety of senior marketing, sales, operations, and management positions with MCI. Taylor holds a B.S. degree in physics from San Francisco State University.

*Francis J. Harkins,* president, Southwest Division. Mr. Harkins is senior vice-president of planning and administration at MCI Telecommunications Corporation. Prior to joining MCI in August 1982, Harkins was executive vice-president of MCI's subsidiary, Western Union International, in charge of special assignments for the president and board of directors. He was formerly a vice-president with North American Phillips and the W. R. Grace Company; group executive and general counsel for ITT's operations in Latin America, and an agent with the Federal Bureau of Investigation. Harkins obtained his law degree from St. Johns College in New York and holds an undergraduate degree from Georgetown University.

*Ronald E. Spears,* president, Midwest Division. Mr. Spears is senior vice-president at Western Union International, a position he assumed in June 1983. He joined MCI in 1979 as a senior manager in the engineering department and became director of network engineering in 1980. In August 1982, he assumed the position of vice-president of operations and engineering at WUI. Prior to joining MCI, he worked at AT&T Longlines. He holds a B.S.E.E. degree from the U.S. Military Academy and an M.A. in public administration from Western Kentucky University.

*Charles M. Skibo,* president, Southeast Division. Mr. Skibo has been vice-president for MCI Telecommunications Corporation since 1982. Previously, he served as MCI's senior vice-president of planning and administration. Prior to joining MCI in 1979, Skibo held senior management positions at Exxon, where he worked for more than 19 years. He holds a B.S. degree from West Virginia University.

*H. Brian Thompson,* president, Mid-Atlantic Division. Mr. Thompson, senior vice-president of corporate development for MCI Communications Corporation, joined MCI in 1981. Since joining the company in 1981, Thompson has guided the developmental work behind MCI's strategy of expanding to offer a full range of telecommunications services. This strategy is exemplified by the acquisition of Western Union International and the creation of the company's time-sensitive delivery system, MCI Mail. Prior to that time, he was president of Subscription Television of America, where he headed the company's entry into the over-the-air pay television industry. He was a senior vice-president of plans and marketing for Resources Sciences Corporation, executive director for the Civilian/Military Institute, and was associated with the consulting firm of McKinsey & Co. for nine years. Thompson holds an M.B.A. degree from Harvard Graduate School of Business Administration and a B.S. degree in chemical engineering from the University of Massachusetts.

*Nathan Kantor,* president, Northeast Division. Mr. Kantor, president of MCI International, was the vice-president of national field operations for MCI. Prior to joining MCI in 1972, Kantor was with Sperry Rand Corporation and an officer in the U.S. Air Force. Kantor holds a B.S. degree in engineering from West Point and an M.S. degree in business management from Florida State University.

Source: *MCI Communicator,* January 1985.

plete all their interstate calls using MCI. By employing Omni-Call, customers could save from 5 percent to 35 percent on every out-of-state call. Since equal access, customers can still save money but the Omni-Call features has been discontinued.

For its business customers, MCI is offering an expanded WATS service and an improved corporate account service. A new TI service was introduced in April 1984 for volume business. Also, MCI offers the MCI Advantage service, which is a small computerized piece of equipment that eliminates the dialing of extra digits for business customers.

Public telephones that allow easy access to the MCI long-distance network are now available in many airports and other high-traffic areas such as hotels, convention centers, and truck stops across the country. Last year, MCI introduced the nation's first public telephone activated by national credit cards. Now, a number of local and regional phone companies are installing their own credit-card-activated phones with the MCI logo prominently displayed. Public phones that do allow travel card holders to access the network are also becoming more common. Currently, more than 1000 such phones are in service throughout the country.

MCI is offering an array of telephone services in the equal-access environment. In an equal-access area, local Bell operating company customers will have two ways to access MCI and other long-distance carriers. The method of accessing a customer's primary long-distance carrier is called Dial 1 or Direct Dial.[6] With Dial 1 service, after choosing a long-distance carrier, a customer may place a long-distance call merely by dialing 1 and the area code and number.

An alternative method of accessing any other long-distance carrier in the area is called 10XXX Dialing.[7] Under this method, even after choosing a long-distance carrier, customers will be able to place calls over other long-distance carriers by dialing five digits, (1, 0, and three other digits) before the area code and phone number. Potential new customers who have rotary dial phones—a market which represents approximately half of the total number of phones in the United States —will for the first time be able to use low-cost MCI service.

In August 1984, MCI began offering its customers a no-fee credit card service to use whenever they are away from home or the office. Previously, credit cards had a subscription fee and could only be used from certain major cities.

In December 1984, MCI took a giant step toward being a full provider of the whole range of telecommunications services with the establishment of DATA-NET, a packet-switched data transmission service. The new service will provide an electronic highway—linking 110 cities—allowing high-volume customers to tie into MCI's data network as though it were their own. The service reduces the need for large users to construct and maintain their own private data networks.

**Marketing.** MCI's prices are competitive. This is one of its competitive advantages. Initially, MCI charged a flat rate per minute. As of July 15, 1983, MCI changed its price structure to be more directly competitive with AT&T's. It now has a higher first-minute charge and lower additional-minute charges.[8] MCI's new pricing structure, which lowered rates, eliminated subscription fees, and provided discounts for volume users, will ensure its competitive position in the transition to full equal access. This innovative pricing, along with such attention-getting and business promotions as free calls on Mother's Day, support MCI's advertising.

MCI has introduced innovative advertising and marketing promotion to the industry. Its target market is the mass market, even though it uses different strategies to reach its residential and commercial prospects. MCI Telecommunications reaches potential new customers through marketing, advertising, direct mailings, and a continuing educational program. Advertisements are usually done via newspapers, business magazines, and television commercials. The commercials featuring Joan Rivers and Merv Griffin were the first in which MCI used celebrity spokespersons.[9]

MCI's business-to-business advertising commercial was one of its biggest and best. Bob Giraldi, director of the production, is also the genius behind many Michael Jackson videos and commercials, as well as the Miller Lite beer series of commercials. Giraldi, who describes MCI's newest commercial as "bigger than most movies and one of the biggest commercials ever made," has also directed commercials for MCI's residential marketing efforts.[10]

In October 1983, MCI negotiated a project with Sears in which customers with Sears charge accounts could have their long-distance calls billed to their Sears accounts. Now, for the first time, Sears is offering in-store sales of Sears long-distance phone service from MCI.

In October 1984, MCI, in conjunction with Procter & Gamble, offered 20 free minutes of long-distance calling to new MCI subscribers. The offer was communicated to prospects via newspaper inserts from October 28 through November 1. Television advertising was also used in many markets to announce the offer.

To help maximize participation in the residential market, MCI entered into an agreement through which American Express markets is services to millions of cardholders and assumes liaison responsibility between the customers and MCI.

Last, General Electric has chosen MCI to provide telecommunications services for GE's new service offering in the emerging market of tenant services for commercial real estate properties. GE defines tenant services as a unique combination of telephone, information processing, office automation, and communications products and services managed by a single source.[11] These products and services are then offered to tenants of multitenant office buildings on a pay-by-use basis.

**Facilities.** When MCI became a serious contender in the telecommunications industry around 1980, its network comprised copper wire leased from the local phone company, microwave radio with an 1800-channel capacity per radio frequency, and a few rudimentary computer switches of limited capacity and sophistication. In 1983, the MCI system incorporated satellites and fiber optics, microwave radio retrofitted to a 5400-channel capacity through single-band technology, and ditigal and analog computer switches.[12] Much of the expansion under way at the alternative long-distance companies today is to reduce their continuing dependence on AT&T. None of them cover all of the United States, so to provide the nationwide access their customers expect, all buy phone lines from AT&T and other carriers at wholesale rates and then resell them to their customers.[13]

MCI's domestic network is the second largest national long-distance network in the world. This network lies at the very center of its business strategy. As MCI has enhanced its capabilities, it has been able to create new services and build the transmission capacity required for the increase in market share that it expects to gain with equal access. Even though its network is not yet the largest, it is the most modern in the world.

Building transmission capacity requires a huge amount of capital. Overall, in fiscal year 1983, MCI expanded its domestic network by approximately one new facility every calendar day, with its capital expansion program reaching an investment rate of $12 million a week. In fiscal year 1984, MCI invested approximately $890 million in its system. In 1985, it planned to invest even more. MCI has already invested approximately $3 billion in its network over the past 14 years and plans to spend an additional $2.5 billion by 1986 to achieve national coverage.[14] In 1986 and 1987, MCI plans to expand its network to handle the volume resulting from equal access. In 1984, MCI spent almost $900 million expanding its communications system, and this year it will invest approximately $1 billion.[15]

Optical fiber, which is the emerging technology for very-high-capacity routes, has almost unlimited capacity. MCI has purchased more than 100,000 miles of optical fiber and leased 4,300 miles of railroad rights-of-way on which to install it.[16]

MCI's first single-mode fiber system was completed between Dominquez Hills and downtown Los Angeles during 1984. In March 1984, MCI put its 229-mile fiber-optic system into service. This system is the world's longest and highest-capacity single-mode fiber-optic system in operation.[17] Single mode is the most advanced fiber-optic technology available.

Satellite is used by MCI to augment its territorial network and to reach remote cities where other means of transmission are not available. MCI is also installing advanced radio technologies—single-sideband and ditigal radio—on its existing microwave systems. Single-sideband radios will boost MCI's current 14,000 circuits to 37,000 circuits per route, capable of carrying voice and data simultaneously. By the end of fiscal 1985, circuit miles will number almost 275 million, an increase of 76 percent over today's capacity. It will soon be a network of more than 27,000 route miles.[18]

**MCI Airsignal**     Paging and cellular technology are also new areas in which MCI has strongly positioned itself. MCI Airsignal has over 103,000 paging and mobile customers.[19] By the end of 1982, MCI Airsignal had applied for cellular franchises in 51 of the nation's top 90 markets. In each market, MCI faces competition on two levels: on the one hand from the local telephone entity, which will be granted a cellular license, and on the other, from the other applicants applying for the non–telephone company franchise. MCI has won a number of cellular franchises.

Cellular technology brings clear transmissions, expanded capacity, a competitive price, and nationwide capacity to car telephone service. As a result of these innovations, the mobile telephone market in the United States is expected to grow from less than 200,000 conventional mobile telephone users in 1984 to more than one million cellular car telephone users by 1990.[20]

Just as cellular technology will actualize the portable telephone concept, so have improvements in paging technology accelerated to the usefulness and flexibility in these devices while simultaneously reducing their cost.

**Services.** MCI Airsignal introduced its newest personal communications service—Express Message Service—in Minneapolis–St. Paul in mid-July 1984. This service combines the ability of MCI Message Service (affiliated with MCI Mail) to alert customers to a call with an answering machine's ability to record, store, and replay messages.

Callers can dial a customer's Express Message number and leave 20-second messages. Express Message Service stores the messages and instantly pages customers to let them know that they have received a message. The device displays telephone numbers of up to four persons trying to reach MCI customers. As customers return their calls, they clear the pager's memory for more numbers.

MCI Airsignal entered two major paging markets in September 1984 with start-up of commercial service in Washington and New York City. Service offerings include tone message, voice message, numeric display message service, and alphanumeric message service, which allows subscribers to view printed messages and numbers on the pager screen.

**Marketing.** Airsignal has recently moved its market penetration westward. In October 1984 it began to offer its paging services in Chicago, and in December 1984 it began to offer service in the Los Angeles area.

MCI Airsignal primarily uses television and print media to advertise. According to its 1983 annual report, MCI has been advertising its new paging services as the "greatest tool for business since telephone."

In 1982, MCI announced an agreement with the Radio Shack division of Tandy Corporation to help develop the consumer paging market. The future is even brighter as paging matures from the traditional "beeper" business to encompass all sorts of electronic message delivery services.

## MCI Digital Information Services Company

MCI Mail, which was introduced in September 1983, is revolutionizing time-sensitive message delivery. Its differential advantage is that it can be used with any electronic communicating device and will deliver a message to anyone, anywhere, electronically or on paper.

MCI Mail is doing exceptionally well. There are over 200,000 subscribers to the service, and MCI expects many more as more people become accustomed to electronic communication, both nationally and internationally.[21] MCI has combined its experience in international and domestic telex, international cablegram, and its innovation in MCI Mail to transmit what has been named MCI World Message Service.

**Services.** Messages can be transmitted within seconds, minutes, or hours depending on the option chosen by customers when they initiate a message. "Instant" delivers a message electronically in seconds for $1. "Four-hour" delivers paper copy to any address in 15 major cities with courier assistance within four hours for $30. "Overnight" delivers paper copy to 20,000 cities in the United States with courier assistance by noon of the following business day for $8. "Next day" delivery is made through the post office.

MCI Mail Link, which was introduced in January 1984, is the industry's first breakthrough in linking organizations previously in compatible electronic mail systems. Messages that once could be sent only internally through a company's electronic mail network will be able to be transmitted externally without great changes to the existing mail system.

With MCI Mail Alert, senders of critical business information can request that their recipients be notified about important mail waiting in their MCI mailbox.

**Marketing.**   MCI Mail has opened a digital post office (DPO) in Honolulu, providing mainland MCI Mail users with four-hour (or less) mail delivery to Hawaii for the first time. Like all of the other MCI Mail DPOs, the new facility in Hawaii uses laser printers to produce high-quality black-and-white printing of letters, characters, and graphic elements—such as logos, letterheads and signatures—on high-quality bond paper.

MCI Mail opened its newest postal center in Miami in October 1984. Residences and businesses within a 35-mile radius of the center can receive MCI mail from anywhere in the continental United States and Hawaii within four hours.

As of January 1, 1985, volume discounts of 10 to 30 percent have been applied to both MCI Letters (U.S. Post Office delivery) and Overnight Letters (guaranteed delivery by noon the next day), when sending the same message to many recipients. Also, subscribers now pay only 45 cents to send an electronic message of up to 500 characters.[22] This represents a 55 percent decrease in the cost of sending a short MCI Mail message.

MCI Mail has begun marketing MCI Mail: ACCESS, a communications software package for IBM and IBM-compatible computers. The package features automatic dialing and sign-on to MCI Mail, as well as the capability to send text files created on personal computers and word processors. The package is available to subscribers through MCI's 800 numbers, business account representatives, MCI Mail agents, and Power Up!, a software catalog.

In order to stimulate customer usage and awareness of the service, MCI Mail conducted a "Letter Perfect Sweepstakes" which offered the winner an all-expense-paid luxury trip to Hawaii or a personal computer with a graphic printer, modem, and five software packages.

**Facilities.**   To support its entry into the data message business, MCI added digital transmission capacity to its existing voice network. Initially, its data system carried 90 megabits. Ultimately, it will handle ten times that volume. This capacity will be used in the provision of such services as digital termination, for which, during 1983, it received authorization in 41 cities, as well as switched data messages.[23]

## MCI International

The $4 billion international voice market is the fastest-growing segment in tele-communications.[24] In worldwide markets, MCI is expanding from telex to international voice. This is a movement toward MCI's goal to become an international communications company. MCI International presently has over 40,000 customers.

**Services.** The extension of direct-dial service overseas opens the way to dramatic expansion for MCI. MCI's purchase of Western Union International from Xerox Corporation on June 23, 1982, gave MCI a valuable understanding of the international marketplace, and an entry into a $4 billion market that it did not serve—a market which is growing at approximately 20 percent a year, faster even than the domestic long-distance market.[25]

MCI International reached another continent for direct-dial telephone service with the addition of agreements for service to Algeria and South Africa. MCI already has direct-dial service to Canada (1983), Belgium, Greece, the German Democratic Republic (East Germany), Argentina, Brazil, and the United Arab Emirates. In early 1985, direct-dial service became available in the United Kingdom.

**Marketing.** MCI's rates are up to 30 percent lower than AT&T's, and include volume discounts. This is one of the strategies that MCI uses to continue to be the most efficient and low-cost supplier of telecommunications services.

## FINANCES

Prior to the divestiture activity, MCI's financial activity in 1983 demonstrated its progress in meeting demand for residential and business services. Revenue increased by 112 percent, from $506.4 million to $1.07 billion. Income from operations grew by 77 percent, from $167 million to $295.1 million. Net income also increased 98 percent, from $86.5 million to $170.8 million.

MCI began to invest more heavily in its own network to reduce its dependence on AT&T. For this reason, annual capital expenditures for network expansion increased from $271.5 million to $623 million. Total investment in plant and equipment grew from $765.3 million to $1.56 billion.

In fiscal year 1984, MCI experienced a period of declining profits in the face of sharply higher access charges. Its revenues for the year increased by 55 percent, from $1.07 billion in 1983 to $1.66 billion in 1984. Net income was $155.7 million, compared with $170.8 million in 1983. MCI's net income did not keep pace with its revenue growth for four reasons: First, the leased-line costs associated with providing universal termination for its customers' calls were exorbitantly high. MCI expects these costs to decline as it continues to expand its network. Second, MCI experienced the first full impact of the higher access fees mandated earlier in 1984 by the Federal Communications Commission. Third, MCI continues to make substantial investments in network expansion to accommodate future growth. Finally, the costs associated with enlarging MCI's customer base through equal-access marketing are high. To help offset these factors, MCI raised prices for certain domestic long-distance service between 1.75 and 5 percent.

Exhibits 16.5 and 16.6 reveal that in 1982 revenue increased by 116 percent, from $234.2 million to $506.4 million. Income from operations increased by 225 percent, from $51.3 million to $167 million. Net income increased phenomenally —309 percent. MCI's expenditures for network expansion increased from $155.7 million to $271.5 million. Also, as an indication of the company's growth in 1982, total investment in plant and equipment increased from $496.3 million to $765.3 million. In light of these increases in network expansion which gave MCI the capacity to handle a larger customer base, its customer base almost tripled. There were 750,000 customers in 1983, compared to 280,000 in 1982.

**Exhibit 16.5** Selected Financial Information (in thousands, except per share amounts)

| Year Ended December 31, | 1984 | 1983 | 1982 | 1981 | 1980 |
|---|---|---|---|---|---|
| **Summary of operations** | | | | | |
| Sales of communications services | $ 1,959,291 | $ 1,521,460 | $  906,596 | $413,379 | $ 205,867 |
| Operating expenses | 1,783,812 | 1,181,888 | 644,525 | 289,254 | 159,616 |
| Income from operations | 175,479 | 339,572 | 262,071 | 124,125 | 46,251 |
| Interest and other expense, net | 124,945[a] | 57,204 | 48,268 | 36,279 | 26,756 |
| Income before extraordinary item | 59,203 | 202,912 | 151,415 | 59,396 | 14,829 |
| Net income | 59,203 | 202,912 | 151,415 | 60,572 | 18,420 |
| **Earnings per common share**[b] | | | | | |
| Primary | | | | | |
| Income before extraordinary item | .25 | .89 | .78 | .30 | .03 |
| Net income | .25 | .89 | .78 | .31 | .06 |
| Assuming full dilution | | | | | |
| Income before extraordinary item | .25 | .88 | .73 | .29 | .03 |
| Net income | .25 | .88 | .73 | .30 | .06 |
| **Balance sheet** | | | | | |
| Total assets | $ 3,893,818 | $ 3,500,080 | $ 1,569,019 | $769,278 | $430,244 |
| Long-term debt | 1,821,138 | 1,697,805 | 603,401 | 408,715 | 220,094 |
| Stockholders' equity | 1,199,121 | 1,119,579 | 605,764 | 201,978 | 143,032 |
| Gross investment in communications system | 3,270,296 | 2,155,112 | 1,406,879 | 647,350 | 451,228 |
| Annual investment in communications system | 1,157,116 | 760,509 | 578,030 | 198,448 | 134,907 |

[a]Includes a provision of $49.8 million to reflect a decline in value of telex-related equipment.
[b]Restated to reflect two-for-one stock splits in August 1983 and September 1982.

*Source:* MCI Communications Corporation 1984 Annual Report.

**Exhibit 16.6** Statement of Operations (in thousands, except per share amounts)

| Year Ended December 31, | 1984 | 1983 | 1982 |
|---|---|---|---|
| **Revenues** | | | |
| Sales of communications services | $ 1,959,291 | $ 1,521,460 | $906,596 |
| **Operating expenses** | | | |
| Local interconnection | 479,658 | 262,012 | 142,972 |
| Facilities leased from other common carriers | 343,257 | 273,663 | 104,438 |
| Communications system engineering, operations and maintenance | 263,276 | 184,942 | 117,420 |
| Sales and marketing | 240,131 | 157,002 | 85,743 |
| Administrative and general | 192,917 | 145,310 | 104,788 |
| Depreciation | 264,573 | 158,959 | 89,164 |
| | 1,783,812 | 1,181,888 | 644,525 |
| **Income from operations** | 175,479 | 339,572 | 262,071 |
| Interest expense | 188,545 | 134,277 | 69,141 |
| Interest (income) | (114,644) | (76,708) | (21,602) |
| Provision for decline in value of telex-related equipment | 49,800 | | |
| Other expense (income), net | 1,244 | (365) | 729 |
| **Income before income taxes** | 50,534 | 282,368 | 213,803 |
| Income tax provision (benefit) | (8,669) | 79,456 | 62,388 |
| **Net income** | $ 59,203 | $ 202,912 | $151,415 |
| Earnings per common share | | | |
| Primary | $.25 | $.89 | $.78 |
| Assuming full dilution | $.25 | $.88 | $.73 |

*Source:* MCI Communications Corporation 1984 Annual Report.

## TELECOMMUNICATIONS INDUSTRY PROFILE

AT&T—the Bell System—had a century-old tradition of service to telephone customers. It was structured to provide end-to-end telecommunications service. AT&T monopolized the telecommunications industry. It provided local service, long-distance service within and between states, and the technology and equipment that helped complete these millions of calls.

But all that has changed. Technology and competition, coupled with new regulatory requirements and the court-ordered breakup of AT&T, created a new telecommunications marketplace in 1984. (See Exhibit 16.7.)

## History

Before 1984, AT&T was composed of American Bell, Advance Mobile Phone Service, Inc., AT&T Long Lines, Western Electric, and Bell Laboratories. AT&T's role in the divestiture was to divest its wholly owned operating compa-

**Exhibit 16.7** Events That Lead to Divestiture

| | |
|---|---|
| 1934 | *Communications Act of 1934.* Established Federal Communications Commission, which replaced the Interstate Commerce Commission as governing body. |

**Principles:**

Prices must be just and reasonable.

Services must be profitable; no cross-subsidization of services.

No discrimination between groups of customers.

Public notices of rate changes required.

| | |
|---|---|
| 1956 | *Consent decree.* AT&T and the U.S. Department of Justice reached agreement on a consent decree involving the Bell System's monopoly status. This agreement, known as the final judgment, spelled out what the various operating companies within the Bell System could and could not do as legal monopolies. The Department of Justice charged that the inclusion of Western Electric in AT&T constituted a violation of Sherman Antitrust Act. Negotiated out of court. |

**Results:**

AT&T kept Western Electric. Western Electric agreed to confine sales to AT&T-type equipment, not other markets.

AT&T agreed to stay in common-carrier communications and "incidental" markets; not to enter deregulated industries; specifically not to enter infant computer industry.

| | |
|---|---|
| 1968 | *Cartefone decision.* Carter Electronics Corporation wanted to connect mobile radio units to telephone network. FCC ruled that customers may use interconnect devices not provided by AT&T so long as they cause no technical harm to the phone company. Created the interconnect industry. |
| 1969 | *MCI decision.* FCC granted MCI permission to construct a St. Louis–Chicago connection to provide long-distance private-line service as an alternative to AT&T. Created specialized common carrier (SCC) industry. |
| 1970 | *Specialized common carrier proceeding.* FCC decision permitted specialized common carriers to operated intercity microwave relay systems for private leased-line telephones. Provided more direct competition with Bell. Required Bell to provide local access/connection. |
| 1974 | *MCI filing of antitrust suit against AT&T in March.* The suit was filed because AT&T refused to provide MCI with some of the local interconnections needed to connect customers with MCI. |
| 1974 | *U.S. Department of Justice filing of antitrust suit against AT&T.* The suit charged that AT&T had attempted to restrict and eliminate competition from other common carriers and manufacturers and suppliers of telecommunications. Settled in 1982. |
| 1978 | *ENFIA (exchange network facilities for interstate access).* Negotiations between Bell and MCI (later other common carriers, or OCCs) to work out the mechanics of and financial arrangements for interconnection with local exchange networks. After negotiations broke down, FCC ruled that all local telephone companies must provide access and interconnections for all authorized OCC services. |
| 1978 | *Execunet decision.* FCC ruled that all OCCs are authorized to participate in fair competition for intercity long-distance market. Expanded OCC horizons beyond private-line services to include shared services. |
| 1980 | *AT&T loss of MCI antitrust suit.* First antitrust suit AT&T lost in court. MCI was awarded $1.8 billion in damages. |
| 1980 | *FCC decision on computer inquiry II.* Under terms of this decision, AT&T may market computer equipment only through a fully separate subsidiary. |

(continued)

**Exhibit 16.7** (continued)

| | |
|---|---|
| 1982 | *Consent decree.* Final agreement on a consent decree was reached in the U.S. government antitrust case against AT&T. This agreement became known as the modification of final judgment because it replaced the final judgment entered in 1956. |

**Results:**

Completed the establishment of fully separate subsidiary (AT&T Information Systems).

Divested AT&T of its local operating companies, effective January 1, 1984. The Bell name was assigned to local operating companies, except for Bell Laboratories and foreign subsidiaries of AT&T. The 22 divested Bell telephone companies were grouped into seven new regional companies known as regional holding companies (RHCs).[26]

nies, retain its Long Lines, Western Electric, and Bell Labs, and acquire past ownership in Cicinnati Bell. AT&T can also manufacture and sell customer premise equipment. However, it cannot engage in electronic publishing until 1991.

The role of the Bell operating companies is to offer cost-based equal access to all long-distance carriers. They are restricted to intra-LATA service, yellow-page service, customer premise equipment sale (not manufacture), and regulated monopoly services. Local access and transport area boundaries (LATAs) define the areas within which Bell operating companies provide service. There are 165 LATAs. Most states are composed of several LATAs. A few LATAs cross state lines, and some of the less populated states constitute a single LATA. Local companies provide service within the LATAs—intra-LATA. AT&T, MCI, and other long-distance carriers now transport information between the LATAs—inter-LATA.

Also, as a result of the divestiture, MCI and other long-distance carriers are allowed equal access where the Bell operating companies offer connections of equal quality to all long-distance carriers. This will allow customers improved phone quality. Currently, AT&T is provided with superior interconnections. Bell will gradually offer equal access to long-distance carriers over the next three years. On September 1, 1984, Bell operating companies began providing equal access. On September 1, 1985, one-third of access line was available, and on September 1, 1986, equal access was available through every end office. (Parts of Mobile and Atlanta were the first areas in MCI's Southeast region to receive equal access in September 1984.)

Equal access essentially means that many users will find it equally as easy to access AT&T Communications or its competitors. Today, AT&T is accessed by dialing 1, the area code, and number that a user is calling. Now, users can access all long-distance companies in precisely the same way. Long-distance carriers will have to pay the Bell operating companies for the extra services those Bell operating companies will provide, such as administering the programs, presenting them with billing information, perhaps doing their billing. On the other hand, the long-distance carriers will pick up customers with rotary phones and those who dislike dialing a lot of extra digits for long-distance calls.

AT&T's competitors spent billions of dollars to increase capacity so that they can handle the increased demand for their services. They are buying heavy-capacity fiber optics. Therefore, railroads are viewing the fiber optics along their roadbed as a great new revenue opportunity.[27]

## Marketing Practices and Market Structure

A lot of marketing activity has gone on in the telecommunications industry in the last several years. Because the divestiture has required local phone companies to ask customers to choose the long-distance carrier they prefer to use, the long-distance carriers have been fighting to get customers to choose their service.

In the 12 years that they have competed with AT&T for the long-distance market, the long-distance carriers—which include MCI Communications, GTE Sprint, and ITT—managed to capture only about 8 percent of the $40 billion market for long-distance services.[28] This performance was due primarily to the fact that customers detested dialing the access number and personal code in addition to the area code and numbers that they were trying to reach. But with equal access, these companies have done much better. Just two of them—GTE Sprint Communications Corporation and MCI Communications Corporation—"are going to take upwards of a third of the market from AT&T in the next several years," predicts Lee L. Franklin, marketing vice-president at Sprint.[29]

In the end, there will probably be few major national long-distance companies—AT&T, MCI, Sprint, Allnet, and maybe a few others. Their services will be similar, but they will try to beat AT&T on certain features, such as price. Second, there will be some regional companies. Most will be resellers, buying circuits from the nationals, including AT&T, and from specialty microwave, satellite, and fiber-optics suppliers. They will offer calling from several cities in a given state or region of the country. Third, there will be the locals, particularly in smaller towns the bigger companies don't want to serve. They can't match the general services of the larger ones, but they can find markets where their special services can be best and/or cheapest. Therefore, entry is relatively easy, but only the fittest survive.

The reason for all of the marketing activity is the fact that the long-distance carriers want customers to choose them the first time around as their primary long-distance carrier. Some local phone companies route all unspecified long-distance calls via AT&T.

The long-distance carriers target sales efforts at each community as its telephone system is converted. Also, consumers and businesses receive enormous amounts of direct mailings, telephone solicitations, and door-to-door salespersons. The carriers have increased their advertising and promotion expenditures tremendously. Other industry practices consist of price discounting, free calls, free gifts, and free installation of phone lines.

## Pricing

There have been a lot of price wars within the telecommunications industry in recent years. Prior to 1984, AT&T claimed that MCI and its other competitors did not pay enough to cover its operating companies for their access. AT&T used its power to set rates for its monopoly services in order to impede competition in the telecommunications industry.

The 1982 consent decree which divested AT&T of its 22 local operating companies required the divested companies to provide the same quality of access to all long-distance carriers. Since alternative carriers have inferior connections to local phone companies, the FCC ruled in January 1984 that the alternative carriers have to pay only 45 percent of what AT&T pays for each minute they are connected to a local network (until they receive access equal in function and quality to AT&T's).[30]

AT&T isn't making money on all parts of its business; for example, in its "Reach Out America" program, customers are charged 16.7 cents a minute, but AT&T pays 16.8 cents to the local phone companies per minute of access, plus 10 cents a call for billing, and its own operating expenses are over and above that.[31] AT&T's competitors will be paying more and more for access to the local companies (as their access quality becomes as good as AT&T's) while AT&T's access charges will drop, allowing AT&T and forcing MCI to lower rates. This means that MCI will have to raise its rates in line with AT&T's and slash promotional outlays.

## Services

Many products and features have been introduced within the past five years. MCI and GTE Sprint began offering accounting codes, which are two-digit codes dialed at the end of the long-distance number called. These codes allow businesses to track the department within the company that placed the call.

As a result of the divestiture, there are equal-access "products" such as primary carriers, alternate carriers, and default carriers. Primary carriers pertain to prescription "dial 1" access where customers are asked to choose a primary carrier through which they can place their long-distance calls. The customer dials "1 plus" to place long-distance calls. Customers may also select a second long-distance company or alternate carrier. The alternative carrier is accessed by dialing 1 plus 0XX. (0XX is the access code assigned to each long-distance carrier. MCI's access code is 1022.) If a customer does not preselect a long-distance carrier, his or her long-distance calls will be carried by "default." Each Bell operating company may give default traffic to the long-distance carrier of its choice. Thus far, Northwestern Bell has agreed to give a percentage of default traffic to MCI.[32]

Recently introduced telecommunications services—including cellular mobile radio telephone, videotex, and video conferences—promise to widen the range of services offered by traditional POTS (plain old telephone service) providers and may usher in a new era of growth for the industry.[33] These new services should pay off for the telecommunications companies in the long run. Construction expenditures for these new services should also pay off for the telephone equipment manufacturers. Because of the increasing competition in this industry, new product development is critical.

Specialized common carriers—MCI Communications Corporation, U.S. Transmission Systems, Inc., and Western Union—have built networks to offer both public and private long-distance service. The revenues of all the long-distance firms reached approximately $2.6 billion in 1984.

Traditional common carriers invested $21.4 billion in new plant and equipment in 1984, a 3 percent increase over the 1983 level. These capital expenditures were made to increase the capacity of the existing network. The domestic telegraph carrier and the international record carriers (IRCs) invested more than $100 million in plant expansion in 1974.

## Competition

The telecommunication industry leaders are AT&T, MCI Telecommunications, GTE Sprint, and Allnet. In 1983, AT&T held approximately 92 percent of the long-distance market, MCI held 3 percent, Sprint held 2.1 percent, Allnet held 0.5 percent, and ITT held 0.48 percent.[34] With equal access, AT&T is losing market share because most customers choose lower-priced vendors as their primary carrier. And so, in those areas where equal access has come, AT&T's market share has dropped quickly, usually to about 75 percent.[35] The long-distance competitors and the service they provide are listed in Exhibit 16.8.

Since the divestiture, MCI is also competing with the local Bell operating companies for intra-LATA service. The seven regional holding companies that form the basis for the local Bell companies are Ameritech, Bell Atlantic, Bell South, Nynex, Pacific Telesis, S.W. Bell, and U.S. West. Most of the regional holding companies are engaged in the furnishing of exchange telecommunications, exchange access service, mobile communications service, directory advertising and publishing, and telecommunications equipment.[36]

On the other hand, the local Bell operating companies provide access to all long-distance carriers. Therefore, all long-distance carriers are customers of the local Bell operating companies. The discount carriers are finding some allies in the regional Bell companies. Nynex Corporation has set up a separate marketing organization just to service the long-distance carriers. Because the increased competition should result in more long-distance traffic and because the local company gets a cut on each long-distance call, Nynex "will share in the competitive stimulation of traffic," says Leo J. Berard, its director for carrier services.[37]

AT&T has had to become more marketing-oriented because of the increased competition afforded by the divestiture. AT&T's recent competitive marketing practices included a multimillion-dollar campaign featuring actor Cliff Robertson in heavily aired commercials that remind viewers that only AT&T offers operator services. AT&T also has an "Opportunity Calling" campaign that allows its customers to win numerous gifts, depending on call volume. Presently, AT&T's "Reach Out America" promotion is offering night and weekend service below cost, which is squeezing dry a market vital to MCI. Also, AT&T will be lowering its rates in the near future. AT&T's revenues, profits, resources (networks, transmission capacity), and established reputation have enabled it to remain successful.

**Exhibit 16.8** Competition at a Glance

| Question | AT&T (DDD) | MCI (Execunet) | GTE (Sprint) | ITT (longer distance) | WU (Metrofone) |
|---|---|---|---|---|---|
| Installation/ start-up fees | None | None | None | None | None |
| Monthly svc. fees | None | None | None | None | $5 (optional) |
| Minimum usage | None | None | $5 | Niteline—$16 Others—none | $10 (optional) $40 (optional) |
| Billing increment minimum | 60 sec 60 sec | 60 sec 60 sec | 60 sec 60 sec | 60 sec 60 sec | 60 sec 60 sec |
| # orig. cities | All U.S. cities | 369 | 277 | 143 | 144 |
| # term. cities on—net | All U.S. cities | 369 | 277 | 149 | 300 |
| Universal term. | Yes | Yes | Yes | Yes (from 42 cities) | Yes |
| Auth. codes | N/A | 1–5/no chg. 6–50/$5/code | 1/no chg. $2/add'l code | $5/code (res.) $10/1st code (bus.) $5/add'l code (bus.) | Regional $5/code National $8/code |
| Account. codes | N/A | $5/99 | Yes Rates N/A | N/A | $15/99 |
| Mag tape | Yes Rates N/A | $50/tape $100/setup | Yes Rates N/A | $50/tape/mo. setup $100/setup | N/A |
| Speed #s | N/A | $5/ea. | Yes Rates N/A | N/A | $4/ten no. grp. $10 setup |
| Auto dialers | N/A | "ADVANTAGE" | "EDGE" | "Longer Distance Dialer" | Yes |
| Corp. billing arrangements | N/A | Yes | Yes | N/A | Yes |
| Inbound service | Yes | N/A | Yes $15/code/mo. $5 install. fee | N/A | Yes $25/mo. |
| Special features | (see company description) | Travel svc. Vol. discounts Internat'l calls Directory assist. | Travel svc. Vol. discounts | Travel svc. | Travel svc. Service restriction Vol. discounts |

GTE Sprint has completely changed its dial-up service in order to make itself look more like AT&T. There is no longer a monthly service fee or start-up fee; all customers can now call 24 hours a day; there is a higher first-minute and lower additional-minute rate; there are automatic volume discounts cut in at $25, $75, and $200 per month (all discounts are retroactive to the first call). In addition, Sprint offers enhanced features such as accounting codes and speed dialing which have monthly fees, but are free if monthly volume exceeds a fixed amount ($200 or $300 depending on the feature).[38] GTE Sprint's newly restructured and therefore more competitive services have contributed to its success.

Most of the companies in the industry are price followers—they follow AT&T's lead. However, since the other discount carriers are gaining more equal access, their access charges will be more while AT&T's will be less. This means that if and when AT&T lowers it rates, thereby forcing its competitors to lower theirs, the other long-distance carriers can begin to lose money. Thus far, price has been the primary marketing tool used by long-distance carriers.

**Operating Conditions**

In order to operate in this industry, long-distance carriers need capacity to handle their long-distance calls. Long-distance companies use optical-fiber cable, microwave transmitters, circuits of satellite capacity, and terminals to route calls from their network to the networks of the local Bell operating companies. Some use a combination of microwave, satellite, and optical-fiber systems to transmit calls. Most companies are moving toward optical-fiber systems which shoot calls at the speed of light through thin, flexible glass strands and become more economical with more traffic. Every railroad in the country is eyeing fiber optics along their roadbed as a great new revenue opportunity. Few want to be in the retail long-distance business. Most seem happy to stay as suppliers.

Equipment makers are also suppliers for this industry, and the divestiture opened up the equipment market. In 1984, AT&T suggested that it may lose equipment sales to the regional holding companies. Most of the regional holding companies announced alternative suppliers to Western Electric for all or part of their requirements.

MCI does not manufacture the equipment it uses. The company has learned from the experience of others that an in-house manufacturer tends to restrain rather than advance the pace of technology. As a concern wholly immersed in a capital-intensive industry, MCI has invested its capital in such a way as to encourage equipment manufacturers not only to enter the common-carrier supply market, but also to carve their way into that market through innovation. This means that MCI pays less for the equipment that it incorporates into its network. This will help MCI achieve, on an incremental basis, a one-for-one relationship between each dollar that it invests in its system and each additional dollar of revenue it garners.

**Industry Outlook**

Revenues for the domestic telephone and telegraph service companies in 1985, measured in constant 1972 dollars, exceeded those of 1984 by 10.8 percent. Over the next five years, revenues are expected to increase at an annual rate of 8 percent. Additionally, international service, the single fastest-growing component of telecommunications, is compounding at an annual rate of over 20 percent. International Telephone and Telegraph service revenues were up 14.3 percent from 1984. Over the next five years, international service revenues will increase by an average of 15 percent annually.

Paging is on the verge of substantial growth as the devices offer their users more information stored, retained, and retrieved. Portable telephoning through cellular technology is another service whose time has come. All of the 90 largest cities in this country should have cellular mobile radios by 1990. This industry is expected to generate more than $3 billion annually in service revenues by 1990.

Data transmission, for computer-to-computer or electronic-mail applications, is also a clearly lucrative industry. Because of the smallness of its base, growth in this market sector will initially appear phenomenal; and, over time, it actually will be. The foundations for this growth are embedded in the transmitting capability of word processors and personal computers. The telephone companies, the U.S. Postal Service, satellite companies, computer firms, specialized and value-added carriers, facsimile companies, and data processing companies will all be using electronic mail.

## NOTES

1. MCI Communications Corporation Annual Report, 1981, p. 12.
2. *Dun's Business Ratings 1984,* p. 1495.
3. Report of the 1984 Meeting of Stockholders and Three Months Ended June 30, p. 7.
4. Ibid., p. 8.
5. Frank Allen and James A. White, "MCI to Cut Its Long-Distance Phone Rates to Keep Pace with AT&T's Proposed Cuts," *Wall Street Journal,* October 6, 1983, p. 25.
6. "Charge It—On Visa or Mastercard . . . or Use AMEX Expressphone," *MCI Communicator,* January 1985, p. 2.
7. Ibid.
8. "MCI Joins GE in Business Venture," *MCI Communicator,* November 1984, p. 1.
9. MCI Communications Corporation Annual Report, 1983, p. 5.
10. "Why AT&T Will Lose More Long-Distance Business," *Business Week,* February 13, 1984, pp. 102–106.
11. Ibid.
12. MCI Communications Corporation Annual Report, 1984, p. 5.
13. Virginia Inman, "Long-Distance War—MCI Races the Clock, Bets Millions of Dollars in Phone Competition," *Wall Street Journal,* June 14, 1983, pp. 1–14.
14. Ibid.
15. MCI Communications Corporation Annual Report, 1984, p. 10.
16. *Dun's Business Rankings,* p. 1567.
17. "Telecommunications Services and Equipment," *Standard and Poor's Industry Survey,* February 16, 1984, p. T.13–T.20.
18. MCI Communications Corporation *Annual Report,* 1983, p. 5.
19. *MCI Communicator,* January 1985, p. 2.
20. Report of the 1984 Meeting of Stockholders and Three Months Ended June 30, p. 13.
21. "Telephone and Telegraph Services: The Outlook," *U.S. Industrial Outlook,* January 1985, p. 3.1–31.8.
22. Ibid.
23. "Lights, Camera, Action! On Wall Street," *MCI Communicator,* June 1983, p. 4.
24. "The Marketing Blitz Begins," *Teleconnect,* March 1984, pp. 33a–38a.
25. "Why AT&T Will Lose More Long-Distance Business," *Business Week,* February 13, 1984, p. 102.
26. "FCC to Delay Access Charges on Some Phones," *Wall Street Journal,* January 20, 1984.

27. "FCC Chief Favors a #4 Access Fee," *The Atlanta Journal and Constitution,* March 1, 1984.
28. "Telecommunications Industry," *Value Line,* January 25, 1985, p. 750.
29. U.S. West-Northwestern Bell, pamphlet, 1984, pp. 3–5.
30. *Standard and Poor's Industry Surveys,* January 1985, pp. T.10–T.30.
31. "Why AT&T Will Lose More Long-Distance Business," p. 102.
32. "Telecommunications Industry," p. 751.
33. Ibid.
34. "Why AT&T Will Lose More Long-Distance Business," p. 106.
35. "The Marketing Blitz Begins," p. 36a.
36. MCI Communications Corporation Annual Report, 1983, p. 10.
37. MCI Communications Corporation Annual Report, 1984, p. 12.
38. Standard and Poor's Corporation, *The Outlook,* March 27, 1985.

# 17 Tandy, Inc.

Sexton Adams
North Texas State University
Adelaide Griffin
Texas Woman's University

The Tandy Corporation, which controls the largest number of retail electronics outlets in the world and produces over $2.4 billion in sales, was, as of 1984, "the world's leading distributor of electronic technology to the individual."[1] The span of products sold through the Tandy system is almost overwhelming, ranging from sophisticated computer and telecommunicative systems at one extreme to diodes and transistors at the other. The incredible size Tandy has achieved becomes that much more amazing when one considers its humble beginnings only a short time ago.

As with any organization that has experienced extraordinary early growth, the environmental forces facing the firm and the resulting choices made in response to those forces require constant review, and Tandy is no exception. Tandy presently faces many challenges in many new markets. How these challenges are dealt with will determine whether Tandy can maintain its past growth rate and remain a "star" or simply become another company, that had been.

**HISTORY**   Since 1960 the Radio Shack chain had grown from a small, money-losing, Boston-based company to an electronics powerhouse whose after-tax income rivals those of the country's largest retailers. The man who oversaw much of that transformation was Charles Tandy, a Harvard Business School dropout who converted common sense, salesmanship, and employee motivation into a spectacular business success.

Tandy had practice at turning local operations into national ones. During the 1950s he had turned his family's small leathercraft business, Tandycrafts, Inc., into a national chain. He then sold Tandycrafts to a leather and sportswear company, but shortly afterwards reacquired it, along with the leather and sportswear firm, in a proxy fight.

In 1960, Tandy bought an option of 51 percent of Radio Shack stock. He paid $5000 cash and took out a $300,000 loan for the option, which allowed him to purchase the stock at book value. Book value, as the auditors later determined, was a negative $1.5 million. The loan was later converted to stock, and Charles

This case was prepared by Paul Trobaugh, Greg Dufour, Michele Little, Alex Blair, Sally Dehaney, and Alan Moore under the supervision of Professor Sexton Adams, North Texas State University, and Professor Adelaide Griffin, Texas Woman's University.

Tandy was left with control of Radio Shack on a personal investment of only $5000.

Some would say that the purchase of a losing proposition at any price is not a bargain. There was little doubt that Radio Shack was a losing proposition. In addition to its huge debts, the chain had posted a $4.0 million loss the year before Tandy took control. Tandy, however, felt that the firm, which at the time was selling electronic equipment to ham operators and other electronics buffs, would complement his recent acquisition of the Electronic Crafts Company of Fort Worth. In addition, Tandy was attracted by the chain's $9.0 million annual sales and by the high quality of its personnel, a characteristic that he considered essential for growth in the electronics area.

Charles Tandy set out to prove his doubters wrong with a vengeance. The first order of business was to reduce the ailing firm's accounts receivable balance. Radio Shack had a policy of selling on a no-money-down, two-years-to-pay basis which had resulted in a large number of bad debts. Tandy quickly eliminated this problem by hiring a legal team to go after Radio Shack's debtors.

Also of concern to Tandy was the excessive number of products offered and high inventory levels. Tandy reduced inventory and whittled the product lines down from over 25,000 to just 2,500 using aggressive direct-mail advertising campaigns and sidewalk sales. Products that had a low turnover were cut, as well as those that generated anything less than a 50 percent gross profit margin. Radio Shack was eventually left with a relatively small group of diverse but highly profitable products.

Tandy also decided to eliminate brand-name items, realizing that larger profits could be made by marketing private-label merchandise. He was particularly successful in negotiations with Japanese manufacturers, who at that time were actively seeking an opening into American markets.

Tandy felt that the company's overhead costs should be spread out over as many stores as possible. That belief led to the rapid expansion of Radio Shack's retail outlets. In less than ten years the company was opening new stores at the rate of one a day. By 1969 the firm was ready to begin producing its own goods, and the first of 26 manufacturing plants was built.

But the development of Radio Shack was not Tandy's only concern during the sixties. The company acquired, developed, and eventually spun off Color Tile, Inc., and Stafford Lowden, Inc., a printing firm. Tandycrafts and Tandy Brands were also spun off. The Radio Shack division, however, remained, and became one of the world's leading distributors of technology to the individual consumer.

The firm was more than ready for the citizens band (CB) radio boom of the mid-1970s. "As consumers stampeded to get the chance to say 'breaker one nine', Tandy saw its net income rise from $26.8 million in 1975 to $69 million in 1977, a 157% increase."[2] But CBs proved to be a passing fad and "Tandy had to scramble in 1977 to switch from its heavy commitment to CB manufacturing."[3]

In 1977 the firm began developing its first home computer. Tandy was among the first companies to enter that market, and the move was to provide much of the firm's growth in the early part of the eighties.

**MANAGE-
MENT**

Tandy had an extremely young management team who relied, for the most part, on Charles Tandy's tried-and-true management techniques. In 1983 the average age of the company's vice-presidents was 48, and more than two-thirds had spent 15 years or more with Tandy.

**Charles Tandy**

Charles Tandy had been described as the founder, architect, and driving force behind the corporation that bore his name.[4] Tandy was still a strong influence at Tandy more than five years after his death. According to one source, "even today, Radio Shack executives characterize their performance by saying, 'Charles Tandy would have been proud of what we've done.' "[5]

Tandy's rise to the top closely paralleled that of his company. "He had no hobbies, no children," said one Tandy executive, "He ate, drank and slept business, from dawn until as late as anyone was willing to talk about his business with him." Executives described him as "larger than life . . . throwing off boundless energy, laughing into his ever-busy phone, while waving a 30-cent cigar with his free hand. . . ."[6]

Tandy, in his own unique style "set the rules and pattern successors have carried on since he died. . . ." Among his favorite Tandyisms were, "You can't sell from an empty wagon" (a conviction that led the firm to stock high levels of inventory in its retail outlets); "Who wants dividends when they can have capital gains?" (thus the firm never paid dividends, using all earnings for growth); and "If you want to catch a mouse, you have to make a noise like a cheese" (the philosophy that justified an exceptionally large advertising budget). He also emphasized gross profit: "Tandy never entered a market or sold a product without a 50% gross margin."[7]

Vertical integration was another important part of Tandy's management philosophy. Everything from production to distribution to retailing to advertising was kept in-house whenever possible. By 1982, one observer was moved to remark, "No retailer—not even Sears—has that kind of vertical integration."[8]

Charles Tandy's real genius was in motivation. Store managers were offered large bonuses and profit sharing plans based on their store's performance. Former chairman Phil North recounted, "Charles would call the employees into a room when it was time to hand out the bonus checks. He wouldn't let them out until they bought Tandy stock."[9] He was so successful at convincing employees to invest into the company that today nearly 25 percent of Tandy's stock is estimated to be owned by employees.

Charles Tandy's fatal heart attack could hardly be said to mark the end of an era at the Tandy Corporation. "I miss him," says one executive, "but the company won't, because he taught enough people to do it right."[10] Another observer agrees: "Tandy's personal influence on the development of the corporation cannot be understated. He developed a top management team that understood and appreciated his business philosophy."[11]

Journalist Harold Seneker described Tandy's death: "Charles D. Tandy, 60, lay down for a nap one Saturday afternoon in November and never got up. He couldn't have timed his passing much better if he had planned it." The firm's directors and top officers were in Fort Worth for a stockholders' meeting, and by the time the stock market opened on Monday they had decided on their course of action, business as usual, and on Charles Tandy's successor, Phil North.[12]

## Phil North

Phil North was named president and chairman of Tandy when his longtime friend and business associate, Charles Tandy, passed away. As a young man, North had been a reporter on his family's newspaper, the *Fort Worth Star Telegram.* During World War II he served as General Douglas McArthur's personal press secretary. In 1964 Tandy convinced him to invest $100,000 in his firm, and in 1966 North became a member of Tandy's board of directors.

North was less than delighted by the prospect of taking control of the firm. "I'd rather be perfecting my duplicate bridge or seeing friends around the world," he said. He agreed to accept the position only "to provide a smooth transition of management for an interim period," saying that it was "one of the last things I can do for Charles, and by God, I'm going to do it."[13]

North, who described himself as "the company philosopher," was described by others as "Charles Tandy's alter ego." He was determined to carry on the Tandy philosophy, saying, "We will achieve the goals Charles set."[14]

As soon as practical, North relinquished the presidency to John Roach, and in 1982 Roach also took over as chairman of the board. Phil North returned to his position as a director and, presumably, to his bridge.

## John Roach

John Roach, chairman and CEO, took charge of Tandy Corp. at the age of 43. Roach was born and raised in Texas, as were the majority of Tandy's executives, and had received his M.B.A. from Fort Worth's Texas Christian University. Roach came to Tandy in 1967 as a data processing specialist and embarked on what was to become his pet project, the development of a home computer. Ten years later, after his rapid rise within the firm, his project was complete. One day in early 1977 Charles Tandy came down to his office to see it and was hooked. The computer was a resounding success and Roach's future with the company assured.

In spite of his youth, Roach was awarded the 1982 Chief Executive of the Year Award by *Financial World.* Roach's management philosophy smacks of Tandy's: "We are continuing to build Tandy's business on the strong fundamentals that have yielded extraordinary operating results for a retailer in one of the most competitive segments of the retail industry. Our basic philosophies of private label merchandising, strong promotion . . . convenient locations, vertical integration and the institutionalization of individual entrepreneurship truly make Tandy and Radio Shack unique."[15]

## The Executive Vice-Presidents

Roach's two primary executives in the Radio Shack division are Bernard Appel, executive vice-president for marketing, and Robert Keto, executive vice-president for operations (see Exhibit 17.1). Appel, who had been with Tandy for 24 years, was also strongly committed to the Tandy philosophy. As Appel puts it, "Charles Tandy was a genius."[16] Appel's approach, like Tandy's, was that "our own product line, sold through our own distribution system via our own marketing plan . . . will enable us to remain the Number One retailer of electronics to the world."[17] Robert Keto added, "Providing our customers with products they want at a convenient location and then giving them the after-the-sale service they have come to expect, is why Radio Shack continues to be the leader in consumer electronics." Keto was 42 years old in 1983 and had been with Radio Shack for 19 years.[18]

## MARKETING

The Tandy marketing effort was a reflection of the size and diversity of the company as a whole. The marketing effort cannot be discussed in terms of stores alone, because to do so would drastically oversimplify the nature of the organization. As a result this section is subdivided into two sections, Internal and External. Each of these is in turn further subdivided into Stores and Products. In this way the major internal operations and external forces affecting those operations are singled out for more thorough analysis.

### Internal

**Store Operations**  John Roach described the Tandy store concept better than anyone else when he said, "Tandy is a distribution system for the products of technology. Sometimes we are innovators, sometimes not, but we do have the capability to move a lot of products."[19] As of 1983 the Tandy distribution system was comprised of more than 6400 individual stores.

Of these 6400 stores approximately 4300 are corporate owned and managed, and some 2000 are privately franchised. In fiscal 1983 Tandy opened the five hundredth full-service computer center worldwide. More than 400 of these are in the United States. In addition to the stand-alone computer centers, more than 775 Radio Shack stores have computer departments. Six hundred of these are in the United States. Through expansion of both stand-alone computer centers and computer departments within Radio Shack stores, Tandy anticipated having more than 1400 computer centers and computer departments by the end of 1984. For many retail organizations, this number of stores would be considered unmanageable. However, Tandy had always considered a large number of stores crucial to their strategy of ensuring distribution.

Although generally lost in the intense interest in computers, Tandy has always been primarily a full-line electronics retailer. As Exhibit 17.2 illustrates, the lines that Tandy stores have carried range from computers to diodes and almost everything in between. Again, reviewing Exhibit 17.2, significant trends appear in these data. The first, and most notable, is that computers and computer-related sales were steadily becoming a much larger and more substantial part of the business. Along with this, areas of historical strength (such as stereos and CBs)

**Exhibit 17.1** Tandy Corporation Organization Chart

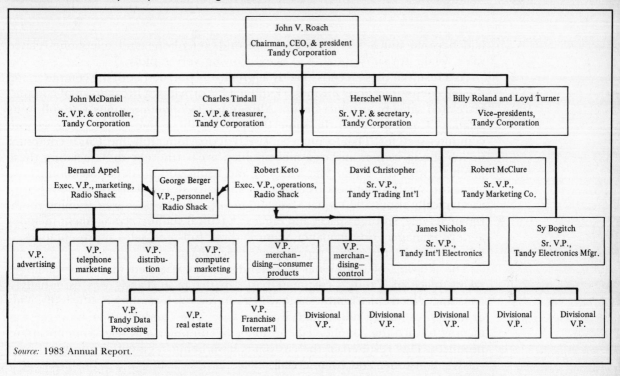

*Source:* 1983 Annual Report.

**Exhibit 17.2** Worldwide Warehouse Shipments (unaudited)

| | Year Ended June 30, | | | | |
| --- | --- | --- | --- | --- | --- |
| **Class of Products** | **1983** | **1982** | **1981** | **1980** | **1979** |
| Radios, phonographs, and televisions | **8.6%** | 9.4% | 11.6% | 12.1% | 13.3% |
| Citizens band radios, walkie-talkies, scanners, and public address systems | **4.9** | 6.0 | 6.8 | 9.3 | 13.2 |
| Audio equipment, tape recorders, and related accessories | **18.2** | 21.5 | 25.4 | 29.5 | 33.8 |
| Electronic parts, batteries, test equipment, and related items | **13.2** | 13.9 | 14.5 | 15.8 | 16.4 |
| Toys, antennas, security devices, timers, and calculators | **12.5** | 12.0 | 14.1 | 12.6 | 10.3 |
| Telephones and intercoms | **8.0** | 6.5 | 5.8 | 5.6 | 3.5 |
| Microcomputers, software, and peripheral equipment | **34.6** | 30.7 | 21.8 | 15.1 | 9.5 |
| | **100.0%** | 100.0% | 100.0% | 100.0% | 100.0% |

*Source:* 1983 Annual Report.

had become much less significant. Second, telephone and telephone-related sales, while not substantial, had been growing very rapidly.

As a result of these trends, Tandy aggressively pursued both the computer and the telecommunications business. Exhibit 17.3 provides a breakdown of computer-related sales by product group. Although telecommunications was still in its infancy, Tandy pursued the same formula for these lines of business as with computer systems. That formula consisted of providing full-line Tandy computer or telephone centers in large metropolitan areas (thereby disassociating these products with the Radio Shack name) and using add-on departments in those areas too small to support freestanding specialty stores. The freestanding store was typically about 3000 square feet and incorporated a sales area, training room, repair service, storage space, and offices. A typical staffing arrangement includes a store manager, one manager trainee, three full-time sales representatives, a full-time instructor, and a repair service technician.

The altering of traditional merchandise lines was tied directly to changes taking place in Tandy's customer base. In the past, Tandy was essentially a consumer electronics hobby shop, which catered to electronics hobby buffs. This group represented a substantial customer base. The Tandy of 1984, however, was moving toward the commercial consumer of computer and telecommunications products. This resulted in the customer base being segmented into two broad classes, consumer and commercial.

Tandy experienced problems with this shift in customer groups stemming from its carefully developed image as an electronics hobby shop. Commercial customers tended to view Radio Shack equipment as more appropriate to the home than the office. For this reason new computer and telecommunications products were marketed under the brand name of Tandy rather than Radio Shack. In addition, freestanding computer and telephone stores carried the name Tandy rather than Radio Shack.

One of Tandy's great strengths had been its ability to hold customers through

**Exhibit 17.3** Computer-related Sales (unaudited)

|  | Year Ended June 30, | | |
|---|---|---|---|
|  | 1983 | 1982 | 1981 |
| Model I/III/4 | 28.1% | 27.2% | 30.5% |
| Model II/12/16 | 21.4 | 25.7 | 25.3 |
| Color computers | 9.8 | 7.2 | 3.3 |
| Portable/pocket computers | 3.1 | 2.5 | 2.7 |
| Printers | 16.5 | 16.7 | 17.5 |
| Software | 9.2 | 8.5 | 7.5 |
| Other | 11.9 | 12.2 | 13.2 |
|  | 100.0% | 100.0% | 100.0% |

*Source:* 1983 Annual Report.

heavy targeted advertising. At the core of the advertising program was the direct-mail catalog. Each month Radio Shack sent a 24-page pamphlet (32-page in November and 48-page in December) to more than 25 million previous customers. The mailing list used for these mailings had been assembled over many years at checkout counters in Radio Shack stores all over the United States. The objective of the catalogs was that the "complex nature of the electronic equipment and gadgetry sold through the Radio Shack stores is distilled and presented in an easy-to-understand form."[20] This philosophy was apparent in the manner that computers were marketed through the catalog. The catalogs stressed a computer for every walk of life, for every use, whether it be a computer for the home or business. This was done in a style that stressed plain English and de-emphasized technical descriptions. The catalogs also served to standardize (or police) pricing in all stores (franchised or company-owned), and promote Radio Shack's nationwide distribution and service network.

Although catalogs were the primary advertising vehicle, they were still only a part of the program. Catalogs were closely linked to freestanding inserts and run-of-the-paper (ROP) newspaper advertising. Freestanding inserts consisted of 8- and 12-page inserts circulated at least 15 times a year. Magazines played an increasing role in advertising to more specialized markets, such as computer and telecommunications users. Television was considered the least important medium, and was used primarily for status or "class" exposure.

An in-house agency named Radio Shack National Advertising Agency was responsible for all advertising programs. This agency, which employed 145 people and took up one floor of the corporate headquarters, was given the company's total advertising budget of over $160 million. Notes Bernard Appel, executive vice-president of marketing, "Keeping the agency inside allows us to have tighter control and ultimately better input over our advertising. It would also be much more costly to go outside."[21] Although the agency was in-house, its relationship to the company was similar to that of an outside agency, with the client being Radio Shack. All of the advertising for a product was the responsibility of the buyer. The buyer acted as the client and the agency had to obtain the client's approval.

The total cost of advertising was $199.1 million in 1983, a 23 percent increase from the expenditure of $160.9 million in 1982. For the first time since 1979 the percentage increase in advertising expense was greater than the sales increase. Even so, the advertising expense as a percent of sales had been declining since 1979. This percentage was 1979, 9.4 percent; 1980, 9.0 percent; 1981, 8.1 percent; 1982, 7.9 percent; and 1983, 8.0 percent.

The merchandising of the Radio Shack stores was guided primarily by information gathered at the store level. One type of information previously noted was the customer names that supported the mailing list. An even more critical type of information was that gathered through the Radio Shack operating system (SOS). Through this system, each retail store was able to transmit daily sales, financial data, payroll, inventory, and merchandise orders. This system has served to provide up-to-date merchandising data, streamline stores and central office accounting and warehouse operations. Through a joint venture with Citibank, Tandy began offering a national credit card good for purchases of more than $225.00 at all Radio Shack stores nationwide. This provided a source of information on large credit purchasers that Tandy had not had access to in the past.

Tandy put this information to good use, judging by the financial status of its stores. Year-to-year sales gains of 22 percent in 1983, 20 percent in 1982, 22 percent in 1981, 14 percent in 1980, and 15 percent in 1979 were recorded. This sales growth came through the expansion of the store system, increases in sales of old stores, new product categories, and international operations. As can be seen from Exhibit 17.4, none of these gains were at the expense of gross profit or general overhead expenses.

Gross profit as a percent of sales remained steady for fiscal 1983 and 1982 after four years of increases. Factors that favorably influenced the gross profit were the continuing increases in the volume of self-manufactured products and the increase in manufacturing profits. The factors that limited gross margins were adverse conditions in international operations caused by the strong dollar and foreign market restrictions.

Through a continuous improvement in financial position, Tandy had become a retail powerhouse rivaling the traditional giants of the industry.

As can be seen from Exhibit 17.5, Tandy's return on equity was still one of the highest of the nation's retail giants.

**Products**  The primary strategy Tandy had pursued was to develop the largest retail distribution system in the electronics industry. The distribution system Tandy developed became enormous, presenting both opportunities and problems. One way that Tandy had chosen to capitalize on these opportunities and cope with these problems had been through self-manufacturing.

Tandy produced some products within all of the product categories sold in the Radio Shack stores. The percentage manufacturered in-house varied by product line, the largest concentration being in the area of computers and related peripheral devices. One area of rapidly increasing production was that of telephone and telecommunications equipment. This was particularly true of those product areas that combined the features of computer and telephone equipment. In addition to production in-house, a large number of products were manufactured under contract in production facilities not owned by Tandy. These products carried private labels, such as Realistic.

Tandy saw many opportunities in self-production. The first was the positive effect manufacturing in-house had on gross profit. As can be seen from Exhibit 17.4, gross margins had been increasing in direct relation to the percentage of private-label merchandise sold through the Radio Shack stores. The percentage of private-label merchandise was limited, however. Since the early eighties Tandy had been mainly building computer-manufacturing capacity, and President John Roach estimated that because of this Tandy might get up to 65 percent self-production, but no further.[22] Margins were assisted through both the ability to control vendor profit and the ability to develop products designed to fit the unique needs of the Radio Shack stores. One of the major advantages of in-house production was the result of one of the problems arising out of maintaining a

**Exhibit 17.4** Gross Profit Percentages and Selling, General, and Administrative Expenses as a Percent of Sales

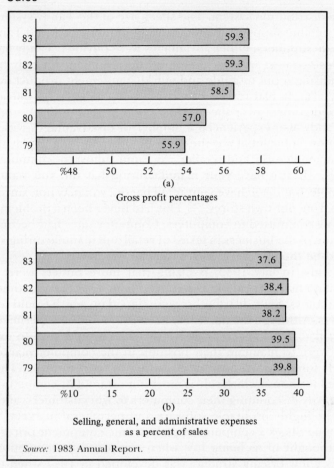

(a)
Gross profit percentages

(b)
Selling, general, and administrative expenses
as a percent of sales

*Source:* 1983 Annual Report.

**Exhibit 17.5**

|  | Twelve Months Ending | Total Sales (millions) | Retail Income (millions) | Return on Equity (%) |
|---|---|---|---|---|
| K-Mart | 10/28/81 | $15,759 | $232 | 9.9 |
| J.C. Penney | 1/31/82 | 11,860 | 156 | 12.9 |
| Sears, Roebuck | 12/31/81 | 27,357 | 285[a] | 6.6 |
| Tandy | 12/31/81 | 1,886 | 200 | 40.8 |
| Toys-R-Us | 11/01/81 | 687 | 36 | 19.4 |
| Wal-Mart | 1/31/82 | 2,445 | 83 | 27.9 |

[a]After capital gains and before unassigned corporate costs of $108 million.

*Source: Forbes,* March 1982.

large distribution system. The sheer size of the Tandy system made it difficult to find suitable suppliers. Manufacturing in-house reduced Tandy's dependence on outside suppliers. Other advantages were obvious. Tandy had the ability to keep in close contact with technological developments. Tandy had continuous merchandising input to guide and quickly implement product development. In summary, Tandy had reduced its overall dependence on outside suppliers and increased control over the products sold in Radio Shack stores.

Tandy also experienced a number of disadvantages with this system. One of the more substantial was the problem of attempting to play the dual roles of both the manufacturer and retailer. As Equil Juliussen, computer marketing analyst, states, "If you have your manufacturing hat on, you want as many outlets as possible; but if you have your retail hat on, you may not, since you could be taking sales from our own stores."[23] This had never been a problem until Tandy became heavily committed to computers. Computer sales had become such a substantial portion of the business in terms of retail and manufacturing sales that neither one could be thought of as subservient to the other.

Tandy, in late 1983, realizing that more outlets were needed in order to maintain market share in computers, began for the first time using independent distributors. Sixty distributors were signed up which would sell to over 2000 retail outlets. Although the move had been promoted as experimental, Tandy management had clearly become aware that they would have to expand distribution if they were to maintain their position in the computer market. Tandy was being slowly forced into a position of having to set priorities. "The company could be forced to choose which role is more important if its competitors pushed strategies of heavily discounting their computers to win customers, and aggressively pursuing the highly profitable software and peripheral markets."[24]

Radio Shack's computer and electronic equipment prices had been traditionally thought of as being low when compared to competitors' products. Radio Shack's low-pricing strategy was developed in 1977 when the TRS-80 was first brought into the market. The primary reason Tandy chose a low-pricing strategy was that in order to sell through their Radio Shack stores, the computer price had to be in line with other consumer electronic products. It was in Radio Shack's strategy to keep the TRS-80 at a reasonable level ($599.95) so that more of its current customers could afford to buy one.

Since that time however, competition in the home and personal computer market had become intense. This had placed extreme pressure on gross margins, which had placed Tandy in a serious dilemma. Tandy's strategy had always been to drop lines that did not produce at least a 50 percent gross margin. Tandy was now far too dependent upon computer systems to simply drop them. This problem was not acute when Tandy never had to compete head-to-head with the products in non–Radio Shack stores. However, with wider distribution, Tandy no longer had this luxury. This problem was further aggravated by the fact that costs had not come down as fast as prices, and that Tandy had a high manufacturing cost. As one article on the subject points out, "It seems no accident that the home computer company with the highest prices in the U.S.—Tandy—also performs most of its assemblies in the U.S."[25] This situation had the effect of forcing price discounting on the independent retailers that were now carrying Tandy computers. This had been unheard of in the past and had the effect of putting more price pressures on Tandy products in Radio Shack stores.

The name Radio Shack corresponded with a hobby-shop image in the minds of many consumers. This was a desirable image for most of the product areas that Tandy serves. However, computer systems was not one of those areas. To many computer buyers, Tandy maintained the image of a peddler of cheap electronics goods. The TRS-80 model 16 was developed primarily to counteract this image. The unit, which initially cost $4999, aimed at sophisticated users, such as large corporations. In further moves to change its image, Tandy was replacing Radio Shack with the Tandy name on all computer products and full-service computer stores. Probably more important was the manner in which Tandy modeled itself after IBM, stressing support and systems as selling points. This had been an area of needed improvement which had become especially apparent to independent retailers, who had complained of weak and indecisive support from Tandy.

## External

**Stores**  Tandy, as discussed earlier, marketed a wide range of electronics products. These products essentially fell into four general areas: consumer electronics (radios, stereos, etc.), electronic components (diodes, transistors, etc.), computer-related products (computers and peripheral devices), and telephone-related products (telephones and related perpheral devices). The first two of these product areas were entered when they were considered high-growth markets. As these markets began to mature and stagnate, efforts were made to replace them with products aimed at new growth markets. It was at this time that Tandy entered the computer market. When growth in the computer markets began to slow and competition became more intense, Tandy began to invest in the development of telephone and telecommunications equipment. This was the pattern that led to the market structure facing Tandy, in addition to providing a basis on which to understand its retail competition.

Tandy's original product line was that of electronic components aimed at the home electronics buff. These components were carried in all Radio Shack stores except those that were full-line computer or telephone stores. Competitors in this area were generally in the form of small independent retailers or small regional chains.

The next market was that for consumer electronics. This category covered a wide range of products from expensive component stereos to walkie-talkies. These products were carried in all stores except those devoted exclusively to computers or telephone systems. Tandy's primary competition in this market could generally be considered the large mass-merchandising chains such as Sears, Penneys, and Target on the one hand and the large stereo/electronics specialty chains such as Pacific Stereo on the other.

The next market, and the one that was responsible for the strongest recent growth and largest percentage of total sales, was that for computers and related equipment. Tandy faced strong competition in three areas: mass merchandisers, computer specialty stores, and manufacturers who sold directly.

It was estimated that in 1983 there were approximately 20,000 mass merchandisers selling lower-priced home computers (less than $1000). As a result, margins on these units had been squeezed to the point where most computer specialty stores were being forced out of this market into professional business systems.

The strongest competition for Tandy came from computer specialty stores. In 1982 there were an estimated 1800 computer dealers in the United States who controlled over 50 percent of the microcomputer market. This number was expected to grow to over 6500 stores in 1988 and control 35 percent of the products in the personal computer market alone. As the number of stores grew their markup was also changing, as can be seen in Exhibit 17.6. Independent retailers were gradually losing ground as chains began to dominate the market. The largest of the competing chains was Computerland, which had over 500 fran-

**Exhibit 17.6**

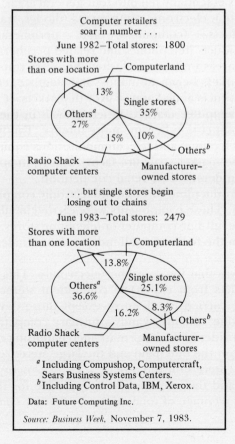

Computer retailers
soar in number . . .

June 1982—Total stores: 1800

Stores with more than one location

Computerland 13%

Single stores 35%

Others[a] 27%

Radio Shack computer centers 15%

Manufacturer-owned stores 10%

Others[b]

. . . but single stores begin losing out to chains

June 1983—Total stores: 2479

Stores with more than one location

Computerland 13.8%

Single stores 25.1%

Others[a] 36.6%

Radio Shack computer centers 16.2%

Manufacturer-owned stores 8.3%

Others[b]

[a] Including Compushop, Computercraft, Sears Business Systems Centers.
[b] Including Control Data, IBM, Xerox.

Data: Future Computing Inc.

*Source: Business Week,* November 7, 1983.

chised stores, followed by Sears with over 100 stores, IBM with over 60 stores, and Computercraft with over 30 stores.

This trend toward chains was being motivated by shifts in market structure. Smaller stores were having a difficult time competing with the same recognition, buying power, capital formation abilities, and advertising of the larger chains. In addition, there was a shift toward standardization and a de-emphasis on technology in favor of marketing, value-added services, and price cutting. This translated into retail chains that operated on minimum margins, maintained outside sales personnel, and provided high levels of service.

One chronic problem of many chains and independent wholesalers alike was lack of adequate cash flow. High-ticket merchandise coupled with a high-growth market had created severe cash flow problems for many dealers. Tandy had not had any serious difficulties with this problem.

Tandy was meeting the competition from other computer retail organizations in several ways. Tandy's primary strategy was to blanket the nation with a large number of stores in order to guarantee stable national distribution. As of 1983 Tandy had 412 freestanding computer centers and 632 Radio Shack stores containing computer departments, in addition to plans to add 100 centers and 50 combined stores by the end of the year. In order to further enhance distribution, Tandy had signed up at least 60 distributors to market its computers to independent retailers. Aware of the need to sell corporate customers directly, Tandy had begun the formation of a direct field sales force. This sales force had embarked upon a campaign of seminars and direct-mail advertising to data processing managers in order to acquaint professional users with the capabilities of Tandy equipment. Last, Tandy was beginning to provide comprehensive service in terms of repair and training throughout the entire Tandy store system.

The last market, and the one that Tandy looked to for future growth, was that for telephones and related equipment. Tandy was, at this time, considered the largest independent retailer of telephones in the United States. Telephones were marketed through all Tandy stores except computer centers. In 1984, Tandy opened a group of experimental telephone centers designed to carry nothing but telephone equipment. The telephone centers were designed to fulfill a similar role to that of the stand-alone computer centers in that they carried lines appropriate to the small business user such as business phones and key systems.

Tandy's interest in telephones was based on two factors. The first was that the telephone market was projected to reach over $5 billion annually by the latter part of the decade. The second was that developing technology was giving the telephone substantial new capabilities that would include integration with such devices as personal computers and home electronics. Last, telephones and related products were the fastest-growing segment of Tandy's business.

Tandy was not alone in its interest in this market. AT&T already had over 461 phone centers and had announced plans to open more in major Sears mall locations. GTE was also a major retailer through freestanding phone centers, as were most other national mass merchandisers.

**Products**   The consumer electronics industry, of which Tandy was a part, represented an estimated $20 billion in 1983. Tandy's sales, while dominated by the computer, had shown comfortable growth in nearly all "traditional" product areas. As a result, only two areas will be reviewed in depth: computers and telecommunications. Computers, because they dominated sales and had become substantially more competitive; telecommunications, because this market represented future growth.

*Computer Systems*   The conditions facing Tandy in the computer markets were the result of the two markets Tandy was in: home, and small-business and personal computers.

The vast majority of people for whom a computer is a necessity already owned a computer. As a result, the order of the day was to create a mass market for home computers. Atari's senior vice-president of marketing, Ted Vass, put the situation clearly when he said, "The people who pioneered this field were technology-oriented. But now the essence of the business is consumer marketing."[26] The drive toward mass merchandising accurately described the nature of the home computer market in 1984.

The most significant factor that faced both the home and small-business computer market was intense competition. The inner workings of most small computers were the same, with key ingredients provided by the same handful of suppliers. Much of the software was also the same. Although manufacturers had tried to distinguish themselves by providing innovative features, these were rapidly copied by competitors. The result was that no computer really had a substantial technological advantage. As a result, the real differences were found in price, service, compatibility, distribution networks, and image.

"Clearly, the industry had grown out of its initial, entreprenurial stage and is reaching for maturity," said David Lawrence, an analyst with Montgomery Securities in San Francisco.[27] With the change from an entreprenurial to a mature market, the critical factors for success also changed. To succeed, personal computer workers would need to monitor these critical areas:

1. *Low-cost production.*   As personal computer hardware became increasingly standardized, the ability to provide the most value for the dollar greatly influenced sales.
2. *Distribution.*   Only those makers that could keep their products in the customer's line of sight would survive.
3. *Software.*   Computer sales would suffer unless a wide choice of software packages was offered to increase the number of applications.[28]

In summary, the market became saturated with undifferentiated manufacturers, crowded distribution channels, and heavy price discounting. As a result, even though worldwide sales were expected to grow from $6.1 billion in 1982 to $21 billion in 1986, there was little doubt that a shakeout would gradually occur over the next three to five years. It had been predicted that by 1986, there could be only a dozen microcomputer vendors left.

Exhibit 17.7 provides an overview of the general position Tandy held as compared to the competition.

**Exhibit 17.7** Picking the Winners in Personal Computers

*Business Week* interviewed more than 40 leading hardware software and peripheral equipment makers, industry consultants and analysts to come up with a list of expected survivors and their current strengths.

| Companies | Applications Software | Brand Image | Depth of Management | Financial Muscle | Low-Cost Production | National Sales Force | Retail Distribution | Service and Support |
|---|---|---|---|---|---|---|---|---|
| | | | | Current Strengths | | | | |
| Apple Computer | * | * | | | | | * | |
| Atari (Warner) | * | * | | * | | | * | |
| Commodore International | | | | | * | | * | |
| Digital Equipment | | | * | * | * | * | | * |
| Fortune Systems | * | | | | | | | |
| International Business Machines | * | * | * | * | * | * | * | * |
| Japan Inc.[a] | | | * | * | * | | | |
| Radio Shack (Tandy) | * | * | | * | | | * | * |
| Texas Instruments | | | * | * | * | | * | * |

[a] At least one Japanese company is expected to succeed, but it is too early to pick which one.

*Source: Business Week,* November 22, 1982

Tandy's strengths were guaranteed distribution, financial muscle, and service through Radio Shack stores. However, as Cleve G. Smith, an analyst for the Yankee Group said, "Tandy's advantage in distribution has disappeared." He further stated that "the company will slip to fourth this year [1982] in home computer sales."[29] Tandy also had a notable weakness in that it lacked a national outside sales force and that it had relied entirely on in-house programmers for software development. Moving to correct these deficiencies, Tandy began to staff full-line computer centers with field sales personnel, in addition to allowing software companies to sell products under the Tandy name. Finally, Tandy had begun to respond to price pressures by reducing prices on many items, particularly those that are more price-sensitive such as low-priced home computers.

Tandy's largest competitor was without a doubt IBM. In fact, it could be said that IBM had virtually defined the competition. As can be seen from Exhibit 17.7, IBM had no obvious weaknesses. IBM was known for its aggressive marketing, superb sales force, financial power, and an impeccable brand image. IBM had combined all of these abilities to create one of the most incredible marketing success stories of this century, the introduction of the IBM PC. As Exhibit 17.8 illustrates, the growth of the PC had been nothing less than phenomenal.

Following the introduction of the PC, IBM had introduced the PC Jr. With both of these, IBM had followed a strategy of aggressive distribution and pricing, designed to make it the dominant producer in these markets. Declared David G. Jackson, president of Altos Computer Systems, "IBM is moving faster than anything I've ever seen. It is being absolutely predatory."[30]

New sales did not necessarily represent the whole picture. IBM, while certainly a powerful new force, was far behind in terms of units in place.

As a result of the IBM PC, Apple Computer was being unseated from the number one spot in personal computers. Apple (referring again to Exhibit 17.7) had many areas of weaknesses, the primary one being its inability to come up with a cohesive product and marketing strategy. However, under the direction of their new president, John Sculley, who resigned as president of PepsiCo to join Apple, these flaws were being rapidly corrected. Apple brought out a whole new series of products aimed directly at IBM, in addition to cutting prices and redirecting marketing efforts on their current lines.

Of the remaining competition, the most significant fell into the area of inexpensive home computers. These makers included Commodore, Atari, and Texas Instruments. Of this group, Commodore was probably the most significant to Tandy. Of the larger computer manufacturers, Commodore alone had yet to be scathed in the home computer price wars. This had largely been a result of the low-cost production Commodore enjoyed in the Far East. Atari, following suit, had completely eliminated assembly operations in the United States, hoping to achieve cost parity through foreign assembly operations.

**Exhibit 17.8** Which Companies Are Taking the Biggest Byte of the Pie?

| Personal computer market shares (%) | | | | |
|---|---|---|---|---|
| | 1980 | 1981 | 1982 | 1983 |
| Apple | 29.3 | 41.8 | 28.5 | 22.0 |
| IBM | 0 | 5.0 | 22.2 | 28.0 |
| Tandy | 37.6 | 22.5 | 10.1 | 7.0 |
| Hewlett-Packard | 5.3 | 6.1 | 4.7 | 3.5 |
| Commodore | 15.9 | 10.6 | 3.6 | 3.5 |
| Franklin | 0 | 0 | 2.5 | 3.5 |
| Others | 11.9 | 12.6 | 20.2 | 29.0 |

*Source: Advertising Age,* March 5, 1984

These computer manufacturers had been at the forefront of the effort to mass merchandise home computers. They had pursued this effort through extensive distribution, low service, and heavy price discounting. It was because of these companies that Tandy decided to begin using independent distributors and a more flexible pricing policy.

*Telecommunications*    Arthur D. Anderson expected the world telecommunications market to grow from $40 billion in 1980 to about $87.5 billion by the end of the decade.[31] The telephone market alone in 1982 was growing at a rate of 40 percent a year. Quite understandably, manufacturers in the United States and abroad were rapidly moving into what was shaping up to be a very lucrative market.

At the heart of this growth were three factors: the breakup of AT&T, demand for new service, and new technology. The breakup of AT&T provided an opening for new competitors in what was once a monopolistic market. Second, much of the future demand would be for services aimed at moving computer data. Third, new technology was providing systems for applications never possible before.

Tandy focused on two markets in this industry: the basic telephone and data systems. Tandy pursued the first market area through products such as telephones, pagers, and answering machines. More focus, however, was being placed on combining computer and communications technologies into a symbiotic connection.

Tandy already faced competition from an array of large corporations. The most significant of these was AT&T. Already AT&T had distribution of its products through 4500 retail stores and at least half of their sales through another group of mail-order houses and catalog companies. In addition, AT&T was developing an entirely new line of small-office, data, and computer systems, all of which integrated telecommunications and data processing functions.

The potential of this market had not been lost on IBM, which had bought a 15 percent interest in Rolm Corp., a maker of telecommunications equipment. Thanks to the IBM connection, Rolm was the safe choice of buyers of telecommunications equipment, the way the phone company used to be. This development, of course, placed Tandy in direct competition with IBM in the telecommunications market as well as the computer market.

The International Telephone and Telegraph Corporation (ITT) was the second largest telephone company in the world. In 1982, it had a net income of $702.8 million and a 21 percent market share in the total electronics industry. ITT was aggressively pursuing the market because of the void created by the deregulation of AT&T. Unlike Tandy, ITT was known for its aggressive pricing policies, and in addition, it spent over $750 million in telecommunication research in 1982.

# PRODUCTION

Tandy operated 29 wholly owned factories in the United States, Asia, and Canada that produced products for Radio Shack stores. This was in addition to the products manufactured under contract by independent producers and sold under private labels through Radio Shack stores.

The company had been consistently increasing the percentage of products made internally over the years (Exhibit 17.9). However, John Roach, the president and CEO, forecasted that Tandy may get up to 65 percent self-production, but no further. This limit was due to the fact that most self-production was dedicated to computer-related products, and there was a limit to the total percentage of these that could be economically produced in-house. Another reason was the criteria applied to in-house production decisions. If Tandy could not offer the best possible product at competitive prices, and make an adequate profit, merchandising would be from the outside sources. If the decision was made to produce in-house, the sampling and quality control procedures were the same that outside vendors were required to follow.

One of the major problems with this arrangement had been the conflict between the needs of the retail and the manufacturing operations. This was particularly true since Tandy had begun selling to independent distributors. In response to this problem Tandy split the top management of its International Manufacturing Operations into Tandy Division. The latter was eventually split, giving one division responsibility for manufacturing of all products sold through the Radio Shack store chain and the other division responsibility for products sold to the general retail market. These divisions were called Tandy Electronics Manufacturing and Tandy Marketing Co., respectively.

Although Tandy's greatest strength was its distribution system, manufacturing operations were taking on much greater importance. Because of this, Tandy was constantly on the lookout for possible acquisitions of manufacturing plants, in order to improve its already high degree of vertical integration and ability to capture additional manufacturing margins. For example, on September 27, 1983, Tandy announced its intentions of acquiring Datapoint's half of a joint disk-manufacturing venture. In fiscal 1982, videotape-manufacturing capabilities were added through the purchase of the domestic portion of the Consumer Products Division of Memorex. The international operations of this division were being acquired on a country-by-country basis. Also, Tandy had agreed to a joint manufacturing venture with Matra S.A. of France in order to produce microcomputers. On August 18, 1983, Tandy made public its plans to acquire O'Sullivan Industries, Inc., a subsidiary of Conroy Inc. O'Sullivan was a manufacturer of consumer electronic stands, racks, desks, and accessories.

These production facilities were supported by the efforts of two major design centers, one in Ft. Worth and one in Tokyo. These design centers, along with those attached to specialized production facilities, were responsible for all product design from car radios to computers. These groups included not only hardware designers but also a team of 180 persons engaged in software development for the Tandy computer line.

Even with this R&D capability, Tandy did not strive to be an innovator, which was revealed by the fact that R&D costs were considered financially immaterial. The Tandy product design effort was set up to create applications, not technologies.

**Exhibit 17.9** Percentage of Private-Label
Merchandise to Total Sales

| Year | 1981 | 1982 | 1983 |
|---|---|---|---|
| Percentage | < 50 | 54 | 57 |

**Exhibit 17.10** Working Capital Provided by Operations
(in millions of dollars)

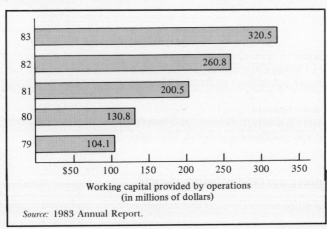

Working capital provided by operations
(in millions of dollars)

*Source:* 1983 Annual Report.

**FINANCIAL**

One of the major tasks of these groups was to reduce production costs. This had become a substantial problem in recent years because of the strong dollar and high domestic production costs. Most of Tandy's computer products came from domestic plants, which were considered high-cost production facilities. At the same time, these products were competing against imports (Commodore) which had a price advantage because of the strong dollar.

**Working Capital**

In 1983 operations generated $321 million in working capital, an increase of over 23 percent as compared to 1982 (see Exhibit 17.10). The 1983 working capital amount was approximately 12 times the amount generated in 1974.

Tandy utilized its working capital for capital expansion as Tandy did not issue any long-term debt in 1983. The total capital expansion budget for 1983 was $75 million. This amount included the expansion of manufacturing facilities, the opening of 350 new retail stores, and the remodeling of 600 existing retail stores.

**Cash Flow**

In 1983 Tandy's net income increased by 24.3 percent on a sales increase of 21.8 percent. (See Exhibits 17.11 and 17.12). Tandy had recorded similar gains, such as the one in 1976 when sales increased 40 percent because of the CB radio craze. The lowest sales increase Tandy ever experienced since 1973 was in 1978, when sales only grew 12 percent after the CB radio craze ended.

**Exhibit 17.11**

## TANDY CORPORATION AND SUBSIDIARIES
### Consolidated Statements of Income (in thousands, except per share amounts.)[a]

| | Year Ended June 30, | | |
| --- | --- | --- | --- |
| | 1983 | 1982 | 1981 |
| Net sales | $2,475,188 | $2,032,555 | $1,691,373 |
| Other income | 38,109 | 28,657 | 15,697 |
| | 2,513,297 | 2,061,212 | 1,707,070 |
| Costs and expenses | | | |
| Cost of products sold | 1,008,187 | 826,842 | 701,777 |
| Selling, general, and administrative, net of amounts allocated to spun-off operations in fiscal 1976 and prior | 930,244 | 780,378 | 645,934 |
| Depreciation and amortization | 38,679 | 29,437 | 23,288 |
| Interest expense, net of interest income, and interest allocated to spun-off operations in fiscal 1976 and prior | 8,905 | 1,168 | 15,454 |
| | 1,986,015 | 1,637,825 | 1,386,453 |
| **Income from continuing operations before income taxes** | 527,282 | 423,387 | 320,617 |
| Provision for income taxes | 248,761 | 199,302 | 151,015 |
| Income from continuing operations | 278,521 | 224,085 | 169,602 |
| Loss from discontinued operations, net of income taxes | — | — | — |
| **Net income before income from operations spun off** | 278,521 | 224,085 | 169,602 |
| Income from operations spun off, net of income taxes | — | — | — |
| **Net income** | $ 278,521 | $ 224,085 | $ 169,602 |
| Income (loss) per average common share and common share equivalent | | | |
| Continuing operations | $2.67 | $2.17 | $1.65 |
| Discontinued operations | — | — | — |
| Spun-off operations | — | — | — |
| **Net income** | $2.67 | $2.17 | $1.65 |
| Average common shares and common share equivalents outstanding | 104,335 | 103,395 | 102,578 |

[a]Per share amounts restated for two-for-one stock splits in May 1981, December 1980, June 1978, and December 1975.
Fiscal 1983 and 1982 amounts reflect the adoption of FAS No. 52, Foreign Currency Translation.

*Source:* 1983 Annual Report.

| | | | Year Ended June 30, | | | |
|---|---|---|---|---|---|---|
| 1980 | 1979 | 1978 | 1977 | 1976 | 1975 | 1974 |
| $ 1,384,637 | $ 1,215,483 | $ 1,059,324 | $ 949,267 | $ 741,722 | $ 528,286 | $ 411,241 |
| 11,360 | 11,403 | 5,629 | 3,763 | 2,649 | 3,963 | 2,153 |
| 1,395,997 | 1,226,886 | 1,064,953 | 953,030 | 744,371 | 532,249 | 413,394 |
| 594,841 | 535,549 | 491,509 | 434,031 | 331,400 | 249,006 | 198,067 |
| 546,325 | 484,249 | 403,173 | 350,878 | 270,308 | 204,107 | 158,792 |
| 19,110 | 17,121 | 13,879 | 11,140 | 8,034 | 7,392 | 5,461 |
| 25,063 | 28,466 | 30,260 | 15,192 | 7,282 | 14,044 | 8,544 |
| 1,185,339 | 1,065,385 | 938,821 | 811,241 | 617,024 | 474,549 | 370,864 |
| 210,658 | 161,501 | 126,132 | 141,789 | 127,347 | 57,700 | 42,530 |
| 98,423 | 78,272 | 59,986 | 69,970 | 63,066 | 29,078 | 20,669 |
| 112,235 | 83,229 | 66,146 | 71,819 | 64,281 | 28,622 | 21,861 |
| — | — | — | (2,777) | — | (1,820) | (7,072) |
| 112,235 | 83,229 | 66,146 | 69,042 | 64,281 | 26,802 | 14,789 |
| — | — | — | — | 3,243 | 7,794 | 5,657 |
| $ 112,235 | $ 83,229 | $ 66,146 | $ 69,042 | $ 67,524 | $ 34,596 | $ 20,446 |
| $1.12 | $.81 | $.69 | $.54 | $.44 | $.20 | $.13 |
| — | — | — | (.02) | — | (.01) | (.04) |
| — | — | — | — | .02 | .05 | .03 |
| $1.12 | $.81 | $.69 | $.52 | $.46 | $.24 | $.12 |
| 103,644 | 106,004 | 96,136 | 132,336 | 144,824 | 145,408 | 169,992 |

# Exhibit 17.12

## TANDY CORPORATION AND SUBSIDIARIES
### Consolidated Balance Sheets
### (in thousands)

|  | June 30, 1983 | June 30, 1982 |
|---|---|---|
| **Assets** | | |
| Current assets | | |
| Cash and short-term investments | $ 279,743 | $ 167,547 |
| Accounts and notes receivable, less allowance for doubtful accounts | 107,530 | 83,616 |
| Inventories | 844,097 | 670,568 |
| Other current assets | 31,928 | 27,000 |
| Total current assets | 1,263,298 | 948,731 |
| Property and equipment, at cost | | |
| Consumer electronics operations, net of accumulated depreciation | 194,004 | 158,678 |
| Tandy Center, net of accumulated depreciation | 63,616 | 66,317 |
|  | 257,620 | 224,995 |
| Other assets | 60,990 | 53,918 |
|  | $1,581,908 | $1,227,644 |
| **Liabilities and stockholders' equity** | | |
| Current liabilities | | |
| Notes payable | $ 55,737 | $ 24,942 |
| Accounts payable | 64,640 | 63,641 |
| Accrued expenses | 115,054 | 92,125 |
| Income taxes payable | 50,668 | 52,160 |
| Total current liabilities | 286,099 | 232,868 |
| Notes payable, due after one year | 15,482 | 20,642 |
| Subordinated debentures, net of unamortized bond discount | 122,938 | 122,666 |
| Store managers' deposits | 8,490 | 9,306 |
| Deferred income taxes | 17,682 | 18,886 |
| Other noncurrent liabilities | 10,345 | 10,599 |
| Total other liabilities | 174,937 | 182,099 |
| Stockholders' equity | | |
| Preferred stock, no par value, 1,000,000 shares authorized, none issued or outstanding | — | — |
| Common stock, $1 par value, 250,000,000 shares authorized with 105,645,000 shares issued | 105,645 | 105,645 |
| Additional paid-in capital | 68,111 | 39,627 |
| Retained earnings | 969,626 | 691,105 |
| Foreign currency translation effects | (16,297) | (12,317) |
| Common stock in treasury, at cost, 976,000 and 1,789,000 shares, respectively | (6,213) | (11,383) |
| Total stockholders' equity | 1,120,872 | 812,677 |
| Commitments and contingent liabilities | | |
|  | $1,581,908 | $1,227,644 |

*Source:* 1983 Annual Report.

The effects of the CB radio craze are shown through an operational cash flow analysis that was performed by Paul Pappadio, a professional analyst. Pappadio defined operational cash flow (OCF) as net income, plus depreciation, plus changes in working capital, less investments in property, plant and equipment, and debt. OCF can be thought of as the uncommitted cash Tandy has on hand at the end of the year.[32]

Through his analysis, Pappadio found that in 1977, when the CB radio craze ended, Tandy's OCF fell to negative $30 million. In the years following, due to Tandy's rebound brought about by entering the microcomputer market. OCF rose to a high of $70 million. Pappadio also found that in 1982 Tandy's OCF fell again to negative $78.5 million. Pappadio credits this drop to the accumulation of huge amounts of inventories.

In response to this OCF analysis, Garland Asher, a Tandy financial officer, stated that by putting cash into inventory, rather than simply holding it, it earns a better return, making it the better strategy. Substantiating this, Asher stated that in 1982 Tandy's after-tax return on noncash assets was 25.5 percent. Further, Asher concluded that the success of the company lay largely in the fact that its customers were never faced with empty shelves.[33]

**International Financial Markets**

The strength of the U.S. dollar in the 1981–1983 period affected Tandy in three major ways. First, foreign-produced products imported into the United States carried a favorable price advantage. In fact, Robert Miller, vice-president of merchandising, Consumer Products, said, "The strong U.S. dollar improved technology and manufacturing efficiencies continue to bring our customers more advanced products at lower retail prices."[34]

Second, the strong dollar raised the costs of Tandy's exported products in the international markets. This meant that exported American-made products carried a price disadvantage abroad.

Third, the profits the international division generated were greatly reduced due to currency translation charges. These charges reflect the costs of translating foreign currency denominated profits into U.S. dollars. In 1983 the international division yielded $527 million of profits but lost over $590 million foreign currency translation.

**NOTES**

1. Tandy Corporation, 1983 10-K, p. 2.
2. Paul Borenstein, "Can Tandy Stay on Top?" *Forbes,* April 11, 1983, p. 43.
3. Ibid., p. 43.
4. "A Computer that Builds Radio Shack Image," *Business Week,* February 1, 1982, p. 23.
5. Bernard Appel, "Advantages of Being Self Contained," *Marketing and Media Decisions,* Spring 1982, special, p. 71.
6. Harold Seneker, "What Do You Do After You Bury the Boss?" *Forbes,* March 5, 1979, p. 7.
7. Harold Rudnitsky, and Toni Mach, "Sometimes We Are Innovators, Sometimes Not," *Forbes,* March 29, 1982, p. 66.
8. Ibid., p. 68.
9. Seneker, "What Do You Do?" p. 7.

10. Rudnitsky and Mach, "Sometimes We Are Innovators," p. 66.
11. Appel, "Advantages of Being Self Contained," p. 71.
12. Seneker, "What Do You Do?" p. 118.
13. "Tandy Man", *Forbes,* December 11, 1978, p. 118.
14. Ibid.
15. 1983 Annual Report, p. 3.
16. Appeal, "Advantages of Being Self Contained," p. 71.
17. 1983 Annual Report, p. 5.
18. Ibid., p. 15.
19. Rudnitsky and Mach, "Sometimes We Are Innovators," p. 66.
20. 1983 Annual Report, p. 14.
21. Madeleine Dreyfack, "Do It Yourself," *Marketing and Media Decisions,* May 1983, p. 60.
22. Rudnitsky and Mach, "Sometimes We Are Innovators," p. 68.
23. *Business Week,* August 30, 1983, p. 30.
24. "Rivals Crowd Tandy's Computer Niches," *Business Week,* August 30, 1982, p. 30.
25. Mark Halper, "Losses Mount in Home Computers as Suppliers Assess 2nd Half," *Electronic News,* 1983, p. 60.
26. "Computer Marketing: No Longer Fun and Games," *Advertising Age,* March 5, 1984, p. M-1.
27. "Painful Adolescence: A Hot Market Meets a Shake-Out," *Electronic Business,* December 1983, p. 30.
28. "The Coming Shakeout in Personal Computers," *Business Week,* November 22, 1982, p. 74.
29. "Rivals Crowd Tandy's Computer Niches," p. 28.
30. "Personal Computers and the Winner Is IBM," *Business Week,* October 3, 1983, p. 78.
31. *World Telecommunications: Study II 1980–1990* (Cambridge, Mass.: A. D. Little, Inc., 1982).
32. "Tandy to Acquire Datapoint's Half of Disk Venture," *Electronic News,* September 27, 1983, p. 16.
33. Ibid.
34. Ibid.

# 18 Corporate Planning at Borg-Warner in the 1980s

William C. Scott
Indiana State University

Borg-Warner is a Chicago-based diversified company operating internationally with total sales of over $3 billion. In 1982, the corporate net profit margin was just over 5 percent. Forty-six percent of that profit came from manufacturing, 34 percent from services, and 20 percent from investments in Hughes Tool Company and other affiliates. This case is the story of what has taken place in strategic management, especially in the early 1980s. Exhibit 18.1 summarizes certain financial data on the company.

Borg-Warner was formed in 1928 with the merger of several automobile industry suppliers. Planning was always an important management activity, even prior to 1950 when many large corporations started taking a formal interest in long-range planning. In 1950 Roy Ingersoll became president of Borg-Warner and began to implement his planning techniques throughout the company.

> The system had many of the features of what later came to be called "strategic planning." Each Borg-Warner Division was asked to actively search for new product areas where the company's strengths would enable it to compete successfully. Each division was asked to develop plans for replacement of existing products and expansion in markets currently occupied. Ingersoll himself concentrated his efforts on a program of acquisitions designed to fill the gap left by the expected loss of the Ford business.[1]

The new planning system led to a 20-year period of strategy by acquisition and divestment to fit corporate purpose and environmental conditions. Starting in the 1970s, the planning horizon was lengthened to five years and wider management participation in strategy decisions began to occur. During this time a strategy process was developed which utilized the business matrix and other analytical techniques. Corporate planners at Borg-Warner were instrumental in the development of the nine-cell matrix plotted on axes of market attractiveness and business strength. Goals began to emphasize return on equity, and strategies reflected not only optimizing the business mix but also efficient operations. Concentrating on a few strategic issues and financial modeling were other techniques incorporated into strategic decision making. "The data available from the PIMS program was integrated into the planning process and used to develop strategic business unit plans, and in 1978 a procedure was developed to define the 'investment in technology' needed by each strategic business unit."[2]

Most of this case was prepared from material published in Annual Reports for 1979–1982 and Investor Facts for 1980, 1981, and 1983.

This case was prepared by William C. Scott of Indiana State University, Terre Haute, Indiana, as a basis for class discussion rather than to illustrate either effective or ineffective organizational practices.

Presented at Midwest Case Writers Association Workshop, 1984.

**Exhibit 18.1** Balance Sheet, December 31 (millions of dollars)

|  | 1982 | 1981 |
|---|---|---|
| **Assets** | | |
| Current assets | | |
| Cash | $ 29.6 | $ 35.5 |
| Marketable securities | 57.0 | 59.8 |
| Receivables | 429.6 | 364.8 |
| Inventories | 300.9 | 377.2 |
| Other current assets | 66.1 | 70.9 |
| Total current assets | 883.2 | 908.2 |
| Investments and advances | 600.9 | 524.8 |
| Property, plant, and equipment | 832.8 | 811.3 |
| Other assets and deferred charges less amortization | 145.7 | 92.2 |
|  | $2,462.6 | $2,336.5 |
| **Liabilities and shareholders' equity** | | |
| Current liabilities | | |
| Notes payable | $ 62.1 | $ 119.1 |
| Accounts payable and accrued expenses | 482.8 | 472.0 |
| Income taxes | 8.4 | 21.3 |
| Total current liabilities | 553.3 | 612.4 |
| Warranties and other liabilities | 138.9 | 138.0 |
| Deferred income | 53.3 | 43.5 |
| Deferred income taxes | 52.6 | 56.7 |
| Long-term debt | 280.6 | 226.2 |
| Minority shareholders' interest in consolidated subsidiaries | 24.2 | 23.8 |
| Shareholders' equity | | |
| Capital stock | | |
| Preferred stock, liquidation preference $4.6 million in 1982, $5.3 million in 1981 | .3 | .3 |
| Common stock, 42,953,308 shares issued in 1982 and 1981 | 107.4 | 107.4 |
| Capital in excess of par value | 101.4 | 57.3 |
| Retained earnings | 1,220.3 | 1,113.3 |
| Currency translation adjustment | (40.5) | (14.0) |
|  | 1,388.9 | 1,264.3 |
| Less treasury common stock, at cost | 29.2 | 28.4 |
| Total shareholders' equity | 1,359.7 | 1,235.9 |
|  | $2,462.6 | $2,336.5 |

*Source:* 1982 Annual Report.

A very effective strategic management system was in place in 1980. It consisted of the following seven related subprocesses:

1. Attention is given to corporate objectives, which are needed to support the entire goal-setting process. At the top, the board of directors and the policy and planning committee are involved.
2. Borg-Warner is organized into six major groups of businesses. They are

air-conditioning, chemicals and plastics, energy and industrial equipment, financial services, protective services, and transportation equipment. Within each group are several separate divisions. Some of the divisions are further divided into several more strategic business units. The second step in the strategy process requires the division managers to identify their SBUs on the basis of market served, products, and competition. Each SBU has uniqueness in all three criteria.

3. Next, the line managers of each SBU analyze their unit's position and develop cost-effective strategies. Expected results for both costs and profit are required.

4. The fourth step is refinement of the proposed strategies at the group level. This step ends strategy formulation and the next step begins strategy implementation.

5. The process of allocating resources by corporate managers is the first part of strategy implementation.

6. Then, SBU managers operationalize the newly formulated strategies, making sure a control system is used to monitor the results.

7. The final part of the strategy process is the reward program, which involves group, division, and SBU levels.

The above strategic management system is used at Borg-Warner to direct its 90–100 strategic business units. The strategy profiles for five of the six major groups of businesses are described next. Data on each group is shown in Exhibit 18.2.

**TRANSPOR-
TATION
EQUIPMENT
GROUP**

The transportation equipment group is heavily dependent upon the production of transmission components for automobiles. However, parts for many other varieties of vehicles including agricultural and marine equipment are manufactured and sold in the United States and other countries. Sales grew to over $900 million in 1979 and have remained near that figure for several years. An off year in the sales growth trend was experienced in 1980 due to poor worldwide economic conditions. The closing of a plant in the United Kingdom was a typical strategy for 1980. A report published in 1981 stated the following:

> The automotive aftermarket operation performed much better than the original equipment units last year. Strong export sales and strength in several of our non-U.S. distribution units kept 1980 sales slightly ahead of 1979. Domestically, however, sales were depressed by the negative effects of high interest rates on the highly leveraged distributors who bring our products to market.[3]

To streamline the organization, the transportation equipment group was reduced to four strategic business units. However, new products continued to be developed in transmissions, carburetors, and electronics. The attention to product mix helped 1981 sales increase in a continuing down market for automobiles. The manufacture and sale of products in later life-cycle stages was hurting the

**Exhibit 18.2** Industry Segment Data (millions of dollars)

|  | 1982 | 1981 | 1980 |
|---|---|---|---|
| **Sales** | | | |
| Air conditioning | $ 596.3 | $ 570.7 | $ 513.7 |
| Chemicals & plastics | 612.8 | 663.9 | 630.9 |
| Energy & industrial equipment | 330.0 | 320.4 | 316.4 |
| Protective services | 589.2 | 363.5 | 292.4 |
| Transportation equipment | 926.5 | 995.8 | 870.4 |
| Sales of segments | 3,054.8 | 2,914.3 | 2,623.8 |
| Discontinued operations | 140.5 | 210.4 | 341.9 |
| Net sales | $3,195.3 | $3,124.7 | $2,965.7 |
| **Operating profit** | | | |
| Air conditioning | $ 33.8 | $ 30.4 | $ 22.8 |
| Chemicals & plastics | 51.8 | 61.2 | 58.8 |
| Energy & industrial equipment | 28.1 | 20.5 | 40.9 |
| Protective services | 45.2 | 33.4 | 21.9 |
| Transportation Equipment | 68.4 | 74.7 | 31.0 |
| Operating profit of segments | 227.3 | 220.2 | 175.4 |
| Discontinued operations | 16.9 | 20.3 | 33.1 |
| General corporate expenses | (41.6) | (44.3) | (35.5) |
| Interest and finance charges | (61.5) | (53.1) | (56.2) |
| Earnings before taxes | 141.1 | 143.1 | 116.8 |
| Income taxes | (43.7) | (66.8) | (54.2) |
| Consolidated earnings | 97.4 | 76.3 | 62.6 |
| Financial services | 36.0 | 32.0 | 27.2 |
| Affiliates at equity | 34.0 | 63.8 | 36.3 |
| Net earnings | $ 167.4 | $ 172.1 | $ 126.1 |
| **Identifiable assets** | | | |
| Air conditioning | $ 260.9 | $ 271.9 | $ 208.4 |
| Chemicals & plastics | 296.7 | 315.9 | 319.9 |
| Energy & industrial equipment | 205.8 | 204.3 | 161.0 |
| Protective services | 426.8 | 284.6 | 246.0 |
| Transportation equipment | 490.8 | 506.5 | 454.9 |
| Identifiable assets of segments | 1,681.0 | 1,583.2 | 1,390.2 |
| Financial services | 270.9 | 234.9 | 202.1 |
| Affiliates at equity | 260.5 | 232.3 | 139.7 |
| General corporate assets | 246.5 | 181.9 | 144.7 |
| Discontinued operations | 3.7 | 104.2 | 148.8 |
| Identifiable assets | $2,462.6 | $2,336.5 | $2,025.5 |

*Source:* 1982 Annual Report.

company's competitive position. There was a need to shift toward high-growth product lines. New products for front-drive cars enabled the company to stay on top of the transportation equipment field. The significant product strategy was described by management as the shift in emphasis away from "products that involve basic metal-fabricating skill and no special technology. Our future concentration will be on component parts where we have a proprietary position or capabilities unique to Borg-Warner."[4] Not only the economics of the market but competitors' vertical integration strategies influenced these changes.

Major shifts in the transportation equipment business continued in 1982. Illustrative of the major changes was the sale of the entire line of automotive aftermarket parts business to Echlin, Inc. This was prompted by governmental objections to acquisitions by Borg-Warner.

Dropping the production of automatic transmissions, and LIFO inventory reductions were other contributions to profits. However, the addition of manual transmissions and other products keeps attention focused on having a viable line of products. In addition to having a market-based strategy, effort is directed at efficiency in both production operations and organization structure.

Thus, transportation equipment components will continue to be a leading product group. The tricky factor in managing strategy here is that the original equipment manufacturer (OEM) is often both major customer and competitor. A principal effect is the lack of pricing flexibility due to the OEM's power in the automotive industry. On the positive side are the large amount of international sales and the updated manufacturing facilities. Some of the economic variables which affect the transportation products market are the following: GNP, car production, gasoline prices, consumer confidence, and farm income.[5]

## CHEMICALS AND PLASTICS GROUP

The second largest group, chemicals and plastics, derives most of its over $600 million revenue from acrylonitrile-butadiene-styrene (ABS) plastic, produced under the trade name Cycolac and sold in the durable goods, automobile, and housing markets. Although costs were increasing rapidly in 1979, demand was strong. Product characteristics can be widely varied, which means that new uses are many. Appliances, plumbing, desktop machines, and telephones are some of the final products using Cycolac. Both increases in existing plant capacities and new plants were recent realities.

European sales weakened in 1981 and 1982, and overcapacity became a problem. However, the development of new markets has offset weak European demand. An acquisition was responsible for additional market expansion. The 1982 Annual Report is positive:

> The reasons for our success: amazing versatility of the ABS family of plastics and the continuing ability of Borg-Warner Chemicals' researchers and marketers to find and promote new product applications for our Cycolac resins. Borg-Warner Chemicals' strategy has been to position itself in the growth markets of the '80s. And Cycolac ABS brands have gained wide acceptance in the electronics, communications and business machine markets. The biggest growth in 1982, for example, was in resins used for personal computer and video game cabinetry. Rapid growth in the use of Cycolac ABS in refrigerator liner bodies is utilizing all current resin capacity at the new Mississippi plant which opened in early 1982.
>
> The recession did take its toll on the industry overall. Two ABS producers discontinued production, leaving only Borg-Warner, Monsanto and Dow as major factors in the U.S. Most national producers in other countries are supported to some extent by subsidies or other protective measures.

Plastics are situated in growth markets, and automotive and housing segments of the economy will influence performance. Recently, several new plastic products have been developed. Even so, relative costs have been kept low.

On the speciality-chemicals side, market share has increased. The markets are wide and they have been growing. Another strong factor in specialty chemicals is that prices follow petroleum prices. The economic variables affecting the plastics and chemicals group are the level of consumer confidence, and sales of appliances, autos, furniture, and houses.

**AIR-CONDITION-ING GROUP**

In 1979 York products were manufactured for three markets: large installations, homes and small buildings, and automobile compressors. A changing product mix toward the larger equipment was prompted by the poor car and housing markets. Also, the international market was weak. The down market continued into the 1980s, but it was offset by the introduction of a new product, the Turbo-Modulator, designed to save energy.

The product mix shift toward large equipment continued in 1981, helped by the elimination of low-profit models of residential units. Manufacturing costs declined and capacity increases came via the acquisition of Westinghouse's smaller commercial and residential air conditioning business.

The above changes helped Borg-Warner become an industry leader. Engineered machinery, the large and technically sophisticated products, enjoyed a 15 percent sales growth in 1982, which resulted in an increase in market share. New products utilizing advanced electronics provide the York divisions with a competitive advantage. However, demand is beginning to decline, partially offset by a good international market. On the other hand, the small-product lines were still awaiting economic recovery.

The air-conditioning group is one of three Borg-Warner groups with sales in the $600 million range. Its strength will be helped by heavy international sales and a high amount of technological innovation resulting in new and high-quality products. However, there is price competition from strong competitors such as GE, Carrier, and Rheem. The economy, particularly construction demand, interest rates, and energy prices, will affect how well the air-conditioning business will perform.

**PROTECTIVE SERVICES GROUP**

In the late 1970s, Borg-Warner's strategy began to turn the company more in the direction of service businesses. This was done for the purpose of contracyclicality. In 1977, Baker Industries was acquired, and the protective services group had its beginning. Both the Wells Fargo (alarms and guards) and the Pony Express (courier) divisions have grown rapidly. Successful strategies prior to 1980 included both product development and market penetration.

Steady growth continues, even though the business environment has several weaknesses. In 1981 Wells Fargo expanded into ten cities and made several small acquisitions. The Pony Express division also expanded geographically in their high-growth industry. However, government regulation is a drawback. The 1981 Annual Report stated that "Baker is the third largest protective service operation in the United States, and the scope of its services is the broadest of all." The 1982 strategy continued to be one of geographic growth, acquisitions, and internal expansion. Although revenues are near $600 million and new products have been developed, profits from foreign operations in Canada, Colombia, Spain, and the United Kingdom are only 10 percent of the group's total profits. Another disadvantage is the group's lack of a dominant competitive strength.

The most well known competitors are Pinkerton, Brinks, and Honeywell, and although markets are growing, prices are inflexible. Thus, inflation is a threat. Additional environmental factors affecting the group are crime rates, gasoline prices, new business starts, property values, and the demand for public protection.

# ENERGY AND INDUSTRIAL EQUIPMENT GROUP

Group sales are relatively small ($300 million) but profits are high. As the 1980s began, a large portion of sales came from the Morse Chain division, where strong sales in the automobile industry helped. Sales of the HyVo transmission chain used in front-wheel-drive cares bolstered performance in a generally sagging industry. In fact, strategic plans called for the building of a manufacturing plant.

On the darker side, "Production of energy-saving AC inverters for motor speed controls was delayed due to component shortages, faulty parts, and some scheduling problems."[6] Technical problems continued.

By 1981 the division had become known as Morse Industrial Products and was involved in "an array of power transmission components for general and process industries."[7] Current strategy was described in the 1981 Annual Report as follows: "Morse raised prices, improved productivity, strengthened its product mix by eliminating several low-volume, low-margin items and concentrated on sales to the petroleum drilling industry." A dramatic strategic change occurred in 1982 when the Morse Industrial operations were sold to Emerson Electric. However, Borg-Warner retained its electronic inverter technology.

During this time, the energy equipment part of the group was narrowed in scope with the sale of Centrilift Inc., a manufacturer of submersible pumps, leaving the Byron Jackson Pump, the Nuclear Valve, and the Mechanical Seal businesses. The assets of Centralift were sold to Hughes Tool Co. for 1.2 million shares of common stock.

Product development occurred in other areas, and although the nuclear power business was entering a weak period, the petroleum industry was strong until 1982. In fact, in 1980, while the nuclear valve market was shifting to aerospace and defense segments, a new plant was being built to manufacture pumps for the petroleum and other process industries.

In 1981 the group's name was changed to its present one and business was bad, particularly so because it was adversely affected by the general economy and capital goods spending. Other important environmental variables are utility construction, the prime interest rate, and crude oil prices. The only bright spot was the petroleum industry, and further product development was being done on the submersible pump.

In 1982, 80 percent of the energy equipment sales were to the petroleum and power generation industries. Business was now very weak in both segments. There was very little utility construction and petroleum exploration. The shift to aerospace markets continued, and other new strategies were new product development and productivity improvements. A new sales organization (facilities and personnel) was created to take advantage of the growing service and replacement businesses.

**CORPORATE STRATEGIC PLANNING**

Effective corporate-level strategic management helped to achieve steady sales and profit growth during the 1970s except for the mid-decade economic recession. One of the major goals around 1980 was to reduce the cyclical nature of corporate financial results. The major strategic move to achieve this was to increase the amount of service business relative to manufacturing for industry. The two groups—protective services and financial services—were expected to become more important in the 1980s. A proposed merger with Firestone, which would have been inconsistent with the service business strategy, did not materialize and was dropped. Acquisitions remain potential strategy alternatives.

To further protect profits, two other strategies were to predominate. First was asset management, and the overall results were to be measured by asset turnover. Second, efficient operations were to be a focus in all operating units.

As the 1980s began, a corporate strategy council was created for top management. Its task was to project environmental changes and design corporate strategic change to fit the new situation. Their analysis would include looking at economic, social, and technological directions worldwide and establishing investment priorities. They would be charged with determining what businesses would be appropriate a decade in the future. Also, they would be responsible for having an effective management structure in place. Corporate structure at Borg-Warner is now designed around many autonomous businesses, and the direction of movement is toward a leaner organization with a greater degree of decentralization. Top management wants its 100 SBU managers to think long-range.

Other representative corporate strategy decisions coming from top management are the following:

1. Add a strong marketing orientation to the existing emphasis on production.
2. Concentrate on U.S. manufacturing relative to production in other countries.
3. Reduce capital spending and restructure the debt.

## NOTES

1. Richard E. Hattwick and William C. Scott, *The Development of Corporate Planning at Borg-Warner: A Case History* (Terre Haute, Indiana, 1984), p. 3.
2. Ibid., p. 7.
3. 1980 Annual Report.
4. 1981 Annual Report, p. 20.
5. Investor Facts, 1983.
6. 1980 Annual Report.
7. 1981 Annual Report.

# 19  The Lincoln Electric Company, 1984

Arthur Sharplin
Northeast Louisiana University

The Lincoln Electric Company is the world's largest manufacturer of welding machines and electrodes. Lincoln employees 2400 workers in two U.S. factories near Cleveland and approximately 600 in three factories located in other countries. This does not include the field sales force of more than 200 persons. It has been estimated that Lincoln's market share (for arc-welding equipment and supplies) is more than 40 percent.

The Lincoln incentive management plan has been well known for many years. Many college management texts make reference to the Lincoln plan as a model for achieving high worker productivity. Certainly, Lincoln has been a successful company according to the usual measures of success.

James F. Lincoln died in 1965 and there was some concern, even among employees, that the Lincoln system would fall into disarray, that profits would decline, and that year-end bonuses might be discontinued. Quite the contrary, 18 years after Lincoln's death, the company appears stronger than ever. Each year, except the recession years 1982 and 1983, has seen higher profits and bonuses. Employee morale and productivity remain high. Employee turnover is almost nonexistent except for retirements. Lincoln's market share is stable. Consistently high dividends continue on Lincoln's stock.

## A HISTORICAL SKETCH

In 1895, after being frozen out of the depression-ravaged Elliott-Lincoln Company, a maker of Lincoln-designed electric motors, John C. Lincoln took out his second patent and began to manufacture his improved motor. He opened his new business, unincorporated, with $200 he had earned redesigning a motor for young Herbert Henry Dow, who later founded the Dow Chemical Company.

Started during an economic depression and cursed by a major fire after only one year in business, Lincoln's company grew, but hardly prospered, through its first quarter century. In 1906, John C. Lincoln incorporated his company and moved from his one-room, fourth-floor factory to a new three-story building he erected in east Cleveland. In his new factory, he expanded his work force to 30 and sales grew to over $50,000 a year. John Lincoln preferred being an engineer and inventor rather than a manager, though, and it was to be left to another Lincoln to manage the company through its years of success.

In 1907, after a bout with typhoid fever forced him from Ohio State University in his senior year, James F. Lincoln, John's younger brother, joined the fledgling company. In 1914 he became the active head of the firm, with the titles of general manager and vice-president. John Lincoln, although he remained president of the company for some years, became more involved in other business ventures and in his work as an inventor.

One of James Lincoln's early actions as head of the firm was to ask the employees to elect representatives to a committee which would advise him on company operations. The advisory board has met with the chief executive officer twice monthly since that time. This was only the first of a series of innovative personnel policies which have, over the years, distinguished Lincoln Electric from its contemporaries.

The first year the advisory board was in existence, working hours were reduced from 55 per week, then standard, to 50 hours a week. In 1915, the company gave each employee a paid-up life insurance policy. A welding school, which continues today, was begun in 1917. In 1918, an employee bonus plan was attempted. It was not continued, but the idea was to resurface and become the backbone of the Lincoln management system.

The Lincoln Electric Employees' Association was formed in 1919 to provide health benefits and social activities. This organization continues today and has assumed several additional functions over the years. In 1923, a piecework pay system was in effect, employees got two-week paid vacations each year, and wages were adjusted for changes in the consumer price index. Approximately 30 percent of Lincoln's stock was set aside for key employees in 1914 when James F. Lincoln became general manager, and a stock purchase plan for all employees was begun in 1925.

The board of directors voted to start a suggestion system in 1929. The program is still in effect, but cash awards, a part of the early program, were discontinued several years ago. Now, suggestions are rewarded by additional points, which affect year-end bonuses.

The legendary Lincoln bonus plan was proposed by the advisory board and accepted on a trial basis by James Lincoln in 1934. The first annual bonus amounted to about 25 percent of wages. There has been a bonus every year since then. The bonus plan has been a cornerstone of the Lincoln management system, and recent bonuses have approximated annual wages.

By 1944, Lincoln employees enjoyed a pension plan, a policy of promotion from within, and continuous employment. Base pay rates were determined by formal job evaluation and a merit rating system was in effect.

In the prologue of James F. Lincoln's last book, Charles G. Herbruck wrote regarding the foregoing personnel innovations, "They were not to buy good behavior. They were not efforts to increase profits. They were not antidotes to labor difficulties. They did not constitute a "do-gooder" program. They were an expression of mutual respect for each person's importance, to the job to be done. All of them reflect the leadership of James Lincoln, under whom they were nurtured and propagated."[1] (Lincoln, 1961, p. 11).

By the start of World War II, Lincoln Electric was the world's largest manufacturer of arc-welding products. Sales of about $4 million in 1934 had grown to $24 million by 1941. Productivity per employee more than doubled during the same period.

During the war, Lincoln Electric prospered as never before. Despite challenges to Lincoln's profitability by the navy's Price Review Board and to the tax deductibility of employee bonuses by the Internal Revenue Service, the company increased its profits and paid huge bonuses.

Certainly since 1935 and probably for several years before that, Lincoln productivity has been well above the average for similar companies. Lincoln claims levels of productivity more than twice those for other manufacturers from 1945 onward. Information available from outside sources tends to support these claims.

## COMPANY PHILOSOPHY

James F. Lincoln was the son of a Congregational minister, and Christian principles were at the center of his business philosophy. The confidence that he had in the efficacy of Christ's teachings is illustrated by the following remark taken from one of his books:

> The Christian ethic should control our acts. If it did control our acts, the savings in cost of distribution would be tremendous. Advertising would be a contract of the expert consultant with the customer, in order to give the customer the best product available when all of the customer's needs are considered. Competition then would be in improving the quality of products and increasing efficiency in producing and distributing them; not in deception, as is now too customary. Pricing would reflect efficiency of production; it would not be a selling dodge that the customer may well be sorry he accepted. It would be proper for all concerned and rewarding for the ability used in producing the product.[2]

There is no indication that Lincoln attempted to evangelize his employees or customers—or the general public for that matter. The current board chairman, Mr. Irrgang, and the president, Mr. Willis, do not even mention the Christian gospel in their recent speeches and interviews. The company motto, "The actual is limited, the possible is immense," is prominently displayed, but there is no display of religious slogans, and there is no company chapel.

## Attitude Toward the Customer

James Lincoln saw the customer's needs as the raison d'être for every company. "When any company has achieved success so that it is attractive as an investment," he wrote, "All money usually needed for expansion is supplied by the customer in retained earnings. It is obvious that the customer's interests, not the stockholder's, should come first."[3] In 1947 he said, "Care should be taken . . . not to rivet attention on profit. Between 'How much do I get?' and 'How do I make this better, cheaper, more useful?' the difference is fundamental and decisive."[4] Mr. Willis still ranks the customer as Lincoln's most important constituency. This is reflected in Lincoln's policy to "at all times price on the basis of cost and at all times keep pressure on our cost. . . ."[5] Lincoln's goal, often stated, is "to build a better and better product at a lower and lower price."[6] "It is obvious,"

James Lincoln said, "that the customer's interests should be the first goal of industry."[7]

## Attitude Toward Stockholders

Stockholders are given last priority at Lincoln. This is a continuation of James Lincoln's philosophy: "The last group to be considered is the stockholders who own stock because they think it will be more profitable than investing money in any other way."[8] Concerning division of the largess produced by incentive management, Lincoln writes, "The absentee stockholder also will get his share, even if undeserved, out of the greatly increased profit that the efficiency produces."[9]

## Attitude Toward Unionism

There has never been a serious effort to organize Lincoln employees. Although James Lincoln criticized the labor movement for "selfishly attempting to better its position at the expense of the people it must serve."[10] he still had kind words for union members. He excused abuses of union power as "the natural reactions of human beings to the abuses to which management has subjected them."[11] Lincoln's idea of the correct relationship between workers and managers is shown by this comment: "Labor and management are properly not warring camps; they are parts of one organization in which they must and should cooperate fully and happily."[12]

## Beliefs and Assumptions About Employees

If fulfilling customer needs is the desired goal of business, then employee performance and productivity are the means by which this goal can best be achieved. It is the Lincoln attitude toward employees, reflected in the following quotations, which is credited by many with creating the record of success the company has experienced:

> The greatest fear of the worker, which is the same as the greatest fear of the industrialist in operating a company, is the lack of income. . . . The industrial manager is very conscious of his company's need of uninterrupted income. He is completely oblivious, evidently, of the fact that the worker has the same need.[13]

> He is just as eager as any manager is to be part of a team that is properly organized and working for the advancement of our economy. . . . He has no desire to make profits for those who do not hold up their end in production, as is true of absentee stockholders and inactive people in the company.[14]

> If money is to be used as an incentive, the program must provide that what is paid to the worker is what he has earned. The earnings of each must be in accordance with accomplishment.[15]

> Status is of great importance in all human relationships. The greatest incentive that money has, usually, is that it is a symbol of success. . . . The resulting status is the real incentive. . . . Money alone can be an incentive to the miser only.[16]

> There must be complete honesty and understanding between the hourly worker and management if high efficiency is to be obtained.[17]

**LINCOLN'S BUSINESS**

Arc welding has been the standard joining method in the shipbuilding industry for decades. It is the predominant way of joining steel in the construction industry. Most industrial plants have their own welding shops for maintenance and construction. Manufacturers of tractors and all kinds of heavy equipment use arc welding extensively in the manufacturing process. Many hobbyists have their own welding machines and use them for making metal items such as patio furniture and barbeque pits. The popularity of welded sculpture as an art form is growing.

Although advances in welding technology have been frequent, arc-welding products, in the main, have hardly changed except for Lincoln's Innershield process. This process, utilizing a self-shielded, flux-cored electrode, has established new cost-saving opportunities for construction and equipment fabrication. The most popular Lincoln electrode, the Fleetweld 5P, has been virtually the same since the 1930s. The most popular engine-driven welder in the world, the Lincoln SA-200, has been a gray-colored assembly including a four-cylinder continental "Red Seal" engine and a 200-ampere direct-current generator with two current-control knobs for at least three decades. A 1980 model SA-200 even weighs almost the same as the 1950 model, and it certainly is little changed in appearance.

Lincoln and its competitors now market a wide range of general-purpose and specialty electrodes for welding mild steel, aluminum, cast iron, and stainless and special steels. Most of these electrodes are designed to meet the standards of the American Welding Society, a trade association. They are thus essentially the same as to size and composition from one manufacturer to any other. Every electrode manufacturer has a limited number of unique products, but these typically constitute only a small percentage of total sales.

Lincoln's research and development expenditures have recently been less than 1.5 percent of sales. There is evidence that others spend several times as much as a percentage of sales.

Lincoln's share of the arc-welding products market appears to have been about 40 percent for many years, and the welding products market has grown somewhat faster than the level of industry in general. The market is highly price-competitive, with variations in prices of standard products normally amounting to only a percent or two. Lincoln's products are sold directly by its engineering-oriented sales force and indirectly through its distributor organization. Advertising expenditures amount to less than one-fourth of one percent of sales, one-third as much as a major Lincoln competitor with whom the casewriter checked.

The other major welding process, flame welding, has not been competitive with arc welding since the 1930s. However, plasma arc welding, a relatively new process which uses a conducting stream of superheated gas (plasma) to confine the welding current to a small area, has made some inroads, especially in metal tubing manufacturing, in recent years. Major advances in technology which will produce an alternative superior to arc welding within the next decade or so appear unlikely. Also, it seems likely that changes in the machines and techniques used in arc welding will be evolutionary rather than revolutionary.

**Products**    The company is primarily engaged in the manufacture and sale of arc-welding products—electric welding machines and metal electrodes. Lincoln also produces electric motors ranging from one-half horsepower to 200 horsepower. Motors constitute about 8 to 10 percent of total sales.

The electric welding machines, some consisting of a transformer or motor and generator arrangement powered by commercial electricity and others consisting of an internal combustion engine and generator, are designed to produce from 30 to 1000 amperes of electrical power. This electrical current is used to melt a consumable metal electrode with the molten metal being transferred in a super hot spray to the metal joint being welded. Very high temperatures and hot sparks are produced, and operators usually must wear special eye and face protection and leather gloves, often along with leather aprons and sleeves.

Welding electrodes are of two basic types: (1) Coated "stick" electrodes, usually 14 inches long and smaller than a pencil in diameter, are held in a special insulated holder by the operator, who must manipulate the electrode in order to maintain a proper arc width and pattern of deposition of the metal being transferred. Stick electrodes are packaged in 6- to 50-pound boxes. (2) Coiled wire, ranging in diameter from 0.035 to 0.219 inch, is designed to be fed continuously to the welding arc through a "gun" held by the operator or positioned by automatic positioning equipment. The wire is packaged in coils, reels, and drums weighing from 14 to 1000 pounds.

**MANUFAC-
TURING
OPERATIONS**    The main plant is in Euclid, Ohio, a suburb on Cleveland's east side. The layout of this plant is shown in Exhibit 19.1. There are no warehouses. Materials flow from the half-mile-long dock on the north side of the plant through the production lines to a very limited storage and loading area on the south side. Materials used on each workstation are stored as close as possible to the workstation. The administrative offices, near the center of the factory, are entirely functional. Not even the president's office is carpeted. A corridor below the main level provides access to the factory floor from the main entrance near the center of the plant. A new plant, just opened in Mentor, Ohio, houses some of the electrode production operations, which were moved from the main plant.

**Manufac-
turing
Processes**    Electrode manufacturing is highly capital-intensive. Metal rods purchased from steel producers are drawn or extruded down to smaller diameters, cut to length, coated with pressed-powder "flux" for stick electrodes or plated with copper (for conductivity), and spun into coils or spools for wire. Some of Lincoln's wire, called Innershield, is hollow and filled with a material similar to that used to coat stick electrodes. Lincoln is highly secretive about its electrode production processes, and the casewriter was not given access to the details of those processes.

**Exhibit 19.1** Lincoln Electric Company Main Factory Layout

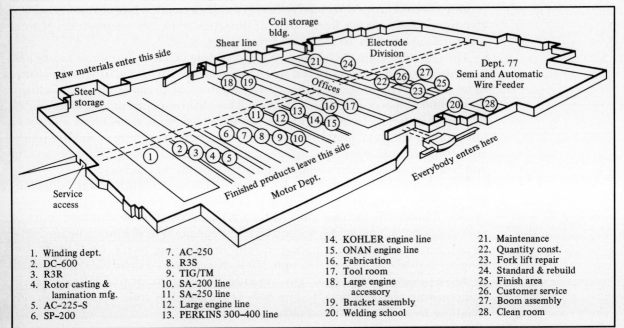

1. Winding dept.
2. DC–600
3. R3R
4. Rotor casting & lamination mfg.
5. AC–225–S
6. SP–200
7. AC–250
8. R3S
9. TIG/TM
10. SA–200 line
11. SA–250 line
12. Large engine line
13. PERKINS 300–400 line
14. KOHLER engine line
15. ONAN engine line
16. Fabrication
17. Tool room
18. Large engine accessory
19. Bracket assembly
20. Welding school
21. Maintenance
22. Quantity const.
23. Fork lift repair
24. Standard & rebuild
25. Finish area
26. Customer service
27. Boom assembly
28. Clean room

Welding machines and electric motors are made on a series of assembly lines. Gasoline and diesel engines are purchased partially assembled, but practically all other components are made from basic industrial products—for example, steel bars and sheets and bar copper conductor wire—in the Lincoln factory.

Individual components, such as gasoline tanks for engine-driven welders and steel shafts for motors and generators, are made by numerous small factories within a factory. The shaft for a certain generator, for example, is made from a raw steel bar by one operator who uses five large machines, all running continuously. A saw cuts the bar to length, a digital lathe machines different sections to varying diameters, a special milling machine cuts a slot for a keyway, and so forth, until a finished shaft is produced. The operator moves the shafts from machine to machine and makes necessary adjustments.

Another operator punches, shapes, and paints, sheet-metal cowling parts. One assembles steel laminations onto a rotor shaft, then winds, insulates, and tests the rotors. Finished components are moved by crane operators to the nearby assembly lines.

**Worker Performance and Attitudes**

Exceptional worker performance at Lincoln is a matter of record. The typical Lincoln employee earns about twice as much as other factory workers in the Cleveland area. Yet the labor cost per sales dollar at Lincoln, currently 23.5 cents, is well below industry averages.

Sales per Lincoln factory employee currently exceed $157,000. An observer at the factory quickly sees why this figure is so high. Each worker is proceeding busily and thoughtfully about his or her task. There is no idle chatter. Most workers take no coffee breaks. Many operate several machines and make a substantial component unaided. The supervisors, some with as many as 100 subordinates, are busy with planning and recordkeeping duties and hardly glance at the people they supervise. The manufacturing procedures appear efficient—no unnecessary steps, no wasted motions, no wasted materials. Finished components move smoothly to subsequent workstations.

Worker turnover at Lincoln is practically nonexistent except for retirements and departures by new employees. The appendix to this case (pp. 642–646) includes summaries of interviews with Lincoln employees.

**ORGANIZA-TION STRUCTURE AND PERSONNEL POLICIES**

Lincoln has never had a formal organization chart.* The objective of this policy is to ensure maximum flexibility. An open-door policy is practiced throughout the company, and personnel are encouraged to take problems to the persons most capable of resolving them.

Perhaps because of the quality and enthusiasm of the Lincoln work force, routine supervision is almost nonexistent. A typical production supervisor, for example, supervises as many as 100 workers, a span of control which does not allow more than infrequent worker-supervisor interaction. Position titles and traditional flows of authority do imply something of an organizational structure, however. For example, the vice-president, sales, and the vice-president, electrode division, report to the president, as do various staff assistants such as the personnel director and the director of purchasing. Using such implied relationships, it has been determined that production workers have two or, at most, three levels of supervision between themselves and the president.

**Recruitment and Selection**

Every job opening at Lincoln is advertised internally on company bulletin boards and any employee can apply for any job so advertised. External hiring is done only for entry-level positions. Selection for these jobs is done on the basis of personal interviews—there is no aptitude or psychological testing. Not even a high school diploma is required except for engineering and sales positions, which are filled by graduate engineers. A committee consisting of vice-presidents and superintendents interviews candidates initially cleared by the Personnel Department. Final selection is made by the supervisor who has a job opening. Out of over 3500 applicants interviewed by the Personnel Department during a recent period, fewer than 300 were hired.

*Once, Harvard Business School researchers prepared an organization chart reflecting the implied relationships mentioned in this section. The chart became available within the Lincoln organization, and present Lincoln management feels that it had a disruptive effect. Therefore, the casewriter was asked not to include any kind of organizational chart in this report.

**Job Security**

In 1958 Lincoln formalized its lifetime employment policy, which had already been in effect for many years. There have been no layoffs at Lincoln since World War II. Since 1958, every Lincoln worker with over one year's longevity has been guaranteed at least 30 hours per week, 49 weeks per year.

The policy has never been so severely tested as during the 1981–1983 recession. As a manufacturer of capital goods, Lincoln's business is highly cyclical. In previous recessions Lincoln has been able to avoid major sales declines. Nineteen eighty-two sales, however, were about one-third below those of 1981. Few companies could withstand such a sales decline and remain profitable. Yet Lincoln not only earned profits, but no employee was laid off, the usual year-end incentive bonuses were paid (averaging $15,600 per worker for 1982), and common shareholders continued to receive about the normal dividend (around $8 per share).

**Performance Evaluations**

Supervisors formally evaluate their subordinates twice a year using the cards shown in Exhibit 19.2. The employee performance criteria, "quality," "dependability," "Ideas and cooperation," and "output," are considered independent of each other. Marks on the cards are converted to numerical scores which are forced to average 100 for each evaluating supervisor. Individual merit rating scores normally range from 80 to 110. Any score over 110 requires a special letter to top management. These scores (over 110) are not considered in computing the required 100-point average for each evaluating supervisor. Suggestions for improvements often result in recommendations for exceptionally high performance scores. Supervisors discuss individual performance marks with the employees concerned. Each warranty claim on a Lincoln product is traced to the individual employee whose work caused the defect. The employee's performance score may be reduced by one point, or the worker may be required to repay the cost of servicing the warranty claim by working without pay.

**Compensation**

Basic wage levels for jobs at Lincoln are determined by a wage survey of similar jobs in the Cleveland area. These rates are adjusted quarterly in accordance with changes in the Cleveland area consumer price index. Insofar as possible, base wage rates are translated into piece rates. Practically all production workers and many others—for example, some forklift operators—are paid by piece rate. Once established, piece rates are never changed unless a substantive change in the way a job is done results from a source other than the worker doing the job. In December of each year, a portion of annual profits is distributed to employees as bonuses. Incentive bonuses since 1934 have averaged about the same as annual wages and somewhat more than after-tax profits. The average bonus for 1981 was about $21,000. Bonuses averaged $15,500 and $10,400, respectively, for the recession years 1982 and 1983. Individual bonuses are proportional to merit rating scores. For example, assume incentive bonuses for the company total 110

## Exhibit 19.2 Merit Rating Cards

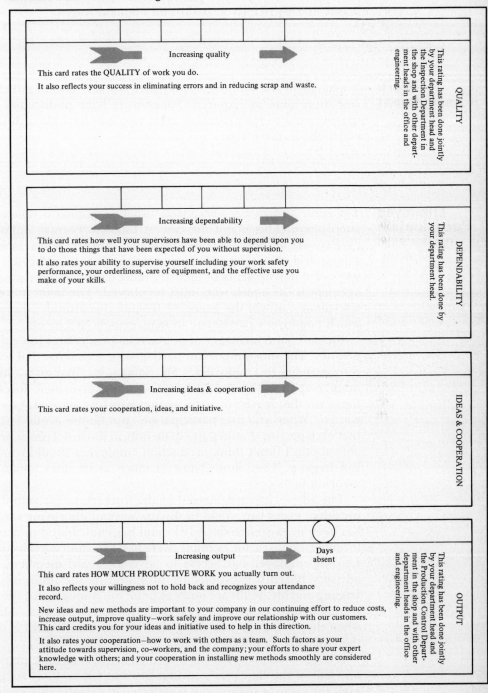

Increasing quality

This card rates the QUALITY of work you do.

It also reflects your success in eliminating errors and in reducing scrap and waste.

This rating has been done jointly by your department head and the Inspection Department in the shop and with other department heads in the office and engineering.

QUALITY

---

Increasing dependability

This card rates how well your supervisors have been able to depend upon you to do those things that have been expected of you without supervision.

It also rates your ability to supervise yourself including your work safety performance, your orderliness, care of equipment, and the effective use you make of your skills.

This rating has been done by your department head.

DEPENDABILITY

---

Increasing ideas & cooperation

This card rates your cooperation, ideas, and initiative.

IDEAS & COOPERATION

---

Increasing output    Days absent

This card rates HOW MUCH PRODUCTIVE WORK you actually turn out.

It also reflects your willingness not to hold back and recognizes your attendance record.

New ideas and new methods are important to your company in our continuing effort to reduce costs, increase output, improve quality—work safely and improve our relationship with our customers. This card credits you for your ideas and initiative used to help in this direction.

It also rates your cooperation—how to work with others as a team. Such factors as your attitude towards supervision, co-workers, and the company; your efforts to share your expert knowledge with others; and your cooperation in installing new methods smoothly are considered here.

This rating has been done jointly by your department head and the Production Control Department in the shop and with other department heads in the office and engineering.

OUTPUT

percent of wages paid. A person whose performance score is 95 will receive a bonus of 1.045 (1.10 $\times$ 0.95) times annual wages.

## Work Assignment

Management has authority to transfer workers and to switch between overtime and short time as required. Supervisors have undisputed authority to assign specific parts to individual workers, who may have their own preferences due to variations in piece rates.

## Employee Participation in Decision Making

The term *participative management* usually suggests a relaxed, nonauthoritarian atmosphere. This is not the case at Lincoln. Formal authority is quite strong. "We're very authoritarian around here," says Mr. Willis. James F. Lincoln placed a good deal of stress on protecting management's authority. "Management in all successful departments of industry must have complete power," he said. "Management is the coach who must be obeyed. The men, however, are the players who alone can win the game."[18] Despite this attitude, there are several ways in which employees participate in management at Lincoln.

Richard Sabo, manager of public relations, relates job enlargement to participation. "The most important participative technique that we use is giving more responsibility to employees." Mr. Sabo says, "We give a high school graduate more responsibility than other companies give their foremen." Lincoln puts limits on the degree of participation which is allowed, however. In Mr. Sabo's words, "When you use 'participation,' put quotes around it. Because we believe that each person should participate only in those decisions he is most knowledgeable about. I don't think production employees should control the decisions of Bill Irrgang. They don't know as much as he does about the decisions he is involved in."

The advisory board, elected by the workers, meets with the chairman and the president every two weeks to discuss ways of improving operations. This board has been in existence since 1914 and has contributed to many innovations. The incentive bonuses, for example, were first recommended by this committee. Every Lincoln employee has access to advisory board members, and answers to all advisory board suggestions are promised by the following meeting. Both Mr. Irrgang and Mr. Willis are quick to point out, though, that the advisory board only recommends actions. "They do not have direct authority," Mr. Irrgang says, "and when they bring up something that management thinks is not to the benefit of the company, it will be rejected."[19]

A suggestion program was instituted in 1929. At first, employees were awarded one-half of the first year's savings attributable to their suggestions. Now, however, the value of suggestions is reflected in performance evaluation scores, which determine individual incentive bonus amounts.

## Training and Education

Production workers are given a short period of on-the-job training and then placed on a piecework pay system. Lincoln does not pay for off-site education. The idea behind this latter policy is that not everyone can take advantage of such a program, and it is unfair to expend company funds for an advantage to which there is unequal access. Sales personnel are given on-the-job training in the plant followed by a period of work and training at one of the regional sales offices.

## Fringe Benefits and Executive Perquisites

A medical plan and a company-paid retirement program have been in effect for many years. A plant cafeteria, operated on a break-even basis, serves meals at about 60 percent of usual costs. An employee association, to which the company does not contribute, provides disability insurance and social and athletic activities. An employee stock ownership program, instituted in about 1925, and regular stock purchases have resulted in employee ownership of about 50 percent of Lincoln's stock.

As to executive perquisites, there are none—crowded, austere offices, no executive washrooms or lunchrooms, and no reserved parking spaces. Even the company president pays for his own meals and eats in the cafeteria.

## FINANCIAL POLICIES

James F. Lincoln felt strongly that financing for company growth should come from within the company—through initial cash investment by the founders, through retention of earnings, and through stock purchases by those who work in the business. He saw the following advantages of this approach:[20]

1. Ownership of stock by employees strengthens team spirit. "If they are mutually anxious to make it succeed, the future of the company is bright."
2. Ownership of stock provides individual incentive because employees feel that they will benefit from company profitability.
3. "Ownership is educational." Owners-employees "will know how profits are made and lost; how success is won and lost. . . . There are few socialists in the list of stockholders of the nation's industries."
4. "Capital available from within controls expansion." Unwarranted expansion will not occur, Lincoln believed, under his financing plan.
5. "The greatest advantage would be the development of the individual worker. Under the incentive of ownership, he would become a greater man."
6. "Stock ownership is one of the steps that can be taken that will make the worker feel that there is less of a gulf between him and the boss. . . . Stock ownership will help the worker to recognize his responsibility in the game and the importance of victory."

Lincoln Electric Company uses a minimum of debt in its capital structure. There is no borrowing at all, with the debt being limited to current payables. Even the new $20 million plant in Mentor, Ohio, was financed totally from earnings.

The unusual pricing policy at Lincoln is succinctly stated by President Willis: "at all times price on the basis of cost and at all times keep pressure on our cost." This policy resulted in Lincoln's price for the most popular welding electrode then in use going from 16 cents a pound in 1929 to 4.7 cents in 1938. More recently, the SA-200 welder, Lincoln's largest-selling portable machine, decreased in price from 1958 through 1965. According to Dr. C. Jackson Grayson of the American Productivity Center in Houston, Texas, Lincoln's prices in general have increased only one-fifth as fast as the consumer price index from 1934 to about 1970. This has resulted in a welding-products market in which Lincoln is the undisputed price leader for the products it manufacturers. Not even the major Japanese manufacturers, such as Nippon Steel for welding electrodes and Asaka Transformer for welding machines, have been able to penetrate this market.

Huge cash balances are accumulated each year preparatory to paying the year-end bonuses. The bonuses totaled $55,718,000 for 1981 and about $41,-000,000 for 1982. This money is invested in short-term U.S. government securities until needed. Financial statements are shown in Exhibit 19.3.

## HOW WELL DOES LINCOLN SERVE ITS PUBLIC?

Lincoln Electric differs from most other companies in the importance it assigns to each of the groups it serves. Mr. Willis identifies these groups, in the order of priority Lincoln ascribes to them, as (1) customers, (2) employees, and (3) stockholders.

Certainly Lincoln customers have fared well over the years. Lincoln prices for welding machines and welding electrodes are acknowledged to be the lowest in the marketplace. Lincoln quality has consistently been so high that Lincoln Fleetweld electrodes and Lincoln SA-200 welders have been the standard in the pipeline and refinery construction industry, where price is hardly a criterion, for decades. The cost of field failures for Lincoln products was an amazing 0.04 percent in 1979. A Lincoln distributor in Monroe, Louisiana, says that he has sold several hundred of the popular AC-225 welders, and though the machine is warranted for one year, he has never handled a warranty claim.

Perhaps best served of all Lincoln constituencies have been the employees. Not the least of their benefits, of course, are the year-end bonuses, which effectively double an already average compensation level. The foregoing description of the personnel program and the comments in Exhibit 19.2 further illustrate the desirability of a Lincoln job.

Although stockholders were relegated to an inferior status by James F. Lincoln, they have done very well indeed. Recent dividends have exceeded $7 a share and earnings per share have exceeded $20. In January 1980, the price of restricted stock committed by Lincoln to employees was $117 a share. By February 4, 1983, the stated value, at which Lincoln will repurchase the stock if tendered, was $166. A check with the New York office of Merrill, Lynch, Pierce, Fenner and Smith on February 4, 1983, revealed an estimated price on Lincoln stock of $240 a share,

Exhibit 19.3

# LINCOLN ELECTRIC COMPANY FINANCIAL STATEMENT
## Summary of Financial Condition ($000's omitted)

| | 1979 | 1980 | 1981 | 1982 | 1983 |
|---|---|---|---|---|---|
| **Assets** | | | | | |
| Cash | $ 2,261 | $ 1,307 | $ 3,603 | $ 1,318 | $ 1,774 |
| Govt. securities and certificates of deposit | 38,408 | 46,503 | 62,671 | 72,485 | 77,872 |
| Notes and accounts receivable | 41,598 | 42,424 | 41,521 | 26,239 | 31,114 |
| Inventories (LIFO basis) | 37,640 | 35,533 | 45,541 | 38,157 | 30,773 |
| Deferred taxes and prepaid expenses | 1,437 | 2,749 | 3,658 | 4,635 | 4,704 |
| | $121,344 | $128,516 | $156,994 | $142,834 | $146,237 |
| Other intangible assets | $ 19,164 | $ 19,723 | $ 21,424 | $ 22,116 | $ 21,421 |
| Investment in foreign subsidiaries | 4,986 | 4,695 | 4,695 | 7,696 | 8,696 |
| | $ 24,150 | $ 24,418 | $ 26,119 | $ 29,812 | $ 30,117 |
| **Property, plant, equipment** | | | | | |
| Land | $ 911 | $ 913 | $ 928 | $ 925 | $ 925 |
| Buildings (after depreciation) | 21,585 | 22,982 | 24,696 | 23,330 | 22,378 |
| Machinery, tools and equipment | 21,250 | 25,339 | 27,104 | 26,949 | 27,146 |
| (after depreciation) | $ 43,746 | $ 49,234 | $ 52,728 | $ 51,204 | $ 50,449 |
| Total assets | $189,240 | $202,168 | $235,841 | $223,850 | $226,803 |
| **Liabilities** | | | | | |
| Accounts payable | $ 16,590 | $ 15,608 | $ 14,868 | $ 11,936 | $ 16,228 |
| Accrued wages | 917 | 1,504 | 4,940 | 3,633 | 3,224 |
| Taxes, including income taxes | 9,620 | 5,622 | 14,755 | 5,233 | 6,675 |
| Dividends payable | 5,889 | 5,800 | 7,070 | 6,957 | 6,675 |
| | $ 33,016 | $ 28,534 | $ 41,633 | $ 27,759 | $ 32,802 |
| Deferred taxes and other long-term liabilities | — | $ 3,807 | $ 4,557 | $ 5,870 | $ 7,805 |
| **Shareholders' equity** | | | | | |
| Common capital stock, stated value | $ 280 | $ 276 | $ 272 | $ 268 | $ 257 |
| Additional paid-in capital | 4,143 | 2,641 | 501 | 1,862 | -0- |
| Retained earnings | 151,801 | 166,910 | 188,878 | 188,392 | 186,318 |
| Equity adjustment from foreign currency translation | | | | (301) | (379) |
| | $156,224 | $169,827 | $189,651 | $190,221 | $186,196 |
| Total liabilities & shareholders' equity | $189,240 | $202,168 | $235,841 | $223,850 | $226,803 |
| **Statement of income and expenses** | | | | | |
| Income | | | | | |
| Net sales | $373,789 | $387,374 | $450,387 | $310,862 | $263,129 |
| Other income | 11,397 | 13,817 | 18,454 | 18,049 | 13,387 |
| | $385,186 | $401,191 | $468,841 | $328,911 | $276,516 |
| Costs and Expenses | | | | | |
| Cost of products sold | $244,376 | $260,671 | $293,332 | $212,674 | $179,851 |
| Selling, administrative, freight Out and general expenses | 33,699 | 37,753 | 42,656 | 37,128 | 36,348 |
| Year-end incentive bonus | 44,068 | 43,249 | 55,718 | 36,870 | 21,914 |
| Payroll taxes related to bonus | 1,349 | 1,251 | 1,544 | 1,847 | 1,186 |
| Pension expense | 6,131 | 6,810 | 6,874 | 5,888 | 5,151 |
| Interest exp. on tax assessments | | | | | 1,946 |
| | $329,623 | $349,734 | $400,124 | $294,407 | $246,396 |

(continued)

**Exhibit 19.3** (continued)

|  | 1979 | 1980 | 1981 | 1982 | 1983 |
|---|---|---|---|---|---|
| Income before income taxes | $55,563 | $51,457 | $68,717 | $34,504 | $30,120 |
| Provision for income taxes |  |  |  |  |  |
| Federal | $22,400 | $20,300 | $27,400 | $13,227 | $14,246 |
| State and local | 3,165 | 3,072 | 3,885 | 2,497 | (989) |
|  | $25,565 | $23,372 | $31,285 | $15,724 | $13,257 |
| Net income | $29,998 | $28,085 | $37,432 | $18,780 | $16,863 |
| Employees (eligible for bonus) | 2,611 | 2,637 | 2,684 | 2,634 | 2,561 |

with none being offered for sale. Technically, this price applies only to the unrestricted stock owned by the Lincoln family, a few other major holders, and employees who have purchased it on the open market, but it gives some idea of the value of Lincoln stock in general. The risk associated with Lincoln stock, a major determinant of stock value, is minimal because of the absence of debt in Lincoln's capital structure, because of an extremely stable earnings record, and because of Lincoln's practice of purchasing the restricted stock whenever employees offer it for sale.

## A CONCLUDING COMMENT

It is easy to believe that the reason for Lincoln's success is the excellent attitude of Lincoln employees and their willingness to work harder, faster, and more intelligently than other industrial workers. However, Mr. Richard Sabo, manager of publicity and educational services at Lincoln, suggests that appropriate credit be given to Lincoln executives, whom he credits with carrying out the following policies:

1. Management has limited research, development, and manufacturing to a standard product line designed to meet the major needs of the welding industry.
2. New products must be reviewed by manufacturing and all production costs verified before being approved by management.
3. Purchasing is challenged to not only procure materials at the lowest cost, but also to work closely with engineering and manufacturing to assure that the latest innovations are implemented.
4. Manufacturing supervision and all personnel are held accountable for reduction of scrap, energy conservation, and maintenance of product quality.
5. Production control, material handling, and methods engineering are closely supervised by top management.
6. Material and finished goods inventory control, accurate cost accounting, and attention to sales cost, credit, and other financial areas have constantly reduced overhead and led to excellent profitability.
7. Management has made cost reduction a way of life at Lincoln, and definite

programs are established in many areas, including traffic and shipping, where tremendous savings can result.

8. Management has established a sales department that is technically trained to reduce customer welding costs. This sales technique and other real customer services have eliminated nonessential frills and resulted in long-term benefits to all concerned.

9. Management has encouraged education, technical publishing, and long-range programs that have resulted in industry growth, thereby assuring market potential for the Lincoln Electric Company.

## NOTES

1. James F. Lincoln, *A New Approach to Industrial Economics* (Old Greenwich, Conn.: Devin-Adair, 1961), p. 11.
2. Ibid., p. 64.
3. Ibid., p. 119.
4. "You Can't Tell What a Man Can Do—Until He Has the Chance," *Reader's Digest,* January 1947, p. 94.
5. George E. Willis, letter to author of September 7, 1978.
6. Lincoln, *A New Approach,* p. 47.
7. Ibid., p. 117.
8. Ibid., p. 38.
9. Ibid., p. 122.
10. Ibid., p. 18.
11. Ibid., p. 76.
12. Ibid., p. 72.
13. Ibid., p. 36.
14. Ibid., p. 75.
15. Ibid., p. 98.
16. Ibid., p. 92.
17. Ibid., p. 39.
18. James F. Lincoln, *Incentive Management* (Cleveland: Lincoln Electric Company, 1951), p. 228.
19. Incentive Management in Action," *Assembly Engineering,* March 1967, p. 18.
20. Lincoln, *A New Approach,* pp. 220–228.

## APPENDIX TO CASE 19: EMPLOYEE INTERVIEWS

During the late summer of 1980, the author conducted numerous interviews with Lincoln employees. Typical questions and answers from those interviews are presented below. In order to maintain each employee's personal privacy, the names used for the interviewees are fictitious.

### I

Interview with Betty Stewart, a 52-year-old high school graduate who had been with Lincoln 13 years and who was working as a cost accounting clerk at the time of the interview.

Q. *What jobs have you held here besides the one you have now?*

A. I worked in payroll for a while, and then this job came open and I took it.

Q. *How much money did you make last year, including your bonus?*

A. I would say roughly around $20,000, but I was off for back surgery for a while.

Q. *You weren't paid while you were off for back surgery?*

A. No.

Q. *Did the Employees Association help out?*

A. Yes. The company doesn't furnish that, though. We pay $6 month into the Employee Association. I think my check from them was $105.00 a week.

Q. *How was your performance rating last year?*

A. It was around 100 points, but I lost some points for attendance with my back problem.

Q. *How did you get your job at Lincoln?*

A. I was bored silly where I was working, and I had heard that Lincoln kept their people busy. So I applied and got the job the next day.

Q. *Do you think you make more money than similar workers in Cleveland?*

A. I know I do.

Q. *What have you done with your money?*

A. We have purchased a better home. Also, my son is going to the University of Chicago, which costs $10,000 a year. I buy the Lincoln stock which is offered each year, and I have a little bit of gold.

Q. *Have you ever visited with any of the senior executives, like Mr. Willis or Mr. Irrgang?*

A. I have known Mr. Willis for a long time.

Q. *Does he call you by name?*

A. Yes. In fact he was very instrumental in my going to the doctor that I am going to with my back. He knows the director of the clinic.

Q. *Do you know Mr. Irrgang?*

A. I know him to speak to him, and he always speaks, always. But I have known Mr. Willis for a good many years. When I did Plant Two accounting I did not understand how the plant operated. Of course you are not allowed in Plant Two, because that's the Electrode Division. I told my boss about the problem one day and the next thing I knew Mr. Willis came by and said, "Come on, Betty, we're going to Plant Two." He spent an hour and a half showing me the plant.

Q. *Do you think Lincoln employees produce more than those in other companies?*

A. I think with the incentive program the way that it is, if you want to work and achieve, then you will do it. If you don't want to work and achieve, you will not do it no matter where you are. Just because you are merit rated and have a bonus, if you really don't want to work hard, then you're not going to. You will accept your ninety points or ninety-two or eighty-five because, even with that, you make more money than people on the outside.

Q. *Do you think Lincoln employees will ever join a union?*

A. I don't know why they would.

Q. *What is the most important advantage of working for Lincoln Electric?*

A. You have an incentive, and you can push and get something for pushing. That's not true in a lot of companies.

Q. *So you say that money is a very major advantage?*

A. Money is a major advantage, but it's not just the money. It's the fact that having the incentive, you do wish to work a little harder. I'm sure that there are a lot of men here who, if they worked some other place, would not work as hard as they do here. Not that they are overworked—I don't mean that—but I'm sure they wouldn't push.

Q. *Is there anything that you would like to add?*

A. I do like working here. I am better off being pushed mentally. In another company if you pushed too hard you would feel a little bit of pressure, and someone might say, "Hey, slow down; don't try so hard." But here you are encouraged, not discouraged.

## II

Interview with Ed Sanderson, 23-year-old high school graduate who had been with Lincoln four years and who was a machine operator in the Electrode Division at the time of the interview.

Q. *How did you happen to get this job?*

A. My wife was pregnant, and I was making three bucks an hour and one day I came here and applied. That was it. I kept calling to let them know I was still interested.

Q. *Roughly what were your earnings last year including your bonus?*

A. $37,000.

Q. *What have you done with your money since you have been here?*

A. Well, we've lived pretty well and we bought a condominium.

Q. *Have you paid for the condominium?*

A. No, but I could.

Q. *Have you bought your Lincoln stock this year?*

A. No, I haven't bought any Lincoln stock yet.

Q. *Do you get the feeling that the executives here are pretty well thought of?*

A. I think they are. To get where they are today, they had to really work.

Q. *Wouldn't that be true anywhere?*

A. I think more so here because seniority really doesn't mean anything. If you work with a guy who has twenty years here, and you have two months and you're doing a better job, you will get advanced before he will.

Q. *Are you paid on a piece rate basis?*

A. My gang does. There are nine of us who make the bare electrode, and the whole group gets paid based on how much electrode we make.

Q. *Do you think you work harder than workers in other factories in the Cleveland area?*

A. Yes, I would say I probably work harder.

Q. *Do you think it hurts anybody?*

A. No, a little hard work never hurts anybody.

Q. *If you could choose, do you think you would be as happy earning a little less money and being able to slow down a little?*

A. No, it doesn't bother me. If it bothered me, I wouldn't do it.

Q. *What would you say is the biggest disadvantage of working at Lincoln, as opposed to working somewhere else?*

A. Probably having to work shift work.

Q. *Why do you think Lincoln employees produce more than workers in other plants?*

A. That's the way the company is set up. The more you put out, the more you're going to make.

Q. *Do you think it's the piece rate and bonus together?*

A. I don't think people would work here if they didn't know that they would be rewarded at the end of the year.

Q. *Do you think Lincoln employees will ever join a union?*

A. No.

Q. *What are the major advantages of working for Lincoln?*

A. Money.

Q. *Are there any other advantages?*

A. Yes, we don't have a union shop. I don't think I could work in a union shop.

Q. *Do you think you are a career man with Lincoln at this time?*

A. Yes.

## III

Interview with Roger Lewis, 23-year-old Purdue graduate in mechanical engineering who had been in the Lincoln sales program for 15 months and who was working in the Cleveland sales office at the time of the interview.

Q. *How did you get your job at Lincoln?*

A. I saw that Lincoln was interviewing on campus at Purdue, and I went by. I later came to Cleveland for a plant tour and was offered a job.

Q. *Do you know any of the senior executives? Would they know you by name?*

A. Yes, I know all of them—Mr. Irrgang, Mr. Willis, Mr. Manross.

Q. *Do you think Lincoln salesmen work harder than those in other companies?*

A. Yes. I don't think there are many salesmen for other companies who are putting in fifty to sixty-hour weeks. Everybody here works harder. You can go out in the plant, or you can go upstairs, and there's nobody sitting around.

Q. *Do you see any real disadvantage of working at Lincoln?*

A. I don't know if it's a disadvantage but Lincoln is a spartan company, a very thrifty company. I like that. The sales offices are functional, not fancy.

Q. *Why do you think Lincoln employees have such high productivity?*

A. Piecework has a lot to do with it. Lincoln is smaller than many plants, too; you can stand in one place and see the materials come in one side and the product go out the other. You feel a part of the company. The chance to get ahead is important, too. They have a strict policy of promoting from within, so you know you have a chance. I think in a lot of other places you may not get as fair a shake as you do here. The sales offices are on a smaller scale, too. I like that. I tell someone that we have two people in the Baltimore office, and they say "You've got to be kidding." It's smaller and more personal. Pay is the most important thing. I have heard that this is the highest-paying factory in the world.

## IV

Interview with Jimmy Roberts, a 47-year-old high school graduate, who had been with Lincoln 17 years and who was working as a multiple-drill press operator at the time of the interview.

Q. *What jobs have you had at Lincoln?*
A. I started out cleaning the men's locker room in 1963. After about a year I got a job in the flux department, where we make the coating for welding rods. I worked there for seven or eight years and then got my present job.
Q. *Do you make one particular part?*
A. No, there are a variety of parts I make—at least twenty-five.
Q. *Each one has a different piece rate attached to it?*
A. Yes.
Q. *Are some piece rates better than others?*
A. Yes.
Q. *How do you determine which ones you are going to do?*
A. You don't. Your supervisor assigns them.
Q. *How much money did you make last year?*
A. $47,000.
Q. *Have you ever received any kind of award or citation?*
A. No.
Q. *Was your rating ever over 110?*
A. Yes. For the past five years, probably. I made over 110 points.
Q. *Is there any attempt to let others know . . . ?*
A. The kind of points I get? No.
Q. *Do you know what they are making?*
A. No. There are some who might not be too happy with their points and they might make it known. The majority, though, do not make it a point of telling other employees.
Q. *Would you be just as happy earning a little less money and working a little slower?*
A. I don't think I would—not at this point. I have done piecework all these years, and the fast pace doesn't really bother me.
Q. *Why do you think Lincoln productivity is so high?*
A. The incentive thing—the bonus distribution. I think that would be the main reason. The paycheck you get every two weeks is important too.
Q. *Do you think Lincoln employees would ever join a union?*
A. I don't think so. I have never heard anyone mention it.
Q. *What is the most important advantage of working here?*
A. Amount of money you make. I don't think I could make this type of money anywhere else, especially with only a high school education.
Q. *As a black person, do you feel that Lincoln discriminates in any way against blacks?*
A. No. I don't think any more so than any other job. Naturally, there is a certain amount of discrimination, regardless of where you are.


**V**

Interview with Joe Trahan, 58-year-old high school graduate who had been with Lincoln 39 years and who was employed as a working supervisor in the tool room at the time of the interview.

Q. *Roughly what was your pay last year?*
A. Over $50,000; salary, bonus, stock dividends.
Q. *How much was your bonus?*
A. About $23,000.
Q. *Have you ever gotten a special award of any kind?*
A. Not really.

Q. *What have you done with your money?*

A. My house is paid for—and my two cars. I also have some bonds and the Lincoln stock.

Q. *What do you think of the executives at Lincoln?*

A. They're really top-notch.

Q. *What is the major disadvantage of working at Lincoln Electric?*

A. I don't know of any disadvantage at all.

Q. *Do you think you produce more than most people in similar jobs with other companies?*

A. I do believe that.

Q. *Why is that? Why do you believe that?*

A. We are on the incentive system. Everything we do, we try to improve to make a better product with a minimum of outlay. We try to improve the bonus.

Q. *Would you be just as happy making a little less money and not working quite so hard?*

A. I don't think so.

Q. *You know that Lincoln productivity is higher than that at most other plants. Why is that?*

A. Money.

Q. *Do you think Lincoln employees would ever join a union?*

A. I don't think they would ever consider it.

Q. *What is the most important advantage of working at Lincoln?*

A. Compensation.

Q. *Tell me something about Mr. James Lincoln, who died in 1965.*

A. You are talking about Jimmy Sr. He always strolled through the shop in his shirt sleeves. Big fellow. Always looked distinguished. Gray hair. Friendly sort of guy. I was a member of the advisory board one year. He was there each time.

Q. *Did he strike you as really caring?*

A. I think he always cared for people.

Q. *Did you get any sensation of a religious nature from him?*

A. No, not really.

Q. *And religion is not part of the program now?*

A. No.

Q. *Do you think Mr. Lincoln was a very intelligent man, or was he just a nice guy?*

A. I would say he was pretty well educated. A great talker—always right off the top of his head. He knew what he was talking about all the time.

Q. *When were bonuses for beneficial suggestions done away with?*

A. About fifteen years ago.

Q. *Did that hurt very much?*

A. I don't think so, because suggestions are still rewarded through the merit rating system.

Q. *Is there anything you would like to add?*

A. It's a good place to work. The union kind of ties other places down. At other places, electricians only do electrical work, carpenters only do carpenter work. At Lincoln Electric we all pitch in and do whatever needs to be done.

Q. *So a major advantage is not having a union?*

A. That's right.

# 20   7-Eleven Stores: Convenience 24 Hours a Day

Jeremy B. Fox and Larry D. Alexander
Virginia Polytechnic Institute and State University

There was little doubt in 1984 that Southland's 7-Eleven stores division continued to be very successful. Approximately 85 percent of Southland's profits were generated by 7-Eleven. Revenues had increased along with earnings per share for the last 22 years. Cash dividends had been declared each of the past 27 years and the annual dividend rate had been raised 12 times in the past 13 years.

Despite this success, 7-Eleven stores were facing heated competition as more firms entered various overlapping segments of the grocery industry. Would 7-Eleven remain the undisputed industry leader and hold on to its 20 percent share of the convenience store segment? How would 7-Eleven stores fare against the minimarkets that gas stations were adding to their franchises? Would supermarkets, superstores, and warehouse stores take away sales by appealing to 7-Eleven's customers in different ways? In sum, how would 7-Eleven address a number of significant threats facing it in the 1980s and beyond?

**HISTORY**    Joe C. Thompson, Jr., was the predominant figure in Southland Corporation's history. He grew up in Dallas and started working for a salary at the age of eight. J. O. Jones, a neighbor who owned the Consumer's Ice Company, initially hired the young Thompson to clean the stalls of the horses that delivered ice throughout the city. After Thompson graduated from the University of Texas at Austin, he went to work full-time at Consumer's Ice in management. In the summer of 1924, Thompson started offering ice-cold watermelon to the public at Consumer's ice dock. By 1927, Thompson was in a key position at Consumers'. When the company was acquired in a merger with several other small ice companies, he was given a full directorship in the new Southland Ice Company.

During the summer of that same year, the convenience store concept came into realization. J. J. Green, owner of a small ice dock in Dallas, began stocking a few grocery items at the urging of a number of customers. As fall came and the demand for ice decreased, he noticed that the demand for his grocery items continued to be strong. He suggested to J. C. Thompson that groceries be continued through the winter, which Thompson would buy, and the profits be split later in the spring. By the spring of 1928, Southland was $1000 richer and the idea of the convenience store became a viable reality.

This case was written by Jeremy B. Fox (doctoral student in management at V.P.I.) and Larry D. Alexander (assistant professor of strategic management), Department of Management, College of Business, Virginia Polytechnic Institute and State University, Blacksburg, Virginia 24061.

Copyright © 1985 by Jeremy B. Fox and Larry D. Alexander.

The Southland Ice Company also continued to grow by acquiring other small, but successful, ice companies throughout Texas. Grocery shelves were installed at many of their ice docks to further develop the convenience store business. Southland soon acquired Tot'em retail stores, which were clearly identified by an Alaskan totem pole standing by the street.

Shortly after being named president of Southland in 1931, the 30-year-old Thompson had to deal with the company's financial problems. The collapse of an affiliate threw Southland into bankruptcy and Thompson was named receiver. Since Southland was in a fair financial situation itself, the receivership freed it from many hindering interest payments caused by its affiliate's bankruptcy.

During the depression years, Thompson and his management team were still able to expand the number of Tot'em ice and grocery stores. In anticipation of further expansion, Southland formed Oak Farms Dairy in 1936 to supply dairy products to the Tot'em stories. Oak Farms also sold to restaurants, hospitals, and grocery chains. Oak Farms initially operated at a loss; however, it became a profitable unit in the Southland group by 1938.

By 1939, there were 60 Tot'em stories in the Dallas–Ft. Worth area alone. World War II brought about the building of Hood Army Base in Temple, Texas. Southland bid and won the contract to supply ice to the base. This proved to be a very significant move, one that stabilized the firm's sales.

At the conclusion of World War II, Thompson decided to put all of Southland's grocery stores and Tot'em stores under the 7-Eleven logo. This name was taken from the extended hours that the stores were open at the time, from 7 A.M. to 11 P.M. The Southland Ice Corporation's name was shortened to Southland Corporation at the same time.

Southland expanded beyond Texas in 1954 by opening a store in Miami, Florida. That same year, the firm's operating profits exceeded $1 million for the first time. Up until 1956, 7-Eleven stores were all located in warmer climates and had an open store front. That year, however, Southland opened its first northern 7-Eleven store. It was located in the Washington, D.C., area and was a fully enclosed building, a necessity in colder climates. This first northern store was such a hit that 20 new stores were opened in the same area within the next 18 months. This milestone hinted at the potential available to the firm. At the 1958 opening of the three hundredth 7-Eleven store, Thompson said, "This new shift toward convenience store shopping is not only evident in Texas, Florida, and Washington, D.C.; it will be evident throughout the United States in the years to come."[1]

These early milestones for 7-Eleven were preliminary to its later expansion that paralleled the American population shift to suburbia and exurbia. This shift caused people to make longer commutes to work by car. With fewer leisure hours, the idea of a convenience store fit perfectly into the American life-style, and by 1961, 7-Eleven stores numbered almost 600. During this period, Southland's dairy and ice divisions had also registered strong gains. When Joe C. Thompson died in mid-1961, control of the company was passed to his oldest son, John Thompson.

All 7-Elevens were owned by Southland up until 1964. Southland was introduced to franchising, however, with its acquisition of California Speedee Marts, which were all franchised. Southland quickly came to realize that there were advantages associated with franchising. Speedee also brought to Southland new methods of owner training and support for franchisees.

Two additional key changes were initiated at 7-Eleven during the 1960s. First, a 7-Eleven store near the University of Texas at Austin frequently started staying open 24 hours a day. This idea spread to many other 7-Eleven stores because the experiment improved the store's sales and profitability. By 1984, approximately 95 percent of all stores were open 24 hours a day. Second was the establishment of an electronic, centrally controlled distribution center in Florida. This started in 1969 but several other centers were added quickly in other regions. These centers helped meet the day-to-day needs of the individual stores in less time and at a lower cost to Southland. Later, Southland started distributing food products to other companies, which by the 1980s included such firms as Bonanza Steak Houses, Arthur Treacher's, Dunkin' Donuts, Rustler Steak House, and even competing convenience store chains.

The number of 7-Eleven stores continued to grow in the 1970s and early 1980s. During 1972, Southland's sales exceeded $1 billion for the first time. There were 4114 stores, and its stock had just been listed on the New York Stock Exchange. Between the years 1972 and 1984, approximately 3000 new stores were opened by Southland in the United States and Canada. In addition, almost 3000 stores were added in foreign countries.

## MARKETING AND SALES

Convenience had always been emphasized in Southland's stores. All early 7-Elevens in the southern states featured curb service. It was literally true that customers could make purchases without leaving their cars. A person came into the old ice dock to buy ice, and the ice was brought out to the vehicle and strapped to the running board. When groceries were added, 7-Eleven decided to provide the same level of convenience. In the 1980s, Southland was still stressing convenience by serving customers who wanted to quickly pick up a few items rather than take more time to go to the supermarket.

7-Eleven's products and product lines continued to evolve through the years. Products or services that no longer sold well, such as television tube testing machines, shotgun shells, and cold watermelon, were discontinued. Conversely, Southland exploited many new ideas that were profitable. For example, when hot coffee was introduced and proved successful, it wasn't long before other hot items were added. The stores had microwave ovens added by the late 1950s. From its emphasis on hot food to go, Southland had become one of the top dozen or so fast-food outlets in the 1980s. Its position was strengthened with such staggering figures as the 50 million burritos that it sold annually.

More recently, Southland became concerned with its stores' image. The image it wanted its stores to project was that of a family store that stood ready to help by providing everyday items for everyday-type people. For example, Southland had removed all cigarette rolling paper from its thousands of stores in 1979 to protect its image. Jere Thompson, Southland's president and second son of J. C. Thompson, ordered this action because he felt that in selling the papers the company gave credibility to the use of drugs, an area in which Thompson didn't want his company associated."[2]

In July 1984, 7-Eleven's image was put to a test. Citizens in a small Pennsylvania town picketed their 7-Eleven store for the removal of *Playboy*-type magazines. Southland considered this a significant threat because it was the nation's largest seller of *Playboy* magazine. After consultation with headquarters, store management complied with the demand and removed all *Playboy*-type magazines. Southland's top management went along with this decision, viewing it as a test market to determine the effect on the store's image, sales, and profits.

Southland initiated various image-building programs that portrayed the firm standing behind America. First, Southland started an annual Jerry Lewis muscular dystrophy fund-raising drive in all of its stores. Second, the firm became one of the top corporate sponsors of the 1984 Olympics. Two new velodromes were constructed for the track bicycling events in Los Angeles at a cost to Southland of over $4 million. In the months before the Olympic Games, its television ads told how various U.S. Olympic hopefuls were getting a chance to become the best because of 7-Eleven's major Olympic sponsorship. Most ads closed by stating that the dream begins with freedom, which clearly sounded very pro-America.

In its stores, 7-Eleven still followed J. C. Thompson's philosophy of giving the customer what he wanted when he wanted it. Exhibit 20.1 shows the major product categories for 7-Eleven stores and their percent of total sales from 1979 through 1983. Each of the new stores was laid out in a similar fashion as other newer 7-Eleven stores, as shown in Exhibit 20.2. Therefore, hurried customers knew that if cold soft drinks were stocked in a particular location in their local 7-Eleven, these items would be in that same location in other 7-Eleven stores they might enter. Southland did this so its hurried customers would not waste time trying to locate items. Southland also stocked only one or two leading brand names for many of its items to help customers quickly decide which brand to purchase. This also helped Southland because its stores averaged only 2,000 square feet compared to over 20,000 square feet for most grocery stores. Other products such as beer had a more extensive selection but they were still limited.

Southland also took action to reduce the number of items carried within a specific brand. For example, although Campbell's made over 20 types of soups, 7-Eleven stocked only the 11 top-selling types on its shelves. 7-Eleven stores had previously carried almost all of Campbell's different types of soup. Surprisingly, 7-Eleven found that when it reduced its Campbell's soup offering to the 11 top sellers, its Campbell's soup sales went up 19.2 percent.

Although approximately 950 daily customers got in and out of the average 7-Eleven store, each in only a couple of minutes, they paid a price for that convenience. In general, 7-Eleven had 10 percent to 30 percent higher prices for most of its products. However, it equaled supermarket prices for a few staples

**Exhibit 20.1** Major Product Categories for 7-Eleven Stores and Their Percent of Total Sales for 1979–1983

**PERCENT CONVENIENCE STORE SALES (BY PRINCIPAL PRODUCT CATEGORY)**

The company does not record sales by product lines, but estimates the percentage of convenience store sales by principal product category based upon total store purchases.

|  | 1983 | 1982 | 1981 | 1980 | 1979 |
|---|---|---|---|---|---|
| Gasoline | 25.5 | 25.3 | 25.3 | 23.0 | 17.2 |
| Tobacco products | 13.8 | 13.1 | 12.1 | 12.3 | 12.9 |
| Beer/wine | 11.8 | 11.9 | 11.7 | 11.7 | 12.4 |
| Groceries | 10.5 | 10.8 | 11.5 | 12.4 | 12.6 |
| Soft drinks | 10.4 | 9.8 | 10.0 | 10.1 | 10.3 |
| Nonfoods | 7.5 | 8.7 | 8.1 | 8.0 | 8.7 |
| Dairy products | 5.7 | 5.9 | 6.3 | 6.7 | 8.4 |
| Other food items | 4.6 | 5.0 | 5.2 | 5.6 | 6.2 |
| Candy | 3.9 | 3.9 | 4.0 | 4.0 | 4.3 |
| Baked goods | 3.5 | 3.0 | 3.2 | 3.4 | 3.8 |
| Health/beauty aids | 2.8 | 2.6 | 2.6 | 2.8 | 3.2 |
| Total | 100.0 | 100.0 | 100.0 | 100.0 | 100.0 |

*Source:* Southland Corporation 1984 Annual Report, p. 12.

such as milk. As a leader, 7-Eleven charged lower prices in the 1980s for gasoline than did many of the national gas station chains.

Store location was another important marketing element for Southland. Proximity to established neighborhoods, traffic flows on the main arteries, and property costs were major considerations. After the oil embargo of 1974 caused many corner gas stations to close, new 7-Eleven stores were almost always located on corner lots. This change was made because Southland discovered that its corner-lot stores typically had 50 percent more sales than did similar mid-block stores.

In September 1978, 7-Eleven opened a store on Manhattan's east side, which initiated its move into city center stores. Whereas 7-Eleven's earlier stores in the suburbs attracted customers who lived nearby, the city center stores appealed primarily to walk-in traffic from customers who worked nearby. Since then, 7-Eleven city center stores were opened in New York, Philadelphia, Boston, Seattle, and San Francisco.

Advertising for Southland and 7-Eleven was handled by the Stanford Agency. Bob Stanford, a Texas radio personality turned advertiser, founded this in-house advertising company. Southland Corporation was the first convenience store that used the media for advertising. In 1965, the Stanford Agency helped 7-Eleven successfully introduce the frozen slurpee drink. Later, it coined the slogan "Thank heaven for 7-Eleven." Stanford Agency's advertising work for other clients, such as its famous "Pepsi Challenge" campaign, helped generate additional profits for Southland. By the 1980s, 7-Eleven still did considerably more advertising in all media than all other convenience stores combined.

**Exhibit 20.2** A Typical 7-Eleven Store Floor Plan

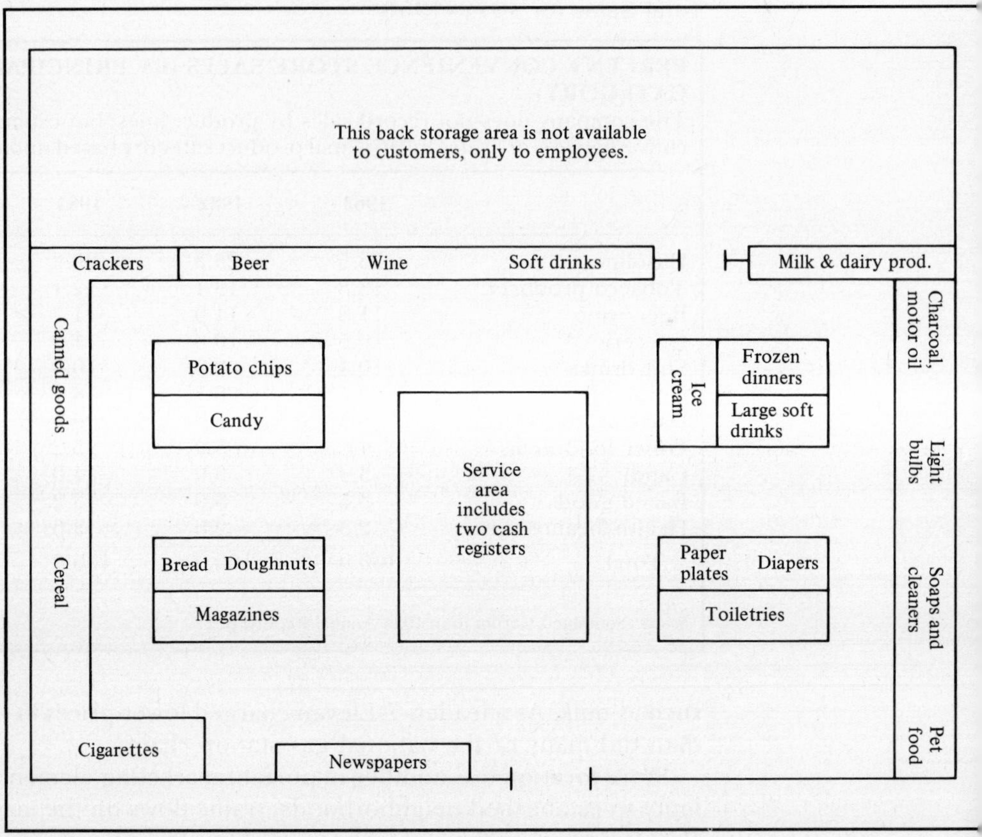

Advertising was directed primarily at the typical male customer. He was under 35, married with two children, lived less than one mile from the store, and earned in the lower-middle-income range. The average customer spent only a couple of dollars per trip and came into the store about 1.25 times per week. Although this customer was considered typical among its 7 million daily customers, 7-Eleven had started to include some advertising directed at the growing number of working women.

In 1981, Bruce W. Krysiak was named marketing vice-president—retail. He immediately started looking for an outside advertising agency which could handle the full-scale network television advertising that was being planned, particularly for the 1984 Olympic Games. Krysiak explained that one reason for this change was that large national agencies had more bargaining power with the television media; thus, 7-Eleven could get more time for the same money. The Stanford Agency, however, still handled radio, print, and any regional advertising used by the stores.

**OPERATIONS**

In 1969, Southland started a small pilot distribution program in Florida which supplied 22 stores. This pilot program was later expanded to establish a massive distribution system that supplied 4900 7-Eleven stores from just four warehouses by 1983. These warehouses were located in Orlando, Florida; Champaign, Illinois; Fredericksburg, Virginia; and Tyler, Texas. They totaled almost 2 million square feet of storage space and served 66 percent of the 7-Eleven stores in 33 states. A new distribution center was scheduled to open in 1984 in Southern California. Southland's distribution center (SDC) operation also supplied products for in-flight meal caterers, several restaurant chains, and even some other convenience store chains.

The operation of Southland's sophisticated computerized distribution centers is shown in Exhibit 20.3. Individual stores prepared and submitted their orders directly to their respective SDC. Hand-held terminals, which read orders from an order book using bar codes, were installed in many 7-Eleven stores in 1982 to make store ordering even easier. This information was transmitted via telephone to a computer at the SDC which received the store's order. At the SDC, the order-filling system was largely automated. Computers helped to decide what to load on which truck and then even determined the route it should travel. Routinely, merchandise arrived within 72 hours at each 7-Eleven store. This quick turnaround permitted stores to place less than case lots orders; thus, they used most of their store space for selling rather than storage.

7-Eleven processed its own fast foods at six food centers. These centers produced about 30 different types of sandwiches, pizzas, burritos, and snack cakes for distribution to 7-Eleven stores and its other customers. These centers operated on high volume. For example, they produced 1.3 million gallons of syrup for Slurpee drinks alone in 1982.

Operations within each 7-Eleven store tended to follow uniform procedures while still permitting individual store freedom. For example, when new products were introduced by Southland, individual stores could accept or reject them. In reality, most stores accepted these new items because they trusted Southland's marketing expertise, which closely monitored the sales of individual items. The majority of stores used Southland distribution centers as the source for most of their goods, which made the ordering operation fairly uniform across most stores.

Over the years, Southland strove to standardize many items within its 7-Eleven stores. All product wrappers, containers, employee uniforms, and company trucks promoted 7-Eleven with this uniformity. This helped 7-Eleven stores become a familiar and recognized part of American life and, in turn, made stopping at a 7-Eleven an ordinary event for millions of customers.

By 1984, approximately 40 percent of the stores were franchise operations. Store profits were split as follows: 52 percent for Southland and 48 percent for the owner. Under this agreement, Southland reserved the right to open new stores at any distance from an existing 7-Eleven store. The average cost of a 7-Eleven franchise was $17,500, which was inexpensive when compared to other chains. Advertising was paid for exclusively by Southland. In addition, although headquarters offered support to an ailing store, it would shut one down rapidly

# Exhibit 20.3 Southland's Sophisticated Computerized Distribution System

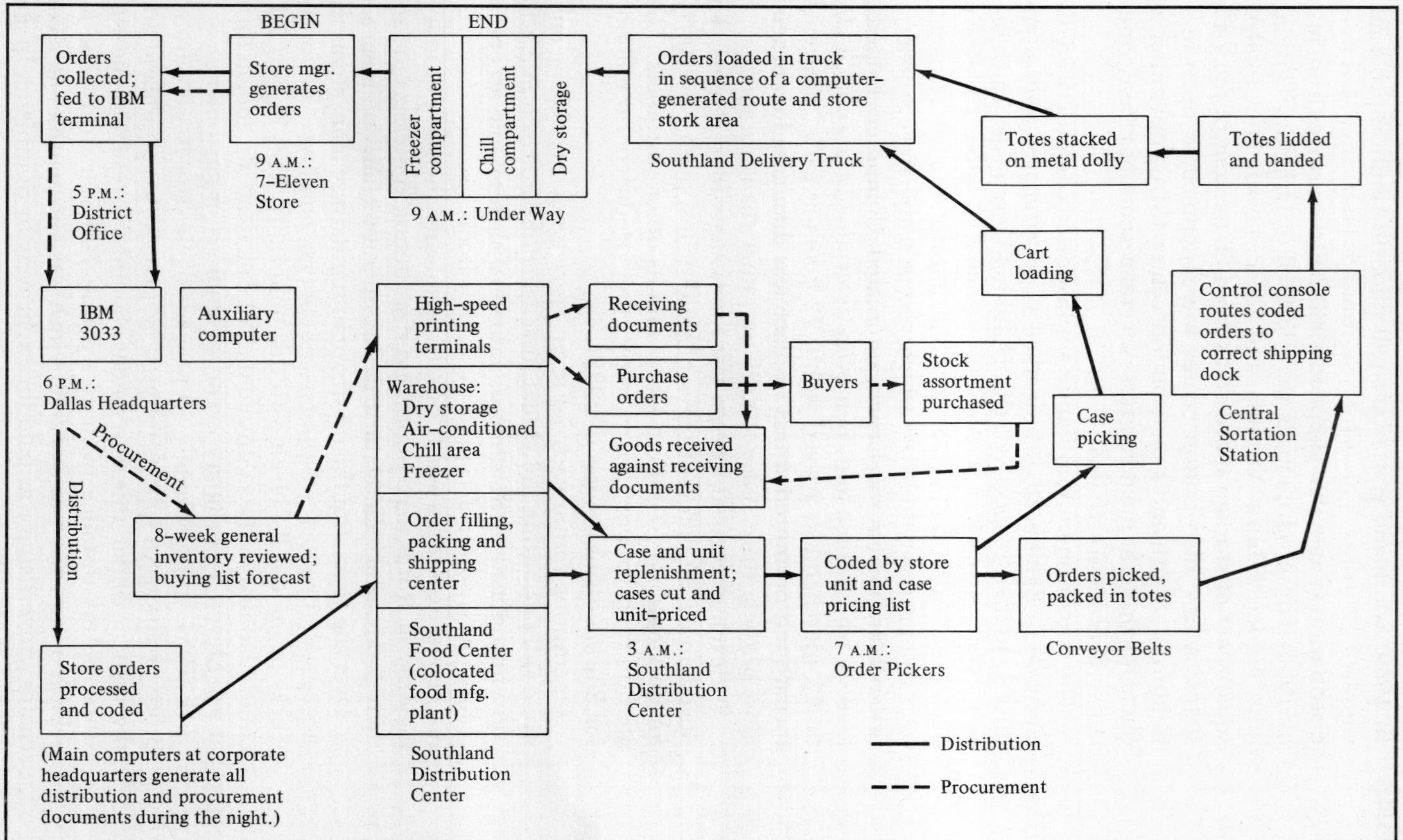

Totes lidded and banded

Control console routes orders to correct shipping dock

Central Sortation Station

Totes stacked on metal dolly

Cart loading

Case picking

Orders picked, packed in totes

Conveyor Belts

Stock assortment purchased

Orders loaded in truck in sequence of a computer-generated route and store stork area

Southland Delivery Truck

Buyers

Goods received against receiving documents

Coded by store unit and case pricing list

7 A.M.: Order Pickers

Receiving documents

Purchase orders

Case and unit replenishment; cases cut and unit-priced

3 A.M.: Southland Distribution Center

Freezer compartment | Chill compartment | Dry storage

END

9 A.M.: Under Way

BEGIN

Store mgr. generates orders

9 A.M.: 7-Eleven Store

High-speed printing terminals

Warehouse: Dry storage Air-conditioned Chill area Freezer

Order filling, packing and shipping center

Southland Food Center (colocated food mfg. plant)

Southland Distribution Center

Orders collected; fed to IBM terminal

5 P.M.: District Office

Auxiliary computer

IBM 3033

6 P.M.: Dallas Headquarters

Procurement

Distribution

8-week general inventory reviewed; buying list forecast

Store orders processed and coded

Distribution ——

Procurement - - - -

(Main computers at corporate headquarters generate all distribution and procurement documents during the night.)

*Source: Restaurants and Institutions*, October 15, 1983, p. 14

654

if there was little hope of making the store profitable. John Thompson bluntly stated that Southland wouldn't carry unprofitable stores." [3] For example, Southland opened 498 new stores in 1983, but it also closed 364 stores during that same year.

Southland basically turned a ready-to-run store over to each newly trained franchisee. The franchisee paid business licenses, permits, and put up cash equal to the value of the stock in the store. Operating expenses were born by the franchisee. The franchisee was not required to purchase merchandise from Southland or to sell the company's merchandise at its suggested prices. If the stores franchise was terminated, Southland repurchased the owner's part of the store stock and equipment.

Headquarters monitored a wide variety of potential store problem areas and brought it to the attention of a store manager when warranted. In addition, Southland headquarters was so interested in learning more about store-level problems that it established the Managers Advisory Council. This committee of store managers came to Dallas periodically to exchange views with top management on various operating problems.

The expansion of new 7-Eleven stores into several European countries, Japan, and other Pacific areas had not been done by either direct ownership or franchising. Rather, this expansion was accomplished by licensing agreements. These licensed stores had little direct contact with Southland. The agreement basically allowed the licensee to use the 7-Eleven logo in exchange for a fee. The profits from these stores were not included in Southland's earnings statement. Royalties from licensees, however, were reported as other income. There were also eight area licensees in the United States which were treated in a similar financial manner.

**FINANCE AND ACCOUNTING**

The consolidated balance sheets for the years ending December 31, 1982 and 1983 are shown in Exhibit 20.4. The consolidated statements of earnings are shown in Exhibit 20.5 for 1981–1983. During 1983, Southland had total revenues of $8,772,067,000 and a net income after taxes of $131,768,000. 7-Eleven stores division represented 76 percent of Southland's revenues in 1983. As a result, Wall Street tended to assess the future of Southland almost entirely upon the outlook for the convenience store industry.

Between the years of 1977 and 1980, 50 percent of capital expenditures and needed working capital were financed from internally generated funds. Southland reinvested 11 percent of its earnings during this same period, of which about 85 percent went into the 7-Eleven stores division. Since the vast majority of purchases at 7-Eleven stores were for small dollar amounts, approximately 85 percent of total sales were cash or check transactions which were quickly converted to cash.

**Exhibit 20.4**

## THE SOUTHLAND CORPORATION AND SUBSIDIARIES
### Consolidated Balance Sheets for 1982 and 1983
### (dollars in thousands)

| | December 31 | |
|---|---|---|
| | 1983 | 1982 |
| **Assets** | | |
| Current assets | | |
| Cash and short-term investments | $ 22,120 | $ 34,685 |
| Accounts and notes receivable | 476,393 | 158,217 |
| Inventories | 954,916 | 309,739 |
| Deposits and prepaid expenses | 55,257 | 36,908 |
| Investment in properties | 76,200 | 76,800 |
| Total current assets | 1,584,886 | 616,349 |
| Investments in affiliates | 84,280 | 31,359 |
| Property, plant, and equipment | 1,437,492 | 990,925 |
| Capital leases | 152,432 | 168,412 |
| Other assets | 50,365 | 35,209 |
| | $3,309,455 | $1,842,254 |
| **Liabilities and shareholders' equity** | | |
| Current liabilities | | |
| Commercial paper and notes payable to banks | $26,438 | $ 11,696 |
| Accounts payable and accrued expenses | 908,802 | 420,294 |
| Income taxes | 8,913 | 43,490 |
| Long-term debt due within one year | 42,813 | 12,052 |
| Capital lease obligations due within one year | 15,065 | 15,805 |
| Total current liabilities | 1,002,031 | 503,337 |
| Deferred credits and other liabilities | 106,819 | 52,589 |
| Long-term debt | 940,878 | 386,304 |
| Capital lease obligations | 184,765 | 196,676 |
| Commitments for operating leases | | |
| Shareholders' equity | | |
| Preferred stock without par value, authorized 5,000,000 shares in 1983, none issued or outstanding | — | — |
| Common stock, $.01 par value, authorized 150,000,000 and 40,000,000 shares, issued and outstanding 46,852,348 and 36,106,841 shares | 469 | 361 |
| Additional capital | 624,483 | 347,786 |
| Retained earnings | 450,010 | 355,201 |
| | 1,074,962 | 703,348 |
| | $ 3,309,455 | $1,842,254 |

*Source:* Southland Corporation 1984 Annual Report, p. 34.

**Exhibit 20.5**

### THE SOUTHLAND CORPORATION AND SUBSIDIARIES
#### Consolidated Statements of Earnings for 1981–1983
#### (dollars in thousands except per share data)

| | Year Ended December 31 | | |
|---|---|---|---|
| | **1983** | **1982** | **1981** |
| Revenues | | | |
| Net sales | $ 8,772,067 | $ 6,756,933 | $ 5,693,636 |
| Other income | 32,943 | 25,450 | 40,524 |
| | 8,805,010 | 6,782,383 | 5,734,160 |
| Cost of sales and expenses | | | |
| Cost of goods sold | 7,177,147 | 5,350,453 | 4,454,774 |
| Selling, general, and administrative expenses | 1,349,574 | 1,174,886 | 1,050,073 |
| Interest expense | 52,636 | 27,390 | 24,539 |
| Imputed interest expense on capital lease obligations | 20,638 | 21,345 | 23,048 |
| Contributions to employees' savings and profit sharing plan | 19,426 | 19,568 | 16,965 |
| | 8,619,421 | 6,593,642 | 5,569,399 |
| Earnings before income taxes | 185,589 | 188,741 | 164,761 |
| Income taxes | 53,821 | 80,690 | 71,901 |
| Net earnings | $   131,768 | $   108,051 | $     92,860 |
| Net earnings per share | | | |
| Primary | $3.26 | $3.02 | $2.61 |
| Fully diluted | $3.21 | $2.94 | $2.54 |

*Source:* Southland Corporation 1984 Annual Report, p. 35.

Conservative fiscal policies at Southland were the result of the Great Depression. John Thompson commented, "Early exposure to the depression era had a lot to do with our understanding of the need to control expenses. We have passed this understanding down to the first-level supervisors."[4]

Investors were concerned over the future of Southland during 1980. Southland's common stock price was down dramatically as was its first-quarter earnings. At that time, a study prepared for the National Association of Convenience Stores on the industry outlook for the eighties was not encouraging. It noted that real sales, adjusted for inflation and ignoring sales of gasoline, showed no gain whatsoever. However, nationwide sales of gasoline had decreased since the first oil embargo in 1974. The report further stated that Southland's sales gains had come exclusively from gasoline, whereas traditional sales leaders such as groceries, dairy products, and candy had shown a decline in sales.

Investors were also concerned about Southland's new Chief Auto Parts group, which had some 300 stores. Some investors and company observers did not see any commonality or synergies between the Auto Parts operations and its more profitable 7-Eleven stores. Interestingly, while Southland's 7-Eleven stores competed on the basis of convenience and didn't worry about price, its Chief Auto Parts stores focused primarily on price competition.

Although Southland wanted to maintain its annual earnings growth at a 15 percent level, its earnings grew by about 20 percent in 1983 alone. Not surprisingly, Southland announced in January 1984 a 9.5 percent dividend rate increase, which was the ninth consecutive year its dividends increased.

## HUMAN RESOURCES AND PERSONNEL

Southland executives frequently referred to themselves as a family. Even its in-house publication that was distributed to its stores was called *Family*. The July 1984 issue of that magazine, for example, was devoted to articles describing how Southland was working with recent emigrants to the United States. Southland also helped these people develop the needed skills to work in a 7-Eleven. This program was aimed at Haitians, but it had focused on Vietnamese and Cubans in the past. Clearly, Southland was a strong believer in the American dream, where all people could have a chance to earn a good living and advance in their job by doing good work.

The 7-Eleven stores group employed about 43,738 regular employees and 1,069 temporary or call-in employees in 1983. This represented more than 80 percent of the employees that worked for Southland. Store personnel were not covered by collective bargaining contracts. In addition, the vast majority of store managers were Southland employees, rather than franchisee owners, which gave headquarters more direct control over store operations. To help stimulate sales, the majority of sales and supervisory staff personnel in 7-Eleven stores were under some form of incentive pay plan.

Southland looked after its existing store managers whether or not they were franchisees. Some 2600 of the 7300 7-Eleven stores were operated by franchisees. Southland originally offered a training program to franchisees which introduced them to the actual nuts and bolts of running a store. Recent programs, however, were aimed at also helping store owners become successful small-business operators. The program started with a mandatory 10- to 12-day training program which dealt with real store problems. After these initial topics, other sessions focused on managerial skills needed to increase a store's profits, time management, auditing store performance, and stress management. Southland felt that these and other topics helped bring about better profits for the franchise holder and Southland itself. This training program was initiated by headquarters at the request of a number of independent owners. Unfortunately, even with this preparation, the average store franchisee lasted only five years. Some industry observers felt this was partially due to the long hours that franchise holders and store managers put in, which averaged 80 hours per week.

Southland's training program had been taken from one developed by Speedee Mart. When Southland acquired that California chain in the 1960s, it adopted Speedee's training methods by developing its own simulated 7-Eleven store. Real store problems were discussed along with ideas about being in business for oneself. This realism was felt to be invaluable for trainees when they finally started their own stores.

## INNOVATION

Southland had always been an innovator. From that day in 1927 when the first additional items were stocked on its ice dock shelves, Southland always looked for new convenience products and services. For example, 7-Eleven tried making money orders available in its stores. This idea was so successful that 7-Eleven was the largest seller of money orders after the Post Office in 1983. Although 7-Eleven welcomed innovation, it quickly dropped products and services that did not work out.

Southland introduced a number of innovations in its 7-Eleven stores over the years. One such innovation was its extended store hours, from 7 A.M. to 11 P.M. Clearly, this helped in its efforts to provide convenience to its customers by being open whenever customers wanted to make a purchase. Later on, 7-Eleven extended this to being open 24 hours a day in most stores. Another innovation was its willingness to expand from just a Texas operation to a national chain of convenience stores.

A major innovation at 7-Eleven stores was installing gasoline pumps outside many of its stores. This was a unique move at the time for a chain of small grocery stores. Yet, by September 1983, Southland became the nation's largest independent gasoline retailer when it purchased Citgo Petroleum from Occidental Petroleum. This was done to secure a reliable source of gasoline.

The gasoline pumps innovation accounted for 25 percent of 7-Eleven's sales from 1981 through 1983. Although gasoline sales accounted for only 8 percent of Southland's profits, 34 percent of the gasoline customers also made other purchases when they went inside the store to pay for their gas. Thus, the real innovation with gasoline perhaps was pricing it lower than many national gas stations so that it drew customers into 7-Eleven stores to purchase higher-priced convenience items.

By 1984, automatic teller machines (ATMs) had been installed at 1680 7-Eleven stores. These ATMs provided 7-Eleven with a monthly rental fee from the bank and an additional transaction-based fee. J. P. Thompson, Southland's chairman, felt that the machines followed the public shift toward more convenience products and services, including self-service ones.

Southland's entry into food distribution through its warehouses was innovative for a convenience store chain. The move helped reduce its dependency on independent suppliers. It also turned a cost center into a profit center and made profits on sales to other retail firms. Sales to these outside concerns increased 50 percent in 1983 alone, which pushed sales of the distribution centers to over $1 billion for the first time.

## MANAGE-MENT

Southland's management team throughout the decades had been family-run. With the death of Joe Thompson, Sr., in 1961, some industry analysts felt that the company might undergo significant changes. However, this did not occur. With John Thompson, as chairman of the board and chief executive officer, and Jere Thompson, as president, the original Thompson philosophy was well maintained. In fact, many actions taken since Joe Thompson's death appeared to be very consistent with what he might have done himself.

Management at Southland practiced promotion from within. Thus, loyal, competent employees were almost always moved up into management positions rather than bringing in outsiders unfamiliar with 7-Eleven. In fact, 24 of the top 29 people in corporate management in 1984 had been with the company for at least ten years.

When there was a need for some hard-to-find expertise, however, Southland did not hesitate to hire someone from the outside. For example, when Southland decided to create its distribution centers, it hired Joseph S. Hardin, head of the U.S. Army's P.X. system to gain the needed expertise. A major task he initially focused on was the establishment of the electronic data processing component of the distribution system. He even hired other outsiders that he felt were needed to handle the day-to-day workings of the data processing system.

## SECURITY

Security was a particular problem at the average 7-Eleven. With the typical store open 24 hours a day, a lone clerk with a cash register full of money was a very attractive target for potential robbers. One clerk, working the night shift, reported first selling rope to two customers who then used it to tie him up in the cooler and rob the store at gunpoint. In one year during the 1970s, Southland had over 17,000 robberies at its 7-Eleven stores.

Southland sought help from a consultant that specialized in robberies. He made a number of changes in day and night operations in its stores. Signs in store windows were removed so the cash register could be seen from the street. Taxis were encouraged to use 7-Eleven parking lots and thereby discourage crime in its stores. Training films were shown to 7-Eleven employees dealing with the topics of robberies and security. Most important, Southland installed a timed-access safe in each store. Called Tidal, these safes accepted deposits and dispensed money in only small quantities after a programmed amount of time had elapsed.

These measures were very successful in reducing robberies. Between 1976 and 1980, the number of robberies was cut about in half and the average amount stolen dropped from $200 to $66. Tidal was so successful that Southland set it up as a separate division for use by its 7-Eleven stores and outside businesses. Southland also created a robbery prevention kit, which contained training materials, that was sold to the public and other convenience stores for $10.

## THE TASK ENVIRON-MENT

The convenience store industry was actually considered a segment of the grocery industry. A convenience store could be defined as an extended-hours retail store that got customers in and out quickly but charged higher prices on most items than did supermarkets. Convenience stores provided groceries, take-out food and beverages, gasoline, dairy products, nonfood merchandise, specialty items, and incidental services.

Convenience stores were facing a growing array of different competitors. They were forced to compete with a variety of national, regional, and independent grocery stores in most cities where they operated. Furthermore, their expanded offerings into nonfood items competed directly with various discount retail stores, such as K-Mart and drug stores. Similarly, their hot foods also competed directly with a whole host of fast-food restaurants. Finally, they were now competing with their mirror image, gas stations that had added food stores. Clearly, competition had become more intense; furthermore, it was coming from a number of different, overlapping industries.

The convenience store segment of the grocery industry faced a periodic common problem or threat: the U.S. economy. When the economy was performing poorly, more and more people started going to grocery stores for all of their food needs. Although they still liked convenience, they were forced to protect their financial resources by searching out the lowest possible prices for food items. Past economic downturns had not significantly hurt the convenience industry, but they had slowed the market growth rate during those periods. However, when the construction of new housing was in a downturn, there had been a corresponding downturn in convenience store sales. This was due to less construction workers out spending money and less suburbs being built for convenience stores to expand into. If future economic downturns were to come more frequently or last longer, then the convenience store industry could be damaged.

The stronger the local market, the less likely a downturn in the economy would have an adverse impact. Irrespective of the health of the economy, most convenience stores continued to stress the idea of convenience to their customers. This meant that the store needed to be in a readily accessible location, with an appropriate range of products (usually this meant little depth), and open long business hours. Most successful convenience stores stayed open 24 hours in the 1980s and had attempted to get corner lots on busy two-way streets. Many stores had added gasoline pumps, which spurred sales of other items and provided up to $1000 per month in profits from gas sales alone.

Two of 7-Eleven's competitors in the convenience stores segment were worth examining. Although these chains were nowhere near the size of 7-Eleven, they did represent a loss of customers. However, as recently as 1978, Southland had sales greater than twice the total sales of the next eight chains.

Munford Inc. was the only other convenience store chain listed on the New York Stock Exchange. Munford was planning a steady expansion of stores, which amounted to some 900 new stores in 1983. There had been no word, however, whether expansion to areas outside Florida and Georgia would be attempted. The company operated and franchised Majik Markets stores, which seemed to be staggering until 1981. Then, Munford took corrective action by closing marginal stores and relocating Majik Markets stores to high-volume gasoline locations. Because of these actions, there was a healthy increase in earnings. Its earnings per share went from 16 cents in 1980 to $2.07 just two years later.

Circle K convenience stores, like Southland and Mumford, espoused the idea of linking convenience stores with gasoline sales. Furthermore, this Phoenix-based firm, which operated in 12 western states, was going about this linking in much the same way as was Southland. Thus, gas pumps were installed at existing convenience stores.

## THREATS TO 7-ELEVEN

One of the biggest threats to 7-Eleven's well-being was the many gas stations that were converting their service bays into convenience stores. The building and necessary space were already there to make the convenience store. Thus, it was easier and cheaper to add convenience foods to a gas station than to do the opposite. For one thing, it cost approximately $80,000 to add gas pumps and storage tanks to an existing convenience store as 7-Eleven did. In addition, most gas station self-service customers were used to going into the station anyway to pay for their gas. Once inside, they could easily get a few needed items before continuing on their way. By 1982, six oil companies had about 2000 convenience stores attached to their stations, whereas 2800 7-Eleven stores had gas pumps.

Southland's Citgo refinery represented another threat. If gas sales at 7-Eleven stores were to decline significantly in the future, Southland would be hurt by its backward vertical integration move into oil refining. Furthermore, if gas sales declined, it would have an adverse impact on impulse items which were marked up much more than was gasoline. Thus, Southland had come to count on gasoline sales to keep up store performance.

Still another threat was supermarkets remaining open 24 hours per day. The fact that, over the years, 7-Elevens had been one of the few businesses open around the clock was a big reason people went to them. However, in the 1980s a customer could choose to go to a 24-hour supermarket late at night and get almost any item cheaper, with a larger brand selection, and not face any delay at the checkout counter. This was obviously cutting into the odd-hour customer base of 7-Eleven and represented a factor that could continue to hurt 7-Eleven increasingly.

Another threat facing Southland was its publicized tax-bribery trial that was litigated in New York in 1984. Apparently a company employee, hoping to save Southland a $1 million back-tax bill, tried to bribe a New York state tax official. The legal issues concerned (1) whether there was actually a conspiracy to bribe and (2) if Southland's corporate management was aware of the attempted bribe.

The resulting conviction on June 11, 1984, made the corporation a felon. In most states that 7-Eleven operated in, felons were not allowed to hold beer or wine licenses, which not only represented 12 percent of its sales but also helped to stimulate the sales of related items. However, Southland felt that the conviction might not have a major impact on the company. Still, it remained to be seen if individual states would place Southland's liquor licenses in jeopardy.

**POSSIBLE NEW PRODUCT/ MARKET OPPORTUN- ITIES**

Over the years, Southland Company had tried, or at least considered, a number of different opportunities. Through acquisition or new start-up ventures, the stores group had tried hardware stores in the late 1950s, candy manufacturing (Loft's and Barricini brands), and grocery stores (Gristede's still operated 124 stores in the New York City area), department stores (Thomas and Hart), and gasoline stations (Super Seven stations on the West Coast). In the 7-Eleven stores themselves, the company had already tried everything from television tube testing machines to garden seeds, from Slurpees to film processing, and from automatic teller machines to cancer insurance. Some worked well, others failed miserably.

One major opportunity for 7-Eleven stores would be to begin keying in on the woman of the house, who traditionally shopped at the supermarket. While its strength with men should not be ignored, women might be attracted to convenience stores by a different mix of products. Southland could advertise the fact that 7-Eleven had what women were looking for when doing last-minute shopping. For example, a *Progressive Grocer* survey identified that the five most important ways women chose a supermarket were (1) cleanliness, (2) prices clearly marked, (3) low prices, (4) accurate and pleasant checkout clerks, and (5) freshness date marked on products.[5] 7-Eleven could match most of these requirements except price. Furthermore, if the price was kept low on key grocery products and advertised as such, perhaps even this factor could be partially overcome. This was not to suggest that 7-Eleven would become the Saturday grocery mecca for women; however, satisfying these five important considerations could help siphon off some customers from supermarkets during the week.

7-Eleven might add new services to its stores. Local 7-Eleven stores could serve as convenient bill-paying centers for common utility and city bills. The unstamped envelopes could be left inside a 7-Eleven store for a small fee. Perhaps it could be done for free just to generate sales on other items. The store could then gather them, sort them, and deliver them daily to the respective utilities.

By the same token, 7-Elevens could be a drop for packages being delivered by one of the overnight freight services. Since the freight company would make one stop to pick up several packages, they might charge less, allowing room for 7-Eleven to make a small profit. Perhaps delivery at the other end could also be to the neighborhood 7-Eleven store. This might be even more convenient, particularly when the receiving party was not at home during delivery hours.

With the emphasis that 7-Eleven puts on fast food, the company might bring out a microwave-ready package of french fries. Southland could work out an agreement with one of the processed-potato companies to develop a product that would equal the quality of french fries available at the local fast-food chains. This product could be made available in single servings at a competitive price. If the french fries were successful, then other fast-food menu items could be added later on.

Along the same lines, 7-Eleven could sell a frozen solid milk shake, available in popular flavors. The product could be thawed in the microwave to a cold but drinkable consistency. Preparation of the drink would be at a food-processing center, shipped by a Southland's delivery truck, and placed in the freezer compartment at the store. Little work by the clerk would be necessary, as was required by the very popular Slurpee drink.

Southland's stores division also operated the Gristede's grocery chain of 50 stores in the New York City area. The company could expand this chain to other east coast metropolitan areas. These stores, which offered premium-quality groceries, might be seen as a good complement to existing 7-Eleven stores. Expanding into more full-scale grocery stores might help Southland directly compete against the supermarket chains.

John Thompson noted, "We're thinking about adding pharmacy items."[6] Since he last mentioned this opportunity back in 1977, it obviously never got off the ground. However, if an all-hours pharmacy could somehow be established in 7-Eleven stores, it might help win the mother of the house over to its convenience stores. The biggest obstacle would be how to process prescription items which would require a doctor's signature. Similarly, a licensed pharmacist would have to fill the prescription. Still, the idea might be workable.

Still another opportunity would be to appeal to nontypical customers. Since 7-Eleven stores appealed to younger and middle-aged men, this clearly suggested that there remained a large untouched customer base that was being ignored or at best poorly served. For example, older citizens were not shopping very frequently at these stores. Women were another nontypical customer for 7-Eleven stores. Perhaps women could be grouped by age to identify patterns and preferences in product offerings. Young schoolchildren were another nontypical customer group that might be exploited. Finally, perhaps Southland could more effectively cater to the concentrations of various minority groups living in major metropolitan areas of the United States.

Over the years, 7-Eleven had succeeded in building a solid business on people spending only a few dollars on an average visit. The nature of the store and pricing structure made it difficult to raise that figure significantly. However, with an increase in store traffic, larger overall sales figures could be generated and increased pressure could be placed on the competition by taking away their potential customers. Both these ends were desirable as 7-Eleven considered which opportunities to pursue in the mid-1980s and beyond.

**CONCLUDING NOTE**

Although 7-Eleven had been very successful in previous decades, the 1980s and beyond would probably not be as hospitable. The numerous competitive threats facing it from different store formats might make a significant dent in its sales and profits. 7-Eleven's success, in part, will rest upon its ability to keep identifying and exploiting new products and services people want in a convenience store. In addition, its future success will also rest upon its ability to develop appropriate responses to a variety of competitive threats, from minimarts to superstores to warehouses.

### NOTES

1. Allen Lilies, *Oh Thank Heaven!* (Dallas: The Southland Corporation, 1977), p. 117.
2. *The Wall Street Journal,* September 13, 1979, p. 1.
3. *Business Week,* March 21, 1977, p. 64.
4. *Restaurants and Institutions,* October 15, 1981, p. 33.
5. *Progressive Grocer,* May, 1984, p. 58.
6. *Business Week,* March 21, 1977, p. 64.

# 21 Wal-Mart Stores, Inc.

Sexton Adams
North Texas State University
Adelaide Griffin
Texas Woman's University

In January 1982, amid the distressed economy, Wal-Mart continued to "pace the discount chain industry, leaving K mart, Target, and Woolco behind."[1] The chain emerged in 1962 with one store serving a small community in Arkansas and had grown to 491 stores serving 13 different states at the close of 1981. Jack Shewmaker, president of Wal-Mart, said the chain "will continue to grow into markets where we can get the right profitability and return on investment."[2]

## HISTORY AND BACKGROUND

Wal-Mart Stores, Inc., headquartered in Bentonville, Arkansas, had its origin in the variety store business. Sam Walton opened his first variety store, under the Ben Franklin franchise, in Newport, Arkansas, in 1945. One year later, he was joined by his brother, J. L. "Bud" Walton, now senior vice-president, who opened a similar store in Versailles, Missouri. The two brothers went on to assemble a group of 15 Ben Franklin stores and subsequently developed the concept of larger discount department stores in communities of small size. This concept emerged in 1962 when the first Wal-Mart Discount City store in Rogers, Arkansas, opened. Wal-Mart Stores, Inc., became a publicly held corporation in October 1970. After the company was listed on the over-the-counter market, stock began trading on the New York Stock Exchange in mid-1972. The founder, Sam Walton, continued to serve as chairman of the board and chief executive officer.

In 1982, Wal-Mart had 491 discount department stores servicing the general-merchandise needs of its customers. The discount stores ranged in size from 30,000 to 90,000 square feet, with the average store size being about 52,000 square feet. Wal-Mart stores were usually organized with 36 departments and carried merchandise such as wearing apparel for the entire family, household furnishings, appliances, and other hard-line merchandise. These stores were located in 13 states across the South and the Southeast.

Unlike many other major discount chains, Wal-Mart devoted itself almost exclusively to serving small towns and medium-sized cities. In their respective communities, Wal-Mart Discount Cities were the largest nonfood retailers. The largest cities in which the company operated in 1982 were Little Rock, Arkansas; Shreveport, Louisiana; Springfield, Missouri; Huntsville, Alabama; and Nashville, Tennessee.

This case was prepared by Monya Giggar, Gregg Gunchick, and David Miller, under the supervision of Professor Sexton Adams, North Texas State University, and Professor Adelaide Griffin, Texas Woman's University, as a basis for class discussion rather than to illustrate either effective or ineffective handling of an administrative situation.

**MANAGE-MENT**

Wal-Mart exercised a highly entrepreneurial, participatory, and goal-oriented style of management. Responsibility for Wal-Mart's style had been attributed to Sam Walton, chief executive officer and chairman of the board. Serving below him were some of the most respected top-level management personnel in the discount store industry. Heading these top-level executives was Jack Shewmaker, president, shown in Exhibit 21.1.

One of the chain's historical strengths, though, had been that it had a single-minded philosophy which had kept it on the straight and narrow path established by Sam Walton 36 years before. Sam's personal attitude was reflected by the

**Exhibit 21.1** Wal-Mart Organization Chart

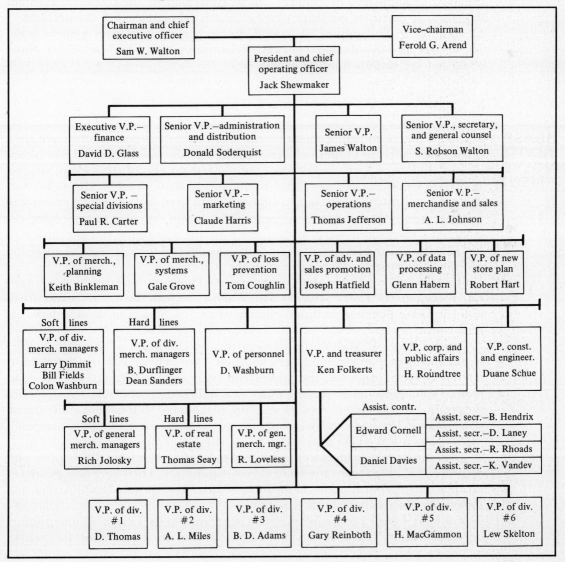

29

manner in which he had established special relationships with many of the employees, which he called associates. In the early years at Wal-Mart, Sam visited all the stores twice a year, exchanging open communication on ideas and problems. Theo Ashcraft, vice-president of the lease department, said that Sam "has always listened to people . . . learning [from them] everyday."[3]

In 1982, the geographical expansion of Wal-Mart made it impossible for Sam Walton to visit and communicate at a personal level with the employees of all 491 stores. Therefore, Jack Shewmaker inherited many responsibilities handed down by the aging Sam Walton. Shewmaker, of the Sam Walton mold, was a strong believer in participatory management. He said, "Wal-Mart's system is people supportive. This is a major factor in our operational strategy. We design programs so systems and procedures can be overriden by the manager, assistant manager, or the store manager who has first hand contact with the problem."[4] In addition to his support of Sam Walton's participatory management style, Shewmaker also maintained a personal relationship with Sam Walton, accompanying him on various hunting expeditions.

## GRASS-ROOTS INVOLVE-MENT

Wal-Mart practiced management objectives called grass-roots involvement. Jack Shewmaker referred to these objectives as being "the involvement of our associates in every aspect of our business and the recognition of their ideas, suggestions, and problems as a key factor to our productivity gains."[5] This policy was designed to provide continuous communication between top management and field operations. Starting at the store level, ideas and thoughts on improving the company's operations were written down by the associates and forwarded to headquarters. The overall corporate plan consolidated these individual goals and objectives to produce Wal-Mart's plan for action.

However, the corporate plans were composed in a centralized fashion at corporate headquarters. Every Saturday Sam Walton met with the top-level executives and corporate planners to discuss future strategies. Sam continued to have the final word.

Another facet of Wal-Mart's strategy was an extension of the participatory management style to get employees involved. "We believe in sharing vital information on sales, expenses, and profits with every associate throughout the company,"[6] said Shewmaker. Among other vital information available, "each month we prepare departmental reports showing percentage to total and comparative performance on sales, markdowns, inventory turnover, and gross margin."[7] "Each person was made to feel that he or she could affect the results."[8]

All of the store managers were evaluated on overall sales from their stores, with consideration given to location and size of community. They were also evaluated on appearance, contributions in the form of ideas to corporate headquarters, and their ability to compete in their region.

Wal-Mart's most successful incentive program was its VPI or volume-producing-item contest. This program allowed individual store departments free rein to price and promote certain merchandise of their own choice. Walton claimed that many faltering products had been revived as a result. "This is another way to keep people involved and thinking. Each month everyone knows where they rank in the chain and what percentage of a store's business they have,"[9] he explained.

The responses of Wal-Mart employees were overwhelmingly in favor of the people-oriented programs. A clerk said that she "had worked for another chain for three years before coming to Wal-Mart, and I started off earning more here and there's no feeling of strain or pressure."[10] A manager stated, "It's so much more open. You know where you stand all the time. You're not left in the dark."[11]

**MERCHAN-DISING**

Consumers' perceptions of Wal-Mart in Russellville, Arkansas, a "typical Wal-Mart market"[12] were very favorable. In a Wal-Mart survey conducted in Russellville, many consumers responded positively to the chain with comments such as "they have better quality merchandise; their prices are lower than K mart's; and they have a big selection."[13] Wal-Mart's merchandising program had found the right combination of brand names, low prices, promotions and presentations, item merchandising, and fashion sense to attract and keep its customers.

Wal-Mart combined a strong brand-name merchandising philosophy with its domination of categories and subcategories. An example of its brand-name appeal was the Wrangler programs. The complete size assortment of Wrangler jeans were displayed in special dark-stained wooden cubicles. Inside the display or adjacent to it in both men's and women's departments, accessories (hats and belts, boots and shirts) were positioned to encourage tie-in sales. Brand programs were also extended to the hard lines. The Wal-Mart strategy was to carry all the usual hard-line brands, but add fringe items to bolster the price or value perception of its shoppers. In health and beauty aids, a line of old-favorite fragrances like Wind Song, Jontue, and Emeraud was joined by a selection of limited semirestricted lines such as Charlie, Cie, Sophia, and Scoundrel. These limited additions were stocked heavily in multiple facings on open shelves, unlike many other chains that keep limited lines under lock-and-key. The philosophy for having the lines accessible was that one cannot sell the lines whenever the shoppers can't get to them.

Another area where perception played a key role was in Wal-Mart's pricing policies. As one consumer stated, "Wal-Mart's prices are lower than K mart's. The selection is better, too."[14] Wal-Mart, T. G. & Y., and K Mart were often locked into intense competition in the markets they all shared (small towns and rural areas). In setting pricing policies, each chain had to devise an assortment strategy. Of the two competitors, T. G. & Y. tended to be overassorted—similar to the variety stores of the past. K Mart, on the other hand, tended to narrow its assortments and fill in the gaps with private-label brands, such as K-Mart toilet tissue and facial tissue. Wal-Mart's strategy called for splitting the difference. First, it out-assorted K Mart, then it beat the prices offered by T. G. & Y. Additionally, much of Wal-Mart's perceived lower prices is revealed in a comparison of shelf prices of the three discount retailers that was conducted in Bartlesville, Oklahoma (1981). The results of the shelf-price study are shown in Exhibit 21.2. There were four random categories chosen and several subcategories within these categories. The total price differential for a 36-item market basket amounted to less than 7½ percent between competitors. These results are indicative of the closeness of the competition.

Much of Wal-Mart's success in developing consumer perceptions was credited to its promotional programs. The program emphasis provided the impact of name brands and good values that made key departments dominant in the marketplace. "Power alley," a Wal-Mart promotional characteristic, was the high-powered promotional racetrack in all the stores. The alley promotions were lined down each aisle in the store's racetrack. In most stores, the power alley had 100 or more promotional tables or platforms. These tables/platforms contained merchandise with average tickets that were sometimes 100 percent lower than at most chains. This promotional effort was the key to the volume production that enabled Wal-Mart to maintain its growth. Included among the 100 or more tables and platforms that made up the total program were assorted 2- by 2-foot cubes, 3- by 3-foot tables, and 5-foot square tables and platforms, occasionally joined together. The $2 \times 2$ cubes were used in health and beauty aids, with 18 to 24 set in a double row down the center of an interior aisle. Requiring lower inventory investments, the small cubes were also used to pull shoppers into the automotive department—located at the right (or left) rear corner of the racetrack aisle.

Wal-Mart's strategy also entailed the use of item merchandising, a concept by which an unusual item was positioned near or adjacent to a department to build category dominance. For example, to create a bigger share of the bed sheet market, and to build brand image, Cannon sheets at attractive prices were promoted on a table adjacent to the domestics department. The item set the scene for the particular department and served as a way to draw shoppers into the department. All Wal-Mart chains practiced this concept with their "million-dollar" items. These were basic everyday needs (sheets, socks, mattress covers) that helped build a category or major-brand-name good that helped build the brand-name image.

The profitable lure of apparel was also becoming increasingly evident in Wal-Mart stores. Over the next five years, Wal-Mart intended to build its stake in soft lines to 35 percent, according to the chain's executives. This intention was evident in the newer stores, where the format was upgraded and total space-to-apparel and major soft lines was as high as 43 percent. Wal-Mart prominently placed large departmental signs that resembled J. C. Penney's signs. Brand emphasis was concentrated more and more on the apparel side of the store as was obvious with the Wrangler brand emphasis in boy's, men's, and women's wear. Most store units also stocked Garan knit sport shirts and displayed them on an eye-catching brand displayer. Also, Wal-Mart was trying to build identity in men's socks by displaying signs that read, "Alder from Burlington." "Overall, Wal-Mart steers clear of no-names, especially in categories where image counts,"[15] said Wal-Mart executives.

**Exhibit 21.2** Shelf-Price Comparison

| BARTLESVILLE, OKLAHOMA, SHELF PRICES | | | |
|---|---|---|---|
| Item | Wal-Mart | T.G. & Y. | K-Mart |
| **Health & beauty aids** | | | |
| Bayer 100s | $ 1.57 | $ 1.60 | $ 1.57 |
| Excedrin X-Strength 100s | 2.58 | 3.37 | 2.06[a] |
| Bufferin 100s | 2.13 | 2.13 | 2.13 |
| Bufferin A.S. | 1.67[a] | 2.09 | 2.43 |
| Tylenol X-Strength 100s | 3.54 | 3.27 | 3.29 |
| Tylenol X-Strength 50s | 2.33 | 2.53 | 2.33 |
| Anacin 200s | 3.68 | 3.97 | 3.68 |
| Anacin 100s | 1.42[a] | 1.99 | 1.97 |
| Flex 16-oz shampoo | 1.68 | 1.68 | 1.74 |
| Suave Baby Shampoo 28 oz | 1.06 | 1.14 | 1.48 |
| Faberge Organic X-tra Body | 1.18 | 1.18 | 1.18 |
| No More Tears 16-oz shampoo | 2.62 | 3.12 | 1.97[a] |
| Wella Balsam 8-oz. shampoo | 1.78 | 1.77 | 1.67 |
| Head & Shoulders 15-oz. tube | 2.97 | 2.99 | 1.58[a] |
| Head & Shoulders 11-oz. bottle | 2.46 | 2.67 | 2.46 |
| Prell tube 5 oz | 1.92 | 1.72 | 1.92 |
| Pert 15 oz | 1.83[a] | 2.44 | 2.13 |
| Silkience 15 oz | 2.56 | 2.78 | 2.16 |
| **Small electrics** | | | |
| Mr. Coffee 10 cup | 22.88 | 22.99 | 24.97 |
| GE automatic percolator | 28.42 | 28.96 | 28.87 |
| Regal Poly-Perk hot pot | 9.96 | 9.99 | 10.62 |
| **Automotive** | | | |
| Rain Dance 16 oz | 5.54 | 5.99 | 5.07 |
| Turtle Zip Wax 18 oz | 1.84 | 2.17 | 2.07 |
| Phillips TropArctic oil | 0.97 | 0.95 | 0.97 |
| Quaker State oil | 0.97 | 0.95 | 0.97 |
| Penzoil 10W-40 | 0.97 | 0.95 | 0.97 |
| PL nondetergent | 0.68 | 0.77 | 0.74 |
| **Hardware** | | | |
| Powerlok II 20 ft | 11.57 | 12.99 | 12.48 |
| Stanley 16-oz | 8.44 | 5.67[a] | 9.97 |
| Steelmaster 16 oz | 12.76 | 14.30 | 11.88 |
| Black & Decker | | | |
| 7104 drill | 16.88 | 17.87 | 15.77 |
| 7004 drill | 12.97 | 12.99 | 11.97 |
| 7504 jigsaw | 12.97 | 11.77 | 13.48 |
| 7580 VSR drill | 42.46 | 34.57 | 33.88 |
| 7308 circular saw | 29.96 | 35.97 | 27.88 |
| 7300 circular saw 5½ in. | 24.97 | 27.77 | 27.97 |
| Total | $284.19 | $290.06 | $268.31 |

[a]Sale item.

*Source: Discount Store News Research,* December 14, 1981, p. 43.

**ADVERTISING**   The advertising policy, displayed in all Wal-Mart stores, was to take sale advertisements from any other store and match the price. Under this policy, historically, it had held advertising expenditures to "1.5 percent of sales or less."[16] Recent expansion, however, was to raise this level to about 1.7 percent of sales or nearly $2.4 billion a year. According to company sources, one-third of that total would be spent on newspaper advertising, and television spots would be increased from $6 million to the $7 million to $8 million-dollar level. The expansion into urban areas had entered Wal-Mart into markets where television time, newspaper space, and radio time were substantially more costly.

In addition to its added level of expansion, Wal-Mart had begun running more expensive, up-scale advertising. In the small town of Fayetteville, Arkansas where it was opening an 85,000-square-foot store, Wal-Mart ran a "36-page, all-four-color, all-photo magazine-size 'catalog' circular."[17] This new style resembled a J. C. Penney's catalog. All 36 pages—11 or so pages of apparel and the remainder of consumables, seasonal merchandise, and hard lines—were full four colors and the circular used models and/or product photography. In contrast to the bigger-store advertisements, smaller units' circulars are usually 10-page broadsheets with "false four-color"[18] on the front and back, and inside, black and white.

Wal-Mart was devising two separate merchandising and advertising strategies: the typical hard-lines-oriented 40,000- to 50,000-square-foot stores and the 85,000- to 90,000-square-foot stores that give greater emphasis to the fashion apparel side. This strategy was important to Wal-Mart's future in the ever-changing marketplace.

**DISTRI- BUTION CENTERS**   A basic practice of Wal-Mart had been to limit its store operations to about a 450- to 500-mile radius of distribution centers, to achieve speed of restocking and savings in delivery costs. As Wal-Mart continued pushing its geographical limits, cost-effective distribution became more critical.

Located near headquarters in Bentonville, a 525,000-square-foot distribution complex handled, in the past, 80 percent of all the goods sold by Wal-Mart.[19] The expansion of the chain had resulted in additional distribution centers being constructed. In Searcy, Arkansas, an equal-capacity center was opened to aid in Wal-Mart's expansion into southern Arkansas. Long-range plans called for the construction of a 512,000-square-foot center in Palestine, Texas. This center fully came on line at the close of 1981. In 1982, a 900,000-square-foot distribution center was to be built in Cullman, Alabama.

The Palestine distribution center helped Wal-Mart penetrate the Texas border and Gulf coast markets. Sam Walton was convinced that he could " 'double, even triple' the size of his company, just with locations in Texas and Louisiana."[20] Shreveport, Louisiana, and Houston, Corpus Christi, and Dallas–Fort Worth, Texas, had been sited for the expansion of Wal-Mart. Management had already sited the Rio Grande Valley and eight more sites in the area for prime expansion moves.

The new Alabama distribution center would perhaps be even more critical to the chain's expansion than the Palestine center. Coming on-stream in 1983, the center would provide overnight delivery into the states where the Big K acquisition brought the chain. It would extend into the Carolinas, Georgia, and Florida. These areas could be potential sites for Wal-Mart expansion.

Wal-Mart distribution centers (existing, as well as those to be built) were mechanized utilizing conveyor systems to expedite the flow of merchandise and each served an approximate proportion of the chain's stores. There were two additional distribution centers in Bentonville that were used for the inspecting and processing of fashion clothing; warehousing for jewelry and sporting goods; operations and accumulation of sale merchandise for shipment to stores as close to the sale as possible. The centers' radius span was to allow Wal-Mart's own trucking fleet to make deliveries in one day.

Wal-Mart trucks were expected to travel about 20 million miles in 1982, at a cost of about $18 million. The distribution centers' total expenses ran "approximately 2.5 percent of the goods shipped through them (now about 85 percent of the chain's total merchandise assortment)."[21] Wal-Mart's move toward establishing distribution centers and trucking fleets in Texas and Alabama was part of its long-range plan to expand its markets outward.

## THE ACQUISITION OF BIG K

Wal-Mart acquired the Kuhn's Big K chain, headquartered in Nashville, Tennessee, in August 1981. The total cost for 92 Big K stores, a large distribution center, headquarters, all of Big K's liabilities, and inventories within each store was about $100 million. It was estimated that each store would cost $125,000 to convert to the Wal-Mart label.

The conversion process (at the close of 1981) was first applied to the five least profitable Big K stores. This served as an acid test of the validity of the acquisition. According to Sam Walton, the average sales gains in these renovated stores had been in excess of 150 percent. In the first quarter as part of the Wal-Mart chain, the renovated stores contributed $70 million in sales volume.

The purchase helped Wal-Mart's future plans become more attainable. With the Big K stores, Wal-Mart gained penetration of Tennessee, Kentucky, and also large clusters in Alabama and Mississippi. It also brought Wal-Mart into the new areas of Georgia and South Carolina. Thus, by purchasing a bargain expansion and getting good locations that were profitable to the chain, Wal-Mart stood ready to face the future.

## FINANCING

The company financed its capital expenditures for expansion primarily through internally generated funds. Funds from operations, $74 million in fiscal 1981, were the primary source of liquidity for the company. For additional externally generated funds, Wal-Mart offered one million shares in 1981 that generated almost $33 million for the company. At fiscal year end 1981, Wal-Mart had access to $176 million of unused short-term credit.

Wal-Mart controlled expenses using several strategies: (1) negotiating harder

**Exhibit 21.3** Consolidated Balance Sheet (dollars in thousands)

|  | January 31, | |
|---|---:|---:|
|  | **1981** | **1980** |
| **Assets** | | |
| Current assets | | |
| Cash | $ 6,927 | $ 5,090 |
| Short-term money market investments | 11,528 | — |
| Receivables | 12,666 | 7,806 |
| Recoverable costs from sale/leaseback | 31,325 | 15,557 |
| Inventories | 280,021 | 235,315 |
| Prepaid expenses | 2,737 | 2,849 |
| Total current assets | 345,204 | 266,617 |
| **Property, plant, and equipment, at cost** | | |
| Land | 5,903 | 15,002 |
| Buildings and improvements | 51,200 | 42,287 |
| Fixtures and equipment | 80,411 | 56,072 |
| Transportation equipment | 12,969 | 9,012 |
|  | 150,483 | 122,373 |
| Less accumulated depreciation | 33,702 | 23,613 |
| Net property, plant, and equipment | 116,781 | 98,760 |
| Property under capital leases | 152,882 | 109,608 |
| Less accumulated amortization | 23,721 | 17,806 |
| Net property under capital leases | 129,161 | 91,802 |
| Other assets and deferred charges | 1,199 | 700 |
| Total assets | $592,345 | $457,879 |
| **Liabilities and stockholders' equity** | | |
| Current liabilities | | |
| Notes payable | $ 15,000 | $ 25,080 |
| Accounts payable | 97,445 | 100,102 |
| Accrued liabilities | | |
| Salaries | 11,229 | 12,889 |
| Taxes, other than income | 9,627 | 6,619 |
| Other | 25,748 | 15,148 |
| Accrued federal and state income taxes | 11,907 | 5,365 |
| Long-term debt due within one year | 3,375 | 2,314 |
| Obligations under capital leases due within one year | 3,270 | 2,704 |
| Total current liabilities | 177,601 | 170,221 |
| Long-term debt | 30,184 | 24,862 |
| Long-term obligations under capital leases | 134,896 | 97,212 |
| Deferred income taxes | 1,355 | 740 |
| Stockholders' equity | | |
| Preferred stock | — | — |
| Common stock | 3,234 | 1,512 |
| Capital in excess of par value | 67,481 | 35,064 |
| Retained earnings | 177,594 | 128,268 |
| Total stockholders' equity | 248,309 | 164,844 |
| Total liabilities and stockholders' equity | $592,345 | $457,879 |

*Source:* 1981 Annual Report.

with landlords for store sites (its occupancy cost was 1.75 percent of sales), (2) keeping store payrolls tight—currently 7.5 percent (store managers worked on smaller base salaries but with richer profit sharing plans), (3) discouraging employee theft by sharing half the savings with employees, (4) maintaining tough bargaining stances on key line items from suppliers, and (5) keeping advertising costs at less than 1.2 percent of sales.

"Wal-Mart's operating, selling, general and administrative expenses (1981) rose 138 percent since 1977, and the cost of goods sold at the chain increased even more by 139.7 percent."[22] Sales of the company rose 142.2 percent during that same period. Earnings for Wal-Mart also had increased 193.8 percent since 1977.

The financial statements that follow detail Wal-Mart's impressive financial record. Exhibit 21.3 is the consolidated balance sheet and Exhibit 21.4 is the

**Exhibit 21.4** Consolidated Statement of Income (dollars in thousands)

| | Years Ended January 31, | | |
| --- | --- | --- | --- |
| | 1981 | 1980 | 1979 |
| Number of stores in operation at the end of the year | 330 | 276 | 229 |
| Revenues | | | |
| Net sales | $1,643,199 | $1,248,176 | $900,298 |
| Rentals from licensed departments | 5,331 | 4,804 | 6,344 |
| Other income—net | 6,732 | 5,288 | 3,271 |
| | 1,655,262 | 1,258,268 | 909,913 |
| Costs and expenses | | | |
| Cost of sales | 1,207,802 | 919,305 | 661,062 |
| Operating, selling and general and administrative expenses | 331,524 | 251,616 | 182,365 |
| Interest costs | | | |
| Debt | 5,808 | 4,438 | 3,119 |
| Capital leases | 10,849 | 8,621 | 6,595 |
| | 1,555,983 | 1,183,980 | 853,141 |
| Income before income taxes | 99,279 | 74,288 | 56,772 |
| Provision for federal and state income taxes | | | |
| Current | 42,982 | 31,649 | 28,047 |
| Deferred | 615 | 1,488 | (722) |
| | 43,597 | 33,137 | 27,325 |
| Net income | $ 55,682 | $ 41,151 | $ 29,447 |
| Net income per share | | | |
| Primary and fully diluted | $1.73 | $1.34[a] | $.97[a] |

[a]Adjusted to reflect the 100% stock dividend paid on December 16, 1980.

*Source:* 1981 Annual Report.

consolidated statement of income. Exhibit 21.5 highlights the two-year comparison and the five-year financial review of Wal-Mart's performance. Exhibit 21.6 provides a review of ten years of growth for Wal-Mart.

**Exhibit 21.5** Wal-Mart's Financial Highlights

**TWO-YEAR COMPARISON**
**(dollar amounts in thousands)**

|  | 1981 | 1980 |
|---|---|---|
| Current assets | $ 345,204 | $ 266,617 |
| Current liabilities | 177,601 | 170,221 |
| Working capital | 167,603 | 96,396 |
| Current ratio | 1.94 | 1.57 |
| Stockholders' equity | $ 248,309 | $ 164,844 |
| Number of shares outstanding | 32,342,445 | 30,242,522[a] |

**FIVE-YEAR FINANCIAL REVIEW**
**(dollar amounts in thousands except per share data)**

|  | 1981 | 1980 | 1979 | 1978 | 1977 |
|---|---|---|---|---|---|
| Net sales | $ 1,643,199 | $ 1,248,176 | $900,298 | $678,456 | $478,807 |
| Income before income taxes | 99,279 | 74,288 | 56,772 | 40,847 | 30,857 |
| Net income | 55,682 | 41,151 | 29,447 | 21,191 | 16,039 |
| Net income per share | | | | | |
|   Primary | $ 1.73 | $ 1.34[a] | $ .97[a] | $ .74[a] | $ .58[a] |
|   Fully diluted | 1.73 | 1.34[a] | .97[a] | .71[a] | .54[a] |
| Number of stores in operation at the end of the period | 330 | 276 | 229 | 195 | 153 |

[a]Adjusted to reflect the 100% stock dividend paid December 16, 1980, to holders of Wal-Mart common stock.

*Source:* 1981 Annual Report.

**Exhibit 21.6** Ten Years of Growth for Wal-Mart.

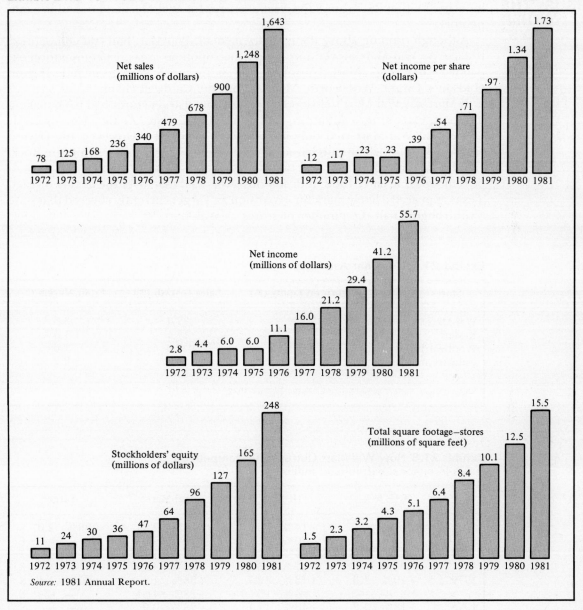

Net sales
(millions of dollars)

| 1972 | 1973 | 1974 | 1975 | 1976 | 1977 | 1978 | 1979 | 1980 | 1981 |
| 78 | 125 | 168 | 236 | 340 | 479 | 678 | 900 | 1,248 | 1,643 |

Net income per share
(dollars)

| 1972 | 1973 | 1974 | 1975 | 1976 | 1977 | 1978 | 1979 | 1980 | 1981 |
| .12 | .17 | .23 | .23 | .39 | .54 | .71 | .97 | 1.34 | 1.73 |

Net income
(millions of dollars)

| 1972 | 1973 | 1974 | 1975 | 1976 | 1977 | 1978 | 1979 | 1980 | 1981 |
| 2.8 | 4.4 | 6.0 | 6.0 | 11.1 | 16.0 | 21.2 | 29.4 | 41.2 | 55.7 |

Stockholders' equity
(millions of dollars)

| 1972 | 1973 | 1974 | 1975 | 1976 | 1977 | 1978 | 1979 | 1980 | 1981 |
| 11 | 24 | 30 | 36 | 47 | 64 | 96 | 127 | 165 | 248 |

Total square footage—stores
(millions of square feet)

| 1972 | 1973 | 1974 | 1975 | 1976 | 1977 | 1978 | 1979 | 1980 | 1981 |
| 1.5 | 2.3 | 3.2 | 4.3 | 5.1 | 6.4 | 8.4 | 10.1 | 12.5 | 15.5 |

*Source:* 1981 Annual Report.

**WAL-MART VERSUS "THE OTHER GUYS"**

Wal-Mart's five-year financial record through 1981 paced the discount store industry. Exhibit 21.7 shows five-year averages for Wal-Mart and two of its competitors.

Although running above the industry median, Wal-Mart had stiff competition to face. As Wal-Mart moved into larger metropolitan areas, its competition expanded from Magic Mart, Gibson's, T.G. & Y., and K Mart to include Dayton Hudson's Target, Woolworth, Murphy, and the Caldwell chain.

K Mart was Wal-Mart's closest competitor, but Target stores had been making moves to expand into Arkansas, Wal-Mart's home state. At the close of 1981, Target and Wal-Mart vied only in Nashville, Tennessee. However, the Dayton Hudson discount chain purchased three shuttered Woolco stores in Little Rock, an 80,000-square-foot unit and two 10,000-square-footers.[23] The stores were to be remodeled in early 1982. Industry observers said that, over the next two years, Texas appeared a likely mark for expansion as Target currently covered that state "with roughly half the number of stores as Wal-Mart."[24]

**Exhibit 21.7** Five-Year Averages

| Stores | Return on Equity (%) | Sales Growth (%) | Profit Margin (%) |
|---|---|---|---|
| Wal-Mart | 30.6 | 37.4 | 3.3 |
| K-Mart | 16.0 | 17.1 | 1.5 |
| Woolworth | 11.8 | 9.6 | 1.6 |
| Industry median | 12.1 | 9.7 | 2.2 |

*Source:* "Sam's Song," as published in *Forbes*, January 1982.

**Exhibit 21.8** How Wal-Mart Outruns the Competition
(sales in billions; earnings in millions)

| | T.G. & Y. | | K Mart | | Wal-Mart | | Target | | |
|---|---|---|---|---|---|---|---|---|---|
| 1981 | — | — | +14% | 16.5 | +28% | 2.44 | +26% | 2.07 | S |
| | — | — | −20% | 210.0 | +30% | 79.5 | — | — | E |
| 1980 | +22% | 1.4 | +14% | 14.2 | +29% | 1.7 | +27% | 1.5 | S |
| | — | — | −27% | 260.5 | +26% | 55.7 | — | — | E |
| 1979 | +19% | 1.3 | +13% | 12.7 | +38% | 1.2 | +20% | 1.1 | S |
| | — | — | +4% | 358.0 | +28% | 41.1 | — | — | E |
| 1978 | +18% | 1.2 | +18% | 11.7 | +28% | 0.9 | — | — | S |
| | — | — | +18% | 343.7 | +17% | 29.4 | — | — | E |
| 1977 | +14% | 1.0 | +18% | 9.9 | +42% | 0.5 | — | — | S |
| | — | — | +12% | 302.9 | +31% | 21.4 | — | — | E |

*Source: Discount Store News Research,* December 14, 1981, pp. 13–14.

The past performance of Wal-Mart in its smaller towns had been aided by its assimilating of technological advances. Exhibit 21.8 provides the data to support Wal-Mart's operational power among its competition. Thus, the expansive strength of Wal-Mart was to be tested by all its competitors in the years to come.

**INDUSTRY TRENDS**

Within the discount store industry as of January 1982, there was a definite trend toward upscaled-merchandise presentation. K Mart was adopting a new merchandising program that, for example, was dropping all synthetic fibers in favor of natural blends. In addition, in view of Wal-Mart's success in rural markets, K Mart was targeting expansion outside of metropolitan areas.[25] Increasing emphasis on promotionally priced goods had caused reductions in many chains' profit margins. According to Kenneth Mache, president of Dayton Hudson (Target), this additional promotional activity would "depress the bottom lines for the major chains by cutting into already reduced margins."[26] To combat these problems, many discounters were turning to more updated apparel lines and cosmetics while at the same time reducing the number of items carried.

Macroeconomic factors have a direct impact on industry strategies. In the recessionary environment of early 1982, for example, discounters were caught in a squeeze between declining real income of consumers due to inflation as well as a very high unemployment rate. As a result, consumers were shopping less frequently and seeking out sale-priced items when they did shop. Of this, a Merrill Lynch analyst, Jeffrey Feiner, remarked, "this pattern may reverse itself following the scheduled 10 percent tax cut in July, 1982. But retailers believe that consumers are settling into the habit of sale shopping and will not change quickly."[27]

Industry merchandisers were becoming more selective on the merchandise carried in their stores. Successful merchants carefully scrutinized inventories, making sure that goods did not sit on shelves by stepping up promotions. The test for discounters in the future will be to combine a low-cost structure with the most innovative merchandising techniques to move the goods.

There was also a trend toward greater similarity between major competitors in the discount store industry. Many of the more successful innovations of one chain were quickly adopted by its competitors. Examples of this included race-track configurations in store layouts, heavy use of promotional tables in merchandising, and upgraded apparel quality and presentation.

**COMPANY OUTLOOK**

The important things had changed very little for Wal-Mart over the years. The company still made strong presentations of basic merchandise, still benefited from Sam Walton's entrepreneurial spirit, and still concentrated on the small towns and surrounding rural areas where the store could be the primary source for shoppers. It also still used the best merchandise techniques and developed or attracted the best merchandise talent, always experimenting with new goods and new ways to present these goods.

Wal-Mart had evolved an intense, high-profile management style that brought together field supervisors and store managers into a chainwide merchandising emphasis, providing new ideas for the company. The best ideas were put into the corporate framework and encouraged to be fulfilled. This was but one of several practices that helped Wal-Mart gain its current status. Others included the perception of everyday low prices by the consumers and commitment to innovative, cost-control systems with the savings passed on to the consumer. The company utilized technological advances in its operations for maximum efficiency and productivity. For example, the main computer in Bentonville talked directly to vendor computers, resulting in lower out-of-stocks.

A quote from Wal-Mart's 1981 annual report reflected its view of the future:

> The retailing environment is constantly changing. Competition will continue to improve and become more intense. Life styles will change, and today's solutions will soon be obsolete. But, with a flow of new programs, with the continuing contribution of our dedicated associates and with our commitment to avoid any short-term strategy that does not enhance our long range goals, we are convinced that improved productivity will be achieved. Our people have truly made the difference, and as they respond to the everchanging environment, we will serve our customers with the "best value in town."[28]

## NOTES

1. "Odds Too Long—Wal-Mart Nixes Kuhn's Deal," *Chain Store Age: General Merchandise Issue,* February 1981, p. 35.
2. Ibid.
3. "Sam Walton's Just Getting Started," *Chain Store Age: General Merchandise Issue,* May 1978, p. 32.
4. "Grassroots: People are Wal-Mart Power," *Chain Store Age: General Merchandise Issue,* February 1981, pp. 36–37, 42.
5. Ibid., p. 36.
6. Ibid., p. 37.
7. Ibid.
8. "How Much Is Too Expensive?" *Financial World,* November 1981, pp. 23–24.
9. "Grassroots: People Are Wal-Mart Power," p. 37.
10. Ibid., p. 42.
11. Ibid.
12. "How Does Wal-Mart Do It?," *Discount Store News,* December 14, 1981, p. 43.
13. "The 'Consumer Grip,'" *Discount Store News,* December 14, 1981, p. 16.
14. Ibid., p. 43.
15. Ibid., p. 15.
16. Ibid.
17. Ibid., p. 73.
18. Ibid.
19. Ibid.

20. Company Profile, Wal-Mart Stores, Inc., p. 72.
21. "How Does Wal-Mart Do It?" p. 72.
22. "How Does Wal-Mart Do It?" p. 19.
23. "2 Targets on Hold; 3 Others to Debut," *Chain Store Age: General Merchandise Issue,* February 1982, p. 12.
24. Ibid.
25. Lynda Shuster, "Wal-Mart Chief's Enthusiastic Approach Infects Employees, Keeps Retailer Growing," *Wall Street Journal,* April 20, 1981, p. 21.
26. "A Grass-Roots Blueprint," *Discount Store News,* December 14, 1981, p. 14.
26. Ibid.
28. Wal-Mart Stores, Inc., Annual Report, 1981, p. 11.

# 22 Mary Kay Cosmetics, Inc.

Sexton Adams
North Texas State University
Adelaide Griffin
Texas Woman's University

Mary Kay Cosmetics, Inc. (MKY) is a relatively small manufacturer of cosmetics and skin care products, marketing its products through an international network of independent sales representatives. Located in Dallas, Texas, the company has five regional distribution centers in the United States, one distribution center in Australia, one in Canada, and one in Argentina. Another distribution center was opened in Santo Domingo on December 1, 1982. Founded in 1963 by Mary Kay Ash, the company has grown from nine sales representatives to over 150,000. Starting with an initial investment of $5500, it had grown to net sales of $235 million in 1981. With a relatively small product line which the independent sales representatives, called beauty consultants, carry with them, Mary Kay Cosmetics, Inc., has a target market of women aged 25 to 44 who are in the middle and above income brackets.

**MARY KAY—
THE WOMAN**
The story of Mary Kay Ash's life is, to a large extent, the story of MKY. Mary Kay was born Mary Kathlyn Wagner in Hot Wells, a small town in south Texas.[1] At age seven she was helping to support her family and her invalid father while her mother ran the family restaurant in a Houston suburb.[2]

Graduation from high school meant the end of formal education, even though she had graduated from Reagan High School in Houston with honors and hoped to attend college. Mary Kay was soon married to Ben Rogers. The marriage lasted 11 years, and resulted in the birth of three children: Marylin in 1935, Ben, Jr., in 1936, and Richard in 1943. World War II meant months at a time of separation from her husband, who had been drafted and was unable to send home more than a few dollars each month. For a while during the time Ben was in the service, Mary Kay attended classes at the University of Houston, but her college career was cut short by the responsibility of the small children.[3]

This case was prepared by Marlene Carle, Robert Carle, Richard Edwards, and Paula Walters, under the supervision of Professor Sexton Adams, North Texas State University, and Professor Adelaide Griffin, Texas Woman's University, as a basis for class discussion rather than to illustrate either effective or ineffective handling of an administrative situation.

**SELLING FOR OTHERS**

To make ends meet, Mary Kay went to work part-time for Stanley Home Products in Houston selling household specialties at parties in homes. She had a natural aptitude for selling and quickly became one of her company's leading sales representatives. Mary Kay learned that people liked to talk to her and that her positive attitude enabled her to overcome most of the obstacles she encountered in sales.[4]

**RETIREMENT**

In 1953 Mary Kay left Stanley after 13 years and went to work for World Gifts Company in Dallas selling decorative accessories. She moved up in this organization to the position of national training director. After ten years with World Gifts, Mary Kay was working 60-hour weeks and making $25,000 a year. A disagreement over proposed policy changes at World Gifts prompted Mary Kay to "retire" in 1963. She had spent almost 25 years in direct selling and intended to spend her time writing.[5]

Mary Kay carefully avoids discussing her age, commenting that a woman who would tell that would tell anything.[6] For this reason there are few times when Mary Kay's age is mentioned by writers and reporters who have interviewed her.

Retirement was very unpleasant for Mary Kay. She was unhappy with nothing to do, and within a few days after leaving World Gifts, she began writing down all the direct-selling techniques she had learned in her 25 years in sales. After spending two weeks on this task, she spent another two weeks compiling a list of problems she had encountered in selling, ways of solving these problems, and how she would do things differently in the future if she had the opportunity. Her initial intent was to put this material in a book which would help women sell.[7]

**DISCOVERY OF THE PRODUCT**

In reviewing and editing the notes she had written, Mary Kay realized that she had prepared everything needed to operate a sales organization. The only thing missing was a product.[8]

Several years earlier, while working for Stanley Home Products, Mary Kay conducted a demonstration of her company's products one evening to a group of approximately 20 women in a home in one of the suburbs of Dallas. The hostess for the party kept the guests after Mary Kay's demonstration to give them little jars of skin treatment, several creams she had prepared using formulas she had been given by her grandfather who had at one time operated a local tannery. The women attending the party were being used to test the formulas. Mary Kay had noticed the beautiful complexions of the women she had met that evening and was anxious to try the skin treatment herself. She took several of the jars, which were of various sizes and shapes and were handed to her in an old shoe box.[9] The creams smelled terrible, but they worked. Mary Kay maintains to this day that her own beautiful complexion is the result of using these creams which were eventually to become the first of the MKY product line.[10]

**THE BEGINNING OF A COMPANY**

Soon after the completion of her writing, Mary Kay and her second husband, George Hallenbeck, whom she had married earlier in 1963, decided to use Mary Kay's sales and problem-solving techniques and to go into business. George's background included sales and administration. The idea of starting a new business appealed to both of them.[11] The formulas for the skin creams Mary Kay had been given several years earlier were purchased for $500. The woman who owned the formulas had been attempting to produce and market them by herself but had not been successful.[12]

The busy process of organizing their new company was under way. Mary Kay's husband was to be the administrator. He was in the process of planning the physical facilities and caring for other matters regarding the operation of the business, while Mary Kay was preparing the final draft of the sales manual, designing and ordering containers, and recruiting sales people. One month before the business was to open, George died of a heart attack.[13]

Mary Kay discussed her situation with her children, and Richard, who was then a 20-year-old insurance salesman in Houston, moved to Dallas and helped his mother start the company in September 1963, with $500 capitalization.[14] Richard, who had attended North Texas State University for a year and a half as a marketing major, was in charge of administration and finance. His mother's duties included training, merchandising, and selling. Six months later Ben, Mary Kay's older son, joined to take care of warehousing and shipping.[15] Ben later became the vice-president for merchandising but left the company in 1978.[16]

The new company, Beauty by Mary Kay, opened with two full-time employees, Mary Kay and Richard, who drew a salary of $250 a month to start, and nine women who sold the initial skin care products which were being made with the formulas purchased for $500.[17] One of MKY's strategies from the beginning was that each sales representative buys her own products at approximately 50 percent of retail, pays for all supplies in advance, and carries a sufficient amount of cosmetics with her to fill all orders on the spot. Thus, the company had no accounts payable and no accounts receivable.[18]

**IMMEDIATE SUCCESS**

The small staff of beauty consultants was successful, both in selling and in recruiting new beauty consultants. The number of people added became so large that a system was established whereby some of the beauty consultants became training directors. An incentive compensation plan was devised which enabled beauty consultants who became training directors to draw an override on the commissions earned by the beauty consultants they recruited and trained.[19] The number of beauty consultants grew from the original nine to 318 in 1964, just one year after the company began operation. Sales for the first year amounted to $198,514. The second year, sales exceeded $800,000. The growth continued at an astonishingly rapid pace both in the number of consultants and sales. MKY went public in 1967.[20]

In 1969 it was necessary to add 102,000 square feet to the manufacturing facility in Dallas. Additional space has been added several times. A new distribution center was added in Dallas, and in the late sixties plans for expansion of sales and distribution centers outside the five-state Texas Southwest were begun.[21] Planning for growth has been necessary from the beginning. The company recently purchased a 177-acre site in another area of North Dallas in order to have the land available for future growth.[22]

## EXPANSION

The rapid growth in the sixties brought MKY to the $6 million sales level and a point where expansion beyond Texas and into the four contiguous states was a logical next step. In the seventies, expansion was first made into the California market with the opening of a branch in Los Angeles designed to serve the western states. The move westward was tremendously successful, and MKY soon had more beauty consultants in California than in Texas. An Atlanta branch was opened in 1972, and a third branch was opened in Chicago in 1975. In 1978 the first office outside the United States was opened in Toronto.[23]

The small regional company of 1970 which had sales of $6 million grew in the decade of the seventies to an international company with sales in 1979 of $91 million. In 1980 sales were $167 million and in 1981 they reached $235 million. The sales force now includes over 150,000 consultants and training directors.[24]

## ANNUAL SEMINAR

One factor that has contributed to MKY's rapid growth is the ability of the company to instill the spirit of winning and the desire for success in the minds of the beauty consultants, the training directors, and the company employees. A major attraction to many of these people is the annual sales meeting, called by MKY a seminar, which is held in Dallas for three days each August. This spectacle is a combination consisting of beauty pageant, awards night, party, the sharing of ideas, classes, goalsetting, leadership training, and even bookkeeping. Each person attends the meeting at her own expense, and they come from all states, Puerto Rico, Canada, Australia, and Argentina. The awards include mink coats, diamond rings, diamond bumblebee pins, watches, luggage, typewriters, pocket calculators, exotic vacations, and the yearlong use of pink Cadillacs and Buick Regals. Some 16,000 MKY beauty consultants and training directors have attended the seminar for each of the past two years.[25]

## INTERNATIONAL OPERATIONS

Attempts to broaden international operations beyond Canada have led to the opening of a subsidiary in Australia, and in 1980, a wholly owned subsidiary in Argentina. These two companies contributed 3 percent of the overall MKY sales in 1981. The Australian company appears to have reasonably good prospects for growth; however, the political and inflationary problems in Argentina, as well as the language barrier, are forcing MKY to examine this operation carefully before deciding whether or not to attempt to expand its efforts in this market.[26] Recruiting is difficult in Argentina, and keeping sales directors in this country is a problem for MKY. As of December 1, 1982, MKY began operations in Santo Domingo.

> In the two where we have a different language, we have a language barrier, that we from the home office standpoint find very difficult to hurdle. . . . We have tried to find someone who not only knows the cosmetic business well, but who is willing to come over here and spend a year to a year and a half learning *our* way of doing business. I don't think we will open any other market until we have someone who can speak the languages and is trained here and goes there.[27]

Not only is language a problem, but brochures must be rewritten in Spanish or the foreign language of that country.

## GOVERN-MENTAL REGULA-TIONS AND LEGAL CONCERNS

The rapid expansion of the business has seen the need for an increase in the number of employees. From the beginning of 1963, with the original two, Mary Kay and Richard Rogers, the company has grown to over 1400 employees.

The beauty consultants and training directors are technically considered independent contractors of MKY, not employees of the company. However, this status of independent contractors has been under investigation by the Internal Revenue Service since 1978. The Revenue Act of 1978 contained provisions for determining an independent-contractor status. With this act, eligible taxpayers, including MKY, were relieved of all liability for ". . . federal income tax, withholding, FICA and FUTA taxes with respect to their sales persons for any period ending before January 1, 1979."[28] Congress extended the interim relief period until July 1, 1982. Any legislation enacted after the period of interim relief could present a financially adverse effect on the company's future operations. This issue has been magnified as a result of other direct-sales companies whose representatives have tried to alter tax deductions.

In 1982 a bill with three provisions was introduced before Congress addressing the status of independent contractors, and was endorsed by MKY and the Direct Selling Association. In a presentation made before the New York Society of Security Analysts on July 22, 1982, Rogers said the bill ". . . would require reporting to the IRS commissions paid to sales people when those commissions exceed $600 per year. Another provision would require reporting to the IRS sales of product to individuals when their sales exceed $5000 per person per year. The third provision which is very important to us is called a safe harbor provision which includes several tests which if met would automatically classify a sales person as an independent contractor rather than an employee."[29] Mary Kay suggested that it would be difficult for her independent contractors to avoid the IRS and not report actual commissions because her company provides the needed information regarding each contractor to the IRS, with this information being maintained on a computer system.[30]

In the third quarter of 1982, the issue was resolved, at least for the time being. The IRS ruled in favor of the independent-contractor status. Said Mary Kay, "We won."[31] Rogers indicated that an adverse effect could have impacted the company in several ways.

The company presently faces a class action suit with regard to the tender offer and purchase of MKY stock from 1979. "Nothing yet has happened," says Mary Kay. "We think, of course, that it's ridiculous. In 1978 and 1979 we as a company had suddenly realized that our directors weren't meeting the test of a salary requirement except on a secretarial basis. They (women) will take the stable salary rather than a 'maybe' commission."[32] From this, management developed the new compensation plan which has contributed to the success of the growth of the company. "In late 1979, we found 60 Minutes on our doorstep; and after nine days of filming, we came out smelling like a rose. Since that program, our sales have quadrupled and our numbers have tripled."[33] For most companies a loss of the suit could negatively affect financial operations and future plans. "It's just for $17 million, and we did $458 million last year in 1981. Anyway, we won't lose it."[34]

## GROWTH

Approximately 40 percent of the 1400 MKY employees are housed in a modern, eight-story office building in North Dallas. This $7 million structure contains approximately 109,000 square feet of office and meeting space and was completed in 1978. The building is now completely free of encumbrance and is a showplace for employees and others; it is a rounded structure of bronzed-gold glass and beige brick, filled with plants, flowers, and trees, and a colorful display of woods, rugs, and paintings.[35]

According to management, the continued and rapid growth of MKY has necessitated the expansion of the physical plant and plans have begun to build a new facility which will be a campus. Land encompassing 177 acres has been purchased over the past year, and in November 1982 ground was broken for the new building. "Almost every department will have its own building, particularly production, distribution, and administrative facilities. We already have our own print shop and legal counsel. In addition, there will be a child care center and possibly in the future plans are to build a hotel."[36] Estimated cost is $100 million for this five-year project, and according to Mary Kay, it will be paid for from funds generated internally.

## PRODUCT LINE

The initial product line at MKY consisted of skin care products for women. Since the introduction of this line in 1963, the line has remained relatively stable. Since 1976, there has been a gradual move toward diversification of products and additions to the Mary Kay line. In 1980, the Skin Care Line was diversified to meet the needs of the different consumers whose skin types were not alike. Colors have been updated to reflect the colors in fashion. The sunscreen has been reformulated, and in 1981, MKY introduced the Body Care System. The line has also been expanded to include toiletry items, accessories, and hair care products. The skin care products for women still account for 50 percent of the sales revenue and will remain the major income producers in all likelihood.[37] Today the products at MKY are still primarily oriented toward skin care rather than the high-fashion market.

Still the line consists of only 45 products. Says Dr. Myra Barker, vice-president for research and development, "our plan is to maintain the present number in our line so that our Beauty Consultants can carry the inventory with them. The best way to service our Consultants is to keep the color line basic when offering the Fashion Forecast for fall and spring." According to Dr. Barker, "this strategy allows the Consultants to sell large numbers of basic colors which sell well to our customers. This allows us to discontinue those colors which don't sell well and provide the necessary flexibility of updating our line. Mary Kay quality is instilled in all employees and products."[38]

An 11-year veteran of the pharmeceutical industry, Dr. Bruce Rudy, former director, quality assurance, for the Burroughs Wellcome Company, had primary responsibility for governmental, technical, and regulatory compliance in the quality control area. Having joined the MKY organization in January 1981 as director of quality assurance, Dr. Rudy is now vice-president of quality assurance of MKY. "We have one of the strongest quality control programs in existence. Each batch of raw materials is tested in our labs. They must meet our chemical, physical, and microbiological specifications. Bulk products and finished packaged products are audited on the line, with final testing in the lab. Last week, we were inspected by the FDA which is the primary governmental agency responsible for the cosmetics industry."[39] Says Myra Barker, "we have one the most sophisticated computer control systems in the industry. Even the FDA was impressed. Our goal is to be the best."[40]

During the past several years, MKY has experimented in the market of skin care products and toiletry items for men. These are marketed under the product name Mr. K. and to date have accounted for 3 percent of the total company's sales in each of the past three years.[41] "Ten years ago, a man would not have gone into a beauty shop to have his hair done. As time goes on, men will find out that skin is skin. With all the emphasis on youth and keeping trim and fit in this country, skin follows right behind it. For men, skin care is a behind the door thing with cosmetics. I don't have a crystal ball," says Mary Kay, "but it's just one more step to creating the total image, even for men."[42]

"We are faced with the problem of growing too fast. We are constantly reviewing our systems and products for control measures. Typically we are understaffed and have to work a lot of overtime. Give me these problems anyday! They are nice problems to have," reflects Dr. Rudy. "With the building of our new MKY campus, we are phasing in buildings for the new facility. For example, the Glamour Products manufacturing facility is working closely with the engineering groups to ensure that we meet the criteria for a drug company and can be approved by the FDA. We are looking at meeting not only present, but future requirements for the industry and our company."[43]

**MANUFAC- TURING, RESEARCH, AND DEVELOP- MENT**

The manufacturing and research and development facilities for MKY are located in Dallas. Products needed in other geographical areas are shipped to the various distribution centers. Raw materials, fuel, and electrical energy are available in the Dallas area at reasonable costs, and there are no plans to relocate any of the manufacturing or research and development facilities at this time, although the company does study energy-related costs. Company officials point out that a continuous research and development program is under way and is geared mainly toward the goal of improving present products; however, only a very small percentage of total income is budgeted for the research and development department.[44]

**MANAGE- MENT AND PHILOSOPHY**

The primary reason for the success of MKY was the motivating reason for starting the company. "This company was really begun to give women an opportunity to advance, which I was denied, when I worked for others." This opportunity to become successful and the rewards provided for hard work are evident in the slogan, "I can, I will, I must," which Mary Kay instills in all her employees, particularly during the training seminars. "I train the sales force by example and by relationships."[45]

Although the sales force is independent, it maintains a strong and intimate relationship with the mother company. The organization of the sales force is the brainchild of Mary Kay herself. One of the more subtle activities which takes place at the home beauty show is the recruitment of new beauty consultants. A portion of each show is reserved for explaining the MKY sales organization, compensation, and incentive plan.

Recognizing a lag in the sales force and a loss of competitive edge in 1978, MKY changed its compensation program.[46] In addition to the markup they receive on the products they sell, sales managers are also eligible for a series of commissions based on their monthly unit sales. To become a sales manager, the beauty consultant must recruit 24 women into the organization to become consultants. The sales manager is then eligible to participate in a training program and later become a sales director. Sales directors spend time on independent sales, but they also manage, train, and recruit other sales consultants. "We expect sales directors to sell a minimum level of $3000 wholesale products per month, which is $6000 retail."[47] Mary Kay says that if a sales director falls short of that goal for two consecutive months, then the company contacts that woman to see how it can help. The chairman of the board doesn't just want sales directors to be minimum. She wants to help them excel. The average sales director earned $30,000 in 1982. New sales managers will come to Dallas for one week of training and return from time to time during the year for special training programs, the highlight of the year being the seminar. It consists of workshops conducted by outstanding beauty consultants and directors. Used not only during seminar but also at other times during the year are training materials such as guides, manuals, tape cassettes, flip charts, films, and other materials developed by MKY staff.[48]

The incentive plan is no small contribution to the motivation strategy employed by MKY. This plan allows sales consultants and managers to set goals for themselves whereby they can earn expensive and extravagant prizes for outstanding sales. Not only is the prize itself a motivator, but its method of presentation provides the recipient extended measures of recognition from her peers. Promotion from sales director to national sales director is also recognized on awards night during the seminar.

Being promoted to national sales director is no small task. Each woman must have already proven what she can do. Each person has at least ten offspring directors that she has brought into the company and nurtured up the ladder. These ten offspring directors must have women who they are working with and motivating, who are called second-line directors. For example, Shirley Hutton earns $32,000 per month and has 26 offspring directors. Rena Tarbet, who is "living with cancer for seven years now" is working on her third million-dollar-year sales.[49]

> Richard and I are the parents of the company. We are really mother and father figures, which I am given the credit for the success, and really Richard deserves as much or at least half of everything that has been done and then some. When I started the company, I didn't know that Richard had an IBM head. I take care of the motivating of the sales force and the public relations work. I don't know the financial condition of the company because I don't have to. Richard knows all of that. I ask for a sales report and the number of recruits that we had for each month. That's all I need. I take it from there.[50]

Communication is considered a high-priority motivational strategy at MKY. Monthly publications with circulations of 150,000, weekly bulletins, personalized letters, and 15,000 telephone calls per month keep sales directors and consultants in touch with the home office.[51] MKY also has a computerized tracking system for keeping up with its complex organization of sales consultants, sales directors, and their respective sales and recruiting data.[52]

**SALES STAFF**   Today there are over 150,000 independent beauty consultants selling MKY products. The company places a great deal of emphasis upon the rapport with others inside the organization; however, company policy is very clear on the requirements which must be fulfilled in order to be a beauty consultant:

- Submit a signed agreement with cashier's check or money order in advance in order to receive the beauty showcase, which is the basic sales kit.
- Attend three beauty shows or sales demonstrations.
- Schedule five beauty shows for the first week's activity.
- Attend training classes conducted by a sales director in the area.

The beauty shows are the company's marketplace and are held in homes with no more than six customers in attendance.

## FUTURE OF MKY

It would seem that MKY would merge or be acquired by another company. Mary Kay's reply: "All the time, but no thanks. These companies believe they can bring in their male executives and take over this 2 × 4 company and show them how to run it. You can't run a direct sales company like that. We must operate in a different way. Right now we are in the top ten in the cosmetics industry. Richard's and my goal is to be the largest and best skin care company in the world. I'm sure we are the best. Now we have to concentrate on becoming the largest."[53]

The future of MKY lies in the hands of the national sales directors (NSDs). These NSDs are carbon copies of Mary Kay herself. She constantly feeds into their computers that they are Mary Kay. "Wherever you go, whatever you do, be careful what you do, because you are Mary Kay. You are the future of the company. When I'm not here anymore, you will be taking over. Each of you are in training to be Mary Kay."[54]

Mary Kay's goal is for every single day that passes, she tries to touch as many of these women's lives as she can. "If I see one more woman today become greater than she ever thought she could be by my persuasion that she is great, then it's a good day."[55]

Richard Rogers, 38-year-old son of Mary Kay Ash, is positioned at the helm of Mary Kay, serving as president and CEO of the company since 1968. He is responsible for setting the tone and direction for the company. (See Exhibit 22.1.)

## THE INDUSTRY

Mary Kay Cosmetics, Inc., is a participant and competitor in two basic industries: the cosmetics and personal-care industry and the direct-sales industry, the latter composed of approximately 2200 direct-sales companies. Among MKY's competitors in the cosmetics industry are Avon, Revlon, Estee Lauder, Gillette's Jafra, Richardson-Vick, Fabergé, Chesebrough-Ponds, Inc., and Noxell Corp. With well over $2 billion in sales in 1981, Avon, Revlon, and Gillette are the industry leaders. Chesebrough-Pond's 1981 sales were $1.5 billion. Ranked within the top ten of the cosmetics industry, sales for MKY were $235 million (net), with Fabergé and Noxell in the same sales category as MKY.[56, 57] Skin care, which is MKY's niche, is the focus of the competition.

With its appeal to older women in middle- to high-income brackets who are entering the work force in record numbers, skin care and quality are the targets for a growing number of women, according to industry analysts. They have more purchasing power but less time to spend their money. They want health, fitness, and value.[58] Appealing to these women with major marketing thrusts are Gillette with Aapri, a facial scrub containing ground apricot pits, and Silkience, a self-adjusting moisture lotion; Richardson-Vick with Oil of Olay moisturizer; Nozell with Raintree Hand and Body Lotion and Noxzema; Chesebrough-Pond's Vaseline Intensive Care; and Estee Lauder's Clinique, as well as a number of products from both Revlon and Avon. Noxell and Chesebrough-Pond's sell the low-cost products. Avon and Revlon products are in the mid-price range, with the Estee Lauder products in the high-price range. MKY's products are in the mid- to

**Exhibit 22.1** Mary Kay Cosmetics, Inc., Organization Chart: President's Staff

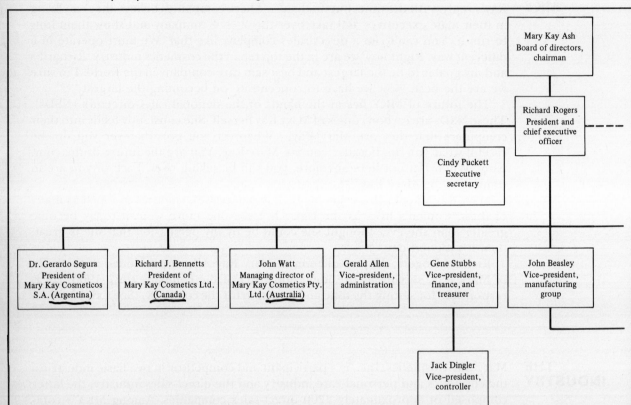

high-priced range. With the exception of Avon and MKY, all of these companies sell their products over the counter in department stores, drug stores, discount stores, and supermarkets.[59]

The cosmetics industry as a whole is seeing a gradual downturn for the first time in its history according to *Forbes'* Richard Stern. What has been classified as a recession-proof industry is now seeing growth that is mainly attributed to inflation. Volume sales are declining and the assumption that growth is eternal is gone. The skin care treatment portion of the industry was the only one with any expectation for growth, with perhaps 2 percent for 1982. Even though the recession is motivating a shift to more reasonably priced products, Avon and Revlon are hurting the most. The industry has survived other recessions because of the increasing numbers of women entering the work force. But the rate of increase has been declining in recent years.[60] To further complicate the volume of sales, virtually every cosmetic company has sales promotions on the concept

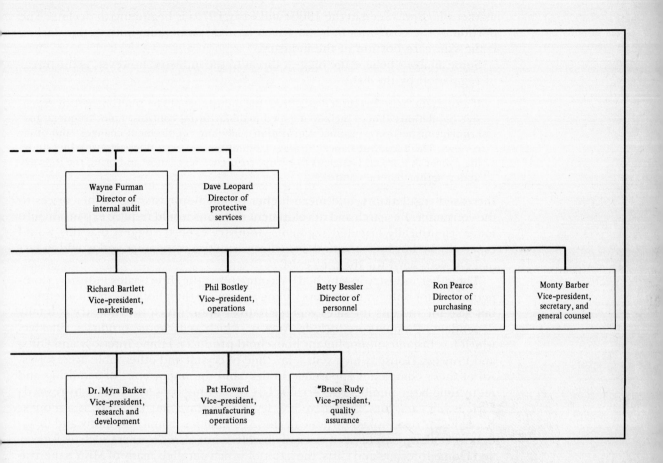

of a free gift with purchase. MKY is different. Says chairman of the Board Ash, "They would love to get out of that business. We don't have to do that. We don't need to."[61]

Both Stern and Mintz of *Sales and Marketing Management* note that Avon's problems stem from a less captive home market and an inadequate compensation program for sales representatives. Retail outlets such as drug stores, mass merchandisers, and food stores are capturing some of Avon's low- to middle-income market. Avon's reward program of gifts and vacations to outstanding sales representatives has failed to improve productivity, which has been in a decline since 1979.[62]

Other industry analysts speculate that the leveling of sales in the cosmetics industry can be attributed to consumers cutting back on purchases traditionally categorized as luxury items because of inflation and recession. Furthermore, the number of women entering careers is leveling off, and the bulge in the teenage market which was seen in the 1960s and early 1970s is beginning to decline. The portion of the cosmetics industry which has had some immunity to this decline is the skin care portion of the industry.

Some analysts believe the biggest threat to the industry, however, is the threat of regulation by the FDA.

> If a cosmetic item is regarded as a drug, the industry could be confronted with expensive regulations. These include detailed manufacturing controls, more frequent government inspections, product registrations, labeling requirement changes, and other reviews. The Toxic Substances Strategy Committee, a special White House panel studying cancer, has asked Congress to review cosmetics legislation and bring the industry under tighter federal control.[63]

Increased regulation would mean higher production costs and higher prices to the consumer. Research and development divisions would require expansion into more scientifically oriented segments. Industry experts suggest that this would especially be burdensome to the smaller cosmetics companies and would in fact make it very hard for them to exist.

The other industry in which MKY competes is the direct-sales industry. Competition is not only for customers willing to provide their home as the marketplace but also for recruits for sales representatives upon which the industry is totally dependent. Competitors include Amway, which sells home products; Shaklee, which has organic, nonpollutant household products; Home Interiors and Gifts; and Princess House, which sells a fine line of crystal and other table accessories. All of these companies apparently understand the importance of acquiring and motivating large numbers of recruits. Use of exciting contests with flashy rewards such as big cars, furs, expensive jewelry, and extravagant vacations is a motivational factor overlooked by none of these companies. Family harmony and devotion to God are emphasized not only by MKY but also by others such as Amway and Home Interiors and Gifts, the latter of which parallels many of MKY's motivational practices and was in fact founded by Mary Kay Ash's former sister-in-law, Mary Crowley.[64]

Another characteristic shared by the direct-sales companies is investigation by the Internal Revenue Service regarding the status of their direct-sales personnel. MKY and many of the others claim that their "beauty consultants" are independent distributors and not employees of MKY. Consequently MKY pays no federal withholding or employment taxes for any of its 150,000 direct-sales representatives. MKY and other direct-sales companies are currently protected from liability under an interim relief act passed by the Congress.[65]

Other pressure being exerted by the Internal Revenue Service on direct-sales organizations such as Amway targets individual sales representatives' use of business expenses as tax shelters. In a copyrighted article appearing in the *Fort Worth Star Telegram,* reporters Bowles, McKinsey, and Magmusson claim that Amway recruiters use the advantage of tax shelters as an enticement to become an Amway distributor. The pitch is to use the Amway distributorship as an excuse to write off new clothes, Christmas gifts, appliances, long-distance calls, new cars, vacation houses, and expensive vacations. In IRS audits of the tax returns of 300

Amway distributors in Baltimore last year, all but two resulted in back taxes and penalties being assessed, the average payment being $1350 not including interest and penalties. Currently 1000 more Amway distributors in Baltimore are undergoing IRS audits. According to Roscoe Edgar, Jr., the IRS commissioner, "It appears that the tax benefit aspects of many of these activities may be the primary reason large numbers of people become involved. Promotional schemes, recruitment methods and other information we have on these activities frequently highlight the anticipated tax benefits above all else. This indicates to us that the individuals involved know full well what they are doing."[66]

## EXTERNAL ENVIRON-MENT

Among the external factors that affect the cosmetics industry are the following: economic forces, technological forces, social forces, and political and legal forces.

## Economic Forces

There are several factors of the economy that impact on the cosmetics industry in general and MKY in particular. Among these factors are consumer demand, competition, and the general state of the national economy. For one reason or another, the once held assumption of eternal growth for the cosmetics industry seems to have vanished. The supposedly recession-proof cosmetics industry has, for the first time in its history, experienced a downturn in business. According to Jack Salyman of Wall Street's Smith, Barney and industry consultant Allan Mottus, unit sales have been flat for years with nearly all of the growth (43 percent) since 1978 attributable to a 39 percent increase in the cost of living. The shakeout appears to be focused on the middle market. This leaves the effect on MKY uncertain.[67]

As in any other retail industry, consumer demand is the key factor that influences a company's business decisions. Competition to meet the consumer's needs has stiffened considerably in the cosmetics industry as evidenced by the fact that many companies formerly in totally unrelated businesses now have lines of cosmetics. Clothes designers are a good example. One economic factor that is affecting consumers and industry alike was the higher cost of borrowing money, the prime lending rate. This made it more expensive for MKY to produce and sell its products and resulted in higher costs to the customer.

## Technological Forces

If a company is not on the leading edge of industry technology, it will be at a competitive disadvantage. The cosmetics industry is not a high-technology industry in the sense of the product produced. But a company needs the latest technology to be able to produce its product cost-effectively, which is instrumental in gaining a competitive advantage. In the cosmetics industry technology revolves around research into how the skin relates to the rest of the body and how it relates to its environment. Of major concern is the safety and efficacy of the product.[68]

**Social Forces**

Two keys to the success of the cosmetics industry, factors that greatly influence MKY's business strategy, are population demographics and sociological changes. As noted by Richard Stern of *Forbes,* "The key is the underlying demographics. The industry rode out previous recessions by riding the skirts of ever more working women. More working women meant increased women's spending and more cosmetics to wear to the office. But the rate of increase in the number of working women has declined in recent years." Stern also sees "sociological changes afoot as well. Working women now seem to prefer convenience to ambience, prompting a shift in distribution channels toward more merchandisers, discount drugstores and even supermarkets and away from department stores."[69] These changes would appear to enhance the appeal of direct marketing because from a convenience standpoint it is much easier to have a product brought to you than it is to have to go get it. Also, the recession seems to have caused a shift in buying habits that may impact the middle-market cosmetics significantly. As in other retail industries, consumers of cosmetics have gone to lower-priced goods in an effort to economize or have switched to higher-priced good for quality.[70] Population distribution is very important to the cosmetics industry in helping determine target markets. There has been a definite change in the distribution of the population. Between 1970 and 1980 the number of people over the age of 30 increased 40 percent while total population grew only 11.4 percent. America is growing older.[71]

**Political and Legal Forces**

The factors that affect MKY politically and legally fall into two categories. First, there are laws that affect the cosmetics industry as a whole. Then there are factors that are concerned just with regulating firms that sell through direct-sales marketing techniques as does MKY. MKY, as is the rest of the industry, is subject to regulation of the FDA and the Alcohol and Tax Unit of the Treasury Department. The FTC regulates the company's advertising and sales practices. Plus, the company's marketing, packaging, package labeling, and product content are regulated by many other federal, state, local, and foreign laws.

Of more immediate concern to MKY and all other companies that use direct sales to market their products was the battle with the IRS over whether the salesperson should be considered an employee or an independent contractor. To quote Richard Rogers, "We (MKY) are sure you can appreciate the administrative overhead and expense that we would incur if we were required to maintain employee-type records, withhold taxes, pay social security taxes, etc. for the over 150,000 persons in our sales force."[72] The Tax Equity and Fiscal Responsibility Act of 1982 contains provisions which classify people in the sales force of direct-sales marketing firms as "statutory non-employees." Thus ended a ten-year battle with the IRS.[73, 74]

## INTERNAL ENVIRON-MENT

Internal factors that affect the cosmetics industry include human resources, physical and production resources, market resources, research and development resources, operations, financial condition, strategic posture, and environmental research.

## Human Resources

Today MKY employs approximately 1400 persons. These employees are nonunionized. Of the 1400, around 40 percent are employed in the management and administrative end of the business. The other 60 percent are employed in areas such as research and development, and manufacturing. Even more important to the organization are the more than 150,000 beauty consultants that operate as independent contractors in selling the MKY products.

When considering human resources, the value of a company's employees must also be considered. In a direct-sales organization such as MKY, motivation is the grease that keeps the wheels turning. In that respect, Mary Kay Ash is the head "cheerleader". She is the one ultimately responsible for the motivation of the over 150,000 beauty consultants. Without the proper motivation, sales would suffer. The company's motivation and communication have already been covered in detail, but the philosophy behind it all is summed up in the following quote by Mary Kay: "Somebody said, if you act enthusiastic, you will become enthusiastic. We try to generate enthusiasm by example."[75]

## Physical and Production Resources

MKY is headquartered in Dallas, Texas, and has facilities in Atlanta; Chicago; Los Angeles; Piscataway, New Jersey; Victoria, Australia; Toronto, Canada; and Buenos Aires, Argentina.

The executive offices are housed in an eight-story, 109,000-square-foot building in Dallas. The company's lone manufacturing facility is housed in a building of some 300,000 square feet, also located in Dallas. This facility is partitioned such that there are approximately 110,300 square feet for manufacturing, 51,300 square feet for office space, and 116,000 square feet for use as a warehouse. This building and the eight-story office tower are owned by the company free of encumbrance. The company leases a third building in Dallas that has approximately 450,600 square feet. This building houses operations for distribution, printing, data processing, and more warehouse space. MKY's office and warehouse facilities in Atlanta, Chicago, Los Angeles, and Australia total approximately 200,000 square feet and are owned free of encumbrance. The office and warehouse facilities in New Jersey, Argentina, and Canada total about 100,000 square feet. These facilities are leased, with an option to purchase the Canadian facility. The manufacturing facilities and equipment are at least modern and in many cases state-of-the-art and well maintained.[76] Every machine that comes in contact with an MKY product is disassembled, cleaned, and sanitized at regular intervals.[77]

In the interest of future growth, MKY has purchased 177 acres in Dallas at a cost of about $6.5 million.[78] The project to develop this land will cost an estimated $100 million, according to Mary Kay.[79] "At the present time," believes

Richard Rogers, "we have in place facilities to support an annual sales volume of approximately $400 million."[80]

**Market Resources**

Market resources are the elements necessary to transfer possession of MKY's products to the consumer. MKY's two most important market resources are channel of distribution and advertising (although it has taken MKY time to understand and properly utilize this resource). MKY's channel of distribution is comprised solely of one element, a sales force of 150,000 beauty consultants who operate as independent contractors. The products are distributed via one wholesale sale and one retail sale channel. The products are transferred from the company to the consultant at wholesale, then from the consultant to the consumer at retail. The beauty consultant's profit is directly derived from the sale of the product to the ultimate consumer. Her profit is the difference between the wholesale price paid MKY for the product and the price the customer paid for the product. Every consultant can sell products wherever she wishes because MKY does not set territories or sell franchises.[81]

Until recently, advertising was used infrequently in MKY's marketing plan. Historically, most advertising was done by word of mouth, relying upon direct-sales personnel to spread the word. In the past, when there was an advertising budget it was set at or below 1 percent of sales. When national advertising was used, ads usually appeared in magazines such as *McCalls, Redbook, Better Homes and Gardens,* and *Ladies' Home Journal.*[82] Since the appearance of Mary Kay Ash on "60 Minutes" in late 1979, the company's view of advertising has been changing. Gerald Allen, MKY's administrative vice-president, said the company learned a lesson in the past two and one-half years thanks to "60 Minutes." He considers the show partially responsible for the tremendous growth of MKY's sales force. Mr. Allen also believes the show to have been worth the equivalent of $40 million worth of national network advertising and says, "That made believers out of us."[83] In the third quarter of 1982, MKY launched its first nationwide television advertising campaign. The advertising budget for the third and fourth quarters of 1982 would total $3 million and raise the total advertising budget for the year to $4 million (more than double the budget for any previous year).[84, 85]

**Research and Development Resources**

According to John Beasley, vice-president of manufacturing for MKY, "Research and Development is the leading edge" in obtaining the corporate goal of being the finest teaching-oriented skin care company in the world with sales of $500 million by 1990. Since 1975, the company's research and development staff has grown from 2 to 47. Mr. Beasley also said, "We go after the top ten percent of the people in the country who have the skills that we're looking for and personal integrity."[86] MKY funds research all over the world in an effort to develop new technology. Again to quote Mr. Beasley, "We [MKY] are having to stretch current technology in establishing some new standards in the industry in the area of comedogenicity, the interaction of the product, the environment and the skin causing comedones [acne]."[87] Of great importance to the company is that research maintain a fast-response attitude because of the rate at which tastes and fashions change.[88] During a recent interview, Mary Kay Ash indicated that the research and development budget would continue to be approximately one percent of sales, as has been the case in recent years.

**Results of
Operations**
In 1981 net sales increased at a rate of 41 percent compared to 83 percent for 1980 and 70 percent in 1979. At the same time, the number of beauty consultants increased 42 percent, 64 percent, and 33 percent in 1981, 1980, and 1979, respectively. During the same period, individual productivity of the beauty consultants declined. In 1979 average annual productivity for a consultant increased 27 percent compared with an increase of 12 percent for 1980 and a decrease of 1 percent for 1981. At the same time, selling and general and administrative expenses held fairly constant at approximately 51 percent of sales. It should also be noted that MKY instituted price increases of 15 percent in 1981 and 5 percent in 1980. As a result of all the above mentioned factors, net income increased from $4.8 million in 1978 to $24.2 million in 1981.[89] (Refer to Exhibit 22.2.)

**Exhibit 22.2** Growth of Mary Kay Cosmetics, Inc.

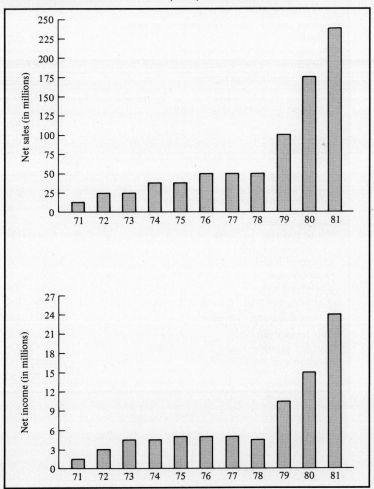

**Exhibit 22.3**

## MARY KAY COSMETICS, INC.
### Consolidated Balance Sheets
### December 31, 1981 and 1980

|  | 1981 | 1980 |
| --- | --- | --- |
| **Assets** | | |
| Current assets | | |
| Cash and cash equivalents | $ 7,953,000 | $ 11,085,000 |
| Accounts and notes receivable | 2,715,000 | 1,109,000 |
| Inventories | | |
| Raw materials | 8,888,000 | 6,380,000 |
| Finished goods | 18,193,000 | 15,218,000 |
|  | 27,081,000 | 21,598,000 |
| Deferred income tax benefits | 2,948,000 | 2,036,000 |
| Prepaid expenses | 1,213,000 | 666,000 |
| Total current assets | 41,910,000 | 36,494,000 |
| Property, plant, and equipment, at cost | | |
| Land | 12,298,000 | 3,793,000 |
| Buildings and improvements | 23,869,000 | 21,348,000 |
| Furniture, fixtures, and equipment | 28,299,000 | 14,963,000 |
| Construction in progress | 4,829,000 | 3,877,000 |
|  | 69,295,000 | 43,981,000 |
| Less accumulated depreciation | 10,519,000 | 7,653,000 |
|  | 58,776,000 | 36,328,000 |
| Notes receivable | — | 1,087,000 |
| Other assets | 290,000 | 522,000 |
|  | $ 100,976,000 | $ 74,431,000 |
| **Liabilities and stockholders' equity** | | |
| Current liabilities | | |
| Note payable to bank | $ 1,260,000 | $ — |
| Accounts payable | 8,061,000 | 8,900,000 |
| Accrued liabilities | 16,659,000 | 13,063,000 |
| Income tax | 5,712,000 | 4,214,000 |
| Deferred sales | 1,321,000 | 4,363,000 |
| Current portion of long-term debt | 1,058,000 | 1,000,000 |
| Total current liabilities | 34,071,000 | 31,540,000 |
| Long-term debt | 2,366,000 | 3,000,000 |
| Deferred income taxes | 2,587,000 | 1,258,000 |
| Stockholders' equity | 61,952,000 | 38,633,000 |
|  | $ 100,976,000 | $ 74,431,000 |

**Financial Condition**

In 1981 *Business Week* ranked MKY as the twelfth fastest-growing company in the country.[90] When asked in a recent interview her opinion concerning the current financial condition of the company, Mary Kay Ash responded, "I think we're doing great!" However, she also admitted that she let her son Richard Rogers, the president and CEO, handle the financial matters of the company.[91]

MKY's total assets grew from $36 million in 1978 to $101 million in 1981. Working capital for the same period was $5.7 million in 1978, $2.3 million in 1979, $4.0 million in 1980, and $7.8 million in 1981. At the same time, capital expenditures were increasing faster than both working capital and total assets. In 1981 capital expenditures were $25.3 million compared to $12.5 million in 1980, $4.7 million in 1979, and $2.1 million in 1978.[92] There were approximately 14.3 million shares of common stock outstanding in 1981.[93] This represented a 25 percent decrease compared to the 19.6 million shares outstanding at the end of 1976.[94, 95] The decrease resulted from MKY tender offers in 1977 and 1979. Other information on the company is detailed in Exhibits 22.3 through 22.5.

**Exhibit 22.4**

**MARY KAY COSMETICS, INC.**
**Consolidated Statements of Income**
**Years Ended December 31, 1981, 1980, and 1979**

|  | 1981 | 1980 | 1979 |
|---|---|---|---|
| Net sales | $ 235,296,000 | $ 166,039,000 | $ 91,400,000 |
| Interest and other income, net | 1,485,000 | 712,000 | 493,000 |
|  | 236,781,000 | 167,650,000 | 91,893,000 |
| Cost and expenses |  |  |  |
| Cost of sales | 71,100,000 | 52,484,000 | 27,574,000 |
| Selling, general, and administrative expenses | 120,880,000 | 86,998,000 | 45,522,000 |
| Interest expense | 1,014,000 | 635,000 | 958,000 |
|  | 192,994,000 | 140,117,000 | 74,054,000 |
| Income before income taxes | 43,787,000 | 27,533,000 | 17,839,000 |
| Provision for income taxes | 19,632,000 | 12,398,000 | 8,207,000 |
| Net income | $ 24,155,000 | $ 15,135,000 | $ 9,632,000 |
| Net income per common and common equivalent share | $1.65 | $1.05 | $.65 |
| Average shares | 14,662,000 | 14,442,000 | 14,720,000 |

**Exhibit 22.5**

**MARY KAY COSMETICS, INC.**
**Consolidated Statements of Changes in Financial Position**
**Years Ended December 31, 1981, 1980, and 1979**

|  | 1981 | 1980 | 1979 |
|---|---|---|---|
| **Source of funds** | | | |
| Operations | | | |
|   Net income | $24,155,000 | $15,135,000 | $ 9,632,000 |
|   Depreciation | 2,866,000 | 1,987,000 | 1,569,000 |
|   Increase in deferred income taxes | 1,329,000 | 351,000 | 177,000 |
|   Gains on sales of real estate not used in business | — | — | (116,000) |
|   Funds provided from operations | 28,350,000 | 17,473,000 | 11,262,000 |
| Proceeds from exercises of stock options | 1,922,000 | 1,338,000 | 164,000 |
| Decrease in notes receivable | 1,087,000 | 120,000 | — |
| Increase in long-term debt | 366,000 | — | 5,442,000 |
| Proceeds from sales of real estate not used in business | — | — | 1,182,000 |
| Other | 325,000 | — | 276,000 |
|  | 32,050,000 | 18,931,000 | 18,326,000 |
| **Application of funds** | | | |
| Additions to property, plant, and equipment, net | 25,314,000 | 12,457,000 | 4,510,000 |
| Dividends declared | 2,851,000 | 2,458,000 | 1,764,000 |
| Reduction of long-term debt | 1,000,000 | 1,000,000 | 5,000,000 |
| Purchase of treasury shares | — | — | 9,422,000 |
| Increase in notes receivable | — | — | 1,047,000 |
| Other | — | 369,000 | — |
|  | 29,165,000 | 16,284,000 | 21,743,000 |
| Increase (decrease) in working capital | $ 2,885,000 | $ 2,647,000 | $ (3,417,000) |

**Present Strategic Posture**

Strategic posture is determined by the answers to questions such as, "What is our product mix?" and "What is our customer mix?" The most important factor in MKY's strategic posture is its niche in the skin care products area of the cosmetics market where larger competitors such as Avon are a minor factor.[96] Also, Mary Kay Ash believes that a limited product line maximizes the sales forces' efficiency.[97] Thus, the company's product line is limited to about 45 items.[98] Also important is the company's target market. The company perceives its prime market to be women aged 25 to 44 who are in or a little above the middle-income bracket, have some college education, and live in suburbia or exurbia.[99, 100]

**Environmental Research**

Environmental research is used to determine if an organization can keep pace with external change. As MKY continues to grow it must be able to recognize and react to changes in competition, consumer demand, and economic conditions. The company believes that to do this it must be capable of supporting rapid sales volume growth with consistently high-quality products and reliable service.[101]

## NOTES

1. Mitchell Gordon, "Mary Kay's Team," *Barron's,* July 9, 1979, pp. 32, 34.
2. "People," *Chemical Week,* August 6, 1975, p. 40.
3. Paul Rosenfield, "The Beautiful Make-up of Mary Kay," *Saturday Evening Post,* October 1981, reprint 2714B82.
4. Ibid.
5. "Flying High on an Idea," *Nation's Business,* August 1978, pp. 41–47.
6. Marcia Froelke Coburn, "Direct's Sleeker Sell," *Advertising Age,* March 1, 1982, pp. 50–51.
7. "Flying High on an Idea," pp. 41–47.
8. "People," p. 40.
9. "Flying High on an Idea," pp. 41–47.
10. Ibid.
11. "People," p. 40.
12. Gordon, "Mary Kay's Team," pp. 32, 34.
13. "People," p. 40.
14. "Mary Kay Finds Incentives that Pay Off," *Chemical Week,* May 13, 1981, pp. 50–51.
15. "People," p. 40.
16. Gordon, "Mary Kay's Team," pp. 32, 34.
17. Mary Kay Cosmetics, Inc., presentation of Mary Kay Cosmetics, Inc., before the New York Society of Security Analysts on July 22, 1982.
18. "Flying High on an Idea," pp. 41–47.
19. "Mary Kay: Some Overriding Reasons for Success," *Sales and Marketing Management/Special Report,* August 23, 1976, pp. 54–55.
20. "Flying High on an Idea," pp. 41–47.
21. Mary Kay Cosmetics, Inc., presentation on July 22, 1982.
22. Mary Kay Cosmetics, Inc., Annual Report 1981.
23. Mary Kay Cosmetics, Inc., presentation of July 22, 1982.
24. Ibid.
25. John Beasley (vice-president, manufacturing), published interview, Mary Kay Cosmetics, Inc., May 1982.
26. Mary Kay Cosmetics, Inc., "Interim Report for Nine Months Ended September 30, 1982."
27. Mary Kay Ash, personal interview given to Paula Walters, Dallas, Texas, November 16, 1982.
28. Securities and Exchange Commission, "Annual Report, Mary Kay Cosmetics, Inc.," year ended December 31, 1981, p. 11.
29. Mary Kay Cosmetics, Inc., presentation on July 22, 1982.
30. Mary Kay Ash, personal interview given to Paula Walters.
31. Ibid.
32. Ibid.
33. Ibid.
34. Ibid.
35. "Flying High on an Idea," pp. 41–47.
36. Mary Kay Ash, personal interview given to Paula Walters.

37. Securities and Exchange Commission, "Annual Report."
38. Myra Barker, telephone interview with Paula Walters, November 22, 1982.
39. Richard Rogers, telephone interview with Paula Walters, November 22, 1982.
40. Myra Barker, telephone interview with Paula Walters.
41. Securities and Exchange Commission, "Annual Report."
42. Mary Kay Ash, personal interview given to Paula Walters.
43. Richard Rogers, telephone interview with Paula Walters.
44. Securities and Exchange commission, "Annual Report."
45. Mary Kay Ash, personal interview given to Paula Walters.
46. Paul Rosenfield, "The Beautiful Make-up of Mary Kay."
47. Mary Kay Ash, personal interview given to Paula Walters.
48. "Analysts Caught off Guard by Mary Kay Profit Spurt," *The Insiders' Chronicle,* November 9, 1979, pp. 1, 17–18.
49. Mary Kay Ash, personal interview given to Paula Walters.
50. Ibid.
51. Mary Kay Cosmetics, Inc., Annual Report 1981.
52. "Flying High on an Idea," pp. 41–47.
53. Mary Kay Ash, personal interview given to Paula Walters.
54. Ibid.
55. Ibid.
56. "Composite Industry Data," *Standard and Poor's Industry Surveys,* 1982, pp. H31–H44.
57. "The *Chemical Week* 300 Companies: 1981 Divisional Results," *Chemical Week,* February 24, 1982, p. 45.
58. Mary McCable English, "Face of the 80's: What's Ahead," *Advertising Age,* March 1, 1982, section 2, p. PM-11.
59. Lori Kesler, "Skincare Penetrates New Layers of Profits," *Advertising Age,* March 1, 1982.
60. Richard L. Stern, "The Grease Trade Skids," *Forbes,* October 25, 1982, pp. 161–164.
61. Mary Kay Ash, personal interview given to Paula Walters.
62. Steven Mintz, "Avon, You're Looking Better," *Sales and Marketing Management,* April 5, 1982, pp. 52–57.
63. "Cosmetics and Personal Care Products," *Standard and Poor's Industry Surveys,* May 20, 1982, p. H28.
64. James Perkins, "Artful Promotions: Key to Direct Selling Success," *Direct Marketing,* April 1980, pp. 55–58.
65. Securities and Exchange Commission, "Annual Report."
66. Billy Bowles, Kitty McKinsey, and Paul Magmusson, "IRS Questions the Use of Tax Shelters by Some of Amway's Distributors," *Fort Worth Star Telegram,* November 10, 1982, pp. B1, B3.
67. Stern, "The Grease Trade Skids."
68. John Beasley, published interview.
69. Stern, "The Grease Trade Skids," p. 162.
70. Ibid.
71. Kesler, "Skincare Penetrates."
72. Mary Kay Cosmetics, Inc., presentation on July 22, 1982.
73. Ibid.
74. Securities and Exchange Commission, "Annual Report."
75. Gerhard Gschwandtner, "The Make-up of Sales Success," *Personal Selling Power,* November 1982, pp. 1, 8.
76. Securities and Exchange Commission, "Annual Report."
77. Rosenfield, "The Beautiful Make-Up of Mary Kay."
78. Securities and Exchange Commission, "Annual Report."
79. Mary Kay Ash, personal interview given to Paula Walters.

80. Mary Kay Cosmetics, Inc., Annual Report 1981.
81. Mary Kay Cosmetics, Inc., "A Business Perspective," 1982.
82. Pat Sloan, "Mary Kay Putting on an Ad Show," *Advertising Age,* March 24, 1980, pp. 36, 44.
83. Tom Bayer, "Mary Kay Tries Net TV," *Advertising Age,* August 2, 1982.
84. Ibid.
85. Mary Kay Cosmetics, Inc., "Interim Report for Nine Months Ended September 30, 1982."
86. John Beasley, published interview.
87. Ibid.
88. Mary Kay Cosmetics, Inc., Annual Report 1981.
89. Ibid.
90. Coburn, "Direct's Sleeker Sell."
91. Mary Kay Ash, personal interview given to Paula Walters.
92. Coburn, "Direct's Sleeker Sell."
93. Mary Kay Cosmetics, Inc., Annual Report 1981.
94. Ibid.
95. Howard Rudnitsky, "The Flight of the Bumblebee," *Forbes,* June 22, 1981, pp. 104–106.
96. Ibid.
97. Coburn, "Direct's Sleeker Sell."
98. Rudnitsky, "The Flight of the Bumblebee."
99. Mary Kay Cosmetics, Inc., Annual Report 1981.
100. Coburn, "Direct's Sleeker Sell."
101. Mary Kay Cosmetics, Inc., Annual Report 1981.

# 23 Mobil Corporation

Robert R. Gardner and M. Edgar Barrett
Maguire Oil and Gas Institute
Southern Methodist University

It was early March 1984. Richard Collier, exploration manager of Mobil Oil Corporation's Rocky Mountain Division, had just heard the news of Mobil Corporation's $5.7 billion offer for Superior Oil Company. This piece of information came as no great surprise to Collier, since it had been well known that Superior had been looking for a merger partner and that its owners had approached Mobil's board of directors several months ago. Also, this type of move was not uncommon for Mobil. This was, in fact, the company's eighth acquisition attempt since 1979 (three were successful). Perhaps understandably in his position, however, Collier wished Mobil would begin placing more emphasis on replacing reserves from its own exploration activities.

## COMPANY OVERVIEW

Mobil Corporation was the third largest industrial company in the United States (behind Exxon and General Motors), with revenue from operations in 1983 of nearly $55 billion. Mobil consisted of one of the world's largest petroleum operations, a growing chemical business, a paperboard packaging business, and a nationwide retailing operation. Mobil companies conducted business in more than 100 countries and employed more than 178,000 people.

The company had total assets in 1983 of $35 billion. Net income was $1.5 billion. Total return to investors in 1983 was 22.39 percent. Over the previous ten years, Mobil averaged a 15.17 percent total return to investors—highest among the major oil companies.[1] With a 5.69 percent share of the domestic market, Mobil ranked as the fifth largest gasoline retailer in 1983. (See Exhibits 23.1–23.9, pp. 708ff.)

## HISTORICAL BACKGROUND

Mobil's corporate roots could be traced in one direction back to the formation of Vacuum Oil in 1866, and in another, to John D. Rockefeller's Standard Oil Trust, which later absorbed the smaller company. Vacuum Oil was founded by

This case was written by Robert R. Gardner, associate director of the Maguire Oil and Gas Institute, under the direction of M. Edgar Barrett, director of the same institute. It was based, in part, on earlier versions written by Bill Clark and Mary Pat Cormack. The character and situation described in the first and last paragraphs of the case are fictional. Data provided elsewhere are drawn entirely from public sources. This case was prepared as the basis for class discussion rather than to illustrate either effective or ineffective handling of an administrative situation.

Copyright © 1985 by M. Edgar Barrett.

Hiram Bond Everest and Matthew Ewing, who had invented in 1865 a new process of distilling crude oil under a vacuum. At that time, a gallon of kerosene sold for twice as much as a barrel of crude oil, and Ewing believed that his vacuum process could produce more kerosene from a barrel of crude than was possible with other known refining methods. Everest, on the other hand, recognized the possibilities of using the oily residue from the distilling process as a petroleum lubricant for machinery and leather. Everest decided to finance the new venture, and Vacuum Oil was founded in 1866.

After some initial consumer resistance, the quality and utility of Everest's lubricants were proven in the marketplace, and Vacuum Oil began growing rapidly. The favorable reputation of Vacuum Oil finally attracted the attention of Rockefeller's Standard Oil Company, and in 1879, Rockefeller bought a controlling interest in the smaller company. Under Standard's aegis, Vacuum Oil evolved into a company whose primary functions were refining, domestic and foreign marketing, domestic manufacturing, and distribution of specialty products. By 1912, Vacuum had become an international lubricating-oil company, two-thirds of whose business volume was outside the United States.

Standard Oil Company of New York (Socony), was the other of Mobil's immediate ancestors. When the huge Standard Oil Trust was broken up in the historical antitrust action of 1911, Socony was one of 33 fragments of the original company. In 1912, Socony had both an extensive export business and a wide marketing outlet system. However, the company had no crude-oil resources, nor was it involved in the lubricating-products business. In fact, after leaving the Standard Oil Trust, neither Socony nor Vacuum Oil had any significant strength in exploration or production. Consequently, both companies began trying to integrate operations in the United States and abroad in order to shore up their respective weaknesses. In 1918, Socony acquired 70 percent of the stock of a Texas oil-producing company called Magnolia Petroleum Company, which had crude-oil production, reserves, refineries, and pipeline in the Southwest. Later, in 1925, Socony, which had assets of $90 million, acquired all of the properties of Magnolia Petroleum Co. Other acquisitions included the General Petroleum Corporation of California (1926), which had production properties, refineries, and marketing facilities on the West Coast, and the White Eagle Oil & Refining Company of Kansas City (1930), which had refineries in Wyoming and Kansas. These acquisitions provided considerable new oil reserves and strengthened the company's marketing network throughout the United States.

Socony and Vacuum Oil merged in 1931, forming Socony-Vacuum, with international capabilities to produce, refine, and market petroleum products. Thus, Socony-Vacuum (later to become Mobil) emerged as the youngest and the smallest of the American "sisters." In 1933, Socony-Vacuum pooled its properties and business operations in the Far East with properties owned by Standard Oil Company of New Jersey. Each company owned 50 percent of the stock of the newly formed company called Standard-Vacuum Oil Company, which handled Far Eastern operations.

**Exhibit 23.1**

## MOBIL CORPORATION
### Income Statement
(millions)

|  | 1983 | 1982 | 1981 | 1980 | 1979 |
|---|---|---|---|---|---|
| **Revenues** | | | | | |
| Sales and services | | | | | |
| Petroleum operations | $43,433 | $49,182 | $53,298 | $49,189 | $35,403 |
| Chemical | 2,230 | 2,034 | 2,235 | 1,812 | 1,562 |
| Paperboard packaging | 1,685 | 1,869 | 1,998 | 1,880 | 1,600 |
| Retail merchandising | 6,003 | 5,584 | 5,742 | 5,497 | 5,251 |
| Services and other | 1,256 | 1,277 | 1,215 | 1,132 | 905 |
| Total sales and services | 54,607 | 59,946 | 64,488 | 59,510 | 44,721 |
| Excise and state gasoline taxes | 3,389 | 3,168 | 3,129 | 3,313 | 2,764 |
| Interest | 513 | 460 | 335 | 414 | 339 |
| Dividends and other income | 92 | 142 | 19 | 22 | 80 |
| Equity in earnings of certain affiliated companies | 397 | 392 | 616 | 467 | 388 |
| Total revenues | 58,998 | 64,108 | 68,587 | 63,726 | 48,292 |
| **Costs and expenses** | | | | | |
| Crude oil, products, merchandise, and operating supplies and expenses | 38,404 | 43,997 | 46,178 | 41,301 | 30,477 |
| Exploration expenses | 618 | 847 | 803 | 524 | 359 |
| Selling and general expenses | 4,967 | 5,312 | 5,181 | 4,957 | 4,265 |
| Depreciation, depletion, and amortization | 1,892 | 1,736 | 1,586 | 1,399 | 1,086 |
| Interest and debt discount expense | 814 | 663 | 608 | 479 | 459 |
| Taxes other than income taxes | | | | | |
| Excise and state gasoline taxes | 3,389 | 3,168 | 3,129 | 3,313 | 2,764 |
| Windfall profit tax | 447 | 630 | 936 | 267 | — |
| Import duties | 3,395 | 3,500 | 3,825 | 4,155 | 3,756 |
| Property, production, payroll, and other taxes | 858 | 949 | 942 | 655 | 564 |
| Total taxes other than income taxes | 8,089 | 8,247 | 8,832 | 8,390 | 7,084 |
| Income taxes | 2,711 | 2,093 | 2,966 | 3,863 | 2,555 |
| Total costs and expenses | 57,495 | 62,895 | 66,154 | 60,913 | 46,285 |
| Income before extraordinary item | 1,503 | 1,213 | 2,433 | 2,813 | 2,007 |
| Extraordinary item—Gain on sale of interest in Belridge Oil Company (less income taxes of $189) | — | — | — | 459 | — |
| Net income | $ 1,503 | $ 1,213 | $ 2,433 | $ 3,272 | $ 2,007 |
| **Memo** | | | | | |
| Income less foreign inventory profits (before extraordinary item) | $ 1,503 | $ 1,213 | $ 2,332 | $ 2,169 | $ 1,707 |

*Source:* Mobil Corporation financial and operating statistics 1983.

**Exhibit 23.2**

## MOBIL CORPORATION
### Balance Sheet
### (millions)

| | December 31, | | | | |
|---|---|---|---|---|---|
| | 1983 | 1982ᵃ | 1981 | 1980 | 1979 |
| **Assets** | | | | | |
| Current assets | | | | | |
| Cash | $ 507 | $ 542 | $ 782 | $ 698 | $ 621 |
| Marketable securities, at cost | 1,046 | 1,133 | 1,262 | 1,220 | 1,257 |
| Accounts and notes receivable | 4,832 | 5,135 | 5,440 | 5,718 | 5,060 |
| Inventories | | | | | |
| Crude oil and petroleum products | 3,070 | 3,678 | 4,320 | 4,518 | 3,114 |
| Chemical products | 317 | 338 | 333 | 315 | 237 |
| Paperboard packaging | 128 | 137 | 172 | 181 | 158 |
| Retail merchandising | 937 | 893 | 937 | 975 | 1,080 |
| Other, including materials and supplies | 626 | 737 | 718 | 474 | 362 |
| Total Inventories | 5,078 | 5,783 | 6,480 | 6,463 | 4,951 |
| Prepaid expenses | 427 | 367 | 256 | 203 | 174 |
| Total current assets | 11,890 | 12,960 | 14,220 | 14,302 | 12,063 |
| Investments and long-term receivables | 2,854 | 2,563 | 2,423 | 2,213 | 2,030 |
| Properties, plants, and equipment, at cost | 31,673 | 30,029 | 27,612 | 24,581 | 20,676 |
| Less accumulated depreciation, depletion, and amortization | 11,795 | 10,714 | 9,902 | 8,741 | 7,573 |
| Net properties, plants, and equipment | 19,878 | 19,315 | 17,710 | 15,840 | 13,103 |
| Deferred charges and other assets | 450 | 378 | 423 | 350 | 310 |
| Total Assets | $35,072 | $35,216 | $34,776 | $32,705 | $27,506 |
| **Liabilities and shareholders' equity** | | | | | |
| Current liabilities | | | | | |
| Notes and loans payable | $ 1,185 | $ 2,187 | $ 1,692 | $ 949 | $ 1,064 |
| Accounts payable and accrued liabilities | 6,847 | 7,332 | 7,604 | 7,880 | 7,113 |
| Income, excise, state gasoline, and other taxes payable | 2,246 | 2,393 | 2,486 | 3,218 | 2,377 |
| Deferred income taxes | 163 | 316 | 704 | 546 | 467 |
| Long-term debt and capital lease obligations maturing within one year | 372 | 198 | 219 | 126 | 170 |
| Total current liabilities | 10,813 | 12,426 | 12,705 | 12,719 | 11,191 |
| Long-term debt | 5,162 | 4,404 | 3,284 | 3,256 | 2,962 |
| Capital lease obligations | 328 | 313 | 320 | 315 | 342 |
| Reserves for employee benefits | 336 | 385 | 410 | 412 | 398 |
| Deferred credits and other noncurrent obligations | 1,074 | 845 | 653 | 605 | 294 |
| Accrued restoration and removal costs | 315 | 265 | 208 | 148 | 114 |
| Deferred income taxes | 3,000 | 2,665 | 2,442 | 2,087 | 1,605 |
| Minority interest in subsidiary companies | 92 | 106 | 97 | 94 | 87 |
| Shareholders' equity | 13,952 | 13,807 | 14,657 | 13,069 | 10,513 |
| Total Liabilities and Shareholders' Equity | $35,072 | $35,216 | $34,776 | $32,705 | $27,506 |

ᵃRestated.

*Source:* Mobil Corporation financial and operating statistics 1983.

Exhibit 23.3

## MOBIL CORPORATION
### Changes in Financial Position
#### (millions)

| | 1983 | 1982[a] | 1981 | 1980 | 1979 |
|---|---|---|---|---|---|
| **Sources of funds** | | | | | |
| Operations | | | | | |
| Income before extraordinary item | $ 1,503 | $ 1,213 | $ 2,433 | $ 2,813 | $ 2,007 |
| Depreciation, depletion, and amortization | 1,892 | 1,736 | 1,586 | 1,399 | 1,086 |
| Deferred income tax charges | 487 | 166 | 425 | 482 | 585 |
| Dividends in excess of (less than) equity in income of unconsolidated companies | (158) | 44 | (41) | 129 | (50) |
| Funds available from operations | 3,724 | 3,159 | 4,403 | 4,823 | 3,628 |
| Extraordinary item | — | — | — | 459 | — |
| Book value of properties, plants, and equipment sold | 140 | 209 | 116 | 99 | 78 |
| Other, net | (30) | 195 | 123 | 410 | 84 |
| Funds available before financing | 3,834 | 3,563 | 4,642 | 5,791 | 3,790 |
| **Application of funds** | | | | | |
| Cash dividends to shareholders | 813 | 836 | 851 | 733 | 541 |
| Capital expenditures | 3,073 | 3,821 | 3,571 | 3,525 | 2,641 |
| Major acquisitions[b] | — | 500 | — | 715 | 792 |
| Increase (decrease) in | | | | | |
| Accounts and notes receivable | (303) | (302) | (278) | 658 | 870 |
| Inventories | (705) | (545) | 17 | 1,512 | 823 |
| Prepaid expenses | 60 | 111 | 53 | 29 | 32 |
| Investments and long-term receivables | 133 | 77 | 169 | 312 | 136 |
| (Increase) decrease in | | | | | |
| Accounts payable and accrued liabilities | 485 | 266 | 276 | (767) | (1,437) |
| Income, excise, state gasoline, and other taxes payable | 147 | 93 | 732 | (841) | (637) |
| Foreign exchange translation effects on working capital, debt, and other items, net | 206 | 203 | — | — | — |
| Application of funds before financing | 3,909 | 5,060 | 5,391 | 5,876 | 3,761 |
| Increase (decrease) in funds before financing | (75) | (1,497) | (749) | (85) | 29 |
| **Total financing[c]** | | | | | |
| Increases in long-term debt | 1,208 | 1,424 | 375 | 525 | 202 |
| Decreases in long-term debt | (450) | (304) | (347) | (231) | (287) |
| Increase (decrease) in capital lease obligations | 15 | (7) | 5 | (27) | (20) |
| Increase (decrease) in notes and loans payable | (1,002) | 495 | 743 | (115) | 461 |
| Increase (decrease) in long-term debt and capital lease obligations maturing within one year | 174 | (21) | 93 | (44) | 1 |
| Purchase of common stock for treasury | (11) | (471) | — | — | — |
| Issuance or sale of common stock | 19 | 12 | 6 | 17 | 10 |
| Total financing increase (decrease) | (47) | 1,128 | 875 | 125 | 367 |

(continued)

**Exhibit 23.3**    (continued)

|  | 1983 | 1982[a] | 1981 | 1980 | 1979 |
|---|---|---|---|---|---|
| **Increase (decrease) in cash and marketable securities** | $ (122) | $ (369) | $ 126 | $ 40 | $ 396 |
| Mobil Oil Credit Corporation | $ (16) | $ (101) | $ — | $ 193 | $ 187 |
| Montgomery Ward Credit Corporation | 36 | (315) | (281) | (99) | 498 |
| Total | $ 20 | $ (416) | $ (281) | $ 94 | $ 685 |

[a]Restated.

[b]Includes acquisition of a working interest in certain holdings of The Anschutz Corp., 1982, and acquisition of operations of TransOcean Oil, Inc., 1980, and General Crude Oil Co., 1979.

[c]Excludes the increase (decrease) in financing of two major unconsolidated subsidiaries.

*Source:* Mobil Corporation financial and operating statistics 1983.

In 1936, Socony-Vacuum and Texaco, Inc., each acquired a 50 percent interest in South American Gulf Oil Co., and a 49.94 percent interest in Columbian Petroleum Company. Mobil sold its interest in these companies in 1972. In 1955, the company changed its name to Socony Mobil Oil Corporation. (The company later dropped "Socony" from its name and was known as Mobil Oil Corporation until 1976, after which time it was known simply as Mobil Corporation.) By this time, Mobil was already heavily dependent on the Middle East, which supplied 50 percent of the company's total crude oil. In 1961, Mobil acquired the oil and gas properties and other assets of Republic Natural Gas Co. In the following year the company transferred its business and assets in the Far East, representing its 50 percent ownership of Standard Vacuum Oil Co., into a new company called Mobil Petroleum Company, Inc. The new firm's affiliates and branches were later brought under the single management of Mobil International Oil Co. (1965).

Other acquisitions in the sixties and seventies included Kordite Corp. (1962); Goliad Corp., a gas processor in Louisiana and Texas (1962); Forum Insurance Company (1963); the worldwide paint and chemical coatings interests of Martin Marietta Corp. (1962); Virginia-Carolina Chemical Corp. (1962); Northern Natural Gas Producing Co. (1962); Industrias Atlas S. A., a manufacturer of industrial and consumer paints in Mexico (1965); Goodling Electric Co., Inc. (1968); Aral Italiana, an Italian subsidiary of Aral AG, West Germany (1971); Pastucol Cos., three Italian firms which manufactured and marketed polyethylene film products (1971); Marcor Corporation, which operated through two subsidiaries, Montgomery Ward & Co., Inc., and Container Corp. of America (1974); W. F. Hall Printing Co. (1979); the oil and gas operations of General Crude Oil Co. (1979); and TransOcean Oil Inc. (1980).

In terms of the petroleum business proper, Mobil spent the three decades following its formation in 1931 consolidating its diverse holdings and subsidiar-

**Exhibit 23.4**

# MOBIL CORPORATION
### Distribution of Earnings and Assets—Segments
### (millions)

|  | 1983 | 1982[a] | 1981 | 1980 | 1979 |
|---|---|---|---|---|---|
| **Total revenues** | | | | | |
| Petroleum—United States | $14,291 | $14,759 | $15,701 | $14,560 | $10,820 |
| —Foreign | 35,745 | 42,073 | 44,827 | 43,226 | 31,814 |
| Chemical | 2,424 | 2,246 | 2,437 | 2,027 | 1,718 |
| Paperboard packaging | 1,779 | 1,953 | 2,068 | 1,946 | 1,647 |
| Retail merchandising | 6,646 | 6,143 | 6,122 | 5,916 | 5,652 |
| Other | 22 | 46 | 24 | 33 | 13 |
| Adjustments and eliminations | (1,909) | (3,112) | (2,592) | (3,982) | (3,372) |
| Total | $58,998 | $64,108 | $68,587 | $63,726 | $48,292 |
| **Segment earnings** | | | | | |
| Petroleum—United States | $   774 | $   877 | $ 1,174 | $   953 | $   689 |
| —Foreign | 979 | 677 | 1,512 | 2,012 | 1,345 |
| Chemical | 8 | 24 | 93 | 119 | 113 |
| Paperboard packaging | 1 | 24 | 57 | 71 | 40 |
| Retail merchandising | 40 | (93) | (160) | (162) | 54 |
| Other | (133) | (136) | (99) | (42) | (83) |
| Corporate expenses | (166) | (160) | (144) | (138) | (151) |
| Income before extraordinary item | $ 1,503 | $ 1,213 | $ 2,433 | $ 2,813 | $ 2,007 |
| **Capital expenditures** | | | | | |
| Petroleum—United States | $ 1,458 | $ 1,617 | $ 1,485 | $ 1,215 | $ 1,160 |
| —Foreign | 1,074 | 1,389 | 1,236 | 1,424 | 825 |
| Chemical | 210 | 328 | 274 | 248 | 146 |
| Paperboard packaging | 129 | 273 | 255 | 180 | 182 |
| Retail merchandising | 121 | 69 | 144 | 322 | 250 |
| Alternative energy | 16 | 68 | 107 | 48 | 27 |
| Corporate and other | 65 | 77 | 70 | 88 | 52 |
| Total | $ 3,073 | $ 3,821 | $ 3,571 | $ 3,525 | $ 2,642 |
| **Depreciation, depletion, and amortization** | | | | | |
| Petroleum—United States | $ 1,045 | $ 1,033 | $   856 | $   751 | $   540 |
| —Foreign | 495 | 394 | 445 | 396 | 334 |
| Chemical | 95 | 82 | 76 | 67 | 58 |
| Paperboard packaging | 107 | 93 | 88 | 79 | 71 |
| Retail merchandising | 106 | 105 | 101 | 88 | 74 |
| Corporate and other | 44 | 29 | 20 | 18 | 9 |
| Total | $ 1,892 | $ 1,736 | $ 1,586 | $ 1,399 | $ 1,086 |
| **Total segment assets at year end** | | | | | |
| Petroleum—United States | $10,878 | $10,560 | $ 9,686 | $ 9,107 | $ 7,651 |
| —Foreign | 15,457 | 16,519 | 17,137 | 16,692 | 13,681 |
| Chemical | 2,266 | 2,044 | 1,797 | 1,547 | 1,160 |
| Paperboard packaging | 1,866 | 1,942 | 1,820 | 1,649 | 1,519 |
| Retail merchandising | 4,183 | 4,076 | 4,154 | 3,942 | 3,746 |
| Other | 410 | 391 | 337 | 275 | 271 |
| Corporate assets | 483 | 483 | 443 | 221 | 115 |
| Adjustments and eliminations | (471) | (799) | (598) | (728) | (637) |
| Total | $35,072 | $35,216 | $34,776 | $32,705 | $27,506 |

[a]Restated.

*Source:* Mobil Corporation financial and operating statistics 1983.

**Exhibit 23.5**

## MOBIL CORPORATION
### Distribution of Earnings and Assets—Geographic
(millions)

|  | 1983 | 1982[a] | 1981 | 1980 | 1979 |
|---|---|---|---|---|---|
| **Total revenues** | | | | | |
| United States | $23,934 | $23,844 | $24,936 | $23,318 | $18,908 |
| Foreign | | | | | |
| Canada | 1,203 | 1,072 | 835 | 850 | 723 |
| Other | 35,399 | 41,898 | 44,901 | 43,189 | 31,806 |
| Total foreign | 36,602 | 42,970 | 45,736 | 44,039 | 32,529 |
| Adjustments and eliminations | (1,538) | (2,706) | (2,085) | (3,631) | (3,145) |
| Total revenues | $58,998 | $64,108 | $68,587 | $63,726 | $48,292 |
| **Geographic earnings** | | | | | |
| United States | $ 659 | $ 660 | $ 1,041 | $ 826 | $ 739 |
| Foreign | | | | | |
| Canada | 104 | 80 | 33 | 97 | 100 |
| Other | 906 | 633 | 1,503 | 2,028 | 1,319 |
| Total foreign | 1,010 | 713 | 1,536 | 2,125 | 1,419 |
| Corporate expenses, net of income taxes | (166) | (160) | (144) | (138) | (151) |
| Income before extraordinary item | $ 1,503 | $ 1,213 | $ 2,433 | $ 2,813 | $ 2,007 |
| **Geographic assets at year end** | | | | | |
| United States | $18,706 | $18,123 | $16,898 | $15,644 | $13,696 |
| Foreign | | | | | |
| Canada | 1,329 | 1,314 | 1,138 | 969 | 788 |
| Other | 15,200 | 16,265 | 17,049 | 16,765 | 13,716 |
| Total foreign | 16,529 | 17,579 | 18,187 | 17,734 | 14,504 |
| Corporate assets | 483 | 483 | 443 | 221 | 115 |
| Adjustments and eliminations | (646) | (969) | (752) | (894) | (809) |
| Total assets | $35,072 | $35,216 | $34,776 | $32,705 | $27,506 |

[a]Restated.

*Source:* Mobil Corporation financial and operating statistics 1983.

ies. Throughout its corporate evolution, Mobil continued to be well known as a manufacturer of high-grade industrial lubricants. In 1969, Albert Nickerson, chief executive officer at Mobil, noted: "In most of the world after World War II, the company had really been just a lubricant marketer. Then we started to expand into one European market after another; we constructed refineries; we improved our crude oil sufficiency."[2]

Even so, Mobil continued to be short of crude-oil reserves relative to the other majors, and its reputation in lubricants had followed the company into more recent times. An article from the August 1978 issue of *Industrial Marketing* high-

**Exhibit 23.6**

## MOBIL CORPORATION
### Capital, Exploration, and Other Outlays
### (millions)

| | 1983 | 1982[a] | 1981 | 1980 | 1979 |
|---|---|---|---|---|---|
| **Segment distribution** | | | | | |
| United States | | | | | |
| Petroleum— | $1,742 | $2,061 | $1,804 | $1,429 | $1,301 |
| —Acquisitions[b] | — | 500 | — | 712 | 700 |
| Chemical | 195 | 311 | 258 | 200 | 130 |
| Paperboard packaging | 101 | 224 | 208 | 131 | 144 |
| Retail merchandising | 121 | 69 | 144 | 322 | 250 |
| Alternative energy | 12 | 82 | 123 | 61 | 40 |
| Corporate and other | 145 | 162 | 165 | 139 | 72 |
| Total | $2,316 | $3,409 | $2,702 | $2,994 | $2,637 |
| Foreign | | | | | |
| Petroleum— | $1,400 | $1,774 | $1,697 | $1,715 | $1,026 |
| —Acquisitions[b] | — | — | — | 3 | 92 |
| Chemical | 15 | 17 | 16 | 48 | 16 |
| Paperboard packaging | 28 | 49 | 47 | 49 | 38 |
| Alternative energy | 12 | 4 | 7 | 6 | 3 |
| Total | $1,455 | $1,844 | $1,767 | $1,821 | $1,175 |
| Worldwide | | | | | |
| Petroleum— | $3,142 | $3,835 | $3,501 | $3,144 | $2,327 |
| —Acquisitions[b] | — | 500 | — | 715 | 792 |
| Chemical | 210 | 328 | 274 | 248 | 146 |
| Paperboard packaging | 129 | 273 | 255 | 180 | 182 |
| Retail merchandising | 121 | 69 | 144 | 322 | 250 |
| Alternative energy | 24 | 86 | 130 | 67 | 43 |
| Corporate and other | 145 | 162 | 165 | 139 | 72 |
| Total | $3,771 | $5,253 | $4,469 | $4,815 | $3,812 |
| **Geographic distribution** | | | | | |
| United States | $2,316 | $3,409 | $2,702 | $2,994 | $2,637 |
| Canada | 153 | 138 | 148 | 222 | 206 |
| Other foreign | 1,302 | 1,706 | 1,619 | 1,599 | 969 |
| Worldwide | $3,771 | $5,253 | $4,469 | $4,815 | $3,812 |
| Research expense | $ 209 | $ 196 | $ 179 | $ 143 | $ 115 |

[a]Restated.

[b]Includes acquisition of a working interest in certain holdings of The Anschutz Corp., 1982, and acquisition of the operations of TransOcean Oil, Inc., 1980, and General Crude Oil Co., 1979.

*Source:* Mobil Corporation financial and operating statistics 1983.

Exhibit 23.7

## MOBIL CORPORATION
### Supplementary Oil- and Gas-Producing Disclosures

**TABLE 1   ESTIMATED QUANTITIES OF NET PROVED CRUDE OIL AND NATURAL GAS LIQUID RESERVES (UNAUDITED) (MILLIONS OF BARRELS)**

| | United States | | Canada | | Foreign Europe | | Other | | Total |
|---|---|---|---|---|---|---|---|---|---|
| | Crude | NGL | Crude | NGL | Crude | NGL | Crude | NGL | |
| **Year ended December 31, 1983** | | | | | | | | | |
| Net proved reserves | | | | | | | | | |
|   Beginning of year | 746 | 160 | 180 | 62 | 506 | 11 | 390 | 200 | 2,255 |
|   Revisions of previous | | | | | | | | | |
|     estimates | 2 | 3 | 4 | (3) | (6) | — | — | 12 | 12 |
|   Improved recovery | 26 | — | 3 | 1 | 8 | — | — | — | 38 |
|   Extensions, discoveries, and | | | | | | | | | |
|     other additions | 18 | 2 | 4 | — | 7 | — | 3 | — | 34 |
|   Production | (86) | (16) | (17) | (2) | (36) | — | (21) | (13) | (191) |
| Net proved reserves | | | | | | | | | |
|   End of year | 706 | 149 | 174 | 58 | 479 | 11 | 372 | 199 | 2,148 |
| Net proved developed reserves | | | | | | | | | |
|   Beginning of year | 670 | 156 | 180 | 62 | 152 | — | 238 | 200 | 1,658 |
|   End of year | 638 | 146 | 174 | 58 | 188 | 1 | 231 | 199 | 1,635 |
| Mobil's share of net proved reserves of investees accounted for on the equity method | — | — | — | — | 6 | — | 431 | — | 437 |
| Quantities under special arrangements in which the company acts as producer | | | | | | | | | |
|   Quantities received during the year | — | — | — | — | — | — | 34 | — | 34 |
|   Estimated future quantities | — | — | — | — | — | — | 14 | — | 14 |
| **Year ended December 31, 1982** | | | | | | | | | |
| Net proved reserves | | | | | | | | | |
|   Beginning of year | 766 | 132 | 189 | 55 | 536 | 8 | 520 | 219 | 2,425 |
|   Revisions of previous | | | | | | | | | |
|     estimates | 34 | 10 | 4 | 9 | (6) | 3 | (124) | (7) | (77) |
|   Improved recovery | 25 | 1 | — | — | 4 | — | — | — | 30 |
|   Purchases (sales) of minerals | | | | | | | | | |
|     in place | — | 33 | — | — | — | — | (1) | — | 32 |
|   Extensions, discoveries, and | | | | | | | | | |
|     other additions | 7 | 1 | 2 | — | 1 | — | 18 | — | 29 |
|   Production | (86) | (17) | (15) | (2) | (29) | — | (23) | (12) | (184) |
| Net proved reserves | | | | | | | | | |
|   End of year | 746 | 160 | 180 | 62 | 506 | 11 | 390 | 200 | 2,255 |
| Net proved developed reserves | | | | | | | | | |
|   Beginning of year | 677 | 127 | 189 | 55 | 167 | 1 | 289 | 158 | 1,663 |
|   End of year | 670 | 156 | 180 | 62 | 152 | — | 238 | 200 | 1,658 |

(continued)

**Exhibit 23.7** (continued)

| | United States | | Canada | | Foreign Europe | | Other | | |
|---|---|---|---|---|---|---|---|---|---|
| | Crude | NGL | Crude | NGL | Crude | NGL | Crude | NGL | Total |
| Mobil's share of net proved reserves of investees accounted for on the equity method | — | — | — | — | 6 | — | 451 | 2 | 459 |
| Quantities under special arrangements in which the company acts as producer | | | | | | | | | |
| Quantities received during the year | — | — | — | — | — | — | 31 | — | 31 |
| Estimated future quantities | — | — | — | — | — | — | 43 | — | 43 |
| **Year ended December 31, 1981** | | | | | | | | | |
| Net proved reserves | | | | | | | | | |
| Beginning of year | 742 | 148 | 199 | 53 | 574 | 10 | 355 | 170 | 2,251 |
| Revisions of previous estimates | 37 | 2 | 5 | 2 | (12) | (3) | 13 | 61 | 105 |
| Improved recovery | 55 | — | 1 | — | 1 | 1 | — | — | 58 |
| Extensions, discoveries, and other additions | 19 | — | — | 1 | — | — | 177 | — | 197 |
| Production | (87) | (18) | (16) | (1) | (27) | — | (25) | (12) | (186) |
| Net proved reserves | | | | | | | | | |
| End of year | 766 | 132 | 189 | 55 | 536 | 8 | 520 | 219 | 2,425 |
| Net proved developed reserves | | | | | | | | | |
| Beginning of year | 624 | 135 | 199 | 53 | 164 | 10 | 280 | 169 | 1,634 |
| End of year | 677 | 127 | 189 | 55 | 167 | 1 | 289 | 158 | 1,663 |
| Mobil's share of net proved reserves of investees accounted for on the equity method | — | — | — | — | 7 | — | 453 | 2 | 462 |
| Quantities under special arrangements in which the company acts as producer | | | | | | | | | |
| Quantities received during the year | — | — | — | — | — | — | 31 | — | 31 |
| Estimated future quantities | — | — | — | — | — | — | 78 | — | 78 |

(continued)

lighted Mobil's current emphasis on industrial lubricants: "Mobil Oil Corp. announced a new print ad campaign . . . that will emphasize the company's service and technological expertise in the industrial lubrication market. . . . the new ads are part . . . of an evolutionary communications effort which for the past ten years has been positioning Mobil as the leader in supplying total lubrication programs to industry."[3]

Exhibit 23.7   (continued)

## TABLE 2   ESTIMATED QUANTITIES OF NET PROVED NATURAL GAS RESERVES (UNAUDITED) (BILLIONS OF CUBIC FEET)

| | United States | Foreign | | | Total |
| --- | --- | --- | --- | --- | --- |
| | | Canada | Europe | Other | |
| **Year ended December 31, 1983** | | | | | |
| Net proved reserves | | | | | |
| Beginning of year | 6,334 | 1,977 | 2,053 | 6,893 | 17,257 |
| Revisions of previous estimates | (13) | (29) | 48 | 1,353 | 1,359 |
| Improved recovery | 3 | 3 | 2 | — | 8 |
| Purchases (sales) of minerals in place | (1) | — | — | — | (1) |
| Extensions, discoveries, and other additions | 400 | 12 | 152 | — | 564 |
| Production | (448) | (67) | (98) | (247) | (860) |
| Net proved reserves | | | | | |
| End of year | 6,275 | 1,896 | 2,157 | 7,999 | 18,327 |
| Net proved developed reserves | | | | | |
| Beginning of year | 5,938 | 1,976 | 1,192 | 6,893 | 15,999 |
| End of year | 5,941 | 1,895 | 1,276 | 7,999 | 17,111 |
| Mobil's share of net proved reserves of investees accounted for on the equity method | — | — | 61 | 93 | 154 |
| **Year ended December 31, 1982** | | | | | |
| Net proved reserves | | | | | |
| Beginning of year | 6,310 | 2,147 | 2,160 | 6,761 | 17,378 |
| Revisions of previous estimates | 251 | (110) | (162) | 348 | 327 |
| Improved recovery | 26 | — | — | — | 26 |
| Purchases (sales) of minerals in place | 133 | — | — | (1) | 132 |
| Extensions, discoveries, and other additions | 220 | 7 | 151 | — | 378 |
| Production | (606) | (67) | (96) | (215) | (984) |
| Net proved reserves | | | | | |
| End of year | 6,334 | 1,977 | 2,053 | 6,893 | 17,257 |
| Net proved developed reserves | | | | | |
| Beginning of year | 5,872 | 2,146 | 1,415 | 3,514 | 12,947 |
| End of year | 5,938 | 1,976 | 1,192 | 6,893 | 15,999 |
| Mobil's share of net proved reserves of investees accounted for on the equity method | — | — | 58 | 208 | 266 |
| **Year ended December 31, 1981** | | | | | |
| Net proved reserves | | | | | |
| Beginning of year | 6,205 | 2,082 | 2,275 | 3,712 | 14,274 |
| Revisions of previous estimates | 508 | 94 | (59) | 3,248 | 3,791 |
| Improved recovery | 88 | 2 | — | — | 90 |
| Extensions, discoveries, and other additions | 170 | 33 | 62 | — | 265 |
| Production | (661) | (64) | (118) | (199) | (1,042) |
| Net proved reserves | | | | | |
| End of year | 6,310 | 2,147 | 2,160 | 6,761 | 17,378 |
| Net proved developed reserves | | | | | |
| Beginning of year | 5,754 | 2,080 | 1,514 | 3,712 | 13,060 |
| End of year | 5,872 | 2,146 | 1,415 | 3,514 | 12,947 |
| Mobil's share of net proved reserves of investees accounted for on the equity method | — | — | 60 | 206 | 266 |

(continued)

**Exhibit 23.7** (continued)

**TABLE 3 CAPITALIZED COSTS RELATED TO OIL- AND GAS-PRODUCING ACTIVITIES (UNAUDITED) (IN MILLIONS)**

| At December 31, | 1983 | 1982 |
|---|---|---|
| Capitalized costs | | |
|   Unproved properties | $ 2,032 | $ 1,928 |
|   Proved properties, wells, plants, and other equipment | 14,259 | 12,848 |
| Total capitalized costs | $16,291 | $14,776 |
| Accumulated depreciation, depletion, and amortization | $ 6,224 | $ 5,360 |
| Mobil's share of net capitalized costs of investees accounted for on the equity method | $ 120 | $ 124 |

**TABLE 4 COSTS INCURRED IN OIL AND GAS PROPERTY ACQUISITION, EXPLORATION, AND DEVELOPMENT ACTIVITIES (UNAUDITED) (IN MILLIONS)**

| | United States | Foreign Canada | Foreign Europe | Foreign Other | Total |
|---|---|---|---|---|---|
| **Year ended December 31, 1983** | | | | | |
| Property acquisition costs | $ 473 | $ 2 | $ — | $ — | $ 475 |
| Exploration costs | 508 | 110 | 158 | 148 | 924 |
| Development costs | 493 | 37 | 463 | 161 | 1,154 |
| Total expenditures | $1,474 | $ 149 | $ 621 | $ 309 | $2,553 |
| Mobil's share of investees' costs of property acquisition, exploration, and development | — | — | $ 12 | $ 37 | $ 49 |
| **Year ended December 31, 1982** | | | | | |
| Property acquisition costs | $ 947 | $ 2 | $ — | $ 15 | $ 964 |
| Exploration costs | 712 | 88 | 168 | 290 | 1,258 |
| Development costs | 608 | 44 | 514 | 218 | 1,384 |
| Total expenditures | $2,267 | $ 134 | $ 682 | $ 523 | $3,606 |
| Mobil's share of investees' costs of property acquisition, exploration, and development | — | — | $ 17 | $ 59 | $ 76 |
| **Year ended December 31, 1981** | | | | | |
| Property acquisition costs | $ 383 | $ 1 | $ — | $ 6 | $ 390 |
| Exploration costs | 633 | 115 | 96 | 396 | 1,240 |
| Development costs | 516 | 19 | 385 | 130 | 1,050 |
| Total expenditures | $1,532 | $ 135 | $ 481 | $ 532 | $2,680 |
| Mobil's share of investees' costs of property acquisition, exploration, and development | — | — | $ 14 | $ 37 | $ 51 |

(continued)

Exhibit 23.7   (continued)

## TABLE 5   RESULTS OF OPERATIONS FOR OIL- AND GAS-PRODUCING ACTIVITIES (UNAUDITED) (IN MILLIONS)

| | United States | Foreign Canada | Foreign Europe | Foreign Other | Total |
|---|---|---|---|---|---|
| **Year ended December 31, 1983** | | | | | |
| Revenues—Trade sales | $ 935 | $ 150 | $ 776 | $ 931 | $ 2,792 |
| —Intercompany sales | 3,059 | 493 | 894 | 1,183 | 5,629 |
| Production (lifting) costs | (1,606) | (213) | (608) | (397) | (2,824) |
| Exploration expenses | (296) | (34) | (119) | (181) | (630) |
| Depreciation, depletion, and amortization | (845) | (39) | (108) | (79) | (1,071) |
| Other operating revenues and (expenses) | (39) | 13 | 45 | (9) | 10 |
| Finance (charges) credits | (75) | (8) | (11) | (1) | (95) |
| Income tax expense | (522) | (258) | (635) | (1,132) | (2,547) |
| Results of operations for producing activities | $ 611 | $ 104 | $ 234 | $ 315 | $ 1,264 |
| Mobil's share of results of operations for producing activities of investees accounted for on the equity method | — | — | $ 20 | $ 29 | $ 49 |
| **Year ended December 31, 1982** | | | | | |
| Revenues—Trade sales | $ 1,132 | $ 135 | $ 552 | $ 947 | $ 2,766 |
| —Intercompany sales | 3,134 | 386 | 954 | 1,197 | 5,671 |
| Production (lifting) costs | (1,600) | (195) | (565) | (554) | (2,914) |
| Exploration expenses | (457) | (45) | (104) | (247) | (853) |
| Depreciation, depletion, and amortization | (802) | (27) | (76) | (49) | (954) |
| Other operating revenues and (expenses) | (21) | 25 | 44 | (5) | 43 |
| Finance (charges) credits | (49) | 30 | (94) | 7 | (106) |
| Income tax expense | (599) | (211) | (509) | (1,054) | (2,373) |
| Results of operations for producing activities | $ 738 | $ 98 | $ 202 | $ 242 | $ 1,280 |
| Mobil's share of results of operations for producing activities of investees accounted for on the equity method | — | — | $ 15 | $ 37 | $ 52 |
| **Year ended December 31, 1981** | | | | | |
| Revenues—Trade sales | $ 1,098 | $ 127 | $ 541 | $ 973 | $ 2,739 |
| —Intercompany sales | 3,422 | 280 | 987 | 1,414 | 6,103 |
| Production (lifting) costs | (1,788) | (152) | (541) | (518) | (2,999) |
| Exploration expenses | (326) | (72) | (61) | (330) | (789) |
| Depreciation, depletion, and amortization | (636) | (31) | (72) | (83) | (822) |
| Other operating revenues and (expenses) | (13) | 25 | 37 | (7) | 42 |
| Finance (charges) credits | (44) | 16 | (15) | 27 | (16) |
| Income tax expense | (803) | (146) | (439) | (1,281) | (2,669) |
| Results of operations for producing activities | $ 910 | $ 47 | $ 437 | $ 195 | $ 1,589 |
| Mobil's share of results of operations for producing activities of investees accounted for on the equity method | — | — | $ 14 | $ 42 | $ 56 |

(continued)

**Exhibit 23.7** (continued)

**TABLE 6   STANDARDIZED MEASURE OF DISCOUNTED FUTURE NET CASH FLOWS RELATING TO PROVED OIL AND GAS RESERVES (UNAUDITED) (IN MILLIONS)**

| | United States | Foreign Canada | Europe | Other | Total |
|---|---|---|---|---|---|
| **At December 31, 1983** | | | | | |
| Future cash inflows | $ 34,939 | $ 9,019 | $ 23,481 | $ 54,091 | $121,530 |
| Future production costs | (13,963) | (3,115) | (6,888) | (3,817) | (27,783) |
| Future development costs | (890) | (7) | (1,124) | (766) | (2,787) |
| Future income tax expenses | (7,593) | (3,663) | (10,926) | (30,359) | (52,541) |
| Future net cash flows | 12,493 | 2,234 | 4,543 | 19,149 | 38,419 |
| 10% annual discount for estimated timing of cash flows | (5,254) | (1,186) | (1,908) | (10,255) | (18,603) |
| Standardized measure of discounted future net cash flows | $ 7,239 | $ 1,048 | $ 2,635 | $ 8,894 | $ 19,816 |
| Mobil's share of standardized measure of discounted future net cash flows of investees accounted for on the equity method | — | — | $ 83 | $ 128 | $ 211 |
| **At December 31, 1982** | | | | | |
| Future cash inflows | $ 37,315 | $ 8,634 | $ 26,727 | $ 59,262 | $131,938 |
| Future production costs | (16,400) | (3,341) | (6,703) | (4,230) | (30,674) |
| Future development costs | (709) | (17) | (1,830) | (963) | (3,519) |
| Future income tax expenses | (7,956) | (3,298) | (12,139) | (33,771) | (57,164) |
| Future net cash flows | 12,250 | 1,978 | 6,055 | 20,298 | 40,581 |
| 10% annual discount for estimated timing of cash flows | (4,875) | (1,051) | (2,319) | (11,111) | (19,356) |
| Standardized measure of discounted future net cash flows | $ 7,375 | $ 927 | $ 3,736 | $ 9,187 | $ 21,225 |
| Mobil's share of standardized measure of discounted future net cash flows of investees accounted for on the equity method | — | — | $ 85 | $ 163 | $ 248 |
| **At December 31, 1981** | | | | | |
| Future cash inflows | $ 39,082 | $ 7,755 | $ 30,946 | $ 58,542 | $136,325 |
| Future production costs | (14,956) | (2,765) | (5,507) | (4,813) | (28,041) |
| Future development costs | (796) | (13) | (1,862) | (1,294) | (3,965) |
| Future income tax expenses | (9,744) | (3,451) | (16,348) | (33,683) | (63,226) |
| Future net cash flows | 13,586 | 1,526 | 7,229 | 18,752 | 41,093 |
| 10% annual discount for estimated timing of cash flows | (6,077) | (758) | (3,343) | (10,404) | (20,582) |
| Standardized measure of discounted future net cash flows | $ 7,509 | $ 768 | $ 3,886 | $ 8,348 | $ 20,511 |
| Mobil's share of standardized measure of discounted future net cash flows of investees accounted for on the equity method | — | — | $ 86 | $ 169 | $ 255 |

(continued)

**Exhibit 23.7** (concluded)

**TABLE 7   CHANGES IN STANDARDIZED MEASURE OF DISCOUNTED FUTURE NET CASH FLOWS (UNAUDITED) (IN MILLIONS)**

| At December 31, | 1983 | 1982 | 1981 |
|---|---|---|---|
| Beginning of year | $21,473 | $20,766 | $19,014 |
| Changes resulting from | | | |
| Sales and transfers of production, net of production costs | (5,597) | (5,523) | (5,843) |
| Net changes in prices, and development and production costs | (6,980) | (3,308) | (5,674) |
| Extensions, discoveries, additions, and purchases less related costs | 919 | 1,363 | 3,118 |
| Development costs incurred during the period | 1,154 | 1,384 | 1,050 |
| Revisions of previous quantity estimates | 3,250 | (833) | 8,658 |
| Accretion of discount | 5,077 | 4,836 | 4,293 |
| Net change in income taxes | 768 | 2,795 | (3,868) |
| Other | (37) | (7) | 18 |
| End of year | $20,027 | $21,473 | $20,766 |

*Source:* Mobil Corporation Annual Report 1983.

Thus, Mobil Corporation, now the second largest oil company in the United States, still retained part of its heritage, which could be traced to Vacuum Oil, a small producer of petroleum lubricants which had been capitalized in 1866 for $10,000.

**CORPORATE STRUCTURE**

Many of the smaller subsidiaries which had been acquired by Socony and Vacuum had not been fully integrated into Mobil's corporate structure. These companies often retained their original staffs, operating procedures, and corporate identities. In 1959, Albert L. Nickerson, chief executive officer of Mobil, initiated an extensive companywide program of reorganization which included the full integration of some of the more independent of Mobil's subsidiaries. Concerted efforts were made to cut fixed costs in the form of redundant staff services, to improve efficiency in exploration and production through better coordination among subsidiaries, and to redefine corporate strategy.

From 1969 until the present, Mobil had been led by two men: Rawleigh Warner, Jr., chairman, and William P. Tavoulareas, president and (later) chief operating officer. Both men rose through the ranks of the company on the financial side. This was somewhat unique, as the engineering ladder was, for most oil companies, the more traditional route. Warner had received a liberal arts degree from Princeton. Tavoulareas started with Mobil in 1947 in the accounting department, and later received a law degree.[4] Tavoulareas was named the first manager of the newly formed planning department in 1959, part of Nickerson's program of reorganization. One oil analyst who worked in planning and finance at Mobil for ten years said, "Mobil is a lawyer-businessman company rather than an oil-man-geologist company. Planning is the real essence of this company."[5]

**Exhibit 23.8** Top 11 Domestic Retail Gasoline Marketers

| | 1983 | | 1982 | | 1981 | | 1980 | | 1979 | | 1978 | | 1977 | |
|---|---|---|---|---|---|---|---|---|---|---|---|---|---|---|
| | Rank | % Share | Rank | % Share | Rank | % Share | Rank | % Share | Rank | % Share | Rank | % Share | Rank | % Share |
| Amoco | 1 | 7.23 | 1 | 7.32 | 1 | 7.28 | 3 | 7.40 | 2 | 7.48 | 2 | 7.70 | 2 | 7.30 |
| Shell | 2 | 6.97 | 2 | 6.77 | 2 | 6.89 | 2 | 7.44 | 3 | 7.30 | 1 | 7.71 | 1 | 7.53 |
| Exxon | 3 | 6.90 | 3 | 6.75 | 3 | 6.81 | 1 | 7.54 | 1 | 7.65 | 3 | 7.28 | 3 | 7.14 |
| Texaco | 4 | 5.80 | 6 | 5.62 | 4 | 5.77 | 5 | 5.95 | 5 | 6.01 | 4 | 6.75 | 4 | 7.11 |
| Mobil | 5 | 5.69 | 5 | 5.68 | 6 | 5.38 | 4 | 6.01 | 6 | 5.78 | 6 | 5.55 | 6 | 5.59 |
| Gulf | 6 | 5.30 | 4 | 5.78 | 5 | 5.69 | 7 | 5.39 | 4 | 6.36 | 5 | 5.83 | 5 | 5.91 |
| Chevron | 7 | 5.06 | 8 | 4.84 | 7 | 5.21 | 6 | 5.77 | 7 | 5.30 | 7 | 4.76 | 7 | 4.75 |
| Arco | 8 | 4.82 | 7 | 4.64 | 8 | 3.80 | 8 | 3.87 | 8 | 3.89 | 8 | 3.79 | 8 | 3.85 |
| Union | 9 | 3.52 | 9 | 3.31 | 9 | 3.31 | 9 | 3.50 | 9 | 3.49 | 9 | 3.28 | 11 | 3.08 |
| Phillips | 10 | 2.61 | 10 | 2.77 | 10 | 2.88 | 10 | 2.83 | 11 | 2.85 | 11 | 3.02 | 10 | 3.15 |
| Sun | 11 | 2.54 | 11 | 2.64 | 11 | 2.55 | 11 | 2.74 | 10 | 3.01 | 10 | 3.20 | 9 | 3.39 |

*Source: 1984 National Petroleum News Factbook, p. 117.*

**Exhibit 23.9** Share Price Data[a]

|      | High            | Low             |
|------|-----------------|-----------------|
| 1974 | $14\frac{1}{4}$ | $7\frac{3}{4}$  |
| 1975 | $12\frac{1}{4}$ | $8\frac{5}{8}$  |
| 1976 | $16\frac{3}{8}$ | $11\frac{7}{8}$ |
| 1977 | $17\frac{7}{8}$ | $14\frac{5}{8}$ |
| 1978 | $18\frac{1}{8}$ | $14\frac{5}{8}$ |
| 1979 | $30\frac{1}{4}$ | 17              |
| 1980 | $44\frac{7}{8}$ | $24\frac{7}{8}$ |
| 1981 | $41\frac{1}{8}$ | $24\frac{1}{8}$ |
| 1982 | $28\frac{5}{8}$ | $19\frac{1}{2}$ |
| 1983 | $34\frac{5}{8}$ | $24\frac{1}{4}$ |

[a]Adjusted for stock splits.

*Source: Standard NYSE Stock Reports,* Standard & Poor's Corp., December 6, 1984.

As head of planning, Tavoulareas set out to shake up a company said to be extremely slothful and badly in need of reorientation. Though incurring the ire of some of Mobil's more traditional executives, Tavoulareas and his planning department set in motion a procedure of carefully scrutinizing all projects and killing those which failed to measure up financially.[6]

Both Warner and Tavoulareas continued the earlier trend toward leaner staffing and greater consolidation. In 1973, Mobil's U.S. marketing force, which had previously been operating through seven divisions, was consolidated into four regional offices, whose greater efficiency was expected to save the company about $10 million a year.[7]

Prior to 1974, Mobil was organized into four operating divisions. The North American Division was Mobil's operating petroleum division for the United States and Canada. The International Division coordinated the petroleum operations of Mobile affiliates outside the United States and Canada. Mobil Chemical Company was an operating division formed in 1960 which coordinated the chemical operations of Mobil affiliates in the United States and several other countries. This division was involved in the manufacture of agricultural and industrial chemicals, plastics, paints, chemical coatings, and petrochemicals. The fourth division, Transportation, was comprised of domestic trucking, pipelines, and deep-sea carriers.

In 1974, the North American Division was reorganized to exclude Canada; the resulting divisions were U.S. Operations and Foreign Operations. Two years later, on July 1, 1976, a holding company was formed called Mobil Corporation, encompassing the Mobil Oil Corporation (which included domestic and foreign energy operations), the Mobil Chemical Company, Montgomery Ward, and Container Corporation. So there were still four operating segments, but they were now distinguished as follows: Energy Operations, including the subdivisions of United States Energy Operations and Foreign Energy Operations; Chemical Operations; Retail Merchandising; and Paperboard Packaging.

Further belt-tightening moves were put into effect in the early 1980s, paralleling efforts made by other industry members. As part of an overall attempt to trim fixed costs, Mobil closed various plants, refineries, and gasoline terminals. The company also scrapped surplus tankers, cut back on travel, and shrank an administrative unit in Europe.

Another reorganization took place in late 1982. This most recent restructuring was said to be setting the stage for the retirement of Warner and Tavoulareas. Warner was scheduled to retire in 1986 and Tavoulareas in 1983. (However, during 1983, the board extended Tavoulareas' tenure until November 1984.)

Two major operating units were established under Mobil Corporation, which remained responsible for overall policy and strategy decisions. All oil- and gas-related activities became the responsibility of Mobil Oil. Allen E. Murray was named president of this unit. All other activities, such as chemicals, paperboard packaging, retailing, and alternative energy interests, became the responsibility of Mobil Diversified Business. The creation of this new division lumped the company's most severely troubled businesses into a single group. Richard F. Tucker was named president of this unit. Warner and Tavoulareas were, in turn, named chairman and vice-chairman of Mobil's executive committee.

Murray and Tucker were often compared to Tavoulareas and Warner and were considered to be heirs apparent. "Murray is a numbers man, and he came in from the bottom, like Tavoulareas. Tucker is extremely effective in public and came to Mobil at a later stage—and at a fairly high level—as Warner did."[8] Shortly after the reorganization, Warner was quoted as saying, "We will rate these individuals on their capacity to meet established plans."[9]

## EXPLORATION AND PRODUCTION

Mobil's commitment to a strong exploration program can be traced back to the Suez crisis in 1956, when Mobil's Middle East oil supplies were seriously disrupted and the company paid dearly to acquire crude. A tangible sign of an increased emphasis on exploration was Mobil's increased acreage position, which doubled to nearly 100 million acres throughout the 1960s.

Despite this apparent strategy, the period of the sixties and early seventies was a frustrating one for the explorationists at Mobil. The company still concentrated a great deal on downstream (refining and marketing) activities. A number of instances could be cited in which Mobil sold or passed up the opportunity to buy into certain prospects, Alaska being the most costly. Mobil's staff was one of the first to perform seismic work on Alaska's North Slope and vigorously encouraged Mobil's participation. However, the company did not bid aggressively on what later became the Prudhoe Bay field. "The financial people in this company did a disservice to the exploration people," Warner was quoted as saying. "The poor people in exploration were adversely impacted by people (in the company) who knew nothing about oil and gas."[10]

Oil prices substantially increased during the 1970s and Mobil, like the other majors, stepped up its exploration activities. By the late 1970s, Mobil's strategy was finally paying off. The company held an interest in nine giant oil and gas fields which were discovered during 1979 and the first half of 1980, each of which could net Mobil the equivalent of at least 100 million barrels of new reserves. "We've hit on some kind of formula in exploration," said Tavoulareas. "We hope we are in a cycle where each year we can find a big field, and if we do, I'm not worried about our future."[11]

**Saudi Arabia**   During the late 1940s, Texaco and Standard Oil Co. of California (Socal), who were then co-owners of Arabian American Oil Company (Aramco), offered 40 percent of Aramco to Jersey Standard and Mobil. Being a bit nervous about its ability to absorb its share of crude oil, Mobil opted for 10 percent rather than the 20 percent it could have bought.

Commented Warner in 1971: "That (decision) cost us a tremendous amount of money. . . . The oil companies that year in and year out make the most money make it because they are balanced. They move their own crude, they refine their own crude, and they sell their own crude."[12] By the mid-1950s, the Middle East was supplying approximately 50 percent of Mobil's crude oil. The company's dependence on Mideast oil was particularly evident during the Arab-Israeli war in 1956. Mobil's earnings suffered much more than its competitors with the closing of the Suez Canal during that conflict.

William Tavoulareas first went to the Middle East on Mobil business in late 1950. He possessed a no-nonsense manner and a determination to build a strong relationship with the Saudis. As his stature in Mobil grew, Tavoulareas's conviction that the company's best prospects lay in enhancing its access to Saudi oil became ingrained in Mobil's strategy. For years this strategy handsomely benefited the traditionally crude-poor oil company. During the mid-1970s, he skillfully negotiated a five-year contract to acquire another 5 percent of Aramco.

Originally, the Aramco partners (Exxon, Mobil, Texaco, and Socal) owned the production and the Saudi government was paid a royalty. During the mid-1970s, however, the Saudis began negotiations to buy out the Aramco partners. This process was completed in 1980. The partners were granted priority access to significant volumes of Saudi Arabian oil. The price of this oil put the partners at both an advantage and a disadvantage compared to their competitors during the four years which followed the buyout.

Saudi Arabia, with its small population and vast reserves, had traditionally possessed sufficient foresight to cut back production in times of surplus. Special access to Saudi crude, therefore, was likely to pay off only in an expanding market.

Access to Saudi oil was especially beneficial from 1979 to 1981, when the Saudis were flooding the market with relatively cheap oil to retain world prices. The so-called Aramco advantage added some $200 million to Mobil's 1980 earnings.[13]

In 1981, the Aramco advantage became a burden. When world oil prices started declining, Saudi oil became among the world's most expensive, because the country adhered rigidly to OPEC's price structure. As other members of Aramco slashed their purchases, Mobil increased its take, buying as much as 35 percent of Aramco's contracted volumes. Tavoulareas explained, "We made a commitment to believing continued reliance on Saudi crude would be a benefit to our company. Every time we set out to lift more than our share, other guys (in Aramco) cut back more . . . so we lifted a bit more than we wanted to."[14] Mobil's European refining and marketing arm, once a principal profit center because it used competitively priced Saudi crude, lost $280 million in 1982, a drop of more than $1 billion from 1980.

To further cement its ties to the Saudis, Mobil, in 1980, agreed to build two vast export facilities for the Saudis: an oil refinery and a petrochemical complex in Yanbu, a new industrial city on the Red Sea. In return, Mobil won the right to buy an extra 1.4 billion barrels of extra crude over 19 years. Tavoulareas defended the deal by pointing to the favorable financing and low-cost materials that the Saudis had promised. However, he stated, "These projects must be judged as part of the Saudi 'insurance policy' rather than by their own economics."[15]

Mobil's bold moves in Saudi Arabia were not without criticism from skeptical industry members. Warned one highly placed industry source: "Mobil's serious risk is that the market won't grow. They made their big, expensive moves in Saudi Arabia in an expansive environment. The expenses they made there have drawn resources that could have been used elsewhere."[16]

Nonetheless, Mobil's Saudi commitment has never waivered. By year-end 1983, $600 million had been spent at Yanbu. In addition, many hours of manpower had been employed to train Saudis to run the complexes. In February 1984, Mobil directors held their board meeting in Saudi Arabia—a first for any U.S. corporation.

In early 1984, Mobil was receiving less than 30 percent of its total crude supply from Saudi Arabia. Though Mobil was lifting the full amount of oil to which it was contractually obligated, the Saudi portion of Mobil's total crude supply was down from some 50 percent in 1982.

**Offshore Activities**

During the early 1970s, Mobil decided to confine most of its domestic exploration to a search for big fields in offshore waters. The Gulf of Mexico was the area in which Mobil spent the most and received the greatest rewards. Between 1970 and 1983, the company spent over $2.5 billion to acquire federal lease bonuses, second in the industry. For the most part, Mobil has been successful in maintaining U.S. reserves through a combination of exploration efforts in the Gulf of Mexico and a series of acquisitions of producing companies.

Mobil acquired 20,000 acres in the Mobile Bay, offshore Alabama, in a state lease sale in 1969 for a low price. The company completed a discovery well in 1979 which flowed 12.2 million cubic feet per day of natural gas. The company then acquired drilling permits for four additional wells, and in 1981, bought two more leases near the discovery. Mobil estimated reserves on the acreage to be between 200 and 600 billion cubic feet. However, industry analysts believed that the potential of the area was much higher—nearly one trillion cubic feet.[17]

Mobil's long record of success in the Gulf of Mexico continued with a significant discovery in the Green Canyon area of the central gulf. In a 1983 central gulf lease sale, Mobil added considerably to its holdings in the area, spending more than $400 million for interests in 38 leases. Some of these tracts were located in the vicinity of the Green Canyon discovery.

The company's exploration efforts in other domestic offshore areas have not been as prosperous. Following the launching of a sophisticated $14 million geophysical vessel in 1978, Mobil bid aggressively in a 1979 federal drilling lease sale for tracts located off Massachusetts. Mobil spent $222 million, more than one-quarter of the money the government took in.[18] People in the industry questioned whether Mobil had simply overbid or had seen more valuable structures in the area because it had better data. Unfortunately for Mobil, the former turned out to be closer to the truth. The company spudded its first well in the area in 1981. As of 1984, no hydrocarbons had been discovered.

Other offshore U.S. areas have also proved to be disappointing. Expenditures in the Baltimore Canyon, where Mobil began drilling in 1978, have been largely written off.

Mobil's partnership with Sohio in a promising offshore Alaska exploration effort ended in further disappointment. Mobil had paid $288 million for 14 federal tracts in the Mukluk area. Failure to discover commercial quantities of oil and gas in the well drilled there caused Mobil to write off its share of the costs to drill the well, as well as part of its investment in tracts in the Mukluk area. This amounted to a $98 million after-tax write-off against 1983 income.

Mobil's efforts to find hydrocarbons in offshore areas in other parts of the world have proved more fruitful, however. In 1971, Mobil discovered Arun, a 13-trillion-cubic-foot gas field in Indonesia which ranked as the second largest gas field of the decade. To exploit the field, Pertamina, the Indonesian state oil company, built a liquefied natural gas plant. Arun has been Mobil's most profitable single property, annually contributing more than $300 million to net income.

Mobil was the holder of the largest private interest in the Statfjord Field. This field had been discovered by Mobil and was located off the coast of Norway in the North Sea. The company's interest in this project was almost 13 percent, the largest of any of the 12 company partners except Statoil, the Norwegian State Oil Company. Production from the Statfjord Field, which had reserves of more than 3 billion barrels of oil and 2.5 trillion cubic feet of natural gas, began in November 1979 and reached a total of 391,000 barrels daily in 1983.

The largest single North Sea addition, however, was the Beryl oil and gas field in the British sector. Mobil held a 50 percent interest in Beryl, and production was expected to begin during the summer of 1984.

Mobil was also active in the offshore areas of Nigeria, where the company produced some 65,000 barrels per day in 1983.

The company paid $37,000 for the rights to 13 million acres off Newfoundland in 1965. It performed seismic activity in the area, which was enough to satisfy the minimal work requirements of the 12-year leases. (Other companies had previously drilled nearly 50 unsuccessful wildcats in the vicinity.) Presumably in an attempt to hold onto their leases, yet unwilling to commit the money needed to drill, Mobil offered farm-outs which eventually reduced its share to 28.1 percent. Then, in 1980, the massive Hibernia field was discovered in the area by a Chevron-operated rig. It was estimated that the field would eventually yield 3 billion to 4 billion barrels of oil.

Another promising find was the Venture gas field near Sable Island off the coast of Nova Scotia. Mobil held a 42 percent share in an estimated 4 trillion cubic feet of natural gas at that location.

Mobil officials announced in early 1984 that the company's 1984 capital budget would total $3.4 billion, about the same as the previous year, and would be funded entirely from cash flow. Some 70 percent of the budget was to be devoted to exploration and development, while some 70 percent of that was earmarked for North American activities. Mobil's attention in the near future was to be focused on four locations—the central Gulf of Mexico, state and federal waters off Alabama, the Canadian Atlantic, and offshore Alaska.[19]

**Domestic Onshore Activities**

With the exception of the large field that Mobil discovered in Mobile Bay, the company's record at finding domestic reserves had been considered only average. While it was "hunting for elephants" offshore, Mobil missed much of the early action in such promising plays as the Rocky Mountain Overthrust, the Williston Basin of the Dakotas, and the Anadarko Basin of Oklahoma.

The company paid dearly during the early 1980s in an attempt to catch up to competitors such as Amoco, Shell, and Chevron. Since 1978, Mobil had devoted 67 percent of its $5 billion exploration budget to the United States. Without acquisitions, however, Mobil would not have managed to replace the reserves it produced. Since 1979, Mobil had made more attempts to purchase other oil companies than any other major.

By and large, Mobil's U.S. hydrocarbon reserves were primarily in the form of natural gas. Price regulation on some of that gas, along with a growing natural gas surplus, had made much of Mobil's domestic reserves uneconomic. In 1983, the company's domestic gas production fell 20 percent (to 1,506,000,000 gross cubic feet per day) as a result of flagging demand. Production in the Hugoton field in Kansas proved to be particularly susceptible.

**REFINING**

With the merger of Socony and Vacuum Oil in 1931, the company emerged as one of the strongest refiners in the industry. In terms of refining capacity, Socony-Vacuum was the second largest refiner in the United States. By 1960, however, Mobil had dropped back to third place, and its U.S. refining capacity relative to the other major oil companies continued to decline in the following years. By 1978, Mobil was in seventh place behind Exxon, Standard of California, Standard of Indiana, Shell, Texaco, and Gulf. In 1960, Mobil's U.S. refining capacity was

**Exhibit 23.10** Refining Statistics (thousands of barrels daily)

|  | 1983 | 1982 | 1981 | 1980 | 1979 |
|---|---|---|---|---|---|
| Domestic runs | 618 | 644 | 639 | 734 | 797 |
| Domestic capacity | 750 | 860 | 860 | 910 | 901 |
| Domestic runs/capacity (%) | 82 | 75 | 74 | 81 | 88 |
| Foreign runs | 976 | 1067 | 1134 | 1225 | 1266 |
| Foreign capacity | 1436 | 1534 | 1647 | 1709 | 1770 |
| Foreign runs/capacity (%) | 68 | 70 | 69 | 72 | 72 |

*Source:* Mobil Corporation financial and operating statistics 1983.

716,700 barrels per day, or 7.4 percent of the U.S. total. By 1983, however, the company's domestic refining capacity had been restored to 750,000 barrels per day.

As of December 31, 1983, Mobil owned or had operating interests in 29 refineries in 17 countries. Mobil's total crude-oil refinery capacity was 2,186,000 barrels per day, 34 percent of which was located in the United States. The company's domestic refineries ran at 82 percent of capacity during 1983, while foreign refineries ran at 68 percent capacity. (See Exhibit 23.10.)

Mobil's petroleum product operations were fairly evenly divided among the United States, Europe, and the Far East. Foreign downstream earnings had suffered during 1982, owing to the relatively high cost of Saudi Arabian crude. Foreign margins recovered somewhat in 1983, following a $5 per barrel price reduction by the Saudis.

At home, Mobil was still seriously short of crude. Just 45 percent of the oil used in its domestic refineries came from Mobil's own wells in the United States.[20] Gasoline markets in 1983 were particularly competitive in the United States. Without inventory profits, Mobil would have lost money on its domestic refining and marketing operations in that year.[21]

Speaking before a group of New York security analysts in early 1984, Tavoulareas said that downstream strategic plans called for Mobil to be "the lowest cost operator wherever we do business or get out."[22] Evidence of this strategy in action was Mobil's announcement in May 1983 that it would close its refinery in Augusta, Kansas, within a year. Accordingly, Mobil would gradually withdraw from marketing gasoline and distillates in Kansas, Nebraska, South Dakota, and parts of Iowa, Missouri, and North Dakota.

**MARKETING**  Between 1950 and 1970, the major oil companies had been competing fiercely to penetrate as many regional markets as possible. Market share, rather than profitability, had been the primary marketing objective. Mobil, on the other hand, had followed a different strategy. Albert L. Nickerson, who was then chairman of Mobil, made the decision to limit domestic marketing expenditures in the effort to develop European markets. In 1969, Nickerson commented on this period of the company's growth: "From 1948 to 1964 we really starved our marketing people in this country.We just said, 'Look, there are many jobs this company has to do. . . . Give us a chance to strengthen some other elements of the company, and the day will come when we can come back to you. . . .' We had a program that almost required us to lose position."[23]

Mobil's domestic market share dropped from 9.9 percent in 1948 to 6.7 percent in 1967. By 1965, when foreign sales were approaching domestic sales, Mobil finally began to increase its domestic marketing expenditures. By 1969, Mobil's European market share was about 5 percent. Since earnings had improved every year since 1958, Nickerson's strategy was viewed as an overall success.

Since the early seventies, however, there had been a steady decline in the number of marketing outlets for all companies. Even as late as 1977, Texaco was marketing to every state in the union. At the same time, Mobil was in 48 states, Exxon in 44, Shell in 40, and Socal and Gulf in 39.

By the late 1970s, Mobil had decided to get out of the Rocky Mountain states because the firm had no refineries in that area. The decision called for pulling out of five states by 1981, and included closing 276 retail outlets which were supplied directly or indirectly by Mobil. As previously mentioned, Mobil later announced its intention to withdraw from several midwestern states. From 1969 to 1983, Mobil decreased the number of its retail outlets nationwide from 25,513 to 15,403.

Both at home and abroad, Mobil's strategy was to close down marginal service stations and to consolidate areas of marketing strength. Part of Mobil's domestic-marketing retrenchment included the introduction of secondary brands, beginning with the Sello brand in the Southwest in 1972, and later with Big-Bi stations in the Midwest and Reelo in North Carolina. Most of these secondary outlets were marginal Mobil stations which were converted to self-serve operations designed to compete with lower-priced private brands. The introduction of these secondary brands caused some confusion among competitors and jobbers, since Mobil was not supplying these outlets with its own product, nor was it closing all of its branded outlets in the areas where secondary brands had been introduced. Amid considerable speculation, Mobil consistently maintained that it did not intend to withdraw the Mobil brand from those areas where secondary outlets had been introduced. The company claimed that it was looking at each of its branded outlets on an individual basis to see if they met various investment criteria.

As of December 31, 1983, Mobil's petroleum products were marketed in more than 100 countries. Worldwide the company had approximately 33,000 retail dealer outlets, 47 percent of which were located in the United States. Thirty-four percent of Mobil's petroleum product sales were in the United States. Mobil ranked as the fifth largest gasoline retailer.

During October 1983, Mobil announced plans to install point-of-sale terminals in 2400 of its outlets around the country.[24] Station attendants would debit or credit cards through a reader on the terminal, allowing the company to benefit from automated credit checks, inventory controls, and electronic funds transfer.

Mobil's announcement followed a 2½ year study and $10 million in testing debit card systems. The move was expected to put Mobil in the lead among the majors in a race toward a national electronic fund transfer system.

In February 1984, Mobil made known its intention to turn as many as possible of its full-service stations into self-service gas islands in combination with convenience stores.[25] The company called them snack shops. Although many of the majors, including Arco, Texaco, Amoco, and Tenneco, had already introduced combination gas stations and convenience stores, none were on the scale reportedly envisioned at Mobil.

## TRANSPORTATION

At year-end 1983, Mobil owned 38 oceangoing tankers and had another 20 vessels under charter. The company also made use of voyage charters. Mobil had traditionally been extremely adept at handling its tanker commitments, thus benefiting from consistently low transportation costs.

Mobil's U.S. pipeline system, including partly owned facilities, consisted in December 1983 of 18,855 miles of crude oil, natural gas liquids, natural gas, and carbon dioxide trunk and gathering lines, and 9158 miles of product lines. The company's pipeline system outside of the United States, including partly owned facilities, consisted of 7969 miles of trunk and gathering lines, and 1893 miles of product lines.

Mobil held a 4 percent interest in the Trans Alaska Pipeline System (TAPS), a 48-inch pipeline system which moved crude oil some 800 miles from the Prudhoe Bay field on Alaska's North Slope to the port of Valdez on the southern coast of Alaska.

## OTHER ENERGY SOURCES

Anticipating the future importance of alternative energy sources, Mobil, in the mid-1970s, began investing more in research and development for new sources of energy. The objectives of Mobil's energy research efforts were to improve technology for finding and extracting current energy resources and to find viable alternatives to petroleum-based energy.

Mobil held proved and probable coal reserves of 4.3 billion tons located in Wyoming, Montana, North Dakota, Colorado, and Illinois. The company first commenced shipments from a mine near Gillette, Wyoming, in late 1982. Production from the mine was soon expected to reach 2.5 million tons annually.

Initially, coal was thought to be a very attractive alternative if it could be economically liquefied or gasified for transportation through the oil industry's huge pipeline system. The major oil companies had, accordingly, increased their ownership of coal reserves since 1970. By the early 1980s, however, serious doubts remained about whether coal liquefication and gasification would ever become economical.

Mobil was a majority shareholder in a venture that began exploration for coal

**Exhibit 23.11** Nonpetroleum Earnings, 1979–1983 (millions)

|  | 1979 | 1980 | 1981 | 1982 | 1983 |
|---|---|---|---|---|---|
| Chemicals | $ 113 | $ 119 | $ 93 | $ 24 | $ 8 |
| Paperboard packaging | 40 | 71 | 57 | 24 | 1 |
| Retail merchandising | 54 | (162) | (160) | (93) | 40 |
| Total | $ 207 | $ 28 | $ (10) | $ (45) | $ 49 |

*Source:* "Company Analysis: Mobil Corporation," Donaldson, Lufkin & Jenrette, March 20, 1984.

in Indonesia in 1983. In Australia, the company was involved in coal exploration, as well, and held reserves of 60 million tons through a joint venture.

The company had had a significant position in oil shale lands for many years and was active in shale research. No commercial oil shale operations had yet begun, however.

In New Zealand, a Mobil synthetic fuel plant, which would manufacture gasoline from locally produced natural gas, was expected to come on stream in late 1985.

Mobil had, as well, devoted considerable effort to researching solar technology. Mobil Solar Energy Corporation, a wholly owned subsidiary, planned to build a solar-powered desalination plant in Abu Dhabi. Mobil Tyco Solar Energy Corporation, another subsidiary, was meanwhile involved in the production of solar panels for use in the residential consumer market.

Mobil held proved and probable uranium reserves of 33.5 million pounds, and sold 207,000 pounds of uranium domestically during 1983.

## NONENERGY DIVERSIFICATION

Mobil's diversification into areas outside of petroleum included operations involving chemicals, real estate, paperboard packaging, and retail merchandising. Like some of the other major oil companies, Mobil found it difficult to achieve profit margins in these businesses which approached those of its core business. In 1983, for instance, Mobil netted just $49 million in net income out of $10 billion in revenues from chemicals, paperboard packaging, and retail merchandising. (See Exhibit 23.11.)

## Chemicals

The Mobil Chemical Company was formed in 1960 to bring the company's worldwide chemical business into one integrated operating division. This division was equipped with its own research and development, manufacturing, and marketing facilities. The primary domestic facilities produced basic petrochemicals such as ethylene, propylene, and butadiene, and aromatics such as benzene and toluene.

Mobil's strategy in chemicals was said to be one of concentrating on selected areas of business with good growth opportunities, primarily in those fields where the company already had a strong competitive position and could profit from its structural integration and traditional expertise. In addition, Mobil Chemical used much of its output of basic petrochemicals in other manufacturing operations. This large degree of internal utilization made the company somewhat less sensitive to the fluctuations of the petrochemical market.

The company owned or had interest in 63 facilities located in ten countries. Mobil's principal chemical products included plastics used in the home and in packaging by industry; basic petrochemicals sold to producers of plastics, synthetic fibers, and other chemical products; phosphate rock and di-ammonium phosphate products sold to fertilizer producers; coatings used in packaging, furniture, shipping, and maintenance applications; and specialty industrial chemicals. Brand names identifying Mobil's chemical products included Hefty, Kordite, and Baggies.

Mobil Chemical was, in fact, the largest manufacturer of plastic packaging in the United States, producing such products as garbage bags, food bags, bread wrapping, and industrial packaging. Another highly successful product of the plastics division was polystyrene foam, which was used in the manufacture of egg cartons, fast-food containers, and disposable tableware. There had also been considerable growth in sales of a product called Mobilrap, which was a heavy-duty polyethylene stretch film used to wrap pallet loads for industrial distribution.

Mobil also produced oriented polypropylene (OPP) under the brand name BICOR, which was a packaging-film replacement for cellophane. This product was receiving rapid acceptance because of its lower cost and higher quality as a cellophane substitute. Mobil was the world's largest producer of this fabricated plastic, and had OPP manufacturing plants in the United States, Canada, and Europe.

Mobil had attained leadership in the field of high-performance chemical coatings, and was the third largest U.S. producer of phosphate rock as well.

The company's chemical earnings were barely break-even in 1983, partly because of $23 million of preoperating expenses related to the Saudi petrochemical facility.

## Real Estate

Mobil made its first significant real estate investment in 1966 when it moved its Hong Kong terminal, thereby vacating a choice 40-acre site. Mobil decided to build a huge middle-class apartment complex rather than sell the land for an estimated $15 million. This complex was completed in 1979 and housed more than 70,000 people.

In 1970, a management team was formed to explore further opportunities in real estate. The company's first U.S. purchase was a residential community comprised of 3300 bay-front acres near San Francisco.

Early in 1977, Mobil began bidding for southern California's Irvine Co., which was the owner of America's largest real estate development. Beginning with an offer of $24 per share (or $202 million), Mobil finally bid more than $336 million for the property before losing out to a private group which included Henry Ford

II, John Irvin Smith, Max M. Fisher (a Detroit industrialist), and others. In July 1978, Mobil purchased the undeveloped half of Reston, Virginia, from Gulf Oil for over $30 million. Gulf previously had sizable interests in real estate, but later divested itself completely of these projects. Gulf maintained that they were not closely enough related to the company's basic business and that they had not made a meaningful contribution to corporate profits.

The majority of Mobil's real estate was owned by Mobil Land Development Company, a nonconsolidated subsidiary located in San Francisco. Mobil's holdings were generally large tracts of land strategically located in high-growth areas and were well suited to large-scale communities of at least 1000 homes.

Despite these investments, real estate remained a relatively minor part of Mobil's overall operations.

## Marcor

In 1968, Mobil made a decision to diversify outside of the energy business in a significant way. A diversification study team was formed to analyze various industries and select individual companies as possible candidates for acquisition. Mobil's objective was not to become a large conglomerate, but to acquire one major diversification subsidiary. Mobil's Rawleigh Warner, Jr., commented on Mobil's motivation: "We had become aware that governments would interfere with our business. We thought they would be oil-producing countries, not consuming nations. But after the oil embargo we realized that the consuming nations would also pay a greater role. That impelled us forward with the diversification program."[26]

Senior management established certain criteria for any potential acquisitions. These criteria required that any company being considered have a strong management team, considerable experience in its own field, good earnings growth and rate of return possibilities, different business cycles and business risks from the oil industry, and a strong competitive position within its own markets.

After reviewing over 100 companies in a five-year period, Mobil began looking very closely at Marcor, Inc., a holding company formed in 1968 which consisted of two main subsidiaries, Montgomery Ward and Container Corp. Montgomery Ward was a retailer in the United States, and Container Corp. was the largest U.S. producer of paperboard packaging.

In 1973, Mobil bought 4.5 percent of Marcor's stock for an average cost of $23 per share. When the Arab oil embargo hit, the stock market fell sharply and oil prices skyrocketed. By 1974, Mobil had a lot of extra cash on hand, and Marcor's stock looked like more of a bargain than ever. In August 1974, Mobil made a tender offer for shares that would give it a majority interest in the smaller company. The price at that time was still below $25 per share. Marcor's price per share rose sharply that same year. Later in 1974, three Marcor executives were elected to Mobil's board of directors, and four officers of Mobil, including Warner and Tavoulareas, were elected directors of Marcor.

In July 1976, Mobil bought the rest of Marcor. The 1976 Annual Report contained the following message to the stockholders: "By merging with Ward and

Container, Mobil effectively realized its major diversification objective. Both firms are extremely well managed and have the growth potential to contribute materially to Mobil's U.S. based earnings. They helped Mobil to increase significantly the percentage of total earnings produced in the U.S. Moreover, they operate in business areas with different cycles and risks from oil's and are not subject to the vagaries of oil industry regulation."[27]

During the period of acquisition, Mobil drew considerable criticism from members of Congress and the Federal Energy Administration (FEA). John C. Sawhill, chief of the FEA, who had previously defended higher oil profits as necessary for capital investment in domestic exploration and production, said the Mobil offer to acquire controlling interest in Marcor was "like having a wet dishrag thrown in your face." Walter F. Mondale (D-Minn.) said in July 1974 that the proposed acquisition "is the best sign yet that the oil industry is engaged in a desperate search for ways in which to get rid of embarrassingly high profits. [It] lends substantial weight to the wisdom of repealing the oil depletion allowance immediately."[28] Senator Thomas J. McIntyre (D-N.H.) called the acquisition plan "irresponsibility at its worst."[29]

Warner's reply to the criticism that the Marcor acquisition siphoned off cash which should have been used in exploration and production (E&P) was that Mobil was already exploiting as many E&P opportunities as it could find.

While Mobil never revealed the total price for Marcor, it was estimated that it must have paid about $1.8 billion, spending around $800 million for the first 54 percent in 1973 and 1974. Mobil put $200 million of cash directly into Marcor's treasury in exchange for new preferred stock, but maintained that it had no plans to pump additional capital into the retailing chain. Ward was definitely expected to pull its own weight, and Mobil emphasized that its new subsidiary would be granted operational autonomy in the conduct of its business.

Although the Marcor acquisition was seen by some analysts as one of the boldest diversification efforts by a major oil company into a nonenergy field, some oil people viewed the acquisition as overly conservative. One oil executive said: "They were far ahead with the idea, but maybe they were too timid. Why not diversify into drugs, instruments, office equipment, electronics, or computers—all of which have higher rates of return?"[30] By 1980, Mobil's management was admitting that the scenario surrounding Marcor had not panned out as they had predicted. "We probably wouldn't buy Marcor this year, right now," conceded Tavoulareas.[31]

In order to maintain Montgomery Ward's bond rating in 1980, Mobil was forced to pump $200 million into the company. Mobil took great care to label the transaction an interest-free loan. At year-end 1980, Montgomery Ward showed a loss of $162 million. Early in 1981, Mobil granted the retailer an additional $155 million in interest-free loans. Earnings, however, continued to deteriorate. (See Exhibit 23.12.)

A 1983 turnaround at Montgomery Ward was attributed to rising retail sales, lower interest rates, more sophisticated merchandising techniques, and cost savings related primarily to a reduction in the number of employees. Credit was also

**Exhibit 23.12** Montgomery Ward Earnings, 1979–1983 (millions)

| 1979 | 1980 | 1981 | 1982 | 1983 |
|------|------|------|------|------|
| $54 | $(162) | $(160) | $(93) | $40 |

*Source:* Mobil Corporation Annual Reports, 1981–1983.

**Exhibit 23.13** Container Corporation Funds Flow (millions)

|  | 1979 | 1980 | 1981 | 1982 | 1983 |
|--|------|------|------|------|------|
| Funds from operations | $128 | $141 | $147 | $117 | $100E |
| Capital expenditures | 116 | 141 | 206 | 229 | 132 |
| Surplus (deficiency) | $12 | $0 | $(59) | $(112) | $(32) |

*Source:* "Company Analysis: Mobil Corporation," Donaldson, Lufkin & Jenrette, March 20, 1984.

widely given to the guidance of Stephen Pistner, who became chief executive of Ward in 1981.

Results at Marcor's Container Corporation of America, meanwhile, were less than encouraging. Though the paperboard packaging firm showed a $1 million profit in 1983, had gains on sales of properties been excluded, Container Corp. would actually have shown a loss. Moreover, the company had proved to be a drain on capital to Mobil for several years. (See Exhibit 23.13.)

Mobil's 1983 annual report stressed that a management reorganization, major cost-cutting programs, and the introduction of more efficient labor practices were expected to lay the groundwork for better margins at Container Corp. in the years ahead.

## PUBLIC RELATIONS

Beginning in the early 1970s, Mobil developed a public relations strategy which was outspoken, controversial, and decidedly atypical compared with other members of the conservative and usually silent oil industry. This strategy did not appear to have resulted from any single decision by senior management. Rather, "Mobil's 'high profile' operation developed gradually," according to *Fortune* magazine, "in response to an increasingly perceived need for the company to become more visible and articulate."[32]

By the late 1970s, Mobil was also well known for its efforts to sponsor and promote cultural events on both public and commercial television networks. Its first grant was made in 1970 to launch the very successful "Masterpiece Theatre."

Another facet of Mobil's public relations strategy was revealed in the company's willingness to address "issue-oriented" or "advocacy" questions in the media. While much of its advocacy advertising was aimed at problems within the oil industry, Mobil also editorialized on other controversial issues which the company thought were of national interest. Mobil was quick to attack any treatment of the oil industry (by the media or the government) which it perceived as unfair. At the same time, many of its views were somewhat surprising when first aired. For example, the endorsement of an effective mass-transit policy for the nation's large metropolitan areas initially surprised many observers. At one time or another, Mobil's readiness to defend its interests had led it into extended public conflicts with such powerful media forces as the CBS and ABC television networks, the *Washington Post,* and the *Wall Street Journal.* Mobil had also not hesitated to break ranks with the other members of the oil industry on particularly sensitive issues, such as the question of oil price controls.

## MOBIL ON THE PROWL

Throughout the late seventies and early eighties, Mobil redirected its exploration and production efforts toward properties in North America. At the same time, Mobil made repeated attempts to bolster its paltry domestic reserves through acquisition—attempts which met with mixed success.

## General Crude Oil Co.

Mobil entered the high-stakes bidding war for General Crude Oil Co. (a subsidiary of International Paper) in the spring of 1979. Gulf had originally reached a tentative agreement to buy General Crude's oil and gas operations, but was later outbid by a joint offer from Tenneco and Southland Royalty Co. Mobil offered in March 1979 to buy the operations for $765 million, thus topping the previous offer. General Crude's reserves, located primarily in the United States, were said to approach 160 million barrels. Mobil eventually raised its offer, and a sale for $792 million was completed in July 1979.

## Belridge Oil Co.

In May 1979, Belridge Oil Co. let it be known that it was actively seeking a merger with a large oil company. Mobil, the largest single shareholder with 18 percent, was thought to have an inside track. Belridge attracted a good deal of interest. This was due in part to Belridge's substantial proven reserves, mostly heavy crude located in California. Some speculated, however, that the interest in Belridge was better explained by the company's vast and largely unexplored reserves of light, high-quality oil located in deep geologic formations. A group of big oil companies (which included Mobil) lost out on the bid for the closely held target to Shell Oil, which ultimately purchased Belridge for $3.6 billion. Mobil, in turn, sold its interest in Belridge in January 1980.

## Texas Pacific Oil Co.

Some months later, Sun Oil bid $2.3 billion for the U.S. oil and gas properties of Texas Pacific Oil, a subsidiary of Joseph E. Seagram & Sons, Inc. Texas Pacific was one of the nation's five largest nonintegrated petroleum producers, with proven U.S. reserves of 120 million barrels of oil and 300 billion cubic feet of natural gas. Sun's bid was a record for proven reserves, and amounted to $12 per barrel. Despite a last-minute, secret effort by Mobil to bid for the properties, Sun and Seagram signed a definitive agreement. Mobil was said to have offered to match Sun's price, but with different terms.

## TransOcean Oil

TransOcean Oil was the exploration unit of Vickers Energy Group, which in turn was a subsidiary of Esmark, Inc. In the summer of 1980, Mobil successfully bid $715 million for TransOcean, which owned considerable property in the Overthrust Belt in the Rockies. The deal was structured so that Esmark would be free of capital gains tax. To accomplish this, Mobil bought Esmark common stock, then swapped those shares with Esmark for TransOcean shares—a tax-free transaction. This arrangement was said to have saved Esmark some $100 million in capital gains taxes.

## Conoco

In July 1981, Mobil made a $7.7 billion tender offer for slightly more than 50 percent of the stock of Conoco, Inc. Mobil thus became Conoco's third major suitor, along with E. I. du Pont de Nemours & Co. and Seagram. Mobil's offer was immediately rebuffed. Conoco filed an antitrust suit against Mobil, while continuing to press for a du Pont merger.

Mobil continued to press its attack, however, quickly raising its offer to $8.2 billion, and later $8.82 billion. Conoco was an attractive target to crude-short Mobil. Conoco offered stable and abundant acreage, half of which was located in the United States and the remainder in Europe and Canada. Moreover, a Mobil-Conoco merger would more than double Mobil's interest in the North Sea's Statfjord field.

In response to continued reference to possible antitrust violations, Mobil offered to dispose of certain U.S. marketing operations in order to speed the purchase.

Ultimately, Mobil lost out to du Pont when a federal appeals court refused to issue a temporary restraining order to delay a du Pont deal. Mobil had been spurned again, despite a final offer which was $1.28 billion more than du Pont's.

## Marathon

In the fall of the same year, still smarting from the failed Conoco takeover attempt, Mobil made a $5.1 billion ($85 a share) bid for Marathon Oil. Like Conoco, Marathon held reserves in politically secure areas. Marathon, the nation's seventeenth largest oil company, actually offered greater reserves in the United States and Canada than did Conoco. A merger with Marathon at Mobil's bid price would have yielded oil and gas reserves at an equivalent of less than $3 a barrel. Moreover, such a merger would boost Mobil's U.S. oil reserves by some 80 percent.

Though Mobil had structured its offer so as to entice Marathon stockholders to tender their shares quickly, Mobil's bid was immediately stalled by a court restraining order. That gave Marathon time to search for a white knight (or friendly suitor). Marathon managed to secure a $100 a share offer from U.S. Steel (subsequently raised to $106 a share).

In a last-ditch effort to salvage the merger attempt, Mobil announced plans to purchase as much as 25 percent of the outstanding stock of U.S. Steel, its rival bidder. Industry observers questioned the sincerity of Mobil's threat. Though many labeled the announcement scare tactics, others speculated that a future attempt to buy all of U.S. Steel was not out of the question. Were that to happen, Mobil would pick up massive mineral reserves and could conceivably write down the target company's steel mills, using the loss to shield oil profits.

In order to counter antitrust concerns in the Marathon takeover bid, Mobil offered to bid jointly for Marathon with Amerada Hess. Mobil would then sell Amerada Hess all of Marathon's existing marketing, refining, and transportation properties. A lower court rejected this plan, however.

Though Mobil eventually raised its offer for Marathon to slightly above the U.S. Steel bid, it finally lost out to the steel company when the U.S. Supreme Court rejected a Mobil appeal. Mobil officials would not rule out a run at U.S. Steel in the future, however.

## Anschutz

In 1982, Mobil acquired a working interest in certain domestic oil and gas reserves and exploration acreage from the Anschutz Corporation. Industry sources estimated the purchase price exceeded $500 million. The acquisition was said to net Mobil some 100 million barrels of oil from a giant field located in Utah and straddling the southwestern corner of Wyoming. Mobil was also said to have received 250,000 acres of undeveloped exploration leases elsewhere. A report from one investment broker called the Anschutz field "potentially one of the most significant finds in North America since the Prudhoe Bay discovery" on the North Slope of Alaska.[33] It was expected that the Anschutz field would be expensive to develop, however.

It had earlier been reported that Anschutz had been seeking a buyer for part of its interest in the field because it was in need of more money to develop the property.

While adding significantly to Mobil's reserves, the acquisition reflected a desire on Mobil's part to bolster its domestic reserves through private, friendly transactions. Mobil thus avoided many of the antitrust complications which hindered earlier takeover attempts.

## Superior

Having twice failed to acquire an integrated oil firm, in March 1984 Mobil turned its attentions to Superior Oil Company, the nation's largest independent. Industry experts viewed Mobil's interest in Superior as a calculated effort to avoid the antitrust accusations of Mobil's previous attempts. Superior owned neither gasoline stations nor refineries. It did possess, however, vast reserves in the United States and Canada.

A Mobil-Superior merger would increase Mobil's U.S. and Canadian oil reserves by 15 percent and 48 percent respectively. Growth in natural gas reserves would be even more dramatic, with U.S. reserves increasing by 29 percent and Canadian reserves by 92 percent. In fact, Superior's 1983 reserve increases would more than offset Mobil's 1983 reserve declines.

In sharp contrast to its maverick reputation, Mobil's strategy in attempting a takeover of Superior was uncharacteristically couched in secrecy and aimed at achieving a friendly deal. Mobil officials first met with members of the founding Keck family, who owned 22 percent of Superior. Mobil's management knew that the Keck family members, who had recently been fighting among themselves, were willing to sell. Mobil offered them $45 a share and received their agreement to make the purchase for the Keck's 22 percent share. While negotiating with the Kecks, Mobil was simultaneously attempting to strike a deal with Superior's top executives.

On March 11, Mobil made public its agreement with the Kecks and announced its intention to purchase the remaining shares at the same $45 price. The total bid of $5.7 billion would make this deal the fifth largest oil merger in history. Mobil would gain reserves of about one billion barrels of oil and oil equivalent at a price of less than $6 a barrel.

## CONCLUSION

Counting up this list of recent Mobil acquisition attempts, Collier continued to feel somewhat frustrated by his company's apparent strategy. He had to admit, however, that over the past 15 years Mobil had become more than just an oil and gas firm. "Maybe it's not so bad after all," he thought to himself, shutting his briefcase and reaching for his coat. "Could be that all these merger attempts really signal a move back toward an emphasis on E&P."

### NOTES

1. "The 500 Largest U.S. Industrial Corporations," *Fortune*, April 30, 1984, pp. 276–277. (As measured by *Fortune*, "total return to investors" includes both price appreciation and dividend yield to an investor in the company's stock.)
2. "How to Rob Peter . . . ," *Forbes*, June 15, 1969, pp. 30–31.
3. "New Mobil Pro Ad Campaign Stresses Expertise in Industrial Lubricants," *Industrial Marketing*, August 1978, p. 22.
4. "What Makes Mobil Run," *Business Week*, June 13, 1977, pp. 80–85.
5. Ibid.
6. "Mobil's Maverick: Tavoulareas Puts Firm on a Separate Course from Most of Big Oil," *Wall Street Journal*, February 14, 1980, p. 18.
7. "Mobil Reshuffle Aims at Cost-Cutting," *National Petroleum News*, September 1973, p. 145.
8. "Mobil's Costly Saudi Strategy," *Business Week*, October 17, 1983, p. 76.
9. Ibid.

10. "Mobil's Successful Exploration," *Business Week,* October 13, 1980, p. 112.
11. Ibid.
12. "The Lively Tortoise," *Forbes,* August 1, 1971, pp. 18–19.
13. "What Makes Mobil Run," pp. 80–85.
14. "Mobil's Costly Saudi Strategy," p. 76.
15. Ibid.
16. Ibid.
17. "Research Brief, Mobil Corporation," Goldman Sachs, April 1, 1981.
18. "Mobil's Successful Exploration," p. 112.
19. "Mobil's Spending to Concentrate on Regions in North America," *Oil and Gas Journal,* February 20, 1984, p. 33.
20. "Mobil's Costly Saudi Strategy," p. 76.
21. "Company Analysis: Mobil Corporation," Donaldson, Lufkin & Jenrette, March 20, 1984.
22. "Mobil's Spending to Concentrate on Regions in North America," p. 33.
23. "How to Rob Peter . . . ," pp. 30–31.
24. "Mobil One-Ups Others with Debit Card System," *National Petroleum News,* December 1983, p. 29.
25. "Mobil Wants to Be Your Milkman," *Forbes,* February 13, 1984, p. 44.
26. "Big Oil's Move into Retailing," *Chain Store Executive,* September 1976, pp. 29–32.
27. Mobil Annual Report, 1976.
28. "Congressional Barbs Hit Mobil-Marcor Deal," *Oil and Gas Journal,* July 1, 1974, p. 32.
29. Ibid.
30. "The New Diversifications Oil Game," *Business Week,* April 24, 1978, pp. 76–88.
31. "Mobil's Successful Exploration," p. 112.
32. Irwin Ross, "Public Relations Isn't Kid-Glove Stuff at Mobil," *Fortune,* September 19, 1976, pp. 106–202.
33. "Mobil Buys Part of Utah Oil Field from Anschutz," *Wall Street Journal,* August 12, 1982, p. 2.

# 24  Kerr-McGee Corporation

Roger M. Atherton
Northeastern University

Mark W. Bushell
University of Oklahoma

It certainly had been a terrific half century. Rising out of the red dust of Oklahoma in the 1920s as a small oil company, Kerr-McGee Corporation had by 1981 sprouted into a $3.8-billion-dollar energy resource business. Kerr-McGee (KM) was different from the many other oil industry hopefuls because the company almost from the beginning had envisioned itself not just as an oil company but as one whose business was the development of natural resources. Oil was still Kerr-McGee's primary business, but its leadership had had the early foresight to push into other resources such as coal, uranium, chemicals, and timber. Dean A. McGee had led the company as either president or CEO for the last four decades. Without a doubt he was one of the most respected businessmen in America in 1981, but McGee would turn 78 years old in 1982. Trained as a geologist and mining engineer, McGee had skillfully guided the company into being one of the strongest midsized integrated oil companies in the market.

Experts agreed that the petroleum industry had reached the threshold of a new frontier where stiffened macroeconomic conditions, increased competition, and slackened demand promised to weed out the weaker competitors either through liquidation or takeovers. Kerr-McGee has been a favorite of takeover speculators because of its financial strength and its expansive and profitable resource base. In 1982, Kerr-McGee was faced with having to give birth to a new management as well as having to determine a strategic response to this new industry environment. Taken together, these events promised that the next few years would be crucial. Kerr-McGee's basic strategy—to develop natural resources—had been sound in the past because of its ability to generate cash from its petroleum operations to fund ventures into other resource markets. Since this cash would be more difficult to obtain in the future, the strategic issue had become one of deciding where to focus resources so that the next 50 years would be as good as the first.

This case was written by Mark W. Bushell of the University of Oklahoma and by Professor Roger M. Atherton of Northeastern University. The primary sources of information were *Value Line*, April 16, 1982, and Kerr-McGee Annual Reports 1978, 1979, 1980, and 1981. It was prepared as a basis for class discussion rather than to illustrate either effective or ineffective handling of an administrative situation.

Copyright © 1983 by Roger M. Atherton.

**PETROLEUM**  Petroleum had been Kerr-McGee's bread and butter since the beginning. In 1981 petroleum exploration, production, refining, and marketing accounted for 77 percent of sales and 72 percent of net income (see Exhibit 24.1).

The majority of KM's petroleum exploration and production expenditures had been concentrated in the fields in the Gulf of Mexico. This particular area has been the most active in the world in terms of number of producing wells and was considered mature with limited growth potential. KM had only recently expanded extensive exploration efforts into the less-developed areas in the North Sea, Arabian Gulf, and offshore Indonesia. In land-based operations, KM was drilling in Texas, Oklahoma, Louisiana, Wyoming, and North Dakota. KM's working interests in both offshore and land sites ranged from 5 percent to 100 percent, with the majority falling in the 50–65 percent range. Because of the risk and capital investment required for oil exploration and production, joint ventures were common.

Exhibit 24.2 indicates KM's oil and gas reserves. Using these reserves and KM's current production of 30,000 barrels a day, assuming no new oil is found, KM's estimated reserves would be depleted in about 13 years. For natural gas, KM's reserves would last about 10 years. (KM's 1981 oil production rate was 27,800

**Exhibit 24.1** Petroleum Products

|                   | 1978 | 1979 | 1980 | 1981 |
| ----------------- | ---- | ---- | ---- | ---- |
| % of total sales  | 76   | 76   | 76   | 77   |
| % of net income   | 68   | 84   | 63   | 72   |

**Exhibit 24.2** Proved Petroleum Reserves

|                                              | 1978    | 1979    | 1980    | 1981    |
| -------------------------------------------- | ------- | ------- | ------- | ------- |
| **Crude/nat. gas liquids (×1000 barrels)**   |         |         |         |         |
| Domestic                                     | 59,430  | 57,063  | 63,082  | 66,795  |
| Foreign                                      | 70,038  | 74,770  | 83,350  | 80,053  |
| Totals                                       | 129,468 | 131,833 | 146,432 | 146,848 |
| **Natural gas (billions of ft³)**            |         |         |         |         |
| Domestic                                     | 886     | 826     | 835     | 747     |
| Foreign                                      | 70      | 81      | 125     | 128     |
| Totals                                       | 956     | 907     | 960     | 875     |

**Exhibit 24.3** Capital Expenditures—Petroleum

|  | 1978 | 1979 | 1980 | 1981 |
|---|---|---|---|---|
| Expenditures (millions) | $ 142.1 | $ 282.8 | $ 426.4 | $ 513.0 |
| As a % of total KM expenditures | 53 | 73 | 81 | 85 |

barrels per day and *Value Line* estimated KM's 1984–1986 production would be closer to 42,000 barrels per day.)

KM's capital expenditures in its major line of business had increased dramatically over the last four years both in real terms and as a percentage of total capital expenditures within the company (see Exhibit 24.3).

KM's capital expenditures over the same period taken as a percentage of total sales have increased from 13 percent to 16 percent. These increases in expenditures represented KM's recent expansion into foreign exploration and acquisition of more domestic onshore and offshore leases, as well as the drilling and equipping of new wells. Additionally, part of these increases represented the four new rigs that were added to KM's contract drilling subsidiary, Transworld Drilling.

Industrywide, the approximate norm for capital expenditures as a percent of sales was about 9 percent. Exxon, the industry leader with sales of $108 billion in 1981, had historically committed about 9 percent, but was expected to increase capital outlays by 20 percent to about $130 billion in 1982.

KM also refined and marketed the oil it produced. In 1981, three crude-oil refineries were operating in the United States. Finished products flowed through either KM's chain of 1519 service stations or KM's wholly owned subsidiary, Triangle Refineries, Inc. Triangle sold gasoline and other distillates at the wholesale level to buyers through major pipeline and waterway terminals. Profits in this area had been off recently owing to low plant utilization rates. The current industry average utilization rate hovered around 74 percent. In 1981, KM's rate averaged 63 percent. In the three years prior to this, KM's plant utilization rates were 80%, 68%, and 62%, respectively. KM had been processing less oil because selling prices had not been high enough to make operations sufficiently profitable. According to the company, the lower profits in refining and marketing were due to narrower margins between crude-oil prices and refined-product prices. Although unit costs rise slightly with lower refinery utilization rates, the major reasons for variations in refinery and marketing profits have been margins. This was one line of business where KM performed extensive processing for consumer sales. At one time, Dean McGee had stated that KM's business definition would never take it into consumer markets. He then saw KM strictly as a company dedicated to getting the resource out of the ground and selling it to those whose expertise lay in the consumer distribution field.

The future did not look rosy for the refining industry as a whole. The industry suffered from severe overcapacity that was not expected to be utilized within the next five years. In the interim, success would depend both on increasing operating efficiencies through larger investments in applied technology and expanding production flexibility. In trying to extricate itself from some of the problems related to industry overcapacity, KM had recently tuned up two of its refineries to better meet changed market conditions (greater product flexibility). Additionally, these plants would better meet the upcoming federal requirements for production of more no-lead and low-lead gasolines as a percentage of total gasoline produced. KM hoped that these modifications, plus the application of more advanced methods of processing petroleum residuum (developed by KM), would improve their deteriorating position in a highly cyclical business, and leave the company more competitive in an increasingly price-sensitive market.

In the natural gas segment of the petroleum market, KM operated six processing plants in the United States with interests in 12 others in the United States and Canada. KM had done reasonably well in this segment of the market, and hopes were high that the continuing decontrol of gas wellhead prices would keep profits buoyant. This decontrol mechanism, begun under the Ford administration and formalized under the 1978 Natural Gas Policy Act (NGPA), mandated that certain gas prices would rise 15–20 percent per year until January 1, 1985, when controls would be lifted altogether. Some experts predicted that the price of $3 or so per thousand cubic feet would triple by the end of the decade. This legislation explained in part the enthusiastic search that continued unabated since decontrol began until the early part of 1982 when prices increased and demand dropped.

The demand for natural gas remained 12 percent under the 1973 peak. As the price of crude oil went up, industrial and private gas hookups increased substantially. However, with higher prices came conservation in all energy consumption, and gas consumers new and old burned their gas frugally and invested in more energy-efficient building designs. The overall result was more customers but less demand. Even more important, however, nearly every community in the United States had been tapped into gas pipelines, leaving very little room for growth through expanded service. In short, the market for natural gas in the United States had become saturated. Additionally, all those incentives discussed earlier with regard to the decontrol of wellhead prices had left utilities (primary users) and gas producers with bulging inventories that demand levels would not burn off for another two years. The business recession was also a major factor in the slowdown in the demand for gas. What precipitated out of this mixed bag of influences was that current short-run conditions would encourage producers to keep their reserves in the ground for the next several years because of excess inventory. In the long run, Kerr-McGee expected to see healthy, stable profits as the excess was burned off, crude-oil prices rose, and petroleum in general became more valuable.

KM's efforts in petroleum also took the form of contract offshore drilling. KM led the industry in shallow-water contract drilling, one of its strongest suits. KM's

Transworld Drilling Company had laid claim to a number of industry firsts including being the first company ever to drill a commercial well out of sight of land (1947). The company also developed the first semisubmersible rig (1955) and pioneered floating platforms that could perform double duty as a drilling rig and processing station (1974). In 1981, the company owned 23 rigs with three more under construction for delivery in 1982. Exhibit 24.4 charts Transworld's progress over the four-year period.

Contract drilling was one of the important segments of the petroleum industry. As current fields were drained and the price of petroleum increased, there would be intense efforts to both find new oil and develop ways to get more oil out of the wells that had already been drilled. In the offshore-drilling business, this search would be especially profitable for those contract firms which had the expertise to secure long-term contracts with larger oil companies and the reputation for completing contracted wells. KM had demonstrated a real talent for operating on the leading edge of drilling technology. Given this and KM's sound reputation, KM was in an excellent position to maintain its market share in a growing market.

By 1982 the oil industry was feeling the pinch of decreased demand and increased supply. It was argued by many that the industry had indeed reached an inflection point in its growth curve because of the enhanced societal value of energy conservation and the increased usage of alternative fuels. The loss to energy conservation is shown in Exhibit 24.5, which compares 1978 demand to that in 1981 for various classes of users.

Exhibit 24.5 shows that homeowners and business people (residential/business) were the quickest to adjust their thermostats and the designs of their homes and offices to the rising price of petroleum. If anything, this −38 percent figure understates the true effect because of the higher demand during this period attributed to two unusually harsh winters. The loss in utilities' demand followed closely behind, dropping 37 percent. This too can be considered relatively permanent as this loss represented conversions to coal-generated energy processes. It was expected that this particular loss would probably grow if petroleum prices were to go up and new ways were devised to make coal a cleaner source of energy. In the transportation sector, more efficient automobile, truck, and aircraft power plants had significantly reduced demand. As more older, less efficient engines were replaced in the coming years, this loss could also be expected to grow. *Value*

**Exhibit 24.4** Transworld

|  | 1978 | 1979 | 1980 | 1981 | 1982 |
|---|---|---|---|---|---|
| No. of rigs | 18 | 18 | 19 | 23 | 26 |
| % of utilization | 99.6 | 97.6 | 98.7 | 96.0 | — |

**Exhibit 24.5** Petroleum Demand ($\times$ 1000 barrels)

| Segment | 1978 | 1981 | % Change |
|---|---|---|---|
| Transportation | 9450 | 8510 | −9 |
| Utilities | 1800 | 1160 | −37 |
| Residential/business | 2960 | 1810 | −38 |
| Industrial | 3700 | 3690 | — |
| Totals | 17910 | 15170 | −16 |

*Line* believed that, although the coming economic recovery would increase demand somewhat, it was reasonable to assume that most of the losses due to conservation and alternative fuels were permanent.

This is not to imply that oil would no longer be black gold. Oil was a scarce resource that was rapidly getting more scarce. However, the environment had changed. Oil would become increasingly more valuable but not by the leaps and bounds projected earlier. Equally important, the current projection that interest rates would remain stubbornly high throughout the rest of the decade (see *Business Week,* April 12, 1982, cover story) meant that the costs and risks inherent to the industry would be higher. Even more importantly from the perspective of the oil industry, banks and lending institutions would draw harder lines on who would and who would not be able to get capital for expansion. As a result, the players that currently made up the industry would decrease in number in favor of those cost-conscious firms which could effectively balance their bread-and-butter operations with their capital ventures. Acquisitions would become increasingly popular as the reserves of small companies became more valuable and they were less financially able to get it out of the ground because of increasing production costs and higher risks.

Exhibit 24.6 shows *Value Line* figures on how KM stacked up against some of its competitors in the petroleum industry in 1981.

**CHEMICALS**

As the second largest division in Kerr-McGee's natural resource business, Kerr-McGee Chemical Corporation manufactured industrial chemicals, fertilizer raw materials, and specialty chemical products. Industrial products included manganese, sodium chlorate (used in the paper industry), boron, soda ash (used in making glass), salt cake, manganese dioxide (for dry-cell batteries), ammonium perchlorate, and titanium dioxide (pigment used in paints). Despite the recession at that time, prices for the majority of these products had kept pace with cost increases. Concurrently, KM had kept most of these lines profitable through

**Exhibit 24.6** *Value Line* Competitive Analysis

| Firm | Present Value Proven Res.[a] | Production (daily)[b] | Sales[a] | Labor Cost % Sales | Employees | RONW (%) | Projected RONW 1984–1986 (%) |
|---|---|---|---|---|---|---|---|
| Exxon | $ 72035 | 3900 | $ 108108 | 5.3 | 180000 | 19.5 | 16.0 |
| Gulf | 25969 | 615 | 38252 | 6.4 | 58500 | 12.3 | 12.5 |
| Diamond Shamrock | 1372 | NA | 3376 | 11.0 | 13500 | 9.0 | 21.0 |
| Kerr-McGee | 2786 | 28 | 3826 | 6.0 | 11200 | 14.1 | 14.5 |
| Murphy Oil | 3532 | NA | 2447 | 6.0 | 4800 | 20.5 | 16.0 |
| Pennzoil | 2790 | 37 | 2682 | 11.0 | 10100 | 19.2 | 21.5 |
| Phillips | 14884 | 409 | 15966 | 8.0 | 34500 | 16.0 | 17.0 |
| Tesoro Oil | 639 | 25 | 3035 | 3.0 | 5300 | 18.0 | 17.5 |

[a]In millions.
[b]Thousands of barrels.

intensive cost-control programs. In early 1982, the company shut down most of the old Trona plant in Searles Valley, California, citing equipment and process obsolescence, high energy consumption, and high maintenance costs. This shutdown effectively halved Kerr-McGee's total production capacity for soda ash and would cost the company an estimated $17 million (one-time charge) against earnings.

Kerr-McGee produced chemically treated railroad ties, utility poles, and hardwood pallets from the company's 265,000 or so acres of timber in the Ohio and Mississippi river valleys. Interestingly enough, Kerr-McGee was the nation's second largest supplier of railroad ties. Sales in this area had been off recently because railroads had postponed maintenance work because of the recession. Sales were expected to reach normal levels as the economy headed toward recovery. Because of the age of the many miles of track in place, Kerr-McGee expected this niche to remain highly profitable through the end of the century.

Exports of industrial products and fertilizers to Europe, South America, Japan, and other Pacific Basin countries represented about a fifth of division sales. Kerr-McGee considered this a potential growth market. It used agents and distributors to push KM products further into existing markets and lay the groundwork for expansion into new markets. Exhibit 24.7 tracks exports over the last four years in terms of percentage of total KM chemical sales and tonnage exported.

Exhibits 24.8, 24.9, and 24.10 summarize production, sales, and capital expenditures as they apply to the chemical manufacturing division.

For 1982, net profits promised lackluster performance primarily due to the $17 million loss resulting from the Trona plant closure. Owing to poor demand in other product lines, KM Chemical was not expected to be able to overcome this loss.

**Exhibit 24.7** Exports—Chemical Corporation

|  | 1978 | 1979 | 1980 | 1981 |
|---|---|---|---|---|
| % of sales | 35[a] | 18 | 20 | 15 |
| Thous. of tons | 1200 | 860 | 583 | 1000 |

[a]Due to the weakness of the dollar which made U.S. goods particularly attractive overseas.

**Exhibit 24.8** Production History

|  | 1978 | 1979 | 1980 | 1981 |
|---|---|---|---|---|
| Industrial ($\times 1000$ tons) | 1168 | 1327 | 1434 | 1627 |
| Agricultural ($\times 1000$ tons) | 1855 | 1880 | 2005 | 1557 |
| Forest Products ($\times 1000$ board ft) | N/A[a] | 283 | 292 | 325 |

[a]N/A—not available.

**Exhibit 24.9** Chemical Corporation Sales/Profits

|  | 1978 | 1979 | 1980 | 1981 |
|---|---|---|---|---|
| Sales (millions) | $375 | $420 | $501 | $543 |
| Net profit margin (%) | 6.2 | 3.4 | 4.0 | 3.0 |
| Return on assets (%) | 3.9 | 2.3 | 3.1 | 2.4 |
| % of total KM sales | 18.1 | 14.2 | 14.4 | 15.6 |
| % of KM net income | 19.7 | 8.9 | 10.9 | 7.6 |

**Exhibit 24.10** Chemical Corporation Capital Expenditures

|  | 1978 | 1979 | 1980 | 1981 |
|---|---|---|---|---|
| Capital expenditures (millions) | $67 | $45.6 | $36.3 | $43.2 |
| % of total KM cap. exp. | 25 | 12 | 7 | 7 |

As a major part of the industry, industrial chemicals were taking a real beating as a result of the then-current global recession. Falling demand on almost all fronts and continued high interest rates had dragged industrial chemical profits to all-time lows. As a smaller competitor, KM competed against such giants as du Pont with 1981 sales reaching $21 billion and Dow Chemical with sales of $11 billion. KM's industrial chemicals cover a wide variety of products. Most of these products were tied to the manufacturing and construction sectors of the economy. Industrial chemical sales rely heavily on the strength of these particular industrial segments. Like many of the companies in these related manufacturing segments, capital expenditures in this part of the chemical industry had been reduced significantly. The principal reasons lined up behind a common problem found in today's marketplace—severe overcapacity. As a consequence of this and the lower demand levels, plant utilization rates had dropped to an average of 74 percent. Estimates showed that considerable market growth was required to move this figure up to the more reasonable rate of 85–90 percent. Equally distressing, foreign demand had fallen off significantly in the last few years. As domestic prices of oil and gas reached worldwide levels, American companies increasingly lost their competitive edge in terms of lower costs of production. (Petroleum normally comprises a significant portion of the raw materials used in producing these chemicals.) Obviously, the global recession had affected a part of this loss, but experts contended that the industry would experience some permanent loss in overseas demand.

For fertilizers, the industry news had gone from bad to worse. Fertilizers were marketed by over half of the companies that compete in the industrial chemical segment of the market. Several macroeconomic factors stood out as the biggest anchors holding this segment down. Domestic farm income was lower in real terms than at any time within the last 45 years. Although the return on investment of fertilizers in terms of bigger yields remained high, the combination of poor profits and high interest rates had precluded farmers from borrowing the necessary cash. On a global scale, demand for fertilizer had been negatively affected over the last few years as it became increasingly popular to use farm exports as political tools. Recent experience with the Soviet grain embargo pointed to the sensitivity of the food and fertilizer industries to political tinkering. Another aspect of this global demand as it applies to U.S. companies was the long-term effect on demand for U.S. fertilizers as American producers lost their lower-cost advantage. (Petroleum also makes up a significant portion of the raw materials used to produce fertilizer.) As with the industrial-chemical producers and their products, the leveling of U.S. petroleum prices to worldwide levels took away one production cost advantage U.S. companies had had over other overseas fertilizer producers.

The fertilizer industry had high hopes that these domestic and international problems would dissipate within the next two years as domestic farm income and interest rates improved significantly and worldwide demand increased as a result of the economic recovery. Certainly, food consumption would increase over the next 20 years as the earth's population grew larger. The key for the fertilizer industry was when this demand would turn into operating profits.

As a subsegment of the chemical industry, speciality chemical products historically had been resilient performers even in times of economic downturn. Currently, this could be seen in several companies that specialized in the very profitable segments dealing in oil-field specialty chemicals and specialty adhesives and sealants. The common denominator throughout this segment was the development and production of products (often proprietary) designed for a specific use. The companies competing in this market generally were not capital-intensive. This in part explained the ability of this segment to stand up against falling demand. Large sales organizations also distinguished this particular segment of the chemical industry. In some of the companies salespeople accounted for more than half the work force. KM did not market products in either specialty oil-field chemicals or specialty adhesives.

**COAL**   Consistent with its commitment to develop natural resources, Kerr-McGee began acquiring coal reserves back in 1957. In 1978, profitable coal production began near Gilette, Wyoming, with the opening of the Jacob's Ranch mine. Since then KM has increased production 700 percent and opened the Clovis Point mine 60 miles from Jacob's. In a move to further increase capacity, KM planned to open its first underground mine near Galatia, Illinois, in 1985. (Construction began in July 1981.) As is the case with many new mines, contracts have already been finalized to market the coal from the Galatia mine to coal-burning utility plants near St. Louis. In 1981 KM had coal reserves of 885 million tons in the Wyoming mines and the Illinois mine. Kerr-McGee also holds leases and fee lands in five other states. Widespread drilling has shown the presence of in-place resources of 2.3 billion tons. The company has also begun aggressive efforts to acquire additional reserves of low-sulfur coal. The selection criteria for these acquisitions included prime access to labor markets, transportation facilities, and utility consumers.

KM's Coal Corporation was both the smallest and the most profitable operating division in the company. Exhibit 24.11 provides data on production, sales, profit margins, and sales and net income as a percentage of overall company sales.

Within the coal industry KM was a small- to medium-sized competitor. Larger

**Exhibit 24.11** Coal

|  | 1978 | 1979 | 1980 | 1981 |
|---|---|---|---|---|
| Coal shipped (thous. of tons) | 1774 | 5067 | 10677 | 12380 |
| Sales (millions) | $14.9 | $50.5 | $101.2 | $128.9 |
| Profit margin (%) | 2.7 | 26.1 | 29.8 | 23.4 |
| Return on assets (%) | 0.5 | 12.1 | 23.9 | 22.2 |
| % of total KM sales | 1.0 | 1.9 | 2.9 | 3.4 |
| % of total KM net income | 0.3 | 8.3 | 16.5 | 14.3 |

producers such as North American Coal controlled significantly larger reserves (5.5 billion tons for North American versus 885 million for KM) and annually marketed about double of what KM did in 1981. In the area of critical-solvent technology, however, KM was the industry leader. Critical-solvent technology involves the process that removes ash, sulfur, and other impurities from coal so that it burns cleanly. The process KM developed was a spinoff of the same type of technology (which KM also pioneered) used in KM's oil refineries to get more product out of crude oil. Under a joint program with the U.S. Department of Energy and the Electric Power Research Institute, the applications of this breakthrough were successfully demonstrated in a pilot plant in Wilsonville, Alabama. Further research was being conducted in a coal liquefaction plant colocated with KM's nuclear facility in Cimarron, Oklahoma. In 1981 the International Coal Refining Company licensed KM's critical-solvent process to be used in the SRC-1 refinery, a government coal liquefaction demonstration plant.

The future for the coal industry looked promising indeed. Increasingly, utility companies in the United States and abroad were turning to coal-based energy generation schemes. In 1981, U.S. utilities used coal to generate 52.4 percent of all electric power compared with 50.8 percent in 1980, 50.5 percent in 1979, and 48 percent in 1978. Several new developments precipitated this trend and promised further gains in coal demand. First, there had been significant progress in developing technologies that processed coal without harming the atmosphere. Untreated coal is notorious in its effects on the atmosphere and indeed the entire environment. Solving these related problems in the past had been cost-prohibitive, but new breakthroughs in technology promised to lower this obstacle in the near future. Technology had also enabled companies to respond to the concerns brought on in the strip-mining process. It had been demonstrated that the land used in strip mining could be "returned" to the environment and, in many documented cases, left better in terms of a more balanced ecosystem.

A second development favoring coal was the rising price of petroleum and the stalled nuclear-energy industry. The petroleum pricing development had the most impact of all of the factors discussed. As oil prices increased, coal had become more attractive as an alternative. A subset of rising oil prices was the question of availability. The United States depended upon the middle East for a significant amount of the petroleum it consumed. Given the volatile politics that governed that area of the world, it is very possible that supply could be severed at any time either by a major war or by another embargo by OPEC. Whatever the case, some of the richest deposits of coal in the world rested within U.S. borders. The case to convert to coal seemed most compelling given the precarious situation from which a significant portion of U.S. oil flowed. There was a problem. The coal industry continued to demonstrate significant overcapacity. In numbers, this means the industry had the capacity to annually produce 100 million to 150 million tons of coal above the level of demand. Naturally, this overcapacity exerted a downward pressure on coal prices. In 1981, this meant that mines were not even considered for opening unless a large long-term sales contract had been signed for the coal still in the ground. It was simply too risky to commit the huge amounts of capital necessary to obtain the coal without the promise of a buyer. In this environment, the keys to success lay in securing long-term utilities contracts and employing technology and strong management to keep production costs down.

## URANIUM

Of all the major industries Kerr-McGee competed in, it was the leader in only one. Over the last 30 years KM had been one of the largest producers of uranium concentrates used by nuclear plants to generate power. In 1981, the industry was reeling from the effects of the Three-Mile Island incident, lagging energy demand, massive nuclear plant cost overruns, and increased government intervention. Of all the companies in the industry, KM was probably in the best position to weather the storm. KM had a substantial backlog of contracts for both uranium concentrates and conversion services. To cut costs, four of the eleven KM mines in New Mexico had been put on standby while three mines in Wyoming remained operating at minimum levels. Exhibit 24.12 shows KM's uranium production, sales, profit margins, and net income as a percentage of overall company sales and net income.

The longer-range projections for nuclear power and the uranium industry revolved around the relative permanency of the financial, environmental, and safety problems. There were 73 plants operating in the United States, with some 80 plants in various stages of construction. Purchase contracts and utility inventories were in place to cover needs until 1985. Additional purchases to replenish inventories and provide uranium for new plants point to a possible growth market in the late 1980s both in the United States and abroad. Additionally, KM anticipated that 45 percent of any additional power requirements for the 1980s and 1990s would be filled by nuclear power. The current market was forcing several competitors out of this business, thereby strengthening the market for those that

**Exhibit 24.12** Uranium

|  | 1978 | 1979 | 1980 | 1981 |
|---|---|---|---|---|
| Production (thousands of pounds) | 5261 | 5100 | 5200 | 5000 |
| Sales (millions) | 115.2 | 163.4 | 238.9 | 201.5 |
| Net profit margin (%) | 18.3 | — | 8.1 | 6.3 |
| Return on assets (%) | 7.8 | — | 6.3 | 4.2 |
| % of total KM sales | 5.6 | 6.1 | 6.9 | 5.2 |
| % of total KM net income | 17.9 | [a] | 10.6 | 6.1 |

[a]Net loss $1.1 million.

could afford to stay. Although some experts believed a turnaround in nuclear power and uranium demand was not likely until 1990, Kerr-McGee believed, as it did in 1952, that the use of nuclear power would continue to grow in the United States and abroad. Given KM's strength in the industry, it was hopeful of reaping the fruits of any growth that did occur.

**ORGANIZA-TION**

Kerr-McGee's most valuable asset was not even listed on the balance sheet. Dean A. McGee first came to the company in 1937 as chief geologist for $700 a month. Five years later, McGee took over the reins as CEO, a position he has held ever since. Under his tutelage, KM had successfully expanded from sales of $2 million in 1942 to $3.8 billion in 1981. Even critics praised McGee's uncanny ability to put the company in the right place at the right time. McGee's philosophy of management was best described by the man himself when he told one interviewer he believed in "pitching, not catching." KM followed this strategy closely, creating opportunities by shrewd acquisitions and expansions. For instance, in its role as an energy company in 1954, KM foresaw the potential in uranium. In 1981, KM was poised ready to reap the benefits of a choice made almost three decades past. Under Dean McGee, the current business cycle was not where KM planned; it was the long-range prognosis that KM spent its money on. KM's success reflected McGee's vision of KM as a company in the business of exploiting natural resources—finding them, processing them, and bringing them to the marketplace.

But KM had a problem. Dean McGee would turn 78 in 1982. In 1977, KM's annual report noted that a succession plan had been initiated. Two candidates were chosen by McGee and the board of directors as possible replacements. J. W. McKenny was in 1981 vice-chairman of the board (see KM organization chart, Exhibit 24.13). He was formerly vice-president of exploration. F. A. McPherson in 1981 was president of KM and has served as Vice President in charge of both coal and nuclear operations. Both men had been with KM throughout their careers and both were considered well qualified. McGee's selection of the two company men was predictable and expected. Replacing McGee would be no easy task, however. McGee was known throughout the business world as a man of remarkable vision. In 1974, *Dun's Review* rated KM as one of the five best managed companies in America, noting that KM best demonstrated the ability to move faster than inflation, outpace recession, and weather a crashing stock market. In 1981, the *Wall Street Transcript* selected Dean McGee as the Bronze award winner among chief executives of the domestic integrated oil companies and The American Petroleum Institute gave him a gold medal for distinguished achievement. In early 1982, the *Financial World* selected him for the 1982 CEO of the Year Certificate of Distinction for the petroleum industry.

Like most integrated oil companies which had interests in other resources or businesses, KM was managed divisionally. Unlike the others, however, KM had separated petroleum exploration from the oil and gas divisions, and likewise separated mineral exploration from the coal, nuclear, and chemical divisions. Given KM's success in discovering petroleum and minerals, one could justify this structure on results alone. The ramifications of such a structure, however, raised some interesting questions. Specifically, taking exploration control out of the hands of the operating divisions in some ways hamstrung the division directors as they turned their thinking to intermediate- and long-range planning. Basically, they had little control over how big their operation would get and how fast it would get there. Obviously, KM's operating division heads did not live in the dark and were kept reasonably well informed of the current plans of the exploration divisions. Yet it seemed to some that it was antithetical to separate exploration from those who must live with its results. Some have speculated that more than anything else this structure represented McGee's way of maintaining tight control over a diverse number of activities.

Major operating decisions were closely controlled by McGee. Recommendations on expansions, cutbacks, etc., were made to McGee through McPherson and McKenny. All major requests for expenditures were processed through the operating committee. Sometimes an issue would be taken to the operating committee for discussion. Additional inputs concerning market forecasts, government regulations, etc., were solicited from the staff. The final decision was McGee's. This mechanism closely mirrored the budget process and also encompassed the strategic planning function, with McGee in the driver's seat.

McGee's decision style was described as innovative, deliberate, and to a certain extent conservative. McGee was particularly noted for his ability to assimilate large amounts of information and identify the important issues and trends as they applied to his company. There is no doubt McGee ran a tight ship. In the area of strategic planning one could say McGee was something of a genius. His foresight had reaped many benefits. KM's strategic planning process had been institutionalized with all the required staff work on projections and all the necessary upper-management discussions. Yet the operational strategic planning process really took place between McGee's ears. So although KM has a recognized vehicle for strategic planning, the process really had never been taken for a serious drive by anyone other than its inventor.

In the staff organization two other areas deserve mention. KM's technology division had been a major contributor to KM's recent growth. This well-funded division had recently gained favorable publicity for the development of the critical-solvent process described in the section on coal. This process, called deashing, represented a real breakthrough in terms of providing cleaner energy from coal. In a related development, the division manufactured another deashing agent that processed petroleum residuum into valuable distillates. Coined ROSE (residuum oil supercritical extraction), this proprietary process had already been licensed to five refineries within the United States.

**Exhibit 24.13** Kerr-McGee Corporation Organization Chart

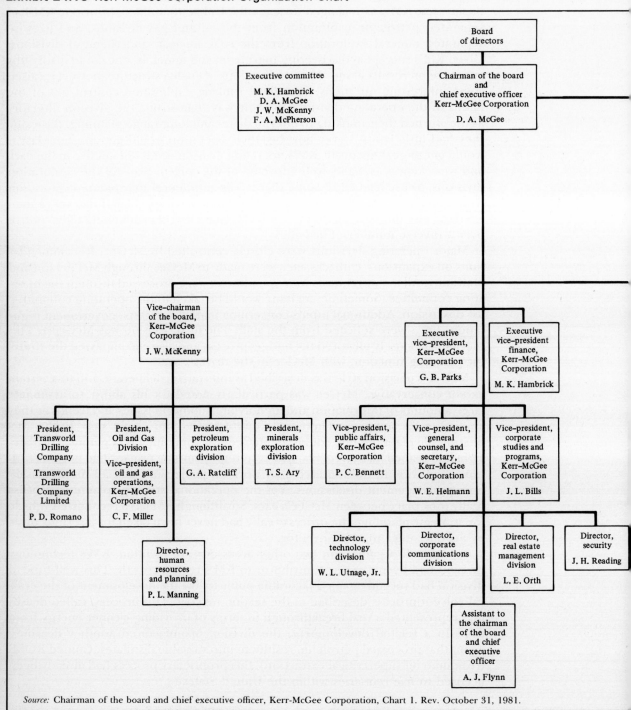

*Source:* Chairman of the board and chief executive officer, Kerr-McGee Corporation, Chart 1. Rev. October 31, 1981.

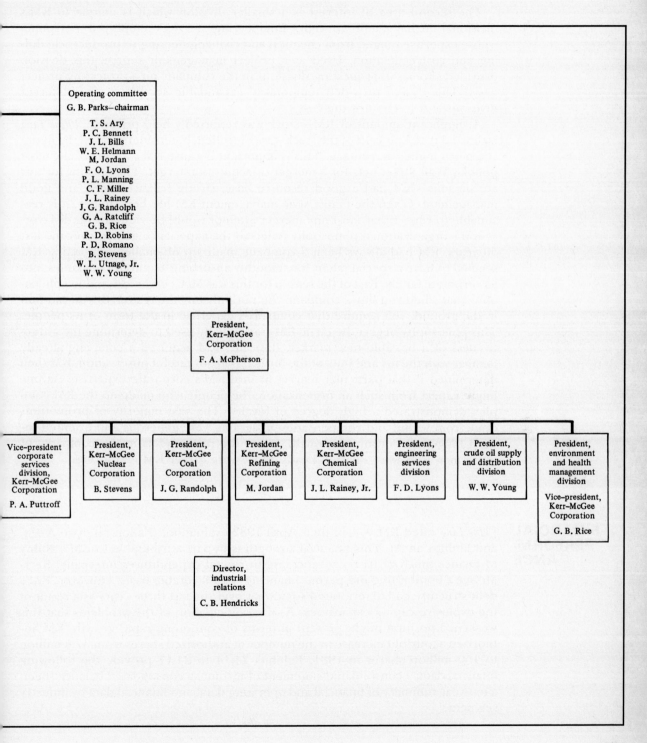

Operating committee

G. B. Parks—chairman

T. S. Ary
P. C. Bennett
J. L. Bills
W. E. Helmann
M. Jordan
F. O. Lyons
P. L. Manning
C. F. Miller
J. L. Rainey
J. G. Randolph
G. A. Ratcliff
G. B. Rice
R. D. Robins
P. D. Romano
B. Stevens
W. L. Utnage, Jr.
W. W. Young

President,
Kerr-McGee
Corporation

F. A. McPherson

Vice-president
corporate
services
division,
Kerr-McGee
Corporation

P. A. Puttroff

President,
Kerr-McGee
Nuclear
Corporation

B. Stevens

President,
Kerr-McGee
Coal
Corporation

J. G. Randolph

President,
Kerr-McGee
Refining
Corporation

M. Jordan

President,
Kerr-McGee
Chemical
Corporation

J. L. Rainey, Jr.

President,
engineering
services
division

F. D. Lyons

President,
crude oil supply
and distribution
division

W. W. Young

President,
environment
and health
management
division

Vice-president,
Kerr-McGee
Corporation

G. B. Rice

Director,
industrial
relations

C. B. Hendricks

The second area of interest is a smaller division which is unique to KM's divisional management concept. Engineering Services employed personnel whose expertise ranged from chemical and civil engineering to product scheduling and cost estimation. Used as a project management source, this division provided experts to requesting divisions in the company on a project-by-project basis. This design provided temporarily expandable services to the different divisions at a fraction of the cost.

A significant amount of KM's stock was reportedly held privately. *Value Line* estimated that 7 percent of the stock was controlled, but insiders placed the figure at a much higher percentage. This is important because KM was one of the most popular Wall Street bets for a merger or acquisition target. The reasons for this are obvious—KM had a good resource base, strong balance sheet, and good management. Given the family-style management KM has been under, it is reasonable to expect that most any merger attempt would be viewed with disfavor.

KM's organizational philosophy reflected the experience gained over the last 50 years. KM had always been a company made up of smaller companies. KM seemed to have a special talent for smoothly absorbing acquired companies into its corporate family. Part of the reason for this was McGee's broad-minded philosophy that when you buy a company you not only buy the resources you can find in the ground, you acquire that company's expertise in the form of its people. This philosophy begets the tactic KM traditionally used to determine the attractiveness of a possible new market. Basically, KM acquired a company already familiar with the ins and outs of the business. From careful observation, KM then determined if that particular market fit into KM's corporate expertise. As one might expect from such an organization, the people who made up the KM complex demonstrated a high degree of loyalty. The vast majority of promotions came from within and compensation programs were generous and oriented toward long-term corporate growth. As for the role models in the company, of those men who were division heads, most were career KM employees.

**FINANCIAL PERFORM-ANCE**

*Value Line* rated KM A+ in their April 1982 evaluation. (Exxon rated an A++ and Phillips an A). This financial strength is in part attributable to KM's ability to finance much of its recent increase in capital expenditures internally. Kerr-McGee's bond rating did permit financing on a favorable basis. However, KM's debt structure had deteriorated somewhat over the last three years as a result of the explosive capital expansions. As if in anticipation of the problems that this weakened position might present in terms of continuing rapid growth, KM authorized a fourfold increase in the number of authorized shares from 37.5 million to 150 million shares in 1981. Exhibits 24.14 to 24.17 provide the following financial data: a consolidated statement of income, a consolidated balance sheet, a ten-year summary of financial and operating data, and financial data by industry segment.

**Exhibit 24.14**

## KERR-McGEE CORPORATION
### Consolidated Statement of Income
### (in thousands of dollars, except per share amounts)

|  | 1981 | 1980 | 1979 |
|---|---|---|---|
| Income |  |  |  |
| Sales and services | $3,826,420 | $3,477,881 | $2,683,469 |
| Costs and expenses |  |  |  |
| Costs and operating expenses | $2,827,253 | $2,705,414 | $2,051,897 |
| Selling, general, and administrative expenses | 130,932 | 100,319 | 96,772 |
| Depreciation, depletion, and amortization | 183,999 | 155,375 | 116,290 |
| Exploration, including dry holes | 83,823 | 62,726 | 47,537 |
| Taxes, other than income taxes | 156,982 | 85,824 | 50,405 |
| Interest and debt expense | 91,027 | 56,005 | 57,620 |
| Total costs and expenses | $3,474,016 | $3,165,663 | $2,420,521 |
|  | $ 352,404 | $ 312,218 | $ 262,948 |
| Other income | 25,344 | 20,273 | 21,137 |
| Net income before income tax provision | $ 377,748 | $ 332,491 | $ 284,085 |
| Provision for income taxes | 166,631 | 150,268 | 124,068 |
| Net income | $ 211,117 | $ 182,223 | $ 160,017 |
| Net income per common share | $ 4.07 | $ 3.51[a] | $ 3.09[a] |

[a]Restated to reflect two-for-one stock split on October 21, 1981.

**Exhibit 24.15**

**KERR-McGEE CORPORATION**
**Consolidated Balance Sheet**
**(in thousands of dollars)**[a]

|  | 1981 | 1980 |
|---|---|---|
| **Assets** | | |
| Current assets | | |
| Cash, including $174,159,000 certificates of deposit in 1981 and $114,688,000 in 1980 | $ 204,577 | $ 152,689 |
| Marketable securities, at cost | 13,371 | 16,872 |
| Notes and accounts receivable | 180,067 | 203,215 |
| Inventories | | |
| Petroleum and other products | 338,583 | 218,514 |
| Materials and supplies | 170,304 | 118,961 |
| Deposits and prepaid expenses | 18,844 | 16,571 |
| Total current assets | $ 925,746 | $ 726,822 |
| Investments and other assets | $ 75,312 | $ 64,976 |
| Property, plant, and equipment, at cost | | |
| Petroleum | $ 2,141,203 | $ 1,648,673 |
| Chemicals | 741,164 | 702,656 |
| Nuclear | 334,655 | 331,605 |
| Coal | 179,074 | 147,049 |
| Other | 83,203 | 82,073 |
|  | $ 3,479,299 | $ 2,912,056 |
| Less reserves for depreciation, depletion, and amortization | 1,113,560 | 949,322 |
|  | $ 2,365,739 | $ 1,962,734 |
| Deferred charges | $ 48,107 | $ 52,027 |
|  | $ 3,414,904 | $ 2,806,559 |

[a]The successful-efforts method of accounting for oil- and gas-producing activities has been followed in preparing this balance sheet.

|                                                | 1981 | 1980 |
|------------------------------------------------|-----:|-----:|
| **Liabilities and stockholders' equity**       |      |      |
| Current liabilities                            |      |      |
| Notes payable                                  | $ 2,300 | $ 22,000 |
| Accounts payable                               | 313,009 | 313,395 |
| Long-term debt due within one year             | 38,314 | 9,058 |
| Taxes on income                                | 87,261 | 91,270 |
| Accrued liabilities                            | 114,733 | 82,854 |
| Total current liabilities                      | $ 555,617 | $ 518,577 |
| Long-term debt                                 | $ 841,509 | $ 520,599 |
| Advances to be repaid from future production   | $ 85,857 | $ 95,659 |
| Deferred credits and reserves                  |      |      |
| Income taxes                                   | $ 324,976 | $ 260,269 |
| Other                                          | 54,972 | 34,173 |
|                                                | $ 379,948 | $ 294,442 |
| Minority interests in subsidiary companies     | $ 50,749 | $ 35,310 |
| Stockholders' equity                           |      |      |
| Common stock, par value $1.00—authorized shares: 150,000,000 in 1981 and 37,500,000 in 1980; shares issued: 52,088,012 in 1981 and 26,009,646 in 1980 | $ 52,088 | $ 26,010 |
| Capital in excess of par value                 | 228,213 | 252,579 |
| Retained earnings                              | 1,222,695 | 1,064,707 |
|                                                | $1,502,996 | $1,343,296 |
| Less common stock in treasury, at cost—224,989 shares in 1981 and 106,840 in 1980 | 1,772 | 1,324 |
| Total stockholders' equity                     | $1,501,224 | $1,341,972 |
|                                                | $3,414,904 | $2,806,559 |

**Exhibit 24.16**

## KERR-McGEE CORPORATION
### Ten-Year Summary of Financial and Operating Data

| | 1981 | 1980 | 1979 | 1978 |
|---|---|---|---|---|
| **Summary of earnings** | | | | |
| (thousands, except per share amounts) | | | | |
| Sales of products, services, etc. | $3,826,420 | $3,477,881 | $2,683,469 | $2,072,443 |
| Operating costs and expenses | $3,382,989 | $3,109,658 | $2,362,901 | $1,853,217 |
| Interest expense | 91,027 | 56,005 | 57,620 | 39,698 |
| Total costs and expenses | $3,474,016 | $3,165,663 | $2,420,521 | $1,892,915 |
| | $ 352,404 | $ 312,218 | $ 262,948 | $ 179,528 |
| Other income | 25,344 | 20,273 | 21,137 | 31,363 |
| Net income before income taxes | $ 377,748 | $ 332,491 | $ 284,085 | $ 210,891 |
| Provision for income taxes | 166,631 | 150,268 | 124,068 | 92,695 |
| Net income | $ 211,117 | $ 182,223 | $ 160,017 | $ 118,196 |
| Common stock outstanding at year end | 51,863 | 25,903 | 25,877 | 25,857 |
| Net income per common share[a] | $ 4.07 | $ 3.51 | $ 3.09 | $ 2.28 |
| Cash dividends paid on common stock | $ 53,129 | $ 46,602 | $ 40,099 | $ 32,320 |
| Cash dividends paid per common share[a] | $ 1.03 | $ .90 | $ .78 | $ .63 |
| **Financial (thousands)** | | | | |
| Working capital | $ 370,129 | $ 208,245 | $ 239,799 | $ 184,140 |
| Long-term debt and production advances | $ 927,366 | $ 616,258 | $ 484,876 | $ 371,566 |
| Common stockholders' equity | $1,501,224 | $1,341,972 | $1,204,768 | $1,084,084 |
| Total assets | $3,414,904 | $2,806,559 | $2,339,165 | $2,021,742 |
| Capital expenditures | $ 606,257 | $ 526,570 | $ 389,195 | $ 270,185 |
| **Operating** | | | | |
| Production (net interest) | | | | |
| Crude oil/condensate produced | | | | |
| (thousands of barrels) | 10,522 | 9,984 | 10,021 | 10,199 |
| Natural gas liquids produced | | | | |
| (thousands of barrels) | 1,885 | 1,920 | 2,175 | 2,458 |
| Natural gas sales | | | | |
| (billions of cubic feet) | 83 | 86 | 89 | 84 |
| Oil and gas wells completed | 65.45 | 79.71 | 55.31 | 44.46 |
| Refining and marketing | | | | |
| (thousands of barrels) | | | | |
| Refinery runs | 41,486 | 41,425 | 44,976 | 52,893 |
| Refined-product sales | | | | |
| (excluding commission sales) | 52,485 | 57,666 | 62,583 | 75,051 |
| Contract drilling (offshore | | | | |
| operations only) | | | | |
| Number of drilling rigs | 23 | 19 | 18 | 18 |
| Number of wells drilled | 107 | 98 | 93 | 91 |
| Number of feet drilled (thousands) | 1,064 | 909 | 921 | 918 |
| Chemicals | | | | |
| Industrial sales (thousands of tons) | 1,627 | 1,434 | 1,327 | 1,168 |
| Wholesale agricultural sales | | | | |
| (thousands of tons) | 1,557 | 2,005 | 1,880 | 1,855 |
| Nuclear | | | | |
| Deliveries of uranium ($U_3O_8$) | | | | |
| (thousands of pounds) | 5,354 | 6,751 | 5,808 | 3,959 |
| Deliveries of uranium ($UF_6$) (uranium | | | | |
| content in thousands of kilograms) | 6,851 | 6,897 | 7,855 | 5,139 |
| Coal | | | | |
| Coal shipped (thousands of tons) | 12,380 | 10,678 | 5,068 | 1,744 |
| Number of employees | 11,202 | 11,286 | 10,823 | 11,148 |

[a]Per share amounts have been adjusted to reflect the two-for-one stock split on October 21, 1981.

| 1977 | 1976 | 1975 | 1974 | 1973 | 1972 |
|---|---|---|---|---|---|
| $2,164,754 | $1,955,058 | $1,798,580 | $1,550,349 | $727,953 | $679,576 |
| $1,951,008 | $1,723,742 | $1,570,089 | $1,353,609 | $632,141 | $607,266 |
| 28,623 | 22,688 | 14,129 | 10,736 | 7,625 | 8,539 |
| $1,979,631 | $1,746,430 | $1,584,218 | $1,364,345 | $639,766 | $615,805 |
| $ 875,123 | $ 208,628 | $ 214,362 | $ 186,004 | $ 88,187 | $ 63,771 |
| 13,654 | 7,165 | 8,517 | 10,174 | 7,412 | 5,099 |
| $ 198,777 | $ 215,793 | $ 222,879 | $ 196,178 | $ 95,599 | $ 68,870 |
| 84,293 | 81,661 | 91,799 | 79,769 | 32,831 | 19,955 |
| $ 114,484 | $ 134,132 | $ 131,080 | $ 116,409 | $ 62,768 | $ 48,915 |
| 25,854 | 25,850 | 25,806 | 25,020 | 24,989 | 24,375 |
| $ 2.21 | $ 2.59 | $ 2.57 | $ 2.32 | $ 1.26 | $ 1.03 |
| $ 32,314 | $ 30,660 | $ 25,415 | $ 21,254 | $ 14,741 | $ 13,984 |
| $ .63 | $ .59 | $ .50 | $ .43 | $ .30 | $ .30 |
| $ 237,699 | $ 273,870 | $ 287,414 | $ 201,673 | $ 204,128 | $ 198,247 |
| $ 377,216 | $ 336,738 | $ 216,409 | $ 158,600 | $ 122,819 | $ 124,427 |
| $ 998,104 | $ 915,766 | $ 810,556 | $ 636,815 | $ 540,738 | $ 463,976 |
| $1,833,301 | $1,625,595 | $1,387,882 | $1,164,432 | $ 866,671 | $ 806,801 |
| $ 269,199 | $ 332,642 | $ 234,734 | $ 227,956 | $ 113,041 | $ 76,054 |
| 11,195 | 11,474 | 10,487 | 11,193 | 11,326 | 12,393 |
| 2,619 | 2,350 | 2,245 | 2,240 | 2,654 | 2,775 |
| 81 | 90 | 89 | 104 | 108 | 109 |
| 40.90 | 20.13 | 34.97 | 22.50 | 23.07 | 19.39 |
| 60,263 | 60,212 | 55,842 | 46,984 | 14,152 | 13,612 |
| 80,255 | 79,388 | 83,693 | 79,201 | 40,820 | 47,808 |
| 18 | 18 | 16 | 15 | 14 | 14 |
| 96 | 99 | 123 | 87 | 85 | 94 |
| 901 | 935 | 984 | 773 | 860 | 968 |
| 1,129 | 1,183 | 1,178 | 853 | 784 | 762 |
| 1,514 | 1,040 | 1,109 | 931 | 1,236 | 1,348 |
| 5,425 | 4,018 | 3,638 | 5,178 | 5,952 | 7,553 |
| 5,067 | 3,527 | 2,162 | 2,379 | 3,818 | 3,157 |
| — | — | — | — | — | 5 |
| 11,271 | 11,427 | 10,305 | 10,105 | 8,966 | 9,217 |

**Exhibit 24.17** Industry Segment Data

| Selected financial data by industry segment for the last three years are summarized below (in millions of dollars). | | | |
|---|---|---|---|
| | **1981** | **1980** | **1979** |
| Sales to unaffiliated customers | | | |
| Petroleum | $2,951.7 | $2,635.7 | $2,049.2 |
| Chemicals | 542.7 | 501.2 | 419.7 |
| Nuclear | 201.5 | 238.9 | 163.4 |
| Coal | 128.9 | 101.2 | 50.5 |
| Other | 1.6 | .9 | .7 |
| Total | $3,826.4 | $3,477.9 | $2,683.5 |
| Operating profit or (loss) | | | |
| Petroleum | $ 379.2 | $ 284.5 | $ 294.6 |
| Chemicals | 35.1 | 36.9 | 31.8 |
| Nuclear | 26.3 | 30.0 | (.2) |
| Coal | 46.6 | 43.8 | 17.3 |
| Other | .5 | .9 | .7 |
| | $ 487.7 | $ 396.1 | $ 344.2 |
| General corporate expenses | (28.3) | (20.3) | (19.5) |
| Interest and debt expense | (91.0) | (56.0) | (57.6) |
| Other income and other expenses—net | 9.3 | 12.7 | 17.0 |
| Provision for income taxes | (166.6) | (150.3) | (124.1) |
| Net income | $ 211.1 | $ 182.2 | $ 160.0 |
| Net income | | | |
| Petroleum | $ 152.3 | $ 113.9 | $ 134.6 |
| Chemicals | 16.1 | 19.8 | 14.2 |
| Nuclear | 12.8 | 19.4 | (1.1) |
| Coal | 30.1 | 30.2 | 13.2 |
| Other | (.2) | (1.1) | (.9) |
| Net income | $ 211.1 | $ 182.2 | $ 160.0 |
| Identifiable assets at December 31 | | | |
| Petroleum | $2,081.9 | $1,537.8 | $1,197.4 |
| Chemicals | 684.7 | 640.6 | 624.4 |
| Nuclear | 304.5 | 304.8 | 288.4 |
| Coal | 135.3 | 126.6 | 109.2 |
| Other | 39.8 | 26.4 | 48.2 |
| | $3,246.2 | $2,636.2 | $2,267.6 |
| Investment in unconsolidated affiliates | 41.2 | 29.6 | 23.1 |
| Corporate assets | 127.5 | 140.8 | 48.5 |
| Total | $3,414.9 | $2,806.6 | $2,339.2 |
| Capital expenditures | | | |
| Petroleum | $ 513.0 | $ 426.4 | $ 282.8 |
| Chemicals | 43.2 | 36.3 | 45.6 |
| Nuclear | 14.2 | 17.9 | 28.8 |
| Coal | 33.2 | 39.7 | 31.2 |
| Other | 2.7 | 6.3 | .8 |
| Total capital expenditures | $ 606.3 | $ 526.6 | $ 389.2 |
| Exploration expenses (excluding abandonment provisions) | 63.9 | 48.5 | 37.5 |
| Total | $ 670.2 | $ 575.1 | $ 426.7 |

# 25 Delta Air Lines: World's Most Profitable Airline

Elizabeth Lavie and Larry D. Alexander
Virginia Polytechnic Institute and State University

It was mid-1982 and the sun was setting over Atlanta. At Hartsfield International Airport, Delta Air Lines' new midfield complex was bustling with activity. More than two dozen jets had come into gates within the last half hour, and they were all scheduled to take off again within the next half hour. David Garrett, Delta's president and chief executive officer, was watching the activities at the gates. The employees were not astonished to see him there. The president, vice-presidents, and other members of the senior management team often came over to the airport from their modest offices to chat with employees or just to watch. Garrett was not surprised by the smoothness of the operation which every employee at Delta had worked hard to perfect in order to improve service and ease connections for the customer.

Garrett walked through the complex and stopped in at the spacious employee lounge. He sat down and thought back over the monumental changes that had occurred in Delta and in the industry since he had become president in 1971. It had all been very dynamic and exciting, especially for Delta, which had remained profitable throughout the changes. Garrett remembered some of the history of his company and how thrilling it must have been for Woolman, who was Delta's founder and chief executive officer until he died in 1966.

## COMPANY HISTORY

Mr. C. E. (Collett Everman) Woolman was born in Indiana in 1889. Even as a child, Woolman exhibited a keen interest in aviation. He and a friend borrowed most of the clothesline available in the neighborhood to help control a giant passenger kite they had built. Fortunately, it got wrecked before anyone attempted to fly in it.

As he grew older, Woolman took advantage of every opportunity to get near airplanes, such as traveling to France to attend aviation meets. Despite this avid interest, Woolman did not pursue a career in aviation in 1908 because its business potential then seemed minimal. Instead, Woolman went to college and earned a bachelor's degree in agriculture from the University of Illinois in 1912. After

This case was prepared by Elizabeth Lavie, M.B.A. from Virginia Polytechnic Institute and State University in June 1982, and Larry D. Alexander, assistant professor of business strategy, Virginia Polytechnic Institute and State University, Blacksburg, Virginia 24061. This case was written as a basis for class discussion rather than to illustrate either effective or ineffective handling of an administrative situation.

Copyright © 1984 by Elizabeth Lavie and Larry D. Alexander.

graduation, Woolman began farming in Louisiana, and soon became an agricultural extension agent there. He moved up to become a district supervisor of the extension service. In his work, Woolman became alarmed by the eating habits of the boll weevil, which was destroying a high percentage of the cotton crop. He tried to develop ways to destroy the creatures, but soon there were other things to worry about. A world war had begun.

During World War I, the airplane and commercial aviation became very important. In fact, the war helped to change attitudes about aviation because the wartime contracts influenced businesses to invest in aviation. Commercial aviation companies sprang up during the war, hoping to capture some of the military business and to capture the new United States postal airmail delivery rights. In 1920, the Huff Daland Company was formed to try to get in on the military business. Because the company achieved little success in its military endeavors, the company officers turned to crop dusting and formed a new division known as the Huff Daland Dusters, Inc. During this period, many small airlines merged to gain the power necessary to win the rights to carry the airmail. Some of these early merged firms were Transcontinental Air Transportation, United Air Lines, Aviation Corporation of America, and the North American Aviation Company. These companies later changed their respective names to World Airlines, United Airlines, American Airlines, and Eastern Airlines.

Woolman was especially interested in Huff Daland Dusters because the firm represented two of the major interests in his life, aviation and killing the boll weevil. In 1925, he joined the firm as a salesman. In 1928, Woolman persuaded a group of Monroe, Louisiana, area businessmen and planters to purchase the firm's American assets. The new company was chartered under the name of Delta Air Services, Inc.

Woolman was dissatisfied with Delta's just being a crop duster and began planning to make his company a more significant operation. Delta Air Services went through mergers, being bought out, and struggles over route rights. It finally restructured and rechartered in Louisiana as the Delta Air Corporation in 1930.

With the dusting operations becoming less significant to total operations every year, Delta became a strong organization under Woolman's leadership. Delta survived the depression, helped out during World War II, and profited under strict government regulation after the war.

When Woolman died in 1966, many industry watchers, officials, and employees wondered about the future of Delta. To these people, C. E. Woolman was Delta, and Delta was C. E. Woolman. Despite the appearance of one-man management, Delta did not lack for managerial talent to replace him. In fact, several inside successors were considered after his death. Regardless of the fact that Delta was now being run by different people, Woolman's personality has continued to influence the organization. His policies and management techniques have still been used, the very principles that have made the company profitable for almost four decades. That is, profitable until 1982.

Because of the silence around him, current President Garrett ended his thoughts, which unfortunately may have been turning into a nightmare. Garrett suddenly realized that he had an evening meeting with you, a leading industry consultant he had hired to help decide what Delta should do in a now turbulent industry. He had collected the following information to help you on this consulting assignment. It should enable you to appreciate Delta's historical development, understand its present environment, and make recommendations about its future strategy.

**INDUSTRY OUTLOOK**

Since the airline industry has changed so much since 1978, it is almost irrelevant to discuss the industry before deregulation. However, a later section will be devoted to a discussion of deregulation and the industry before deregulation.

**1978**

Despite the uncertainty and all the changes that occurred, 1978 was still a boom year for the airlines. In fact, 1978 was the best year ever for the U.S. airlines, with passenger traffic and financial records being set. Revenues for the 11 major airlines were $19.6 billion, which represented an increase of 13.8 percent over the 1977 total. The resulting profits hit an all-time industry high of $1.06 billion, which was 71.6 percent higher than 1977.

Other important indicators of success in the airline industry besides the bottom line have been passenger boardings, traffic, revenue passenger kilometers, load factors, and freight ton kilometers. Load factors indicate the percentage of available seats on an airline's average flight that were occupied by paying customers. All of these indicators demonstrated that 1978 was successful for the airlines. Passenger boardings increased 13.1 percent over 1977 to 220 million boardings, and the traffic growth rate was almost double that of 1977. Revenue passenger kilometers were up 14.4 percent, which was double what the analysts had expected, and load factors rose from 56 percent to 61.7 percent in 1978.

It is important to note here that 1977 had also been considered a successful year for the airlines. Much of the success in 1978 was attributed to the Airline Deregulation Act, which was signed by President Carter on October 24, 1978, and the generally good economic condition which prevailed. Deregulation allowed the airlines to begin their low-fare revolution, which resulted in a great increase in traffic. The airlines were helped out in this traffic surge and able to take advantage of it because of their wide-bodied jets and their computerized reservation systems. The airlines learned that if the price was right, then the customers would be willing to put up with indignities and inconveniences.

Two divisions of the U.S. airline industry which were not as successful were the charter and cargo divisions. Charter passenger boardings fell 22.9 percent from the level of 1977. This decrease was attributed to the low fares which became available on the regular flights. Cargo traffic grew only 0.71 percent in 1978. This low growth was attributed to the growth of the emerging cargo specialists, such as Flying Tigers and Federal Express.

Despite all the success, some dark clouds were forming by the end of 1978.

One cloud was formed by the OPEC (Organization of Petroleum Exporting Countries) nations. Fuel prices were expected to increase dramatically. The other dark cloud was the airlines' labor unions, which were looking at the nice profits the airlines were achieving and thinking about making higher wage demands.

**1979**    As was expected, earnings for the U.S. major airlines spiraled downward throughout 1979 from their peak in 1978. For the ten major airlines (also down in number from 1978 owing to the merger of Pan Am and National), revenues increased 15.5 percent over 1978 to $22.6 billion. However, this increase was due to fare increases of nearly 30 percent. Profits declined 75 percent from the lofty $1.06 billion of 1978 to a sad $262 million. One of the culprits was the 22.6 percent increase in operating expenses. A large factor in the increasing expenses was the large increase in the price of jet fuel.

Passenger traffic increased by 8.1 percent, but this indicated a decline in the traffic growth rate. Revenue passenger kilometers climbed by 10.6 percent, but this also indicated a declining growth rate. Load factors only increased by 1.6 percent to 63.3 percent in 1979.

Charter traffic continued to decline in 1979 with the number of charter passengers plunging 27.4 percent. This continued decline was still attributed to low fares on the regularly scheduled flights. The cargo divisions of the major U.S. airlines reported zero growth in 1979. This figure was affected by the labor strikes and the grounding of the DC-10 fleet.

The blame for what happened was being placed on a number of factors. The increases in operating expenses, especially for fuel cost, certainly hurt the airlines. Many airlines blamed the Civil Aeronautics Board (CAB), which still had authority over fare increases despite deregulation. The airlines claimed that the CAB did not grant fare increases fast enough or high enough to offset increasing expenses. Another factor which hurt the airlines was the 38-day grounding of the DC-10 jets after the crash of an American Airlines DC-10. Major portions of six of the major airlines' fleets were made up of DC-10s. Individual airlines were hurt by poor weather in the first quarter and by strikes. Many of the airlines were beginning to blame deregulation, but a stronger force was the beginning of a lengthy, severe recession. By the end of 1979, there was widespread concern in the airline industry about what 1980 would bring.

**1980**    Some forecasts for the U.S. major airlines segment were particularly bleak. Revenues, expenses, and profits were expected to climb equally, and traffic growth was expected to be flat in 1980. However, a few forecasts did predict that 1980 might be a good year.

Operating revenues in 1980 increased by 15.6 percent, almost the same percentage as the previous year. Operating expenses also increased by about the same percentage as in 1979. However, the industry suffered combined net losses of $9.5 million. Thus, none of the forecasts came close to predicting the size of the actual loss.

Total passenger traffic decreased 6.31 percent from 1979's level, and revenue passenger kilometers decreased by about 5 percent. Load factors decreased by 4.1 percent, resulting in an industry average load of 59.1 percent. Charter traffic also continued to decline, with the number of charter passenger boardings down by 37.8 percent.

Things were obviously not getting better. The poor performance in 1980 was again the result of many factors. Some of the factors were the same as those affecting performance in 1979, only more intensified. In 1980, deregulation was beginning to affect the major airlines. New competitors were entering the industry because of the new freedom of entry, and the majors were not prepared to handle the extra competition. Prices declined and many fare wars resulted, at a time when prices should have increased to offset increasing expenses. The recession also took a greater hold in 1980 and resulted in dampening traffic a great deal. As a result of all these factors, the airlines were juggling routes to find the most profitable, furloughing large numbers of employees, and reducing operations. At the same time, they were beginning to worry about how they would be able to finance the acquisition of much-needed new equipment, especially aircraft.

Needless to say, there was extreme pessimism among the U.S. majors as to what 1981 would have to offer.

**1981**   Substantial losses swamped the airlines in 1981. Amazingly, a few of the U.S. majors experienced their worst year ever, even though a couple of years earlier they had enjoyed their best year ever. Operating revenues for the U.S. majors increased by the same 15 percent in 1981, amounting to revenues of $31.9 billion. Net losses increased, which resulted in an industry loss of $462 million. Passenger boardings decreased 8.6 percent, and revenue passenger kilometers decreased by 6.7 percent in 1981.

Thus, things not only did not get any better; in fact, everything got worse. The same factors from the previous two years hurt the industry, along with a few surprises during 1981.

Many more new airlines entered the industry, and the ones that had entered in 1980 surprisingly survived the year. These new airlines caused many problems for the established airlines through increased competition and more fare wars. The newer airlines typically had lower operating expenses than the majors and thus could afford to lower their prices. Many labor union issues arose during 1981, as many contracts came up for renegotiation. Costs continued to rise for the majors, and their debts mounted. Many of the majors began to search out novel ways to finance their equipment purchases. Most airlines preferred to purchase the more fuel-efficient aircraft, which helped reduce their operating expenses, but they had not generated the revenues and the capacity to do so. Taken together, it seemed like a vicious cycle, especially when a staggering economy and high interest rates were considered.

An additional problem cropped up in August 1981. The Professional Air Traffic Controllers Organization (PATCO) struck and many strikers were fired as

**Exhibit 25.1** Industry Summary (000,000)

|                     | 1977      | 1978      | 1979      | 1980      | 1981      |
|---------------------|-----------|-----------|-----------|-----------|-----------|
| Revenue             | $17,200   | $19,600   | $22,600   | $26,100   | $31,900   |
| Profit              | 620       | 1,060     | 262       | −9        | −462      |
| Passenger boardings | 194       | 220       | 238       | 223       | 204       |

a result of their actions. The Federal Aviation Administration responded by cutting back flights and service, which prevented airlines from operating at full capacity. Many industry experts believed that the airlines were pulling out of their slump earlier in 1981, but that the PATCO strike destroyed any hopes of a profitable year.

Some sources indicated that 1981 was not all bad because the airlines were learning from their losses. The airlines began to strive for efficiency and cooperation from their suppliers of labor and materials. They were learning the complexities of pricing in a more competitive environment and were learning to define and capitalize on their strengths. By the end of 1981, there were signs that the airlines that survived the economic downturn would be much stronger competitors than had existed before.

A summary of the yearly data for the industry which was discussed in this section appears in Exhibit 25.1.

# INDUSTRY TRENDS AND PROBLEMS

Before Delta is examined, it might help to understand more of the details of the trends and problems in the airline industry that were mentioned in the previous discussions.

## Deregulation: Changing the Industry Structure

The Airline Deregulation Act of 1978 ended 40 years of federal protection for the airlines. The purpose of the law was to open up the industry to increased competition and to maintain a high level of safety while protecting profitability, providing small-community service, and preventing unreasonable industry concentration. Within certain limits, any airline that was ready, willing, and able could fly practically anywhere it wanted if the transportation was consistent with public convenience and necessity. All the airline had to do was inform the CAB that they intended to add a route, and then do it within 60 days. Airlines could only protect one of their routes from competitors per year, and they could discontinue service to a route provided that there was still another airline covering that route. The airlines were gaining the power to adjust rates up and down, and the industry was no longer closed to new entrants. The law called for the powers of the CAB to gradually be decreased and then eliminated in 1985. After 1985, the Justice Department would still oversee antitrust issues, the Department of Transportation would handle subsidies, and the Federal Aviation Agency would monitor safety matters.

As implied earlier, deregulation may have caused more problems than it solved, especially when one considers the profitability objective of deregulation. In many cases, deregulation has resulted in a bitter dogfight over routes, rates, and passengers that has caused increased competition and confusion.

Since deregulation, various problems arose concerning the airports themselves. The most critical problem has been a shortage of landing slots and physical space for new entrants at many airports. This problem quickly became known as the slot crisis as well as the airport access problem. Established carriers, who had made large investments in their airport facilities, were threatened with charges of rights to free and equal access by various government agencies, who represented the new entrants. Warnings had also been made to the airports by the agencies about noise pollution, ground congestion, and other environmental concerns. The aviation community fought to save small existing airports and to use military bases as possible reliever airports. However, then even the reliever airports were getting crowded.

Besides competition from the new entrants, competition was enhanced between the established major carriers as they entered and exited markets chasing efficiency and customers. The result of several airlines operating on the same route has been terrible fare wars. These fare wars were going on in 1978 on the transcontinental routes, and then moved to shorter-haul routes. The Florida fare war in 1981 and 1982 was a more recent example. When the airlines were regulated, they could not compete on the basis of price, but rather on their service. After deregulation, as soon as one airline on a route cut a fare, most of the others were forced to follow. This price competition was destructive because the airlines' yields suffered, owing to the fact that the majority of the passengers were flying at discounts of up to 70 percent. In addition, these price wars started alienating the full-fare group of passengers, especially business travelers, since they were not able to take advantage of the low fares.

Between October 24, 1978, and mid-1980, the combined total of new markets added by airlines and existing markets vacated was 1313. The result was mass confusion for the customers, with the airlines flying all over the place and changing schedules all the time. With all these changes, airlines themselves took on an air of instability rather than reliability.

Service was improved in small communities and large markets, but medium-sized cities started protesting service cuts since deregulation became effective. A strong group formed, composed of representatives of medium-sized cities, and demanded that some form of reregulation be legislated.

In-flight service also deteriorated since deregulation. Some of the airlines made in-flight service cuts to try to offset reduced fares. These service cuts included such things as no meals on flights, few contacts with cabin personnel, being jammed into small spaces with many other people, and restrictions on carry-on luggage. As a result, many customers, again especially the business travelers, started getting fed up with the service they received.

As a result of deregulation and the problems with the economy, pricing became a very important tool. However, many industry experts claimed that management of the various airlines did not understand the complexities of pricing and that the discount fare was not always the answer, regardless of what your competitors were doing. Clearly, marketing as a whole had become a more important function within the organization since deregulation.

While a deregulation turnabout has appeared unlikely under the Reagan administration, the long-term future of deregulation was not as crystal clear. An early 1980 report indicated that there was increasing discontent over the state of the airline industry, and that the new issue might be reregulation. Several reports brought out the benefits that the airlines had already gained from deregulation. Some of these suggested benefits were more efficient airlines, faster responses to the environment, and learning to exercise their options.

**Increasing Expenses**

One trend that continued from 1978 through 1981 was an alarming increase in expenses in the industry. One of the most critical expenses in the airline industry was jet fuel. The real cost of jet fuel increased threefold since the beginning of the worldwide oil crisis in 1973. The cost of aviation fuel 20 years ago represented only 25 percent of an airline's operating cost; however, in 1980 fuel represented 55 percent of operating costs. Since 1978, the average price per gallon for jet fuel has increased as follows: $.38 in 1978, $.56 in 1979, $.86 in 1980, $.99 in February 1981, and $1.40 in October 1981. Since fuel has represented such a large portion of expenses, many of the airlines have blamed their losses or low profits on the cost of fuel.

As a result of these increasing costs, many of the major airlines began fuel conservation programs and started purchasing new fuel-efficient aircraft. Other responses by the airlines were to get deeper into the ownership and control of distribution and storage facilities and to form their own energy exploration ventures. The airlines also began to line up more suppliers and to form consortiums to gain power in negotiating with the suppliers.

**Computerization**

The airlines themselves have already made a substantial investment in computerization, and many expected to spend much more on computers in the future. Many airlines even offered computer services and software for sale to other airlines and travel agents. Some examples of these programs were maintenance control systems, reservation systems, and price management systems.

Many airlines started exploring ways to get involved in the telecommunications revolution. Many industry specialists speculated that businesses that spent a lot of money on traveling would move towards electronic conferences. This trend could damage the airlines because 55 percent of their traffic historically came from business travelers, the very customer group that was becoming disenchanted with airline service.

**Flight Equipment**

In order to remain competitive, the U.S. major airlines needed to buy the most advanced and fuel-efficient aircraft or to modify their present aircraft. Generally, the majors have preferred to finance these acquisitions out of internally generated funds, but because of the losses they had encountered in recent years, this was almost impossible for them. Paying for aircraft acquisition became a real challenge for many airlines because of the price of the aircraft and size of the capital cost involved. The capital cost of an acquisition used to run about 10 percent of the total cost; this percentage was up to 25 percent by 1982. As a result, finance departments began searching for alternative ways to fund acquisitions to update their fleet. Aircraft manufacturers started stepping up their financial assistance to airlines, but the manufacturers were beginning to have financial problems of their own.

Financing was also available from foreign export banks if they were purchasing the aircraft from foreign firms. Many of the airlines became attracted by the low interest rates in other countries, such as Japan, and got loans from trading firms in those countries. The big disadvantage of this method was that the firms had to play the exchange rate gamble. Several new leasing opportunities for airlines also were introduced, including the Safe Harbor Lease, which was a tax benefit transfer. However, industry experts pointed out that there was a limit to how many planes an airline could obtain with lease financing, if their equity and earnings were not high enough.

Each airline had to decide whether it was strong enough then or would be in the future to buy new airplanes or to modify its existing planes. Each airline also had to decide which type of financing was best for its situation.

## Labor and Management Relations

Labor has been one of the airlines' top two expenses for a long time. Recently, the airlines started making demands on their employees to accept concessions. The airlines needed these concessions in order to help keep their operating expenses down in a time when they were in trouble. Unfortunately, most of the U.S. major airlines were heavily unionized and existing contracts would have to be renegotiated. The airlines threatened that they would have to lay off some employees if concessions were not made. Some unions took this threat seriously and granted various concessions such as pay cuts, wage freezes, and less restrictive work rules. However, some industry experts felt that in 1982, the unions would put up more resistance to any concessions being offered. Thus, if the recession continued, the airlines could not decrease their ticket prices unless the unions cut their wages.

The newer entrants to the airline industry were more fortunate because their employees were not unionized; thus, they had lower operation costs. For example, in 1981 "captains flying DC-9-30s at New York Air were being paid $30,000 per year and were flying about 75 hours per month, while captains flying the same airplanes at the airline's parent company, Texas International, were being paid $62,000 per year for flying 55 hours per month."[1] Unionized airlines needed to be especially careful to avoid a strike because a strike in the deregulation environment could be fatal for them.

## PATCO Strike

On August 3, 1981, the Professional Air Traffic Controllers Organization went on strike. Because of their subsequent refusal to return to work, 12,500 of the air traffic controllers were fired. The initial traffic impact was disastrous, with very large numbers of passenger no-shows. For the first few days, the U.S. airlines lost about $34 million per day. However, once the reduced schedules were established, traffic picked up. The overall traffic figures for the month of August were less than 13 percent off, which was far less than expected.

Capacity constraints were put into effect at 22 high-density airports. Many of these were key airports in the majors' hub and spoke route systems. This reduced capacity squelched expansion plans that many airlines had, and it was expected to last until late 1982 or early 1983. The airlines affected by the constraints at those airports were able to resume 75 percent of their previous operations by rescheduling their flights to off-peak times.

The FAA then developed an $8.5 billion plan to revamp air traffic control. This plan called for the use of computers to do many of the jobs formerly performed by controllers. This new plan also involved giving more responsibility to the pilots in the cockpit. If the plan was approved, airlines would have to equip their aircraft with a number of new devices. However, the airlines would reap one big benefit from this plan. The pilots would no longer have to follow the presently inefficient long-distance routes.

Now that you're equipped with a pretty good overview of the industry and recent changes in it, it's time to get inside Delta and see how it operates. With all this information, you should be in a good position to develop your consulting recommendations.

**DELTA AIR LINES**

Delta Air Lines was primarily in the business of providing scheduled air transportation for passengers, freight, and mail over a network of routes throughout the United States and abroad. Delta was one of the few major airlines that had not diversified into other businesses to improve their profits. Since deregulation and the uncertainty of the economy developed, many airlines began searching for other revenue sources. One study indicated that 70 percent of the world's airlines provided airframe maintenance for others, 60 percent were involved in outside engine and component maintenance, many offered training services and computer services to other airlines, and others were involved in totally unrelated businesses. Exhibit 25.2 indicates what Delta and some of its competitors were involved with.

Delta had always operated under the philosophy that running an airline required the undivided attention of top management and the undivided resources of the organization. Furthermore, Delta had been so strong financially that it could afford not to diversify, since it could weather out periodic economic downturns.

Delta certainly had financial strength through the years. Cliches that had been passed around in the industry, such as "Flying high at Delta," and "A wing and a cash register," indicated that Delta had been doing something right for quite some time.

By 1976, Delta broke into the big five of the U.S. airlines, after being known as the big little airline for years. Actually, the industry only had a big four,

**Exhibit 25.2** Airlines' Activities and Related Businesses

| Airline | Hotel | Restaurant/ Catering | Travel Tour Operations | Ground Support | Training | Computer |
|---|---|---|---|---|---|---|
| American | x | x | x | x | x | |
| Braniff | x | x | x | x | x | |
| Continental | x | x | x | x | | |
| Delta | | | | | | |
| Eastern | x | x | | | | |
| National | | | | | | |
| Pan Am | x | x | x | x | x | x |
| TWA | x | x | x | x | x | x |
| United | x | x | x | x | | |

*Source:* "World Airline Ancillary Activity—1978," *Air Transport World,* June 1979, pp. 38–39.

consisting of American, Eastern, TWA, and United, but Delta changed all that. For example, Delta's cumulative net earnings from 1971 through 1981 were $857 million compared to $448 million for United, the world's largest airline. For the year 1981, Delta was in the number two spot for passenger boardings and sixth in revenue passenger kilometers among the U.S. airlines. This was a far cry from the crop duster of the 1930s. Some experts and observers of the industry have even predicted that by 1990 Delta will be the biggest airline in the United States.

So, what is it that Delta has done that the other airlines have not done? Unfortunately, the following facts will not provide an easy answer.

**Management**

Delta had been organized along a functional basis for quite some time. Exhibit 25.3 shows the eight basic divisions that reported to President Garrett in June 1981. Those functional divisions were finance, marketing, flight operations, legal, corporate affairs, technical operations, personnel, and passenger service. In turn, many divisions were further subdivided into departments.

Delta had always been very centralized. Clearly, David Garrett and his senior management group had always made the key decisions. The senior management group acted as a unit. All members were involved in consensus decision making regardless of what department they were from. Each morning, this group attended a short briefing session to uncover any problems and to touch base with each other. While no one likes to meet for the sake of meeting, Delta senior management felt that these daily short meetings helped to quickly identify problems as well as opportunities. It also helped educate the senior management team about what was going on in all other functional departments. More lengthy weekly meetings were held where actual decision making took place.

Although the organization was very centralized, the senior management group had never been inaccessible to the rest of the company. Delta maintained very open and often informal communications channels. Employees were encouraged to air their gripes and problems directly with senior management.

More informally, the senior vice-presidents' doors usually were open to the

**Exhibit 25.3** Organization Chart (as of June 1981)

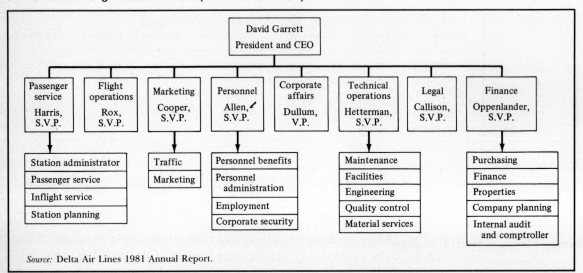

*Source:* Delta Air Lines 1981 Annual Report.

employees in their divisions. One Delta executive declared, "You can tell from the state of my carpet that mechanics come in here all the time to talk to me—look at the grease stains on that carpet."[2] Senior management also developed the policy of making themselves visible and available to employees by walking around their divisions and stopping to talk.

The atmosphere at Delta was more like a family business, a close-knit family of 36,790 people. Family members were invited to participate in management as much as possible. This family atmosphere resulted in a spirit of cooperation between labor and management.

These policies were instilled into Delta by Woolman, the founder of the airline. Woolman was known as a master of personnel relations, and as shown here, Delta has retained this mastery despite its strong centralization.

**Marketing Division**

The marketing division at Delta fell under the direction of Mr. Joe Cooper, and was further subdivided into the traffic and marketing departments. Delta's marketing efforts had been described as consistently innovative and aggressive since Delta's first days of operation. Starting with Woolman himself, Delta executives never minded spending money on sales promotion and media advertising as long as they were convinced that it would pay off financially. The marketing division also handled promotion, pricing, and the analysis of new route possibilities. Final route scheduling and the maintenance of the route system were the responsibility of the flight operations division.

Delta's advertising had always been highly pragmatic, both in content and form. Delta concentrated on reaching local markets as opposed to nationwide recognition, and the messages focused on information about destinations, fares, arrival times, and its image of reliability and professionalism. Since deregulation, many of the other major airlines shifted the focus of their advertising from the

**Exhibit 25.4** Ad Expenditures and Revenues

| Airline | 1980 Ad Expense (000) | Pass. Rev. per Ad |
|---|---|---|
| American | $50,948 | $ 53.80 |
| Braniff | 16,536 | 55.05 |
| Continental | 16,291 | 49.39 |
| Delta | 36,480 | 79.91 |
| Eastern | 44,864 | 60.49 |
| Northwest | 10,974 | 86.38 |
| Pan Am | 23,494 | 36.08 |
| Republic | 6,065 | 136.47 |
| TWA | 38,817 | 51.60 |
| United | 62,776 | 59.64 |
| US Air | 9,930 | 89.65 |
| Western | 13,535 | 60.08 |

*Source:* "U.S. Airline Advertising Analysis: 1980," *Air Transport World,* June 1981, p. 85.

traditional focus on image to a focus on price, new routes, better routes, better food, and free drinks. Delta only got involved in such advertising wars if they were forced to do so. For the most part, Delta continued to emphasize its businesslike atmosphere, its solidness, and its efficiency.

For 1980, Delta spent almost $40 million on advertising. It broke down in the following manner: 50 percent for newspapers, 16 percent for radio, 15 percent for magazines, 11 percent for television, and 8 percent for outdoor billboards. Delta spent more for newspaper advertising than the other airlines. It did so because it had found that the newspapers provided quick local coverage, a link to business, and a matter-of-fact content that was consistent with their style of advertising. Delta's passenger revenues per advertising dollar were higher than some of the other majors, but were also much lower than some of the competitors, as shown in Exhibit 25.4.

After deregulation, the airlines had a lot more control over their prices. As a result, severe price competition developed in many markets. In 1979, Delta refused to lower its coach fares and its economy fares because such a reduction would alienate its regular customers, especially its business customers. Delta viewed these price wars as misguided efforts to achieve competitive advantage, but in a policy statement issued in 1981, Delta stated that it would not allow any other carrier to maintain a price advantage in any market in which Delta had a meaningful amount of traffic participation.

So Delta became involved in some price wars, which of course resulted in lost revenues because traffic was not growing. Delta established a frequent-flyer program in an effort to provide some way for its business and regular passengers to take advantage of the reduced fares. It offered a free trip after a certain number of paid flights flown.

Since deregulation, Delta moved at a deliberate pace to strengthen and extend its route system. Exhibit 25.5 shows what Delta's route system was as of June 30, 1981.

New routes were studied and analyzed for a long time by the route develop-

**Exhibit 25.5** Delta Route Map—June 30, 1981

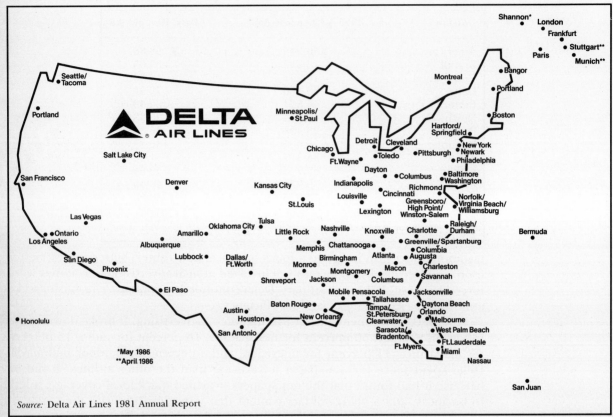

Source: Delta Air Lines 1981 Annual Report

ment committee, co-chaired by Mr. Bob Oppenlander, senior vice-president of finance, and Mr. Cooper. The new routes or cities had to be very strong for Delta to consider them. Delta was willing to take risks on new routes, but through the route development committee, these risks were well calculated.

Cooper described the expansion of Delta's system as a slow expansion. Since 1978, Dallas–Ft. Worth and Cincinnati were developed as new hubs, and plans were being made to develop Denver as another hub. In 1981, Delta added non-stop operations in 39 markets between cities already receiving its service. In 1980, Delta added 8 new cities and 13 new nonstop routes to already serviced cities.

**Passenger Service**

In 1982, the passenger service division was headed by Mr. Hollis Harris. For nine of the past ten years that the CAB had compiled consumer complaint records, Delta had the best complaint record. For 1980, Delta had only 1.4 complaints per 100,000 passengers. Pan Am had the worst record out of the U.S. major airlines with a complaint rate of 13.0 complaints per 100,000 customers.

However, Delta consistently scored poorly (ninth or tenth) among the ten majors for on-time performance. Delta officials explained that this poor perform-ance was due to its policy of holding departing flights until all incoming flights were in, which was done to accommodate passengers connecting to other flights. This was one of the reasons Delta's complaint record was so low.

Woolman instilled the friendly and helpful approach into Delta during his years as president. Employees were instructed to treat customers the way they would want to be treated as customers. Woolman took this policy to an extreme and even told reservation clerks to suggest a competitor's flight if it fit the customer's needs better than the Delta flight.

For the last few years, it cost more to serve fewer passengers, because the number of total passengers was decreasing. The cost of Delta's passenger service—which included food expenses, cabin expenses, and cabin attendant salaries—increased. Fortunately, costs went up for the other major airlines as well. In addition, Delta had a large number of passengers who were denied boarding because of overbooking in 1980. This resulted in an extra expense of $3 million, which was paid out to customers in compensation.

In one aspect of its passenger service, Delta had been at a competitive disadvantage when compared with other airlines. Delta always assigned seats by hand, so that on every change of plane, the customer waited at the gate to receive a seat assignment. Many of the other airlines had used computerized seat assignments for some time.

## Technical Operations

The technical operations division was under the direction of Mr. Don Hetterman, who had responsibility for the maintenance and engineering of all of Delta's equipment. It was also responsible for developing specifications for fleet purchases and for the planning of new facilities.

Delta's maintenance and engineering expenses were increasing by 17.4 percent each year, while the industry average increased yearly by about 15 percent. There were 6100 employees in the division in 1982, of which 68 were considered management. Only three other airlines had more employees in this division, but remember that Delta did more of its own maintenance and engineering work than any other major airline.

Hetterman claimed that this fact had been one of the many keys to Delta's success. He described his division as being self-contained. Delta had not sold its services, and it had tried to buy as little as possible from the outside. Only 3 percent of Delta's maintenance burden went to outside suppliers. This "make rather than buy" attitude resulted in this department's developing and producing everything from test units for aircraft to plastic decorative items for the airplanes. The next project planned was to produce plastic meal trays.

Hetterman claimed that he operated a no-budget division. Forecasts were made for planning purposes, but no budgets were ever set for expenditures. Delta apparently just spent what was necessary for this department as needed. The beauty of this method was that when justifiable expenditures were turned in, Hetterman could approve or disapprove them quickly. Also, this method did away with the end-of-year rush to spend the allocated funds that had not been spent yet.

One other Delta attitude revealed in this division was that salvage means money. Delta never threw anything away that could be turned into a penny. Even the cardboard shipment boxes were collected to be sold.

**Personnel**  Mr. Ron Allen headed up the personnel division. As was mentioned previously, Delta treated its employees like family members. As a result, Delta enjoyed high morale, high productivity, and low unionism. From the day it started business, Delta's top management recognized that Delta's employees could be its greatest asset. Some of the personnel policies established by Delta have been very interesting.

Delta's employees had the best job security in the industry. In fact, no permanent employee had been furloughed or laid off at Delta, even during severe economic times, in over 25 years. During deregulation's rough times and the recessions, other airlines laid off thousands of employees, but not Delta. Delta found something for its employees to do during reduced-traffic periods. President Garrett discussed this policy:

> In the 1973 fuel crisis we had to cut back on our flying by 20% within sixty days. That meant we had about 200 pilots and 400 flight attendants that were surplus. But we put them to work everywhere we could—loading cargo, cleaning airplanes, selling tickets, making reservations. Sure that was a blow to the size of their paychecks, especially in the case of the pilots, but they still got paychecks and they kept their seniority and all their medical benefits.[3]

All job openings were filled from within when possible. Many firms have claimed to do that, but Delta actually followed it. Also, with the exception of various specialists, all employees started at the bottom of the ladder. We can see that this policy had been enforced by looking at the top-management team. Garrett started as a reservationist, Hetterman started as a mechanic, and Harris started as a transportation agent.

Delta established a policy that every employee must meet with a member of the senior management at least once every 18 months. The employee's immediate supervisor was usually asked to leave during part of this meeting so subordinates could voice any concerns they had about their boss.

Delta's salaries were always kept above the union scale. Furthermore, its employee benefit plan was known as one of the most generous in U.S. industry.

All these aspects of its personnel policies helped Delta to develop an excellent reputation. At one point in 1978, Delta's employment files were bulging with 250,000 job applications that were less than six months old.

This reputation helped develop a nonunionism philosophy at Delta. By 1982, only the pilots and the dispatchers had been organized. The other employees apparently felt that they did not need a union. This fact provided Delta with a great deal of flexibility, which in turn lowered its expenses. Since Delta did not have to abide by union work rules, it assigned people temporarily to different jobs when needed. This helped Delta achieve flexibility in assignments and in scheduling. On busy days, it was not rare to find flight attendants making seat assignments or mechanics handling luggage.

Hetterman reasoned that not having unions and their work rules helped productivity in his division. He commented, "When we get jammed up with a lot of mechanical problems at once, I can pull people out of one part of the shop and put them in another, or I can even pull in people from other stations."[4] Union work rules in other firms forbade such action. Generally, union employees performed very narrowly defined job responsibilities.

The nonunionism philosophy resulted in increased flexibility and decreased labor costs. It also had one other big advantage for Delta, namely no costly labor strikes.

Almost all training at Delta was on-the-job training. There was no formal management training program, but Delta's personnel system helped create an environment where knowledge and expertise were passed on from old to new employees. This informal training was monitored by managers who were required to submit a yearly plan for the upgrading of their people and for their own replacement.

Senior management at Delta were encouraged to become familiar with all aspects of the operations, not just their own. At Delta, this was known as the theory of interchangeable parts. Garrett observed, "We have a group of senior officers who are almost interchangeable because lines of communication are so short you never have to worry about someone not knowing what is going on."[5] Oppenlander further added, "We do respond very quickly to fires that develop. We've all been working here together for a long time so we can work together very quickly. We're also not cluttered with a great deal of committee type or staff-type operations around this company. People can get to us and get to us very quickly."[6]

## Flight Operations

The senior vice-president of flight operations was Mr. Frank Rox. This division was responsible for flight personnel, communications, and flight control.

As mentioned previously, the rising cost of jet fuel was a great problem to the airlines. Many of the airlines, such as American, got involved in oil exploration and had begun to take more control of the fuel distribution. Delta tried changing suppliers and tried the spot market, but it resisted deeper involvement in the fuel or storage domain. Delta believed that these ventures would be cost-prohibitive.

Instead, Delta was taking every step possible to conserve fuel. They had begun to purchase fuel-efficient equipment, to modify their current equipment, and to analyze their flight operations to see where conservation could be achieved. But fuel conservation can only help so much. Antiquated flight routes that air traffic controllers required jet pilots to follow and the design of the airports also wasted a lot of fuel. As a result, Delta got involved in lobbying Congress and the FAA to try to have some say in these two causes of wasted fuel.

Another key to its success was that Delta had learned how to schedule its short flights so that they interconnected. Delta accomplished this through its hub-and-spoke system. All flights either originated from or led to one of the hubs. The cities or markets that the flights, which had generated from a hub, flew to were known as spokes. Delta currently had its major hub in Atlanta, and two lesser ones operating in Dallas–Ft. Worth and Cincinnati. Delta was also looking at Denver for a fourth hub.

The spoke-and-hub system worked this way. Jets departed early each morning from the new terminal in Atlanta and flew in all directions along spokes of a wheel to end point cities. At the same time, other jets flew from these end points along the spokes toward Atlanta. The in-bound flights were then scheduled to land in rapid succession so that 30 or more jets would be at the terminal at the same time. The jets then roared off, one after the other along a different spoke to another endpoint city.

This method of scheduling allowed passengers traveling on Delta to go to any point on the airline's route by connecting at a hub. In fact, during the first six months of 1980, 88.3 percent of Delta's passengers on flights to Atlanta continued their journey on Delta.

Many of the other airlines have tried to copy Delta's efficient hub-and-spoke system. Eastern Airlines, Delta's archrival, also established a hub in Atlanta. Because of the amount of connections that go on in Atlanta, the joke has grown among southerners that when you die, you may not know for sure whether you're going to heaven or hell, but you know for sure that you'll have to change planes in Atlanta.

**Finance**

The finance division, under the direction of Mr. Bob Oppenlander, had been very crucial to Delta since the planning division was also located under it. For the thirty-fourth consecutive year, Delta reported a profitable year in 1981. Delta's balance sheets, income statements, and other relevant data appear in Exhibits 25.6, 25.7, and 25.8. Financial information for some of Delta's competitors appears in Exhibit 25.9. Delta even remained profitable during the difficult years when other airlines were suffering severe losses. Indeed, many industry observers have felt that Delta has the best balance sheet in the industry. It has been so good that banks periodically have gone to Delta and asked if they wanted to borrow some money.

Some of Delta's financial policies have helped to maintain its health as well as independence. Delta has tried to stay away from external debt and has financed its fleet acquisition with 85–90 percent internally generated funds. This percentage has been much higher than those of other airlines, which were only able to cover 50–60 percent of their debt with internally generated funds. In fact, a former chief executive at Eastern said: "When I came to work every January 2, I would say to myself, I am $15 million behind in our battle with Delta before we even start. That's how much more interest we have to pay."[7] Furthermore, when Delta has turned to long-term debt for financing, it has repaid the debt as fast as banks would allow it.

Delta has also avoided leasing aircraft, preferring to buy the aircraft itself and conservatively depreciating its values down in ten years. While these policies may have been costly over the short run, they provided a hedge against the possibility that the aircraft might become obsolete more quickly than expected and have enabled Delta to sell the planes while they could still command a favorable price.

Although Delta did not have a formal planning department, advance planning was administered by Mr. Arthur Ford, assistant vice-president—long-range planning. Senior management, however, was very involved in the planning function on an ongoing basis. Planning at Delta was viewed as a line rather than staff function. Given its financial strength, Delta has been one of the few airlines to stick with long-range plans, even when uncontrollable events such as fuel shortages and a PATCO strike occurred. Delta has looked 15 years ahead for its fleet programs, and has been in the enviable position of being able to complete its program despite all the problems in the industry.

Delta has been willing to spend money on fleet modernization which has given it a competitive edge. This edge arose from the new technologies of aircraft—fuel efficiency, low noise, and lower emissions. Because Delta has kept its fleet up to date technologically, it has one of the youngest fleets in the industry. In 1980,

**Exhibit 25.6** Income Statements, 1981–1979 (in thousands of dollars)

| | 1981 | 1980 | 1979 |
|---|---|---|---|
| Operating revenues | | | |
| Passenger | $3,287,511 | $2,733,820 | $2,213,024 |
| Cargo | 213,431 | 190,490 | 167,904 |
| Other, net | 32,384 | 32,650 | 46,918 |
| Total operating revenues | 3,533,326 | 2,956,960 | 2,427,846 |
| Operating expenses | | | |
| Salaries and related costs | 1,306,359 | 1,161,487 | 1,014,144 |
| Aircraft fuel | 1,070,057 | 857,165 | 475,633 |
| Aircraft maintenance materials and repairs | 76,631 | 64,325 | 52,689 |
| Rentals and landing fees | 98,530 | 89,760 | 82,634 |
| Passenger service | 121,502 | 115,996 | 106,038 |
| Agency commissions | 157,710 | 114,304 | 79,183 |
| Other cash costs | 307,364 | 267,192 | 225,106 |
| Depreciation and amortization | 220,979 | 194,004 | 183,287 |
| Total operating expenses | 3,359,132 | 2,864,323 | 2,218,814 |
| Operating income | 174,194 | 92,637 | 209,032 |
| Other expense (income) | | | |
| Interest expense | 23,135 | 21,852 | 16,178 |
| Less interest capitalized | 15,539 | 10,790 | 6,717 |
| | 7,596 | 11,062 | 9,461 |
| Gain on disposition of aircraft | (30,078) | (36,091) | (20,514) |
| Realized and unrealized (gain) loss on foreign currency translation, net | (6,227) | 3,735 | 7,110 |
| Miscellaneous income, net | (19,917) | (10,687) | (9,069) |
| | (48,626) | (31,981) | (13,012) |
| Income before income taxes | 222,820 | 124,618 | 222,044 |
| Income taxes provided | 101,447 | 54,433 | 104,429 |
| Amortization of investment tax credits | (25,101) | (22,973) | (19,129) |
| Net income | $ 146,474 | $ 93,158 | $ 136,744 |
| Net income per common share | $7.37 | $4.69 | $6.88 |

*Source:* Delta Air Lines 1981 Annual Report.

**Exhibit 25.7** Balance Sheets 1981–1978 (in thousands of dollars)

|  | 1981 | 1980 | 1979 | 1978 |
|---|---|---|---|---|
| **Assets** | | | | |
| Current assets | | | | |
| Cash | $ 6,899 | $ 38,064 | $ 25,712 | $ 7,347 |
| Short-term investments | | | 3,216 | 116,764 |
| Acct. receivable | 308,168 | 283,039 | 229,284 | 116,764 |
| Supplies | 52,648 | 37,836 | 16,275 | 12,892 |
| Prepaid expense | 20,808 | 37,836 | 16,275 | 12,892 |
| Total current assets | 388,523 | 369,497 | 284,183 | 325,130 |
| Property and equipment | | | | |
| Cost less depreciation | 1,734,901 | 1,552,829 | 1,419,393 | 1,240,552 |
| Advance payments | 149,628 | 90,952 | 78,420 | 71,983 |
| Total prop./equip. | 1,884,529 | 1,643,781 | 1,497,813 | 1,312,532 |
| Other assets | 31,275 | 29,261 | 6,329 | 9,018 |
| Total assets | $2,304,327 | $2,042,539 | $1,788,325 | $1,646,683 |
| **Liabilities and stockholder equity** | | | | |
| Current liabilities | | | | |
| Current portion of long-term debt | $ 11,137 | $ 15,225 | $ 14,832 | $ 9,731 |
| Note payable | 44,487 | 30,934 | 30,104 | |
| Other | 532,627 | 504,405 | 363,453 | 363,063 |
| Total current liabilities | 588,251 | 550,564 | 408,389 | 372,794 |
| Long-term debt | 198,411 | 147,901 | 125,483 | 167,331 |
| Deferred credit | 477,054 | 422,105 | 401,785 | 369,759 |
| Stockholder equity | | | | |
| Common stock, par $3 per share | | | | |
| Authorized 25,000,000 | | | | |
| Outstanding 19,880,577 | 59,642 | 59,642 | 59,642 | 59,642 |
| Additional paid in capital | 80,088 | 80,088 | 80,088 | 80,088 |
| Retained earnings | 900,881 | 782,239 | 712,938 | 597,069 |
| Total stockholder equity | $1,040,611 | $ 921,969 | $ 852,668 | $ 736,799 |
| Total liabilities | $2,304,327 | $2,042,539 | $1,788,325 | $1,646,683 |

*Source:* Delta Air Lines 1981 Annual Report.

Delta bought 60 Boeing 757s valued at $3 billion. This was the largest aircraft order in history. In 1978, Delta ordered 20 Boeing 767s which were valued at $1.5 billion. The total value of this fleet program was $4.5 billion. These new planes will burn about 40 percent less fuel per seat than the planes they have replaced. However, Delta would like to buy more planes, if it could only find someone to build what it wants. Delta has developed specifications for a plane it calls the Delta III, and it has said it would buy 100 of these planes if someone would build them. Garrett noted that by developing the Delta III, Delta would be ready for the twenty-first century. The Delta III would burn even less fuel than the 757s and 767s and would provide other economies as well. However, none of the aircraft

**Exhibit 25.8** Other Relevant Data

| | 1981 | 1980 | 1979 | 1978 | 1977 |
|---|---|---|---|---|---|
| Long-term debt | $ 198,411 | $ 147,901 | $ 125,483 | $ 167,331 | $ 237,497 |
| Stockholder equity | $ 1,040,611 | $ 921,969 | $ 852,668 | $ 736,799 | $ 620,583 |
| Stockholder equity per share | $52.34 | $46.38 | $42.89 | $37.06 | $31.22 |
| Shares of common stock outstanding | 19,880,577 | 19,880,577 | 19,880,577 | 19,880,577 | 19,880,577 |
| Revenue passengers enplaned | 36,743,214 | 39,713,904 | 39,360,368 | 33,007,670 | 28,811,966 |
| Available seat miles (000) | 45,428,277 | 43,217,372 | 39,826,891 | 35,135,046 | 32,614,260 |
| Revenue passenger miles (000) | 25,192,531 | 26,171,197 | 25,518,520 | 20,825,722 | 18,042,339 |
| Passenger load factor (%) | 55.46 | 60.56 | 64.07 | 59.27 | 55.32 |
| Break-even load factor (%) | 52.52 | 58.51 | 58.02 | 52.74 | 50.36 |
| Available ton miles (000) | 6,037,476 | 5,748,143 | 5,357,995 | 4,743,778 | 4,478,038 |
| Revenue ton miles (000) | 2,845,425 | 2,934,375 | 2,916,585 | 2,426,265 | 2,113,798 |
| Passenger revenue per passenger mile | 13.05¢ | 10.45¢ | 8.67¢ | 8.94¢ | 8.73¢ |
| Operating expenses per available seat mile | 7.39¢ | 6.63¢ | 5.57¢ | 5.25¢ | 4.84¢ |
| Operating expenses per available ton mile | 55.64¢ | 49.83¢ | 41.41¢ | 38.91¢ | 35.25¢ |

*Source:* Delta Air Lines 1981 Annual Report.

**Exhibit 25.9** Financial Information on Competitors for 1981 (000,000)

| Company | Sales | Profit | Current Ratio |
|---|---|---|---|
| American | $4,108.7 | $ 16.8 | 1.0 |
| Braniff | $1,204.0 | $ −160.6 | 0.6 |
| Continental | $1,090.8 | $ −60.4 | 0.9 |
| Eastern | $3,727.1 | $ −65.9 | 0.9 |
| Trans World | $5,265.5 | $ 45.0 | 0.8 |
| United | $5,141.2 | $ −70.5 | 0.8 |
| US Air | $1,110.5 | $ 51.1 | 1.1 |

*Source:* "Corporate Scoreboard," *Business Week,* March 1, 1982, p. 53, March 15, 1982, p. 74.

manufacturers have banged down Delta's door to get the order. Furthermore, it just would not make sense for Delta to try to manufacture the plane itself.

In planning for fleets in earlier years, Delta has maintained a wait-and-see attitude about new technology. Now, however, Delta has been doing just the opposite. It wants the new technology of the Delta III, so it has designed it. Delta's financial position has helped tremendously with its fleet programs. It can tread where other airlines do not in this day of deregulation, recession, and air traffic constraints.

Delta has never backed off on a fleet improvement program because of financial limitations. Year after year, Delta has stayed on course with its long-term plans, regardless of external financial threats or internal problems. Oppenlander commented on this point:

> If you didn't consistently apply the financial principles, you could have generated a lot of wealth during good times and blown it. Some people have. Because we have been consistent, we are poised to attack the next growth period for the industry while the rest of the industry has laid off a lot of people and restricted its fleet improvement program because of financial limitations. We jumped off in strength after the recession in 1971 with all our people, with all their training and skills intact, and with a modern fleet. We did it again in 1975. And when the air traffic control situation returns to normal and traffic turns up again, we'll do it again.[8]

Delta's plans for the coming years have included growth and competitiveness. Deregulation threw a kink into many of the airlines' expansion plans because of the extra competition it caused. But deregulation also gave the airlines the freedom to enter and exit as they pleased. When deregulation was official, many of the airlines jumped right in and started expanding. Not so with Delta, which was content to expand slowly. Delta planned any move it might make very carefully, and then it made that move cautiously. Delta had intense competition on many routes and recently began to feel the pressure from Piedmont Airlines, another carrier that had been successful in the last few years. Delta was at a disadvantage on many of its routes because it was basically a short-haul airline and many of its competitors flew the more profitable long-haul routes.

The air traffic controllers also threw a kink into the airlines' expansion plans because they were required to cut back their service, and service is still cut back. Although the impact of the strike was very painful at many other airlines, things at Delta were under control and Oppenlander went on vacation. Delta's reaction to the strike was to downsize, while trying to maintain as much of the hub-and-spoke system as intact as possible. Delta simply flew less frequently, and found something else for surplus employees to do.

## FICTIONAL-IZED CONCLUSION

It was now two weeks later and you were having another meeting with President Garrett. He looked somewhat concerned. As you looked on his desk, you saw a report entitled "Outlook for 1982." You also saw the headlines of a recent newspaper which read "Braniff Terminates Operations."

The outlook report indicated that industry leaders and experts did not anticipate any improvements in the economy or in traffic until mid-1982 at the earliest. The outlook on the entire year was not very optimistic. Estimates showed only a 3 percent expected increase in traffic.

Worse than this, Garrett had the first quarter 1982 result shown in Exhibit 25.10 and Delta had posted a loss, along with most of the other airlines. He told you that although the first quarter is usually poor, he was disappointed in the results. Moreover, he mentioned to you that the final results for 1981 were in, and that Delta's profits had decreased 30 percent from the year before. Delta

**Exhibit 25.10** First Quarter, 1982
(000,000)

| Company | Sales | Profits |
|---|---|---|
| American | 956.9 | −41.6 |
| Delta | 881.3 | −18.4 |
| Eastern | 908.4 | −51.4 |
| Trans World | 1,087.5 | −102.7 |
| United | 1,203.6 | −129.3 |
| US Air | 279.2 | 10.8 |

*Source:* "Corporate Scoreboard," *Business Week,* May 17, 1982, p. 61.

seemed to be losing traffic in its established markets, and gains were not being made in the new markets.

Delta was losing a lot of traffic to strong competitors, mainly Piedmont, Ozark, and U.S. Air. These airlines used to provide Delta with feed traffic, but now they had expanded their routes with hubs and spokes of their own to directly compete with Delta.

Also, Delta had pretty much saturated the Atlanta market, and wherever they might move, there was either some airline already there or another one was sure to follow. As one competitor's chief officer said: "Delta is just beginning to look a little more like everyone else. What's worrisome is that it can afford to bleed a little more than anyone else."[9]

Garrett paused and looked you square in the eyes and said "Well, consultant, what do you recommend we do to cope with this changing industry?" President Garrett further asked, "What threats and major problems do you feel we need to be addressing?" He further commented, "I know that we've concentrated pretty much on running just an airline. I'm sure there are opportunities within this industry and there are probably other related opportunities outside of it that we might try to exploit. What do you recommend?"

## NOTES

1. "Deregulation and Recession Realities Causing Major Shifts in Labor Relations," *Air Transport World,* December 1981, p. 45.
2. "Delta's Flying Money Machine," *Business Week,* May 9, 1977, p. 88.
3. "Delta: The World's Most Profitable Airline," *Business Week,* August 31, 1981, p. 70.
4. Ibid., p. 71.
5. "Flying High at Delta Airlines," *Dun's Review,* December 1977, p. 60.
6. "Delta: The World's Most Profitable Airline," p. 72.
7. "Delta's Flying Money Machine," p. 85.
8. "Delta: The World's Most Profitable Airline," p. 72.
9. "Delta Adjusts to Flying at Less Lofty Heights," *Business Week,* January 25, 1982, p. 30.

# 26   Waste Management, Inc.

Robert G. Wirthlin and James Kendrix
Butler University

"In light of the myriad events of 1983, the year might be expressed as the best of times and the worst of times." Although this sentiment was expressed by the CEO of the country's largest waste disposal organization, the implications of this statement transcend the environment of his firm to encompass the entire waste disposal industry.

The 1980–1982 period introduced the Clean Air Act as the number one environmental issue, but a multiplicity of new waste disposal regulations ranked a close second on the environmental "worry list."

The year 1983 proved to be tumultuous for both the waste industry and its regulators. The Environmental Protection Agency (EPA) captured the media's attention on a daily basis. We witnessed the resignation of EPA Administrator Ann Burford and the ousting of Toxics Chief Rita M. Lavelle. President Reagan ordered the Justice Department to open a full investigation of EPA's management of the cleanup of abandoned chemical dumps. As a result of this flurry of accusations and investigations relating to the EPA and its handling of the "superfund," public outcry put the government in the position of having to prove its responsibility to the public.

The management of waste moved to the forefront of domestic policy issues in 1984—a year in which seven major environmental laws were up for reauthorization in a presidential election year. When the Reagan administration took office in 1980, it promised revisions that would have undermined major environment laws governing clean air, clean water, and hazardous waste. However, the public outcry against these proposals—and the EPA mismanagement—reversed the politics on a number of environmental issues to the point where Congress, with new White House support, would undoubtedly stiffen many laws to respond to public demand.

**HIGHLIGHTS OF THE 1984 SITUATION**   During the first quarter, the EPA developed two programs to force more than 1700 public sewage treatment plants to comply with clean-water standards. Ocean incineration of hazardous waste created political pressures in Washington, and the EPA recommended rejection of long-term incineration permits for two vessels operating in the Gulf of Mexico. The agency also recommended delaying permits for smaller-scale test burns of hazardous wastes aboard incineration ships.

In March, the first industrywide effort to finance cleanup of abandoned toxic-waste sites around the country was initiated. This action was developed by a group including major chemical producers.

The second quarter saw the EPA, for the second time in less than a year, substantially increase its estimated total amount of hazardous chemical waste generated by American industry. The Supreme Court agreed to decide whether the EPA could legally grant some companies waivers from national standards for the treatment of toxic wastes that were to be discharged into sewage systems and declined to hear Mobil Corporation's challenge to the EPA to sample water before it was treated and discarded into public sewage streams. Investigations concerning hazardous-waste disposal were under way all over the country. John Ruckelshaus, the new EPA administrator, was appointed to bring new luster to the tarnished EPA image.

During July, the EPA was facing the dilemma of where to relocate toxins it required to be removed from more than 20 waste sites and announced that it was developing an array of more stringent operating, monitoring, and inspection standards for the largest operating hazardous-waste landfills. The Senate approved major environmental legislation which tightened hazardous-waste regulations and attempted to minimize the industry's use of risky land-disposal sites. In August, the House Ways and Means Committee approved legislation that would extend "superfund" toxic-waste programs through fiscal 1990 and substantially augmented its funding by increasing the excise tax on crude oil. The House overwhelmingly voted to expand and extend the "superfund" toxic-waste disposal program. "Superfund" financing would increase more than sixfold during the five-year period 1985–1990 from $1.6 billion to $10.2 billion.

## WASTE MANAGEMENT, INC.

Waste Management, Inc. (WMI) was incorporated in Delaware on September 23, 1968. WMI provides integrated solid- and chemical-waste management services consisting of storage and collection, transfer, interim processing, and disposal to commercial, industrial, and municipal customers, to other waste management companies, and solid-waste management services to residences.

Recently, WMI has offered street-sweeping services to municipalities in the United States. WMI is developing solid- and chemical-waste resources recovery operations where economically feasible. Since 1977, during which WMI entered into a five-year contract to operate the department of streets and sanitation for a major city in Saudi Arabia, WMI has been involved with international street-cleaning projects. As of March 1984, WMI had interests in projects in Jeddah, Saudi Arabia; Brisbane, Australia; Buenos Aires and Cordoba, Argentina; and Caracas, Venezuela. WMI intends to aggressively pursue such foreign business opportunities.

WMI has been providing low-level radioactive-waste services, primarily to utilities with nuclear reactors, since 1982 and is also engaged in the sale of industrial minerals mined and processed by the company from its reserves. As of December 31, 1984, WMI had solid- and chemical-waste management operations in 33 states and in Ontario, Canada. During 1983, operations in Florida and Illinois accounted for approximately 33 percent of North American operations revenue. Fees paid by collection customers (including charges for interim processing and disposal) accounted for approximately 72 percent of North American operations revenue during 1981–1983. Transfer, interim processing, and disposal services provided to municipalities, countries, and other waste management companies accounted for approximately 26 percent of such revenue. (See Exhibits 26.1 through 26.7.)

Developments in environmental and ecological regulations may require companies engaged in the waste management business to modify, supplement, or replace equipment and facilities at costs which may be substantial. Because the business is intrinsically connected with the protection of the environment and the potential discharge of materials into the environment, a material portion of WMI's capital is related to such items.

Early in 1983, WMI was the subject of allegations that certain of its activities relating to its chemical-waste service were not conducted in accordance with applicable laws and regulations. As a result of these allegations, management retained independent environmental legal counsel to conduct an investigation of activities and policies and procedures in the chemical-waste area and make recommendations. Although the investigation found many of the more serious allegations to be without merit, the investigation did identify instances of infractions. WMI carefully reviewed the results of the investigation and implemented appropriate action.

## 1984 HIGHLIGHTS OF WMI

- Applied Technology sued WMI in federal court, seeking damages of $45 million for alleged anticompetitive behavior. Suit charged that WMI made it difficult for Applied Technology trucks to enter a landfill in Emelle, Alabama.
- Political pressure to put ocean incineration of hazardous waste in dry dock for a while continued to persist. Such action would adversely affect WMI's efforts to obtain a permit to burn toxic waste on U.S. waters utilizing its oceangoing incineration ship.
- The Emelle, Alabama, chemical-waste storage facility, where large amounts of polychlorinated biphenyls (PCBs) were stored, was under investigation concerning its storage and recordkeeping practices. EPA proposed a $321,000 fine against WMI for violating a January deadline to dispose of the PCBs.
- An Ohio EPA study concluded that hazardous waste leaked at a Vickery, Ohio, site operated by WMI.

**Exhibit 26.1**

## WASTE MANAGEMENT, INC., AND SUBSIDIARIES
### Consolidated Statement of Income
#### For the Years Ended December 31 (000's omitted except per share amounts)

|  | 1981 | 1982 | 1983 |
|---|---|---|---|
| Revenue | $772,690 | $966,548 | $1,039,989 |
| Costs and expenses |  |  |  |
|   Operating | $492,512 | $593,149 | $ 657,536 |
|   Selling and administrative | 116,960 | 160,201 | 171,477 |
|     Income from operations | $163,218 | $213,198 | $ 210,976 |
| Other (income) expense |  |  |  |
|   Interest, net | $ (587) | $ 3,947 | $ 3,337 |
|   Sundry, net, including minority interest | 9,333 | 13,619 | (1,676) |
|     Income Before Income Taxes | $154,472 | $195,632 | $ 209,315 |
| Provision for income taxes | 70,439 | 89,108 | 88,868 |
| Net income for the year | $ 84,033 | $106,524 | $ 120,447 |

**Exhibit 26.2** Summary Operating Data by Business Group, 1981, 1982, and 1983

|  | Waste Management of North America | Chemical Waste Management | Waste Management International | Chem-Nuclear Systems, Inc. | Industrial Minerals |
|---|---|---|---|---|---|
| **Year ended December 31, 1981** |  |  |  |  |  |
| Revenue | $483,927 | $119,126 | $130,238 | $ — | $39,399 |
| Income before income taxes | $ 98,358 | $ 37,076 | $ 18,414 | $ — | $ 624 |
| % of revenue | 20.3 | 31.1 | 14.1 | — | 1.6 |
| **Year ended December 31, 1982** |  |  |  |  |  |
| Revenue | $536,753 | $125,257 | $240,061 | $27,035 | $37,442 |
| Income before income taxes | $121,674 | $ 29,751 | $ 36,969 | $ 4,640 | $ 2,598 |
| % of revenue | 22.7 | 23.8 | 15.4 | 17.2 | 6.9 |
| **Year ended December 31, 1983** |  |  |  |  |  |
| Revenue | $622,794 | $148,134 | $156,773 | $72,290 | $39,998 |
| Income before income taxes | $150,581 | $ 12,883 | $ 23,252 | $19,876 | $ 2,723 |
| % of revenue | 24.2 | 8.7 | 14.8 | 27.5 | 6.8 |

**Exhibit 26.3**

## WASTE MANAGEMENT, INC., AND SUBSIDIARIES
### Consolidated Balance Sheets As of December 31 ($000's omitted)

|  | 1982 | 1983 |
|---|---|---|
| **Current assets** | | |
| Cash | $ 1,812 | $ 966 |
| Short-term investments | 84,101 | 51,064 |
| Accounts receivable, less reserve of $4,500 in 1982 and $4,967 in 1983 | 144,150 | 190,156 |
| Employee receivables | 2,244 | 4,950 |
| Contract costs incurred in excess of unrecognized revenue billed | 78,884 | 90,800 |
| Parts and supplies | 26,477 | 28,951 |
| Prepaid expenses | 19,976 | 19,644 |
| Total current assets | $ 357,644 | $ 386,531 |
| | | |
| **Property and equipment, at cost** | | |
| Land, primarily disposal sites | $ 224,873 | $ 285,515 |
| Buildings | 66,844 | 78,360 |
| Vehicles and equipment | 569,739 | 671,557 |
| Leasehold improvements | 17,209 | 16,625 |
| | $ 878,665 | $1,052,057 |
| Less accumulated depreciation and amortization | (253,890) | (308,948) |
| Total property and equipment, net | $ 624,775 | $ 743,109 |
| | | |
| **Other assets** | | |
| Intangible assets relating to acquired businesses, net | $ 116,138 | $ 140,001 |
| Funds held by trustees for acquisition or construction | 28,766 | 6,180 |
| Sundry, including investments | 42,358 | 62,142 |
| Total other assets | $ 187,262 | $ 208,323 |
| Total assets | $1,169,681 | $1,337,963 |

|  | 1982 | 1983 |
|---|---:|---:|
| **Current liabilities** | | |
| Portion of long-term debt payable within one year | $ 31,793 | $ 43,623 |
| Accounts payable | 60,837 | 83,491 |
| Accrued expenses | 49,489 | 58,958 |
| Unearned revenue | 42,219 | 38,270 |
| Income taxes | 13,558 | 8,563 |
| Total current liabilities | $ 197,896 | $ 232,905 |
| | | |
| **Deferred items** | | |
| Income taxes | $ 63,658 | $ 81,787 |
| Investment credit | 20,643 | 21,574 |
| Other, including unearned revenue, noncurrent portion, and minority interest in subsidiaries | 57,310 | 65,892 |
| Total deferred items | $ 141,611 | $ 169,253 |
| | | |
| **Long-term debt, less portion payable within one year** | $ 166,338 | $ 167,940 |
| **Stockholders' equity** | | |
| Preferred stock, $1 par value (issuable in series); 500,000 shares authorized; none outstanding during the years | $ — | $ — |
| Common stock, $1 par value; 150,000,000 shares authorized; 47,127,117 shares issued in 1982 and 47,952,421 in 1983 | 47,127 | 47,952 |
| Additional paid-in capital | 294,849 | 309,711 |
| Retained earnings | 321,860 | 410,202 |
| Total Stockholders' Equity | $ 663,836 | $ 767,865 |
| Total Liabilities and Stockholders' Equity | $1,169,681 | $1,337,963 |

**Exhibit 26.4** Summary Operating Data by Service Provided

| | Solid Waste | Chemical Waste | Nuclear Waste | Industrial Minerals | Consolidated |
|---|---|---|---|---|---|
| **1981** | | | | | |
| Revenue | $614,165 | $119,126 | $ — | $39,399 | $ 772,690 |
| Income from operations | $124,218 | $ 36,270 | $ — | $ 2,730 | $ 163,218 |
| Interest income, net | | | | | (587) |
| Sundry expense, net, including minority interest | | | | | 9,333 |
| Income before income taxes | | | | | $ 154,472 |
| Identifiable assets | $657,175 | $145,892 | $ — | $29,634 | $ 832,701 |
| Depreciation and amortization expense | $ 53,685 | $ 8,348 | $ — | $ 2,378 | $ 64,411 |
| Capital expenditures | $110,268 | $ 30,619 | $ — | $ 3,925 | $ 144,812 |
| **1982** | | | | | |
| Revenue | $776,814 | $125,257 | $ 27,035 | $37,442 | $ 966,548 |
| Income from operations | $172,800 | $ 29,053 | $ 6,275 | $ 5,070 | $ 213,198 |
| Interest expense, net | | | | | 3,947 |
| Sundry expense, net, including minority interest | | | | | 13,619 |
| Income before income taxes | | | | | $ 195,632 |
| Identifiable assets | $797,066 | $228,734 | $110,458 | $33,423 | $1,169,681 |
| Depreciation and amortization expense | $ 61,363 | $ 10,506 | $ 1,651 | $ 2,682 | $ 76,182 |
| Capital expenditures | $128,257 | $ 58,087 | $ 28,347 | $ 5,154 | $ 219,845 |
| **1983** | | | | | |
| Revenue | $779,567 | $148,134 | $ 72,290 | $39,998 | $1,039,989 |
| Income from operations | $165,497 | $ 15,237 | $ 25,496 | $ 4,746 | $ 210,976 |
| Interest expense, net | | | | | 3,337 |
| Sundry income, net, including minority interest | | | | | (1,676) |
| Income before income taxes | | | | | $ 209,315 |
| Identifiable assets | $920,406 | $270,699 | $115,567 | $31,291 | $1,337,963 |
| Depreciation and amortization expense | $ 69,305 | $ 12,315 | $ 4,865 | $ 2,479 | $ 88,964 |
| Capital expenditures | $158,017 | $ 53,148 | $ 5,141 | $ 2,620 | $ 218,926 |

**Exhibit 26.5** Summary Operating Data by Geographic Area

| | United States | Foreign | Consolidated |
|---|---|---|---|
| **1981** | | | |
| Revenue | $ 619,549 | $153,141 | $ 772,690 |
| Income from operations | $ 125,076 | $ 38,142 | $ 163,218 |
| Interest income, net | | | (587) |
| Sundry expense, net, including minority interest | | | 9,333 |
| Income before income taxes | | | $ 154,472 |
| Identifiable assets | $ 679,533 | $153,168 | $ 832,701 |
| **1982** | | | |
| Revenue | $ 704,474 | $262,074 | $ 966,548 |
| Income from operations | $ 151,760 | $ 61,438 | $ 213,198 |
| Interest expense, net | | | 3,947 |
| Sundry expense, net, including minority interest | | | 13,619 |
| Income before income taxes | | | $ 195,632 |
| Identifiable assets | $ 963,178 | $206,503 | $1,169,681 |
| **1983** | | | |
| Revenue | $ 858,085 | $181,904 | $1,039,989 |
| Income from operations | $ 171,685 | $ 39,291 | $ 210,976 |
| Interest expense, net | | | 3,337 |
| Sundry income, net, including minority interest | | | (1,676) |
| Income before income taxes | | | $ 209,315 |
| Identifiable assets | $1,097,570 | $240,393 | $1,337,963 |

**Exhibit 26.6** Capital Plans

Capital additions for 1983 were $218,926,000, including $29,473,000 of assets from businesses acquired in purchase transactions. The company continued to invest heavily in disposal and processing facilities for both solid- and chemical-waste operations as well as normal replacements and additions to vehicles and equipment.

The following is a summary of capital expenditures for the last three years:

|  | 1981 | 1982 | 1983 |
| --- | --- | --- | --- |
| Land (primarily disposal sites) | $ 30,971 | $ 66,448 | $ 72,920 |
| Buildings | 15,399 | 15,474 | 12,421 |
| Vehicles | 33,719 | 43,761 | 52,076 |
| Containers | 17,654 | 19,946 | 27,284 |
| Other equipment | 41,050 | 69,096 | 51,106 |
| Leasehold improvements | 6,019 | 5,120 | 3,119 |
|  | $144,812 | $219,845 | $218,926 |

A capital appropriation of $250 million has been approved by the board of directors for 1984. A portion of that amount, $180 million, is allocated to replacements and additions to existing business units and the balance of $70 million to acquisitions and special projects.

- Senior EPA officials, responding to widespread congressional and public opposition to WMI plans to burn toxic waste at sea, recommended rejection of long-term incineration permits for two company vessels slated to operate in the Gulf of Mexico; decision set back effort to get a head start on ocean incineration of hazardous chemicals.
- WMI agreed to pay $10.5 million over the next ten years to settle charges that it violated state and federal environmental laws at the Vickery, Ohio, disposal site. A separate agreement with the EPA called for WMI to pay the EPA a fine totaling $50,000 annually for the next ten years.
- WMI failed to dispose of an undetermined amount of hazardous military DDT wastes, even though it had certified to the Defense Department that all pesticides were incinerated.
- Alabama ordered WMI to dispose of 2.8 million gallons of toxic waste containing PCBs stored in its Emelle landfill as "expeditiously as practicable." WMI had filed a disposal plan that called for disposal over a two-year period. WMI contended that its agreement with the EPA superseded the state's authority and sought an injunction against the state. The injunction was issued in favor of WMI.
- EPA stated that WMI was being investigated for possible criminal violations in storage and disposal of PCBs. Separately, WMI and EPA reached a tentative settlement on civil charges that WMI violated federal deadlines the previous January for disposing of PCBs stored in Emelle. WMI agreed to pay $100,000 in fines.
- WMI proposed to acquire SCA Services Inc. for about $300 million in a

merger that would combine the nation's largest and third largest waste disposal firms.

- EPA dictated a WMI unit, Chem-Waste Management, to accelerate the closing of a landfill outside Denver. EPA also stated that WMI must remove all 34,000 drums of hazardous waste from the landfill and ship them to an approved site. (WMI had planned to ship only 14,000 drums.)
- A Florida federal grand jury indicted an executive of United Sanitation Services, a WMI unit, on charges of conspiring to allocate customers of waste disposal services in the Miami area.
- SCA was acquired by a new company formed by WMI and Genstar Corp. for $423 million. The acquiring firms divided SCA's assets, strengthening WMI's domination in waste disposal. SCA gave WMI a head start in the hazardous-waste management business, which is expected to be spurred by emerging federal regulations.

**SOLID-WASTE OPERATIONS**

WMI provides storage and collection services to approximately 232,000 commercial and industrial customers. Collection services are also provided to approximately 3,064,000 homes and apartment units. WMI's commercial and industrial customers utilize containers to store solid waste. These containers, ranging from 1 to 45 cubic yards in size, are provided to customers as part of the company's services. Stationary compactors, which reduce volume of the stored waste prior to collection, are frequently installed on the premises of large customers. Containerization enables WMI to service most of its commercial and industrial customers with collection vehicles operated by a single employee. Compaction serves to decrease the frequency of collection.

Commercial and industrial storage and collection services are generally performed under agreements or arrangements cancellable on short notice by either party, and fees are determined by such factors as collection frequency, type of equipment furnished, and type and volume or weight. WMI employs 2860 persons in its commercial and industrial collection operations.

Most home collection services are performed under contracts with municipalities giving the company exclusive rights to service homes in their respective jurisdiction. Such contracts range in duration from one to five years. WMI employs 1895 persons in providing residential collection services.

In order to reduce transportation costs to disposal sites, WMI operates 16 transfer stations, employing 175 people, where solid waste is transferred from collection vehicles to large specially constructed trailers which compact it for transportation to disposal or resource recovery facilities. This procedure reduces costs by improving utilization of collection personnel and equipment. Transfer stations are operated in seven states and Ontario, Canada.

WMI currently operates two solid-waste shredding facilities for interim processing and is participating in a variety of resource recovery projects. Interim processing involves changing characteristics of solid waste to facilitate disposal

**Exhibit 26.7** Summary Financial Data

| For the Ten Years Ended December 31 | 1974 | 1975 | 1976 |
|---|---|---|---|
| Revenue | $ 160,413 | $ 166,650 | $ 189,656 |
| Costs and expenses | 134,430 | 141,636 | 160,534 |
| Income from operations | $ 25,983 | $ 25,014 | $ 29,122 |
| Other expense | 8,684 | 7,838 | 6,581 |
| Income before income taxes | $ 17,299 | $ 17,176 | $ 22,541 |
| Provision for income taxes | 7,951 | 7,995 | 10,537 |
| Net income for the year | $ 9,348 | $ 9,181 | $ 12,004 |
| Average shares | 30,146 | 31,198 | 31,388 |
| Earnings per common and common equivalent share | $.31 | $.29 | $.38 |
| Dividends per share | $— | $— | $.05 |
| December 31, | | | |
|   Property and equipment, net | $ 140,611 | $ 148,643 | $ 158,987 |
|   Total assets | $ 209,449 | $ 218,808 | $ 225,346 |
|   Long-term debt | $ 98,378 | $ 84,049 | $ 74,428 |
|   Stockholders' equity | $ 74,645 | $ 84,239 | $ 92,659 |

or resource recovery. Resource recovery involves the reclamation of marketable materials from solid wastes (ferrous and nonferrous metals, paper, and glass) or the conversion of solid waste into usable forms of energy feedstock, such as methane gas or refuse-derived fuel. Many advanced resource recovery operations require that the solid waste be shredded prior to further processing.

WMI operates a solid-waste reduction center at its Pompano Beach, Florida, sanitary-landfill site. Through shredding, solid waste is converted into material suitable for surface spreading. This process reduces the need for excavation of the landfill site and helps avoid contamination of underground water sources—a particular problem in this area of Florida because of the high water table. WMI is also exploring the feasibility of recovering, purifying, and marketing methane gas generated in selected sanitary-landfill sites it operates.

In late 1976, reduction and disposal operations commenced at WMI's Recovery 1 facility in New Orleans, where it receives at least 650 tons of municipal waste per day for shredding and landfill disposal.

Since 1978, WMI has had North American market rights for System Volund, a Danish mass-combustion/energy technology which significantly reduces the volume of waste requiring disposal while generating valuable energy in the form of steam or hot water. Pursuant to a contract between WMI and the city of Tampa, construction began in May 1983 on a waste-to-energy facility of a rated capacity of 1000 tons per day utilizing the System Volund technology. The facility is scheduled to be operational in 1986 and the $60 million cost is being financed by Tampa via revenue bonds. Upon completion, WMI will operate for a 25-year period and will share in revenues received from the sale of the energy generated in addition to its operating fees.

WMI operates 71 solid-waste sanitary-landfill facilities in 22 states and Ontario, Canada. Of this number, 39 are company-owned and the remainder are

| 1977 | 1978 | 1979 | 1980 | 1981 | 1982 | 1983 |
|---|---|---|---|---|---|---|
| $237,953 | $393,785 | $486,100 | $655,966 | $772,690 | $ 966,548 | $ 1,039,98 |
| 192,876 | 323,135 | 397,023 | 531,306 | 609,472 | 753,350 | 829,01 |
| $ 45,077 | $ 70,650 | $ 89,077 | $124,660 | $163,218 | $ 213,198 | $ 210,97 |
| 9,373 | 11,259 | 12,141 | 17,258 | 8,746 | 17,566 | 1,66 |
| $ 35,704 | $ 59,391 | $ 76,936 | $107,402 | $154,472 | $ 195,632 | $ 209,31 |
| 16,970 | 28,098 | 35,028 | 48,424 | 70,439 | 89,108 | 88,86 |
| $ 18,734 | $ 31,293 | $ 41,908 | $ 58,978 | $ 84,033 | $ 106,524 | $ 120,44 |
| 31,730 | 36,304 | 39,179 | 41,063 | 43,172 | 44,432 | 48,23 |
| $.59 | $.86 | $1.07 | $1.44 | $1.95 | $2.40 | $2.5 |
| $.097 | $.158 | $.217 | $.283 | $.375 | $.49 | $.6 |
| | | | | | | |
| $167,032 | $277,177 | $326,562 | $415,799 | $491,271 | $ 624,775 | $ 743,109 |
| $290,259 | $444,045 | $496,250 | $662,138 | $832,701 | $1,169,681 | $1,337,963 |
| $ 64,475 | $129,669 | $110,779 | $132,090 | $128,099 | $ 166,338 | $ 167,940 |
| $109,906 | $214,077 | $237,222 | $344,391 | $417,637 | $ 663,836 | $ 767,865 |

leased from or operated under contract with others. Suitable landfills have become increasingly difficult to obtain because of scarcity of land, local resident opposition, and expanding governmental regulations. The scarcity of sites and increased volume of wastes have resulted in more intensive use of existing sanitary landfills. As existing sites become filled, solid-waste disposal operations will continue to be materially dependent on WMI's ability to purchase or lease such sites and obtain necessary permits from regulatory authorities to operate them. WMI's management believes that sites currently available are sufficient to meet the needs of its operations for the foreseeable future.

In 1981–1983, approximately 55 percent of the solid waste collected by WMI was disposed of in company-operated landfills.

## CHEMICAL-WASTE OPERATION

WMI has also acquired a number of companies which, together with the facilities it has developed in the Midwest, enable it to provide integrated chemical-waste management services consisting of collection, interim processing, and disposal. Prior to entering into an agreement with a customer, WMI has the chemical wastes in question (which may be either in solid or liquid state) analyzed by company-owned laboratories or independent labs so that the best method of transportation, processing, and disposal may be determined. In addition, WMI also processes and disposes of chemicals collected by other waste service companies.

Interim processing of chemical waste is accomplished by a procedure involving the transformation of chemicals into inert materials which can be readily disposed of in conventional solid- or chemical-waste landfills. Solar evaporation is also utilized. Chemical waste is then disposed of by various methods including burial, landfill, high-temperature incineration and deep-well injection. A landfill for chemical-waste is designed, constructed, and operated in a manner so as to provide long-term containment. Geological and hydrological conditions in parts of the country effectively preclude disposal of certain chemicals and landfills.

Chemical-waste service operations are subject to extensive governmental regulation. It is difficult to obtain permits for landfills which may accept chemical waste—extensive geological studies and testing are required before permits may be issued. The chemical-waste services performed expose WMI to risks not associated with its solid-waste management operations. In addition, WMI is required to monitor and maintain closed solid or chemical landfill sites, or undertake corrective measures at open or closed disposal sites.

In October 1980, the company acquired Ocean Combustion Service (OCS) BV, a company with extensive experience in disposing of a broad spectrum of chlorinated liquid wastes on its incineration vessel *Vulcanus I*. Although OCS has primarily served markets outside the United States, it successfully completed a burn of PCBs in U.S. waters in 1981 and again in late 1982, with destruction and combustion efficiencies exceeding required levels. *Vulcanus II* was delivered to WMI in late 1982 and has been operating in European waters.

Through its Environmental Remedial Action division, WMI is engaged in the cleanup and restoration of problem hazardous-waste sites and facilities, some of which have been designated by the EPA as "superfund" sites.

At mid-1984, WMI operated eight processing/transfer facilities and nine disposal sites which have received necessary permits to accept chemical waste. Also in 1984, 1490 employees were employed in chemical-waste service operations, including approximately 130 performing analytical or engineering services.

**LOW-LEVEL RADIO-ACTIVE-WASTE OPERATIONS**

Through its acquisition of Chem-Nuclear, WMI has become one of the leading companies providing low-level radioactive-waste (LLRW) management services for utilities with nuclear reactors. These services include the collection and treatment of waste at customers' facilities, transportation of waste to burial sites, and operation of a licensed burial site in Barnwell, South Carolina. Chem-Nuclear's activities include decommissioning and support services for nuclear power plants and the design and engineering of waste treatment systems.

Wastes with varying degrees of radioactivity and contamination are generated by nuclear reactors and by medical and industrial use of radioactive isotopes. At the present time, Chem-Nuclear's business is solely connected with LLRW, which decays more quickly than high-level waste. LLRW waste generated by nuclear power plants largely consists of dry compressible waste, such as gloves, paper, tools, clothing, and resin filters which have been contaminated with radioactive substances.

Since electric utilities operate at higher capacities during the peak demand periods in winter and summer, waste management operations are generally postponed until spring and fall when reactors are shut down or operating at lower capacity. Consequently, WMI's nuclear-waste business may be subject to seasonal variations, with potentially greater activity occurring in spring and fall months. Additionally, cold weather may reduce all disposal activities for a period of time, and severe weather conditions such as unusually heavy rainfall can interrupt such activities.

Chem-Nuclear's licensed radioactive-waste disposal site at Barnwell has been in operation since 1970 and is one of three presently operating in the United States. Barnwell includes approximately 183 acres for burial of waste. At the present rate of utilization (100,000 cubic feet per month), Barnwell contains space for 32 more years of operation. Regulatory or legislative developments, including possible adoption of an interstate compact, may limit the period of actual operation of the Barnwell site to approximately nine years. The portion to be used for burial of waste has been deeded to South Carolina's Department of Health and Environmental Control, and Chem-Nuclear has leased back the deeded portions.

South Carolina amended Chem-Nuclear's license for Barnwell in 1979 to reduce the maximum annual volume of radioactive waste which could be processed for disposal. These limits, unlike the limitations they replaced, were lower than the actual volume received in prior periods. The present maximum volume which may be buried at the site, 100,000 cubic feet per month, is approximately one-half the actual volume received immediately prior to the 1979 amendment. As a result of volume limitations, Chem-Nuclear has instituted a volume allocation plan to allocate the available space among waste generators.

Regulatory requirements adopted by South Carolina pertaining to the character of the treated waste which may be accepted at the Barnwell site have necessitated substantial research and development relating to hardening agents and high-integrity disposal containers.

The Low-Level Radioactive-Waste Policy Act of 1980 has resulted in the states of Alabama, Florida, Georgia, Mississippi, North Carolina, South Carolina, Tennessee, and Virginia joining together to form the Southeast Interstate Low-level Radioactive-waste Management Compact. In the event the compact is endorsed by Congress, the volume restrictions on Barnwell will be limited to those generated within the states which are parties to the compact. Also the commission provided for in the compact may prohibit the exportation of LLRW from the eight-state region. The compact envisions that the Barnwell site will serve as the disposal facility for the region until 1992. After this date, LLRW generated in the region will be disposed of at a site in a state which is a member of the compact other than South Carolina.

Chem-Nuclear is currently exploring opportunities to develop sites in other states. Presently, commercial LLRW sites are located in Hanford, Washington, and Beatty, Nevada—both operated by a division of a major U.S. corporation. Because licensed disposal sites require considerable capital expenditures, and since licenses are difficult to obtain, companies which have licensed sites enjoy a competitive advantage.

At December 31, 1983, WMI had interests in city cleaning contracts in Saudi Arabia, Argentina, Venezuela, and Australia:

- *Jeddah.* Service contract became operational April 1982 and is scheduled to end in April 1987. The contract amounted to $387 million (consisting of $45 million for facilities construction, $34 million for equipment, $212 million for cleaning services, and $87 million for street maintenance) paid in U.S. dollars.
- *Buenos Aires.* Contractual services commenced in February 1980 and total $400 million over a ten-year term. This contract requires monthly payments, based on tonnage of waste collected, to be made in Argentine pesos. Prices are adjusted quarterly pursuant to a formula reflecting variations in an index published by the Argentina National Institute of Statistics and Census.
- *Córdoba.* Contractual services began in December 1981 and end in December 1986. Monthly payments (in Argentine pesos) are to be made on the basis of tonnage handled and kilometers serviced to a formula reflecting such factors as minimum wage and labor rates and the cost of living. During the first two years of the contract annual revenue averaged $11.9 million.
- *Brisbane.* Early in 1984, a subsidiary of WMI was awarded a seven-year contract initially valued at $7.25 million per year and subject to adjustment for inflation during its term. This contract is for residential solid-waste collection services.

Revenue from these projects, along with Canadian and ocean incineration operations, accounted for 17 percent of total revenues in 1983.

## WASTE MANAGEMENT PARTNERS, INC.

In 1983, the company implemented a program through a new subsidiary, Waste Management Partners, which forms joint-venture companies with the owners of solid-waste collection companies in selected metropolitan areas. In each transaction, the joint-venture company purchases the customer accounts of the local solid-waste collection company. The joint-venture company then enters into a long-term operating agreement with the local collection company.

In order to provide the local company with an incentive to continue to develop waste management services, a series of agreements are entered into at the time the customer accounts are purchased by the joint-venture company. First, Waste Management Partners is granted the right, upon termination of the operating agreement, to purchase the local owner's interest in the joint-venture company as well as the local company's operating equipment. Additionally, each local collection company in the program becomes eligible to receive a broad range of operational support services. Twenty-five local collection companies operating in 17 states participate in the Management Partners Programs.

**INDUSTRIAL MINERALS**

WMI is also engaged in the extraction, processing, and sale of industrial minerals —lime and aggregates—through its wholly owned subsidiary, Warner Company. These operations were acquired in 1981.

Lime products are extracted and processed at two locations in Pennsylvania. At one site, dolmitic-high-magnesium lime is mined. Magnesium is used primarily for steel fluxing, masonry mortar, and acid-waste treatment. The second location produces a metallurgical limestone that is processed into high-calcium products which are used by the glass industry, steel fluxing in basic oxygen furnances, steel wire drawing, and acid-waste neutralization.

Aggregates are produced from mineral reserves located in Pennsylvania and New Jersey; two quarries in Pennsylvania supply hard rock for railroad ballast and highway construction. A third Pennsylvania quarry supplies construction material products. Industrial mineral products are marketed principally in the eastern United States.

# 27 Nike, Inc.

Robert G. Wirthlin and Anthony P. Schlichte
Butler University

In June 1984, the senior management met to review the events of the past fiscal year that ended May 31. Although the company reported a net income of $40.6 million, this represented a 29 percent decrease from the previous year despite a 6 percent increase in revenues. All were aware of the problems facing the company. The athletic-footwear industry had become keenly competitive, forcing price reductions. In addition, the domestic market for athletic shoes was decreasing. Consumers were changing their preference from the athletic look to a more fashionable and traditional style. Furthermore, the demand for running shoes, the company's leading revenue producer, was declining very rapidly. This was partly due to demographics. The industry's primary market was the baby boomers born between 1946 and 1964. With that market saturated and its leading-edge age approaching 40, the industry was hard-pressed to maintain the substantial early growth it enjoyed.

At the beginning of fiscal 1984, NIKE was caught in this changing market with an all-time-high inventory of 22 million pairs of shoes. Although by year end the inventory level had been reduced to 17 million pairs, this buildup was costly. The effects of price cutting, slow-moving merchandise, and inventory write-downs to market value decreased the gross margin by 3.5 percent. This translated into $32 million of additional costs.

No one was happy. Fiscal 1984 was the first year since the company was founded that had failed to produce an increase in net income.

## COMPANY HISTORY

In 1958, Phil Knight was an aspiring miler at the University of Oregon. His coach, Bill Bowerman, was considered by many to be the premier track coach in the United States. In 1960, Knight went on to Stanford's Graduate School of Business. While fellow students were doing their market research papers on computers and electronics, Knight was only interested in running. His research paper asserted that there was an enormous potential in the United States for athletic shoes. Furthermore, he concluded the Japanese could become a dominent market force in athletic shoes. Following his graduation in 1962, Knight celebrated with a trip around the world. He stopped in Japan and placed his first shoe order with Onitsuka, which manufactured Tiger running shoes. When his shipment of 300 pairs of shoes finally arrived in December 1963, nearly 14 months after the order, Knight took the shoes to his former coach for his opinion. Bowerman was enthusiastic and joined Knight in a partnership called Blue Ribbon Shoes (BRS). They each put up $500 to order more shoes. In the first year, BRS sold 1300 pairs of shoes for a total revenue of $8000. Within two years, BRS had opened its first office and warehouse in Tigard, a Portland suburb. Then in 1969, Knight resigned his accounting position with Coopers and Lybrand to devote his full time to the company. Now employing 20, and having three retail outlets, BRS attained $100,000 in revenues.

In 1972, a dispute over their distribution agreement led to litigation between BRS and Onitsuka. BRS launched a new shoe line under its own label. The name Nike, after the Greek goddess of victory, was chosen. Bowerman was selected as head track and field coach for the U.S. Olympic team. Several members of his team wore Nike shoes in competition. Sales for the first year were $1.90 million.

In 1973, John Anderson won the Boston Marathon wearing Nike shoes. Ilie Nastase, playing in Nike, was ranked number 1 tennis player in the world. One year later, the company opened its first manufacturing facility in Exeter, New Hampshire. Nike also expanded its sales overseas to Australia. Worldwide revenues reached $4.8 million.

In 1975, taking a clue from his traditional Sunday breakfast, Bill Bowerman created the first "waffle" sole using raw rubber and a kitchen waffle iron. The resulting studded design revolutionized running by providing a high-traction, lightweight, durable outsole. This invention was patented and the design was quickly grasped by the emerging jogging boom. Sales for the year shot to $8.3 million.

In 1977, Nike made a commitment to amateur sports by organizing Athletics West (AW). This club was the first track and field training club for Olympic contenders. AW members included Mary Decker, Alberto Salazar, Willie Banks, and Carl Davis. In the same year, Nike established factory sources in Taiwan and Korea. Nike shoes were sold for the first time in Asia. Sales more than doubled over 1976 to $28.7 million.

By 1979, Nike had signed agreements with distributors in all European countries. In that same year, Nike shoes became the most popular athletic shoes in the United States and Canada. In 1980, the Company went public and offered 2 million shares of common stock. In 1980, the company also signed new manufacturing contracts in Thailand, Malaysia, and the Philippines.

In October 1981, the company formed a 51 percent owned subsidiary in Japan with Nissho Iwai Corporation to market Nike products in Japan. The company continued its explosive growth in sales, and by May 1984, revenues had grown to $919 million. In just 12 years, the company's revenues went from $1.96 million to $919 million and the company was in a strong financial position to continue this growth. (See financial statements, Exhibits 27.1–27.3.)

## PRODUCTS

The company produces a broad line of athletic shoes for men, women, and children for competitive and recreational wear. The majority of the footwear products are designed for a specific athletic use. However, more and more shoes are being purchased and worn for casual or leisure purposes.

**Exhibit 27.1**

NIKE, INC.
Consolidated Statement of Income
(in thousands except per share data)

| | Year Ended May 31 | | |
| --- | --- | --- | --- |
| | 1983 | 1982 | 1981 |
| Revenues | $867,212 | $693,582 | $457,742 |
| Costs and expenses | | | |
|    Cost of sales | 589,986 | 473,885 | 328,133 |
|    Selling and administrative | 132,400 | 94,919 | 60,953 |
|    Interest | 25,646 | 24,538 | 17,859 |
|    Other expenses | 1,057 | 435 | 92 |
| | 749,089 | 593,777 | 407,037 |
| Income before provision for income taxes and minority interest | 118,123 | 99,805 | 50,705 |
| Provision for income taxes | 60,922 | 50,589 | 24,750 |
| Income before minority interest | 57,201 | 49,216 | 25,955 |
| Minority interest | 197 | 180 | — |
| Net income | $ 57,004 | $ 49,036 | $ 25,955 |
| Net income per common share | $      1.53 | $      1.37 | $      .76 |
| Average number of common and common equivalent shares | 37,158 | 35,708 | 34,031 |

The company also manufactures a line of active-sports apparel including running shoes and shirts, tennis clothing, warmup suits, socks, jackets, athletic bags, and accessories. Apparel and accessories are designed to complement the company's footwear products featuring the "swoosh" design and the Nike trademark.

Shown in Exhibit 27.4 is a breakdown of revenues in the United States by product category, and revenues from foreign markets.

The company's products are designed for the high-quality market. At the end of 1984, the company's product line included 235 basic footwear models. Running, basketball, racquet, and children's shoes were expected to continue to account for the majority of the company's shoe sales in the near future. However, the company planned to continue to place significant emphasis on the development and production of a broader line of leisure shoes.

**DOMESTIC SALES AND MARKETING**

Nearly 83 percent of the company's sales in fiscal 1984 were made in the United States to approximately 12,000 retail accounts consisting of department stores, shoe stores, sporting good stores, specialty stores, tennis shops, and other retail

**Exhibit 27.2**

## NIKE, INC.
### Consolidated Balance Sheet
### (in thousands)

|  | May 31 1983 | May 31 1982 |
|---|---|---|
| **Assets** | | |
| Current assets | | |
| Cash | $ 13,038 | $ 4,913 |
| Accounts receivable, less allowance for doubtful accounts of $3,751 and $3,877, respectively | 151,581 | 130,438 |
| Inventories | 283,788 | 202,817 |
| Deferred income taxes and purchased tax benefits | 10,503 | 2,145 |
| Prepaid expenses | 6,625 | 5,198 |
| Total current assets | 465,535 | 345,511 |
| Property, plant, and equipment | 61,359 | 41,407 |
| Less accumulated depreciation | 21,628 | 12,485 |
|  | 39,731 | 28,922 |
| Other assets | 2,762 | 1,040 |
|  | $508,028 | $375,473 |
| **Liabilities and shareholders' equity** | | |
| Current liabilities | | |
| Current portion of long-term debt | $ 2,347 | $ 3,936 |
| Notes payable to banks | 132,092 | 112,673 |
| Accounts payable | 91,102 | 74,064 |
| Accrued liabilities | 19,021 | 22,894 |
| Income taxes payable | 11,102 | 19,774 |
| Total current liabilities | 255,664 | 233,341 |
| Long-term debt | 10,503 | 9,086 |
| Commitments and contingencies | — | — |
| Minority interest in consolidated subsidiary | 948 | −86 |
| Redeemable preferred stock | 300 | 300 |
| Shareholders' equity | | |
| Common stock at stated value | | |
| Class A convertible—18,837 and 11,976 shares outstanding | 225 | 166 |
| Class B—18,434 and 5,555 outstanding | 2,646 | 1,414 |
| Capital in excess of stated value | 77,457 | 27,020 |
| Unrealized translation gain (loss) | 70 | (67) |
| Retained earnings | 160,215 | 103,427 |
|  | 240,613 | 131,960 |
|  | $508,028 | $375,473 |

# Exhibit 27.3

## NIKE, INC.
### Consolidated Statement of Changes in Financial Position
#### (in thousands)

| | Year Ended May 31 | | |
|---|---|---|---|
| | **1983** | **1982** | **1981** |
| **Financial resources were provided by** | | | |
| Net income | $ 57,004 | $ 49,036 | $ 25,955 |
| Income charges (credits) not affecting working capital | | | |
| Depreciation | 9,421 | 5,135 | 3,774 |
| Minority interest | 197 | 180 | — |
| Other | (188) | 194 | 131 |
| Working capital provided by operations | 66,434 | 54,545 | 29,860 |
| Net proceeds from sale of class B common stock in October 1982 and December 1980 | 51,442 | — | 27,890 |
| Purchased tax benefits becoming current | 14,270 | — | — |
| Additions to long-term debt | 4,135 | 4,477 | 4,392 |
| Disposal of property, plant, and equipment | 584 | 343 | 134 |
| Proceeds from exercise of stock options | 100 | — | 450 |
| Minority shareholder contribution | — | 648 | — |
| | 136,965 | 60,013 | 62,726 |
| **Financial resources were used for** | | | |
| Additions to property, plant, and equipment | 21,031 | 18,228 | 9,914 |
| Purchase of tax benefits | 15,277 | — | — |
| Long-term debt becoming current | 2,368 | 4,002 | 7,049 |
| Additions to other assets | 527 | 161 | 670 |
| Unrealized loss from translation of statements of foreign operations, including minority interest | 31 | 109 | — |
| Dividends on redeemable preferred stock | 30 | 30 | 30 |
| | 39,264 | 22,530 | 17,663 |
| Increase in working capital | $ 97,701 | $ 37,483 | $ 45,063 |
| **Analysis of changes in working capital** | | | |
| Increase (decrease) in current assets | | | |
| Cash | $ 8,125 | $ 3,121 | $ (35) |
| Accounts receivable | 21,143 | 43,202 | 23,375 |
| Inventories | 80,971 | 82,588 | 64,288 |
| Deferred income taxes and purchased tax benefits | 8,358 | 845 | 1,165 |
| Prepaid expenses | 1,427 | 2,711 | 336 |
| | 120,024 | 132,467 | 89,129 |
| Increase (decrease) in current liabilities | | | |
| Current portion of long-term debt | (1,589) | (2,684) | 2,753 |
| Notes payable to banks | 19,419 | 51,483 | 24,690 |
| Accounts payable | 17,038 | 31,572 | 5,560 |
| Accrued liabilities | (3,873) | 7,493 | 5,102 |
| Income taxes payable | (8,672) | 7,120 | 5,961 |
| | 22,323 | 94,984 | 44,066 |
| Increase in working capital | $ 97,701 | $ 37,483 | $ 45,063 |

**Exhibit 27.4**

| | 1981 | | 1982 | | 1983 | | 1984 | |
|---|---|---|---|---|---|---|---|---|
| | | | | **Year Ended May 31**[a] | | | | |
| U.S. Revenues | | | | | | | | |
| Footwear | | | | | | | | |
| Running | $149,300 | 33% | $236,300 | 34% | $267,600 | 31% | $240,200 | 26% |
| Court | | | | | | | | |
| Basketball | 104,500 | 23 | 144,400 | 21 | 122,400 | 14 | 125,100 | 14 |
| Racquet | 60,700 | 13 | 58,600 | 9 | 62,100 | 7 | 81,400 | 9 |
| Field | | | | | | | | |
| sports | 8,700 | 2 | 13,600 | 2 | 41,300 | 5 | 42,200 | 5 |
| Other | | | | | | | | |
| Children's | 64,300 | 14 | 106,100 | 15 | 120,800 | 14 | 97,100 | 10 |
| Leisure/other | 11,400 | 2 | 21,300 | 3 | 52,300 | 6 | 53,600 | 6 |
| | 398,900 | 87 | 580,300 | 84 | 666,500 | 77 | 639,600 | 70 |
| Apparel | 33,100 | 7 | 70,300 | 10 | 107,400 | 12 | 121,800 | 13 |
| Total United States | 432,000 | 94 | 650,600 | 94 | 773,900 | 89 | 761,400 | 83 |
| Foreign revenues | 25,700 | 6 | 43,000 | 6 | 93,300 | 11 | 158,400 | 17 |
| Total revenues | $457,700 | 100% | $693,600 | 100% | $867,200 | 100% | $919,800 | 100% |

[a]Dollars in thousands.

outlets. During fiscal 1984, no single customer accounted for more than 9.0 percent of the company's sales, and the three largest customers accounted for only 17 percent of sales.

Sales are solicited in the United States by 24 independent regional sales representative firms which are compensated on a commission basis. These firms do not take title to the inventory. Additionally, the company supports its reps with in-house sales personnel. Company sales and credit personnel review all orders and new accounts and are responsible for collecting receivables. Bad-debt losses have been minimal.

The company operates seven Nike retail stores which carry a full line of products. One store carries primarily close-out merchandise. The company feels these stores are valuable for promotional purposes as well as a training ground for employees.

During 1984, nearly 60 percent of the company shipments were made under the "futures" program. This program, started in 1982, allows dealers to order six months in advance of delivery and be guaranteed that 90 percent of their order will be shipped within 15 days of the requested delivery date at a specified price. Retailers benefit from this program because prices are fixed, promotional activities are planned in advance, and sufficient inventories are assured to meet seasonal peak demands. These orders can be cancelled with penalties.

The company distributes its footwear products in the United States through three large warehouse facilities. The western United States is served from Portland; the East is served from Greenland, New Hampshire; and, the Midwest and South by Memphis, Tennessee. Apparel products are distributed from Beaverton, Oregon, and Memphis, Tennessee.

**FOREIGN SALES**

Nike products are sold in 50 countries in addition to the United States. In most countries, Nike is represented by independent distributors, several of whom are licensed to manufacture and sell Nike brand products. Licensing arrangements provide for the company's approval of product lines and on-site quality control inspection.

In larger foreign markets, Nike has become directly responsible for the marketing of its products by opening its own branches and acquiring subsidiaries (Nissho Iwai Corporation to market Nike products in Japan and the acquisition of the Canadian distributorship).

**PROMOTION AND ADVERTISING**

Since 1972, the company has spent the majority of its annual promotion and advertising budget on having athletes wear and endorse Nike products. Shoes and equipment are provided to outstanding athletes and teams, athletes are hired as consultants, and product endorsements are obtained from leading professional athletes. The company uses this form of promotion to establish product creditability with customers.

The company founded Athletics West in 1972 to provide coaching, training, and financial support for postgraduate athletes. Presently there are 80 athletes in this club. During 1984, the company sponsored or assisted in nearly 1000 road races, marathons, and other sporting events across the United States.

Although the company spends the majority of its advertising budget on promotional activities, it does limited advertising on television and in athletic and trade magazines, and it assists retailers with local advertising. The company supplies dealers with brochures, posters, and other point-of-purchase promotional material.

**MANUFAC-TURING**

Nearly 95 percent of the footwear produced for the company is manufactured by 35 foreign suppliers, primarily in South Korea and Taiwan. The remaining portion is manufactured by three contract suppliers in the United States and its own plants in Massachusetts, Ireland, and England. The U.S. facilities produce approximately 100,000 pairs of shoes per month, or roughly 2 percent of the current requirements. U.S. production is concentrated on the most expensive models. In fiscal 1984, South Korean and Taiwanese suppliers accounted for 63 percent and 15 percent respectively of total footwear production for the company. The company also obtains production from contract suppliers in the People's Republic of

China, Spain, Yugoslavia, Malaysia, the Philippines, Brazil, and Italy. No single supplier accounted for more than 12 percent of that 1984 production.

All foreign and domestic contract manufacturing is performed to detailed specifications furnished by the company. The company closely monitors such production to ensure compliance with such specifications. Foreign operations are subject to the usual risks such as revaluation of currency, export duties, quotas, restrictions on the transfer of funds, and political instability. To date, Nike has not been materially affected by any such risk. However, the company has developed alternative sources of supply for such products.

Since 1972, Nissho Iwai American Corporation (NIAC), a subsidiary of Nissho Iwai Corporation, a large Japanese trading company, has performed significant financing and export-import services for the company. The company purchases through NIAC substantially all of the athletic shoes and apparel it acquires from overseas suppliers for sale in the United States. The company's agreements with NIAC expired on September 30, 1985.

## COMPETITION

There are approximately 50 companies worldwide that produce athletic footwear and apparel. The industry has experienced substantial growth the past ten years and is becoming increasingly competitive. Adidas is the leader in worldwide sales. Nike is the largest producer in the United States and second largest in the world and estimates it has 30 percent of the worldwide market. Although there is no comprehensive independent trade statistics, Nike believes its running, basketball, and tennis shoes have the highest sales volume in the United States. (See Exhibit 27.5.)

## RESEARCH AND DEVELOPMENT

Nike has always relied heavily on its technical competence and innovation and feels its success will depend on continued emphasis on research and development for the elimination of injury and performance maximization of its products. Many of the 150 people employed in R&D hold degrees in biochemics, exercise physiology, engineering, industrial design, and chemistry. The company also utilizes advisory boards, which include coaches, athletes, trainers, equipment managers, podiatrists, and orthopedists to review designs and concepts aimed at improving shoes.

## TRADEMARKS AND PATENTS

The Nike trademark and "swoosh" design are two of the company's most valuable assets. Both are registered in over 70 countries.

The company has an exclusive worldwide license to manufacture and sell

**Exhibit 27.5**

**CONVERSE INC.**

| | Year Ended December 31 | | Ten-Month Period Ended December 31, 1982 |
| --- | --- | --- | --- |
| | **1984** | **1983** | **1982** |
| Net revenues | $265,598,000 | $209,470,000 | $150,844,000 |
| Cost of sales | 179,730,000 | 137,580,000 | 97,824,000 |
| Gross profit on sales | 85,868,000 | 71,890,000 | 53,020,000 |
| Other expenses | | | |
| Marketing, general, and administrative | 52,910,000 | 44,043,000 | 27,548,000 |
| Research and development | 2,107,000 | 1,588,000 | 1,031,000 |
| Income from operations | 30,851,000 | 26,259,000 | 24,441,000 |
| Other income, net | 842,000 | 236,000 | 141,000 |
| Interest expense | (7,581,000) | (7,601,000) | (10,207,000) |
| Income before income taxes | 24,112,000 | 18,894,000 | 14,375,000 |
| Income taxes | 9,645,000 | 7,784,000 | 6,564,000 |
| Net income | 14,467,000 | 11,110,000 | 7,811,000 |
| Less cumulative preferred dividends and amortization | — | (309,000) | (707,000) |
| Net income available to common stockholders | $ 14,467,000 | $ 10,801,000 | $ 7,104,000 |
| Net income per common share | $ 2.54 | $ 2.07 | $ 1.63 |

**HYDE ATHLETIC INDUSTRIES, INC.**

| | **1984** | **1983** | **1982** |
| --- | --- | --- | --- |
| Net sales | $ 47,313,237 | $ 44,556,716 | $ 36,877,503 |
| Costs and expenses | | | |
| Cost of sales | 28,176,286 | 27,381,355 | 23,663,233 |
| Depreciation and amortization | 487,516 | 316,948 | 279,813 |
| Selling and administrative expenses | 13,160,584 | 10,557,907 | 6,939,945 |
| Total costs and expenses | 41,824,386 | 38,256,210 | 30,882,991 |
| Operating income | 5,488,851 | 6,300,506 | 5,994,512 |
| Interest expense | 890,104 | 492,656 | 1,065,482 |
| Income before income taxes | 4,598,747 | 5,807,850 | 4,929,030 |
| Income taxes | 1,917,721 | 2,944,111 | 2,440,000 |
| Net income | $ 2,681,026 | $ 2,863,739 | $ 2,489,030 |
| Net income per share of common stock based on the average number of shares outstanding | $ .92 | $ 1.06 | $ 1.01 |

footwear using the patented Nike-Air midsole unit. This unit utilizes pressurized gas encapsulated in a polyurethane midsole. The company also has a number of patents covering component features used in various athletic shoes.

**MANAGE-MENT AND EMPLOYEES**

Nike management in 1984 is shown in Exhibit 27.6.

Nike employs 4100 people. Approximately 1300 are engaged in footwear production, 600 in apparel operations, 375 in sales and marketing, 100 in retail stores, 500 in footwear warehousing, 150 in product research and development, 600 in foreign operations, and 475 in general management and administration. Except for 120 employees in Ireland, none of the company's employees are represented by a union.

**Exhibit 27.6**

| Name | Age | Title | Years with NIKE | Background |
|------|-----|-------|-----------------|------------|
| Philip Knight | 46 | Chairman & president | 14 | Accountant |
| William J. Bowerman | 73 | Vice-chairman & vice-president | 14 | Track coach |
| Robert L. Woodell | 40 | Executive vice-president | 14 | Salesman |
| Delbert J. Hayes | 49 | Executive vice-president | 9 | Accountant |
| Henry C. Carsh | 45 | Vice-president and manager—international operations | 7 | Accountant |
| David P. C. Chang | 54 | Vice-president—foreign production | 3 | Architect |
| Neil Goldschmidt | 43 | Vice-president—international marketing | 3 | Former sec. of treas. under Pres. Carter & Portland mayor |
| John E. Jaqua | 63 | Secretary | 14 | Attorney |
| Gary D. Kurtz | 38 | Treasurer | 3 | Banker |
| James L. Manns | 46 | Vice-president—finance | 5 | Accountant |
| Ronald E. Nelson | 41 | Vice-president—apparel division | 8 | Accountant |
| George E. Porter | 53 | Vice-president—footwear division | 2 | Accountant |
| Robert J. Strasser | 36 | Vice-president—marketing and planning | 8 | Attorney |
| Richard H. Werschkul | 38 | Vice-president and counsel | 1 | Attorney |

# 28  Community Mental Health Center

E. R. Worthington
West Texas State University

"Well, that just about does it. Tonight I'll take all of this stuff home and you can move your things in tomorrow any time you want. Yes sir, tomorrow all of this will be yours." Dr. Steve West, psychiatrist and outgoing director of the Community Mental Health Center (CMHC), was packing his possessions in boxes and talking to Dr. Ron Elliott, psychologist and incoming director of CMHC.

As Ron watched Steve remove the books from the shelves, examine titles, blow dust away, or leaf through pages before carefully placing them neatly in one or another of several open boxes, he reflected on what Steve said: "Tomorrow, all of this will be yours."

**DEPARTMENT OF PSYCHIATRY**

"Tomorrow" actually began in September, a year before. Dr. Elliott was then chief of Psychology Service, Department of Psychiatry, at City Medical Center. City Medical Center had been experiencing a shortage of psychiatrists. Of the five facilities in the Department of Psychiatry, two were headed by psychologists. The department was authorized ten psychiatrists (to include the chief) and four psychologists. The staff actually had only six psychiatrists and three psychologists. (See Exhibit 28.1.)

Dr. George Samuels, chief of the Department of Psychiatry, had discussed the matter at length with his staff, hoping some would know of psychiatrists who were qualified and interested in joining the staff. Dr. West expressed a desire to leave his position at CMHC and join the hospital staff. Dr. Elliott knew a psychologist in Hawaii who had indicated an interest in seeking employment at the medical center. Elliott presented the idea to Samuels of having a community psychologist assume the CMHC director's position, a job that had been filled only by a psychiatrist. Because mental health clinics/centers treat psychiatric disorders, the directors have traditionally been psychiatrists. George Samuels was very much aware that unless he filled the staff vacancies somehow, he would have to terminate some of the services currently provided by his department; this would not be favorably received on the part of the medical center chief of staff. Obviously something had to be done.

**CITY MEDICAL CENTER**

City Medical Center is a 600-bed medical center consisting of three major hospital complexes and 12 separate outpatient facilities. This medical center is a joint city-county facility and one of four teaching medical centers located in this city

Copyright © 1984 by E. R. Worthington.

**Exhibit 28.1**

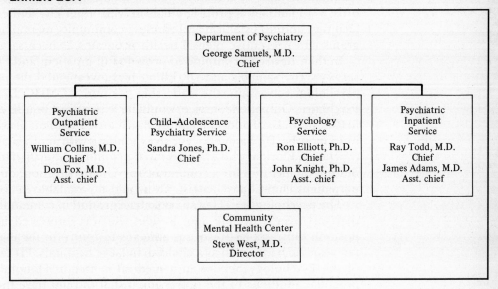

**Exhibit 28.2**

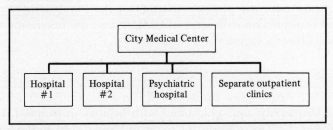

of over one million people. Within the medical center is the Department of Psychiatry, one of the numerous medical departments found in most hospitals. In this case the department is actually a separate psychiatric hospital with a geographically separate Community Mental Health Center. (See Exhibit 28.2.)

The Community Mental Health Center is a semiautonomous outpatient clinic in that its director is dependent on the Department of Psychiatry for both administrative support and medical supervision. The director is additionally responsible to the medical center chief of staff for the overall management of the mental health center. The mission of the Community Mental Health Center is to provide psychiatric, psychological, social work, and consultation services as appropriate to maintain the mental health of those eligible city or county citizens residing within the Community Mental Health Center catchment area. The functions of the clinic include (1) operate an outpatient mental health facility to provide the diagnosis, care, treatment, and proper medical disposition of patients; (2) provide mental health consultation services to the community; (3) conduct in-service training programs as necessary; (4) evaluate medical care as prescribed by the medical center chief of staff or the chief of the Department of Psychiatry; (5) conduct research relevant to the field of mental health; (6) initiate, maintain, complete, and store patient medical (mental health portion only) records; (7) maintain appropriate liaison with other city and county mental health facilities; and (8) establish and conduct community mental health education programs and preventive mental health programs as necessary.

In their desire to continue to provide full inpatient and outpatient psychiatric services, Dr. Samuels and Dr. Elliott had investigated the possibility of hiring a psychologist to assume the leadership position at CMHC. Dr. Collins, chief of the Psychiatric Outpatient Service, would be leaving in a year to enter private practice in Colorado. Dr. Todd, chief of the Psychiatric Inpatient Service, was due to retire in 15 months. Dr. Samuels was corresponding with another psychiatrist, in private practice in Florida, who was interested in joining the staff. This man's background did not qualify him for a community psychiatry position, only as an inpatient or outpatient clinical psychiatrist. He would be available in six to nine months.

The psychologist in Hawaii had a background in community mental health but that was over a decade ago; besides, he was interested in the mental health position only as a last resort as a means to return to the mainland. For the past ten years he had served as a clinician in large hospitals. Presently he was the chief of the Psychology Service in a medical center in Honolulu. Because the two potential additions to the professional staff did not have the ideal backgrounds (or desire) to be assigned to CMHC, Dr. Samuels had another idea. Dr. West could take over the position of chief of the Psychiatric Outpatient Service, Dr. Elliott could become director of CMHC, and the psychologist from Hawaii could fill Dr. Elliott's vacancy.

## TWO MENTAL HEALTH PROFESSIONALS

*Steve West, M.D.,* grew up in North Carolina, obtained a football scholarship to Duke University, and graduated with honors in premed. He earned a medical degree at the Texas Medical Center in Houston from Baylor University of Medicine and completed his internship at the University of Texas Health Science Center in San Antonio. Young Dr. West served as an army physician assigned as a general medical officer. He ended his army tour as a staff physician in the army hospital at Fort Devens, Massachusetts, outside of Boston. After being discharged, Dr. West joined a family practice group in Boston, where he saw as many psychiatric complaints as he did physical. His interest grew, and he entered a three-year psychiatric residency program at Peter Bent Brigham Hospital (an affiliate of the Massachusetts General Hospital System). By the time the residency was completed, Steve had secured a staff position at the University of Texas Health Science Center in San Antonio, Texas. Four years later the director's position at CMHC became open and Steve was selected to fill the vacancy. Steve is 42, married, and has two teenage children.

The general medical and family practice experience provided Steve with a broad background in medicine. His exposure to all kinds of people and problems proved its worth in his three years at CMHC. Although he had both the training and practical experience of community psychiatry, he preferred to work in a clinical outpatient setting.

In-service training, supervision, and treatment programs under Dr. West were all aimed at providing the best outpatient clinical service possible. Community mental health, as he viewed it, was to establish a clinical practice where the customers lived and worked, not in the hospital setting but in the neighborhood where the client was. In time, Dr. West recognized that as close as he was to the source of his patients, he was unable to reach many of them. In the hospital setting, waiting rooms were always overflowing with people in need. In the community setting this was not always the case. This was an important factor in Steve's decision to return to the hospital clinic.

*Ron Elliott, Ph.D.,* grew up in Connecticut and earned a liberal arts degree from Dartmouth College in New Hampshire. A commission in the U.S. Marine Corps led to a variety of leadership positions culminating with a tour as an infantry unit commander. After service as a marine officer, Ron elected to accept a civil service position in the U.S. foreign service. While serving in an overseas post, Ron found himself giving counsel and advice to other foreign service employees and discovered he not only enjoyed this but was good at it. When his tour was over, he left the government and entered graduate school at Northern Arizona University in Flagstaff. After receiving a master's degree in psychology Ron worked half-time as a Veteran's Administration (VA) counselor at the university and half-time as an outreach counselor in a local mental health clinic. A year later he entered the doctoral program in psychology at the University of Utah. Before receiving his Ph.D. he completed his clinical psychology internship at the VA hospital in Salt Lake City. Dr. Elliott next obtained a one-year postgraduate fellowship in community psychology at Beaumont Medical Center in El Paso, Texas, before taking a position in New Orleans. Excellent service as a staff psychologist in a hospital in New Orleans (half-time in the clinic and half-time in the community) led to his being appointed as assistant chief of the service. Three years later he learned of an opening at City Medical Center as chief of the Psychology Service; Ron applied and received the appointment. Ron is 42, married, and has three teenage children. Testimony to the manner in which he served as chief of the Psychology Service at City Medical Center is indicated by the following excerpts from his annual evaluation reports. Each report covers a one-year period; all were written by Dr. Samuels.

> Dr. Elliott has functioned in an outstanding manner as chief, Psychology Service. He pursued his duties energetically, enthusiastically, and methodically with much initiative. He developed a consultation program for the Adolescent Medicine Clinic, conducted specialized group therapy for couples, developed a 15-week practicum for graduate psychology students from two local universities, and served as coordinator for a U.S. Olympic team psychological research program. Requests for psychological evaluations from both inpatient and outpatient services were answered expeditiously. His written patient reports, being concise and thorough, revealed high professional skill and sound judgment. He constantly improved the physical facilities and procedures. He related well with patients, staff, and others. He presented a variety of in-service training throughout the hospital and his research has been published in professional journals. His excellent volunteer program to augment the regular staff is an outstanding example of how to train and use paraprofessionals.

Dr. Elliott has performed his duties in an outstanding manner, supervising the Psychology Service, providing psychological evaluation and treatment and conducting highly successful liaison efforts with other elements of the hospital and the medical community. He conducted a weight control clinic using behavioral methods, presented monthly seminars to the staff of the Clinical Dietetics Service, directed a psychology graduate program, and served as sports psychologist to a U.S. Olympic team. His outstanding volunteer paraprofessional program has become a model for the hospital to use to augment understaffed clinics. He is an adjunct professor on the faculty of three local universities and over the past year has presented two research papers and authored five professional articles.

Dr. Elliott has incorporated his skills as a researcher, author, and clinician into the provision of expert consultative services not only locally but on a regional level. His expertise and accomplishments have been recognized by inclusion in the *Who's Who of the South and Southwest* and *Men of Achievement.* He is a superb clinician and professional who cares about people, especially the patients he treats. Under his leadership the Psychology Service has simultaneously provided unparalleled quality health care and preventive education services to his patients. The volunteer paraprofessional concept he developed has served as a means for this medical center to continue to provide sorely needed clinical services in spite of reductions in our regular clinical professional staffs.

With this background, Dr. Elliott was appointed director of Community Mental Health Center, effective September 15.

## COMMUNITY MENTAL HEALTH CENTER STAFF

The mental health center, under Dr. West, was organized primarily as an outpatient clinic. (See Exhibit 28.3.) In addition to normal clinical duties, each staff member was assigned to a consultation team. The CMHC catchment area was split in half with Sally Malone as one team chief (Frank Gilroy and Chuck Masters were the other team members), and Ed Jenkins as the other team chief assisted by the remaining two counselors. In actuality, very little community consultation was accomplished except for liaison work or visits to follow up in the community on patients being seen in the clinic. (See Exhibit 28.4.)

Steve West's staff consisted of the following people:

*Sally Malone,* R.N., psychiatric nurse clinician, 27, married, no children. Her husband was in his last year of law school and would graduate in December. Sally had given notice to leave in December as her husband had a job in Chicago, to begin in January. As a psychiatric nurse, Sally was responsible for the day-to-day administration of the outpatient clinic (under the supervision of Dr. West). Most of the work consisted of psychiatric screening and evaluation, treatment, and/or disposition of patients. Most treatments were primarily once- or twice-a-week individual counseling sessions or group therapy sessions. Very seldom were psychiatric medications prescribed by the clinic because behavioral intervention (e.g., one-to-one counseling) was seen as the treatment of choice. Helping the patients recognize where their problems were and learning how to control and be responsible for their behavior was favored over using chemicals to alter behavior patterns. Medicine was used, of course, as a stabilizer for the more seriously

**Exhibit 28.3**

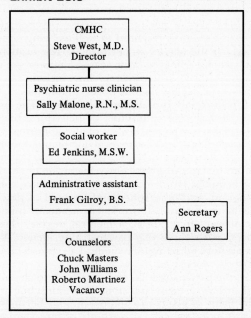

ill patients. Sally had a B.S. degree in nursing and had earned an M.S. in community psychiatric nursing. She felt she was not allowed to fully utilize her skills as a community nurse.

*Ed Jenkins,* M.S.W., social worker, 33, married, one nine-year-old daughter. Ed's training was primarily in the field of family and community counseling, beginning as a social worker teaching family counseling in an undergraduate university program in Oregon. For six years he worked for a community mental health center in Kansas, a nonclinical position where he was responsible for providing social services to low-income families. While in Kansas, Ed learned of an M.S.W. opening at the CMHC. He applied for the position, was accepted, and left Kansas. Since arriving at CMHC in August, Ed had not had his role defined. Although his expertise lay in community consultation, he found that most of his time was occupied doing clinical evaluations (i.e., seeing walk-in patients, conducting initial interviews to ascertain their problems/complaints, and conducting follow-up counseling sessions). He viewed this as both good and bad. He needed the experience in this area as his exposure to clinical evaluation was limited to his graduate training, yet he was not receiving any supervision. Since Ed joined the staff, Dr. West had been too preoccupied with leaving to be able to spend any time with Ed. Ed felt he needed this experience, but he also recognized a need for the community consultation services he had been doing all along but that were sadly lacking at CMHC.

*Frank Gilroy,* B.S., administrative assistant, 31, married, no children. Frank had completed one year of college and enlisted in the army. He served as a mental health counselor and after being discharged returned to college to obtain a B.S.

**Exhibit 28.4** Description of Mental Health Titles, Positions, and Services

I. *Clinical psychologist:* For a person to practice psychology, a doctoral degree (Ph.D., Ed.D., or Psy.D.) is required as well as being certified and licensed by the state in which the service is performed. The academic training typically required is a bachelor's degree (four years), a master's degree (two years), and a doctoral degree (three to five years) which includes a one-year internship.

   A clinical psychologist is trained to observe and evaluate (using interviews and psychological testing) abnormal human behavior. The psychologist is further trained to use a variety of counseling or behavioral therapeutic intervention techniques to make the patient aware of the abnormal behavior and how to change. The psychologist is not a medical doctor and does not prescribe medication.

II. *Psychiatrist:* For a person to practice psychiatry, he or she must have a doctor's degree in medicine (M.D.) or osteopathy (O.D.), have completed a psychiatric residency program, and be certified and licensed to practice medicine by the state in which he or she wants to work. The academic training typically requires a bachelor's degree (four years), a medical degree (three years), an internship (one year), and a three-year psychiatric residency. A psychiatrist, being a physician, is authorized to render medical diagnoses and to prescribe medication.

   Historically, the psychiatrist has resorted more to chemical means of treating psychiatric disorders (using medication) than counseling or behavioral intervention. With the fields of psychiatry and psychology becoming more eclectic, less medication and more behavioral methods of intervention are being used by psychiatrists.

III. *Psychiatric nurse clinician:* This title is awarded to a registered nurse (R.N.) who possesses a bachelor's degree and has a master's degree in nursing and extensive training as a psychiatric nurse. A nurse must pass a national certification exam to be able to practice nursing.

   The nurse clinician gives psychiatric medicine as prescribed by a psychiatrist, serves as a medical assistant to a psychiatrist or as a medical consultant to a psychologist, interviews patients, and provides counseling and therapeutic intervention.

IV. *Social worker:* A social worker must have a bachelor's degree and then earn a master of social work degree (two years). The social worker, in addition to providing counseling and therapeutic intervention, is trained to provide a liaison between the patient, the clinic or center, and the community. Special em-

in psychology. He worked in a state mental health agency as a counselor for three years before being transferred, doing essentially the same job in another state agency. A year later a counselor position became available at Community Mental Health Center. Frank applied and was accepted. When Dr. West assumed the director's position, he and Frank became good friends. About a year later the administrative assistant left and Frank was promoted into that position. Frank entered the administrative position with about six years' experience as a counselor, but he had neither formal nor informal training as an administrator. His performance furthermore suggested that he lacked any interest in learning how to be an effective administrator. When Dr. West became aware of his transfer to chief of the Psychiatric Outpatient Service, he told Frank he would see if Frank could also move to a position in the psychiatric hospital.

*Chuck Masters,* counselor, 29, married, two small children. Chuck had a high

phasis is placed on knowing what community services are available to help a patient and then arranging to make those services available to the patient.

V. *Psychological testing assistant:* This position requires a bachelor's degree and special training in administering psychological tests and gathering psychological data from observations and interviews (as a part of the testing process). The collected raw data is then given to the psychologist for interpretation. A psychological testing assistant cannot work independently or for a professional other than a doctoral-level psychologist.

VI. *Counselor:* This title may apply to almost any person in the mental health field who sees patients. For the purpose of this case, the counselors are people who have high school degrees but not college degrees. They have completed special mental health courses in which they have been trained to interview patients, gather patient background data and complaints, and conduct limited therapeutic counseling under the supervision of a mental health professional (i.e., psychologist, psychiatrist, nurse, or social worker). The position of counselor, as used in this case, refers to a paraprofessional position in which the counselor typically is indigenous to the community or client population served.

VII. *Outpatient services:* This refers to evaluation or treatment provided to patients when they come to a clinic or center for an appointment. The opposite of this, inpatient services, refers to care received as a hospitalized patient.

VIII. *Community consultation services:* Consultation services occur when the mental health professionals and counselors go into the community to bring their expertise to the people (as opposed to the people going to a center or clinic for outpatient services).

An example would be having a mental health team visit a large business in the community which is experiencing high rates of substance abuse turnover and absenteeism. The mental health team, working with the business executives, would try to find out what kind of stress is affecting the workers and what can be done to change the situation.

The emphasis of consultation services is to work with the community to recognize and deal with problems or situations adversely affecting mental health.

IX. *Educational services:* This involves providing education and training to the community showing how to cope with life's problems to enhance positive mental health. In the above example, stress management training for executives and employees could be an effective educational service.

school education plus vocational schooling. He was certified as an electronics repairman and worked in the field about six years. Recently Chuck returned to school to become a mental health counselor. He had no experience, having just joined the staff out of school in July.

*John Williams,* counselor, 28, married, one child. John had a high school education plus vocational schooling. He spent eight years as an auto mechanic and then went to school this past spring to be a counselor. John joined the staff in July without previous experience. He was the only black person on the staff.

*Roberto Martinez,* counselor, 24, single, one semester of college. After high school Robert served four years overseas in the air force. He then returned to the United States, obtained counselor training, and was hired in August. Roberto was the only Mexican-American on the staff.

*Ann Rogers,* secretary/receptionist, 35, single. Ann had been a secretary since graduating from high school. She had been in her present position for ten years. Ann was an excellent typist and secretary, but under the supervision of Frank Gilroy, she had limited opportunity to fully exercise her skills and talents. At this point Ann was the most knowledgeable person in the CMHC regarding administrative procedures, especially in the area of maintaining patient records. Since both Dr. West and Frank Gilroy had an immense dislike for paperwork, little emphasis was placed on the administrative aspect of the clinic.

**COMMUNITY MENTAL HEALTH CENTER SERVICES**

Prior to assuming his new job, Dr. Elliott had several talks with the chief of the Department of Psychiatry. Dr. Samuel's last talk summed up his concerns for the CMHC and what he hoped Elliott could accomplish. "Steve West is a good man; he has a wide range of medical experience and is one of the best psychiatric clinicians in City Medical Center. Like most people he also has some limitations; first, being a top-notch clinician he prefers to do what he does best, treat patients. Second, he is not an administrator; he leaves the paperwork to Frank, who unfortunately is no better. CMHC needs someone who can manage the clinic as both an administrator and a clinician. In the past few months several new counselors have joined the staff, and there is a lack of depth in experience among the counselors. CMHC has always enjoyed an excellent reputation for the quality of its health care; I expect you to carry on this tradition."

A major mission of CMHC was the servicing of a contract with a local medical vocational training school, the Health Sciences Institute. CMHC was responsible for providing all mental health services to the institute. This consisted primarily of counseling services for the young students who would encounter difficulty coping with classwork, interpersonal relationships, or being away from home. The institute had about 5000 students, most of whom lived on campus. The curriculum consisted mostly of vocational-level training for all medical fields such as dental assistants, medical technicians, lab technicians, emergency medical specialists, medical-dental secretaries, counselors, practical nurses, and medical administrative assistants. The school also provided short courses for hospital administrators and, in conjunction with a private university, had a limited-enrollment master's degree program in hospital administration.

Dr. Elliott spoke on several occasions with the institute staff and administrators regarding what CMHC could do to better meet their needs. Dr. Clark, dean of students, felt that, although CMHC provided excellent outpatient care, the CMHC staff was not very knowledgeable about the functions of the institute or the demands placed upon the students. Dr. Clark remarked, "Your clinic remains a part of the hospital and for many students, visiting a shrink is not seen as the best way to become popular with your classmates."

Mrs. Jordan, coordinator for women's activities at the institute, said, "My biggest concern is the increasing reports of sexual assaults. As you know, about 30 to 40 percent of our students are 19- to 21-year-old single females who are away from home for the first time." Dr. Elliott was aware of the problems in this area. In New Orleans he was codeveloper of a citywide sexual-assault treatment program for the hospital he worked in.

Before moving to CMHC Ron arranged to have the administrative assistant he had in the Psychology Service, Tom Edwards, also move with him. (Frank Gilroy and Tom Edwards just switched positions.) Tom Edwards was an able administrator and very knowledgeable about recordkeeping and supervising counselors. He was 36, married with four children, and has been in the mental health field for ten years. He had gone from high school into the navy. Four years later, he used his navy clerical experience to obtain a clerical position in a hospital. Working in the Psychiatric Service led to his return to school to earn a B.S. degree and become a counselor and psychological testing assistant. Over the years Tom gained a reputation as being an excellent trainer and supervisor of young counselors. His psychological testing skills were so good he trained psychology graduate students (doing their practicum at City Medical Center) in testing procedures.

Steve West had warned Ron of problems he might encounter with Ann. She tended to remain aloof and distant. Frank had experienced difficulty with her in that she seemed to want to do things her way and was reluctant to follow instructions. If Steve had his way he would have fired her long ago, but they needed someone to answer the phone, schedule appointments, and greet the patients when they entered the clinic. Steve had almost no contact with Ann as she worked directly under Frank.

Steve's and Frank's feelings about Ann bothered Ron. He felt the secretary of a clinic was a most vital position. Patients would form an impression of the clinic based primarily on their interaction with the receptionist-secretary, in this case Ann. Ron had depended, in the past, on the secretary to be a key person in the management team. She would handle many of the small administrative details, which would relieve Ron of making many time-consuming routine decisions. Ron's concerns did not become less confused when other secretaries in the Department of Psychiatry reported just the opposite. They saw Ann as a highly competent, responsible worker who was being misused by Frank and Dr. West.

By visiting community leaders Ron learned that, indeed, as Dr. Samuels has stated, CMHC enjoyed an enviable reputation as a clinic providing quality mental health care. As one man put it, "Now, I don't need it; but the mental clinic is the best place for messed-up minds; they fix you up real good there." When asked if they or their families had used the services offered, all professed they had not because the clinic was mostly for people who had severe mental problems.

## PERSONAL AMBITIONS AND CAREER DESIRES

During the first week on the job Ron set out to have an individual appointment with every member of CMHC. He began with Ann, then Sally and Ed, and then the counselors. He asked two major questions, "If you were in charge of CMHC what changes would you make to improve the clinic?" and, "What would you like to do or have happen to you in the next year at CMHC?"

Ann spoke of her inability to do her job. She was a qualified secretary but relegated by Frank to being only a receptionist. She took Dr. Elliott to a back room and showed him four years of old, unfiled patient records which had been dumped there at the end of the year. Two directors had allowed this to happen despite her protests. She hoped to be able to regain the ability to do what she had been trained for and not just greet patients.

Sally reminded Ron that she had no future at CMHC since she was leaving in three months. She did offer her observations. The new counselors came to CMHC eager to work and were highly motivated. There had been no formal training for them and they were limited to only conducting intake interviews; they had not been able to do any counseling with patients. Sally felt they were mature, intelligent people who could do an excellent counseling job if only given the chance and the proper training.

Ed related that his major talents lay in family and community work but he had done very little since he was hired. When asked why, he remarked, "No one knows what we have to offer. People in the community who have family problems don't see us as a provider of those kinds of services; they go to their church or to a private counselor; they see us as only helping 'crazy people.' Part of the problem is our image; we are seen as a clinic where mentally ill people come to us. We do not go out in the community; we wait for sick people to come to us."

Chuck Masters expressed disappointment with his job. He had come to CMHC to help normal people who were experiencing some problems coping with life. Instead, all he was doing was interviewing people who had problems even he had difficulty understanding.

John Williams said he felt inadequate. He had learned just enough in school to know what should be done, but he lacked the clinical skills to know how to do anything.

Roberto expressed confusion. He was not sure where he fit in. Sally had been very helpful in teaching the counselors, but her time was so limited because of her own patient load. He also mentioned in passing something he had heard. He was dating a young woman who was a technician in the emergency room. One night she was feeling down when they had a date. When Roberto asked why, she explained what had happened to her on the shift she just finished. An 18-year-old female student was brought to the emergency room, the victim of a sexual assault. The ER was trained and equipped to provide excellent treatment, but they felt stymied because the hospital had no official follow-up procedures. All they could do was recommend that the woman seek counseling and give her the phone number of CMHC. Roberto knew that no sexual victims had contacted CMHC in the six weeks he had been there. His date said the ER had seen three women in that period.

**WHAT NOW?**   One day after the clinic had closed and everyone else had gone home, Ron and Tom were discussing what to do. Tom said that there was a lot of work for both of them. He felt Ann knew a great deal more than either Frank or Dr. West gave her credit for. When it came to hospital rules and regulations, she was an expert. She was also a very friendly person, eager to help out wherever she could and willing to assume a more responsible role than she had previously been allowed. The counselors were not happy with their jobs. They were bright and motivated but had received almost no training since they arrived. They had not been allowed to do much more than see patients when they first came to the clinic, collecting background information and finding out why they were seeking help. Ron acknowledged that the future didn't look too bright either. Sally was leaving and the hospital said they would not be able to get a replacement until next spring. This would leave Ed as the number two professional in the clinic and he had no clinical background. Ron would then be the only clinical expert. The clinic was authorized four counselors but they only had three and all of these were males. He recalled that the institute had between 1500 and 2000 female students. Ron, with feet propped on his desk, leaned back in his swivel chair, glanced at Tom, and said, "Well, Tom, what do we do now?"

Tom stood up, moved to the doorway, turned around, and replied, "I don't know; you're the boss; you tell me." He continued to look at Ron, then shrugged his shoulders and said, "Ron, I've got to go; you think on it tonight and tomorrow tell all of us what direction we should head in." With that said, he left the clinic.

It was late; Ron turned on his desk light as the fading September sun no longer provided sufficient illumination to read. Ron hunched over his desk, scrutinizing his notes, thinking of what he had to do. Ron recalled what one of his graduate school professors had preached over and over, "A good community mental health program has two primary objectives: The first is to recognize the needs of the people and the second is to design a system to go into the community and meet these needs."

Ron thought, "Boy, we sure don't do that; in fact, with the staff we now have and the lack of trained personnel, will we ever be able to do that?"

# Section B   Small Business

## 29   Circuit Services North

Harriett Stephenson and Patrick Koeplin
Seattle University

In 1971 Neil Christie and Jim Beall decided to form their own printed-circuit-board manufacturing company, calling it Circuit Services. They decided to locate the company in Sunnyvale, California, the heart of the fast-growing electronics industry in Silicon Valley. After getting friends, relatives, and business associates to invest in their small company, they opened their doors for business in August 1971. Since Neil had previous experience in manufacturing printed-circuit boards and Jim had experience in sales of printed-circuit boards, the new company was well suited to meet the demands of a rapidly growing market.

The company prospered over the next five years, increasing sales from $120,000 in the first year to over $1 million per year by 1976. Its customer base expanded not only to include companies in the Silicon Valley area but also to encompass the emerging electronics industry located in the Pacific Northwest. Having survived the 1974–1975 recession that had disastrous consequences for much of the industry and seeing a strong resurgence in business, Neil and Jim decided to form another printed-circuit manufacturing company, this time locating it in the Seattle area. They chose Seattle because in doing business with electronics companies there, Neil and Jim had seen the tremendous demand for a quality printed-circuit company to be located in the area. Unlike their first company, however, the new company could be financed by Neil and Jim themselves. They decided to include only one other person, Steve Spero, who was their CPA, as partial owner.

Circuit Services North (CSN) began operations in April 1976 with a ready-made customer base who had been doing business with the California company. (See Exhibit 29.1.) Because there were only two other very small companies in the area, competition was almost nonexistent. A manager with ten years' experience in manufacturing printed-circuit boards was hired away from a California competitor to run the new company. Because Neil, Jim, and Steve wanted to start

**Exhibit 29.1** Background Information

In 1976, when Circuit Services North was first started, there were two other printed-circuit-board companies in the Seattle area. Both were very small, doing under $400,-000 annually, and both continue to exist today.

Between 1976 and 1979, the industry grew from 2 companies to over 30 companies. Between 1979 and the present, the number of firms in the industry has been reduced to 22. Most firms were offshoots of the first five companies in the area. The largest privately held firm in the industry is presently doing approximately $5 million annually, and 90 percent of the firms have annual sales of under $1 million.

The largest customers are involved in telecommunications, electronic equipment for banks, and computers and computer accessories. Other customers are involved in aircraft equipment and medical instrumentation.

Much of the industry management can be characterized as nonprofessional managers who worked in printed-circuit shops before opening their own companies. Other managers started in production and were promoted to management positions. Established management techniques such as budgeting, strategic planning, and cost accounting are almost nonexistent.

From 1976 to 1979 the industry experienced a dramatic expansion phase which allowed all companies in the industry to have more than enough work at profitable prices. Lead times stretched to 8–10 weeks. As business began to contract from the end of 1979 to 1981, most companies reduced prices to maintain sales levels. This led to increasing price competition for a smaller amount of available business. The result was reduced profits and, for some companies, bankruptcy. Lead times went to two to four weeks.

the company with minimal investment, all the equipment was either handed down from the California company or purchased at auctions from companies that had gone out of business. The philosophy of the owners was to get into the market as inexpensively as possible, establish a reputation for high quality and excellent service at mid to high prices, and from the profits of the company gradually upgrade the facilities and equipment. They also believed in leaving all day-to-day operating decisions to the general manager. The owners only got involved in decisions concerning sales goals, profit goals, capital investment decisions, and financing decisions.

This philosophy was very successful for the first few years. By the end of the second fiscal year, in March 1978, sales had grown to $1 million per year. The company was able to begin replacing some of the outdated equipment and everything seemed to be going according to expectations. In April 1978, however, the general manager of the facility quit to form his own locally competitive printed-circuit-board company, taking with him many of the key people of the company. Even though the company survived, it was not adequately prepared to deal with a change in leadership. It had no plan of action to fall back on in such cases and had to rely on the owners taking over day-to-day control until a new general manager could be found.

The second general manager for the company was again hired from a California competitor, this time having previous experience in sales of printed-circuit boards. By the time the new general manager established control, in June 1978, customer relations had badly deteriorated, the 25 employees were unsure of their own future with the company, and delivery commitment had gone unkept. Fortunately, the industry was in the midst of an expansion period which allowed the company to maintain 1977–1978 sales and profit levels. This same expansion period, however, also led to an increase in competition, with the number of printed-circuit-board companies in the Seattle area going from 4 to 30 between 1976 and 1979.

The new manager of the company was under tremendous pressure from Neil, Jim, and Steve to maintain a sales level of $125,000 per month and gross profits of 30 percent (gross profit = sales minus cost of goods). Each month would be reviewed as to profit and sales objectives. As long as the industry was in the midst of expansion this policy worked out fine. However, by mid-1979 the expansion was over and serious cutbacks in the industry were beginning to be made. As the amount of business began to contract, price competition began to increase. This put further pressure on the general manager to continue hitting his monthly sales and profit goals. By the end of 1979 he was able to do this only by forgoing much-needed repair and replacement of equipment facilities and by cutting back on wages.

By the end of the first quarter of 1980 the company was in serious difficulties. As business continued its downward spiral, prices were being cut by competitors below break-even levels and delivery requirements were getting shorter and shorter. The company, however, was in the worst shape of its history to deal with the situation. Because wages were so low most workers were inexperienced, working with equipment that was continually breaking down and with delivery commitments that put them under tremendous pressure. The owners, having put strong emphasis on profit and sales goals as a means of evaluating performance, had neglected to institute any strong financial and administrative controls that would have alerted them earlier to the developing situation.

In April 1980, sales dropped to $55,000 and the company lost $40,000. Since the California company had continued growing, both in sales and profitability, Neil, Jim, and Steve were perplexed about what was happening in Seattle. By mid-May the owners, believing that the general manager was not capable of turning the company around, decided to fire him and began looking for his replacement. They found him within their own California company working as a middle-level manager.

Paul Levinson was 25 years old when he was hired by the California company in 1976. He was brought on as a purchasing agent but within two years had been put in charge of production control, shipping-receiving, and maintenance as well. He was the only person in the company with a college degree, having received his diploma in philosophy and psychology, and was attending night school to get his MBA. He seemed attractive to the owners not only because of his accomplishments with the California company and his education but also because he was thoroughly familiar with the philosophy of the owners in operating a company, had seen how successful that philosophy could be, and had worked briefly with Circuit Services North on setting up some internal systems for purchasing and production control. After a quick trip up with his wife and two children, Paul accepted the position and by June 1, 1980, the third general manager in four years for Circuit Services North was on the job.

By the time Paul started, the company had already lost $80,000 and many of the approximately 50 customers were ready to disqualify the company for poor quality and poor performance on delivery commitments. Worker morale was very low, and the equipment and facilities were in a state of continual breakdown. There was no organized production control or purchasing system because everything had been done on a crisis-to-crisis basis. The accounting system for payables and receivables was about the only area that wasn't in need of immediate attention.

Drawing on his four years' experience with the California company, and after spending a couple of days assessing the situation, Paul made his first significant change. He instituted a production control system that allowed him to see on a daily basis where each job was in the process, when it was due, how much had been shipped for the month, how much had been booked from sales, and which jobs were especially critical to complete on time. This allowed Paul the opportunity to see exactly where bottlenecks were occurring in the production process as well as the ability to make more accurate delivery commitments to the customer. Once he was able to pinpoint production bottlenecks, Paul then got together with the supervisor of the responsible department to discuss ways of correcting the situation.

The first six months Paul spent reestablishing credibility with customers and improving the internal organization of the company. Customers especially had to be assured that Circuit Services North could be a reliable and competitive source for their printed-circuit-board needs. By the end of 1980 sales had risen to $107,000 per month but, because of continued pricing pressure, gross profits were still well below owners' expectations, averaging just 15 percent of sales.

The second major change Paul made was to increase the wage level to make it more competitive with other printed-circuit companies. Although department supervisors evaluated on a regularly scheduled basis all of their employees, Paul was responsible for deciding the amount of any raise to be given. He was also responsible for the evaluation and raises of department supervisors, office manager, and production manager. The average hourly wage for all production workers, supervisors included, when Paul started was $4.50 per hour. By the time Paul had finished reevaluating all personnel, six months later, the average hourly wage had gone to $5.20 per hour. This increase seemed necessary in order to attract and hold on to more experienced workers. It also stabilized the work force, giving workers the chance to stay with the company for long periods of time instead of using the company as a training ground for competitors. Finally, it allowed the company the stability of having key people, especially department supervisors, stay with their jobs and train the less experienced workers. The problem with this strategy was that as the amount spent on labor went up, profits continued to go down. In fiscal year ending March 31, 1981, labor was 35 percent of sales when it should have been 25 percent. Paul was under increasing pressure from the owners to somehow reduce labor costs, bringing them in line with owners' expectations.

By April 1981 the company had reestablished credibility with its customers, had lifted the wages and morale of workers, and had stabilized turnover in the work force. However, gross profits were still around 15 percent of sales and much of the equipment was badly in need of repair. When the company only shipped $87,000 in April 1981 and lost $30,000, Paul was called down to California to meet with the owners and explain what was happening. Much of the problem revolved around equipment breakdowns and price competition. The owners, not being involved on a day-to-day basis, insisted the problems revolved around manufacturing inefficiencies. It was decided to send the general manager of the California company to Seattle for two weeks to evaluate the situation and report back to the owners. When his report essentially confirmed Paul's analysis of the situation, the owners decided that they were going to have to spend money to improve the facility and equipment if they expected to continue business. By the end of 1981 much of the outdated equipment had been replaced, yet profits were still well below the owners' expectations.

By February 1, 1982, Circuit Services North had shipped an average of $128,000 per month, exceeding the goal for shipments set by Paul and the owners at the start of the fiscal year. The customer base of the company continued to expand and the reputation of the company for high quality and reliable service at competitive prices was firmly established. Equipment and facilities were updated to prevent continual breakdowns, leading not only to reduced downtime but also to improved quality. The company had made great progress in overcoming many of the problem areas that existed two years earlier. The one crucial area where little progress was made, however, was in profitability. Though by February 1, 1982, the company was able to exceed its goal for shipments, it was unable to even come close to profitability goals, having a year-to-date gross profit of under 10 percent. The owners, though encouraged by the progress made, found the situation intolerable and decided, against Paul's strong recommendation, to cut back the work force by laying people off and reducing the monthly shipment goal to $100,000. Of the seven people mandated by the owners to be laid off (approximately 20 percent of the work force at the time) Paul could decide which five hourly workers were to be let go and was ordered to lay off two particular supervisors out of six. The two supervisors let go were the two highest-paid employees working for Paul at the time. The layoff reduced the total work force from 34 to 27 and monthly labor costs by $8000. The idea behind the layoff and reduction in shipments goal was to allow Paul to pick and choose the more profitable work without having to take all the business available by reducing prices and consequently reducing profits.

The strategy worked very well. Not only did profitability exceed owners' expectations, but shipments during the next five months averaged just under $128,000 per month. By cutting back on the number of workers, raising prices, eliminating unprofitable customers, and updating facilities and equipment, Circuit Services

North had regained the position it had achieved during its first two years and was prepared to profit from the expected business upswing.

In April 1983, CSN found itself with a very bright future. Sales had increased the past fiscal year (ending March 31) to an average $155,000 per month compared with $128,000 per month average for fiscal 1981–1982, a 21 percent increase. The last four months of fiscal 1982–1983 saw average monthly shipments go to $183,000, with March 1983 hitting $235,000. More importantly, gross profitability exceeded 35 percent, well above owners' expectations, making the year the most successful one in the company's history.

There were four basic reasons for this success. First, two major local competitors withdrew from the market. Second, three large customers reoriented their marketing strategy, requiring them to use low quantities of many different types of printed-circuit boards, giving much of their work to CSN. Third, the commission schedule was revised for in-house salespeople, giving them greater incentive to increase bookings. Fourth, the owners' philosophy of taking a portion of earnings and plowing it back into the company in updating facilities and modernizing equipment was successful.

In April 1983, Paul Levinson and the owners were faced with making decisions on the future direction of the company. They could attempt to maintain their current sales and profit goals, keeping utilization of existing plant equipment at 85 percent, or they could attempt to increase sales goals by adding more salespeople and adding to plant facilities and equipment as sales increased.

The decision Paul and the owners made in April 1983 was to try to maintain the previous year's performance for fiscal 1983–1984. If Paul wanted CSN to continue its growth rate, he could do so as long as profit margins remained at or above owners' expectations. If he wanted to consolidate his position and keep sales at 1982–1983 levels, the owners would go along with that decision as long as profit margins were maintained.

Paul decided that if business demand remained strong he would attempt to continue increasing monthly shipping goals without jeopardizing profitability. For the first six months of fiscal 1983–1984 Paul was very successful with this strategy. Shipments had increased to $209,000 per month (an increase of over 50 percent from the first six months of fiscal 1982–1983), and profitability was even higher than the owners or Paul thought possible. However, over the remaining six months, even as shipments continued to increase (averaging $248,000 per month), gross profit margins were seriously eroded, falling below owners' expectations in February and March 1984.

Even though fiscal 1983–1984 broke shipments and profit records, CSN was in deep trouble. Profitability had declined for the previous six months below acceptable levels. CSN was setting monthly shipping records, but many delivery commitments were not met and the in-house reject rates as well as customer returns were increasing. CSN had overextended it resources in trying to take advantage of favorable business conditions. In an effort to deal with this situation, Paul made major purchases of expensive equipment and leased another 4000 square feet of space down the street to house the numerically controlled (NC) machines used in the manufacturing process. By increasing equipment and space, Paul thought, he could continue to maintain growth in shipments as well as regain previous levels of profitability. However, Paul found that in acquiring more space and adding new equipment he also had to increase his work force, especially in areas that did not directly manufacture the boards (i.e., shipping/receiving, office staff, production scheduling, and maintenance). Also, because the NC areas were physically separate from the rest of manufacturing, Paul now had logistics problems of transporting work back and forth as well as communications between the two areas. Finally, during this time the Environmental Protection Agency had finalized requirements for chemical-waste dischargers (such as printed-circuit-board companies). In order to comply with these requirements, CSN spent over $150,000 on new pollution control equipment as well as $50,000 on installation, start-up, and maintenance of equipment.

All of these factors—added costs for equipment, space, labor, and pollution control combined with logistics problems between two distinct manufacturing areas—led to greater problems for Paul and CSN. By the end of fiscal 1984–1985, monthly shipments began to level off while costs continued to rise. Delivery commitments went largely unmet, and quality, although still high, was gradually deteriorating. Most importantly, profitability was well below owners' expectations, causing serious concerns by the owners over what was happening with Paul and CSN.

During the first six months of fiscal 1984–1985, Paul continued to struggle with the problems of growing profitably. Because business demand had remained strong (monthly shipments were now averaging $303,000), profitability continued to be below acceptable levels. By October 1984, the owners began to become more involved in developing solutions to CSN's problems. Their primary action consisted of bringing in a new production manager who had experience working with larger-volume shops. They especially wanted someone whom they felt could be tough in a deteriorating situation—primarily in dealings with employees, wage raises, productivity, and increasing manufacturing efficiency. The previous production manager was then put in charge of quality assurance. The real effect of this move was to increase costs, increase dissension among employees, and send the company into even deeper trouble. During this time (October 1984–January 1985) Paul attempted to resolve the problem of having two distinct manufacturing areas by leasing space adjacent to existing manufacturing areas. This eliminated many of the logistical and communications problems inherent in having separate manufacturing areas. However, in making the new space usable CSN spent a lot of money in improvements, which in the short term continued to drive up costs without increasing revenue.

It was during this period that the one bright area in the past 24 months began to fade—demand turned abruptly down. Although for the past six months CSN's monthly shipments continued to increase, its lead time and overall backlog were decreasing. In November–December (1984) to January (1985), monthly shipments averaged $226,000, a drop of 28 percent from the previous three months. To deal with this new problem, Paul instituted a wage freeze, a hiring freeze, and a 32-hour work week. By early January, when the owners were informed that CSN had actually lost money, the decision was made to take more drastic steps to prevent further decline. Included in these actions were layoffs of 35 people (one-third of the work force), letting go of the new and the old production managers and one department supervisor, and the hiring of a second in-house direct salesperson. Remaining workers were put back on a 40-hour work week and the wage freeze and hiring freeze were lifted. By reducing the size of the work force and cutting out expensive managers and supervisors, the owners hoped to bring some of CSN's costs in line with sales and relieve some of the pressure on Paul to maintain unrealistically high shipping goals. Paul was then left to regroup with the remaining employees to develop a strategy that could take a demoralized work force in a declining market with costs still too high and return the company to its former excellence.

The first action Paul took was to reorganize some of the job functions of his key people. He promoted one to manufacturing manager and another to manufacturing engineer in charge of process technology, quality assurance, and facilities upkeep. Daily meetings were held to discuss objectives to be met that day and that week. The NC department was split into two distinct departments with a supervisor for each department. A thorough examination of each manufacturing area was undertaken to determine its relationship to overall quality, delivery, and profitability. The second action Paul took was to limit wage raises to 5 percent and to mandate that all new hires be trainees rather than more costly experienced workers.

By March 1985, shipments had stabilized at $250,000 per month although profitability was still below owners expectations—even though it had begun moving in an upward direction. During this time Paul and his manufacturing manager had completed their evaluation of the company's personnel and the potential for increased profitability. On the basis of this evaluation, Paul knew that changes would have to continue to be made and decided to lay off two more supervisors and four hourly workers. This helped to reduce costs without having a serious impact on quality or delivery. Also on the basis of this evaluation, Paul and the manufacturing manager made a comprehensive one-year plan that outlined goals and objectives as well as a time line for implementation of future changes. By matching up resources with goals and objectives, Paul was able to prioritize courses of action that would enable CSN to return to an acceptable level of profitability.

Out of this planning process Paul arrived at two major conclusions. First, although costs were still out of line with pricing, any further cost reduction would have to come from areas outside of direct labor costs. Specifically what Paul had in mind was to begin a campaign to reduce costs by reducing mistakes and making workers responsible for quality. If in-house reject rates could be substantially reduced then the amount of overage needed could also be reduced, eliminating a major source of added cost. Paul thought to do this by increasing the amount of training given each employee and by meeting personally with small groups of employees. These small groups met with Paul and discussed the history of the company, its goals, and its plan on meeting those goals. Paul then gave the group an extensive tour of the manufacturing areas, stressing the importance of doing things right the first time and the role each employee plays in how well or how poorly the company does. Within one month of instituting these changes, in-house reject rates dropped from 12.4 percent to 4.5 percent. Profitability continued to increase although it still fell short of acceptable levels.

The second major conclusion Paul came to was that the pricing structure for single- and double-sided boards was too low to allow Paul to meet owners' profit expectations. As business demand began to decline in November 1984, pricing also fell sharply. Though there were no available statistics, Paul believed that his local competitors were probably doing less well then he was, primarily because of their very low prices but also because of the necessity for many of these competitors to make the investment for pollution control equipment that Paul had made in 1984. Even though Paul felt that most of the competition would either drop out of the market or begin raising their prices by third-quarter 1985, Paul could not wait that long to get profitability to where the owners wanted it. To deal with this problem Paul evaluated business demands and supplier capability for the local printed-circuit market and decided that CSN should get into the business of supplying printed-circuit boards for the United States Defense Department. This meant in the short term added costs for necessary testing procedures (that were very expensive and difficult to pass) as well as more formal documentation of manufacturing processes and calibration of equipment. In July 1985, CSN was informed that it had passed all tests and could start taking mil-spec orders in September 1985, making CSN the only local job shop capable of building mil-spec boards.

In July 1985, Paul and the owners found themselves at yet another crossroads for CSN. Profitability was getting better but was still below owners' expectations (as it had been since November 1983). Business had stabilized but at prices that were below what Paul needed to make his goals for profitability, and there were no indications of when this might turn around although Paul felt it could happen as early as September 1985. Paul and his key managers had developed a plan of action that they felt would return them to previous profit levels—especially in doing work with the Defense Department, although this was far from certain. The work force was stable even though they had been through a wage freeze, layoffs, reorganizations, intensive training, and educational meetings all within the past nine months. Although no major piece of equipment was currently needed, some of the NC machines were beginning to show signs of extensive wear and tear and would probably require replacement in the next six to nine months.

# 30 Hines Industries, Inc.

Robert P. Crowner
Eastern Michigan University

In June 1984, Gordon Hines, the president of Hines Industries, Inc., reflected upon the first quarter of the 1985 fiscal year with mixed feelings. His marketing strategy of "niching" had been successful. He had started his second company in 16 years when he began Hines Industries in 1979. The first three years were characterized by rapid growth in sales, but the recession took its toll in 1983. Exhibits 30.1, 30.2, and 30.3 show the balance sheet, income statement, and expense statements for the fiscal years 1981 through 1984. The first quarter of 1985 looked as if it would be near the entire sales of 1984 and a profit of 12 percent to 15 percent should be produced. Maybe this high growth rate would produce a new set of problems.

Gordon Hines is not new to the entrepreneur ranks. In February 1968 he founded Balance Technology, Inc. (Bal Tec) in Ann Arbor, Michigan, which manufactures and markets balancing equipment and vibration instruments. Bal Tec grew rapidly but Gordon lost absolute control of the company when he needed outside money, a mistake he is determined not to make again. Eventually he was squeezed out of the management and finally sold his stock at a considerable profit to an outsider who in turn squeezed out the management that followed Gordon.

Gordon Hines has an unusual background in relation to the businesses he founded. He has a degree in psychology and at one time was a social worker for the Chicago YMCA. Later, while selling insurance, he successfully sold policies to two partners in a balancing-equipment company who really did not have the funds to buy insurance. They were so impressed by Gordon's sales ability that they made him an offer to enter their business. Gordon accepted and soon was successfully selling machines and became involved in redesigning and improving them as well.

Gordon, who is 54, has a natural aptitude for visualizing how things look and work and can quickly conceptualize his ideas. He is a problem solver. His father was an engineer and took Gordon into work on weekends with him so that Gordon learned early about machinery and the engineering behind machinery. He completed two years of engineering work at the University of Illinois before his intense interest in people drew him toward psychology.

The research and written case information were presented at a Case Research Symposium and were evaluated by the Case Research Association's Editorial Board. This case was prepared by Robert P. Crowner, associate professor of management of Eastern Michigan University, as a basis for class discussion.

Copyright © 1984 by Robert P. Crowner.

Distributed by the Case Research Association. All rights reserved to the author and the Case Research Association. Permission to use this case should be obtained from the Case Research Association.

**Exhibit 30.1**

**HINES INDUSTRIES, INC.**
**Balance Sheet**
**Years Ending February 28**

|  | 1981 | 1982 | 1983 | 1984 |
|---|---|---|---|---|
| **Current assets** | | | | |
| Cash | $ 9,005 | $ 5,027 | $ 11,361 | $ 26,707 |
| Accounts receivable | 96,509 | 124,905 | 129,413 | 215,222 |
| Inventories | | | | |
| Materials | 60,448 | 33,715 | 83,176 | 269,268 |
| Work in process | 35,656 | 135,031 | 21,794 | 45,219 |
|  | 96,104 | 168,746 | 104,970 | 314,487 |
| Loan receivable, officer | | | | 49,935 |
| Total current assets | 201,618 | 298,678 | 245,744 | 606,351 |
| **Property & equipment** | | | | |
| Leasehold improvements | 7,386 | 7,386 | 7,386 | 7,386 |
| Machinery & equipment | 21,894 | 38,871 | 52,358 | 96,188 |
| Office equipment | 5,451 | 7,680 | 13,604 | 29,557 |
| Transportation equipment | 0 | 19,933 | 30,247 | 58,768 |
| Leasehold interest in communication equipment | 5,060 | 5,060 | 5,060 | 5,060 |
|  | 39,791 | 78,930 | 108,655 | 196,959 |
| Less depreciation | 6,485 | 20,747 | 42,084 | 82,258 |
|  | 33,306 | 58,183 | 66,571 | 114,701 |
| Intangible assets | 108 | 81 | 596 | 27 |
|  | 235,032 | 356,942 | 312,911 | 721,079 |
| **Current liabilities** | | | | |
| Notes payable, bank | 40,000 | 0 | 69,300 | 170,000 |
| Current portion of long-term debt | 6,632 | 2,626 | 12,100 | 27,353 |
| Accounts payable | 77,273 | 88,765 | 72,432 | 181,684 |
| Accrued expenses | 13,896 | 28,150 | 29,630 | 49,047 |
| Accrued taxes | 5,930 | 8,579 | 6,748 | 20,288 |
| Customer deposits | 30,074 | 117,513 | 10,000 | 218,091 |
| Total current liabilities | 173,805 | 245,633 | 200,210 | 666,463 |
| Long-term debt | 6,051 | 67,131 | 25,178 | 24,641 |
| **Stockholder's equity** | | | | |
| Common stock, $1 par value, 100,000 shares, 70,000 issued | 70,000 | 70,000 | 70,000 | 70,000 |
| Retained earnings | (14,824) | (25,822) | 17,523 | (40,025) |
|  | 55,176 | 44,178 | 87,523 | 29,975 |
|  | 235,032 | 356,942 | 312,911 | 721,079 |

**Exhibit 30.2**

**HINES INDUSTRIES, INC.**
**Income Statement**
**Years Ending February 28**

|  | 1981 | 1982 | 1983 | 1984 |
|---|---|---|---|---|
| Net sales | $394,498 | $634,767 | $1,114,201 | $1,434,912 |
| Cost of sales |  |  |  |  |
|   Material | 158,364 | 269,957 | 373,713 | 381,268 |
|   Direct labor | 36,345 | 107,362 | 174,321 | 209,747 |
|   Subcontract | 63,842 | 27,514 | 8,288 | 7,063 |
|   Drafting | 3,716 | 7,335 | 11,078 | 43,322 |
|   Installation | 0 | 2,900 | 3,567 | 18,100 |
|   Manufacturing overhead | 27,605 | 80,317 | 207,173 | 281,656 |
|  | 289,872 | 495,385 | 778,140 | 941,156 |
| Gross profit | 104,626 | 139,382 | 336,061 | 493,756 |
| Operating expenses |  |  |  |  |
|   Research & development | 10,945 | 5,506 | 25,750 | 53,449 |
|   Selling expenses | 36,498 | 54,084 | 131,851 | 302,048 |
|   General & adm. expense | 68,204 | 79,000 | 128,123 | 173,892 |
|  | 115,647 | 138,590 | 285,724 | 529,389 |
| Operating income | (11,021) | 792 | 50,337 | (35,633) |
| Nonoperating income (exp) |  |  |  |  |
|   Interest income | 0 | 0 | 0 | 790 |
|   Interest expense | (4,473) | (11,790) | (6,992) | (22,705) |
|   Miscellaneous | 670 | 0 | 0 | 0 |
|  | (3,803) | (11,790) | (6,992) | (21,915) |
| Income before taxes | (14,824) | (10,998) | 43,345 | (57,548) |

It is certainly fair to say that Gordon Hines is Hines Industries. His creativity is in evidence everywhere—marketing, design, manufacturing, and even finance.

**PRODUCTS** Hines Industries presently has five basic product lines. These machines are known as hard-bearing balancing machines. They come in a number of different models with different features. All of the lines are available with microprocessor analyzers. The DL, driveline balancing machine, and the HC, hard crankshaft balancing machine, were the products which were first developed. The HC500A model has been sold to more than 120 customers in 33 states and 4 foreign countries. The HC balancer is sold primarily to the automotive aftermarket for high-performance and racing cars.

The DL line is used to balance the drive shaft for cars and trucks. Because of the heavy weights and usage given to trucks, their drive shafts, unlike cars, have

**Exhibit 30.3**

## HINES INDUSTRIES, INC.
### Expense Statements
### Years Ending February 28

|  | 1981 | 1982 | 1983 | 1984 |
|---|---|---|---|---|
| **Manufacturing overhead** | | | | |
| Supervisory labor | $ 0 | $ 0 | $ 47,103 | $ 67,654 |
| Indirect labor | 2,638 | 2,829 | 8,635 | 12,640 |
| Payroll taxes | 2,995 | 8,827 | 22,476 | 43,585 |
| Insurance | 2,662 | 6,469 | 26,642 | 37,200 |
| Depreciation | 3,469 | 10,874 | 15,019 | 22,710 |
| Freight | 4,799 | 14,118 | 13,657 | 30,099 |
| Utilities | 2,169 | 5,288 | 7,438 | 9,453 |
| Maintenance | 79 | 272 | 789 | 2,117 |
| Tools | 1,150 | 2,414 | 5,408 | 12,398 |
| Rent | 13,172 | 36,252 | 41,404 | 44,929 |
| Supplies | 4,618 | 4,442 | 7,885 | 10,584 |
| Overhead variance | (10,146) | (11,468) | 10,717 | (11,713) |
| Total | 27,605 | 80,317 | 207,173 | 281,656 |
| **Selling expense** | | | | |
| Advertising | $ 0 | $ 0 | $ 0 | $ 8,175 |
| Commissions | 13,509 | 33,150 | 75,082 | 184,879 |
| Payroll | 0 | 0 | 20,990 | 35,747 |
| Sales promotion | 11,616 | 11,158 | 18,018 | 49,460 |
| Payroll taxes | 0 | 0 | 2,101 | 4,382 |
| Travel & entertainment | 11,373 | 9,776 | 15,660 | 19,405 |
| Total | 36,498 | 54,084 | 131,851 | 302,048 |
| **General & administrative expenses** | | | | |
| Auto operation | $ 8,171 | $ 6,275 | $ 6,473 | $ 2,439 |
| Airplane | 510 | 3,408 | 3,688 | 1,876 |
| Bad debts | 0 | 0 | 15,616 | 4,255 |
| Contributions | 0 | 270 | 394 | 3,741 |
| Depreciation | 1,332 | 3,388 | 8,586 | 17,464 |
| Dues & subscriptions | 32 | 128 | 253 | 434 |
| Equipment rental | 0 | 647 | 5,053 | 6,459 |
| Insurance | 1,785 | 724 | 8,641 | 13,956 |
| Professional fees | 3,111 | 4,990 | 3,764 | 12,468 |
| Maintenance & repairs | 0 | 382 | 0 | 1,048 |
| Miscellaneous | 942 | 1,761 | 2,175 | 2,511 |
| Office supplies | 3,127 | 4,047 | 7,455 | 7,110 |
| Clerical payroll | 24,781 | 35,046 | 39,083 | 65,275 |
| Payroll taxes | 4,473 | 4,628 | 4,509 | 7,746 |
| Sales tax | 406 | 273 | 715 | 667 |
| Michigan single-business tax | 219 | 960 | 3,900 | 4,100 |
| Other taxes | 220 | 185 | 2,246 | 1,586 |
| Telephone | 8,515 | 11,888 | 15,572 | 20,757 |
| Officer salary | 10,580 | 0 | 0 | 0 |
| Total | 68,204 | 79,000 | 128,123 | 173,892 |

to be replaced about every 50,000–75,000 miles and, of course, require balancing at that time. Dana Corporation is the exclusive sales agent for the Dana High Tech Driveline Package. In September 1983, Dana placed a large order for ten units totaling $600,000. Shipments against this order began in February 1984 and $321,000 remained in backlog as of April 30, 1984. A second order from Dana for $600,000 was received in June, 1984.

The other three product lines, which are sold in several sizes, are the HO or horizontal overhung machine, the HVR or hard vertical rotator machine, and the HVS or hard vertical static machine. Balancing is important in parts which rotate in order to minimize or eliminate vibration. Parts which are not balanced create noise and excessive wear. These machines are sold to industrial customers to balance fans, pump impellers, pulleys, etc. These machines sell for about $22,000 each, but the HVR machine can reach $66,000.

Basically, balancing can be done in one or two planes depending upon the size or shape of the part to be balanced. The balancing equipment finds the center of the mass and determines how much weight must be added to or removed from a determined point or points on the part to balance it. Elapsed time for balancing varies between 15 minutes to 1½ hours in the case of engine balancing plus time for loading and unloading the part. The heart of a balancing machine is the microprocessor which quickly senses and performs the necessary calculations.

## ORGANIZA-TION

Hines Industries is organized along functional lines. Exhibit 30.4 depicts the organization as of June 1984. Gordon Hines is the president and sole owner of the company. There are 46 employees, including 18 temporary or part-time employees. Temporary employees do not receive all of the fringe benefits and are subject to being laid off first should a cutback be necessary. Five of the key employees—Ron Anderson, Ken Cooper, Joann Huff, Mike Myers, and Len Salenbien—were with Gordon Hines at Balance Technology and came to Hines Industries at various times after Gordon organized his new venture.

## MARKETING

Marketing is managed in an overall way by Gordon Hines through three employees. Joann Huff is responsible for the automotive aftermarket. She joined Hines in June 1980 after being with Bal Tec in secretarial and sales positions for nine years. She supervises 20 manufacturer's representatives employing 45 salesmen who sell the products to the ultimate customers. Mike Myers is responsible for the DL machines, which are sold through several manufacturer's representatives. Industrial sales are handled by John Ramer through three manufacturer's representatives and some direct sales to customers. Bob Edwards was recently hired to cover the Ohio and West Virginia territory directly for the company since it is difficult to get qualified general reps for this market.

Manufacturer's representatives are paid on a commission basis. A 15 percent

**Exhibit 30.4** Hines Industries, Inc., Organization Chart

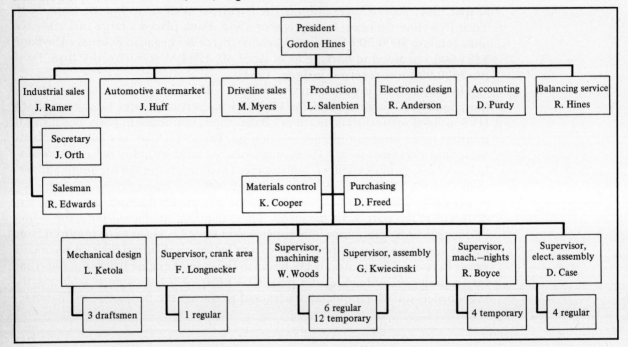

**Exhibit 30.5**

**HINES INDUSTRIES, INC.**
**Sales Analysis**
**Month Ending**

|  | 4/84 | 3/84 | 2/84 | 1/84 | 12/83 | 11/83 |
|---|---|---|---|---|---|---|
| **Billings** | | | | | | |
| Automotive | 74,510 | 120,111 | 191,071 | 68,368 | 128,572 | 112,594 |
| Industrial | 112,707 | 117,705 | | 300 | 162,725 | 52,630 |
| Driveline | 125,610 | 124,770 | 55,555 | | | |
| Parts & Service | 2,373 | 1,159 | 2,372 | 1,281 | 1,201 | 1,269 |
| Total | 315,200 | 363,745 | 248,998 | 69,949 | 292,498 | 166,493 |
| **Bookings** | | | | | | |
| Automotive | 96,432 | 21,019 | 109,888 | (22,942) | 280,141 | 188,781 |
| Industrial | 31,808 | 29,652 | 132,100 | 83,470 | 85,190 | 114,739 |
| Driveline | | 4,250 | 33,725 | 26,900 | | |
| Parts & Service | 2,373 | 1,159 | 2,372 | 1,281 | 1,201 | 1,269 |
| Total | 130,613 | 56,080 | 278,085 | 88,709 | 366,532 | 304,780 |
| Backlog | 792,904 | 977,491 | 1,285,156 | 1,256,069 | 1,237,309 | 1,163,275 |

commission is paid on the basic machine and 10 to 15 percent is paid on added components for the basic machine. Advertising support is provided in trade magazines to get inquiries.

Products are built to order, so no finished products are stocked. A substantial backlog of orders is considered desirable as an indicator of future sales and as an aid to scheduling production. Exhibit 30.5 is a sales analysis for the 12 months ending in April 1984. It shows the monthly billings and bookings by product line and the backlog.

## Automotive Aftermarket

The automotive aftermarket for balancing has been primarily for high-performance cars. It is believed to include the potential for 100 to 150 balancers per year. Hines HC500 balancer for this market sells for about $16,500. The market potential has improved since the EPA and OSHA have backed off interfering with racing.

The automotive aftermarket has two other competitors: Winona VanNorman, which is now a foreign-made copy of Hines equipment, and Stewart Warner, who is now engaging in an aggressive promotional campaign to overcome the Hines advantage.

To aid the marketing by manufacturer's reps, who also handle other machinery for rebuilding engines, Joann Huff advertises in five trade journals for the performance and rebuilding industry: *Automotive Rebuilder, Specialty and Custom Dealer, Jobber Retailer, National Dragster,* and *Circle Track.* Six half-page two-color advertisements were placed in 1983, costing between $1200 and $2000 depending on the publication. She has increased advertising in 1984 to one per month including some full-page ads which are 1½ times the cost of the half-page ads. She would like to increase advertising to two per month in the latter part of 1984. She gets

| 10/83 | 9/83 | 8/83 | 7/83 | 6/83 | 5/83 | 4/83 | 3/83 |
|---|---|---|---|---|---|---|---|
| 42,305 | 59,193 | | | | | | |
| 47,070 | 105,510 | | | | | | |
| 2,231 | 1,268 | | | | | | |
| 91,606 | 165,971 | 111,202 | 87,012 | 94,507 | 10,822 | 41,224 | 99,559 |
| 78,964 | 87,560 | | | | | | |
| 129,615 | 54,310 | | | | | | |
| | 600,000 | | | | | | |
| 2,231 | 1,268 | | | | | | |
| 210,810 | 743,138 | 165,471 | 114,821 | 142,277 | 35,772 | 182,654 | 39,444 |
| 1,024,979 | 905,775 | 328,608 | 274,339 | 246,530 | 198,760 | 173,810 | 32,380 |

opinions from respected users as to which journals are most effective and tries to time Hines ads with articles about balancing, editorials about balancing, or issues preceding trade shows. Extra copies of the journals preceding trade shows are often distributed free at the shows.

Special mailings and telephone campaigns are conducted to promote to the automotive aftermarket. Mailings typically range between 200 and 600 but have gone as high as 2500. The membership lists of associations such as Automotive Engine Rebuilders Association (AERA), Automotive Service Industries Association, and Specialty Engine Machine Association are used for the mailings.

The company attends at least six trade shows per year. A balancing machine is displayed, and Joann Huff as well as area manufacturer's reps are in attendance. Brochures describing the various machines made by Hines are available for use at trade shows as well as for use by manufacturer's reps and company sales personnel. Gordon Hines also attended the important Las Vegas AERA show in June 1984. Seven orders totaling $175,000 were obtained as a result of the show. Other shows of the associations previously mentioned are held in March and October, respectively. The National Dragster show is held in September, the Oval Track show in February, and the Pacific Automotive Show in March. Other wholesaler shows in individual states are attended by manufacturer's reps, and a balancer is sent.

Joann Huff sees her job as being an educational process—first manufacturer's reps and then customers. She said, "The market is there but needs to be made. About half of the rebuilders always balance and the other half never balance." An engine will last 50 percent longer if balanced, which is an important cost factor because the initial cost of engines is causing more and more to be rebuilt rather than replaced.

Diesel engine rebuilding is a new market which the company will be emphasizing. It is estimated by Gordon Hines that 5 percent of all truck engines are rebuilt each year and that more than 20 million trucks are on the road. Joanne plans to use the trade journal *Renews* for advertising, which costs $2600 for a full page. A heavy-duty HC machine with extra bed length will be used for this market. Better driveline tooling has helped the servicing of this market.

Another market which has potential is rebuilding shops which also wish to do some industrial work such as repairing and rebuilding electric motor armatures, pump impellers, fans, and blowers. A microprocessor can be added to the balancers for shops doing this kind of work. The machines are designed and built in a modular form. Therefore, by the simple addition or changing of certain components, it is possible to culture whole new products which can be assembled to satisfy customer requirements. New market segments could be entered in this same way.

The company has a tabletop version of the HC500 called the HC10TC for turbo charger balancing. The machine sells for $10,000. The only competitor is a company which curiously is called Heins. One trade show, Automotive Diesel Specialists, can be used.

Another market is the 100 firms making up the Production Engine Rebuilders

Association (PERA). A typical firm rebuilds as many as 70 engines per day using used parts obtained from tearing down used engines. Their business is increasing because the smaller engines used in production cars do not last as long because of higher speeds used in the engines.

Still another market is the clutch rebuilder. An HVR balancer without all of the "bells and whistles" is used for this job and costs about $11,000 versus the normal HVR price of $20,000. The size of this market is not known but is more like the PERA described previously. The trade group, Automotive Parts Rebuilder Association, puts on one show each year. Hines has three competitors in this business segment.

## Driveline Market

The DL balancer is used primarily to balance truck drive shafts, which have to be replaced frequently because of the heavy weights involved and the many miles of use each year. The current DL balancer was redesigned from the original version to bring it into conformance with the other balancers Hines makes. It is similar to the crankshaft machine, HC series.

Gordon Hines, as he typically does, sold the original concept to Dana Corporation, which is now the exclusive sales agent for the Dana High Tech Drive Line Package. Gordon has been intensively involved in the initial design and marketing of a new product for six months or so, often spending long hours at it, and then, he "eases back so his whole body can come back up". Mike Myers, who sells about one DL balancer to other customers a month, also tries to handle the big Dana account but really needs some help. Mike has a B.A. degree from the University of Michigan including 2½ years of engineering and worked at Bal Tec for 15 years in mechanical design, computer programming, and sales before joining Hines in December 1983. Mike is the internal computer expert for Hines and often provides help for those using the three Hines computers. He also is somewhat involved in mechanical design, although Gordon provides the major mechanical design concepts. Gordon Hines believes the Dana account has a potential for $2 million per year, with another $500,00 of DL balancers sold to others.

In addition to the DL balancer, Hines makes two other products which are related to the balancer and sold as part of the package Dana buys for $60,000–$75,000. These are a push-up press and a specialty lathe. This group of machines allows Dana to do eight specific jobs essential to rebuilding shafts—weld cutoff, tube cut and chamfer, push up, pull out, straighten, weld, straighten, and balance. The package includes specialized tooling designed and built to Dana's specifications. Dana, in turn, sells the unit to the ultimate customer.

## Industrial Market

The industrial market includes sales of the HO, HVR, and HVS products with several size models of each to industrial producers of original equipment (OEM) using impellers, fans, blowers, pulleys, etc. John Ramer heads this activity, and he and Bob Edwards personally sell the products along with the three manufacturer's reps. John Ramer has a degree in business administration from the University of Michigan and is an artist. He joined Hines in 1982 as his first full-time job. It is believed that there is a great deal of business to be had within a 300- to 500-mile radius, and therefore, company sales personnel can be very effective.

Both John and Bob try to stay off the road and do most of their selling by telephone and by sending out literature. They use lists of pump and blower manufacturers obtained from their trade association, as well as referrals, to make their calls. Thus they make only "hot calls." Gordon Hines believes the market is too narrow to advertise in publications like the *American Machinist,* so he prefers the "rifle" rather than "shotgun" approach. He believes the HVR market is $4 million per year, and if the balancing could be done automatically, the market could be $20 million. HC balancers are also being sold for industrial use. Hines is being successful against established competitors.

**Balancing Service**

The company offers a balancing service for local customers who need relatively small quantities balanced. The idea behind this venture is to provide a service to smaller customers, gain experience with other items needing balancing, and, hopefully, sell balancers to the service customers when they grow large enough to warrant their own machine. For instance, Hines is now balancing 2000 specialized parts per week for a Ford Motor supplier. This activity is managed by Robin Hines, Gordon's daughter. This activity will be housed in a third building, along with demo units, containing 3200 square feet which will be available July 1. This move will free up some of the space in the main building.

**MANUFAC-TURING**

Leonard Salenbien, 40 years old, is the manager of production. Prior to joining Hines he served in the same position at Balance Technology. He worked at Bal Tec for 11 years, starting as a checkout technician and progressing to head of the service department before he became production manager there.

Hines Industries rents two buildings located in the light industrial area north of the Ann Arbor Airport. The main facility consists of 9600 square feet on one floor plus 1600 square feet on the second floor. The second building, which is located nearby, contains 3200 square feet. It is used for painting machines, storage of large parts, lumber storage, fabrication of pallets for shipping machines, and storage of concrete bases for machines. Both buildings are quite crowded, and thought has been given to the need for additional space. Unfortunately, the present buildings that are available or being built in the area are not big enough to house all Hines activities in one area.

The production area uses general-purpose machines for the fabrication work. Most of the machinery was purchased used at auctions at very favorable prices. Later these machines were reworked by Hines to bring them up to the standards required. Some have been converted to numerical control using the microprocessors which Hines produces. The production equipment includes four lathes, two horizontal milling machines, six vertical milling machines, one jig borer, one radial-arm drilling machine, one cylindrical ID/OD grinder, one cylindrical ID grinder, one face grinder, a Burgemaster machining center which is being retrofit for numerical control (NC), and a lathe retrofit to CNC. Hines makes many of its own parts and does the mechanical and electrical assembly work. Electronics assembly, including the building of microprocessors, is done on the second floor of the main building, which also includes mechanical drafting.

One of the unique features of the machines produced by Hines is the use of a precision-formed concrete base to provide the mass needed to support and dampen the balancing machines. These concrete bases are purchased locally from a company which uses the forms which were designed and built by Hines. Delivery time on the bases is a week, so it is not necessary to have many of the bulky units in stock.

All machines are thoroughly tested at Hines using customer parts before they are shipped. Len Salenbien is often involved in the testing if trouble is encountered. An automotive aftermarket type of machine such as the HC takes about two days to assemble and test if all of the parts are available. Hines also trains the customer's maintenance people at the Hines plant so that little field repair by Hines is required.

Purchasing of standard parts from vendors is the responsibility of Dave Freed, who has been with Hines since August 1983. He worked as a refrigeration contractor until three years ago when he was injured while water skiing. He subsequently took training on computers at Washtenaw Community College before joining Hines.

Dave gets verbal or written lists of materials required from seven or eight people who keep track of their own stock and determine what they need. These people and their areas of responsibility are as follows:

- Fran Longnecker—crankshaft machines
- Willie Woods—shop materials and supplies
- Gary Kwiecinski—industrial machines, skidding, and shipping
- Dave Bloom (part time)—industrial machines
- Keith Kwiecinski—painting
- Larry Ketola—special tooling and special parts for each machine
- Kay Lamay (Doug Case's employee)—electronics

Dave orders all of his parts by telephone. No purchase orders are sent to vendors. Dave maintains a list of purchase orders by number on the computer, including all of the pertinent data on each order. Orders are placed by description of the part. No part numbers have been assigned by Hines and vendor part numbers are not used. Although engineering is beginning to assign part numbers to mechanical parts required for the company's products, it has not yet decided if company part numbers will be assigned to standard purchased parts. A bill of material is not generated for each machine, although the company wants to do this. In fact, the company does not presently have a comprehensive part numbering system.

Dave does not know how many different parts are in the products but believes there are at least 1000 purchased parts, not counting internally manufactured parts. Partial inventories may be taken every six months or so. Parts are not actually counted, but the quantity is estimated. There is no definite stockroom used but rather a series of stock locations by product assembly area. Parts may be stocked in more than one area. Sometimes parts are ordered a second time if an item is on back order. No production schedule is available.

Most of the parts Dave orders are available within a short time. Motors require a week and IC (integrated circuit) chips usually require a month. However, ICs could require four to six months if not in stock. Dave orders from vendors, with whom Hines is on good financial terms, based upon price, first, and delivery, second. Quality is important on some items.

Dave believes the company is "moving away from chaos" but not fast enough. He describes the big upswing in business in December 1983 (Dana) as like a "cobra trying to swallow a pig." Although everyone knows basically how they fit in, what their job is, and how they do it, they are not enough aware of the company's goals and objectives, Dave believes. Items seem to be ordered on an emergency basis half of the time.

The big upswing in business created some cash flow problems, although Gordon Hines believes the worst is over. Since May, Dave has been required to check the price before ordering and he may be required to get approval for cash reasons. Sometimes he has ordered smaller quantities at a higher price in order to conserve cash. Sometimes he has delayed orders or challenged the size of orders. Sometimes, if a vendor requires COD, Dave has had to find a new vendor because Gordon has said no COD shipments will be accepted.

Gordon and Len sometimes disagree on product design and ordering. Dave feels caught in the middle. About half of the time Gordon discusses the issue directly with Dave, thus resolving it. Dave would like to see more formal planning. Purchase requisition forms are on order which presumably will be used for preapproval before Dave sees them. The forms will be two-part—one for accounting and one for purchasing. If the originator wants a copy, a Xerox copy will be made.

Dave gets a copy of the Sales Order Information Form-Partial Release but is not sure why he gets it since he cannot order even long-delivery items based on this information. The form is used primarily by Ken Cooper to order outside mechanical items, he says.

Ken Cooper, whose responsibility is materials control, joined Hines in March 1984. He worked at Bal Tec for 13 years and was purchasing manager when he left. Prior to Bal Tec, he worked in the machine shop at Bendix for 20 years. Ken orders some material directly and gets his purchase order numbers from Dave Freed. He subcontracts some of the mechanical parts work to outside firms on a time and material basis.

Ken schedules the shop and is supposed to schedule electronics, but Doug Case really does it. Ken keeps a cardex inventory system of common manufactured parts. Based upon this information, he initiates orders for parts through machining or through outside suppliers. The lot size ordered is based on previous experience, with input from Willie Woods and Fran Longnecker. An inventory may be taken on individual items. Ken is trying to set up inventories by production area. He decides whether to make or buy an item.

Ken's goal is to get things running smoothly. He is getting shop costs by using the average actual hours secured from job tickets times $25 per hour, which includes burden. The actual cost of labor is about $7 per hour. If an item has not been made before, he estimates the cost based upon his previous experience.

Ken is concerned that production always seems to be behind and is "playing catch-up." He believes the workers are learning but are operators and not machinists in that they can not do setups well. Only Willie Woods and Bob Boyce can do setups. There is no formal training program. The last thing that gets made is customer tooling, which is what often creates the delays. He also believes more space may be needed soon now that the second Dana order has been received. He estimates that under ideal conditions two or three Dana machines, three HCs, and three HVRs or HOs could be assembled simultaneously if parts were available (maybe requiring multiple shifts) and if moves were carefully checked.

Ken describes the delivery commitment process in this way. Len Salenbien makes a tentative commitment to a salesperson who has a potential order. If and when the order is actually received, it may be different than originally described. Also, other orders may have been received after the tentative commitment and be loaded into the shop. Thus the delivery commitment is frequently a problem. On the average, it takes two weeks from the beginning of assembly until the product is shipped, but shipment can be delayed six to eight weeks because of production planning problems, inadequate pretesting of components, and delays in securing information and samples of customer parts for tooling fabrication.

## ELECTRONIC DESIGN

The electronic design activity is conducted by Ron Anderson, who is 49 years old. Ron Anderson, who also worked for Gordon at Bal Tec, began working for Hines on a part-time basis but now is full-time. He has known Gordon personally for many years and began his work at Bal Tec as a consultant. He has a degree in electrical engineering and has specialized in electronic design. He had ten years' previous experience at the University of Illinois as director of electronics for the Chemistry Department, which involved developing specialized instrumentation. Ron tries to use standard techniques and approaches in designing the electronics for the products so that common modules are used in the various models whenever possible. Ron is happiest when there is some new design to be developed and admits to being bored when things are too routine.

## ACCOUNTING

Dean Purdy, who is 55 years old, was hired in late March 1984 as controller. Dean had previously worked for Fansteel for 17 years. His last position was controller of their V. R. Wesson Division plant at Ferndale, Michigan, which made tungsten carbide cutting tools. The Ferndale plant had 125 employees and 50,000 square feet of floor area. He also had previous experience with Midwest Machine Company, an OEM for the auto industry. Thus Dean's background in the machining business fits well with Hines.

During his three months with Hines, Dean has learned the product line and internal workings of the company. He believes he has made progress in stabilizing the cash flow from receivables to payables. His personal priority is "to establish systems to do things in an orderly fashion" including inventory and production control and cost control.

The company presently uses two Altos computers, one with a 10-megabyte hard disk and one with 1-megabyte dual 8-inch floppy disks. The latter unit together with a small 64K dual 4½-inch floppy-disk computer is used by purchasing. Thought has been given to buying a Radio Shack 30-megabyte hard-disk computer for additional applications including accounting. Such a computer would cost about $15,000 including software.

Because the equipment for the industrial market and Dana typically have a longer delivery cycle than other products, Hines offers these customers, after receiving their order, a 2 to 5 percent discount if the customer will make an initial 30 percent down payment and will pay the balance within ten days after delivery. Gordon Hines believes this policy gives the company a competitive advantage in addition to improving the cash flow.

## MANAGE-MENT

Gordon Hines began to draw a $40,000 per year salary in May 1984. Prior to that he was living off his proceeds from selling his Bal Tec stock. When asked how he spends his time at the company, he estimated the following: sales, 20 percent; design, 20 percent; general business, 20 percent; production, 25 percent; and new business planning, 15 percent. Gordon expects Dean Purdy to pick up a major share of his general business activities, which will free up some of Gordon's time to move into sales/design activities of other products or to develop new large accounts.

Gordon has also contemplated the need for a mechanical engineer who could handle design activities and manufacturing engineering activities. Such a person would be difficult to find and could be quite expensive in salary and relocation expenses. However, such a move would free Gordon from mechanical design activities which do require a substantial amount of his time.

Gordon also would like to see all of the company's activities in a common location. He would continue to rent because he does not want to put scarce cash into bricks and mortar. The location would need to be near the present location for the convenience of employees. The airport location is also convenient since Gordon shares an airplane with two other businessmen. Fortunately, the business which occupied the 3200 square feet immediately adjoining Hines Industries is relocating to another part of the industrial park in July and Hines will be able to rent this space and combine it with the main plant area.

Gordon sees a strong growth potential for the company over the next two years barring another prolonged recession. He thinks fiscal 1985 should see $4 million in sales, with the following year increasing another 50 percent. His overall management priorities are to manage cash first and profits second. In his view, the October through December 1984 period will set the stage for the following year.

# 31 Rainbow Food Company

Thomas M. Bertsch
James Madison University

Ms. Kate Caldwell, the manager and sole proprietor of Rainbow Food Company, is considering her future business strategy. Although she is very pleased with the 8 percent increase in sales over last year, she is still unsatisfied with one particular aspect of her marketing approach.

Ever since she took over the store in 1979 she has attempted to reach the student population at the nearby university. She feels that the sizable student body of over 9000 can be a profitable market segment for her "natural" food store. The modern concern for health and fitness among young adults seems to encourage the use of natural foods as an alternative to the packaged, preservative-ridden foods generally found in supermarkets. Yet she has not been able to capitalize on this product difference. She is still trying to find a way to make Rainbow Food Company known to the students of James Madison University at an expense her limited marketing budget can afford.

## PRODUCT OFFERING

Rainbow Food Company carries a complete line of spices, teas, medicinal herbs, grains, and grain flours. It also carries some dairy products, vitamins, and juices. Lately, shampoos and clothing have been added, with good sales results. All of the food products offered are pesticide- and preservative-free and are manufactured and distributed by lesser-known "natural" food companies.

## MARKET AREA

Rainbow Food Company is located approximately half a mile north of Harrisonburg, Virginia. Harrisonburg is a town in central Virginia with a population of approximately 25,000. However, it has a market area of more than 200,000, which extends into West Virginia. The town is remarkably diverse considering its size. Its inhabitants range from the members of the austere Mennonite religious sect to the cosmopolitan residents of James Madison University. Although Rainbow Food Company is located directly across from Eastern Mennonite College, it is considerably outside the downtown shopping area and out of the way for most area residents.

Ms. Caldwell is not considering expansion in the near future because of poor

This case was prepared by Tim Hays and Michael Ratcliffe, research associates, and Thomas M. Bertsch, associate professor of marketing, at James Madison University. It was designed as a basis for class discussion rather than to illustrate either effective or ineffective handling of a management situation. Confidential information has been disguised.

economic conditions in the area and the fact that she has no one to assist her. However, she would consider expansion into a combination natural food snack bar and natural food store if a good downtown location were available and conditions were favorable.

## PERSONAL PHILOSOPHY

Ms. Caldwell thinks of Rainbow Food Company as more than simply a profitable business venture; it is very much a way of life for her. Ever since becoming a vegetarian in 1973, she has tried to learn more about the preservative- and pesticide-free foods that could make up a "natural" diet. Basically, she endorses a vegetarian diet, because she feels it is a healthier diet and makes use of primary protein (like soybeans) as opposed to the very wasteful secondary source—meat. (Cattle consume ten times more protein than they provide.) She sees her store as a way of providing this philosophy to others while making a good living for herself. She views her customers as those who are "changing their diet and possibly life-style." Ms. Caldwell also feels very strongly about supporting other local businesses and does so herself whenever possible. She attributes her success to her total commitment and belief in what she sells.

## INDUSTRY DEVELOP-MENT

The natural food industry has grown rapidly in recent years. In 1977, annual sales of natural food products in the United States were only $140 million. However, sales increased to $1.1 billion in 1978, and they are expected to reach $3.1 billion by 1987. There are several reasons cited by researchers for this dramatic increase: increased consumer awareness of environmental issues, questionable food additives, and concern over pesticides and drugs used in "nonnatural" food preparation. In addition, the number of people in the age groups of 24 to 34, 34 to 44, and over 65 is increasing. Researchers feel that people in these age groups are the ones who most often buy natural foods.

Along with this growing market for natural foods have come an increasing variety of natural foods and many new brands. These changes have aggravated the display space problem for conventional supermarkets. Even though the demand for natural foods is increasing, the volume in individual stores is not yet large enough to justify the allocation of much space to such products. As a result, most supermarkets do not carry a full line of natural food products or a wide choice of brands. This moderate level of demand has left the market open for natural food stores to open all over the United States.

## HISTORY OF RAINBOW FOODS

When Ms. Caldwell took over the store, it was a full-service business, much like an old-time general store. After taking over the store, she converted it to self-service and doubled the stock. She also increased the lines of tea, cheeses, and bath care products. In addition, she obtained new distributors, local to the area. Ms. Caldwell notes that if she had stayed with her past distributors, she probably would be out of business because of problems related to quality, of which she is very conscious.

In order to raise the $12,000 capital needed to buy the store, Ms. Caldwell's parents cosigned a loan for $9,000. She provided the additional $3,000 from her own money.

The advantage of Rainbow Food's location is the rent, which is only $180 per month and includes the store area and upstairs living quarters. The rent is very reasonable compared to rents of $600 to $800 per month for store locations of equivalent size in downtown Harrisonburg, which do not even include a living area. Her electric bill averages about $155 per month, and the water cost is $8.00 per month for both the store and house. Also, Ms. Caldwell burns wood for fuel, which costs her only $200 per year.

Ms. Caldwell feels that the herbs, teas, and spices are the most successful part of her business from both a sales volume and a customer point of view. These items are priced at one-half the price charged by supermarkets for comparable items.

Ms. Caldwell believes that she does not have any direct competition in the area. A natural food store in the nearby regional shopping mall is not considered a real competitor, because it is primarily a vitamin store. Also, a nutrition store in downtown Harrisonburg is not considered a major competitor, because it does not carry the same items as Rainbow Food. A co-op store in Harrisonburg is her strongest competitor, but it does not specialize in natural foods. Ms. Caldwell feels there is no other store like Rainbow Food within a 70-mile radius of Harrisonburg.

Rainbow Food has never operated at a loss since Ms. Caldwell bought it in 1979. Her annual sales last year were about $75,000 with a markup on cost of about 100 percent, giving her a gross margin of $37,500 and a net profit before taxes of $26,000 (see Exhibit 31.1). Typical of most new businesses, Rainbow Foods maintains a low cash reserve; only 2.5 percent of total assets are in cash (see Exhibit 31.2). At this time, Ms. Caldwell has set her marketing budget for the current year at 2.5 percent of last year's gross sales, which amounts to $1875.

**Exhibit 31.1**

### RAINBOW FOOD COMPANY
**Comparative Income Statement for Past Two Years**

|  | Last Year | Two Years Ago |
|---|---|---|
| Sales | $75,000 | $69,000 |
| Cost of goods sold | 37,500 | 34,500 |
| Gross margin | 37,500 | 34,500 |
| Variable cost | 4,900 | 4,200 |
| Fixed cost | 6,000 | 6,000 |
| Total cost | 10,900 | 10,200 |
| Profit (before taxes) | $26,600 | $24,300 |

**Exhibit 31.2**

## RAINBOW FOOD COMPANY
### Projected Balance Sheet for This Year

| | |
|---|---:|
| Assets | |
| Cash | $ 500 |
| Inventory | 13,500 |
| Equipment | 6,000 |
| Total assets | $ 20,000 |
| Liabilities | |
| Accounts payable | $ 1,700 |
| Current maturities on long-term debt | 900 |
| Interest payable | 500 |
| Taxes payable | 4,700 |
| Notes payable | 7,200 |
| Total liabilities | $ 15,050 |
| Owner's equity | 4,950 |
| Total liabilities and equity | $ 20,000 |

**CUSTOMER TYPES**

In Ms. Caldwell's opinion, the customers of Rainbow Food Company represent a wide cross section of the population, and most are repeat customers. Examples of those who shop at the store are

- Young professionals who seek top-quality natural foods and vitamins
- Low-income shoppers desiring inexpensive bulk items (grains, for example)
- Mennonite families seeking foodstuffs without preservatives or fancy packaging
- Older shoppers who seek natural foods and herbs to alleviate their digestive problems
- Young athletes desiring fresh juices, vitamins, and sources of potent energy

**PROMOTION**

Ms. Caldwell has used a variety of means to get public attention for her store. Her first promotional effort involved the use of dated discount coupons that appeared in the local newspaper, the *Daily News Record*. This was quite effective in reaching the local price-oriented shopper but somewhat expensive (see Exhibits 31.3 and 31.4).

In May, Ms. Caldwell had a Harrisonburg-based music house named Ad Sound write and produce a package of three jingles to be used on the local radio stations, WSVA and WQPO. She felt she needed a commercial with a simple folk sound to promote her store. So far the indications seem to be positive. She is now getting some customers from outlying areas, and her local base of repeat customers is increasing. Feedback usually comes in the form of customer requests for specials advertised on the radio spots.

Lately, Ms. Caldwell also feels that she has gotten good results from her use of the Welcome Wagon (see Exhibit 31.5). The Welcome Wagon distributes discount coupons and promotional items that describe local businesses and services available to area newcomers.

**Exhibit 31.3** Newspaper Advertisement

## You Are What You Eat

Autumn leaves are in the air and prices at Rainbow Food Company are "falling" as well. Bring this ad for a special discount on the items below:

| | |
|---|---|
| **Peanuts** | **99¢/lb.** |
| **Popcorn** | **49¢/lb.** |
| **Raisins** | **$1.29/lb.** |
| **Raisin Granola** | **$1.39/lb.** |
| **Trail Mix** | **$1.94/lb.** |

We also carry 100% cotton clothing and a variety of books.

*Rainbow Food Company – Wholesome, Natural foods at student prices.*

**Just North of Harrisonburg on Rt. 42 (Across from the Mennonite Nursing Home), approximately 2 miles from the University.**

**Store hours: Monday through Friday 10-6**
**Saturday:10-5**
**Phone:434-6078**

**Exhibit 31.4** Local Media Rates

| Media | Rates |
|---|---|
| Radio stations | |
| WSVA | $ 16.00 per 30-second spot |
| WQPO | $ 16.00 per 30-second spot |
| Newspapers | |
| *Daily News Record* | $338.00 per half page |
| (regional) | $178.00 per quarter page |
| | $ 88.80 per eighth page |
| *Breeze* | $ 95.00 per half page |
| (for students at the university) | $ 48.00 per quarter page |
| | $ 28.00 per eighth page |

**Exhibit 31.5** Welcome Wagon Announcement

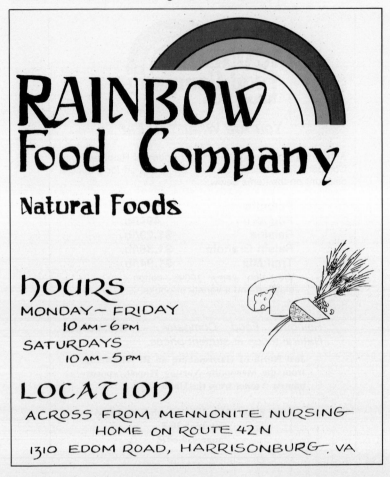

At the store itself there are handouts concerning the use of medicinal herbs and recipes for natural foods. These handouts are provided free by the manufacturers and have been very popular with steady customers.

Although she has run ads in the school newspaper, posted announcements, and mailed promotional flyers, most students at James Madison University have still not visited Rainbow Food Company. Ms. Caldwell feels that the key problem is awareness, because it has been her experience that the students are still unaware of the store rather than simply choosing not to shop at it.

# Section C   International Business Cases

# 32   Ford of Europe and Local-Content Regulations

H. Landis Gabel and Anthony E. Hall
INSEAD

In mid-1983, the management committee of Ford of Europe (the company's senior decision-making committee) was once again examining the trends, opportunities, and threats offered by the European market. The principal threat perceived by management was the growing Japanese presence in Europe. Japanese manufacturers had increased their car sales in Western Europe from 750,000 units in 1979 to almost one million units in 1983 and they were beginning to establish a manufacturing foothold in Europe. Nissan, for example, was just beginning to produce automobiles in Italy. It would soon increase its production of vehicles for Europe from a Spanish plant, and, most worrisome, the company was expected to announce imminently a decision to proceed with a previously shelved plan to construct a new and very large assembly plant in the United Kingdom. Although Ford competed very successfully against the other European producers—and for the first time had captured the number one European market share position in the second quarter of 1983—Japanese producers' plants in Europe would constitute a new and severe challenge. What especially worried Ford was the possibility that Nissan's new U.K. plant would import major automobile components into Europe from Japan, assemble them into finished vehicles, and then claim that the vehicles were European in origin and thus not subject to any existing European-Japanese trade agreements or understandings.

This worry had led Ford executives back in 1981 to consider seriously local-content regulations as a way of reducing this risk and helping to stem the growth of the Japanese producers' share of the European market. Local-content regulations, most commonly employed by developing countries against multinational

This case study was developed after discussions with certain Ford personnel but it does not necessarily reflect the actual scope or manner of deliberations undertaken by Ford management or the conclusions of Ford management.

Address reprint requests to H. Landis Gabel, Associate Professor of Industrial Economics, INSEAD, Boulevard de Constance, 77305 Fontainebleau Cedex, France.

© H. Landis Gabel and Anthony E. Hall, 1985.

Reprinted with permission from *The Journal of Management Case Studies*, vol. 1 (1985), pp. 38–59.

firms based in developed countries, defined the percentage of a product that must be produced in a specified geographical region as a precondition of sale in that region.

Although local-content regulations had been discussed occasionally in the management committee for the past two years, no conclusions had been reached, and pressure was building to push the discussion through to a definitive policy stance. If the committee were to decide to favor local-content regulations, it would then have to decide on strategy and tactics. Regulations could take various forms, some of which might be more advantageous to Ford than others. And, of course, Ford would have to decide how to represent its position to the governmental bodies that would have to introduce, monitor, and enforce the regulations.

**FORD OF EUROPE** Ford's European headquarters are based at Warley near Brentwood in southeast England. The sixth floor of its 2500-person office building houses Ford of Europe's executive suites, where trade policy is a frequent—and often emotional—topic of conversation. The Ford Motor Company had a long tradition of favoring unrestricted international trade. Henry Ford declared in 1928, "I don't believe in anything else than free trade all 'round." Indeed, he exported the sixth car he made (to Canada). But the international trade environment of the 1920s was not that of the 1970s and 1980s, and although Henry Ford II was a strong free-trader like his grandfather, Ford U.S. had altered its official policy position in 1980 away from free trade toward fair trade with an element of protectionism. The management of Ford of Europe could follow this lead by lobbying for local-content regulations, but they did not feel obliged to do so. They were sufficiently independent of their American parent that the decision was theirs to make.

Ford of Europe was a product of the Ford Motor Company's traditional internationalism. It was created in 1967 when the managing director of Ford of Germany, John Andrews, convinced Henry Ford II of the need to coordinate the design, development, production, and marketing operations of the Ford European national operating companies within the framework of the European Economic Community (EEC).

Ford now has 25 manufacturing sites in six European countries, and it is the most geographically integrated car producer in Europe. In the last five years the company spent more than $5 billion on automation and common design of its European cars, with the objective of making at least half the parts used in its European line interchangeable. Ford's European integration and focus and its image as a national producer in each national market give it an important advantage in the growing trend of nationalistic car buying. The company proudly claims that 95 percent of the content of its European cars is European in origin.

Ford of Europe had sales of $9.9 billion in 1981 and would have ranked thirty-fourth on the *Fortune* 500 listing. From 1980 through 1982—one of the worst periods for the auto industry since the 1950s—Ford of Europe earned $1 billion in profit. (See Exhibits 32.1, 32.2, and 32.3.)

**Exhibit 32.1**

# FORD MOTOR COMPANY AND CONSOLIDATED SUBSIDIARIES
## Consolidated Balance Sheet at December 31, 1982 ($ millions)

|  | 1982 | 1981 |
|---|---|---|
| **Assets** | | |
| Current assets | | |
| Cash and cash items | $ 943.7 | $ 1,176.5 |
| Marketable securities (including $500 million of commercial paper of Ford Motor Credit Company in 1981), at cost and accrued interest (approximates market) | 611.7 | 923.5 |
| Receivables | 2,376.5 | 2,595.8 |
| Inventories | 4,123.3 | 4,642.9 |
| Other current assets | 743.7 | 838.2 |
| Total current assets | 8,798.9 | 10,176.9 |
| Equities in net assets of unconsolidated subsidiaries and affiliates | 2,413.4 | 2,348.2 |
| Property | | |
| Land, plant, and equipment, at cost | 17,014.9 | 16,395.7 |
| Less accumulated depreciation | 9,546.9 | 8,959.4 |
| Net land, plant and equipment | 7,468.0 | 7,436.3 |
| Unamortized special tools | 2,668.3 | 2,410.1 |
| Net property | 10,136.3 | 9,846.4 |
| Other assets | 613.1 | 649.9 |
| Total assets | $21,961.7 | $23,021.4 |
| **Liabilities and stockholders' equity** | | |
| Current liabilities | | |
| Accounts payable | | |
| Trade | $ 3,117.5 | $ 2,800.2 |
| Other | 1,002.1 | 1,089.8 |
| Total accounts payable | 4,119.6 | 3,890.0 |
| Income taxes | 383.0 | 208.9 |
| Short-term debt | 1,949.1 | 2,049.0 |
| Long-term debt payable within one year | 315.9 | 128.7 |
| Accrued liabilities | 3,656.4 | 3,663.7 |
| Total current liabilities | 10,424.0 | 9,940.3 |
| Long-term debt | 2,353.3 | 2,709.7 |
| Other liabilities | 1,922.7 | 1,856.2 |
| Deferred income taxes | 1,054.1 | 1,004.8 |
| Minority interests in net assets of consolidated subsidiaries | 130.1 | 148.2 |
| Guarantees and commitments | — | — |
| Stockholders' equity | | |
| Capital stock, par value $2.00 a share | | |
| Common stock, shares issued: 1982—108,870,062; 1981—107,859,065 | 217.8 | 215.7 |
| Class B stock, shares issued: 1982—11,717,738; 1981—12,717,003 | 23.4 | 25.5 |
| Capital in excess of par value of stock | 522.4 | 526.1 |
| Foreign-currency translation adjustments | (623.2) | — |
| Earnings retained for use in the business | 5,937.1 | 6,594.9 |
| Total stockholders' equity | 6,077.5 | 7,362.2 |
| Total liabilities and stockholders' equity | $21,961.7 | $23,021.4 |

*Source:* Ford of Europe.

**Exhibit 32.2** Ford Motor Company and Consolidated Subsidiaries
Ten-Year Financial Summary ($ millions)

| Summary of operations | 1982[a] | 1981 | 1980 |
|---|---|---|---|
| Sales | $37,067.2 | 38,247.1 | 37,085.5 |
| Total costs | 37,550.8 | 39,502.9 | 39,363.8 |
| Operating income (loss) | (483.6) | (1,255.8) | (2,278.3) |
| Interest income | 562.7 | 624.6 | 543.1 |
| Interest expense | 745.5 | 674.7 | 432.5 |
| Equity in net income of unconsolidated subsidiaries and affiliates | 258.5 | 167.8 | 187.0 |
| Income (loss) before income taxes | (407.9) | (1,138.1) | (1,980.7) |
| Provision (credit) for income taxes | 256.6[b] | (68.3)[b] | (435.4)[c] |
| Minority interests | (6.7) | (9.7) | (2.0) |
| Income (loss) before cumulative effect of an accounting change | (657.8) | (1,060.1) | (1,543.3) |
| Cumulative effect of an accounting change[d] | — | — | — |
| Net income (loss) | (657.8) | (1,060.1) | (1,543.3) |
| Cash dividends | — | 144.4 | 312.7 |
| Retained income (loss) | $ (657.8) | (1,204.5) | (1,856.0) |
| Income before minority interests as percentage of sales[e] | | | |
| Stockholders' equity at year end | $ 6,077.5 | 7,362.2 | 8,567.5 |
| Assets at year end | $21,961.7 | 23,021.4 | 24,347.6 |
| Long-term debt at year end | $ 2,353.3 | 2,709.7 | 2,058.8 |
| Average number of shares of capital stock outstanding (in millions) | 120.4 | 120.3 | 120.3 |
| A share (in dollars) | | | |
| Income (loss) before cumulative effect of an accounting change | $ (5.46) | (8.81) | (12.83) |
| Cumulative effect of an accounting change[d] | — | — | — |
| Net income (loss)[f] | $ (5.46) | (8.81) | (12.83) |
| Net income assuming full dilution | — | — | — |
| Cash dividends | — | $ 1.20 | 2.60 |

| 1979 | 1978 | 1977 | 1976[b] | 1975 | 1974 | 1973 |
|---|---|---|---|---|---|---|
| 43,513.7 | 42,784.1 | 37,841.5 | 28,839.6 | 24,009.1 | 23,620.6 | 23,015.1 |
| 42,596.7 | 40,425.6 | 35,095.9 | 27,252.7 | 23,572.7 | 23,015.4 | 21,446.1 |
| 917.0 | 2,358.5 | 2,745.6 | 1,586.9 | 436.4 | 605.2 | 1,569.0 |
| 693.0 | 456.0 | 299.1 | 232.6 | 155.8 | 171.4 | 189.9 |
| 246.8 | 194.8 | 192.7 | 216.6 | 301.0 | 281.5 | 174.7 |
| 146.2 | 159.0 | 150.0 | 136.3 | 107.0 | 58.5 | 48.5 |
| 1,509.4 | 2,778.7 | 3,002.0 | 1,739.2 | 398.2 | 553.6 | 1,632.7 |
| 330.1 | 1,175.0 | 1,325.6 | 730.6 | 151.9 | 201.5 | 702.1 |
| 10.0 | 14.8 | 3.6 | 25.5 | 18.8 | 25.0 | 24.1 |
| 1,169.3 | 1,588.9 | 1,672.8 | 983.1 | 227.5 | 327.1[d] | 906.5[d] |
| — | — | — | — | 95.2 | — | — |
| 1,169.3 | 1,588.9 | 1,672.8 | 983.1 | 322.7 | 327.1 | 906.5 |
| 467.6 | 416.6 | 359.3 | 263.4 | 242.6 | 298.1 | 317.1 |
| 701.7 | 1,172.3 | 1,313.5 | 719.7 | 80.1 | 29.0 | 589.4 |
| 2.7% | 3.7% | 4.4% | 3.5% | 1.4% | 1.5% | 4.0% |
| 10,420.7 | 9,686.3 | 8,456.9 | 7,107.0 | 6,376.5 | 6,267.5 | 6,405.1 |
| 23,524.6 | 22,101.4 | 19,241.3 | 15,768.1 | 14,020.2 | 14,173.6 | 12,954.0 |
| 1,274.6 | 1,144.5 | 1,359.7 | 1,411.4 | 1,533.9 | 1,476.7 | 977.0 |
| 119.9 | 119.0 | 118.1 | 117.6 | 116.6 | 116.8 | 124.1 |
| 9.75 | 13.35 | 14.16 | 8.36 | 1.95 | 2.80[d] | 7.31[d] |
| — | — | — | — | 0.82 | — | — |
| 9.75 | 13.35 | 14.16 | 8.36 | 2.77 | 2.80 | 7.31 |
| $ 9.15 | 12.42 | 13.08 | 7.74 | 2.65 | 2.69[d] | 6.86[d] |
| 3.90 | 3.50 | 3.04 | 2.24 | 2.08 | 2.56 | 2.56 |

(continued)

**Exhibit 32.2** (continued)

| Summary of operations | 1982[a] | 1981 | 1980 | 1979 |
|---|---|---|---|---|
| Stockholders' equity at year-end | $ 50.40 | 61.06 | 71.05 | 86.46 |
| Common stock price range (NYSE) | $ 41½ | 26 | 35¾ | 45⅜ |
| | $ 16¾ | 15¾ | 18⅛ | 29⅜ |

*Pro forma* amounts assuming the investment tax credits accrued after 1970 flowed through to

| | | | | |
|---|---|---|---|---|
| Net income (in millions) | — | — | — | — |
| Net income a share | — | — | — | — |
| Assuming full dilution | — | — | — | — |

**Facility and tooling data**

| | | | | |
|---|---|---|---|---|
| Capital expenditures for expansion, modernization and replacement of facilities (excluding special tools) | $ 1,605.8 | 1,257.4 | 1,583.8 | 2,152.3 |
| Depreciation | $ 1,200.8 | 1,168.7 | 1,057.2 | 895.9 |
| Expenditures for special tools | $ 1,361.6 | 970.0 | 1,184.7 | 1,288.0 |
| Amortization of special tools | $ 955.6 | 1,010.7 | 912.1 | 708.5 |

**Employee data—worldwide**

| | | | | |
|---|---|---|---|---|
| Payroll | $ 8,863.0 | 9,380.1 | 9,519.0 | 10,169.1 |
| Total labor costs | $ 11,756.7 | 12,238.3 | 12,417.3 | 13,227.2 |
| Average number of employees | 379,229 | 404,788 | 426,735 | 494,579 |

**Employee data—U.S. operations**

| | | | | |
|---|---|---|---|---|
| Payroll | $ 5,352.7 | 5,507.5 | 5,248.5 | 6,262.6 |
| Average hourly labor costs per hour worked[h] (in dollars) | | | | |
| Earnings | $ 13.57 | 12.75 | 11.45 | 10.35 |
| Benefits | 9.80 | 8.93 | 8.54 | 5.59 |
| Total | $ 23.37 | 21.68 | 19.99 | 15.94 |
| Average number of employees | 155,901 | 170,806 | 179,917 | 239,475 |

[a] See Note 1 of Notes to Financial Statements.
[b] Change to LIFO reduced net income by $81 million.
[c] See Note 5 of Notes to Financial Statements.
[d] Cumulative effect of change (as of January 1, 1975) to flow-through method of accounting for investment tax credit.
[e] 1982, 1981, and 1980 results were a loss.
[f] See Note 7 of Notes to Financial Statements.
[g] Excludes effect of UAW strike.
[h] Excludes data for subsidiary companies.
Share data have been adjusted to reflect the five-for-four stock split that became effective May 24, 1977.

*Source:* Ford of Europe.

| 1978 | 1977 | 1976[b] | 1975 | 1974 | 1973 |
|---|---|---|---|---|---|
| 80.77 | 71.15 | 60.14 | 54.09 | 53.58 | 51.66 |
| 51⅞ | 49¼ | 49½ | 36¼ | 43½ | 65⅞ |
| 39 | 41⅜ | 34⅞ | 25⅞ | 23 | 30⅞ |

income in the year the assets were placed in service

| 1978 | 1977 | 1976[b] | 1975 | 1974 | 1973 |
|---|---|---|---|---|---|
| — | — | — | — | $ 363.9 | 938.9 |
| — | — | — | — | $ 3.12 | 7.57 |
| — | — | — | — | $ 2.98 | 7.10 |
| 1,571.5 | 1,089.6 | 551.0 | 614.2 | 832.5 | 891.7 |
| 735.5 | 628.7 | 589.7 | 583.8 | 530.8 | 485.1 |
| 970.2 | 672.7 | 503.7 | 342.2 | 618.7 | 594.3 |
| 578.2 | 487.7 | 431.0 | 435.3 | 392.7 | 463.1 |
| 9,774.9 | 8,338.3 | 6,639.2 | 5,629.2 | 5,892.6 | 5,769.2 |
| 12,494.0 | 10,839.2 | 8,653.3 | 7,165.7 | 7,317.3 | 7,108.2 |
| 506,531 | 479,292 | 443,917[g] | 416,120 | 464,731 | 474,318 |
| 6,581.2 | 5,653.4 | 4,380.4 | 3,560.5 | 3,981.9 | 4,027.0 |
| 9.73 | 8.93 | 8.03 | 7.10 | 6.61 | 6.12 |
| 4.36 | 3.91 | 3.98 | 3.86 | 2.88 | 2.31 |
| 14.09 | 12.84 | 12.01 | 10.96 | 9.49 | 8.43 |
| 256,614 | 239,303 | 219,698[g] | 203,691 | 235,256 | 249,513 |

**Exhibit 32.3**

# FORD MOTOR COMPANY AND CONSOLIDATED SUBSIDIARIES
## Ten-Year Summary of Vehicle Factory Sales

| | 1982 | 1981 | 1980 | 1979 | 1978 |
|---|---|---|---|---|---|
| **U.S. and Canadian cars and trucks**[a] | | | | | |
| Cars | | | | | |
| United States | 1,270,519 | 1,385,174 | 1,397,431 | 2,044,461 | 2,632,190 |
| Canada | 118,721 | 148,515 | 162,576 | 236,437 | 248,285 |
| Total cars | 1,389,240 | 1,533,689 | 1,560,007 | 2,280,898 | 2,880,475 |
| Trucks[b] | | | | | |
| United States | 803,484 | 716,648 | 753,195 | 1,183,016 | 1,458,132 |
| Canada | 70,120 | 104,136 | 109,006 | 160,160 | 153,955 |
| Total trucks | 873,604 | 820,784 | 862,201 | 1,343,176 | 1,612,087 |
| Total cars and trucks | 2,262,844 | 2,354,473 | 2,422,208 | 3,624,074 | 4,492,562 |
| **Cars and trucks outside the United States and Canada**[b] | | | | | |
| Germany | 797,850 | 737,383 | 657,258 | 880,325 | 847,529 |
| Britain | 423,073 | 418,629 | 468,472 | 555,496 | 433,191 |
| Spain | 229,839 | 254,006 | 266,522 | 252,917 | 247,408 |
| Brazil | 145,110 | 125,346 | 165,703 | 169,631 | 158,935 |
| Australia | 141,990 | 127,181 | 93,490 | 115,148 | 107,389 |
| Mexico | 90,478 | 107,312 | 84,668 | 74,703 | 68,009 |
| South Africa | 59,171 | 66,962 | 52,671 | 40,447 | 46,201 |
| Argentina | 52,764 | 78,671 | 106,463 | 89,669 | 52,702 |
| Other countries | 51,790 | 43,225 | 10,995 | 7,894 | 8,139 |
| Total outside United States and Canada | 1,992,065 | 1,958,715 | 1,906,242 | 2,186,230 | 1,969,503 |
| Total worldwide—cars and trucks | 4,254,909 | 4,313,188 | 4,328,450 | 5,810,304 | 6,462,065 |
| Tractors[b] | | | | | |
| United States | 24,258 | 31,517 | 35,286 | 51,361 | 35,789 |
| Overseas | 48,905 | 57,757 | 62,415 | 82,267 | 59,448 |
| Total worldwide—tractors | 73,163 | 89,274 | 97,701 | 133,628 | 95,237 |
| Total worldwide factory sales | 4,328,072 | 4,402,462 | 4,426,151 | 5,943,932 | 6,557,302 |

## FORD SHARES OF MAJOR CAR AND TRUCK MARKETS

| | Cars | | | |
|---|---|---|---|---|
| | 1982 | | 1981 | |
| | Industry Unit Sales | Ford Market Share | Industry Unit Sales | Ford Market Share (%) |
|---|---|---|---|---|
| United States | 7,955,970 | 16.9 | 8,514,956 | 16.6 |
| Canada | 713,005 | 15.8 | 903,536 | 15.2 |
| Germany | 2,091,297 | 11.3 | 2,264,634 | 11.8 |
| United Kingdom | 1,552,926 | 30.5 | 1,484,250 | 30.9 |
| Other European markets[c] | 6,171,231 | 8.2 | 5,913,692 | 7.8 |
| Brazil | 556,596 | 17.6 | 448,256 | 19.2 |
| Mexico | 288,253 | 12.9 | 342,724 | 15.9 |
| Argentina | 114,455 | 33.9 | 172,640 | 31.8 |
| Other Latin American markets[c] | 288,423 | 15.9 | 439,635 | 11.1 |
| Australia | 454,250 | 26.0 | 453,806 | 23.0 |
| South Africa | 283,427 | 14.5 | 301,528 | 16.7 |
| All other markets[c] | 4,673,287 | 2.0 | 4,630,160 | 1.8 |
| Worldwide total[c] | 25,143,120 | 12.5% | 25,869,817 | 12.4 |

[a]Factory sales are by source of manufacture, except that Canadian exports to the United States are included as U.S. vehicle sales and U.S. exports to Canada are included as Canadian vehicle sales. Prior year data have been restated for reclassification of Club Wagons from cars to trucks.
[b]Includes units manufactured by other companies and sold by Ford.
[c]1982 data estimated.

*Source:* Ford of Europe.

| 1977 | 1976 | 1975 | 1974 | 1973 |
|---|---|---|---|---|
| 2,625,485 | 2,197,039 | 1,867,713 | 2,336,415 | 2,685,423 |
| 247,427 | 210,049 | 225,293 | 258,980 | 231,598 |
| 2,872,912 | 2,407,088 | 2,093,006 | 2,595,395 | 2,917,021 |
| | | | | |
| 1,345,282 | 1,017,736 | 809,360 | 991,447 | 1,086,281 |
| 149,756 | 131,186 | 131,104 | 143,079 | 98,326 |
| 1,495,038 | 1,148,922 | 940,464 | 1,134,526 | 1,184,607 |
| 4,367,950 | 3,556,010 | 3,033,470 | 3,729,921 | 4,101,628 |
| | | | | |
| | | | | |
| 891,390 | 815,279 | 636,799 | 496,780 | 728,514 |
| 563,384 | 515,368 | 468,255 | 559,534 | 615,276 |
| 212,855 | 16,448 | — | — | — |
| 129,466 | 169,707 | 172,235 | 177,698 | 144,739 |
| 112,376 | 108,549 | 124,600 | 131,393 | 130,881 |
| 49,216 | 45,498 | 55,909 | 54,649 | 44,242 |
| 34,156 | 33,638 | 36,878 | 40,155 | 35,473 |
| 52,466 | 35,318 | 39,793 | 53,810 | 61,373 |
| 9,042 | 8,629 | 9,833 | 14,993 | 8,902 |
| 2,054,351 | 1,748,434 | 1,544,302 | 1,529,012 | 1,769,400 |
| 6,422,301 | 5,304,444 | 4,577,772 | 5,258,933 | 5,871,028 |
| | | | | |
| 39,650 | 34,643 | 38,342 | 41,090 | 40,223 |
| 90,880 | 83,177 | 73,981 | 68,202 | 61,624 |
| 130,530 | 117,820 | 112,323 | 109,292 | 101,847 |
| 6,552,831 | 5,422,264 | 4,690,095 | 5,368,225 | 5,972,875 |

## Trucks

| 1982 | | 1981 | |
|---|---|---|---|
| Industry Unit Sales | Ford Market Share | Industry Unit Sales | Ford Market Share (%) |
|---|---|---|---|
| 2,584,989 | 30.6 | 2,281,879 | 31.4 |
| 205,409 | 26.7 | 287,290 | 30.2 |
| 187,789 | 8.1 | 214,261 | 7.7 |
| 229,346 | 36.6 | 213,832 | 30.5 |
| 874,626 | 6.1 | 842,626 | 7.0 |
| 134,621 | 23.2 | 132,677 | 17.9 |
| 181,948 | 27.7 | 230,939 | 25.6 |
| 29,484 | 54.1 | 56,965 | 46.4 |
| 171,138 | 17.5 | 249,266 | 13.8 |
| 162,104 | 13.0 | 152,476 | 13.1 |
| 142,696 | 10.3 | 152,013 | 10.7 |
| 3,288,457 | 1.0 | 3,437,096 | 0.8 |
| 8,192,607 | 14.6 | 8,251,320 | 14.0 |

**THE GROWING JAPANESE PRESENCE IN EUROPE**

Ford of Europe had identified Japanese automotive products as the principal threat in the 1980s. To respond to that threat, Ford's European companies launched a major education and development program in the late 1970s called "After Japan." The program had started with trips by management to Japan to tour Japanese automobile assembly plants. By 1983, "After Japan" was well established with emphasis on robotics, quality circles, "just-in-time" inventory controls, and other work practices imported from Japan. Already, over 700 robots were at work in Ford's European plants, with 1500 planned by 1986.

Ford's top management believed, however, that it would still take at least five to ten years for their European plants to establish the cost and productivity levels necessary to match the landed price of Japanese imports. The Japanese cost advantage has been estimated to be about $1500 ex-works per automobile.

A series of bilateral trade agreements between individual European countries and Japan currently capped Japanese automobile imports into Europe. A reciprocal trade treaty between Italy and Japan (ironically initiated by the Japanese in the 1950s) restricted exports to each other's market to 2200 units annually. Japan's shares of the French and U.K. markets were informally limited to 3 percent and 11 percent, respectively. The French quota was imposed by President Valéry Giscard d'Estaing in 1976 after an abrupt increase in Japan's share of the French market. The U.K. quota was negotiated with the Japanese Ministry of International Trade and Industry (MITI) in 1978 after a previous, less formal agreement on export restraint failed. The Benelux countries and West Germany were technically open to the Japanese after the lapse of a 1981 informal one-year agreement in those countries establishing a maximum share of 10 percent of each market for the Japanese. Although there was no evidence that the Japanese were moving quickly to exploit this opening into Europe, Ford executives feared that the whole structure of trade understandings was very fragile.* (See Exhibits 32.4–32.9.)

It was not only by exporting vehicles that the Japanese were making their presence felt in Europe, threatening European producers, and prompting European government concern. In 1981, British Leyland launched its Triumph Acclaim. The Acclaim was a Honda Ballade assembled under license from Honda. Mechanical components were imported from Japan, and a royalty was paid to Honda on each car. The Acclaim was introduced to plug a gap in British Leyland's model range, and it precipitated a considerable outcry by some European governments. For example, although British Leyland argued that 70 percent of the car was British in origin, the Italian government refused to allow the first consignment of Acclaims to enter their country from Britain in 1982. The Italians classified the car as Japanese and thus subject to the strict quota agreement between Italy and Japan. British Leyland successfully mobilized support from the U.K. government and the EEC, and the Italians eventually backed down. Nonetheless, the nature of the future battle was becoming clear.

---

*Ford also perceived an import threat from the emerging automobile industries of Eastern Europe. Many of the countries of Eastern Europe had established their industries with the help of Western European producers (e.g., Fiat in the Soviet Union and Poland, and Renault in Romania). The cars now produced in Eastern Europe were of outdated design, however, and with rapidly growing domestic demand, Eastern European countries were not expected to be a challenge in Western European markets on a scale close to that of the Japanese.

In August 1983, the French government announced that starting in 1984 the Acclaim would be subject to the French "voluntary" agreement with Japan; or rather 40 percent of it would be. That was the percentage that the French government deemed to be of Japanese origin. Again the threat to the Acclaim was withdrawn after a visit to Paris by the U.K. trade minister, Cecil Parkinson, in August 1983.

The United Kingdom also experienced a similar situation on the import side. In 1983 a Mitsubishi automobile named the Lonsdale was imported for the first time into the United Kingdom from Australia, where it was assembled from Japanese components. Strong industry concern was again expressed about hidden loopholes in the network of orderly marketing agreements, but no action was taken.

**Exhibit 32.4** Automobile Production by Producer, 1975, 1980, 1982 (thousands of units)

| Producer | 1975 | 1980 | 1982 |
|---|---|---|---|
| 1. General Motors (U.S.) | 4,649 | 4,753 | 4,069 |
| 2. Toyota (Japan) | 2,336 | 3,293 | 3,144 |
| 3. Gr. Nissan (Nissan-Fuji) | 2,280 | 3,117 | 2,958 |
| 4. Volkswagen-Audi | 1,940 | 2,529 | 2,108 |
| 5. Renault-RVI (France) | 1,427 | 2,132 | 1,965 |
| 6. Ford (U.S.) | 2,500 | 1,888 | 1,817 |
| 7. Peugeot-Talbot-Citroën (France) | 659 | 1,408 | 1,574 |
| 8. Ford (Europe) | 1,099 | 1,395 | 1,450 |
| 9. Fiat-Autobianchi-Lancia-OM | 1,231 | 1,554 | 1,170 |
| 10. Toyo—Kogyo (Mazda) | 642 | 1,121 | 1,110 |
| 11. Honda | 413 | 956 | 1,020 |
| 12. Mitsubishi | 520 | 1,104 | 969 |
| 13. Chrysler Co. (U.S.–Canada) | 1,508 | 882 | 967 |
| 14. Opel (General Motors) | 675 | 833 | 961 |
| 15. Lada (Fiat-USSR) | 690 | 825 | 800 |
| 16. Daimler-Benz | 556 | 717 | 700 |
| 17. Suzuki | 184 | 468 | 603 |
| 18. General Motors (Canada) | 598 | 763 | 560 |
| Talbot (France, U.K., Europe) | 719 | 642 | — |
| 19. British Leyland | 738 | 525 | 494 |
| 20. Isuzu | 244 | 472 | 404 |
| 21. BMW | 221 | 341 | 378 |
| 22. Ford Canada | 481 | 434 | 374 |
| 23. Volvo (Sweden-Netherlands) | 331 | 285 | 335 |
| 24. Seat (Fiat) | 332 | 297 | 246 |
| 25. Polski Fiat | 135 | 330 | 240 |
| 26. Moskvitch | 300 | 230 | 205 |
| 27. American Motors | 463 | 252 | 194 |
| 28. Alfa Romeo | 191 | 221 | 189 |
| 29. Vauxhall | 190 | 151 | 164 |
| 30. Saporoskje (USSR) | 130 | 150 | 150 |

*Source: L'Argus de l'Automobile.*

**Exhibit 32.5** Automobile Industry in Leading Countries (data in thousands of units)

|  | 1973 | 1980 | 1982[a] |
|---|---|---|---|
| Worldwide production | 29,793 | 29,244 | 27,197 |
| **Federal Republic of Germany** | | | |
| New car registrations | 2,031 | 2,426 | 2,156 |
| Imports | 763 | 1,013 | 824 |
| Exports | 2,173 | 1,873 | 2,194 |
| to Europe | 1,150 | 1,381 | 1,785 |
| to United States | 786 | 335 | 257 |
| Production | 3,650 | 3,521 | 3,761 |
| **France** | | | |
| New car registrations | 1,746 | 1,873 | 2,056 |
| Imports | 461 | 675 | 972 |
| Exports | 1,446 | 1,530 | 1,464 |
| to Europe | 1,222 | 1,203 | 1,095 |
| Production | 2,867 | 2,939 | 2,777 |
| **United Kingdom** | | | |
| New car registrations | 1,664 | 1,516 | 1,557 |
| Imports | 505 | 863 | 934 |
| Exports | 599 | 359 | 313 |
| to Europe | 296 | 143 | 140 |
| Production | 1,747 | 959 | 888 |
| **Italy** | | | |
| New car registrations | 1,449 | 1,530 | 1,900 |

[a]Figures are partly estimated.
[b]From 1978 on, actual figures are given, excluding major components.
[c]Including exports to Canada.

*Source:* Daimler-Benz.

**Exhibit 32.6** EEC Market Share Analysis, 1973, 1980, 1982 (percent of total registrations)

|  | Germany | Belgium | Denmark |
|---|---|---|---|
| Fiat[a] | 7.2/3.6/4.3 | 9.1/5.4/5.7 | 7.1/8.7/4.9 |
| Ford[b] | 12.8/10.4/11.3 | 14.7/8.5/8.6 | 11.7/10.6/16.1 |
| General Motors[c] | 21.6/16.9/18.2 | 13.4/10.2/10.3 | 12.8/11.6/14.3 |
| Renault | 7.1/4.7/3.9 | 9.7/8.9/9.4 | 5.3/1.9/1.0 |
| Peugeot[d] | 6.7/4.7/4.0 | 24.3/15.2/13.8 | 11.6/8.6/7.4 |
| Volkswagen[e] | 24.9/21.7/23.5 | 10.3/8.9/10.4 | 19.1/5.1/5.3 |
| Nissan | —/2.1/2.0 | —/3.8/3.7 | —/5.0/5.2 |
| Honda | —/1.8/1.5 | —/4.4/3.3 | —/2.4/0.9 |
| Mazda | —/1.9/1.9 | —/3.2/3.6 | —/8.9/9.4 |
| Mitsubishi (Colt) | —/1.7/1.9 | —/3.5/3.4 | —/3.4/1.2 |
| Toyota | —/2.4/1.9 | —/9.1/6.1 | —/8.2/7.1 |
| For 1973 all Japanese vehicles | 0.8 | 13.4 | 7.1 |

[a]Fiat includes Lancia and Autobianchi.
[b]Ford includes all sourced vehicles (e.g., Spain and Belgium).
[c]General Motors includes both Vauxhall and Opel.
[d]Peugeot includes 1973 Chrysler and Citroen, bought in 1979 and 1974, respectively.
[e]Includes Audi.
[f]Ireland and Luxembourg figures (about 100,000 units) are not included.

*Source: L'Argus de l'Automobile.*

|  | 1973 | 1980 | 1982[a] |
|---|---|---|---|
| Imports | 419 | 908 | 868 |
| Exports | 656 | 511 | 437 |
|   to Europe | 505 | 385 | 383 |
| Production | 1,823 | 1,445 | 1,297 |
| Spain |  |  |  |
| Exports | 158 | 492 | 495 |
| Production | 706 | 1,029 | 928 |
| USSR |  |  |  |
| Production | 917 | 1,327 | 1,307 |
| Japan[b] |  |  |  |
| New car registrations | 2,919 | 2,854 | 3,038 |
| Import | 37 | 46 | 35 |
| Exports | 1,451 | 3,947 | 3,770 |
|   to Europe | 357 | 1,003 | 896 |
|   to United States | 601 | 1,887 | 1,741 |
| Production | 4,471 | 7,038 | 6,882 |
| United States |  |  |  |
| New car registrations | 11,351 | 8,761 | 7,754 |
| Imports | 2,437 | 3,248 | 3,091 |
| Exports[c] | 579 | 560 | 353 |
|   to Europe | 15 | 24 | 6 |
| Production | 9,667 | 6,376 | 5,073 |

| France | United Kingdom | Italy | Holland | Total[f] |
|---|---|---|---|---|
| 4.8/3.7/4.9 | 3.0/3.3/3.0 | 64.6/49.4/51.7 | 8.8/4.1/5.5 | 16.9/12.2/14.9 |
| 4.6/3.7/6.5 | 24.2/30.7/30.1 | 3.6/4.8/5.6 | 9.3/9.1/10.4 | 11.5/11.4/12.1 |
| 2.5/1.8/2.5 | 9.8/8.8/12.0 | 3.3/3.5/3.7 | 13.0/15.3/16.1 | 10.4/9.1/9.5 |
| 28.9/40.5/39.1 | 3.6/5.8/4.1 | 3.3/10.5/11.1 | 7.5/8.7/8.0 | 10.6/14.3/14.4 |
| 51.8/36.4/30.2 | 12.4/5.1/4.4 | 10.2/11.0/8.5 | 27.8/12.9/11.8 | 20.6/14.1/12.2 |
| 2.4/4.0/4.9 | 4.1/3.4/4.5 | 3.8/4.4/5.3 | 8.4/7.5/8.2 | 9.9/9.6/10.0 |
| —/0.9/0.9 | —/6.1/5.9 | —/0.03/0.01 | —/5.3/4.6 | —/2.5/2.2 |
| —/0.4/0.4 | —/1.5/1.1 | —/0.03/0.01 | —/5.5/3.5 | —/1.4/1.0 |
| —/0.7/0.7 | —/1.0/1.0 | —/0.02/0.01 | —/3.9/3.7 | —/1.4/1.3 |
| —/0.2/0.2 | —/0.7/0.6 | —/0.02/0.02 | —/4.8/3.5 | —/1.1/0.9 |
| —/0.7/0.7 | —/2.3/1.8 | —/0.02/0.03 | —/6.0/4.4 | —/2.1/1.5 |
| 0.6 | 4.6 | 0.1 | 10.1 | 2.5 |

**Exhibit 32.7** European Motor Industry, Net Profits in Millions of British Pounds (unless otherwise stated)

|  | 1977 | 1978 | 1979 | 1980 | 1981 | 1982 |
|---|---|---|---|---|---|---|
| Peugeot | 226 | 526 | 1,800 | −150 | −184 | −336 |
| Renault | 31[b] | 19[b] | 133[b] | 140 | −55 | −112 |
| Ford U.K. | 116 | 144 | 347 | 204 | 165 | 192 |
| Ford Werke | 143 | 143 | 124 | 11 | 32 | 76 |
| Ford Europe[a] | 1,045 | 1,271 | 1,219 | 323 | 289 | 451 |
| Vauxhall | −2 | −2 | −31 | −183 | −57 | −29 |
| Opel | 84 | 128 | 65 | −97 | −130 | 22 |
| General Motors Europe[a] | 277 | 376 | 338 | −359 | −427 | 6 |
| British Leyland | −52 | −28 | −145 | −536 | −497 | −293 |
| VAG | 103 | 149 | 172 | 76 | 20 | −11 |
| Daimler Benz | 145 | 154 | 164 | 261 | 181 | 217 |
| BMW | 31 | 39 | 45 | 28 | 32 | 47 |
| MAN | — | 17 | 18 | 13 | 12 | 7 |
| Alfa-Romeo | −98 | −77 | −52 | −28 | −51 | −29 |
| Fiat | 41 | 46 | 22 | 26 | 39 | 58 |
| Seat | NA[c] | NA[c] | NA[c] | −106.6 | −104.7 | −122.6 |
| Motor Iberica | 5.8 | 6.6 | 4.2 | −2.3 | −13.4 | −17.2 |
| Volvo | 25 | 36 | 46 | 4 | 45 | 45 |
| Saab | 23 | 23 | 26 | 36 | 39 | 43 |

[a]Millions of U.S. dollars.
[b]Unconsolidated.
[c]NA = Not available.

*Source:* Company accounts and University of East Anglia, finance and accountancy department; Krish Bhaskar.

**Exhibit 32.8** Share of Japanese Exports in Registrations by Importing Country in Europe (percent)

| Country | 1966 | 1970 | 1975 | 1979 | 1981 |
|---|---|---|---|---|---|
| Belgium | 0.3 | 4.9 | 16.5 | 18.0 | 28 |
| France | 0 | 0.2 | 1.6 | 2.2 | 2 |
| Germany | 0 | 0.1 | 1.7 | 5.6 | 10 |
| Italy | 0 | 0 | 0.1 | 0.1 | — |
| Netherlands | 0.6 | 3.2 | 15.5 | 19.5 | 26 |
| United Kingdom | 0.1 | 0.4 | 9.0 | 10.8 | 10 |
| Denmark | 0.5 | 3.4 | 14.7 | 18.1 | 28 |
| Ireland | 0 | 0 | 8.9 | 25.2 | 30 |
| Austria | 0 | 0.9 | 5.4 | 12.4 | 23 |
| Switzerland | 0.1 | 5.6 | 8.4 | 16.0 | 26 |
| Portugal | 0 | 10.7 | 11.8 | 7.8 | 11 |
| Finland | 14.4 | 18.3 | 20.8 | 23.9 | 26 |
| Norway | 1.9 | 11.4 | 28.4 | 24.2 | 36 |
| Sweden | 0.2 | 0.7 | 6.5 | 10.0 | 14 |

*Source:* G. Sinclair, *The World Car.*

**Exhibit 32.9** Restrictions on Japanese Car Sales in Developed Countries, 1981–1982

| | |
|---|---|
| United Kingdom | 10–11 percent market share ceiling, dating from 1975 package to nationalize British Leyland |
| Federal Republic of Germany | Growth limit of 10 percent per annum on 1980 sales (252,000 units) |
| Netherlands | No increase on 1980 level |
| Luxembourg | No increase on 1980 level |
| Italy | Quota of 2200 units |
| France | 3 percent market share ceiling |
| Belgium | Reduction of 7 percent on 1980 sales |
| EEC as a whole | Common external tariff is 10.9 percent |
| Canada | Shipments of "around 174,000" units as against 158,000 in 1980 |
| Australia | All imports restricted to 20 percent of market; tariff of 57 percent; local content must be 85 percent to count as home-produced |
| United States | Shipments of 1.68 million for 1981 (Japanese fiscal year); subsequent shipment limits to be calculated taking account of U.S. market conditions; tariff is 2.9 percent |
| Denmark, Greece, Ireland | No restrictions |
| Japan | No quotas or tariffs on assembled cars, but internal taxes, depending on engine size; distribution and administrative checking systems alleged to operate as nontariff barriers |

The Benelux and Canadian restrictions are supposed to last only for 1981. The others appear to be more permanent.

*Source:* G. Sinclair, *The World Car.*

Japanese components were also beginning to appear on the European market in the 1980s in what had been until then strictly European automobiles. In Milan, Innocenti replaced the old British Leyland miniengine in its small car with a Japanese Daihatsu engine. And in 1981 General Motors started to purchase gearboxes from Japan for its Cavalier (U.K.) and Rekord (Germany) models. General Motors was thought by many industry observers to be pursuing a policy of increasing the percentage of Japanese components in its European and U.S. models.

In addition to their direct export of vehicles, and their indirect exports through cooperative agreements with some European producers, the Japanese were beginning to explore direct foreign investment in Europe. Nissan (Datsun) had for some time been actively looking at sites for overseas automobile assembly plants. In 1981, Nissan commissioned the consulting firm of McKinsey and Co. to undertake a feasibility study for the location of an assembly plant in the United Kingdom. It was to produce up to 200,000 units annually by 1986, rising possibly to 500,000 by 1990. Employment on a greenfield site was to be 4,000–5,000, rising to perhaps 12,000 workers. The scheme would be eligible for government grants of £50–£100 million.

Included in the negotiations between Nissan and the U.K. government was a discussion of the degree of voluntary local content. It was widely rumored at the time that Nissan was prepared to accept an EEC content level of 60 percent by value from the outset, rising to 80 percent later. The U.K. Department of Industry was rumored to want these percentages to apply to the ex-works price, after classifying Nissan's profit after tax on the operation as an import. British Leyland and Ford lobbied hard for an immediate 80 percent local content. Further uncertainty revolved around the impact of the new plant on the understanding between the U.K. Society of Motor Manufacturers and Traders and the Japanese Association of Motor Assemblers, which restrained the Japanese share of the U.K. market to 11 percent. The project had been temporarily shelved in 1982 because of uncertainty about future car sales, possible hostility from European governments (notably Italy and France), and fears of poor labor relations. It now threatened to come off the shelf.

Although the U.K. project was at least temporarily stalled, the first cars had just begun to roll off the line from a factory in southern Italy that Nissan built jointly with Alfa Romeo.* The production rate planned was 60,000 units annually. The Italian government was said to be satisfied that no more than 20 percent of the value of the cars was being imported into Italy.

Finally, Nissan was sending four-wheel-drive vehicles into the EEC from a Spanish plant in which it held a two-thirds share. Next year, panel vans would follow.†

## THE U.S. SITUATION

Much of what might be envisioned in Europe's future was already taking place in the United States. Japanese imports had been taking a progressively larger share of the market until a voluntary limit of 1.68 million vehicles was negotiated between Washington and Tokyo in 1981. That agreement was due to expire in March 1984, and there was widespread speculation that the Japanese wanted at least a substantially higher ceiling in the future. In the meantime, Ford's share of the U.S. market had dropped alarmingly from 26 percent in 1976 to 16 percent in 1982. Analysts blamed much of this on a 1975 decision by Henry Ford II to postpone a major U.S.-based small-car program. (A U.S.-based Fiesta had been planned.) Ford reengineered and restyled their existing Pinto line instead and relied on that for the small-car market.

Regardless of the question of fault, Ford's deteriorating position in the late 1970s led the company in 1980 to reverse its historic free-trade policy, arguing for what was called fair trade instead. Fair trade was defined by its proponents as trade between countries with similar social and industrial infrastructures and similar national trade policies (for example, similar wage rates, indirect tax burdens, and export incentives).

---

*This plant was a 50-50 joint venture in which Alfa Romeo mechanical components were installed in a Nissan Cherry body coming from Japan. Alfa Romeo ran the assembly operation. Half the finished vehicles went to Alfa Romeo and half to Nissan.

†In 1980 Nissan bought 36 percent of Motor Iberica and later increased that share to 66 percent.

In November 1980, Ford and the United Auto Workers Union lost a petition they had filed in June with the U.S. International Trade Commission* seeking protection from imports. A three-to-two majority of the commissioners ruled that imports were not the major cause of the industry's problems. The causes, according to the majority, were the recession and Detroit's own mistakes.

Ford had requested in its statement to the International Trade Commission that imports from Japan be limited to 1.7 million cars—the 1976 import level. Ford's setback by the commission was short-lived, however. In April 1981, President Reagan announced the voluntary export restraint agreement with the Ministry of International Trade and Industry. Automobile imports would not exceed 1.68 million units for the next three years.

In spite of the voluntary export restraint, Ford continued lobbying for legislative relief from the pressure of Japanese imports. Ford favored a policy that combined a continuing cap on Japanese imports, a better yen-dollar exchange rate, and tax incentives. The United Auto Workers Union, fearful of the threat to American jobs, was lobbying hard for domestic-content legislation. (See Exhibit 32.10.)

In February 1983, a bill was introduced in Congress entitled the Fair Practices and Procedures in Automotive Products Act. If passed, the bill would impose a graduated minimum domestic-content percentage for automobile importers dependent on the total volume of the importer's sales. The percentages ranged from zero for foreign producers with U.S. sales of fewer than 100,000 units per year to an upper limit of 90 percent for those with annual sales of more than 500,000 units.

The conflicting positions on trade policy of General Motors (GM) on the one hand and Ford, Chrysler, and the American Motor Company on the other were brought into the open by the proposed bill. (See Exhibit 32.11.) General Motors lobbied against the bill, arguing that any moves toward protectionism could cause a cascade of restrictive measures that would threaten global traders such as itself. Said Thomas R. Atkinson, GM's director of international economic policy (*New York Herald Tribune,* June 29, 1983), "Local content and other performance regulations decrease our flexibility as a corporation, and force us to do things we otherwise might not be doing. We wish these laws had never been invented, and would not like to see them increased or created in countries where they don't exist now."

General Motors' position was particularly suspect in the eyes of the other major U.S. manufacturers, given the 1982 announcement by GM and Toyota of a cooperative plan to produce 450,000 small cars annually by 1985 from a mothballed GM plant in Freemont, California. General Motors and Toyota would have equal shares in the venture, and half the output would be sold under the Toyota name, half under the GM name (to replace GM's Chevette). Ford and other U.S. manufacturers were strongly opposed to the deal, fearing that it was a precedent

*The International Trade Commission is an advisory commission that determines whether a given industry has been substantially injured by foreign imports, and if so, makes recommendations to the president. Traditionally, the commission has been viewed as a valuable ally in the executive branch of the government of beleaguered U.S. industries. Thus its decision in this case was a surprise to everyone.

**Exhibit 32.10** Foreign Sourcing—Recently Announced Commitments by U.S. Automobile Manufacturers to Purchase Foreign-made Components for Use in Domestic Vehicles Production

| Automobile Manufacturer | Description of Component | Intended Use | Manufacturing Source | Approximate Number of Components | Period |
|---|---|---|---|---|---|
| General Motors | 2-8 lit V-6 | Cars | GM Mexico | <400,000/year | 1982– |
| | 2-0 lit L-4 with transmission | Minitrucks | Isuzu (Japan) | 100,000/year | 1981– |
| | 1-8 lit diesel L-4 | Chevette | Isuzu (Japan) | Small numbers | 1982– |
| | 1-8 lit L-4 | J-car | GM Brazil | 250,000/year | 1979– |
| | THM 180 automatic transmission | Chevette | GM Strasbourg (France) | ~250,000/year | 1979– |
| Ford | 2-2 lit L-4 | Cars | Ford Mexico | <400,000/year | 1983– |
| | Diesel L-4 | Cars | Toyo Kogyo | 150,000/year | 1983– |
| | 2-0 lit L-4 | Minitrucks | Toyo Kogyo | <100,000/year | 1982– |
| | 2-3 lit L-4 | Cars | Ford Brazil | ~50,000/year | 1979– |
| | Diesel 6 cyl. | Cars | BMW/Steyr | 100,000/year | 1983– |
| | Turbo-diesel/ 4 cyl. | Cars | BMW/Steyr | — | 1985– |
| | Manual transaxles | Front-disc cars | Toyo Kogyo | 100,000/year | 1980– |
| | Aluminum cylinder heads | 1-6 lit L-4 | Europe, Mexico | — | 1980– |
| | Electronic engine control devices | Cars | Toshiba | 100,000 +/year | 1978– |
| | Ball joints | Cars | Musashi Seimibu | 1,000,000/year | 1980–1984 |
| Chrysler | L-6 and V-8 engines | Cars | Chrysler Mexico | <100,000/year | Early 1970 |
| | 2-2 lit L-4 | K-body | Chrysler Mexico | <270,000/year | 1981 |
| | 2-6 lit L-4 | K-body | Mitsubishi | 1 million | 1981–1985 |
| | 1-7 lit L-4 | L-body (Omni) | Volkswagen | 1–2 million | 1978–1982 |
| | 1-6 lit L-4 | L-body | Talbot (Peugeot) | 400,000 total | 1982–1984 |
| | 2-0 lit diesel V-6 | K-body | Peugeot | 100,000/year | 1982– |
| | 1-4 lit L-4 | A-body (Omni replacement) | Mitsubishi | 300,000/year | 1984– |
| | Aluminum cylinder heads | 2-2 lit L-4 | Fiat | | |
| AMC | Car components and power train | AMC-Renault | Renault in France and Mexico | 300,000/year | 1982– |
| VW of America | Radiators, stampings | Rabbit | VW Mexico | 250,000/year | 1979– |
| | L-4 diesel and gas | Cars | VW Mexico | 300,000 +/year | 1982– |

*Source:* Bulletin of the European Communities, *The European Automobile Industry: Commission Statement.*

**Exhibit 32.11** Selected Testimony on Fair Practices and Procedures in Automotive Products Act of 1983

Over one million jobs have been lost in the auto industry and its supplier industries since 1978. In many parts of our country, this has contributed to unemployment unheard of since the Great Depression.

Quite simply, this bill requires that the more cars a company wants to sell in our country, the more they would be required to build here. If a company takes advantage of the biggest automobile market in the world, it ought to make some effort to put some of its manufacturing in that market—the economic times demand it, and so does the American worker.

These are tough times—and much of the industrial base of our country has eroded. Without reviving this base, our national security is jeopardized and economic recovery will be stifled. We must act now, before our jobs and industrial base are permanently lost.

*Congressman Richard Ottinger (D–N.Y.) (sponsor of the bill)*

It is our belief that this legislation will (1) have a negative effect on U.S. employment, (2) impose substantial costs on consumers, (3) violate our international agreements, (4) invite retaliation by our trading partners against United States exports, (5) undermine the competitiveness of the domestic auto manufacturers, and (6) discourage foreign investment in the United States.

When the Congressional Budget Office reviewed this legislation last September, it determined that, by 1990, this legislation would create 38,000 auto jobs but 104,000 jobs would be lost in the U.S. export sector. This would mean a net loss in American jobs of 66,000.

The direct effect of H.R. 1234 would be to increase substantially the automobile prices paid by American consumers by reducing both the number of automobile imports and the competitive pressures that they exert on domestic manufacturers.

A 1980 Commission staff analysis—commenting on a proposal to reduce foreign car imports from 2.4 million to 1.7 million units per year—estimated that prices of small cars would increase by between $527 and $838 per unit, and increase total consumer expenditures on the purchase of automobiles by $1.9 to $3.6 billion per year.

*Statements by opposing Congressmen*

[The Bill] would severely damage America's trading position, flout our international obligations under the General Agreement on Tariffs and Trade (GATT), subject us to challenge under bilateral Treaties of Friendship, Commerce and Navigation with many of our trading partners, and be of great cost to the American consumer and to the nation.

*Secretary of State George Schultz*

In addition to competitive pressures on price, foreign competition has also provided important incentives for U.S. manufacturers to engage in research efforts and to invest in new technologies. American car makers have been moving rapidly toward smaller "world cars" that are very similar to those produced abroad, and United States companies are already importing engines, transmissions, and other components. Confronted with the enormous cost of downsizing American cars and the lower production costs of many foreign companies, United States auto makers are reportedly planning even greater reliance on foreign sources for major components. The enactment of legislation requiring vehicles sold in the United States to be 90 percent "American-made" by 1987 would disrupt established supply lines and aggravate the demands upon scarce domestic capital resources now faced by the United States automobile industry and the economy as a whole. The resulting supply effects would increase car prices, leading to reduced sales and employment in the auto industry.

*United States Federal Trade Commission*

The difficulties of our industry ultimately will not be resolved in legislative halls, but rather in the marketplace where success is earned by offering superior products at competitive prices. Rather than seek shelter from competition—even temporarily—in laws and regulations, U.S. automakers must continue their efforts to meet and exceed foreign competition.

*General Motors Corporation*

873

that could end up threatening the native U.S. industry. The implications of a joint venture by the world's first and third largest automobile manufacturers were obvious to all their competitors.

Of course, there were other risks involved in the proposed U.S. domestic-content law that went beyond those cited by GM. The more restrictive the import regulations in the United States, for example, the greater the pressure on Europe from Japanese exports diverted from U.S. shores. And some analysts within Ford felt that the bill would stimulate Japanese direct investment in the United States, perhaps constituting a greater threat to the U.S. manufacturers than some limited degree of imports. On this point the interest of the U.S. labor unions and manufacturers could conflict. Finally, there was the general realization that the government could exact a price in return for protectionist favors granted the industry.

## LOCAL-CONTENT REGULATIONS

Local-content regulations have long been a device used by developing countries to force multinational companies to increase the rate at which they transfer technology and employment to their local operations. With respect to automobiles, these regulations typically require that a certain percentage of a vehicle's content be produced in the country of sale. This percentage may be defined by value or by weight. Weight is generally thought to be a stricter criterion because it is not susceptible to manipulation by transfer pricing. Yet it can lead to only low-technology, high-weight items being produced locally (e.g., steel castings and chassis components).

Although simple in concept, local-content regulations can often be quite complicated in practice. The treatment of overhead and profit is often a problem. Some countries apply the regulations on the basis of fleet averaging, others to specific models. Mexico, where at least 50 percent of the value of all cars sold must be produced locally, strengthened its regulations by also requiring that the value of all component imports must be matched by component exports for each assembler. This led to a flurry of investments by Chrysler and Ford in engine facilities in Mexico.

Until recently, Spain had a 95 percent domestic-content rule. All component imports were assessed a 30 percent customs duty, and 50 percent of all local manufacturing operations had to be Spanish-owned. All this was changed in the 1975 negotiations between the Spanish government and Ford over Ford's Bobcat (or Fiesta) project in Valencia. Contemplating the attractive prospect of a plant producing 225,000 cars annually, the Spanish government settled for 100 percent Ford ownership, 75 percent Spanish content, and 5 percent import duty on component parts. Concessions on import duty were also granted for machine tools and equipment unavailable in Spain. But two-thirds of automobile production had to be exported from Spain, and Ford's sales in Spain could not exceed 10 percent of the previous year's total Spanish market size. General Motors arranged a similar deal for a plant in Zaragoza, Spain, producing 280,000 small

S cars (Corsas) annually. Spanish accession to the EEC would phase out much of its protective legislation.

Local-content regulations did not exist in any EEC or European Free Trade Association (EFTA) country except Portugal and Ireland. (The European Community's trade regime did have a scheme for defining local assembly with the EFTA countries for the purpose of trade classification—60 percent of value added had to be locally produced.) Nevertheless, there was a variety of statutory powers in the EEC and the General Agreement on Tariffs and Trade (GATT) that could protect specific industries. For example, Regulation No. 926 of the EEC allowed for the protection of specific industries and could be triggered by the Commission of the EEC after advice from the Council of Ministers.

At the GATT level, any member country could ask for temporary protection from imports from another member (under Articles 19–23) if those imports severely endangered national industry. These escape clause articles were difficult for EEC countries to use, however, because each country delegated responsibility for all trade negotiations to the EEC Commission in Brussels. Thus the European automobile industry would have to coordinate campaigns in a number of EEC member countries before it could approach the EEC Commission. Even then, there was no guarantee that the commission would agree to take a case to the GATT. Not surprisingly, existing import restrictions were essentially bilateral diplomatic agreements—varying widely from country to country—rather than statutory enactments.

## FORD'S DELIBERA-TIONS

At least on the surface, informal local-content regulations in Europe looked very attractive to Ford's executives. The Japanese threat was surely very real. Production levels in Europe in 1980 were about the same as they had been in 1970, and in the last decade, while European exports to non-European markets fell 42 percent, Japanese worldwide exports rose 426 percent. Ford's market analysts forecast slow growth for the European market in the future, indicating that higher Japanese sales in Europe would come directly from those of the established European producers. The existing structure of voluntary agreements to limit Japanese imports into individual European countries was fragile. Although *voluntary* was clearly a euphemism, any cracks in the agreements could quickly lead to more Japanese imports before new and possibly more lenient agreements were negotiated. West Germany and Belgium were thought to be the weak spots.

If a European local-content rule were to be established on the basis of local sales (i.e., if a specified percentage of each manufacturer's European sales had to be produced in Europe), then the existing system of individual national voluntary trade agreements would become redundant. Alternatively, if a local-content rule were to be applied to local production (i.e., if a specified percentage of the content of each manufacturer's cars assembled in Europe had to be sourced in Europe), then some controls on automobile imports would still be needed. A local-content rule of this type would prevent the Japanese from circumventing the intent of import controls by importing the bulk of their components from Japan while establishing only token assembly operations in Europe.

Yet there were many potential negative consequences for European producers if local-content regulations spread across Europe. It was not obvious that European producers should object to Japanese imports, even at a substantially higher level than at present, if the alternative was to be new Japanese greenfield plants in Europe. Even if they complied scrupulously with local-content rules, these new plants, employing the most advanced production technology and work methods, could be tough competitors, unshackled from any form of constraint. At the very least, they would add production capacity to a market already suffering from 20 percent excess capacity. A price war was certainly not impossible to imagine. And Ford, among others, was worried about the impact that these plants could have on fleet sales, particularly in the high-margin U.K. market, if nationalistic customers began to think of Nissan, for example, as a national producer.

Another problem was that local-content rules could limit Ford's own manufacturing flexibility. The key new concept in the automobile industry in the 1970s was that of a world car. A world car is assembled in local markets (tailored to local consumers' tastes) from a common set of components. Each component is produced in very high volume at one site, where it can be done least expensively, and then shipped around the world to the scattered assembly plants. Local-content rules and world cars were seemingly incompatible.

Ford's Erika project (the 1981 Escort) was the first of the world cars. In actual practice, the world car concept was of questionable success. The Escort that was marketed in the United States differed so much in style and design from its European sibling that there was little parts commonality, and transportation costs ate away at the efficiency gains from large-scale production of the common parts. The result was that although there was some international trade in components within Ford, most movement of parts was either within Europe or within the United States.

General Motors had similar problems with its J-car (the Vauxhall Cavalier in the United Kingdom and Opel Rekord in West Germany) and X-car (the Vauxhall Royale in the United Kingdom and Opel Senator in Germany). General Motors seemed to have been more successful than Ford, however, in standardizing components, and whereas Ford had primarily maintained an approach of European sourcing for European markets, GM had already moved to exploit its global reach.

To make matters even more complex, Ford had a 25 percent share in Toyo Kogyo (Mazda) and thus an option of working with Mazda to import inexpensive Japanese vehicles. Indeed, a Mazda pickup truck was sold in the United States and Greece as a Ford truck, and the very successful Ford Laser in the Far East was a version of the Mazda 626 made in Japan. (In July 1983, Ford was threatening such a policy to counteract the proposed GM-Toyota production plant in California.)

# TECHNICAL ASPECTS OF LOCAL-CONTENT REGULATIONS

If the management of Ford of Europe were to support local-content regulations, they felt they would have to answer four technical questions:

1. How should *local* be defined geographically?
2. How was local content to be measured?
3. To what should local-content regulations be applied—individual cars, models, or a producer's entire fleet?
4. What should the minimum percentage of local content be?

The company had already done some thinking about each question.

Of all the producers, Ford was the most geographically integrated in Europe. It would therefore be important to encompass most or all of Europe in the term *local.* A definition restricted to the EEC would exclude Ford's big Valencia plant in Spain and a 200,000-unit-per-year plant contemplated for Portugal. These plants represented critical low-cost sources for small cars for the other European markets. (Both Spain and Portugal had applied for admission to the EEC, however.) Ford regarded a nation-state definition as impractical and intolerable.

Defining local content was a very difficult task. One proposal was to define content by weight. This had the advantage of being difficult to manipulate by transfer pricing, but it might allow the importation of high-value, high-technology components that were light in weight.

The other common definition of local content was by value. Essentially the percentage of local content was established by subtracting the value of the imported components as declared on customs documentation from (1) the distributor's price, (2) the ex-works price, or (3) the ex-works price minus the labor and overhead content of the car. Then the local-content residue was divided by the corresponding denominator. (See Exhibit 32.12.)

Clearly the percentage of the imported components gets larger from (1) to (3) as the value of the domestic content gets smaller. Ford had not decided its position with regard to this issue, except that it did not want specific components identified for mandatory local production. It was also possible to devise other hybrid methods of valuing local content, but they were generally not under discussion.

Regarding the question of to what the local-content rules should be applied, Ford favored applying them to the average of a producer's entire line of cars, rather than to each individual car or model. The former would jeopardize Ford's current importation from South Africa of small quantities of their P100 pickup truck (based on the Cortina).

There was also a related question of whether automobile production or regional sales should form the basis of measurement. Ford preferred that a specified percentage of a producer's European sales be made in Europe, since such a rule was insurance against circumvention of the current import quotas. A production-based local-content rule would only prevent circumvention of the intent of import quotas by token local final assembly.

Finally there was the question of what the appropriate percentage should be.

**Exhibit 32.12** Analysis of Automobile Construction Cost[a]

|  | | Percentage of Ex-works Price[b] |
|---|---|---|
| Freight | | 2 |
| Administration, selling cost, warranty, and profit | | 7 |
| Production and assembly overheads | | 22 |
| Variable manufacturing costs[c] | | |
| Engine | 10.4 | |
| Gearbox | 4.8 | |
| Axles | 6.9 | |
| Other mechanical parts | 8.3 | |
| Body stamping | 5.5 | |
| Body assembly | 6.9 | |
| Accessories and seating | 7.6 | |
| Final assembly and painting | 18.6 | |
| | | 69 |
| Total | | 100% |

[a]For a typical medium-sized salon at a production level of 200,000 annually.
[b]Final retail price is usually 22 percent higher than the ex-works price.
[c]The labor content of variable manufacturing costs accounts for 14 percent of the total ex-works price.

*Source:* Yves Doz, "Internationalization of Manufacturing in the Automobile Industry," unpublished paper; and Ford of Europe estimates.

Figures currently under discussion ranged from 60 to 80 percent, although the percentage clearly depended on the format of the specific proposals. Of particular significance in terms of these percentages was that a 60 percent rule might allow importation of engines and major parts of the drive train that would all be excluded by an 80 percent rule. Also, it might be very difficult for the Japanese to start up a new plant with an immediate 80 percent local content (even if that percentage were to be achieved with more time). Start-up at 60 percent would be substantially easier.

**THE POLITICAL OPTIONS**

Should Ford decide to support local-content regulations and then find answers to the technical questions, it would still have to determine the best way to carry its case to the appropriate government body. And here again, the way was not clear.

Ford definitely did not want to act on its own. It would be much better to act in concert with the other European producers. (Despite the all-American image of the founder and his name, Ford of Europe unquestionably considered itself European.) Not only was this desirable on general principles, but for one quite specific reason Ford preferred not to lobby the EEC directly. It had recently fought and was currently fighting other battles with the European Commission. In 1982, the commission had issued an interim order to Ford under Article 85 of the Treaty of Rome (an antitrust statute) requiring the company to offer right-hand-drive cars to the West German market. The background to this directive was that most European automobile producers charged significantly higher prices in the United Kingdom than on the Continent. To prevent consumers from ordering right-hand-drive cars in Germany and importing them to the United Kingdom, Ford had refused to make the models available on the Continent. This provoked a consumer response to which the EEC Commission reacted.

In June 1983 the commission issued a draft regulation applicable to the distribution systems of all motor manufacturers operating in Europe. The regulation aimed at harmonizing vehicle availability and prices across Europe. Any model of vehicle sold in any EEC member state would have to be made available in all other member states. And if price differences exceeded 12 percent (net of taxes) between any EEC markets, new importers (not authorized by the manufacturer) could enter the market. Ford, along with all other European motor manufacturers, was opposing this proposal vigorously.

Although Ford preferred to have a common industry position to press on the governmental authorities, there was little likelihood of unanimity among the European producers even on the most basic question of whether local-content rules were desirable. General Motors was an almost certain opponent to local-content rules despite the fact that it too might welcome relief from Japanese competition. Fiat, Renault, and British Leyland, on the other hand, might be strong allies who could perhaps rally the support of their respective governments. They appeared to have much to gain from local-content rules because they had most of their operations in Europe and they purchased most of their components locally.

There were a number of sourcing arrangements, however, which could undermine the support of some of these firms. Japanese cars assembled in Australia were entering the United Kingdom with a certificate of origin from Australia. British Leyland's Acclaim was of questionable origin. Fiat was bringing in Pandas from Brazil, and Volkswagen "beetles" came into Europe from Mexico. Renault had extensive operations in the United States that could alter the company's outlook. And on July 27, 1983, the *Wall Street Journal* reported that Fiat was being indicted by the Italian authorities for selling cars made in Spain and Brazil under the guise of Italian manufacture. Fiat denied the charge.

Ford executives believed, nonetheless, that with the exception of GM, Ford was likely to find general support within the industry. In fact, in a 1981 draft paper, the CLCA* stated:

The establishment of Japanese motor vehicle manufacturing plants should be subject to the following durable conditions:

a. The CIF value of the components not originating from the EEC should not exceed 20 percent of the price ex-works of the vehicle.
b. The manufacturing and assembly of mechanical components (engines, gearboxes and drivetrain) should be performed within the EEC.

*Comité de Liaison des Constructeurs Associations. The CLCA was basically a political liaison committee of the national automotive trade associations of France, the United Kingdom, Germany, Belgium, Holland, and Italy.

**THE EUROPEAN COMMISSION**

Ford executives believed that the European Commission was prepared to take some action on the automobile imports issue. In January 1983 the commission had held discussions with the Japanese in Tokyo and had obtained a nonbinding commitment to moderate vehicle exports to the EEC. The commission was currently monitoring the agreement. Beyond this it was unclear what action the European Commission was considering. In principle, the EEC should be expected to favor relatively free trade between its member countries and the rest of the world. The history of international trade since World War II—a history in which the EEC featured prominently—was one of declining tariffs (from an average of 20 percent on manufactured goods in the 1950s to 8 percent in the mid-1970s), dramatically growing trade volumes, and greater interdependence of national economies. Two other principles dear to the EEC were that all member countries maintain a *common* trade policy vis-à-vis non-EEC countries, and that there be no barriers to trade between member countries. Clearly, the existing set of nonuniform bilateral trade agreements with the Japanese offended these principles.

Although the principles underlying the EEC were relatively unambiguous, the EEC often resorted to protective policies, and it was not immune to pressures to maintain jobs in the automotive sector. But granted this observation, it was still not evident just how job preservation might best be achieved. Formal local-content rules would be inconsistent with EEC law and would violate the GATT. Thus any local-content measures would have to be informal such as those that currently existed between the Japanese and the British. Would the EEC prefer to see a uniform (albeit informal) external quota and internal production-based local-content rule? Or would it rather see a uniform internal sales-based content rule and no quota? Would its preference in either case be less restrictive than the status quo, shaky though it might be? And was it realistic to expect that an informal negotiating process could create a common position among the different EEC member states? A weak, contentious, and nonuniform set of local-content rules established and enforced by each EEC member country could be the worst of all the imaginable alternatives.

The Japanese, of course, would have some influence on EEC thinking on this matter. Any EEC action would probably come in the context of trade negotiations —not simply unilaterally imposed trade sanctions. And what position might the Japanese take? It is conceivable that they might agree to some reasonable export restraints into the EEC in return for open markets within the EEC. That would give them access to the two big markets from which they were currently virtually excluded—France and Italy. But would those two countries agree? Each would face greater Japanese competition in its home market but less in its export markets in other EEC countries.

The executives on the management committee considered their alternatives. If they were to have any role in determining the public policies that would undoubtedly have a significant impact on their company, they would have to act quickly.

# 33 Nitrofix Ghana

William A. Stoever

Craig Michael Lee, the project advisor to the vice-president of Nitrofix Inc.'s international division, had a long meeting in mid-1982 with Bawol Cabiri, the commercial consul at the Ghana Trade and Investment Office in New York City. Lee hoped that the talk would enable him to write a report to the vice-president recommending whether to pursue an investment opportunity in Ghana.

A Ghanaian government representative had first approached Nitrofix about establishing a fertilizer plant in 1981, two years after Dr. Hilla Limann became the country's first democratically elected president in over a decade. The Limann government was actively seeking foreign investment, reversing previous governments' socialist practices and antipathy to private investment. However, Nitrofix was hesitant to enter an agreement because of Ghana's past political instability and economic chaos, and negotiations had proceeded fitfully. Then the Limann government was overthrown in a military coup on December 31, 1981. Lee had assumed that was the end of the matter until the Ghana Trade and Investment Office contacted him again in mid-1982 and mentioned that some very favorable terms might now be possible for the investment. His recent meeting with Cabiri focused on the possibility that Nitrofix might invest in a plant in Ghana to be operated as a joint venture with either private Ghanaian entrepreneurs or with the government. A tentative name was agreed upon: Nitrofix (Ghana) Ltd. Lee had been impressed by Cabiri's knowledge and understanding and by the potential profitability of the project. However, he knew that he had to evaluate a number of issues of vital importance including

- The condition of the Ghanaian economy
- The political climate in Ghana and West Africa
- The existence of a Ghanaian and/or African market for fertilizer
- Ghana's policies toward foreign investment
- The financial arrangements

He also knew that if his company decided to follow up on the possibility, it would have to prepare for negotiations on a wide range of matters.

The author acknowledges inspiration from the "Ghana Fertilizers" case prepared by John M. Stopford, which appears in Vernon and Wells, *Manager in the International Economy*, 3rd edition.
   This case is based on a real situation but all names are disguised.

Address reprint requests to William A. Stoever, 228 Hudson Street, Hoboken, N.J. 07030. A teaching note is available from the author.

© W. A. Stoever, 1985.

Reprinted with permission from *The Journal of Management Case Studies*, vol. 1 (1985), pp. 205–217.

## NITROFIX, INC.

Nitrofix was a medium-sized U.S. manufacturer of nitrogenous fertilizers that had made a specialization of setting up plants to serve the local markets in smaller countries. In the 1960s its first international ventures had gone into the smaller countries of Western Europe, but in the 1970s it had expanded into friendly third world countries such as the Philippines, Indonesia, Thailand, and Venezuela. The company thoroughly analyzed its overseas investments, and they had generally planned out well, contributing most of Nitrofix's growth in sales and profits for two decades. In the 1960s Nitrofix had usually insisted on 100 percent ownership of each overseas subsidiary, but in the 1970s it had come to recognize both the necessity and the desirability of entering into joint ventures with local partners when terms and conditions were suitable.

## THE POLITICAL ECONOMY OF GHANA

After a day of library research, Lee pieced together the following information about Ghana's political and economic situation. The country had received independence from Great Britain in 1957, the first black colony in Africa to become independent. Its first prime minister (later president) was Dr. Kwame Nkrumah, an eloquent spokesman and leader for the emerging aspirations of Africa. Thanks largely to its position as the world's largest cocoa exporter, Ghana was the richest country in Africa at the time of independence. Continuing a British colonial tradition, the new government invested a substantial part of its revenues in education at all levels from primary school through university. As a result Ghana had a high level of literacy and more college graduates than the country could absorb. But economic policy moved from one disaster to the next. The Nkrumah government embarked on a series of expensive projects such as grandiose industrialization schemes and public buildings that drained the country's coffers while contributing little to its growth. The government's policies toward private enterprise (both Ghanaian and foreign) reflected a basic ambiguity that has persisted for two decades. On the one hand, the Ghanaians recognized their need for the capital, entrepreneurial initiative, managerial know-how, and technology that domestic and foreign companies could supply; but on the other hand, they were impressed with the socialist state-directed model of development and were concerned that private capitalists, if left unchecked, would accumulate most of the country's wealth and benefits of development for themselves. Nkrumah's solution was to attempt to channel and control private investment by establishing four categories of enterprises:

1. State enterprises: wholly government-owned, supposed to include most large businesses
2. Private enterprises: owned by Ghanaians or foreign investors or joint Ghanaian-foreign ventures
3. Joint state-private enterprises: partnerships, generally between the government and foreign investors
4. Cooperatives

A government agency was to supervise domestic and foreign investments to ensure that they complied with the requirements of their assigned categories.

A Capital Investments Act was passed in 1963. It set up a scheme of priorities and incentives to attract foreign investment, provided such investment conformed to the conditions set down by the government. Initially a fair amount of investment was attracted, but a lot of it went into capital-intensive, high-technology plants that were inefficient and expensive producers for the small Ghanaian market. Meanwhile agricultural development was neglected.

Nkrumah was overthrown by military coup in 1966. The military regime attempted to liberalize the economy, reduce import and currency controls, increase the role of the market in allocating resources, and create a more attractive climate for foreign investment. In spite of their efforts, however, the economy remained largely stagnant.

The military stepped aside as promised in 1969, and a former university professor, Dr. Kofi Busia, was elected president. Buoyed by a boom in cocoa prices during his first year in office, Busia initiated an expansionary program intended to increase the rates of domestic savings and investment. But imports of consumer items swelled, world cocoa prices fell, inflation heated up, and the balance-of-payments deficit worsened.

Another military coup was staged in January 1972, bringing to power a group calling itself the National Reconciliation Council (NRC). This group set out to undo the liberalization of the previous five and a half years. They clamped on wage, price, and rent controls; vastly increased import and currency controls; reasserted the program of state enterprises; nationalized 55 percent of most of the larger domestic- and foreign-owned businesses; and held down prices paid to cocoa farmers in an attempt to increase the state share of agricultural revenues. The consequences were disastrous. Cocoa production fell off, and farmers began smuggling their crops to neighboring Ivory Coast and Togo, where they could obtain much higher prices. Once one of the most abundant food producers in Africa, the country now had to import canned goods and staples from Europe and the United States, and it was caught in the vise of spiraling oil prices. Inflation, the government deficit, the money supply, and the balance-of-payments deficit ballooned. Corruption and mismanagement in the government machinery and the state enterprises were rampant. Skilled and educated people fled to jobs in Nigeria, England, and the United States. The cumbersome administrative procedures prevented the government from utilizing even the foreign aid that was given to it. Some factories were operating at less than 25 percent of capacity because the shortage of foreign exchange made it impossible to import necessary raw materials and spare parts. Foreign companies faced a proliferation of controls and hindrances; for example, one company applied in 1972 for permission to repatriate a dividend and was still waiting in 1979 for the foreign-exchange allocation to come through. Some foreign companies pulled out, and virtually no new investment came into the country. Meanwhile, the military rulers divided into factions and struggled among themselves for control of the government, with the result of paralysis and continuous crisis in the country's political leadership.

In June 1979 a group of junior air force officers overthrew the NRC regime and installed as president flight lieutenant Jerry Rawlings, the son of a British father and a Ghanaian mother. Rawlings stepped aside three months later, after the election of Hilla Limann, a former diplomat and economist, as president. In spite of his lack of political experience, Limann proved to be an adept politician. He neutralized some potential coupmakers in the military and lined up enough support in the newly reconstituted Parliament to institute a program of economic reforms. His government imposed severe austerity measures, enabling the country to meet its obligations on its foreign debts for the first time in five years and to regain a measure of international creditworthiness. Prices paid to cocoa farmers were trebled, reversing the declining production figures and reducing the amount of smuggling. Many problems remained, however. The inflation rate was still above 50 percent a year, shortages of food and spare parts continued, and the country's best managers continued deserting the inefficient state industries in favor of higher-paying jobs abroad. The government hesitated to take one of the most necessary but politically risky steps, devaluation of the Ghanaian currency, the cedi. The International Monetary Fund (I.M.F.) tried to impose devaluation as a condition for the granting of further credits, but Limann feared that such a move might trigger another coup, and the I.M.F. relented somewhat. In spite of an increase in cocoa production, the country's export revenues declined because of a steep fall in the world price.

President Limann made clear his intention to seek new foreign investment for Ghana. His government enacted a new Investment Code designed to "encourage foreign investments in Ghana by the provision of incentives, to promote the development of Ghanaian entrepreneurs, to indicate enterprises in which the State and Ghanaians are required to participate in any investment and the extent of such participation, to make provision for the registration of technology transfer contracts. . . ." The code assured foreign investors of "protection" and a fair return on their investment. It specifically eliminated any restrictions on transfers out of Ghana of fees, charges, capital, and profits to the investor's country of origin. It established a Ghana Investing Centre chaired by the vice-president of Ghana to dismantle regulatory and administrative barriers to investment and to review investment projects; the centre could decide which projects should quality for special incentives. All approved enterprises were to receive five-year exemptions from customs duties for machinery and equipment imported for use in the enterprises, three years' customs exemption for spare parts, guaranteed manufacturing or establishment licenses, guaranteed immigration of necessary expatriate personnel, and certain tax exemptions and remittance guarantees for such personnel. In the manufacturing sector the government sought industries in which the country had a raw material advantage, underutilized existing plant capacity, or the capacity to conserve and/or earn foreign exchange. Projects qualifying for investment included agro-based industries, those processing raw materials originating in Ghana, animal feed, and fertilizer, among others. Companies in the export sector could be exempted from company income tax during an initial period provided they declared no dividends during that period.

Evidently the new Investment Code made a favorable impression on at least a few potential investors, because Lee recalled seeing a couple of items in the newspapers during 1981 mentioning that a few American and European companies were exploring possibilities for new investments in Ghana. Lee himself was attracted by the country's advantages—rich soil, adequate rainfall, an educated and energetic population, potential mineral wealth, and the beginnings of a national development program. Lee thought it would be very desirable for Nitrofix to be the first fertilizer producer in Ghana and thus secure an entrenched position in what could become a very prosperous market. But he knew that many problems remained. The country was still deeply in debt, its currency vastly overvalued, its foreign exchange reserves close to zero, its economy dependent on the vagaries of the world cocoa market, its borrowing power from the I.M.F. and private lenders essentially exhausted, and its record of economic mismanagement still needing much improvement. If only they could get their act together. . . .

On New Year's Day 1982, Lee was shocked to learn that the Limann government had been overthrown in yet another military coup, Ghana's fifth in 15 years. This one too was led by Jerry Rawlings, then 34 years old. In radio broadcasts Rawlings claimed that Limann had been incapable of solving Ghana's economic problems, and he announced his intention to retain the presidency "as long as necessary." It soon became apparent, however, that he did not enjoy much popular support and did not have many ideas on how to improve the country's economic situation. Ghana appeared to have suffered another political and economic setback, at least temporarily.

Exhibit 33.1 gives the most recent statistics Lee could find on the Ghanaian economy. Exhibits 33.2, 33.3, and 33.4 give some statistics on the world production, consumption, and price of cocoa. Exhibits 33.5, 33.6, and 33.7. show the consumption of fertilizer in Ghana and other countries.

## MARKET FOR FERTILIZER

Agriculture is a way of life for the people of Ghana, employing 60 percent of the labor force and producing 42 percent of the gross domestic product in 1980. However, out of the 23 million hectares suitable for farming, only 3 million hectares, or 13 percent, were under cultivation. Methods of cultivation were divided into two general categories: traditional (or subsistence) and new improved practices. Traditional methods were characterized by the use of simple tools; they relied almost entirely on human labor, resulting in inefficient processing and storage methods and low crop yields. The new methods stressed the use of chemicals (fertilizers and pesticides) as well as farm machinery and implements.

Over 90 percent of farming was undertaken by subsistence-level private farmers cultivating small plots of land, generally between three and four hectares. Soil fertility on these farms was generally maintained by crop rotation and burning of vegetation cover; the latter practice returned potash and some minerals to the

**Exhibit 33.1** Statistics on the Ghanaian Economy (millions of cedis at official exchange rate)

|  | 1974 | 1975 | 1976 | 1977 | 1978 | 1979 | 1980 | 1981 |
|---|---|---|---|---|---|---|---|---|
| Total exports | 840 | 929 | 952 | 1,106 | 1,645 | 1,201 | — | — |
| Exports of cacao | 866 | 551 | 516 | 680 | 1,033 | — | — | — |
| Imports | 944 | 909 | 969 | 1,176 | 1,653 | 1,299 | — | — |
| Foreign debt (claims on government) | 574 | 881 | 1,513 | 2,527 | 4,287 | 4,413 | 5,724 | 9,494 |
| Official reserves | 92 | 149 | 203 | 162 | 288 | 300 | 216 | 196 |
| **(Figures in U.S. dollars per cedi)** | | | | | | | | |
| Official exchange rate | .8696 | .8696 | .8696 | .8696 | .3636 | .3636 | .3636 | .3636 |
| Black market exchange rate[a] | .65 | .52 | .23 | .13 | .10 | .07 | .04 | .02 |
| **1975 = 100** | | | | | | | | |
| Consumer price index | 77.0 | 100.0 | 156.1 | 337.8 | 584.8 | 903.0 | 1,355.4 | 2,934 |

[a] *Pick's Currency Yearbook,* 1977–1979; 1980 and 1981 rates from current news articles.

Source: *International Financial Statistics,* except where noted otherwise.

**Exhibit 33.2** World Production of Cocoa Beans in Principal Exporting Countries (thousand metric tons)

| Crop Year | Brazil | Ghana | Ivory Coast | Nigeria | World Total |
|---|---|---|---|---|---|
| 1967–1968 | 145 | 422 | 147 | 239 | 1,352 |
| 1968–1969 | 165 | 339 | 145 | 192 | 1,242 |
| 1969–1970 | 201 | 416 | 181 | 223 | 1,435 |
| 1970–1971 | 182 | 392 | 180 | 308 | 1,499 |
| 1971–1972 | 167 | 464 | 226 | 255 | 1,583 |
| 1972–1973 | 162 | 418 | 181 | 241 | 1,398 |
| 1973–1974 | 246 | 350 | 209 | 215 | 1,448 |
| 1974–1975 | 273 | 377 | 242 | 214 | 1,549 |
| 1975–1976 | 258 | 397 | 231 | 216 | 1,509 |
| 1976–1977 | 234 | 320 | 230 | 165 | 1,340 |
| 1977–1978 | 283 | 268 | 304 | 205 | 1,502 |
| 1978–1979 | 314 | 250 | 312 | 137 | 1,480 |
| 1979–1980 | 294 | 290 | 373 | 169 | 1,617 |
| 1980–1981 | 350 | 255 | 352 | 165 | 1,584 |

Source: *Commodity Yearbook,* 1981, p. 85.

soil, but it caused the loss of important organic matter and other minerals. Burning was especially damaging if done too frequently or at the wrong season, conditions likely to result as land use intensifies.

While the cultivation of tree crops (cocoa, coffee, rubber, and palm oil) was labor-intensive, mechanization had been introduced in the cultivation of field crops such as maize and rice. Mechanical cultivation leads to rapid deterioration

**Exhibit 33.3**
Consumption of
Cocoa (thousand
metric tons)

| Year | World Total |
|------|-------------|
| 1967 | 1,366 |
| 1968 | 1,410 |
| 1969 | 1,353 |
| 1970 | 1,355 |
| 1971 | 1,438 |
| 1972 | 1,565 |
| 1973 | 1,556 |
| 1974 | 1,478 |
| 1975 | 1,462 |
| 1976 | 1,525 |
| 1977 | 1,367 |
| 1978 | 1,391 |
| 1979 | 1,437 |
| 1980 | 1,468 |

*Source: Commodity Yearbook, 1981.*

**Exhibit 33.4** Spot Cocoa Bean Prices
(yearly/monthly average, New York)

| Year | U.S. Cents per Pound |
|------|----------------------|
| 1975 | 75.9 |
| 1976 | 109.2 |
| 1977 | 214.4 |
| 1978 | 174.2 |
| 1979 | 160.4 |
| 1980 | 135.4 |
| 1981 | 108.5 |
| 1982 Jan. | 116.0 |
| Feb. | 107.0 |
| Mar. | 102.0 |
| Apr. | 99.0 |
| May | 94.0 |

*Source:* Figures for 1967–1980 from *Commodity Year-book,* 1981; figures for 1981–1982 from *Survey of Current Business.*

of the organic matter in the soil and the depletion of soil nutrients. Therefore fertilizers must be used to replenish lost minerals, or else crop yields decline.

The Limann government declared that agriculture would be the number one priority for development and investment. The government encouraged the development of large-scale commercial farming, which requires the use of modern techniques. In order to boost overall productivity and expand agricultural output, the government supplied many inputs including hoes, seed rice, and groundnuts (peanuts). It also distributed over one million bags of fertilizer to small producers, commercial farms, and parastate organizations.

These steps alone would not be sufficient to improve productivity or increase the usage of fertilizers, however; raising the educational level of the farm population is a fundamental necessity to boost the understanding and acceptance of fertilizers. Such an educational program would require a massive effort by the government, but the more energetic and literate younger generation who might be more amenable to adopting new practices have been leaving the countryside for the cities. Furthermore, the archaic land tenure system is based on traditions and customs that discourage innovation and thus constitute a formidable obstacle to the acceptance of fertilizer by small farmers.

Cocoa is raised both by small farmers who convert a portion of their subsistence holdings to production of the cash crop and by larger plantations and state farms. The cocoa industry is the main source of Ghana's foreign exchange earnings, accounting for approximately 65 percent in an average year. It employs 11 percent of the nation's labor force and is believed to account for a large part of its fertilizer usage. However, cocoa production has declined steadily since the early 1960s, and by 1980 Ghana had fallen from first to third place among the world's major exporters. The factors responsible for the decline in output include low producer prices, poor maintenance of cocoa farms, aging of cocoa trees and cocoa farmers, scarcity of farm labor in the major producing areas, and ineffective control of pests and diseases. Poor transportation and a lack of infrastructure are problems, as well as smuggling to neighboring countries where better prices are obtainable. Storage facilities have also deteriorated.

After reviewing the preceding information, Lee concluded that there would be many imponderables in any effort to estimate the growth potential of the Ghanaian fertilizer market. So much would depend on noneconomic factors such as the effort and expense the government might decide to put into promoting the use of fertilizer and the pace at which Ghanaian farmers would accept it. Lee did find some tables apparently indicating that the use of fertilizers was growing in Ghana and enabling comparisons with other countries (see Exhibits 33.5 and 33.6). However, he also found another source that said that Ghanaian consumption of nitrogenous fertilizers had peaked at 11.0 thousand metric tons in 1975–1976 and had declined somewhat for several years thereafter. Consumption of potash and phosphate fertilizers had also decreased since 1975–1976.

Lee also wondered whether some Ghanaian fertilizer production might be exportable to other West African countries. Ghana had joined the Economic Community of West African States (ECOWAS) at its inception in 1975. This community had a total of 16 member states,* many of which were even smaller and poorer than Ghana. It was supposed to become a common market with the elimination of trade barriers among its members and a common external tariff. Members were supposed to cooperate for agricultural development, the construction of infrastructure to improve regional transportation and communications, and industrial growth. However, most of the members could not afford to lower their own tariff barriers or to take any concrete steps to implement the regional integration plans. Furthermore, Nigeria, with its oil wealth and naphtha feedstocks, would be likely to grab the lead as the dominant nitrogenous fertilizer exporter in the region.

**PLANT TYPE AND SIZE**  Lee knew that the technical and economic factors involved in the choice of plant size and production methods for nitrogenous fertilizers were very complex and subject to change depending on the price of the primary input, naphtha, a petroleum derivative. Nonetheless, he knew that Nitrofix had three basic choices of technology and that significant economies of scale could be achieved in both construction and per unit production costs as plants were made larger and more

---

*Benin, Cape Verde, Gambia, Ghana, Guinea, Guinea-Bissau, Ivory Coast, Liberia, Mali, Mauritania, Niger, Nigeria, Senegal, Sierra Leone, Togo, Upper Volta (now Burkina Faso).

**Exhibit 33.5** World Fertilizer Usage (kilograms of inorganic fertilizers[a] per hectare of land under arable cultivation and permanent crops)

| | 1961–1965 (yearly average) | 1967 | 1972 | 1977 |
|---|---|---|---|---|
| World | 27.9 | 39.9 | 54.3 | 68.0 |
| Africa | 4.7 | 6.3 | 10.0 | 12.4 |
| N. and C. America | 41.2 | 61.3 | 69.7 | 83.2 |
| S. America | 8.4 | 11.2 | 24.7 | 38.8 |
| Asia | 11.8 | 18.5 | 31.0 | 45.4 |
| Europe | 103.9 | 139.6 | 188.7 | 210.3 |
| Oceania | 34.0 | 34.1 | 37.4 | 36.2 |
| USSR | 18.0 | 33.7 | 53.2 | 77.6 |
| **Selected countries** | | | | |
| Africa | | | | |
| Egypt | 109.9 | 100.2 | 146.7 | 187.5 |
| Ghana | 0.6 | 0.5 | 1.7 | 10.9 |
| Kenya | 9.6 | 17.2 | 24.9 | 22.7 |
| Nigeria | 0.1 | 0.3 | 0.8 | 3.1 |
| South Africa | 23.4 | 32.9 | 47.6 | 59.6 |
| Sudan | 3.7 | 6.3 | 8.0 | 4.3 |
| Uganda | 0.7 | 0.8 | 1.5 | 0.5 |
| Zaire | 0.2 | 0.5 | 0.7 | 1.4 |
| N. and C. America | | | | |
| Canada | 12.4 | 20.4 | 23.2 | 34.3 |
| Cuba | 94.0 | 169.3 | 76.2 | 132.7 |
| Mexico | 11.3 | 18.5 | 29.3 | 46.0 |
| U.S. | 52.2 | 77.4 | 86.2 | 99.5 |
| S. America | | | | |
| Argentina | 0.9 | 2.2 | 2.5 | 2.2 |
| Brazil | 9.1 | 13.8 | 45.2 | 77.4 |
| Asia | | | | |
| Bangladesh | 4.4 | 10.6 | 20.0 | 37.1 |
| China | 13.2 | 24.1 | 45.5 | 74.3 |
| India | 3.7 | 7.1 | 16.7 | 25.3 |
| Indonesia | 8.4 | 8.6 | 28.9 | 35.0 |
| Japan | 305.2 | 387.4 | 389.5 | 428.1 |
| Thailand | 2.2 | 7.7 | 10.8 | 15.6 |
| Turkey | 3.9 | 10.6 | 22.4 | 46.5 |
| Europe | | | | |
| France | 133.9 | 191.6 | 284.5 | 277.6 |
| Netherlands | 534.9 | 626.2 | 719.5 | 737.3 |
| Hungary | 52.9 | 91.3 | 182.7 | 278.7 |
| Italy | 60.2 | 73.8 | 125.3 | 140.9 |
| Poland | 65.2 | 117.9 | 201.1 | 241.0 |
| Romania | 7.8 | 27.4 | 40.1 | 54.2 |
| U.K. | 198.9 | 254.2 | 240.0 | 287.6 |
| Oceania | | | | |
| Australia | 24.5 | 26.6 | 26.1 | 24.5 |
| New Zealand | 737.6 | 720.3 | 1319.5 | 1296.3 |

[a]Inorganic nitrogenous, phosphatic, and potash fertilizers.

*Source: The World Food Book (1981),* pp. 214–215.

**Exhibit 33.6** Kilograms of Inorganic
Fertilizers per Hectare of Land Under Arable
Cultivation and Permanent Crops (log scale),
1977

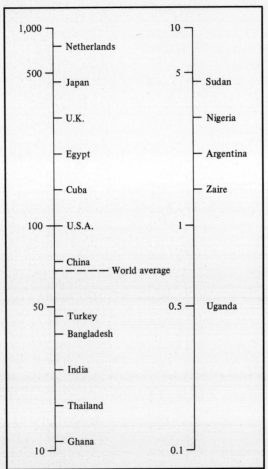

**Exhibit 33.7**

| Annual Production Capacity (tons) | Production Technology | Factor Proportions | Construction Cost (U.S. $) | Production Cost per Ton of Ammonia |
|---|---|---|---|---|
| 20,000 | Steam-reforming | Relatively labor-intensive | $20 million | $130 |
| 80,000 | Reciprocating compressor | Relatively capital-intensive | $60 million | $120 |
| 160,000 | Centrifugal compressor | More capital-intensive | $90 million | $100 |

advanced. He obtained some ballpark figures from one of the company engineers (Exhibit 33.7).

The ammonia (from whatever source) would then be converted into ammonium nitrate—the actual fertilizer—in a technologically simple process. This diluted the value of the ammonia by about 50 percent: one ton of ammonia made two tons of ammonium nitrate. Lee was aware that construction and production costs had a way of soaring when plants were put into developing countries because of shortages of materials and the added costs and inefficiencies of trying to train and use unskilled labor. The steam-reforming production technique was outdated and inefficient, but it was easier to learn, and used equipment could be obtained from other LDCs (lesser-developed countries).

Another alternative was for the Ghanaians to import U.S. or European ammonium nitrate. The world price was rather volatile, fluctuating between $50 and $90 per ton during the previous five years. Lee established that a good average would be $65 per ton (the equivalent of paying $130 per ton of ammonia). In all likelihood importing fertilizer would be cheaper than trying to produce it in Ghana because of the added expenses and hassles of operating in a faraway LDC. (Lee figured that transportation costs would approximately even out regardless of whether unprocessed naphtha or processed ammonium nitrate was shipped to Ghana.) By producing it themselves, however, the Ghanaians *might* save some foreign exchange, raise the skills and industrial experience of some workers, and add to the foundation for the country's industrial development. A shiny new plant would also make the government leaders look good.

**THE FINANCIAL AND OWNERSHIP ARRANGE-MENTS**

The Investment Code required any foreign investment in fertilizer to be a joint venture, 55 percent Ghanaian and 45 percent foreign. All other things being equal, Nitrofix might have prefered 100 percent ownership and control, but they also knew that there were some advantages to having a local partner. Lee noted that in spite of the apparent rigidity of the code, the 1979 constitution allowed some room for further negotiations. If the enterprise was cast as a joint venture, he assumed that each partner would put in equity capital proportional to its percentage ownership. This was not a rule cast in stone, however, and considerable flexibility might be achieved by negotiating the valuation of whatever machinery Nitrofix contributed, the rate at which contributions in cedis were valued, and the mixture of equity and debt contributed by each partner.

If the partners agreed to go with the 20,000-ton plant employing steam-reforming technology, it would be ideal from Nitrofix's point of view to make its entire contribution in the form of used equipment. The valuation of such equipment would be quite arbitrary: its value as scrap might be $100,000, but it might produce several millions of dollars worth of output per year for somebody who could keep it running. Lee suspected the Ghanaians were too sophisticated to accept such outdated technology or at least to give it a very high valuation, however.

As to choice of partner, Nitrofix would probably have preferred a private businessman or group, but Lee doubted that private citizens would be capable of raising that kind of money in Ghana, and Nitrofix was most reluctant to take on a partner that didn't contribute a fair share of the risk capital. Realistically, therefore, they would probably have to go with the government.

Another question was the matter of debt versus equity. In order to minimize their exposure in a country like Ghana, Nitrofix would have preferred to put in a relatively small amount of its own capital as equity and to obtain most of the financing in the form of loans. On a $20-million project, for example, Lee wondered whether Nitrofix could put in as little as $4.5 million, the Ghanaian partner $5.5 million, and the remaining $10 million come from outside lenders. But it was questionable whether outside lenders would put up this large a percentage on such a risky venture, and Nitrofix might end up having to pay for a much higher percentage of a much larger project. What's more, interest rates in the Eurodollar market were then running about 15 percent, which would make them think carefully about taking on a hard-currency debt. And there wasn't a lot of money available for soft loans at this time, either.

Cabiri said the government would help arrange local financing for plant construction and local supplies and would try to help obtain hard-currency financing for necessary imports. It might offer to guarantee any borrowings from international banks, for example. But in view of the country's desperate financial straits, Lee seriously doubted whether the banks would give much weight to such guarantees. Furthermore, he was most reluctant to have Nitrofix bear the entire foreign-exchange risk of the project; the Ghanaians were going to have to come up with a decent share of the dollars.

Overhead expenses and taxes were other imponderables. Lee made the optimistic assumption that overhead expenses might run only 10 percent of gross sales, although he was aware that red tape, delays, and corruption often ate up a much larger percent of the profits in LDCs. Ghana imposed a 50 percent tax on corporate income, but Lee assumed Nitrofix could get a holiday from all taxes for at least the first five years of production, and maybe for ten. However, he knew the Bank of Ghana and the Ministry of Finance would object if the tax abatement was too generous.

It was obvious from all these considerations that the problems of financing and risk might be enough to discourage Nitrofix from the venture. But Lee's preliminary calculations suggested the possibility of some very handsome returns if everything went right. Nitrofix would of course seek tariff protection against fertilizer imports. If they got a 100 percent tariff, they might be able to sell their Ghanaian production for as much as $260 per ton. He recognized that the higher the tariff, the less the net economic benefit to the host country. But he calculated that if they went ahead with the 160,000-ton plan *and* obtained 50 percent financing at 15 percent *and* were able to sell their entire output at $260 per ton *and* were able to hold their overhead costs to 10 percent of sales *and* could get a complete tax holiday, Nitrofix Inc. might earn $6.6 million per year on a $20 million investment—a handsome return. And the returns could be even higher if they could get subsidized loans, a subsidized plant site, payments for training workers, and the like. Perhaps if they waited a year or two they could get a lower rate on their hard-currency borrowings. On the other hand, the returns would be lower as soon as the tax holiday ran out or was canceled, or if they decided to go with the 80,000-ton plant, or if Lee's assumptions regarding the size of the market or the low amount of overhead did not pan out. (Lee also calculated that they would need at least 22 percent tariff protection in order for the plant to break even if all his optimistic assumptions held true.)

In some ways the 20,000-ton plant seemed the most attractive for both Nitrofix and Ghana, despite its badly outdated technology. Lee wondered if Nitrofix Inc. could get a 45 percent stake in exchange for some obsolescent steam-reforming equipment from their Greek or Philippine subsidiaries plus a promise to provide technical assistance and train Ghanaians to run the plant. The Ghanaian partner would get 55 percent in exchange for supplying 15 million cedis ($5.5 million at the official exchange rate); this money would pay local expenses for setting up the plant. They would seek a $10-million Eurodollar loan to cover the hard-currency expenses. With a 100 percent tariff, this plant should produce a pretax profit of $580,000 if everything went right. Nitrofix Inc.'s share would be $261,-000—not bad considering that it would be an essentially costless investment for them.

Another factor that could help make the investment more attractive would be if Nitrofix could find a way of reducing some of the risks. Lee wondered whether they could bargain the Ghanaians into giving Nitrofix's shares a priority claim to dividends, for example. Maybe Nitrofix could cast part of its compensation in the form of a management fee or licensing payment off the top—say 1 or 2 percent of gross revenues. They might be able to obtain insurance from the Overseas Private Investment Corporation (OPIC) against the risks of expropriation, war, and currency inconvertibility; the premiums on such insurance could run up to 1.5 percent of the amount of coverage (0.6 percent for expropriation, 0.6 percent for war, revolution, or insurrection, and 0.3 percent for currency inconvertibility, if Nitrofix elected to take the full coverage).

Reviewing all this information, Lee realized he faced a daunting task in trying to evaluate it and recommend a decision. But he also looked forward to it as an interesting challenge.

# 34 Multiquimica do Brasil

Mary Pat Cormack and M. Edgar Barrett

Maguire Oil and Gas Institute
Southern Methodist University

"I'm really concerned about our position in Brazil. Our pharmaceutical products are being hurt by both local and foreign producers and our foreign exchange policies may well be to blame." So said Don Howard, controller of the foreign operations of the pharmaceutical group of Multichemical Industries, Inc. "Look at Levadol, for example, our sales are falling while those of Hoffman et Cie are up."*

This conversation took place in February 1983 as Don was reviewing the 1982 results of the foreign operations of the pharmaceutical group with the group's general manager, Paul McConnell. The men were in the company's corporate offices in Houston, Texas.

**BACK-GROUND** Multichemical Industries, Inc., sold 75 different products in over 50 countries during 1982. Sales for the year were $3.1 billion (see Exhibit 34.1 for financial data). The company's principal product groups were pharmaceuticals, industrial chemicals, agricultural chemicals, and petrochemicals. Multichemical's overseas subsidiaries accounted for 35 percent of sales in 1982, with the majority of the activity taking place in Europe.

Multiquimica do Brasil (MB) was responsible for all sales and manufacturing which took place in Brazil. Thus, its managers had responsibility for products in several of the firm's product groups. Sales during the year were $65 million, 6 percent of foreign sales. This wholly owned subsidiary was formed in 1977 with the initial purpose of establishing manufacturing facilities for agricultural chemical, industrial chemical, and pharmaceutical products in Brazil. Prior to that time, Multichemical had been active in Brazil through export sales. In other words, products which were manufactured in the United States had been sold in Brazil through local, independent importers. Multichemical did not operate either manufacturing facilities or a division office in the country until 1977.

The new subsidiary began manufacturing and selling herbicides in 1977. MB did not show a profit until 1980. The losses which were incurred were primarily attributable to two factors: the large start-up costs associated with a new business

---

*Hoffman et Cie was a large multinational firm based in Bern, Switzerland.

This case was prepared by Mary Pat Cormack and Professor M. Edgar Barrett as a basis for class discussion. It is not intended to illustrate either effective or ineffective handling of an administrative situation.

Copyright © 1983 by M. Edgar Barrett.

**Exhibit 34.1**

### MULTIQUIMICA DO BRASIL
### Financial Data: Consolidated Corporate Results
### (in millions of dollars)

| | 1982 | 1981 |
|---|---|---|
| **Income statement** | | |
| Sales | | |
|   Agricultural chemicals | $ 658 | $ 600 |
|   Industrial chemicals | 583 | 513 |
|   Petrochemicals | 652 | 585 |
|   Pharmaceutical products | 1,210 | 1,086 |
|   Subtotal | $3,103 | $2,784 |
| Cost of goods sold | 1,300 | 1,169 |
| Selling and administrative expense | 884 | 793 |
| Depreciation | 296 | 262 |
| Research expense | 292 | 250 |
|   Subtotal | $2,772 | $2,474 |
| Operating income | $ 331 | $ 310 |
| Interest expense | 45 | 42 |
| Other income—net | 41 | 30 |
|   Subtotal | $ 4 | $ 12 |
| Income before taxes | 327 | 298 |
| Income taxes | 126 | 110 |
|   Net income | $ 201 | $ 188 |
| **Balance sheet** | | |
| Current assets | $1,016 | $1,001 |
| Net property, plant, and equipment | 1,536 | 1,338 |
| Other assets | 241 | 139 |
|   Total assets | $2,793 | $2,478 |
| Current liabilities | 363 | 297 |
| Long-term debt | 394 | 309 |
| Deferred income taxes | 140 | 124 |
| Stockholders' equity | 1,896 | 1,748 |
|   Total liabilities and stockholders' equity | $2,793 | $2,478 |

*Source:* Multichemical Industries, Inc., 1982 Annual Report.

and a weak economic period in Brazil. As a result of the losses sustained during the 1977–1980 period, MB was entitled to a substantial amount of tax loss carryforwards on its Brazilian tax return.*

In late 1979, the company installed a manufacturing plant to process Levadol, an aspirin-free pain reliever. Such facilities were included in the original operat-

*The term *tax loss carryforward* refers to the fact that net operating losses, to the extent that they exceed taxable income of the preceding three years, can be carried forward, thus reducing future taxable income.

ing plans for MB. They were scheduled, however, for the early 1980s. They went onstream sooner than originally planned due to an increase in the amount of duty on imports.

The manufacture of this product involved shipping the raw materials in bulk form from the United States. The raw materials were formulated, converted into tablet form, and packaged in the Brazilian plant and then sold to distributors. MB sales of Levadol in 1982 were $6.8 million.

## PRODUCT AND PRICING FLOW FOR LEVADOL

The raw materials for Levadol were shipped from a domestic subsidiary of Multi-chemical to MB. The invoiced price for the transferred goods during 1982 averaged $60 per case equivalent. The invoice was denominated in U.S. dollars.

The cost of goods sold on MB's books for Levadol averaged $131 per case. This figure included the $60 per case raw material costs, plus $31 per case for import duty and $40 per case to formulate, convert, and package it.

The product was sold to wholesalers serving both drug stores and chain stores, usually on 90-day payment terms, for a price of approximately $218 per case. The $87-per-case difference between the sales price and the cost of goods sold consisted of marketing costs (roughly 20 percent of sales), administration, distribution, and interest expenses and approximately a 5 percent profit margin before taxes. The distributors, in turn, usually added a 10–20 percent margin. This was designed to both cover their costs and provide a profit margin.

## DOLLAR LINKAGE BILLING

On their tax and fiscal books, MB benefited from a system known as dollar linkage billing. A statement on the invoice which was sent from the domestic subsidiary to MB said "payable at the exchange rate in effect on the date of the receipt of goods." (Management books, on the other hand, were kept on the assumption that the invoice was to be paid in dollars—thus, effectively, using the exchange rate in effect at the time of payment.)

Brazilian law, at the time, required 180-day payment terms on imports. Since the Brazilian cruzeiro lost value in relation to the dollar on a more or less continuous basis, a foreign exchange loss would normally show up on a Brazilian firm's cruzeiro-denominated books. Given the above system, however, the foreign exchange loss showed up on the U.S. tax books.

## DOMESTIC SALES WITHIN BRAZIL

Even within the context of the Brazilian domestic market, MB's reported profit in dollar terms was affected by the more or less continuous devaluation of the cruzeiro. The major problem here was tied to the fact that competition had forced MB to offer 90-day payment terms to their customers. Given the fact that the cruzeiro was formally devalued approximately once every 10 days, any domestic subsidiary with terms of 90 days was faced with a translation loss whenever its books were translated back into dollar terms.*

In an attempt to deal with the situation, MB put into place a method known as forward pricing. Under the assumptions of this method, MB's management predicted the amount of cruzeiro devaluation which would occur during the forthcoming 90 days. This estimate then served as the basis for raising the then current sales price. In other words, they passed along the expected loss due to the devaluation of the cruzeiro to the customer. As a result of this policy, product prices were revised at least monthly.

## HEDGING POLICIES

From 1977 to 1979, the annual inflation rate in Brazil was in the general range of 30–50 percent. In 1979, however, Brazil—which imported the vast majority of its crude oil—began to feel the effects of the increasing price of crude oil. As a result, the domestic inflation rate took off and the cruzeiro was devalued by 30 percent during the year. MB reacted by pushing up its prices, a policy which it continued to adhere to throughout 1982.

Beginning in late 1979, the corporate treasurer's office of Multichemical began to "encourage" MB to borrow locally. Such a policy was designed to match assets and liabilities in cruzeiro terms and thus offset the translation loss on assets with a translation gain on liabilities. By having the subsidiaries borrow locally, the corporate treasurer was hoping to eliminate the risk of having to report large translation losses on the corporate income statement. Local borrowing, in essence, helped to smooth the corporation's reported income stream by substituting a periodic interest expense for less frequent, but presumably larger, losses due to translation. There was a cost, however. The nominal interest rate in Brazil in 1982 was approximately 160 percent. (See Exhibit 34.2 for foreign exchange and inflation rate data.)

## PERFORM-ANCE MEASURE-MENT POLICIES

Multichemical had recently changed its internal reporting system. Before the change, operating managers had been held responsible for the performance of their units as measured by the operating-income figures. This meant that items such as other income, other expense, interest expense, and translation gains and losses were not focused upon in the quarterly business results review meetings. Over time, the senior management at the corporate level had come to feel that this system of performance measurement ignored the impact of some business decisions which could (or should) be taken by some of the operating managers in question.

After a thorough study of both the then-existing internal reporting system and a set of alternative systems, a new system was designed and introduced. "Full

---

*This translation loss would be caused by the fact that the dollar value of the original cruzeiro-denominated sale would exceed the dollar value of the actual cruzeiro-denominated collection of the account receivable some 90 days later.

**Exhibit 34.2**

**YEAR-END FOREIGN EXCHANGE RATES (PER U.S. DOLLAR)**

| Year | Brazilian Cruzeiro | Swiss Franc |
|------|--------------------|-------------|
| 1976 | 12.34 | 2.45 |
| 1977 | 16.05 | 2.00 |
| 1978 | 20.92 | 1.62 |
| 1979 | 42.53 | 1.58 |
| 1980 | 65.50 | 1.76 |
| 1981 | 127.80 | 1.80 |
| 1982 | 252.67 | 1.99 |

Source: *International Financial Statistics,* International Monetary Fund.

**CONSUMER PRICE INDEX NUMBERS AND YEARLY PERCENTAGE CHANGES**

| Year | Brazil | | Switzerland | | U. S. | |
|------|--------|------|-------------|------|-------|------|
| 1976 | 254.3 | | 147.3 | | 146.6 | |
| 1977 | 357.3 | 0.41 | 149.2 | 0.01 | 156.1 | 0.06 |
| 1978 | 494.2 | 0.38 | 150.8 | 0.01 | 167.9 | 0.08 |
| 1979 | 742.5 | 0.50 | 156.2 | 0.04 | 187.2 | 0.11 |
| 1980 | 1321.2 | 0.78 | 162.5 | 0.04 | 212.4 | 0.13 |
| 1981 | 2584.9 | 0.96 | 173.1 | 0.07 | 234.1 | 0.10 |
| 1982 | 6394.7[a] | 1.47 | 182.8 | 0.06 | 248.2 | 0.06 |

[a]Estimated.

Source: *Monthly Bulletin of Statistics,* United Nations, February 1983, p. 200.

responsibility accounting," as the new system was called, was made effective with the 1983 data. Under the terms of this new system, both individual product managers and product group managers were to be held responsible for the relationship between their profit-after-tax figures and the net assets under their control on both a worldwide and a major-country basis. The term *net assets* for a particular subunit of the overall corporation was defined as net property (gross property less accumulated depreciation) plus net working capital. Thus, both individual product managers and product group managers now bore some of the responsibility for such items as interest expense, translation gains and losses, and the amount and composition of both short- and long-term assets.

The new system was designed with the intention that it would, among other things, force top management to delegate expansion and curtailment decisions to lower levels. The individual product managers and their superiors (the product group managers), sometimes in conjunction with an (geographic) area manager, were to have total responsibility for the assets which they employed in the process of producing, distributing, and selling their particular product. The firm's capital budgeting and operational budgeting systems were to be altered such that the full year's capital expenditures would be approved at once and there would be agreement reached during the operational budgeting cycle as to the appropriate levels for inventories and receivables for the budget year in question.

Although the new system was very focused upon a return-on-assets figure, two other measures were to receive emphasis under the terms of the new program. Both net income and cash flow were to be measured and monitored. The former would be measured against a budgeted target and the latter would be assessed in respect to an understanding of the underlying strategy for the subunit. Thus a subunit with a growth strategy might be expected to generate little or no cash (or indeed, even use cash) over a short- to medium-term time period.

Of particular concern to product group managers, such as Paul McConnell, was the fact that they were now responsible for both translation gains and losses *and* interest expense, the latter of which could be very high in the case of local borrowing. Fortunately, the translation losses that were to be reported were to be highly specific in nature. That is, they were to be directly traced to specific items on the local subsidiary balance sheets and thus would be tied to items directly related to the pharmaceutical group's products. Interest expense and translation gains, on the other hand, were not easily identified with such specific items. This lack of easy identification was caused by the fact that the corporate treasurer would sum all of the Brazilian borrowings and then allocate both translation gains and interest expense to each product group based on a formula tied primarily to sales.

**COMPETI-TION**

MB had been able to successfully position Levadol such that a significant amount of the population asked for Levadol when they wanted an aspirin-free pain reliever. This had become an important issue as the product became more widely stocked by the various grocery chains and cooperatives (with their open freestanding shelves). Every year MB sold a greater amount of Levadol through grocery stores than it had the year before. During 1982, it was estimated that 60 percent of the retail sales of all aspirin-free pain relievers in Brazil took place in grocery stores, and the remaining 40 percent were sold through some type of drug-related outlet.

During 1982, MB lost both volume and market share on Levadol. Over 36,000 cases of Levadol were sold in 1980. Less than 32,000 were sold in 1982 (see Exhibit 34.3 for volume and market share data). Although it was considered a premium product, an increasing number of distributors were reacting to the recession by substituting lower-cost products.

MB's primary competition during 1982 was the Swiss firm Hoffman et Cie, which sold a similar, but not identical, product. Hoffman's product was priced slightly lower than Levadol. The Swiss franc (in relation to the cruzeiro) had not revalued as fast as the U.S. dollar over the most recent two-year period (see Exhibit 34.2). Thus, the apparent incentive for Hoffman to raise its price to cover a translation loss was not as great as MB's. Also, Hoffman had been known to be somewhat more concerned with market share than with short-term reported profit.

**Exhibit 34.3** Aspirin-free Pain Relievers
(percentage of market share by major competitors)

| Year | MB | Hoffman | Generic | All Other | Total Volume (thousands of cases) |
|------|------|---------|---------|-----------|-----------------------------------|
| 1977 | 3 | 7 | 31 | 59 | 125 |
| 1978 | 8 | 12 | 25 | 55 | 152 |
| 1979 | 9 | 17 | 21 | 53 | 202 |
| 1980 | 15 | 25 | 17 | 43 | 240 |
| 1981 | 13 | 32 | 13 | 42 | 287 |
| 1982 | 10 | 32 | 15 | 43 | 320 |

**Exhibit 34.4** Average Wholesale Price of
Aspirin-free Pain Relievers
(U.S. dollars per case)

| Year | MB | Hoffman | Generic |
|------|-------|---------|---------|
| 1980 | $ 182 | $ 180 | $ 172 |
| 1981 | 201 | 198 | 187 |
| 1982 | 218 | 212 | 200 |

Other reasons for Hoffman's strength had to do with the company's size in Brazil. In addition to having a large percentage of the pharmaceutical market, it also had a very large share of the market in agricultural chemicals. Its field sales force was about three to four times the size of MB's. Also, Hoffman gave somewhat longer payment terms. Hoffman's management apparently felt that they could squeeze the profit margin in pharmaceuticals a bit because of their strong position and high profits with agricultural chemicals.

In addition to Hoffman and other foreign-based firms, two local producers sold a generic substitute. The raw materials for the generic product were sourced in Brazil. The local patent covering this product had already expired. One result of this was that the industry was currently afflicted with an overcapacity of manufacturing facilities for products such as generic-brand pain relievers. The price of the generic aspirin-free pain reliever had risen 16 percent in the past two years. On the other hand, the price of Levadol had risen 20 percent, making the price difference $18 per case (see Exhibit 34.4).

## CONCLUSION

"My greatest fear at this moment in Brazil is that we're being finessed by firms with a better knowledge of international business. Levadol should not be losing market share to Hoffman," said Paul McConnell. "I could understand some loss of market to the locals, but even there we should be able to sell the customer on our product superiority. Hoffman has a premium product. But it's not as good as ours."

# Section D   Social Responsibility

# 35   Union Carbide of India, Ltd. (1985)

Arthur Sharplin
Northeast Louisiana University

December 2, 1984, began as a typical day in the central Indian city of Bhopal. Shoppers moved about the bustling open-air market. Here and there a customer haggled with a merchant. Beasts of burden, donkeys and oxen, pulled carts or carried ungainly bundles through the partly paved streets. Children played in the dirt. In the shadow of a Union Carbide pesticide plant, tens of thousands of India's poorest citizens milled about the shanty town they called home. A few miles away, wealthy Indians lived in opulence rivaling that of the first-class districts of London or Paris. Inside the plant, several hundred Indian workers and managers went about their duties, maintaining and operating the systems which produced the mildly toxic pesticide Sevin. Most of the plant was shut down for maintenance and it was operating at far below capacity.

At about 11 o'clock that evening, one of the operators noticed that the pressure in a methyl isocyanate (MIC) storage tank read 10 pounds per square inch—four times normal. The operator was not concerned, thinking that the tank may have been pressurized with nitrogen by the previous shift. Around midnight several of the workers noticed that their eyes had begun to water and sting, a signal experience had taught them indicated an MIC leak. The leak, a small but continuous drip, was soon spotted. The operators were still not alarmed because minor leaks at the plant were quite common. It was time for tea and most of the crew retired to the company canteen, resolving to correct the problem afterwards.

By the time the workers returned it was too late. The MIC tank pressure gauge was pegged. The leak had grown much larger and the entire area of the MIC tanks was enveloped in the choking fumes. The workers tried spraying water on the leak to break down the MIC. They sounded the alarm siren and summoned the fire

The research assistance of Aseem Shukla is gratefully acknowledged.

brigade. As the futility of their efforts became apparent, many of the workers panicked and ran upwind—some scaling the chain-link and barbed-wire fence in their frantic race for survival.

By one o'clock, only a supervisor remained in the area. He stayed upwind, donning his oxygen breathing apparatus every few minutes to check the various gauges and sensors. By that time the pressure in the MIC tank had forced open a relief valve and the untreated MIC vapor could be seen escaping from an atmospheric vent line 120 feet in the air.

The cloud of deadly white gas was carried by a southeasterly wind toward the Jai Prakash Nagar shanties. The cold temperature of the December night caused the MIC to settle towards the ground (in the daytime, or in the summer, convection currents probably would have raised and diluted the MIC).

As the gaseous tentacles reached into the huts there was panic and confusion. Many of the weak and elderly died where they lay. Some who made it into the streets were blinded. "It was like breathing fire," one survivor said. As word of the gas leak spread, many of Bhopal's affluent were able to flee in their cars. But most of the poor were left behind. When the gas reached the railroad station, supervisors who were not immediately disabled sent out word along the tracks and incoming trains were diverted. This cut off a possible means of escape but may have saved hundreds of lives. Because the whole station was quickly enveloped in gas, arriving trains would have been death traps for passengers and crews.

Of Bhopal's total population of about 1 million, an estimated 500,000 fled that night, most on foot. The surrounding towns were woefully unprepared to accept the gasping and dying mass of people. Thousands waited outside hospitals for medical care. There was no certainty about how to treat the gas victims and general-purpose medical supplies were in hopelessly short supply. Inside the hospitals and out, screams and sobs filled the air. Food supplies were quickly exhausted. People were even afraid to drink the water, not knowing if it was contaminated.

During the second day, relief measures were better organized. Several hundred doctors and nurses from nearby hospitals were summoned to help medical personnel in Bhopal. Just disposing of the dead was a major problem. Mass cremation was necessary. Islamic victims, whose faith allows burial rather than cremation, were piled several deep in hurriedly dug graves. Bloated carcasses of cattle and dogs littered the city. There was fear of a cholera epidemic. Bhopal's mayor said, "I can say that I have seen chemical warfare. Everything so quiet. Goats, cats, whole families—father, mother, children—all lying silent and still. And every structure totally intact. I hope never again to see it."

By the third day, the city had begun to move toward stability, if not normalcy. The Union Carbide plant had been closed and locked. A decision was made to consume the 30 tons of MIC that remained by using it to make pesticide. Most of the 2000 dead bodies had been disposed of, however inappropriately. The more than 100,000 injured were being treated as rapidly as the limited medical facilities would allow, although many simply sat in silence, blinded and maimed by an enemy they had never known well enough to fear. For them, doctors predict an increased risk of sterility, kidney and liver infections, tuberculosis, vision problems, and brain damage. The potential for birth defects and other long-term effects is not clear. However, months after the incident newspapers reported a high incidence of stillbirths and congenital deformities among the population which was affected by the gas.

**COMPANY BACK-GROUND**

The Ever-Ready Company, Ltd. (of Great Britain), began manufacturing flashlight batteries in Calcutta in 1926. The division was incorporated as the Ever-Ready Company (India), Ltd. in 1934 and became a subsidiary of Union Carbide Corporation of New York. The name of the Indian company was changed to National Carbide Company (India), Ltd., in 1949 and to Union Carbide (India), Ltd. (UCIL), in 1959. The 1926 capacity of 40 million dry-cell batteries per year was expanded to 767 million by the 1960s. In 1959, a factory was set up in India to manufacture the flashlights themselves.

By the 1980s, UCIL was involved in five product areas: batteries, carbon and metals, plastics, marine products, and agricultural chemicals. Exhibit 35.1 provides production statistics for UCIL products. The company eventually operated 14 plants at 8 locations, including the headquarters operation in Calcutta. Union

**Exhibit 35.1** Production Statistics

| Class of Goods | 1983 Capacity | Production Levels | | | | | |
|---|---|---|---|---|---|---|---|
| | | 1983 | 1982 | 1981 | 1980 | 1979 | 1978 |
| Batteries (millions of pieces) | 792 | 510.4 | 512.2 | 411.3 | 458.8 | 460.3 | 430.3 |
| Flashlight cases (millions of pieces) | 7.5 | 6.7 | 6.7 | 7.4 | 6.9 | 6.4 | 5.7 |
| Arc carbons (millions of pieces) | 9.0 | 7.5 | 7.0 | 7.0 | 6.7 | 6.2 | 6.1 |
| Industrial carbon electrodes and shapes (millions of pieces) | 2.5 | 0.5 | 0.5 | 0.5 | 0.3 | 0.5 | 0.2 |
| Photoengravers' plates/strips for printing (tonnes)[a] | 1,200 | 412.0 | 478.0 | 431.0 | 399.0 | 469.0 | 506.0 |
| Stellite castings, head facings, and tube rods (tonnes) | 150 | 17.5 | 12.7 | 16.4 | 14.5 | 15.8 | 18.2 |
| Electrolytic manganese dioxide (tonnes) | 4,500 | 3,335 | 3,085 | 3,000 | 2,803 | 2,605 | 2,700 |
| Chemicals (tonnes) | 13,600 | 7,349 | 6,331 | 6,865 | 7,550 | 8,511 | 8,069 |
| Polyethylene (tonnes) | 20,000 | 18,144 | 17,290 | 19,928 | 19,198 | 16,324 | 12,059 |
| MIC-based pesticides (tonnes) | 5,000 | 1,647 | 2,308 | 2,704 | 1,542 | 1,496 | 367 |
| Marine products (tonnes) | 5,500 | 424 | 649 | 642 | 601 | 648 | 731 |

[a]One tonne = 1000 kilograms = 2214 pounds. One British long ton = 2240 pounds. One U.S. ton = 2000 pounds.

*Source:* The Stock Exchange Foundation, Bombay, India, *The Stock Exchange Official Directory*, vol. XVII/29, July 18, 1983.

Carbide's petrochemical complex, established in Bombay in 1966, was India's first.

UCIL began its marine products operation with two shrimping ships in 1971. The business is completely export-oriented and employs 15 deep-sea trawlers. Processing facilities are located off the east and west coasts of India. The trawlers now harvest deep-sea lobsters in addition to shrimp.

In 1979, UCIL initiated a letter of intent to manufacture dry-cell batteries in Nepal. A 77.5 percent-owned subsidiary was set up in Nepal in 1982 and construction of a Rs18-million plant was begun.

The agricultural products division of UCIL was started in 1966 with only an office in Bombay. Agreement was reached with the Indian government in 1969 to set up a pesticide plant at Bhopal. Land was rented to UCIL for about $40 per acre per year. The initial investment was small, only $1 million, and the process was simple. Concentrated Sevin powder was imported from the United States, diluted with nontoxic powder, packaged, and sold. Under the technology transfer provisions of its agreement with UCIL, Union Carbide Corporation (USA) was obligated to share its more advanced technologies with UCIL. Eventually the investment at Bhopal grew to exceed $25 million and the constituents of Sevin were made there. Another Union Carbide insecticide, called Temik, was made in small quantities at Bhopal.

UCIL's assets grew from Rs558 million in 1974 to Rs1234 million in 1983 (the conversion rate stayed near 9 rupees to the dollar during this period, moving to about 12.50 as the dollar strengthened worldwide during 1984 and 1985). The *Economic Times* of India ranks UCIL number 21 in terms of sales among Indian companies. Union Carbide Corporation (USA) owns 50.9 percent of UCIL's stock and Indian citizens and companies own the remainder. When Indira Gandhi was voted out of office in 1977, the Janata (Peoples') Party strengthened the Foreign Exchange Regulation Act (FERA) (see Exhibit 35.2). As a result, IBM and Coca-Cola pulled out of India. IBM's business in India was taken over by ICIM (International Computers Indian Manufacturers), a domestic firm. Another similar firm performs the maintenance services for the existing IBM computers.

Since 1967 the chairman of the board of UCIL has been an Indian and foreign membership on the 11-member board of directors has been limited to four. One expert on Indian industry affairs said, "Though the foreigners on the board are down to four from six in previous years, they continue to hold sway over the affairs of the company." Major capital expenditures by UCIL were required to be approved by Union Carbide Corporation. Also, the Bhopal plant submitted monthly reports to U.S. corporate headquarters detailing operations and safety procedures. And inspections of the plant were carried out from time to time by Union Carbide technical specialists.

## OPERATIONS AT BHOPAL

On the surface, the UCIL insecticide factory is a typical process plant. A wide diversity of storage tanks, hoppers, and reactors are connected by pipes. There are many pumps and valves and a number of tall vent lines and ducts. Ponds and

**Exhibit 35.2** The Foreign Exchange Regulation Act

The act was originally enacted as a temporary measure in 1947 and made permanent in 1957. It was revised and redrafted in 1973. It covers various aspects of foreign exchange transactions, including money changing, buying or selling foreign exchange in India or abroad, having an account in a bank outside India, and remitting money abroad.

The purpose of the act is to restrict outflow of foreign exchange and to conserve hard-currency holdings in India. One requirement of the act is that any company in which the nonresident interest is more than 40 percent "shall not carry on in India or establish in India any branch or office without the special permission of the Reserve Bank of India." But the Reserve Bank of India has authority to exempt a company from the provisions of the act. The 40 percent requirement was changed to 49 percent by Rajiv Gandhi's government.

High-technology companies are frequently exempted from the equity ownership provisions of the act. Other companies which have operated in India for many years are sometimes exempted if they agree not to expand their Indian operations.

Policies in India regarding nationalization of foreign-owned companies have varied. A number of major oil companies have been nationalized. For example, Indian Oil Corporation, Bharat Petroleum, and Hindustan Petroleum used to be, respectively, Burmah Shell, Mobil, and Stanvae (Standard Vacuum Oil Company, an Esso unit). More typically, a multinational company is asked to reduce its holdings to 49 percent or less by offering shares to the Indian public and Indian financial institutions. Multinationals which have diluted equity to meet the 49 percent requirement include CIBA-GEIGY, Parke-Davis, Bayer (aspirin), Lever Brothers (which operates as Hindustan Lever in India), Lipton, and Brooke-Bond.

pits are used for waste treatment and several railway spur lines run through the plant. Exhibit 35.3 is a diagram of the factory and Exhibit 35.4 is a schematic of the MIC process. The plant was designed and supplied by Union Carbide Corporation, which sent engineers to India to supervise construction.

Sevin is made through a controlled chemical reaction involving alpha-naphthol and MIC. Alpha-naphthol is a brownish granular material and MIC is a highly reactive liquid which boils and becomes a gas at usual daytime temperatures. When plans were first made to begin production of alpha-naphthol at Bhopal in 1971, a pilot plant was set up to manufacture the product. Because the pilot plant was successful, a full-size alpha-naphthol plant (in fact, the world's largest) was constructed and placed in operation in 1977.

In the meantime, work had begun on the ill-fated MIC plant. But even before the MIC plant was completed in 1979, problems began to crop up with the alpha-naphthol plant, resulting in a shutdown for modifications in 1978. In February 1980, the MIC plant was placed into service. The alpha-naphthol plant continued in various stages of shutdown and partial operation through 1984. Mr. V. P. Gokhale, managing director of UCIL, called the alpha-naphthol plant a "very large mistake." But he said the company was forced to build it to keep its operating license from the Indian government. The Bhopal factory was designed to produce 5000 tons per year of Sevin but never operated near capacity. UCIL has generally been the third largest producer of pesticides in India, sometimes slipping to number four.

**Exhibit 35.3** The Union Carbide Pesticide Factory in Bhopal

The Union Carbide pesticide factory in Bhopal is a collection of buildings and equipment on 80 acres at the edge of Bhopal's old city. At the heart of the factory is the plant that makes methyl isocyanate, or MIC, which is used to make all the pesticides produced there. There are three key areas in the MIC plant: the production facility, the control room, and the area housing the three storage tanks—nos. 610, 611, and 619. The MIC in tank no. 610 leaked on December 3, killing more than 2000 people and injuring 200,000 others in the worst industrial accident in history.

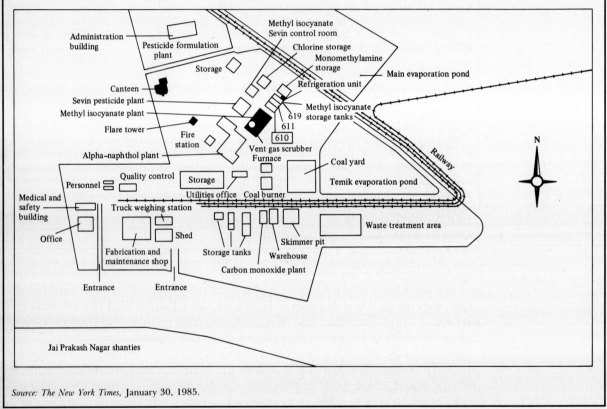

*Source: The New York Times,* January 30, 1985.

**FINANCE** Exhibits 35.5, 35.6, 35.7, and 35.8 provide financial facts and figures for UCIL. As mentioned earlier, Union Carbide Corporation (USA) holds 50.9 percent of UCIL's common shares. The remainder are publicly traded on major Indian stock exchanges. Most of these shares are held by about 24,000 individuals. However, a number of institutional investors own substantial blocks. The Indian government does not directly own any UCIL stock, although the Life Insurance Corporation of India, the country's largest insuror and owner of many UCIL shares, is owned by the Indian Government. During the months before the Bhopal disaster, UCIL's common shares hovered around Rs30, but dropped to a low of Rs15.8 on December 11, recovering only slightly in succeeding weeks.

In 1975, the United States Export-Import bank in cooperation with First National Citibank of New York agreed to grant loans of $2.5 million to buy equip-

**Exhibit 35.4** The MIC Manufacturing Process

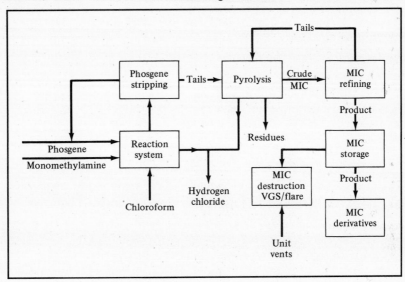

**Exhibit 35.5** Summary of Income Statements (Rs000, except per share data)

|  | 1983 | 1982 | 1981 | 1980 | 1979 |
|---|---|---|---|---|---|
| Net sales | 2,100,682 | 2,075,282 | 1,854,214 | 1,615,926 | 1,449,664 |
| Cost of goods sold | 1,733,999 | 1,720,303 | 1,518,538 | 1,307,042 | 1,190,242 |
| Operating expenses | 138,509 | 136,834 | 115,550 | 103,318 | 83,501 |
| Profit from operations | 228,174 | 218,145 | 220,126 | 205,566 | 175,921 |
| Other income | 24,684 | 27,426 | 26,955 | 23,528 | 13,685 |
| Profit from operations plus other income | 252,858 | 245,571 | 247,081 | 229,094 | 189,606 |
| Interest expense | 57,529 | 57,082 | 30,950 | 31,468 | 19,871 |
| Depreciation expense | 47,579 | 41,614 | 40,913 | 36,524 | 32,016 |
| Earnings before taxes | 147,750 | 146,875 | 175,218 | 161,102 | 137,719 |
| Provisions for taxes | 54,520 | 50,200 | 80,300 | 80,000 | 73,000 |
| Net earnings | 93,230 | 96,675 | 94,918 | 81,102 | 64,719 |
| Earnings per share | 2.86 | 2.95 | 2.91 | 2.49 | 2.98 |
| Earnings as % of price | 11.31 | 11.73 | 10.96 | 10.20 | 11.46 |
| Cash dividends per share | 1.50 | 1.50 | 1.50 | 1.40 | 1.60 |

*Note:* The conversion rate was fairly stable from 1978 to 1982 at about $1 = Rs9.00. From 1983 to 1985 the rupee weakened steadily. In mid-1985, the conversion rate was about $1 = Rs12.50. Within the country, inflation from 1978 to 1984 proceeded at rates of about 2 percentage points below the corresponding U.S. rates.

Average conversion rate for 1978–1982, $1 = Rs9.00; for 1985, $1 = Rs12.50.

ment for the MIC project. Also, the Industrial Credit and Investment Corporation of India (ICICI) authorized a Rs21.5 million loan, part of which was drawn in 1980. Finally, long-term loans were provided by several Indian financial institutions and insurance companies. Some of these loans were guaranteed by the State Bank of India.

**Exhibit 35.6** Summary of Balance Sheets (December 25, respective years, Rs000)

|  | 1983[a] | 1982 | 1981 | 1980 | 1979 |
|---|---|---|---|---|---|
| **Assets** | | | | | |
| Current assets | | | | | |
|   Cash | 58,234 | 52,285 | 52,173 | 56,589 | 53,026 |
|   Receivables | 410,000 | 375,672 | 244,158 | 169,015 | 121,718 |
|   Inventories | 369,172 | 327,317 | 368,606 | 311,612 | 292,935 |
|   Other current assets | 6,000 | 6,088 | 9,230 | 9,277 | 11,237 |
|     Total current assets | 843,406 | 761,362 | 674,167 | 546,493 | 478,916 |
| Net fixed assets | 465,806 | 449,546 | 393,516 | 405,890 | 401,422 |
| Miscellaneous assets | 21 | 21 | 21 | 57 | 57 |
|   Intangible assets | 3,000 | 3,000 | 3,000 | 3,000 | 3,000 |
|     Total assets | 1,312,233 | 1,213,929 | 1,070,704 | 955,440 | 883,395 |
| **Liabilities & owners' equity** | | | | | |
| Current liabilities | | | | | |
|   Accounts payable & accruals | 590,667 | 530,641 | 390,990 | 341,956 | 320,942 |
|   Provision for taxes | 51,839 | 57,739 | 63,266 | 60,216 | 49,000 |
|     Total current debt | 642,506 | 588,380 | 454,256 | 402,172 | 369,942 |
| Long-term liabilities | | | | | |
|   Debentures | 30,000 | 29,340 | 54,823 | 31,315 | 20,300 |
|   Long-term loans | 20,000 | 20,836 | 34,049 | 40,420 | 46,306 |
|     Total long-term debt | 50,000 | 50,176 | 88,872 | 71,735 | 66,606 |
| Stockholders' equity | | | | | |
|   Common stock | 325,830 | 325,830 | 325,830 | 325,830 | 217,220 |
|   Retained earnings & surplus | 293,897 | 249,543 | 201,746 | 155,703 | 229,627 |
|     Total owners' Equity | 619,727 | 575,373 | 527,576 | 481,533 | 446,847 |
|     Total liabilities & owners' equity | | 1,213,929 | 1,070,704 | 955,440 | 883,395 |

[a]Due to an apparent change in accounting procedure, some 1983 amounts could not be determined from available reports and have been estimated.

Profits of several million dollars from the Bhopal facility were originally predicted for 1984. Several factors kept these expectations from being realized. First, an economic recession made farmers more cost-conscious and caused them to search for less-expensive alternatives to Sevin. Second, a large number of small-scale producers were able to undersell the company, partly because they were exempt from excise and sales taxes. Seventeen of these firms bought MIC from UCIL and used it to make products virtually identical to Sevin and Temik. Finally, a new generation of low-cost pesticides was becoming available. With sales collapsing, the Bhopal plant became a money loser in 1981. By late 1984, the profit estimate for that year had been adjusted downward to a $4 million *loss* on the basis of 1000 tons of output, one-fifth of capacity.

To forestall what may have seemed inevitable economic failure, extensive cost-cutting efforts were carried out. The staff at the MIC plant was cut from

**Exhibit 35.7** Summary of Common Stock Issues

| | Paid-up Common Stock | | | |
|---|---|---|---|---|
| Year | # of Shares | Paid up per Share (Rs) | Total Amount (Rs) | Remarks |
| 1959–1960 | 2,800,000 | 10 | 28,000,000 | 800,000 right shares issued premium Rs2.50 per share in the proportion 2:5. |
| 1964 | 3,640,000 | 10 | 36,400,000 | 840,000 right shares issued at a premium of Rs4 per share in the proportion 3:10. |
| 1965 | 4,095,000 | 10 | 40,950,000 | 455,000 bonus shares issued in the proportion 1:8. |
| 1968 | 8,190,000 | 10 | 81,900,000 | 2,047,500 right shares issued at par in the proportion 1:2. 2,047,500 bonus shares issued in the proportion 1:2. |
| 1970 | 12,285,000 | 10 | 122,850,000 | 4,095,000 bonus shares issued in the proportion 1:2. |
| 1974 | 18,427,500 | 10 | 184,275,000 | 6,142,500 bonus shares issued in the proportion 1:2. |
| 1978 | 21,722,000 | 10 | 217,220,000 | 3,294,500 shares issued at a premium of Rs6 per share to resident Indian shareholders, the company's employees, and financial institutions. |
| 1980 | 32,583,000 | 10 | 325,830,000 | 10,861,000 bonus shares issued in the proportion 1:2. |

twelve operators on a shift to six. The maintenance team was reduced in size. In a number of instances, faulty safety devices remained unrepaired for weeks. Because a refrigeration unit that was designed to keep the methyl isocyanate cool continued to malfunction, it was shut down. Though instrumentation technology advanced at Union Carbide's other pesticide plants, the innovations were only partly adopted at Bhopal.

# PERSONNEL

Until 1982, a cadre of American managers and technicians worked at the Bhopal plant. The Americans were licensed by the Indian government only for fixed periods. While in India they were expected to train Indian replacements. From

**Exhibit 35.8** Union Carbide of India, Ltd., Financial Charts

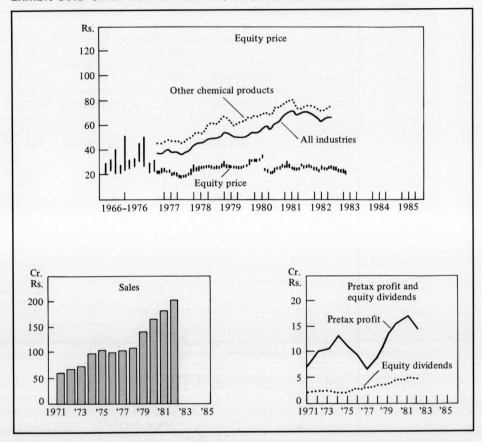

1982 onward, no American worked at Bhopal. Although major decisions such as approval of the annual budget were cleared with Union Carbide (USA), day-to-day details such as staffing and maintenance were left to the Indian officials.

In general, the engineers at the Bhopal plant were among India's elite. Most new engineers were recruited from the prestigious Indian Institutes of Technology and paid wages comparable with the best offered in Indian industry. Successful applicants for engineering jobs with UCIL were provided two years of training before being certified for unsupervised duty.

Until the late seventies, only first-class science graduates or persons with diplomas in engineering were employed as operators at Bhopal. New hires were given six months of theoretical instruction followed by on-the-job training. As cost-cutting efforts proceeded in the eighties, standards were lowered significantly. Some operators with only a high school diploma were employed and training was much less rigorous than before. In addition, the number of operators on a shift was reduced by about half and many supervisory positions were eliminated.

The Indian managers developed strong ties with the local political establishment. A former police chief became the plant's security contractor and a local political party boss got the job as company lawyer. *Newsweek* reports that a luxurious guest house was maintained and lavish parties thrown there for local dignitaries.

In general, wages at the Bhopal plant were well above those available in domestic firms. A janitor, for example, earned Rs1000 per month compared to less than Rs500 elsewhere. Still, as prospects continued downward after 1981, a number of senior managers and the best among the plant's junior executives began to abandon ship. The total work force at the plant dropped from a high of about 1500 to 950. This reduction was accomplished through voluntary departures rather than layoffs. An Indian familiar with operations at Bhopal said, "The really competent and well trained employees, especially managers and supervisors, got sick of the falling standards and indifferent management and many of them quit despite high salaries at UCIL. Replacements were made on an ad hoc basis. Even guys from the consumer products division, who only knew how to make batteries, were drafted to run the pesticide plant."

## MARKETING

The population of India is over 700 million persons, but its land area is only about one-third that of the United States. Three-fourths of India's people depend on agriculture for a livelihood. Fewer than one-third are literate. Modern communications and transportation facilities connect the major cities, but the hundreds of villages are largely untouched by twentieth-century technology. English tends to be at least a second language for most Indian professionals but not for ordinary Indians. There are 16 officially recognized languages in the country. The national language is Hindi, which is dominant in five of India's 22 states. The working classes speak hundreds of dialects, often unintelligible to citizens just miles away.

India's farmers offer at best a challenging target market. They generally eke out a living from small tracts of land. Most have little more than subsistence incomes and are reluctant to invest what they have in such modern innovations as pesticides. They are generally ignorant of the right methods of application and, given their linguistic diversity and technological isolation, are quite hard to educate. To advertise its products, UCIL has used billboards and wall posters as well as newspaper and radio.

Radio is the most widely used advertising medium in India. The state-owned radio system includes broadcasts in local languages. Companies can buy advertising time on the stations, but it is costly to produce commercials in so many dialects. Much of the state-sponsored programming, especially in rural areas, is devoted to promoting agriculture and instructing farmers about new techniques. Often the narrators mention products such as Sevin and Temik by name.

Movies provide another popular promotional tool. Most small towns have one or more cinema houses and rural people often travel to town to watch the shows. Advertisements appear before and after main features and are usually produced in regional languages (though not in local dialects).

**Exhibit 35.9** India

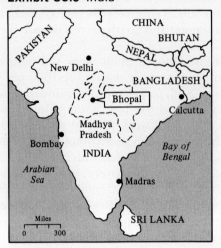

Until recently, television was available only in the cities. During 1984, a government program spread TV relay stations at the rate of more than one each day, with the result that 80 percent of the population was within the range of a television transmitter by the end of the year. Still, few rural citizens had access to television receivers.

Pesticide sales are highly dependent on agricultural activity from year to year. In years of drought, like 1980 and 1982, UCIL's pesticide sales have suffered severe setbacks. In 1981, abundant rains helped spur pesticide sales.

Exhibit 35.9 is a map of India. India has a very extensive network of railways. The total track mileage in India is second only to the USSR. The road and highway system crisscrosses the areas between railway lines. The railway system was especially significant to UCIL's pesticide operation because Bhopal lies near the junction of the main east-west and north-south tracks in India. Bhopal is also just south of the vast Indo-Gangetic plain, the richest farming area in India. An Indian familiar with the agricultural economy remarked, "Overall, physical distribution of pesticides is not too monumental a task. Getting farmers to use them and teaching them how are the real problems."

The marketing division for agricultural products was headquartered in Hyderabad. Under the headquarters were eight branch offices scattered all over the country. Sales were through a network of distributors, wholesalers, and retailers. Sales representatives from the branch offices booked orders from the distributors and wholesalers. Retailers got their requirements from wholesalers, who, in turn, were supplied by distributors. The distributors got their stocks from the branch offices. The branch office "godowns" (warehouses) were supplied directly from the Bhopal plant. The retailers' margin was 15 percent. Wholesalers and distributors each received about 5 percent. Most of the retailers were individually or family-owned, although some of UCIL's pesticides were sold through government agricultural sales offices.

**EVENTS OF 1985**

In early 1985, the government of India canceled the operating license of the Bhopal plant, clearing the way for the plant's dismantlement. The likelihood that this would happen provoked a Bhopal political leader to remark, "We've lost 2,000 lives, now must we lose 2,000 jobs?"

Manslaughter and other charges were filed against UCIL executives. Union Carbide Corporation chairman Warren Anderson had been briefly detained by Indian officials when he went to India shortly after the incident. Still, both companies continued for months to enjoy good relations with the Indian government. This may have been true in part because many leading Indian citizens and institutions have a financial interest in UCIL. And, except for the Bhopal incident, Union Carbide had an excellent safety record in India.

Warren Anderson said, "The name of the game is not to nail me to the wall but to provide for the victims of the disaster." He said he expected to be mainly concerned with the incident for the rest of his working life. In keeping with these ideas, Union Carbide Corporation helped provide funding for a hospital to treat the Bhopal victims. The company also contributed at least $2 million to a victims' relief fund and offered to build a new plant, one that would use nontoxic inputs, on the Bhopal site.

Within months after the incident, Union Carbide (USA) faced lawsuits in amounts far exceeding the company's net worth. That company's stock dropped from its mid-fifties trading range to the low thirties. A dozen or more American attorneys signed up thousands of Bhopal victims and relatives of victims and filed suits in America purporting to represent them. The attorney general of India was authorized to sue Union Carbide in an American court. He stated that compensation had to be in accordance with American standards. A Minneapolis law firm which specializes in product liability cases was retained to represent India.

By March 1985, the streets of Bhopal were bustling again. There were cars, cattle, and crowds of people. But everywhere there were reminders of the disaster. Many wore dark glasses and covered their faces with shrouds to protect their injured eyes from the sunlight or to keep others from seeing their blindness. At the city's main police station, women and children continued to seek help. Vegetables shriveled by the poison gas were putting forth green shoots here and there. Occasionally, someone still fell sick from eating fish contaminated by MIC.

In the modern masonry-and-glass headquarters in Danbury, Connecticut, Union Carbide officials looked out on the beautiful Connecticut countryside and wondered how best to manage the company's public affairs and how to grapple with the needs in India. Half a world away, in spatial as well as philosophical distance, the poor of Jai Prakash Nagar, now poorer than ever, peered out from their shanties on dusty streets and pondered quite different questions: From where would tomorrow's food come? How long would the pain inside and the dimming of vision last? And, just as importantly, what source of wealth would replace the pesticide plant? And how long would it be before its effects were felt?

In late June 1985, a lawsuit consolidating about 100 claims was filed in the United States by famed attorney F. Lee Bailey and his associates. The Indian government continued to press its lawsuit and to engage in out of court negotiations with Union Carbide. As the lawsuits in America moved forward, the legal issues involved became clearer: (1) Should the cases be tried in U.S. courts or in Indian courts? Both legal systems are based on English common law, but punitive damages are almost unheard of in Indian courts and compensatory damage awards are much lower than in America. (2) Should settlements be based on American standards simply because Union Carbide, the 51 percent parent of UCIL, is an American company, or on the much lower standards in India? (3) Who is responsible for the incident—Union Carbide, the Indian managers at Bhopal, the mostly Indian board of directors of UCIL, or the Indian government? (4) Which victims should be represented by the Indian government and which by the U.S. attorneys who went to India after the incident and signed up clients? (5) Did Union Carbide fail to properly warn the Indian managers at UCIL of the dangers posed by MIC? (6) Did Union Carbide fail to ensure that appropriate safety equipment was installed at the Bhopal facility?

Negotiations between Union Carbide and Asoke K. Sen, the Indian law minister, seemed to have broken down in June 1985. Union Carbide had made a $230 million offer, with payment to be spread over 20 years. Mr. Sen said the offer was worth only $100 million in current terms and continued, "Union Carbide's offer is based on a total lack of appreciation of the magnitude of the problem, so is hardly worth consideration." He said that doctors have treated 200,000 Indians injured by the gas leak and that the government is having to build 15,000 housing units and a 100-bed hospital to care for the most seriously ill.

On the other hand, a Union Carbide spokesperson said that $100 million could "pay the heirs of each dead person 100 years' annual income . . . and the seriously injured 20 years' annual income," leaving funds left over. The U.S. district judge under whom the Indian court cases were consolidated requested that Union Carbide pay $5 million in emergency aid, but that was rejected by the Indian officials. Mr. Sen said that India had already spent several times more than that on relief and that $5 million would not serve a critical need.

As Union Carbide (USA) struggled to recover from the disaster and restore its favorable public image, four events thrust the company back to the forefront of national and international news coverage. In June 1985, hundreds of persons were poisoned by California watermelons grown on soil to which the Union Carbide pesticide Temik had been improperly applied. In August a leak of the chemical intermediate aldecarb oxime at the company's Institute, West Virginia, plant, the only U.S. facility to make MIC, sent 135 people to hospitals. A few days later another accidental discharge of chemicals at a Union Carbide plant just miles from the Institute facility caused a public health scare. Finally, a group of investors headed by corporate takeover specialist Carl Icahn increased their holdings of Union Carbide stock and were rumored to be seeking control of the corporation. Even though West Virginia governor Arch Moore publicly criticized Union Carbide's handling of the aldecarb oxime leak and CEO Warren Anderson admitted that the company had waited too long to warn residents, Union Carbide stock moved above $50 a share for the first time since the Bhopal incident.

# 36  Manville Corporation

Arthur Sharplin
Northeast Louisiana University

Asbestos is an insidious poison. Microscopic fibers, as small as a human cell, cause progressive, irreversible, incurable disease. Asbestos causes scarring of the small airways and further scarring of the lung tissue itself, parenchymal asbestosis. Asbestos causes scarring, thickening and calcification of the lung linings, pleural asbestosis. Asbestos causes an always fatal cancer, mesothelioma, in the tissue surrounding the lungs. Asbestos causes lung cancer. Asbestosis causes an abnormally high level of lung infections which are unusually hard to treat.

For eight years in the boiler rooms of the USS Santa Fe, the USS Antietam and the USS Thomas F. Nickel, Ed Janssens used and repaired thermal insulation. He never knew he was planting a time-bomb deep within his lungs. Twenty years passed before he first felt its toxic effects. He was sick, but he didn't know why.

Ed Janssens has asbestosis. To be more specific, his asbestos exposure from 1943 through 1951 has caused thickening and calcification of the lining of his lungs, small airways disease, complication of his asthma, life-threatening lung infections, and a progressive decrease in lung function. He will require close medical surveillance forever. If Ed Janssens, an asbestotic, does not die sooner of cancer, mesothelioma or massive lung infection, the inexorable march of asbestosis will eventually block his blood flow, swell his heart and cause death by coronary pulmonale.

In 1981, 30 years after his last exposure to its asbestos, Ed Janssens brought Johns-Manville to trial. For ten years, his asbestosis has been stealing his breath, complicating his asthma, retarding treatment for lung infections, keeping him out of work, making him lonely and reclusive, causing him depression and frustration, reducing the length of his natural life, and keeping him from sleeping in even the same bedroom with his wife, Patsy, the mother of his eight children. For years, he had to sit up in a chair to get any sleep; now, under more effective medical care, he can sleep lying down—sometimes.

It was 1978 when Ed Janssens, 35 years too late, first learned of the asbestos hazard. Who knew the death-dealing hazards of the asbestos fibers? Johns-Manville knew. Who knew in 1929, when Ed Janssens was just five years old? Johns-Manville did. Who exercised editorial prerogative over Dr. A. J. Lanza's 1935 United States Public Health Service report entitled "Effects of Inhalation of Asbestos Dust on the Lungs of Asbestos Workers"? Johns-Manville did. And who rushed on Christmas Eve 1934, to make sure "additions, omissions or changes . . . beneficial from the industry viewpoint" would be included in Dr. Lanza's official report? Johns-Manville did.

When an asbestos manufacturer's health credo was "our interests are best served by having asbestosis receive the minimum of publicity," it is no surprise to learn that no hazard warning besmirched [Manville's] asbestos bags and boxes until 30 years after Dr. Lanza acceded to his benefactor's demands; and, even then, only because Dr. Irving Selikoff had "held the smoking gun aloft"—publicly in 1964 [ellipses omitted].—*Wayne Hogan, counsel for asbestos victims*

Ed and Patsy Janssens filed suit against Manville in 1979 and were eventually awarded $1,757,600 in compensatory and punitive damages. But Manville moved

915

for a judgment notwithstanding the verdict, then for a new trial, then for a return of part of the adjudged damages (none of which had been paid). When all of these motions were denied in December 1981, Manville initiated the formal appeal process. The appeal had not been heard—and Ed Janssens had not been paid—when the Manville board of directors met secretly on August 25, 1982 to decide whether to file for protection under Chapter 11 of the U.S. Bankruptcy Code.

Manville Corporation (Johns-Manville until 1981) is a diversified mining, timber, and manufacturing company. In 1982, the company employed about 30,000 people at more than 125 facilities (plants, mines, and sales offices), most in the United States. For many years, the company had been the world's largest producer of asbestos and asbestos-based products. In 1976, sales of asbestos fiber alone (mostly to manufacturers outside the United States) provided 52 percent of Manville's income from operations, although it constituted only about 11 percent of sales. In addition, asbestos was used by the company in making hundreds of products such as floor tile, textiles, filters, pipe, and roofing materials. Altogether, asbestos and asbestos products clearly accounted for more than one-half of Manville's sales and probably for three-fourths of operating profit. Exhibit 36.1 describes asbestos.

In 1957, the Industrial Health Foundation proposed a study on asbestos and cancer to be funded by the Asbestos Textile Institute (made up of asbestos manufacturers). The proposal was rejected by Manville and the others at the

**Exhibit 36.1** What Is Asbestos?

This is taken from the *Encyclopedia Britannica:*

> *Asbestos,* mineral fibre occurring in nature in fibrous form. It is obtained from certain types of asbestos rock, chiefly the chrysotile variety of the serpentine groups of minerals, by mining or quarrying. Valued since ancient times for its resistance to fire, asbestos fibre achieved commercial importance in the 19th century.
>
> The fibre is freed by crushing the rock and is then separated from the surrounding material, usually by a blowing process.

This is from an article by Bruce Porter in *Sunday Review of the Society:*

> Perhaps no other mineral is so woven into the fabric of American life as is asbestos. Impervious to heat and fibrous—it is the only mineral that can be woven into cloth—asbestos is spun into fireproof clothing and theater curtains, as well as into such household items as noncombustible drapes, rugs, pot holders, and ironing-board covers. Mixed into slurry, asbestos is sprayed onto girders and walls to provide new buildings with fireproof insulation. It is used in floor tiles, roofing felts, and in most plasterboards and wallboards. Asbestos is also an ingredient of plaster and stucco and of many paints and putties. This "mineral of a thousand uses"—an obsolete nickname: the present count stands at around 3,000 uses—is probably present in some form or other in every home, school, office building, and factory in this country. Used in brake linings and clutch facings, in mufflers and gaskets, in sealants and caulking, and extensively used in ships, asbestos is also a component of every modern vehicle, including space ships.

March 1957 meeting of the institute. The minutes report, "There is a feeling among certain members that such an investigation would stir up a hornets' nest and put the whole industry under suspicion."

In 1963, Dr. I. J. Selikoff of Mt. Sinai Medical Center in New York completed an extensive study of asbestos and health. Minutes of the Asbestos Textile Institute's Air Hygiene Committee meeting of June 6, 1963 includes the following: "The committee was advised that a Dr. Selikoff will read at the next meeting of the AMA in about 30 days a paper on a study he has made of about 1,500 workers, largely in asbestos insulation application, showing a very large incidence of lung cancer over normal expectations."

Dr. Selikoff's report and the symposia and publications which followed revealed, for the first time to those outside the industry, the magnitude and character of the asbestos problem: Thousands had already died of asbestos diseases and hundreds of thousands more would become disabled and die in the decades to follow. Breathing asbestos dust causes a progressive thickening and stiffening of lung tissue (asbestosis) and sometimes causes the always fatal asbestos cancer (mesothelioma), either of which diseases may disable the victim 20 to 40 years after exposure.

The dangers of ingesting asbestos fibers began to be widely publicized in the 1960s and 1970s. Beginning in 1978, there were hundreds of newspaper stories, magazine articles, and television documentaries relating to the problem. Health, Education and Welfare (HEW) Secretary Califano estimated that between 8.5 million and 11 million workers had been exposed to asbestos since World War II. In April 1978, HEW announced it was warning present and former asbestos workers and their doctors about the hazards of asbestos and the U.S. surgeon general sent 400,000 warning letters to the nation's doctors. In June, the Environmental Protection Agency established limits for airborne asbestos caused by building demolition. Then, in December, the Environmental Defense Fund claimed that millions of schoolchildren had been exposed to cancer-causing levels of asbestos because of use of the product in school construction.

## MANVILLE'S LEGAL DEFENSES WEAKEN

The dozens of asbestos injury lawsuits against Manville in the twenties and thirties, scores during the forties and fifties, and hundreds in the sixties and early seventies became thousands in the late seventies. Although the asbestos litigation was not mentioned in Manville's 1977 Annual Report, it was described, as the law required, in the company's 1977 Form 10K, submitted to the Securities and Exchange Commission in April 1978. The 10K reports 623 asbestos lawsuits against Manville, some of them multiplaintiff cases involving many claimants. The claims for which amounts are given total $2.79 billion.

For nearly 50 years, Manville had been able to hide the fact that company executives knew the dangers of breathing asbestos dust from about 1930 onward and suppressed research and publicity about asbestos diseases. But, in April 1978, plaintiffs in a South Carolina asbestos tort case obtained what have come to be called the "Raybestos-Manhattan papers." These documents consist of asbestos industry correspondence and reports from the 1930s and 1940s. Coupled with the publications of Selikoff and other researchers, the Raybestos-Manhattan papers made a compelling case. Exhibit 36.2 gives excerpts from a few of the papers.

In ordering a new trial, the South Carolina judge wrote,

> The Raybestos-Manhattan correspondence reveals written evidence that Raybestos-Manhattan and Johns-Manville exercised an editorial prerogative over the publication of the first study of the asbestos industry which they sponsored in 1935. It further reflects a conscious effort by the industry in the 1930s to downplay, or arguably suppress, the dissemination of information to employees and the public for fear of the promotion of law suits. . . .
>
> On two separate occasions, September 1977, pursuant to subpoena duces tecum, and December 1977, pursuant to a Request to Produce, plaintiff sought to discover the Raybestos correspondence in question. . . . It is uncontroverted that the same documents were produced in April 1977, in a New Jersey asbestos lawsuit. . . .
>
> It is also clear that the defendant, Johns-Manville, upon whom the December Request to Produce was also served, had in its possession since April 1977 the Raybestos correspondence, which also involved its corporate agents.

During the late seventies, asbestos plaintiff lawyers were able to obtain depositions from a number of retired Manville executives. Dr. Kenneth W. Smith (mentioned in Exhibit 36.2) had been Manville's physician and medical director from 1945 to 1966 (except for one year). In a 1976 deposition, Dr. Smith testified that he became "knowledgeable of the relationship between the inhalation of asbestos fibers and the lung condition known as asbestosis" during his internship in 1941–1942, before he went to work for Manville. Following are other excerpts from Dr. Smith's testimony:

Q. *Did you [tell other employees of Johns-Manville] of the relationship between the inhalation of asbestos fiber and the lung condition known as asbestosis?*

A. Many people at Canadian Johns-Manville in supervisory positions already knew about the association of inhalation of asbestos fibers and disease. I just amplified that [and] made much more explicit the disease process.

Q. *Did you or did you not have discussions with Mr. A. R. Fisher with respect to the relationship between the inhalation of asbestos fiber and the pulmonary lung condition known as asbestosis, both with respect to employees of Johns-Manville and what you defined as the civilian population? [Mr. Fisher had been involved in the asbestos litigation in the 1930s and was president in the 1950s and 1960s.]*

A. Definitely, we discussed the whole subject many times, about dust and what it does to people, whether they are employed or not employed. . . . The good Lord gave us all the same breathing apparatus and if the asbestos fiber is present and the housewife and the asbestos worker, and the fireman, and the jeweler, and doctor, and everybody else are all in the same room, they are all going to breath the same dust. . . . So wherever there is dust and people are breathing dust they are going to have a potential hazard.

Q. *Did you at any point . . . make any recommendations to anyone at Johns-Manville in respect to the utilization of a caution label for the asbestos-containing products?*

**Exhibit 36.2** Excerpts from the Raybestos-Manhattan Papers

From a December 15, 1934, letter by George Hobart, Manville's chief counsel, to Vandiver Brown, Manville's corporate secretary and legal vice-president:

> ...It is only within a comparatively recent time that asbestosis has been recognized by the medical and scientific professions as a disease—in fact, one of our principal defenses in actions against the company on the common law theory of negligence has been that the scientific and medical knowledge has been insufficient until a very recent period to place on the owners of plants or factories the burden or duty of taking special precautions against the possible onset of the disease in their employees.

From a 1935 letter to Sumner Simpson, president of Raybestos-Manhattan Corporation, by Anne Rossiter, the editor of *Asbestos,* an industry trade journal:

> You may recall that we have written you on several occasions concerning the publishing of information, or discussion of, asbestosis.... Always you have requested that for obvious reasons, we publish nothing, and, naturally your wishes have been respected.

From an October 3, 1935, letter by Vandiver Brown to Sumner Simpson, commenting on the Rossiter letter:

> I quite agree that our interests are best served by having asbestosis receive the minimum of publicity.

From a report by Dr. Kenneth Smith, Manville physician and medical director, on a 1949 study of 708 men who worked in a Manville asbestos mine (the report shows that only four of the 708 were free of lung damage and those four had less than four years' exposure to asbestos dust):

> Of the 708 men, seven had X-ray evidence of early asbestosis.... They have not been told of this diagnosis. For it is felt that as long as the man feels well, is happy at home and at work, and his physical condition remains good, nothing should be said.... The fibrosis of this disease is irreversible and permanent....
>
> There are seven cases of asbestosis and 52 cases in a "preasbestosis group." These 59 cases are probable compensation claims.... There are 475 men with [fibrosis extending beyond the lung roots] all of whom will show progressive fibrosis if allowed to continue working in dusty areas.

A. Hugh Jackson and I sat down with many people in other divisions suggesting that similar caution labels should be put on products which when used could create airborne dust that could be inhaled.

Q. *When did you sit down with Hugh Jackson and come to that conclusion?*

A. It would be late 1952 and early 1953.

Q. *What was the reason . . . the asbestos containing products were not labeled with a caution label back in 1952?*

A. It was business decision as far as I could understand . . . application of a caution label identifying a product as hazardous would cut out sales. There would be serious financial implications.

Q. *Did you at any time recognize the relationship between the inhalation of asbestos fibers and pulmonary malignancies, as you phrased it, or lung cancer, or pleural cancer?*

A. Yes, I have recognized the alleged and sometimes factual association of malignancy with the inhalation of asbestos fibers.

Q. *When would that have been, Doctor, for the first time?*
A. The first time would be in the late 1940s.
Q. *Had there not been studies in Britain and perhaps even in the United States prior to the beginning of the Saranac Lake Laboratories studies [1936] which had indicated [that fibrous asbestos dust caused lung disease]?*
A. Very definitely. As I recall, Merriweather and his cohorts studied the effects of the asbestos textile dust many years prior to 1935 and their publications are well-documented and available worldwide.

Dr. Smith died in 1977. In 1981, a Manville lawyer (appealing a $1.9 million damage award to asbestos victim Edward Janssens) argued that the Smith deposition should not have been admitted in court. The attorney said, "J-M made a conscious policy decision not to cross-examine Dr. Smith as fully as it otherwise would have. For example, Johns-Manville decided against examining Dr. Smith regarding the fact that he was an alcoholic and under psychiatric care."

Another Manville executive, Wilbur L. Ruff, who had worked for Manville from 1929 through 1972, much of the time as plant manager at a number of Manville plants, gave an extensive deposition in 1979. Excerpts follow:

Q. *Do you know whether, in fact, abnormal chest findings ever were discussed with any employee of the Johns-Manville plant? . . .*
A. I know of no specific cases.
Q. *Was there a policy at that time not to talk to the employees about chest findings, findings that suggested asbestosis, pneumoconiosis, or mesothelioma [asbestos cancer]?*
A. That was the policy.
Q. *When did the policy change?*
A. In the early 1970s.
Q. *Have you on other occasions, Mr. Ruff, referred to this policy that we have been discussing as a hush-hush policy?*
A. Yes.
Q. *Were you aware that it was company policy back in the late forties that if a man had asbestosis or industrial lung diseases that nothing would be said to him until he actually became disabled?*
A. That's the way it was done.
Q. *You were aware that was the company policy?*
A. Whether it was policy or not, it was somebody's decision.

In 1964, Manville placed the first caution labels on its asbestos products. The labels read,

This product contains asbestos fiber.
Inhalation of asbestos in excessive quantities over long periods of time may be harmful.
If dust is created when the product is handled, avoid breathing the dust.
If adequate ventilation control is not possible, wear respirators approved by the U.S. Bureau of Mines for pneumoconiosis-producing dust.

In upholding a landmark 1972 district court decision against Manville and other asbestos defendants, the New Orleans U.S. Court of Appeals stated,

Asbestosis has been recognized as a disease for well over fifty years. . . . By the mid-1930s the hazard of asbestos as a pneumoconiotic dust was universally accepted.

Cases of asbestosis in insulation workers were reported in this country as early as 1934.
. . . The evidence . . . tended to establish that none of the defendants ever tested its
product to determine its effect on industrial insulation workers. . . . Indeed the evidence
tended to establish that the defendants gave no instructions or warnings at all.

The court quoted Manville's caution label (above) and continued,

It should be noted that none of these so called "cautions" intimated the gravity of the
risk: the danger of a fatal illness caused by asbestosis and mesothelioma or other
cancers. The mild suggestion that inhalation of asbestos in excessive quantities over a
long period of time may be harmful conveys no idea of the extent of the danger.

## NEW DIRECTIONS FOR THE 1970S

In the 1960s, several of Manville's older directors had died or retired. Among
them were A. R. Fisher and E. M. Voorhees, senior Manville officials since before
1930. (Both Fisher and Voorhees were involved in the early asbestos lawsuits.
Also, Fisher was chief executive in the fifties and early sixties.) Compared to the
1966 board of directors, the 1969 board contained a majority of new members.
Departing from a tradition of promotion from within, in 1969 Manville brought
in an outsider, psychologist Richard Goodwin, to a top management position.
The next year, the board of directors voted to move longtime president C. B.
Burnett to chairman and install Goodwin as president and chief executive officer.
Goodwin led the company through at least 20 acquisitions and several divestitures, increasing the company's profit and sales but also increasing long-term
debt, from zero in 1970 to $196 million in 1975.

Goodwin arranged to purchase the 10,000-acre Ken-Caryl Ranch near Denver
in 1971, moved the company there from New York, and made plans to build a
luxurious world headquarters. The first phase of the project was to cost $182.2
million, 45 percent of Manville's net worth. The magazine *Industrial Development*
called the Manville plan "a study in corporate environmental concern." *Fortune*
magazine quotes Goodwin as saying, "A company's headquarters is its signature.
I wanted a new signature for J-M that, frankly, would attract attention—that
would tell everybody, including ourselves, that things were changing."

Things did change. With the asbestos problem growing out of control, and
with the company having lost the first of many asbestos lawsuits, Manville turned
back to one of its own—its chief legal officer—for leadership. In what *Fortune*
magazine called "The Shoot-Out at the J-M Corral," the board of directors
deposed Goodwin without explanation and J. A. McKinney was installed as president in September 1976. McKinney charted the new course in his 1977 "President's Review":

We believe we can further improve the fundamental economics of a number of our
operations and we will be working toward that end in the year to come. . . .

   Asbestos fiber, while contributing substantially to earnings, has assumed a less
important position with the earnings growth of our other basic businesses. Although
its profitability is expected to improve in the long term with reviving European econo-

mies, we do not expect asbestos fiber to dominate J-M earnings to the extent that it has in the past. . . .

We have also consolidated and repositioned some businesses for more profitable growth and phased out others not important to the future direction of the company. . . .

We have begun aggressively to seek out opportunities for growth. One example is the previously announced $200 million capital expansion program which will, by 1980, double U.S. fiber glass capacity over the 1976 levels. . . . We continue seeking still other growth possibilities that would markedly change the Johns-Manville profile, possibly through substantial acquisitions. . . .

Our main thrust in 1978 will be to continue improving profitability by maintaining our expense control and pricing vigilance, by adding volume to below-capacity businesses, by better utilizing existing capacity, and by adding capacity in sold-out businesses.

When that was written, Manville had already begun to seek a large merger candidate—a "substantial acquisition"—employing the services of the investment banking firm of Morgan Stanley to assist in the search. Manville quickly identified Olinkraft Corporation, a forest products manufacturer and timber company (owning 580,000 acres of timberland), as a likely prospect. After a brief bidding war, Olinkraft and Manville completed their merger agreement. The purchase price was $595 million. This was 2.24 times Olinkraft's June 1978 book value and over twice the average total market value of Olinkraft's stock in 1978's first half.

Approximately half of the purchase price was paid in cash and the other half with preferred stock. That preferred stock was described in the 1978 annual report:

On January 19, 1979, the Company issued 4,598,327 shares of cumulative preferred stock, $5.40 series, to consummate the acquisition of Olinkraft. . . .

Under a mandatory sinking fund provision, the Company is required to redeem the $5.40 preferred series between 1987 and 2009 at $65 per share plus accrued dividends. The annual redemption requirements will consist of varying percentages applied to the number of outstanding shares on October 20, 1986, as follows: 5% annually from 1987 through 1996, 4% annually from 1997 through 2007, and 3% in 2008. All remaining outstanding shares are required to be redeemed in 2009.

While the Olinkraft merger was being negotiated, Manville common stock declined in market value to a low of $22.125, a total decrease of over $225 million. Olinkraft's stock rose to approximate the proposed acquisition price of $65 a share.

The merger was consummated on January 19, 1979. The purchase method of accounting was used. Essentially, the book values of Olinkraft's assets were adjusted upward by the amount by which the purchase price exceeded net worth. Exhibit 36.3 shows the adjusted and unadjusted balance sheet values for Olinkraft.

After the mergers and divestitures engineered by Goodwin and McKinney,

**Exhibit 36.3** Purchase Method Merger Accounting Olinkraft Balance Sheets

|  | Adjusted | Unadjusted |
|---|---|---|
| Current assets | $ 137,557 | $ 119,610 |
| Investments in and advances to associated companies | 6,886 | 6,078 |
| Property, plant, and equipment | 700,633 | 372,761 |
| Deferred charges and other assets | 799 | 3,513 |
|  | $ 845,857 | $ 501,962 |
| Current liabilities | $ 83,912 | $ 67,793 |
| Long-term debt | 141,258 | 141,295 |
| Other noncurrent liabilities | 25,159 | 26,678 |
|  | $ 250,329 | $ 235,766 |
| Net worth | $ 596,546 | $ 266,196 |

*Source:* December 31, 1978, Manville-Olinkraft Joint Proxy Statement and Manville 1978 Annual Report.

Manville's mix of businesses (as described in the 1978 and 1979 annual reports) was as follows:

Fiberglass products: Residential insulations account for the largest portion of the product line, with commercial and industrial insulations and fiber glass making up the rest. . . . New home construction represented 55 percent of the total market while [insulation for existing homes] . . . accounted for 45 percent. . . .

Non-fiberglass insulations: This business segment includes roof insulations, refractory fibers, calcium silicate insulation, and a broad range of other commercial and industrial insulating products. . . .

Pipe products and systems: Major products in this business segment are polyvinyl chloride (PVC) plastic pipe and asbestos cement (A-C) pipe. . . .

Roofing products: The roofing products segment includes residential shingles and built-up roofing for commercial and industrial structures. New construction accounts for 40 percent of sales. Reroofing represents 60 percent. . . .

Asbestos fiber: Asbestos fiber is sold in markets throughout the world. A major portion of the fiber sold is used as a raw material in products where the fiber is locked in place by cement, rubber, plastics, resins, asphalts, and similar bindings. Products include asbestos cement products, brake linings, resilient flooring, roofing, and other products that require strength and fire protection, heat resistance, dimensional stability, and resistance to rust and rot. . . .

Industrial and specialty products and services: A diverse group of businesses that has as its principal areas: Holophane lighting systems, filtration and minerals [comprised of diatomite, perlite, and fiber glass filter products] and industrial specialties. . . . Perlite is . . . used by J-M in the manufacture of Fesco Board roof insulation. Other uses are in acoustical ceiling tile, horticultural applications, and in cryogenic insulations.

Forest products: Forest products include clay-coated unbleached Kraft and other paperboards: corrugated containers; beverage carriers and folding cartons; Kraft bags; pine lumber, plywood, and particleboard; and hardwood veneer and flooring.

**STRATEGIC MANAGE- MENT IN THE 1980s**

After Richard Goodwin was expulsed, top-management continuity was maintained through the late seventies and eighties. The chairman of the board and chief executive officer, J. A. McKinney, the president and chief operating officer, Fred L. Pundsack, and all ten senior vice-presidents listed in the 1981 annual report also appear in the 1977 annual report. In fact, the five most highly paid executives of Manville, as shown in the March 1982 proxy statement, had all been with the company for 29 or more years. Only three of Manville's outside directors joined the board after the sixties. Except for brief service by John D. Mullins, former president of Olinkraft, no new director was added after 1976. Then, in May 1982, the existing directors were renominated.

Manville's asbestos health costs were relatively insignificant (less than one-half percent of sales through 1981). But asbestos use, especially in the United States, declined sharply after 1978. The Interior Department reported a 36 percent drop from 1979 to 1980 alone. With a virtual U.S. monopoly in asbestos sales, Manville was hardest hit. The loss of asbestos profits was compounded by a deep recession in housing and other construction which began in mid-1978 and was to last through 1982.

Attempts to expand and diversify Manville had begun in 1970, when net sales totaled $578 million. The sixties had seen growth at only a 1.5 percent real rate, less than the rate of GNP growth. Because of the purchases of businesses by Goodwin and McKinney, the company had surpassed $1 billion sales in 1974 and $2 billion in 1978. However, on an inflation-corrected basis, sales declined from 1978 onward, despite the contribution of $500 million in annual sales by Olinkraft. Exhibit 36.4 illustrates Manville's sales and earnings patterns from 1977 through 1982. The corresponding financial statements and a record of Manville's common stock prices are included as Exhibits 36.5, 36.6, 36.7, and 36.8.

Six pages of Manville's 1978 annual report and over half of J. A. McKinney's "Chairman's Message" were devoted to the personal injury lawsuits. Excerpts from these documents follow:

> During the past year a great deal of publicity has appeared in the media about asbestos health hazards—most of it attacking the corporation and nearly all of it needlessly inflammatory. Your corporation has acted honorably over the years and has led the asbestos industry, medical science and the federal government in identifying and seeking to eliminate asbestos health problems. . . .

> Individuals exposed to asbestos-containing insulation materials are particular victims of the incomplete knowledge of earlier years. . . . It was not until 1964 that the particular risk to this category of worker [insulation workers] was clearly identified by Dr. Irving J. Selikoff of Mt. Sinai Hospital in New York City. . . .

> Media representatives and some elected officials have consistently ignored J-M's intensive efforts to solve asbestos health problems and, in fact, have untruthfully portrayed those efforts. . . .

> Litigation is based upon a finding of fault, and with respect to asbestos-related disease, there simply is no fault on the part of J-M, a fact increasingly recognized by juries throughout the nation. Litigation is, of course, favored and fostered by lawyers in search of lucrative fees and by "media personalities" in search of sensational stories. . . .

**Exhibit 36.4** Manville Corporation Sales and Earnings, 1978–1982 (constant 1981 dollars)

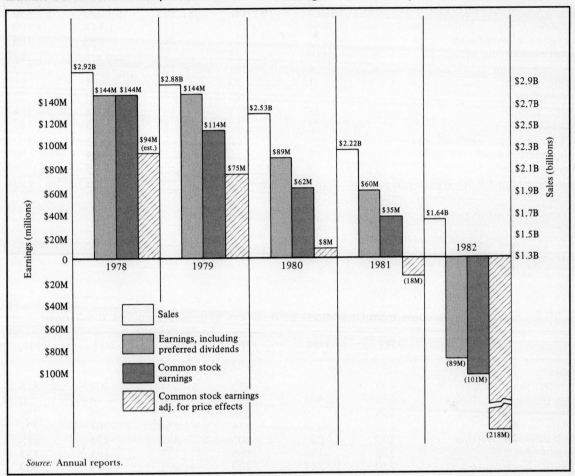

*Source:* Annual reports.

Despite the worsening financial situation and though beseiged by thousands of asbestos victims seeking billions of dollars in damages, Manville was publicly optimistic. The 1979 annual report states, "Johns-Manville has a strategy for the early 80's . . . and the commitment to succeed. . . . J-M's strategic plan embraces three major goals:"

Goal 1: To rebuild our financial reserves. . . . As expected, the Olinkraft acquisition burdened our financial resources. . . . For this reason, our most immediate short-term goal is to improve and increase the financial strength of J-M's balance sheet. We will accomplish this by increasing productivity and using the better levels of cash flow that result to provide for most of our new capital needs.

Goal 2: To improve productivity and cost efficiencies. . . . We will look for ways to increase the output of our manufacturing processes, concentrating first on those projects promising the shortest payback periods. . . .

Goal 3: To reaffirm J-M's position as a technological leader in terms of product

**Exhibit 36.5** Manville Corporation Income Statements (amounts in millions)[a]

|  | 1982 (6 mos) | 1981 | 1980 | 1979 | 1978 |
|---|---|---|---|---|---|
| Sales | $949 | $2,186 | $2,267 | $2,276 | $1,649 |
| Cost of sales | 784 | 1,731 | 1,771 | 1,747 | 1,190 |
| Selling, gen., & admin. exp. | 143 | 271 | 263 | 239 | 193 |
| R&D and engineering exp. | 16 | 34 | 35 | 31 | 33 |
| Operating income | 6 | 151 | 197 | 259 | 232 |
| Other income, net | 1 | 35 | 26 | 21 | 28 |
| Interest expense | 35 | 73 | 65 | 62 | 22 |
| Total income | (28) | 112 | 157 | 218 | 238 |
| Income taxes | 2 | 53 | 77 | 103 | 116 |
| Net income before extraordinary items | (25) | 60 | 81 | 115 | 122 |
| Div. on preferred stock | 12 | 25 | 25 | 24 | 0 |
| Extraordinary item | 0 | 0 | 0 | 0 | 0 |
| Net income available for common stock | $ (37) | $ 35 | $ 55 | $ 91 | $ 122 |

[a]Totals may not check due to rounding.

*Source:* Annual Reports and June 30, 1982, 10Q Report.

**Exhibit 36.6** Revenues and Income from Operations by Business Segment (amounts in millions)[a]

|  | 1981 | 1980 | 1979 | 1978 | 1977 | 1976 |
|---|---|---|---|---|---|---|
| **Revenues** | | | | | | |
| Fiberglass products | $ 625 | $ 610 | $ 573 | $ 514 | $ 407 | $ 358 |
| Forest products | 555 | 508 | 497 | 0 | 0 | 0 |
| Nonfiberglass insulation | 258 | 279 | 268 | 231 | 195 | 159 |
| Roofing products | 209 | 250 | 273 | 254 | 204 | 171 |
| Pipe products & systems | 199 | 220 | 305 | 303 | 274 | 218 |
| Asbestos fiber | 138 | 159 | 168 | 157 | 161 | 155 |
| Industrial & spec. prod. | 320 | 341 | 309 | 291 | 301 | 309 |
| Corporate revenues, net | 12 | 9 | 11 | 20 | 12 | (22) |
| Intersegment sales | (95) | (84) | (106) | (94) | (74) | (56) |
| Total | $2,221 | $2,292 | $2,297 | $1,677 | $1,480 | $1,291 |
| **Income from operations** | | | | | | |
| Fiberglass products | $ 90 | $ 91 | $ 96 | $ 107 | $ 82 | $ 60 |
| Forest products | 39 | 37 | 50 | 0 | 0 | 0 |
| Nonfiberglass insulation | 20 | 27 | 27 | 35 | 28 | 18 |
| Roofing products | (17) | 9 | 14 | 23 | 14 | 8 |
| Pipe products & systems | 0 | (5) | 18 | 26 | 24 | (3) |
| Asbestos fiber | 37 | 35 | 56 | 55 | 60 | 60 |
| Industrial & spec. prod. | 50 | 55 | 43 | 36 | 25 | 19 |
| Corporate expense, net | (23) | (38) | (23) | (23) | (24) | (49) |
| Eliminations & adjustments | 3 | 11 | (2) | 1 | 3 | 2 |
| Total | $ 198 | $ 223 | $ 280 | $ 260 | $ 212 | $ 116 |

[a]Totals may not check due to rounding.

*Source:* Annual Reports and June 30, 1982, 10Q Report.

**Exhibit 36.7** Manville Corporation Balance Sheets
(amounts in millions)[a]

| | June 30 1982 | 1981 | 1980 | 1979 | 1978 |
|---|---|---|---|---|---|
| **Assets** | | | | | |
| Cash | $ 10 | $ 14 | $ 20 | $ 19 | $ 28 |
| Marketable securities | 17 | 12 | 12 | 10 | 38 |
| Accounts & notes receivable | 348 | 327 | 350 | 362 | 328 |
| Inventories | 182 | 211 | 217 | 229 | 219 |
| Prepaid expenses | 19 | 19 | 20 | 31 | 32 |
| Total current assets | $ 576 | $ 583 | $ 619 | $ 650 | $ 645 |
| Property, plant, & equipment | | | | | |
| Land & land improvements | | 119 | 118 | 114 | 99 |
| Buildings | | 363 | 357 | 352 | 321 |
| Machinery & equipment | | 1,202 | 1,204 | 1,161 | 1,043 |
| | | $1,685 | $1,679 | $1,627 | $1,462 |
| Less Accum. depreciation & depletion | | (525) | (484) | (430) | (374) |
| | | $1,160 | $1,195 | $1,197 | $1,088 |
| Timber & timber land, less cost of timber harvested | | 406 | 407 | 368 | 372 |
| | $1,523 | $1,566 | $1,602 | $1,565 | $1,460 |
| Invest. & adv. to assoc. cos. | | 0 | 0 | 0 | 0 |
| Real est. sub. invest. & adv. | | 0 | 0 | 0 | 0 |
| Other assets | 148 | 149 | 117 | 110 | 113 |
| Total assets | $2,247 | $2,298 | $2,338 | $2,324 | $2,217 |
| **Liabilities** | | | | | |
| Short-term debt | $ | $ 29 | $ 22 | $ 32 | $ 23 |
| Accounts payable | 191 | 120 | 126 | 143 | 114 |
| Comp. & employee benefits | | 77 | 80 | 54 | 45 |
| Income taxes | | 30 | 22 | 51 | 84 |
| Other liabilities | 149 | 58 | 61 | 50 | 63 |
| Total current liabilities | $ 340 | $ 316 | $ 310 | $ 329 | $ 329 |
| Long-term debt | 499 | 508 | 519 | 532 | 543 |
| Other noncurrent liabilities | 93 | 86 | 75 | 73 | 60 |
| Deferred income taxes | 186 | 185 | 211 | 195 | 150 |
| Total liabilities | $1,116 | $1,095 | $1,116 | $1,129 | $1,083 |
| **Stockholders' equity** | | | | | |
| Preferred ($1.00 par) | $ 301 | $ 301 | $ 300 | $ 299 | $ 299 |
| Common ($2.50 par) | 60 | 59 | 58 | 208 | 197 |
| Capital in excess of par | 178 | 174 | 164 | 0 | 0 |
| Retained earnings | 642 | 695 | 705 | 692 | 643 |
| Cum. currency translation adj. | (47) | (22) | 0 | 0 | 0 |
| Less cost of treasury stock | (3) | (3) | (4) | (4) | (6) |
| Total stockholders' equity | $1,131 | $1,203 | $1,222 | $1,196 | $1,134 |
| Total liab. & stockholders' equity | $2,247 | $2,298 | $2,338 | $2,324 | $2,217 |

[a]Totals may not check due to rounding.

*Source:* Annual Reports and June 30, 1982 10Q Report.

**Exhibit 36.8** Manville Corporation Monthly Common Stock Trading Range, 1976 through July 1982

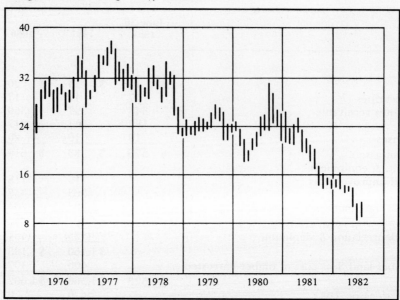

performance and cost of production . . . to increase the effort and money spent on improving manufacturing methods, enhancing the competitive strengths of present product lines and developing new products.

In 1981 Manville accelerated efforts to avoid the asbestos claims. Mr. McKinney wrote to his shareholders, "You can be assured that we will continue to be aggressive in asserting our defenses." By spending millions on the defense efforts, Manville was able to avoid or delay payment of most tort judgments and to settle many for cents on the dollar. The company was reorganized into a parent corporation and a number of operating subsidiaries, with the asbestos businesses in one subsidiary.

**THE DAY OF DECISION APPROACHES**

It quickly became apparent that courts would see through the new corporate structure and treat the companies as one for asbestos liability purposes. Further, as the number and amounts of asbestos tort judgments skyrocketed, Manville's ability to avoid paying them grew increasingly questionable.

Manville's mid-year 1982 10Q report (to the Securities and Exchange Commission) described the worsening situation with regard to the asbestos claims:

During the first half of 1982, J-M [Manville] received an average of approximately 425 new cases per month brought by an average of approximately 495 new plaintiffs per month. . . .

J-M was, for the first time in 1981, found liable by juries for punitive damages in five separate asbestos-related actions. [Punitive damages are payments above the actual damages sustained—intended to punish defendants.] All of these cases are presently subject to post-trial motions or appeals filed by J-M. The average of the punitive damages awarded against J-M in these five cases (one of which involved eleven plaintiffs) and the five cases decided during the first half of 1982 and discussed below is approximately $616,000 per case. . . .

*Hansen v. Johns-Manville:* $1,060,000 in compensatory damages and $1,000,000 in punitive damages were assessed against J-M. . . .

*Bunch v. Johns-Manville Corp.* A jury verdict of $420,000 in compensatory damages and $220,000 in punitive damages. . . . *Dorell v. Johns-Manville Corp.* The jury awarded the plaintiff $100,000 in compensatory damages and $1,000,000 in punitive damages. . . . *Jackson v. Johns-Manville.* A jury verdict of $195,000 in compensatory damages and $500,000 in punitive damages. . . . *Cavett v. Johns-Manville Corp.* The jury awarded the plaintiff $800,000 in compensation damages and $1,500,000 in punitive damages.

Aside from actual and anticipated tort claims, Manville was in much worse condition in 1982 than the financial statements indicate. This is true for four reasons. First, $340 million of Manville's net worth resulted from purchase method accounting in the Olinkraft merger. Second, the $300 million in preferred stock shown on the balance sheet is essentially equivalent to 16 percent long-term debt. Third, Manville had endured several years of negative cash flows requiring certain cash-producing strategies which tended to reduce asset values. For example, the 580,000 acres of timber farms obtained in the Olinkraft purchase were converted to a 30-year planned life from a 40-year life. This rationalized immediate cutting of about one-fourth of the timber and continuing removal of one-thirtieth of that remaining each year instead of one-fortieth. Finally, the desire of Manville executives to show profits each year has resulted in "creative accounting," which tended to inflate reported earnings. The following are examples from the 1981 annual report: (1) a $9 million increase in "Other Revenues" which resulted largely from the sale of mineral exploration rights on 580,000 acres of timberland; (2) a $2.7 million increase in reported earnings due to the "reversal of a portion of the litigation reserves established at the time of the Olinkraft, Inc. acquisition"; (3) a $9.8 million increase in reported earnings because of a new way of reporting foreign currency transactions; (4) an unspecified amount due to "the sale during 1981 of eight container plants [which] occurred as part of [the] asset management program;" and (5) an $8.4 million increase in reported earnings brought about by "changes in certain actuarial assumptions in computing pension expense."

If Manville were to fail, not only would managers and directors lose their salaries, benefits, and perquisites, but they would lose their corporate indemnification against personal liability for the asbestos claims. Undoubtedly each one would then be subject to hundreds, perhaps thousands, of tort lawsuits.

In December 1981, Manville formed a ten-member committee of inside and outside lawyers, the Litigation Analysis Group (LAG), to study the firm's situation with regard to the asbestos liabilities. LAG employed a number of consultants to research various aspects of the issue and met each month to hear reports and discuss developments. The conclusion of LAG, arrived at in mid-1982, was that

**Exhibit 36.9** Usual Effects of Filing for Reorganization Under Chapter 11

---

All debts are stayed until a "plan of reorganization" is confirmed or special approval of the bankruptcy court is obtained.

The bankrupt corporation, with prefiling management, is declared to be the "Debtor in Possession" (DIP).

The DIP can carry out the "ordinary course of business," e.g., hiring and firing employees, incurring and repaying debts, making and executing contracts, selling and buying assets.

The DIP is allowed to enforce all claims against others, by filing lawsuits if necessary.

Lawsuits against the DIP are stayed.

Unsecured creditors, and common and preferred stockholders, are represented by committees appointed by the bankruptcy judge.

The DIP is allowed to cancel contracts, including collective bargaining agreements and leases, to the extent that they have not been carried out.

The DIP is allowed 120 days to file a plan of reorganization and 60 days to seek the required approval of each creditor class (half in number holding two-thirds in amount) and equity class (holders of two-thirds in amount), either of which periods may be extended.

The plan of reorganization typically provides for

1. Payment of postfiling debt, including costs of administering the case
2. Payment of secured prefiling debt up to the value of the liened property
3. Payment of some or all of unsecured debt over some period into the future, with or without interest
4. Discharge of all claims not provided for in the plan

---

Manville would eventually have to pay about $2 billion to present and future asbestos victims.

In a subsequent lawsuit it has been alleged that the $2 billion figure was contrived so as to be high enough to justify a filing for reorganization under Chapter 11 of the U.S. bankruptcy code, but not high enough to appear to require liquidation of the company. At a board of directors meeting on August 4, 1982, J. A. McKinney (chairman of the board and chief executive officer) appointed four outside directors to a special committee to determine what Manville should do. Members of the special committee were briefed on Chapter 11 by company executives. A limited overview of the practical effects of a Chapter 11 reorganization is provided in Exhibit 36.9.

A special meeting of the board of directors was called for August 25, 1982. The special committee was expected to present its recommendation at that meeting.

Academic journals, 239
Accounts payable, 203
Accounts receivable, 202
Accrued expenses payable, 203
Accumulated retained earnings, 204–205
Acquisitions, 78–84
Adams, Robert, 379
Adams, Sexton, 592, 666, 682
Additional paid-in capital, 204
Administrative expenses, 208
Agricultural information, 227
Aguilar, Francis J., 94–95
Airline Deregulation Act (1978), 767, 770
Albert, Kenneth J., 107
Alexander, Larry D., 351, 529, 647, 765
Alfa Romeo, 870
Allen, Ron, 780
Allstate, 73
Almanacs, 232
Alternatives, strategic, 62–63
Altman, Edward I., 185
American Accounting Association, 176–177
American Airlines, 775
American Broadcasting Company, 468, 472
American Express Company, 55, 71, 183
American Motors Corporation, 422, 426, 430, 437, 447, 871

Analyses, organizational (internal), 15, 37, 39–43
Analyzers, 114
Anderson, Arthur D., 609
Anderson, John, 805
Anderson, Ron, 839, 847
Anderson, Warren, 913–914
Andrews, John, 856
Anheuser, Eberhard, 320
Anheuser-Busch, 316, 320–321
Anschutz Corporation, 739
Ansoff, H. Igor, 146
Antonini, M. H., 375
Appel, Bernard, 595–596, 599
Apple Computer, 52–53
Applied research, 152
Aquilano, Nicholas J., 151
Arbitrageurs, 82
Arkansas Power & Light Company, 179
Armstrong World Industries, 10
Arroyo, Tony, 293
Asbestos Textile Institute, 916–917
Ash, Mary Kay, 682–691, 697–699, 701–702
Ashcraft, Theo, 668
Asher, Garland, 615
Assets, 200–203
  capital, 148–149
  current, 200
AT&T, 54–55, 568–569, 576, 582–587, 609
Atherton, Roger M., 742

Atkinson, Thomas R., 871
Atlantic Richfield, 49
Audit committees, 133
Audits
  as control methods, 176–179
  strategy, 181–182
Austin, J. Paul, 256, 275
Australia, 8
Avon, 691–693
Ayoub, Sam, 258

Backward integration, 67–69
Bagehot, Walter, 144
Bailey, Bob, 293
Bailey, F. Lee, 913
Baird, Lloyd, 153
Balance sheets, 200–207
Bank Holding Company Act (1956), 499
Bankruptcy, 75–76
Banks, R. S., 375
Barker, Myra, 688
Barnard, Chester I., 122
Barnes, Steven J., 515
Barnhardt, William M., 494
Barrett, M. Edgar, 706, 894
Basic research, 152
Battery Street Enterprises, 282
Beall, Jim, 826–834
"Bear hugs," 82
Beasley, John, 698
Beatrice Foods Company, 7, 12, 81
Belk, Thomas M., 494

Bell, Griffin, 485
Belridge Oil Company, 737
Bemelmans, T., 155
Benjamin, Wanda, 552
Bertsch, Thomas M., 849
Bet-your-company cultures, 54
Bevans, Bill, 468
Bibliographies, 235–237
Bikerstaff, George, 169
Biographies, 246
Black & Decker, 78–79
Blaine, Charley, 82
Blumenfeld, Seth D., 571
Boards of directors, 130–134
Bonds, 209
Book value, of securities, 206
Booz, Allen & Hamilton, 180, 464
Boren, W. C., III, 494
Borg-Warner, 617–625
Boston Consulting Group, 92–94,
    96
Bouette, Alvin J., 296–297
Bowerman, Bill, 804–805
Boy Scouts of America, 55
Brainstorming, 32
Brazil, 894–900
Bricker, William, 132
Brigham, Eugene F., 177
Brinker, Norman, 531
British Leyland, 864, 869–870
Broken Hill Proprietary, 75
Brookings Institute, 30
Brown, James K., 15
Buchele, Robert B., 40
Budgeting
    capital, 148–149
    program, 157–158
    program planning and, 157
    resource deployment through,
        154, 156–159
Budget Rent-a-Car, 73
Budgets
    as control methods, 176
    flexible, 156–157
Burford, Ann, 788
Burger King Corporation, 518,
    521, 529–551
Busch, Adolphus, 320
Bushell, Mark W., 742
Busia, Kofi, 883
Business facts, sources of, 213–250
Business judgment rule, 134
Business periodicals, 239–240
Business policy, 8–9, 12
Business portfolio analyses
    growth-share matrix, 92–97
    industry attractiveness–business
        strength matrix, 97–104
    life-cycle approach, 104–108
Business portfolios, 92

Business reference librarians, 230
Business services/guides, 240–243
Business unit strategies, 62–63,
    77–79, 103–108
*Business Week*, 30
Buy-backs, stock, 83
Buy-outs, leveraged, 82
Byars, Lloyd L., 156, 280, 336,
    489, 511, 552, 568

Cabiri, Bawol, 881, 892
Cable News Network, 468–470,
    480–482, 486
Caldwell, Kate, 849–854
Califano, Joseph, 917
Callahan, Michael J., 556
Cameron, Bruce B., 494
Campbell, J. Jeffrey, 529, 538, 544,
    550–551
Canada, 456
Candler, Asa, 255
Candler, Howard, 256
Canning, Richard G., 183
Canon, 379
Cannon, J. Thomas, 123
Capital assets, 148–149
Capital budgeting, 148–149
Capitalization ratio, 206–207
Capital stock, 204
Caputa, Michael D., 314
Carlson, Chester, 373
Carroll, Lewis, 62
Carter, Jimmy, 451, 767
Carter, Wilbur L., Jr., 494
Cary, Frank T., 9
Case analyses, 189–191
Cases, 189
Cash, 200
"Cash cows," 93
Cash flow analyses, 149
Cason, Marilynn J., 296
Catch-up research and
    development strategies, 154
Celler-Kefauver amendment (1950),
    70
Census Bureau, U.S., 33, 217–218
Census data, 217–220
Certified public accountants, 178
Chandler, Alfred D., Jr., 123
Changes in financial position,
    statements of, 211–212
Chase, Richard B., 151
Chase Econometrics, 33
Chase Manhattan Bank, 33
Chevron Corporation, 81
Chicago Ice Company, 15
Chief executive officers, 114
Chollot, Richard, 556
Christie, Neil, 826–834
Chrysler, Walter P., 447

Chrysler Corporation, 29, 422,
    424–426, 428, 430, 432–434,
    443, 446–467, 871
Chrysler Loan Guarantee Act
    (1979), 432–434, 443,
    446–447, 451–459
Circuit Services North, 826–834
CIT Financial, 75
Clark, Johnnie L., 199
Clayton Antitrust Act (1914), 70
Clean Air Act (1970), 440, 788
Cleary, Russell, 325–326
Close, Darwin B., 185
Cluster analyses, 110–111
Coca-Cola Company, 6–7, 13, 66,
    69–70, 113, 255–279
Coker, Charles W., Jr., 494
Coldwell Banker & Company, 73
Collier, Richard, 706
Collins, William, 816
Columbia Broadcasting System,
    472, 486–488
Columbia Pictures Industries,
    267–270
Combination strategies, 76–77, 154
Commerce Department, U.S., 33,
    214
Committees, board of directors,
    132–133
Common Market. *See* European
    Economic Community
Common stock, 204
Community Mental Health Center,
    814–825
Community Reinvestment Act
    (1977), 504
Compensation committees, 133
Competition considerations, 11, 70,
    114–115
Competitive analyses, 34–39, 43
Competitive strategy analyses,
    108–110
Compustat, 172
Computer-aided design, 184
Computer-integrated manufacturing,
    184
Computerized data bases, 172
Computer-Land, 604–605
Computer programs, 181
Concentration, single
    product/service, 66–67
Concentric acquisitions, 78
Concentric diversification, 67
Concentric mergers, 78
Conference Board, 30
Conflict tolerance, and
    organizational culture, 51
Conglomerate acquisitions, 78
Conglomerate diversification, 71–72
Conglomerate mergers, 78

Congress, U.S., 222, 788–789. *See also specific acts*
Conoco, 738
Conquest, Thomas, 372
Consumer Credit Protection Act (1968), 504
Consumer income, 26
Consumer information, 229
Container Corporation of America, 734–736
Continental Banking Company, 16
Contingency approach, to organizing, 122–126
Contingency structures, 125–127
Control methods, 176–181
Control process, 168–184
Control systems, 174–177
Cooper, Joe, 776, 778
Cooper, Ken, 839, 846–847
Coors, Adolphus, 326, 351
Coors, Jeff, 353, 359, 362
Coors, Joseph, 327, 352–354, 369
Coors, Peter, 353
Coors, William, 353–354, 362, 369
Coors (Adolphus) Company, 316, 326–327, 351–371
Copyright Office, U.S., 10, 13
Cormack, Mary Pat, 894
Corner, David N., 296
Corning Glass, 152–153
Corporate responsibility committees, 133
Corporate strategies, 62–63, 77–79, 103
Correlation analyses, 33
Cost of goods sold, 208
Cox, Tench, 468
Creecy, Deirdre, 568
Creeping tender offers, 82
Critical path method, 180
Critical success factors, 98–103
Cromwell, Henry, 552, 555–556
Crowley, J. S., 375
Crowner, Robert P., 835
Crum & Forster, 389–394
Culbreath, H. L., 494
Culture. *See* Organizational culture
Cunningham, Gary M., 159
Current assets, 200
Current liabilities, 203
Customer service, and organizational objectives, 55

Damon, E. K., 375
Dana, 129
Daniels, William, 485
Darcy, Jack, 383
Data bases, 172, 228–229, 233–235
Data Research, 30
Data Resources, 33

Davidson, William H., 468
Davis, Hugh, 399–400
Deal, Terrence, E., 53
Dean Witter, 73
Debbie's School of Beauty Culture, 297, 299
Decentralization growth stage, 124
Decisions, strategic, 18–19
Decision support systems, 184
Defenders, 113
Defense Department, U.S., 6, 157, 180
Deferred charges, 202
DeGive, Ghislaine, 153
Deihl, Lincoln W., 255
DeLorean, John, 169
DeLorean Motor Company, 169
Delphi technique, 31
Delta Air Lines, 7, 49, 765–787
Depository Institutions Act (1982), 499, 502
Depreciation, 202, 208
Development research, 152
Dhaliwal, Tehsel S., 296
Diab, John, 537
Diamond Shamrock Corporation, 132
Dickson, Alan T., 494
Dictionaries, 230–231
Differentiation strategies, 78–79
Digital Equipment Corporation, 49, 381
Directories, 237, 240, 243–246
Directors, 130–134
Disney, Walt, 50–51
Dissertations, doctoral, 246–247
Diversification
  concentric, 67
  conglomerate, 71–72
  horizontal, 70–71
Diversification marketing strategies, 146
Divestment strategies, 74–76
Doctoral dissertations, 246–247
Dr. Pepper, 263
"Dogs," 93
Dow, Herbert Henry, 626
Dowd, W. Frank, Jr., 494
Drimmer, Melvin, 160
Drucker, Peter F., 48, 65, 126, 128, 162
Due care, 134
Dun and Bradstreet, 33, 172
*Dun's Review*, 172–173
du Pont, 177, 180

Earnings per share, 209
Eastern Airlines, 775
Easton, Alan, 332, 334
Econometric models, 32–34

Economic barriers, to divestment, 76
Economic Community of West African States, 888
Economic forces, scanning of, 26–27
Economic forecasting, 32–34
Economic indicators, 33, 221–222
Edgerton, David R., 529–530, 539
Edwards, Bob, 839, 843–844
Eidenberg, Eugene, 574
Electronic data processing, 181
Electronic Data Systems, 81
Elliott, Ron, 814, 816–818, 822
Ellis, A. L., 494
Ellis, Perry, 285
Emerson Electric, 129
Employees, organization relationship with, 9, 11
Employers Reinsurance, 75
Encyclopedias, 231–232
Endgame strategies, 72–74
Energy Policy and Conservation Act (1975), 421, 440, 448–449
Energy Tax Act (1978), 440
Entrepreneurial cultures, 52
Entrepreneurial growth stage, 123
Environment. *See* Organizational environment
Environmental forecasting, 31–34, 43
Environmental information, 229
Environmental Protection Agency, 440, 788–789, 796–797, 917
Environmental scanning, 26–31, 43
Equal Credit Opportunity Act (1974), 504
Ernest, Robert C., 52
Erwin, Dennis C., 543
Esmark, 81
European Economic Community, 27, 856, 870, 875, 877–880
Evaluation criteria, 170–175
Everest, Hiram Bond, 707
Everett, Ed, 266
Ewing, Matthew, 707
Executive committees, 132
External organizational environment, 15, 26–43
Exxon Corporation, 744

Family Financial Services, 75
Federal Aviation Administration, 770, 774, 781
Federal Communications Commission, 28, 472, 568–569
Federal Deposit Insurance Corporation, 499, 502
Federal Energy Administration, 735
Federal Express, 7

Federal government publications, 214–229
Federal income tax payable, 203
Federal Reserve System, 82, 499, 504
Federal Trade Commission, 28
Feedback, 174–175
Feiner, Jeffrey, 679
Fiat, 149
Finance committees, 133
Financial resources, and organizational objectives, 56
Financial services/guides, 240–243
Financial statements, 199–212
Financial strategies, 147–149
Firth, Robert D., 375, 378
Fisher, A. R., 921
Fisher, Max M., 734
Fisher-Price Toys, 559, 566
Fleming, Foy B., 494
Flexible budgets, 156–157
Focus strategies, 78–79
Food and Drug Administration, 29
*Forbes*, 30, 173
Ford, Arthur, 782
Ford, Henry, II, 114, 733–734, 856, 870
Ford Foundation, 6
Ford Motor Company, 53, 114, 422, 424, 426, 428, 430, 434–435, 447, 459, 856, 871
Ford of Europe, 855–880
Forecasting, environmental, 31–34, 43
Foreign business, 27, 29, 86, 222–223, 249–250
Foreign exchange rates, 27
*Fortune*, 30, 33, 173
Forward integration, 67–69
Fox, Jeremy B., 647
Foxboro Company, 163
France, 864–865
Fraser, Douglas, 433
Freed, Dave, 845–846
Friendly acquisitions, 79
Friendly mergers, 80
Friendly takeovers, 82
Fujitsu, 379
Functional development growth stage, 123–124
Functional strategies, 62, 104, 144–155
Furek, Robert M., 267

Gardner, Robert R., 706
Garrett, David, 765–767, 775, 781, 784, 786–787
Geneen, Harold, 114
General Accounting Office, 178–179

General Crude Oil Company, 737
General Electric, 18, 75, 97, 111, 576
Generally accepted accounting principles, 178
Generally accepted auditing standards, 178
General Mills, 12
General Motors Corporation, 6, 81, 115, 130–131, 150, 422, 424, 426, 428, 430, 436–437, 443, 447, 449, 459, 869, 871
Generic strategies, 77–79
George, Claude S., Jr., 168
Georgia Institute of Technology, 6
Gerot, Paul S., 530
Getty Oil Company, 81
Ghana, 881–893
Giganti, Jorge, 272
Gilroy, Frank, 819–820
Giraldi, Bob, 576
Giscard d'Estaing, Valéry, 864
Glantz, Richard H., 556
Glass-Steagall Banking Act (1933), 499
Glavin, W. F., 375
Glazer, Eugene C., 378
"Go together–split" strategies, 85
Goeken, Jack, 568
Goizueta, Roberto C., 13, 256–257, 266, 279
Gokhale, V. P., 905
Golden parachutes, 82
Goldman, Jack E., 375, 388
Goodwin, Richard, 921–922, 924
Government auditors, 178–179
Government publications, 214–230
Government regulation, 11, 28–29
Grace (W. R.) & Company, 337–338
Grant (W. T.), 7
Grayson, C. Jackson, 638
Great Britain, 27, 31, 125, 146, 864–865
Green, J. J., 647
Greenberg, Jack M., 514–515
Greene, Harold H., 569
"Greenmail," 82
Greenwood Trust Company, 73
Griffin, Adelaide, 592, 666, 682
Griffith, Timothy, 257
Gross national product, 26
Gross profit, 208
Growth rate, 26
Growth-share matrix, 92–97
Growth stage, organizational, 123–124
Growth strategies, 64–73
GTE Sprint, 588–589
Guides, business, 240–243

Gulf + Western, 12, 71
Gulf Corporation, 81
Guthrie, Michael J., 296

Haas, Peter E., 280, 282
Haas, Robert D., 283
Haas, Walter A., Jr., 283
Hammer, Armand, 132
Handbooks, 232–233
Harcharik, J. Robert, 571
Hardin, Joseph S., 660
Hardware, 181
Harkins, Francis J., 574
Harley State Bank, 73
Harrigan, Kathryn Rudie, 73
Harris, Hollis, 778
Harvard Business School, 65
Harvest strategies, 74
Harvey, C. Felix, 494
Hax, Arnoldo C., 97, 99–102
Heileman, Gottlieb, 325
Heileman (G.) Brewing Company, 316, 325–326
Herbruck, Charles G., 627
Hertz, 20, 75
Hessler, Marian, 293
Hetterman, Don, 779
Hewlett-Packard, 122–123, 381
Hines, Gordon, 835, 839, 842–844, 846, 848
Hines, Robin, 844
Hines Industries, 835–848
History, organizational, 50–51
Hofer, Charles W., 107, 109
Hoffman et Compagnie, 899–900
Holiday Inns, 77
Honda, 423, 466
Honeywell, 379
Horizontal acquisitions, 78
Horizontal integration, 70–71
Horizontal mergers, 78
Horrigan, Edward A., Jr., 494
Hostile acquisitions, 80
Hostile mergers, 80
Howard, Don, 894
Howard, M., 375
Howell, Jesse L., 297
Howell, William K., 339, 341, 343–344, 348
Hudson Institute, 30
Huff, Joann, 839, 841–842
Human resource/personnel strategies, 151–153
Human resources, and organizational objectives, 56
Hunger, J. David, 372
Hunter, Jan, 293
Husky Oil, 75
Hussey, David E., 40
Hutton (E. F.) & Company, 486

Iacocca, Lee, 425, 446, 448, 464
IBM, 6–7, 9, 11, 18–19, 49–51, 53,
    81, 114, 123, 154, 376, 379,
    381, 607–609
Icahn, Carl, 914
Identification, and organizational
    culture, 51
Implementation, strategy, 9, 17
    budgeting, 154, 156–159
    functional strategies, 144–155
    mergers/acquisitions, 78–86
    motivational systems, 160–163
Incentive pay plans, 162
Income
    net, 209
    statements of, 207–210
Income taxes, 203, 208
Independent auditors, 178
Independent business units, 19
Indexes, 215, 217, 237–238, 240,
    247–248
India, 901–914
Indicators, leading, 33, 221–222
Individual autonomy, and
    organizational culture, 51
Industrial information, 223–226,
    248
Industry attractiveness–business
    strength matrix, 97–104
Inflation rate, 26
Information systems, management,
    181, 183–184
Ingersoll, Roy, 617
Innovation, and organizational
    objectives, 56
Innovative research and
    development strategies, 153
"In play," 82
Intangibles, 203
Integrated cultures, 52
Integration
    backward, 67–69
    forward, 67–69
    horizontal, 70–71
    successive, 85
    vertical, 67–70
Intel, 129, 381
Interactive cultures, 52
Interdependence barriers, to
    divestment, 76
Interest
    bond, 209
    paid by corporations, 26
Interior Department, U.S., 924
Internal auditors, 179
Internal organizational analyses, 15,
    37, 39–43
Internal organizational environment,
    15, 26–43
Internal Revenue Service, 29, 179

International business. See Foreign
    business
International Monetary Fund, 884
Interstate Commerce Commission,
    28
Inventories, 202, 205–206
Irrgang, William, 628, 636
Isotalo, Leo P., 283
Isuzu, 437
Italy, 864, 870
ITT, 12, 16, 71, 114, 609

Jackson, David G., 608
Janssens, Ed, 915–916, 920
Japan, 27, 86, 150, 155, 376–377,
    379, 421–423, 426–427, 432,
    436–437, 439, 442, 467, 593,
    804, 855, 864–865, 869–871,
    874–880
Jaquith, Richard D., 556
Jay, Anthony, 144
Jeans Company, 281
Jefferson, Melvin D., 297
Jenkins, Ed, 819
John, Harry G., Jr., 337
Johns-Manville Corporation,
    915–930
Johnson, George E., 293–297, 299,
    303, 306
Johnson, Joan B., 296–297
Johnson, Robert Wood, 50
Johnson & Johnson, 50, 67–68
Johnson Controls, 13
Johnson Products Company,
    293–313
Joint ventures, 84–86
Jones, Jack, 378
Jones, J. O., 647
Jones, Patricia E., 137
Journals, 239–240
Judges, 92
Juliussen, Equil, 602
Junk bonds, 82
Justice Department, U.S., 70, 465,
    568–569, 770, 788

Kalmanowitz, Paul, 326, 328
Kantor, Nathan, 574
Kearns, David, 372–376, 378,
    392–393
Keck family, 740
Kendrix, James, 788
Kennedy, Allan A., 53
Kentucky Fried Chicken, 547
Keough, Donald R., 258
Kerin, Roger A., 147
Kerr-McGee Corporation, 742–764
Keto, Robert, 595–596
Key factors for success, 171
Khalil, Ezzat N., 296

Killen, Michael, 381
King, John W., 381
King, Martin Luther, Jr., 160
King, William R., 39, 185
Kiwanis International, 6
Klopman, William A., 494
Klug, Norman R., 337
K Mart, 669, 678–679
Knight, Phil, 804–805
Kodak, 376
Koeplin, Patrick, 826
Korn, Steven, 468
Kozel, Frank J., Jr., 571
Kroc, Ray, 67, 178, 511–514, 523
Krysiak, Bruce W., 652

Labor information, 227–228
Lanza, A. J., 915
Latin American Integration
    Association, 27
Lauenstein, Milton, 182, 185
Lavelle, Rita M., 788
Lavie, Elizabeth, 765
Lawrence, David, 606
Leadership, organizational,
    159–160
Leadership strategies, 73
Leading indicators, 33, 221–222
Lean staffs, 129
Lee, Craig Michael, 881–882, 885,
    888, 891–893
Legal considerations, 133–134
Lelewer, David K., 283
Levadol, 894, 896, 899–900
Leveraged buy-outs, 82
Levine, Aaron M., 404, 408
Levinson, Paul, 828–834
Levi Strauss & Company, 280–292
Liabilities, 201, 203–204
    current, 203
    long-term, 203–204
Librarians, business reference, 230
Liddle, David E., 380–381
Life-cycle approach, 104–108
Limann, Hilla, 881, 884–885, 887
Lincoln, James F., 626–629,
    636–637
Lincoln, John C., 626
Lincoln Electric Company, 626–646
Linear regression, 33
Liquidation strategies, 76
Little (Arthur D.), Inc., 104
Lockheed Corporation, 29, 180
Lockups, 82
Lockyer, Roy, 274
Lole, Chris, 325
Lomiuta, Azusa, 155
Long-range objectives, 8, 14–15,
    17, 48
Long-term liabilities, 203–204

Loune, Donald B., 555
Low-Level Radioactive Waste Policy
    Act (1980), 801
LTV, 71
Luke, 6

MacAvoy, R. E., 38
McColl, Hugh L., 491, 495
McColough, C. Peter, 374,
    376–377, 380, 387
McConnell, Paul, 894, 900
McConner, Dorothy, 296
McCormick & Company, 13
McDonald, Richard and Maurice,
    511–513, 546
McDonald's Corporation, 53–54,
    67, 178, 511–529, 532–534,
    544, 546–547, 551
McGarrell, Edmond J., Jr., 153
McGee, Dean A., 742, 744, 754
McGowan, William, 568, 571
McGraw-Hill, 33
Mache, Kenneth, 679
McIlhenny (E. L.) & Company, 64
McIntyre, Thomas J., 735
McKenny, J. W., 754–755
McKinney, J. A., 921–922, 924, 930
McKinney, Luther C., 556
McLamore, James W., 529–530
MacMillan, Ian C., 137
McPherson, F. A., 754–755
Maim, Jeremy, 55
Majluk, Nicholas S., 97, 99–102
Malone, Sally, 818–819
Management. See Strategic
    management
Management audits, 179
Management by objectives,
    180–181
Management information systems,
    181, 183–184
Managerial barriers, to divestment,
    76
Manuals, 232–233
Manufacturers Hanover, 75
Manville Corporation, 915–930
Marathon Oil Company, 738–739
Marcor, 734–736
Marketable securities, 200
Market development strategies,
    145
Marketing, 145
Marketing information, 248–249
Marketing Science Institute, 65
Marketing strategies, 145–147
Market penetration strategies, 145
Markets, and organizational
    objectives, 56
Martinez, Roberto, 821
Martini, Herbert, 293–294

Mary Kay Cosmetics, 50, 54,
    682–705
Mason, Kenneth, 555–556
Massaro, Donald, 380–381
Masters, Chuck, 820–821
Mayo Clinic, 6
Mazda, 435
MCI Communications, 568–591
Mead Corporation, 94–95
Mechanic systems, 124
Mergers, 78–84
Merhige, Robert R., Jr., 419
Merrill Lynch, 53
Meshoulam, Ilan, 153
Metzler, Richard J., 179
Miller, Carl A., 336
Miller, Charles W., 337
Miller, Ernest, 336–337
Miller, Frederic, 321, 336
Miller, Frederic C., 337
Miller, Robert, 615
Miller, William (case writer), 372
Miller, William (Treasury
    Secretary), 451–452
Miller Brewing Company, 316,
    321–324, 336–350
Milutinovich, Jugoslav S., 213–216
Miner, Jeffrey M., 351
Minute Maid, 264
Mission, organizational, 12–15, 17
Mitchell, Ralph C., 179
Mitsubishi, 432, 434, 449–450,
    865
Mobil Corporation, 81, 706–741,
    789
Models, econometric, 32–34
Moder, Joseph J., 185
Mondale, Walter F., 735
Monopolies, 70
Montgomery Ward, 734–736
Moore, Arch, 914
Morgan, Frank J., 556
Morgan Stanley, 51
Motivational systems, 160–163
Mottus, Allan, 695
Mullins, John D., 924
Multinational organizations. See
    Foreign business
Multiple regression, 33
Multiquimica do Brasil, 894–900
Murphy, John A., 338, 348–350
Murray, Allan E., 724
Murray, Denise, 511
Myers, Mike, 839, 843

Nabisco, 71
Nader, Ralph, 450
Naisbitt, John, 26
Narod, Susan, 50
National Association for the

Advancement of Colored
    People, 6
National Broadcasting Company,
    472
National Traffic and Motor Vehicle
    Safety Act (1966), 441
Natural Gas Policy Act (1978), 745
NCNB Corporation, 489–510
Neeb, Louis P., 544
Neil, Thomas C., 255, 336
Nelson, Gaylord, 398
Nelson, Orville, 293
Net income, 209
Net sales, 208
Net working capital, 205
New Jersey Bell Telephone
    Company, 122
Newsletters, 240
Newspaper indexes, 240
Niche strategies, 73–74
Nickerson, Albert L., 713, 721,
    729–730
Nielsen (A. C.) Company, 474–475,
    479
Nike, 804–813
Nippon Steel, 154–155
Nissan, 423, 466, 855, 869–870
Nitrofix Ghana, 881–893
Nixon, Robert L., 293
Nkrumah, Kwame, 882–883
Nominating committees, 133
Nonparticipative budgeting process,
    154, 156
Nordtvedt, Ernest R., 421, 446
North, Phil, 594–595
Northside Presbyterian Church, 159
Notes payable, 203

Objectives
    long-range, 8, 14–15, 17, 47
    organizational, 48, 55–59
    short-range, 14–15, 17, 48
Occidental Petroleum Corporation,
    132
Occupational Safety and Health
    Administration, 11
On-line data bases, 233–235
Operating profit, 208
Operations planning and control,
    150
Operators, 181
Opinion, statements of, 199–200
Oppenlander, Bob, 778, 781–782,
    786
Optimum strategy reports, 111
Organic systems, 124
Organizational analyses, internal,
    15, 37, 39–43
Organizational culture, 15, 48–50
    changes in, 54–55

defined, 48
identification/classification, 51–54
origin, 50–51
and power relationships, 114
Organizational environment, 15
 contingency approach to
  organizing, 124–125
 internal/external, 26–43
 strategy evaluation/selection,
  113–114
Organizational growth stage,
 123–124
Organizational leadership, 159–160
Organizational mission, 12–15, 17
Organizational objectives, 48
 cascade approach, 58–59
 mix of, 55–57
Organizational philosophy, 9–11,
 17
Organizational rewards, 162
Organizational size, 123–124
Organizational structure
 assessment, 126–128
 boards of directors, 130–134
 contingency approach to
  organizing, 122–126
 and culture, 51
 effective designs, 128–129
 and objectives, 56
 restructuring, 130–131
 strengths/weaknesses of types,
  137–140
Organization of African Unity, 27
Organization of Petroleum
 Exporting Countries (OPEC),
 27, 768
Organizations, 122
Organizing
 contingency approach, 122–126
 defined, 122
Osell, Roger R., 107
Other income/expenses, 208
Overall cost leadership strategies,
 78–79
Ozark Airlines, 787

Pabst Brewing Company, 316,
 327–328
"Pac-man defense," 82
Pappadio, Paul, 615
Parkinson, Cecil, 865
Par reports, 111
Participative budgeting process,
 154, 156
Patents, 228
Patton, Phil, 64
Payables, 203
Pay plans, incentive, 162
Pemberton, John Styth, 255
Penney, J. C., 9

Penney (J. C.) Company, 10, 50, 57
PepsiCo, 262, 338
Performance
 evaluation of, 173–174
 and rewards, organizational
  culture for, 51
Periodical indexes/directories,
 237–238
Periodicals, 239–240
Personnel management, 151
Peters, Thomas J., 9, 11–12, 67,
 129, 163
Peterson, Robert A., 147
Philadelphia Saving Fund Society,
 75
Philip Morris, 338–339, 344
Phillips, Cecil R., 185
Philosophy, organizational, 9–11,
 17
Physical facilities, and
 organizational objectives, 56
Piedmont Airlines, 786–787
Pillsbury, 530–531, 538, 544, 551
PIMS analysis, 111–112
Pinkney, William, 307
Pipp, F. J., 375
Pippitt, R. M., 375
Pistner, Stephen, 736
Pizza Hut, 548
Planning, strategic, 8, 17
Planning committees, 133
Poison pills, 83
Policy formulation, and strategy, 8,
 11
Political forces, scanning of, 28–29
Porter, Bruce, 916
Porter, Michael E., 35–36, 73, 79,
 108–110
Portfolio analyses. See Business
 portfolio analyses
Power, 114
Preferred dividend coverage, 209
Preferred stock, 204
Prepayments, 202
Price, Paul E., 556
Price-earnings ratio, 209–210
"Problem children," 93
Process cultures, 54
Procter, Harley, 50
Procter & Gamble Company,
 50–51, 179, 576
Product development strategies,
 145
Production/operations strategies,
 150–151
Productivity, and organizational
 objectives, 56
Product positioning, 147
Products, and organizational
 objectives, 56

Professional Air Traffic Controllers
 Organization, 769–770,
 773–774
Profitability, and organizational
 objectives, 14, 56
Profit impact of market strategies,
 65, 111–112
Profit margins, 209
Profits, 208–209
Program budgeting, 157–158
Program evaluation and review
 technique, 180
Programmers, 181
Program planning, and budgeting,
 157
Property, plant, and equipment, 56,
 202
Prospectors, 113–114
Protective research and
 development strategies, 154
Puckett, Roscoe E., 419
Pundsack, Fred L., 924
Purdy, Dean, 847–848

Quaker Oats Company, 552–567
Qualitative evaluation criteria,
 170–172
Qualitative factors, strategy
 evaluation/selection, 112–115
Quantitative evaluation criteria,
 172–173
Quick divestment strategy, 74
Quinlan, Michael R., 514–515, 519
Quinn, James Brian, 185

Radford, K. J., 185
Radio Shack, 592–596, 598–600,
 602–603, 607
Raiders, 83
Rainbow Food Company, 849–854
Ralston Purina, 16
Ramer, John, 839, 843–844
Rawlings, Jerry, 884–885
RCA, 75, 479
Reactors, 114
Reader's Digest, 50
Reagan, Ronald, 438, 442–443,
 465, 788, 871
Receivables, 202
Recentralization growth stage,
 124
Reemsynder, H., 159
Regulatory forces, scanning of,
 28–29
Remington Rand Univac, 180
Renault, 437
Rensi, Edward H., 515
Reports, strategy, 111
Research, and organizational
 objectives, 56

Research and development
strategies, 152–154
Restructuring, 130–131
Retained earnings, 204–205, 210
Retrenchment strategies, 74–76
Returns on investment, 111
Revlon, 691–692
Rewards, organizational, 162
Rheingold, Paul, 400
Riccardo, John, 446
Richardson, H. Smith, Jr., 495
Ripp, Thomas W., 529
Risk, organizational tolerance of,
51, 112–113
Ritchie, Dan, 485
Roach, John, 595–596, 610
Roberts, Bert, 571
Robins, Albert Hartley, 397
Robins, Claiborne, 397
Robins (A. H.), 397–420
Rockefeller, John D., 706–707
Rockefeller Foundation, 122
Rockwell, Willard F., 81, 84
Rockwell International Corporation,
81, 84
Rogers, Ann, 821–822
Rogers, Richard, 682, 684,
686–687, 690–691, 696, 698,
701
ROLM Corporation, 81, 129, 609
Roman Catholic Church, 179
Ross, S. B., 375
Rothschild, William E., 18
Rox, Frank, 781
Royal Crown, 263–264
Roys, Ruben, 272
Rucklehaus, John, 789
Rudy, Bruce, 688
Rue, Leslie W., 156
Ruff, Wilbur L., 920

Sabo, Richard, 636, 640
Salenbien, Len, 839, 844–847
Sales, net, 208
Salyman, Jack, 695
Sampsell, R. Bruce, 556
Samuels, George, 814, 816, 822
Sanders, Harland, 547
Saudi Arabia, 725–726
Sawhill, John C., 735
SCANA, 10
Scanning, environmental, 26–30, 43
Scanning programs, 30–31
Scenarios, 32
Schendel, Dan, 109
Schiller, S. David, 419
Schlichte, Anthony, 804
Schlumberger, 129
Schmidt, Charles E., 495
Schmitt, Edward H., 514–515

Schneider, Georg, 320
Schueler, Jacob, 351
Schumacher, Ferdinand, 552,
555–556
Scott, William C., 617
Sculley, John, 608
Sears, Roebuck and Company, 53,
72–73, 576
Sears Savings Bank, 73
Securities, 200, 206
Securities and Exchange
Commission, 11, 29, 83, 485,
917
Self-tender offers, 83
Selikoff, Irving, 915, 917, 924
Selling expenses, 208
Sen, Asoke K., 914
Seneker, Harold, 594
Sequential strategies, 77
Services, business, 240–243
7-Eleven stores, 647–665
Seven-Up Company, 263
Seybold, Patricia, 393
Shanken, Marvin, 266
Shark repellent, 83
Sharplin, Arthur, 626, 901, 915
Shewmaker, Jack, 666–668
Short-range objectives, 14–15, 17,
48
Shriver, John T., 296
Simca, 449
Simple organizational structures,
128–129
Simultaneous strategies, 77
Size, organizational, 123–124
Skibo, Charles M., 574
Skislock, Kevin B., 256
Slacik, Karl F., 283
Slane, John C., 495
Sloan, Albert F., 495
Small Business Administration,
452, 465
Small business information, 228
Smith, Cleve G., 607
Smith, Donald N., 544, 548
Smith, John Irvin, 734
Smith, Kenneth W., 918–919
Smith, Lee, 283
Smith, Lucin, 256
Smith, Roger, 131, 150
Smithburg, William, 555–557
*Smith* v. *Van Gorkom*, 134
Snyder, Neil H., 280, 293, 397, 486
Social forces, scanning of, 29–30
Socialization process, 51
Social responsibility, and
organizational objectives,
56–57
Software, 181
Soles, W. Roger, 495

Souders, W. F., 375
South Carolina Electric & Gas
Company, 10, 34
Southern Christian Leadership
Conference, 160
Southern Railway Company, 14
Southland Corporation, 647–665
Spain, 874–875
Spangler, C. D., Jr., 495
Spears, Ronald E., 574
Spero, Steve, 826–834
"Spider's web" strategies, 85
Spilman, Robert H., 495
SRI International, 30
Stable growth strategies, 63–64
Staffing process, 51
Staff proliferation growth stage,
124
Staffs, lean, 129
Stakeholders
and boards of directors, 130
organization relationship with, 9,
11
Standard and Poor's Corporation
and Value Line, 172
Standard Brands, 71
Standstill agreement, 83
Stanford, Bob, 651
"Stars," 93
State government publications,
229–230
Statements, financial, 199–212
Statements of changes in financial
position, 211–212
Statements of income, 207–210
Statements of opinion, 199–200
Statements of retained earnings,
210
Statistical indicators, 33, 221–222
Statistical sources, 247–250
Stephenson, Harriett, 826
Stern, Richard, 692–693, 696
Stock, 204, 209
Stock buy-backs, 83
Stockholders' equity, 201, 204–205
Stockman, David, 506–507
Stoever, William A., 881
Stokes, Colin, 495
Storrs, Thomas I., 495
Strategic alternatives, 62–63
Strategic business units, 17–19
Strategic control process, 168–169
effective systems, 174–176
elements, 170–174
management information
systems, 181, 183–184
methods, 176–181
and other management
processes, 170
strategy audits, 181–182

Strategic management
  decision making, 18–19
  defined, 6, 17
  integration of process
      components, 16–17
  and organizational success, 6, 8
  process. *See* Strategic
      management process
  SBUs, 17–18
Strategic management process, 8
  long- and short-range objectives,
      14–15
  organizational mission, 12–15
  organizational philosophy, 9–11
  strategy selection, 16
Strategic planning, 8, 17
Strategic Planning Institute, 111
Strategy(ies)
  business unit, 62–63, 77–79
  catch-up R&D, 154
  combination, 76–77, 154
  corporate, 62–63, 77–79
  defined, 16–17
  differentiation, 78–79
  diversification marketing, 146
  divestment, 74–76
  endgame, 72–74
  evaluation/selection, 92–115
  financial, 147–149
  focus, 78–79
  functional, 62, 104, 144–155
  generic, 77–79
  go together–split, 85
  growth, 64–73
  harvest, 74
  human resource/personnel,
      151–153
  implementation, 9, 17, 78–86,
      144–163
  innovative R&D, 153
  leadership, 73
  liquidation, 76
  market development, 145
  marketing, 145–147
  market penetration, 145
  niche, 73–74
  and organizational structure,
      122–134
  overall cost leadership, 78–79
  and policy formulation, 8
  previous, influence of, 115
  product development, 145
  production/operations, 150–151
  protective R&D, 154
  quick divestment, 74
  research and development,
      152–155
  retrenchment, 74–76
  selection, 16–17
  sequential, 77

  simultaneous, 77
  "spider's web," 85
  stable growth, 63–64
  successive integration, 85
  turnaround, 74–75
Strategy audits, 181–182
Strategy reports, 111
Strauss, Levi, 280
Stroh Brewery, 316, 324–325
Structural barriers, to divestment,
      76
Structure. *See* Organizational
      structure
Stuart, Douglas, 555–556
Stuart, John, 555–556
Stuart, Robert, 552, 555–556
Stuart, Robert D., Jr., 555–556
Sturzenegger, Otto, 495
Successive integration strategies, 85
Superior Oil Company, 81, 706,
      739–740
Support, and organizational
      culture, 51
Supreme Court, U.S., 160, 789
Surveys, 33
Suzuki, 437
Sym-Smith, Alan N., 296
Synergy, 71–72
Systematized cultures, 52
System design, 150
Systems analysts, 181

Takeover acquisitions, 80
Takeover mergers, 80
Takeovers, friendly, 82
Tandy, Charles, 592–595
Tandy Corporation, 592–616
Target companies, 80, 83
Targett, David, 146
Tariffs, 27
Tavoulareas, William P., 721–726
Taxes, income, 203, 208
Taylor, Gerald H., 574
Technological factors
  contingency approach to
      organizing, 125
  scanning of forces, 28
Ten-day window, 83
Tender offers, 81–83
Texaco, 75, 81
Texas Pacific Oil Company,
      737–738
Textron, 71
Thigpen, Peter, 283
Thompson, Debra, 489
Thompson, H. Brian, 574
Thompson, J. P., 659
Thompson, Jere, 650, 660
Thompson, Joe C., Jr., 647–648,
      650

Thompson, John, 648, 655, 657,
      660
Thornhill, William T., 185
Thurston, Robert N., 556
Time-related control methods,
      179–180
Timing considerations, 115
Titsworth, J. V., 375
Todd, Ray, 816
"Tough-guy macho" cultures,
      53–54
Toyota, 436, 443, 871
Trademarks, 228
Trailways, 77
TransOcean Oil, 738
Transportation Department, U.S.,
      770
Trans Union Corporation, 134
Transworld Drilling Company, 746
Trapani, Cosmo S., 158
Treasury Department, U.S., 451
Trend analyses, 33
Trend-impact analyses, 32
Tucker, Richard F., 724
Turnaround strategies, 74–75
Turner, Fred, 513–515
Turner, Robert ("Ted"), 468–469,
      486
Turner Broadcasting System,
      468–488
Turnover, inventory, 205–206
Tusher, Thomas W., 283
TWA, 775
Two-tiered tender offers, 83

Union Carbide Corporation,
      903–905, 910, 913–914
Union Carbide of India, 901–914
United Airlines, 20, 75, 775
United Auto Workers, 433, 454,
      456, 871
U.S. Air, 787
U.S. Industries, 12
U.S. Steel, 75, 739
United Way, 57
Utah International, 75

Value Line, 172
Vass, Ted, 606
Vertical acquisitions, 78
Vertical integration, 67–70
Vertical mergers, 78
Volkswagen, 423, 438–439
Voorhees, E. M., 921

Wallin, Winston, 533
Wal-Mart Stores, 666–681
Walt Disney Productions, 50–51
Walton, J. L. ("Bud"), 666
Walton, Sam, 666–668, 672–673

Warner, Rawleigh, Jr., 721, 724, 734
Waste Management, 788–803
Waterman, Robert H., Jr., 9, 11–12, 67, 129, 163
Watson, Thomas J., Jr., 9, 11, 50
Watson, Thomas J., Sr., 9, 114
Wendy's, 532–533, 547–548
West, Steve, 814, 816–817, 822
Western Union International, 570
West Germany, 438–439, 864
Westinghouse Electric Corporation, 468, 483, 485
Weston, J. Fred, 177

Wharton Econometric Forecasting Associates, 33
Wheelen, Thomas L., 293
White Knights, 83
Williams, John, 821
Williams, Lauren, 341
Willis, George E., 628, 636, 638
Wilson, Joseph C., 373
Wine Spectrum, 265–267
Wirthlin, Robert G., 788, 804
Wittmer, Donald G., 556
Wohl, Amy, 393
Woodruff, Ernest, 256
Woodruff, Robert W., 256, 270
Woolman, C. E., 765–766, 776, 779

Work force, 29–30
Work hard/play hard cultures, 54
Working capital, net, 205
Worthington, E. R., 814
Wright, Robert V., 107
Wright, V. Orville, 571
WTBS, 479–481

Xerox Corporation, 54, 372–396

Yearbooks, 232

Zero-based budgeting, 157–158
Ziff-Davis Publishing Company, 33